Psychological Testing

Third Edition

Psychological Testing

History, Principles, and Applications

Robert J. Gregory

Wheaton College, Wheaton, Illinois

Allyn and Bacon

Boston London Toronto Sydney Tokyo Singapore

Editor: *Rebecca Pascal*
Editor-in-Chief, Social Sciences: *Karen Hanson*
Editorial Assistant: *Susan Hutchinson*
Production Administrator: *Deborah Brown*
Editorial-Production Service: *P. M. Gordon Associates*
Composition Buyer: *Linda Cox*
Manufacturing Buyer: *Megan Cochran*
Cover Administrator: *Linda Knowles*

Copyright © 2000, 1996, 1992
Allyn & Bacon, Inc.
A Pearson Education Company
160 Gould Street
Needham Heights, MA 02494

Internet: www.abacon.com

Library of Congress Cataloging-in-Publication Data

Gregory, Robert J., 1943–
    Psychological testing : history, principles, and applications /
Robert J. Gregory. — 3rd ed.
      p. cm.
    Includes bibliographical references and index.
    ISBN 0–205–30479–6
    1. Psychological tests. 2. Psychological tests—History.
I. Title.
BF176.G74   2000
150′.28′7—dc21
                                             99-25926
                                             CIP

Printed in the United States of America

10 9 8 7 6 5 4 3 2   04 03 02 01 00

Brief Contents

Contents

CHAPTER 4   Validity and Test Development   95

CHAPTER 5   Intelligence Testing I: Theories and Preschool Assessment   138

CHAPTER 6   Intelligence Testing II: Individual and Group Tests   176

CHAPTER 7   Test Bias and Testing Special Populations   218

CHAPTER 8   Group Tests of Aptitude and Achievement   267

CHAPTER 9   Neuropsychological and Geriatric Assessment   302

CHAPTER 12   Vocational and Values Assessment   440

CHAPTER 13   Origins of Personality Testing   480

CHAPTER 14   Structured Personality Assessment   514

CHAPTER 15   Special Topics and Issues in Testing   552

Preface

Psychological testing began as a timid enterprise in the scholarly laboratories of nineteenth-century European psychologists. From this inauspicious birth, the practice of testing proliferated throughout the industrialized world at an ever accelerating pace. As the reader will discover within the pages of this book, psychological testing now impacts virtually every corner of modern life, from education to vocation to remediation.

PURPOSE OF THE BOOK

The third edition of this book is based upon the same assumptions as earlier versions. Its ambitious purpose is to provide the reader with knowledge about the characteristics, objectives, and wide-ranging effects of the consequential enterprise, psychological testing. In pursuit of this goal, I have incorporated certain well-worn traditions but proceeded into some new directions as well. For example, in the category of customary traditions, the book embraces the usual topics of norms, standardization, reliability, validity, and test construction. Furthermore, in the standard manner, I have assembled and critiqued a diverse compendium of tests and measures in such traditional areas as intellectual, achievement, industrial-organizational, vocational, and personality testing.

Special Features

In addition to the traditional topics previously listed, I have emphasized certain issues, themes, and concepts that are, in my opinion, essential for an in-depth understanding of psychological testing. For example, the book opens with a chapter on the history of psychological testing. The placement of this chapter underscores my view that the history of psychological testing is of substantial relevance to present-day practices. Put simply, a mature comprehension of modern testing can be obtained only by delving into its heritage. Of course, students of psychology typically shun historical matters because these topics are often presented in a dull, dry, and pedantic manner, devoid of relevance to the present. However, I hope the skeptical reader will approach my history chapter with an open mind—I have worked hard to make it interesting and relevant.

Psychological testing represents a contract between two persons. One person—the examiner—usually occupies a position of power over the other person—the examinee. For this reason, the examiner needs to approach testing with utmost sensitivity to the needs and rights of the examinee. To emphasize this crucial point, I have devoted an early chapter to the subtleties of the testing process, including such issues as establishing rapport and watching for untoward environmental influences upon test results. The last topic in the book also emphasizes the contractual nature of assessment by reviewing professional issues and ethical standards in testing.

Another topic emphasized in this book is neuropsychological assessment, a burgeoning subfield of clinical psychology that is now a well-established specialty in its own right. Neuropsychological assessment is definitely a growth area and now constitutes one of the major contemporary applications of psychological testing. I have devoted an entire chapter to this important subject. So that the reader can better appreciate the scope and purpose of neuropsychological assessment, I begin the chapter with a succinct review of neurological principles before discussing specific instruments. Tangentially, this review introduces important concepts in neuropsychological assessment such as the relationship between localized brain dysfunction and specific behavioral symptoms. Nonetheless, readers who need to skip the section on neurological underpinnings of behavior may do so with minimal loss—the section on neuropsychological tests and procedures is comprehensible in its own right.

This is more than a book about tests and their reliabilities and validities. I also explore numerous value-laden issues bearing on the wisdom of testing. Psychological tests are controversial precisely because the consequences of testing can be harmful, certainly to individuals and perhaps to the entire social fabric as well. I have not ducked the controversies surrounding the use of psychological tests. Separate topics explore genetic and environmental contributions to intelligence, origins of race differences in IQ, test bias and extra-validity concerns, cheating on group achievement tests, courtroom testimony, and ethical issues in psychological testing.

Note on Case Exhibits

This edition continues the use of case histories and brief vignettes that feature testing concepts and illustrate the occasionally abusive application of psychological tests. These examples are "boxed" and referred to as Case Exhibits. Most are based on my personal experience rather than scholarly undertakings. All of these case histories are real. The episodes in question really happened—I know because I have direct knowledge of the veracity of each anecdote. These points bear emphasis because the reader will likely find some of the vignettes to be utterly fantastical and almost beyond belief. Of course, to guarantee the privacy of persons and institutions, I have altered certain unessential details while maintaining the basic thrust of the original events.

CHANGES FROM THE SECOND EDITION

Of course, a revised edition should strive to add the latest findings about specific tests and incorporate new thinking on old concepts. I have done both. For example, many tests have been revised in the last few years (e.g., WAIS-III, Leiter-R, SIB-R, to name just a few), and I have described the newest editions and reviewed the relevant research. Also, some venerable concepts have undergone reinterpretation, and I have included the newest views on these concepts. A case in point is Cronbach's alpha, usually interpreted as an index of the unidimensionality of a test or scale, but now seen as an index of item homogeneity (and not necessarily a measure of test or scale unidimensionality).

In addition to updating tests and concepts, the third edition features a few shifts in topical coverage. The most prominent changes are as follows:

1. The varieties of school-based assessment have been assembled in a single place, Topic 10A: School-Based Assessment.
2. The coverage of forensic assessment has been increased and relegated to a single topic, Topic 10B: Forensic Applications of Assessment.
3. Spiritual and religious assessment has been included for the first time in Topic 12B: Values in Moral, Spiritual, and Religious Development.
4. Predictions as to the future of testing have been included in Topic 15A: Computerized Assessment and the Future of Testing.
5. The coverage of ethical and social issues has been expanded in Topic 15B: Ethical and Social Issues in Testing.

OUTLINE OF THE BOOK

Topical Organization

To accommodate the widest possible audience, I have incorporated an outline that splits the gargantuan field of psychological testing—its history, principles, and applications—into 30 small, manageable, modular topics. I was intrigued to discover that the 30 topics generally fell into natural pairings. Thus, the reader will notice that the book is also organized as an ordered series of 15 chapters of two topics each. The chapter format helps identify pairs of topics that are more or less contiguous and reduces the need for redundant preambles to each topic.

The most fundamental and indivisible unit of the book is the topic. Each topic stands on its own. In each topic, the reader encounters a manageable number of concepts and reviews a modest number of tests. To the student, the advantage of topical organization is that the individual topics are small enough to read at a single sitting. To the instructor, the advantage of topical organization is that subjects deemed of lesser importance can be easily excised from the reading list. Of course, I would prefer that every student read every topic, but I am a realist, too. Often, a foreshortened textbook is necessary for practical reasons such as the length of the school term. In those instances, the instructor will find it easy to fashion a subset of topics to meet the curricular needs of almost any course in psychological testing.

Basic Outline

The 15 chapters break down into six broad areas, as follows:

History
Chapter 1: The History of Psychological Testing
Topic 1A: The Origins of Psychological Testing
Topic 1B: Early Testing in the United States

Foundations
Chapter 2: Tests and The Testing Process
Topic 2A: The Nature and Uses of Psychological Tests
Topic 2B: The Testing Process
Chapter 3: Norms and Reliability
Topic 3A: Norms and Test Standardization
Topic 3B: Concepts of Reliability

Chapter 4: Validity and Test Development
Topic 4A: Basic Concepts of Validity
Topic 4B: Test Construction

Intell ectual and Ability Testing
Chapter 5: Intelligence Testing I: Theories and Preschool Assessment
Topic 5A: Theories and the Measurement of Intelligence
Topic 5B: Assessment of Infant and Preschool Abilities
Chapter 6: Intelligence Testing II: Individual and Group Tests
Topic 6A: Individual Tests of Intelligence
Topic 6B: Group Tests of Intelligence
Chapter 7: Test Bias and Testing Special Populations
Topic 7A: Testing Special Populations
Topic 7B: Test Bias and Other Controversies
Chapter 8: Group Tests of Aptitude and Achievement
Topic 8A: Aptitude Tests and Factor Analysis
Topic 8B: Group Tests of Achievement

Specialized Applications
Chapter 9: Neuropsychological and Geriatric Assessment
Topic 9A: A Primer of Neuropsychology
Topic 9B: Neuropsychological and Geriatric Assessment
Chapter 10: Special Settings for Psychological Assessment
Topic 10A: School-Based Assessment
Topic 10B: Forensic Applications of Assessment
Chapter 11: Industrial and Organizational Assessment
Topic 11A: Personnel Assessment and Selection
Topic 11B: Appraisal of Work Performance
Chapter 12: Vocational and Values Assessment
Topic 12A: Assessment of Interests and Work Values
Topic 12B: Values in Moral, Spiritual, and Religious Development

Personality Testing
Chapter 13: Origins of Personality Testing
> Topic 13A: Theories and the Measurement of Personality
> Topic 13B: Projective Techniques

Chapter 14: Structured Personality Assessment
> Topic 14A: Self-Report Inventories
> Topic 14B: Behavioral Assessment and Related Approaches

Computer-Aided Assessment and Professional Issues
Chapter 15: Special Topics and Issues in Testing
> Topic 15A: Computerized Assessment and the Future of Testing
> Topic 15B: Ethical and Social Issues in Testing

The book also features an extensive glossary, appendices for locating tests and publishers, and a table for converting percentile ranks to standard and standardized-score equivalents. In addition, an important feature is Appendix A, titled Major Landmarks in the History of Testing. Of course, to meet personal needs, readers and course instructors will pick and choose from these topics as they please.

ACKNOWLEDGMENTS

I would like to express my gratitude to several persons for helping the third edition become a reality. Sean Wakely and Sue Hutchinson provided encouragement and tactical advice in the various phases of revision. Deborah Brown guided the book through the production phase and helped to determine the design of the book. Dozens of psychologists and educators permitted me to reproduce tables, figures, and artwork from their research and scholarship. Rather than gathering these names in an obscure appendix that few readers would view, I have cited the contributors in the context of their tables and figures.

In addition, these individuals helped with earlier editions and their guidance has carried forward to the current version:

George M. Alliger, University of Albany
Linda J. Allred, East Carolina University
Kay Bathurst, California State University, Fullerton
Fred Brown, Iowa State University
Michael L. Chase, Quincy University
Milton J. Dehn, University of Wisconsin-La Crosse
Timothy S. Hartshorne, Central Michigan University
Herbert W. Helm, Jr., Andrews University
Ted Jaeger, Westminster College
Richard Kimball, Worcester State College
Haig J. Kojian
Phyllis M. Ladrigan, Nazareth College
Terry G. Newell, California State University, Fresno
Walter L. Porter, Harding University
Linda Krug Porzelius, SUNY, Brockport
Robert W. Read, Northeastern University
Robert A. Reeves, Augusta College
James R. Sorensen, Northeastern University
Billy Van Jones, Abilene Christian University

Thanks are due to the many publishers who granted permission for reproduction of materials. Administrators and colleagues at Wheaton College (Illinois) helped with the book by providing excellent resources and a supportive atmosphere. Three graduate assistants deserve special thanks for finding relevant references quickly: Timothy Chaddock, John Laskowski, and Kevin Novotny.

Finally, special thanks to Mary, Sara, and Anne, who continue to support my preoccupation with textbook writing. For at least a few years, I promise not to mention "the book" when my loved ones ask me how things are going.

Psychological Testing

CHAPTER 1

The History of Psychological Testing

The history of psychological testing is a fascinating story and has abundant relevance to present-day practices. After all, contemporary tests did not spring from a vacuum; they evolved slowly from a host of precursors introduced over the last one hundred years. Accordingly, Chapter 1 features a review of the historical roots of present-day psychological tests. In Topic 1A, The Origins of Psychological Testing, we focus largely on the efforts of European psychologists to measure intelligence during the late nineteenth century and pre-World War I era. These early intelligence tests and their

successors often exerted powerful effects upon the examinees who took them, so the first topic also incorporates a brief digression documenting the pervasive importance of psychological test results. Topic 1B, Early Testing in the United States, catalogues the profusion of tests developed by American psychologists in the first half of the twentieth century.

Psychological testing in its modern form originated little more than one hundred years ago in laboratory studies of sensory discrimination, motor skills, and reaction time. The British genius Francis

Galton (1822–1911) invented the first battery of tests, a peculiar assortment of sensory and motor measures which we review in the following. The American psychologist James McKeen Cattell (1860–1944) studied with Galton and then, in 1890, proclaimed the modern testing agenda in his classic paper entitled "Mental Tests and Measurements." He was tentative and modest when describing the purposes and applications of his instruments:

> Psychology cannot attain the certainty and exactness of the physical sciences, unless it rests on a foundation of experiment and measurement. A step in this direction could be made by applying a series of mental tests and measurements to a large number of individuals. The results would be of considerable scientific value in discovering the constancy of mental processes, their interdependence, and their variation under different circumstances. Individuals, besides, would find their tests interesting, and, perhaps, useful in regard to training, mode of life or indication of disease. The scientific and practical value of such tests would be much increased should a uniform system be adopted, so that determinations made at different times and places could be compared and combined (Cattell, 1890).

Cattell's conjecture that "perhaps" tests would be useful in "training, mode of life or indication of disease" must certainly rank as one of the prophetic understatements of all time. Anyone reared in the Western world knows that psychological testing has emerged from its timid beginnings to become a big business and a cultural institution that permeates modern society. To cite just one example, consider the number of standardized achievement and ability tests administered in the school systems of the United States. Although it is difficult to obtain exact data on the extent of such testing, an estimate of 200 million per year is probably not extreme (Medina & Neill, 1990). Of course, the total number of tests administered yearly also includes millions of personality tests and untold numbers of the thousands of other kinds of tests now in existence (Conoley & Kramer, 1989, 1992; Mitchell, 1985; Sweetland & Keyser, 1987). There is no doubt that testing is pervasive. But does it make a difference?

THE IMPORTANCE OF TESTING

Tests are used in almost every nation on earth for counseling, selection, and placement. Testing occurs in settings as diverse as schools, civil service, industry, medical clinics, and counseling centers. Most persons have taken dozens of tests and thought nothing of it. Yet, by the time the typical individual reaches retirement age, it is likely that psychological test results will help shape his or her destiny. The deflection of the life course by psychological test results might be subtle, such as when a prospective mathematician qualifies for an accelerated calculus course based on tenth-grade achievement scores. More commonly, psychological test results alter individual destiny in profound ways. Whether a person is admitted to one college and not another, offered one job but refused a second, diagnosed as depressed or not—all such determinations rest, at least in part, on the meaning of test results as interpreted by persons in authority. Put simply, psychological test results change lives. For this reason it is prudent—indeed, almost mandatory—that students of psychology learn about the contemporary uses and occasional abuses of testing. In Case Exhibit 1.1, the life-altering aftermath of psychological testing is illustrated by means of several true case history examples.

The importance of testing is also evident from historical review. Students of psychology generally regard historical issues as dull, dry, and pedantic, and sometimes these prejudices are well deserved. After all, many textbooks fail to explain the relevance of historical matters and provide only vague sketches of early developments in mental testing. As a result, students of psychology often conclude incorrectly that historical issues are boring and irrelevant.

In reality, the history of psychological testing is a captivating story that has substantial relevance to present-day practices. Historical developments are pertinent to contemporary testing for the following reasons:

1. A review of the origins of psychological testing helps explain current practices that might other-

THE CONSEQUENCES OF TEST RESULTS

The importance of psychological testing is best illustrated by example. Consider these brief vignettes:

- A shy, withdrawn seven-year-old girl is administered an IQ test by a school psychologist. Her score is phenomenally higher than the teacher expected. The student is admitted to a gifted and talented program where she blossoms into a self-confident and gregarious scholar.
- Three children in a family living near a lead smelter are exposed to the toxic effects of lead dust and suffer neurological damage. Based in part on psychological test results which demonstrate impaired intelligence and shortened attention span in the children, the family receives an $8 million settlement from the company that owns the smelter.
- A candidate for a position as police officer is administered a personality inventory as part of the selection process. The test indicates that the candidate tends to act before thinking and resists supervision from authority figures. Even though he has excellent training and impresses the interviewers, the candidate does not receive a job offer.
- A student, unsure of what career to pursue, takes a vocational interest inventory. The test indicates that she would like the work of a pharmacist. She signs up for a prepharmacy curriculum but finds the classes to be both difficult and boring. After three years she abandons pharmacy for a major in dance, frustrated that she still faces three more years of college to earn a degree.
- An applicant to graduate school in clinical psychology takes the Minnesota Multiphasic Personality Inventory (MMPI). His recommendations and grade point average are superlative, yet he must clear the final hurdle posed by the MMPI. His results are reasonably normal but slightly defensive; by a narrow vote, the admissions committee extends him an invitation. Ironically, this is the only graduate school to admit him—nineteen others turn him down. He accepts the invitation and becomes enchanted with the study of psychological assessment. Many years later, he writes this book.

wise seem arbitrary or even peculiar. For example, why do many current intelligence tests incorporate a seemingly nonintellective capacity, namely, short-term memory for digits? The answer is, in part, historical inertia—intelligence tests have always included a measure of digit span.

2. The strengths and limitations of testing also stand out better when tests are viewed in historical context. The reader will discover, for example, that

modern intelligence tests are exceptionally good at predicting school failure—precisely because this was the original and sole purpose of the first such instrument developed in Paris, France, at the turn of the century.

3. Finally, the history of psychological testing contains some sad and regrettable episodes that help remind us not to be overly zealous in our modern-day applications of testing. For example, based upon the misguided and prejudicial

application of intelligence test results, several prominent psychologists helped insure passage of the Immigration Restriction Act of 1924.

In later chapters, we examine the principles of psychological testing, investigate applications in specific fields (e.g., personality, intelligence, neuropsychology), and reflect upon the social and legal consequences of testing. However, the reader will find these topics more comprehensible when viewed in historical context. So, for now, we begin at the beginning by reviewing rudimentary forms of testing that existed over four thousand years ago in imperial China.

RUDIMENTARY FORMS OF TESTING IN CHINA IN 2200 B.C.

Although the widespread use of psychological testing is largely a phenomenon of the twentieth century, historians note that rudimentary forms of testing date back to at least 2200 B.C. when the Chinese emperor had his officials examined every third year to determine their fitness for office (Chaffee, 1985; DuBois, 1970; Franke, 1963; Lai, 1970; Teng, 1942–43). Such testing was modified and refined over the centuries until written exams were introduced in the Han dynasty (202 B.C.–200 A.D.). Five topics were tested: civil law, military affairs, agriculture, revenue, and geography.

The Chinese examination system took its final form about 1370 when proficiency in the Confucian classics was emphasized. In the preliminary examination, candidates were required to spend a day and a night in a small isolated booth, composing essays on assigned topics and writing a poem. The 1 to 7 percent who passed moved up to the district examinations which required three separate sessions of three days and three nights.

The district examinations were obviously grueling and rigorous, but this was not the final level. The 1 to 10 percent who passed were allowed the privilege of going to Peking for the final round of examinations. Perhaps 3 percent of this final group passed and became mandarins, eligible for public office.

Although the Chinese developed the external trappings of a comprehensive civil service exami-

nation program, the similarities between their traditions and current testing practices are, in the main, superficial. Not only were their testing practices unnecessarily grueling, the Chinese also failed to validate their selection procedures. Nonetheless, it does appear that the examination program incorporated relevant selection criteria. For example, in the written exams beauty of penmanship was weighted very heavily. Given the highly stylistic features of Chinese written forms, good penmanship was no doubt essential for clear, exact communication. Thus, penmanship was probably a relevant predictor of suitability for civil service employment. In response to widespread discontent, the examination system was abolished by royal decree in 1906 (Franke, 1963).

PSYCHIATRIC ANTECEDENTS OF PSYCHOLOGICAL TESTING

Most historians trace the beginnings of psychological testing to the experimental investigation of individual differences that flourished in Germany and Great Britain in the late 1800s. There is no doubt that early experimentalists such as Wilhelm Wundt, Francis Galton, and James McKeen Cattell laid the foundations for twentieth-century testing, and we will review their contributions in detail. But psychological testing owes as much to early psychiatry as it does to the laboratories of experimental psychology. In fact, the examination of the mentally ill around the middle of the nineteenth century resulted in the development of numerous early tests (Bondy, 1974). These early tests featured the absence of standardization and were consequently relegated to oblivion. They were nonetheless influential in determining the course of psychological testing, so it is important to mention a few typical developments from this era.

In 1885, the German physician Hubert von Grashey developed the antecedent of the memory drum as a means of testing brain-injured patients. His subjects were shown words, symbols, or pictures through a slot in a sheet of paper which was moving slowly over the stimuli. Grashey found that many patients could recognize stimuli in their totality but could not identify them when shown through the moving slot. Shortly thereafter, the German psychiatrist Conrad Rieger developed an excessively ambitious test battery for brain damage. His battery took over 100 hours to administer and soon fell out of favor.

In summary, early psychiatry contributed to the mental test movement by showing that standardized procedures could help reveal the nature and extent of symptoms in the mentally ill and brain-injured patients. Most of the early tests developed by psychiatrists faded into oblivion, but a few procedures were standardized and perpetuate themselves in modern variations (Bondy, 1974).

THE BRASS INSTRUMENTS ERA OF TESTING

Experimental psychology flourished in the late 1800s in continental Europe and Great Britain. For the first time in history, psychologists departed from the wholly subjective and introspective methods that had been so fruitlessly pursued in the preceding centuries. Human abilities were instead tested in laboratories. Researchers used objective procedures that were capable of replication. Gone were the days when rival laboratories would have raging arguments about "imageless thought," one group saying it existed, another group saying that such a mental event was impossible.

Even though the new emphasis on objective methods and measurable quantities was a vast improvement over the largely sterile mentalism that preceded it, the new experimental psychology was itself a dead end, at least as far as psychological testing was concerned. The problem was that the early experimental psychologists mistook simple sensory processes for intelligence. They used assorted brass instruments to measure sensory thresholds and reaction times, thinking that such abilities were at the heart of intelligence. Hence, this period is sometimes referred to as the Brass Instruments era of psychological testing.

In spite of the false start made by early experimentalists, at least they provided psychology with an appropriate methodology. Such pioneers as Wundt, Galton, Cattell, and Wissler showed that it was possible to expose the mind to scientific scrutiny and measurement. This was a fateful change in the axiomatic assumptions of psychology, a change that has stayed with us to the current day.

Most sources credit Wilhelm Wundt (1832–1920) with founding the first psychological laboratory in 1879 in Leipzig, Germany. It is less well recognized that he was measuring mental processes years before, at least as early as 1862, when he experimented with his thought meter (Diamond, 1980). This device was a calibrated pendulum with needles sticking off from each side. The pendulum would swing back and forth, striking bells with the needles. The observer's task was to take note of the position of the pendulum when the bells sounded. Of course, Wundt could adjust the needles beforehand and thereby know the precise position of the pendulum when each bell was struck. Wundt thought that the difference between the observed pendulum position and the actual position would provide a means of determining the swiftness of thought of the observer.

Wundt's analysis was relevant to a longstanding problem in astronomy. The problem was that two or more astronomers simultaneously using the same telescope (with multiple eyepieces) would report different crossing times as the stars moved across a grid line on the telescope. Even in Wundt's time, it was a well-known event in the history of science that Kinnebrook, an assistant at the Royal Observatory in England, had been dismissed in 1796 because his stellar crossing times were nearly a full second too slow (Boring, 1950). Wundt's analysis offered another explanation that did not assume incompetence on the part of anyone. Put simply, Wundt believed that the speed of thought might differ from one person to the next:

> For each person there must be a certain speed of thinking, which he can never exceed with his given mental constitution. But just as one steam engine can go faster than another, so this speed of thought will probably not be the same in all persons (Wundt, 1862, as translated in Rieber, 1980).

This analysis of telescope reporting times seems simplistic by present-day standards and overlooks the possible contribution of such factors as attention, motivation, and self-correcting feedback from prior trials. On the positive side, this was at least an empirical analysis that sought to explain individual differences instead of trying to explain them away. And that is the relevance to current practices in psychological testing. However crudely, Wundt measured mental processes and begrudgingly acknowledged individual differences.[1]

Galton and the First Battery of Mental Tests

Sir Francis Galton (1822–1911) pioneered the new experimental psychology in nineteenth-century Great Britain. Galton was obsessed with measurement, and his intellectual career seems to have been dominated by a belief that virtually anything was measurable. His attempts to measure intellect by means of reaction time and sensory discrimination tasks are well known. Yet, to appreciate his wide-ranging interests, the reader should be apprised that Galton also devised techniques for measuring beauty, personality, the boringness of lectures, and the efficacy of prayer, to name but a few of the endeavors that his biographer has catalogued in elaborate detail (Pearson 1914, 1924, 1930ab).

Galton was a genius who was more interested in the problems of human evolution than in psychology per se (Boring, 1950). His two most influential works were *Hereditary Genius* (1869), an empirical analysis purporting to prove that genetic factors were overwhelmingly important for the attainment of eminence, and *Inquiries into Human Faculty and its Development* (1883), a disparate series of essays which emphasized individual differences in mental faculties.

Boring (1950) regards *Inquiries* as the beginning of the mental test movement and the advent of the scientific psychology of individual differences. The book is a curious mixture of empirical research and speculative essays on topics as diverse as "just perceptible differences" in lifted weight and diminished fertility among inbred animals. There is,

nonetheless, a common theme uniting these diverse essays; Galton demonstrates time and again that individual differences not only exist but are objectively measurable.

Galton borrowed the time-consuming psychophysical procedures practiced by Wundt and others on the European continent and adapted them to a series of simple and quick sensorimotor measures. Thus, he continued the tradition of brass instruments mental testing but with an important difference: his procedures were much more amenable to the timely collection of data from hundreds if not thousands of subjects. Because of his efforts in devising practicable measures of individual differences, historians of psychological testing usually regard Galton as the father of mental testing (Goodenough, 1949; Boring, 1950).

To further his study of individual differences, Galton set up a psychometric laboratory in London at the International Health Exhibition in 1884. It was later transferred to the London Museum, where it was maintained for six years. Various anthropometric and psychometric measures were arranged on a long table at one side of a narrow room. Subjects were admitted at one end for threepence and given successive tests as they moved down the table. At least 17,000 individuals were tested during the 1880s and 1890s. About 7,500 of the individual data records have survived to the present day (Johnson, McClearn, Yuen, Nagoshi, Ahern, & Cole, 1985).

The tests and measures involved both the physical and behavioral domains. Physical characteristics assessed were height, weight, head length, head breadth, armspan, length of middle finger, and length of lower arm, among others. The behavioral tests included strength of hand squeeze determined by dynamometer, vital capacity of the lungs measured by spirometer, visual acuity, highest audible tone, speed of blow, and reaction time (RT) to both visual and auditory stimuli.

Ultimately, Galton's simplistic attempts to gauge intellect with measures of reaction time and sensory discrimination proved fruitless. Nonetheless, he did provide a tremendous impetus to the testing movement by demonstrating that objective tests could be devised and that meaningful scores could be obtained through standardized procedures.

---

1. This emphasis upon individual differences was rare for Wundt. He is more renown for proposing common laws of thought for the average adult mind.

Cattell Imports Brass Instruments to the United States

James McKeen Cattell (1860–1944) studied the new experimental psychology with both Wundt and Galton before settling at Columbia University where, for twenty-six years, he was the undisputed dean of American psychology. With Wundt, he did a series of painstakingly elaborate RT studies (1880–1882), measuring with great precision the fractions of a second presumably required for different mental reactions. He also noted, almost in passing, that he and another colleague had small but consistent differences in RT. Cattell proposed to Wundt that such individual differences ought to be studied systematically. Although Wundt acknowledged individual differences, he was philosophically more inclined to study general features of the mind, and he offered no support for Cattell's proposal (Fancher, 1985).

But Cattell received enthusiastic support for his study of individual differences from Galton, who had just opened his psychometric laboratory in London. After corresponding with Galton for a few years, Cattell arranged for a two-year fellowship at Cambridge so that he could continue the study of individual differences. Cattell opened his own research laboratory and developed a series of tests that were mainly extensions and additions to Galton's battery.

Cattell (1890) invented the term *mental test* in his famous paper entitled "Mental Tests and Measurements." This paper described his research program, detailing ten mental tests he proposed for use with the general public. These tests were clearly a reworking and embellishment of the Galtonian tradition:

Strength of hand squeeze as measured by dynamometer

Rate of hand movement through a distance of 50 centimeters

Two-point threshold for touch—minimum distance at which two points are still perceived as separate

Degree of pressure needed to cause pain—rubber tip pressed against the forehead

Weight differentiation—discern the relative weights of identical-looking boxes varying by one gram from 100 to 110 grams

Reaction time for sound—using a device similar to Galton's

Time for naming colors

Bisection of a 50-centimeter line

Judgment of 10 seconds of time

Number of letters repeated on one hearing

Strength of hand squeeze seems a curious addition to a battery of mental tests, a point that Cattell (1890) addressed directly in his paper. He was of the opinion that it was impossible to separate bodily energy from mental energy. Thus, in Cattell's view, an ostensibly physiological measure such as dynamometer pressure was an index of one's mental power as well. Clearly, the physiological and sensory bias of the entire test battery reflects its strongly Galtonian heritage (Fancher, 1985).

In 1891, Cattell accepted a position at Columbia University, at that time the largest university in the United States. His subsequent influence on American psychology was far in excess of his individual scientific output and was expressed in large part through his numerous and influential students (Boring, 1950). Among his many famous doctoral students and the years of their degrees were E. L. Thorndike (1898) who made monumental contributions to learning theory and educational psychology; R. S. Woodworth (1899) who was to author the very popular and influential *Experimental Psychology* (1938); and E. K. Strong (1911) whose Vocational Interest Blank—since revised—is still in wide use. But among Cattell's students, it was probably Clark Wissler (1901) who had the greatest influence on the early history of psychological testing.

Wissler obtained both mental test scores and academic grades from more than 300 students at Columbia University and Barnard College. His goal was to demonstrate that the test results could predict academic performance. With our late twentieth century perspective on research and testing, it seems amazing that the early experimentalists waited so long to do such basic validational research. Wissler's (1901) results showed virtually no tendency for the mental test scores to correlate with academic achievement. For example, class standing correlated .16 with memory for number lists, −.08

with dynamometer strength, .02 with color naming, and –.02 with reaction time. The highest correlation (.16) was statistically significant because of the large sample size. However, so humble a correlation carries with it very little predictive utility.[2]

Also damaging to the brass instruments testing movement was the very modest correlations between the mental tests themselves. For example, color naming and hand movement speed correlated only .19, while RT and color naming correlated –.15. Several physical measures such as head size (a holdover measure from the Galton era) were, not surprisingly, also uncorrelated with the various sensory and RT measures.

With the publication of Wissler's (1901) discouraging results, experimental psychologists largely abandoned the use of RT and sensory discrimination as measures of intelligence. From one standpoint, this turning away from the brass instruments approach was a desirable development in the history of psychological testing. The way was thereby paved for immediate acceptance of Binet's more sensible and useful measures of higher mental processes.

But in other respects, the abandonment of RT and sensory measures was premature and unfortunate. After all, by contemporary standards Wissler's research methods revealed an extraordinary psychometric naivete. By using only bright college students as subjects, Wissler had inadvertently introduced an extreme restriction of range which would invariably reduce the size of his correlations. If a more heterogeneous sample of subjects had been used, the correlations would have been substantially larger. In addition, certain measures such as RT were inherently unreliable because of the small number of trials per subject. Such unreliability in a measure also places a severe restriction on the upper bounds of correlation coefficients.

If Wissler's (1901) negative findings had been more skeptically scrutinized, it might not have been a full 70 years later until RT was resurrected as a potentially useful intellectual measure. Correlations of –.40 between complex forms of RT and intelligence are not at all uncommon (Jensen, 1982).[3]

But that is getting ahead of the story. The more common reaction among psychologists in the early 1900s was to begrudgingly conclude that Galton had been wrong in attempting to infer complex abilities from simple ones. Goodenough (1949) has likened Galton's approach to "inferring the nature of genius from the nature of stupidity or the qualities of water from those of the hydrogen and oxygen of which it is composed." The academic psychologists apparently agreed with her, and American attempts to develop intelligence tests virtually ceased at the turn of the century. For his own part, Wissler was apparently so discouraged by his results that he immediately switched to anthropology where he became a strong environmentalist in explaining differences between ethnic groups.

The void created by the abandonment of the Galtonian tradition did not last for long. In Europe, Alfred Binet was on the verge of a major breakthrough in intelligence testing. Binet introduced his scale of intelligence in 1905 and shortly thereafter H. H. Goddard imported it to the United States where it was applied in a manner that Gould (1981) has described as "the dismantling of Binet's intentions in America." Whether early twentieth century American psychologists subverted Binet's intentions is an important question that we review in the next topic. First, we examine the social changes in nineteenth-century Europe that created the necessity for practical intelligence tests.

CHANGING CONCEPTIONS OF MENTAL RETARDATION IN THE 1800S

Many great inventions have been developed in response to the practical needs created by changes in societal values. Such is the case with intelligence

---

2. We discuss the correlation coefficient in more detail in Topic 3B, Concepts of Reliability. By way of quick preview, correlations can range from –1.0 to +1.0. Values near zero indicate a weak, negligible linear relationship between the two variables. For example, correlations between –.20 and +.20 are generally of minimal value for purposes of individual prediction. Note also that negative correlations indicate an inverse relationship.

3. The correlations are negative because *low* scores on RT are associated with high scores on intelligence tests.

tests. To be specific, the first such tests were developed by Binet in the early 1900s to help identify children in the Paris school system who were unlikely to profit from ordinary instruction. Prior to this time, there was little interest in the educational needs of retarded children. A new humanism toward the retarded thus created the practical problem—identifying those with special needs—that Binet's tests were to solve.

The western world of the late 1800s was just emerging from centuries of indifference and hostility toward the psychiatrically and mentally impaired. Medical practitioners were just beginning to acknowledge a distinction between the emotionally disabled and the mentally retarded. For centuries, all such social outcasts were given similar treatment. In the Middle Ages, they were occasionally "diagnosed" as witches and put to death by burning. Later on, they were alternately ignored, persecuted, or tortured. In his comprehensive history of psychotherapy and psychoanalysis, Bromberg (1959) has an especially graphic chapter on the various forms of maltreatment toward the mentally and emotionally disabled, from which only one example will be provided here. In 1698, a prominent physician wrote a gruesome book, *Flagellum Salutis,* in which beatings were advocated as treatment "in melancholia; in frenzy; in paralysis; in epilepsy; in facial expression of feebleminded" (Bromberg, 1959).

By the early 1800s, saner minds began to prevail. Medical practitioners realized that some of those with psychiatric impairment had reversible illnesses that did not necessarily imply diminished intellect, whereas other exceptional persons, the mentally retarded, showed a greater developmental continuity and invariably had impaired intellect. In addition, a newfound humanism began to influence social practices toward the psychologically and mentally disabled. With this humanism there arose a greater interest in the diagnosis and remediation of mental retardation. At the forefront of these developments were two French physicians, J. E. D. Esquirol and O. E. Seguin, each of whom revolutionized thinking about the mentally retarded, thereby helping to create the necessity for Binet's tests.

Esquirol and Diagnosis in Mental Retardation

Around the beginning of the nineteenth century, many physicians had begun to perceive the difference between mental retardation (then called *idiocy*) and mental illness (often referred to as *dementia*). J. E. D. Esquirol (1772–1840) was the first to formalize the difference in writing. His diagnostic breakthrough was noting that mental retardation was a lifelong developmental phenomenon whereas mental illness usually had a more abrupt onset in adulthood. He thought that mental retardation was incurable, whereas mental illness might show improvement (Esquirol, 1845/1838).

Esquirol placed great emphasis upon language skills in the diagnosis of mental retardation. This may offer a partial explanation as to why Binet's later tests and the modern-day descendents from them are so heavily loaded on linguistic abilities. After all, the original use of the Binet scales was, in the main, to identify mentally retarded children who would not likely profit from ordinary schooling.

Esquirol also proposed the first classification system in mental retardation and it should be no surprise that language skills were the main diagnostic criteria. He recognized three levels of mental retardation: (1) those using short phrases, (2) those using only monosyllables, and (3) those with cries only, no speech. Apparently, Esquirol did not recognize what we would now call *mild mental retardation,* instead providing criteria for the equivalents of the modern-day classifications of moderate, severe, and profound mental retardation.

Seguin and Education of the Mentally Retarded

Perhaps more than any other pioneer in the field of mental retardation, O. Edouard Seguin (1812–1880) helped establish a new humanism toward the retarded in the late 1800s. He had been a student of Esquirol and had also studied with J. M. G. Itard (1774–1838) who is well known for his five-year attempt to train the Wild Boy of Aveyron, a feral child who had lived in the woods for his first 11 or 12 years (Itard, 1932/1801).

Seguin borrowed from techniques used by Itard and devoted his life to developing educational programs for the retarded. As early as 1838, he had established an experimental class for the mentally retarded. His treatment efforts earned him international acclaim and he eventually came to the United States to continue his work. In 1866, he published *Idiocy, and Its Treatment by the Physiological Method,* the first major textbook on the treatment of mental retardation. This book advocated a surprisingly modern approach to education of the retarded and even touched on what would now be called *behavior modification.*

Such was the social and historical background that allowed intelligence tests to flourish. We turn now to the invention of the modern-day intelligence test by Alfred Binet. We begin with a discussion of the early influences which shaped his famous test.

INFLUENCE OF BINET'S EARLY RESEARCH UPON HIS TEST

As most every student of psychology knows, Alfred Binet (1857–1911) invented the first modern intelligence test in 1905. What is less well known, but equally important for those who seek an understanding of his contributions to modern psychology, is that Binet was a prolific researcher and author long before he turned his attentions to intelligence testing. The character of his early research had a material bearing on the subsequent form of his well-known intelligence test. For those who seek a full understanding of his pathbreaking influence, brief mention of Binet's early career is mandatory. For more details the reader can consult DuBois (1970), Fancher (1985), Goodenough (1949), Gould (1981), and Wolf (1973).

Binet began his career in medicine, but was forced to drop out because of a complete emotional breakdown. He switched to psychology where he studied the two-point threshold and dabbled in the associationist psychology of John Stuart Mill (1806–1873). Later, he selected an apprenticeship with the neurologist J. M. Charcot (1825–1893) at the famous Salpetriere Hospital. Thus, for a brief time Binet's professional path paralleled that of Sigmund Freud, who also studied hysteria under Charcot. At the Salpetriere Hospital, Binet coauthored (with C. Fere) four studies supposedly demonstrating that reversing the polarity of a magnet could induce complete mood changes (e.g., from happy to sad) or transfer of hysterical paralysis (e.g., from left to right side) in a single hypnotised subject. In response to public criticism from other psychologists, Binet later published a recantation of his findings. This was a painful episode for Binet, and it sent his career into a temporary detour. Nonetheless, he learned two things through his embarrassment. First, he never again used sloppy experimental procedures that allowed for unintentional suggestion to influence his results. Second, he became skeptical of the Zeitgeist (spirit of the times) in experimental psychology. Both of these lessons were applied when he later developed his intelligence scales.

In 1891, Binet went to work at the Sorbonne as an unpaid assistant and began a series of studies and publications that were to define his new "individual psychology" and ultimately to culminate in his intelligence tests. Binet was an ardent experimentalist, often using his two daughters to try out existing and new tests of intelligence. Early on, he flirted with a Cattellian approach to intelligence testing, using the standard measures of reaction time and sensory acuity on his two daughters. The results were annoyingly inconsistent and difficult to interpret. As might be expected, he found that the reaction times of his children were, on average, much slower than for adults. But on some trials his daughters' performance approached or exceeded adult levels. From these findings, Binet concluded that attention was a key component of intelligence, which was itself a very multifaceted entity. Furthermore, he became increasingly disenchanted with the brass instruments approach to measuring intelligence, which probably explains his subsequent use of measures of higher mental processes.

In addition, Binet's sensory-perceptual experiments with his children greatly influenced his views on proper testing procedures:

> The experimenter is obliged, to a point, to adjust his method to the subject he is addressing. There are certain rules to follow when one experiments

on a child, just as there are certain rules for adults, for hysterics, and for the insane. These rules are not written down anywhere; each one learns them for himself and is repaid in great measure. By making an error and later accounting for the cause, one learns not to make the mistake a second time. In regard to children, it is necessary to be suspicious of two principal causes of error: suggestion and failure of attention. This is not the time to speak on the first point. As for the second, failure of attention, it is so important that it is always necessary to suspect it when one obtains a negative result. One must then suspend the experiments and take them up at a more favorable moment, restarting them 10 times, 20 times, with great patience. Children, in fact, are often little disposed to pay attention to experiments which are not entertaining, and it is useless to hope that one can make them more attentive by threatening them with punishment. By particular tricks, however, one can sometimes give the experiment a certain appeal (Binet, 1895, quoted in Pollack, 1971).

It is interesting to contrast modern-day testing practices—which go so far as to specify the exact wording the examiner should use—with Binet's advice to exercise nearly endless patience and use entertaining tricks when testing children.

BINET AND TESTING FOR HIGHER MENTAL PROCESSES

In 1896, Binet and his Sorbonne assistant, Victor Henri, published a pivotal review of German and American work on individual differences. In this historically important paper, they argued that intelligence could be better measured by means of the higher psychological processes rather than the elementary sensory processes such as reaction time. After several false starts, Binet and Simon eventually settled on the straightforward format of their 1905 scales, discussed subsequently.

The character of the 1905 scale owed much to a prior test developed by Dr. Blin (1902) and his pupil, M. Damaye. They had attempted to improve the diagnosis of mental retardation by using a battery of assessments in 20 areas such as spoken language; knowledge of parts of the body; obedience to simple commands; naming common objects; and

ability to read, write, and do simple arithmetic. Binet criticized the scale for being too subjective, for having items reflecting formal education, and for using a yes or no format on many questions (DuBois, 1970). But he was much impressed with the idea of using a battery of tests, a feature which he adopted in his 1905 scales.

In 1904, the Minister of Public Instruction in Paris appointed a commission to decide upon the educational measures that should be undertaken with those children who could not profit from regular instruction. The commission concluded that medical and educational examinations should be used to identify those children who could not learn by the ordinary methods. Furthermore, it was determined that these children should be removed from their regular classes and given special instruction suitable to their more limited intellectual prowess. This was the beginning of the special education classroom.

It was evident that a means of selecting children for such special placement was needed, and Binet and his colleague Simon were called upon to develop a practical tool for just this purpose. Thus arose the first formal scale for assessing the intelligence of children.

Goodenough (1949) has outlined the four ways in which the 1905 scale differed from those which had been previously constructed.

1. It made no pretense of measuring precisely any single faculty. Rather, it was aimed at assessing the child's general mental development with a heterogeneous group of tasks. Thus, the aim was not measurement, but classification.
2. It was a brief and practical test. The test took less than an hour to administer and required little in the way of equipment.
3. It measured directly what Binet and Simon regarded as the essential factor of intelligence—practical judgment—rather than wasting time with lower-level abilities involving sensory, motor, and perceptual elements. They took a pragmatic view of intelligence:

   There is in intelligence, it seems to us, a fundamental agency the lack or alteration of which has the greatest importance for practical life; that is judgement, otherwise known as good sense, practical sense, initiative, or the faculty of adapting oneself. To judge well, to understand well, to reason well—these are the essential wellsprings of intelligence (Binet and Simon, 1905; as translated in Fancher, 1985).

4. The items were arranged by approximate level of difficulty instead of content. A rough standardization had been done with 50 normal children ranging in age from three to 11 years and several subnormal and retarded children as well.

The 30 tests on the 1905 scale ranged from utterly simple sensory tests to quite complex verbal abstractions. Thus, the scale was appropriate for assessing the entire gamut of intelligence—from severe mental retardation to high levels of giftedness. The entire scale is outlined in Table 1.1.

TABLE 1.1   The 1905 Binet-Simon Scale

1. Follows a moving object with the eyes.
2. Grasps a small object which is touched.
3. Grasps a small object which is seen.
4. Recognizes the difference between a square of chocolate and a square of wood.
5. Finds and eats a square of chocolate wrapped in paper.
6. Executes simple commands and imitates simple gestures.
7. Points to familiar named objects, e.g., "Show me the cup."
8. Points to objects represented in pictures, e.g., "Put your finger on the window."
9. Names objects in pictures, e.g., "What is this?" [examiner points to a picture of a sign].
10. Compares two lines of markedly unequal length.
11. Repeats three spoken digits.
12. Compares two weights.
13. Shows susceptibility to suggestion.
14. Defines common words by function.
15. Repeats a sentence of 15 words.
16. Tells how two common objects are different, e.g., "paper and cardboard."
17. Names from memory as many as possible of 13 objects displayed on a board for 30 seconds. [This test was later dropped because it permitted too many possibilities for distraction.]
18. Reproduces from memory two designs shown for 10 seconds.
19. Repeats a longer series of digits than in item 11 to test immediate memory.
20. Tells how two common objects are alike, e.g., "butterfly and flea."
21. Compares two lines of slightly unequal length.
22. Compares five blocks to put them in order of weight.
23. Indicates which of the previous five weights the examiner has removed.
24. Produces rhymes, e.g., "What rhymes with 'school'?"
25. A word completion test based on those proposed by Ebbinghaus.
26. Puts three nouns, e.g., "Paris, river, fortune" (or three verbs) in a sentence.
27. Responds to 25 abstract (comprehension) questions, e.g., "When a person has offended you, and comes to offer his apologies, what should you do?"
28. Reverses the hands of a clock.
29. After paper folding and cutting, draws the form of the resulting holes.
30. Defines abstract words by designating the difference between, e.g., "boredom and weariness."

Source: Based on translations in Jenkins and Paterson (1961) and Jensen (1980).

Except for the very simplest tests, which were designed for the classification of very low-grade *idiots* (an unfortunate diagnostic term that has since been dropped), the tests were heavily weighted toward verbal skills, reflecting Binet's departure from the Galtonian tradition.

An interesting point that is often overlooked by contemporary students of psychology is that Binet and Simon did not offer a precise method for arriving at a total score on their 1905 scale. It is well to remember that their purpose was classification, not measurement, and that their motivation was entirely humanitarian, namely, to identify those children who needed special educational placement. By contemporary standards, it is difficult to accept the fuzziness inherent in such an approach, but that may reflect a modern penchant for quantification more than a weakness in the 1905 scale. In fact, their scale was popular among educators in Paris. And, even with the absence of precise quantification, the approach was successful in selecting candidates for special classes.

THE REVISED SCALES
AND THE ADVENT OF IQ

In 1908, Binet and Simon published a revision of the 1905 scale. In the earlier scale, more than half the items had been designed for the very retarded, yet the major diagnostic decisions involved older children and those with borderline intellect. To remedy this imbalance, most of the very simple items were dropped and new items were added at the higher end of the scale. The 1908 scale had 58 problems or tests, almost double the number from 1905. Several new tests were added, many of which are still used today: reconstructing scrambled sentences, copying a diamond, and executing a sequence of three commands. Some of the items were absurdities which the children had to detect and explain. One such item was amusing to French children: "The body of an unfortunate girl was found, cut into 18 pieces. It is thought that she killed herself." However, this item was very upsetting to some American subjects, demonstrating the importance of cultural factors in intelligence (Fancher, 1985).

The major innovation of the 1908 scale was the introduction of the concept of mental level. The tests had been standardized on about 300 normal children between the ages of 3 and 13 years. This allowed Binet and Simon to order the tests according to the age level at which they were typically passed. Whichever items were passed by 80 to 90 percent of the 3-year-olds were placed in the 3-year level, and similarly on up to age 13. Binet and Simon also devised a rough scoring system whereby a basal age was first determined from the age level at which not more than one test was failed. For each five tests that were passed at levels above the basal, a full year of mental level was granted. Insofar as partial years of mental level were not credited and the various age levels had anywhere from three to eight tests, the method left much to be desired.

In 1911, a third revision of the Binet-Simon scales appeared. Each age level now had exactly five tests. The scale was also extended into the adult range. And with some reluctance, Binet introduced new scoring methods that allowed for one-fifth of a year for each subtest passed beyond the basal level. In his writings, Binet emphasized strongly that the child's exact mental level should not be taken too seriously as an absolute measure of intelligence.

Nonetheless, the idea of deriving a mental level was a monumental development that was to influence the character of intelligence testing throughout the twentieth century. Within months, what Binet called mental level was being translated as mental age. And testers everywhere, including Binet himself, were comparing a child's mental age with his chronological age. Thus, a nine-year-old who was functioning at the mental level (or mental age) of a six-year-old was retarded by three years. Very shortly, Stern (1912) pointed out that being retarded by three years had different meanings at different ages. A five-year-old functioning at the two-year-old level was more impaired than a 13-year-old functioning at the 10-year-old level. Stern suggested that an intelligence quotient computed from the mental age divided by the chronological age would give a better measure of the relative functioning of a subject compared to his or her same-aged peers.

In 1916, Terman and his associates at Stanford revised the Binet-Simon scales, producing the Stanford-Binet, a successful test that will be discussed in a later chapter. Terman suggested multiplying the Intelligence Quotient by 100 to remove fractions; he was also the first person to use the abbreviation *IQ*. Thus was born one of the most popular and controversial concepts in the history of psychology. Binet died in 1911 before the IQ swept American testing, so we will never know what he would have thought of this new development based on his scales. However, Simon, his collaborator, later called the concept of IQ a "betrayal" of their scale's original objectives (Fancher, 1985, p. 104), and we can assume from Binet's humanistic concern that he might have held a similar opinion.

SUMMARY

1. For better or for worse, psychological test results possess the power to alter lives. A review of historical trends is crucial if we desire to comprehend the contemporary influence of psychological tests.

2. Rudimentary forms of testing date back to 2200 B.C. in China. The Chinese emperors used grueling written exams to select officials for civil service.

3. In the mid- to late 1800s, several physicians and psychiatrists developed standardized procedures to reveal the nature and extent of symptoms in the mentally ill and brain-injured. For example, in 1885, Hubert von Grashey developed the precursor to the memory drum to test the visual recognition skill of brain-injured patients.

4. Modern psychological testing owes its inception to the era of brass instruments psychology that flourished in Europe during the late 1800s. By testing sensory thresholds and reaction times, pioneer test developers such as Sir Francis Galton demonstrated that it was possible to measure the mind in an objective and replicable manner.

5. Wilhelm Wundt founded the first psychological laboratory in 1879 in Leipzig, Germany. Included among his earlier investigations was his 1862 attempt to measure the speed of thought with the thought meter, a calibrated pendulum with needles sticking off from each side.

6. The first reference to mental tests occurred in 1890 in a classic paper by James McKeen Cattell, an American psychologist who had studied with Galton. Cattell imported the brass instruments approach to the United States.

7. One of Cattell's students, Clark Wissler, showed that reaction time and sensory discrimination measures did not correlate with college grades, thereby redirecting the mental testing movement away from brass instruments.

8. In the late 1800s, a newfound humanism toward the mentally retarded, reflected in the diagnostic and remedial work of French physicians Esquirol and Seguin, helped create the necessity for early intelligence tests.

9. Alfred Binet, who was to invent the first true intelligence test, began his career by studying hysterical paralysis with the French neurologist Charcot. Binet's claim that magnetism could cure hysteria was, to his pained embarrassment, disproved. Shortly thereafter, he switched interests and conducted sensory-perceptual studies, using his children as subjects.

10. In 1905, Binet and Simon developed the first useful intelligence test in Paris, France. Their simple 30-item measure of mainly higher mental functions helped identify schoolchildren who could not profit from regular instruction. Curiously, there was no method for scoring the test.

11. In 1908, Binet and Simon published a revised 58-item scale which incorporated the concept of mental level. In 1911, a third revision of the Binet-Simon scales appeared. Each age level now had exactly five tests; the scale extended into the adult range.

12. In 1912, Stern proposed dividing the mental age by the chronological age to obtain an Intelligence Quotient. In 1916, Terman suggested multiplying the Intelligence Quotient by 100 to remove fractions. Thus was born the concept of IQ.

TOPIC 1B Early Testing in the United States

The Binet-Simon scales helped solve a practical social quandary, namely, how to identify children who needed special schooling. With this successful application of a mental test, psychologists realized that their inventions could have pragmatic significance for many different segments of society. Almost immediately, psychologists in the United States adopted a utilitarian focus. Intelligence testing was embraced by many as a reliable and objective response to perceived social problems such as the identification of mentally retarded immigrants and the quick, accurate classification of Army recruits.

Whether these early tests really solved social dilemmas—or merely exacerbated them—is a fiercely debated issue reviewed in the following sections. One thing is certain: The profusion of tests developed early in this century helped shape the character of contemporary tests. A review of these historical trends will aid in the comprehension of the nature of modern tests and a better appreciation of the social issues raised by them.

EARLY USES AND ABUSES OF TESTS IN AMERICA

First Translation of the Binet-Simon Scale

In 1906, Henry H. Goddard was hired by the Vineland Training School in New Jersey to do research on the classification and education of "feebleminded" children. He soon realized that a diagnostic instrument would be required and was therefore pleased to read of the 1908 Binet-Simon scale. He quickly set about translating the scale, making minor changes so that it would be applicable to American children (Goddard, 1910a).

Goddard (1910b) tested 378 residents of the Vineland facility and categorized them by diagnosis and mental age. He classified 73 residents as *idiots* because their mental age was 2 years or lower; 205 residents were termed *imbeciles* with mental age of 3 to 7 years; and, 100 residents were deemed *feebleminded* with mental age of 8 to 12 years. It is instructive to note that originally neutral and descriptive terms for portraying levels of mental retardation—idiot, imbecile, and feebleminded—have made their way into the everyday lexicon of pejorative labels. In fact, Goddard made his own contribution by coining the diagnostic term *moron* (from the Greek *moronia,* meaning "foolish").

Goddard (1911) also tested 1,547 normal children with his translation of the Binet-Simon scales. He considered children whose mental age was four or more years behind their chronological age to be feebleminded—these constituted 3 percent of his sample. Considering that all of these children were found outside of institutions for the retarded, 3 percent is rather an alarming rate of mental deficiency. Goddard (1911) was of the opinion that these children should be segregated so that they would be prevented from "contaminating society." These early studies piqued Goddard's curiosity about "feebleminded" citizenry and the societal burdens they imposed. He also gained a reputation as one of the leading experts on the use of intelligence tests to identify persons with impaired intellect. His talents were soon in heavy demand.

The Binet-Simon and Immigration

In 1910, Goddard was invited to Ellis Island by the commissioner of immigration to help make the examination of immigrants more accurate. A dark and foreboding folklore had grown up around mental deficiency and immigration in the early 1900s:

> It was believed that the feebleminded were degenerate beings responsible for many if not most social problems; that they reproduced at an alarming rate and menaced the nation's overall biological fitness; and that their numbers were being incremented by undesirable "new" immigrants from southern and eastern European countries who had largely supplanted the "old" immigrants from northern and western Europe (Gelb, 1986).

Initially, Goddard was unconcerned about the supposed threat of feeblemindedness posed by the immigrants. He wrote that adequate statistics did not exist and that the prevalent opinions about undue percentages of mentally defective immigrants were "grossly overestimated" (Goddard, 1912). However, with repeated visits to Ellis Island,

Goddard became convinced that the rates of feeblemindedness were much higher than estimated by the physicians who staffed the immigration service. Within a year, he reversed his opinions entirely and called for congressional funding so that Ellis Island could be staffed with experts trained in the use of intelligence tests. In the following decade, Goddard became an apostle for the use of intelligence tests to identify feebleminded immigrants. Although he wrote that the rates of mentally deficient immigrants were "alarming," he did not join the popular call for immigration restriction (Gelb, 1986).

The story of Goddard and his concern for the "menace of feeblemindedness," as Gould (1981) has satirically put it, is often ignored or downplayed in books on psychological testing. The majority of textbooks on testing do not mention or refer to Goddard at all. The few books that do mention him usually state that Goddard ". . . used the tests in institutions for the retarded . . ." which is surely an understatement. In his influential *History of Psychological Testing,* DuBois (1970) has a portrait of Goddard but devotes less than one line of text to him.

The fact is that Goddard was one of the most influential American psychologists of the early 1900s. Any thoughtful person must therefore wonder why so many contemporary authors have ignored or slighted the person who first translated and applied Binet's tests in America. We will attempt an answer here, based in part on Goddard's original writing, but also relying upon Gould's (1981) critique of Goddard's voluminous writings on mental deficiency and intelligence testing. We refer to Gelb's (1986) more sympathetic portrayal of Goddard as well.

Perhaps Goddard has been ignored in the textbooks because he was a strict hereditarian who conceived of intelligence in simple-minded Mendelian terms. No doubt his call for colonization of "morons" so as to restrict their breeding has won him contemporary disfavor as well. And his insistence that much undesirable behavior—crime, alcoholism, prostitution—was due to inherited mental deficiency also does not sit well with the modern environmentalist position.

However, the most likely reason that modern authors have ignored Goddard is that he exemplified a large number of early, prominent psychologists who engaged in the blatant misuse of intelligence testing. In his efforts to demonstrate that high rates of retarded immigrants were entering the United States each day, Goddard sent his assistants to Ellis Island to administer his English translation of the Binet-Simon tests to newly arrived immigrants. The tests were administered through a translater, not long after the immigrants walked ashore. We can guess that many of the immigrants were frightened, confused, and disoriented. Thus, a test devised in French, then translated to English was, in turn, retranslated back to Yiddish, Hungarian, Italian, or Russian; administered to bewildered farmers and laborers who had just endured an Atlantic crossing; and interpreted according to the original French norms.

What did Goddard find and what did he make of his results? In small samples of immigrants (22 to 50), his assistants found 83 percent of the Jews, 80 percent of the Hungarians, 79 percent of the Italians, and 87 percent of the Russians to be feebleminded, that is, below age 12 on the Binet-Simon scales (Goddard, 1917). His interpretation of these findings is, by turns, skeptically cautious and then provocatively alarmist. In one place he claims that his study "makes no determination of the actual percentage, even of these groups, who are feebleminded." Yet, later in the report he states that his figures would only need to be revised by "a relatively small amount" in order to find the actual percentages of feeblemindedness among immigrant groups. Further, he concludes that the intelligence of the average immigrant is low, "perhaps of moron grade" but then goes on to cite environmental deprivation as the primary culprit. Simultaneously, Goddard appears to favor deportation for low IQ immigrants but also provides the humanitarian perspective that we might be able to use "moron laborers" if only "we are wise enough to train them properly."

There is much, much more to the Goddard era of early intelligence testing, and the interested reader is urged to consult Gould (1981) and Gelb (1986). The most important point that we wish to stress here is that—like many other early psychologists—Goddard's scholarly views were influenced by the social ideologies of his time. Finally, Goddard was a complex scholar who refined and contradicted his professional opinions on numerous occasions. One ironic example: After the damage was done and his writings had helped restrict immigration, Goddard (1928) recanted, concluding that feeblemindedness was not incurable, and that the feebleminded did not need to be segregated in institutions.

The Goddard chapter in the history of testing serves as a reminder that even well-meaning persons operating within generally accepted social norms can misuse psychological tests. We need be ever mindful that disinterested "science" can be harnessed to the goals of a pernicious social ideology.

THE INVENTION OF NONVERBAL TESTS IN THE EARLY 1900S

Because of the heavy emphasis of the Binet-Simon scales upon verbal skills, many psychologists realized that this new measuring device was not entirely appropriate for non-English-speaking subjects, illiterates, and the speech and hearing impaired. A spate of performance scales therefore arose in the decade following Goddard's 1908 translation of the Binet-Simon. Only a brief chronology of nonverbal tests will be supplied here. The interested reader should consult DuBois (1970). In this listing of early performance tests, the reader will surely recognize many instruments and subtests that are still used today.

The earliest of the performance measures was the Seguin form board, an upright stand with depressions into which ten blocks of varying shapes could be fitted. This had been used by Seguin as a training device for the retarded, but was subsequently developed as a test by Goddard, and then standardized by R. H. Sylvester (1913). This identical board is still used, with the subject blindfolded, in the Halstead-Reitan neuropsychological test battery (Reitan & Wolfson, 1985).

Knox (1914) devised several performance tests for use with Ellis Island immigrants. His tests required absolutely no verbal responses from subjects. The examiner demonstrated each task nonverbally to insure that the subjects understood the instructions. Included in his tests were a simple wooden puzzle (which Knox referred to as the "moron" test) and the same digit-symbol substitution test which is now found on most of the Wechsler scales of intelligence.

Several other early performance tests are worthy of brief mention because they have survived to the present day in revised form. Pintner and Paterson (1917) invented a 15-part scale of performance tests that used several form boards, puzzles, and object assembly tests. The object assembly test—reassembling cut-up cardboard versions of common objects such as a horse—is a mainstay of several contemporary intelligence tests. The Kohs Block Design test (Kohs, 1920), which required the subject to assemble painted blocks to resemble a pattern, is well known to any modern tester who uses the Wechsler scales. The Porteus Maze Test (Porteus, 1915) is a graded series of mazes for which the subject must avoid dead ends while tracing a path from beginning to end. This is a fine instrument that is still available today, but underused.

THE STANFORD-BINET: THE EARLY MAINSTAY OF IQ

While it was Goddard who first translated the Binet scales in America, it was Stanford professor Lewis M. Terman (1857–1956) who popularized IQ testing with his revision of the Binet scales in 1916. The new Stanford-Binet, as it was called, was a substantial revision, not just an extension, of the earlier Binet scales. Among the many changes that led to the unquestioned prestige of the Stanford-Binet was the use of the now familiar IQ for expressing test results. The number of items was increased to 90, and the new scale was suitable for the mentally retarded, children, and both normal and "superior" adults. In addition, the Stanford-Binet had clear and well-organized instructions for administration and scoring. Great care had been taken in securing a representative sample of subjects for use in the standardization of the test. As Goodenough (1949) notes: "The publication of the Stanford Revision marked the end of the initial period of experimentation and uncertainty. Once and for all, intelligence testing had been put on a firm basis."

The Stanford-Binet was the standard of intelligence testing for decades. New tests were always validated in terms of their correlations with this measure. It continued its preeminence through revisions in 1937, and 1960, by which time the Wechsler Scales (Wechsler, 1949, 1955) had begun to compete with it. The latest revision of the Stanford-Binet was completed in 1986. This test and the Wechsler scales are discussed in detail in a later chapter. It is worth mentioning here that the Wechsler scales became a quite popular alternative to the Stanford-Binet mainly because they provided more than just an IQ score. In addition to Full Scale IQ, the Wechsler scales provided ten to twelve subtest scores, and a Verbal and Performance IQ. By contrast, the earlier versions of the Stanford-Binet supplied only a single overall summary score, the global IQ.

GROUP TESTS AND THE CLASSIFICATION OF WWI ARMY RECRUITS

Given the American penchant for efficiency, it was only natural that researchers would seek group mental tests to supplement the relatively time-consuming individual intelligence tests imported from France. Among the first to develop group tests was Pyle (1913) who published schoolchildren norms for a battery consisting of such well-worn measures as memory span, digit-symbol substitution, and oral word association (quickly writing down words in response to a stimulus word). Pintner (1917) revised and expanded Pyle's battery, adding to it a timed cancellation test in which the child crossed out the letter *a* wherever it appeared in a body of text.

But group tests were slow to catch on, partly because the early versions still had to be scored laboriously by hand. The idea of a completely objective test with a simple scoring key was inconsistent with tests such as logical memory for which the judgment of the examiner was required in scoring. Most amazing of all—at least to anyone who has spent any time as a student in American schools—the multiple choice question was not yet in general use.

The slow pace of developments in group testing picked up dramatically as the United States entered World War I in 1917. It was then that Robert M. Yerkes, a well-known psychology professor at Harvard, convinced the U.S. government and the Army that all of its 1.75 million recruits should be given intelligence tests for purposes of classification and assignment (Yerkes, 1919). Immediately upon being commissioned into the Army as a colonel, Yerkes assembled a Committee on the Examination of Recruits, which met at the Vineland school in New Jersey to develop the new group tests for the assessment of Army recruits. Yerkes chaired the committee; other famous members included Goddard and Terman.

Two group tests emerged from this collaboration: the Army Alpha and the Army Beta. It would be difficult to overestimate the influence of the Alpha and Beta upon subsequent intelligence tests. The format and content of these tests inspired developments in group and individual testing for decades to come. We will discuss these tests in some detail so that the reader can appreciate their influence on modern intelligence tests.

The Army Alpha and Beta Examinations

The Alpha was based on the then unpublished work of Otis (1918) and consisted of eight verbally loaded tests for average and high-functioning recruits. The eight tests were: (1) following oral directions, (2) arithmetical reasoning, (3) practical judgment, (4) synonym-antonym pairs, (5) disarranged sentences, (6) number series completion, (7) analogies, and (8) information. Figure 1.1 lists some typical items from the Army Alpha examination.

The Army Beta was a nonverbal group test designed for use with illiterates and recruits whose first language was not English. It consisted of various visual-perceptual and motor tests such as tracing a path through mazes and visualizing the correct number of blocks depicted in a three-dimensional drawing. Figure 1.2 depicts the blackboard demonstrations for all eight parts of the Beta examination.

In order to accommodate illiterate subjects and recent immigrants who did not comprehend English, Yerkes instructed the examiners to use largely pictorial and gestural methods for explaining the tests to the prospective Army recruits. The examiner and his assistant stood atop a platform at the front of the class and engaged in pantomime to explain each of the seven tests. We will reproduce here the exact instructions for one test so that the reader can appraise the likely effects of the testing procedures upon Beta results. Keep in mind that many recruits could not see or hear the examiner well, and that some had never taken a test before. Here is how the examiners introduced test 6, picture completion, to each new roomful of potential recruits:

> "This is test 6 here. Look. A lot of pictures." After everyone has found the place, "Now watch." Examiner points to hand and says to demonstrator, "Fix it." Demonstrator does nothing, but looks puzzled. Examiner points to the picture of the hand, and then to the place where the finger is missing and says to demonstrator, "Fix it; fix it." Demonstrator then draws in finger. Examiner says "That's right." Examiner then points to fish and place for eye and says, "Fix it." After demonstrator has drawn missing eye, examiner points to each of the four remaining drawings and says, "Fix them all." Demonstrator works samples out slowly and with apparent effort. When the samples are finished examiner says, "All right. Go head. Hurry up!" During the course of this test the orderlies walk around the room and locate individuals who are doing nothing, point to their pages and say, "Fix it. Fix them," trying to set everyone working. At the end of 3 minutes examiner says, "Stop! But don't turn over the page." (Yerkes, 1921).

The Army testing was intended to help segregate and eliminate the mentally incompetent, to

FOLLOWING ORAL DIRECTIONS

Mark a cross in the first and also the third circle:

○   ○   ○   ○   ○

ARITHMETICAL REASONING

Solve each problem:

How many men are 5 men and 10 men?   Answer (   )

If 3 1/2 tons of coal cost $21, what will 5 1/2 tons cost?   Answer (   )

PRACTICAL JUDGMENT

Why are high mountains covered with snow? Because
☐   they are near the clouds
☐   the sun shines seldom on them
☐   the air is cold there

SYNONYM-ANTONYM PAIRS

Are these words the same or opposite?

largess—donation   same? or opposite?

accumulate—dissipate   same? or opposite?

DISARRANGED SENTENCES

Can these words be rearranged to form a sentence?

envy bad malice traits are and   true? or false?

NUMBER SERIES COMPLETION

Complete the series: 3   6   8   16   18   36   ...   ...

ANALOGIES

Which choice completes the analogy?

tears—sorrow :: laughter—   joy   smile   girls   grin

granary—wheat :: library—   desk   books   paper   librarian

INFORMATION

Choose the best alternative:

The pancreas is in the   abdomen   head   shoulder   neck

The Battle of Gettysburg was fought in   1863   1813   1778   1812

Note: Examinees received verbal instructions for each subtest.

FIGURE 1.1   **Sample Items from the Army Alpha Examination**
Source: Reprinted from Yerkes, R. M. (ed.) (1921). *Psychological examining in the United States Army. Memoirs of the National Academy of Sciences, Volume 15.* With permission from the National Academy of Sciences, Washington, DC.

classify men according to their mental ability, and to assist in the placement of competent men in responsible positions (Yerkes, 1921). However, it is not really clear whether the Army made much use of the masses of data supplied by Yerkes and his eager assistants. A careful reading of his memoirs reveals that Yerkes did little more than produce favorable testimonials from high-ranking officers. In the main, his memoirs say that the Army could have saved millions of dollars and increased its efficiency, if the testing data had been used.

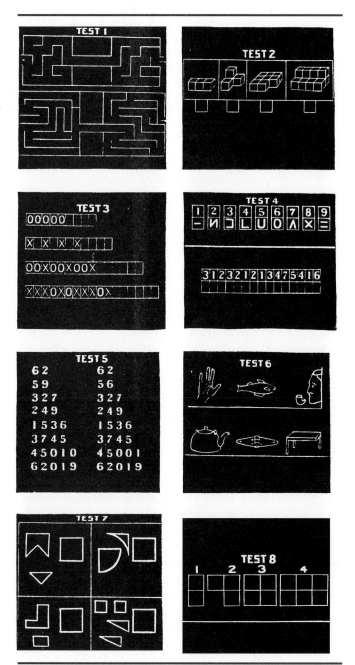

FIGURE 1.2
**The Blackboard Demonstrations for All
Eight Parts of the Beta Examination**
Source: Reprinted from Yerkes, R. M. (Ed.) (1921).
*Psychological examining in the United States Army.
Memoirs of the National Academy of Sciences, Volume 15.* With permission from the National Academy of Sciences, Washington, DC.

To some extent, the mountains of test data had little practical impact on the efficiency of the Army because of the resistance of the military mind to scientific innovation. However, it is also true that the Army brass had good reason to doubt the validity of the test results. For example, an internal memorandum described the use of pantomime in the instructions to the nonverbal Beta examination:

> For the sake of making results from the various camps comparable, the examiners were ordered to follow a certain detailed and specific series of ballet antics, which had not only the merit of being perfectly incomprehensible and unrelated to mental testing, but also lent a highly confusing and distracting mystical atmosphere to the whole performance, effectually preventing all approach to the attitude in which a subject should be while having his soul tested (cited in Samelson, 1977).

In addition, the testing conditions left much to be desired, with wave upon wave of recruits ushered in one door, tested, and virtually shoved out the other side. Tens of thousands of recruits received a literal zero for many subtests, not because they were retarded but because they couldn't fathom the instructions to these enigmatic new instruments. Many recruits fell asleep while the testers gave esoteric and mysterious pantomime instructions.

On the positive side, the Army testing provided psychologists with a tremendous amount of experience in the psychometrics of test construction. Thousands of correlation coefficients were computed, including the prominent use of multiple correlations in the analysis of test data. Test construction graduated from an art to a science in a few short years.

The Army Tests and Ethnic Differences

Unfortunately, the Army test results were sometimes used to substantiate prejudices about various racial and ethnic groups rather than to dispassionately investigate the causes of group differences. For example, in his influential book *A Study of American Intelligence,* Brigham (1923) undertook a massive analysis of Alpha and Beta scores for Nordic, Mediterranean, and Alpine immigrants. The text is stuffed with ostensibly objective tables and charts comparing racial and ethnic groups. For example, one curious figure in his book depicts the proportion of each immigration sample at or below the average of the African-American draft. Brigham concluded that African Americans, Mediterranean

immigrants, and Alpine immigrants were intellectually inferior. He sounded a dire warning that racial intermixture would inevitably cause a deterioration of American intelligence. For example, the caption to one graph reads, in part:

> The distributions of the intelligence scores of the entire Nordic group, the combined Mediterranean and Alpine groups, and the negro draft. The process of racial intermixture cannot result in anything but an average of these elements, with the resulting deterioration of American intelligence (Brigham, 1923).

Seven years later, Brigham (1930) forthrightly disavowed his earlier views. He cited cultural and language differences as the likely cause of ethnic and racial disparities on the Army tests. He asserted that comparative studies of national and racial groups could not be made with existing tests and concluded that his earlier findings were "without foundation" (Brigham, 1930).

EARLY EDUCATIONAL TESTING

For good or for ill, Yerkes's grand scheme for testing Army recruits helped to usher in the era of group tests. After WWI, inquiries rushed in from industry, public schools, and colleges about the potential applications of these straightforward tests that almost anyone could administer and score (Yerkes, 1921). The psychologists who had worked with Yerkes soon left the service and carried with them to industry and education their newfound notion of paper-and-pencil tests of intelligence.

The Army Alpha and Beta were also released for general use. These tests quickly became the prototypes for a large family of group tests and influenced the character of intelligence tests, college entrance examinations, scholastic achievement tests, and aptitude tests. To cite just one specific consequence of the Army testing, the National Research Council, a government organization of scientists, devised the National Intelligence Test, which was eventually given to 7 million children in the United States during the 1920s. Thus, such well-known tests as the Wechsler scales, the

Scholastic Aptitude Tests, and the Graduate Record Exam actually have roots that reach back to Yerkes, Otis, and the mass testing of Army recruits during WWI.

The College Entrance Examination Board (CEEB) was established at the turn of the century to help avoid duplication in the testing of applicants to American colleges. The early exams had been of the short answer essay format, but this was to change quickly when C. C. Brigham, a disciple of Yerkes, became CEEB secretary after WWI. In 1925, the College Board decided to construct a scholastic aptitude test for use in college admissions (Goslin, 1963). The new tests reflected the now familiar objective format of unscrambling sentences, completing analogies, and filling in the next number in a sequence. Machine scoring was introduced in the 1930s, making objective group tests even more efficient than before. These tests then evolved into the present College Board tests, in particular, the Scholastic Aptitude Tests, now known as the Scholastic Assessment Tests.

The functions of the CEEB were later subsumed under the nonprofit Educational Testing Service (ETS). The ETS directed the development, standardization, and validation of such well-known tests as the Graduate Record Examination, the Law School Admissions Test, and the Peace Corps Entrance Tests.

Meanwhile, Terman and his associates at Stanford were busy developing standardized achievement tests. The Stanford Achievement Test (SAchT) was first published in 1923; a modern version of it is still in wide use today. From the very beginning, the SAchT incorporated such modern psychometric principles as norming the subtests so that within-subject variability could be assessed and selecting a very large and representative standardization sample.

THE DEVELOPMENT OF APTITUDE TESTS

Aptitude tests measure more specific and delimited abilities than intelligence tests. Traditionally, intelligence tests assess a more global construct such as general intelligence, although there are exceptions to this trend that will be discussed later. By contrast, a single aptitude test will measure just one ability domain, and a multiple aptitude test battery will provide scores in several distinctive ability areas.

The development of aptitude tests lagged behind that of intelligence tests for two reasons, one statistical, the other social. The statistical problem was that a new technique, factor analysis, was often needed to discern which aptitudes were primary and therefore distinct from each other. Research on this question had been started quite early by Spearman (1904) but was not refined until the 1930s (Spearman, 1927; Kelley, 1928; Thurstone, 1938). This new family of techniques, factor analysis, allowed Thurstone to conclude that there were specific factors of primary mental ability such as verbal comprehension, word fluency, number facility, spatial ability, associative memory, perceptual speed, and general reasoning (Thurstone, 1938; Thurstone & Thurstone, 1941). More will be said about this in the later chapters on intelligence and ability testing. The important point here is that Thurstone and his followers thought that global measures of intelligence did not, so to speak, "cut nature at its joints." As a result, it was felt that such measures as the Stanford-Binet were not as useful as multiple aptitude test batteries in determining a person's intellectual strengths and weaknesses.

The second reason for the slow growth of aptitude batteries was the absence of a practical application for such refined instruments. It was not until WWII that a pressing need arose to select candidates who were highly qualified for very difficult and specialized tasks. The job requirements of pilots, flight engineers, and navigators were very specific and demanding. A general estimate of intellectual ability, such as provided by the group intelligence tests used in WWI, was not sufficient to choose good candidates for flight school. The armed forces solved this problem by developing a specialized aptitude battery of 20 tests which was administered to men who passed preliminary screening tests. These measures proved invaluable in selecting pilots, navigators, and bombadiers, as reflected in the much lower washout rates of men selected by test battery instead of the old methods (Goslin, 1963). Such tests are still used widely in the armed services.

PERSONALITY AND VOCATIONAL TESTING AFTER WWI

While such rudimentary assessment methods as the free association technique had been used before the turn of the century by Galton, Kraepelin, and others, it was not until WWI that personality tests emerged in a form resembling their contemporary appearance. As has happened so often in the history of testing, it was once again a practical need that served as the impetus for this new development. Modern personality testing began when Woodworth attempted to develop an instrument for detecting Army recruits who were susceptible to psychoneurosis. Virtually all the modern personality inventories, schedules, and questionnaires owe a debt to Woodworth's Personal Data Sheet (1919).

The Personal Data Sheet consisted of 116 questions which the subject was to answer by underlining *Yes* or *No*. The questions were exclusively of the "face obvious" variety and, for the most part, involved fairly serious symptomatology. Representative items included:

- Do ideas run through your head so that you cannot sleep?
- Were you considered a bad boy?
- Are you bothered by a feeling that things are not real?
- Do you have a strong desire to commit suicide?

Readers familiar with the Minnesota Multiphasic Personality Inventory (MMPI) must surely recognize the debt that this more recent inventory has to Woodworth's instrument.

From his account of how the Personal Data Sheet was developed (Woodworth, 1951), it is clear that Woodworth took great care in the selection of items. In other respects, though, this instrument embodies a large dose of psychometric credulity. The most serious problem is simply that a disturbed subject motivated to look good could do so without detection; likewise, a normal subject with a *fake bad* mentality might be categorized as unfit for service. Modern instruments such as the MMPI have incorporated various validity scales for detecting such response tendencies. The Personal Data Sheet, by contrast, was predicated on the assumption that subjects would be honest when responding to the questions.

The next major development was an inventory of neurosis, the Thurstone Personality Schedule (Thurstone & Thurstone, 1930). After first culling hundreds of items answerable in the yes-no-? manner from Woodworth's inventory and other sources, Thurstone rationally keyed items in terms of how the neurotic would typically answer them. Reflecting Thurstone's penchant for statistical finesse, this inventory was one of the first to use the method of internal consistency whereby each prospective item was correlated with the total score on the tentatively identified scale to determine if it belonged on the scale.

From the Thurstone test sprang the Bernreuter Personality Inventory (Bernreuter, 1931). It was a little more refined than its Thurstone predecessor, measuring four personality dimensions: neurotic tendency, self-sufficiency, introversion-extroversion, and dominance-submission. A major innovation in test construction was that a single test item could contribute to more than one scale.

The Allport-Vernon Study of Values was also published in 1931 (Allport & Vernon, 1931). This test was quite different from the others in that it measured values instead of psychopathology. Furthermore, it adopted a new scoring method, the ipsative approach, in which the respondent was compared only with himself or herself regarding the balance of importance given to six basic values: theoretical, economic, aesthetic, social, political, and religious. The test was devised in such a manner that subjects were required to make choices between the six values in specific situations. As a consequence, the average on the six scales was always the same for each subject. A weakness in one value was compensated for by a strength in some other value. Thus, only the relative peaks and valleys were of interest.

Any chronology of self-report inventories must surely include the Minnesota Multiphasic Personality Inventory or MMPI (Hathaway & McKinley, 1940). This test and its revision, the MMPI-2, will be discussed in detail later. It will suffice for now to point out that the scales of the MMPI were constructed by the method that Woodworth pioneered, contrasting the responses of normal and psychiatrically disturbed subjects. In addition, the MMPI introduced the use of validity scales to determine fake bad, fake good, and random response patterns.

THE ORIGINS OF PROJECTIVE TESTING

The projective approach originated with the word association method pioneered by Francis Galton in the late 1800s. Galton gave himself four seconds to come up with as many associations as possible to a stimulus word, and then categorized his associations as parrotlike, image-mediated, or histrionic representations. This latter category convinced him that mental operations "sunk wholly below the level of consciousness" were at play. Some historians have even speculated that Freud's application of free association as a therapeutic tool in psychoanalysis sprang from Galton's paper published in *Brain* in 1879 (Forrest, 1974).

Galton's work was continued in Germany by Wundt and Kraepelin, and finally brought to fruition by Jung (1910). Jung's test consisted of 100 stimulus words. For each word, the subject was to reply as quickly as possible with the first word coming to mind. Kent and Rosanoff (1910) gave the association method a distinctively American flavor by tabulating the reactions of 1,000 normal subjects to a list of 100 stimulus words. These tables were designed to provide a basis for comparing the reactions of normal and "insane" subjects.

While the Americans were pursuing the empirical approach to objective personality testing, a young Swiss psychiatrist, Hermann Rorschach (1884–1922), was developing a completely different vehicle for studying personality. Rorschach was strongly influenced by Jungian and psychoanalytic thinking, so it was natural that his new approach focused on the tendency of patients to reveal their innermost conflicts unconsciously when responding to ambiguous stimuli. The Rorschach and other projective tests discussed subsequently were predicated upon the projective hypothesis: When responding to ambiguous or unstructured stimuli, we inadvertently disclose our innermost needs, fantasies, and conflicts.

Rorschach was convinced that people revealed important personality dimensions in their responses to inkblots. He spent years developing just the right set of ten inkblots and systematically analyzed the responses of personal friends and different patient groups (Rorschach, 1921). Unfortunately, he died only a year after his monograph was published, and it was up to others to complete his work. Developments in the Rorschach are reviewed later in the text.

While Rorschach's test was originally developed to reveal the innermost workings of the abnormal subject, the TAT, or Thematic Apperception Test (Morgan & Murray, 1935), was developed as an instrument to study normal personality. Of course, both have since been expanded for testing with the entire continuum of human behavior.

The TAT consists of a series of pictures which largely depict one or more persons engaged in an ambiguous interaction. The subject is shown one picture at a time and told to make up a story about it. He or she is instructed to be as dramatic as possible, to discuss thoughts and feelings, and to describe the past, present, and future of what is depicted in the picture.

Murray (1938) believed that underlying personality needs, such as the need for achievement, would be revealed by the contents of the stories.

Although numerous scoring systems were developed, clinicians in the main have relied upon an impressionistic analysis to make sense of TAT protocols. Modern applications of the TAT are discussed in a later chapter.

The sentence completion technique was also begun during this era with the work of Payne (1928). There have been numerous extensions and variations on the technique, which consists of giving subjects a stem such as "I am bored when _____," and asking them to complete the sentence. Some modern applications are discussed later, but it can be mentioned now that the problem of scoring and interpretation, which vexed early sentence completion test developers, is still with us today.

An entirely new approach to projective testing was taken by Goodenough (1926) who tried to determine not just intellectual level, but also the interests and personality traits of children by analyzing their drawings. Buck's (1948) test, the House-Tree-Person, was a little more standardized and structured, and required the subject to draw a house, a tree, and a person. Machover's (1949) *Personality Projection in the Drawing of the Human Figure*, was the logical extension of the earlier work. Figure drawing as a projective approach to understanding personality is still used today, and a later chapter discusses modern developments in this practice.

Meanwhile, projective testing in Europe was dominated by the Szondi Test, a wacky instrument based on wholly faulty premises. Lipot Szondi was a Hungarian-born Swiss psychiatrist who believed that major psychiatric disorders were caused by recessive genes. His test consisted of 48 photographs of psychiatric patients divided into six sets of the following eight types: homosexual, epileptic, sadistic, hysteric, catatonic, paranoiac, manic, and depressive (Deri, 1949). From each set of eight pictures, the subject was instructed to select the two pictures he or she liked best and the two disliked most. A person who consistently preferred one kind of picture in the six sets was presumed to have some recessive genes which made him or her have sympathy for the pictured person. Thus, projective preferences were presumed to reveal recessive genes predisposing the individual for specific psychiatric disturbances.

Deri (1949) imported the test to the United States and changed the rationale. She did not argue for a recessive genetic explanation of picture choice but explained such preferences on the basis of unconscious identification with the characteristics of the photographed patients. This was a more palatable theoretical basis for the test than the dubious genetic theories of Szondi. Nonetheless, empirical research cast doubt on the validity of the Szondi Test, and it shortly faded into oblivion (Borstelmann & Klopfer, 1953).

THE DEVELOPMENT OF INTEREST INVENTORIES

While the clinicians were developing measures for analyzing personality and unconscious conflicts, other psychologists were devising measures for guidance and counseling of the masses of more normal persons. Chief among such measures was the interest inventory which has roots going back to Thorndike's (1912) study of developmental trends in the interests of 100 college students. In 1919–1920, Yoakum developed a pool of 1,000 items relating to interests from childhood through early maturity (DuBois, 1970). Many of these items were incorporated in the Carnegie Interest Inventory. Cowdery (1926–27) improved and refined previous work on the Carnegie instrument by increasing the number of items, comparing responses of three criterion groups (doctors, engineers, and lawyers) with control groups of nonprofessionals, and developing a weighting formula for items. He was also the first psychometrician to realize the importance of cross validation. He tested his new scales on additional groups of doctors, engineers, and lawyers to insure that the discriminations found in the original studies were reliable group differences rather than capitalizations on error variance.

Edward K. Strong (1884–1963) revised Cowdery's test and devoted 36 years to the development of empirical keys for the modified instrument known as the Strong Vocational Interest Blank (SVIB). Persons taking the test could be scored on separate keys for several dozen occupations, providing a series of scores of immeasurable value in vocational guidance. The SVIB became one of the most widely used tests of all time (Strong, 1927). Its modern version, the Strong Interest Inventory, is still widely used by guidance counselors.

For decades the only serious competitor to the SVIB was the Kuder Preference Record (Kuder, 1934). The Kuder differed from the Strong by forcing choices within triads of items. The Kuder was an ipsative test, that is, it compared the relative strength of interests within the individual, rather than comparing his or her responses to various pro-

fessional groups. More recent revisions of the Kuder Preference Record include the Kuder General Interest Survey and the Kuder Occupational Interest Survey (Kuder, 1966; Kuder & Diamond, 1979; Zytowski, 1985).

SUMMARY OF MAJOR LANDMARKS IN THE HISTORY OF TESTING

We conclude our historical survey of psychological testing with a brief tabular summary of landmark events up to 1950 (Table 1.2). The interested reader can find a more detailed listing—including a chronology of post-1950 developments—in Appendix A.

TABLE 1.2   A Summary of Early Landmarks in the History of Testing

2200 B.C.	Chinese begin civil service examinations.
1862	Wilhelm Wundt uses a calibrated pendulum to measure the "speed of thought."
1884	Francis Galton administers the first test battery to thousands of citizens at the International Health Exhibit.
1890	James McKeen Cattell uses the term *mental test* in announcing the agenda for his Galtonian test battery.
1901	Clark Wissler discovers that Cattellian "brass instruments" tests have no correlation with college grades.
1905	Binet and Simon invent the first modern intelligence test.
1914	Stern introduces the IQ, or intelligence quotient: the mental age divided by chronological age.
1916	Lewis Terman revises the Binet-Simon scales, publishes the Stanford-Binet. Revisions appear in 1937, 1960, and 1986.
1917	Robert Yerkes spearheads the development of the Army Alpha and Beta examinations used for testing WWI recruits.
1917	Robert Woodworth develops the Personal Data Sheet, the first personality test.
1920	Rorschach Inkblot test published.
1921	Psychological Corporation—the first major test publisher—founded by Cattell, Thorndike, and Woodworth.
1927	First edition of the Strong Vocational Interest Blank published.
1939	Wechsler-Bellevue Intelligence Scale published. Revisions published in 1955, 1981, and 1997.
1942	Minnesota Multiphasic Personality Inventory published.
1949	Wechsler Intelligence Scale for Children published. Revisions published in 1974, 1991.

SUMMARY

1. In 1910, Henry Goddard translated the 1908 Binet-Simon scale. In 1911, he tested more than a thousand schoolchildren with the test, relying upon the original French norms. He was disturbed to find that 3 percent of the sample was "feebleminded" and recommended segregation from society for these children.

2. Nonverbal intelligence tests were invented in the early 1900s to facilitate testing of non-English-speaking immigrants. For example, Knox published a wooden puzzle test in 1914 and also used the now familiar digit-symbol substitution test.

3. In 1916, Lewis Terman released the Stanford-Binet, a revision of the Binet scales. This well-designed and carefully normed test placed intelligence testing on a firm footing once and for all.

4. During WWI, Robert Yerkes headed a team of psychologists who produced the Army Alpha, a verbally loaded group test for average and superior recruits, and the Army Beta, a nonverbal group test for illiterates and non-English-speaking recruits.

5. Early testing pioneers such as C. C. Brigham used results of individual and group intelligence tests to substantiate ethnic differences in intelligence and thereby justify immigration restrictions. Later, some of these testing pioneers disavowed their prior views.

6. Educational testing fell under the purview of the College Entrance Examination Board (CEEB) founded at the turn of the century. In 1947, the CEEB was replaced by the Educational Testing Service (ETS) which supervised the release of such well-known tests as the Scholastic Aptitude Tests and the Graduate Record Exam.

7. The advent of multiple aptitude test batteries was made possible with the development of factor analysis by L. L. Thurstone and others. Later, the improvement of these test batteries was spurred on by the practical need for selecting WWII recruits for highly specialized positions.

8. Personality testing began with Woodworth's Personal Data Sheet, a simple yes-no checklist of symptoms used to screen WWI recruits for psychoneurosis. Many later inventories, including the popular Minnesota Multiphasic Personality Inventory, borrowed content from the Personal Data Sheet.

9. Projective testing began with the word association technique pioneered by Francis Galton and brought to fruition by C. G. Jung in 1910. Hermann Rorschach published his famous inkblot test in 1921.

10. The Thematic Apperception Test (TAT), a picture storytelling test introduced in 1935 by Morgan and Murray, was based upon the projective hypothesis: When responding to ambiguous or unstructured stimuli, examinees inadvertently disclose their innermost needs, fantasies, and conflicts.

11. The assessment of vocational interest began with Yoakum's Carnegie Interest Inventory developed in 1919–1920. After several revisions and extensions, this instrument emerged as E. K. Strong's Vocational Interest Blank.

CHAPTER 2

Tests and the Testing Process

The historical introduction in the preceding chapter has acquainted the reader with only a small fraction of the many types and uses of psychological tests. These early tests were used predominantly for two purposes: to measure intelligence and to detect personality disorders. It is understandable, then, that the average citizen equates psychological testing with IQ scores, inkblots, and personality inventories. Certainly there is more than a grain of truth to this common view: Measures of personality and intelligence are still the essential mainstays of psychological testing. However, psychometricians have developed many other kinds of tests for diverse and imaginative purposes that the early testing pioneers might never have an-

ticipated. This chapter provides a panoramic survey of psychological tests and their numerous applications. In Topic 2A, The Nature and Uses of Psychological Tests, we summarize the different types and varied applications of modern tests. In Topic 2B, The Testing Process, we emphasize that testing is a transaction between tester and examinee, not a sterile process of measurement.

From birth to old age, we encounter tests at almost every turning point in life. The baby's first test, conducted immediately after birth is the Apgar test, a quick, multivariate assessment of heart rate, respiration, muscle tone, reflex irritability, and color (Clarke-Stewart & Friedman, 1987). The total Apgar score (0 to 10) helps determine the need for any immediate medical attention. Later, a toddler who previously received a low Apgar score might be a candidate for developmental disability assessment. The preschool child may take school-readiness tests. Once a school career is begun, each student endures hundreds, perhaps thousands of academic tests before graduation. Not to mention possible tests for learning disability, giftedness, vocational interest, and college admission. After graduation, adults may face tests for job entry, driver's license, security clearance, personality function, marital compatibility, developmental disability, brain dysfunction—the list is nearly endless. Some persons even encounter one final indignity in the frailness of their later years: a test to determine their competency to manage financial affairs.

The idea of a test is thus a pervasive element of our culture, a feature we take for granted. However, the layperson's notion of a test does not necessarily coincide with the more restrictive view held by psychometricians. A **psychometrician** is a specialist in psychology or education who develops and evaluates psychological tests. Because of widespread misunderstandings about the nature of tests, it is fitting that we begin this topic with a fundamental question, one that defines the scope of the entire book: What is a test?

DEFINITION OF A TEST

A **test** is a standardized procedure for sampling behavior and describing it with categories or scores. In addition, most tests have norms or standards by which the results can be used to predict other, more important, behaviors. We elaborate these characteristics in the sections that follow, but first it is instructive to portray the scope of the definition. Included in this view are traditional tests such as personality questionnaires and intelligence tests, but the definition also subsumes diverse procedures which the reader might not recognize as tests. For example, all of the following could be tests according to the definition used in this book: a checklist for rating the social skills of a retarded youth; a

nontimed measure of mastery in adding pairs of three-digit numbers; microcomputer appraisals of reaction time; and even situational tests such as observing an individual working on a group task with two "helpers" who are obstructive and uncooperative.

In sum, tests are enormously varied in their formats and applications. Nonetheless, most tests possess these defining features:

- Standardized procedure
- Behavior sample
- Scores or categories
- Norms or standards
- Prediction of nontest behavior

In the sections that follow, we examine each of these characteristics in more detail. The portrait that we draw pertains especially to norm-referenced tests—tests that use a well-defined population of persons for their interpretive framework. However, the defining characteristics of a test differ slightly for the special case of criterion-referenced tests—tests that measure what a person can do rather than comparing results to the performance levels of others. For this reason, we provide a separate discussion of criterion-referenced tests.

Standardized procedure is an essential feature of any psychological test. A test is considered to be *standardized* if the procedures for administering it are uniform from one examiner and setting to another. Of course, standardization depends to some extent upon the competence of the examiner. Even the best test can be rendered useless by a careless, poorly trained, or ill-informed tester, as the reader will discover in Topic 2B, The Testing Process. However, most examiners are competent. Standardization therefore rests largely upon the directions for administration found in the instructional manual that typically accompanies a test.

The formulation of directions is an essential step in the standardization of a test. In order to guarantee uniform administration procedures, the test developer must provide comparable stimulus materials to all testers, specify with considerable precision the oral instructions for each item or subtest, and advise the examiner how to handle a wide range of queries from the examinee.

To illustrate these points, consider the number of different ways a test developer might approach the assessment of *digit span*—the maximum number of orally presented digits a subject can recall from memory. An unstandardized test of digit span might merely suggest that the examiner orally present increasingly long series of numbers until the subject fails. The number of digits in the longest series recalled would then be the subject's digit span. Most readers can discern that such a loosely defined test will lack uniformity from one examiner to another. If the tester is free to improvise any series of digits, what is to prevent him or her from presenting, with the familiar inflection of a television announcer, "1-800-325-3535"? Such a series would be far easier to recall than a more random set, such as, "7-2–8-1-9-4-6-3-7-4-2." The speed of presentation would also crucially affect the uniformity of a digit span test. For purposes of standardization, it is essential that every examiner present each series at a constant rate, for example, one digit per second. Finally, the examiner needs to know how to react to unexpected responses such as a subject asking "Could you repeat that again?" For obvious reasons, the usual advice is "No."

The test developer may even go so far as to recommend a desired demeanor in the examiner such as maintaining a neutral facial expression when recording a subject's response. These seemingly subtle influences can have a serious impact upon the uniformity of testing procedures. For example, an examiner who smirks when recording answers might cause the subject to become anxious and fail an easy task. We discuss the potential influence of the examiner upon test results in the next topic, The Testing Process.

A psychological test is also a limited sample of behavior. Neither the subject nor the examiner has sufficient time for truly comprehensive testing, even when the test is targeted to a well-defined and finite behavior domain. Thus, practical constraints dictate that a test is only a sample of behavior. Yet, the sample of behavior is of interest only insofar as

it permits the examiner to make inferences about the total domain of relevant behaviors. For example, the purpose of a vocabulary test is to determine the examinee's entire word stock by requesting definitions of a very small but carefully selected sample of words. Whether the subject can define the particular 35 words from a vocabulary subtest (e.g., on the WAIS-R) is of little direct consequence. But the indirect meaning of such results is of great import because it signals the examinee's general knowledge of vocabulary.

An interesting point—and one little understood by the lay public—is that the test items need not resemble the behaviors which the test is attempting to predict. The essential characteristic of a good test is that it permit the examiner to predict other behaviors—not that it mirror the to-be-predicted behaviors. If answering "true" to the question "I drink a lot of water" happens to help predict depression, then this seemingly unrelated question is a useful index of depression. Thus, the reader will note that successful prediction is an empirical question answered by appropriate research. While most tests do sample directly from the domain of behaviors they hope to predict, this is not a psychometric requirement.

A psychological test must also permit the derivation of scores or categories. Thorndike (1918) expressed the essential axiom of testing in his famous assertion that "Whatever exists at all exists in some amount." McCall (1939) went a step further, declaring "Anything that exists in amount can be measured." Testing strives to be a form of measurement akin to procedures in the physical sciences whereby numbers represent abstract dimensions such as weight or temperature. Every test furnishes one or more scores or provides evidence that a person belongs to one category and not another. In short, psychological testing sums up performance in numbers or classifications.

The implicit assumption of the psychometric viewpoint is that tests measure individual differences in traits or characteristics that exist in some vague sense of the word. In most cases, all people are assumed to possess the trait or characteristic being measured, albeit in different amounts. The purpose of the testing is to estimate the amount of the trait or quality possessed by an individual.

In this context, two cautions are worth mentioning. First, every test score will always reflect some degree of measurement error. The imprecision of testing is simply unavoidable: Tests must rely upon an external sample of behavior to estimate an unobservable and therefore inferred characteristic. Psychometricians often express this fundamental point with an equation:

$$X = T + e$$

where X is the observed score, T is the true score, and e is a positive or negative error component. The best that a test developer can do is make e very small. It can never be completely eliminated, nor can its exact impact be known in the individual case. We discuss the concept of measurement error in Topic 3B, Concepts of Reliability.

The second caution is that test consumers must be wary of reifying the characteristic being measured. Test results do not represent a *thing* with physical reality. Typically, they portray an abstraction which has been shown to be useful in predicting nontest behaviors. For example, in discussing a person's IQ, psychologists are referring to an abstraction that has no direct, material existence but which is, nonetheless, useful in predicting school achievement and other outcomes.

A psychological test must also possess norms or standards. An examinee's test score is usually interpreted by comparing it with the scores obtained by others on the same test. For this purpose, test developers typically provide **norms**—a summary of test results for a large and representative group of subjects (Petersen, Kolen, & Hoover, 1989). The norm group is referred to as the standardization sample.

The selection and testing of the **standardization sample** is crucial to the usefulness of a test. This group must be representative of the population for whom the test is intended or else it is not possible to determine an examinee's relative standing. In the extreme case where norms are not provided, the examiner can make no use of the test results at all. An exception to this point occurs in the case of criterion-referenced tests, discussed later.

Norms not only establish an average performance, but also serve to indicate the frequency with which different high and low scores are obtained. Thus, norms allow the tester to determine the degree to which a score deviates from expectations. Such information can be very important in predicting the nontest behavior of the examinee. Norms are of such overriding importance in test interpretation that we will consider them at length in a separate section later in this text.

Finally, tests are not ends in themselves. In general, the ultimate purpose of a test is to predict additional behaviors, other than those directly sampled by the test. Thus, the tester may have more interest in the nontest behaviors predicted by the test than in the test responses per se. Perhaps a concrete example will clarify this point. Suppose an examiner administers an inkblot test to a patient in a psychiatric hospital. Assume that the patient responds to one inkblot by describing it as "eyes peering out." Based on established norms, the examiner might then predict that the subject will be highly suspicious and a poor risk for individual psychotherapy. The purpose of the testing is to arrive at this and similar predictions—not to determine if the subject perceives eyes staring out from the blots.

The ability of a test to predict nontest behavior is determined by an extensive body of validational research, most of which is conducted after the test is released. But there are no guarantees in the world of psychometric research. It is not unusual for a test developer to publish a promising test, only to read years later that other researchers find it deficient. There is a lesson here for test consumers: The fact that a test exists and purports to measure a certain characteristic is no guarantee of truth in advertising. A test may have a fancy title, precise instructions, elaborate norms, attractive packaging, and preliminary findings—but if in the dispassionate study of independent researchers the test fails to predict appropriate nontest behaviors, then it is useless.

FURTHER DISTINCTIONS IN TESTING

The chief features of a test previously outlined apply especially to norm-referenced tests, which constitute the vast majority of tests in use. In a **norm-referenced test,** the performance of each examinee is interpreted in reference to a relevant standardization sample (Petersen, Kolen, & Hoover, 1989). However, these features are less relevant in the special case of criterion-referenced tests, since these instruments suspend the need for comparing the individual examinee with a reference group. In a **criterion-referenced test,** the objective is to determine where the examinee stands with respect to very tightly defined educational objectives (Berk, 1984). For example, one part of an arithmetic test for 10-year-olds might measure the accuracy level in adding pairs of two-digit numbers. In an untimed test of 20 such problems, accuracy should be nearly perfect. For this kind of test, it really does not matter how the individual examinee compares to others of the same age. What matters is whether the examinee meets an appropriate, specified criterion—for example, 95 percent accuracy. Because there is no comparison to the normative performance of others, this kind of measurement tool is aptly designated a criterion-referenced test. The important distinction here is that, unlike norm-referenced tests, criterion-referenced tests can be meaningfully interpreted without reference to norms. We discuss criterion-referenced tests in more detail in Topic 3A, Norms and Test Standardization.

Another important distinction is between testing and assessment, which are often considered equivalent. However, they do not mean exactly the same thing. Assessment is a more comprehensive term, referring to the entire process of compiling information about a person and using it to make inferences about characteristics and to predict behavior. **Assessment** can be defined as appraising or estimating the magnitude of one or more attributes in a person. The assessment of human characteristics involves observations, interviews, checklists, inventories, projectives, and other psychological tests. In sum, tests represent only one source of information used in the assessment process. In assessment, the examiner must compare and combine data from different sources. This is an inherently subjective process which requires the examiner to sort out conflicting information and make predictions based on a complex gestalt of data.

The term *assessment* was invented during World War II to describe a program to select men for secret service assignment in the Office of Strategic Services (OSS Assessment Staff, 1948). The OSS staff of psychologists and psychiatrists amassed a colossal amount of information on candidates during four grueling days of written tests, interviews, and personality tests. In addition, the assessment process included a variety of real-life situational tests based on the realization that there was a difference between know-how and can-do:

> . . . we made the candidates actually attempt the tasks with their muscles or spoken words, rather than merely indicate on paper how the tasks could be done. We were prompted to introduce realistic tests of ability by such findings as this: that men who earn a high score in Mechanical Comprehension, a paper-and-pencil test, may be below average when it comes to solving mechanical problems with their hands (OSS Assessment Staff, 1948).

The situational tests included group tasks of transporting equipment across a raging brook and scaling a 10-foot-high wall, as well as individual scrutiny of the ability to survive a realistic interrogation and to command two uncooperative subordinates in a construction task.

On the basis of the behavioral observations and test results, the OSS staff rated the candidates on dozens of specific traits in such broad categories as leadership, social relations, emotional stability, effective intelligence, and physical ability. These ratings served as the basis for selecting OSS personnel.

TYPES OF TESTS

Tests can be broadly grouped into two camps: group tests versus individual tests. **Group tests** are largely pencil-and-paper measures suitable to the testing of large groups of persons at the same time. **Individual**

tests are instruments which by their design and purpose must be administered one on one. An important advantage of individual tests is that the examiner can gauge the level of motivation of the subject and assess the relevance of other factors (e.g., impulsiveness or anxiety) upon the test results.

For convenience, we will sort tests into the eight categories depicted in Table 2.1. Each of the categories contains norm-referenced, criterion-referenced, individual, and group tests. The reader will note that any typology of tests is a purely arbitrary determination. For example, we could argue for yet another dichotomy: tests that seek to measure maximum performance (e.g., an intelligence test) versus tests that seek to gauge a typical response (e.g., a personality inventory).

In a narrow sense, there are hundreds—perhaps thousands—of different kinds of tests, each measuring a slightly different aspect of the individual. For example, even two tests of intelligence might be arguably different types of measures. One test might reveal the assumption that intelligence is a biological construct best measured through brain waves, whereas another might be rooted in the traditional view that intelligence is exhibited in the capacity to learn acculturated skills such as vocab-ulary. Lumping both measures under the category of *intelligence tests* is certainly an oversimplification, but nonetheless a useful starting point.

As the reader will recall from the first chapter, **intelligence tests** were originally designed to sample a broad assortment of skills in order to estimate the individual's general intellectual level. The Binet-Simon scales were successful, in part, because they incorporated heterogeneous tasks, including word definitions, memory for designs, comprehension questions, and spatial visualization tasks. The group intelligence tests that blossomed with such profusion during and after WWII also tested diverse abilities—witness the Army Alpha with its eight different sections measuring practical judgment, information, arithmetic, and reasoning, among other skills.

Modern intelligence tests also emulate this historically established pattern by sampling a wide variety of proficiencies deemed important in our culture. In general, the term *intelligence test* refers to a test that yields an overall summary score based on results from a heterogeneous sample of items. Of course, such a test might also provide a profile of subtest scores as well, but it is the overall score that generally attracts the most attention.

TABLE 2.1   The Main Types of Psychological Tests

Intelligence Tests: measure an individual's ability in relatively global areas such as verbal comprehension, perceptual organization, or reasoning and thereby help determine potential for scholastic work or certain occupations.

Aptitude Tests: measure the capability for a relatively specific task or type of skill; aptitude tests are, in effect, a narrow form of ability testing.

Achievement Tests: measure a person's degree of learning, success, or accomplishment in a subject or task.

Creativity Tests: assess novel, original thinking, and the capacity to find unusual or unexpected solutions especially for vaguely defined problems.

Personality Tests: measure the traits, qualities, or behaviors that determine a person's individuality; such tests include checklists, inventories, and projective techniques.

Interest Inventories: measure an individual's preference for certain activities or topics and thereby help determine occupational choice.

Behavioral Procedures: objectively describe and count the frequency of a behavior, identifying the antecedents and consequences of the behavior.

Neuropsychological Tests: measure cognitive, sensory, perceptual, and motor performance to determine the extent, locus, and behavioral consequences of brain damage.

An **aptitude test** measures one or more clearly defined and relatively homogeneous segments of ability. Such tests come in two varieties: single aptitude tests and multiple aptitude test batteries. A single aptitude test appraises, obviously, only one ability, whereas a multiple aptitude test battery provides a profile of scores for a number of aptitudes.

Aptitude tests are often used to predict success in an occupation, training course, or educational endeavor. For example, the Seashore Measures of Musical Talents (Seashore, 1938), a series of tests covering pitch, loudness, rhythm, time, timbre, and tonal memory, can be used to identify children with potential talent in music. Specialized aptitude tests also exist for the assessment of clerical skills, mechanical abilities, manual dexterity, and artistic ability. These tests are reviewed in Topic 8A, Aptitude Tests and Factor Analysis.

The most common use of aptitude tests is to determine college admissions. Most every college student is familiar with the SAT (Scholastic Assessment Test, previously called the Scholastic Aptitude Test) of the College Entrance Examination Board. This test contains a Verbal section stressing word knowledge and reading comprehension and a Mathematics section stressing algebra, geometry, and insightful reasoning. In effect, colleges that require certain minimum scores on the SAT for admission are using the test to predict academic success.

Achievement tests measure a person's degree of learning, success, or accomplishment in a subject matter. The implicit assumption of most achievement tests is that the schools have taught the subject matter directly. The purpose of the test is then to determine how much of the material the subject has absorbed or mastered. Achievement tests commonly have several subtests, such as reading, mathematics, language, science, and social studies. These tests are reviewed in Topic 8B, Group Tests of Achievement.

The distinction between aptitude and achievement tests is more a matter of use than content (Gregory, 1994a). In fact, any test can be an aptitude test to the extent that it helps predict future performance. Likewise any test can be an achieve-

ment test insofar as it reflects how much the subject has learned. In practice, then, the distinction between these two kinds of instruments is determined by their respective uses. On occasion, one instrument may serve both purposes, acting as an aptitude test to forecast future performance and an achievement test to monitor past learning.

Creativity tests assess a subject's ability to produce new ideas, insights, or artistic creations that are accepted as being of social, aesthetic, or scientific value. Thus, measures of **creativity** emphasize novelty and originality in the solution of fuzzy problems or the production of artistic works. A creative response to one problem is illustrated in Figure 2.1.

Tests of creativity have a checkered history. In the 1960s, they were touted as a useful alternative to intelligence tests and used widely in American school systems. Educators were especially

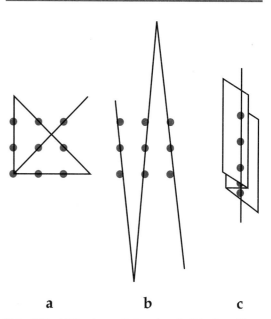

a   b   c

Note: Without lifting the pencil, draw through all the dots with as few straight lines as possible. The usual solution is shown in *a*. Creative solutions are depicted in *b* and *c*.

FIGURE 2.1   Solutions to the Nine-Dot Problem as Examples of Creativity

impressed that creativity tests required divergent thinking—putting forth a variety of answers to a complex or fuzzy problem—as opposed to convergent thinking—finding the single correct solution to a well-defined problem. For example, a creativity test might ask the examinee to imagine all the things that would happen if clouds had strings trailing from them down to the ground. Students who could come up with a large number of consequences were assumed to be more creative than their less-imaginative colleagues. However, some psychometricians are skeptical, concluding that creativity is just another label for applied intelligence (e.g., McNemar, 1964).

Personality tests measure the traits, qualities, or behaviors that determine a person's individual-ity; this information helps predict future behavior. These tests come in several different varieties, including checklists, inventories, and projective techniques such as sentence completions and inkblots (Table 2.2).

Interest inventories measure an individual's preference for certain activities or topics and thereby help determine occupational choice. These tests are based upon the explicit assumption that interest patterns determine and therefore also predict job satisfaction. For example, if the examinee has the same interests as successful and satisfied accountants, it is thought likely that he or she would enjoy the work of an accountant. The assumption that interest patterns predict job satisfaction is largely born out by empirical studies, as we will re-

---

TABLE 2.2   Examples of Personality Test Items

(a) An Adjective Checklist:

Check those words which describe you:

( ) relaxed	( ) assertive
( ) thoughtful	( ) curious
( ) cheerful	( ) even-tempered
( ) impatient	( ) skeptical
( ) morose	( ) impulsive
( ) optimistic	( ) anxious

(b) A True-False Inventory:

Circle true or false as each statement applies to you:

T   F   I like sports magazines.
T   F   Most people would lie to get a job.
T   F   I like big parties where there is lots of noisy fun.
T   F   Strange thoughts possess me for hours at a time.
T   F   I often regret the missed opportunities in my life.
T   F   Sometimes I feel anxious for no reason at all.
T   F   I like everyone I have met.
T   F   Falling asleep is seldom a problem for me.

(c) A Sentence Completion Projective Test:

Complete each sentence with the first thought that comes to you:

I feel bored when
What I need most is
I like people who
My mother was

view in Topic 12A, Assessment of Interests and Work Values.

Many kinds of **behavioral procedures** are available for assessing the antecedents and consequences of behavior, including checklists, rating scales, interviews, and structured observations. These methods share a common assumption that behavior is best understood in terms of clearly defined characteristics such as frequency, duration, antecedents, and consequences. Behavioral procedures tend to be highly pragmatic in that they are usually interwoven with treatment approaches.

Neuropsychological tests are used in the assessment of persons with known or suspected brain dysfunction. *Neuropsychology* is the study of brain-behavior relationships. Over the years, neuropsychologists have discovered that certain tests and procedures are highly sensitive to the effects of brain damage. Neuropsychologists use these specialized tests and procedures to make inferences about the locus, extent, and consequences of brain damage.

Although neuropsychological tests and procedures are helpful in arriving at a neurological diagnosis, their primary purpose is to evaluate the sensory, motor, cognitive, and behavioral strengths and weaknesses of the neurologically impaired patient.[1] The evaluation of strengths and weaknesses in these patients is crucial for documenting improvement, charting the extent of decline in degenerative diseases, and planning effective remediation for specific disabilities. A full neuropsychological assessment typically requires three to eight hours of one-on-one testing with an extensive battery of measures. Examiners must undergo comprehensive advanced training in order to make sense out of the resulting mass of test data. We review individual

---

1. Advanced radiological techniques such as Computerized Tomography (CT) scan, Magnetic Resonance Imaging (MRI), and Positron Emission Tomography (PET) scan now allow neurologists to make exceedingly accurate inferences about the presence, location, and causes of brain damage. However, this does not diminish the importance of neuropsychological testing in determining the *functional consequences* of brain damage in the life of the individual patient.

tests and the major test batteries in Topic 9B, Neuropsychological and Geriatric Assessment.

USES OF TESTING

By far the most common use of psychological tests is to make decisions about persons. For example, educational institutions frequently use tests to determine placement levels for students, and universities ascertain who should be admitted, in part, on the basis of test scores. State, federal, and local civil service systems also rely heavily upon tests for purposes of personnel selection.

Even the individual practitioner exploits tests, in the main, for decision making. Examples include the consulting psychologist who uses a personality test to determine that a police department hire one candidate and not another, and the neuropsychologist who employs tests to conclude that a client has suffered brain damage.

But simple decision making is not the only function of psychological testing. It is convenient to distinguish five uses of tests:

- Classification
- Diagnosis and treatment planning
- Self-knowledge
- Program evaluation
- Research

These applications frequently overlap and, on occasion, are difficult to distinguish one from another. For example, a test that helps determine a psychiatric diagnosis might also provide a form of self-knowledge. Let us examine these applications in more detail.

The term **classification** encompasses a variety of procedures that share a common purpose: assigning a person to one category rather than another. Of course, the assignment to categories is not an end in itself but the basis for differential treatment of some kind. Thus, classification can have important effects such as granting or restricting access to a specific college or determining whether a person is hired for a particular job. There are many variant forms of classification, each emphasizing a particular purpose in assigning persons to categories. We will distinguish placement, screening, certification, and selection.

Placement is the sorting of persons into different programs appropriate to their needs or skills. For example, universities often use a mathematics placement exam to determine whether students should enroll in calculus, algebra, or remedial courses.

Screening refers to quick and simple tests or procedures to identify persons who might have special characteristics or needs. Ordinarily, psychometricians acknowledge that screening tests will result in many misclassifications. Examiners are therefore advised to do follow-up testing with additional instruments before making important decisions on the basis of screening tests. For example, to identify children with highly exceptional talent in spatial thinking, a psychologist might administer a 10-minute paper-and-pencil test to every child in a school system. Students who scored in the top 10 percent might then be singled out for more comprehensive testing.

Certification and selection both have a pass/fail quality. Passing a certification exam confers privileges. Examples include the right to practice psychology or to drive a car. Thus, certification typically implies that a person has at least a minimum proficiency in some discipline or activity. Selection is similar to certification in that it confers privileges such as the opportunity to attend a university or to gain employment.

Another use of psychological tests is for diagnosis and treatment planning. **Diagnosis** consists of two intertwined tasks: determining the nature and source of a person's abnormal behavior, and classifying the behavior pattern within an accepted diagnostic system. Diagnosis is usually a precursor to remediation or treatment of personal distress or impaired performance.

Psychological tests often play an important role in diagnosis and treatment planning. For example, intelligence tests are absolutely essential in the diagnosis of mental retardation. Personality tests are helpful in diagnosing the nature and extent of emotional disturbance. In fact, some tests such as the MMPI were devised for the explicit purpose of increasing the efficiency of psychiatric diagnosis.

Diagnosis should be more than mere classification, more than the assignment of a label. A proper diagnosis conveys information—about strengths, weaknesses, etiology, and best choices for remediation/treatment. Knowing that a child has received a diagnosis of **learning disability** is largely useless. But knowing in addition that the same child is well below average in reading comprehension, is highly distractible, and needs help with basic phonics can provide an indispensable basis for treatment planning.

Psychological tests also can supply a potent source of self-knowledge. In some cases, the feedback a person receives from psychological tests can change a career path or otherwise alter a person's life course. Of course, not every instance of psychological testing provides self-knowledge. Perhaps in the majority of cases the client already knows what the test results divulge. A high-functioning college student is seldom surprised to find that his IQ is in the superior range. An architect is not perplexed to hear that she has excellent spatial reasoning skills. A student with meager reading capacity is usually not startled to receive a diagnosis of "learning disability."

Another use for psychological tests is the systematic evaluation of educational and social programs. We will have more to say about the evaluation of educational programs when we discuss achievement tests in a later chapter. We focus here upon the use of tests in the evaluation of social programs. Social programs are designed to provide services that improve social conditions and community life. For example, Project Head Start is a federally funded program which supports nationwide preschool teaching projects for underprivileged children (Cicerelli, 1969; McKey and others, 1985). Launched in 1965 as a precedent-setting attempt to provide child development programs to low-income families, Head Start has provided educational enrichment and health services to millions of at-risk preschool children.

But exactly what impact does the multi-billion-dollar Head Start program have on early childhood development? Congress wanted to know if the program improved scholastic performance and reduced school failure among the enrollees. But the centers vary by sponsoring agencies, staff characteristics, coverage, content, and objectives, so the effects of Head Start are not easy to ascertain. Psychological tests provide an objective basis for answering these questions that is far superior to anecdotal or impressionistic reporting. In general, Head Start children show immediate gains in IQ, school readiness, and academic achievement, but these gains dissipate in the ensuing years (Figure 2.2).

So far we have discussed the practical application of psychological tests to everyday problems such as job selection, diagnosis, or program evaluation. In each of these instances, testing serves an immediate, pragmatic purpose: helping the tester make decisions about persons or programs. But tests also play a major role in both the applied and theoretical branches of behavioral research. As an example of testing in applied research, consider the problem faced by neuropsychologists who wish to investigate the hypothesis that low-level lead absorption causes behavioral deficits in children. The only feasible way to explore this supposition is by testing normal and lead-burdened children with a battery of psychological tests. Needleman, Gunnoe, Leviton, Reed, Peresie, Maher, and Barrett (1979) used an array of traditional and innovative tests to conclude that low-level lead absorption causes decrements in IQ, impairments in reaction time, and escalations of undesirable classroom behaviors. Their conclusions inspired a tumultuous and bitter exchange of opinions that we will not review here (Needleman et al., 1990). However, the passions inspired by this study epitomize an instructive point: Academicians and public policymakers respect psychological tests. Why else would they engage in lengthy, acrimonious debates about the validity of testing-based research findings?

On occasion, tests serve a less-worldly role by helping scientists investigate theoretical matters that have no immediate or obvious practical applications. For example, to analyze perceptual field dependence, Witkin (1949) invented the tilting-room-tilting-chair tests (TRTC). The apparatus for these tests consists of a boxlike room, suspended on ball-bearing pivots so that it can be tilted by any amount to left or right. Inside the room is a chair for the subject which can also be tilted independent of the room. The subject's task is to bring his or her body to a position that is perceived as upright. Field dependent subjects align their bodies somewhat to the room rather than the perceived force of gravity. Field independent subjects are less affected by the misaligned room, more attuned to their internal perceptual signals; that is, their perceptual judgments are relatively independent of the distorting visual information. The TRTC inspired a lifetime of research on personality development, but was seldom applied to any practical problems of testing.

WHO MAY OBTAIN TESTS

Test developers, publishers, and psychological examiners generally release psychological tests only to qualified persons who have a legitimate need to study or use these materials. There are three reasons why access to psychological tests is restricted:

1. In the hands of unqualified persons, psychological tests can cause harm.
2. The selection process is rendered invalid for persons who preview test questions.
3. Leakage of item content to the general public completely destroys the efficacy of a test.

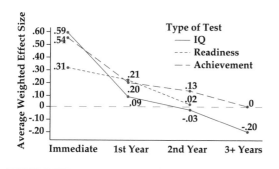

FIGURE 2.2   **Longitudinal Test Results from the Head Start Project**
Source: From McKey, R. H. and others (1985). *The impact of Head Start on children, families and communities.* Washington, DC: U.S. Government Printing Office. In the public domain.

We examine each of these points in more detail.

An unqualified examiner may err in the selection, administration, scoring, or interpretation of psychological tests, which could cause harm to the subject. The possibilities for error and harm are almost limitless, so we will provide only a typical example here. A common mistake among inexperienced examiners is the failure to give credit to an older subject for the easier, unadministered items on a subscale. For example, on a hypothetical 20-item subscale of intelligence, the test manual might specify that an older subject should encounter only items 11 through 20, on the assumption that the easier items (1 through 10) would surely be answered correctly. Nonetheless, the test instructions might specify that the examinee should receive point credit for items 1 through 10. Failure to tally these points would cause the score to be drastically low, with negative consequences for the subject.

Another reason for limiting the availability of tests is that illicit access to their content undermines the effectiveness of selection processes. Put simply, examinees who have prior access to a selection test can learn to produce the desired test results. Finally, it should be obvious that leakage of test items to the public renders a test completely useless. If individuals can memorize the answers to test questions, their performance on the test will be artificially inflated. To give an extreme example, a blind person could pass a color vision test by memorizing the correct responses.

SOURCES OF INFORMATION ON TESTS

A textbook on psychological testing cannot begin to survey all the tests of potential interest to readers. There are simply too many tests! Furthermore, dozens of new and useful tests are developed each year. The serious student of psychological tests will need guidelines and strategies for learning about tests, not a static list of recommendations.

Information about psychological tests is available from four sources: reference books, publisher's catalogues, journals, and test manuals. We will cite a few prominent examples from each category, but we hope the reader will assimilate a strategy for knowledge acquisition rather than relying exclusively on these specific citations.

The best single reference source for information on mainstream tests is the *Mental Measurements Yearbook* (*MMY*) published by the Buros Institute for Mental Measurement at the University of Nebraska. A new edition of the *MMY* is issued periodically (Buros, 1978; Conoley & Impara, 1995; Conoley & Kramer, 1989, 1992; Mitchell, 1985). The *MMY* includes critical reviews of tests and a listing of important references.

The Test Corporation of America publishes several excellent reference books and critiques of testing. *Tests*, edited by Sweetland and Keyser (1987), is a comprehensive listing of instruments for assessments in psychology, education, and business. *Test Critiques* (Volumes I–VI), edited by Keyser and Sweetland (1984–1988), provides in-depth evaluations of psychological, educational, and business tests. In addition, the same publisher offers a series of books on testing children, adolescents, adults, and older persons (Weaver, 1984; Harrington, 1986; Swiercinsky, 1985). Another excellent source of short, straightforward clinical measures is *Measures for Clinical Practice: A Sourcebook,* by Corcoran and Fischer (1994). In this compendium, instruments for adults, children, couples, and families are cross-indexed by problem area.

Another way to learn about tests is to request catalogs from the major test publishers. Appendix B (Test Publisher Addresses) lists the names and addresses of prominent American publishers and distributors of tests. Appendix C (Major Tests and Their Publishers) provides a categorized list of notable tests and their publishers. The latest *MMY* contains a more comprehensive directory of publishers and tests.

Many psychological journals publish articles on the reliability and validity of better-known tests. The best way to locate studies on a specific test is through *Psychological Abstracts,* a prominent monthly digest of major journals in psychology and related fields. Larger libraries will usually carry PsychLit on CD-ROM. This is the computerized version of *Psychological Abstracts.* If the reader is merely interested in perusing recent studies of psychological tests, it is worth consulting the latest issues of the following journals:

Assessment
Advances in Personality Assessment
The Journal of Psychoeducational
   Assessment
Psychology in the Schools
The Journal of School Psychology

Educational and Psychological
   Measurement
Psychological Assessment
The Journal of Clinical Neuropsychology
The Journal of Clinical Psychology
The Journal of Personality Assessment

Finally, an important and often overlooked source of information about any specific test is its manual. A good manual contains essential information about norms, standardization, administration, reliability, and validity.

SUMMARY

1. A test can be defined as a standardized procedure for sampling behavior and describing it with categories or scores. In addition, most tests have norms or standards by which the results can be used to predict other, more important, behaviors.

2. Tests always constitute a sample of behavior, never the totality of that which the examiner seeks to measure. For this reason, test results always incorporate some degree of measurement error.

3. In a norm-referenced test, the examinee's test score is interpreted in relation to scores obtained by others on the same test. In a criterion-referenced test, the emphasis is on what the examinee can do with respect to very tightly defined educational criteria.

4. Assessment is the process of compiling information about a person and using it to make inferences about characteristics and to predict behavior. Assessment incorporates testing but is more comprehensive and may include observations, interviews, and other sources of information.

5. Group tests are pencil-and-paper measures suitable to testing large groups of persons at one time. Individual tests are designed for one-on-one administration; the examiner can thereby observe motivation and other characteristics of the examinee.

6. An arbitrary but useful classification of psychological tests is as follows: intelligence, aptitude, achievement, creativity, personality, interest, behavioral, and neuropsychological. The characteristics of these tests are outlined in Table 2.1.

7. Five uses of tests may be distinguished: classification, diagnosis and treatment planning, self-knowledge, program evaluation, and research.

8. Classification can be further broken down into: placement, the sorting of persons into appropriate programs; screening, quick identification of persons with special characteristics or needs; and certification (e.g., for a driver's license) and selection (e.g., for college).

9. Access to psychological tests is strictly controlled so that only persons with appropriate training may gain access to them. Many test publishers divide tests into three levels of complexity that require increasing degrees of expertise for their application.

10. Sources of information about tests include the *Mental Measurements Yearbook* series and the *Test Critiques* volumes. Some journals such as *Assessment* and *The Journal of Psychoeducational Assessment* also feature information about psychological tests.

KEY TERMS AND CONCEPTS

psychometrician   p. 30

test   p. 30

standardized procedure   p. 30

norms   p. 32

standardization sample   p. 32

norm-referenced test   p. 33

criterion-referenced test   p. 33

assessment   p. 33

group tests   p. 33

individual tests   p. 33–34

intelligence tests   p. 34

aptitude tests   p. 35

achievement tests   p. 35

creativity tests   p. 35

creativity   p. 35

personality tests   p. 36

interest inventories   p. 36

behavioral procedures   p. 37

neuropsychological tests   p. 37

classification   p. 37

placement   p. 38

screening   p. 38

certification   p. 38

diagnosis   p. 38

learning disability   p. 38

T O P I C **2B** The Testing Process

Psychological testing is a dynamic process influenced by many factors. Although examiners strive to insure that test results accurately reflect the traits or capacities being assessed, many extraneous factors can sway the outcome of psychological testing. In this section, we review the potentially crucial impact of several sources of influence: the manner of administration, the characteristics of the tester, the context of the testing, the motivation and experience of the examinee, and the method of scoring.

The sensitivity of the testing process to extraneous influences is obvious in those rare, egregious spectacles of nonstandard testing that are reported from time to time (Case Exhibit 2.1). However, invalid test results do not originate only from obvious sources such as blatantly nonstandard administration, hostile tester, noisy testing room, scared examinee, or careless scoring. In addition, there are numerous, subtle ways in which method, examiner, context, motivation, or scoring can alter test results. We provide a comprehensive survey of these extraneous influences in the remainder of this topic.

STANDARDIZED PROCEDURES IN TEST ADMINISTRATION

The interpretation of a psychological test is most reliable when the measurements are obtained under the standardized conditions outlined in the publisher's test manual. Nonstandard testing procedures can alter the meaning of the test results, rendering them invalid and therefore misleading. Standardized procedures are so important that they are listed as an essential criterion for valid testing in the *Standards for Educational and Psychological Testing* (1985, 1999), a reference manual published jointly by the American Psychological Association and other groups:

> In typical applications, test administrators should follow carefully the standardized procedures for administration and scoring specified by the test publisher. Specifications regarding instructions to test takers, time limits, the form of item presentation or response, and test materials or equipment should be strictly observed. Exceptions should be made only on the basis of carefully considered professional judgment, primarily in clinical applications (AERA, APA, NCME, 1985).

Suppose the instructions to the vocabulary section of a children's intelligence test specify that the examiner should ask "What does *sofa* mean, what is a sofa?" If a subject were to reply "I've never heard that word," an inexperienced tester might be tempted to respond, "You know, a couch—what is a couch?" This may strike the reader as a harmless form of fair play, a simple rephrasing of the original question. Yet, by straying from standardized

CASE EXHIBIT	THE IMPACT OF NONSTANDARD TESTING
2.1	

A psychology graduate student with unkempt, frizzy hair and full beard approaches a six-year-old girl in the waiting room and requests that she follow him. The graduate student speaks brusquely with a Brooklynese accent that is unfamiliar to the small girl. She is visibly frightened and remains seated until her mother pushes her forward with the not too comforting admonition to "Hurry now, or your dad's gonna be real angry." It is 8:30 in the evening and the young girl has just completed an extensive battery of medical tests. Just an hour before, a nurse stuck a large needle in the girl's right arm and withdrew a syringe of blood. Dutifully but with hesitation, the young girl follows the examiner into a dimly lit room. The constant roar of nearby freeway traffic makes it difficult for her to hear the tester's instructions. The examiner is tired—as part of a massive epidemiological research project he has been testing children since 7:30 that morning. Nonetheless, he administers the Wechsler Intelligence Scale for Children (WISC) at a torrid pace, completing it in 25 minutes. Later that night, he scores the test in his motel room. He neglects to give the girl credit for several simple items and also makes a clerical error in adding the standard scores together. The young girl is reported to have an IQ of 69, possibly indicative of mild mental retardation. Fortunately, on the following day the testing supervisor spots the scoring errors and questions the graduate student about the conditions of testing. Recognizing that the results are not valid, the supervisor readministers the test a month later under favorable conditions; the young girl scores much higher, in the low average range. Comparing the first and second test protocols, the graduate examiner learns a valuable lesson: Valid testing is more than a simple matter of posing questions, recording responses, and nonchalantly adding scores.

procedures, the examiner has really given a different test. The point in asking for a definition of *sofa* (and not *couch*) is precisely that *sofa* is harder to define and therefore a better index of high-level vocabulary skills.

Even though standardized testing procedures are normally essential, there are instances in which flexibility in procedures is desirable or even necessary. As suggested in the APA Standards, such deviations should be reasoned and deliberate. An analogy to the spirit of the law versus the letter of the law is relevant here. An overly zealous examiner might capture the letter of the law, so to speak, by adhering literally and strictly to testing procedures outlined in the publisher's manual. But is this really what most test publishers intend? Is it even how the test was actually administered to the normative sample? Most likely publishers would prefer that examiners capture the spirit of the law even if, on occasion, it is necessary to adjust testing procedures slightly.

Consider the following situation which arose when a psychologist administered a standardized intelligence test to an anxious and overly concrete college student. When asked "How much is four dollars and five dollars?" the student replied, "Four dollars is four dollars and five dollars is five dollars." A literal interpretation of the test manual would require that the examiner record zero credit and proceed to the next item. However, the question was intended to test arithmetical skills, not concreteness of thinking. Thus, the examiner asked the question again with a slight change in emphasis: "How much is four dollars *and* five dollars?" The subject guffawed loudly and answered immediately, "Nine dollars—I didn't realize it was an arithmetic question."

The need to adjust standardized procedures for testing is especially apparent when examining persons with certain kinds of disabilities. A subject with a speech impediment might be allowed to write down the answers to orally presented questions or to use gesture and pantomime in response to some items. For example, a test question might ask "What shape is a ball?" The question is designed to probe the subject's knowledge of common shapes, not to examine whether the examinee can verbalize "round." The written response *round* and the gestured response (a circular motion of the index finger) are equally correct, too.

Minor adjustments in procedures which heed the spirit in which a test was developed occur on a regular basis and are no cause for alarm. These minor adjustments do not invalidate the established norms—on the contrary, the appropriate adaptation of procedures is necessary so that the norms remain valid. After all, the testers who collected data from the standardization sample did not act like heartless robots when posing questions to subjects. Examiners who wish to obtain valid results must likewise exercise a reasoned flexibility in testing procedures.

However, considerable clinical experience is needed to determine whether an adjustment in procedure is minor or so substantial that existing norms no longer apply. This is why psychological examiners normally receive extensive supervised experience before they are allowed to administer and interpret individual tests of ability or personality.

In certain cases an examiner will knowingly depart from standard procedures to a substantial degree; this practice precludes the use of available test norms. In these instances, the test is used to help formulate clinical judgments rather than to determine a quantitative index. For example, when examining aphasic patients it may be desirable to ignore time limits entirely and accept roundabout answers (Eisenson, 1954). The examiner might not even calculate a score. In these rare cases, the test becomes, in effect, an adjunct to the clinical interview. Of course, when the examiner does not adhere to standardized procedures, this should be stated explicitly in the written report.

DESIRABLE PROCEDURES OF TEST ADMINISTRATION

A small treatise could be written on desirable procedures of test administration, but we will have to settle for a brief listing of the most essential points. For more details, the interested reader can consult Sattler (1988) on the individual testing of children and Clemans (1971) on group testing. We discuss individual testing first, then briefly list some important points about desirable procedures in group testing.

An essential component of individual testing is that examiners must be intimately familiar with the materials and directions before administration begins. Largely this involves extensive rehearsal and anticipation of unusual circumstances and the appropriate response. A well-prepared examiner has memorized key elements of verbal instructions and is ready to handle the unexpected.

The uninitiated student of assessment often assumes that examination procedures are so simple and straightforward that a quick once-through reading of the manual will suffice as preparation for testing. Although some individual tests are exceedingly rudimentary and uncomplicated, many of them have complexities of administration that, unheeded, can cause the examinee to fail items unnecessarily. For example, Choi and Proctor (1994) found that 25 of 27 graduate students made serious errors in the administration of the Stanford-Binet: Fourth Edition, even though the sessions were videotaped and the students knew their testing skills were being evaluated. Appropriate attention to the details of administration is essential for valid results.

The necessity for intimate familiarity with testing procedures is well illustrated by the Block Design subtest of the WAIS-III (Wechsler, 1997). The materials for the subtest include nine blocks (cubes) colored red on two sides, white on two sides, and red/white on two sides. The examinee's task is to use the blocks to construct patterns depicted on cards. For the initial designs, four blocks are needed, while for more difficult designs, all nine blocks are provided (Figure 2.3).

Bright examinees have no difficulty comprehending this task and the exact instructions do not influence their performance appreciably. However, persons whose intelligence is average or below average need the elaborate demonstrations and corrections that are specified in the WAIS-III Manual (Wechsler, 1997). In particular, the examiner demonstrates the first two designs and responds to the examinee's success or failure on these according to a complex flow of reaction and counterreaction, as outlined in *three pages* of instructions. Woe to the tester who has not rehearsed this subtest and anticipated the proper response to examinees who falter on the first two designs.

Sensitivity to Disabilities

Another important ingredient of valid test administration is sensitivity to disabilities in the examinee. Impairments in hearing, vision, speech, or motor

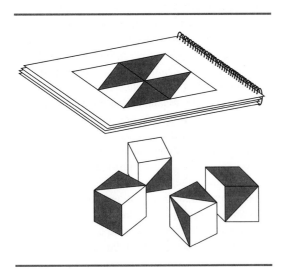

FIGURE 2.3 **Materials Similar to WAIS-III Block Design Subtest**

control may seriously distort test results. If the examiner does not recognize the physical disability responsible for the poor test performance, a subject may be branded as intellectually or emotionally impaired when, in fact, the essential problem is a sensory or motor disability.

Vernon and Brown (1964) reported the tragic case of a young girl who was relegated to a hospital for the mentally retarded as a consequence of the tester's insensitivity to physical disability. The examiner failed to notice that the child was deaf and concluded that her Stanford-Binet IQ of 29 was valid. She remained in the hospital for five years, but was released after she scored an IQ of 113 on a performance-based intelligence test! After dismissal from the hospital she entered a school for the deaf and made good progress.

Persons with disabilities may require specialized tests for valid assessment. The reader will encounter a lengthy discussion of available tests for exceptional examinees in Topic 7A (Testing Special Populations). In this section, we concentrate on the vexing issues raised when standardized tests for normal populations are used with mildly or moderately disabled subjects. We include separate discussions of the testing process for examinees with a hearing, vision, speech, or motor control problem. However, the reader needs to know that many exceptional examinees have multiple disabilities (Tweedie & Shroyer, 1982).

Valid testing with a hearing-impaired subject requires first of all that the examiner detect the existence of the disability! This is often more difficult than it seems. Many persons with mild hearing loss learn to compensate for this disability by pretending to understand what others say and waiting for further conversational cues to help clarify faintly perceived words or phrases. As a result, other persons—including psychologists—may not perceive that a mildly hearing-impaired individual has any disability at all.

Failure to notice a hearing loss is particularly a problem with young examinees, who are usually poor informants about their disability. Young children are also prone to fluctuating hearing losses due to the periodic accumulation of fluid in the middle ear during intervals of mild illness (Vernon & Alles, 1986). A child with a fluctuating hearing loss may have normal hearing in the morning, but perceive conversational speech as a whisper just a few hours later.

Indications of possible hearing difficulty include lack of normal response to sound, inattentiveness, difficulty in following oral instructions, intent observation of the speaker's lips, and poor articulation (Sattler, 1988). In all cases where hearing impairment is suspected, referral for an audiological examination is crucial. If a serious hearing problem is confirmed, then the examiner should consider using one of the specialized tests discussed in Topic 7A, Testing Special Populations. In persons with a mild hearing loss, it is essential for the examiner to face the subject squarely, speak loudly, and repeat instructions slowly. It is also important to find a quiet room for testing. Ideally, a testing room will have curtains and textured wall surfaces to minimize the distracting effects of background noises.

In contrast to the hearing-impaired, subjects with visual disabilities generally attend well to verbally presented test materials. The visually impaired examinee introduces a different kind of challenge to the examiner: detecting that a visual impairment exists, and then insuring that the subject can see the test materials well.

Detecting visual impairment is a straightforward matter with adult subjects—in most cases, a mature examinee will freely volunteer information about visual impairment, especially if asked. However, children are poor informants about their visual capacities, so testers need to know the signs and symptoms of possible visual impairment in a young examinee. Common sense is a good starting point: Children who squint, blink excessively, or lose their place when reading may have a vision problem. Holding books or testing materials up close is another suspicious sign. Blurred or double vision may signify visual problems, as may headaches or nausea after reading. In general, it is so common for children to require corrective lenses that examiners should be on the lookout for a vision problem in any young subject who does not wear glasses and has not had a recent vision exam.

Depending upon the degree of visual impairment, examiners need to make corresponding adjustments in testing. If the child's vision is of no practical use, special instruments with appropriate norms must be used. For example, the Hays-Binet and Perkins-Binet are available for testing blind children. These tests are discussed in Topic 7A (Testing Special Populations). For obvious reasons, only the verbal portions of tests should be administered to sighted children with an uncorrected visual problem.

Speech impairments present another problem for diagnosticians. The verbal responses of speech-impaired subjects are difficult to decipher. Owing to the failed comprehension of the examiner, subjects may receive less credit than is due. Sattler (1988) relates the lamentable case of Daniel Hoffman, a speech-impaired youngster who spent his entire youth in classes for the mentally retarded because his Stanford-Binet IQ was 74. In actuality, his intelligence was within the normal range, as revealed by other performance-based tests. In another tragic miscarriage of assessment, a patient in England was mistakenly confined to a ward for the severely retarded because cerebral palsy rendered his speech incomprehensible. The patient was wheelchair-bound and had almost no motor control, so his performance on nonverbal tests was also grossly impaired. The staff assumed he was severely retarded, so the patient remained on the back ward for decades. However, he befriended a fellow resident who could comprehend the patient's gutteral rendition of the alphabet. The friend was severely retarded but could nonetheless recognize keys on a typewriter. With laborious letter-by-letter effort, the patient with incapacitating cerebral palsy wrote and published an autobiography, using his retarded friend as a conduit to the real world.

Even if their disability is mild, persons with cerebral palsy or other motor impairments may be penalized by timed performance tests. When testing a person with a mild motor disability, examiners may wish to omit timed performance subtests, or to discount these results if they are consistently lower than scores from untimed subtests. If a subject has an obvious motor disability—such as a difficulty in manipulating the pieces of a puzzle—then standard instruments administered in the normal manner are largely inappropriate. A number of alternative instruments have been developed expressly for examinees with cerebral palsy and other motor impairments, and standard tests have been cleverly adapted and renormed (Topic 7A, Testing Special Populations).

Desirable Procedures of Group Testing

Psychologists and educators commonly assume that almost any adult can accurately administer group tests, so long as he or she has the requisite manual. Administering a group test would appear to be a simple and straightforward procedure of passing out forms and pencils; reading instructions; keeping time; and collecting the materials.

In reality, conducting a group test requires as much finesse as administering an individual test, a point recognized years ago by Traxler (1951):

> It is doubtful if any educational institution would trust the administration and scoring of the individual Stanford-Binet Scale to anyone other than a trained psychometrician, but there is a rather general impression among school people that almost anyone can administer and score a group test if only he has a manual at hand. As a matter of fact, however, the administration of a group test to a class of pupils in one sense is a far more exacting procedure than the giving of an individual test to one pupil. The routine is more rigid and the penalty for error is multiplied by the number of individuals in the group. In the administration of an individual test a certain amount of leeway may be allowed in order to create a situation favorable for the eliciting of responses from that particular individual, but when testing a group, complete fidelity to all details of the prescribed procedure is imperative if the examiner is to avoid wasting the time of many individuals and if the results are to have the same meaning for all.

There are numerous ways in which careless administration and scoring can impair group test results, causing bias for the entire group or affecting only certain individuals. We outline only the more important inadequacies and errors in the following paragraphs, referring the reader to Traxler (1951) and Clemans (1971) for a more complete discussion.

Undoubtedly the greatest single source of error in group test administration is incorrect timing of tests that require a time limit. Examiners must allot sufficient time for the entire testing process: setup, reading instructions out loud, and the actual test taking by examinees. Allotting sufficient time requires foresightful scheduling. For example, in many school settings, children must proceed to the next class at a designated time, regardless of ongoing activities. Inexperienced examiners might be tempted to cut short the designated time limit for a test so that the school schedule can be maintained. Of course, reduced time on a test renders the norms completely invalid and likely lowers the score for most subjects in the group.

Allowing too much time for a test can be an equally egregious error. For example, consider the impact of receiving extra time on the Miller Analogies Test (MAT), a high-level reasoning test once required by many universities for graduate school application. Since the MAT is a speeded test that requires quick analogical thinking, extra time would allow most examinees to solve several extra problems. This kind of testing error would likely lower the validity of the MAT results as a predictor of graduate school performance.

A second source of error in group test administration is lack of clarity in the directions to the examinees. Examiners must read the instructions slowly in a clear, loud voice that commands the attention of the subjects. Instructions must not be paraphrased. Where allowed by the manual, examiners must stop and clarify points with individual examinees who are confused.

Variations in the physical conditions under which tests are given is a third source of potential error in group test administration. Examiners must insure that the testing room is well illuminated and, if needed, heated or air-conditioned to control extreme variations in temperature and humidity. Clemans (1971) has noted that test authors seldom go into detailed specifications concerning illumination, temperature, and humidity, since examiner and subjects, with few exceptions, will have to put up with the conditions that exist. Nonetheless, it is obvious that examinees cannot perform optimally if tested in a dimly lit room that is too cold or oppressively hot and humid. Foresightful test administrators should do their examinees a favor by scheduling important group tests in a pleasant and well-illuminated environment.

The quality of the writing surface can be crucially important for valid group testing, especially for young subjects. Traxler's (1951) point that schools vary widely in their facilities for the administration of group tests is valid even today:

> In the matter of writing space alone, some schools use large, comfortable tables, others use desks, others armchairs, and still others give their tests in the auditorium with each pupil writing on a portable beaverboard "desk," or even on his lap. It is not reasonable to expect fully comparable results under such varying conditions.

The importance of the writing surface is magnified by the current tendency to use separate answer sheets. Subjects need a wider desk space when employing separate answer sheets than otherwise. Although few test publishers do so, it would be wise to specify in test manuals the permissible variations in writing surfaces that still allow for comparable test results.

Noise is another factor that must be controlled in group testing. It has been known for some time that noise causes a decrease in performance, especially for tasks of high complexity (e.g., Boggs & Simon, 1968). Surprisingly, there is little research on the effects of noise on psychological tests. However, it seems almost certain that loud noise, especially if intermittent and unpredictable, will cause test scores to decline substantially. Elementary schoolchildren should not be expected to perform well while a construction worker jackhammers a cement wall in the next room. In fairness to the examinees, there are times when the test administrator should reschedule the test.

A fourth source of error in the administration of a group test is failure to explain when and if examinees should guess. Perhaps more frequently than any other question, examiners are asked "Is there a penalty if I guess wrong?" In most instances, test developers anticipate this issue and provide explicit guidance to subjects as to the advantages and/or

pitfalls of guessing. Examiners should not give supplementary advice on guessing—this would constitute a serious deviation from standardized procedure.

Most test developers incorporate a **correction for guessing** based on established principles of probability. Consider a multiple choice test that has four alternatives per item. On those items that the subject makes a wild, uneducated guess, the odds on being correct are 1 out of 4, while the odds on being wrong are 3 out of 4. Thus, for every three wrong guesses, there will be one correct guess that reflects luck rather than knowledge. Suppose a young girl answers correctly on 35 questions from a 50-item test but answers erroneously on 9 questions. In all she has answered 44 questions, leaving 6 blank. The fact that she selected the wrong alternative on 9 questions suggests that she also gained 3 correct answers due to luck rather than knowledge. Remember, on wild guesses we expect there to be, on average, 3 wrong answers for every correct answer, so for 9 wrong guesses we would expect 3 correct guesses on other questions. The subject's corrected score—the one actually reported and compared to existing norms—would then be 32, that is, 35 minus 3. In other words, she probably knew 32 answers but by guessing on 12 others she boosted her score another 3 points.

The scoring correction outlined in the preceding paragraph pertains only to wild, uneducated guesses. The effect of such a correction is to eliminate the advantage otherwise bestowed on unabashed risk takers. However, not all guesses are wild and uneducated. In some instances, an examinee can eliminate one or two of the alternatives, thereby increasing the odds of a correct guess among the remaining choices. In this situation, it may be wise for the examinee to guess.

Whether an educated guess is really to the advantage of the examinee depends partly on the diabolical skill of the item writer. Traxler (1951) notes that:

> In effect, the item writer attempts to make each wrong response so plausible that every examinee who does not possess the desired skill or ability will select a wrong response. In other words, the

item writer's aim is to make all or nearly all considered guesses wrong guesses.

A skilled item writer can fashion questions so that the correct alternative is completely counterintuitive and the wrong alternatives are persuasively appealing. For these items an educated guess is almost always wrong.

Nonetheless, many test developers now advise subjects to make educated guesses, but warn against wild guesses. For example, a recent edition of the test preparation manual *Taking the SAT* advises:

> Because of the way the test is scored, haphazard or random guessing for questions you know nothing about is unlikely to change your score. When you know that one or more choices can be eliminated, guessing from among the remaining choices should be to your advantage.

Whether or not a group test uses a scoring correction, the important point to emphasize in this context is that the administrator should follow standardized procedure and never offer supplementary advice about guessing. In group testing, deviations from the instructions manual are simply unacceptable.

INFLUENCE OF THE EXAMINER

The Importance of Rapport

Test publishers urge examiners to establish **rapport**—a comfortable, warm atmosphere which serves to motivate examinees and elicit cooperation. Initiating a cordial testing milieu is a crucial aspect of valid testing. A tester who fails to establish rapport may cause a subject to react with anxiety, passive-aggressive noncooperation, or open hostility. Failure to establish rapport distorts test findings: Ability is underestimated and personality is misjudged.

Rapport is especially important in individual testing and particularly so when evaluating children. Wechsler (1974) has noted that establishing rapport places great demands on the clinical skills of the tester:

He must put the child at ease, keep him interested in the tasks at hand, and encourage him to do his best. There is no magic formula for "reaching" a child; approaches that succeed with some children may antagonize others. With experience, the examiner will develop a perceptiveness enabling him to establish sympathetic relations with children and to adapt to the specific needs of each one. The general suggestions below are offered to aid the examiner in this endeavor.

To put the child at ease in his surroundings, the examiner might engage him in some informal conversation before getting down to the more serious business of giving the test. Talking to him about his hobbies or interests is often a good way of breaking the ice, although it may be better to encourage a shy child to talk about something concrete in the environment—a picture on the wall, an animal in his classroom, or a book or toy (not a test material) in the examining room. In general, this introductory period need not take more than 5 to 10 minutes, although the testing should not start until the child seems relaxed enough to give his maximum effort.

A study by Gregory, Lehman, and Mohan (1976) illustrates the importance of establishing rapport when testing children. These researchers sought to determine the effects of low-level lead exposure on IQ by administering the WISC to 193 children living near a lead smelter. Children were assigned to five different graduate-student testers on a quasi-random, first-come, first-served rotational basis. The groups of children tested by each of the five psychometricians did not differ in average age, lead exposure, or social class. Moreover, the sample sizes were substantial, ranging from 30 to 45. Hence, the average tested IQs of the five groups should have been highly similar.

However, the differences between tested IQs of the five groups were distressingly large, with average scores varying by as much as 14 points. Ranked from low to high, the average scores for the five groups were 90, 94, 95, 96, and 104. The tester whose subjects tested at an average IQ of 90 was very formal, precise, cold, and hurried. In fact, he tested the most subjects by far (45, compared to 37 for the next-most prolific tester) and was usually finished with a child much sooner. At the other extreme was the tester whose subjects obtained an average IQ of 104. He went beyond good rapport to offer support and encouragement that bordered on leading the subjects to the correct answer. For example, on Block Design he urged one child to "Come on, get the blocks in the corners and go forward from there."

Testers, then, may differ in their abilities to establish rapport. Cold testers will likely obtain less cooperation from their subjects resulting in reduced performance on ability tests or distorted, defensive results on personality tests. Overly solicitous testers may err in the opposite direction, giving subtle (and occasionally blatant) cues to correct answers. Both extremes should be avoided.

Examiner Sex, Experience, and Race

A wide body of research has sought to determine if certain characteristics of the examiner cause examinee scores to be raised or lowered on ability tests. For example, does it matter if the examiner is male or female? Experienced or novice? Same or different race from the examinee? We will contain the urge to review these studies—with a few exceptions—for one simple reason: The results are contradictory and therefore inconclusive. Most studies find that sex, experience, and race of the examiner make little, if any, difference. Furthermore, the few studies that report a large effect in one direction (e.g., female examiners elicit higher IQ scores) are contradicted by other studies showing the opposite trend. The interested reader can consult Sattler (1988) for a discussion and extensive listing of references.

Yet, it would be unwise to conclude that sex, experience, or race of the examiner never affect test scores. In isolated instances, a particular examiner characteristic might very well have a large effect on examinee test scores. For example, Terrell, Terrell, and Taylor (1981) ingeniously demonstrated that the race of the examiner interacts potently with the trust level of African-American examinees in IQ testing. These researchers identified African-American college students with high

and low levels of mistrust of whites; half of each group was then administered the WAIS by a white examiner, the other half by an African-American examiner. The high-mistrust group with an African-American examiner scored significantly higher than the high-mistrust group with a white examiner (average IQs of 96 versus 86, respectively). In addition, the low-mistrust group with a white examiner scored slightly higher than the low-mistrust group with an African-American examiner (average IQs of 97 versus 92, respectively). In sum, the authors concluded that mistrustful African Americans do poorly when tested by white examiners. Data bearing on this type of racial effect are meager, and there is certainly room for additional research.

BACKGROUND AND MOTIVATION OF THE EXAMINEE

Examinees differ not only in the characteristics that examiners desire to assess, but also in other extraneous ways that might confound the test results. For example, a bright subject might perform poorly on a speeded ability test because of test anxiety; a sane murderer might seek to appear mentally ill on a personality inventory to avoid prosecution; a student of average ability might undergo coaching to perform better on an aptitude test. Some subjects utterly lack motivation and don't care if they do well on psychological tests. In all of these instances, the test results may be inaccurate due to the filtering and distorting effects of certain examinee characteristics such as anxiety, malingering, coaching, or cultural background.

Test Anxiety

Test anxiety refers to those phenomenological, physiological, and behavioral responses that accompany concern about possible failure on a test. There is no doubt that subjects experience different levels of test anxiety ranging from a carefree outlook to incapacitating dread at the prospect of being tested.

Several true-false questionnaires have been developed to assess individual differences in test anxiety (e.g., Sarason, 1980; Morris, Davis, & Hutchings, 1981). Following, we list characteristic items and their direction of keying (*T* for True, *F* for False):

(T) When taking an important examination I sweat a great deal.
(T) I freeze up when I take intelligence tests or school exams.
(F) I really don't understand why some people get so upset about tests.
(T) I dread courses where the instructor likes to give "pop" quizzes.

An extensive body of research has confirmed the commonsense notion that test anxiety is negatively correlated with school achievement, aptitude test scores, and measures of intelligence (Naveh-Benjamin, McKeachie, & Lin, 1987; McKeachie, 1984). However, the interpretation of these correlational findings is not straightforward. One possibility is that students develop test anxiety because of a history of performing poorly on tests. That is, the decrements in performance may precede and cause the test anxiety. In support of this viewpoint, Paulman and Kennelly (1984) found that—independent of their anxiety—many test-anxious students also display ineffective test taking in academic settings. Such students would do poorly on tests whether or not they were anxious. Moreover, Naveh-Benjamin, McKeachie, and Lin (1987) determined that a large proportion of test-anxious college students have poor study habits that predispose them to poor test performance. The test anxiety of these subjects is partly a byproduct of lifelong frustration over mediocre test results.

Other lines of research indicate that test anxiety has a directly detrimental effect on test performance. That is, test anxiety is likely both cause and effect in the equation linking it with poor test performance. Consider the seminal study on this topic by Sarason (1961) who tested high- and low-anxious subjects under neutral or anxiety-inducing instructions. The subjects were college students required to memorize two-syllable words low in meaningfulness—a difficult task. Half of the subjects performed under neutral instructions—they were simply told to memorize the lists. The remaining subjects were told to memorize the lists and told that the task was an intelligence test. They were urged to perform as well as possible. The two groups did not differ significantly in performance when the instructions were neutral and nonthreatening. However, when the instructions aroused anxiety, performance levels for the high-anxious subjects dropped markedly, leaving them at a huge disadvantage compared to low-anxious subjects. This indicates that test-anxious subjects show significant decrements in performance when they perceive the situation as a test. In contrast, low-anxious subjects are relatively unaffected by such a simple redefinition of the context.

Tests with narrow time limits pose a special problem to persons with high levels of test anxiety. Time pressure seems to exacerbate the degree of personal threat, causing significant reductions in the performance of test-anxious persons. Siegman (1956) demonstrated this point many years ago by comparing performance levels of high- and low-anxious medical/psychiatric patients on timed and untimed subtests from the WAIS. The WAIS consists of eleven subtests, including six subtests for which the examiner uses a stopwatch to enforce strict time limits, and five subtests for which the subject has unlimited time to respond. Interestingly, the high- and low-anxious subjects were of equal overall ability on the WAIS. However, each group excelled on different kinds of subtests in predictable directions. In particular, the low-anxious subjects surpassed the high-anxious subjects on timed subtests, whereas the reverse pattern was observed on untimed subtests (Figure 2.4).

Motivation to Deceive

Test results may be inaccurate if the subject has reasons to perform in an inadequate or unrepresentative manner. Overt faking of test results is rare, but it does happen. A small fraction of persons

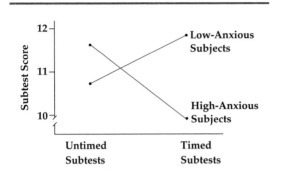

FIGURE 2.4 Influence of Timing and Anxiety Level on WAIS Subtest Results

Source: Based on data from Siegman, A. W. (1956). The effect of manifest anxiety on a concept formation task, a nondirected learning task, and on timed and untimed intelligence tests. *Journal of Consulting Psychology, 20,* 176–178.

seeking benefits from rehabilitation or social agencies will consciously fake bad on personality and ability tests. Occasionally, persons who anticipate criminal prosecution will fake mental illness on personality tests. Consider the case of the psychotherapy client who took a personality test at the behest of his therapist. The therapist desired an accurate assessment of the client's seemingly mild depression. The results were ambiguous, indicating either a monumental degree of psychological disturbance or a conscious attempt to exaggerate symptoms. Two weeks later the therapist inadvertently discovered that the client was about to be charged with child molestation. Apparently, he had faked the test results, anticipating that legal charges would soon be filed against him. He planned to defend himself, in part, by claiming that mental illness was a mitigating factor in his behavior.

In most cases, a well-trained psychometrician can detect conscious faking by asking two questions: (1) Does the client have motivation to perform deceitfully on the tests? (2) Is the overall pattern of test results suspicious in light of other information known about the client? If the answer to both questions is "yes," then the examiner is well advised to approach the test results with skepticism.

Effects of Coaching on Test Results

The influence of coaching on test scores has been widely studied by psychologists and educators. **Coaching** may include several components: extra practice on testlike materials, review of fundamental concepts likely to be covered by the test, and advice about optimal test-taking strategies. We can do no more than mention a few highlights here, with special emphasis on aptitude tests. Readers who wish more detail can consult Anastasi (1981) and Bond (1989).

There is no doubt that coaching can improve scores significantly on certain kinds of aptitude tests containing "coachable" test item types. For example, Powers and Swinton (1984) mailed various sets of test preparation materials to random samples of Graduate Record Examination (GRE) candidates approximately five weeks before the test administration.[1] The test preparation materials included extra practice tests, explanations to practice test questions, and hints or strategies for answering different item types. Incidentally, GRE test scores generally range from 200 to 800 with a national average of approximately 500. The general test includes three sections: Verbal, Quantitative, and Analytical. By comparing the performance of the experimental subjects with control subjects who received no supplementary test preparation materials, Powers and Swinton (1984) were able to deduce that four hours of special self-tutored preparation yielded a dividend of a 53-point increase on the GRE Analytical Test scale. This finding was comparable to a 66-point increase in an earlier instructor-based intervention that entailed seven hours of direct contact (Swinton & Powers, 1983).

However, the effects observed in these studies were highly specific. The special preparation materials for analytical items acted only on the analytical scores, not on verbal or quantitative scores. In fact, the effects were restricted only to the par-

---

1. The GRE is required by many graduate school admission committees. During the period when Powers and Swinton (1984) studied the GRE, it consisted of verbal, quantitative, and analytical portions.

ticular kinds of analytical items that were *coachable*—items involving analysis of explanations and logical diagrams. Performance on other kinds of analytical items—for example, analytical reasoning—was unaffected.

Coaching presents a serious problem to test developers because it can inflate an examinee's score without correspondingly improving his or her overall abilities in the domain being tested. If this occurs, the score is no longer a valid representation of an examinee's ability. Thus, coaching may invalidate existing norms. Certainly, coaching raises the spectre of privileged test preparation for rich or savvy students at the expense of those who are poor or uninformed. After all, privately established coaching schools abound, but they may charge hundreds of dollars for a day or two of preparation for aptitude exams.

Fortunately, there is a partial solution to the problem of coaching that many test developers are embracing: Make self-tutored coaching available to everyone. Most major testing programs, including the Graduate Record Examinations, now provide sample test materials so that examinees can become familiar with the nature of the questions. Of course, this does not guarantee that everyone will make use of the materials, but at least the opportunity is immediately available at no cost. Students who refuse to inspect test familiarization materials do so at their own risk.

ISSUES IN SCORING

Group tests generally employ a multiple-choice format for which the examinee pencils in responses on a separate answer sheet which is then machine scored with total objectivity and accuracy. Consequently, group tests seldom present an opportunity for human error in scoring. However, scoring errors can creep in with machine-scored group tests if examinees do not sufficiently darken the response areas with a soft lead pencil or if they leave extraneous marks on the answer sheet. To guard against this source of error, testers must inspect every answer sheet and correct any irregularities in pencil markings before submitting materials for machine scoring.

Scoring errors occur mainly with individual tests for which the examiner must make scoring judgments, add columns of numbers, and consult tables that convert raw scores into IQs or other summary statistics. Contrary to popular belief, examiner judgments about scoring—whether a certain response on an IQ test merits one or two raw score points, for example—are almost never a significant source of scoring errors. We will illustrate this point with individual IQ testing, but it applies to most other individual tests as well. Even when examiners blatantly err in a conservative direction, consistently giving a subject less credit than deserved for ambiguous or borderline answers, the net effect on Full Scale IQ is minimal, perhaps one or two points at most. The reason that judgment errors seldom make a serious difference is simple: Scoring criteria on most tests are spelled out in such detail that the examiner is seldom required to make a judgment call.

Clerical scoring errors are another matter altogether. These kinds of errors occur far more often than even psychologists want to admit. As we shall see, clerical scoring errors can have disastrous effects.

Ryan, Prifitera, and Powers (1983) asked 19 psychologists and 20 graduate students to score the WAIS-R protocols of two vocational counseling clients. For one client whose Full Scale IQ was 110, the practicing psychologists tallied scores ranging from 107 to 115, and the graduate students obtained scores ranging from 108 to 117. The variations in scoring were due largely to **clerical scoring errors,** not judgmental differences about credit due for ambiguous or borderline answers. Gregory (1987) has illustrated much the same point with a group of advanced graduate students who erred by as much as 30 points when scoring a standard Wechsler IQ test protocol. We may surmise, then, that scoring errors do occur frequently and do seriously compromise the accuracy of IQ assessment and other forms of psychological testing. This problem does not disappear merely because of increased experience. The only way to avoid clerical scoring errors is to publicize how widespread the problem is and encourage examiners to exercise great care when scoring protocols.

SUMMARY

1. Standardized testing procedures are essential to valid testing. The use of nonstandard procedures may alter the meaning of the test results, rendering them invalid and misleading.

2. Flexibility in testing procedures is nonetheless appropriate when it is reasoned and deliberate. In determining whether a flexible shift in testing procedures is acceptable, the examiner should surmise how the test was most likely administered to the normative sample.

3. In individual testing, it is desirable for the examiner to become highly familiar with the test materials. Tests need to be rehearsed so that the examiner can anticipate the appropriate responses to the numerous contingencies of testing.

4. Another important ingredient of valid testing is sensitivity to disabilities in the examinee. When disabilities go unrecognized, serious errors of test interpretation may occur; for example, a deaf examinee may be misdiagnosed as retarded.

5. In the administration of group tests, examiners must adhere strictly to oral instructions and defined time limits. In addition, the physical conditions of testing must be appropriate, such as, proper lighting and minimal noise.

6. Especially in the administration of individual tests, examiners are urged to establish rapport. In testing, rapport is a comfortable, warm atmosphere which serves to motivate examinees and elicit cooperation.

7. Contrary to popular expectation, most studies find that the sex, experience, and race of the examiner have little effect upon psychological test results. Nonetheless, there may be specialized cases in which examiner-examinee interactions produce a detrimental effect upon test scores.

8. Test anxiety refers to those phenomenological, physiological, and behavioral responses that accompany concern about possible failure on a test. Test anxiety has been shown to correlate negatively with school achievement, aptitude test scores, measures of intelligence, and performance on timed tests.

9. Faking of test results is rare, but does occur. In most cases, a well-trained examiner can detect conscious faking by asking whether the client has motivation to perform deceitfully on the tests and whether the overall pattern of test results is suspicious in light of other information.

10. Coaching can improve examinee test scores for certain kinds of coachable items such as the analytical portion of the Graduate Record Examination (GRE). Practice with sample test items and learning hints or strategies can boost a GRE subtest score by 50 to 60 points on the 800-point scale.

11. In scoring individual tests, differences in personal judgment—for example, assigning a certain test response one raw score point versus two points—rarely influence the overall test score to any appreciable extent, such as one or two Full Scale IQ points at most.

12. Clerical scoring errors—such as adding columns of scores incorrectly or consulting the wrong reference table—pose a serious problem in individual psychological testing. These kinds of errors can cause test scores to be wildly inaccurate.

KEY TERMS AND CONCEPTS

correction for guessing   p. 49

rapport   p. 50

test anxiety   p. 51

coaching   p. 53

clerical scoring errors   p. 54

CHAPTER 3

Norms and Reliability

TOPIC 3A Norms and Test Standardization

This chapter concerns two basic concepts needed to facilitate the examiner's interpretation of test scores: norms and reliability. In most cases, scores on psychological tests are interpreted by reference to norms which are based upon the distribution of scores obtained by a representative sample of examinees. In Topic 3A, Norms and Test Standardization, we review the process of standardizing a test against an appropriate norm group so that test users can make sense out of individual test scores. Since the utility of a test score is also determined by the consistency or repeatability of test results, we introduce the essentials of reliability theory and measurement in Topic 3B, Concepts of Reliability. The next chapter flows logically

from the material presented here and investigates the complex issues of validity—does a test measure what it is supposed to measure? First, we begin with the more straightforward issues of establishing a comparative frame of reference (norms) and determining the consistency or repeatability of test results (reliability).

The initial outcome of testing is typically a raw score such as the total number of personality statements endorsed in a particular direction or the total number of problems solved correctly, perhaps with bonus points added in for quick solutions. In most cases, the initial score is useless by itself. For test results to be meaningful, examiners must be able to convert the initial score to some form of derived

| OUTMODED TESTS AND OUTDATED NORMS | CASE EXHIBIT 3.1 |

A consulting psychologist worked with a high school system that boasted a respected program for the gifted and talented. Entry into this program could be earned in several ways, including documentation from a psychologist that the applicant had an IQ of 130 or higher. School officials expressed surprise when the number of qualified students increased sharply in the early 1980s. Most of the newfound high-IQ students had been tested by the school psychologist, an honest and competent person who had no apparent motivation to fudge his results. The school principal commented to the consulting psychologist that the community seemed to be fostering a higher and higher proportion of gifted and talented students. When asked which tests were used for program screening, the principal replied that the WAIS (Wechsler, 1955) was the instrument of choice for older students.

The consultant pointed out that the WAIS was a good test in its time but that the test had been revised (the WAIS-R was published in 1981) and its old norms were no longer relevant. In fact, the WAIS is much easier than its revision (Kaufman, 1990; Mishra & Brown, 1983) and tends to yield IQs that are up to eight points higher! It was little wonder that so many students were achieving superior IQs. The effect of using an obsolete test was that, on average, each applicant had eight points added to his or her real IQ. Upon hearing these facts, the principal resolved to buy a copy of the WAIS-R so that the school psychologist would have the updated instrument with norms appropriate for assessing applicants to the special program.

score based upon comparison to a standardization or norm group. The vast majority of tests are interpreted by comparing individual results to a norm group performance; criterion-referenced tests are an exception, discussed subsequently.

A **norm group** consists of a sample of examinees who are representative of the population for whom the test is intended. Consider a word knowledge test designed for use with prospective college freshmen. In this case, the performance of a large, heterogenous, nationwide sampling of such persons might be collected for purposes of standardization. The essential objective of test standardization is to determine the distribution of raw scores in the norm group so that the test developer can publish derived scores known as norms. Norms come in many varieties, for example, percentile ranks, age equivalents, grade equivalents, or standard scores, as discussed in the following. In general, norms indicate an examinee's standing on the test relative to the performance of other persons of the same age, grade, sex, and so on.

To be effective, norms must be obtained with great care and constructed according to well-known precepts discussed in the following. Furthermore, norms may become outmoded in just a few years, so periodic renorming of tests should be the rule, not the exception (Case Exhibit 3.1). We approach the topic of norms indirectly, first providing the reader with a discussion of raw scores and then reviewing statistical concepts essential to an understanding of norms.

RAW SCORES

The most basic level of information provided by a psychological test is the **raw score.** For example, in personality testing, the raw score is often the number of questions answered in the keyed direction for a specific scale. In ability testing, the raw score commonly consists of the number of problems answered correctly, often with bonus points added for quick performance. Thus, the initial outcome of testing is almost always a numerical tally such as 17 out of 44 items answered in the keyed direction on a depression scale, or 29 of 55 raw score points earned on the block design subscale of an intelligence test.

However, it should be obvious to the reader that raw scores, in isolation, are absolutely meaningless. For example, what use is it to know that a subject correctly solved 12 of 20 abstract reasoning questions? What does it mean that an examinee responded in the keyed direction to 19 out of 33 true-false questions from a psychological-mindedness scale?

It is difficult to even think about such questions without resorting to comparisons of one variety or another. We want to know how others have done on these tests, whether the observed scores are high or low in comparison to a representative group of subjects. In the case of ability tests, we are curious whether the questions were easy or hard, especially in relation to the age of the subject.

In fact, it seems almost a truism that a raw score becomes meaningful mainly in relation to norms, an independently established frame of reference derived from a standardization sample. We will have much to say about the derivation and use of norms later in this unit. For now it will suffice to know that norms are empirically established by administering a test to a large and representative sample of persons. An examinee's score is then compared to the distribution of scores obtained by the standardization sample. In this manner, we determine from the norms whether an obtained score is low, average, or high.

The vast majority of psychological tests are interpreted by consulting norms; as noted, these instruments are called *norm-referenced tests.* However, the reader is reminded that other kinds of instruments do exist. In particular, criterion-referenced tests help determine whether a person can accomplish an objectively defined criterion such as adding pairs of two-digit numbers with 97 percent accuracy. In the case of criterion-referenced tests, norms are not essential. We elaborate upon criterion-referenced tests at the end of this topic.

There are many different kinds of norms, but they share one characteristic in common: Each incorporates a statistical summary of a large body of scores. Thus, in order to understand norms, the reader needs to master elementary descriptive statistics. We take a modest digression here to review essential statistical concepts.

ESSENTIAL STATISTICAL CONCEPTS

Suppose for the moment that we have access to a high-level vocabulary test appropriate for testing the verbal skills of college professors and other professional persons (Gregory & Gernert, 1990). The test is a multiple choice quiz of 30 difficult words such as *welkin, halcyon,* and *mellifluous.* A curious professor takes the test and chooses the correct alternative for 17 of the 30 words. She asks how her score compares to others of similar academic standing. How might we respond to her question?

One manner of answering the query would be to give her a list of the raw scores from the preliminary standardization sample of 100 representative professors at her university (Table 3.1). However, even with this relatively small norm sample (thousands of subjects is more typical), the list of test scores is an overpowering display.

When confronted with a collection of quantitative data, the natural human tendency is to summarize, condense, and organize it into meaningful patterns. For example, in assessing the meaning of the curious professor's vocabulary score, the reader might calculate the average score for the entire sample, or tally the relative position of the professor's score (17 correct) among the 100 data points found in Table 3.1. We will review these and other

TABLE 3.1   Raw Scores of 100 Professors on a 30-Item Vocabulary Test

6,	10,	16,	16,	17,	14,	19,	14,	16,	15
17,	17,	19,	20,	20,	22,	17,	24,	14,	25
13,	20,	11,	20,	21,	11,	20,	16,	18,	12
13,	7,	20,	27,	21,	7,	15,	18,	18,	25
20,	27,	28,	13,	21,	17,	12,	18,	12,	15
9,	24,	25,	9,	17,	17,	9,	19,	24,	15
20,	21,	22,	12,	21,	12,	19,	19,	23,	16
8,	12,	12,	17,	13,	19,	13,	11,	16,	16
7,	19,	14,	17,	19,	14,	18,	15,	15,	15
14,	14,	17,	18,	18,	22,	11,	15,	13,	9

Source: Based on data from Gregory, R. J., and Gernert, C. H. (1990). *Age trends for fluid and crystallized intelligence in an able subpopulation.* Unpublished manuscript.

TABLE 3.2   Frequency Distribution of Scores of 100 Professors on a Vocabulary Test

Class Interval	Frequency
4–6	1
7–9	8
10–12	12
13–15	21
16–18	24
19–21	21
22–24	7
25–27	5
28–30	1
	$N = 100$

approaches to organizing and summarizing quantitative data in the following sections.

Frequency Distributions

A very simple and useful way of summarizing data is to tabulate a frequency distribution (Table 3.2). A **frequency distribution** is prepared by specifying a small number of usually equal-sized class intervals and then tallying how many scores fall within each interval. The sums of the frequencies for all intervals will equal *N*, the total number of scores in the sample. There is no hard and fast rule for determining the size of the intervals. Obviously, the size of the intervals depends upon the number of intervals desired. It is common for frequency distributions to include between 5 and 15 class intervals. In the case of Table 3.2, there are 9 class intervals of 3 scores each. The table indicates that one professor scored 4, 5, or 6, eight professors scored 7, 8, or 9, and so on.

A **histogram** provides a graphic representation of the same information contained in the frequency distribution (Figure 3.1A). The horizontal axis portrays the scores grouped into class intervals, whereas the vertical axis depicts the number of scores falling within each class interval. In a histogram, the height of a column indicates the num-

ber of scores occurring within that interval. A **frequency polygon** is similar to a histogram, except that the frequency of the class intervals is represented by single points rather than columns. The single points are then joined by straight lines (Figure 3.1B).

The graphs shown in Figure 3.1 constitute visual summaries of the 100 raw score data points from the sample of professors. In addition to visual summaries of data, it is also possible to produce

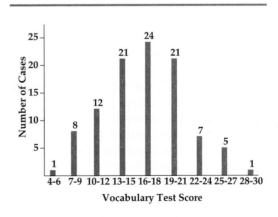

FIGURE 3.1A   A Histogram Representing Vocabulary Test Scores for 100 Professors

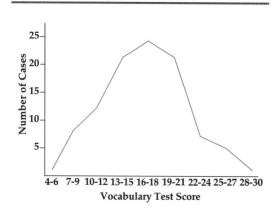

FIGURE 3.1B A Frequency Polygon of Vocabulary Test Scores for 100 Professors

numerical summaries by computing statistical indices of central tendency and dispersion.

Measures of Central Tendency

Can we designate a single, representative score for the 100 vocabulary scores in our sample? The mean (*M*), or arithmetic average, is one such measure of central tendency. We compute the **mean** by adding all the scores up and dividing by *N*, the number of scores. Another useful index of central tendency is the **median**, the middlemost score when all the scores have been ranked. If the number of scores is even, the median is the average of the middlemost two scores. In either case, the median is the point that bisects the distribution so that half of the cases fall above it, half below. Finally, the **mode** is simply the most frequently occurring score. If two scores tie for highest frequency of occurrence, the distribution is said to be bimodal.

The mean of the scores listed in Table 3.1 is 16.8; the median and mode are both 17. In this instance, the three measures of central tendency are in very good agreement. However, this is not always so. The mean is sensitive to extreme values and can be misleading if a distribution has a few scores that are unusually high or low. Consider an extreme case where nine persons earn $10,000 and a tenth person earns $910,000. The mean income for this group is $100,000 yet this income level is not typical of anyone in the group. The median income of $10,000 is much more representative. Of course, this is an extreme example but it illustrates a general point: If a distribution of scores is skewed (that is, asymmetrical), the median is a better index of central tendency than the mean.

Measures of Variability

Two or more distributions of test scores may have the same mean, yet differ greatly in the extent of dispersion of the scores about the mean (Figure 3.2). To describe the degree of dispersion, we need a statistical index that expresses the variability of scores in the distribution.

The most commonly used statistical index of variability in a group of scores is the **standard deviation**, designated as *s* or abbreviated as SD. From a conceptual standpoint, the reader needs to know that the standard deviation reflects the degree of dispersion in a group of scores. If the scores are tightly packed around a central value, the standard deviation is small. In fact, in the extreme case

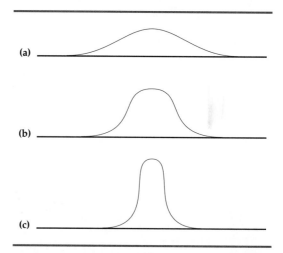

FIGURE 3.2 Three Distributions with Identical Means but Different Variability

where all the scores are identical, the standard deviation is exactly zero. As a group of scores becomes more spread out, the standard deviation becomes larger. For example, in Figure 3.2, distribution *a* would have the largest standard deviation, distribution *c* the smallest.

The standard deviation or *s* is simply the square root of the variance, designated as s^2. The formula for the **variance** is

$$s^2 = \frac{\Sigma(X - \bar{X})^2}{(N - 1)}$$

where Σ designates "the sum of," *X* stands for each individual score, $\bar{X}$ is the mean of the scores, and *N* is the total number of scores. As the name suggests, the variance is a measure of variability. However, psychologists usually prefer to report the standard deviation, which is computed by taking the square root of the variance. Of course, the variance and the standard deviation convey interchangeable information—one can be computed from the other by squaring (of the standard deviation to obtain the variance) or taking the square root (of the variance to obtain the standard deviation). The standard deviation is nonetheless the preferred measure of variance in psychological testing because of its direct relevance to the normal distribution, as discussed in the next section.

The Normal Distribution

The frequency polygon depicted in Figure 3.1B is highly irregular in shape, a typical finding with real-world data based upon small sample sizes. What would happen to the shape of the frequency polygon if we increased the size of the normative sample and also increased the number of class intervals by reducing their size? Possibly, as we added new subjects to our sample, the distribution of scores would more and more closely resemble a symmetrical, mathematically defined, bell-shaped curve called the **normal distribution** (Figure 3.3).

Psychologists prefer a normal distribution of test scores, even though many other distributions are theoretically possible. For example, a rectangular

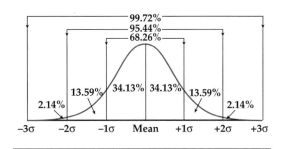

FIGURE 3.3   The Normal Curve and the Percentage of Cases within Certain Intervals

distribution of test scores—an equal number of outcomes in each class interval—is within the realm of possibility. Indeed, many laypersons might even prefer a rectangular distribution of test scores on the egalitarian premise that individual differences are thereby less pronounced. For example, a higher proportion of persons would score in the superior range if psychological tests conformed to a rectangular rather than normal distribution of scores.

Why, then, do psychologists prefer a normal distribution of test scores, even to the point of selecting test items that help produce this kind of distribution in the standardization sample? There are several reasons, including statistical considerations and empirical findings. We digress briefly here to explain the psychometric fascination with normal distributions.

One reason that psychologists prefer normal distributions is that the normal curve has useful mathematical features that form the basis for several kinds of statistical investigation. For example, suppose we wished to determine if the average IQs for two groups of subjects were significantly different. An inferential statistic such as the *t*-test for a difference between means would be appropriate. However, many inferential statistics are based upon the assumption that the underlying population of scores is normally distributed, or nearly so. Thus, in order to facilitate the use of inferential statistics, psychologists prefer that test scores in the general population follow a normal or near-normal distribution.

Another basis for preferring the normal distribution is its mathematical precision. Since the normal distribution is precisely defined in mathematical terms, it is possible to compute the area underneath different regions of the curve with great accuracy. Thus, a useful property of normal distributions is that the percentage of cases falling within a certain range or beyond a certain value is precisely known. For example, in a normal distribution, a mere 2.14 percent of the scores will exceed the mean by two standard deviations or more (Figure 3.3). In like manner, we can determine that the vast bulk of scores—more than 68 percent—fall within one standard deviation of the mean in either direction.

A third basis for preferring a normal distribution of test scores is that the normal curve often arises spontaneously in nature. In fact, early investigators were so impressed with the ubiquity of the normal distribution that they virtually deified the normal curve as a law of nature. For example, Galton (1888) wrote:

> It is the supreme law of Unreason. Whenever a large sample of chaotic elements are taken in hand and marshalled in the order of their magnitude, an unsuspected and most beautiful form of regularity proves to have been latent all along.

Certainly there is no "law of nature" regarding the form that frequency distributions must take. Nonetheless, it is true that many important human characteristics—both physical and mental—produce a close approximation to the normal curve when measurements for large and heterogeneous samples are graphed. For example, a near-normal distribution curve is a well-known finding for physical characteristics such as birth weight, height, and brain weight (Jensen, 1980).

An approximately normal distribution is also found with numerous mental tests, even for tests constructed entirely without reference to the normal curve. To illustrate this point, we refer to early tests devised before the current psychometric fixation upon the normal distribution. Wechsler (1944) chose items for the original Wechsler-Bellevue Intelligence Scale largely on the basis of variety of item types, paying no heed to the resulting distribution of scores. In fact, he considered the belief that mental measures must distribute themselves according to the normal curve to be "mistaken." Yet, when he graphed the distribution of Full Scale IQs on his test, the predictably near-normal distribution emerged (Figure 3.4). Lindvall (1967) found the same thing when plotting data from the 1923

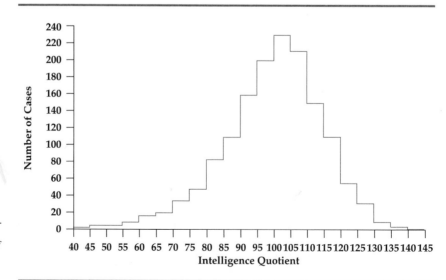

FIGURE 3.4
Near-Normal Distribution of 1,508 Full Scale IQs on the Wechsler-Bellevue
Source: Reprinted with permission from Wechsler, D. (1944). *The measurement of adult intelligence* (3rd ed.). Baltimore: Williams & Wilkins.

Pintner Ability Test. We see, then, that even in the absence of psychometric tinkering, the distribution of mental test scores in standardization samples typically approximates a normal curve.

Skewness

Skewness refers to the symmetry or asymmetry of a frequency distribution. If test scores are piled up at the low end of the scale, the distribution is said to be positively skewed. In the opposite case, when test scores are piled up at the high end of the scale, the distribution is said to be negatively skewed (Figure 3.5).

In psychological testing, skewed distributions usually signify that the test developer has included too few easy items or too few hard items. For example, when scores in the standardization sample are massed at the low end (positive skew), the test probably contains too few easy items to make effective discriminations at this end of the scale. In this case, examinees who obtain zero or near-zero scores might actually differ with respect to the dimension measured. However, the test is unable to elicit these differences, since most of the items are too hard for these examinees. Of course, the opposite pattern holds as well. If scores are massed at the high end (negative skew), the test probably contains too few hard items to make effective discriminations at this end of the scale.

When initial research indicates that an instrument produces skewed results in the standardization sample, test developers typically revamp the test at the item level. The most straightforward solution is to add items or modify existing items so that the test has more easy items (to reduce positive skew) or more hard items (to reduce negative skew). If it is too late to revise the instrument, the test developer can use a statistical transformation to help produce a more normal distribution of scores (see the following). However, the preferred strategy is to revise the test so that skewness is minimal or nonexistent.

RAW SCORE TRANSFORMATIONS

Making sense out of test results is largely a matter of transforming the raw scores into more interpretable and useful forms of information. In the preceding discussion of normal distributions, we hinted at transformations by showing how knowledge of the mean and standard deviation of such distributions can help us determine the relative standing of an individual score. In this section we continue this theme in a more direct manner by introducing the formal requirements for several kinds of raw score transformations.

Percentiles and Percentile Ranks

A **percentile** expresses the percentage of persons in the standardization sample who scored below a specific raw score. For example, on the vocabulary

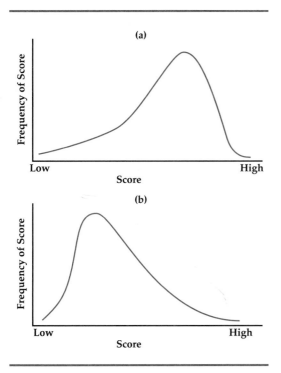

FIGURE 3.5 **Skewed Distribution Curves**
(a) Negative Skew
(b) Positive Skew

test depicted in Table 3.2, 94 percent of the sample fell below a raw score of 25. Thus, a raw score of 25 would correspond to a percentile of 94, denoted as P_{94}. Note that higher percentiles indicate higher scores. In the extreme case, an examinee who obtained a raw score that exceeded every score in the standardization sample would receive a percentile of 100 or P_{100}.

The reader is warned not to confuse percentiles with percent correct. Remember that a percentile indicates only how an examinee compares to the standardization sample and does not convey the percentage of questions answered correctly. Conceivably, on a difficult test, a raw score of 50 percent correct might translate to a percentile of 90, 95, or even 100. Conversely, on an easy test, a raw score of 95 percent correct might translate to a percentile of 5, 10, or 20.

Percentiles can also be viewed as ranks in a group of 100 representative subjects, with 1 being the lowest rank and 100 the highest. Note that percentile ranks are the complete reverse of usual ranking procedures. A percentile rank (PR) of 1 is at the bottom of the sample, while a PR of 99 is near the top.

A percentile of 50 (P_{50}) corresponds to the median or middlemost raw score. A percentile of 25 (P_{25}) is often denoted as $Q1$ or the first quartile because one-quarter of the scores fall below this point. In like manner, a percentile of 75 (P_{75}) is referred to as $Q3$ or the third quartile because three-quarters of the scores fall below this point.

Percentiles are easy to compute and intuitively appealing to laypersons and professionals alike. It is not surprising, then, that percentiles are the most common type of raw score transformation encountered in psychological testing. Almost any kind of test result can be reported as a percentile, even when other transformations are the primary goal of testing. For example, intelligence tests are used to obtain IQ scores—a kind of transformation discussed subsequently—but also yield percentile scores, too. Thus, an IQ of 130 corresponds to a percentile of 98, meaning that the score is not only well above average but, more precisely, exceeds 98 percent of the standardization sample.

Percentile scores do have one major drawback: They distort the underlying measurement scale, especially at the extremes. A specific example will serve to clarify this point. Consider a hypothetical instance where four persons obtain the following percentiles on a test: 50, 59, 90, and 99. (Remember that we are speaking here of percentiles, not percent correct.) The first two persons differ by 9 percentile points (50 versus 59) and so do the last two persons (90 versus 99). The untrained observer might assume, falsely, that the first two persons differed in underlying raw score points by the same amount as the last two persons. An inspection of Figure 3.6 reveals the fallacy of this assumption. The difference in underlying raw score points between percentiles of 90 and 99 is far greater than between percentiles of 50 and 59.

Standard Scores

Although percentiles are the most popular type of transformed score, standard scores exemplify the most desirable psychometric properties. A standard score uses the standard deviation of the total distribution of raw scores as the fundamental unit of measurement. The **standard score** expresses the distance from the mean in standard deviation units. For example, a raw score that is exactly one standard deviation above the mean converts to a stan-

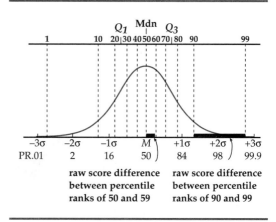

FIGURE 3.6   Percentile Ranks in a Normal Distribution

dard score of +1.00. A raw score that is exactly one-half a standard deviation below the mean converts to a standard score of – 0.50. Thus, a standard score not only expresses the magnitude of deviation from the mean, but the direction of departure (positive or negative) as well.

Computation of an examinee's standard score (also called a z score) is simple: Subtract the mean of the normative group from the examinee's raw score and then divide this difference by the standard deviation of the normative group. Table 3.3 illustrates the computation of z scores for three subjects of widely varying ability on a hypothetical test.

Standard scores possess the desirable psychometric property of retaining the relative magnitudes of distances between successive values found in the original raw scores. This is because the distribution of standard scores has exactly the same shape as the distribution of raw scores. As a consequence, the use of standard scores does not distort the underlying measurement scale. This fidelity of the transformed measurement scale is a major advantage of standard scores over percentiles and percentile ranks. As previously noted, percentile scores are very distorting, especially at the extremes.

A specific example will serve to illustrate the nondistorting feature of standard scores. Consider four raw scores of 55, 60, 70, and 80 on a test with

---

TABLE 3.3 Computation of Standard Scores on a Hypothetical Test

For the normative sample: $M = 50$, $SD = 8$

Standard Score $= z = \dfrac{X - M}{SD}$

Person A: raw score of 35 (below average)

$$z = \frac{35 - 50}{8} = -1.88$$

Person B: raw score of 50 (exactly average)

$$z = \frac{50 - 50}{8} = 0.00$$

Person C: raw score of 70 (above average)

$$z = \frac{70 - 50}{8} = +2.50$$

---

mean of 50 and standard deviation of 10. The first two scores differ by 5 raw score points, while the last two scores differ by 10 raw score points—twice the difference of the first pair. When the raw scores are converted to standard scores, the results are +0.50, +1.00, +2.00, and +3.00, respectively. The reader will notice that the first two scores differ by 0.50 standard scores, while the last two scores differ by 1.00 standard scores—twice the difference of the first pair. Thus, standard scores always retain the relative magnitude of differences found in the original raw scores.

Standard score distributions possess important mathematical properties that do not exist in the raw score distributions. When each of the raw scores in a distribution is transformed to a standard score, the resulting collection of standard scores always has a mean of zero and a variance of 1.00. Because the standard deviation is the square root of the variance, the standard deviation of standard scores ($\sqrt{1.00}$) is necessarily 1.00 as well.

One reason for transforming raw scores into standard scores is to depict results on different tests according to a common scale. If two distributions of test scores possess the same form, we can make direct comparisons on raw scores by transforming them to standard scores. Suppose, for example, that a college freshman earned 125 raw score points on a spatial thinking test where the normative sample averaged 100 points (with SD of 15 points). Suppose, in addition, he earned 110 raw score points on a vocabulary test where the normative sample averaged 90 points (with SD of 20 points). In which skill area does he show greater aptitude, spatial thinking or vocabulary?

If the normative samples for both tests produced test score distributions of the same form, we can compare spatial thinking and vocabulary scores by converting each to standard scores. The spatial thinking standard score for our student is (125 – 100)/15 or +1.67, whereas his vocabulary standard score is (110 – 90)/20 or +1.00. Relative to the normative samples, the student has greater aptitude for spatial thinking than vocabulary.

But a word of caution is appropriate when comparing standard scores from different distributions.

If the distributions do not have the same form, standard score comparisons can be very misleading. We illustrate this point with Figure 3.7, which depicts two distributions: one markedly skewed with average score of 30 (SD of 10) and another normally distributed with average score of 60 (SD of 8). A raw score of 40 on the first test and a raw score of 68 on the second test both translate to identical standard scores of +1.00. Yet, a standard score of 1.00 on the first test exceeds 92 percent of the normative sample, while the equivalent standard score on the second test exceeds only 84 percent of the normative sample. When two distributions of test scores do not possess the same form, equivalent standard scores do not signify comparable positions within the respective normative samples.

T Scores and Other Standardized Scores

Many psychologists and educators appreciate the psychometric properties of standard scores but regard the decimal fractions and positive/negative signs (e.g., $z = -2.32$) as unnecessary distractions. In response to these concerns, test specialists have de-

vised a number of variations on standard scores that are collectively referred to as *standardized scores.*

From a conceptual standpoint, standardized scores are identical to standard scores. Both kinds of scores contain exactly the same information. The shape of the distribution of scores is not affected, and a plot of the relationship between standard and standardized scores is always a straight line. However, standardized scores are always expressed as positive whole numbers (no decimal fractions or negative signs), so many test users prefer to depict test results in this form.

Standardized scores eliminate fractions and negative signs by producing values other than zero for the mean and 1.00 for the standard deviation of the transformed scores. The mean of the transformed scores can be set at any convenient value such as 100 or 500, and the standard deviation at, say, 15, or 100. The important point about standardized scores is that we can transform any distribution to a preferred scale with predetermined mean and standard deviation.

One popular kind of standardized score is the **T score,** which has a mean of 50 and a standard de-

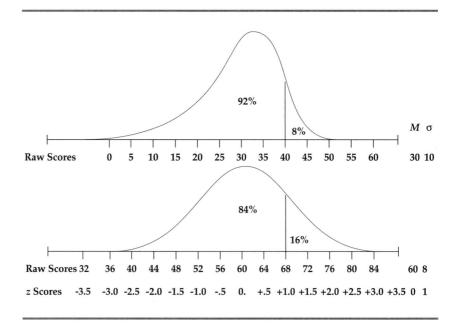

FIGURE 3.7
Relationships between Raw Scores, z Scores, and Relative Standing for Two Distributions of Markedly Different Form

viation of 10. *T* score scales are especially common with personality tests. For example, on the MMPI, each clinical scale (e.g., Depression, Paranoia) is converted to a common metric where 50 is the average score and 10 is the standard deviation for the normative sample.

To transform raw scores to *T* scores, we use the following formula:

$$T = \frac{10(X - M)}{SD} + 50$$

The term $(X - M)/SD$ is, of course, equivalent to *z*, so we can rewrite the formula for *T* as a simple transformation of *z*:

$$T = 10z + 50$$

For any distribution of raw scores, the corresponding *T* scores will have an average of 50. In addition, for most distributions the vast majority of *T* scores will fall between values of 20 and 80, that is, within three standard deviations of the mean. Of course, *T* scores outside this range are entirely possible and perhaps even likely in special populations. In clinical settings it is not unusual to observe very high *T* scores—even as high as 90—on personality inventories such as the MMPI.

Standardized scores can be tailored to produce any mean and standard deviation. However, to eliminate negative standardized scores, the preselected mean should be at least five times as large as the standard deviation. In practice, test developers rely upon a few preferred values for means and standard deviations of standardized scores, as outlined in Table 3.4.

Normalizing Standard Scores

As previously noted, psychologists and educators prefer to deal with normal distributions because the statistical properties of the normal curve are well known and standard scores from these distributions can be directly compared. Perhaps the reader has wondered what recourse is available to test developers who find that their tests produce an asymmetrical distribution of scores in the normative sample. Fortunately, distributions of scores which are skewed or otherwise nonnormal can be transformed or normalized to fit a normal curve. Although test specialists have devised several methods for transmuting a nonnormal distribution into a normal one, we will discuss only the most popular approach—the conversion of percentiles to normalized standard scores. Oddly enough, it is easier to explain this approach if we first describe the reverse process: conversion of standard scores to percentiles.

We have noted that a normal distribution of raw scores has, by definition, a distinct, mathematically defined shape (Figure 3.3). In addition, we have pointed out that transforming a group of raw scores to standard scores leaves the original form of a distribution unchanged. Thus, if a collection of raw scores is normally distributed, the resulting standard scores will obey the normal curve, too.

We also know that the mathematical properties of the normal distribution are precisely calculable. Without going into the details of computation, it should be obvious that we can determine the percentage of cases falling below any particular standard score. For example, in Figure 3.6, a standard

TABLE 3.4   Means and Standard Deviations of Common Standardized Scores

Type of Measure	Specific Examples	Mean	Standard Deviation
Full Scale IQ	WAIS-III	100	15
IQ Test Subscales	Vocabulary, Block Design	10	3
Personality Test Scales	MMPI-2 Depression, Paranoia	50	10
Aptitude Tests	Graduate Record Exam, Scholastic Assessment Tests	500	100

score of –2.00 (designated as –2σ) exceeds 2.14 percent of the cases. Thus, a standard score of –2.00 corresponds to a percentile of 2.14. In like manner, any conceivable standard score can be expressed in terms of its corresponding percentile. Appendix D lists percentiles for standard scores and several other transformed scores.

Producing **normalized standard scores** is accomplished by working in the other direction. Namely, we use the percentile for each raw score to determine its corresponding standard score. If we do this for each and every case in a nonnormal distribution, the resulting distribution of standard scores will be normally distributed. Notice that in such a normalized standard score distribution, the standard scores are not calculated directly from the usual computational formula, but are determined indirectly by first computing the percentile and then ascertaining the equivalent standard score.

The conversion of percentiles to normalized standard scores might seem an ideal solution to the problem of unruly test data. However, there is a potentially serious drawback: Normalized standard scores are a nonlinear transformation of the raw scores. Thus, mathematical relationships established with the raw scores may not hold true for the normalized standard scores. In a markedly skewed distribution, it is even possible that a raw score that is significantly below the mean might conceivably have a normalized standard score that is above the mean.

In practice, normalized standard scores are used sparingly. Such transformations are appropriate only when the normative sample is large and representative and the raw score distribution is only mildly nonnormal. Incidentally, the most likely cause of these nonnormal score distributions is inappropriate difficulty level in the test items, such as too many difficult or easy items.

There is a Catch-22 here, in that mildly nonnormal distributions are not changed much when they are normalized, so little is gained in the process. Ironically, normalized standard scores produce the greatest change with markedly nonnormal distributions. However, when the raw score distribution is markedly nonnormal, test developers are better advised to go back to the drawing board and adjust the difficulty level of test items so as to produce a normal distribution, rather than succumb to the partial statistical fix of normalized standard scores.

Stanines, Stens, and C Scale

Finally, we give brief mention to three raw score transformations which are mainly of historical interest. The stanine (standard nine) scale was developed by the United States Air Force during World War II. In a **stanine scale,** all raw scores are converted to a single-digit system of scores ranging from 1 to 9. The mean of stanine scores is always 5, and the standard deviation is approximately 2. The transformation from raw scores to stanines is simple: The scores are ranked from lowest to highest, and the bottom 4 percent of scores convert to a stanine of 1, the next 7 percent convert to a stanine of 2, and so on (see Table 3.5). The main advantage of stanines is that they are restricted to single-digit numbers. This was a considerable asset in the premodern computer era in which data was keypunched on Hollerith cards which had to be physically carried and stored on shelves. Because a stanine could be keypunched in a single column, far fewer cards were required than if the original raw scores were entered.

Statisticians have proposed several variations on the stanine theme. Canfield (1951) proposed the 10-unit **sten scale,** with 5 units above and 5 units

TABLE 3.5 Distribution Percentages for Use in Stanine Conversion

Percentage	4	7	12	17	20	17	12	7	4
Stanine	1	2	3	4	5	6	7	8	9

below the mean. Guilford and Fruchter (1978) proposed the **C scale** consisting of 11 units. Although stanines are still in widespread use, variants such as the sten and C scale never roused much interest among test developers.

A Summary of Statistically Based Norms

We have alluded several times to the ease with which standard scores, *T* scores, stanines, and percentiles can be transformed into each other, especially if the underlying distribution of raw scores is normally distributed. In fact, the exact form in which scores are reported is largely a matter of convention and personal preference. For example, a WAIS-III IQ of 115 could also be reported as a standard score of +1.00, or a *T* score of 60, or a per-

centile rank of 84. All of these results convey exactly the same information.[1] Figure 3.8 summarizes the relationships that exist between the most commonly used statistically based norms.

This ends the brief introduction to the many techniques by which test data from a normative sample can be statistically summarized and transformed. We should never lose sight of the overriding purpose of these statistical transmutations, namely, to help the test user make sense out of one

---

1. A WAIS-III IQ of 115 also can be expressed as a stanine of 7. However, it is worth noting that some information is lost when scores are reported as stanines. Note that IQs in the range of 111 to 119 *all* convert to a stanine of 7. Thus, if we are told only that an individual has achieved at the 7th stanine on an intelligence test, we do not know the exact IQ equivalent.

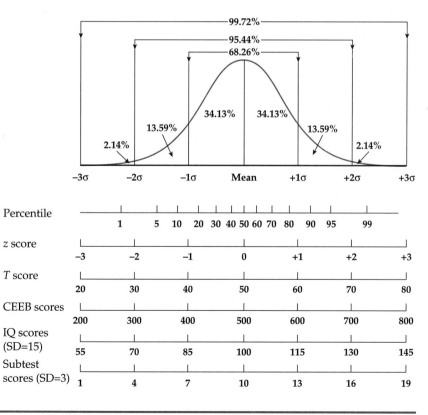

FIGURE 3.8
Equivalencies between Common Raw Score Transformation in a Normal Distribution

individual's score in relation to an appropriate comparison group.

But what is an appropriate comparison group? What characteristics should we require in our norm group subjects? How should we go about choosing these subjects? How many subjects do we need? These are important questions that influence the relevance of test results just as much as proper item selection and standardized testing procedure. In the remainder of this topic, we examine the procedures involved in selecting a norm group.

SELECTING A NORM GROUP

When choosing a norm group, test developers strive to obtain a representative cross section of the population for whom the test is designed (Petersen, Kolen, & Hoover, 1989). In theory, obtaining a representative norm group is straightforward and simple. Consider a scholastic achievement test designed for sixth graders in the United States. The relevant population is all sixth graders coast to coast and in Alaska and Hawaii. A representative cross section of these potential subjects could be obtained by computerized random sampling of 10,000 or so of the millions of eligible children. Each child would have an equal chance of being chosen to take the test, that is, the selection strategy would be simple **random sampling.** The results for such a sample would comprise an ideal source of normative data. With a large random sample, it is almost certain that the diversities of ethnic background, social class, geographic location, and urban versus rural setting, and so on would be proportionately represented in the sample.

In the real world, obtaining norm samples is never as simple and definitive as the hypothetical case previously outlined. Researchers do not have a complete list of every sixth grader in the nation, and even if they did, test developers could not compel every randomly selected child to participate in the standardization of a test. Questions of cost arise, too. Psychometricians must be paid to administer the tests to the norm group. Test developers may opt for a few hundred representative subjects instead of a larger number.

To help insure that smaller norm groups are truly representative of the population for which the test was designed, test developers employ **stratified random sampling.** This approach consists of stratifying, or classifying, the target population on important background variables (e.g., age, sex, race, social class, educational level) and then selecting an appropriate percentage of persons at random from each stratum. For example, if 12 percent of the relevant population is African American, then the test developer chooses subjects randomly, but with the constraint that 12 percent of the norm group is also African American.

In practice, very few test developers fully emulate either random sampling or stratified random sampling in the process of selecting the norm group. What is more typical is a good faith effort to pick a diverse and representative sample from strong and weak schools, minority and white neighborhoods, large and small cities, and north, east, central, and southern communities. If this sample then embodies about the same percentage of minorities, city dwellers, upper- and lower-class families, as the national census, then the test developer feels secure that the norm group is representative.

There is an important lesson in the uncertainties, compromises, and pragmatics of norm group selection, namely, psychological test norms are not absolute, universal, or timeless. They are relative to one historical era and the particular normative population from which they were derived. We will illustrate the ephemeral nature of normative statistics in a later section when we show how a major IQ test normed at a national average of 100 in 1974 yielded a national average of 107 in 1988. Even norms that are selected with great care and based on large samples can become obsolete in a decade—sometimes less.

Age and Grade Norms

As we grow older, we change in measurable ways, for better or worse. This is obviously true in childhood when intellectual skills improve visibly from one month to the next. In adulthood, personal change is slower but still discernible. We expect, for example, that adults will show a more mature level of vocabulary with each passing decade (Gregory & Gernert, 1990).

An **age norm** depicts the level of test performance for each separate age group in the normative sample. The purpose of age norms is to facilitate same-aged comparisons. With age norms, the performance of an examinee is interpreted in relation to standardization subjects of the same age. The age span for a normative age group can vary from a month to a decade or more, depending upon the degree to which test performance is age-dependent. For characteristics that change quickly with age—such as intellectual abilities in childhood—test developers might report separate test norms for narrowly defined age brackets, such as four-month intervals. This allows the examiner, for example, to compare test results of a child who is 5 years and 2 months old (age 5-2) to the normative sample of children ranging from age 5-0 to age 5-4. By contrast, adult characteristics change more slowly and it might be sufficient to report normative data by five- or 10-year age intervals.

Grade norms are conceptually similar to age norms. A **grade norm** depicts the level of test performance for each separate grade in the normative sample. Grade norms are rarely used with ability tests. However, these norms are especially useful in school settings when reporting the achievement levels of schoolchildren. Since academic achievement in many content areas is heavily dependent upon grade-based curricular exposure, comparing a student against a normative sample from the same grade is more appropriate than using an age-based comparison.

Local and Subgroup Norms

With many applications, local or subgroup norms are needed to suit the specific purpose of a test. **Local norms** are derived from representative local examinees, as opposed to a national sample. Likewise, **subgroup norms** consist of the scores obtained from an identified subgroup (African Americans, Hispanics, females), as opposed to a diversified national sample. As an example of local norms in action, the admissions officer of a junior college that attracts mainly local residents might prefer to consult statewide norms rather than national norms on a scholastic achievement test.

As a general rule, whenever an identifiable subgroup performs appreciably better or worse on a test than the more broadly defined standardization sample, it may be helpful to construct supplementary subgroup norms. The subgroups can be formed with respect to sex, ethnic background, geographical region, urban versus rural environment, socioeconomic level, and many other factors.

Whether local or subgroup norms are beneficial depends on the purpose of testing. For example, ethnic norms for standardized intelligence tests may be superior to nationally based norms in predicting competence within the child's nonschool environment. However, ethnic norms may not predict how well a child will succeed in mainstream public school instructional programs (Mercer & Lewis, 1978). Thus, local and subgroup norms must be used cautiously.

Expectancy Tables

One practical form that norms may take is an expectancy table. An **expectancy table** portrays the established relationship between test scores and expected outcome on a relevant task (Harmon, 1989). Expectancy tables are especially useful with predictor tests used to forecast well-defined criteria. For example, an expectancy table could depict the relationship between scores on a scholastic aptitude test (predictor) and subsequent college grade point average (criterion).

Expectancy tables are always based on the previous predictor and criterion results for large samples of examinees. The practical value of tabulating normative information in this manner is that new examinees receive a probabilistic preview of how well they are likely to do on the criterion. For example, high school examinees who take a scholastic aptitude test can be told the statistical odds of achieving a particular college grade point average.

Based on 7,835 previous examinees who subsequently attended a major university, the expectancy table in Table 3.6 provides the probability of achieving certain first-year college grades as a function of score on the American College Testing (ACT) examination. The ACT test is typically given to high school seniors who have expressed an interest in attending college. The first column of the table shows ACT test scores, divided into 10 class intervals. The second column gives the number of students whose scores fell into each interval. The remaining entries in each row show the percentage of students within each test-score interval who subsequently received college grade points within a designated range. For example, of the 117 students who scored 31 to 33 points on the ACT, only 2 percent received a first-year college grade point average below 1.50, while 64 percent earned superlative grades of 3.50 up to a perfect A or 4.00. At the other extreme, of the 102 students who scored below 10 points on the ACT, fully 80 percent (60 percent plus 20 percent) received first-year college grades below a C average of 2.00.

Of course, expectancy tables do not foreordain how new examinees will do on the criterion. In an individual case, it is conceivable that a low–ACT scoring student might beat the odds and earn a 4.00 college grade point average. More commonly, though, new examinees discover that expectancy tables provide a broadly accurate preview of criterion performance.

But there are some exceptional instances in which expectancy tables can become inaccurate. An expectancy table is always based on the previous performance of a large and representative sample of examinees whose test performances and criterion outcomes reflected existing social conditions and institutional policies. If conditions or policies change, an expectancy table can become obsolete and misleading. Consider the expectancy table in Figure 3.9 which depicts the likelihood of finishing high school as a function of seventh grade IQ (Dillon, 1949, cited in Matarazzo, 1972, p. 283). Notice that in the 1940s only 4 percent of seventh-grade students with IQs below 85 went on to finish high school. However, social policies and school environments have changed since the 1940s. There is currently a strong emphasis on special services for disabled students, with the aim of retention and eventual graduation. As a result, the expectancy table in Figure 3.9 surely would be pessimistically erroneous if applied to contemporary seventh-grade students with low IQs.

TABLE 3.6 Expectancy Table Showing Relation between ACT Composite Scores and First-Year College Grades for 7,835 Students at a Major State University

ACT Test Score	Number of Cases	Grade Point Average (4.00 Scale)					
		0.00–1.49	1.50–1.99	2.00–2.49	2.50–2.99	3.00–3.49	3.50–4.00
34–36	3	0	0	33	0	0	67
31–33	117	2	2	4	9	19	64
28–30	646	10	6	10	17	23	35
25–27	1,458	12	10	16	19	24	19
22–24	1,676	17	10	22	20	20	11
19–21	1,638	23	14	25	18	16	4
16–18	1,173	31	17	24	15	11	3
13–15	690	38	18	25	12	6	1
10–12	332	54	16	20	6	3	1
below 10	102	60	20	13	8	0	0

Note: Some rows total to more than 100 percent because of rounding errors.

Source: Courtesy of Archie George, Management Information Services, University of Idaho.

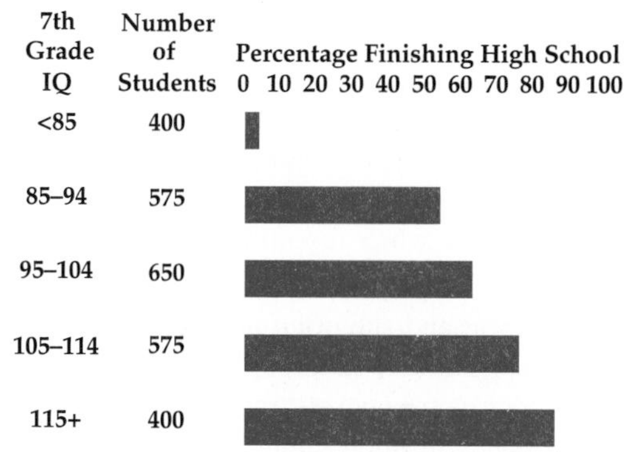

7th Grade IQ	Number of Students	Percentage Finishing High School 0 10 20 30 40 50 60 70 80 90 100
<85	400	
85–94	575	
95–104	650	
105–114	575	
115+	400	

FIGURE 3.9 **Expectancy of High School Graduation as a Function of Seventh-Grade IQ**
Source: Based on data from Dillon, H. J. (1949). *Early school leavers: A major educational problem.* New York: National Child Labor Committee. Cited in Matarazzo (1972).

CRITERION-REFERENCED TESTS

We close this unit with brief mention of an alternative to norm-referenced tests, namely, criterion-referenced tests (Frechtling, 1989; Glaser, 1963; Popham, 1978; Berk, 1984). Whereas a norm-referenced test uses a representative sample of persons as its interpretive framework, a criterion-referenced test compares an examinee's accomplishments to a well-defined content domain. For example, the test taker's performance might be reported as a specific skill level in arithmetic (adds two 3-digit numbers correctly 100 percent of the time, but has only 70 percent accuracy when adding three 3-digit numbers).

Criterion-referenced tests represent a fundamental shift in perspective. The focus is on what the test taker can do rather than on comparisons to the performance levels of others. Thus, criterion-referenced tests identify an examinee's absolute mastery (or nonmastery) of specific behaviors. In the main, these tests have been used in educational settings to help classroom teachers determine what ought to be taught and also to evaluate the precise effects of curricular efforts.

Criterion-referenced tests are best suited to the testing of basic academic skills (e.g., reading level, computation skill) in educational settings. However, these kinds of instruments are largely inappropriate for testing higher-level abilities because it is difficult to formulate specific objectives for such content domains. Consider a particular case: How could we develop a criterion-referenced test for expert computer programming? It would be difficult to propose specific behaviors which all expert computer programmers would possess, and therefore nearly impossible to construct a criterion-referenced test for this high-level skill. Berk (1984) discusses the technical problems in the construction and evaluation of criterion-referenced tests.

SUMMARY

1. A norm group consists of a sample of examinees who are representative of the population for whom the test is intended. A frequency distribution is useful in portraying the distribution of test scores within certain score intervals for a norm group. A histogram is a graphic representation of a frequency distribution.

2. Measures of central tendency for collections of scores include the mean or arithmetic average; the median or middlemost of the ranked scores; and the mode, which is the most frequently occurring score.

3. Measures of variability for a group of scores include the variance and its square root, the standard deviation, which is the preferred measure in psychological testing. These indices help gauge the dispersion of scores by incorporating the sums of squared deviations from the mean score in their formulas.

4. The distribution of test scores for large groups of heterogeneous examinees often resembles the normal distribution, a symmetrical, mathematically defined, bell-shaped curve. Psychologists prefer to deal with normally distributed test scores because the statistical characteristics of the normal distribution are well known.

5. A skewed distribution is one in which the scores pile upon at the low end (positive skew) or the high end (negative skew). On psychological tests, the most common cause of positive skew is too few easy items, whereas the most common cause of negative skew is too few hard items.

6. A percentile expresses the percentage of persons in the standardization sample who scored below a specific raw score. Percentiles vary from 0 to 100. It is important to distinguish percentile (a relative measure) from percent correct (an absolute measure).

7. A standard score expresses an examinee's raw score in terms of its distance from the mean in standard deviation units. The formula for a standard score is $z = (X - M)/SD$. A T score is a standardized score with mean of 50 and standard deviation of 10. The formula for a T score is

$$T = 10(X - M)/SD + 50$$

8. The most common approach to selecting a norm group is through stratified random sampling. In this procedure, the target population is stratified or classified on important background variables (e.g., age, sex, race, social class, educational level) and then an appropriate percentage of persons is chosen at random within each stratum.

9. For many tests, it is important to provide separate age and grade norms. Age norms are necessary for characteristics that change quickly with developing age—for example, intellectual abilities in childhood. Grade norms are commonly used in school settings when reporting the achievement levels of school children.

10. Local and subgroup norms may be valuable if an identifiable subgroup performs appreciably better or worse on a test than the more broadly defined standardization sample.

11. An expectancy table—one form of test standardization—portrays the established relationship between test scores and expected outcome on a relevant task. For example, an expectancy table might depict the relationship between scores on a scholastic aptitude test and subsequent college grade point average.

12. A criterion-referenced test compares an examinee's test accomplishments to a well-defined content domain. These tests help identify an examinee's mastery or nonmastery of specific behaviors. For example, results of a criterion-referenced test might specify that the examinee can add two 3-digit numbers correctly 100 percent of the time.

KEY TERMS AND CONCEPTS

Topic 3B Concepts of Reliability

Reliability refers to the attribute of consistency in measurement. However, reliability is seldom an all-or-none matter; more commonly it is a question of degree. Very few measures of physical or psychological characteristics are completely consistent, even from one moment to the next. For example, a person who steps on a scale twice in quick succession might register a weight of 145½ pounds the first time and 145¾ pounds the second. The same individual might take two presumably equivalent forms of an IQ test and score 114 on one and 119 on the other. Two successive measures of speed of response—pressing a key quickly whenever the letter *X* appears on a microcomputer screen—might produce a reaction time of 223 milliseconds on the first trial and 341 milliseconds on the next. We see in these examples a pattern of consistency—the pairs of measurements are not completely random—but different amounts of inconsistency are evident, too. In the short run, measures of weight are highly consistent, intellectual test scores are moderately stable, but simple reaction time is somewhat erratic.

The concept of **reliability** is best viewed as a continuum ranging from minimal consistency of measurement (e.g., simple reaction time) to near perfect repeatability of results (e.g., weight). Most psychological tests fall somewhere in between these two extremes. With regard to tests, an acceptable degree of reliability is more than an academic matter. After all, it would be foolish and unethical to base important decisions upon test results that are not repeatable (Case Exhibit 3.2).

Psychometricians have devised several statistical methods for estimating the degree of reliability of measurements, and we will explore the computation of such reliability coefficients in some detail. But first we examine a more fundamental issue to help clarify the meaning of reliability: What are the sources of consistency and inconsistency in psychological test results?

CASE EXHIBIT

3.2

TEST RELIABILITY AND COURTROOM TESTIMONY

The reliability of test findings may have a decisive impact on the outcome of legal proceedings. Consider the issues raised by a rape trial in which the alleged victim was a mentally disabled 22-year-old woman. In most rape trials, the defendant is accused of using force or threat of force in commission of a sexual act. This case was unusual because the defendant was accused of statutory rape, even though the victim was of legal age. The prosecuting attorney maintained that because of her mental disability the acquiescent victim was incapable of giving meaningful consent to a sexual act.

Everyone who knew the woman realized that she was "slow"; in fact, two mental health professionals described her as mildly retarded. Based in part upon the WAIS-R, a consulting psychologist arrived at an official diagnosis of mental retardation, too. The woman obtained a Verbal IQ of 68, Performance IQ of 75, and Full Scale IQ of 71. An IQ below 70 (or 75 in exceptional cases) is but one of several criteria of mental retardation, as discussed further in 7A, Testing Special Populations. Thus, the scores were just barely within the range of mild mental retardation and became a focal point of pretrial negotiations between the prosecuting attorney and the defense lawyer, who wanted to make his own arrangements for independent testing. No doubt the defense lawyer was hoping that a second round of testing would yield higher IQ scores and thereby rebut the damaging evidence that the young woman was mentally retarded.

What could the consulting psychologist tell the prosecuting attorney about the likely outcome of a second WAIS-R administration? It is well known that IQ test results are usually consistent in the short run, but how consistent? Was it likely that the young woman would score in the retarded range on the second administration? The answer to this last question was fraught with legal significance. If the second test results confirmed the original findings, then the prosecutor's trial strategy was secure. However, if the alleged victim scored substantially higher the second time, such findings would cast doubt on a diagnosis of mental retardation. As a result, the prosecutor would be obliged to substantially revise his courtroom tactics—almost literally overnight. Psychometric theory had left the clouds of scholastic abstraction and touched earth in the courtroom: Pretrial maneuverings in a rape case hinged in part on the potential repeatability or reliability of a psychological test result.

The consulting psychologist informed the prosecuting attorney that the odds were 2 to 1 in favor of the second Full Scale IQ falling between 68 and 74, assuming that sufficient time had passed to eliminate any practice effects from the first administration. The prediction proved correct. A second psychologist, hired by the defense, found the young woman to have a Full Scale IQ of 72, only a single point higher than the original findings. How was it possible to predict this outcome in advance? This question is central to the concepts of reliability presented in this topic. Incidentally, the defendant was found guilty of rape and sentenced to 15 years in prison. This outcome hinged, in part, on the consistency or reliability of a psychological test result.

CLASSICAL THEORY AND THE SOURCES OF MEASUREMENT ERROR

The theory of measurement introduced here has been called the classical theory because it was developed from simple assumptions made by test theorists since the inception of testing. This approach is also called the *theory of true and error scores,* for reasons explained below. Charles Spearman (1904) laid down the foundation for the theory which was subsequently extended and revised by contemporary psychologists (Feldt & Brennan, 1989; Gulliksen, 1950; Lord & Novick, 1968; Kline, 1986). We should mention that a rival model does exist. The theory of domain sampling arose with Tryon's (1957) reformulation and was more recently extended by Cronbach, Gleser, Nanda, and Rajaratnam (1972) in a variant called generalizability theory. In the following, we will make brief reference to the domain sampling viewpoint. However, the classical theory is still the prevailing psychometric viewpoint. Accordingly, we concentrate our coverage on this model.

The basic starting point of the **classical theory of measurement** is the idea that test scores result from the influence of two factors:

1. Factors that contribute to consistency. These consist entirely of the stable attributes of the individual which the examiner is trying to measure.
2. Factors that contribute to inconsistency. These include characteristics of the individual, test, or situation which have nothing to do with the attribute being measured, but which nonetheless affect test scores.

It should be clear to the reader that the first factor is desirable because it represents the true amount of the attribute in question, while the second factor represents the unavoidable nuisance of error factors that contribute to inaccuracies of measurement. We can express this conceptual breakdown as a simple equation:

$$X = T + e$$

where X is the obtained score, T is the **true score,** and e represents errors of measurement.

Errors in measurement thus represent discrepancies between the obtained scores and the corresponding true scores:

$$e = X - T$$

Notice in the preceding equations that errors of measurement e can be either positive or negative. If e is positive, the obtained score X will be higher than the true score T. Conversely, if e is negative, the obtained score will be lower than the true score. Although it is impossible to eliminate all **measurement error,** test developers do strive to minimize this psychometric nuisance through careful attention to the sources of measurement error outlined in the following section.

Finally, it is important to stress that the true score is never known. As the reader will discover, we can obtain a probability that the true score resides within a certain interval and we can also derive a best estimate of the true score. However, we can never know the value of a true score with certainty.

SOURCES OF MEASUREMENT ERROR

As indicated by the formula $X = T + e,$ measurement error e is everything other than the true score that makes up the obtained test score. Errors of measurement can arise from innumerable sources (Feldt & Brennan, 1989). Stanley (1971) provides an unusually thorough list. We will outline only the most important and likely contributions here: item selection, test administration, test scoring, and systematic errors of measurement.

Item Selection

One source of measurement error is the instrument itself. A test developer must settle upon a finite number of items from a potentially infinite pool of test questions. Which questions should be included? How should they be worded? Item selection is crucial to the accuracy of measurement.

Although psychometricians strive to obtain representative test items, the particular set of questions chosen for a test might not be equally fair to all persons. A hypothetical and deliberately extreme example will serve to illustrate this point: Even a well-prepared student might flunk a classroom test that emphasized the obscure footnotes in the text-book. By contrast, an ill-prepared but curious student who studied only the footnotes might do very well on such an exam. The scores for both persons would reflect massive amounts of measurement error. Remember in this context that the true score is what the student really knows. For the conscientious student, the obtained score would be far lower than the true score, due to a hefty dose of negative measurement error. For the serendipitous second student, the obtained score would be far higher than the true score, owing to the positive measurement error.

Of course, in a well-designed test the measurement error from item sampling will be minimal. However, a test is always a sample and never the totality of a person's knowledge or behavior. As a result, item selection is always a source of measurement error in psychological testing. The best a psychometrician can do is minimize this unwanted nuisance by attending carefully to issues of test construction. We discuss technical aspects of item selection in Topic 4B, Test Construction.

Test Administration

Although examiners usually provide an optimal and standardized testing environment, numerous sources of measurement error may nonetheless arise from the circumstances of administration. Examples of general environmental conditions that may exert an untoward influence on the accuracy of measurement include uncomfortable room temperature, dim lighting, and excessive noise. In some cases it is not possible to anticipate the qualities of the testing situation that will contribute to measurement error. Consider this example: An otherwise lackluster undergraduate correctly answers a not very challenging information item, namely, "Who wrote *Canterbury Tales*?" When queried later whether he had read any Chaucer, the student replies "No, but you've got that book right behind you on your bookshelf."

Momentary fluctuations in anxiety, motivation, attention, and fatigue level of the test taker may also introduce sources of measurement error. For example, an examinee who did not sleep well the night before might lack concentration and therefore misread questions. A student distracted by temporary emotional distress might inadvertently respond in the wrong columns of the answer sheet. The classic nightmare in this regard is the test taker who skips a question—let us say, question number 19—but forgets to leave the corresponding part of the answer sheet blank. As a result, all the subsequent answers are off by one, with the response to question 20 entered on the answer sheet as item 19, and so on.

The examiner, too, may contribute to measurement error in the process of test administration. In an orally administered test, an unconscious nod of the head by the tester might convey that the examinee is on the right track, thereby guiding the test taker to the correct response. Conversely, a terse and abrupt examiner may intimidate a test taker who would otherwise volunteer a correct answer.

Test Scoring

Whenever a psychological test uses a format other than machine-scored multiple-choice items, some degree of judgment is required to assign points to answers. Fortunately, most tests have well-defined criteria for answers to each question. These guidelines help minimize the impact of subjective judgment in scoring (Gregory, 1987). However, subjectivity of scoring as a source of measurement error can be a serious problem in the evaluation of projective tests or essay questions. With regard to projective tests, Nunnally (1978) points out that the projective tester might undergo an evolutionary change in scoring criteria over time, coming to regard a particular type of response as more and more pathological with each encounter.

Systematic Measurement Error

The sources of inaccuracy previously discussed are collectively referred to as *unsystematic measure-*

ment error, meaning that their effects are unpredictable and inconsistent. However, there is another type of measurement error that constitutes a veritable ghost in the psychometric machine. A **systematic measurement error** arises when, unknown to the test developer, a test consistently measures something other than the trait for which it was intended. Suppose, for example, that a scale to measure social introversion also inadvertently taps anxiety in a consistent fashion. In this case, the equation depicting the relationship between observed scores, true scores, and sources of measurement error would be

$$X = T + e_s + e_u$$

where X is the obtained score, T is the true score, e_s is the systematic error due to the anxiety subcomponent, and e_u is the collective effect of the unsystematic measurement errors previously outlined.

Because by definition their presence is initially undetected, systematic measurement errors may constitute a significant problem in the development of psychological tests. However, if psychometricians use proper test development procedures discussed in Topic 4B, Test Construction, the impact of systematic measurement errors can be greatly minimized. Nonetheless, systematic measurement errors serve as a reminder that it is very difficult, if not impossible, to truly assess a trait in pure isolation from other traits.

We have furnished the barest outline of the numerous and varied sources of measurement error in this section. The reader may wish to review Topic 2B, The Testing Process, which provides more detail on the multitudinous factors that can sway the outcome of psychological testing and thereby introduce measurement error.

MEASUREMENT ERROR AND RELIABILITY

Perhaps at this point the reader is wondering what measurement error has to do with reliability. The most obvious connection is that measurement error

reduces the reliability or repeatability of psychological test results. In fact, we will show here that reliability bears a precise statistical relationship to measurement error. Reliability and measurement error are really just different ways of expressing the same concern: How consistent is a psychological test? The interdependence of these two concepts will become clear if we provide a further sketch of the classical theory of measurement.

A crucial assumption of classical theory is that unsystematic measurement errors act as random influences. This does not mean that the sources of measurement error are completely mysterious and unfathomable in every individual case. We might suspect for one person that her score on digit span reflected a slight negative measurement error caused by the auditory interference of someone coughing in the hallway during the presentation of the fifth item. Likewise, we could conjecture that another person received the benefit of positive measurement error by glimpsing in the mirror behind the examiner to see the correct answer to the ninth item on an information test. Thus, measurement error is not necessarily a mysterious event in every individual case.

However, when we examine the test scores of groups of persons, the causes of measurement error are incredibly complex and varied. In this context, unsystematic measurement errors behave like random variables. The classical theory accepts this essential randomness of measurement error as an axiomatic assumption.

Because they are random events, unsystematic measurement errors are equally likely to be positive or negative and will therefore average out to zero across a large group of subjects. Thus, a second assumption is that the mean error of measurement is zero. Classical theory also assumes that measurement errors are not correlated with true scores. This makes intuitive sense: If the error scores were related to another score, it would suggest that they were systematic rather than random, which would violate the essential assumption of classical theory. Finally, it is also assumed that measurement errors are not correlated with errors on other tests.

We can summarize the main features of classical theory as follows (Gulliksen, 1950, chap. 2):

1. Measurement errors are random.
2. Mean error of measurement = 0.
3. True scores and errors are uncorrelated: $r_{Te} = 0$.
4. Errors on different tests are uncorrelated: $r_{12} = 0$.

Starting from these assumptions, it is possible to develop a number of important implications for reliability and measurement. (The points that follow are based on the optimistic assumption that systematic measurement errors are minimal or nonexistent for the instrument in question.) For example, we know that any test administered to a large group of persons will show a variability of obtained scores which can be expressed statistically as a variance, that is, σ^2. The value of classical theory is that it permits us to partition the variance of obtained scores into two separate sources. Specifically, it can be shown that the variance of obtained scores is simply the variance of true scores plus the variance of errors of measurement:

$$\sigma_X^2 = \sigma_T^2 + \sigma_e^2$$

We will refer the interested reader to Gulliksen (1950, chp. 3) for the computational details.

The preceding formula demonstrates that test scores vary as the result of two factors: variability in true scores, and variability due to measurement error. The obvious implication of this relationship is that errors of measurement contribute to inconsistency of obtained test scores; results will not remain stable if the test is administered again.

THE RELIABILITY COEFFICIENT

We are finally in a position to delineate the precise relationship between reliability and measurement error. By now the reader should have discerned that reliability expresses the relative influence of true and error scores on obtained test scores. In more precise mathematical terms, the **reliability coefficient** (r_{XX}) is the ratio of true score variance to the total variance of test scores. That is:

$$r_{XX} = \frac{\sigma_T^2}{\sigma_X^2}$$

or equivalently:

$$r_{XX} = \frac{\sigma_T^2}{\sigma_T^2 + \sigma_e^2}$$

Note that the range of potential values for r_{XX} can be derived from analysis of the preceding formula. Consider what happens when the variance due to measurement error (σ_e^2) is very small, close to zero. In that event, the reliability coefficient (r_{XX}) approaches a value of (σ_T^2/σ_T^2) or 1.0. At the opposite extreme where the variance due to measurement error is very large, the value of the reliability coefficient becomes smaller, approaching a theoretical limit of 0.0. In sum, a completely unreliable test (large measurement error) will yield a reliability coefficient close to 0.0 while a completely reliable test (no measurement error) will produce a reliability coefficient of 1.0. Thus, the possible range of the reliability coefficient is between 0 and 1.0. In practice, all tests produce reliability coefficients somewhere in between, but the closer the value of r_{XX} to 1.0 the better.

In a literal sense, r_{XX} indicates the proportion of variance in obtained test scores which is accounted for by the variability in true scores. However, the formula for the reliability coefficient r_{XX}, indicates an additional interpretation of it as well. The reader will recall that obtained scores are symbolized by Xs. In like manner, the subscripts in the symbol for the reliability coefficient signify that r_{XX} is an index of the potential or actual consistency of obtained scores. Thus, tests which capture minimal amounts of measurement error produce consistent and reliable scores; their reliability coefficients are near 1.0. Conversely, tests which reflect large amounts of measurement error produce inconsistent and unreliable scores; their reliability coefficients are closer to 0.0.

Up to this point, the discussion of reliability has been conceptual rather than practical. We have pointed out that reliability refers to consistency of measurement; that reliability is diminished to the extent that errors of measurement dominate the obtained score; and, that one statistical index of reliability, the reliability coefficient, can vary between 0.0 and 1.0. But how is a statistical measure of reliability computed? We approach this topic indirectly, first reviewing an essential statistical tool, the correlation coefficient. The reader will discover that the correlation coefficient, a numerical index of the degree of linear relationship between two sets of scores, is an excellent tool for appraising the consistency or repeatability of test scores. We provide a short refresher on the meaning of correlation before proceeding to a summary of methods for estimating reliability.

THE CORRELATION COEFFICIENT

In its most common application, a **correlation coefficient** (r) expresses the degree of linear relationship between two sets of scores obtained from the same persons. Correlation coefficients can take on values ranging from −1.00 to +1.00. A correlation coefficient of +1.00 signifies a perfect linear relationship between the two sets of scores. In particular, when two measures have a correlation of +1.00, the rank ordering of subjects is identical for both sets of scores. Furthermore, when arrayed on a scatterplot (Figure 3.10a), the individual data points (each representing a pair of scores from a single subject) conform to a perfectly straight line with an upward slope. A correlation coefficient of −1.00 signifies an equally strong relationship, but with inverse correspondence: the highest score on one variable corresponding to the lowest score on the other, and vice versa. In this case, the individual data points conform to a perfectly straight line with a downward slope (Figure 3.10b). Correlations of +1.00 or −1.00 are extremely rare in psychological research and usually signify a trivial finding. For example, if on two occasions in quick succession we counted the number of letters in the last name of 100 students, these two sets of "scores" would show a correlation of +1.00.

Negative correlations usually result from the manner in which one of the two variables was scored. For example, scores on the Category Test (Reitan & Wolfson, 1993) are reported as errors, whereas results on the Raven Progressive Matrices (Raven, Court, & Raven, 1983, 1986) are reported as number of items correct. Persons who obtain a high score on the Category Test (many errors) will most likely obtain a low score on the Progressive Matrices test (few correct). Thus, we would expect a substantial negative correlation for scores on these two tests.

Consider the scatterplot in Figure 3.10c which might depict the hypothetical height and weight of a group of persons. As the reader can see, height and weight are strongly but not perfectly related to one another. Tall persons tend to weigh more, short persons less, but there are some exceptions. If we were to compute the correlation coefficient between height and weight—a simple statistical task outlined in the following—we would obtain a value of about +0.80, indicating a strong, positive relationship between these measures.

When two variables have no relationship, the scatterplot takes on an undefined bloblike shape and the correlation coefficient is close to 0.00 (Figure 3.10d). For example, in a sample of adults, the correlation between reaction time and weight would most likely be very close to zero.

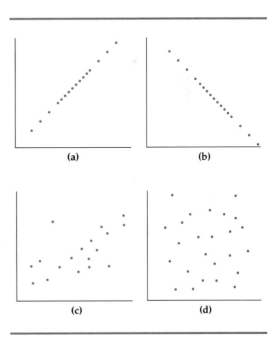

FIGURE 3.10 Scatterplots Depicting Different Degrees of Correlation

Finally, it is important to understand that the correlation coefficient is independent of the mean. For example, a correlation of +1.00 can be found between two administrations of the same test even when there are significant mean differences between pretest and posttest. In sum, perfect correlation does not imply identical pre- and posttest scores for each examinee. However, perfect correlation does imply perfectly ordered ranking from pretest to posttest, as discussed previously.

THE CORRELATION COEFFICIENT AS A RELIABILITY COEFFICIENT

One use of the correlation coefficient is to gauge the consistency of psychological test scores. If test results are highly consistent, then the scores of persons taking the test on two occasions will be strongly correlated, perhaps even approaching the theoretical upper limit of +1.00. In this context, the correlation coefficient is also a reliability coefficient. Even though the computation of the Pearson *r* makes no reference to the theory of true and error scores, the correlation coefficient does, nonetheless, reflect the proportion of variance in obtained test scores accounted for by the variability in true scores. Thus, in some contexts a correlation coefficient is a reliability coefficient.

This discussion introduces one method for estimating the reliability of a test: Administer the instrument twice to the same group of persons and compute the correlation between the two sets of scores. The test-retest approach is very common in the evaluation of reliability, but several other strategies exist as well. As we review the following methods for estimating reliability, the reader may be temporarily bewildered by the apparent diversity of approaches. In fact, the different methods fall into two broad groups, namely, temporal stability approaches which directly measure the consistency of test scores, and internal consistency approaches which rely upon a single test administration to gauge reliability. Keep in mind that one common theme binds all the eclectic methods together: Reliability is always an attempt to gauge the likely accuracy or repeatability of test scores.

RELIABILITY AS TEMPORAL STABILITY

Test-Retest Reliability

The most straightforward method for determining the reliability of test scores is to administer the identical test twice to the same group of heterogeneous and representative subjects. If the test is perfectly reliable, each person's second score will be completely predictable from his or her first score. On many kinds of tests, particularly ability and achievement tests, we might expect subjects generally to score somewhat higher the second time because of practice, maturation, schooling, or other intervening effects that take place between pretest and posttest. However, so long as the second score is strongly correlated with the first score, the existence of practice, maturation, or treatment effects does not cast doubt upon the reliability of a psychological test.

An example of a reliability coefficient computed as a **test-retest** correlation coefficient is depicted in Figure 3.11. In this case, 60 subjects were adminis-

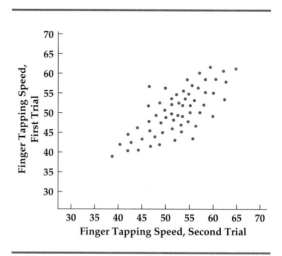

FIGURE 3.11 Scatterplot Revealing a Reliability Coefficient of .80
Source: Based on data from Morrison, M. W., Gregory, R. J., and Paul, J. J. (1979). Reliability of the Finger Tapping Test and a note on sex differences. *Perceptual and Motor Skills, 48,* 139–142.

tered the Finger Tapping Test (FTT) on two occasions separated by a week (Morrison, Gregory, & Paul, 1979). The FTT, one component of the Halstead-Reitan neuropsychological test battery (Reitan & Wolfson, 1985), is a relatively pure measure of motor speed. Using a standardized mechanical counting apparatus, the subject is instructed to tap with the index finger as fast as possible for 10 seconds. This procedure is continued until five trials in a row reveal consistent results. The procedure is repeated for the nondominant hand. The score for each hand is the average of the five consecutive trials.

The correlation between scores from repeated administrations of this test works out to be about 0.80. This is at the low end of acceptability for reliability coefficients, which usually fall in the .80s or .90s. We discuss standards of reliability in more detail subsequently.

Alternate-Forms Reliability

In some cases test developers produce two forms of the same test. These alternate forms are independently constructed to meet the same specifications, often on an item-by-item basis. Thus, **alternate forms** of a test incorporate similar content and cover the same range and level of difficulty in items. Alternate forms of a test possess similar statistical and normative properties. For example, when administered in counterbalanced fashion to the same group of subjects, the means and standard deviations of alternate forms are typically quite comparable.

Estimates of alternate-form reliability are derived by administering both forms to the same group and correlating the two sets of scores. This approach has much in common with test-retest methods—both strategies involve two test administrations to the same subjects with an intervening time interval. For both approaches, we would expect that intervening changes in motivation and individual differences in amount of improvement would produce fluctuations in test scores and thereby reduce reliability estimates somewhat. Thus, test-retest and alternate-forms reliability estimates share considerable conceptual similarity.

However, there is one fundamental difference between these two approaches. The alternate-forms methodology introduces item-sampling differences as an additional source of error variance. That is, some test takers may do better or worse on one form of a test because of the particular items sampled. Even though the two forms may be equally difficult on average, some subjects may find one form quite a bit harder (or easier) than the other because supposedly parallel items are not equally familiar to every person. Notice that item-sampling differences are not a source of error variance in the test-retest approach because identical items are used in both administrations.

Alternate forms of a test are also quite expensive—nearly doubling the cost of publishing a test and putting it on the market. Because of the increased cost and also the psychometric difficulties of producing truly parallel forms, fewer and fewer tests are being released in this format.

RELIABILITY AS INTERNAL CONSISTENCY

We turn now to some intriguing ways of estimating the reliability of an individual test without developing alternate forms and without administering the test twice to the same examinees (Feldt & Brennan, 1989). The first approach correlates the results from one-half of the test with the other half and is appropriately termed split-half reliability. The second approach examines the internal consistency of individual test items. In this method, the psychometrician seeks to determine whether the test items tend to show a consistent interrelatedness. Finally, insofar as some tests are less than perfectly reliable due to differences among scorers, we also take up the related topic of interscorer reliability.

Split-Half Reliability

We obtain an estimate of **split-half** reliability by correlating the pairs of scores obtained from equivalent halves of a test administered only once to a representative sample of examinees. The logic of split-half reliability is straightforward: If scores on two half tests from a *single* test administration show a strong correlation, then scores on two whole tests from two *separate* test administrations (the traditional approach to evaluating reliability) also should reveal a strong correlation.

Psychometricians typically view the split-half method as supplementary to the gold standard approach, which is the test-retest method. For example, in the standardization of the WAIS-III, the reliability of most scales was established by the test-retest approach *and* the split-half approach. These two estimates of reliability are generally similar although split-half approaches often yield higher estimates of reliability.

One justification for the split-half approach is that logistical problems or excessive cost may render it impractical to obtain a second set of test scores from the same examinees. In this case, a split-half estimate of reliability is the only thing available, and it is certainly better than no estimate at all. Another justification for the split-half approach is that the test-retest method is potentially misleading in certain cases. For example, some ability tests are prone to large but inconsistent practice effects—such as when examinees learn concepts from feedback given as part of the standardized testing procedure. When practice effects are large and variable, the rank order of scores from a second administration will at best sustain only a modest association to the rank order of scores from the first administration. For these kinds of instruments, test-retest reliability coefficients could be misleadingly low. Finally, test-retest approaches also will yield misleadingly low estimates of reliability if the trait being measured is known to fluctuate rapidly (e.g., certain measures of mood).

The major challenge with split-half reliability is dividing the test into two nearly equivalent halves. For most tests—especially those with the items ranked according to difficulty level—the first half is easier than the second half. We would not expect examinees to obtain equivalent scores on these two portions, so this approach to splitting a test rarely is used. The most common method for obtaining split halves is to compare scores on the odd items versus the even items of the test. This procedure works particularly well when the items are arranged in approximate order of difficulty.

In addition to calculating a Pearson *r* between scores on the two equivalent halves of the test, the computation of a coefficient of split-half reliability entails an additional step: adjusting the half-test reliability using the Spearman-Brown formula.

The Spearman-Brown Formula

Notice that the split-half method gives us an estimate of reliability for an instrument half as long as the full test. Although there are some exceptions, a shorter test generally is less reliable than a longer test. This is especially true if, in comparison to the shorter test, the longer test embodies equivalent content and similar item difficulty. Thus, the Pearson *r* between two halves of a test will usually underestimate the reliability of the full instrument. We need a method for deriving the reliability of the whole test based on the half-test correlation coefficient.

The **Spearman-Brown formula** provides the appropriate adjustment:

$$r_{SB} = \frac{2r_{hh}}{1 + r_{hh}}$$

In this formula, r_{SB} is the estimated reliability of the full test computed by the Spearman-Brown method, while r_{hh} is the half-test reliability. Table 3.7 shows conceivable half-test correlations alongside the cor-

TABLE 3.7 Comparison of Split-Half Reliabilities and Corresponding Spearman-Brown Reliabilities

Split-Half Reliability	Spearman-Brown Reliability
.5	.67
.6	.75
.7	.82
.8	.89
.9	.95

responding Spearman-Brown reliability coefficients for the whole test. For example, using the Spearman-Brown formula, we could determine that a half-test reliability of .70 is equivalent to an estimated full-test reliability of .82.

Critique of the Split-Half Approach

Although the split-half approach is widely used, nonetheless it has been criticized for its lack of precision:

> Instead of giving a single coefficient for the test, the procedure gives different coefficients depending on which items are grouped when the test is split into two parts. If one split may give a higher coefficient than another, one can have little faith in whatever result is obtained from a single split (Cronbach, 1951).

Why rely on a single split? Why not take a more typical value such as the mean of the split-half coefficients resulting from all possible splittings of a test? Cronbach (1951) advocated just such an approach when proposing a general formula for estimating the reliability of a psychological test.

Coefficient Alpha

As proposed by Cronbach (1951) and subsequently elaborated by others (Novick & Lewis, 1967; Kaiser & Michael, 1975), **coefficient alpha** may be thought of as the mean of all possible split-half coefficients, corrected by the Spearman-Brown formula. The formula for coefficient alpha is

$$r_\alpha = \left(\frac{N}{N-1} \right) \left(1 - \frac{\Sigma \sigma_j^2}{\sigma^2} \right)$$

where r_α is coefficient alpha, N is the number of items, σ_j^2 is the variance of one item, $\Sigma \sigma_j^2$ is the sum of variances of all items, and σ^2 is the variance of the total test scores. As with all reliability estimates, coefficient alpha can vary between 0.00 and 1.00.

Coefficient alpha is an index of the internal consistency of the items, that is, their tendency to correlate positively with one another. Insofar as a test or scale with high internal consistency will also tend to show stability of scores in a test-retest approach, coefficient alpha is therefore a useful estimate of reliability.

Traditionally, coefficient alpha has been thought of as an index of unidimensionality, that is, the degree to which a test or scale measures a single factor. Recent analyses by Cortina (1993) and Schmitt (1996) serve to dispel this misconception. Certainly coefficient alpha is an index of the interrelatedness of the individual items, but this is not synonymous with the unidimensionality of what the test or scale measures. In fact, it is possible for a scale to measure two or more distinct factors and yet still possess a very strong coefficient alpha. Schmitt (1996) gives the example of a 6-item test in which the first three items correlate .8 one with another, the last three items also correlate .8 one with another, whereas correlations across the two 3-item sets are only .3 (Table 3.8). Even though this is irrefutably a strong two-factor test, the value for coefficient alpha works out to be .86! For this kind of test, coefficient alpha probably will overestimate test-retest reliability. This is why psychometricians look to test-retest approaches as essential to the evaluation of reliability. Certainly the split-half approach in general, and coefficient alpha in particular, are

TABLE 3.8   A Six-Item Test with Two Factors and Strong Coefficient Alpha

Variable	1	2	3	4	5	6
1	—					
2	.8	—				
3	.8	.8	—			
4	.3	.3	.3	—		
5	.3	.3	.3	.8	—	
6	.3	.3	.3	.8	.8	—

Note: coefficient alpha = .86

Source: Reprinted with permission from Schmitt, N. (1996). Uses and abuses of coefficient alpha. *Psychological Assessment, 8,* 350–353.

valuable approaches to reliability, but they cannot replace the common sense of the test-retest approach: When the same test is administered twice to a representative sample of examinees, do they obtain the same relative placement of scores?

The Kuder-Richardson Estimate of Reliability

Cronbach (1951) has shown that coefficient alpha is the general application of a more specific formula developed earlier by Kuder and Richardson (1937). Their formula is generally referred to as **Kuder-Richardson formula 20** or, simply, **KR-20**, in reference to the fact that it was the twentieth in a lengthy series of derivations. The KR-20 formula is relevant to the special case where each test item is scored 0 or 1 (e.g., wrong or right). The formula is

$$\text{KR-20} = \left(\frac{N}{N-1}\right)\left(1 - \frac{\Sigma pq}{\sigma^2}\right)$$

where

N = the number of items on the test,
σ^2 = the variance of scores on the total test,
p = the proportion of examinees getting each item correct,
q = the proportion of examinees getting each item wrong.

Coefficient alpha extends the Kuder-Richardson method to types of tests with items that are not scored as 0 or 1. For example, coefficient alpha could be used with an attitude scale in which examinees indicate on each item whether they strongly agree, agree, disagree, or strongly disagree.

Interscorer Reliability

Some tests leave a great deal of judgment to the examiner in the assignment of scores. Certainly projective tests fall into this category, as do tests of moral development and creativity. Insofar as the scorer can be a major factor in the reliability of these instruments, a report of interscorer reliability is imperative. Computing **interscorer reliability** is a very straightforward procedure. A sample of tests is independently scored by two or more examiners and scores for pairs of examiners are then correlated. Test manuals typically report the training and experience required of examiners and then list representative interscorer correlation coefficients.

Interscorer reliability supplements other reliability estimates, but does not replace them. It would still be appropriate to assess the test-retest or other type of reliability in a subjectively scored test. We provide a quick summary of methods for estimating reliability in Table 3.9.

TABLE 3.9 Brief Synopsis of Methods for Estimating Reliability

Method	No. Forms	No. Sessions	Sources of Error Variance
Test-Retest	1	2	Changes over time
Alternate-Forms (immediate)	2	1	Item sampling
Alternate-Forms (delayed)	2	2	Item sampling Changes over time
Split-Half	1	1	Item sampling Nature of split
Coefficient Alpha	1	1	Item sampling Test heterogeneity
Interscorer	1	1	Scorer differences

Which Type of Reliability Is Appropriate?

As noted, even when a test has only a single form, there are still numerous methods available for assessing reliability: test-retest, split-half, coefficient alpha, and interscorer methods. For tests which possess two forms, we can add a fifth method: alternate-forms reliability. Which method is best? When should we use method but not another? To answer these questions, we need to know the nature and purpose of the individual test in question.

For tests designed to be administered to individuals more than once, it would be reasonable to expect that the test demonstrate reliability across time—in this case test-retest reliability is appropriate. For tests which purport to possess factorial purity, coefficient alpha would be essential. In contrast, factorially complex tests such as measures of general intelligence would not fare well by measures of internal consistency. Thus, coefficient alpha is not an appropriate index of reliability for all tests, but applies only to measures which are designed to assess a single factor. Split-half methods work well for instruments which have items carefully ordered according to difficulty level. Of course, interscorer reliability is appropriate for any test which involves subjectivity of scoring.

It is common for test manuals to report multiple sources of information about reliability. For example, the WAIS-III Manual (Tulsky, Zhu, & Ledbetter, 1997) reports split-half reliabilities for most subtests and also provides test-retest coefficients for all subtests and IQ scores. The manual also cites information akin to alternate-forms reliability—it reports the correlations between the WAIS-III and its predecessor, the WAIS-R.

In order to analyze the error variance into its component parts, a number of reliability coefficients will need to be computed. Although it is difficult to arrive at precise data in the real world, on a theoretical basis we can partition the variability of scores into true and error components as depicted in Figure 3.12.

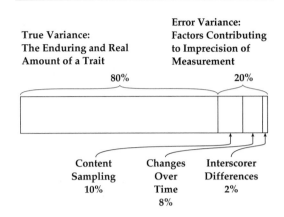

Note: The results are similar to what might be found if alternative forms of an individual intelligence test were administered to the same person by different examiners.

FIGURE 3.12   Sources of Variance in a Hypothetical Test

THE DOMAIN SAMPLING MODEL AND GENERALIZABILITY THEORY

The classical theory previously summarized is the basis for most analyses of reliability cited in research reports and test manuals. Another approach known as domain sampling provides an alternative and thought-provoking conceptualization of reliability and error components in measurement (Tryon, 1957). We discuss here the essentials of one domain sampling approach known as generalizability theory (Cronbach et al., 1972; Feldt & Brennan, 1989; Shavelson & Webb, 1991).

According to **generalizability theory,** when psychologists or educators set out to measure a variable, they almost always have a domain or universe of behaviors in mind (Cronbach, 1984). For example, when assessing typing speed the relevant domain or universe might be the examinee's average speed of all typing conducted during a particular month. If we could observe and calculate the average typing speed of one examinee for an entire month, then we would possess a universe score for that examinee. Of course, since universe scores typically refer to huge samples of behavior, from a practical standpoint we must settle for a finite sample of behavior. For example, we might compute the typing speed from one typing test—conducted by a particular examiner for a specified time period on a certain day. From this finite sample of behavior, we hope to generalize to the larger universe of possible outcomes—hence the appellation of generalizability theory.

Some parallels to classical theory are evident here. The finite sample of behavior in generalizability theory is akin to the observed score in classical theory. Furthermore, the universe score in generalizability theory is like the true score in classical theory. Just as a sample may or may not be an accurate representation of the domain (generalizability theory), an obtained score may or may not be an accurate representation of the true score (classical theory). So, these two approaches do share certain components in common.

The difference is that generalizability theory recognizes that there may be several viable and alternative universes of generalization, each containing distinctive sources of measurement error. To acknowledge the existence of alternative universes of generalization, Cronbach et al. (1972) introduce the notion of *facets*. Alone or in combination, facets define universes:

> We classify conditions of observation with respect to facets; for example, test forms, observers, and occasions. This does much to sharpen the definition of the universe of generalization and brings to attention the importance of the universe definition. Investigators often choose procedures for evaluating reliability that implicitly define a universe narrower than their substantive theory calls for. When they do so, they underestimate the "error" of measurement, that is, the error of generalization.

For example, in one instance we may want to know how an examinee responds on a typing test when confronted with a stern supervisor. In this case, using a stern examiner to conduct the typing test does not introduce measurement error. In another instance, we may want to know how an examinee responds on a typing test in a more typical office milieu. For this case, using a stern examiner would introduce an unwanted source of measurement error. The essential point of generalizability theory is that we cannot specify sources of measurement error until the relevant universe of generalization is defined.

Cronbach (1970) expresses the heart of generalizability theory in the following selection:

> When we use a single observation as if it represented the universe, we are generalizing. We generalize over scorers, over selections typed, perhaps over days. If the observed scores from a procedure agree closely with the universe score, we can say that the observation is "accurate," or "reliable," or "generalizable." And since the observations then also agree with each other, we say that they are "consistent" and "have little error variance." To have so many terms is confusing, but not seriously so. The term most often used in the literature is "reliability." The author prefers "generalizability" because that term immediately implies "generalization to what?" . . . There is a different degree of generalizability for each universe. The older methods of analysis do not separate the sources of variation. They deal with a single source of variance, or leave two or more sources entangled.

The classical theory of measurement is still the dominant model in psychometrics. However, generalizability theory has served a valuable function by reminding examiners that reliability is not a static quality that resides within the test per se; rather, reliability is an emergent property of the test in conjunction with the circumstances of use. In particular, reliability always hinges upon the manner in which we define the universe of potential behaviors, the universe of generalization.

SPECIAL CIRCUMSTANCES IN THE ESTIMATION OF RELIABILITY

Traditional approaches to estimating reliability may be misleading or inappropriate for some applications. Some of the more problematic situations involve unstable characteristics, speed tests, restriction of range, and criterion-referenced tests.

Unstable Characteristics

Some characteristics are presumed to be ever changing in reaction to situational or physiological variables. Emotional reactivity as measured by electrodermal or galvanic skin response is a good example. Such a measure fluctuates quickly in reaction to loud noises, underlying thought processes, and stressful environmental events. Even just talking to another person can arouse a strong electrodermal response. Because the true amount of emotional reactivity changes so quickly, test and retest must be nearly instantaneous in order to provide an accurate index of reliability for unstable characteristics such as an electrodermal measure of emotional reactivity.

Speed and Power Tests

A **speed test** typically contains items of uniform and generally simple level of difficulty. If time permitted, most subjects should be able to complete most or all of the items on such a test. However, as the name suggests, a speeded test has a restrictive time limit which guarantees that few subjects complete the entire test. Since the items attempted tend to be correct, an examinee's score on a speeded test largely reflects speed of performance.

Speed tests are often contrasted with power tests. A **power test** allows enough time for test takers to attempt all items, but is constructed so that no test taker is able to obtain a perfect score. Most tests contain a mixture of speed and power components.

The most important point to stress about the reliability of speed tests is that the traditional split-half approach (comparing odd and even items) will yield a spuriously high reliability coefficient. Consider one test taker who completes 60 of 90 items on a speed test. Most likely, the odd-even approach would show 30 odd items correct and 30 even items correct. With similar data from other subjects, the correlation between scores on odd and even items necessarily would approach +1.00. The reliability of a speed test should be based on the test-retest method or split-half reliability from two, separately timed half tests. In the latter instance, the Spearman-Brown correction is needed.

Restriction of Range

Test-retest reliability will be spuriously low if it is based on a sample of homogeneous subjects for whom there is a **restriction of range** on the characteristic being measured. For example, it would be inappropriate to estimate the reliability of an intelligence test by administering it twice to a sample of college students. This point is illustrated by the hypothetical but realistic scatterplot shown in Figure 3.13, where the reader can see a strong test-retest correlation for the entire range of diverse subjects, but a weak correlation for brighter subjects viewed in isolation.

Reliability of Criterion-Referenced Tests

The reader will recall from the first topic of this chapter that criterion-referenced tests evaluate performance in terms of mastery rather than assessing a continuum of achievement. Test items are designed to identify specific skills that need remediation; therefore, items tend to be of the "pass/fail" variety.

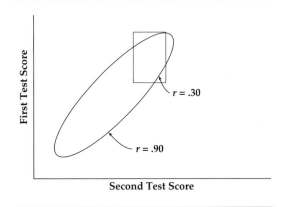

FIGURE 3.13   Sampling a Restricted Range of Subjects Causes Test-Retest Reliability To Be Spuriously Low

The structure of criterion-referenced tests is such that the variability of scores among examinees is typically quite minimal. In fact, if test results are used for training purposes and everyone continues training until all test skills are mastered, variability in test scores becomes nonexistent. Under these conditions, traditional approaches to the assessment of reliability are simply inappropriate.

With many criterion-referenced tests, results must be almost perfectly accurate to be useful. For example, any classification error is serious if the purpose of a test is to determine a subject's ability to drive a manual transmission or stick shift automobile. The key issue here is not whether test and retest scores are close to one another, but whether the classification ("can do/can't do") is the same in both instances. What we really want to know is the percentage of persons for whom the same decision is reached on both occasions—the closer to 100 percent, the better. This is but one illustration of the need for specialized techniques in the evaluation of nonnormative tests. Berk (1984) and Feldt and Brennan (1989) discuss approaches to the reliability of criterion-referenced tests.

THE INTERPRETATION OF RELIABILITY COEFFICIENTS

The reader should now be well versed in the different approaches to reliability and should possess at least a conceptual idea of how reliability coefficients are computed. In addition, we have discussed the distinctive testing conditions which dictate the use of one kind of reliability method as opposed to others. No doubt, the reader has noticed that we have yet to discuss one crucial question: What is an acceptable level of reliability?

Many authors suggest that reliability should be at least .90 if not .95 for decisions about individuals (e.g., Salvia & Ysseldyke, 1988; Nunnally & Bernstein, 1994). However, there is really no hard and fast answer to this question. We offer the loose guidelines suggested by Guilford and Fruchter (1978):

> There has been some consensus that to be a very accurate measure of individual differences in some characteristic, the reliability should be above .90. The truth is, however, that many standard tests with reliabilities as low as .70 prove to be very useful. And tests with reliabilities lower than that can be useful in research.

On a more practical level, acceptable standards of reliability hinge upon the amount of measurement error the user can tolerate in the proposed application of a test. Fortunately, reliability and measurement error are mutually interdependent concepts. Thus, if the test user can specify an acceptable level of measurement error, then it is also possible to determine the minimum standards of reliability required for that specific application of a test. We pursue this topic further by introducing a new concept: standard error of measurement.

RELIABILITY AND THE STANDARD ERROR OF MEASUREMENT

To introduce the concept of standard error of measurement we begin with a thought experiment. Suppose we could administer thousands of equivalent IQ tests to one individual. Suppose further that each test session was a fresh and new experience for our cooperative subject; in this hypothetical experiment, practice and boredom would have no effect on later test scores. Nonetheless, because of the kinds of random errors discussed in this chapter, the scores of our hapless subject would not be identical across test sessions. Our examinee might score a little worse on one test because he stayed up late the night before; the score on another test might be better because the items were idiosyncratically easy for him. Even though such error factors are random and unpredictable, it follows from the classical theory of measurement that the obtained scores would fall into a normal distribution with a precise mean and standard deviation. Let us say that the mean of the hypothetical IQ scores for our subject worked out to be 110, with a standard deviation of 2.5.

In fact, the mean of this distribution of hypothetical scores would be the estimated true score for our examinee. Our best estimate, then, is that our subject has a true IQ of 110. Furthermore, the standard deviation of the distribution of obtained scores would be the **standard error of measurement** (SEM). Note that while the true score on a test likely differs from one person to the next, the SEM is regarded as constant, an inherent property of the test. If we repeated this hypothetical experiment with another subject, the estimated true score would probably differ, but the SEM should work out to be a similar value.[1]

As its name suggests, the SEM is an index of measurement error which pertains to the test in question. In the hypothetical case where SEM = 0 there would be no measurement error at all. A subject's obtained score would then also be his or her true score. However, this outcome is simply impossible in real-world testing. Every test exhibits some degree of measurement error. The larger the SEM the greater the typical measurement error. However, the accuracy or inaccuracy of any individual score is always a probabilistic matter and never a known quantity.

As noted, the SEM can be thought of as the standard deviation of an examinee's hypothetical obtained scores on a large number of equivalent tests, under the assumption that practice and boredom effects are ruled out. Like any standard deviation of a normal distribution, the SEM has well-known statistical uses. For example, 68 percent of the obtained scores will fall within one SEM of the mean, just as 68 percent of the cases in a normal curve fall within one SD of the mean.

The reader will recall from earlier in this chapter that about 95 percent of the cases in a normal distribution fall within two SDs of the mean. For this reason, if our examinee were to take one more IQ test, we could predict with 95 percent odds that the obtained score would be within two SEMs of the estimated true IQ of 110. Knowing that the SEM is 2.5, we would therefore predict that the obtained IQ score would be 110 ± 5, that is, the true score would very likely (95 percent odds) fall between 105 and 115.

---

1. This would hold true for subjects of similar age. The SEM may differ from one age group to the next—see Wechsler (1997) for an illustration with the WAIS-III.

Unfortunately, in the real world we do not have access to true scores and we most certainly cannot obtain multiple IQs from large numbers of equivalent tests; nor for that matter do we have direct knowledge of the SEM. All we typically possess is a reliability coefficient (e.g., a test-retest correlation from normative studies) plus one obtained score from a single test administration. How can we possibly use this information to determine the likely accuracy of our obtained score?

Computing the Standard Error of Measurement

We have noted several times in this chapter that reliability and measurement error are intertwined concepts, with low reliability signifying high measurement error, and vice versa. It should not surprise the reader, then, that the SEM can be computed indirectly from the reliability coefficient. The formula is

$$SEM = SD \sqrt{1 - r}$$

where SD is the standard deviation of the test scores and r is the reliability coefficient, both derived from a normative sample or other large and representative group of subjects.

We can use WAIS-R Full Scale IQ to illustrate the computation of the SEM. The SD of WAIS-R scores is known to be about 15, and the reliability coefficient is .97 (Wechsler, 1981). The SEM for Full Scale IQ is therefore

$$SEM = 15 \sqrt{1 - .97}$$

which works out to be about 2.5.

The SEM and Individual Test Scores

Let us consider carefully what the SEM tells us about individual test results, once again using WAIS-R IQs to illustrate a general point. What we would really like to know is the likely accuracy of IQ. Let us say we have an individual examinee who obtains a score of 90, and let us assume that the test was administered in competent fashion. Nonetheless, is the obtained IQ score likely to be accurate?

In order to answer this question, we need to rephrase it. In the jargon of classical test theory, questions of accuracy really involve comparisons between obtained scores and true scores. Specifically, when we inquire whether an IQ score is accurate, we are really asking: How close is the obtained score to the true score?

The answer to this question may seem perturbing at first glance. It turns out that, in the individual case, we can never know precisely how close the obtained score is to the true score! The best we can do is provide a probabilistic statement based on our knowledge that the hypothetical obtained scores for a single examinee would be normally distributed with a standard deviation equal to the SEM. Based on this premise, we know that the obtained score is accurate to within plus or minus 2 SEMs in 95 percent of the cases. In other words, Full Scale IQ is 95 percent certain to be accurate within ±5 IQ points. This range of plus or minus 5 IQ points corresponds to the 95 percent **confidence interval** for WAIS-R Full Scale IQ, because we can be 95 percent confident that the true score is contained within it.

Testers would do well to report test scores in terms of a confidence interval, because this practice would help place scores in proper perspective (Sattler, 1988). An examinee who obtains an IQ of 90 should be described as follows: "Mr. Doe obtained a Full Scale IQ of 90 which is accurate to +/-5 points with 95 percent confidence." This wording helps forewarn others that test scores always incorporate some degree of measurement error.

The SEM and Differences between Scores

Testers are often expected to surmise if an examinee has scored significantly higher in one ability area than another. For example, it is usually germane to report whether an examinee is stronger at verbal or performance tasks or to say that no real difference exists in these two skill areas. The issue is not entirely academic. An examinee who has a relative superiority in performance intelligence might be counseled to pursue practical, hands-on careers. In contrast, a strength in verbal intelligence

might result in a recommendation to pursue academic interests. How is an examiner to determine whether one test score is significantly better than another?

Keep in mind that every test score incorporates measurement error. It is therefore possible for an examinee to obtain a verbal score higher than his or her performance score when the underlying true scores—if only we could know them—would reveal no difference or even the opposite pattern! (See Figure 3.14). The important lesson here is that when each of two obtained scores reflects measurement error, the difference between these scores is quite volatile and must not be overinterpreted.

The **standard error of the difference** between two scores is a statistical measure that can help a test user determine whether a difference between scores is significant. The standard error of the difference between two scores can be computed from

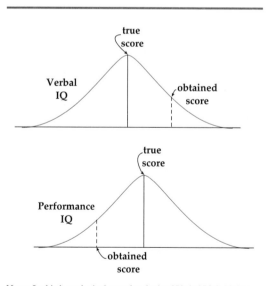

Note: In this hypothetical case the obtained Verbal IQ is higher than the obtained Performance IQ, whereas the underlying true scores show the opposite pattern.

FIGURE 3.14 **Obtained Scores Reflect Measurement Error and May Therefore Obscure the Relationship between True Scores**

CHAPTER 4

Validity and Test Development

TOPIC 4A Basic Concepts of Validity

As most every student of psychology knows, the merit of a psychological test is determined first by its reliability but then ultimately by its validity. In the preceding chapter we pointed out that reliability can be appraised by many seemingly diverse methods ranging from the conceptually straightforward test-retest approach to the theoretically more complex methodologies of internal consistency. Yet, regardless of the method used, the assessment of reliability invariably boils down to a simple summary statistic, the reliability coefficient. In this chapter, the more difficult and complex issue of validity—what a test score means—is

investigated. The concept of validity is still evolving and therefore stirs up a great deal more controversy than its staid and established cousin, reliability (AERA, APA, & NCE, 1999). In Topic 4A, Basic Concepts of Validity, we introduce essential concepts of validity, including the standard tripartite division into content, criterion-related, and construct validity. We also discuss extra-validity concerns, which include side effects and unintended consequences of testing. Extra-validity concerns have fostered a wider definition of test validity that extends beyond the technical notions of content, criteria, and constructs. In Topic 4B, Test

CASE EXHIBIT
4.1

RESEARCH AS THE ESSENTIAL PROOF OF TEST VALIDITY

In collaboration with his faculty adviser, a psychology graduate student sought to devise a paper-and-pencil measure of shyness. The student went through the appropriate steps of item selection and scale construction discussed in the next section (Topic 4B, Test Construction), and then attempted to validate his instrument by correlating it with existing measures such as the 10 clinical scales from the MMPI. Unfortunately, this new measure, tentatively named the Shyness Index, proved to have a whoppingly high correlation with the MMPI Depression scale ($r = .65$) and essentially no correlation with the MMPI Social Introversion Scale ($r = .08$). The graduate student's measure of *shyness* was apparently an index of social ineptitude and resulting depression. There is a moral in this brief tale: The trait measured by a given test is defined by validational research, not by what the developer chooses to name the instrument.

Construction, we stress that validity must be built into the test from the outset rather than being limited to the final stages of test development.

Put simply, the validity of a test is the extent to which it measures what it claims to measure. Psychometricians have long acknowledged that validity is the most fundamental and important characteristic of a test. After all, validity defines the *meaning* of test scores. Reliability is important, too, but only insofar as it constrains validity. To the extent that a test is unreliable, it cannot be valid. We can express this point from an alternative perspective: Reliability is a necessary but not a sufficient precursor of validity.

Test developers have a responsibility to demonstrate that new instruments fulfill the purposes for which they are designed. However, unlike test reliability, test validity is not a simple issue that is easily resolved on the basis of a few rudimentary studies. Test validation is a developmental process that begins with test construction and continues indefinitely:

> After a test is released for operational use, the interpretive meaning of its scores may continue to be sharpened, refined, and enriched through the gradual accumulation of clinical observations and through special research projects. . . . Test validity

is a living thing; it is not dead and embalmed when the test is released (Anastasi, 1986).

Test validity hinges upon the accumulation of research findings (Case Exhibit 4.1). In the sections that follow, we examine the kinds of evidence sought in the validation of a psychological test.

VALIDITY: A DEFINITION

We begin with a definition of **validity,** paraphrased from the influential *Standards for Educational and Psychological Testing* (AERA, APA, & NCME, 1985, 1999):

> A test is valid to the extent that inferences made from it are appropriate, meaningful, and useful.

Notice that a test score per se is meaningless until the examiner draws inferences from it based on the test manual or other research findings. For example, knowing that an examinee has obtained a slightly elevated score on the MMPI-2 Depression scale is not particularly helpful. This result becomes valuable only when the examiner infers behavioral characteristics from it. Based upon existing research, the examiner might conclude that "The elevated Depression score suggests that the examinee has little energy and has a pessimistic outlook on life." The MMPI-2 Depression scale possesses psychometric validity to the extent that such inferences are appropriate, meaningful, and useful.

Unfortunately, it is seldom possible to summarize the validity of a test in terms of a single, tidy statistic. Determining whether inferences are appropriate, meaningful, and useful typically requires numerous studies of the relationships between test performance and other independently observed behaviors. Validity reflects an evolutionary, research-based judgment of how adequately a test measures the attribute it was designed to measure. Consequently, the validity of tests is not easily captured by neat statistical summaries but is instead characterized on a continuum ranging from *weak* to *acceptable* to *strong*.

Traditionally, the different ways of accumulating validity evidence have been grouped into three categories:

- Content validity
- Criterion-related validity
- Construct validity

We will expand on this tripartite view of validity shortly, but first a few cautions. The use of these convenient labels does not imply that there are distinct types of validity or that a specific validation procedure is best for one test use and not another:

> An ideal validation includes several types of evidence, which span all three of the traditional categories. Other things being equal, more sources of evidence are better than fewer. However, the quality of the evidence is of primary importance, and a single line of solid evidence is preferable to numerous lines of evidence of questionable quality. Professional judgment should guide the decisions regarding the forms of evidence that are most necessary and feasible in light of the intended uses of the test and any likely alternatives to testing (AERA, APA, NCME, 1985).

We may summarize these points by stressing that validity is a unitary concept determined by the extent to which a test measures what it purports to measure. The inferences drawn from a valid test are appropriate, meaningful, and useful. In this light, it should be apparent that virtually any empirical study that relates test scores to other findings is a potential source of validity information (Anastasi, 1986; Messick, 1995).

CONTENT VALIDITY

Content validity is determined by the degree to which the questions, tasks, or items on a test are representative of the universe of behavior the test was designed to sample. In theory, content validity is really nothing more than a sampling issue (Bausell, 1986). The items of a test can be visualized as a sample drawn from a larger population of potential items that define what the researcher really wishes to measure. If the sample (specific items on the test) is representative of the population (all possible items), then the test possesses content validity.

Content validity is a useful concept when a great deal is known about the variable that the researcher wishes to measure. With achievement tests in particular, it is often possible to specify the relevant universe of behaviors in advance. For example, when developing an achievement test of spelling, a researcher could identify nearly all possible words that third graders should know. The content validity of a third-grade spelling achievement test would be assured, in part, if words of varying difficulty level were randomly sampled from this preexisting list.

However, test developers must take care to specify the relevant universe of responses as well. All too often, a multiple-choice format is taken for granted:

> If the constructor thinks about his aims with an open mind he will often decide that the task should call for a response constructed by the student— written open-end responses or, if inhibitions are to be minimized, oral responses. Nor are the directions to the subject and the social setting of the test to be neglected in defining the task (Cronbach, 1971).

In reference to spelling achievement, it cannot be assumed that a multiple-choice test will measure the same spelling skills as an oral test or a frequency count of misspellings in written compositions. Thus, when evaluating content validity, response specification is also an integral part of defining the relevant universe of behaviors.

Content validity is more difficult to assure when the test measures an ill-defined trait. How could a test developer possibly hope to specify the universe of potential items for a measure of anxiety? In these cases where the measured trait is less tangible, no test developer in his or her right mind would try to construct the literal universe of potential test items. Instead, what usually passes for content validity is the considered opinion of expert judges. In effect, the test developer asserts that "a panel of experts reviewed the domain specification carefully and judged the following test questions to possess content validity." Figure 4.1 reproduces a sample judge's item rating form for determining the content validity of test questions.

Quantification of Content Validity

Lawshe (1975), Martuza (1977), and others have discussed statistical methods for determining the overall content validity of a test from the judgments of experts. These methods tend to be very specialized and have not been widely accepted. Nonetheless, their approaches can serve as a model for a commonsense viewpoint on interrater agreement as a basis for content validity.

When two expert judges evaluate individual items of a test on the four-point scale proposed in Figure 4.1, the ratings of each judge on each item can be dichotomized into weak relevance (ratings of 1 or 2) versus strong relevance (ratings of 3 or 4). For each item, then, the conjoint ratings of the two judges can be entered into the two-by-two agreement table depicted in Figure 4.2. For example, if both judges believed an item was quite relevant (strong relevance), it would be placed in cell D. If the first judge believed an item was very relevant (strong relevance) but the second judge deemed it be only slightly relevant (weak relevance), the item would be placed in cell B.

Notice that cell D is the only cell that reflects valid agreement between judges. The other cells involve disagreement (cells B and C) or agreement that an item doesn't belong on the test (cell A). We have reproduced hypothetical results for a 100-item test in Figure 4.3. A coefficient of content validity can be derived from the following formula:

$$\text{content validity} = \frac{D}{(A + B + C + D)}$$

For example, on our 100-item test both judges concurred that 87 items were strongly relevant (cell D), so the coefficient of content validity would be 87/(4 + 4 + 5 + 87) or .87. If more than two judges are used, this computational procedure could be completed with all possible pair-wise combinations of judges, and the average coefficient reported. An important note: A coefficient of content validity is just one piece of evidence in the evaluation of a test. Such a coefficient does not by itself establish the validity of a test.

Reviewer:_____ Date: _____

FIGURE 4.1

Sample Judges Item Rating Form for Determining Content Validity
Source: Based on Martuza (1977), Hambleton (1984), Bausell (1986).

Please read carefully through the domain specification for this test. Next, please indicate how well you feel each item reflects the domain specification. Judge a test item solely on the basis of match between its content and the content defined by the domain specification. Please use the four-point rating scale shown below:

| *1* | *2* | *3* | *4* |
| *not relevant* | *somewhat relevant* | *quite relevant* | *very relevant* |

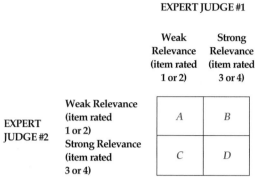

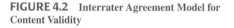

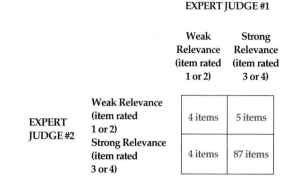

FIGURE 4.2   Interrater Agreement Model for Content Validity

FIGURE 4.3   Hypothetical Example of Agreement Model of Content Validity for a 100-Item Test

The commonsense approach to content validity advocated here serves well as a flagging mechanism to help cull out existing items that are deemed inappropriate by expert raters. However, it cannot identify nonexistent items that should be added to a test to help make the pool of questions more representative of the intended domain. A test could possess a robust coefficient of content validity and still fall short in subtle ways. Quantification of content validity is no substitute for careful selection of items.

Face Validity

We digress briefly here to mention face validity, which is not really a form of validity at all. Nonetheless, the concept is encountered in testing and therefore needs brief explanation. A test has **face validity** if it looks valid to test users, examiners, and especially the examinees. Face validity is really a matter of social acceptability, and not a technical form of validity in the same category as content, criterion-related, or construct validity (Nevo, 1985). From a public relations standpoint, it is crucial that tests possess face validity—otherwise those who take the tests may be dissatisfied and doubt the value of psychological testing. How-

ever, face validity should not be confused with objective validity, which is determined by the relationship of test scores to other sources of information. In fact, a test could possess extremely strong face validity—the items might look highly relevant to what is presumably measured by the instrument—yet produce totally meaningless scores with no predictive utility whatever.

CRITERION-RELATED VALIDITY

Criterion-related validity is demonstrated when a test is shown to be effective in estimating an examinee's performance on some outcome measure. In this context, the variable of primary interest is the outcome measure, called a *criterion*. The test score is useful only insofar as it provides a basis for accurate prediction of the criterion. For example, a college entrance exam that is reasonably accurate in predicting the subsequent grade point average of examinees would possess criterion-related validity.

Two different approaches to validity evidence are subsumed under the heading of criterion-related validity. In **concurrent validity,** the criterion measures are obtained at approximately the same time as the test scores. For example, the current psychiatric diagnosis of patients would be an appropriate criterion measure to provide validation evidence for a paper-and-pencil psychodiagnostic test. In **predictive validity,** the criterion measures are obtained in the future, usually months or years after the test scores are obtained, as with the college grades predicted from an entrance exam. Each of these two approaches is best suited to different testing situations, discussed in the following sections. However, before we review the nature of concurrent and predictive validity, let us examine a more fundamental question: What are the characteristics of a good criterion?

Characteristics of a Good Criterion

As noted, a *criterion* is any outcome measure against which a test is validated. In practical terms, a criterion can be most anything. Some examples will help to illustrate the diversity of potential criteria. A simulator-based driver skill test might be validated against a criterion of "number of traffic citations received in the last twelve months." A scale measuring social readjustment might be validated against a criterion of "number of days spent in a psychiatric hospital in the last three years." A test of sales potential might be validated against a criterion of "dollar amount of goods sold in the preceding year." The choice of criteria is circumscribed, in part, by the ingenuity of the test developer. However, criteria must be more than just imaginative, they must also be reliable, appropriate, and free of contamination from the test itself.

The criterion must itself be reliable if it is to be a useful index of what the test measures. If you recall the meaning of reliability—consistency of scores—the need for a reliable criterion measure is intuitively obvious. After all, unreliable means unpredictable. An unreliable criterion will be inherently unpredictable, regardless of the merits of the test.

Consider the case where scores on a college entrance exam (the test) are used to predict subsequent grade point average (the criterion). The validity of the entrance exam could be studied by computing the correlation (r_{xy}) between entrance exam scores and grade point averages for a repre-

sentative sample of students. For purposes of a validity study, it would be ideal if the students were granted open or unscreened enrollment so as to prevent a restriction of range on the criterion variable. In any case, the resulting correlation coefficient is called a *validity coefficient.*[1]

The theoretical upper limit of the validity coefficient is constrained by the reliability of both the test and the criterion:

$$r_{xy} = \sqrt{(r_{xx})(r_{yy})}$$

The validity coefficient is always less than or equal to the square root of the test reliability multiplied by the criterion reliability. In other words, to the extent that the reliability of either the test or the criterion (or both) is low, the validity coefficient is also diminished. Returning to our example of an entrance exam used to predict college grade point average, we must conclude that the validity coefficient for such a test will always fall far short of +1.00, owing in part to the unreliability of college grades and also in part to the unreliability of the test itself.

A criterion measure must also be appropriate for the test under investigation. The *Standards for Educational and Psychological Testing* sourcebook (AERA, APA, NCME, 1985) incorporates this important point as a separate standard:

> All criterion measures should be described accurately, and the rationale for choosing them as relevant criteria should be made explicit.

For example, in the case of interest tests, it is sometimes unclear whether the criterion measure should indicate satisfaction, success, or continuance in the activities under question. The choice between these subtle variants in the criterion must be made carefully, based on an analysis of what the interest test purports to measure.

A criterion must also be free of contamination from the test itself. Lehman (1978) has illustrated

---

1. We have purposefully refrained from referring to such a statistic as *the* validity coefficient. Remember that validity is a unitary concept determined by multiple sources of information which may include the correlation between test and criterion.

this point in a criterion-related validity study of a life change measure. The Schedule of Recent Events (SRE, Holmes & Rahe, 1967) is a widely used instrument that provides a quantitative index of the accumulation of stressful life events (e.g., divorce, job promotion, traffic tickets). Scores on the SRE correlate modestly with such criterion measures as physical illness and psychological disturbance. However, many seemingly appropriate criterion measures incorporate items that are similar or identical to SRE items. For example, screening tests of psychiatric symptoms often check for changes in eating, sleeping, or social activities. Unfortunately, the SRE incorporates questions that check for the following:

> change in eating habits
> change in sleeping habits
> change in social activities

If the screening test contains the same items as the SRE, then the correlation between these two measures will be artificially inflated. This potential source of error in test validation is referred to as *criterion contamination,* since the criterion is "contaminated" by its artificial commonality with the test.

Criterion contamination is also possible when the criterion consists of ratings from experts. If the experts also possess knowledge of the examinees' test scores, this information may (consciously or unconsciously) influence their ratings. When validating a test against a criterion of expert ratings, the test scores must be held in strictest confidence until the ratings have been collected.

Now that the reader knows the general characteristics of a good criterion, we will review the application of this knowledge in the analysis of concurrent and predictive validity.

Concurrent Validity

In a concurrent validation study, test scores and criterion information are obtained simultaneously. Concurrent evidence of test validity is usually desirable for achievement tests, tests used for licensing or certification, and diagnostic clinical tests.

An evaluation of concurrent validity indicates the extent to which test scores accurately estimate an individual's present position on the relevant criterion. For example, an arithmetic achievement test would possess concurrent validity if its scores could be used to predict, with reasonable accuracy, the current standing of students in a mathematics course. A personality inventory would possess concurrent validity if diagnostic classifications derived from it roughly matched the opinions of psychiatrists or clinical psychologists.

A test with demonstrated concurrent validity provides a shortcut for obtaining information that might otherwise require the extended investment of professional time. For example, the case assignment procedure in a mental health clinic can be expedited if a test with demonstrated concurrent validity is used for initial screening decisions. In this manner, severely disturbed patients requiring immediate clinical workup and intensive treatment can be quickly identified by paper-and-pencil test. Of course, tests are not intended to replace mental health specialists, but they can save time in the initial phases of diagnosis.

Correlations between a new test and existing tests are often cited as evidence of concurrent validity. This has a Catch-22 quality to it—old tests validating a new test—but is nonetheless appropriate if two conditions are met. First, the criterion (existing) tests must have been validated through correlations with appropriate nontest behavioral data. In other words, the network of interlocking relationships must touch ground with real-world behavior at some point. Second, the instrument being validated must measure the same construct as the criterion tests. Thus, it is entirely appropriate that developers of a new intelligence test report correlations between it and established mainstays such as the Stanford-Binet and Wechsler scales.

Predictive Validity

In a predictive validation study, test scores are used to estimate outcome measures obtained at a later date. Predictive validity is particularly relevant for entrance examinations and employment tests. Such tests share a common function—determining who is likely to succeed at a future endeavor. A relevant criterion for a college entrance exam would be freshman year grade point average, while an employment test might be validated against supervisor ratings after six months on the job. In the ideal situation, such tests are validated during periods of open enrollment (or open hiring) so that a full range of results is possible on the outcome measures. In this manner, future use of the test as a selection device for excluding low-scoring applicants will rest on a solid foundation of validational data.

When tests are used for purposes of prediction, it is necessary to develop a regression equation. A **regression equation** describes the best-fitting straight line for estimating the criterion from the test. We will not discuss the statistical approach to fitting the straight line, except to mention that it minimizes the sum of the squared deviations from the line (Ghiselli, Campbell, & Zedeck, 1981). For current purposes, it is more important to understand the nature and function of regression equations.

Ghiselli, Campbell, and Zedeck (1981) provide a simple example of regression in the service of prediction, summarized here. Suppose we are trying to predict success on a job, *Y* (evaluated by the supervisor on a 7-point scale ranging from poor to excellent performance) from scores on a preemployment test, *X* (with scores that range from a low of 0 to a high of 100). The regression equation

$$Y = .07X + .2$$

might describe the best-fitting straight line and therefore produce the most accurate predictions. For an individual who scored 55 on the test, the predicted performance level would be 4.05 (that is, .07(55) + .2). A test score of 33 yields a predicted performance level of 2.51 (that is, .07(33) + .2). Additional predictions are made likewise.

Validity Coefficient and the Standard Error of the Estimate

The relationship between test scores and criterion measures can be expressed in several different ways. Perhaps the most popular approach is to compute the correlation between test and criterion (r_{xy}). In this context, the resulting correlation is known as a **validity coefficient.** The higher the validity coefficient r_{xy}, the more accurate is the test in predicting the criterion. In the hypothetical case where r_{xy} is 1.00, the test would possess perfect validity and allow for flawless prediction. Of course, no such test exists, and validity coefficients are more commonly in the low- to midrange of correlations and rarely exceed .80. But how high should a validity coefficient be? There is no general answer to this question. However, we can approach the question indirectly by investigating the relationship between the validity coefficient and the corresponding error of estimate.

The **standard error of estimate** (SE_{est}) is the margin of error to be expected in the predicted criterion score. The error of estimate is derived from the following formula:

$$SE_{est} = SD_y \sqrt{1 - r_{xy}^2}$$

In this formula, r_{xy}^2 is the square of the validity coefficient and SD_y is the standard deviation of the criterion scores. Perhaps the reader has noticed the similarities between this index and the standard error of measurement (SEM). In fact, both indices help gauge margins of error. The SEM indicates the margin of measurement error caused by unreliability of the test, whereas SE_{est} indicates the margin of prediction error caused by the imperfect validity of the test.

The SE_{est} helps answer the fundamental question: "How accurately can criterion performance be predicted from test scores?" (AERA, APA, NCME, 1985). Consider the common practice of attempting to predict college grade point average from high school scores on a scholastic aptitude test. For a specific aptitude test, suppose we determine that the SE_{est} for predicted grade point average is .2 (on the usual 0.0 to 4.0 grade point scale). What does this mean for the examinee whose college grade point is predicted to be 3.1? As is the case with all standard deviations, the standard error of the estimate can be used to bracket predicted outcomes in a probabilistic sense. Assuming that the frequency distribution of grades is normal, we know that the chances are about 68 in 100 that the examinee's predicted grade point will fall between 2.9 and 3.3 (plus or minus one SE$_{est}$). In like manner, we know that the chances are about 95 in 100 that the examinee's predicted grade point will fall between 2.7 and 3.5 (plus or minus two SE$_{est}$).

What is an acceptable standard of predictive accuracy? There is no simple answer to this question. As the reader will discern from the discussion that follows, standards of predictive accuracy are, in part, value judgments. To explain why this is so, we need to introduce the basic elements of decision theory (Taylor & Russell, 1939; Cronbach & Gleser, 1965).

Decision Theory Applied to Psychological Tests

Proponents of **decision theory** stress that the purpose of psychological testing is not measurement per se but measurement in the service of decision making. The personnel manager wishes to know who to hire; the admissions officer must choose who to admit; the parole board desires to know which felons are good risks for early release; and, the psychiatrist needs to determine which patients require hospitalization.

The link between testing and decision making is nowhere more obvious than in the context of predictive validation studies. Many of these studies use test results to determine who will likely succeed or fail on the criterion task so that, in the future, examinees with poor scores on the predictor test can be screened from admission, employment, or other privilege. This is the rationale by which admissions officers or employers require applicants to obtain a certain minimum score on an appropriate entrance or employment exam—previous studies of predictive validity can be cited to show that candidates scoring below a certain cutoff face steep odds in their educational or employment pursuits.

Psychological tests frequently play a major role in these kinds of institutional decision making. In a typical institutional decision, a committee—or sometimes a single person—makes a large number of comparable decisions based on a cutoff score on

one or more selection tests. In order to present the key concepts of decision theory, let us oversimplify somewhat and assume that only a single test is involved.

Even though most tests produce a range of scores along a continuum, it is usually possible to identify a cutoff or pass/fail score that divides the sample into those predicted to succeed versus those predicted to fail on the criterion of interest. Let us assume that persons predicted to succeed are also selected for hiring or admission. In this case, the proportion of persons in the "predicted-to-succeed" group is referred to as the *selection ratio*. The selection ratio can vary from 0 to 1.0, depending on the proportion of persons who are considered good bets to succeed on the criterion measure.

If the results of a selection test allow for the simple dichotomy of "predicted to succeed" versus "predicted to fail," then the subsequent outcome on the criterion measure likewise can be split into two categories, namely, "did succeed" and "did fail." From this perspective, every study of predictive validity produces a two-by-two matrix, as portrayed in Figure 4.4.

Certain combinations of predicted and actual outcomes are more likely than others. If a test has good predictive validity, then most persons predicted to succeed will succeed; and most persons

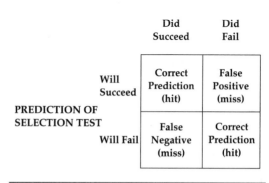

PERFORMANCE ON CRITERION MEASURE

		Did Succeed	Did Fail
PREDICTION OF SELECTION TEST	Will Succeed	Correct Prediction (hit)	False Positive (miss)
	Will Fail	False Negative (miss)	Correct Prediction (hit)

FIGURE 4.4   Possible Outcomes When a Selection Test Is Used To Predict Performance on a Criterion Measure

predicted to fail will fail. These are examples of correct predictions and serve to bolster the validity of a selection instrument. Outcomes in these two cells are referred to as *hits* because the test has made a correct prediction.

But no selection test is a perfect predictor, so two other types of outcomes are also possible. Some persons predicted to succeed will, in fact, fail. These cases are referred to as **false positives.** And some persons predicted to fail would, if given the chance, succeed. These cases are referred to as **false negatives.** False positives and false negatives are collectively known as misses, because in both cases the test has made an inaccurate prediction. Finally, the hit rate is the proportion of cases in which the test accurately predicts success or failure, that is, hit rate = (hits)/(hits + misses).

False positives and false negatives are unavoidable in the real-world use of selection tests. The only way to eliminate such selection errors would be to develop a perfect test, an instrument which has a validity coefficient of +1.00, signifying a perfect correlation with the criterion measure. A perfect test is theoretically possible, but none has yet been observed on this planet. Nonetheless, it is still important to develop selection tests with very high predictive validity, so as to minimize decision errors.

Proponents of decision theory make two fundamental assumptions about the use of selection tests:

1. The value of various outcomes to the institution can be expressed in terms of a common utility scale. One such scale—but by no means the only one—is profit and loss. For example, when using an interest inventory to select salespersons, a corporation can anticipate profit from applicants correctly identified as successful, but will lose money when, inevitably, some of those selected do not sell enough even to support their own salary (false positives). The cost of the selection procedure must also be factored in to the utility scale as well.

2. In institutional selection decisions, the most generally useful strategy is one which maximizes the average gain on the utility scale (or minimizes average loss) over many similar decisions. For example, which selection ratio produces the largest average gain on the utility scale? Maximization is thus the fundamental decision principle.

The application of decision theory is much more complicated than illustrated here, mainly because of the difficulty of finding a common utility scale for different outcomes. Consider the plight of the admissions officer at any large university. If the selection ratio is quite strict, then most of the admitted students will also succeed. But some students not admitted might have succeeded, too, and their financial support to the university (tuition, fees) is therefore lost. However, if the selection ratio is too lenient, then the percentage of false positives (students admitted who subsequently fail) skyrockets. How is the cost of a false positive to be calculated? The financial cost can be estimated— for example, advisers dedicate a certain number of hours at a known pay rate counseling these students. But no single utility scale can encompass the other diverse consequences such as the need for additional remedial services (which require money), the increase in faculty cynicism (an issue of morale), and the dashed hopes of misled students (whose heartbreak affects public perception of the university and may even influence future state funding!). Clearly, the neat statistical notions of decision theory oversimplify the complex influences that determine utility in the real world.

Nonetheless, in large institutional settings where a common utility scale can be identified, principles of decision theory can be applied to selection problems with thought-provoking results. For example, Schmidt, Hunter, McKenzie, and Muldrow (1979) analyzed the potential impact of using the Programmer Aptitude Test (PAT, Hughes & McNamara, 1959) in the selection of computer programmers by the federal government. They based their analysis on the following facts and assumptions:

1. PAT scores and measures of later on-the-job programming performance correlate quite substantially; the validity coefficient of the PAT is .76 (fact).

2. The government hires 600 new programmers each year (fact).
3. The cost of testing is about $10 per examinee (fact).
4. Programmers stay on the job for about nine years and receive pay raises according to a known pay scale (fact).
5. The yearly productivity in dollars of low-performing, average, and superior programmers can be accurately estimated by supervisors (assumption).

Based on these facts and assumptions, Schmidt et al. (1979) then compared the hypothetical use of the PAT against other selection procedures of lesser validity. Since the usefulness of a test is partly determined by the percentage of applicants who are selected for employment, the researchers also looked at the impact of different selection ratios on overall productivity. In each case, they estimated the yearly increase in dollar-amount productivity from using the PAT instead of an alternative and less efficacious procedure. In general, the use of the PAT was estimated to increase productivity by tens of millions of dollars. The specific estimated increase depended on the selection ratio and the validity coefficient of hypothetical alternative procedures (Table 4.1). For example, if 80 percent of the applicants were hired (selection ratio of .80), using the PAT would increase the productivity of the federal government by at least $5.6 million (if the alternative procedure had a validity coefficient of .50) and possibly as much as $16.5 million (if the alternative procedure had no validity at all). If the selection ratio were quite small, the use of the PAT for selection boosted productivity even more—possibly as much as nearly $100 million. Schmidt et al. (1979) concluded that "the impact of valid selection procedures on work-force productivity is considerably greater than most personnel psychologists have believed."

In general, large organizations that make dozens or hundreds of similar hiring decisions each year can profit from the application of decision theory to selection procedures, whereas smaller employers may not possess a sufficient database to apply the complex methodologies inherent to this

TABLE 4.1   Estimated Productivity Increase (in Millions of Dollars) from One Year's Use of the Programmer Aptitude Test

Selection Ratio	True Validity of Previous Selection Procedure				
	.00	.20	.30	.40	.50
.05	97.2	71.7	58.9	46.1	33.3
.10	82.8	60.1	50.1	39.2	28.3
.20	66.0	48.6	40.0	31.3	22.6
.30	54.7	40.3	33.1	25.9	18.7
.40	45.6	34.6	27.6	21.6	15.6
.50	37.6	27.7	22.8	17.8	12.9
.60	30.4	22.4	18.4	14.4	10.4
.70	23.4	17.2	14.1	11.1	8.0
.80	16.5	12.2	10.0	7.8	5.6

Source: Reprinted with permission from Schmidt, F. L., Hunter, J. E., McKenzie, R. C., and Muldrow, T. W. (1979). Impact of valid selection procedures on work-force productivity. *Journal of Applied Psychology, 64,* 609–626.

approach. When it is possible to use the maximization principle in conjunction with a measurable scale of utility, decision theory holds great promise. For example, Schmidt, Hunter, Outerbridge, and Trattner (1986) estimated that using valid measures of cognitive ability instead of nontest procedures (e.g., requiring a specific degree) for employee selection could increase the productivity of federal government workers by $8 billion over the course of a typical 13-year occupational tenure.

Taylor-Russell Tables

In the context of decision theory, we should describe the statistical tables published by Taylor and Russell (1939) which permit a test user to determine the expected proportion of successful applicants selected with use of a test. For obvious reasons, these guides are known as Taylor-Russell tables. In order to use the Taylor-Russell tables, the tester must specify (1) the predictive validity of the test, (2) the selection ratio, and (3) the base rate for successful applicants. A change in any of these factors will alter the selection accuracy of the test.

The predictive validity of a test is usually known from previous studies and consists of r_{xy}, the correlation between test and criterion. The selection ratio is the proportion of applicants who are selected (usually because they are predicted to succeed). The **base rate** is the proportion of successful applicants who would be selected using current methods, without benefit of the new test. (In the extreme case, the base rate is the proportion of successful applicants who would be chosen at random without benefit of any selection procedure.) When all three of these factors are known, the Taylor-Russell tables can be consulted to determine the proportion of successes expected through the application of the test. In this manner, the test user can determine the extent to which using a new test would improve selection over the base rate obtained from existing methods.

Perhaps a specific example will clarify the potential application of the Taylor-Russell tables (Table 4.2). Assume that the base rate for successful applicants is .60, meaning that 60 percent of ap-

TABLE 4.2   The Expected Proportion of Successes for a Selection Test of Given Validity, with Given Selection Ratio, for Base Rate .60

| | | | | | *Selection Ratio* | | | | | | |
Validity	.05	.10	.20	.30	.40	.50	.60	.70	.80	.90	.95
.00	.60	.60	.60	.60	.60	.60	.60	.60	.60	.60	.60
.05	.64	.63	.63	.62	.62	.62	.61	.61	.61	.60	.60
.10	.68	.67	.65	.64	.64	.63	.63	.62	.61	.61	.60
.15	.71	.70	.68	.67	.66	.65	.64	.63	.62	.61	.61
.20	.75	.73	.71	.69	.67	.66	.65	.64	.63	.62	.61
.25	.78	.76	.73	.71	.69	.68	.66	.65	.63	.62	.61
.30	.82	.79	.76	.73	.71	.69	.68	.66	.64	.62	.61
.35	.85	.82	.78	.75	.73	.71	.69	.67	.65	.63	.62
.40	.88	.85	.81	.78	.75	.73	.70	.68	.66	.63	.62
.45	.90	.87	.83	.80	.77	.74	.72	.69	.66	.64	.62
.50	.93	.90	.86	.82	.79	.76	.73	.70	.67	.64	.62
.55	.95	.92	.88	.84	.81	.78	.75	.71	.68	.64	.62
.60	.96	.94	.90	.87	.83	.80	.76	.73	.69	.65	.63
.65	.98	.96	.92	.89	.85	.82	.78	.74	.70	.65	.63
.70	.99	.97	.94	.91	.87	.84	.80	.75	.71	.66	.63
.75	.99	.99	.96	.93	.90	.86	.81	.77	.71	.66	.63
.80	1.00	.99	.98	.95	.92	.88	.83	.78	.72	.66	.63
.85	1.00	1.00	.99	.97	.95	.91	.86	.80	.73	.66	.63
.90	1.00	1.00	1.00	.99	.97	.94	.88	.82	.74	.67	.63
.95	1.00	1.00	1.00	1.00	.99	.97	.92	.84	.75	.67	.63
1.00	1.00	1.00	1.00	1.00	1.00	1.00	1.00	.86	.75	.67	.63

Source: Reprinted from Taylor, H. C., and Russell, J. T. (1939). The relationship of validity coefficients to the practical effectiveness of tests in selection. *Journal of Applied Psychology, 23,* 565–578. In the public domain.

plicants accepted by current methods turn out to be successful. Assume also that the selection ratio is .50, meaning that 50 percent of all applicants are selected. Further, assume that a new test has a validity coefficient of .40, which specifies the correlation between test scores and criterion. Under these assumptions, the Taylor-Russell tables provide the expected proportion of successes through the use of the new test. The expected proportion of successes turns out to be .73, a substantial improvement over the existing base rate of .60 for successful selection.

The most intriguing conclusion to emerge from the Taylor-Russell tables is that tests with "poor" validity can, nonetheless, substantially improve selection accuracy—if the selection ratio is low enough. Consider a test with validity of merely .20, which doesn't sound very impressive; for most tests, validity coefficients are commonly much higher. Assume also that the base rate for successful selection is .60, which is probably a realistic base rate for many forms of personnel selection. Further, assume that the selection ratio is very stringent, say .05, meaning that only 5 percent of the applicants are deemed acceptable and therefore selected. Under these assumptions, the proportion of successes expected through use of the test is .75, a net improvement of 15 percent above the base rate of .60.

CONSTRUCT VALIDITY

The final type of validity discussed in this unit is construct validity, and it is undoubtedly the most difficult and elusive of the bunch. A **construct** is a theoretical, intangible quality or trait in which individuals differ (Messick, 1995). Examples of constructs include leadership ability, overcontrolled hostility, depression, and intelligence. Notice in each of these examples that constructs are inferred from behavior, but are more than the behavior itself. In general, constructs are theorized to have some form of independent existence and to exert broad but to some extent predictable influences on human behavior. A test designed to measure a construct must estimate the existence of an inferred,

underlying characteristic (e.g., leadership ability) based on a limited sample of behavior. Construct validity refers to the appropriateness of these inferences about the underlying construct.

All psychological constructs possess two characteristics in common:

1. There is no single external referent sufficient to validate the existence of the construct, that is, the construct cannot be operationally defined (Cronbach & Meehl, 1955).
2. Nonetheless, a network of interlocking suppositions can be derived from existing theory about the construct (AERA, APA, NCME, 1985).

We will illustrate these points by reference to the construct of psychopathy (Cleckley, 1976), a personality constellation characterized by antisocial behavior (lying, stealing, and occasionally violence), a lack of guilt and shame, and impulsivity.[2] Psychopathy is surely a construct, in that there is no single behavioral characteristic or outcome sufficient to determine who is strongly psychopathic and who is not. On average we might expect psychopaths to be frequently incarcerated, but so are many common criminals. Furthermore, many successful psychopaths somehow avoid apprehension altogether (Cleckley, 1976). Psychopathy cannot be gauged only by scrapes with the law.

Nonetheless, a network of interlocking suppositions can be derived from existing theory about psychopathy. The fundamental problem in psychopathy is presumed to be a deficiency in the ability to feel emotional arousal—whether empathy, guilt, fear of punishment, or anxiety under stress (Cleckley, 1976). A number of predictions follow from this appraisal. For example, psychopaths should: lie convincingly, have a greater tolerance for physical pain, show less autonomic arousal in the resting state, and get into trouble because of their lack of behavioral inhibition. Thus, to validate a measure of psychopathy, we would need to

---

2. The construct of psychopathy is very similar to what is now designated as antisocial personality disorder (American Psychiatric Association, 1994).

check out a number of different expectations based on our theory of psychopathy.

Construct validity pertains to psychological tests that claim to measure complex, multifaceted, and theory-bound psychological attributes such as psychopathy, intelligence, leadership ability, and the like. The crucial point to understand about construct validity is that "no criterion or universe of content is accepted as entirely adequate to define the quality to be measured" (Cronbach & Meehl, 1955). Thus, the demonstration of construct validity always rests upon a program of research using diverse procedures outlined in the following sections. To evaluate the construct validity of a test, we must amass a variety of evidence from numerous sources.

Although the construct validation of a test is a lengthy and complex process, the diverse procedures are designed to answer one crucial question: Based on the current theoretical understanding of the construct which the test claims to measure, do we find the kinds of relationships with nontest criteria that the theory predicts? Consider the concept of psychopathy, discussed previously, as measured by the Psychopathic deviate (Pd) scale of the MMPI and MMPI-2. One small piece of evidence supporting the construct validity of this scale is the finding that hunters who had "carelessly" shot someone were significantly elevated on Pd when compared with other hunters (Cronbach & Meehl, 1955). Such a finding fits well with the theoretical notion of psychopathy, especially as regards a lack of behavioral inhibition. Of course, many other lines of evidence would be needed to confirm the construct validity of the Pd scale. We see, then, that the investigation of construct validity is not essentially different from the general scientific procedures for confirming a theory.

Many psychometric theorists regard construct validity as the unifying concept for all types of validity evidence (Cronbach, 1988; Guion, 1980; Messick, 1995). According to this viewpoint, individual studies of content, concurrent, and predictive validity are regarded merely as supportive evidence in the cumulative quest for construct validation.

APPROACHES TO CONSTRUCT VALIDITY

How does a test developer determine whether a new instrument possesses construct validity? As previously hinted, no single procedure will suffice for this difficult task. Evidence of construct validity can be found in practically any empirical study which examines test scores from appropriate groups of subjects. Most studies of construct validity fall into one of the following categories:

- Analysis to determine whether the test items or subtests are homogeneous and therefore measure a single construct.
- Study of developmental changes to determine whether they are consistent with the theory of the construct.
- Research to ascertain whether group differences on test scores are theory-consistent.
- Analysis to determine whether intervention effects on test scores are theory-consistent.
- Correlation of the test with other related and unrelated tests and measures.
- Factor analysis of test scores in relation to other sources of information.

We examine these sources of construct validity evidence in more detail in the following.

Test Homogeneity

If a test measures a single construct, then its component items (or subtests) likely will be homogeneous (also referred to as *internally consistent*). In most cases, homogeneity is built into the test during the development process discussed in more detail in the next unit. The aim of test development is to select items that form a **homogeneous scale.** The most commonly used method for achieving this goal is to correlate each potential item with the total score and select items which show high correlations with the total score. A related procedure is to correlate subtests with the total score in the early phases of test development. In this manner, wayward scales that do not correlate to some minimum degree with the total test score can be revised before the instrument is released for general use.

Homogeneity is an important first step in certifying the construct validity of a new test, but standing alone it is weak evidence. Kline (1986) has pointed out the circularity of the procedure:

> If all our items in the item pool were wide of the mark and did not measure what we hoped, they would be selecting items by the criterion of their correlation with the total score, which can never work. It is to be noted that the same argument applies to the factoring of the item pool. A general factor of poor items is still possible. This objection is sound and has to be refuted empirically. Having found by item analysis a set of homogeneous items, we must still present evidence concerning their validity. Thus to construct a homogeneous test is not sufficient, validity studies must be carried out.

In addition to demonstrating the homogeneity of items, a test developer must provide multiple other sources of construct validity, discussed subsequently.

Appropriate Developmental Changes

Many constructs can be assumed to show regular age-graded changes from early childhood into mature adulthood and perhaps beyond. Consider the construct of vocabulary knowledge as an example. It has been known since the inception of intelligence tests at the turn of the century that knowledge of vocabulary increases exponentially from early childhood into late childhood. More recent research demonstrates that vocabulary continues to grow, albeit at a slower pace, into old age (Gregory & Gernert, 1990). For any new test of vocabulary, then, an important piece of construct validity evidence would be that older subjects score better than younger subjects, assuming that education and health factors are held constant.

Of course, not all constructs lend themselves to predictions about developmental changes. For example, it is not clear whether a scale measuring "assertiveness" should show a pattern of increasing, decreasing, or stable scores with advancing age. Developmental changes would be irrelevant to the construct validity of such a scale. We should also mention that appropriate developmental changes are but one piece in the construct validity puzzle. This approach does not provide information about how the construct relates to other constructs.

THEORY-CONSISTENT GROUP DIFFERENCES

One way to bolster the validity of a new instrument is to show that, on average, persons with different backgrounds and characteristics obtain theory-consistent scores on the test. Specifically, persons thought to be high on the construct measured by the test should obtain high scores, whereas persons with presumably low amounts of the construct should obtain low scores.

Crandall (1981) developed a social interest scale which illustrates the use of theory-consistent group differences in the process of construct validation. Borrowing from Alfred Adler, Crandall (1984) defined *social interest* as an "interest in and concern for others." To measure this construct, he devised a brief and simple instrument consisting of 15 forced-choice items. For each item, one of the two alternatives includes a trait closely related to the Adlerian concept of social interest (e.g., helpful) whereas the other choice consists of an equally attractive but nonsocial trait (e.g., quick-witted). The subject is instructed to "choose the trait which you value more highly." Each of the 15 items is scored 1 if the social interest trait is picked, 0 otherwise; thus total scores on the Social Interest Scale (SIS) can range from 0 to 15.

Table 4.3 presents average scores on the SIS for 13 well-defined groups of subjects. The reader will notice that individuals likely to be high in social interest (e.g., nuns) obtain the highest average scores on the SIS, whereas the lowest scores are earned by presumably self-centered persons (e.g., models) and those who are outright antisocial (felons). These findings are theory-consistent and support the construct validity of this interesting instrument.

TABLE 4.3   Mean Scores on the Social Interest Scale for Selected Groups

Group	N	Mean Score
Ursuline sisters	6	13.3
Adult church members	147	11.2
Charity volunteers	9	10.8
High-school students nominated for high social interest	23	10.2
University students nominated for high social interest	21	9.5
University employees	327	8.9
University students	1,784	8.2
University students nominated for low social interest	35	7.4
Professional models	54	7.1
High-school students nominated for low social interest	22	6.9
Adult atheists and agnostics	30	6.7
Convicted felons	30	6.4

Source: Adapted with permission from Crandall, J. (1981). *Theory and measurement of social interest: Empirical tests of Alfred Adler's concept.* New York: Columbia University Press.

Theory-Consistent Intervention Effects

Another approach to construct validation is to show that test scores change in appropriate direction and amount in reaction to planned or unplanned interventions. For example, the scores of elderly persons on a spatial orientation test battery should increase after these subjects receive cognitive training specifically designed to enhance their spatial orientation abilities. More precisely, if the test battery possesses construct validity, we can predict that spatial orientation scores should show a greater increase from pretest to posttest than found on unrelated abilities not targeted for special training (e.g., inductive reasoning, perceptual speed, numerical reasoning, or verbal reasoning). Willis and Schaie (1986) found just such a pattern of test results in a cognitive training study with elderly subjects, supporting the construct validity of their spatial orientation measure.

Convergent and Discriminant Validation

Convergent validity is demonstrated when a test correlates highly with other variables or tests with which it shares an overlap of constructs. For example, two tests designed to measure different types of intelligence should, nonetheless, share enough of the general factor in intelligence to produce a hefty correlation (say, .5 or above) when jointly administered to a heterogeneous sample of subjects. In fact, any new test of intelligence that did not correlate at least modestly with existing measures would be highly suspect, on the grounds that it did not possess convergent validity.

Discriminant validity is demonstrated when a test does not correlate with variables or tests from which it should differ. For example, social interest and intelligence are theoretically unrelated, and tests of these two constructs should correlate negligibly, if at all.

In a classic paper often quoted but seldom emulated, Campbell and Fiske (1959) proposed a systematic experimental design for simultaneously confirming the convergent and discriminant validity of a psychological test. Their design is called the *multitrait-multimethod matrix,* and it calls for the assessment of two or more traits by two or more methods. Table 4.4 provides a hypothetical example of this approach. In this example, three

TABLE 4.4   Hypothetical Multitrait-Multimethod Matrix

	Traits	Method 1			Method 2			Method 3		
		A_1	B_1	C_1	A_2	B_2	C_2	A_3	B_3	C_3
Method 1	A_1	(89)								
	B_1	51	(89)							
	C_1	38	37	(76)						
Method 2	A_2	**57**	22	09	(93)					
	B_2	22	**57**	10	68	(94)				
	C_2	11	11	**46**	59	58	(84)			
Method 3	A_3	**56**	22	11	67	42	33	(94)		
	B_3	23	**58**	12	43	66	34	67	(92)	
	C_3	11	11	**45**	34	32	58	58	60	(85)

Note: Letters *A, B,* and *C* refer to traits; subscripts 1, 2, and 3 refer to methods. The matrix consists of correlation coefficients (decimals omitted). See text.

Source: Reprinted with permission from Campbell, D. T., and Fiske, D. W. (1959). Convergent and discriminant validation by the multitrait-multimethod matrix. *Psychological Bulletin, 56,* 81–105.

traits (*A, B,* and *C*) are measured by three methods (1, 2, and 3). For example, traits *A, B,* and *C* might be social interest, creativity, and dominance. Methods 1, 2, and 3 might be self-report inventory, peer ratings, and projective test. Thus, *A*1 would represent a self-report inventory of social interest, *B*2 a peer rating of creativity, *C*3 a dominance measure derived from projective test, and so on.

Notice in this example that nine tests are studied (three traits are each measured by three methods). When each of these tests is administered twice to the same group of subjects and scores on all pairs of tests are correlated, the result is a **multitrait-multimethod matrix** (Table 4.4). This matrix is a rich source of data on reliability, convergent validity, and discriminant validity.

For example, the correlations along the main diagonal (in parentheses) are reliability coefficients for each test. The higher these values, the better, and preferably we like to see values in the .80s or .90s here. The correlations along the three shorter diagonals (in boldface) supply evidence of convergent validity—the same trait measured by different methods. These correlations should be strong and positive, as shown here. Notice that the

table also includes correlations between different traits measured by the same method (in solid triangles) and different traits measured by different methods (in dotted triangles). These correlations should be the lowest of all in the matrix, insofar as they supply evidence of discriminant validity.

The Campbell and Fiske (1959) methodology is an important contribution to our understanding of the test validation process. However, the full implementation of this procedure typically requires too monumental a commitment from researchers. It is more common for test developers to collect convergent and discriminant validity data in bits and pieces, rather than producing an entire matrix of intercorrelations. Meier (1984) provides one of the few real-world implementations of the multitrait-multimethod matrix in an examination of the validity of the "burnout" construct.

Factor Analysis

Factor analysis is a specialized statistical technique that is particularly useful for investigating construct validity. We discuss factor analysis in substantial detail in Topic 8A, Aptitude Tests and

Factor Analysis; here, we provide a quick preview so that the reader can appreciate the role of factor analysis in the study of construct validity. The purpose of **factor analysis** is to identify the minimum number of determiners (factors) required to account for the intercorrelations among a battery of tests. The goal in factor analysis is to find a smaller set of dimensions, called *factors,* that can account for the observed array of intercorrelations among individual tests. A typical approach in factor analysis is to administer a battery of tests to several hundred subjects and then calculate a correlation matrix from the scores on all possible pairs of tests. For example, if 15 tests have been administered to a sample of psychiatric and neurological patients, the first step in factor analysis is to compute the correlations between scores on the 105 possible pairs of tests.[3] Although it may be feasible to see certain clusterings of tests that measure common traits, it is more typical that the mass of data found in a correlation matrix is simply too complex for the unaided human eye to analyze effectively. Fortunately, the computer-implemented procedures of factor analysis search this pattern of intercorrelations, identify a small number of factors, and then produce a table of factor loadings. A **factor loading** is actually a correlation between an individual test and a single factor. Thus, factor loadings can vary between –1.0 and +1.0. The final outcome of a factor analysis is a table depicting the correlation of each test with each factor.

A table of factor loadings helps describe the factorial composition of a test and thereby provides information relevant to construct validity. We will illustrate this point with factor analytic data from a study of the Category Test. The Category Test is a relatively complex concept formation test designed to be different from traditional psychometric measures of intelligence, and superior to them at detecting neurological disorders (Reitan & Wolfson, 1985). If the Category Test does, indeed, measure something different from traditional tests

of intelligence, then it should load strongly on one or more factors not represented by the subtests of the WAIS. Such a finding would strengthen the construct validity of the Category Test by distinguishing it from traditional measures of intelligence.

Lansdell and Donnelly (1977) administered the 11 subtests of the Wechsler Adult Intelligence Scale, the Category Test, and the Finger Tapping Test to 94 psychiatric and neurological patients. The test scores were factor analyzed, producing the factor loadings shown in Table 4.5. Notice that the verbal subtests from the WAIS have the highest loadings on factor I which is surely a factor of verbal comprehension. The Category Test has a minimal loading on this factor, indicating that verbal abilities are not particularly important for good performance on this test. Factor II has its strongest loadings on Block Design (.74) and Object Assembly (.73) and is typically labeled a perceptual orga-

TABLE 4.5 Factor Loadings for the Category Test, Finger Tapping Test, and WAIS Subtests

Test	*Factor Loading*			
	I	*II*	*III*	*IV*
Information	.88	.15	.07	.07
Comprehension	.83	–.03	.06	–.09
Arithmetic	.43	.26	.67	–.12
Similarities	.78	.30	.17	.02
Digit Span	.23	.08	.83	.12
Vocabulary	.92	.07	.06	.01
Digit Symbol	.25	.31	.21	.61
Picture Completion	.64	.50	–.24	–.01
Block Design	.39	.74	.06	.20
Picture Arrangement	.50	.60	.12	–.01
Object Assembly	.29	.73	.00	.31
Category	.19	.82	.11	–.18
Finger Tapping Test	.07	–.08	.18	.76

Source: Adapted with permission from Lansdell, H., and Donnelly, E. F. (1977). Factor analysis of the Wechsler Adult Intelligence Scale Subtests and the Halstead-Reitan Category and Tapping Tests. *Journal of Consulting and Clinical Psychology, 45,* 412–416.

---

3. The general formula for the number of pairings among *N* tests is $N(N – 1)/2$. Thus, if 15 tests are administered, there will be $15 \times 14/2$ or 105 possible pairings of individual tests.

nization factor.[4] Unfortunately, the Category Test has a substantial loading (.82) on this factor, and this factor alone. At least for this sample of subjects, it appears that the Category Test is merely an alternative measure of perceptual organizational skills and not a new and different test, as many of its users might like to claim. Incidentally, factor III seems to measure freedom from distractibility, and factor IV appears to be a pure measure of motor speed.

EXTRA-VALIDITY CONCERNS AND THE WIDENING SCOPE OF TEST VALIDITY

We begin this section with a review of **extra-validity concerns,** which include side effects and unintended consequences of testing. By acknowledging the importance of the extra-validity domain, psychologists confirm that the decision to use a test involves social, legal, and political considerations that extend far beyond the traditional questions of technical validity. In a related development, we will also review how the interest in extra-validity concerns has spurred several theorists to broaden the concept of test validity. As the reader will discover, value implications and social consequences are now encompassed within the widening scope of test validity.

Even if a test is valid, unbiased, and fair, the decision to use it may be governed by additional considerations. Cole and Moss (1989) outline the following factors:

- What is the purpose for which the test is used?
- To what extent are the purposes accomplished by the actions taken?
- What are the possible side effects or unintended consequences of using the test?
- What possible alternatives to the test might serve the same purpose?

We survey only the most prominent extra-validity concerns here and show how they have served to widen the scope of test validity. Readers who wish more detail on these topics should consult AERA, APA, NCME (1999), Cole and Moss (1989), Cronbach (1988), and Jensen (1980, ch. 15).

Unintended Side Effects of Testing

The intended outcome of using a psychological test is not necessarily the only consequence. Various side effects also are possible, indeed, they are probable. The examiner must determine whether the benefits of giving the test outweigh the costs of the potential side effects. Furthermore, by anticipating unintended side effects, the examiner might be able to deflect or diminish them.

Cole and Moss (1989) cite the example of using psychological tests to determine eligibility for special education. Although the intended outcome is to help students learn, the process of identifying students eligible for special education may produce numerous negative side effects:

- The identified children may feel unusual or dumb.
- Other children may call the children names.
- Teachers may view these children as unworthy of attention.
- The process may produce classes segregated by race or social class.

A consideration of side effects should influence an examiner's decision to use a particular test for a specified purpose. The examiner might appropriately choose not to use a test for a worthy purpose if the likely costs from side effects outweigh the expected benefits.

Consider the common practice in years past of using the Minnesota Multiphasic Personality Inventory (MMPI) to help screen candidates for peace officer positions such as police officer or sheriff's deputy. Although the MMPI was originally designed as an aid in psychiatric diagnosis, subsequent research indicated that it is also useful in the identification of persons unsuited to a career in law enforcement (Hargrave, 1985; Hiatt &

---

4. Notice that humans provide the label for a factor, based on an analysis of the tests that load most strongly on it. Two investigators might conceivably use different names for the same factor—for example, referring to factor II as either *perceptual organization* or *visuospatial analysis*.

Hargrave, 1988). In particular, peace officers who produce MMPI profiles with mild elevations (e.g., T-score 65 to 69) on Scales F (Frequency), Masculinity-Femininity, Paranoia, and Hypomania tend to be involved in serious disciplinary actions; peace officers who produce more "defensive" MMPI profiles with fewer clinical scale elevations tend not to be involved in such actions. Thus, the test possessed modest validity for the worthy purpose of screening law enforcement candidates. But no test, not even the highly respected MMPI, is perfectly valid. Some good applicants will be passed over because their MMPI results are marginal. Perhaps their Paranoia Scale is at T-score of 66, or the Hypomania Scale is at T-score of 68. On the MMPI, a T-score of 70 is often considered the upper limit of the "normal" range.

One unintended side effect of using the MMPI for evaluation of peace officer applicants is that job candidates who are unsuccessful with one agency may be tagged with a pathological label such as psychopathic, schizophrenic, or paranoid. The label may arise in spite of the best efforts of the consulting psychologist, who may never have used any pejorative terms in the assessment report on the candidate. Typically, the label is conceived when administrators at the referring department look at the MMPI profile and see that the candidate obtained his/her highest score on a scale with a horrendous title such as Psychopathic Deviate, Schizophrenia, Hypochondriasis, or Paranoia. Unfortunately, the law enforcement community can be a very closed fraternity. Police chiefs and sheriffs commonly exchange verbal reports about their job applicants, so a pejorative label may follow the candidate from one setting to another, permanently barring the applicant from entry into the law enforcement profession. The repercussions are not only unfair to the candidate, they also raise the specter of lawsuits against the agency and the consulting psychologist. All things considered, the consulting psychologist may find it preferable to use a technically less valid test for the same purpose, particularly if the alternative instrument does not produce these unintended side effects.

The renewed sensitivity to extra-validity issues has caused several test theorists to widen their definition of test validity. We review these recent developments in the following section, cautioning the reader that a final consensus about the nature of test validity is yet to emerge.

The Widening Scope of Test Validity

By now the reader is familiar with the narrow, traditionalist perspective on test use, which states that a test is valid if it measures "what it purports to measure." The implicit implication of this perspective is that technical validity is the most essential basis for recommending test use. After all, valid tests provide accurate information about examinees—and what could be wrong with that?

Recently, several psychometric theoreticians have introduced a wider, functionalist definition of validity which asserts that a test is valid if it serves the purpose for which it is used (Cronbach, 1988; Messick, 1995). For example, a reading achievement test might be used to identify students for assignment to a remedial section. According to the functionalist perspective, the test would be valid—and its use therefore appropriate—if the students selected for remediation actually received some academic benefit from this application of the test.

The functionalist perspective explicitly recognizes that the test validator has an obligation to determine whether a practice has constructive consequences for individuals and institutions, and especially to guard against adverse outcomes (Messick, 1980). Test validity, then, is an overall evaluative judgment of the adequacy and appropriateness of inferences *and actions* that flow from test scores.

Messick (1980, 1995) argues that the new, wider conception of validity rests on four bases. These are (1) traditional evidence of construct validity, for example, appropriate convergent and discriminant validity, (2) an analysis of the value implications of the test interpretation, (3) evidence for the usefulness of test interpretations in particular applications, and (4) an appraisal of the potential and actual social consequences, including side effects, from test use. A valid test is one that answers well to all four facets of test validity.

This wider conception of test validity is admittedly controversial, and some theorists prefer the traditional view that consequences and values are important but nonetheless separate from the technical issues of test validity. Everyone can agree on one point: Psychological measurement is not a neutral endeavor, it is an applied science that occurs in a social and political context.

SUMMARY

1. The validity of a test is the degree to which it measures what it claims to measure. A test is valid to the extent that inferences made from it are appropriate, meaningful, and useful. Reliability is a necessary but not a sufficient precursor to validity.

2. Traditionally, the different ways of accumulating validity evidence have been grouped into three categories: content validity, criterion-related validity, and construct validity. However, validity is a unitary concept and any empirical study may bear upon the validity of a test.

3. Content validity is determined by the degree to which the questions, tasks, or items on a test are representative of the universe of behavior the test was designed to sample. Content validity is easy to assure for well-defined traits such as spelling ability, but more difficult to specify for inexplicit traits such as anxiety.

4. A test has face validity if it looks valid to test users, examiners, and especially the examinees. Face validity is important for social acceptability of a test but is irrelevant for psychometric purposes.

5. Criterion-related validity is demonstrated when a test is effective in predicting performance on an appropriate outcome measure. Criterion-related validity subsumes concurrent validity, in which the criterion measures are obtained at approximately the same time as the predictor test scores, and predictive validity, in which the criterion measures are obtained in the future.

6. When tests are used for purposes of prediction, it is necessary to develop a regression equation. A regression equation describes the best-fitting straight line (one that minimizes the sum of the squared deviations from the line) for estimating the criterion from the test. For example, the equation $Y = .07X + .2$ might be used to predict job ratings from an employment test.

7. The correlation between test and criterion (r_{xy}) is known as a validity coefficient. The higher the correlation, the more accurate is the test in estimating the criterion.

8. The standard error of estimate (SE_{est}) is the margin of error to be expected in the predicted criterion score. The error of estimate is derived from the following formula:

$$SE_{est} = SD_y \sqrt{1 - r_{xy}^2}$$

where r_{xy} is the validity coefficient.

9. Proponents of decision theory stress that a test must aid in accurate decision making. The accurate prediction of success versus failure on an outcome measure is essential. Tests should avoid two kinds of errors: false positives, in which subjects are predicted to succeed but fail, and false negatives, in which subjects are predicted to fail but succeed.

10. Decision theory assumes that the costs of accurate and inaccurate predictions can be measured on a common utility scale such as profit/loss. A fundamental assumption of decision theory is maximization: In institutional selection decisions, the most appropriate test-use strategy is one that maximizes the average gain or minimizes the average loss.

11. A construct is a theoretical, intangible quality or trait in which individuals differ. Construct validity pertains to psychological tests that claim to measure complex, multifaceted, and theory-bound psychological attributes such as leadership ability, overcontrolled hostility, and intelligence.

12. Studies of construct validity generally fall into one of these categories: analysis of item homogeneity; assessment of developmental and group changes on the test; analysis of intervention effects; correlation and factor analysis of test scores in relation to other sources of information. In each case, the crucial question is whether the results are consistent with the underlying theory of the construct that is measured.

13. Extra-validity concerns include the side effects and unintended consequences of testing. For example, a valid assessment for special education placement may nonetheless cause identified children to feel unusual or dumb. A consideration of side effects should influence an examiner's decision to use a particular test for a specific purpose.

14. The new, wider, functionalist perspective on test validity asserts that a test is valid if it serves the purposes for which it is used. For example, the validity of a reading achievement test might be linked to successful remediation of the reading-impaired students identified by the test.

KEY TERMS AND CONCEPTS

validity   p. 96

content validity   p. 97

face validity   p. 99

criterion-related validity   p. 99

concurrent validity   p. 99

predictive validity   p. 100

regression equation   p. 102

validity coefficient   p. 102

standard error of estimate   p. 102

decision theory   p. 103

false positive   p. 104

false negative   p. 104

base rate   p. 106

construct   p. 107

construct validity   p. 108

homogeneous scale   p. 108

convergent validity   p. 110

discriminant validity   p. 110

multitrait-multimethod matrix   p. 111

factor analysis   p. 112

factor loading   p. 112

extra-validity concerns   p. 113

T O P I C **4B** Test Construction

Creating a new test involves both science and art. A test developer must choose strategies and materials, and then make day-to-day research decisions that will affect the quality of his or her emerging instrument. The purpose of this section is to discuss the process by which psychometricians create valid tests. Although we will discuss many separate topics, they are united by a common theme: Valid tests do not just materialize upon the scene in full maturity—they emerge slowly from an evolutionary, developmental process that builds in validity from the very beginning. We will emphasize the basics of test development here; readers who desire a more advanced presentation should consult Kline (1986) and Nunnally (1978).

Test construction consists of six intertwined stages:

Defining the test
Selecting a scaling method
Constructing the items
Testing the items
Revising the test
Publishing the test

By way of preview, we can summarize these steps as follows: defining the test consists of delimiting its scope and purpose, which must be known before the developer can proceed to test construction. Selecting a scaling method is a process of setting the rules by which numbers are assigned to test results. Constructing the items is as much art as science, and it is here that the creativity of the test developer may be required. Once a preliminary version of the test is available, the developer usually administers it to a modest-sized sample of subjects in order to collect initial data about test item characteristics. Testing the items entails a variety of statistical procedures referred to collectively as item analysis. The purpose of *item analysis* is to determine which items should be retained, which revised, and which thrown out. Based on item analysis and other sources of information, the test is then revised. If the revisions are substantial, new items and additional pretesting with new subjects may be required. Thus, test construction involves a feedback loop whereby second, third, and fourth drafts of an instrument might be produced (Figure 4.5). Publishing the test is the final step. In addition to releasing the test materials, the developer must produce a user-friendly test manual. Let us examine each of these steps in more detail.

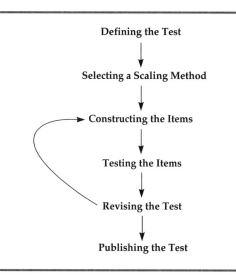

Defining the Test

Selecting a Scaling Method

Constructing the Items

Testing the Items

Revising the Test

Publishing the Test

FIGURE 4.5 The Test Construction Process

DEFINING THE TEST

In order to construct a new test, the developer must have a clear idea of what the test is to measure and how it is to differ from existing instruments. Insofar as psychological testing is now entering its second century, and insofar as thousands of tests have already been published, the burden of proof clearly rests upon the test developer to show that a proposed instrument is different from, and better than, existing measures.

Consider the daunting task faced by a test developer who proposes yet another measure of general intelligence. With dozens of such instruments already in existence, how could a new test possibly make a useful contribution to the field? The answer is that contemporary research continually adds to our understanding of intelligence and impels us to seek new and more useful ways to measure this multifaceted construct.

Kaufman and Kaufman (1983) provide a good model of the test definition process. In proposing the Kaufman Assessment Battery for Children (K-ABC), a new test of general intelligence in children, the authors listed six primary goals which

define the purpose of the test and distinguish it from existing measures:

1. Measure intelligence from a strong theoretical and research basis
2. Separate acquired factual knowledge from the ability to solve unfamiliar problems
3. Yield scores that translate to educational intervention
4. Include novel tasks
5. Be easy to administer and objective to score
6. Be sensitive to the diverse needs of preschool, minority group, and exceptional children (Kaufman & Kaufman, 1983)

As the reader will discover in a later topic, the K-ABC represents an interesting departure from traditional intelligence tests. For now, the important point is that the developers of this recent instrument explained its purpose explicitly and proposed a fresh focus for measuring intelligence, long before they started constructing test items.

SELECTING A SCALING METHOD

The immediate purpose of psychological testing is to assign numbers to responses on a test so that the examinee can be judged to have more or less of the characteristic measured. The rules by which numbers are assigned to responses define the scaling method. Test developers select a scaling method that is optimally suited to the manner in which they have conceptualized the trait(s) measured by their test. No single scaling method is uniformly better than the others. For some traits, ordinal ranking of expert judges might be the best measurement approach; for other traits, complex scaling of self-report data might yield the most valid measurements.

There are so many distinctive scaling methods available to psychometricians that we will be satisfied to provide only a representative sample here. Readers who wish a more thorough and detailed review should consult Gulliksen (1950), Nunnally (1978), or Kline (1986). However, before reviewing selecting scaling methods, we need to introduce a related concept, levels of measurement, so that the reader can better appreciate the differences between scaling methods.

Levels of Measurement

According to Stevens (1946), all numbers derived from measurement instruments of any kind can be placed into one of four hierarchical categories: nominal, ordinal, interval, or ratio. Each category defines a level of measurement; the order listed is from least to most informative.

In **nominal scales,** the numbers serve only as category names. For example, when collecting data for a demographic study, a researcher might code males as "1" and females as "2." Notice that the numbers are arbitrary and do not designate "more" or "less" of anything. In nominal scales the numbers are just a simplified form of naming.

Ordinal scales constitute a form of ordering or ranking. If college professors were asked to rank order four cars as to which they would prefer to own, the preferred order might be "1" Cadillac, "2" Chevrolet, "3" Volkswagen, "4" Hyundai. Notice here that the numbers are not interchangeable. A ranking of "1" is "more" than a ranking of "2," and so on. The "more" refers to the order of preference. However, ordinal scales fail to provide information about the relative strength of rankings. In this hypothetical example, we do not know if college professors strongly prefer Cadillacs over Chevrolets, or just marginally so.

An **interval scale** provides information about ranking, but also supplies a metric for gauging the differences between rankings. To construct an interval scale, we might ask our college professors to rate on a scale from 1 to 100 how much they would like to own the four cars previously listed. Suppose the average ratings work out as follows: Cadillac, 90; Chevrolet, 70; Volkswagen, 60; Hyundai, 50. From this information we could infer that the preference for a Cadillac is much stronger than for a Chevrolet which, in turn, is mildly stronger than the preference for a Volkswagen. More important, we can also make the assumption that the intervals

between the points on this scale are approximately the same: The difference between professors' preference for a Chevrolet and Volkswagen (10 points) is about the same as that between a Volkswagen and a Hyundai (also 10 points). In short, interval scales are based on the assumption of equal-sized units or intervals for the underlying scale.

A **ratio scale** has all the characteristics of an interval scale, but also possesses a conceptually meaningful zero point in which there is a total absence of the characteristic being measured. The essential characteristics of the four levels of measurement are summarized in Figure 4.6.

Ratio scales are rare in psychological measurement. Consider whether there is any meaningful sense in which a person can be thought to have zero intelligence. Not really. The same is true for most constructs in psychology: Meaningful zero points just do not exist. However, a few physical measures used by psychologists qualify as ratio scales. For example, height and weight qualify, and perhaps some physiological measures such as electrodermal response qualify, too. But by and large the best a psychologist can hope for is interval-level measurement.

Levels of measurement are relevant to test construction because the more powerful and useful parametric statistical procedures (e.g., Pearson *r*, analysis of variance, multiple regression) should be used only for scores derived from measures that meet the criteria of interval or ratio scales. For

Level	*Characteristics*			
	Allows for Categorizing	*Allows for Ranking*	*Uses Equal Intervals*	*Possesses Real Zero Point*
Nominal	X			
Ordinal	X	X		
Interval	X	X	X	
Ratio	X	X	X	X

FIGURE 4.6 Essential Characteristics of Four Levels of Measurement

scales that are only nominal or ordinal, less-powerful nonparametric statistical procedures (e.g., chi-square, rank order correlation, median tests) must be employed. In practice, most major psychological testing instruments (especially intelligence tests and personality scales) are assumed to employ approximately interval-level measurement even though, strictly speaking, it is very difficult to demonstrate absolute equality of intervals for such instruments (Bausell, 1986). Now that the reader is familiar with levels of measurement, we introduce a representative sample of scaling methods, noting in advance that different scaling methods yield different levels of measurement.

REPRESENTATIVE SCALING METHODS

Expert Rankings

Suppose we wanted to measure the depth of coma in patients who had suffered a recent head injury that rendered them unconsciousness. A depth of coma scale could be very important in predicting the course of improvement, because it is well known that a lengthy period of unconsciousness offers a poor prognosis for ultimate recovery. In addition, rehabilitation personnel have a practical need to know whether a patient is deeply comatose or in a partially communicative state of twilight consciousness.

One approach to scaling the depth of coma would be to rely on the behavioral **rankings of experts.** For example, we could ask a panel of neurologists to list patient behaviors associated with different levels of consciousness. After the experts had submitted a large list of diagnostic behaviors, the test developers—preferably experts on head injuries—could rank the indicator behaviors along a continuum of consciousness ranging from deep coma to basic orientation. Using precisely this approach, Teasdale and Jennett (1974) produced the Glasgow Coma Scale. Instruments similar to this scale are widely used in hospitals for the assessment of traumatic brain injury (Figure 4.7).

The Glasgow Coma Scale is scored by observing the patient and assigning the highest level of functioning on each of three subscales. On each

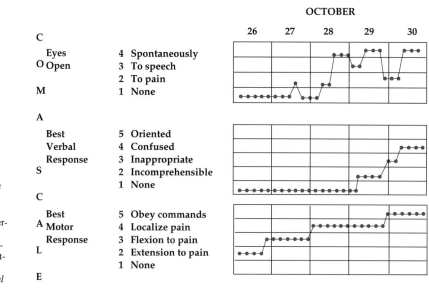

FIGURE 4.7

Example of the Use of Glasgow Coma Scale for Recording Depth of Coma

Source: Reprinted with permission from Jennett, B., Teasdale, G. M., and Knill-Jones, R. P. (1975). Predicting outcome after head injury. *Journal of the Royal College of Physicians of London, 9,* 231–237.

subscale, it is assumed that the patient displays all levels of behavior below the rated level. Thus, from a psychometric standpoint, this scale consists of three subscales (eyes, verbal response, and motor response) each yielding an ordinal ranking of behavior.

In addition to the rankings, it is possible to compute a single overall score that is something more than an ordinal scale, although probably less than true interval-level measurement. If numbers are attached to the rankings (e.g., for eyes open a coding of "none" = 1, "to pain" = 2, and so on), then the numbers for the rated level for each subscale can be added, yielding a maximum possible score of 14. The Total Score on the Glasgow Coma Scale predicts later recovery with a very high degree of accuracy (Jennett, Teasdale, & Knill-Jones, 1975). We see, then, that quite plain psychological tests derived from the very simplest scaling methods can, nonetheless, provide valid and useful information.

Method of Equal-Appearing Intervals

Early in this century, L. L. Thurstone (1929) proposed a method for constructing interval-level scales from attitude statements. His **method of equal-appearing intervals** is still used today, marking him as one of the giants of psychometric theory. The actual methodology of constructing equal-appearing intervals is somewhat complex and statistically laden, but the underlying logic is easy to explain (Ghiselli, Campbell, & Zedeck, 1981). To illustrate the method, we summarize the steps involved in constructing a scale of attitudes toward church membership:

1. Collect as many true-false statements as possible reflecting a variety of positive and negative attitudes toward the church. Two extreme examples might be:

   "I feel that church services give me inspiration and help me to live up to my best during the following week."

   "I think that churches seek to impose a lot of worn-out dogmas and medieval superstitions."

Of course, many moderate items would be collected as well.

2. Next, have 10 or so known experts or judges rate these statements to determine the degree of favorability/unfavorability toward the attitude. The judges should be qualified for the task at hand; ministers might be used for a church membership attitude scale. Usually, each judge is requested to sort each statement into 1 of 11 categories that range from "extremely favorable" to "extremely unfavorable." Judges are told to disregard their own biases and to regard the 11 categories as equidistant.

3. After the judges have completed the evaluation process, the mean favorability rating (from 1 to 11) and standard deviation for each item is determined. For example, 10 judges may have given an average favorability rating of 9.2 to the first item previously noted; but ratings would likely differ from one judge to another, as reflected in a standard deviation of 1.1 for this item.

4. Because the standard deviation of an item favorability rating reflects ambiguity, items with large standard deviations are therefore dropped. Usually, about 20 to 30 items are chosen such that the statements cover the range of the dimension (favorable to unfavorable). It is assumed that the differences between items on the final scale fulfill the properties of an interval scale.

5. Persons who take the attitude scale are asked to mark all the statements with which they agree. Their score is determined by averaging the scale values of those items endorsed.

Ghiselli, Campbell, and Zedeck (1981) note that the preceding scaling method merely produces the attitude scale. Reliability and validity analyses of the scale are still needed to determine its appropriateness and usefulness.

A study by Russo (1994) illustrates a modern application of the Thurstone method. She used a Thurstone scaling approach to evaluate 216 items from three prominent self-report depression inventories. The judges included 527 undergraduates and 37 clinical faculty members at a medical school. The 216 items were randomized and rated with respect to depressive severity from 1 representing no depression to 11 representing extreme depression. She discovered that all three self-report inventories lacked items and response options typical of mild depression. The distribution of the 216 items was bimodal with many items bunched near the bottom (no depression) and many items bunched near the middle (moderate depression). A characteristic finding for one set of items from a prominent depression scale was as follows:

Rated Depression	Original Scoring	Item Content
1.0	1	I never feel downhearted or sad.
3.4	2	I sometimes feel downhearted or sad.
4.1	3	I feel downhearted or sad a good part of the time.
4.4	4	I feel downhearted or sad most of the time.

The reader will notice that the original scoring on these items deviates substantially from the depression ratings provided by the panel of students and clinical faculty. It is also evident that the actual scale values are discontinuous, jumping from 1.0 to 3.4 and higher. A similar pattern was observed for many items on all three inventories, leading Russo (1994) to conclude:

> The present results suggest that if the original scoring is used for the three scales examined here, then the distinctions between well-being and absence of depression as well as between moderate and severe will be difficult to make. Such imprecision will make it difficult to assess the efficacy of treatments for depression, because a lack thereof must be a function of added measurement error due to ordinal measures. Such error could also wreak havoc in longitudinal studies, especially in those in which memory is involved.

We see in this example that Thurstone's approach to item scaling has powerful applications in test development. Based upon these findings, researchers are now in a position to develop improved self-report scales which assess the full range of symptomatology in depression.

Method of Absolute Scaling

Thurstone (1925) also developed the **method of absolute scaling,** a procedure for obtaining a measure of absolute item difficulty based upon results for different age groups of test takers. The methodology for determining individual item difficulty on an absolute scale is quite complex, although the underlying rationale is not too difficult to understand. Essentially, a set of common test items is administered to two or more age groups. The relative difficulty of these items between any two age groups serves as the basis for making a series of interlocking comparisons for all items and all age groups. One age group serves as the anchor group. Item difficulty is measured in common units such as standard deviation units of ability for the anchor group. The method of absolute scaling is widely used in group achievement and aptitude testing (*STEP*, 1980; Donlon, 1984).

Thurstone (1925) illustrated the method of absolute scaling with data from the testing of 3,000 schoolchildren on the 65 questions from the original Binet test. Using the mean of Binet test intelligence of 3½-year-old children as the zero point and the standard deviation of their intelligence as the unit of measurement, he constructed a scale that ranged from –2 to +10 and then located each of the 65 questions on that scale. Thurstone (1925) found that the scale "brings out rather strikingly the fact that the questions are unduly bunched at certain ranges [of difficulty] and rather scarce at other ranges." A modern test developer would use this kind of analysis as a basis for dropping redundant test items (redundant in the sense that they measure at the same difficulty level) and adding other items that test the higher (and lower) ranges of difficulty.

Likert Scales

Likert (1932) proposed a simple and straightforward method for scaling attitudes that is widely used today. A **Likert scale** presents the examinee with five responses ordered on an agree/disagree or approve/disapprove continuum. For example, one item on a scale to assess attitudes toward church membership might read:

Church services give me inspiration and help me to live up to my best during the following week.

Do you:

Strongly Agree	Agree	Undecided	Disagree	Strongly Disagree

Depending on the wording of an individual item, an extreme answer of "strongly agree" or "strongly disagree" will indicate the most favorable response on the underlying attitude measured by the questionnaire. Likert (1932) assigned a score of 5 to this extreme response, 1 to the opposite extreme, and 2, 3, and 4 to intermediate replies. The total scale score is obtained by adding the scores from individual items. For this reason, a Likert scale is also referred to as a *summative scale.*

Guttman Scales

On a **Guttman scale,** respondents who endorse one statement also agree with milder statements pertinent to the same underlying continuum (Guttman, 1944, 1947). Thus, if the examiner knows an examinee's most extreme endorsement on the continuum, it is possible to reconstruct the intermediate responses as well. Guttman scales are produced by selecting items that fall into an ordered sequence of examinee endorsement. A perfect Guttman scale is seldom achieved due to errors of measurement, but is nonetheless a fitting goal for certain types of tests.

Although the Guttman approach was originally devised to determine whether a set of attitude statements is unidimensional, the technique has been used in many different kinds of tests. For example, Beck used Guttman-type scaling to produce the individual items of the Beck Depression Inventory (BDI, Beck, Steer, & Garbin, 1988; Beck et al., 1961). Items from the BDI resemble the following:

( ) I occasionally feel sad or blue.
( ) I often feel sad or blue.

( ) I feel sad or blue most of the time.
( ) I always feel sad and I can't stand it.

Clients are asked to "check the statement from each group that you feel is most true about you." A client who endorses an extreme alternative (e.g., "I always feel sad and I can't stand it") almost certainly agrees with the milder statements as well.

Method of Empirical Keying

The reader may have noticed that most of the scaling methods discussed in the preceding section rely upon the authoritative judgment of experts in the selection and ordering of items. It is also possible to construct measurement scales based entirely on empirical considerations devoid of theory or expert judgment. In the **method of empirical keying,** test items are selected for a scale based entirely on how well they contrast a criterion group from a normative sample. For example, a Depression scale could be derived from a pool of true-false personality inventory questions in the following manner:

1. A carefully selected and homogeneous group of persons experiencing major depression is gathered to answer the pool of true-false questions.
2. For each item, the endorsement frequency of the depression group is compared to the endorsement frequency of the normative sample.
3. Items which show a large difference in endorsement frequency between the depression and normative samples are selected for the Depression scale, keyed in the direction favored by depression subjects (true or false, as appropriate).
4. Raw score on the Depression scale is then simply the number of items answered in the keyed direction.

The method of empirical keying can produce some interesting surprises. A common finding is that some items selected for a scale may show no obvious relationship to the construct measured. For example, an item such as "I drink a lot of water" (keyed true) might end up on a Depression scale. The momentary rationale for including this item is simply that it works. Of course, the challenge posed to researchers is to determine why the item works. However, from the practical standpoint of empirical scale construction, theoretical considerations are of secondary importance. We discuss the method of empirical keying further in Topic 14A, Self-Report Inventories.

Rational Scale Construction (Internal Consistency)

The rational approach to scale construction is a popular method for the development of self-report personality inventories. The name *rational* is somewhat of a misnomer, insofar as certain statistical methods are essential to this approach. Also, the name implies that other approaches are nonrational or irrational, which is untrue. The heart of the **method of rational scaling** is that all scale items correlate positively with each other and also with the total score for the scale. An alternative and more appropriate name for this approach is internal consistency, which emphasizes what is actually done. Gough and Bradley (1992) explain how the rational approach earned its descriptive title:

> The idea of rationality enters the scene in that the central theme or unifying dimension around which the items cluster is one that was conceptually articulated beforehand by the developer of the measure and from which the scoring of each item is determined in a logical and understandable way.

We will follow their presentation to illustrate the features of the rational approach.

Suppose a test developer desires to develop a new self-report scale for leadership potential. Based upon a review of relevant literature, the researcher might conclude that leadership potential is characterized by self-confidence, resilience under pressure, high intelligence, persuasiveness, assertiveness, and the ability to sense what others are thinking and feeling. These notions suggest that the following true-false items might be useful in the assessment of leadership potential (Gough & Bradley, 1992):

- I generally feel sure of myself and self-confident. (T)
- When others disagree with me, I usually just keep quiet or else give in. (F)
- I believe that I am distinctly above average in intellectual ability. (T)
- I often feel that I have a poor understanding of how other people will react to things. (F)
- My friends would probably describe me as a strong, forceful person. (T)

The *T* and *F* after each statement indicate the rationally keyed direction for leadership potential.

Of course, additional items with similar intentions also would be proposed. The test developer might begin with 100 items which appear—on a rational basis—to assess leadership potential. These preliminary items would be administered to a large sample of individuals similar to the target population for whom the scale is intended. For instance, if the scale is designed to identify college students with leadership potential, then it should be administered to a cross section of several hundred college students. For scale development, very large samples are desirable. In this hypothetical case, let us assume that we obtain results for 500 college students.

The next step in rational scale construction is to correlate scores on each of the preliminary items with the total score on the test for the 500 subjects in the tryout sample. Because scores on the items are dichotomous (1 is arbitrarily assigned to an answer corresponding to the scoring key, 0 to the alternative), a biserial correlation coefficient r_{bis} is needed. Once the correlations are obtained, the researcher scans the list in search of weak correlations and reversals (negative correlations). These items are discarded because they do not contribute to the measurement of leadership potential. Up to half of the initial items might be discarded. If a large proportion of items is initially discarded, the researcher might recalculate the item-total correlations based upon the reduced item pool to verify the homogeneity of the remaining items. The items which survive this iterative procedure constitute the leadership potential scale. The reader should keep in mind that the rational approach to scale construction merely produces a homogeneous scale thought to measure a specified construct. Additional studies with new subject samples would be needed to determine the reliability and validity of the new scale.

CONSTRUCTING THE ITEMS

Constructing test items is a painful and laborious procedure that taxes the creativity of test developers. The item writer is confronted with a profusion of initial questions:

- Should item content be homogeneous or varied?
- What range of difficulty should the items cover?
- How many initial items should be constructed?
- Which cognitive processes and item domains should be tapped?
- What kind of test item should be used?

We will address the first three questions briefly before turning to a more detailed discussion of the last two topics which are commonly referred to under the rubrics of table of specifications and item formats.

Initial Questions in Test Construction

The first question pertains to the homogeneity versus heterogeneity of test item content. In large measure, whether item content is homogeneous or varied is dictated by the manner in which the test developer has defined the new instrument. Consider a culture-reduced test of general intelligence. Such an instrument might incorporate varied items, so long as the questions do not presume specific schooling. The test developer might seek to incorporate novel problems equally unfamiliar to all examinees. On the other hand, with a theory-based test of spatial thinking, subscales with homogeneous item content would be required.

The range of item difficulty must be sufficient to allow for meaningful differentiation of examinees at both extremes. The most useful tests, then, are those that include a graded series of very easy items passed by almost everyone as well as a group of incrementally more difficult items passed by virtually no one. A ceiling effect is observed when significant numbers of examinees obtain perfect or near-perfect scores. The problem with a ceiling effect is that distinctions between high-scoring examinees are not possible, even though these examinees might differ substantially on the underlying trait measured by the test. A floor effect is observed when significant numbers of examinees obtain scores at or near the bottom of the scale. For example, the WAIS-R has a serious floor effect in that it fails to discriminate between moderate, severe, and profound levels of mental retardation—all persons with significant developmental disabilities fail to answer virtually every question.

Test developers expect that some initial items will prove to make ineffectual contributions to the overall measurement goal of their instrument. For this reason, it is common practice to construct a first draft that contains excess items, perhaps double the number of questions desired on the final draft. For example, the 550-item MMPI originally consisted of more than 1,000 true-false personality statements (Hathaway & McKinley, 1940).

Table of Specifications

Professional developers of achievement and ability tests often use one or more item-writing schemes to help insure that their instrument taps a desired mixture of cognitive processes and content domains. For example, a very simple item-writing scheme might designate that an achievement test on the Civil War should consist of 10 multiple-choice items and 10 fill-in-the-blank questions, half of each on factual matters (e.g., dates, major battles) and the other half on conceptual issues (e.g., differing views on slavery).

Before development of a test begins, item writers usually receive a table of specifications. A **table of specifications** enumerates the information and cognitive tasks on which examinees are to be assessed. Perhaps the most common specification table is the content-by-process matrix which lists the exact number of items in relevant content areas and details the precise composite of items which must exemplify different cognitive processes (Millman & Greene, 1989).

Consider a science achievement test suitable for high school students. Such a test must cover many different content areas and should require a mixture of cognitive processes ranging from simple recall to inferential reasoning. By providing a table of specifications prior to the item-writing stage, the test developer can guarantee that the resulting instrument contains a proper balance of topical coverage and taps a desired range of cognitive skills. A hypothetical but realistic table of specifications is portrayed in Table 4.6.

Item Formats

When it comes to the method by which psychological attributes are to be assessed, the test developer is confronted with dozens of choices. Indeed, it would be easy to write an entire chapter on this topic alone. For reviews of item formats, the interested reader should consult Bausell (1986), Jensen (1980), and Wesman (1971). In this section, we will quickly survey the advantages and pitfalls of the more common varieties of test items.

For group-administered tests of intellect or achievement, the technique of choice is the multiple-choice question. For example, an item on an American history achievement test might include this combination of stem and options:

The president of the United States during the Civil War was

a. Washington
b. Lincoln
c. Hamilton
d. Wilson

Proponents of multiple-choice methodology argue that properly constructed items can measure conceptual as well as factual knowledge. Multiple choice tests also permit quick and objective machine scoring. Furthermore, the fairness of multiple-choice questions can be proved (or occasionally disproved!) with very simple item analysis procedures discussed subsequently. The major shortcomings of multiple-choice questions are, first, the difficulty of writing good distractor options and, second, the possibility that the presence of the response may cue a half-knowledgeable respondent to the correct answer. Guidelines for writing good multiple-choice items are listed in Table 4.7.

TABLE 4.6 Example of a Content-by-Process Table of Specifications for a Hypothetical 100-Item Science Achievement Test

| Content Area | *Process* | | |
	Factual Knowledge[a]	*Information Competence[b]*	*Inferential Reasoning[c]*
Astronomy	8	3	3
Botany	6	7	2
Chemistry	10	5	4
Geology	10	5	2
Physics	8	5	6
Zoology	8	5	3
Totals	50	30	20

[a]Factual Knowledge: Items can be answered based on simple recognition of basic facts.

[b]Information Competence: Items require usage of information provided in written text.

[c]Inferential Reasoning: Items can be answered by making deductions or drawing conclusions.

TABLE 4.7 Guidelines for Writing Multiple-Choice Items

Choose words that have precise meanings.
Avoid complex or awkward word arrangements.
Include all information needed for response selection.
Put as much of the question as possible in the stem.
Do not take stems verbatim from textbooks.
Use options of equal length and parallel phrasing.
Use "none of the above" and "all of the above" rarely.
Minimize the use of negatives such as *not*.
Avoid the use of nonfunctional words.
Avoid unessential specificity in the stem.
Avoid unnecessary clues to the correct response.
Submit items to others for editorial scrutiny.

Matching questions are popular in classroom testing, but suffer serious psychometric shortcomings. An example of a matching question:

Using the letters on the left, match the name to the accomplishment:

A. Binet ＿＿＿ translated a major intelligence test

B. Woodworth ＿＿＿ no correlation between grades and mental tests

C. Cattell ＿＿＿ developed true/false personality inventory

D. McKinley ＿＿＿ battery of sensorimotor tests

E. Wissler ＿＿＿ developed first useful intelligence test

F. Goddard ＿＿＿ screening test for emotional disturbance

The most serious problem with matching questions is that responses are not independent—missing one match usually compels the examinee to miss another. Another problem is that the options in a matching question must be very closely related or the question will be too easy.

For individually administered tests, the procedure of choice is the short answer objective item. Indeed, the simplest and most straightforward types of questions often possess the best reliability and validity. A case in point is the Vocabulary subtest from the WAIS-III, which consists merely of asking the examinee to define words. This subtest has very high reliability (.96) and is usually considered the single best measure of overall intelligence on the WAIS-III (Gregory, 1999).

Personality tests often use true-false questions because they are easy for subjects to understand. Most people find it simple to answer true or false to items such as:

T   F
＿＿＿ ＿＿＿ I like sports magazines.

Critics of this approach have pointed out that answers to such questions may reflect social desirability rather than personality traits (Edwards, 1961). An alternative format designed to counteract this problem is the **forced-choice methodol-**

ogy where the examinee must choose between two equally desirable (or undesirable) options:

Which would you rather do:
＿＿＿ Mop a gallon of syrup from the floor.
＿＿＿ Volunteer for a half-day at a nursing home.

Although the forced-choice approach has many desirable psychometric properties (Zavala, 1965), personality test developers have not rushed to embrace this interesting methodology.

TESTING THE ITEMS

Psychometricians expect that numerous test items from the original tryout pool will be discarded or revised as test development proceeds. For this reason, test developers initially produce many, many excess items, perhaps double the number of items they intend to use. So how is the final sample of test questions selected from the initial item pool? Test developers use item analysis, a family of statistical procedures, to identify the best items. In general, the purpose of item analysis is to determine which items should be retained, which revised, and which thrown out. In conducting a thorough item analysis, the test developer might make use of item-difficulty index, item-reliability index, item-validity index, item-characteristic curve, and an index of item discrimination. We turn now to a brief review of these statistical approaches to item analysis. Readers who wish an in-depth discussion and critique of these topics should consult Hambleton (1989) and Nunnally (1978).

Item-Difficulty Index

The item difficulty for a single test item is defined as the proportion of examinees in a large tryout sample who get that item correct. For any individual item i, the index of item difficulty is p_i, which varies from 0.0 to 1.0. An item with difficulty of .2 is more difficult than an item with difficulty of .7, because fewer examinees answered it correctly.

The **item-difficulty index** is a useful tool for identifying items that should be altered or discarded. Suppose an item has a difficulty index near 0.0, meaning that nearly everyone has answered it incorrectly. Unfortunately, this item is psychometrically unproductive because it does not provide information about differences between examinees. For most applications, the item should be rewritten or thrown out. The same can be said for an item with difficulty index near 1.0, where virtually all subjects provide a correct answer.

What is the optimal level of item difficulty? Generally, item difficulties that hover around .5, ranging between .3 and .7, maximize the information the test provides about differences between examinees. However, this rule of thumb is subject to one important qualification and one very significant exception.

For true-false or multiple-choice items, the optimal level of item difficulty needs to be adjusted for the effects of guessing. For a true-false test, a difficulty level of .5 can result when examinees merely guess. Thus, the optimal item difficulty for such items would be .75 (halfway between .5 and 1.0). In general, the optimal level of item difficulty can be computed from the formula $(1.0 + g)/2$ where g is the chance success level. Thus, for a four-option multiple-choice item, the chance success level is .25, and the optimal level of item difficulty would be $(1.0 + .25)/2$ or about .63.

If a test is to be used for selection of an extreme group by means of a cutting score, it may be desirable to select items with difficulty levels outside the .3 to .7 range. For example, a test used to select graduate students for a university that admits only a select few of its many applicants should contain many very difficult items. A test used to designate children for a remedial-education program should contain many extremely easy items. In both cases, there will be useful discrimination among examinees near the cutting score—a very high score for the graduate admissions and a very low score for students eligible for remediation—but little discrimination among the remaining examinees (Allen & Yen, 1979).

Item-Reliability Index

A test developer may desire an instrument with a high level of internal consistency in which the items are reasonably homogeneous. A simple way to determine if an individual item "hangs together" with the remaining test items is to correlate scores on that item with scores on the total test. However, individual items are typically right or wrong (often scored 1 or 0) whereas total scores constitute a continuous variable. In order to correlate these two different kinds of scores it is necessary to use a special type of statistic called the *point-biserial correlation coefficient.* The computational formula for this correlation coefficient is equivalent to the Pearson *r* discussed earlier, and the point-biserial coefficient conveys much the same kind of information regarding the relationship between two variables (one of which happens to be dichotomous and scored 0 or 1). In general, the higher the point-biserial correlation r_{iT} between an individual item and the total score, the more useful is the item from the standpoint of internal consistency.

The usefulness of an individual dichotomous test item is also determined by the extent to which scores on it are distributed between the two outcomes of 0 and 1. Although it sounds incongruous, it is possible to compute the standard deviation for dichotomous items; as with a continuously scored variable, the standard deviation of a dichotomous item indicates the extent of dispersion of the scores. If an individual item has a standard deviation of zero, everyone is obtaining the same score (all right or all wrong). The more closely the item approaches a 50–50 split of right and wrong scores, the greater is its standard deviation. In general, the greater the standard deviation of an item, the more useful is the item to the overall scale. Although we will not provide the derivation, it can be shown that the item-score standard deviation s_i for a dichotomously scored item can be computed from

$$s_i = \sqrt{p_i(1 - p_i)}$$

We may summarize the discussion up to this point as follows: The potential value of a dichotomously scored test item depends jointly upon its internal consistency as indexed by the correlation with the total score (r_{iT}) and also its variability as indexed by the standard deviation (s_i). If we compute the product of these two indices, we obtain $s_i r_{iT}$, which is the **item-reliability index.** Consider the characteristics of an item which possesses a relatively large item-reliability index. Such an item must exhibit strong internal consistency and produce a good dispersion of scores between its two alternatives. The value of this index in test construction is simply this: by computing the item-reliability index for every item in the preliminary test, we can eliminate the "outlier" items that have the lowest value on this index. Such items would possess poor internal consistency or weak dispersion of scores and therefore not contribute to the goals of measurement.

Item-Validity Index

For many applications, it is important that a test possess the highest possible concurrent or predictive validity. In these cases, one overriding question governs test construction: How well does each preliminary test item contribute to accurate prediction of the criterion? The **item-validity index** is a useful tool in the psychometrician's quest to identify predictively useful test items. By computing the item-validity index for every item in the preliminary test, the test developer can identify ineffectual items, eliminate or rewrite them, and produce a revised instrument with greater practical utility.

The first step in figuring an item-validity index is to compute the point-biserial correlation between the item score and the score on the criterion variable. In general, the higher the point-biserial correlation r_{iC} between scores on an individual item and the criterion score, the more useful is the item from the standpoint of predictive validity. As previously noted, the utility of an item also depends upon its standard deviation s_i. Thus, the item-validity index consists of the product of the standard deviation and the point-biserial correlation: $s_i r_{iC}$.

Item-Characteristic Curves

An **item-characteristic curve** (ICC) is a graphical display of the relationship between the probability of a correct response and the examinee's position on the underlying trait measured by the test. However, we do not have direct access to underlying traits, so observed test scores must be used to estimate trait quantities.

A separate ICC is graphed for each item, based upon a plot of the total test scores on the horizontal axis versus the proportion of examinees passing the item on the vertical axis (Figure 4.8). An ICC is actually a mathematical idealization of the relationship between the probability of a correct response and the amount of the trait possessed by test respondents. Different ICC models use different mathematical functions, based upon initial assumptions. The simplest ICC model is the Rasch model, based upon the item-response theory of the Danish mathematician Georg Rasch (1966). The Rasch model is the simplest model because it makes just two assumptions: (1) test items are unidimensional and measure one common trait, and (2) test items vary upon a continuum of difficulty level.

In general, a good item has a positive ICC slope. If the ability to solve a particular item is normally distributed, the ICC will resemble a **normal**

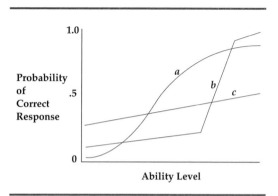

FIGURE 4.8 Some Sample Item-Characteristic Curves

ogive (curve *a* in Figure 4.8). The normal ogive is simply the normal distribution graphed in cumulative form.

The desired shape of the ICC depends upon the purpose of the test. Psychometric purists would prefer that test item ICCs approximate the normal ogive, because this curve is convenient for making mathematical deductions about the underlying trait (Lord & Novick, 1968). However, for selection decisions based on cutoff scores, a step function is preferred. For example, when combined with other similar items, the item which produced curve *b* in Figure 4.8 would be the best for selecting examinees with high levels of the measured trait.

ICCs are especially useful for identifying items that perform differently for subgroups of examinees (Allen & Yen, 1979). For example, a test developer may discover that an item performs differently for men and women. A sex-biased question involving football facts comes to mind here. For men, the ICC for this item might have the desired positive slope, whereas for women the ICC might be quite flat (such as curve *c* in Figure 4.8). Items with ICCs that differ among subgroups of examinees can be revised or eliminated.

The underlying theory of ICC is also known as *item response theory* and *latent trait theory*. The usefulness of this approach has been questioned by Nunnally (1978) who points out that the assumption of test unidimensionality (implied in the ICC curve which plots percentage passing against the unidimensional horizontal axis of trait value) is violated when many psychological tests are considered. If there were no serious technical and practical problems involved, "one wonders why ICC theory was not adopted long ago for the actual construction and scoring of tests" (Nunnally, 1978).

The merits of the ICC approach are still debated. ICC theory seems particularly appropriate for certain forms of computerized adaptive testing (CAT) in which each test taker responds to an individualized and unique set of items which are then scored on an underlying uniform scale (Weiss, 1983). The CAT approach to assessment would not

be possible in the absence of an ICC approach to measurement. CAT is discussed in Topic 15A, Computerized Assessment and the Future of Testing. Readers who wish a more detailed discussion of ICC and other latent trait models should consult Anastasi (1988), Hambleton (1989), and Wright and Stone (1979).

Item-Discrimination Index

It should be clear from the discussion of ICCs that an effective test item is one which discriminates between high scorers and low scorers on the entire test. An ideal test item is one which most of the high scorers pass and most of the low scorers fail (see curve *a* in Figure 4.8). Simple visual inspection of the ICC provides a coarse basis for gauging the discriminability of a test item: If the slope of the curve is positive and the curve is preferably ogive-shaped, the item is doing a good job of separating high and low scorers. But visual inspection is not a completely objective procedure; what is needed is a statistical tool that summarizes the discrimination power of individual test items.

An **item-discrimination index** is a statistical index of how efficiently an item discriminates between persons who obtain high and low scores on the entire test. There are many indices of item discrimination, including such indirect measures as r_{iT}, the point-biserial correlation between scores on an individual item and the total test score. However, we will restrict our discussion here to a direct measure, the item-discrimination index, symbolized by the lowercase, italicized letter *d*. On an item-by-item basis, this index compares the performance of subjects in the upper and lower regions of total test score. The upper and lower ranges are generally defined as the upper- and lower-scoring 10 percent to 33 percent of the sample. If the total test scores are normally distributed, the optimal comparison is the highest-scoring 27 percent versus the lowest-scoring 27 percent of the examinees. If the distribution of total test scores is flatter than the normal curve, the optimal percentage is larger, approaching 33 percent. For most applications, any percentage between 25 and 33 will yield similar estimates of d (Allen & Yen, 1979).

The item-discrimination index for a test item is calculated from the formula:

$$d = (U - L)/N$$

where U is the number of examinees in the upper range who answered the item correctly, L is the number of examinees in the lower range who answered the item correctly, and N is the total number of examinees in the upper or lower range.

Let us illustrate the computation and use of d with a hypothetical example. Suppose that a test developer has constructed the preliminary version of a multiple-choice achievement test and has administered the exam to a tryout sample of 400 high school students. After computing total scores for each subject, the test developer then identifies the high-scoring 25 percent and low-scoring 25 percent of the sample. Since there are 100 students in each group (25 percent of 400), N in the preceding formula will be 100. Next, for each item, the developer determines the number of students in the upper range and the lower range who answered it correctly. To compute d for each item is a simple matter of plugging these values into the formula $(U - L)/N$. For example, suppose on the first item that 49 students in the upper range answered it correctly, whereas 23 students in the lower range answered it correctly. For this item, d is equal to $(49 - 23)/100$ or .26.

It is evident from the formula for d that this index can vary from -1.0 to $+1.0$. Notice, too, that a negative value for d is a warning signal that a test item needs revision or replacement. After all, such an outcome indicates that more of the low-scoring subjects answered the item correctly than did the high-scoring subjects. If d is zero, exactly equal numbers of low- and high-scoring subjects answered the item correctly; since the item is not discriminating between low- and high-scoring subjects at all, it should be revised or eliminated. A positive value for d is preferred, and the closer to $+1.0$ the better. Table 4.8 illustrates item-discrimination indices for six items from the hypothetical test proposed here.

A test developer can supplement the item-discrimination approach by inspecting the number of examinees in the upper- and lower-scoring groups who choose each of the incorrect alternatives. If a multiple-choice item is well written, the incorrect alternatives should be equally attractive to subjects who do not know the correct answer. Of course, we expect that high-scoring examinees will choose the correct alternative more often than low-scoring examinees—that is the purpose in computing item-discrimination indices. But, in addition, a good item should show proportional dispersion of incorrect choices for both high- and low-scoring subjects.

Assume that we investigate the choices of 100 high- and 100 low-scoring subjects on a hypothetical multiple-choice test. Correct choices are indicated by an asterisk (*). Item 1 demonstrates the

TABLE 4.8   Item-Discrimination Indices for Six Hypothetical Items

Item	U	L	(U − L)/N	Comment
1	49	23	.26	Very good item with high difficulty
2	79	19	.60	Excellent item but rarely achieved
3	52	52	.00	Poor item which should be revised
4	100	0	1.00	Ideal item but never achieved
5	20	80	−.60	Terrible item which should be eliminated
6	0	100	−1.00	Theoretically worst possible item

desired pattern of answers, with incorrect choices about equally dispersed

Item 1	Alternatives				
	a	*b*	*c**	*d*	*e*
High Scorers	5	6	80	5	4
Low Scorers	15	14	40	16	15

On item 2, we notice that no examinees picked alternative *d*. This alternative should be replaced with a more appealing distractor:

Item 2					
	a	*b**	*c*	*d*	*e*
High Scorers	5	75	10	0	10
Low Scorers	21	34	20	0	25

Item 3 is probably a poor item in spite of the fact that it discriminates effectively between high- and low-scoring subjects. The obvious problem is that high-scoring examinees prefer alternative *a* to the correct alternative, *d:*

Item 3					
	a	*b*	*c*	*d**	*e*
High Scorers	43	6	5	37	9
Low Scorers	20	19	22	10	29

Perhaps by rewriting alternative *a,* this item could be rescued. In any case, the main point here is that test developers should pry into every corner of every test item by every means possible, including visual inspection of the pattern of answers.

Reprise: The Best Items

From all the methods of item analysis previously portrayed, which ones should the test developer use to identify the best items for a test? The answer to this question is neither simple nor straightforward. After all, the choice of "best" items depends upon the objectives of the test developer. For example, a theoretically inclined research psychologist might desire a measurement instrument with the highest possible internal consistency; item-reliability indices are crucial to this goal. A practically minded college administrator might wish for an instrument with the highest possible criterion validity; item-validity indices would be useful for this purpose. A remediation-oriented mental retar-

dation specialist might desire an intelligence test with minimal floor effect; item-difficulty indices would be helpful in this regard. In sum, there is no single preferred method for item selection ideally suited to every context of assessment and test development.

REVISING THE TEST

The purpose of item analysis, discussed previously, is to identify unproductive items in the preliminary test so that they can be revised, eliminated, or replaced. Very few tests emerge from this process unscathed. It is common in the evolutionary process of test development that many items are dropped, others refined, and new items added. The initial repercussion is that a new and slightly different test emerges. This revised test likely contains more discriminating items with higher reliability and greater predictive accuracy—but these improvements are known to be true only for the first tryout sample.

The next step in test development is to collect new data from a second tryout sample. Of course, these examinees should be similar to those for whom the test is ultimately intended. The purpose of collecting additional test data is to repeat the item analysis procedures anew. If further changes are of the minor fine-tuning variety, the test developer may decide the test is satisfactory and ready for cross-validational study, discussed in the following section. If major changes are needed, it is desirable to collect data from a third and even perhaps a fourth tryout sample. But at some point, psychometric tinkering must end; the developer must propose a finalized instrument and proceed to the next step, cross validation.

Cross Validation

When a tryout sample is used to ascertain that a test possesses criterion-related validity, the evidence is quite preliminary and tentative. It is prudent practice in test development to seek fresh and independent confirmation of test validity before proceeding to publication. The term **cross valida-tion** refers to the practice of using the original re-gression equation in a new sample to determine if the test predicts the criterion as well as it did in the original sample. Ghiselli, Campbell, and Zedeck (1981) outline the rationale for cross validation:

> Whether items are chosen on the basis of empirical keying or whether they are corrected or weighted, the obtained results should, unless additional data are collected, be viewed as specific to the sample used for the statistical analyses. This is necessary because the obtained results have likely capitalized on chance factors operating in that group and there-fore are applicable only to the sample studied.

Validity Shrinkage

A common discovery in cross-validation research is that a test predicts the relevant criterion less ac-curately with the new sample of examinees than with the original tryout sample. The term **validity shrinkage** is applied to this phenomenon. For ex-ample, a biographically based predictor of sales potential might perform quite well for the sample of subjects used to develop the instrument, but demonstrate less validity when applied to a new group of examinees. Mitchell and Klimoski (1986) studied validity shrinkage of an instrument de-signed to foretell which students will succeed in real estate, as measured by the real-world criterion of obtaining a real estate license two years later. In one analysis based on the sample used to derive the test, the biographically based predictor test cor-related .6 with the criterion. But when this same test was tried out on a new sample of real estate students, the correlation with the criterion was lower, about .4, demonstrating typical validity shrinkage.

Validity shrinkage is an inevitable part of test development and underscores the need for cross validation. In most cases, shrinkage is slight and the instrument withstands the challenge of cross validation. However, shrinkage of test validity can be a major problem when derivation and cross-val-idation samples are small, the number of potential

test items is large, and items are chosen on a purely empirical basis without theoretical rationale.

A classic paper by Cureton (1950) demon-strates a worst-case scenario: using a very small sample to select empirically keyed items from a large item pool, then validating the test on the same sample. The criterion in his study was grade point average, artificially dichotomized into grades of B or better and grades below B. His "test" items con-sisted of 85 tags, numbered on one side. For each of 29 students, the tags were shaken in a container and dropped on the table. All tags that fell with numbers up were recorded as indicating the pres-ence of that "item" for the student. Next, Cureton conducted an item analysis, using the di-chotomized grades as the criterion. Based on this analysis, 24 items were found to be maximally pre-dictive of students' grades. Nine items occurred more often among students with the higher grades and these items were weighted +1. Fifteen items occurred more often among students with the lower grades and these items were weighted −1. The score on this test (facetiously named the "B-Projective Psychokinesis Test") consisted of the sum of these 24 item weights.

In spite of the nonsensical nature of his test, Cureton (1950) found that test scores correlated .82 with grades. Of course, the strength of this cor-relation was due entirely to capitalization upon chance. If we were to conduct a series of cross-val-idation studies using new samples of students, the correlation between the B-Projective Psychokinesis Test and grades would likely hover right around zero, because this test is completely devoid of pre-dictive validity. There is an important lesson here that applies to serious tests as well: Demonstrate validity through cross validation, do not assume it based merely on the solemn intentions of a new in-strument.

Feedback from Examinees

In test revision, feedback from examinees is a po-tentially valuable source of information that is nor-mally overlooked by test developers. We can illustrate this approach with research by Nevo (1992). He developed the Examinee Feedback Questionnaire (EFeQ) to study the Inter-University Psychometric Entrance Examination, a major requirement for admission to the six universities in Israel. The Inter-University entrance exam is a group test consisting of five multiple-choice subtests: General Knowledge, Figural Reasoning, Comprehension, Mathematical Reasoning, and English. The EFeQ was designed as an anonymous posttest administered immediately after the Inter-University entrance exam.

The EFeQ is a short and simple questionnaire designed to elicit candid opinions from examinees as to these features of the test-examiner-respondent matrix:

- Behavior of examiners
- Testing conditions
- Clarity of exam instructions
- Convenience in using the answer sheet
- Perceived suitability of the test

- Perceived cultural fairness of the test
- Perceived sufficiency of time
- Perceived difficulty of the test
- Emotional response to the test
- Level of guessing
- Cheating by the examinee or others

The final question on the EFeQ is open-ended essay: "We are interested in any remarks or suggestions you might have for improving the exam." Some examples of feedback questions in the EFeQ tradition are provided in Figure 4.9.

Nevo (1992) determined that the EFeQ questionnaire possesses modest reliability, with a test-retest reliability of about .70. Regardless of the psychometric properties of his scale, the tradition of asking examinees for feedback about tests has proved invaluable. The Inter-University entrance exam was modified in numerous ways in response to feedback: The answer sheet format was modified in ways suggested by examinees; the time limit was increased for specific tests reported to be

FIGURE 4.9

Examples of Examinee Feedback Questionnaire Items

Source: Based upon Nevo, B. (1992). Examinee feedback: Practical guidelines. In M. Zeidner and R. Most (Eds.), *Psychological testing: An inside view.* Palo Alto, Calif.: Consulting Psychologists Press.

What is your opinion of the amount of time alloted for each test? Mark each box with a number from 1 to 5 according to these ratings:

5	4	3	2	1
Way too much time	Too much time	Adequate time	Too little time	Way too little time

☐ General Knowledge
☐ Figural Reasoning
☐ Comprehension
☐ Mathematical Reasoning
☐ English

Did you or others cheat on this exam? Please check the boxes that apply. You can check more than one box.

☐ Yes—I obtained a copy of the test.
☐ Yes—one of the testers illegally helped me.
☐ Yes—one of the examinees helped me during the test.
☐ Yes—I helped one of the other examinees.
☐ Yes—I used hidden notes during the test.
☐ Yes—I saw another person cheating.
☐ No—I did not cheat in any way.
☐ No—I did not see anyone else cheating.

---

too speeded; certain items perceived as culturally biased or unfair were deleted. In addition, security measures were revised and tightened in order to minimize cheating, which was much more prevalent than examiners had anticipated. Nevo (1992) also cites a hidden advantage to feedback questionnaires: They convey the message that someone cares enough to listen, which reduces postexamination stress. Examinee feedback questionnaires should become a routine practice in group standardized testing.

PUBLISHING THE TEST

The test construction process does not end with the collection of cross-validation data. The test developer also must oversee the production of the testing materials, publish a technical manual, and produce a user's manual. A number of relevant guidelines can be offered for each of these final steps, as outlined in the following sections. Finally, we close this chapter with a provocative comment on the conservatism of modern test publishers.

Production of Testing Materials

Testing materials must be user-friendly if they are to receive wide acceptance by psychologists and educators. Thus, a first guideline for test production is that the physical packaging of test materials must allow for quick and smooth administration. Consider the challenge posed by some performance tests, where the examiner must wrestle with pencil, clipboard, test form, stopwatch, test manual, item shield, item box, and a disassembled cardboard object, all the while maintaining conversation with the examinee. If it is possible for the test developer to simplify the duties of the examiner while leaving examinee task demands unchanged, the resulting instrument will have much greater acceptability to potential users. For example, if the administration instructions can be summarized on the test form, the examiner can put the test manual aside while setting out the task for the examinee. Another welcome addition to psychological test

packaging is the stand-up ring binder which shows the test question on the side facing the examinee and provides instructions for administration on the reverse side facing the examiner.

Technical Manual and User's Manual

Technical data about a new instrument are usually summarized with appropriate references in a **technical manual.** Here, the prospective user can find information about item analyses, scale reliabilities, cross-validation studies, and the like. In some cases, this information is incorporated in the **user's manual** which gives instructions for administration and also provides guidelines for test interpretation.

Test manuals should communicate information to many different groups, ranging in background and training from measurement specialist to classroom teacher. Test manuals serve many purposes, as outlined in the *Standards for Educational and Psychological Testing* (AERA, APA, NCME, 1985, 1999). The influential *Standards* manual suggests that test manuals accomplish the following goals:

- Describe the rationale and recommended uses for the test.
- Provide specific cautions against anticipated misuses of a test.
- Cite representative studies regarding general and specific test uses.
- Identify special qualifications needed to administer and interpret the test.
- Provide revisions, ammendations, and supplements as needed.
- Use promotional material that is accurate and research-based.
- Cite quantitative relationships between test scores and criteria.
- Report on the degree to which alternative modes of response (e.g., booklet versus an answer sheet) are interchangeable.
- Provide appropriate interpretive aids to the test taker.
- Furnish evidence of the validity of any automated test interpretations.

Finally, test manuals should provide the essential data on reliability and validity rather than referring the user to other sources—an unfortunate practice encountered in some test manuals.

Testing Is Big Business

By now the reader should appreciate the intimidating task faced by anyone who sets out to develop and publish a new test. Aside from the gargantuan proportions of the endeavor, test development is extraordinarily expensive, which means that publishers are inherently conservative about introducing new tests. Jensen (1980) provides the following provocative view on this topic:

To produce a new general intelligence test that would be a really significant improvement over existing instruments would be a multimillion-dollar project requiring a large staff of test construction experts working for several years. Today we possess the necessary psychometric technology for producing considerably better tests than are now in popular use. The principal hindrances are copyright laws, vested interests of test publishers in the established tests in which they have already made enormous investments, and the market economy for tests. Significant improvement of tests is not an attractive commercial venture initially and would probably have to depend on large-scale and long-term subsidies from government agencies and private foundations.

SUMMARY

1. Test construction consists of six intertwined stages: defining the test, selecting a scaling method, constructing the items, testing the items, revising the test, and publishing the test.

2. Test developers need to select a scaling method that is optimally suited to the manner in which they have conceptualized the trait(s) measured by the test. The notion of levels of measurement is highly relevant in this context.

3. Four levels of measurement are recognized: Nominal scales constitute mere naming or categorizing; ordinal scales allow for ranking; interval scales possess equal intervals; ratio scales incorporate all the previous characteristics and also introduce an absolute zero point.

4. Dozens of scaling methods exist. Representative examples include the method of absolute scaling, in which item difficulty is located on an axis or baseline and measured in standard deviation units of an anchor group; Likert scales, which present items with five responses ordered on an agree/disagree continuum; and, the rational scaling approach in which rationally derived items are correlated with total test scores.

5. Constructing test items is a laborious and time-consuming procedure. Test developers should seek to avoid ceiling and floor effects. In a ceiling

effect, significant numbers of examinees obtain perfect or near-perfect scores. In a floor effect, significant numbers of examinees obtain scores at or near the bottom of the scale.

6. A table of specifications enumerates the information and cognitive tasks on which examinees are to be assessed. With achievement and ability tests, item writers usually work from a table of specifications to insure that the emerging instrument taps the desired mixture of cognitive processes and item contents.

7. Test items can be written in many different formats, including multiple choice, open-ended response, true-false, and forced-choice. Matching questions, popular in classroom testing, are psychometrically questionable since the choices are not independent of one another.

8. The purpose of item analysis is to determine which initial items should be retained, which revised, and which thrown out. Many statistical procedures are available for item analysis, including item-difficulty index, item-reliability index, item-validity index, item-characteristic curve, and item-discrimination index.

9. The term *cross validation* refers to the practice of revalidating a test on a new sample of examinees. *Validity shrinkage* refers to the common phenomenon wherein a test predicts the relevant criterion less accurately with a new sample than with the original tryout sample.

10. Tests must be user-friendly if they are to receive wide acceptance by psychologists and educators. For example, stand-up ring binders that show instructions on one side and display the test stimuli on the other side are especially desirable. Test users also welcome a thorough technical manual that summarizes technical data and validation research.

KEY TERMS AND CONCEPTS

nominal scale   p. 119

ordinal scale   p. 119

interval scale   p. 119

ratio scale   p. 119

expert rankings   p. 120

method of equal-appearing intervals   p. 121

method of absolute scaling   p. 122

Likert scale   p. 123

Guttman scale   p. 123

method of empirical keying   p. 123

method of rational scaling   p. 124

table of specifications   p. 125

forced-choice methodology   p. 127

item-difficulty index   p. 128

item-reliability index   p. 129

item-validity index   p. 129

item-characteristic curve   p. 129

normal ogive   pp. 129–130

item-discrimination index   p. 130

cross validation   p. 133

validity shrinkage   p. 133

technical manual   p. 135

user's manual   p. 135

CHAPTER 5

Intelligence Testing I: Theories and Preschool Assessment

This chapter opens an extended discussion of intelligence testing, a topic so important and immense that we devote the next two chapters to it as well. In order to understand contemporary intelligence testing, the reader will need to assimilate certain definitions, theories, and mainstream assessment practices. The goal of Topic 5A, Theories and the Measurement of Intelligence, is to investigate the various meanings given to the term *intelligence* and to discuss how definitions and theories have influenced the structure and content of intelligence tests. An important justification for this topic is that an understanding of theories of intelligence is crucial for establishing the construct validity of IQ measures. In Topic 5B, Assessment of

Infant and Preschool Abilities, we review the nature and application of prominent infant assessment devices and then investigate a fundamental issue: What is the practical utility of these instruments? We begin with a review of early, traditional, and contemporary theories of intelligence.

Intelligence is one of the most highly researched topics in psychology. Thousands of research articles are published each year on the nature and measurement of intelligence. New journals such as *Intelligence* and *The Journal of Psychoeducational Assessment* have flourished in response to the scholarly interest in this topic. Despite this burgeoning research literature, the definition of intelligence remains elusive, wrapped in controversy and mystery. In fact, the discussion that follows will illustrate a major paradox of modern testing: Psychometricians are better at measuring intelligence than conceptualizing it!

Even though defining intelligence has proved to be a frustrating endeavor, there is much to be gained by reviewing historical and contemporary efforts to clarify its meaning. After all, intelligence tests did not materialize out of thin air. Most tests are grounded in a specific theory of intelligence and most test developers offer a definition of the construct as a starting point for their endeavors. For these reasons, we can better understand and evaluate the multifaceted character of contemporary tests if we first review prominent definitions and theories of intelligence.

DEFINITIONS OF INTELLIGENCE

Before we discuss definitions of intelligence, we need to clarify the nature of definition itself. Sternberg (1986) makes a distinction between operational and "real" definitions that is important in this context. An **operational definition** defines a concept in terms of the way it is measured. Boring (1923) carried this viewpoint to its extreme when he defined intelligence as "what the tests test." Believe it or not, this was a serious proposal, designed largely to short-circuit rampant and divisive disagreements about the definition of intelligence.

Operational definitions of intelligence suffer from two dangerous shortcomings (Sternberg, 1986). First, they are circular. Intelligence tests were invented to measure intelligence, not to define it. The test designers never intended for their instruments to define intelligence. Second, operational definitions block further progress in understanding the nature of intelligence, because they foreclose discussion on the adequacy of theories of intelligence.

This second problem—the potentially stultifying effects of relying upon operational definitions of intelligence—casts doubt upon the common practice of affirming the concurrent validity of new tests by correlating them with old tests. If established tests serve as the principal criterion against which new tests are assessed, then the new tests will be viewed as valid only to the extent that they correlate with the old ones. Such a conservative practice drastically curtails innovation. The operational definition of intelligence does not allow for the possibility that new tests or conceptions of intelligence may be superior to the existing ones.

We must conclude, then, that operational definitions of intelligence leave much to be desired. In contrast, a **real definition** is one that seeks to tell us the true nature of the thing being defined (Robinson, 1950; Sternberg, 1986). Perhaps the most common way—but by no means the only way—of producing real definitions of intelligence is to ask experts in the field to define it.

Expert Definitions of Intelligence

Intelligence has been given many real definitions by prominent researchers in the field. Following, we list several examples, paraphrased slightly for editorial consistency. The reader will note that many of these definitions appeared in an early but still influential symposium, "Intelligence and its Measurement," published in the *Journal of Educational Psychology* (Thorndike, 1921). Other definitions stem from a modern update of this early symposium, *What Is Intelligence?,* edited by Sternberg and Detterman (1986). Intelligence has been defined as the following:

Spearman (1904, 1923): a general ability which involves mainly the eduction of relations and correlates.

Binet and Simon (1905): the ability to judge well, to understand well, to reason well.

Terman (1916): the capacity to form concepts and to grasp their significance.

Pintner (1921): the ability of the individual to adapt adequately to relatively new situations in life.

Thorndike (1921): the power of good responses from the point of view of truth or fact.

Thurstone (1921): the capacity to inhibit instinctive adjustments, flexibly imagine different responses, and realize modified instinctive adjustments into overt behavior.

Wechsler (1939): The aggregate or global capacity of the individual to act purposefully, to think rationally, and to deal effectively with the environment.

Humphreys (1971): the entire repertoire of acquired skills, knowledge, learning sets, and generalization tendencies considered intellectual in nature that are available at any one period of time.

Piaget (1972): a generic term to indicate the superior forms of organization or equilibrium of cognitive structuring used for adaptation to the physical and social environment.

Sternberg (1985a, 1986): the mental capacity to automatize information processing and to emit contextually appropriate behavior in response to novelty; intelligence also includes metacomponents, performance components, and knowledge-acquisition components (discussed later).

Eysenck (1986): error-free transmission of information through the cortex.

Gardner (1986): the ability or skill to solve problems or to fashion products which are valued within one or more cultural settings.

Ceci (1994): multiple innate abilities which serve as a range of possibilities; these abilities develop (or fail to develop, or develop and later atrophy) depending upon motivation and exposure to relevant educational experiences.

The preceding list of definitions is representative although definitely not exhaustive. For one thing, the list is exclusively Western and omits several cross-cultural conceptions of intelligence. Eastern conceptions of intelligence, for example, emphasis benevolence, humility, freedom from conventional standards of judgment, and doing what is right as essential to intelligence. Many African conceptions of intelligence place heavy emphasis upon social aspects of intelligence such as maintaining harmonious and stable intergroup relations (Sternberg & Kaufman, 1998). The reader can consult Bracken and Fagan (1990), Sternberg (1994), and Sternberg and Detterman (1986) for additional ideas. Certainly this sampling of views is sufficient to demonstrate that there appear to be as many definitions of intelligence as there are experts willing to define it!

In spite of this diversity of viewpoints, two themes recur again and again in expert definitions of intelligence. Broadly speaking, the experts tend to agree that intelligence is (1) the capacity to learn from experience, and (2) the capacity to adapt to one's environment. That learning and adaptation are both crucial to intelligence stands out with poignancy in certain cases of mental disability where persons fail to possess one or the other capacity in sufficient degree (Case Exhibit 5.1).

How well do intelligence tests capture the experts' view that intelligence consists of learning from experience and adaptation to the environment? The reader should keep this question in mind as we proceed to review major intelligence tests in the topics that follow. Certainly there is cause for concern: Very few contemporary intelligence tests appear to require the examinee to learn something new or to adapt to a new situation as part and parcel of the examination process. At best, prominent modern tests provide indirect measures of the capacities to learn and adapt. How well they capture these dimensions is an empirical question that must be demonstrated through validational research.

Layperson and Expert Conceptions of Intelligence

Another approach to understanding a construct is to study its popular meaning. This method is more scientific than it may appear. Words have a common meaning to the extent that they help provide an effective portrayal of everyday transactions. If laypersons can agree on its meaning, a construct such as intelligence is in some sense "real" and therefore potentially useful. Thus, asking persons on the street "What does intelligence mean to you?" has much to recommend it.

Sternberg, Conway, Ketron, and Bernstein (1981) conducted a series of studies to investigate

LEARNING AND ADAPTATION AS CORE FUNCTIONS OF INTELLIGENCE	**CASE EXHIBIT** **5.1**

Persons with mental disability often demonstrate the importance of experiential learning and environmental adaptation as key ingredients of intelligence. Consider the case history of a moderately retarded 61-year-old newspaper vendor well known to local mental health specialists. He was an interesting if not eccentric gentleman who stored canned goods in his freezer and cursed at welfare workers who stopped by to see how he was doing. In spite of his need for financial support from a state agency, he was fiercely independent and managed his own household with minimal supervision from case workers. Thus, in some respects he maintained a tenuous adaptation to his environment. To earn much-needed extra income, he sold a local 25-cent newspaper from a streetside newsstand. He recognized that a quarter was proper payment, and had learned to give three quarters in change for a dollar bill. He refused all other forms of payment, an arrangement that his customers could accept. But one day the price of the newspaper was increased to 35 cents, and the retarded newspaper vendor was forced to deal with nickels and dimes as well as quarters and dollar bills. The amount of learning required by this slight shift in environmental demands exceeded his intellectual abilities and, sadly, he was soon out of business. His failed efforts highlight the essential ingredients of intelligence: learning from experience and adaptation to the environment.

conceptions of intelligence held by American adults. In the first study, people in a train station, entering a supermarket, and studying in a college library were asked to list behaviors characteristic of different kinds of intelligence. In a second study—the only one discussed here—both laypersons and experts (mainly academic psychologists) rated the importance of these behaviors to their concept of an "ideally intelligent" person.

The behaviors central to expert and lay conceptions of intelligence turned out to be very similar, although not identical. In order of importance, experts saw verbal intelligence, problem-solving ability, and practical intelligence as crucial to intelligence. Laypersons regarded practical problem-solving ability, verbal ability, and social competence to be the key ingredients in intelligence. Of course, opinions were not unanimous; these conceptions represent the consensus view of each group. The components of intelligence and representative descriptors are shown in Table 5.1.

In their conception of intelligence, experts placed more emphasis upon verbal ability than problem solving whereas laypersons reverse these priorities. Nonetheless, experts and laypersons alike consider verbal ability and problem solving to be essential aspects of intelligence. As the reader will see, most intelligence tests also accent these two competencies. Prototypical examples would be vocabulary (verbal ability) and block design (problem solving) from the Wechsler scales, discussed later. We see then that everyday conceptions of intelligence are, in part, mirrored quite faithfully by the content of modern intelligence tests.

Some disagreement between experts and laypersons is also evident. Experts consider practical intelligence (sizing up situations, determining how to achieve goals, awareness and interest in the

TABLE 5.1   Factors and Sample Items Underlying Conceptions of Intelligence for Laypersons and Experts

Laypersons	*Experts*
Practical Problem-Solving Ability	*Verbal Intelligence*
Reasons logically and well	Displays a good vocabulary
Identifies connections among ideas	Reads with high comprehension
Sees all aspects of a problem	Displays curiosity
Keeps an open mind	Is intellectually curious
Verbal Ability	*Problem-Solving Ability*
Speaks clearly and articulately	Able to apply knowledge to problems at hand
Is verbally fluent	Makes good decisions
Converses well	Poses problems in an optimal way
Is knowledgeable about a particular field of knowledge	Displays common sense
Social Competence	*Practical Intelligence*
Accepts others for what they are	Sizes up situations well
Admits mistakes	Determines how to achieve goals
Displays interest in the world at large	Displays awareness to world
Is on time for appointments	Displays interest in the world at large

Note: For each factor, only the four items with the highest loading are listed here. Factor names were provided by the researchers.

Source: Reprinted with permission from Sternberg, R. J., Conway, B. E., Ketron, J. L., and Bernstein, M. (1981). People's conceptions of intelligence. *Journal of Personality and Social Psychology, 41,* 37–55.

world) an essential constituent of intelligence whereas laypersons identify social competence (accepting others for what they are, admitting mistakes, punctuality, and interest in the world) as a third component. Yet, these two nominations do share one property in common: Contemporary tests generally make no attempt to measure either practical intelligence or social competence. Partly, this reflects the psychometric difficulties encountered in devising test items relevant to these content areas. However, the more influential reason intelligence tests do not measure practical intelligence or social competence is inertia: Test developers have blindly accepted historically incomplete conceptions of intelligence. Up until recently, the development of intelligence testing has been a conservative affair, little changed since the days of Binet and the Army Alpha and Beta tests for World War I recruits. There are some signs that testing

practices may soon evolve, however, with the development of innovative instruments. For example, Sternberg and colleagues have proposed innovative tests based upon his model of intelligence. Another interesting instrument based upon a new model of intelligence is the Everyday Problem Solving Inventory (Cornelius & Caspi, 1987). In this test, examinees must indicate their typical response to everyday problems such as failing to bring money, checkbook, or credit card when taking a friend to lunch.

We turn now to a review of major theories of intelligence. A reminder: The justification for reviewing theories is to illustrate how they have influenced the structure and content and intelligence tests. In addition, the construct validity of IQ tests depends upon the extent to which they embody specific theories of intelligence, so a review of theories is pertinent to test validation as well.

THEORIES OF INTELLIGENCE

Galton and Sensory Keenness

The first theories of intelligence were derived in the brass instruments era of psychology at the turn of the century. The reader will recall from Topic 1A that Sir Francis Galton and his disciple J. McKeen Cattell thought that intelligence was underwritten by keen sensory abilities. This incomplete and misleading assumption was based on a plausible premise:

> The only information that reaches us concerning outward events appears to pass through the avenues of our senses; and the more perceptive the senses are of difference, the larger is the field upon which our judgment and intelligence can act (Galton, 1883).

The sensory keenness theory of intelligence promoted by Galton and Cattell proved to be largely a psychometric dead end. However, we do see vestiges of this approach in modern chronometric analyses of intelligence such as the Reaction Time-Movement Time (RT-MT) apparatus, an experimental method favored by Jensen (1980) for the culture-reduced study of intelligence (Figure 5.1).

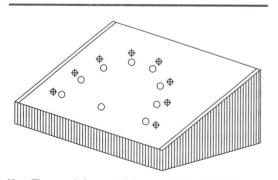

Note: The open circles are push buttons; the crossed circles are green signal lights.

FIGURE 5.1   The Reaction Time-Movement Time Apparatus
Source: Reprinted with permission from Jensen, A. R. (1980). *Bias in mental testing.* New York: Free Press. Copyright © 1980 by Arthur R. Jensen. Reprinted with permission of The Free Press, a Division of Simon & Schuster.

In RT-MT studies, the subject is instructed to place the index finger of the preferred hand on the home button; then an auditory warning signal is sounded, followed (in 1 to 4 seconds) by one of the eight green lights going on, which the subject must turn off as quickly as possible by touching the microswitch button directly below it. RT is the time the subject takes to remove his or her finger from the home button after a green light goes on. MT is the interval between removing the finger from the home button and touching the button that turns off the green light. Jensen (1980) reported that indices of RT and MT correlated as high as .50 with traditional psychometric tests of intelligence.[1] P. A. Vernon has also reported substantial relationships— as high as .70 for multiple correlations—between speed-of-processing RT-type measures and traditional measures of intelligence (Vernon, 1994; Vernon & Mori, 1990). These findings suggest that speed-of-processing measures such as RT might be a useful addition to standardized intelligence test batteries. In general, test developers have resisted the implications of this line of research.

Spearman and the *g* Factor

Based on extensive study of the patterns of correlations between various tests of intellectual and sensory ability, Charles Spearman (1904, 1923, 1927) proposed that intelligence consisted of two kinds of factors: a single **general factor** *g* and numerous **specific factors** s_1, s_2, s_3, and so on. As a necessary adjunct to his theory, Spearman helped invent factor analysis to aid his investigation of the nature of intelligence. Spearman used this statistical technique to discern the number of separate underlying factors that must exist to account for the observed correlations between a large number of tests.

In Spearman's view, an examinee's performance on any homogeneous test or subtest of intellectual ability was determined mainly by two

---

1. Actually, the raw correlation coefficient is negative because *faster* reaction times (*lower* numerical scores) are associated with *higher* intelligence scores.

influences: *g*, the pervasive general factor, and *s*, a factor specific to that test or subtest. (An error factor *e* could also sway scores, but Spearman sought to minimize this influence by using highly reliable instruments.) Because the specific factor *s* was different for each intellectual test or subtest and was usually less influential than *g* in determining performance level, Spearman expressed less interest in studying it. He concentrated mainly on defining the nature of *g*, which he likened to an "energy" or "power" which serves in common the whole cortex. In contrast, Spearman considered *s*, the specific factor, to have a physiological substrate localized in the group of neurons serving the particular kind of mental operation demanded by a test or subtest. Spearman (1923) wrote that "These neural groups would thus function as alternative 'engines' into which the common supply of 'energy' could be alternatively distributed."

Spearman reasoned that some tests were heavily loaded with the *g* factor whereas other tests—especially purely sensory measures—were representative mainly of a specific factor. Two tests each heavily loaded with *g* should correlate quite strongly. In contrast, psychological tests not saturated with *g* should show minimal correlation with one another. Much of Spearman's research was aimed at demonstrating the truth of these basic propositions derived from his theory. We have illustrated these points graphically in Figure 5.2. In this figure, each circle represents an intelligence test and the degree of overlap between circles indicates the strength of correlation. Notice that tests *A*

and *B*, each heavily loaded on *g*, correlate quite strongly. Tests *C* and *D* have weak loadings on *g* and subsequently do not correlate well.

Spearman (1923) believed that individual differences in *g* were most directly reflected in the ability to use three principles of cognition: apprehension of experience, eduction of relations, and eduction of correlations. Incidentally, the little-used term *eduction* refers to the process of figuring things out. These three principles can be explained by examining how we solve analogies of the form *A*:*B*::*C*:?, that is, *A* is to *B* as *C* is to? A simple example might be HAMMER:NAIL::SCREWDRIVER:? To solve this analogy, we must first perceive and understand each term based on past experience, that is, we must have apprehension of experience. If we have no idea what a hammer, nail, and screwdriver are, there is little chance we can complete the analogy correctly. Next, we must infer the relation between the first two analogy terms, in this case, HAMMER and NAIL. Using a somewhat stilted phrase, Spearman referred to the ability to infer the relation between two concepts as eduction of relations. The final step, eduction of correlates, refers to the ability to apply the inferred principle to the new domain, in this case, applying the rule inferred to produce the correct response, namely, SCREWDRIVER:SCREW.

Although Spearman's physiological speculations have been largely dismissed, the idea of a general factor has been a central topic in research on intelligence and is still very much alive today (Jensen, 1979). The correctness of the *g* factor viewpoint is more than an academic issue. If it is true that a single, pervasive, general factor is the essential wellspring of intelligence, then psychometric efforts to produce factorially pure subtests (e.g., measuring verbal comprehension, perceptual organization, short-term memory, and so on) are largely misguided. To the extent that Spearman is correct, test developers should forego subtest derivation and concentrate on producing a test that best captures the general factor.

The most difficult issue faced by Spearman's two-factor theory is the existence of group factors. As early as 1906, Spearman and his contemporaries

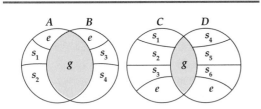

Note: Tests *A* and *B* correlate strongly whereas *C* and *D* correlate weakly. See text.

FIGURE 5.2   **Spearman's Two-Factor Theory of Intelligence**

noted that relatively dissimilar tests could have correlations higher than the values predicted from their respective *g* loadings (Brody & Brody, 1976). This finding raised the possibility that a group of diverse measures might share in common a unitary ability other than *g*. For example, several tests might share a common unitary memorization factor that was halfway between the *g* factor and the various *s* factors unique to each test. Of course, the existence of group factors is incompatible with Spearman's meticulous two-factor theory.

Thurstone and the Primary Mental Abilities

Thurstone (1931) developed factor-analysis procedures capable of searching correlation matrices for the existence of group factors. His methods permitted a researcher to discover empirically the number of factors present in a matrix and to define each factor in terms of the tests that loaded on it. In his analysis of how scores on different kinds of intellectual tests correlated with each other, Thurstone concluded that several broad group factors—and not a single general factor—could best explain empirical results. At various points in his research career, he proposed approximately a dozen different factors. Only seven of these factors have been frequently corroborated (Thurstone, 1938; Thurstone & Thurstone, 1941) and they have been designated **primary mental abilities** (PMAs). They are as follows:

- Verbal Comprehension: the best measure is vocabulary, but this ability is also involved in reading comprehension and verbal analogies.
- Word Fluency: measured by such tests as anagrams or quickly naming words in a given category (e.g., foods beginning with the letter *S*).
- Number: virtually synonymous with the speed and accuracy of simple arithmetic computation.
- Space: such as the ability to visualize how a three-dimensional object would appear if it was rotated or partially disassembled.
- Associative Memory: skill at rote memory tasks such as learning to associate pairs of unrelated items.

- Perceptual Speed: involved in simple clerical tasks such as checking for similarities and differences in visual details.
- Inductive Reasoning: the best measures of this factor involve finding a rule, as in a number series completion test.

Thurstone (1938) published the Primary Mental Abilities Test consisting of separate subtests each designed to measure one PMA. However, he later acknowledged that his primary mental abilities correlated moderately with each other, proving the existence of one or more second-order factors. Ultimately, Thurstone acknowledged the existence of *g* as a higher-order factor. By this time, Spearman had admitted the existence of group factors representing special abilities, and it became apparent that the differences between Spearman and Thurstone were largely a matter of emphasis (Brody & Brody, 1976). Spearman continued to believe that *g* was the major determinant of correlations between test scores and assigned a minor role to group factors. Thurstone reversed these priorities.

P. E. Vernon (1950) provided a rapprochement between these two viewpoints by proposing a hierarchical group factor theory. In his view, *g* was the single factor at the top of a hierarchy that included two major group factors labeled verbal-educational (V:ed) and practical-mechanical-spatial-physical (k:m). Underneath these two major group factors were several minor group factors resembling the PMAs of Thurstone; specific factors occupied the bottom of the hierarchy (Figure 5.3).

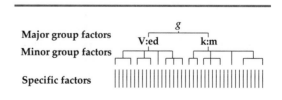

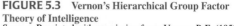

FIGURE 5.3 Vernon's Hierarchical Group Factor Theory of Intelligence
Source: Reprinted with permission from: Vernon, P. E. (1950). *The structure of human abilities.* London: Methuen.

Thurstone's analysis of PMAs continues to influence test development even today. Schaie (1983, 1985) has revised and modified the Primary Mental Abilities Test and used these measures in an enormously influential longitudinal study of adult intelligence. If intelligence were mainly a matter of *g,* then the group factors should change at about the same rate with aging. In support of the group factor approach to intellectual testing, Schaie (1983) reports that some PMAs show little age-related decrement (Verbal Comprehension, Word Fluency, Inductive Reasoning) whereas other PMAs decline more rapidly in old age (Space, Number). Thus, there may be practical real-world reasons for reporting group factors and not condensing all of intelligence into a single general factor.

R. Cattell and the Fluid/Crystallized Distinction

Raymond Cattell (1941, 1971) proposed an influential theory of the structure of intelligence that has been revised and extended by John Horn (1968, 1994). As did their predecessors, Cattell and Horn used factor analysis to study the structure of intelligence. But instead of finding a single general factor or a half-dozen group factors, Cattell and Horn identified two major factors which they labeled fluid intelligence (g_f) and crystallized intelligence (g_c).

Fluid intelligence is a largely nonverbal and relatively culture-reduced form of mental efficiency. It is related to a person's inherent capacity to learn and solve problems. Thus, fluid intelligence is used when a task requires adaptation to a new situation. By contrast, crystallized intelligence represents what one has already learned through the investment of fluid intelligence in cultural settings (e.g., learning algebra in school). **Crystallized intelligence** is highly culturally dependent and is used for tasks which require a learned or habitual response. Since crystallized intelligence arises when fluid intelligence is applied to cultural products, we would expect these two kinds of intelligence to be correlated. In fact, it is commonly found that measures of crystallized and fluid intelligence correlate moderately ($r = .5$).

The abilities that make up fluid intelligence are nonverbal and not heavily dependent upon exposure to a specific culture. For these reasons, Cattell (1940) believed that measures of fluid intelligence were culture-free. Based on this assumption, he devised the Culture Fair Intelligence Test in an attempt to eliminate cultural bias in testing. Of course, calling a test culture-fair does not make it necessarily so. In fact, the goal of a completely culture-free intelligence test has proved elusive. We discuss the CFIT in more detail in Topic 6B, Group Tests of Intelligence.

In later versions of the fluid/crystallized theory of intelligence, Cattell (1971) and Horn (1982, 1994) expanded and elaborated on the previously discussed concepts. Today their approach might better be called a theory of many intelligences, but the g_f-g_c designation has become so well known that it will not easily be phased out. In the latest revisions, the authors have proposed a hierarchical, interlocking model of intelligence with fluid and crystallized components at the top. These capacities are subserved by identified subcomponents of intelligence including visual organization, perceptual speed, auditory organization, several memory capacities, and specific sensory reception components as well. The revised model is labyrinthine; interested readers should consult Horn (1994).

Piaget and Adaptation

The Swiss psychologist Jean Piaget (1896–1980) devised a theory of cognitive development that has a number of implications for the design of children's intelligence tests (Ginsburg & Opper, 1988). Piaget (1926, 1952, 1972) used interviews and informal tests with children to develop a series of provocative and revolutionary views about intellectual development. His new perspective included the following points:

- Children's thought is qualitatively different from adults' thought.
- Psychological structures called *schemas* are the primary basis for gaining new knowledge about the world.

- Four stages of cognitive development can be identified.

We examine each of these points in more detail in the following.

By studying the development of conservation, Piaget concluded that a child's construction of the world is fundamentally different from the adult perspective. **Conservation** refers to the awareness that physical quantities do not change in amount when they are superficially altered in appearance. For example, most adults know that two matching rows of 10 pennies are still equivalent if one row is spread out—adults possess conservation of number. But a young child will be easily misled by the superficial change in appearance and may insist that the second row now has more pennies. In a similar manner, it can be shown that young children do not possess conservation of continuous quantity, substance, weight, or volume.

In order to explain how infants and children gain new knowledge about the world, Piaget suggested that they form psychological structures called schemas. A **schema** is an organized pattern of behavior or a well-defined mental structure that leads to knowing how to do something. Perhaps a few examples will help clarify this difficult concept. Young infants possess schemas that are mainly sensorimotor in nature, such as the grasp-and-pull schema that allows a baby to retrieve a desired object and bring it up to the mouth. As we get older, we add mental structures to our collection of sensorimotor schemas. For example, teenagers usually possess the alphabetizing schema that permits them to find a word in a dictionary by repeatedly applying the simple rule that entries are alphabetical by first letter, then second letter, and so on.

Piaget's genius was in suggesting a mechanism by which schemas evolve toward greater and greater levels of complexity thereby transforming into the more mature level of intellectual skill observed in most adults. The mechanism by which schemas become more mature is called the process of **equilibration.** To understand equilibration, the reader needs to know three additional Piagetian concepts: assimilation, accommodation, and equilibrium.

Assimilation is the application of a schema to an object, person, or event. For example, assimilation is involved when an infant uses the grasp-and-pull schema to retrieve a baby rattle and bring it to the mouth. If assimilation works to achieve the desired goals of the person, a state of harmony or equilibrium exists. But what happens if the application of the schema doesn't work? Suppose the grasp-and-pull schema is unsuccessful because the baby rattle snags on the vertical side bars of the crib as the infant seeks to bring the toy to the mouth. A state of dynamic tension will then arise, requiring the infant to adjust the schema so that it works. The adjustment of an unsuccessful schema so that it works is called **accommodation.** In our example of the infant using the grasp-and-pull schema to retrieve a baby rattle, the schema might be modified and become the grasp-and-pull-and-turn schema. If the modified schema is successful and allows the infant to bring the rattle to the mouth, a state of equilibrium exists once again. Note the distinction between equilibrium, the state of temporary harmony, and equilibration, the entire process of assimilation, accommodation, and equilibrium. Piaget believed that the striving toward equilibrium was an inherited characteristic of the human species.

Piaget also proposed four stages of cognitive development. According to his view, each stage is qualitatively different from the others and characterized by distinctive patterns of thought (Table 5.2). In the next topic (5B, Assessment of Infant and Preschool Abilities), we discuss an infant test based on a Piagetian analysis of cognitive development. In general, tests based upon these concepts seek to ascertain whether a child has passed certain cognitive milestones (e.g., conservation of volume) proposed by Piaget.

Guilford and the Structure-of-Intellect Model

After World War II, J. P. Guilford (1967, 1985) continued the search for the factors of intelligence that had been initiated by Thurstone. Guilford soon concluded that the number of discernible mental

TABLE 5.2   Piaget's Stages of Cognitive Development

Stage and Age Span	Characteristics of Thought
Sensorimotor: birth to 2 years	Infants experience the world mainly through their senses and motor abilities, act as if an object ceases to exist if it is not in sight, but develop object permanence by the end of this stage.
Preoperational: 2 to 6 years	Conservation concepts not yet developed, but these children do understand the idea of a functional relationship—for example, you pull on a cord to open a curtain, and the farther you pull the more the curtain opens. Ability to mentally symbolize things with words and images also develops.
Concrete Operational: 7 to 12 years	Children typically develop conservation and demonstrate limited capacities of logical reasoning. For example, concept of reversibility develops—the knowledge that one action can reverse or negate another.
Formal Operational: 12 years and up	The systematic problem solving that we associate with adult thought usually develops in this stage. There is a greater capacity to generate hypotheses and test them.

abilities was far in excess of the seven proposed by Thurstone. For one thing, Thurstone had ignored the category of creative thinking entirely, an unwarranted oversight in Guilford's view. Guilford also found that if innovative types of tests were included in the large batteries of tests he administered his subjects, then the pattern of correlations between these tests indicated the existence of literally dozens of new factors of intellect. Furthermore, Guilford noticed that some of these new factors had recurring similarities with respect to the kinds of mental processes involved, the kinds of information featured, or the form that the items of information took. As a result of these recurring similarities in the newly discovered factors of intellect, he became convinced that these multitudinous factors could be grouped along a small number of main dimensions. Guilford (1967) proposed an elegant structure-of-intellect (SOI) model to summarize his findings. Visually conceived, Guilford's SOI model classifies intellectual abilities along three dimensions called operations, contents, and products.

By *operations*, Guilford has in mind the kind of intellectual operation required by the test. Most test items emphasize just one of the operations listed here:

Cognition	Discovering, knowing, or comprehending
Memory	Committing items of information to memory, such as a series of numbers
Divergent production	Retrieving from memory items of a specific class, such as naming objects that are both hard and edible
Convergent production	Retrieving from memory a correct item, such as a crossword puzzle word
Evaluation	Determining how well a certain item of information satisfies specific logical requirements

Contents refers to the nature of the materials or information presented to the examinee. The five content categories are as follows:

Visual	Images presented to the eyes
Auditory	Sounds presented to the ears
Symbolic	Such as mathematical symbols that stand for something
Semantic	Meanings, usually of word symbols
Behavioral	The ability to comprehend the mental state and behavior of other persons

The third dimension in Guilford's model, *products,* refers to the different kinds of mental structures that the brain must produce to derive a correct answer. The six kinds of products are as follows:

Unit	A single entity having a unique combination of properties or attributes
Class	What it is that similar units have in common, such as a set of triangles or high-pitched tones
Relation	An observed connection between two items, such as two tones an octave apart
System	Three or more items forming a recognizable whole, such as a melody or a plan for a sequence of actions
Transformation	A change in an item of information, such as a correction of a misspelling
Implication	What an individual item implies, such as to expect thunder following lightning

In total, then, Guilford (1985) identified five types of operations, five types of content, and six types of products, for a total of $5 \times 5 \times 6$ or 150 factors of intellect. Each combination of an operation (e.g., memory), a content (e.g., symbolic), and a product (e.g., units) represents a different factor of intellect. Guilford claims to have verified over 100 of these factors in his research.

The SOI model is often lauded on the grounds that it captures the complexities of intelligence. However, this is also a potential Achilles' heel for the theory. Consider one factor of intellect, memory for symbolic units. A test that requires the examinee to recall a series of *spoken* digits (e.g., Digit Span on the WAIS-III) might capture this factor of intellect quite well. But so might a *visual* digit span test and perhaps even an analogous test with *tactile* presentation of symbols, such as vibrating rods applied to the skin. Perhaps we need a separate cube for hearing, vision, and touch; such an expanded model would incorporate 450 factors of intellect, surely an unwieldy number.

Although it seems doubtful that intelligence could involve such a large number of unique abilities, Guilford's atomistic view of intellect nonetheless has caused test developers to rethink and widen their understanding of intelligence. Prior to Guilford's contributions, most tests of intelligence required mainly convergent production—the construction of a single correct answer to a stimulus situation. Guilford raised the intriguing possibility that **divergent production**—the creation of numerous appropriate responses to a single stimulus situation—is also an essential element of intelligent behavior. Thus, a question such as "List as many consequences as possible if clouds had strings hanging down from them" (divergent production) might assess an aspect of intelligence not measured by traditional tests.

Theory of Simultaneous and Successive Processing

Some modern conceptions of intelligence owe a debt to the neuropsychological investigations of the Russian psychologist Aleksandr Luria (1902–1977). Luria (1966) relied primarily upon individual case studies and clinical observations of brain-injured soldiers to arrive at a general theory of cognitive processing. The heart of his theory is as follows:

> Analysis shows that there is strong evidence for distinguishing two basic forms of integrative activity of the cerebral cortex by which different aspects of the outside world may be reflected. . . . The first of these forms is the integration of the individual stimuli arriving in the brain into simultaneous, and primarily spatial groups, and the second is the integration of individual stimuli arriving consecutively in the brain into temporally organized, successive series (Luria, 1966).

Since this approach focuses upon the mechanics by which information is processed, it is often called an information-processing theory.

Simultaneous processing of information is characterized by the execution of several different mental operations simultaneously. Forms of thinking and perception which require spatial analysis, such as drawing a cube, require simultaneous information processing. In drawing, the examinee must simultaneously apprehend the overall shape and guide hand and fingers in the execution of the shape. A sequential approach to drawing a cube (if one were even possible) would be horrifically complex. In effect, the examinee would have to draw individual lines of highly specific lengths and angular orientations, and just hope that everything would line up. In the absence of a simultaneous mental gestalt to guide the drawing, a distorted production is almost guaranteed. Luria discovered that simultaneous processing is associated with the occipital and parietal lobes in the back of the brain.

Successive processing of information is needed for mental activities in which a proper sequence of operations must be followed. This is in sharp contrast to simultaneous processing (such as drawing), for which sequence is unimportant. Successive processing is needed in remembering a series of digits, repeating a string of words (e.g., shoe, ball, egg), and imitating a series of hand movements (fist, palm, fist, fist, palm). Luria localized successive processing to the temporal lobe and the frontal regions adjacent to it.

Most forms of information processing require an interplay of simultaneous and successive mechanisms. Das (1994) cites the example of reading an unfamiliar word such as *taciturn*:

> The single letters are to be recognized, and that involves simultaneous coding. The reader matches the visual shape of the letter with a mental dictionary and comes up with a name for it. The letter sequences, then, have to be formed (successive coding) and blended together as a syllable (simultaneous). Then the string of syllables has to be made into a word (successive), the word is recognized (simultaneous), and a pronunciation program is then assembled (successive), leading to oral reading (successive and simultaneous).

Das admits that this may be a simplified view of what occurs when a reader is confronted with a word. The essential point is that higher-level information processing relies upon an interplay of specific, anatomically localizable forms of information processing.

The challenge of a simultaneous-successive approach to the assessment of intelligence is to design tasks which tap relatively pure forms of each approach to information processing. Tests that use this strategy are the Kaufman Assessment Battery for Children (K-ABC), discussed in the next topic, and the Das-Naglieri Cognitive Assessment System (Das & Naglieri, 1993). The Das-Naglieri battery includes successive tasks that involve rapid articulation (such as "Say *can, ball, hot* as fast as you can 10 times") and simultaneous measures of both verbal and nonverbal tasks. The battery also assesses planning and attention, which leads to the acronym PASS (planning, attention, simultaneous, successive) (Das, Naglieri, & Kirby, 1994).

Intelligence as a Biological Construct

Most investigators have studied intelligence in the traditional manner by developing tests of intellect and correlating scores with external criteria (e.g., school grades) or other test results. But a few researchers have sought to discern the nature of intelligence by looking at the properties of the brain itself. For example, Hynd and Willis (1985) provide an excellent survey of the neurological foundations of intelligence.

One important property of the brain required for intelligent behavior is the well-patterned and synchronized electrical activity of brain cells. Neurons must transmit precisely calibrated electrochemical impulses in order for sensation, perception, and higher thought processes to occur. The collective electrical activity of brain cells can be measured by placing electrodes on a person's scalp. The ongoing record of electrical activity shows spontaneous fluctuations over time but also demonstrates predictable patternings in response to certain stimuli. For example, an evoked potential can be measured by noting the pattern of brain waves that occurs in the quarter second or so after a light is flashed in a subject's eyes. An average evoked potential (AEP) is usually obtained from hundreds of such trials for a single individual. In this manner, an extremely consistent and distinctive pattern can be obtained for any individual.

Ertl and Schafer (1969) were among the first researchers to study the brain wave correlates of intelligence. They discovered that the waveform of the AEP has many more peaks and troughs for high-IQ subjects than for low-IQ subjects. Eysenck (1982) published similar findings which we have reproduced here (Figure 5.4). Two colleagues of Eysenck, A. E. Hendrickson (1982) and D. E. Hendrickson (1982) noticed that the total length of the sinuous waveform of the AEP could be used as a biological index of intelligence. They laid a piece of string over each of the AEP waveforms reported by Ertl and Shafer (1969). The beginnings and ends of the strings were cut, the strings were tightly stretched into straight lines, then measured for length. The researchers were then able to compute the correlation between the string lengths and the published IQ scores. The result was an impressive value of $r = .77$. This correlation is as high as those reported between any two psychometric tests of intelligence. A purely biological measure of brain function (AEP waves) turns out to be an excellent predictor of intelligence as measured by traditional IQ tests.

In spite of these promising research findings, several investigators remain skeptical about the electrocortical correlates of intelligence. The correlations arise only under certain conditions, and attempts to replicate the results do not always succeed (Eysenck, 1994; Vernon & Mori, 1990). Gale and Edwards (1983) argue that mere correlational studies are not enough; we need a more theory-bound orientation that links intelligence as a trait with information processing at the neural level. Efforts to formulate such a theory have been attempted (Deary, Hendrickson, & Burns, 1987). These and similar studies (e.g., Shucard & Horn, 1972) serve as a reminder that intelligence is somehow bound up in the physiological properties of the brain, even though we don't yet understand the precise biological characteristics that account for intelligence.

Haier and his colleagues have pursued a different path in their study of biological intelligence (Haier, Nuechterlein, Hazlett, and others, 1988; Haier, Siegel, Tang, and others, 1992). They measured cortical glucose metabolic rates as revealed by positron emission tomography (PET) scan analysis of volunteers solving intellectual problems. Brain cells use glucose and oxygen for fuel, so a PET scan will reveal "hot spots" at the most

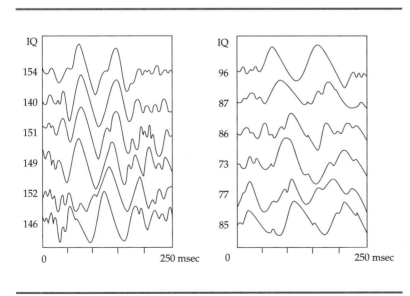

FIGURE 5.4
Averaged Evoked Potential (AEP) Waveforms for High- and Low-IQ Subjects
Source: Reprinted with permission from Eysenck, H. J. (1982). *A model for intelligence.* Heidelberg: Springer. Used by permission of Springer Publishing Company, Inc., 536 Broadway, New York, NY 10012

active brain sites (where glucose is being metabolized). Intriguingly, more-intelligent persons showed *less* brain activity when solving geometric analogy problems and when playing the Tetris computer game than less-intelligent persons. What remains unclear in this line of research is the causal direction: Are people smart because they use less glucose or do they use less glucose because they are smart? Another possibility is that both high IQ and low glucose metabolism are related to a third causal variable (Sternberg & Kaufman, 1998).

Gardner and the Theory of Multiple Intelligences

Howard Gardner (1983, 1993) has proposed a theory of multiple intelligences based loosely upon the study of brain-behavior relationships. He argues for the existence of several relatively independent human intelligences, although he admits that the exact nature, extent, and number of the intelligences has not yet been definitively established. Gardner (1983) outlines the criteria for an autonomous intelligence as follows:

- Potential isolation by brain damage—the faculty can be destroyed, or spared in isolation, by brain injury.
- Existence of exceptional individuals such as savants—the faculty is uniquely spared in the midst of general intellectual mediocrity.
- Identifiable core operations—the faculty relies upon one or more basic information-processing operations.
- Distinctive developmental history—the faculty possesses an identifiable developmental history, perhaps including critical periods and milestones.
- Evolutionary plausibility—admittedly speculative, a faculty should have evolutionary antecedents shared with other organisms (e.g., primate social organization).
- Support from experimental psychology—the faculty emerges in laboratory studies in cognitive psychology.
- Support from psychometric findings—the faculty reveals itself in measurement studies and is susceptible to psychometric measurement.

- Susceptibility to symbol encoding—the faculty can be communicated via symbols including (but not limited to) language, picturing, and mathematics.

Based upon these criteria, Gardner (1983, 1993) proposes that the following seven natural intelligences have been substantially confirmed. The seven intelligences are linguistic, logical-mathematical, spatial, musical, bodily-kinesthetic, interpersonal, and intrapersonal. Three of these seven types of intelligence are well known—linguistic (i.e., verbal) intelligence, logical-mathematical intelligence, spatial intelligence—and numerous formal tests have been devised to measure them, so we will not discuss them further here. The other four variations of intelligence are somewhat novel and therefore require more detailed presentation.

Bodily-kinesthetic intelligence includes the types of skills used by athletes, dancers, mime artists, typists, or "primitive" hunters. Although Western cultures are generally loath to consider the body as a form of intelligence, this is not the case in much of the rest of the world, nor was it true in our evolutionary history. Indeed, persons who could skillfully avoid predators, climb trees, hunt animals, and prepare tools, were more likely to survive and pass on their genes to succeeding generations.

The personal intelligences include the capacity to have access to one's own feeling life (intrapersonal) as well as the ability to notice and make distinctions about the moods, temperaments, motivations, and intentions of others (interpersonal). Thus, personal intelligence encompasses both an intrapersonal and an interpersonal version. The former is found in great novelists who can write introspectively about their feelings, while the latter is often seen in religious and political leaders (e.g., Mahatma Ghandi or Lyndon Johnson) who can fathom the intentions and desires of others and use this information to influence them and form useful alliances.

Musical intelligence is perhaps the least understood of Gardner's intelligences. Persons with good musical intelligence easily learn to perform an instrument or to write their own compositions. Although knowledge of the structural aspects of melody, rhythm, and timbre is important to musical intelligence, Gardner notes that many experts place the affective or feeling aspects of music at its core. He believes that when the neurological underpinnings of music are finally unravelled, we will have "an explanation of how emotional and motivational factors are intertwined with purely perceptual ones" (Gardner, 1983).

The savant phenomenon provides strong support for the existence of separate intelligences, including musical intelligence.[2] A **savant** is a mentally deficient individual who has a highly developed talent in a single area such as art, rapid calculation, memory, or music. An example is the extraordinary case of Leslie Lemke, who was born blind, retarded, and with cerebral palsy. He was not supposed to live. His adoptive mother had to coax him to suck milk from a bottle. Later, she strapped him to her back to help him learn to walk. In spite of his severe disabilities, Leslie became enamored of the piano and showed incredible precocity at picking out melodies on it. Within a few years, at the age of 18, he could listen to a piece of classical piano music a single time and then play it back flawlessly (Patton, Payne, & Beirne-Smith, 1986). The reader can find additional savant case studies in Miller (1989), and Treffert (1989).

Recently, Gardner (1998) has added three tentative candidates to his list of intelligences. These are naturalistic, spiritual, and existential intelligences. Naturalistic intelligence is the kind shown by people who are able to discern patterns in nature. Charles Darwin would be a prime example of such a person. Gardner believes that the evidence for this kind of intelligence is relatively strong. In contrast, spiritual intelligence (a concern with cosmic and spiritual issues in one's development) and existential intelligence (a concern with ultimate issues, including the meaning of life) are less well proven as independent intelligences. In general, the theory of multiple intelligence is compelling in its simplicity, but there is little empirical investigation of its validity.

[2]Historically, savants have also been called *idiot savants,* which refers, literally, to a person who is both profoundly retarded and yet "wise" at the same time. For obvious reasons, the prefix has been dropped.

Sternberg and the Triarchic Theory of Intelligence

Sternberg (1985b, 1986, 1996) takes a much wider view on the nature of intelligence than most previous theorists. In addition to proposing that certain mental mechanisms are required for intelligent behavior, he also emphasizes that intelligence involves adaptation to the real-world environment. His theory emphasizes what he calls successful intelligence or "the ability to adapt to, shape, and select environments to accomplish one's goals and those of one's society and culture" (Sternberg & Kaufman, 1998, p. 494).

Sternberg's theory is called *triarchic* (ruled by three) because it deals with three aspects of intelligence: componential intelligence, experiential intelligence, and contextual intelligence. Each of these types of intelligence has two or more subcomponents. The entire theory is outlined in Table 5.3.

Componential intelligence consists of the internal mental mechanisms that are responsible for intelligent behavior. The components of intelligence serve three different functions. *Metacomponents* are the executive processes that direct the

TABLE 5.3   An Outline of Sternberg's Triarchic Theory of Intelligence

Componential intelligence
  Metacomponents or executive processes (e.g., planning)
  Performance components (e.g., syllogistic reasoning)
  Knowledge-acquisition components (e.g., ability to acquire vocabulary words)

Experiential intelligence
  Ability to deal with novelty
  Ability to automatize information processing

Contextual intelligence
  Adaptation to real-world environment
  Selection of a suitable environment
  Shaping of the environment

Source: Summarized from Sternberg, R. J. (1986). *Intelligence applied: Understanding and increasing your intellectual skills.* San Diego, CA: Harcourt Brace Jovanovich.

activities of all the other components of intelligence. They are responsible for determining the nature of an intellectual problem, selecting a strategy for solving it, and making sure that the task is completed. The metacomponents receive constant feedback as to how things are going in problem solving. Persons who are strong on the metacomponential aspect of intelligence are very good at allocating their intellectual resources.

In a problem-solving study using novel forms of analogies, Sternberg (1981) found that higher intelligence is associated with spending relatively more time on global or higher-order planning, and relatively less time on local or lower-order planning. For example, consider this analogy problem:

Man: Skin:: (Dog, Tree): (Bark, Cat)

The examinee must choose the two correct terms on the right that will complete the analogy. (The correct choices are Tree and Bark). Using reaction time measures for a series of such novel or nonentrenched problems, Sternberg (1981) found that persons of higher intelligence spend more time in global planning—forming a macrostrategy that applies to this and similar problems—than did persons of lower intelligence. Thus, a crucial aspect of intelligence is knowing when to step back and allocate intellectual effort instead of obtusely attacking a difficult problem.

Performance components are the well-entrenched mental processes that might be used to perform a task or solve a problem. These aspects of intelligence are the ones that are probably measured the best by existing intelligence tests. Examples of performance components include short-term memory and syllogistic reasoning.

Knowledge-acquisition components are the processes used in learning. Sternberg has emphasized that in order to understand what makes some people more skilled than others, we must understand their increased capacity to acquire those skills in the first place. A case in point is vocabulary knowledge which is learned mainly in context rather than through direct instruction. More-intelligent persons are better able to use surrounding contexts to figure out what a word means, that is,

they have greater knowledge-acquisition skills. Their increased vocabulary is due, in large measure, to their increased ability to "soak up" the meanings of words they see and hear in their environment. Thus, vocabulary is an excellent measure of intelligence because it reflects people's ability to acquire information in context.

The second aspect of Sternberg's theory involves experiential intelligence. According to the theory, a person with good **experiential intelligence** is able to deal effectively with novel tasks. This aspect of his theory explains why Sternberg is so critical of most intelligence tests. For the most part, the existing tests measure things already learned by presenting tasks that the subject has already encountered. According to Sternberg, intelligence also involves the capacity to learn and think within new conceptual systems, not just to deal with tasks already encountered. A second aspect of experiential intelligence is the ability to automatize or "make routine" tasks that are encountered repeatedly. An example of automatizing that applies to most of us is reading, which is carried out largely without conscious thought. But any task or mental skill can be automatized, if it is practiced enough. Playing music is an example of an extremely high-level skill that can become automatized with enough practice.

The third aspect of Sternberg's theory involves contextual intelligence. **Contextual intelligence** is defined as "mental activity involved in purposive adaptation to, shaping of, and selection of real-world environments relevant to one's life" (Sternberg, 1986, p. 33). This aspect of Sternberg's theory appears to acknowledge that human behavior has been shaped by selective pressures during our evolutionary history. Contextual intelligence has three parts: adaptation, selection, and shaping.

Adaptation refers to developing skills required by one's particular environment. Successful adaptation will differ from one culture to the next. In the pygmy cultures of Africa, adaptation might involve the ability to track elephants and kill them with poison-tipped spears. In the Western industrial nations, adaptation might involve presenting oneself favorably in a job interview.

Selection might be called niche finding. This aspect of contextual intelligence involves the ability to leave the environment we are in and to select a different environment more suitable to our talents and needs. Feldman (1982) has illustrated how selection can operate in the career choices of gifted children, thereby determining whether they are highly accomplished as adults. She followed up on the Quiz Kids who were featured in radio and television shows of the 1950s. These were extremely bright children by conventional standards, most with IQs of 140 and higher. A few became highly successful as adults. However, most of them led rather ordinary lives, devoid of the spectacular accomplishments that might have been predicted from their childhood precocity. Those who were most successful had found occupations highly suited to their abilities and interests. In sum, they had selected environmental niches that fitted them well. Sternberg would argue that the ability to select such environments is an important aspect of intelligence.

Shaping is another way to improve the fit between oneself and the environment, especially when selection of a new environment is not practical. In this application of contextual intelligence, we shape the environment itself so that it better fits our needs. An employee who convinces the boss to do things differently has used shaping to make the work environment more suited to his or her talents.

Although Sternberg's triarchic theory is the most comprehensive and ambitious model yet proposed, not all psychometric researchers have rushed to embrace it. Detterman (1984) cautions that we should investigate the basic cognitive components of intelligence before introducing higher-order constructs that may be unnecessary. Rogoff (1984) questions whether the three subtheories (componential, experiential, contextual) are sufficiently linked. Other comments on the triarchic theory can be found in *Behavioral and Brain Sciences* (1984, pp. 287–304).

Whatever the final verdict on the triarchic theory of intelligence, Sternberg's insistence that intelligence has several components not measured by traditional tests rings true to anyone who has studied or administered these tests. He cites the case of a colleague who was asked to test a number of residents at an institution for the mentally retarded. These residents had just planned and successfully executed an escape from the security-conscious school, a feat requiring high levels of practical intelligence. Yet, when administered the Porteus Maze Test (Porteus, 1965), a standardized test reputed to involve planning ability, they could not solve even the simplest maze correctly. Sternberg (1986) has made it clear that intelligence just has too many components to be measured by any single test.

SUMMARY

1. In spite of symposia and scholarly analysis, the concept of "intelligence" has eluded consensual definition. Yet, two themes recur with some frequency in expert definitions of intelligence. According to the scholars, intelligence encompasses (1) the capacity to learn from experience, and (2) the capacity to adapt to one's environment.

2. Lay and expert conceptions of intelligence are very similar. In order of importance, laypersons regard practical problem-solving ability, verbal ability, and social competence as the key ingredients; experts see verbal intelligence, problem-solving ability, and practical intelligence as crucial.

3. The first theories of intelligence, proposed in the late 1800s, emphasized sensory acuity. Sir Francis Galton and J. McKeen Cattell both believed that intelligence was underwritten by keen sensory abilities. They developed several sensory measures in unsuccessful attempts to measure intelligence.

4. In the early 1900s, Charles Spearman proposed that intelligence consisted of two kinds of factors: a single general factor *g* and numerous specific factors s_1, s_2, s_3, and so on. He helped invent factor analysis to aid his investigations into the nature of intelligence.

5. L. L. Thurstone favored the view that intelligence consists of approximately seven group factors rather than a single general factor. These factors were verbal comprehension, word fluency, number, space, associative memory, perceptual speed, and inductive reasoning. Ultimately, Thurstone acknowledged the existence of g as a higher-order factor.

6. Raymond Cattell proposed that intelligence consists of two major factors, fluid intelligence (g_f) and crystallized intelligence (g_c). Fluid intelligence is a largely nonverbal and relatively culture-reduced form of mental efficiency. Crystallized intelligence is highly culturally dependent and is used for tasks which require a learned or habitual response.

7. Jean Piaget proposed a developmental theme in his theory of intelligence. He suggested that schemas—organized patterns of behavior or mental structures that lead to knowing how to do something—evolve toward greater and greater maturity through a process called equilibration.

8. In Piaget's theory, assimilation is the application of a schema to an object, person, or event. If a schema works, a state of equilibrium arises, if not the result is disequilibrium—a state of dynamic tension. In the latter case, the person must adjust the schema so that it works—a process called accommodation.

9. J. P. Guilford proposed a structure-of-intellect (SOI) model to summarize his views on the multifaceted nature of intelligence. He classified intellectual abilities along three dimensions called operations (5 kinds), contents (5 kinds), and products (6 kinds). Thus, in all, Guilford proposed 150 different kinds of intelligence.

10. According to the theory of simultaneous and successive processing, the human brain has two distinct forms of information processing: simultaneous, in which primarily spatial groups of information are processed all at once, and successive, in which information is temporally organized in a linear series.

11. A few researchers have investigated the biological underpinnings of intelligence. For example, several studies indicate that psychometric intelligence correlates with aspects of brain wave patterns. In some studies the complexity of an evoked brain wave (the average evoked potential, or AEP) correlates in the .70s with measured IQ.

12. H. Gardner has proposed a theory of multiple intelligences based loosely upon the study of brain-behavior relationships. He argues for the existence of several relatively independent intelligences, including linguistic, musical, logical-mathematical, spatial, bodily-kinesthetic, and personal.

13. R. Sternberg proposes a triarchic theory of intelligence with these aspects: componential intelligence (the internal mental mechanisms that are responsible for intelligent behavior); experiential intelligence (the ability to deal effectively with novel tasks); and contextual intelligence (adaptation to, shaping of, and selection of real-world environments).

KEY TERMS AND CONCEPTS

operational definition   p. 139

real definition   p. 139

general factor   p. 143

specific factors   p. 143

primary mental abilities   p. 145

fluid intelligence   p. 146

crystallized intelligence   p. 146

conservation   p. 147

schema   p. 147

equilibration   p. 147

assimilation   p. 147

accommodation   p. 147

divergent production   p. 149

simultaneous processing   p. 149

successive processing   p. 150

savant   p. 153

componential intelligence   p. 153

experiential intelligence   p. 154

contextual intelligence   p. 154

TOPIC 5B Assessment of Infant and Preschool Abilities

Assessment of Infant Ability
Assessment of Preschool Intelligence
Practical Utility of Infant and Preschool Assessment
Summary

The infant and preschool period extends from birth to roughly six years of age. The changes that occur during this period are obviously profound. The infant develops basic reflexes, masters developmental milestones (grasping, crawling, sitting, standing, and so forth), learns a language, and establishes the capacity for symbolic thought. For most children, the pattern and pace of development is visibly within normal limits.

However, parents and professionals trained in the assessment of infants and preschoolers occasionally encounter children whose development seems to be slow, delayed, or even overtly retarded. These children elicit a flurry of anxious questions: How delayed is this child? What are the prospects for normal functioning in school? Will this child achieve personal independence in the adult years?

At the opposite extreme are those precocious children who achieve developmental milestones months or years ahead of the normative schedule. In these cases, the proud parents have a different set of concerns: How advanced is my child? What are the strongest and weakest areas of intellectual functioning? Will this child be a gifted adult?

Infant and preschool assessment devices can help answer questions about children at both extremes of the spectrum—those who might be developmentally delayed, and those who might be intellectually gifted. Of course, these tests also provide useful information about the vast majority of

children who fall in the middle of the distribution. In this topic, we review the nature and application of prominent infant and preschool measures. These tools include individual tests, developmental schedules, and rating scales. We begin with a description of several prominent instruments and then investigate the fundamental question of purpose or utility. What is the use of these measures? What is the meaning of a score on a developmental schedule or preschool intelligence test? To what extent do these procedures allow us to prognosticate adult abilities or, for that matter, help us to predict early school performance? These questions will be more meaningful if we first review the relevant instruments.

We divide the review into two parts: infant measures for children from birth to age 2½, and preschool tests for children from age 2½ to age 6. The division is somewhat arbitrary, but not entirely so. Infant tests tend to be multidimensional and to load significantly on sensory and motor development. Beginning at age 2½, standardized measures such as the Stanford-Binet: Fourth Edition, Kaufman Assessment Battery for Children, Differential Ability Scales, and McCarthy Scales of Children's Abilities are typically used in the assessment of preschool children. These tests load heavily upon cognitive skills such as verbal comprehension and spatial thinking. Thus, infant scales and preschool tests measure somewhat different components of intellectual ability.

ASSESSMENT OF INFANT ABILITY

Gesell Developmental Schedules

Designed to measure the developmental progress of babies and children from 4 weeks to 60 months of age, the Gesell Developmental Schedules were first introduced in 1925 and then revised periodically (Gesell, Ilg, & Ames, 1974; Knobloch, Stevens, & Malone, 1987). Virtually all infant tests have borrowed or adapted items from the original schedules devised by Arnold Gesell (1880–1961), so it is fitting and proper that we begin our review with this instrument.

The Gesell Developmental Schedules provide a standardized procedure for observing and evaluating the developmental attainment of children in five areas: gross-motor, fine-motor, language development, adaptive behavior, and personal-social behaviors. Most of the 144 items in the schedule are purely observational, based on the direct inspection of the child's responses to toys and standard situations. For example, here are some illustrative items typically passed by a 40-week-old infant:

> Adaptive
>> Points at a pellet in a glass
>> Pulls a string to obtain a ring
> Gross-motor
>> "Cruises" a rail using two hands
>> Lets self down with control
> Fine-motor
>> Grasps a pellet promptly
>> Uses "scissors" grasp on string
> Language
>> Uses "da da" with meaning
>> Responds to "no no" word
> Personal-Social
>> Extends toy, no release
>> Pushes arms through dress, if started

The age range of the Gesell Developmental Schedules is birth to 60 months. The genius of Gesell was in identifying naturally occurring situations in the home or clinic and in using objects or tasks with high appeal for infants and preschoolers. In some cases, information from a parent or caretaker is needed to score individual items. In spite of the naturalistic testing environment, well-trained observers can attain interexaminer reliabilities in the middle .90s (Knobloch, Stevens & Malone, 1987).

The Gesell Developmental Schedules are used mainly by pediatricians and other child specialists to identify infants and children at risk for neurological impairment and mental retardation. Gesell never intended his schedule to be an intelligence test. He brought a strong biological orientation to his research and assumed that normal development was a maturational unfolding that occurred in a predictable sequence. Gesell determined that normal development is a time-bracketed phenomenon: The age variability for attaining developmental milestones in infancy is generally small, on the order of a few weeks for many tasks. Therefore, serious delay in meeting his painstakingly chronicled developmental milestones may indicate neurological impairment or mental retardation (Honzik, 1983; Lewis & Sullivan, 1985). Several studies indicate that the Gesell Developmental Schedules function well in the screening of at-risk infants (Knobloch, Stevens, & Malone, 1987).

Even though the Gesell Developmental Schedules are used mainly for clinical screening and diagnosis, Knobloch, Stevens, and Malone (1987) provide a loosely defined basis for obtaining Developmental Quotients for the five areas and overall development. The formula is as follows:

$$DQ = \frac{\text{Maturity Age}}{\text{Chronologic Age}} \times 100$$

The Maturity Age is based on the "total clinical picture" of developmental milestones passed and failed in each area. Although precise criteria are not provided, the Maturity Age for an infant appears to be the developmental age at which most items are passed. Since its technical properties are not well studied, the Developmental Quotient should be used mainly as a research tool.

The Gesell tests are widely respected because they provide detailed descriptions of infant developmental milestones which are unequaled in the child assessment literature (Nuttall, Romero, & Kalesnik, 1992). However, the use of the Gesell as a psychometric instrument has been sharply criticized in recent years. The basic problem appears to be a lack of attention to formal criteria for reliability and validity. For example, early Gesell manuals rarely if ever reported test-retest reliabilities. When contemporary researchers examined this property of the Gesell tests, the results were surprising. Lichtenstein (1990) reported a test-retest correlation of only .73 with a sample of 46 children, which falls well below the recommended level of .90 for making decisions about individuals (Nunnally, 1978; Salvia & Ysseldyke, 1991). Banerji (1992) concluded that the Gesell tests functioned poorly as a screening device for school readiness. In general, educational specialists are wary of using the Gesell for decisions about school placement or retention.

Ordinal Scales of Psychological Development

The Ordinal Scales of Psychological Development, hereafter called the Ordinal Scales, were designed as a Piagetian-based tool for measuring intellectual development between the ages of 2 weeks and 2 years (Uzgiris & Hunt, 1989). The Ordinal Scales consist of six scales, each designed to measure a specific ability that arises during Piaget's first stage of sensorimotor intelligence. Each scale consists of 5 to 15 separate ordinal steps, that is, the items are arranged in a normally invariant developmental sequence.

The scales are as follows:

- Visual pursuit and permanence of objects
- Development of means-ends
- Vocal and gestural imitation
- Development of operational causality
- Construction of object relations in space
- Development of schemes for relating to objects

In light of the many adversities that arise when testing infants—they may cry, regurgitate, crawl away, ignore the task, fall asleep, or fixate on the tester's beard—the scales of this instrument possess surprisingly strong psychometric properties. In one study of 84 infants, the Ordinal Scales showed excellent interobserver reliability (mean of 96 percent), good test-retest consistency, respectable ordinality, and very strong correlations with age (Uzgiris, 1976). In short, this instrument appears to be a psychometrically sound index of sensorimotor intelligence.

Uzgiris (1983) believes that intellectual functioning in infancy is qualitatively different and "needs to be understood in its own right." The Ordinal Scales were developed as a means of investigating infant intelligence within the theoretical framework developed by Piaget. For this reason, Uzgiris makes no pretense of prediction for her instrument. In general, correlations between scale scores and later IQ are very low until infants are at least 18 months of age. Very few clinicians use the instrument for developmental screening. However, Dunst (1980) has argued for using the Ordinal Scales as a basis for designing a developmentally sound curriculum for disabled children. More recently, Auer and Reisberg (1996) have raised the intriguing possibility that the Ordinal Scales can be used for the cognitive assessment of severe dementia in the elderly.

Bayley Scales of Infant Development-II

After decades of prominence in the field of infant assessment, the Bayley Scales of Infant Development have been recently revised (Bayley, 1969, 1993). The format of the scale is the same—the Mental Scale and the Motor Scale provide quantitative normalized standard scores with mean of 100 and standard deviation of 16—but the Bayley-II covers a wider age range, extending from ages 1 month to 42 months. The third component, the Behavior Rating Scale, consists of 30 items designed to assess attention, orientation, emotional regulation, and motor quality. The Bayley-II has been renormed on a stratified random sample of 1,700 children who closely parallel the 1988 U.S. Census statistics on age, sex, ethnicity, region, and parental education.

The Mental Scale measures the following abilities:

- Sensory/perceptual acuities
- Acquisition of object constancy
- Memory, learning, and problem solving
- Vocalization, verbal communication
- Early evidence of abstract thinking
- Habituation
- Mental mapping
- Complex language
- Mathematical concept formation

The Motor Scale assess the following skills:

- Degree of bodily control
- Coordination of large muscles
- Fine motor control of hands and fingers
- Dynamic movement
- Dynamic praxis
- Postural imitation
- Stereognosis

The technical quality and excellent standardization of the Bayley Scales mark this test as the psychometric pinnacle of its field (Sattler, 1988). Although the Bayley-II has only a modest amount of validational research, this instrument strongly resembles its predecessor, for which a huge amount of validity evidence can be cited. Thus, the validity of the Bayley-II rests, in part, upon its resemblance to the Bayley. Regarding validity, the Bayley manual reports a correlation of .57 between the Mental Scale and Stanford-Binet IQ for 120 children ages 24 to 30 months. Self and Horowitz (1979) reviewed the voluminous literature on correlates of Bayley Scale scores. The Bayley shows strong relationships with the Stanford-Binet, Wechsler

scales, Piagetian task performance, social class, and environmental factors. Also, very low scores on the Bayley predict poor developmental outcome in later childhood (VanderVeer & Schweid, 1974). Rhodes, Bailey, and Yow (1983) cite additional validation evidence.

A recent validational study of the BSID-II with premature infants found strong agreement between this test and the first edition, supporting the clinical validity of the revision (Goldstein, Fogle, Wieber, & O'Shea, 1995). A study with healthy Australian infants reported that BSID-II scores were appropriately lower than BSID scores, indicating that the norms for the first edition truly were outdated (Tasbihsazan, Nettelbeck, & Kirby, 1997). In spite of these supportive studies, Nellis and Gridley (1994) suggest caution with the BSID-II until further research is available.

The Bayley Scales require more skill to administer and interpret than comparable instruments such as the Denver-2. It also takes longer (45 to 75 minutes). Consequently, the Bayley Scales are reserved for special assessments and research applications; they are not commonly used as a routine screening instrument.

In Brief: Additional Measures of Infant Ability

The assessment of infants is so important and yet so difficult. Infants do not ordinarily follow directions and they may not be able to verbalize what they know. The assessment of infant abilities is an extraordinary challenge. Nonetheless, dozens of test developers have risen to the summons. Even a brief review of alternative instruments would be chapter-length. We provide a quick summary of better-known approaches in Table 5.4. Most of these instruments involve observation or the presentation of simple tasks to the examinee. For additional reviews of infant assessment, the reader is encouraged to read Nuttall, Romero, and Kalesnik (1992), Ricciuti (1994), and Salvia and Ysseldyke (1991).

TABLE 5.4   Additional Measures of Infant Ability

Battelle Developmental Inventory (BDI) (Newborg, Stock, Wnek, Guidubaldi, & Svinicki, 1984). Birth to age 8; the 341 items assess Personal-Social, Adaptive, Motor, Communication, Cognitive, and Total domains. The full battery takes 1–2 hours to administer; a screening version of the BDI (96 items) has been severely criticized.

Developmental Assessment of Young Children (DAYC) (Voress & Maddox, 1998). Birth to age 6; assessment in five domains (cognition, communication, social-emotional, physical, and adaptive) is completed through observation, interview of caregivers, and direct assessment. DAYC provides a brief assessment (20 minutes) based upon outstanding normative data (1,300 children divided into 23 age groups approximating the 1996 census). The resulting 5 indices and global index are highly reliable (coefficients ranging from .90 to .99).

Developmental Indicators for the Assessment of Learning-3 (DIAL-3) (Mardell-Czudnowski & Goldenberg, 1998). Ages 3 through 6; domains assessed include Motor (e.g., catching, cutting, writing), Concepts (e.g., naming, counting, sorting), and Language (e.g., nouns/verbs, problem solving, sentence length). The test-retest reliability in the high .80s is extraordinary for an instrument of this type. English and Spanish versions are available in the same kit.

Early Screening Inventory (ESI) (Meisels, Wiske, & Tivnan, 1984). Ages 3 to 6; a brief screening instrument which provides scores in four areas—Draw-a-Person, Visual-Motor/Adaptive, Language and Cognition, and Gross Motor/Body Awareness. The total score is used to classify children into one of three referral groups: "OK" (above average to minus 1 SD), "rescreen" (between minus 1 and minus 2 SDs), and "refer" (below minus 2 SDs).

Early Screening Profiles (ESP) (Harrison, Kaufman, Kaufman, and others, 1990). Ages 2 through 6; domains assessed include Cognitive/Language, Motor, and Self-Help/Social; four Surveys (Articulation, Behavior, Health History, and Home) supplement the assessment. This instrument has strong psychometric qualities; the manual reports detailed information on seven validation studies completed independently of the standardization study. Barnett (1995) offers a skeptical review; Telzrow (1995) is more positive.

Gesell Child Development Age Scale (GCDAS) (Cassel, 1990). 18 months through 10 years; this test attempts to operationalize Gesell's stage theory of child development by asking a mother, teacher, or clinician to respond true-false to 100 age-appropriate items from a larger set of 240 total items. Up to three raters can be used to evaluate a child; results include a graphic printout of chronological versus developmental age across 10 developmental areas. The GCDAS is a promising test that needs further research as to psychometric qualities (Lang, 1995).

ASSESSMENT OF PRESCHOOL INTELLIGENCE

Preschool children exhibit wide variability in emotional maturity and responsiveness to adults. One child may warm up to the examiner and strive for optimal performance on all questions. Another child may stare mutely at the floor rather than attempt a simple block design task. For the first child, we can rest assured that the test results are an appropriate index of cognitive functioning. But for the second child, uncertainty prevails. Does the nonresponsiveness signal a lack of skill or a lack of cooperation? With preschool children, a large measure of humility is required of the examiner. Scarr (1981) has expressed this sentiment as follows:

> Whenever one measures a child's cognitive functioning, one is also measuring cooperation, attention, persistence, ability to sit still, and social responsiveness to an assessment situation.

The special danger in preschool assessment is that the examiner may infer that a low score indicates low cognitive functioning when, in truth, the child is merely unable to sit still, attend, cooperate, and so forth. Preschool assessment needs to be approached with unusual caution to avoid negative consequences of labeling and overdiagnosis of disabling conditions.

There are several individually administered intelligence tests suitable for preschool children. Schakel (1986) has dubbed the following tests as "the big 4":

- Wechsler Preschool and Primary Scale of Intelligence (WPPSI-R)
- Stanford-Binet: Fourth Edition (SB:FE)
- Kaufman Assessment Battery for Children (K-ABC)
- McCarthy Scales of Children's Abilities (MSCA)

These are the most commonly used intelligence tests for preschool children. The last of the four is rapidly approaching obsolescence (it was published in 1972). Unless it is revised, school psychologists will soon speak of "the big 3." Of course, some of these instruments extend beyond the preschool age range into early childhood. The SB:FE is used for adults as well. We review these tests and an additional, promising test:

- Differential Ability Scales

The Wechsler Preschool and Primary Scale of Intelligence-Revised (WPPSI-R)

The WPPSI-R is very similar to its predecessor, but offers updated norms and application to a wider age range—ages 3 years to 7 years and 3 months (Wechsler, 1989). In addition, several dated and biased items were revised, and a version of Object Assembly was added to the original 11 subtests. Reliability and validity data for the WPPSI-R are

very similar to the earlier version of this test. Salvia and Ysseldyke (1991) summarize split-half reliabilities from several sources as follows: Verbal IQ (.86 to .96), Performance IQ (.85 to .93) and Full Scale IQ (.90 to .97). Reliabilities for the WPPSI-R subtests are substantially weaker; interpretations of the WPPSI-R should be restricted to the composite IQ scores. Norms for the WPPSI-R are based upon a carefully stratified sample of 1,700 children. The sample was stratified on age, sex, geographic region, ethnicity, and parental education and occupation. The validity of the WPPSI-R is predicated, in part, upon its resemblance to the WPPSI, which earned high praise from reviewers. Sattler (1988) reviewed several dozen studies supporting the concurrent and predictive validity of the WPPSI and concluded that the test serves as an excellent long-term predictor of intelligence and school performance in adolescence.

Initial research with the WPPSI-R confirms the predictive validity of this instrument for later school performance. For example, Kaplan (1996) determined that preschool WPPSI-R results strongly predict elementary school achievement scores for children in kindergarten through third grade. Results for the third graders are summarized in Table 5.5 and reveal that Verbal and Full Scale IQs were much more powerful predictors of later achievement than Performance IQ.

The WPPSI-R subtests include the following:

Verbal	Performance
Information	Object Assembly
Comprehension	Geometric Design
Arithmetic	Block Design
Vocabulary	Mazes
Similarities	Picture Completion
Sentences	Animal Pegs

Three of these twelve subtests (Sentences, Geometric Design, and Animal Pegs) are found only on the WPPSI-R and are briefly summarized here. (The other nine subtests, common to all the Wechsler scales, are discussed in Topic 6A: Individual Tests of Intelligence). Sentences is a supplementary subtest on the WPPSI-R. This subtest requires the

TABLE 5.5   Correlations between Preschool WPPSI-R IQs and Later Achievement Test Results for 72 Third Graders

Comprehensive Testing Program-III Scores	WPPSI-R Scores		
	VIQ	PIQ	FSIQ
Verbal Ability	.62*	.24	.52*
Auditory Comprehension	.46*	.02	.30
Reading Comprehension	.48*	−.03	.28
Writing Mechanics	.54*	.16	.42
Writing Process	.45*	.08	.32
Quantitative Ability	.44	.17	.36
Mathematics	.62*	.34*	.58*

*$p < .005$

Source: Reprinted with permission from Kaplan, C. (1996). Predictive validity of the WPPSI-R: A four year follow-up study. *Psychology in the Schools, 33,* 211–219.

child to repeat verbatim a sentence which has been read out loud by the examiner. The easiest item is on a par with "John had a green car" while the most difficult item is much longer and consists of two connected sentences like these:

> "This Friday we will visit the farmer's garden.
> Bring a quarter so you can buy a pumpkin."

The Geometric Design subtest consists of 10 designs—including a circle, a square, and a diamond—that the child is asked to copy. This subtest is a measure of perceptual and visual-motor organization abilities. Finally, the Animal Pegs subtest requires the child to place a cylinder of the designated color (black, white, blue, yellow) in a hole underneath the appropriate animal (dog, chicken, fish, and cat, respectively). There are 25 animals randomly sequenced in a 5 × 5 array. The initial score on this subtest is the amount of time needed to place a cylinder underneath each animal. Errors detract from the overall score. Success on Animal Pegs requires learning ability, manual dexterity, and sustained attention for the several minutes that might be needed to place an appropriate cylinder under each of the 25 animals.

The extension of age coverage downward to age 3 is a welcome addition to the WPPSI-R, insofar as the early identification of developmental difficulties is essential to their remediation. Also, the IQ norms for the WPPSI-R extend downward to a score of 41, which is about 3.9 standard deviations below the population mean. Especially when used in conjunction with an assessment of adaptive behavior, the WPPSI-R is an essential tool in the diagnosis of mild to severe mental deficiency in preschool and early school-aged children. The IQ norms for this test also extend well beyond the range necessary for identification of giftedness in most school settings. These features have made the WPPSI-R very popular with school psychologists and early development specialists.

Stanford-Binet: Fourth Edition

With an age range of 2 years through adulthood, the Stanford-Binet: Fourth Edition (SB:FE) is one of those rare tests designed for use with preschoolers, children, and adults alike (Thorndike, Hagen, & Sattler, 1986). We present a detailed discussion of SB:FE psychometric properties in the next chapter on individual and group tests of intelligence. A few comments here will briefly summarize its value in preschool assessment.

The SB:FE consists of 15 subtests, but not all subtests are administered to each age group. The subtests and those typically administered to preschool children (up to age 5) are listed in Table 5.6. The reader will notice that the SB:FE yields a number of subtest scores, four area scores, and an overall composite score, which is no longer called an IQ. Unfortunately, with preschoolers the four content areas are not sampled to the same depth. The Verbal Reasoning area is well represented by three subtests, but the Quantitative score is based upon a single subtest. The other two areas (Abstract/Visual Reasoning and Short-term Memory) are based upon results from only two subtests. As discussed in the next chapter, Sattler (1988) advocates a two-factor solution to the reporting of SB:FE scores (Verbal Comprehension and Nonverbal

TABLE 5.6   Subtests and Areas of the Stanford-Binet: Fourth Edition

Verbal Reasoning
>   Vocabulary*
>   Comprehension*
>   Absurdities*
>   Verbal Relations

Abstract/Visual Reasoning
>   Pattern Analysis*
>   Copying*
>   Matrices
>   Paper Folding and Cutting

Quantitative Reasoning
>   Quantitative*
>   Number Series
>   Equation Building

Short-Term Memory
>   Bead Memory*
>   Memory for Sentences*
>   Memory for Digits
>   Memory for Objects

*Denotes a subtest commonly used with preschool children.

Reasoning/Visualization) which is certainly the preferred approach with preschoolers.

An essential feature of the SB:FE is that the overall composite score is highly comparable with other mainstays of preschool assessment such as the WPPSI-R and the WISC-III. For example, the WPPSI-R manual reports similar global scores for 115 children, four to seven years of age, tested with both instruments: average WPPSI-R IQ of 105.3 versus SB:FE composite score of 107.2 (Wechsler, 1989). In a study of 30 preschool children, the average WPPSI-R IQ was 94.1, while the SB:FE composite score was 95.8 (McCrowell & Nagle, 1994). However, the verbal components of the two tests differed significantly: 95.5 for VIQ on the WPPSI-R and 101.6 for Verbal Reasoning on the SB:FE. Rust and Lindstrom (1996) found comparable scores on the SB:FE and the WISC-III for 57 volunteers (ages 6 to 17 years), with overall scores differing less than 2 points, on average. Lavin

(1996) also reported nearly identical overall scores on these two instruments for 40 children ages 6 to 16 years. However, in testing children with known developmental problems, Lukens and Hurrell (1996) found that WISC-III scores were lower in 29 of 31 cases, indicating that the SB:FE may underdiagnose mental retardation. A thorough discussion of the SB:FE in the context of preschool assessment can be found in Nuttall, Romero, and Kalesnik (1992). A review of validity research with the SB:FE is provided by Laurent, Swerdlik, and Ryburn (1992).

Kaufman Assessment Battery for Children (K-ABC)

The K-ABC is a combined measure of intelligence and achievement that was constructed loosely within the theoretical framework of modern neuropsychology (Luria, 1966; Das, Kirby, & Jarman, 1979). Many of the K-ABC subtests resemble neuropsychological tests, which we discuss in more detail in a later topic. Even so, the K-ABC is oriented primarily toward psychoeducational assessment and educational planning (Kaufman & Kaufman, 1983). Proponents of the K-ABC claim that it possesses greater relevance to psychoeducational planning than traditional tests such as the Wechsler scales and the Stanford-Binet.

Designed for examinees ages 2½ to 12½, the K-ABC consists of 16 subtests, with no more than 13 administered to any one child (Figure 5.5). Ten of the subtests yield the Mental Processing Composite which is normed to generate the familiar average of 100 and standard deviation of 15. The other six subtests make up the Achievement Scale. The ten mental processing subtests are broken down into two global scales: the Simultaneous Processing Scale (7 subtests) and the Sequential Processing Scale (3 subtests).

One goal of the K-ABC is to yield scores that translate to educational intervention. Based loosely upon neuropsychological concepts, the Sequential and Simultaneous scales are hypothesized to reflect the child's style of problem solving and information processing. The Sequential Processing subtests

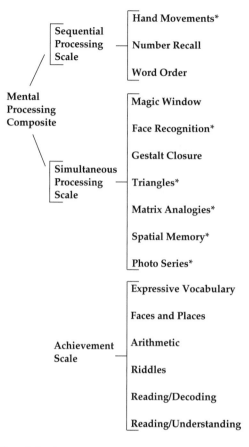

*Nonverbal scale.

FIGURE 5.5   Subtests and Scales on the Kaufman Assessment Battery for Children

require serial or temporal arrangement of verbal, numerical, or visuo-perceptual content. Children who score high on this scale—sequential learners—are presumed to learn best by encountering small amounts of information in consecutive, step-by-step order, such as a series of clearcut verbal instructions. In contrast, the Simultaneous Processing subtests require the child to synthesize and organize visuo-perceptual or spatial content in an immediate or wholistic fashion. Children who score high on this scale—simultaneous learners—are presumed to learn best by integrating and synthe-

sizing many related pieces of information at the same time, such as found in visual media (pictures, maps, or charts).

Kaufman, Kaufman, and Goldsmith (1984) provide guidelines and examples for teaching reading, spelling, and arithmetic to children with K-ABC-based sequential or simultaneous processing strengths. Although the theory is compelling, support for the hypothesized K-ABC aptitude-treatment interaction is mixed at best. For example, Fisher, Jenkins, Bancroft, and Kraft (1988) matched teaching strategies to sequential/simultaneous cognitive styles (as determined from the K-ABC) for 57 elementary schoolchildren enrolled in a learning disability clinic. Although the results generally supported the predicted aptitude-treatment interaction, the effects were small and not of any practical significance.

Both scales in the Mental Processing Composite (MPC) were designed to reduce the effects of sex and race bias, and by most reports the test developers succeeded in these goals (Nolan, Watlington, & Willson, 1989). Based on the standardization data, Kaufman, Kamphaus, and Kaufman (1985) reported small differences (on the order of 5 points) between MPC scores obtained by white and minority group members on the K-ABC. This is a much smaller difference than typically found with tests such as the WISC-III or Stanford-Binet, where differences on the order of 15 IQ points, favoring whites, are common.

Valencia and Rankin (1988) tested 76 white and 90 Mexican-American fifth and sixth graders and reported almost no difference on the Mental Processing Composite (100 versus 98, respectively), although a large difference was found on the Achievement Scale (103 versus 91). Knight, Baker, and Minder (1990) report a comparable difference between the K-ABC and the SB:FE for 30 African-American, learning-disabled elementary schoolchildren (MPC of 83 versus SB:FE Composite of 84).

The K-ABC scales and subtests are described in Table 5.7. In addition to the Simultaneous, Sequential, and Achievement Scales, a supplemental Nonverbal Scale can be computed with six subtests

---

TABLE 5.7 A Description of K-ABC Subtests

Sequential Processing Scale

Hand Movements: The child must copy the precise sequence of taps on the table with the fist, palm, or side of the hand as performed by the examiner.

Number Recall: Very similar to the traditional digit span test, except the examiner is instructed not to drop his/her voice after saying the last digit.

Word Order: Measures the child's ability to point to silhouettes of common objects in the same order as these objects were named by the examiner.

Simultaneous Processing Scale

Magic Window: Requires the child to identify and name an object whose picture is rotated behind a narrow slit so that only a fraction of the picture is exposed at any point in time.

Face Recognition: The child must attend closely to one or two faces in a photograph shown briefly and then select the correct face(s) in a group photograph.

Gestalt Closure: The child must name or accurately describe a partially completed inkblotlike drawing. This subtest measures the ability to mentally fill in gaps to form a gestalt.

Triangles: The child must assemble several identical rubber triangles (yellow on one side, blue on the other) to match a picture of an abstract design.

Matrix Analogies: Using vinyl chips, the child must select the picture or design that best completes a 2×2-inch matrix that expresses a visual analogy.

Spatial Memory: The child must recall the locations of pictures arranged randomly on a page.

Photo Series: The child must order a randomly arranged array of photographs in their proper time sequence. This subtest is similar to Picture Arrangement on the Wechsler scales, except that the task must be solved without physical manipulation, thereby eliminating an unwanted stress on visual-motor feedback.

Achievement Scale

Expressive Vocabulary: The child must name the object pictured in a photograph.

Faces and Places: The child must name a well-known person, fictional character, or place depicted in a photograph.

Arithmetic: A test of basic computational skills and school-related arithmetic abilities.

Riddles: The child must infer the name of a concrete or abstract concept based on a list of its characteristics.

Reading/Decoding: A test of letter identification and word recognition/pronunciation.

Reading/Understanding: The child must demonstrate reading comprehension by following commands given in sentences.

(from the simultaneous and sequential groups) that do not require words. The subtests of the Nonverbal Scale include the following:

Hand Movements
Face Recognition
Triangles
Matrix Analogies
Spatial Memory
Photo Series

For the Nonverbal subtests, the examiner demonstrates each task by example or pantomime. The Nonverbal Scale is appropriate for the testing of recent immigrants or bilingual children whose English language skills might be weak. In addition, children who are hearing impaired, speech disordered, or language disordered can be tested fairly with this scale.

The K-ABC was standardized on a stratified national sample of 8,000 children carefully selected to represent the 1980 U.S. Census on sex, geographic region, parental education, community size, and ethnic category (white, African American, Hispanic, other). An unusual and welcome feature of the standardization sample is the emphasis upon children in special education placements and programs for the gifted and talented (about 7 percent of the norm sample). In addition, supplementary sociocultural norms for race and parental education were derived from test results on 469 African-American and 119 white children.

The reliability of the K-ABC is generally quite good, although some subtests possess marginally acceptable internal consistency coefficients, especially for younger subjects. For preschool subjects, mean values ranged from .72 for Magic Window to .88 for Number Recall. For school-age children, mean values ranged from .71 for Gestalt Closure to .85 for Matrix Analogies. On the other hand, reliability of the Scale scores and the composite score is very robust. For example, the test-retest reliability of the Achievement Scale is .93 for preschool children and .97 for school-aged children; the Mental Processing Composite has a reliability of .90 for preschool children and .95 for school-aged children.

Validity studies of the K-ABC present a mixed picture, with good support for convergent/discriminant validity, strong confirmation of criterion-related validity, and good support for age-appropriate changes in test scores (relevant to construct validity). However, factor-analytic studies of construct validity show mixed and conflicting outcomes. Kamphaus, Beres, Kaufman, and Kaufman (1996) provide a thorough review of the literally dozens of validational studies of the K-ABC.

The Simultaneous and Sequential Scales show the expected pattern of correlations with simultaneous and successive factors on other test batteries (e.g., Das & Mensink, 1989), indicating good convergent and discriminant validity for these global scales on the K-ABC. Cooley and Ayres (1985) found appropriately strong correlations between K-ABC scores and achievement measures (convergent validity), and appropriately negligible relations between K-ABC scores and measures of childhood anxiety (discriminant validity). A somewhat curious finding also emerged: The K-ABC Mental Processing Composite correlated $-.51$ with the Hyperactivity scale from the Achenbach Child Behavior Checklist (the correlation is negative because a high score on Hyperactivity indicates dysfunctional behavior). This well-validated checklist consists of items rated by the parents (e.g., child cannot concentrate, cannot pay attention for long, not liked by other children). Apparently, the K-ABC taps attentional capacities to some extent. Perhaps the overlap is indirect, with poor attentional abilities leading to reduced attainment of intellectual skills measured by the K-ABC.

The validity of the K-ABC is also buttressed by the 43 studies cited and summarized in the Interpretive Manual, including numerous correlational studies with other tests (Kaufman & Kaufman, 1983). These correlations vary widely but are generally supportive of K-ABC validity, at least as regards the mental processing composite. The findings of Obrzut, Obrzut, and Shaw (1984) and Naglieri (1985) are typical in this regard. Using independent samples of learning disabled and educable mentally retarded students, these two studies reported nearly identical correlations of .80 and .83, respectively, between WISC-R IQ and K-ABC composite scores.

As the reader will recall from the chapter on validity, one way to demonstrate the construct validity of a test is to show that age changes in raw scores are orderly, sensible, and theory-consistent. Reynolds, Willson, and Chatman (1984) correlated age and raw scores for the standardization sample (N = 2,000) and an additional sample of African Americans and whites (N = 615). All correlations between age and raw scores were highly significant.

More important, no significant differences occurred in the magnitude of these relationships as a function of race or sex grouping, which supports the construct validity of the K-ABC as a developmental measure of aptitude and achievement.

Factor-analytic studies of the sequential and simultaneous dimensions on which the K-ABC is based have produced conflicting results (Kamphaus, 1990). On the positive side, the test developers cite findings from the standardization sample that seem to confirm the sequential/simultaneous distinction (Kaufman & Kaufman, 1983; Kaufman, Kaufman, Kamphaus, & Naglieri, 1982). Some independent studies have also reported similar findings (e.g., McCallum, Karnes, & Oehler-Stinnett, 1985).

Critics acknowledge that the K-ABC is a good measure of general intelligence, but cast doubt on the distinction between simultaneous and sequential processing as a basis for understanding test performance. For example, Strommen (1988) undertook a confirmatory factor analysis of the K-ABC specifically to test the hypothesis that the factors that make up the test are only moderately correlated, a key assertion of the test authors (Kaufman & Kaufman, 1983). He concluded that the factors that underlie the K-ABC are substantially intercorrelated at all age levels, casting doubt on the separate existence of sequential and simultaneous processes on the test. These modern constructs may well turn out to be old wine in new bottles, nothing more than a relabeling of the familiar dichotomy between highly intercorrelated forms of verbal and nonverbal reasoning. For a more positive interpretation of K-ABC factor-analytic studies, see the review article by Kamphaus et al. (1996).

A second criticism surrounds the designation of six subtests as achievement tests. Anastasi (1985) points out that a test can be properly labeled an achievement test only when it is closely tied to specific instructional content. However, the authors of the K-ABC made special efforts to dissociate the achievement tests from any particular curricular content. These subtests more closely resemble traditional measures of intelligence than academic achievement. In fact, based on factor loadings on the unrotated first factor, many researchers have concluded that the Achievement subtests provide a better measure of general intelligence than do the mental processing subtests! (Kline, Guilmette, Snyder, & Castellanos, 1992). This controversy rests, in part, upon differing philosophical positions as to the nature of intelligence and is not likely to be resolved by research (Reynolds, 1994b).

Another concern is that the K-ABC does not tap verbal skills sufficiently (Sattler, 1988). In spite of these controversies, the K-ABC offers a unique and appealing approach to the assessment of children's intelligence and possesses very high standards of technical quality. As long as examiners include the Achievement subtests—which tap general intelligence to a substantial degree—the K-ABC can provide a new and valuable approach to psychoeducational assessment.

McCarthy Scales of Children's Abilities

The McCarthy Scales of Children's Abilities is an individually administered intelligence test designed for children ages 2½ to 8½ years of age (McCarthy, 1972). The test consists of 18 separate subtests, as listed in Table 5.8. The subtests contribute to scores on five scales, each scale derived from three to seven subtests: Verbal, Perceptual-Performance, Quantitative, Memory, and Motor. In addition, a General Cognitive Index with mean of 100 and SD of 16 is computed from 15 of the subtests. The test is designed to provide a better understanding of both normal children and those with learning disabilities. McCarthy (1972) emphasized functional considerations such as the desire to identify clinically and educationally relevant cognitive weaknesses as the primary criteria for item selection and subtest groupings on the McCarthy Scales.

The standardization sample of 1,032 children consisted of approximately 100 subjects at half-year increments from ages 2½ through 5½ and full-year increments from 5½ through 8½. At each age

TABLE 5.8   Subtests and Scales of the McCarthy Scales of Children's Abilities

	Scales					
Subtests	Verbal	Perceptual Performance	Quantitative	Memory	Motor	General Cognitive Index
Pictorial Memory	V			Mem		GCI
Word Knowledge	V					GCI
Verbal Memory	V			Mem		GCI
Verbal Fluency	V					GCI
Opposite Analogies	V					GCI
Block Building		P				GCI
Puzzle Solving		P				GCI
Tapping Sequence		P		Mem		GCI
Right-Left Orientation		P				GCI
Draw-A-Design		P			Mot	GCI
Draw-A-Child		P			Mot	GCI
Conceptual Grouping		P				GCI
Number Questions			Q			GCI
Numerical Memory			Q	Mem		GCI
Counting and Sorting			Q			GCI
Leg Coordination					Mot	
Arm Coordination					Mot	
Imitative Action					Mot	

level, the sample was roughly stratified on the following variables in accordance with the 1970 U.S. Census: sex, race (white-nonwhite), geographic region, father's occupational level, and urban-rural residence. Children with severe mental or emotional problems were excluded, and bilingual subjects were included only if they could speak and understand English. Of course, a potential problem with the McCarthy Scales is that the normative data, collected in the early 1970s, are quite dated.

Reliability findings for the McCarthy Scales present a mixed picture. The General Cognitive Index performs well, with split-half reliabilities averaging about .93 and one-month test-retest coefficients averaging about .90. Split-half reliabilities for the five scales range from .79 to .88, while test-retest coefficients range from .69 to .89. Reli-

abilities for the 18 individual subtests are substantially lower, so examiners are cautioned not to place too much emphasis upon subtest patterns and differences.

Unfortunately, the clinically based derivation of the five McCarthy scales has not been confirmed by factor-analytic studies, casting doubt on the construct validity of this instrument. Although five factors (corresponding to the five scales) were found at most age groups in the standardization sample (Kaufman, 1975), later studies have not replicated the original findings. For example, Forns-Santacana and Gomez-Benito (1990) found 5 factors in a sample of 141 four- and five-year-olds, but these factors did not correspond to the breakdown proposed by McCarthy. Other researchers report similar instances of failure to confirm the original distribution of the subtests. For example, Keith and Bolen (1980) found only three factors in a sample of 300 children ages 6 to 8½: general cognitive, verbal, and motor.

The confusion about the factorial structure of the McCarthy Scales indicates that examiners should be wary of profile analysis that relies upon the five scales previously listed (Verbal, Perceptual-Performance, Quantitative, Memory, and Motor). In many samples and for some age groups, the scales may be better measures of general cognitive ability than of the specific abilities designated by the names of the scales (Sattler, 1988).

On the positive side, the McCarthy Scales function very well as a predictor of school readiness and later scholastic achievement for kindergarten children. Massoth and Levenson (1982) tested 33 children with the MSCA in the fall term of kindergarten and correlated these scores with results of a reading-readiness test administered one year later and also with achievement levels upon completion of first grade. Curiously, the strongest correlations were with the Quantitative Scale, whereas the Verbal Scale fared poorly as a predictor of school readiness or reading achievement (Table 5.9). The perceptual and analytical abilities measured by the McCarthy Scales appear to be better predictors of reading readiness and achievement than are the verbal tasks. A six-year follow-up of the same subjects revealed surprisingly high correlations between McCarthy Scales administered in kindergarten and scholastic achievement in the sixth grade (Massoth, 1985). The Quantitative Scale showed the strongest correlation with course grades ($r = .60$) whereas the Verbal Scale was a weak predictor ($r = .40$). The Quantitative Scale would appear to be an excellent screening test for preschool children.

In sum, the McCarthy Scales provide a valuable and predictive index of intellectual functioning, especially for children in the five- to six-year-old range. The instrument is also an excellent tool for assessing general intelligence, although it may underestimate functioning in preschoolers, learning-disabled, and retarded children. The norms for the

TABLE 5.9   Correlations between McCarthy Scale Scores and Reading Readiness and Achievement for 33 Kindergarten Children

McCarthy Scale	Macmillan Reading Readiness	Metropolitan Achievement Test
Verbal	.33	.16
Perceptual-Performance	.39*	.37*
Quantitative	.64**	.50**
General Cognitive	.53**	.39*
Memory	.39*	.28
Motor	.31	.35*

*$p < .05$.

**$p < .01$.

Source: Adapted with permission from Massoth, N. A., and Levenson, R. L. (1982). The McCarthy Scales of Children's Abilities as a predictor of reading readiness and reading achievement. *Psychology in the Schools, 19,* 293–296.

test are now badly outdated. In spite of this, overall scores on the MSCA correspond very closely to Full Scale IQs on the WPPSI-R (Karr, Carvajal, Elser, & Bays, 1993). Even so, the McCarthy Scales need to be revised and restandardized.

Differential Ability Scales

The Differential Ability Scales (DAS) are a recent addition to individual intelligence testing that deserve brief mention (Elliott, 1990, 1997). The DAS covers an age range of 2½ years to 18 years in three overlapping batteries: lower preschool (ages 2:6–3:5), upper preschool (ages 3:6–5:11), and school-age (ages 6:0–17:11). We present the upper preschool battery here.

The subtests of the preschool battery consist of "core" and "diagnostic" subtests. The core subtests are heavily saturated with the g factor and are used to derive two area scores (Verbal and Nonverbal) and an overall composite score known as General Conceptual Ability (GCA). The area scores and the GCA are based upon a mean of 100 and standard deviation of 15. The diagnostic subtests measure short-term memory and speed of information processing. They are used for clinical analysis only. The diagnostic subtests are less dependent upon the *g* factor and therefore do not figure in the overall composite. The subtests of the DAS are described in Table 5.10.

The reliability of the DAS scores is commendable for an instrument used at the preschool level. For preschoolers, GCA reliability is reported to be .90 to .94. For older preschoolers (3½ to 6 years of age) the Verbal and Nonverbal cluster scores show reliabilities of .88 and .89, respectively. Concurrent validity studies are highly supportive of the DAS, with correlations in the .70s and .80s with other

preschool measures of intelligence and achievement (Elliott, 1990ab). A study by Dumont, Cruse, Price, and Whelley (1996) provides very strong support for DAS validity by providing a confirmatory pattern of correlations between this instrument and the WISC-III for 53 children identified as learning disabled. The results are summarized in Table 5.11 and show that similar components correlate more strongly than dissimilar components for the two tests. Also, the table reveals that overall scores are very similar, on average, for the DAS (mean GCA of 87.2) and the WISC-III (mean IQ of 89.7). Elliott (1997) describes additional validity studies for this fine instrument.

TABLE 5.10   Subtests of the DAS Preschool Battery

Subtest	Abilities Measured	Contribution to Composite
Core subtests:		
Verbal Comprehension	Receptive language, understanding oral instructions	Verbal, GCA
Naming Vocabulary	Expressive language, knowledge of names	Verbal, GCA
Picture Similarities	Nonverbal reasoning, matching pictures with common themes	Nonverbal, GCA
Pattern Construction	Nonverbal, spatial visualization with colored blocks and squares	Nonverbal, GCA
Copying	Design copying, fine-motor coordination, visual-spatial matching	Nonverbal, GCA
Early Number Concepts	Knowledge of number and quantitative concepts	GCA
Diagnostic subtests:		
Block Building	Spatial orientation, visual-perceptual matching with blocks	n/a
Matching Letterlike Forms	Spatial relationships, visual discrimination of similar forms	n/a
Recall of Digits	Short-term auditory memory for sequences of numbers	n/a
Recall of Objects	Short-term learning and verbal recall of pictures	n/a
Recognition of Pictures	Short-term visual memory, recognition of familiar objects	n/a

n/a = not applicable.

TABLE 5.11   Correlations between DAS and WISC-III Composites for 53 LD Children

	WISC-III Composite			DAS	
DAS Composite	*VIQ*	*PIQ*	*FSIQ*	*Mean*	*SD*
Verbal	.77	.52	.72	90.2	12.0
Nonverbal Reasoning	.55	.65	.67	83.5	12.5
Spatial	.50	.67	.64	93.6	17.0
GCA	.68	.71	.78	87.2	14.8
WISC-III Mean	89.4	93.2	89.7		
WISC-III SD	13.8	14.2	13.2		

Source: Reprinted with permission from Dumont, R., Cruse, C., Price, L., & Whelley, P. (1996). The relationship between the Differential Ability Scales (DAS) and the Wechsler Intelligence Scale for Children-Third Edition (WISC-III) for students with learning disabilities. *Psychology in the Schools, 33,* 203–209.

PRACTICAL UTILITY OF INFANT AND PRESCHOOL ASSESSMENT

The history of child assessment has shown time and again that, in general, test scores earned in the first year or two of life show minimal predictive validity. For example, in her review of infant intelligence testing, Goodman (1990) concluded:

> If the successful prediction of adolescent and adult intelligence from early childhood scores is one of the great accomplishments of applied psychology, then the failure to predict intelligence from infancy to early childhood ranks as one of its greatest failures.

Given this dismal record of repeated failures of predictive validity, we must ask a difficult question: What is the purpose and practical utility of infant assessment? In fact, infant tests do have an important but limited role to play. We return to that issue after a review of predictive studies.

Predictive Validity of Infant and Preschool Tests

With heterogeneous samples of normal children, the general finding is that infant test scores correlate positively but unimpressively with childhood test scores (Goodman, 1990; McCall, 1979). A few studies are more optimistic in tone (e.g., Wilson, 1983), but most researchers agree with McCall's (1976) conclusion:

> Generally speaking, there is essentially no correlation between performance during the first six months of life with IQ score after age 5; the correlations are predominantly in the 0.20s for assessments made between 7 and 18 months of life when one is predicting IQ at 5–18 years; and it is not until 19–30 months that the infant test predicts later IQ in the range of 0.40–0.55.

McCall (1979) reconfirmed his original conclusion in a later review which we have summarized here. The reader will notice in Table 5.12 that the correlations between infant and school-age test scores do not exceed .40 until the subjects are at least 19 months of age for the initial testing.

The findings with preschool tests are somewhat more positive in tone. The correlation between preschool test results and later IQ is typically strong, significant, and meaningful. The simplest way to investigate this question is to measure the stability of IQ results in longitudinal studies. In Table 5.13, we have summarized the age-to-age stability of children's IQ scores on the Stanford-Binet from the Fels Longitudinal Study, an early, classic

TABLE 5.12 Summary of Correlations between Infant and Childhood Intelligence Test Scores in Normal Subjects

Age of Initial Infant Test (Months)	Age of Childhood Test (Years)		
	3–4	5–7	8–18
1–6	.21	.09	.06
7–12	.32	.20	.25
13–18	.50	.34	.32
19–30	.59	.39	.49

Source: Adapted by permission from McCall, R. B. (1979). The development of intellectual functioning in infancy and the prediction of later IQ. In J. D. Osofsky (Ed.), *Handbook of infant development.* New York: John Wiley.

follow-up investigation of children's intellectual and emotional development (Sontag, Baker, & Nelson, 1958). The lowest correlation in this table is .43, and that is between IQ tested at age 4 and again at age 12. What stands out in the table is the robustness of the link between IQ in preschool and later childhood. The older the child at initial testing, the stronger the relationship with later IQ. In

fact, the results suggest that IQ becomes reasonably stable, on average, by 8 years of age.

Collectively, these findings confirm that infant tests generally have poor prognostic value, whereas preschool tests are moderately predictive of later intelligence. This brings us back to the question posed at the beginning of this section: What is the purpose and practical utility of infant assessment?

Practical Utility of the Bayley-II and Other Infant Scales

The most important and justifiable use of infant tests is in screening for developmental disabilities. Although existing infant tests are poor predictors of childhood intelligence, an exception to this rule is encountered for infants who obtain a very low score on the Bayley-II or other screening devices. For example, infants who score two standard deviations below the mean on the Bayley, particularly on the Mental Scale, have a high probability of testing in the retarded ranges later in life (Self & Horowitz, 1979; Goodman, Malizia, Durieux-Smith, MacMurray, & Bernard, 1990).

TABLE 5.13 Stability of IQ from 3 to 12 Years of Age

Age at Initial Testing	Age at Retesting								
	4	5	6	7	8	9	10	11	12
3	.83	.72	.73	.64	.60	.63	.54	.51	.46
4		.80	.85	.70	.63	.66	.55	.50	.43
5			.87	.83	.79	.80	.70	.63	.62
6				.83	.79	.81	.72	.67	.67
7					.91	.83	.82	.76	.73
8						.92	.90	.84	.83
9							.90	.82	.81
10								.90	.88
11									.90

Source: Adapted with permission from Sontag, L. W., Baker, C., and Nelson, V. (1958). Mental growth and personality development: A longitudinal study. *Monographs of the Society for Research in Child Development, 23* (Whole No. 68). Copyright © by The Society for Research in Child Development, Inc.

With at-risk children, the correlation between infant test scores and later childhood IQ is much stronger than for samples of normal children. Mc-Call (1983) determined that the median correlation between infant test scores and childhood IQ at seven-year follow-up was a healthy .48. The most consistent finding is that a very low score on an infant test—two standard deviations below the mean and lower—accurately prognosticates low IQ in childhood (Frankenburg, 1985). For example, studies with the Denver Developmental Screening Test-Revised (since revised and published as the Denver-II) revealed a false positive rate of only 5 to 11 percent, meaning that infants and preschoolers identified as at-risk rarely achieve normal range functioning. Studies with the Bayley Scales also conform to this pattern (e.g., VanderVeer & Schweid, 1974).

New Approaches to Infant Assessment

Lewis has argued that traditional infant tests overlook early information processing behaviors, such as recognition memory and attentiveness to the environment, that might better predict childhood cognitive function (Lewis & Sullivan, 1985). In one study, simple visual habituation to a novel stimulus (measured by the duration of fixation) assessed at three months of age correlated .61 with the Bayley Mental score at 24 months of age (Lewis & Brooks-Gunn, 1981). Using a similar paradigm, Fagan has reported comparable findings (Fagan, 1984; Fagan & Shepherd, 1986). For example, in one study he tested infant recognition memory at four to seven months with the habituation method (Fagan & McGrath, 1981). In this approach, the infants first observed a picture of a baby's face for a short period of time and were then shown the same picture alongside an unfamiliar picture (e.g., picture of a bald-headed man). The investigators kept careful track of which picture the infants looked at most. The logic of the procedure is simple: Staring mainly at the new picture signifies that an infant recognizes the old picture, that is, an infant with good recognition memory prefers to look at something new. Preference for novelty—as measured by visual fixation

time on the new picture—thus becomes an index of early recognition memory. Years later, the investigators administered the Peabody Picture Vocabulary Test (PPVT) to gauge early childhood intelligence. Infant recognition memory scores and early childhood PPVT scores correlated .37 at four years of age and .57 at seven years of age. These correlations probably underestimate the predictive validity of infant memory tests, insofar as the index of infant memory was an unreliable procedure based upon a small number of test items. Furthermore, the researchers assessed normal infants which attenuated the correlations between predictor and criterion.

Infant cognitive measures possess a great deal of promise as predictors of childhood intelligence (Bornstein, 1994; Fagan & Haiken-Vasen, 1997). In the years ahead, we may witness the emergence of entirely new types of infant assessment devices based on the measurement of early memory, habituation, and attentional capacities instead of sensorimotor abilities. A first step in this direction is Fagan's Test of Infant Intelligence (Fagan & Shepherd, 1986), a simple instrument based upon the methods previously outlined for measuring infant novelty preference and recognition memory. The FTII yields a composite score that is based upon preference for novelty—as measured by visual fixation time on a new picture—averaged over several trials. The procedure shows very high interrater agreement (O'Neill, Jacobson, & Jacobson, 1994).

Initial validity studies of the FTII as a predictor of childhood intelligence are mixed in outcome. In one sample of 200 infants, the FTII scores obtained at 7 to 9 months correlated only .32 with Stanford-Binet IQ at age 3 (DiLalla, Thompson, Plomin, and others, 1990). In another recent study, overall correlations between FTII scores obtained at 7 to 9 months and WPPSI-R IQ at age 5 were around .2 for two Norwegian samples of healthy children (Andersson, 1996). These correlations do not support the use of the test as a screening tool in non-risk populations. However, the test may function better when used with at-risk infants. Nonetheless, further research is needed before we abandon traditional infant measures in favor of the Fagan test and similar measures.

SUMMARY

1. The infant and preschool period extends from birth to about age 6. An important application of infant and preschool tests is to help answer questions about developmental delay. Most infant tests (ages birth to 2½) load heavily on sensory and motor skills. Preschool tests (ages 2½ to 6) tend to tap cognitive skills to a significant degree.

2. The Gesell Developmental Schedules (GDS) gauge the developmental progress of babies from 4 weeks to 60 months of age.

3. The Ordinal Scales of Psychological Development were designed as a Piagetian-based measure of intellectual development (ages 2 weeks to 2 years). The scales measure development of object permanence, means-ends, vocal and gestural imitation, operational causality, object relations in space, and schemes for relating to objects.

4. The Bayley Scales of Infant Development-II assess mental and motor development of children from 1 month to 42 months of age. The Bayley is very carefully standardized and highly reliable. Like other infant tests, very low scores predict an intellectually disabled outcome in later childhood, while near-normal and higher scores possess little predictive validity.

5. The Wechsler Preschool and Primary Scale of Intelligence-Revised (WPPSI-R) is designed for children ages 3 years to 7 years and 3 months. The WPPSI-R contains three subtests not found on other Wechsler Scales: Sentences (oral memory); Geometric Designs (design copying); and, Animal Pegs (coded placement of pegs).

6. The SB:FE is a useful instrument for preschool assessment. Although the test is designed to yield four factor scores, Sattler's (1988) two-factor solution to the reporting of SB:FE scores (Verbal Comprehension and Nonverbal Reason-ing/Visualization) is the preferred approach with preschoolers.

7. The Kaufman Assessment Battery for Children (K-ABC), used for children ages 2:6 through 12:5 years, is a combined measure of intelligence and achievement based upon the distinction between sequential processing (serial or temporal arrangement of stimuli) and simultaneous processing (synthesis and organization of stimuli in an immediate or wholistic fashion).

8. The McCarthy Scales of Children's Abilities are designed for children ages 2:6 to 8:6 years. The 18 subtests produce five different subscores and a General Cognitive Index (GCI) akin to an IQ. The subscores include verbal, perceptual-performance, quantitative, memory, and motor. Unfortunately, these five areas are not confirmed by independent factor analyses.

9. Designed for children ages 2 years, 6 months through 17 years, 11 months, the Differential Ability Scales consists of 17 cognitive subtests and 3 co-normed achievement tests for school-aged children. Initial research indicates that the DAS yields reliable and reasonably independent subtest scores useful in the assessment of learning disability.

10. In general, infant test scores correlate positively but weakly with childhood test scores. Infant test scores must be interpreted with caution. An exception is very low infant test scores on such devices as the Bayley-II, which reliably predict developmental disability in childhood.

11. Tests of infant recognition memory show promise as predictors of childhood intelligence. For example, in Fagan's studies, indices of simple visual habituation in infancy correlated .57 with picture vocabulary scores at age seven.

CHAPTER 6

Intelligence Testing II: Individual and Group Tests

TOPIC 6A Individual Tests of Intelligence

Intelligence testing is one of the major achievements of psychology in this century. In response to the success of the Binet-Simon scales in the early 1900s, psychologists developed and refined dozens of individual tests of intelligence patterned after this pathbreaking instrument. Explosive growth was also observed in group tests of intelligence, fostered by the enthusiastic acceptance of the Army Alpha and Beta tests during and after World War I. With only a few exceptions, contemporary individual and group tests of intelligence owe their lineage to Binet, Simon, and the Army testing program.

The purpose of this chapter is to provide an overview of noteworthy approaches to the testing of individual and group intelligence. We survey prominent individual tests in Topic 6A and then close the chapter with a review of group intelligence tests in Topic 6B. Even though this text devotes three full chapters to the fascinating and emotionally charged topic of intelligence testing, we make no pretext that the coverage is comprehensive. An exhaustive analysis of intelligence testing is simply beyond the scope of this or any other basic reference. New and revised tests appear practically every month, and thousands of new research findings are published every year. We have chosen to review tests that are widely used or that illustrate interesting developments in theory or method. Readers can find information on additional tests in the *Mental Measurements Yearbook* series, now published every three or four years by the Buros Institute (e.g., Mitchell, 1985; Conoley & Impara, 1995; Conoley & Kramer, 1989, 1992). *The Encyclopedia of Human Intelligence* (Sternberg, 1994) is also a good source of information on individual and group tests of intelligence.

ORIENTATION TO INDIVIDUAL INTELLIGENCE TESTS

The individual intelligence tests reviewed in this topic include the following:

- Wechsler Adult Intelligence Scale-III (WAIS-III)
- Wechsler Intelligence Scale for Children-III (WISC-III)
- Stanford-Binet: Fourth Edition (SB:FE)
- Detroit Test of Learning Aptitude-4 (DTLA-4)
- Kaufman Brief Intelligence Test (K-BIT)

Another promising test that we do not review in depth is the Kaufman Adolescent and Adult Intelligence Test (KAIT). Published in 1992, the KAIT is a recent arrival on the testing scene (Dumont & Hagberg, 1994; Shaughnessy & Moore, 1994). Kaufman and Kaufman (1997) list several advantages of the KAIT, including its psychometric foundation in the G_c-G_f distinction proposed by John Horn and his followers. The KAIT also is appealing because of its brevity: The test provides highly reliable indices of intelligence in two-thirds the time needed for most batteries. Along with the preschool tests presented in the previous topic, the previously listed instruments probably account for 98 percent of the intellectual assessments conducted in the United States.

The Wechsler scales have dominated intelligence testing in recent years, but they are by no means the only viable choices for individual assessment. Many other instruments measure general intelligence just as well—some would say better. Consider the implications of a now familiar observation: For large, heterogeneous samples, scores on any two mainstream instruments (e.g., Wechsler, Stanford-Binet, McCarthy, Kaufman scales, etc.) typically correlate 0.80 to 0.90. Often, the correlation between two mainstream instruments is nearly as high as the test-retest correlation for either instrument alone. For purposes of producing a global score, it would appear that any well-normed mainstream intelligence test will suffice.

But producing an overall score is not the only goal of assessment. In addition, the examiner usually desires to gain an understanding of the subject's intellectual functioning. For this purpose, the overall IQ is important, but there are instances where the global score may be irrelevant or even misleading. To understand a referral's intellectual functioning, the examiner should also inspect the subtest scores in search of hypotheses that might explain the unique functioning of that individual. Of course, examiners need to undertake subtest analysis cautiously, armed with research-based findings on the nature and meaning of subtest scatter for the test in use (Gregory, 1994b; McLean, Kaufman, & Reynolds, 1989; McDermott, Fantuzzo, & Glutting, 1990).

If the examiner's goal is to understand intellectual functioning and not merely to determine an overall score, the differences between tests become quite real. Every instrument approaches the measurement of intelligence from a different perspective and yields a distinctive set of subtest scores. Furthermore, a test well suited for one referral issue might perform abysmally in another context. For example, the WAIS-R performs admirably in the testing of mild mental retardation, but contains too few simple items for the effective assessment of persons with moderate or severe developmental disability.

A central axiom of assessment is that the choice of a testing instrument should be based on knowledge of its strengths and weaknesses as they pertain to the referral question. Put simply, the skilled examiner does not blindly rely upon a single test for every referral! Instead, the skilled examiner flexibly chooses one or more instruments in light of the perceived assessment needs of the examinee. Each of the tests discussed in this topic has its special merits and also its particular shortcomings. The test user must know these strong and weak facets in order to choose the instruments best suited for each unique referral.

THE WECHSLER SCALES OF INTELLIGENCE

Beginning in the 1930s, David Wechsler, a psychologist at Bellevue Hospital in New York City, conceived a series of elegantly simple instruments that virtually defined intelligence testing in the mid- to late twentieth century. His influence on intelligence testing is exceeded only by the path-breaking contributions of Binet and Simon. It is fitting that we begin the survey of individual tests with a historical summary of the Wechsler tradition, followed by a discussion of individual instruments.

Origins of the Wechsler Tests

Wechsler began work on his first test in 1932, seeking to devise an instrument suitable for testing the diverse patients referred to the psychiatric section of Bellevue Hospital in New York (Wechsler, 1932). In describing the development of his first test, he later wrote that "Our aim was not to produce a set of brand new tests but to select, from whatever source available, such a combination of them as would meet the requirements of an effective adult scale" (Wechsler, 1939). In fact, the content of his scales was largely inspired by earlier efforts such as the Binet scales and the Army Alpha and Beta tests (Frank, 1983). Readers who peruse *Psychological Examining in the United States*

Army, a volume edited by Yerkes (1921) just after World War I, might be astonished to discover that Wechsler purloined dozens of test items from this source, many of which have survived to the present day in contemporary revisions of the Wechsler tests. Wechsler was not so much a creative talent as a pragmatist who fashioned a new and useful instrument from the spare parts of earlier, discontinued attempts at intelligence testing.

The first of the Wechsler tests, named the Wechsler-Bellevue Intelligence Scales, was published in 1939. In discussing the rationale for his new test, Wechsler (1941) explained that existing instruments such as the Stanford-Binet were woefully inadequate for assessing adult intelligence. The Wechsler-Bellevue was designed to rectify several flaws noted in previous tests:

- The test items possessed no appeal for adults.
- Too many questions emphasized mere manipulation of words.
- The instructions emphasized speed at the expense of accuracy.
- The reliance upon mental age was irrelevant to adult testing.

To correct these shortcomings, Wechsler designed his test specifically for adults, added performance items to balance verbal questions, reduced the emphasis upon speeded questions, and invented a new method for obtaining the IQ. Specifically, he replaced the usual formula

$$IQ = \frac{\text{mental age}}{\text{chronological age}}$$

with a new age-relative formula

$$IQ = \frac{\text{attained or actual score}}{\text{expected mean score for age}}$$

This new formula was based on the interesting presumption—stated in the form of an axiom—that IQ remains constant with normal aging, even though raw intellectual ability might shift or even decline. The assumption of **IQ constancy** is basic to the Wechsler scales. As Wechsler (1941) put it:

The constancy of the I.Q. is the basic assumption of all scales where relative degrees of intelligence are defined in terms of it. It is not only basic, but absolutely necessary that I.Q.'s be independent of the age at which they are calculated, because unless the assumption holds, no permanent scheme of intelligence classification is possible.

Although Wechsler's view has been largely accepted by contemporary test developers, it is important to stress that the assumption of IQ invariance with age is really a statement of values, a philosophical choice, and not necessarily an inherent characteristic of human nature.

Wechsler also hoped to use his test as an aid in psychiatric diagnosis. In pursuit of this goal, he divided his scale into separate verbal and performance sections. This division allowed the examiner to compare an examinee's facility in using words and symbols (verbal subtests) versus the ability to manipulate objects and perceive visual patterns (performance subtests). Large differences between verbal ability (V) and performance ability (P) were thought to be of diagnostic significance. Specifically, Wechsler believed that organic brain disease, psychoses, and emotional disorders gave rise to a marked $V > P$ pattern, whereas adolescent psychopaths and mildly retarded persons yielded a strong $P > V$ pattern. Subsequent research demonstrated many exceptions to these simple diagnostic rules. Nonetheless, the distinction between verbal and performance skills has proved valid and useful for other purposes, such as analyzing brain-behavior relationships and studying age effects on intelligence. Wechsler's armchair division of subtests into verbal and performance sections ranks as perhaps his most enduring contribution to contemporary intelligence testing.

General Features of the Wechsler Tests

Including revisions, David Wechsler and his followers produced 10 intelligence tests in a span of about 60 years. A major reason for the success of these instruments was that each new test or revision remained faithful to the familiar content and format first introduced in the Wechsler-Bellevue. By sticking with a single successful formula, Wechsler insured that examiners could switch from one Wechsler test to another with minimal retraining. This was not only good psychometrics but also shrewd marketing, insofar as it guaranteed several generations of faithful test users.

The various versions and editions of the Wechsler tests possess the following common features:

- Ten to fourteen subtests. The multi-subtest approach allows the examiner to analyze intraindividual strengths and weaknesses rather than just to compute a single global score. As the reader will learn subsequently, the pattern of subtest scores may convey useful information not evident from the overall level of performance.

- A Verbal Scale composed of five or six subtests and a Performance Scale composed also of five or six subtests. With this division, the examiner can assess verbal comprehension and perceptual organization skills separately. The pattern of abilities on these two factors of intelligence may have a bearing on the functional integrity of the left and right hemispheres of the brain, as well as indicating vocational strengths and weaknesses, as discussed in the following.

- A common metric for IQ and Index scores. The mean for IQ and Index scores is 100 and the standard deviation is 15 for all tests and all age groups. In addition, the scaled scores on each subtest have a mean of 10 and a standard deviation of approximately 3, which permits the examiner to analyze the subtest scores of the examinee for relative strengths and weaknesses.

- Common subtests for different ages. For example, the preschool, child, and adult Wechsler tests (WPPSI-R, WISC-III, and WAIS-III) all contain a common core of the same eight subtests (Table 6.1). An examiner who masters the administration of one core subtest on any of the Wechsler tests (such as the Information subtest on the WAIS-III) easily can transfer this skill within the Wechsler family of intellectual measures.

TABLE 6.1 Subtest Composition of the Wechsler Scales

	WPPSI-R	WISC-III	WAIS-III
Verbal Scales			
Information	X	X	X
Digit Span		X	X
Vocabulary	X	X	X
Arithmetic	X	X	X
Comprehension	X	X	X
Similarities	X	X	X
Sentences	X		
Letter-Number Sequencing			X
Performance Scales			
Picture Completion	X	X	X
Picture Arrangement		X	X
Block Design	X	X	X
Matrix Reasoning			X
Object Assembly	X	X	X
Coding/Digit Symbol		X	X
Mazes	X	X	
Geometric Design	X		
Symbol Search		X	X
Animal Pegs	X		

Note: The "core" subtests common to all Wechsler scales are in boldface.

THE WECHSLER SUBTESTS: DESCRIPTION AND ANALYSIS

Wechsler (1939) defined intelligence as "the aggregate or global capacity of the individual to act purposefully, to think rationally and to deal effectively with his environment." He also believed that we can only know intelligence by what it enables a person to do. In designing his tests, then, Wechsler selected components to represent a wide array of underlying abilities so as to estimate the global capacity of intelligence. Furthermore, he asked his subjects to do things, not merely to answer questions. The Wechsler subtests are quite diverse and often rely upon what Wechsler referred to as "mental productions."

We present here a description of subtests from the WISC-III and WAIS-III. We also analyze the abilities tapped by each subtest and offer research-based comments. The reader is referred to Topic 5B for a description of three subtests unique to the WPPSI-R (Sentences, Geometric Designs, and Animal Pegs). The verbal subtests are listed first.

Information

Factual knowledge of persons, places, and common phenomena is tested here. Questions for children are like the following:

> "How many eyes do you have?"
> "Who invented the telephone?"
> "What causes a solar eclipse?"
> "Which is the largest planet?"

Questions for adults are similar, but progress to higher levels of difficulty. Difficult questions on the adult Information subtest resemble:

> "Which is the most common element in air?"
> "What is the population of the world?"
> "How does fruit juice get converted to wine?"
> "Who wrote *Madame Bovary*?"

Information items test general knowledge normally available to most persons raised in the cultural institutions and educational systems of Western industrialized nations. Indirectly, this subtest measures learning and memory skills insofar as subjects must retain knowledge gained from formal and informal educational opportunities in order to answer the Information items.

Information is usually regarded as one of the best measures of general ability among the Wechsler subtests (Kaufman, McLean, & Reynolds, 1988). For example, the WAIS-III Manual reveals that Information typically has the second or third highest correlation with Full Scale IQ across the 13 age groups (Tulsky, Zhu, & Ledbetter, 1997). Information consistently loads strongly on the first factor identified in factor analyses of the WAIS-III subtest correlations (see below). The first factor is labeled Verbal Comprehension. However, Information tends to reflect formal education and motivation for academic achievement and may therefore yield spuriously high ability estimates for perpetual students and avid readers.

Digit Span

Digit Span consists of two separate sections, Digits Forward and Digits Backward. In Digits Forward, the examiner reads a series of digits at one per second, then asks the subject to repeat them. If the subject answers correctly on two consecutive trials of the same length, the examiner proceeds to the next series which is one digit longer, up to a maximum length of nine digits. For Digits Backward, a similar procedure is used, except the examinee must repeat the digits in reverse order, up to a maximum length of eight digits. For example, the examiner reads:

"6–1–3–4–2–8–5"

and the subject tries to repeat the numbers in the reverse order:

"5–8–2–4–3–1–6."

Digit Span is a measure of immediate auditory recall for numbers. Facility with numbers, good attention, and freedom from distractibility are required. Performance on this subtest may be affected by anxiety or fatigue, and many clinicians have noted that patients hospitalized for medical or psychiatric reasons frequently perform poorly on Digit Span.

Digits Forward and Digits Backward may assess fundamentally different abilities. Digits Forward seems to require the examinee to access an auditory code in sequential fashion. In contrast, to perform Digits Backward, the examinee must form an internal visual memory trace from the orally presented numerical sequences and then visually scan from end to beginning. Digits Backward is clearly the more complex test; not surprisingly, it loads higher on general intelligence than does Digits Forward (Jensen & Osborne, 1979). Gardner (1981) argues that examiners should supplement standard reporting procedures and list separate subscores for

Digit Span. He presents separate means, standard deviations, and percentile ranks on Digits Forward and Backward for children ages 5 to 15.

Vocabulary

The subject is asked to define up to several dozen words of increasing difficulty while the examiner writes down each response verbatim. For example, on an easy item the examiner might ask "What is a cup?" and the examinee would get partial credit for answering "You drink with it" and full credit for answering "It has a handle, holds liquids, and you drink from it." For adults and bright children, the advanced items on the Wechsler Vocabulary subtests can be very challenging, on a par with: *tincture, obstreperous,* and *egregious.*

Vocabulary is learned largely in context from reading books and listening to others. It is a rare individual who picks up vocabulary by reading the dictionary or memorizing word lists from the "Building Your Wordpower" section of popular magazines. In the main, a person's vocabulary is a measure of sensitivity to new information and the ability to decipher meanings based on the context in which words are encountered. Precisely because the acquisition of word meaning depends upon contextual inference, the Vocabulary subtest turns out to be the single best measure of overall intelligence on the Wechsler scales (Gregory, 1999). This is a surprise to many laypersons who regard vocabulary as merely synonymous with educational exposure and therefore a mediocre index of general intelligence. However, there is simply no denying the empirical evidence: Vocabulary has the highest subtest correlation with Full Scale IQ on both the WISC-III (combined age groups) and also the WAIS-III (for 12 of the 13 age groups).

Arithmetic

Except for the very easiest items for young or mentally retarded persons, the Arithmetic subtest consists of orally presented mathematics problems. The examinee must solve the problems without paper or pencil within a time limit (usually 30 to 60 seconds). The simple items stress fundamental operations of addition or subtraction, for example:

> "If you have fifteen apples and give seven away, how many are left?"

The more difficult items require proper conceptualization of the problem and the application of two arithmetic operations, for example:

> "John bought a stereo that was marked down 15 percent from the original sales price of $600. How much did John pay for the stereo?"

Although the mathematical requirements of the Arithmetic items are not excessively demanding, the necessity of solving the problems mentally within a time limit makes this subtest quite challenging for most examinees. In addition to rudimentary arithmetic skills, successful performance on Arithmetic requires high levels of concentration and the ability to maintain intermediate calculations in short-term memory. In factor analyses of the WISC-III and WAIS-III, Arithmetic often loads on a third factor variously interpreted as Freedom from Distractibility or Working Memory.

Comprehension

The Comprehension subtest is an eclectic collection of items that require explanation rather than mere factual knowledge. The easy questions stress common sense, whereas the more difficult questions require an understanding of social and cultural conventions. On the WAIS-III, the two most difficult questions require the examinee to interpret proverbs.

An easy item on Comprehension is of the form "Why do people wear clothes?" Difficult items resemble the following:

> "What does this saying mean: 'A bird in the hand is worth two in the bush.'"
> "Why are supreme court judges appointed for life?"

Comprehension would appear to be, in part, a measure of "social intelligence" in that many items tap the examinee's understanding of social and cul-

tural conventions. Sipps, Berry, and Lynch (1987) found that Comprehension scores were moderately related to measures of social intelligence on the California Psychological Inventory. Of course, a high score signifies only that the examinee is knowledgeable about social and cultural conventions; choosing right action may or may not flow from this knowledge. However, recent studies by Campbell and McCord (1996) and Lipsitz, Dworkin, and Erlenmeyer-Kimling (1993) provide no support for the commonly accepted clinical lore that Comprehension scores are sensitive to social functioning.

Similarities

In this subtest, the examinee is asked questions of the type "In what way are shirts and socks alike?" The Similarities subtest evaluates the examinee's ability to distinguish important from unimportant resemblances in objects, facts, and ideas. Indirectly, these questions assess the assimilation of the concept of likeness. The examinee must also possess the ability to judge when a likeness is important rather than trivial. For example, "shirts" and "socks" are alike in that both begin with the letter *s* but this is not the essential similarity between these two items. The important similarity is that shirts and socks are both exemplars of a concept, namely, "clothes." As this example illustrates, Similarities can be thought of as a test of verbal concept formation.

We turn now to a description and analysis of Wechsler performance subtests. With the exception of Matrix Reasoning on the WAIS-III, all of the performance subtests are timed, and for most the examinee earns bonus points for quick performance.

Letter-Number Sequencing

This is a new subtest found only on the WAIS-III. The examiner orally presents a series of letters and numbers that are in random order. The examinee must reorder and repeat the list by saying the numbers in ascending order and then the letters in alphabetical order. For example, if the examiner says

"R-3-B-5-Z-1-C," the examinee should respond "1-3-5-B-C-R-Z." This test measures attention, concentration, and freedom from distractibility. Together with Arithmetic and Digit Span, this subtest contributes to the Working Memory Index score on the WAIS-III (see below).

Picture Completion

For this subtest, the examiner asks the subject to identify the "important part" that is missing from a picture. For example, a simple item might be of this type: a picture of a table with one leg missing. The items get harder and harder; testing continues until the examinee misses several in a row. Figure 6.1 depicts an item similar to those found on the WAIS-III.

Although Picture Completion is included on the performance half of each Wechsler test, the abilities required for this subtest overlap only modestly with the classic measures of performance intelligence (e.g., Block Design). For one thing, successful per-

formance on Picture Completion largely involves access to long-term memory rather than perceptual-manipulative skill. True, the examinee must have good attention to visual detail. But high scores mainly reflect the ability to compare each drawing with similar items or situations stored in long-term memory. In sum, Picture Completion really doesn't require a performance component. The examinee needs to verbalize the missing element or merely point to the section of the drawing that is anomalous. The Picture Completion subtest presupposes that the examinee has been exposed to the object or situation represented. For this reason, Picture Completion may be inappropriate for culturally disadvantaged persons.

Picture Arrangement

In this subtest, several panels of nonverbal cartoon strips are laid down out of order by the examiner. The examinee's task is to put the panels together in the correct order to tell a sensible story. Figure 6.2 depicts a picture arrangement task, such as might be found on the WAIS-III.

Although Picture Arrangement is grouped with the Performance tasks, it loads about equally on the verbal and performance components revealed in factor-analytic studies of subtest intercorrelations (e.g., Silverstein, 1982a). The abilities tapped by Picture Arrangement are complex and multifaceted. Before sorting the pictures, the examinee must be able to decipher the gestalt of the entire story from its disarranged elements. This subtest also measures sequential thinking and the ability to see relationships between social events. On the WAIS-III, several of the Picture Arrangement stories have humorous themes. As a result, social sophistication and a sense of humor are required for successful performance.

Block Design

On the Block Design subtest, the examinee must reproduce two-dimensional geometric designs by proper rotation and placement of three-dimensional colored blocks. This subtest was depicted in Topic

FIGURE 6.1 **Picture Completion Item Similar to Those Found on the WAIS-III**

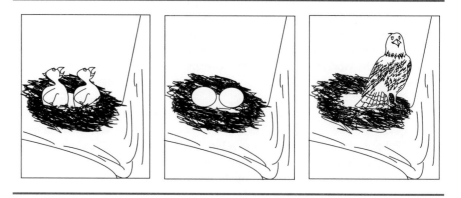

FIGURE 6.2 Picture Arrangement Item Similar to Those Found on the WAIS-III

2B, The Testing Process. For all of the Wechsler scales, the first few Block Design items can be solved through trial and error. However, the more difficult items require the analysis of spatial relations, visual-motor coordination, and the rigid application of logic. Block Design demands much more problem-solving and reasoning ability than most of the Performance subtests in which memory and prior experience are more heavily weighted. In factor analyses of the Wechsler scales, Block Design typically has the highest loading of all the Performance subtests on the second factor. This factor is variously identified as nonverbal, visuospatial, or perceptual-organizational intelligence (Fowler, Zillmer, & Macciocchio, 1990; Silverstein, 1982a). On the WISC-III and WAIS-III, Block Design has the highest correlation with Performance IQ for all but a few of the standardization groups between ages 6 and 89. For this reason, Block Design is generally recognized as the quintessential index of nonverbal intelligence on the Wechsler tests (Gregory, 1999).

Block Design is a strongly speeded test. Consider the WAIS-R version which consists of 14 designs of increasing difficulty. To obtain a high score on this subtest, adults must not only reproduce each of the designs correctly, they must also earn bonus points on the last eight designs by completing them quickly. An examinee who solves all the designs within the time limit but who fails to garner any

bonus points will test out at just slightly above average on this subtest. Block Design scores may be misleading for examinees who do not value speeded performance.

Matrix Reasoning

Matrix Reasoning is a new subtest found only on the WAIS-III. It was added to enhance the assessment of nonverbal reasoning on the adult test. The subtest consists of 26 figural reasoning problems arranged in increasing order of difficulty (Figure 6.3). Finding the correct answer requires the examinee to identify a recurring pattern or relationship between figural stimuli drawn along a straight line (simple items) or in a 3 × 3 grid (hard items) in which the last item is missing. Based upon nonverbal reasoning about the patterns and relationships, the examinee must infer the missing stimulus and select it from five choices provided at the bottom of the card.

Matrix Reasoning was designed to be a measure of fluid intelligence, which is the capacity to perform mental operations such as manipulation of abstract symbols. The items tap pattern completion, reasoning by analogy, and serial reasoning. Overall, the subtest is an excellent measure of inductive reasoning based on figural stimuli. Matrix Reasoning is the only untimed performance subtest on the WAIS-III.

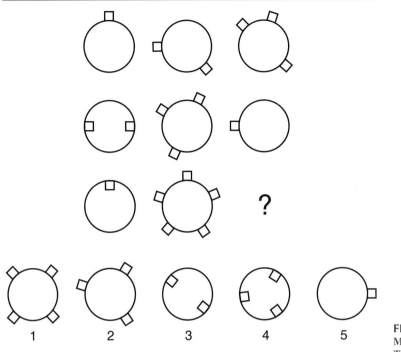

FIGURE 6.3
Matrix Reasoning Item Similar to
Those Found on the WAIS-III

Object Assembly

For each item, the examinee must assemble the pieces of a jigsaw puzzle to form a common object (Figure 6.4). For example, Object Assembly on the WAIS-III consists of five puzzles: a manikin (6 pieces), a profile (7 pieces), an elephant (6 pieces), a house (9 pieces), and a butterfly (7 pieces). The examiner does not identify the items, so the examinee must first discern the identity of each item from its disarranged parts. Success on this subtest requires high levels of perceptual organization, that is, the examinee must grasp a larger pattern or gestalt based on perception of the relationships among the individual parts.

Object Assembly is one of the least reliable of the Wechsler subtests. For example, on the WAIS-III this subtest has an average split-half reliability of only .70 (Tulsky, Zhu, & Ledbetter,1997). Among the WAIS-III subtests, only Picture Arrangement with a value of .74 approaches the unreliability of Object Assembly. These two subtests stand apart from the other, more reliable, Wechsler subtests. The modest reliability of Object Assembly may reflect, in part, the small number of items as well as the role of chance factors in solving jigsaw puzzles.

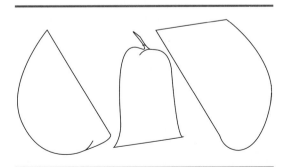

FIGURE 6.4   Object Assembly Item Similar to Those
Found on the WAIS-III

Coding/Digit Symbol

Although the tasks are nearly identical, this subtest is called Coding on the WISC-III and Digit Symbol-Coding on the WAIS-III. The WISC-III version consists of two separate and distinct parts, one for examinees under age 8 (Coding A) and another for those 8 years of age and over (Coding B). In Coding A, the child must draw the correct symbol inside a series of randomly sequenced shapes. The task utilizes five shapes (star, circle, triangle, cross, and square) and each shape is assigned a unique symbol (vertical line, two horizontal lines, single horizontal line, circle, and two vertical lines, respectively). After a brief practice session, the child is told to draw the correct symbol inside 43 of the randomly sequenced shapes. However, since there is a two-minute time limit, high scores require rapid performance.

Coding B on the WISC-III and Digit Symbol-Coding on the WAIS-III are identical in format (Figure 6.5). For both subtests, the examinee must associate one symbol with each of the digits 0 through 9 and quickly draw the appropriate symbol underneath a long series of random digits. The time limit for both versions is two minutes. Very few examinees manage to code all the stimuli in this amount of time.

Estes (1974) analyzed the Digit Symbol subtest from the standpoint of learning theory and concluded that efficient performance requires the ability to quickly produce distinctive verbal codes to represent each of the symbols in memory. For example, in Figure 6.5, the examinee might code the symbol underneath the number 2 as an "inverted T." Verbal coding mediates quick performance by simplifying a difficult task. Efficient performance also demands immediate learning of the digit-symbol pairings so that the examinee need not look from each digit to the reference table to determine the correct response. In this regard, Digit Symbol is unique: It is the only Wechsler subtest that necessitates on-the-spot learning of an unfamiliar task.

Digit Symbol scores show a steep decrement with advancing age. In cross-sectional studies, raw scores on Digit Symbol decline by as much as 50 percent from age 20 to age 70 (Wechsler, 1981). The decrement is approximately linear and not easily explained by superficial references to motivational differences or motor slowing. Of course, cross-sectional results are not necessarily synonymous with longitudinal trends. However, the age decrement on Digit Symbol is so steep that it must indicate, in part, a real age change in the speed of basic information processing skills. Digit Symbol is one of the most sensitive subtests to the effects of organic impairment (Lezak, 1995).

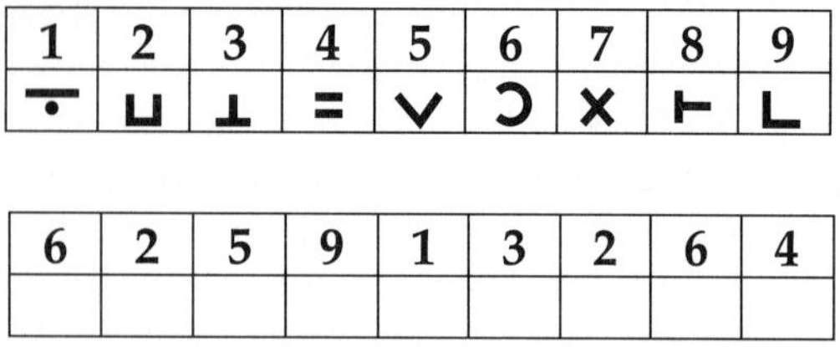

Mazes

This subtest appears only on the WPPSI-R and WISC-III and consists of paper-and-pencil mazes which the child must solve within a time limit. The examinee is told not to lift the pencil and counseled "try not to enter any blind alleys." Full credit for each maze is given if the child solves it within the time limit (30 seconds to 150 seconds, depending upon difficulty) without entering any blind alleys. One raw score point is deducted for each blind alley entered.

Mazes taps perceptual-motor skills, motor speed, visual planning, and the ability to inhibit impulsive responding. This subtest is a poor measure of general intelligence, but measures perceptual organization reasonably well. On the WISC-III, Mazes is a supplementary subtest not used in computation of the IQ.

1	2	3	4	5	6	7	8	9
÷	⊔	⊥	=	∨	⊃	×	⊢	∟

6	2	5	9	1	3	2	6	4

FIGURE 6.5 Digit Symbol Items Similar to Those Found on the WAIS-III

Note: The examinee's task is to determine whether either shape at the left occurs among the five shapes to the right

FIGURE 6.6   **Symbol Search Item Similar to Those Found on the WISC-III**

Symbol Search

Symbol Search is a performance measure found on the WISC-III and the WAIS-III. This is a highly speeded subtest in which the examinee looks at a target group of symbols, then quickly examines a search group of symbols, and finally marks a "YES" or "NO" box to indicate whether one or more of the symbols in the target group occurred within the search group. A Symbol Search item is depicted in Figure 6.6. This subtest would appear to be a measure of processing speed.

⬛ WECHSLER ADULT INTELLIGENCE SCALE-III

The WAIS-III is a significant revision of the WAIS-R, even though many of the previous items were retained. The most significant changes include the addition of three subtests and the inclusion of an alternative model for scoring the test (four Index scores to supplement the traditional approach of Verbal, Performance, and Full Scale IQ). Other important improvements over its predecessor include updating and expanding the normative samples, extending coverage to age 89, adding easy items to improve the assessment of mental retardation, and co-norming with the Wechsler Memory Scale-III

(Gregory, 1999). Due to changes in the WAIS-III protocol forms (e.g., prominent display of discontinue rules) this test is somewhat easier to administer than the WAIS-R. Sattler and Ryan (1999) provide an outstanding overview of the WAIS-III in clinical practice.

The WAIS-III is comprised of 14 subtests, but one (Object Assembly) is now optional and used only as a substitute for spoiled subtests under rare circumstances (Wechsler, 1997). From the main body of 13 subtests, 11 are needed for computation of the traditional IQs (Verbal, Performance, and Full Scale). The IQ scores are normed to the conventional average of 100 and standard deviation of 15 in the general population. The breakdown of subtests for the IQ scores is as follows:

> Verbal IQ
> > Vocabulary
> > Similarities
> > Arithmetic
> > Digit Span
> > Information
> > Comprehension
> Performance IQ
> > Picture Completion
> > Digit Symbol-Coding
> > Block Design
> > Matrix Reasoning
> > Picture Arrangement

All 11 subtests are used in the computation of Full Scale IQ. The Verbal-Performance breakdown of subtests on the WAIS-III is nearly identical to that found on the WAIS-R. The single difference is the addition of Matrix Reasoning in place of Object Assembly.

In addition to the traditional IQ scores, the WAIS-III can be scored for four Index scores, each based on 2 or 3 of the 13 subtests. These are derived from factor analysis of the subtests, which revealed four domains: Verbal Comprehension, Perceptual Organization, Working Memory, and Processing Speed. The Index scores are also based upon the familiar mean of 100 and standard deviation of 15.

The breakdown of subtests for the four Index scores is as follows:

> Verbal Comprehension Index
>> Vocabulary
>> Similarities
>> Information
> Perceptual Organization Index
>> Picture Completion
>> Block Design
>> Matrix Reasoning
> Working Memory Index
>> Arithmetic
>> Digit Span
>> Letter-Number Sequencing
> Processing Speed Index
>> Digit Symbol-Coding
>> Symbol Search

The reader will notice that the Verbal Comprehension Index (VCI) is similar to Verbal IQ but does not include the subtests sensitive to attention (i.e., Digit Span and Arithmetic). For this reason, the VCI is a more direct measure of verbal comprehension than is Verbal IQ. The Perceptual Organization Index (POI) is similar to Performance IQ but is less dependent on speed (because Matrix Reasoning is untimed). For this reason, the POI is a more refined measure of fluid reasoning and visual-spatial problem solving than is Performance IQ. In these respects, VCI and POI are more "pure" measures than Verbal IQ and Performance IQ, respectively.

The Working Memory Index (WMI) is comprised of subtests sensitive to attention and immediate memory (Arithmetic, Digit Span, and Letter-Number Sequencing). A relatively low score on this index may signify that the examinee has an attentional or memory problem, especially with verbally presented materials. The Processing Speed Index (PSI) is comprised of subtests that require the *highly* speeded processing of visual information (Digit Symbol-Coding, Symbol Search). The PSI is sensitive to a wide variety of neurological and neuropsychological conditions (Tulsky, Zhu, & Ledbetter, 1997).

WAIS-III Standardization

The standardization of the WAIS-III was undertaken with great care and based on data gathered by the U.S. Bureau of the Census in 1995. The total sample of 2,450 adults (ages 16 to 89) was carefully stratified on these variables: sex, race/ethnicity, educational level, and geographic region. Census figures from 1995 were used as the target values for the stratification variables. For example, of persons in the 55- to 64-year-old range, the Census Bureau found that 3.47 percent are African Americans with high school education. Hence, 3.5 percent of the standardization subjects in this age range were African Americans with high school education.

The standardization sample was divided into 13 age bands: 16–17, 18–19, 20–24, 25–29, 30–34, 35–44, 45–54, 55–64, 65–69, 70–74, 75–79, 80–84, 85–89. Except for the two oldest age groups, each sample included 200 participants carefully stratified on the demographic variables noted above; the 80–84 age group included 150 participants, and the 85–89 age group included 100 participants. The resulting sample bears a very close correspondence to the U.S. Census proportions. However, persons suspected of even mild cognitive impairment were excluded, so the standardization sample is probably healthier than its Census counterparts. Specifically, several exclusionary criteria were used in the standardization sample, including color blindness, uncorrected hearing or visual impairment, evidence of drug/alcohol problems, upper extremity impairment, use of antianxiety or antidepressant drugs, and a variety of potentially brain-impairing conditions (head injury, stroke, epilepsy, Alzheimer's disease, schizophrenia).

Although the WAIS-III is similar to the WAIS-R and has a substantial item overlap, the two tests do not yield analogous IQs. In counterbalanced studies comparing scores of 192 adults on the two tests, WAIS-III scores are lower by 1 point for Verbal IQ, 5 points for Performance IQ, and 3 points for Full Scale IQ (Tulsky, Zhu, & Ledbetter, 1997). In short, the WAIS-III is a harder test than the

WAIS-R. There is a troubling enigma here: Why does the normative sample for the WAIS-III appear to be smarter than the normative sample for the WAIS-R? We take up this point in more detail in Topic 7B, Test Bias and Other Controversies.

Reliability

The reliability of the WAIS-III is exceptionally good. Composite split-half reliabilities averaged across all age groups are Verbal IQ, .97; Performance IQ, .94; and Full Scale IQ, .98. Stability coefficients on test-retest for 394 examinees confirm much the same picture: Verbal IQ, .96; Performance IQ, .91; and Full Scale IQ, .96. Reliabilities and stability coefficients for the four Index scores tend to be slightly lower, but still at or near .90 in all cases.

For Full Scale IQ, the standard error of measurement is in the range of 2 to 2½ IQ points, depending upon the age group. Consider what this means: 95 percent of the time, an examinee's *true* Full Scale IQ will be within ±5 points (2 standard errors of measurement) of the obtained value. In common parlance, psychometrists would say that WAIS-III IQ has about a 10-point band of error, that is, IQ scores are accurate to within about ±5 points.

In contrast to the strong reliabilities found for IQs and Index scores, the reliabilities of the 14 individual subtests are generally much weaker. The only subtests with stability coefficients in excess of .90 are Information (.94) and Vocabulary (.91). For the remaining subtests, reliability values range from the low .70s to the mid .80s. The most important implication of these weaker reliability findings is that examiners should approach subtest profile analysis with extreme caution. Subtest scores that appear discrepantly high (or low) for an individual examinee might be a consequence of the generally weak reliability of certain subtests rather than indicating true cognitive strengths or weaknesses. Some reviewers conclude that profile analysis (the identification of specific cognitive strengths and weaknesses based upon analysis of peaks and valleys in the subtest scores) is not justified by the evidence (Gregory, 1994b).

Validity

Based on a number of different lines of evidence reviewed here, the validity of the WAIS-III appears to be quite satisfactory. Good criterion-related validity has been demonstrated in several studies correlating the WAIS-III with mainstream intelligence tests and also with measures of academic achievement. For example, the WAIS-III Full Scale IQ correlates strongly with global scores on other measures: .93 with the WAIS-R, .88 with the WISC-III (for 16-year-olds in the overlapping age groups), .64 with the Standard Progressive Matrices, and .88 with the Stanford-Binet: Fourth Edition. The WAIS-III IQs also correlate strongly with the eight subtests from the Wechsler Individual Achievement Test, revealing a median correlation of .70 (Tulsky, Zhu, & Ledbetter, 1997). There is no doubt that the WAIS-III captures the same aspects of global intelligence measured by other widely used instruments.

The validity of the WAIS-III is also buttressed by its strong overlap with the WAIS-R and the WAIS, both of which rest upon an impressive array of validity data. For a full review of these findings the reader should consult Matarazzo (1972) and Kaufman (1990). We will present one representative and provocative study here, a correlational analysis of academic standing and intelligence scores. Conry and Plant (1965) correlated WAIS scores with high school rank at graduation for 98 students. They also correlated WAIS scores with grade point average at the end of the freshman year of college for 335 students in a second sample. The results are portrayed in Table 6.2. Notice that Verbal IQ predicts academic success just as well as Full Scale IQ, whereas Performance IQ bears a weaker relationship to achievement levels. Notice also that Vocabulary yields the highest overall correlation (0.65) with academic standing in the entire table. This finding speaks forcefully in favor of including vocabulary measures in intelligence tests.

TABLE 6.2 Correlations between High School Rank, College Grades, and WAIS Scores

WAIS Subtests and IQs	High School (N = 98)	College (N = 335)
Information	0.54	0.48
Comprehension	0.55	0.33
Arithmetic	0.45	0.19
Similarities	0.50	0.39
Digit Span	0.37	0.04
Vocabulary	0.65	0.46
Digit Symbol	0.34	0.15
Picture Completion	0.33	0.20
Block Design	0.29	0.19
Picture Arrangement	0.22	0.07
Object Assembly	0.17	0.12
Verbal IQ	0.63	0.47
Performance IQ	0.43	0.24
Full Scale IQ	0.62	0.44

Source: Adapted with permission from Conry, R., and Plant, W. T. (1965). WAIS and group test predictions of an academic success criterion: High school and college. *Educational and Psychological Measurement, 25,* 493–500.

Several studies bolster the construct validity of the WAIS-III by showing that test scores in various groups are theory-consistent. For example, Sattler (1982, 1988) has pointed out that age trends on the WAIS-R subtests (which strongly resemble the WAIS-III subtests) conform closely to the Cattell-Horn theory of fluid and crystallized intelligence. The reader will recall from the previous unit in this chapter that fluid intelligence is used to solve novel problems whereas crystallized intelligence requires the retrieval of learned or habitual responses. According to the theory, fluid intelligence declines sharply in old age, whereas crystallized intelligence remains constant or increases slightly (Horn, 1985).

An analysis of the WAIS-R and the WAIS-III indicates that the verbal subtests draw more heavily upon crystallized intelligence (retrieving learned responses) whereas the performance subtests require high levels of fluid intelligence (solving novel problems). Conforming to theoretical expectations, an inspection of normative data reveals that raw scores on the verbal subtests show minimal decrement with advancing age, whereas raw scores on the performance subtests drop off precipitously for the older subjects (Wechsler, 1981, 1997). Of course, these data are cross-sectional and therefore do not constitute definitive proof of longitudinal decline. Nonetheless, the age decrements on performance subtests are so striking that it strains credulity to attribute them to cohort differences or other artifacts. More likely, a significant proportion of this decrement is a real age-related decline that corroborates the Cattell-Horn theory of intelligence.

Another theory-consistent expectation borne out by empirical findings is a strong relationship between educational attainment and IQ scores (Kaufman, 1990). These two variables should be highly correlated, based on two assumptions, namely, that education boosts intelligence and that more-intelligent persons will generally seek a higher level of education. Apparently, analyses of the relationship between WAIS-III IQ scores and educational attainment have not yet been completed. However, research on the previous edition is relevant here because of the strong resemblance between the two instruments. Matarazzo and Herman (1984) analyzed the total years of schooling against the Verbal IQ, Performance IQ, and Full Scale IQ of the 1,880 individuals used in the WAIS-R standardization sample. Excluding younger subjects aged 16 to 24, many of whom had not yet completed their education, the correlation between years of school completed and Full Scale IQ was 0.63 for the 500 subjects aged 25–44, and 0.62 for the 730 subjects aged 45–74. These findings reveal a very strong correlation between educational attainment and IQ scores. Finally, Wechsler IQ and occupational attainment also are strongly linked (Reynolds, Chastain, Kaufman, & McLean, 1987), which further supports the validity of the WAIS-III as a measure of general intelligence.

WECHSLER INTELLIGENCE SCALE FOR CHILDREN-III

The WISC was published in 1949 as a downward extension of the original Wechsler-Bellevue. Although used widely in the next two decades, psychometricians perceived a number of flaws in the WISC: absence of nonwhites in the standardization sample, ambiguities of scoring, inappropriate items for children (e.g., reference to "cigars"), and absence of females and African Americans in the pictorial content of items. The WISC-R (Wechsler, 1974) and the WISC-III (Wechsler, 1991) corrected these flaws.

The WISC-III consists of 10 subtests and 3 supplementary subtests. The verbal and performance subtests are administered in alternating order:

Verbal Subtests	Performance Subtests
Information	Picture Completion
Similarities	Coding
Arithmetic	Picture Arrangement
Vocabulary	Block Design
Comprehension	Object Assembly
Digit Span	Symbol Search
	Mazes

Digit Span, Symbol Search, and Mazes are supplementary subtests not normally included in the computation of IQ. However, these subtests are usually administered because of the diagnostic information they provide. In the event that a subtest is disrupted during administration and therefore spoiled, or must be omitted because of special disabilities, Digit Span (for verbal subtests) or Mazes (for performance subtests) may be substituted. Symbol Search can be used as a substitute only for the Coding subtest.

The standardization of the WISC-III is exceptionally good, based on 100 boys and 100 girls at each year of age from 6½ through 16½ (total N = 2,200). These cases were carefully selected and stratified on the basis of the 1988 U.S. Census with respect to race/ethnicity (White, African American, Native American, Eskimo, Aleut, Asian, Pacific Islander, and Other), geographic region, and parent education. Although not a formal stratification variable, community size for the WISC-III standardization sample resembled census data closely. The standardization sample was drawn from both public and private schools, including children in special service programs. A desirable feature of the sample is that 7 percent of the children were categorized as learning disabled, emotionally disturbed, speech/language impaired, and so forth, and 5 percent of the sample consisted of children in programs for the gifted and talented. The reliability of the WISC-III is comparable to the WAIS-R: The three IQ scores (Verbal, Performance, and Full Scale) show split-half and test-retest reliabilities in the .90s, whereas the individual subtests possess somewhat lower split-half coefficients ranging from .69 (Object Assembly) to .87 (Vocabulary and Block Design). Test-retest reliabilities tend to be slightly lower.

The validity of the WISC-III rests, in part, upon its overlap with the WISC-R, for which dozens of supportive studies could be cited. We do not want to overwhelm with excessive detail, so we refer the interested reader to Sattler (1988) for a good review of earlier studies. The WISC-III Manual cites an impressive array of validity studies, which we summarize here. The preliminary studies indicate strong correlations with WISC-R scores (r = .90 for VIQ, .81 for PIQ, and .89 for FSIQ), strong correlations with WAIS-R scores for 16-year-olds (r = .90 for VIQ, .80 for PIQ, and .86 for FSIQ), and slightly lower but confirmatory correlations with WPPSI-R scores for a sample of 6-year-old children. These correlations are virtually as high as the reliabilities of the respective scales would allow. An interesting finding, discussed in the next chapter, is that WISC-III IQs are an average of about 5 points lower than WISC-R IQs (Vance, Maddux, Fuller, & Awadh, 1996).

The WISC-III also shows theory-confirming correlations with numerous cognitive, ability, and achievement tests (Wechsler, 1991). For example, in a study of 27 children ages 7 to 14 years who were administered both the WISC-III and the Differential Ability Scales (DAS, Elliott, 1990),

WISC-III VIQ scores correlated .87 with Verbal Ability scores from the DAS, but only .58 with Nonverbal Reasoning scores from the DAS. Conversely, WISC-III PIQ scores correlated .78 with Nonverbal Reasoning scores, but only .31 with Verbal Ability. The Manual cites theory-consistent correlations—appropriately high for similar constructs, low for dissimilar constructs—with the Otis-Lennon School Ability Test, the Benton Revised Visual Retention Test, subtests from the Halstead-Reitan neuropsychological test battery, and the Wide Range Achievement Test-Revised. Studies with special groups of children—gifted, retarded, learning disabled, hyperactive, conduct disordered, speech/language delayed—also provide strong support for WISC-III validity.

Factor-analytic studies of the standardization sample provided additional evidence for the utility of the WISC-III in diagnostic assessment of children. The results of numerous factor analyses, including separate analyses for four age-group subsamples (ages 6–7, 8–10, 11–13, and 14–16), strongly indicated a four-factor solution. The first two factors are familiar from previous studies of the Wechsler Scales:

Verbal Comprehension	**Perceptual Organization**
Information	Picture Completion
Similarities	Picture Arrangement
Vocabulary	Block Design
Comprehension	Object Assembly

The third factor on the WISC-III is slightly different from the third factor on its predecessor, whereas the fourth factor is a new one:

Freedom from Distractibility	**Processing Speed**
Arithmetic	Coding
Digit Span	Symbol Search

One subtest, Mazes, revealed an inconsistent assignment to factors, loading weakly on Freedom from Distractibility for 6–7-year-olds and weakly on Perceptual Organizational for children 8 years and older.

The four-factor solution holds up in other samples as well, including child psychiatry inpatients (Tupa, Wright, & Fristad, 1997), Canadian children selected at random (Roid & Worrall, 1997), and children receiving special education (Konold, Kush, & Canivez, 1997). In a dissenting note, Riccio, Cohen, Hall, and Ross (1997) found that the third and fourth factors were not clinically meaningful, that is, they showed minimal relationship with independent measures of attention in a sample of children with presumed attentional problems.

The four-factor solution to the WISC-III provides for the optional reporting of Index Scores (similar to IQ scores) for each of the four factors. These scores are based upon the familiar mean of 100 and standard deviation of 15. The Index Scores (Verbal Comprehension Index or VCI, Freedom from Distractibility Index or FDI, etc.) are derived from the allocation of subtests previously listed and serve to supplement Verbal IQ and Performance IQ. This factorial breakdown of the WISC-III is particularly helpful in the assessment of learning disabilities and related disorders. Learning-disabled children are particularly likely to obtain low scores on the third factor, suggesting that distractibility may underlie some forms of this disorder (Farnham-Diggory, 1978; Smith, 1983). Parker and Atkinson (1994) provide a rationale and specific methods for precise calculation (as opposed to estimation) of WISC-III factor scores.

STANFORD-BINET INTELLIGENCE SCALE: FOURTH EDITION

With a lineage that goes back to the Binet-Simon scale of 1905, the Stanford-Binet: Fourth Edition (SB:FE) has the oldest and perhaps the most prestigious pedigree of any individual intelligence test. In Table 6.3, we outline some important milestones in the development of the Stanford-Binet and its predecessors. The SB:FE incorporates major revisions in the theoretical rationale and content of intelligence testing. While many item types from earlier Stanford-Binet scales have been retained,

TABLE 6.3   Milestones in the Development of the Stanford-Binet and Predecessor Tests

Year	Test/Authors	Comment
1905	Binet and Simon	Simple 30-item test
1908	Binet and Simon	Introduced the mental age concept
1911	Binet and Simon	Expanded to include adults
1916	Stanford-Binet Terman and Merrill	Introduced the IQ concept
1937	Stanford-Binet-2 Terman and Merrill	First use of parallel forms (L and M)
1960	Stanford-Binet-3 Terman and Merrill	Modern item-analysis methods used
1972	Stanford-Binet-3 Thorndike	SB-3 Restandardized on 2,100 persons
1986	Stanford-Binet-4 Thorndike, Hagen, and Sattler	Complete restructuring into 15 subtests

the SB:FE is really a new test that shares only a modest overlap with its predecessors.

The SB:FE Model of Intelligence

Foremost among the SB:FE alterations is a multiple subtest hierarchical model of intelligence. In previous editions of the Stanford-Binet, the examiner obtained only a composite IQ. Although the pattern of right and wrong answers could be analyzed qualitatively, the earlier Stanford-Binet tests did not provide a basis for quantitative analysis of the subcomponents of the entire scale. This shortcoming is corrected with a vengeance in the SB:FE, which consists of 15 subtests designed to assess ability in four areas: verbal, abstract/visual, quantitative, and short-term memory. Because different subtests are suitable for different ages, an examinee is administered only eight to ten subtests. The SB:FE therefore produces up to ten subtest scores, four area scores, and a composite score (no longer called an IQ) based on the entire test.

The authors of the SB:FE adopted a three-level hierarchical model of the structure of cognitive abilities to guide in the construction of this test (Figure 6.7). The first level is general ability, or *g*,

which the authors define as "the cognitive assembly and control processes that an individual uses to organize adaptive strategies for solving novel problems" (Thorndike, Hagen, & Sattler, 1986). By sampling broadly from a wide range of cognitive tasks, factors specific to any particular subtest diminish in importance, and the examinee's standing on the composite performance becomes an indirect reflection of the *g* factor of intelligence.

The second level seems to acknowledge an acceptance of a modified Cattell-Horn view of intelligence (e.g., Horn & Cattell, 1966) by the authors of the SB:FE. However, in addition to the crystallized/fluid distinction originally proposed by Cattell and Horn, the test developers have added a separate short-term memory factor based on four subtests. The SB:FE emphasizes memory skills to a far greater extent than any other test of general intelligence. When the examiner desires a comprehensive assessment of short-term memory, the SB:FE may very well be the instrument of choice. The crystallized-abilities factor represents school-related skills such as vocabulary and quantitative skills. The fluid-analytic-abilities factor is largely synonymous with the Cattell-Horn construct of fluid intelligence and typifies the cognitive skills

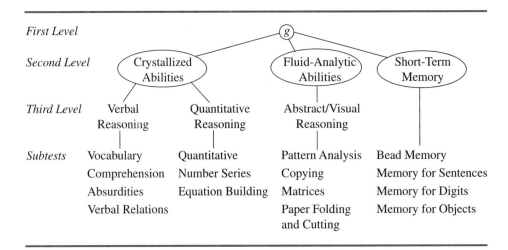

FIGURE 6.7 Cognitive Abilities Factors and Subtests of the Stanford-Binet: Fourth Edition

necessary for solving new problems that involve nonverbal and figural stimuli.

The third level is really only pertinent to the crystallized-abilities factor, which the SB:FE authors split off into two areas: verbal reasoning and quantitative reasoning. At this level, the fluid-analytic abilities are given the alternative label of *abstract/visual reasoning.* The authors note that these factors are more specific and more content-dependent than factors at the first and second levels. These factors are included in the model because they have special meaning to clinicians and educators (Thorndike, Hagen, & Sattler, 1986). In summary, the examiner obtains up to ten subtest scores, four area scores (Verbal Reasoning, Quantitative Reasoning, Abstract/Visual Reasoning, and Short-Term Memory), and an overall composite score.

Subtests on the SB:FE

The latest edition of the Stanford-Binet consists of 15 subtests, but not all subtests are administered to every age group. For example, Verbal Relations and Equation Building are too difficult for younger subjects and are normally administered only to persons 8 years of age and over. In contrast, Absurdities and Copying are too easy for older subjects and are normally administered only to persons under 10 years

of age. Six subtests span all age groups: Vocabulary, Comprehension, Quantitative, Pattern Analysis, Bead Memory, and Memory for Sentences.

Nine of the SB:FE subtests are based on the types of items that appeared in previous editions of the test. However, similar items are grouped into subtests for the first time. In previous editions of the Stanford-Binet, items were grouped by age level, not content. Six of the SB:FE subtests are new and help redress the heavy verbal emphasis of earlier versions of this test. The new subtests provide a more representative coverage of quantitative, spatial, and short-term memory tasks. The subtests of the SB:FE are described in Table 6.4.

SB:FE Standardization and Psychometric Properties

The standardization sample consisted of 5,013 subjects, ranging from ages 2 to 24. Data from the 1980 U.S. Census were used to derive proportional representation on five variables: geographic region, community size, ethnic group, age, and sex. Social class data were also collected. Because there was an excess of children whose parents were from upper socioeconomic categories (43 percent of the sample versus 19 percent of the population), weighting procedures were used to balance the

TABLE 6.4 A Description of the Subtests from the Stanford-Binet: Fourth Edition

Verbal Reasoning

Vocabulary: Begins with 14 picture vocabulary items in which the young child's task is to identify the pictured object; continues with 32 words the subject must define. Difficult vocabulary words are similar to

reluctant   teratogen   pusillanimous

Comprehension: Simple items include identifying parts of the human body, whereas difficult items require social judgment, reasoning, and evaluation. Example of a difficult item: "What are some reasons why a new worker should be required to join the labor union that represents co-workers?"

Absurdities: This subtest extends only to age 9 and requires the examinee to identify the incongruity in pictures. This task requires perception of detail, concentration, and social understanding. A characteristic item might depict a person clearly walking forward in the sand, with footprints in front, but none behind.

Verbal Relations: The examinee is read (and also views) a list of four words, with instructions to state what is similar about the first three things but different about the fourth. This subtest requires verbal concept formation and reasoning. Example: "How are a porpoise, dolphin, and whale different from a shark?"

Abstract/Visual Reasoning

Pattern Analysis: Easy items involve placing cut-out forms into a form-board, whereas difficult items require the examinee to reproduce complex designs with blocks. The difficult items require perceptual organization and spatial visualization, whereas the form-board items test visual-motor and manipulatory abilities.

Copying: For examinees under age 10; the subject must reproduce a simple model of solid blocks (very young examinees) or copy a design with paper and pencil. This subtest requires the examinee to integrate perceptual and motor processes.

Matrices: The examinee's task is to select the object, design, or letter that best completes the matrix. This subtest requires perceptual reasoning and loads heavily on fluid intelligence.

Paper Folding and Cutting: A multiple-choice test, the examinee must identify how a piece of paper that has been folded and cut will look when unfolded. This subtest taps visualization, spatial thinking, and attention to visual clues. Paper Folding and Cutting contributes substantially to the Nonverbal Reasoning/Visualization factor.

Quantitative Reasoning

Quantitative: The tasks on this subtest range from simple counting to more complex arithmetical concepts and operations. This subtest is similar to Arithmetic on the Wechsler scales, but less dependent upon formal education. Example of a difficult item: "How many 4 inch by 4 inch tiles will be needed to cover a section of floor that is 4 feet by 4 feet?"

Number Series: The examinee must complete a number sequence with the next logical number. This subtest measures logical reasoning and requires persistence, flexibility, and a trial-and-error approach to difficult problems. Example of a difficult item: "What two numbers come next?" 5, 10, 9, 18, 17, 34, 33, ___, ___.

Equation Building: The examinee must correctly rearrange a scrambled arithmetic equation. As with Number Series, this subtest taps logic, flexibility, and persistence. Example of a difficult item: ¼ 4 6 10 $-$ / =

continued

TABLE 6.4 (Continued)

Short-Term Memory

Bead Memory: Using four bead shapes in three different colors (a total of 12 kinds of beads), the examinee must reproduce a photographed design by stacking real beads on a stick. However, the design is viewed for only 5 seconds, so the task must be completed from memory. There is no time limit.

Memory for Sentences: The examinee must repeat orally presented sentences exactly. This subtest loads strongly on Verbal Comprehension at ages 2 through 7, but is a good measure of the Memory factor for older subjects. Example of a difficult sentence: "As professors grow older they generally find it less and less valuable to publish several short articles every year."

Memory for Digits: This subtest is essentially identical to Digit Span on the Wechsler tests. It measures short-term auditory memory and freedom from distractibility. It includes digits forward and digits reversed.

Memory for Objects: On this subtest the examinee is shown a series of pictures of individual objects at one per second. After all cards for an item have been displayed, the examinee must pick out the objects shown from a card containing 5 to 13 items. To obtain full credit, the examinee must point to the correct items in the exact order in which they were shown. This subtest contributes substantially to the Memory factor at all age levels.

Note: These items resemble those from the Stanford-Binet, but are not actually on the test.

standardization data. Children from higher socioeconomic backgrounds were counted as only a fraction of a case (as little as 0.28 for some age groups) to adjust for the oversampling from the upper socioeconomic categories. This is a reasonable and recognized statistical procedure that improves standardization data. In general, it appears that normative data for the SB:FE are quite representative of the target population.

With the exception of Memory for Objects, the reliability of the SB:FE subtests is good, judging from Kuder-Richardson internal consistency coefficients in the .80s and .90s for virtually every age group. The reliability of Memory for Objects was only fair, with internal consistency coefficients generally in the low .70s. The reliability of the area scores is outstanding, especially when a full complement of subtests is used to obtain an area score (internal consistency coefficients in the high .90s). The composite score is exceptionally reliable, with KR-20 coefficients ranging from .95 at age 2 to .99 at ages 18 to 23. Test-retest reliability was examined in samples of 5- and 8-year-old children. With an average interval of 16 weeks between sessions,

retest reliabilities were in the .90s for the composite, while the area scores and subtest scores demonstrated a more variable pattern. For example, many of the retest reliabilities were in the .60s and .70s, which is too low for individual decision making. In a few cases, subtest reliabilities were strikingly low: .28 for Quantitative, .46 for Copying, and .51 for Quantitative Reasoning in the 8-year-old sample; and .56 for Bead Memory in the 5-year-old sample. Examiners would be well advised to interpret scores on these subtests with caution.

Administration and Scoring of the SB:FE

The SB:FE uses the first subtest, Vocabulary, as a routing test for the remainder of the examination. The purpose of a routing test is to minimize the total number of items administered by skipping easy subtest items that the examinee would almost surely pass anyway. Based on chronological age and Vocabulary score, the examiner consults a table to determine the entry level for all remaining subtests. In addition, the examiner must establish a basal level and a ceiling level for each subtest. For tests like the SB:FE in which subtest items are ranked from easiest to hardest, the basal level is the level below which the examinee would almost certainly answer all questions correctly. The basal level is found when all four items on two consecutive levels are passed. On occasion, the examiner must go downward from the entry level in order to find the basal level. The ceiling level is the level above which the examinee would almost certainly fail all remaining items. Testing is discontinued at the ceiling level which is found when the examinee fails three out of four or all four items on two consecutive levels.

Every item is either passed or failed in accordance with very specific standards. Expanded scoring guides are provided for five subtests: Vocabulary, Comprehension, Absurdities, Copying, and Verbal Relations. These subtests require "free" responses (as opposed to multiple choice), and some judgment may be required in scoring unusual answers. The SB:FE authors do not report interscorer reliability estimates. However, based upon experience with other tests, examiner differences in the interpretation of scoring guidelines are unlikely to be a common source of measurement error (Gregory, 1999).

Validity of the SB:FE

The criterion-related validity of the SB:FE has been the subject of numerous investigations which correlate scores on this instrument with scores on other intelligence and achievement tests. The Technical Manual is unusually fertile in this regard, reporting study after study that compares or correlates SB:FE scores with other measures. In general, the SB:FE correlates quite robustly with other individual intelligence tests. Furthermore, the pattern of correlations between SB:FE area scores and subscores from other tests is generally confirmatory—similar subscales show higher correlations than dissimilar ones. For example, Wechsler Verbal IQs correlate better with the SB:FE Verbal Comprehension score (a similar measure) than with the SB:FE Abstract/Visual Reasoning score (a dissimilar measure).

Several studies have investigated the construct validity of the SB:FE with confirmatory factor analysis designed to determine whether the test corresponds to the theory that guided its construction (Kline, 1989; Laurent, Swerdlik, & Ryburn, 1992; Kaplan & Alfonso, 1997; Thorndike, Hagen, & Sattler, 1986). In general, the studies provide weak support for the existence of the four factors posited in the construction of the test (verbal reasoning, quantitative reasoning, abstract/visual reasoning, and short-term memory). For example, Kline (1989) concluded that Sattler's (1988) two-factor solution works best for ages 2 through 6, whereas a three-factor solution fits best for the older age groups. Based upon a comprehensive review of validity studies, Laurent, Swerdlik, and Ryburn (1992) also concluded that the SB:FE is a two-factor test for ages 2 through 6 (verbal, nonverbal) and a three-factor test for ages 7 years and older (verbal, nonverbal, memory). Nonetheless, Thorndike (1990) defends the original four-factor model. In part, the debate boils down to the choice of the "right" factor analysis (McCallum, 1990).

The SB:FE is unquestionably better than the previous editions of this test. One of the major changes—the breakdown of overall performance into subtest and area scores—is a welcome and useful addition to intelligence testing. Furthermore, the SB:FE incorporates a good supply of very easy items on most subscales. Consequently, the examiner obtains a much more precise picture of low-level functioning in children and young adults.[1] For the assessment of mental retardation or significant brain damage, the SB:FE is superior to most competing instruments, especially those such as the WAIS-R that "bottom out" at Full Scale IQs in the mid-50s. Another advantage of the SB:FE is that four subtests tap short-term memory. When the referral issue involves short-term memory, the SB:FE is probably the instrument of choice.

---

1. As Sattler (1988) has pointed out, the SB:FE may not yield valid scores with low-functioning examinees under 4 years of age. The "floor" of the test seems artificially high for very young examinees. For example, a two-year-old who failed to answer every question would still earn a composite score of 95!

The SB:FE does have a number of shortcomings. The most serious problem is the nonuniformity of composite scores. The highest and lowest possible scores fluctuate quite dramatically across the different age groups. For example, the highest possible composite score for ages 2 through 12 is 164, but after this age the ceiling drops as low as 149. Another significant problem is the lack of a comparable battery throughout the age levels covered by this test. Young examinees are not administered the same subtests as older examinees. Another problem with the SB:FE is the confusion about its factorial structure. How many factors exist—two, three, or four? A consensus seems to be emerging that the four factors proposed by Thorndike et al. (1986) are not supported by the evidence, and that a two-factor solution describes test performance for preschoolers, whereas a three-factor solution works best for subjects seven years of age and older (Laurent et al., 1992). Another concern is comparability of SB:FE results with other intelligence tests. Prewett and Matavich (1994) found that SB:FE test composite scores were an average of 7 points higher than the WISC-III IQ in a sample of referred children. Worse yet, the SB:FE Verbal Reasoning score was an average of 12 points higher than the WISC-III Verbal IQ. The large difference in verbal scores is troublesome because it indicates that the two tests would give vastly different diagnostic impressions in individual cases. However, it is unclear whether the SB:FE scores are too high or the WISC-III scores are too low (or perhaps both effects are at play).

DETROIT TESTS OF LEARNING APTITUDE-4

The Detroit Tests of Learning Aptitude-4 (DTLA-4, Hammill, 1999) is a recent revision of an instrument first published in 1935. The test is individually administered and designed for schoolchildren from 6 through 17 years of age. The DTLA-4 consists of 10 subtests which form the basis for computing 16 composites, including general intelligence, optimal level, and 14 ability areas. The subtests are largely within the Binet-Wechsler tradition, although there are a few surprises such as the inclusion of Story Construction, a measure of story-telling ability (Table 6.5).

The General Mental Ability composite is formed by combining standard scores for all 10 subtests in the battery. The Optimal Level composite is based upon the highest 4 standard scores earned by the subject and is thought to represent how well the examinee might perform under optimal circumstances. Each of the remaining 14 composite scores is derived from a combination of several subtests thought to measure a common attribute. For example, subtests that involve knowledge of words and their use are combined to form the Verbal Composite, whereas subtests that do not involve reading, writing, or speech comprise the Nonverbal Composite. Several of the composite scores are designed to represent major constructs within contemporary theories of intelligence. In addition to the General Mental Ability composite and

TABLE 6.5 Brief Description of the DTLA-4 Subtests

Subtest	Task
Word Opposites	Provide antonyms—word opposites.
Design Sequences	Discriminate and remember nonsensical graphic material.
Sentence Imitation	Repeat orally presented sentences.
Reversed Letters	Short-term visual memory and attention.
Story Construction	Create a logical story from several pictures.
Design Reproduction	Copy designs from memory.
Basic Information	Knowledge of everyday facts and information.
Symbolic Relations	Select from a series of designs the part that was missing from a previous design.
Word Sequences	Repeat a series of unrelated words.
Story Sequences	Organize pictorial material into meaningful sequences.

the Optimal Level composite, the remaining 14 DTLA-3 composite scores are as follows:

Verbal	Nonverbal	(Linguistic)
Attention-enhanced	Attention-reduced	(Attentional)
Motor-enhanced	Motor-reduced	(Motoric)
Fluid	Crystallized	(Horn & Cattell)
Simultaneous	Successive	(Das)
Associative	Cognitive	(Jensen)
Verbal	Performance	(Wechsler)

The 16 composite scores are based upon the familiar mean of 100 and standard deviation of 15. The 10 subtests are normed for a mean of 10 and standard deviation of 3.

The composites were designed to offer contrasting assessments such that a difference between scores may be of diagnostic significance. For example, an examinee who scored well on Attention-Reduced aptitude but poorly on Attention-Enhanced aptitude (in the Attentional domain) presumably experiences difficulty with immediate recall, short-term memory, or focused concentration.

The DTLA-4 was standardized on 1,350 students whose backgrounds closely matched census data for sex, race, urban/rural residence, family income, educational attainment of parents, and geographic area. The reliability of this instrument is similar to other individual tests of intelligence, with internal consistency coefficients generally exceeding .80 for the subtests and .90 for the composites, and test-retest coefficients for the subtests and the composites in the .80s and .90s. Criterion-related validity is well established through correlational studies with other mainstream instruments such as the WISC-III, K-ABC, and Woodcock-Johnson.

A concern with the DTLA-4 is that the conceptual breakdown into composites is not sufficiently supported by empirical evidence. For example, while it may be true that the Simultaneous composite does measure the simultaneous cognitive processes proposed by Das, Kirby, and Jarman (1979), there is scant empirical support to buttress this claim. Another problem with this instrument is that there are more composites than

there are subtests! Inevitably, the composites will be highly intercorrelated, because each subtest occurs in several composites. In sum, DTLA-4 may be a good measure of general intelligence, but the use of composite scores for purposes of psychoeducational planning requires additional empirical study. Schmidt (1994) provides a thorough review of the previous edition, the DTLA-3.

KAUFMAN BRIEF INTELLIGENCE TEST (K-BIT)

The individual intelligence tests previously discussed in this and the preceding topic are excellent measures of intellectual ability, but they are not without their drawbacks. One problem is the time required to administer them. Testing sessions with the Wechsler scales, Kaufman Assessment Battery for Children, and the Stanford-Binet easily can last one hour, and two hours is not unusual if the examinee is bright and highly verbal. A second disadvantage to these mainstream tests is the amount of training required to administer them. Proper administration of most individual intelligence tests is based upon the assumption that the examiner has an advanced degree in psychology or a related field and has received extensive supervised experience with the instruments in question.

Alan Kaufman responded to the need for a brief, easily administered, screening measure of intelligence by developing the Kaufman Brief Intelligence Test (K-BIT, Kaufman & Kaufman, 1990; Kaufman & Wang, 1992). The K-BIT consists of a Vocabulary section and a Matrices section. The Vocabulary test contains two parts: Expressive Vocabulary (naming pictures) and Definitions (providing a word based upon a brief phrase and a partial spelling). The Matrices test requires solving 2×2 and 3×3 analogies using figural stimuli.

The K-BIT is normed for subjects ages 4 to 90 years and can be administered in 15 to 30 minutes. The test yields standard scores with mean of 100 and SD of 15 for Vocabulary, Matrices, and the combination of two, called the IQ Composite. In spite of the comparability of these scoring dimensions with well-known intelligence tests, the K-BIT authors make it clear that their instrument is not intended as a substitute for traditional approaches (e.g., WPPSI-R, K-ABC, WISC-III, or SB:FE). The K-BIT is mainly a screening test useful in signalling the need for more extensive assessment. The brevity of this instrument also makes it a natural choice for research on intelligence.

Reliability findings for the K-BIT are exceptionally strong. Split-half reliability and test-retest coefficients for a variety of samples were in the .90s for Vocabulary, the .80s and .90s for Matrices, and .90s for IQ Composite. The normative sample of 2,022 individuals was within 1 to 3 percentage points of the 1990 U.S. Census figures for gender, geographic region, race or ethnic group, and educational attainment of the parents (for subjects 4 to 19 years of age) or examinees themselves (20 years of age and above).

The K-BIT Manual reports highly supportive validity data from 20 correlational studies. These results are similar to a recent concurrent validity study which compared K-BIT results and WAIS-R scores for 200 referrals to a neuropsychological assessment center (Naugle, Chelune, & Tucker, 1993). The patient sample included persons with seizure disorders, head injuries, substance abuse, psychiatric disturbance, stroke, dementia, and other neurological conditions. The heterogeneity of the referral sample guaranteed a wide range of functional ability, a desirable feature in a validation study. Although the K-BIT scores tended to be about 5 points higher than their WAIS-R counterparts, the correlations between these two instruments were extremely high and theory-confirming. Vocabulary IQ (K-BIT) and Verbal IQ (WAIS-R) correlated .83; Matrices IQ (K-BIT) and Performance IQ (WAIS-R) correlated .77; and, overall IQs from the two instruments correlated an amazing .88. In a study comparing the K-BIT and the WISC-III scores for 50 referred students, Prewett (1995) also reported strong correlations ($r = .78$ for overall scores) and also discovered that the K-BIT scores tended to be about 5 points higher than their WISC-III counterparts. Canivez (1995) found comparable scores between the K-BIT and the WISC-III for 137 elementary- and middle-school children and also reported very strong correlations between the two tests, especially for overall scores ($r = .87$). Eisenstein and Engelhart (1997) found that the K-BIT performed well in estimating IQs in adult neuropsychology referrals, but Donders (1995) recommends caution when using the test with brain-injured children. The reason for caution is that K-BIT scores show a negligible relationship with length of coma, that is, the test is not a good index of neuropsychological status in children. Even so, the K-BIT is an outstanding screening measure of general intelligence for use in research or when time constraints preclude use of a longer measure.

SUMMARY

1. For purposes of estimating general intelligence, any well-normed mainstream instrument will suffice. However, for purposes of individualized assessment, examiners need to consider the particular strengths and weaknesses of potential instruments.

2. David Wechsler was a pragmatist who borrowed heavily from the Army Alpha and Beta tests in fashioning many of the subtests from the various Wechsler scales. For each of his intelligence tests, Wechsler used 10 to 13 subtests—about half verbal and half performance.

3. The first Wechsler test was the Wechsler-Bellevue, published in 1939 and updated in 1946. Other tests and their dates of revision are Wechsler Preschool and Primary Scale of Intelligence-Revised (1967, 1989); Wechsler Intelligence Scale for Children-III (1949, 1974, 1991); and, Wechsler Adult Intelligence Scale-III (1955, 1981, 1997).

4. All of the Wechsler scales use the same format: 10 to 13 subtests about equally divided between verbal and performance emphasis; a common metric for IQ, with mean of 100 and standard deviation of 15; a common core of subtests, so that examiners can easily transfer their test-giving skills from one Wechsler scale to another.

5. The Wechsler Adult Intelligence Scale-III (WAIS-III) is the most widely used individual test of adult intelligence. The test has excellent reliability, well-established validity, and adds a new subtest: Matrix Reasoning.

6. Factor analysis of the Wechsler Intelligence Scale for Children-III (WISC-III, for children ages 6 to 16½) often yields a four-factor solution: Verbal Comprehension (mainly verbal subtests), Perceptual Organization (mainly performance subtests), Freedom from Distractibility (Arithmetic and Digit Span), and Processing Speed (Coding and Symbol Search).

7. The Stanford-Binet: Fourth Edition (SB:FE) adopts a hierarchical model of intelligence. The general factor is gauged by the overall score. Subcomponents of the general factor include a crystallized-abilities factor (verbal reasoning and quantitative reasoning), a fluid-analytic-abilities factor, and a short-term memory factor.

8. The SB:FE consists of 15 subtests, but not all subtests are administered to every age group. The standardization of the test was excellent. The SB:FE correlates quite robustly with other individual intelligence tests. However, confirmatory factor analyses of the SB:FE do not always support the four-factor model of the test.

9. The SB:FE contains a good supply of very easy items and is therefore especially useful in the assessment of mental retardation. One problem with the SB:FE is the nonuniformity of composite scores, which fluctuate widely across age groups. Another problem is the lack of a comparable battery throughout the age levels covered by this test.

10. The Detroit Tests of Learning Aptitude-4 (DTLA-4) consists of 10 subtests which form the basis for computing 16 composites. The DTLA-4 is a good measure of general intelligence, but the conceptual breakdown into 14 ability areas needs empirical support.

11. The Kaufman Brief Intelligence Test (K-BIT) is a well-normed screening test of general intellectual ability which consists of Vocabulary and Matrices. Although the K-BIT yields IQs about 5 points higher than the WAIS-R, the exceedingly strong correlation between these two instruments ($r = .88$) is highly supportive of K-BIT validity.

KEY TERMS AND CONCEPTS

IQ constancy   p. 178

verbal comprehension   p. 192

perceptual organization   p. 192

freedom from distractibility   p. 192

processing speed   p. 192

A group intelligence test allows for the quick and efficient testing of dozens or hundreds of examinees at the same time. In this topic we introduce the reader to a sampling of prominent group tests. For better or for worse, the number of group tests currently marketed is simply astonishing— scores of them are available. Several dozen entries are reviewed in recent issues of the *Mental Measurements Yearbook* (Mitchell, 1985; Conoley & Kramer, 1989, 1992) and the *Test Critiques* series (Keyser & Sweetland, 1984–1988), and new instruments are published every year. Comprehensive coverage of this burgeoning field is simply not feasible. Consequently, we focus here on issues raised by group tests and then review an eclectic assortment of these diverse instruments.

ORIGINS AND CHARACTERISTICS OF GROUP TESTS

Origins of Group Tests

The first useful group intelligence tests were developed early in the twentieth century in the United States. Nonetheless, the origins of these instruments can be traced to the efforts of nineteenth-century European psychologists. The modern group intelligence test owes a debt especially to the completion technique developed in the 1890s by Ebbinghaus (1896). His test consisted of several passages of text with words or parts of words omitted, as in the following brief example:

Little Red Riding Hood

_____ there was a sweet young _____, beloved by every _____ who _____ eyes on her. Her _____ mother gave her a little cap of _____ silk, which she wore _____ the time. The _____ was known as _____ Red Riding Hood. One _____ her mother told her "Your _____ is ill and weak. _____ take this cake and wine to her. Do not stray from the _____ and do not _____ to strangers."

The student's task was to fill in as many blanks as possible (for several selections) in a five-minute time limit. The completion test was commonly administered to an entire class by one person. The task was highly speeded: Only four times in several thousand cases did a student fill in all of the blanks. Ebbinghaus used the total number correct as a basis for comparing individuals as to their intellectual ability (DuBois, 1970).

A few years later, the practical success of the Binet scales inspired psychologists to develop intelligence tests that could be administered simultaneously to large numbers of examinees. We have noted in a previous chapter that the need to quickly test thousands of Army recruits for WWI inspired psychologists in the United States, led by Robert M. Yerkes, to make rapid advances in psychometrics and test development. Parallel developments occurred in school systems where administrators desired an efficient means for testing and placing students. However, fill-in-the-blank and open-ended questions severely limited the efficiency of assessment. Group testing quickly evolved into its modern design: the multiple-choice format.

Differences between Group and Individual Tests

Group tests differ from individual tests in five ways:

- Multiple choice versus open-ended format
- Objective machine scoring versus examiner scoring
- Group versus individualized administration
- Applications in screening versus remedial planning
- Huge versus merely large standardization samples

We discuss each of these points in turn.

The most obvious difference is that group tests generally employ a multiple-choice format. Although early group tests did use open-ended questions, this feature was quickly dropped because of the excessive amounts of time required for scoring. As a result of the multiple-choice format, group tests can be quickly and objectively scored by an optical scanning device hooked up to a computer. Computer scoring eliminates examiner errors and halo effects that may occur in the scoring of individual tests. In addition, psychometricians gain nearly instant access to item analyses and test data banks, so computer scoring promotes the quick development and revision of group tests.

Group tests also differ from individual tests in the mode of administration. In a group test, the examiner plays a minimal role that is restricted largely to reading instructions and enforcing time limits. There is negligible opportunity for one-on-one interaction between the test giver and the test taker. For most examinees this will not matter, but for a few—the shy, the confused, the unmotivated—the absence of examiner rapport can have disastrous results.

Traditional intelligence tests excel as aids in the diagnosis and remediation of individual learning difficulties, whereas group intelligence tests are more commonly used for mass screening in the furtherance of institutional decision making. Thus, group tests might be used in school systems to "flag" children in need of academic remediation or enrichment; in industrial settings to identify good candidates for specific jobs; or, in military settings to help cull out mentally impaired recruits.

Group tests are generally standardized on ultra-large samples—hundreds of thousands of subjects instead of just the few thousand carefully selected cases used with individual tests. Of course, the suitability of a standardization sample must never be taken for granted. Whether using huge standardization samples for group testing, or smaller standardization samples for individual testing, it is still important to determine the degree to which the sample is representative of the population at large.

Advantages and Disadvantages of Group Testing

Although the early psychometric pioneers embraced group testing wholeheartedly, they recognized fully the nature of their Faustian bargain: Psychologists had traded the soul of the individual examinee in return for the benefits of mass testing. Whipple (1910) summed up the advantages of group testing but also pointed to the potential perils:

> Most mental tests may be administered either to individuals or groups. Both methods have advantages and disadvantages. The group method has, of course, the particular merit of economy of time; a class of 50 or 100 children may take a test in less than a fiftieth or a hundredth of the time needed to administer the same test individually. Again, in certain comparative studies, e.g., of the effects of a week's vacation upon the mental efficiency of school children, it becomes imperative that all S's should take the tests at the same time. On the other hand, there are almost sure to be some S's in every group that, for one reason or another, fail to follow instructions or to execute the test to the best of their

ability. The individual method allows E to detect these cases, and in general, by the exercise of personal supervision, to gain, as noted above, valuable information concerning S's attitude toward the test.

In sum, group testing poses two interrelated risks: (1) some examinees will score far below their true ability, owing to motivational problems or difficulty following directions, and (2) invalid scores will not be recognized as such, with undesirable consequences for these atypical examinees. There is really no simple way to entirely avoid these risks, which are part of the trade-off for the efficiency of group testing. However, it is possible to minimize the potentially negative consequences if examiners scrutinize very low scores with skepticism and recommend individual testing for these cases.

We turn now to an analysis of several prominent group intelligence tests. The reader is reminded that, owing to the sheer number of these instruments, our review is necessarily selective. We present a balance of older, established instruments and newer, promising additions to the field, beginning with a test that attempts to bridge the gap between individual and group tests of intelligence.

MULTIDIMENSIONAL APTITUDE BATTERY (MAB)

The Multidimensional Aptitude Battery (MAB; Jackson, 1984a) is a recent group intelligence test designed to be a paper-and-pencil equivalent of the WAIS-R (Krieshok & Harrington, 1985). As the reader will recall, the WAIS-R is a highly respected instrument (now replaced by the WAIS-III), in its time the most widely used of the available adult intelligence tests. Kaufman (1983) noted that the WAIS-R was "the criterion of adult intelligence, and no other instrument even comes close." However, a highly trained professional needs about 1½ hours just to administer the Wechsler adult test to a single person. Because professional time is at a premium, a complete Wechsler intelligence assessment—including administration, scoring, and report writing—easily can cost hundreds of dollars. Many examiners have long suspected that an appropriate

group test, with the attendant advantages of objective scoring and computerized narrative report, could provide an equally valid and much less expensive alternative to individual testing for most persons.

Background and Description

The MAB was designed to produce subtests and factors parallel to the WAIS-R, but employing a multiple-choice format capable of being computer scored. The apparent goal in designing this test was to produce an instrument that could be administered to dozens or hundreds of persons by one examiner (and perhaps a few proctors) with minimal training. In addition, the MAB was designed to yield IQ scores with psychometric properties similar to those found on the WAIS-R. Appropriate for examinees from age 16 to 74, the MAB yields 10 subtest scores, as well as Verbal, Performance, and Full Scale IQs.

Although it consists of original test items, the MAB is mainly a sophisticated subtest-by-subtest clone of the WAIS-R. The 10 MAB subtests are listed as follows:

Verbal	**Performance**
Information	Digit Symbol
Comprehension	Picture Completion
Arithmetic	Spatial
Similarities	Picture Arrangement
Vocabulary	Object Assembly

The reader will notice that Digit Span from the WAIS-R is not included on the MAB. The reason for this omission is largely practical: There would be no simple way to present a Digit Span-like subtest in paper-and-pencil format. In any case, the omission is not serious. Digit Span has the lowest correlation with overall WAIS-R IQ, and it is widely recognized that this subtest makes a minimal contribution to the measurement of general intelligence.

The only significant deviation from the WAIS-R is the replacement of Block Design with a Spatial subtest on the MAB. In the Spatial subtest, examinees must mentally perform spatial rotations of figures and select one of five possible rotations presented as their answer (Figure 6.8). Only

Picture Completion — Choose the letter that begins the word describing the missing part of the picture.

A. L
B. E
C. B
D. W
E. F

The answer is **Light,** so **A** should be marked.

Spatial — Choose one figure to the right of the vertical line which is the same as the figure on the left. One figure can be turned to look like the figure on the left; the others would have to be flipped over.

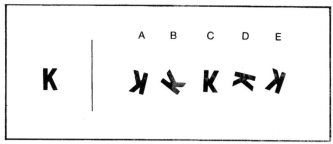

The correct answer is **A,** so **A** should be marked. The others **BCDE** would have to be flipped over.

Object Assembly — Choose the order, from left to right, in which these parts should be placed to form the object.

A. 3 2 1
B. 2 1 3
C. 1 3 2
D. 2 3 1
E. 3 1 2

The correct answer is **C-132** so **C** should be marked. Only this order would create the object **teacup.**

FIGURE 6.8 Demonstration Items from Three Performance Tests of the Multidimensional Aptitude Battery (MAB)

Source: Reprinted with permission from Jackson, D. N. (1984a). *Manual for the Multidimensional Aptitude Battery.* Port Huron, MI: Sigma Assessment Systems, Inc. (800) 265-1285.

mental rotations are involved (although "flipped over" versions of the original stimulus are included as distractor items). The advanced items are very complex and demanding.

The items within each of the 10 MAB subtests are arranged in order of increasing difficulty, beginning with questions and problems that most adolescents and adults find quite simple and proceeding upward to items that are so difficult that very few persons get them correct. There is no penalty for guessing and examinees are encouraged to respond to every item within the time limit. Unlike the WAIS-R in which the verbal subtests are untimed power measures, every MAB subtest incorporates elements of both power and speed: Examinees are allowed only seven minutes to work on each subtest. Including instructions, the Verbal and Performance portions of the MAB each take about 50 minutes to administer.

Technical Features

The first release of the MAB (Jackson, 1984a) was not standardized in the traditional manner in which scores are tied to the performance of large, representative samples stratified on such variables as sex, race, urban/rural residence, parental occupation, geographic region, and the like. Instead, the test developers pursued a strategy of calibrating MAB scores to the WAIS-R as an anchor test. To derive the linear calibrating formula, the WAIS-R and MAB were both administered, in counterbalanced fashion, to a sample consisting of university students ($n = 18$), senior high school students ($n = 74$), hospitalized psychiatric patients ($n = 58$), and probationers ($n = 10$). The subjects, 117 males and 43 females, ranged in age from 16 to 35. The correlation coefficients between MAB and WAIS-R IQs were found to be .82, .65, and .91, for Verbal, Performance, and Full Scale IQ, respectively. The norm tables reported in the *Manual* actually reflect a simple linear transformation from MAB raw scores to WAIS-R IQs for this initial sample of 160 subjects.

The *Manual* reports several studies of internal consistency and test-retest reliability; the results are generally quite impressive. For example, in one study of over 500 adolescents ranging in age from 16 to 20, the internal consistency reliability of Verbal, Performance, and Full Scale IQs was in the high .90s. In a test-retest study of 52 young psychiatric patients, the individual subtests showed reliabilities that ranged from .83 to .97 (median of .90) for the Verbal scale and from .87 to .94 (median of .91) for the Performance scale. These results compare quite favorably with the psychometric standards reported for the WAIS-R (Wechsler, 1981).

Factor analyses of the MAB offer strong support for the construct validity of this instrument (Lee, Wallbrown, & Blaha, 1990; Wallbrown, Carmin, & Barnett, 1988). In a factor analysis of scores for 3,121 male and female high school students, the *Manual* reports a general factor with moderate to high loadings for all subtests (ranging from .53 to .82). In a separate factor analysis of data for the standardization subjects, Lee, Wallbrown, and Blaha (1990) found two orthogonal factors after the first general factor. These two rotated factors are clearly identifiable as Verbal and Performance factors. In addition, other researchers have noted the extremely strong congruence between factor analyses of the WAIS-R (with Digit Span removed) and the MAB. In a large sample of inmates, Ahrens, Evans, and Barnett (1990) observed validity-confirming changes in MAB scores in relation to education level. Thus, there is good justification for the use of separate Verbal and Performance scales on this test.

In general, the validity of the MAB rests upon its very strong physical and empirical resemblance to its parent test, the WAIS-R. Correlational data between MAB and WAIS-R scores are crucial in this regard. For 145 persons administered the MAB and WAIS-R in counterbalanced fashion, correlations between subtests ranged from .44 (Spatial/Block Design) to .89 (Arithmetic and Vocabulary), with a median of .78. WAIS-R and MAB IQ correlations were very healthy, namely, .92 for Verbal IQ, .79 for Performance IQ, and .91 for Full Scale IQ (Jackson, 1984a). With only a few exceptions, correlations between MAB and WAIS-R scores exceed those between the WAIS and the WAIS-R.

Comment on the MAB

Jackson (1984a) exercised great care in the development of the MAB, continually refining it over a period of some 10 years prior to release. During this time, items were selected, revised, and deleted, according to stringent psychometric criteria regarding difficulty level, discriminatory power, and efficiency of distractor alternatives. Not surprisingly, the resulting instrument is a technical tour de force of psychometric excellence. Reliability indices are strong, factor analyses confirm the verbal/performance dichotomy, and subtest scores and overall IQs correlate exceptionally well with corresponding measures from the WAIS-R.

Nonetheless, several reviewers have raised cautions and concerns about the MAB that deserve mention. Krieshok and Harrington (1985) note that the *Manual* does not provide readability estimates for the instructions or for the items themselves. The *Manual* does state vaguely that the MAB "presupposes language skills necessary to read and understand written directions and to comprehend spoken directions." However, it does not recommend a minimum reading level for valid administration. This may lead the examiner to assume that anyone who meets the minimum age level of 16 can take the MAB, a patently unsafe presumption. In fact, Krieshok and Harrington (1985) subjected the MAB to a computerized readability analysis and concluded that some verbal items required a tenth-grade reading level. Because of the relatively high reading level required by parts of this test, it seems likely that an otherwise very bright student with a reading disability might score artificially low on the MAB.

The MAB shows great promise in research, career counseling, and personnel selection. In addition, this test could function as a screening instrument in clinical settings, so long as the examiner viewed low scores as a basis for follow-up testing with the WAIS-R. Examiners must keep in mind that the MAB is a group test and therefore carries with it the potential for misuse in individual cases. The MAB should not be used in isolation for diagnostic decisions or for placement into programs such as classes for the intellectually gifted.

SHIPLEY INSTITUTE OF LIVING SCALE (SILS)

The Shipley Institute of Living Scale (SILS) is also known as the Shipley-Hartford because of its inception in Hartford, Connecticut, decades ago (Shipley, 1940, 1983). The SILS was originally proposed as an **index of intellectual deterioration,** in an attempt to gauge the effects of dementia, brain damage, and other organic conditions. However, the test has been used primarily as a short screening test of intelligence, particularly within the mental health system of the Veterans Administration.

Background and Description

The SILS consists of two subtests, vocabulary and abstractions. The original intention of the test was to detect organic intellectual deterioration by contrasting performance on the vocabulary and abstractions sections. Vocabulary was thought to be relatively unaffected by organic deterioration, whereas it was believed that abstraction ability would show significant decline. A large discrepancy favoring vocabulary over abstractions therefore would appear to signify the presence of organic impairment. However, numerous studies and reviews concluded that the SILS performs poorly as an index of brain damage (e.g., Yates, 1954; Johnson, 1987) and the instrument is seldom used for this purpose.

The SILS consists of 40 multiple-choice vocabulary items and 20 abstract-thinking items. Each item is scored right or wrong. The abstract items count double, so the maximum score on each half of the test is 40 points. A composite score is also reported. The test is self-administered with a 10-minute limit for each of the two sections. Some users favor an untimed use of the test, and separate norms have been developed for this approach (Heinemann, Harper, Friedman, & Whitney, 1985). Few persons require more than 10 minutes per section; most examiners consider the SILS to be entirely a power measure. A microcomputer version of the test is also available. The computer administers and scores the test, and produces a narrative report and graphic depiction of scores.

The examinee's task on the vocabulary section is to select the synonym of a word from four alternatives. The 40 items resemble the following:

- SHIP   house   tree   fork   boat
- INANE   fat   timely   silly   dry

The vocabulary score is the number correct plus one point for every four items omitted. Adding points for items omitted provides a correction for the refusal to guess. As a result of this correction factor, the minimum score is about 10 out of the 40 points.

The intention of the abstractions items was that they should require the examinee to infer a principle common to a given series of components and then to demonstrate this understanding of the principle by finishing the series. Each item is a series of letters or numbers followed by blanks to indicate the number of characters in the answer. The 20 items resemble the following:

- A B D G K ____
- bog hob   mars tram   2 6 8 ____ ____ ____
- 135 341 52 12 ____

The examinee must complete each series and place the appropriate answer in the blanks. (Answers to the preceding items are P, 962, and 3). Of course, to derive the correct answer the examinee must infer the rule that governs the progression of stimuli in each item and then use that rule to determine the continuation. (In item 1 the distance between letters increases arithmetically; in item 2 the pairs are mirror images of each other, except for last and first letters which increment by one—g to h, s to t; in item 3, each group of numbers sums to one less than the previous group—9, 8, 7, . . .).

Technical Features

Zachary (1986) has published norms for the SILS based on 290 mixed psychiatric patients who had also taken the WAIS. The sample contains approximately equal numbers of men and women. This norm sample is young: Most are between the ages of 16 and 54, with a median age of 30. Based on this sample, the manual contains tables of age-corrected T-scores (mean of 50, SD of 10) for vocabulary and abstractions. Against the better advice of numerous prior researchers, the author of the SILS *Manual* also introduced the Abstraction Quotient (AQ), a new impairment index based on the difference between Vocabulary and Abstraction scores. The AQ is obtained by comparing the predicted abstractions score to the obtained abstractions score. The predicted score is derived from a regression equation that uses vocabulary score, age, and educational level. The AQ is an improvement over previous impairment indices in that naturally occurring age decrements are accounted for in its computation. Persons with schizophrenia and other individuals with diminished intellectual efficiency tend to obtain low AQs. Nonetheless, there are nonpathological causes of a low AQ (e.g., a distaste for abstract concepts) and the utility of this index is therefore open to question. Mason, Lemmon, Wayne, and Schmidt (1991) have attempted to revive the AQ approach to the use of the Shipley by publishing regression equations for computing Abstraction Quotients that use age, sex, and social class as moderating variables. However, they do not provide any evidence for the validity of the AQ as an index of brain impairment.

The reliability of the SILS is marginal. Typical internal consistency measures (odd-even correlations) are .87 (vocabulary), .89 (abstractions), and .92 (total score). However, as noted by the *Standards for Educational and Psychological Testing* (AERA, APA, & NCME, 1985), split-half coefficients of the odd-even variety produce inflated reliability estimates for highly speeded tests. To the extent that scores on the SILS are based upon speed instead of power, these reliabilities will be artificially high. Test-retest reliabilities are probably more appropriate for the SILS. These reliabilities vary considerably in the literature, but approach .80 for the total score in larger and more heterogeneous samples (Johnson, 1987).

Insofar as the SILS is used primarily as a screening test of intelligence, the validity of this instrument is strongly linked to its ability to predict Full Scale IQ from individual tests such as the WAIS or WAIS-R. As reviewed by Johnson (1987), literally dozens of correlational studies have investigated the accuracy of the SILS as a predictor of Wechsler IQ (e.g., Zachary, Crumpton, & Spiegel, 1985). Correlations between the SILS and the Wechsler-Bellevue or WAIS range from .65 to .90 with a median of .76 (Johnson, 1987). Based on these studies, Johnson (1987) reports that the 95 percent confidence interval for SILS-estimated IQ is about ±11 IQ points. For example, a Shipley total score of 60 for a 40-year-old man converts to an estimated WAIS-R IQ of 102; in 95 percent of such cases the examinee's actual WAIS-R IQ will fall in the range of 91 to 113 (Zachary, 1986).

Comment on the SILS

The venerable SILS is a reasonably good measure of general intelligence that has found widespread use in research. In addition, the instrument continues to be quite popular as a screening test for general intelligence and possible intellectual inefficiency (Bowers & Pantle, 1998). While the SILS is useful for very broadband intellectual screening, it should not be used to make more fine-grained discriminations. Responsible clinicians will use an individual intelligence test (e.g., K-BIT, WAIS-III) when a more precise individual assessment is needed.

Even though it is a passable screening test, the SILS possesses a number of significant limitations:

1. The SILS is inappropriate for low-IQ persons or those with significant language disabilities.
2. The test has a low ceiling, especially on the abstractions section, and does not spread high-IQ examinees.

3. The SILS has a band of error approaching 11 IQ points, which may be too excessive for many applications.

A MULTILEVEL BATTERY: THE COGNITIVE ABILITIES TEST (CogAT)

One important function of psychological testing is to assess students' abilities that are prerequisite to traditional classroom-based learning. In designing tests for this purpose, the psychometrician must contend with the obvious and nettlesome problem that school-aged children differ hugely in their intellectual abilities. For example, a test appropriate for a sixth grader will be much too easy for a tenth grader, yet impossibly difficult for a third grader.

The answer to this dilemma is a multilevel battery, a series of overlapping tests. In a multilevel battery, each group test is designed for a specific age or grade level, but adjacent tests possess some common content. Because of the overlapping content with adjacent age or grade levels, each test possesses a suitably low floor and high ceiling for proper assessment of students at both extremes of ability. In addition, multilevel batteries usually provide a much desired continuity in the abilities measured. Furthermore, multilevel batteries generally employ highly comparable normative samples at the successive levels. For all of these reasons, multilevel batteries are considered ideal for gauging student readiness for school learning. Virtually every school system in the United States uses at least one nationally normed multilevel battery.

The Cognitive Abilities Test (CogAT) is one of the best school-based test batteries in current use (Thorndike & Hagen, 1993). A recent revision of the test is the CogAT Multilevel Edition, Form 5, released in 1993. We discuss this instrument in some detail and then provide a brief summary of competing tests.

Background and Description

The CogAT evolved from the Lorge-Thorndike Intelligence Tests, one of the first group tests of intelligence intended for widespread use within school systems. The CogAT is primarily a measure of scholastic ability, but also incorporates a nonverbal reasoning battery with items that bear no direct relation to formal school instruction. The two primary batteries, suitable for students in kindergarten through third grade, are briefly discussed at the end of this section. Here we review the multilevel edition intended for students in third through twelfth grade.

The nine subtests of the multilevel CogAT are grouped into three batteries as follows:

Verbal Battery	**Quantitative Battery**	**Nonverbal Battery**
Verbal Reasoning	Quantitative Relations	Figure Classification
Sentence Completion	Number Series	Figure Analogies
Verbal Analogies	Equation Building	Figure Analysis

For each CogAT subtest, items are ordered by difficulty level in a single test booklet. However, entry and exit points differ for each of eight overlapping levels (A through H). In this manner, grade-appropriate items are provided for all examinees. All subtests except one use a multiple-choice format. The exception is Figure Analysis, in which the examinee responds yes or no to a series of alternatives.

The subtests are strictly timed, with limits that vary from eight to twelve minutes. Each of the three batteries can be administered in less than an hour. However, the manual recommends three successive testing days for younger children. For older children, two batteries should be administered the first day, with a single testing period the next.

Many subtests of the CogAT bear a striking resemblance to portions of the Stanford-Binet: Fourth Edition. For example, both tests include paper-folding items. Common parentage is the explanation: Both tests were developed by Robert Thorndike and Elizabeth Hagen; both tests were published by Riverside Publishing Company. We see once again the hybrid character of modern intelligence tests, in which new tests incorporate the best features of their predecessors.

Raw scores for each battery can be transformed into an age-based normalized standard score with mean of 100 and standard deviation of 16. In addition, percentile ranks and stanines for age groups and grade level are also available. Interpolation was used to determine fall, winter, and spring grade-level norms.

Technical Features

The CogAT was co-normed (standardized concurrently) with three achievement tests, the Iowa Tests of Basic Skills, the Tests of Achievement and Proficiency, and the Iowa Tests of Educational Development. Concurrent standardization with achievement measures is a common and desirable practice in the norming of multilevel intelligence tests. The particular virtue of joint norming is that the expected correspondence between intelligence and achievement scores is determined with great precision. As a consequence, examiners can more accurately identify underachieving students in need of remediation or further assessment for potential learning disability.

The reliability of the CogAT is exceptionally good. In previous editions, the Kuder-Richardson-20 reliability estimates for the multilevel batteries averaged .94 (Verbal), .92 (Quantitative), and .93 (Nonverbal) across all grade levels. The six-month test-retest reliabilities for alternate forms ranged from .85 to .93 (Verbal), .78 to .88 (Quantitative), and .81 to .89 (Nonverbal).

The *Manual* provides a wealth of information on content, criterion-related, and construct validity of the CogAT; we summarize only the most pertinent points here. Correlations between the CogAT and achievement batteries are substantial. For example, the CogAT verbal battery correlates in the .70s to .80s with achievement subtests from the Iowa Tests of Basic Skills and the Tests of Achievement and Proficiency.

The CogAT batteries predict school grades reasonably well. Correlations range from the .30s to the .60s, depending upon grade level, sex, and ethnic group. There does not appear to be a clear trend as to which battery is best at predicting grade point average. Correlations between the CogAT and individual intelligence tests are also substantial, typically ranging from .65 to .75. These findings speak well for the construct validity of the CogAT, insofar as the Stanford-Binet is widely recognized as an excellent measure of individual intelligence.

Comment on the CogAT

The CogAT multilevel edition is a highly reliable group test of intelligence that is carefully normed for students in grades three through twelve. The concurrent standardization with three achievement tests is a welcome and practical feature. In support of CogAT validity, correlations with grades, achievement, and other measures of intelligence are quite robust. Recently a German version of the CogAT has been produced (Perleth, Hofmann, Schauer, & Wernberger, 1994).

Ansorge (1985) has questioned whether all three batteries are really necessary. He points out that correlations among the Verbal, Quantitative, and Nonverbal batteries are substantial. The median values across all grades are as follows:

Verbal and Quantitative	.78
Nonverbal and Quantitative	.78
Verbal and Nonverbal	.72

Since the Quantitative battery offers little uniqueness, from a purely psychometric point of view there is no justification for including it. Nonetheless, the test authors recommend use of all batteries in hopes that differences in performance will assist teachers in remedial planning. However, the test authors do not make a strong case for doing this.

A recent study by Stone (1994) provides a notable justification for using the CogAT as a basis for student evaluation. He found that CogAT scores for 403 third graders provided an unbiased prediction of student achievement that was more accurate than teacher ratings. In particular, teacher ratings

showed bias against caucasian and Asian-American students by underpredicting their achievement scores.

CULTURE FAIR INTELLIGENCE TEST (CFIT)

The Culture Fair Intelligence Test (Cattell, 1940; IPAT, 1973) is a nonverbal measure of fluid intelligence first conceived in the 1920s by the prominent measurement psychologist, Raymond B. Cattell. The goal of the CFIT is to measure fluid intelligence—analytical and reasoning ability in abstract and novel situations—in a manner that is as "free" of cultural bias as possible. This test was originally called the Culture Free Intelligence Test. The name was changed when it became evident that cultural influences cannot be completely extirpated from tests of intelligence.

Background and Description

The CFIT has undergone several revisions, emerging in its current form in 1961. The test consists of three versions: Scale 1 is for use with mentally defective adults and children ages four to eight; Scale 2 is for adults in the average range of intelligence and children ages eight to thirteen; Scale 3 is for high-ability adults and for high school and college students. Scale 1 involves considerable interaction between tester and examinee—four of the subtests must be administered individually. Thus, in some respects Scale 1 is more of an individual intelligence test than a group test. We discuss only Scales 2 and 3 here, because they are truly group tests of intelligence. These two tests differ mainly in difficulty level.

Two equivalent forms, called Form A and Form B, are available for each scale. The test developers recommend administering both forms to each subject to obtain what is called the full test. Each form by itself is referred to as a short test. In spite of the recommendation to use both forms as a combined test, it is very common for CFIT users to rely upon a single, brief form for purposes of screening.

Each form consists of four subtests: Series, Classification, Matrices, and Conditions. Sample items are shown in Figure 6.9. Of course, each subtest is preceded by several practice items. The entire test is neatly packaged in an eight-page booklet.

The CFIT is a highly speeded test. Each form of Scales 2 and 3 takes about 30 minutes to administer, but only 12.5 minutes is devoted to actual test taking. Results can therefore be misleading for persons who place no premium on speed of performance in problem solving. Fortunately, Scale 2 can

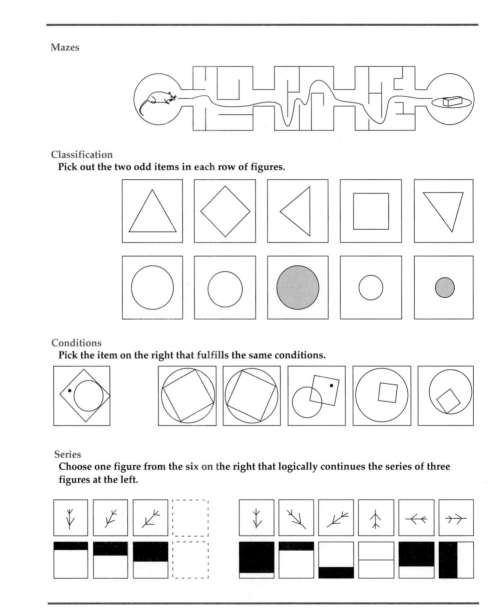

Mazes

Classification
Pick out the two odd items in each row of figures.

Conditions
Pick the item on the right that fulfills the same conditions.

Series
Choose one figure from the six on the right that logically continues the series of three figures at the left.

FIGURE 6.9 **Sample Items from the Culture Fair Intelligence Test**
Source: Copyright © by the Institute for Personality and Ability Testing, Inc. Reproduced by permission.

be used as an untimed power test. However, the norms for this manner of administration are limited (IPAT, 1973).

Technical Features

Standardization samples for Scales 2 and 3 were respectably large, but not described in sufficient detail to determine the extent to which they mirror the general population. The standardization samples were characterized as follows:

> The standardization group for Scale 2 consists of 4,328 males and females sampled from varied regions of the United States and Britain. Scale 3 norms are based on 3,140 cases, consisting of American high school students equally divided among freshmen, sophomores, juniors, and seniors, and young adults in a stratified job sample (IPAT, 1973).

Raw scores are converted to normalized standard score IQs with mean of 100 and standard deviation of 16.

Test-retest, alternate forms, and internal consistency reliabilities are generally in the .70s for individual forms of Scales 2 and 3. The reliabilities of the full test are higher, generally in the mid-.80s. These results are based on dozens of studies with thousands of subjects and indicate a respectable degree of reliability for such a short instrument (IPAT, 1973).

The validity of the CFIT as a measure of general intelligence is established beyond any reasonable skepticism. CFIT scores correlate in the mid-.80s with the general factor of intelligence and show consistently robust relationships—largely in the .70s and .80s—with other mainstream measures of intelligence (WAIS, WISC, Raven Progressive Matrices, Stanford-Binet, Otis, and General Aptitude Test Battery; see IPAT, 1973, p. 11). There is no doubt that the CFIT is a well-designed, useful, and valid test of intelligence.

But is the CFIT a **culture-fair test,** as its title proclaims? One professed goal of this instrument was to "minimize irrelevant influences of cultural learning and social climate" and thereby produce a "cleaner separation of natural ability from specific learning" (IPAT, 1973). Unfortunately, the available evidence indicates that the CFIT is no more successful than traditional measures in the pursuit of a culturally fair method for measuring intelligence (Koch, 1984). For example, Willard (1968) found that 83 culturally disadvantaged African-American children scored about the same on the Stanford-Binet ($M = 68.1$) as on the CFIT ($M = 70.0$). Moreover, 14 of the children hit the CFIT "floor" and received the lowest possible CFIT IQ score of 57, whereas Stanford-Binet IQs scores were dispersed in a pattern more like a bell-shaped curve.

Comment on the CFIT

The CFIT is an excellent brief, nonverbal measure of general intelligence. Even when Form A and Form B are both used to obtain what is referred to as the full test, the CFIT can be administered to large groups in less than an hour. An important caution to test users is that the laudable goal of producing a culture-fair test has not been accomplished by the CFIT. Moreover, the goal itself may be chimerical:

> . . . cultures differ with respect to the importance they place on competition with peers in performing tasks or solving problems, on speed or quality of performance, and on a variety of other test-related behaviors. Some cultures emphasize concrete rather than abstract problem solving, often to the extent that a problem has no meaning except in a concrete setting. The very notion of taking some artificially contrived test is nonsensical in such situations (Koch, 1984).

It is doubtful that a truly culture-fair test is even possible. In future editions, the CFIT developers would be well advised to rename their test so that unsophisticated users do not invest this instrument with imaginary properties.

Even though the CFIT is a worthy test, it is badly in need of revision and renorming. The test is rather old-fashioned in appearance. Some of the test item drawings are so small that only persons with perfect vision can infer the figural relations depicted in the item components. Previous standardization samples have been poorly specified and would appear to be convenience samples rather than carefully selected stratified representations of the population at large.

RAVEN'S PROGRESSIVE MATRICES (RPM)

First introduced in 1938, Raven's Progressive Matrices (RPM) is a nonverbal test of inductive reasoning based on figural stimuli (Raven, Court, & Raven, 1986, 1992). This test has been very popular in basic research and is also used in some institutional settings for purposes of intellectual screening.

Background and Description

RPM was originally designed as a measure of Spearman's *g* factor (Raven, 1938). For this reason, Raven chose a special format for the test that presumably required the exercise of *g*. The reader is reminded that Spearman defined *g* as the "eduction of correlates." The term *eduction* refers to the process of figuring out relationships based on the perceived fundamental similarities between stimuli. In particular, to correctly answer items on the RPM, examinees must identify a recurring pattern or relationship between figural stimuli organized in a 3 × 3 matrix. The items are arranged in order of increasing difficulty, hence the reference to progressive matrices.

Raven's test is actually a series of three different instruments. Much of the confusion about validity, factorial structure, and the like, stems from the unexamined assumption that all three forms should produce equivalent findings. The reader is encouraged to abandon this unwarranted hypothesis. Even though the three forms of the RPM resemble one another, there may be subtle differences in the problem-solving strategies required by each.

The Coloured Progressive Matrices is a 36-item test designed for children from 5 to 11 years of age. Raven incorporated colors into this version of the test to help hold the attention of the young children. The Standard Progressive Matrices is normed for examinees from 6 years and up, although most of the items are so difficult that the test is best suited for adults. This test consists of 60 items grouped into 5 sets of 12 progressions. The Advanced Progressive Matrices is similar to the Standard version, but has a higher ceiling. The Advanced version consists of 12 problems in Set I and 36 problems in Set II. This form is especially suitable for persons of superior intellect.

Technical Features

Large sample U.S. norms for the Coloured and Standard Progressive Matrices are reported in Raven and Summers (1986). Separate norms for Mexican-American and African-American children are included. Although there was no attempt to use a stratified random-sampling procedure, the selection of school districts was so widely varied that the American norms for children appear to be reasonably sound. Sattler (1988) summarizes the relevant norms for all versions of the RPM. Recently, Raven, Court, and Raven (1992) produced new norms for the Standard Progressive Matrices, but Gudjonsson (1995) has raised a concern that these data are compromised because the testing was not monitored.

For the Coloured Progressive Matrices, split-half reliabilities in the range of .65 to .94 are reported, with younger children producing lower values (Raven, Court, & Raven, 1986). For the Standard Progressive Matrices, a typical split-half reliability is .86, although lower values are found with younger subjects (Raven, Court, & Raven, 1983). Test-retest reliabilities for all three forms vary considerably from one sample to the next (Burke, 1958; Raven, 1965; Raven et al., 1986). For normal adults in their late teens or older, reliability coefficients of .80 to .93 are typical. However, for preteen children, reliability coefficients as low as .71 are reported. Thus, for younger subjects, RPM may not possess sufficient reliability to warrant its use for individual decision making.

Factor-analytic studies of the RPM provide little, if any, support for the original intention of the test to measure a unitary construct (Spearman's *g* factor). Several studies of the Coloured Progressive Matrices reveal three orthogonal factors (Carlson & Jensen, 1980; Wiedl & Carlson, 1976). Factor I consists largely of very difficult items and might be termed closure and abstract reasoning by analogy. Factor II is labeled pattern completion through identity and closure. Factor III consists of the easiest items and is defined as simple pattern completion (Carlson & Jensen, 1980). In sum, the very easy and the very hard items on the Coloured Progressive Matrices appear to tap different intellectual processes.

The Advanced Progressive Matrices breaks down into two factors which may have separate predictive validities (Dillon, Pohlmann, & Lohman, 1981). The first factor is composed of items in which the solution is obtained by adding or subtracting patterns (Figure 6.10a). Individuals performing well on these items may excel in rapid decision making and in situations where part-whole relationships must be perceived. The second factor is composed of items in which the solution is based on the ability to perceive the progression of a pattern (Figure 6.10b). Persons who perform well on these items may possess good mechanical ability as well as good skills for estimating projected movement and performing mental rotations. However, the skills represented by each factor are conjectural at this point and in need of independent confirmation.

A huge body of published research bears on the validity of the RPM. The early data is well summarized by Burke (1958) while more recent findings are compiled in the current RPM manuals (Raven & Summers, 1986; Raven, Court, & Raven, 1983, 1986, 1992). In general, validity coefficients with achievement tests range from the .30s to the .60s. As might be expected, these values are somewhat lower than found with more traditional (verbally loaded) intelligence tests. Validity coefficients with other intelligence tests range from the .50s to the .80s. Also, as might be expected, the correlations tend to be higher with performance than with verbal tests. In a massive study involving thousands of schoolchildren, Saccuzzo and Johnson (1995) concluded that the Standard Progressive Matrices and the WISC-R showed approximately equal predictive validity and no evidence of differential validity across eight different ethnic groups.

Johnson, Saccuzzo, and Guertin (1994) accomplished the (nearly) impossible by developing a

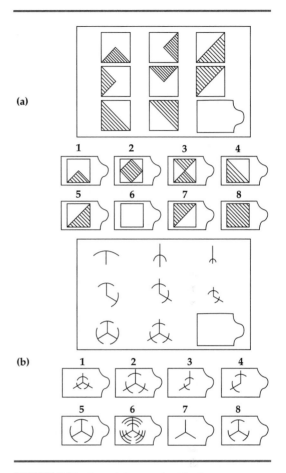

FIGURE 6.10   Raven's Progressive Matrices: Typical Items

truly comparable alternate form of the 60-item Standard Progressive Matrices. For each of the original 60 items, they developed a similar item that was comparable in terms of difficulty level and underlying cognitive strategy required for solution. An alternate-form reliability analysis on a diverse group of 449 children who took both tests in counterbalanced order revealed a reliability coefficient of .90, which is on a par with immediate test-retest data. In this same sample, the distribution of scores showed no differences for standard deviation, skewness, and rank order of item difficulties. The mean number correct was 36.1 on the SPM and 35.5 on the new test. In sum, the two versions of the test are nearly identical in overall psychometric characteristics and also in difficulty level. The new test promises to serve an important role in research studies that require retesting.

Comment on the RPM

Even though the RPM has not lived up to its original intentions of measuring Spearman's *g* factor, the test is nonetheless a useful index of nonverbal, figural reasoning. The recent updating of norms was a much-welcomed development for this well-known test, in that many American users were leary of the outdated and limited British norms. Nonetheless, adult norms for the Standard and Advanced Progressive Matrices are still quite limited.

The RPM is particularly valuable for the supplemental testing of children and adults with hearing, language, or physical disabilities. Often, these examinees are difficult to assess with traditional measures that require auditory attention, verbal expression, or physical manipulation. In contrast, the RPM can be explained through pantomime, if necessary. Moreover, the only output required of the examinee is a pencil mark or gesture denoting the chosen alternative. For these reasons, the RPM is ideally suited for testing persons with limited command of the English language. In fact, the RPM is about as culturally reduced as possible: The test protocol does not contain a single word in any language. Mills & Tissot (1995) found that the Advanced Progressive Matrices identified a higher proportion of minority children as gifted than did a more traditional measure of academic aptitude (The School and College Ability Test).

A final note of caution: Some very bright and high-functioning persons perform abysmally on the RPM. Gregory and Gernert (1990) tested nearly 100 university faculty members with a variant of the RPM. One participant, an accomplished researcher who had risen to a vice presidential level, hadn't the slightest clue how to solve the RPM problems, and scored at a chance level. Some persons of above-average intelligence simply do not perform well on figural-reasoning tasks. Examiners would be well advised to question the validity of a

low score obtained by an otherwise accomplished individual.

PERSPECTIVE ON CULTURE-FAIR TESTS

Cattell's Culture-Fair Intelligence Test (CFIT) and Raven's Progressive Matrices (RPM) are often cited as examples of culture-fair tests, a concept with a long and confused history. We will attempt to clarify terms and issues here.

The first point to make is that intelligence tests are merely samples of what people know and can do. We must not reify intelligence and overvalue intelligence tests. Tests are never samples of innate intelligence or culture-free knowledge. All knowledge is based in culture and acquired over time. As Scarr (1994) notes, there is no such thing as a culture-free test.

But what about a culture-fair test, one that poses problems that are equally familiar (or unfamiliar) to all cultures? This would appear to be a more realistic possibility than a culture-free test, but even here the skeptic can raise objections. Consider the question of what a test *means*, which differs from culture to culture. In theory, a test of matrices would appear to be equally fair to most cultures. But in practice, issues of equity arise. Persons reared in Western cultures are trained in linear, convergent thinking. We know that the purpose of a test is to find the single, best answer and to do so quickly. We examine the 3 × 3 matrix from left to right and top to bottom, looking for the logical principles invoked in the succession of forms. Can we assume that persons reared in Nepal or New Guinea or even the remote, rural stretches of Idaho will do the same? The test may mean something different to them. Perhaps they will approach it as a measure of aesthetic progression rather than logical succession. Perhaps they will regard it as so much silliness not worthy of intense intellectual effort. To assume that a test is equally fair to all cultural groups merely because the stimuli are equally familiar (or unfamiliar) is inappropriate. We can talk about degrees of cultural fairness (or unfairness), but the notion that any test is absolutely culture-fair surely is mistaken.

SUMMARY

1. Group intelligence tests differ from individual tests in five ways: multiple-choice versus open-ended format, objective machine scoring versus examiner scoring, group versus individualized administration, applications in screening versus remedial planning, and huge versus merely large standardization samples.

2. The obvious advantage of group testing is that large numbers of examinees can be tested quickly and efficiently. The disadvantage of group testing is that examinees may score far below their true ability because of motivational problems or difficulty following directions.

3. The Multidimensional Aptitude Battery (MAB) is a multiple-choice group intelligence test designed to be a paper-and-pencil equivalent of the WAIS-R. MAB and WAIS-R IQs correlate .82, .65, and .91, for Verbal, Performance, and Full Scale IQ, respectively. Test-retest reliability of the instrument is excellent, and factor analyses support its construct validity.

4. The Shipley Institute of Living Scale (SILS) was originally proposed as an index of intellectual deterioration. The SILS consists of a 40-item multiple choice vocabulary section and a 20-item fill-in-the-blank abstractions section. The test has not functioned well as an index of organicity, but does meet a need as a brief screening device for general intelligence.

5. The Cognitive Abilities Test (CogAT) is representative of the many multilevel, school-based test batteries in current use. The nine subtests of the CogAT include a Verbal Battery, a Quantitative Battery, and a Nonverbal Battery. The test is co-normed with two achievement tests, the Iowa Test of Basic Skills and the Tests of Achievement and Proficiency.

6. The Culture Fair Intelligence Test (CFIT) is a nonverbal measure of fluid intelligence which attempts to minimize cultural bias. The CFIT is suited for ages four through adult and comes in three versions, each consisting of two equivalent forms. Each form consists of four subtests: Series, Classification, Matrices, and Conditions.

7. The reliability of the CFIT is superb and scores correlate very strongly with other respected tests of intelligence. The CFIT is a good test of intelligence, but is probably as culturally bound as most traditional tests. The test needs revision and restandardization.

8. Originally designed as a measure of Spearman's *g* factor, Raven's Progressive Matrices (RPM) is a nonverbal test of inductive reasoning based on figural stimuli which comes in three different versions: Coloured Progressive Matrices (ages 5 to 11), Standard Progressive Matrices (ages 6 through adult), and Advanced Progressive Matrices.

9. Although the RPM is a reliable and valid index of intelligence, there is little support for the test as a unitary measure of the *g* factor. Factor analyses usually reveal two or three factors, including reasoning by analogy and simple pattern completion. The RPM is useful for the supplemental testing of persons with hearing, language, or physical disabilities.

10. Culture-fair testing is an idealized abstraction that is never achieved in the real world. Even the meaning of a test may differ among cultural groups, which will affect the validity of comparisons. Some tests are more culture-fair than others, but it is not possible for any test to be equally fair to all cultural groups.

KEY TERMS AND CONCEPTS

index of intellectual deterioration   p. 207

culture-fair test   p. 213

CHAPTER 7

Test Bias and Testing Special Populations

The individual and group intelligence tests reviewed in previous chapters are suitable for persons with normal or near-normal capacities in speech, hearing, vision, movement, and general intellectual ability. However, not every examinee falls within the ordinary spectrum of physical and mental abilities. By reason of youthful age, physical disability, diminished intellect, or language disadvantage, a large proportion of the population falls outside the reach of traditional tests and procedures. According to the U.S. Census Bureau, about 25 million Americans (one in ten) have a *severe* disability that prevents them from performing one or more activities or roles (www.census.gov, 1998). This estimate does not include persons living in institutions. In these special cases, novel tests are needed for valid assessment. In Topic 7A, Testing Special Populations, we discuss instruments designed for exceptional and difficult consultations, such as persons with sensory/motor impairment, recent immigrants from non-English-speaking countries, and individuals with significant intellectual deficiencies. In Topic 7B, Test Bias and Other Controversies, we continue a circumspect theme by raising a number of concerns about the use and meaning of intelligence test scores.

ORIGINS OF TESTS FOR SPECIAL POPULATIONS

Beginning in the 1950s, a renewed commitment to the needs and rights of physically and mentally disabled persons arose in the United States (Maloney & Ward, 1979; Patton, Payne, & Beirne-Smith, 1986). Societal attitudes toward those with special needs shifted from outright disdain to a more supportive stance that favored new programs and initiatives on behalf of the disabled. Progress has been slow, but we are no longer surprised to see bathroom facilities with wheelchair access for persons with physical disability, large-print books for persons with visual impairments, or closed-captioned television programs for persons with hearing disabilities. Furthermore, the special needs of mentally retarded citizens are increasingly served by small community care facilities instead of massive, impersonal institutions.

In the early 1970s, the renewed concern for the needs of disabled persons was translated into federal legislation. In 1973, **Public Law 93-112** was passed, serving as a "Bill of Rights" for disabled individuals. This legislation outlawed discrimination on the basis of disability. Two years later, the landmark Education for All Handicapped Children Act (Public Law 94–142) was enacted. This legislation mandated that disabled schoolchildren receive appropriate assessment and educational opportunities. In particular, psychologists were directed to assess children in all areas of possible disability—mental, behavioral, and physical—and to use instruments validated for those express purposes.

In this topic, we examine tests that can be used for the assessment of persons with sensory, motor, or mental disabilities. However, before discussing specific tests, we review certain distinctions between the types of tests that are available for exceptional assessments. The reader also will appreciate a brief summary of the legal mandates that have shaped assessment practices with disabled individuals.

Approaches to Assessment of Special Populations

Special tests were first devised in the early 1900s to test non-English-speaking immigrants, the deaf, and persons with speech defects (DuBois, 1970). These early special instruments were largely performance or nonlanguage tests that could be administered by pantomime. The examinee manipulated objects or used paper and pencil to complete easy-to-understand tasks such as tracing a path through a maze.

Special instruments also have been devised for nonreading examinees who possess some ability to understand spoken English. These nonreading tests are intended for young children and other illiterate persons who nonetheless can comprehend and follow oral instructions. Many nonreading tests involve the manipulation of objects. However, a nonreading test also can assess language comprehension skills by using a picture vocabulary format: The examiner says a word and the examinee points to the one picture from an array of pictures that depicts the word. Several picture vocabulary tests are discussed subsequently.

A motor-reduced test requires the barest minimum of motor output for a response. In a motor-reduced test, the examinee merely points or gestures to the correct answer from among several alternatives. For example, an examinee with cerebral palsy might respond to picture vocabulary items by placing his hand over the chosen alternative. Some nonreading tests—particularly those that use a picture vocabulary format—are also motor-reduced tests.

Finally, we should mention that several important assessment devices are not really tests at all. A developmental schedule is a standardized device for observing and evaluating the behavioral development of infants and young children. These instruments usually inquire into major developmental milestones such as sitting alone, standing unaided, and so forth. It is characteristic of such tools that the "examinee" doesn't take a test per se or, for that matter, do anything out of the ordinary. A developmental schedule is really just a structured form of observation. Likewise, a behavior scale is an instrument for determining the profile of be-havioral skills (and perhaps excesses) exhibited by a child or retarded adult. Behavior scales are usu-ally filled out by a knowledgeable adult (parent, teacher, or psychologist).

THE LEGAL MANDATE FOR ASSESSING PERSONS WITH DISABILITIES

Many practices in the assessment of persons with disabilities are the direct result of legislation and court cases. As background to the discussion of specific tests and procedures, we offer a quick re-view of public laws relevant to the assessment of persons with disabilities. The coverage is purpose-fully brief. Readers can find lengthier discussions in Bruyere and O'Keeffe (1994), Salvia and Ys-seldyke (1991), and Sattler (1988).

Public Law 94-142

In 1975, the U.S. Congress passed a compulsory special education law, **Public Law 94-142,** known as the Education for All Handicapped Children Act.[1] According to Ballard and Zettel (1977) this law was designed to meet four major goals:

1. To insure that special education services are available to children who need them.
2. To guarantee that decisions about services to disabled students are fair and appropriate.
3. To establish specific management and auditing requirements for special education.
4. To provide federal funds to help the states edu-cate disabled students.

Many practices in the assessment of disabled persons stem directly from the provisions of Pub-lic Law 94-142. For example, the law specifies that each disabled student must receive an individual-ized education plan (IEP) based on a comprehen-sive assessment by a multidisciplinary team. The

IEP must outline long-term and short-term objec-tives and specify plans for achieving them. In ad-dition, the IEP must indicate how progress toward these objectives will be evaluated. The parents are intimately involved in this process and must ap-prove the particulars of the IEP.

Pertinent to testing practices, PL 94-142 includes a number of provisions designed to in-sure that assessment procedures and activities are fair, equitable, and nondiscriminatory. Salvia and Ysseldyke (1988) summarize these provisions as follows:

1. Tests are to be selected and administered in such a way as to be racially and culturally nondis-criminatory.
2. To the extent feasible, students are to be as-sessed in their native language or primary mode of communication.
3. Test must have been validated for the specific purpose for which they are used.
4. Tests must be administered by trained personnel in conformance with the instructions provided by the test producer.
5. Tests used with students must include those de-signed to provide information about specific ed-ucational needs, and not just a general intelligence quotient.
6. Decisions about students are to be based on more than performance on a single test.
7. Evaluations are to be made by a multidiscipli-nary team that includes at least one teacher or other specialist with knowledge in the area of suspected disability.
8. Children must be assessed in all areas related to a specific disability, including—where ap-propriate—health, vision, hearing, social and emotional status, general intelligence, academic performance, communicative skills, and motor skills.

PL 94-142 also contains a provision that dis-abled students should be placed in the least restric-tive environment—one that allows the maximum possible opportunity to interact with nonimpaired students. Separate schooling is to occur only when the nature or the severity of the disability is such

---

1. Each congressional law receives two numbers, one referring to the particular Congress that passed it, the other referring to the law itself. Thus, Public Law 94-142 is the 142nd law passed by the 94th Congress.

that instructional goals cannot be achieved in the regular classroom. Finally, the law contains a due process clause that guarantees an impartial hearing to resolve conflicts between the parents of disabled children and the school system.

In general, the provisions of PL 94-142 have provided strong impetus to the development of specialized tests that are designed, normed, and validated for children with specific disabilities. For example, in the assessment of a child with visual impairment, the provisions of PL 94-142 virtually dictate that the examiner must use a well-normed test devised just for this population rather than relying upon traditional instruments.

Public Law 99-457

In 1986, Congress passed several amendments to the Education for All Handicapped Children Act, expanding the provisions of PL 94–142 to include disabled preschool children. **Public Law 99-457** requires states to provide free appropriate public education to disabled children ages 3 through 5. The law also mandates financial grants to states that offer interdisciplinary educational services to disabled infants, toddlers, and their families, thus establishing a huge incentive for states to serve children with disabilities from birth through age 2. Public Law 99–457 also provides a major impetus to the development and validation of infant tests and developmental schedules. After all, the early and accurate identification of at-risk children would appear to be the crucial first step in effective interdisciplinary intervention.

Americans with Disabilities Act

The 1990 **Americans with Disabilities Act** (ADA) forbids discrimination against qualified individuals with disabilities in both the public sector (e.g., government agencies and entities receiving federal grants) and the private sector (e.g., corporations and other for-profit employers). An important provision of the Act in regard to psychological testing is that agencies must make reasonable testing accommodations for persons with disabilities. The relevant accommodations include changes in the testing medium, the time limits, and even (rarely) the test content. An example of an appropriate accommodation in the testing medium is the audiotaped presentation of test items for visually impaired persons. On the other hand, changing a test from a printed version into a sign language version for hearing-impaired persons would be considered translation into another language, not a simple change of medium.

In most testing accommodations mandated by the ADA, it is necessary to change the time limits, usually by providing extra time. This raises problems of test interpretation, especially when a strict time limit is essential to the validity of a test. For example, Willingham, Ragosta, Bennett, and others (1988) found that extended time limits on the SAT significantly reduced the validity of the test as a predictor of first-year college grades. This was especially true for examinees with learning disabilities, whose freshman grades were subsequently overpredicted by their SAT scores. Thus, although it seems fair to provide extra time on a test when the testing medium has been changed (e.g., audiotaped questions replacing the printed versions), from a psychometric standpoint, the challenge is to determine *how much* extra time should be provided so that the modified test is comparable to the original version. Nester (1994) and Phillips (1994) provide thoughtful perspectives on the range of reasonable accommodations required by the ADA.

The implications of ADA with respect to personality testing are still unclear, but could be substantial. One provision of ADA is that medical tests may not be administered prior to an offer of employment. If personality tests are construed as "medical" in nature, this could sharply curtail the use of these tests in any employment-related testing of persons with disabilities (Klimoski & Palmer, 1994). As of this writing, the interpretation of ADA is still being shaped by legal challenges and administrative guidelines.

Now that we have summarized the legal background to the assessment of persons with special needs, we turn to a review of typical instruments used for the testing of individuals with disabilities.

We organize the review around the following topics: nonlanguage tests, nonreading and motor-reduced tests, tests for visually impaired persons, and the assessment of adaptive behavior in mental retardation.

NONLANGUAGE TESTS

As the reader will recall, nonlanguage tests require little or no written or spoken language from examiner or examinee. Thus, they are particularly suited for assessment of non-English-speaking persons, referrals with speech impairments, and examinees with weak language skills. These instruments can also be used as supplementary tests for examinees who have no disabilities.

Leiter International Performance Scale-Revised

The Leiter International Performance Scale-Revised (Roid & Miller, 1997) is a recent revision of a classic and highly praised test of nonverbal intelligence and cognitive abilities (Leiter, 1948, 1979). Leiter devised an experimental edition of the test in 1929 to assess the intelligence of hearing-impaired, speech-impaired, bilingual, or non-English-speaking examinees. The scale was field-tested with several ethnic groups in Hawaii, including children of Japanese and Chinese descent. The first edition was based upon test results for American children, high school students, and WWII Army recruits. Although highly praised and widely used after its initial release, this test received strong criticism in recent years because of poor illustrations and outdated norms. The revised Leiter answers all criticisms handily, and the LIPS-R deserves wide use as a culture-reduced measure of nonverbal intelligence.

A remarkable feature of the Leiter is the complete elimination of verbal instructions. The Leiter-R does not require a single spoken word from the examiner or the examinee. With an age range of 2 years to 20 years and 11 months, the Leiter-R is particularly suitable for children and adolescents whose English language skills are weak. This includes children with any of these features: non-English-speaking, autism, traumatic brain injury, speech impairment, hearing problems, or an impoverished environment. The test is also useful in the assessment of attentional problems, as described in the following.

Testing is performed by the child or adolescent matching small laminated cards underneath corresponding illustrations on an easel display (Figure 7.1). The test is untimed. Because the initial items are transparently obvious, most examinees catch on quickly without need of pantomime demonstration. The Leiter-R contains 20 subtests organized into four domains: Reasoning, Visualization, Memory, and Attention. Not all subtests are administered to every child. For example, the figure rotation subtest is too difficult for two-year-olds and the immediate recognition subtest is too easy for adolescent examinees. The four Reasoning subtests include classification and design analogies. The six Visualization subtests include matching, figure-ground, paper folding, and figure rotation. The eight Memory subtests include memory span, spatial memory, associative memory, and delayed recognition memory. The two Attention subtests consist of an underlining test (e.g., marking all squares printed on a page full of geometric shapes) and a measure of divided attention (e.g., observing a moving display and simultaneously sorting cards correctly).

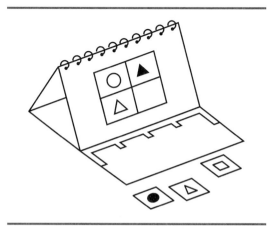

FIGURE 7.1 A Characteristic Item from the Leiter International Performance Scale-Revised

The Leiter-R yields a composite IQ with the familiar mean of 100 and standard deviation of 15. The test also produces subtest scaled scores with a mean of 10 and standard deviation of 3, as well as a variety of composite scores useful in clinical diagnosis. The test was normed on over 2,000 children and adolescents, from 2 to 21 years of age. Using 1993 census statistics, these subjects were carefully stratified according to race, age, gender, social class, and geographic region. Internal consistency reliability for subtests, domain scores, and IQ scores is excellent. Typical coefficient alphas are in the high .80s for subtests and the low .90s for domain scores and IQ scores. Extensive studies of item bias reveal that the items appear to function similarly in separate racial groups (white, African-American, and Hispanic samples), that is, there is no evidence of bias (defined as differential item functioning). Coupled with the fact that the test is completely nonverbal, the absence of test bias indicates that the Leiter-R is a good choice for culture-reduced testing of minority children.

Although correlational research with the Leiter-R is scant at this time, studies with the first edition indicate strong relationships with other intelligence test scores. For example, the Leiter and the WISC Performance IQ correlated near the .80s; correlations with the WISC Verbal IQ are more typically in the .60s (Arthur, 1950; Matey, 1984). Reeve, French, & Hunter (1983) compared the Leiter and the Stanford-Binet: Form L-M as predictors of Metropolitan Achievement Test scores for 60 kindergartners. Correlations were .77 between Stanford-Binet and MAT total, and .61 between Leiter and MAT total. The authors note that although the Stanford-Binet proved to be a marginally better predictor of standard achievement, children with hearing and/or speech problems may require the Leiter or other nonverbal instruments.

The Leiter-R is a welcome revision of an obsolete test. In the hands of a careful clinician, the test is helpful in the intellectual assessment of children with weak skills in English. Other uses for the revised test include the assessment of Attention-Deficit/Hyperactivity Disorder (comparisons of the Attention subtests with the other domains are cru-

cial here) and the evaluation of giftedness in young children (the extremely high ceiling of the test proves invaluable for this application). Whereas reviewers warned against using the original Leiter for placement or decision-making purposes (Sattler, 1988; Salvia & Ysseldyke, 1991), the revised Leiter is a huge improvement in regards to psychometric quality and standardization excellence.

Human Figure Drawing Tests

Most children enjoy drawing human figures and do so routinely and spontaneously. Since the early 1900s, psychologists have tried to tap into this almost instinctive behavior as a basis for measuring intellectual development. The first person to use human figure drawing (HFD) as a standardized intelligence test was Florence Goodenough (1926). Her test, known as the Draw-A-Man test, was revised by Harris (1963) and renamed the Goodenough-Harris Drawing Test. More recently, the HFD technique has been adapted by Naglieri (1988). An additional approach by Gonzales (1986) is not reviewed here. We should also mention that human figure drawings are *widely* used as measures of emotional adjustment, but we do not discuss that application here.

The Goodenough-Harris Drawing Test is a brief, nonverbal test of intelligence that can be administered individually or in a group. Goodenough (1926) published the first edition of this test, while Harris (1963) provided important refinements in scoring and standardization, including the use of a deviation IQ. Strictly speaking, the Goodenough-Harris test doesn't fit the criteria for nonlanguage tests insofar as the examiner must convey certain instructions in English or through a translator. However, the instructions are brief and basic ("I want you to draw a picture of a man [or woman]; make the very best picture you can"). The Goodenough-Harris test is, for all practical purposes, a nonlanguage test.

The purpose of the Goodenough-Harris Drawing Test is to measure intellectual maturity, not artistic skill. Thus, the scoring guide emphasizes accuracy of observation and the development of conceptual thinking. The child receives credit for including body parts and details, as well as for providing perspective, realistic proportion, and implied freedom of movement.

The 73 scorable items were selected according to the following criteria:

1. The items should show a regular and fairly rapid increase with age, in the percentage of children passing the point.
2. The items should show a relationship to some general measure of intelligence.
3. The items should differentiate between children scoring high on the scale as a whole and those scoring low on the scale as a whole (Harris, 1963).

A sample drawing with item-by-item scoring is depicted in Figure 7.2.

In addition to the Man scale, the Harris (1963) revision also includes two additional forms: the Woman scale and the Self scale. For these last two scales, examinees are instructed to draw a picture of a woman and of themselves. Scores on the Man and Woman scales are very highly correlated for examinees of either sex ($r = .91$ to .98). These two versions can be considered equivalent forms. The Self scale was intended as a projective test of self-concept. However, self-concept is a fuzzy construct that is difficult to objectify. The Self scale has largely fallen by the wayside, although some psychologists use it purely as an unscored extension of the clinical interview.

The standardization sample for Goodenough-Harris Drawing Test was large ($N = 2,975$ children), geographically varied (from urban and rural areas throughout the United States), and carefully selected to match U.S. population values for parental occupational status. The test covers ages 3 to 16, but the norms are best for ages 5 to 12. Beyond age 12, examinees begin to approach an asymptote of performance and age differences are reduced. The Man scale yields a deviation IQ-like standard score with mean of 100 and standard deviation of 15. One concern is simply that Drawing Test norms are now quite dated.

Draw a picture of a man. Make the very best picture you can. Be sure to make the whole man, not just his head and shoulders.

Note: This effort by an eight-year-old girl converts to a Standard Score of 118 and a percentile rank of 88.

FIGURE 7.2 Goodenough-Harris Drawing Test with Item-by-Item Scoring
Source: Reprinted with permission from Harris, D. B. (1963). *Children's drawings as measures of intellectual maturity.* New York: Harcourt, Brace & World. Copyright © 1963 by The Psychological Corporation. Reproduced by permission. All rights reserved.

The reliability of the test has been assessed by split-half procedures, test-retest studies, and inter-scorer comparisons (Anastasi, 1975; Frederickson, 1985; Harris, 1963). Split-half reliabilities near .90 are common. However, stability coefficients seldom exceed the .70s, even when the test-retest interval is only a few weeks. This suggests that scores on the Goodenough-Harris Drawing Test possess a sizable band of measurement error. On the other hand, scoring is quite objective: Interscorer correlations are typically in the .90s.

Examiners who have mastered the elaborate point scoring system may then use a simpler global method called the Quality Scale. The Quality Scale consists of 24 drawings (12 for the Man scale and 12 for the Woman scale) used as standardized reference points. The examiner matches the examinee's drawing to one of the 12 reference drawings, then consults a table to determine the corresponding standard score. The Quality score is quicker, but slightly cruder: Interscorer reliabilities are typically in the low .80s.

The Goodenough-Harris test is often used as a nonverbal measure of cognitive ability with language-disabled, minority, or bilingual children. Oakland and Dowling (1983) view the Drawing Test test as a culturally reduced test that is appropriate for initial screening of minority children. The test works best with younger children, particularly those with lower intellectual ability (Scott, 1981). For samples of five-year-old children at a daycare center for lower socioeconomic families, Frederickson (1985) reported correlations between Goodenough-Harris Drawing Test scores and WPPSI Full Scale IQ in the range of .72 to .80. In several other studies, correlations with individual IQ tests are more variable, but the majority are over .50 (Abell, Briesen, & Watz, 1996; Anastasi, 1975).

In response to criticisms of the Goodenough-Harris Drawing Test, Naglieri (1988) developed a quantitative scoring system and renormed the human figure drawing procedure. His scoring system, The Draw A Person: A Quantitative Scoring System (DAP), was normed on a sample of 2,622 individuals ages 5 through 17 years who were representative of the 1980 U.S. Census data on age, sex, race, geographic region, ethnic group, social class, and community size. The DAP yields standard scores with the familiar mean of 100 and standard deviation of 15. In a study of 61 subjects ages 6 to 16 years, the DAP correlated .51 with WISC-R IQ and produced similar overall scores, with a mean IQ of 100 versus mean DAP score of 95 (Wisniewski & Naglieri, 1989). Lassiter and Bardos (1995) found that the DAP score underestimated IQ scores obtained from the WPPSI-R and the K-BIT in a sample of 50 kindergartners and first graders.

Reviewers praise the DAP for its clear scoring system, strong reliability, and careful standardization (Cosden, 1992). However, results of validity studies are more cautionary. Harrison and Schock (1994) note that the accumulated evidence with HFD tests indicates low to moderate predictive validity. In spite of their popularity and appeal, HFD tests do not effectively identify children with learning difficulties or developmental disabilities, and they may not be valid for use even as screening measures.

Hiskey-Nebraska Test of Learning Aptitude

The Hiskey-Nebraska Test of Learning Aptitude (H-NTLA) is a nonlanguage performance scale for use with children ages 3 to 17 years (Hiskey, 1966). This test can be administered entirely through pantomime and requires no verbal response from the examinee. However, verbal instructions can be used with normal and mild hearing-impaired children. The H-NTLA consists of 12 subtests:

Bead Patterns	Block Patterns
Memory for Color	Completion of Drawings
Picture Identification	Memory for Digits
Picture Association	Puzzle Blocks
Paper Folding	Picture Analogies
Visual Attention Span	Spatial Reasoning

Raw scores on the subtests are converted into a Deviation Learning Quotient (LQ) with mean of 100 and standard deviation of 16. H-NTLA scores correlate quite robustly with achievement scales for grades 2 through 12 (median $r = .49$) and also with WISC-R Performance IQ ($r = .85$). Although the LQ yields average scores that are remarkably close to WISC-R Performance IQ for samples of hearing-impaired and deaf children, the H-NTLA scores are substantially more variable (Watson & Goldgar, 1985; Phelps & Ensor, 1986). Thus, use of the H-NTLA may increase the risk of false positive misclassification—labeling children as gifted when they are only bright, or as retarded when they are merely borderline.

The H-NTLA is useful with children who are deaf, speech- or language-impaired, mentally retarded, or bilingual. An interesting feature of this test is the development of parallel norms: The H-NTLA was standardized on 1,079 deaf and 1,074 normal-hearing children ages 2½ to 17½. However, the chief weakness of the instrument is the inadequacy of these norms. For example, the representativeness of the deaf sample—picked on an opportunistic basis from schools for the deaf—is largely unknown. Standardization of the normal-hearing sample was based on occupational level of parents according to the 1960 U.S. Census. A contemporary and more detailed restandardization of the test would be quite helpful.

Test of Nonverbal Intelligence-3

The Test of Nonverbal Intelligence-3 (TONI-3) is a language-free measure of cognitive ability designed for disabled or minority populations (Brown, Sherbenou, & Johnsen, 1998). In particular, the authors recommend the test for assessing persons with aphasia, non-English speakers, the hearing-impaired, and persons who have experienced a variety of severe neurological traumas. The test instructions are pantomimed by the examiner and the examinee answers by pointing to one of six possible responses. The test consists of two equivalent forms of 50 abstract/figural problem-solving items. These items were carefully selected from an initial pool of items according to item-total correlations, appropriate difficulty level, and acceptabil-

ity to potential users and technical experts. The TONI-3 items fall into several categories, including the following:

Simple matching
Analogies
Classification
Intersection
Progressions

Except for the simple-matching items, the TONI-3 items require the examinee to solve problems by identifying relationships among abstract figures. Many of the items are similar in format to those found on the Raven Progressive Matrices. The test yields two kinds of scores: percentile ranks and TONI-3 quotients (mean of 100 and standard deviation of 15).

The TONI-3 was carefully standardized on over 3,000 subjects ranging in age from 6 through 89. Sample characteristics paralleled census data for sex, race, ethnicity, urban-suburban-rural residence, grade, parental education/occupation, and geographic region. Reliability data are quite satisfactory, with internal consistency coefficients typically exceeding .90 and alternate forms reliability in the range of .80 to .95.

Validity studies of the TONI-3 are scant, but investigation of prior editions (which are highly similar in content) are supportive of this test as a culture-reduced index of general intelligence. Nonetheless, research does not support the view that the TONI-3 is a nonverbal test, except in the trivial sense that verbal responses are not required. For example, the TONI-2 *Manual* reports correlation coefficients in the .70s between TONI-2 scores and the Language Arts subtest of the SRA Achievement Series. In general, research studies with precursors to the TONI-3 indicate that it is a good measure of general intelligence, but they do not support the view that it is mainly a measure of *nonverbal* intelligence (Murphy, 1992). Overall, the TONI-3 is highly regarded as a brief nonlanguage screening device for subjects with impaired language abilities (e.g., non-English-speaking, mentally retarded, deaf, or aphasic). The test is more carefully standardized than most and possesses excellent reliability. A useful feature of the TONI-3 is that the untimed administration seldom exceeds 20 minutes.

Two instruments discussed earlier in the text also qualify as nonlanguage tests. Raven's Progressive Matrices and the Cattell Culture Fair Intelligence Test utilize nonverbal items and require essentially no language-based interactions between examiner and examinee. A new and promising language-free test is the Universal Nonverbal Intelligence Test (UNIT), a comprehensive and multidimensional measure of nonverbal intelligence (McCallum & Bracken, 1997; Reed & McCallum, 1995). This test is designed for children who are hearing-impaired or limited in English proficiency. The UNIT provides a good measure of *g* and several subscores, including clear, factor-based scores on memory and reasoning.

NONREADING AND MOTOR-REDUCED TESTS

As the reader will recall, nonreading tests are designed for illiterate examinees who can, nonetheless, understand spoken English well enough to follow oral instructions. Nonreading tests of intelligence are well suited to young children, illiterate examinees, and persons with speech or expressive-language impairments. These tests need not be specialized or esoteric: The performance subtests of most mainstream instruments qualify as nonreading tests. For example, examiners may use the WISC-III performance subtests to estimate the intelligence of language-disabled examinees.

However, clients with cerebral palsy or other orthopedically impairing conditions will score very poorly on nonreading tests that require manipulatory responses. Obtaining valid test results from such persons can present an enormous challenge (Case Exhibit 7.1). The motor deficits, increased tendency to fatigue, and inexactness of purposive movements common to persons with cerebral palsy

will negatively affect their performance on cognitive assessment tools. Orthopedically impaired clients need tests that are both nonreading and motor-reduced. In particular, tests which permit a simple pointing response are well suited to the assessment of children and adults with cerebral palsy or other motor-impairing conditions.

Peabody Picture Vocabulary Test-III

The Peabody Picture Vocabulary Test-III (PPVT-III) is the best known and most widely used of the nonreading, motor-reduced tests (Dunn & Dunn, 1998). The PPVT-III is used to obtain a rapid measure of listening vocabulary with deaf persons, neurologically impaired patients, and speech-impaired individuals. Although the PPVT-III is useful with any examinee who cannot verbalize well, the test is especially useful with examinees who also manifest motor-impairing conditions such as cerebral palsy or stroke.

The PPVT-III comes in two parallel versions, each consisting of 4 practice plates and 204 testing plates. Each plate contains four line drawings of objects or everyday scenes. The examiner presents a plate, states the stimulus word orally, and asks the examinee to point to the one picture that best depicts the stated word. The test items are precisely ordered according to difficulty level, arranged in 17 sets of 12 items each for efficient identification of basal and ceiling levels. The entry level is determined by age, and examinees continue until they reach their ceiling level. Although the test is untimed, administration seldom exceeds 15 minutes. Raw scores are converted to age equivalents or standard scores (mean of 100, standard deviation of 15).

The PPVT-R was standardized on a representative national sample of several thousand individuals ranging from 2½ to 90 or more years of age. Based on earlier editions, split-half reliability coefficients are weak for younger subjects (e.g., .67 at the 2½-year level), but acceptable for older examinees (e.g., .88 at the 18-year level). For the adult sample, the median split-half reliability coefficient is .82. Alternate-form reliabilities are quite variable

CASE EXHIBIT 7.1 THE CHALLENGE OF ASSESSMENT IN CEREBRAL PALSY

The challenges inherent to special consultations are well typified by a client with cerebral palsy recently tested by a consulting psychologist. The young examinee was totally confined to a battery-powered wheelchair, except when a live-in attendant would transfer him to a bed or chair. Even a dispassionate observer would have to agree that the client didn't look very capable, sitting hunched over in his chair, unable to control his drooling, one arm arched out at an awkward angle. Yet, in spite of his disability, he had achieved a fair degree of personal independence. Using a simple joystick control device, he could guide his wheelchair to the grocery store, library, and community center where he would complete simple transactions by pointing to appropriate words and phrases in a plastic-bound spiral notebook. Because of his poor motor control, interactions with this client took quite a long time. Nonetheless, he was very efficient with short communications. Here is a typical exchange, with the client's notebook-designated responses shown in capital letters:

"I understand you have a new synthesized-voice communication box, how do you like it?" YOU ASKED TWO QUESTIONS. "You're right. I'll bet that happens a lot. Do you have a communication box?" YES. "What do you think of it?" IT'S NOT EASY. "Now that we are done testing, should I find your driver?" NO, I'LL WAIT. HE IS COMING BACK.

How intelligent is this client? What is his level of verbal comprehension? How well does he understand abstract concepts? For example, is he capable of understanding the essentials of microcomputer usage such as data entry, file storage, and directory commands? Could he learn to program a microcomputer? These are precisely the referral questions asked by a vocational rehabilitation counselor who was contemplating huge expenditures—thousands of dollars—to purchase a computer system for this disabled client.

Certainly it would be easy to underestimate the potential of this young man with severe motor and language disabilities because—in a quite literal sense—his intelligence was hidden away, trapped inside his incapacitated body. The task of the examiner was to find the able mind inside the disabled body, a formidable challenge indeed. Using the Test of Nonverbal Intelligence-2 and the Peabody Picture Vocabulary Test-Revised, the examiner determined that the young client possessed at least average intelligence and could likely learn the fundamentals of data processing with microcomputers.

from one sample to another (values from .50 to .90) but tend to hover around .80 (Bracken, Prasse, & McCallum, 1984; Dunn & Dunn, 1981; Umberger, 1987).

Several lines of evidence support the validity of the Peabody test, but only as a narrow measure of vocabulary, not as a general measure of intelligence (Altepeter, 1989; Altepeter & Johnson, 1989).

Dunn and Dunn (1981) sought to insure content validity by searching Webster's New Collegiate Dictionary for all words whose meanings could be represented by a picture. Thus, the authors had a specific content universe in mind, and the items from the Peabody appear to be a fair sampling from this domain. In addition, the authors used sophisticated item selection techniques based on the Rasch-Wright latent-trait model to help build construct validity into the test. This model enables researchers to construct a growth curve for the latent trait being measured (hearing vocabulary) and to select items which best fit the curve. Using tryout and calibration data, the curve was drawn repeatedly on a computer. If an item did not fit the Rasch-Wright latent-trait model (too flat or too steep an item-characteristic curve) it was discarded from consideration.

Using a sophisticated structural equation model, Miller and Lee (1993) demonstrated that an earlier edition, the PPVT-R, can be assumed to reflect true developmental level of vocabulary. These researchers were able to predict rank order of the PPVT-R stimulus words reasonably well based upon complex word characteristics (date of entry into the English language, word length, number of separate meanings, frequency of occurrence). The predictor variables provided a reasonable theoretical account of the word ordering in the PPVT-R, that is, they confirmed the construct validity of the test.

Concurrent and predictive validity data for the Peabody are somewhat limited, but promising. Several investigators have correlated the PPVT-R with achievement measures, where modest relationships (rs from .30 to .60) are common (Naglieri, 1981; Naglieri & Pfeiffer, 1983). Correlations with reading achievement tend to be higher than with spelling and arithmetic achievement, suggesting that the PPVT-R has appropriate discriminant validity (Vance, Kitson, & Singer, 1985).

Several investigators have correlated earlier versions of the Peabody with intelligence measures, particularly the WISC-R and WAIS-R, and healthy correlations (near .70) are the rule (e.g.,

Haddad, 1986; Naglieri & Yazzie, 1983). As might be expected, correlations tend to be higher with Verbal IQ than Performance IQ.

In a very important and ingenious study, Maxwell and Wise (1984) investigated the vocabulary loading of the Peabody in a sample of 84 inpatients from psychiatry and psychology wards. Their study utilized the PPVT, but this earlier edition is similar to the PPVT-III, so that the conclusions are pertinent here. The researchers investigated the hypothesis that the PPVT assesses more than vocabulary in adults. In addition to the PPVT, the researchers collected data on the following: WAIS-R, Wechsler Memory Scale, name-writing speed, and years of education. Name-writing speed is simply the number of seconds required for the examinee to write his or her full name. Even though all variables had significant correlations with PPVT IQ, WAIS-R Vocabulary had by far the strongest correlation ($r = .88$). More important, when the variance accounted for by Vocabulary was removed, none of the remaining variables had any predictive relationship with the PPVT. In short, the Peabody is a good measure of vocabulary (hearing vocabulary, in particular) but could be misleading if used as a global measure of intellect.

The PPVT-III is a very recent revision, so independent research with the test is nonexistent. One caution with the previous edition, the PPVT-R, is that standard scores may be substantially lower than Wechsler IQs, particularly with retarded persons and minority examinees. In a sample of 21 mildly mentally retarded adults, Prout and Schwartz (1984) found the PPVT-R standard scores (mean of 56) to be an average of 9 points lower than the WAIS-R IQ (mean of 65). Naglieri and Yazzie (1983) found a huge 26-point difference with a sample of Navajo Indian children who averaged a standard score of 61 on the PPVT-R in contrast to WISC-R IQ of 87.

Overall, we may conclude that the Peabody is a well-normed measure of hearing vocabulary that is useful with nonreading and motor-impaired examinees. However, the instrument is not a substitute for a general intelligence test and prior editions vastly underestimated intellectual functioning in minorities and retarded persons.

Columbia Mental Maturity Scale

The Columbia Mental Maturity Scale (CMMS) is an untimed test of reasoning ability designed for young children with sensory, motor, or speech deficits (Burgemeister, Blum, & Lorge, 1972). Now in its third edition, the test was originally devised for young children with cerebral palsy. The CMMS has found wide acceptance with other disabilities, including deafness and speech impediments. The format for the test is pristinely simple: From a group of three, four, or five drawings, the child is required to "point out the one that does not belong." Thus, the CMMS does not depend upon reading skills. The test is normed for subjects from age 3½ to age 10.

The 92 cards on the CMMS test perceptual discrimination (e.g., color, shape, size, use, number, missing parts), classifications, and abstract manipulation of symbolic concepts. The test takes 15 to 20 minutes to administer. Raw scores are converted into age deviation scores with mean of 100 and standard deviation of 16. An age-equivalent score called the Maturity Index can also be obtained. Several characteristic CMMS items are depicted in Figure 7.3.

The standardization sample consists of 2,600 children selected from 25 states so as to resemble the 1960 census data for geographic region, race, parental occupation, age, and sex. The reliability of the instrument is good, with test-retest and split-half coefficients in the high .80s. The concurrent validity of the instrument is adequate: Correlations with other instruments are typically in the .50s. The *Manual* reports a correlation of .67 with the Stanford-Binet: Form L-M.

The CMMS does possess two serious shortcomings. The first is the obvious fact that the norms, obtained in the 1960s, are now badly outdated. Based upon what has been observed with other dated tests, the CMMS probably overestimates functioning of contemporary children (see discussion of the Flynn effect in the next topic). An-

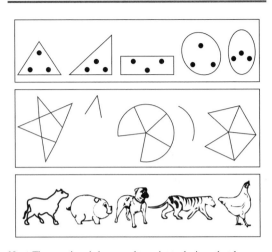

Note: The examinee is instructed to point to the item that does not belong.

FIGURE 7.3 **Examples of Characteristic CMMS Items**

other problem is that when testing very young children the scale is highly vulnerable to random guessing. Kaufman (1978) points out that a young child who merely guesses will, on average, obtain a score of 82. With a little bit of lucky guessing, a retarded five-year-old might score in the average range. Thus, the CMMS is of limited value in testing very young children suspected of intellectual deficiency. However, with older children, guessing has a minimal effect due to the larger number of alternatives and the greater number of items typically administered. Overall, the CMMS is a useful non-language measure of reasoning ability for school-aged children, but new normative data are badly needed.

TESTS FOR VISUALLY IMPAIRED PERSONS

In assessing the intellectual functioning of the visually impaired, examiners have historically relied upon adaptations of the Stanford-Binet. The Hayes-Binet revision for testing the visually impaired was based on the 1916 Stanford-Binet; this instrument has since undergone several revisions. The most recent adaptation is the Perkins-Binet (Davis, 1980). The Perkins-Binet retains most of the verbal items from the Stanford-Binet, but also adapts other items to a tactual mode. The Perkins-Binet possesses acceptable split-half reliability and shows high correlations with verbal scales of the WISC-R (Coveny, 1972; Teare & Thompson, 1982). The developers of the Perkins-Binet have acknowledged that visual problems exist on a continuum by developing separate norms for children with usable vision (Form U) and no usable vision (Form N).

Test developers have also succeeded in modifying the Wechsler Performance scales for use with the visually impaired. The Haptic Intelligence Scale for the Adult Blind (HISAB) consists of six subtests, four of which resemble the Digit Symbol, Block Design, Object Assembly, and Picture Completion tests of the WAIS Performance scale (Shurrager, 1961; Shurrager & Shurrager, 1964). The remaining two subtests consist of Bead Arithmetic, which involves the use of an abacus to solve arithmetic problems, and a Pattern Board, which requires the examinee to reproduce the pattern felt on a board that has rows of holes with pegs in them. The reliability of the HISAB is excellent and the authors provide normative data on a sample of visually impaired adults. Most encouraging of all, HISAB scores correlate .65 with the WAIS Verbal IQ (Shurrager & Shurrager, 1964).

Another interesting instrument is the Blind Learning Aptitude Test (BLAT), a tactile test for blind children from 6 to 16 years of age (Newland, 1971). The BLAT items are in bas-relief form, consisting of dots and lines similar to Braille. The items consist of six different types: recognition of differences, recognition of similarities, identification of progressions, identification of the missing element in a 2 × 2 matrix, completion of a figure, and identification of the missing element in a 3 × 3 matrix. Most of the items were adapted from Raven's Progressive Matrices and the Cattell Culture Fair Intelligence Test. The BLAT is standardized on 760 visually impaired children, but the norms are outdated and the test manual is incomplete and somewhat slipshod (Herman, 1988).

Nonetheless, the test possesses exceptional reliability and correlates very well with the Hayes-Binet ($r = .74$) and the WISC Verbal Scale ($r = .71$). In conjunction with a verbal test, the BLAT is a promising instrument for testing the intelligence of children with visual disabilities. However, the test would profit substantially from minor revisions, updated norms, and a more thorough test manual.

ASSESSMENT OF ADAPTIVE BEHAVIOR IN MENTAL RETARDATION

The assessment of mental retardation is a complex and multifaceted concern which rightfully deserves a chapter or book on its own. Owing to space limitations, our coverage is necessarily abridged; interested readers are referred to American Association on Mental Retardation (1992), Nihira (1985), and Sattler (1988, chps. 15 and 21). Here, we briefly summarize the diagnostic criteria for mental retardation, then review two contrasting assessment instruments in modest detail. We close with a tabular summary of several prominent measures of adaptive behavior.

Definition of Mental Retardation

The most authoritative source for the definition of mental retardation is the manual of terminology and classification of the American Association on Mental Retardation (AAMR, 1992). This manual defines **mental retardation** as follows:

> Mental retardation refers to substantial limitations in present functioning. It is characterized by significantly subaverage intellectual functioning, existing concurrently with related limitations in two or more of the following applicable adaptive skill areas: communication, self-care, home living, social skills, community use, self-direction, health and safety, functional academics, leisure, and work. Mental retardation manifests before age 18 (AAMR, 1992).

The manual further specifies that significantly subaverage intellectual functioning is an IQ of 70 to 75 or below on scales with a mean of 100 and a standard deviation of 15. On tests such as the Stanford-Binet: Fourth Edition which possess a standard deviation of 16, the approximate range for retarded intellectual functioning would be an IQ of 68 to 73 or below. The manual also explicitly affirms the importance of professional judgment in individual cases.

A low IQ by itself is an insufficient foundation for the diagnosis of mental retardation. The AAMR definition also specifies a second criterion, that of limitations in two or more of the relevant adaptive skill areas. A diagnosis of mental retardation is warranted only when an individual displays a sufficiently low IQ and limitations in adaptive skill. Further, these deficits in intellect and adaptive functioning must have arisen during the developmental period—defined as between birth and the eighteenth birthday.

This most recent AAMR *Manual* represents a departure from previous terminology which recognized four levels of retardation: mild, moderate, severe, and profound. Instead of focusing upon the shortcomings of the person, the *Manual* introduces a hierarchy of "Intensities of Needed Supports," which redirects attention to the rehabilitation needs of the client. The four levels of needed supports are intermittent, limited, extensive, and pervasive. However, the previous terminology referring to levels of retardation will likely prevail for quite some time, so we have chosen to blend the old and the new approach in Table 7.1. The reader will notice a zone of uncertainty between levels of retardation, which signifies that clinical judgment about all sources of information is required in diagnosis. Furthermore, even though these levels are calibrated by IQ ranges, we remind the reader that the examinee must also show corresponding deficit in two or more areas of adaptive skill. Under no circumstances is an IQ test a sufficient basis for diagnosing mental retardation.

Limitations in adaptive skill are more difficult to confirm than a low IQ. The AAMR *Manual* lists 10 different areas of adaptive skill and specifies that the client must show substantial limitations in two or more of them:

- Communication
- Self-care
- Home living
- Social skills
- Community use
- Self-direction
- Health and safety
- Functional academics
- Leisure
- Work

As to how these limitations are to be assessed, the *Manual* proposes that well-normed measures of adaptive skills are desirable, but the final determination is always a matter of clinical judgment.

A test developer faces major problems in calibrating limitations in adaptive skill. About the only hard fact we have in this domain is that environmental expectations for adaptive behavior increase sharply from birth through young adulthood. In addition, the expression of adaptive behavior changes

---

TABLE 7.1   Four Levels of Mental Retardation

Mild Mental Retardation: IQ of 50–55 to 70–75+, ***Intermittent Support*** required. Reasonable social and communication skills; with special education, attain 6th grade level by late teens; achieve social and vocational adequacy with special training and supervision; partial independence in living arrangements.

Moderate Mental Retardation: IQ of 35–40 to 50–55, ***Limited Support*** required. Fair social and communication skills but little self-awareness; with extended special education, attain 4th grade level; function in a sheltered workshop but need supervision in living arrangements.

Severe Mental Retardation: IQ of 20–25 to 35–40, ***Extensive Support*** required. Little or no communication skills; sensory and motor impairments; do not profit from academic training; trainable in basic health habits.

Profound Mental Retardation: IQ below 20–25, ***Pervasive Support*** required. Minimal functioning; incapable of self-maintenance; need constant nursing care and supervision.

Source: Based on AAMR (1992) and Patton, Payne, and Beirne-Smith (1986).

character throughout. In childhood, adaptive behaviors may be reflected in sensory-motor skills and facility with language. In adulthood, vocational attainment and social responsibility become important. Just as with intellectual assessment, tools for appraising adaptive behavior must be carefully age-graded.

The first standardized instrument for assessing adaptive behavior was the Vineland Social Maturity Scale (Doll, 1935, 1936). Somewhat simplistic and coarse-grained by modern standards, the original Vineland scale consisted of 117 discrete items arranged in a year-scale format. An informant familiar with the examinee would check off applicable items. From these results the examiner would calculate an equivalent social age, helpful in the diagnosis of mental retardation. Still a respected instrument, the Vineland has undergone several revisions and is now known as the Vineland Adaptive Behavior Scales (Sparrow, Balla & Cicchetti, 1984).

Since the release of the original Vineland scale, over 100 scales of adaptive behavior have been published (Nihira, 1985; Reschly, 1990; Walls, Werner, Bacon, & Zane, 1977). These instruments vary greatly in structure, intended purpose, and targeted population. Broadly speaking, we can distinguish two types of instruments designed for two different purposes. One group of mainly norm-referenced scales is used largely to assist in diagnosis and classification. Another group of mainly criterion-referenced scales is used largely to assist in training and rehabilitation. We have chosen one representative instrument from each group for more detailed analysis.

Scales of Independent Behavior-Revised

The Scales of Independent Behavior-Revised (SIB-R, Bruininks, Woodcock, Weatherman, & Hill, 1996) is an ambitious, multidimensional measure of adaptive behavior that is highly useful in the assessment of mental retardation. The instrument consists of 259 adaptive behavior items organized into 14 subscales. The scale is completed with the help of a parent, caregiver, or teacher well acquainted with the examinee's daily behaviors. For

each subscale, the examiner reads a series of items and for each item records a score from 0 (never or rarely does task) to 3 (does task very well). A useful feature of the SIB-R is that examiners need a minimum of training and experience. Of course, a much higher level of competence is required to evaluate results and make decisions about placement or treatment.

The 14 subscales of the SIB are arranged into 4 clusters, as outlined in Table 7.2. In turn, these 4 clusters constitute the Broad Independence Scale. Each subscale consists of a small number of discrete, developmentally ordered items. For example, the subscale on Eating and Meal Preparation has 19 graded items, including spearing food with a fork, eating soup with a spoon, taking appropriate-sized portions, and preparing snacks that do not require cooking. For each subscale, items are administered until a predetermined ceiling is reached (e.g., 3 of 5 consecutive items scored 0).

Raw scores for a subtest are added to obtain a part score. The part scores for each cluster are then added to obtain the cluster score. The score for the Broad Independence Scale is derived from the four cluster scores. The subtest scores, cluster scores, and the Broad Independence score can then be converted to a variety of normative scores to permit comparison of the examinee's performance with the performance of the national norming sample. The normative scales include age scores, percentile ranks, standard scores, stanines, and normal curve equivalents.

A separate, unique part of the SIB-R also assesses maladaptive behavior by measuring the frequency and severity of problem behaviors. The Problem Behaviors Scale includes eight major categories of personal and social maladjustment that could affect adaptive behavior: Hurtful to Self, Hurtful to Others, Destructive to Property, Disruptive Behavior, Unusual or Repetitive Habits, Socially Offensive Behavior, Withdrawal or Inattentive Behavior, and Uncooperative Behavior. Examples of problem behaviors are listed, and the respondent must indicate the behaviors displayed by the examinee. In addition, the respondent

TABLE 7.2 The Subscales and Clusters of the Scales of Independent Behavior-Revised

1. *Motor Skills*

   Gross Motor—19 large muscle skills such as sitting without support or taking part in strenuous physical activities.

   Fine Motor—19 small muscle skills such as picking up small objects or assembling small objects.

2. *Social and Communication Skills*

   Social Interaction—18 skills requiring interaction with other people such as handing toys to others or making plans with friends to attend social activities.

   Language Comprehension—18 skills involving the understanding of spoken and written language such as looking toward a speaker or reading.

   Language Expression—20 tasks involving talking such as making sounds to get attention or explaining a written contract.

3. *Personal Living Skills*

   Eating and Meal Preparation—19 skills related to eating and meal preparation, ranging from drinking from a glass to planning a meal.

   Toileting—17 skills necessary to bathroom and toilet use.

   Dressing—18 skills related to dressing, ranging from holding out arms and legs while being dressed to arranging for clothing alterations.

   Personal Self-Care—16 tasks involved in basic grooming and health maintenance, for example, washing hands and making a medical appointment.

   Domestic Skills—18 tasks needed to maintain a home, ranging from putting empty dishes in the sink to selecting appropriate housing.

4. *Community Living Skills*

   Time and Punctuality—19 tasks involving time concepts and time management such as keeping appointments.

   Money and Value—20 skills related to money concepts, such as saving money and using credit.

   Work Skills—20 skills related to prevocational and work habits, for example, indicating that an assigned task is completed.

   Home-Community Orientation—18 skills involved in getting around the home and neighborhood and traveling in the community, for example, locating a dentist.

describes the one most serious behavior in each category and rates it according to frequency of occurrence, severity, and typical management.

The standardization of the SIB-R was well conceived and executed. The norm group consisted of 2,182 persons sampled to reflect the 1990 Census characteristics. The normative data cover persons from age 3 months to adults over age 80. An additional sample of retarded, learning-disabled, behavior-disordered, and hearing-impaired persons

was also tested. The value of the SIB-R was further strengthened by anchoring it to the norms for the Woodcock-Johnson Psycho-Educational Battery-Revised. The SIB-R is one component of this larger test battery, but can be used on its own.

The reliability of the SIB-R is generally respectable, but somewhat variable from subscale to subscale and from one age group to another. The individual subscales tend to show split-half reliabilities in the vicinity of 0.80; the four clusters have median composite reliabilities around 0.90; the Broad Independence Scale has a very robust reliability in the high .90s (Bruininks, Woodcock, Weatherman, & Hill, 1996).

Initial validity data for the SIB-R are very promising. For example, the mean scores of various samples of disabled and nondisabled subjects show confirmatory relationships: SIB-R scores are lowest among those persons known to be most severely impaired in learning and adjustment. For disabled examinees, SIB-R scores correlate very strongly with intelligence scores (in the .80s), whereas with nondisabled examinees, the relationship is minimal (Bruininks, Woodcock, Weatherman, & Hill, 1996).

In sum, the SIB-R is an excellent tool for providing insights into an examinee's current level of functioning in real-life situations in the home, school, and community settings. Although this instrument does not have a one-to-one correspondence with the 10 areas of adaptive skill listed in the definition of mental retardation, there is substantial similarity. For example, the following areas of AAMR-listed adaptive skills are well covered by subscales or clusters of the SIB-R: communication, self-care, home living, social skills, community use, health and safety, and work. The SIB-R or a similar instrument ranks as a mandatory supplement to individual intelligence testing in the diagnosis and assessment of mental retardation.

Independent Living Behavior Checklist (ILBC)

The Independent Living Behavior Checklist (ILBC) is an extensive list of 343 independent living skills classified and presented in six categories: mobility, self-care, home maintenance and safety, food, social and communication, and functional academic (Walls, Zane, & Thvedt, 1979). Unlike

---

TABLE 7.3   A Sampling of ILBC Items

Rubber Scraper   35

Condition: Given a bowl containing ingredients, a pan, and a rubber scraper

Behavior: Client pours the ingredients into the pan and scrapes the sides of the bowl

Standard: Behavior within 2 minutes. No ingredients must be spilled. All ingredients must be removed from the bowl

Compliments   30

Condition: Given a role play or natural situation in which the client is complimented

Behavior: Client accepts the compliment(s) (e.g., says "Thank you.")

Standard: In the role play or natural situation, all persons interviewed must independently state that the client accepted the compliment(s) politely and was not overly gracious or vain

Address   38

Condition: Given a piece of paper with an address of place located within 3 blocks of the client

Behavior: Client finds the appropriate location with or without assistance

Standard: Behavior within one hour. The appropriate location must be found. The location may be found by the client alone or by the client with assistance (e.g., asking directions from others such as a policeman)

Source: Reprinted with permission from Walls, R. T., Zane, T., and Thvedt, J. E. (1979). *The Independent Living Behavior Checklist.* Dunbar, WV: West Virginia Research and Training Center.

most of the instruments discussed so far in this text, the ILBC is completely non-normative. The sole purpose of the ILBC is to facilitate the training of the individual examinee in the skills required for independent living. For this purpose, a collection of carefully selected criterion-referenced skills works better than a group of norm-based scores. The ILBC focuses on what the examinee can do, not on how the examinee compares to other persons. An exact age range is not specified, but the instrument appears to be suitable for persons 16 years of age through adulthood.

For each skill, the ILBC specifies a condition, a behavior, and a standard. Table 7.3 lists a sample of ILBC items. The reader will notice that all three components (condition, behavior, and standard) are defined with enough precision that reasonable observers would likely agree when a skill has been mastered. In fact, test-retest and interobserver agreement for ILBC skills range from .96 to a perfect 1.00.

The items within each ILBC category were carefully selected to encompass the important and relevant skills for independent living. Apparently, the authors succeeded in identifying essential skills, insofar as their instrument has a 100 percent overlap with another—initially unknown—checklist for independent living (Schwab, 1979). In addition, the ILBC items were carefully ordered from easiest to hardest. When used on a continuing basis over a several-year training period, the ILBC thus provides a checklist of skills mastered and also furnishes guidance for further rehabilitation.

Additional Measures of Adaptive Behavior

We remind the reader that measures of adaptive behavior vary greatly. Some scales are designed mainly for diagnosis, others for remediation. Some scales are useful with severely and profoundly retarded persons who will never be employed, others with mildly retarded individuals seeking vocational training. Some scales are useful exclusively with children, others with adults. These instruments are not interchangeable and the potential user must study their strengths and limitations carefully. In Table 7.4, we have summarized a salient feature or two for several of the better-known measures of adaptive behavior. Additional scales are reviewed by Reschly (1990).

TABLE 7.4   Adaptive Behavior Measures

Adaptive Behavior Inventory For Children (ABIC)

Ages 5–0 to 11–11

The ABIC is a part of the System of Multicultural Pluralistic Assessment (SOMPA). Six areas of adaptive behavior measure role behavior in the home, neighborhood, and community. Sattler (1988) warns that the ABIC makes no provision for consideration of the child's opportunities to learn the adaptive behaviors.
Mercer and Lewis (1978)

AAMR Adaptive Behavior Scales—
Residential and Community, 2nd Edition (ABS-RC:2)

Ages 18–0 through 80–0

This instrument is a psychometric tour de force that borders on overkill. The normative sample includes more than 4,000 persons with developmental disabilities from 43 states, residing in the community or in residential settings. Internal consistency and test-retest reliabilities exceed .80 for all domain scores. The instrument has been extensively validated and clearly distinguishes persons independently classified at different adaptive behavior levels.
Nihira, Leland, and Lambert (1993)

AAMR Adaptive Behavior Scales—School, 2nd Edition (AAMR-ABS)

Ages 3–0 to 18–11

This instrument is useful with preschool and school-aged children suspected of mental retardation. The scale is filled out by a parent or caretaker. The current AAMR school scale is divided into two parts. Part one consists of nine behavior domains having to do with personal independence. Part two focuses upon the evaluation of socially maladaptive behaviors. The scale produces five factor scores as well as an overall independence score.
Lambert, Nihira, and Leland (1993)

Vineland Adaptive Behavior Scales (VABS)

Ages birth to 19–11

The VABS is a widely respected instrument with good concurrent validity, such as correlations of .50 to .80 with WISC-R and Stanford-Binet. However, some items require knowledge informants may not possess (e.g., whether child says 100 recognizable words). Silverstein (1986) faults the normative data, noting discontinuous jumps in standard scores from one age group to another.
Sparrow, Balla, and Cicchetti (1984)

T.M.R. School Competency Scales

Two Forms: 5 to 10–11 and 11 and older

Designed to assess social and personal skills of trainable mentally retarded children in a school setting. The five scales include Perceptual-Motor, Initiative-Responsibility, Cognition, Personal-Social, and Language. The teacher chooses among four levels of competence for each item. Validity data are lacking.
Levine, Elzey, Thormahlen, and Cain (1976)

Balthazar Scales of Adaptive Behavior

Ages 5 to adult

A useful instrument for evaluating the effectiveness of training programs with the severely and profoundly retarded. The Balthazar Scales provides a very fine grained analysis of eating, dressing, and toileting behaviors.
Balthazar (1976)

Camelot Behavioral Checklist

Adult

The Camelot consists of 399 behavior descriptions grouped into 40 subdomains and 10 domains. Examples of the items include "pours liquids," "waxes floors," "can boil food," and "can do stapling jobs." The 10 domain scores yield norm-referenced percentiles based on a sample of 624 developmentally disabled persons. The Camelot has excellent reliability and correlates .70 to .86 with Wechsler tests and Stanford-Binet.
Foster (1974)

Bruininks-Oseretsky Test of Motor Proficiency

Ages 4–6 to 14–6

This specialized test was developed to help educators and clinicians identify and evaluate motor dysfunctions in persons with mental retardation or other developmental disabilities. Eight subtests examine running speed and agility, balance, bilateral coordination, strength, upper-limb coordination, response speed, visual-motor control, and upper-limb speed and dexterity.
Bruininks (1978)

SUMMARY

1. In the 1970s, a renewed societal concern for the needs of persons with disabilities was translated into federal legislation. Public Law 93-112 outlawed discrimination on the basis of disability. Public Law 94-142 mandated that disabled school-children receive appropriate assessment and educational opportunities.

2. Public Law 94-142, the Education for All Handicapped Children Act, has had dramatic impacts upon assessment practices with the disabled. The law specifies nondiscriminatory assessment, native language testing, validated testing by appropriately trained personnel, and ancillary procedures, such as health, hearing, vision, and emotional assessment.

3. Public Law 99-457 requires states to provide a free appropriate public education to disabled children ages 3 through 5. Furthermore, the law mandates financial grants for states that serve disabled infants, toddlers, and their families.

4. The Americans with Disabilities Act (ADA) of 1990 mandates that agencies must make reasonable testing accommodations for persons with disabilities, including such provisions as increased time on timed tests for persons with learning disabilities and related disorders.

5. The Leiter International Performance Scale-Revised is an untimed measure of perceptual organization and reasoning ability. The test can be administered completely by pantomime—the examinee matches small laminated cards underneath corresponding illustrations on an easel display.

6. The Goodenough-Harris Drawing Test is a brief screening test of intelligence in which the examinee is encouraged to draw a good picture of a man. The 73 scorable items include body parts, details, perspective, proportion, and implied freedom of movement. The Draw A Person test of Naglieri (1988) is an updated version of the Drawing Test.

7. The Hiskey-Nebraska Test of Learning Aptitude is a nonlanguage performance scale for use with children ages 3 to 17 years. The test is used with children who are deaf, speech- or language-impaired, mentally retarded, or bilingual. Originally normed in 1960, the test is in need of restandardization.

8. The Test of Nonverbal Intelligence-3 (TONI-3) is a language-free multiple-choice measure of cognitive ability designed for special populations and carefully standardized for ages 5 through 85. Most items require the examinee to identify relationships among abstract figures. The TONI-3 is a good index of general—as opposed to nonverbal—intelligence.

9. The Peabody Picture Vocabulary Test-III (PPVT-III) is suitable for obtaining a rapid measure of hearing vocabulary with deaf or disabled persons (e.g., from stroke or cerebral palsy). The examiner says a word and the examinee tries to select from four pictures the one which depicts the word.

10. The Columbia Mental Maturity Scale (CMMS), normed in the 1960s for subjects from age 3½ to 10, is a psychometrically sound test of reasoning ability designed for children with sensory, motor, or speech impairments. From a group of three to five drawings, the child is asked to "point out the one that does not belong." The CMMS needs to be restandardized.

11. Respected tests for visually impaired subjects include the Perkins-Binet, an adaptation of the Stanford-Binet; the Haptic Intelligence Scale for the Adult Blind (HISAB), a modification of the Wechsler performance subtests; and the Blind Learning Aptitude Test (BLAT), a Braille-like measure of concept formation and abstract reasoning.

12. Mental retardation is defined by three criteria: significantly subaverage general intellectual functioning, typically defined as an IQ under 70 (or 75 in exceptional cases); limitations in two or more adaptive skill areas; and onset prior to the eighteenth birthday.

13. The Scales of Independent Behavior-R (SIB-R) is a measure of adaptive behavior that is highly useful in the assessment of mental retardation. A parent, caregiver, or teacher completes a series of 14 subscales pertaining to motor skills, social and communication skills, personal living skills, and community living skills.

14. The Independent Living Behavior Checklist (ILBC) is a criterion-referenced, treatment-oriented

compendium of 343 independent living skills. Test-retest reliability and interobserver agreement for ILBC skills are exceptionally high. The ILBC helps guide the continued rehabilitation of developmentally disabled persons.

KEY TERMS AND CONCEPTS

Public Law 93-112   p. 219

Public Law 94-142   p. 220

Public Law 99-457   p. 221

Americans with Disabilities Act   p. 221

mental retardation   p. 231

Topic **7B** Test Bias and Other Controversies

An intelligence test is a neutral, inconsequential tool until someone assigns significance to the results derived from it. Once meaning is attached to a person's test score, that individual will experience many repercussions, ranging from superficial to life-changing. These repercussions will be fair or prejudiced, helpful or harmful, appropriate or misguided—depending upon the meaning attached to the test score.

Unfortunately, the tendency to imbue intelligence test scores with inaccurate and unwarranted connotations is rampant. Laypersons and students of psychology commonly stray into one thicket of harmful misconceptions after another. Tests results are variously overinterpreted or underinterpreted, viewed by some as a divination of personal worth but devalued by others as trivial and unfair.

The purpose of this topic is to further clarify the meaning of intelligence test scores in the light of relevant behavioral research. Specifically, we will pursue five issues—some would say controversies—which bear on the meaning of intelligence test scores:

- The question of test bias
- Genetic and environmental effects on intelligence
- Origins of IQ differences between African Americans and caucasian Americans
- The fate of intelligence in middle and old age
- Generational changes in intelligence test scores

The underlying theme of this section is that intelligence test scores are best understood within the framework of modern psychological research. The reader is warned that the research issues pursued here are complex, confusing, and occasionally contradictory. However, the rewards for grappling with these topics are substantial. After all, the meaning of intelligence tests is demarcated, sharpened, and refined entirely by empirical research.

THE QUESTION OF TEST BIAS

Beyond a doubt, no practice in modern psychology has been more assailed than psychological testing. Commentators reserve a special and often vehement condemnation for ability testing in particular. In his wide-ranging response to the hundreds of criticisms aimed at mental testing, Jensen (1980) concluded that test bias is the most common rallying point for the critics. In proclaiming **test bias,** the skeptics assert in various ways that tests are culturally and sexually biased so as to discriminate unfairly against racial and ethnic minorities, women, and the poor. We cite here a sampling of verbatim criticisms (Jensen, 1980):

- Intelligence tests are sadly misnamed because they were never intended to measure intelligence and might have been more aptly called CB (cultural background) tests.

- Persons from backgrounds other than the culture in which the test was developed will always be penalized.
- There are enormous social class differences in a child's access to the experiences necessary to acquire the valid intellectual skills.
- IQ scores reported for African Americans and low socioeconomic groups in the United States reflect characteristics of the test rather than of the test takers.
- The poor performance of African-American children on conventional tests is due to the biased content of the tests, that is, the test material is drawn from outside the African-American culture.
- Women are not so good as men at mathematics only because women have not taken as much math in high school and college.

Are these criticisms valid? The investigation of this question turns out to be considerably more complicated than the reader might suppose. A most important point is that appearances can be deceiving. As we will explain subsequently, the fact that test items "look" or "feel" preferential to one race, sex, or social class does not constitute proof of test bias. Test bias is an objective, empirical question, not a matter of personal judgment.

Although critics may be loath to admit it, dispassionate and objective methods for investigating test bias do exist. One purpose of this section is to present these methods to the reader. However, an aseptic discussion of regression equations and statistical definitions of test bias would be incomplete, only half of the story. Conceptions of test bias are irretrievably intermingled with notions of test fairness. A full explanation of the story surrounding the test-bias controversy requires that we investigate the related issue of test fairness, too.

Differences in terminology abound in this area, so it is important to set forth certain fundamental distinctions before proceeding. Test bias is a technical concept amenable to impartial analysis. The most salient methods for the objective assessment of test bias are discussed in the following. In contrast, test fairness reflects social values and philosophies of test use, particularly when test use extends

to selection for privilege or employment. Much of the passion that surrounds the test-bias controversy stems from a failure to distinguish test bias from test fairness. To avoid confusion, it is crucial to draw a sharp distinction between these two concepts. We include separate discussions of test bias and test fairness, beginning with an analysis of why test bias is such a controversial topic.

The Test-Bias Controversy

The test-bias controversy has its origins in the observed differences in average IQ among various racial and ethnic groups. For example, African Americans score, on average, about 15 points lower than white Americans on standardized IQ tests. This difference reduces to 7–12 IQ points when socioeconomic disparities are taken into account. The existence of marked racial/ethnic differences in ability test scores has fanned the fires of controversy over test bias. After all, employment opportunities, admission to college, completion of a high school diploma, and assignment to special education classes are all governed, in part, by test results. Biased tests could perpetuate a legacy of racial discrimination. Test bias is deservedly a topic of intense scrutiny by both the public and the testing professions.

One possibility is that the observed IQ disparities indicate test bias rather than meaningful group differences. In fact, most laypersons and even some psychologists would regard the magnitude of race differences in IQ as prima facie evidence that intelligence tests are culturally biased. This is an appealing argument, but a large difference between defined subpopulations is not a sufficient basis for proving test bias. The proof of test bias must rest upon other criteria outlined in the following section.

Racial and ethnic differences are not the only foundation for the test-bias controversy. Significant sex differences also exist on some ability measures, most particularly in the area of spatial thinking (Maccoby & Jacklin, 1974; Halpern, 1986). In one study (Gregory, Alley, & Morris, 1980), males outscored females on the spatial reasoning component of the Differential Aptitude Test by a full standard deviation. Such findings raise the possibility that spatial reasoning tests may be biased in favor of males. But how can we know? When do test score differences between groups signify test bias? We begin by reviewing the criteria that should be used to investigate test bias of any kind, whether for race, sex, or any other defining characteristic.

Criteria of Test Bias and Test Fairness

The topic of test bias has received wide attention from measurement psychologists, test developers, journalists, test critics, legislators, and the courts. Cole and Moss (1989) underscore an unsettling consequence of the proliferation of views held on this topic, namely, concepts of test bias have become increasingly intricate and complex. Furthermore, the understanding of test bias is made difficult by the implicit and often emotional assumptions—held even by scholars—that may lead honest persons to view the same information in different ways.

In part, disagreements about test bias are perpetuated because adversaries in this debate fail to clarify essential terminology. Too often, terms such as *test bias* and *test fairness* are considered interchangeable and thrown about loosely, without definition. We propose that test bias and test fairness commonly refer to markedly different aspects of the test-bias debate. Careful examination of both concepts will provide a basis for a more reasoned discussion of this controversial topic.

As interpreted by most authorities in this field, *test bias* refers to objective statistical indices which examine the patterning of test scores for relevant subpopulations. Although experts might disagree about nuances, on the whole there is a consensus about the statistical criteria that indicate when a test is biased. We will expand this point later but we can provide the reader with a brief preview here: In general, a test is deemed biased if it is differentially valid for different subgroups. For example, a test would be considered biased if the scores from appropriate subpopulations did not fall upon the same regression line for a relevant criterion.

In contrast to the narrow concept of test bias, *test fairness* is a broad concept that recognizes the importance of social values in test usage. Even a test that is unbiased according to the traditional technical criteria of homogeneous regression might still be deemed unfair because of the social consequences of using it for selection decisions. The crux of the debate is this: Test bias (a statistical concept) is not necessarily the same thing as test fairness (a values concept). Ultimately, test fairness is based on social conceptions such as one's image of a just society. In the assessment of test fairness, subjective values are of overarching importance; the statistical criteria of test bias are merely ancillary. We will return to this point later when we analyze the link between social values and test fairness. But let us begin with a traditional presentation of technical criteria for test bias.

The Technical Meaning of Test Bias: A Definition

One useful way to examine test bias is from the technical perspective of test validation. The reader will recall from an earlier chapter that a test is valid when a variety of evidence supports its utility and when inferences derived from it are appropriate, meaningful, and useful. One implication of this viewpoint is that test bias can be equated with differential validity for different groups:

> Bias is present when a test score has meanings or implications for a relevant, definable subgroup of test takers that are different from the meanings or implications for the remainder of the test takers. Thus, bias is differential validity of a given interpretation of a test score for any definable, relevant subgroup of test takers (Cole & Moss, 1989).

Perhaps a concrete example will help clarify this definition. Suppose a simple word problem arithmetic test were used to measure youngsters' addition skills. The problems might be of the form "If you have two six-packs of pop, how many cans do you have altogether?" Suppose, however, the test is used in a group of primarily Spanish-speaking seventh graders. With these children, low scores might indicate a language barrier, not a problem with arithmetic skills. In contrast, for English-speaking children low scores would most likely indicate a deficit in arithmetic skills. In this example, the test has differential validity, predicting arithmetic deficits quite well for English-speaking children, but very poorly for Spanish-speaking children. According to the technical perspective of test validation, we would conclude that the test is biased.

Although the general definition of test bias refers to differential validity, in practice the particular criteria of test bias fall under three main headings: content validity, criterion-related validity, and construct validity. We will review each of these categories, discussing relevant findings along the way. The coverage is illustrative, not exhaustive. Interested readers should consult Jensen (1980), Cole and Moss (1989), and Reynolds and Brown (1984b).

Bias in Content Validity

Bias in content validity is probably the most common criticism of those who denounce the use of standardized tests with minorities (Hilliard, 1984). Typically, critics rely upon their own expert judgment when they expound one or more of the following criticisms of the content validity of ability tests:

1. The items ask for information that minority or disadvantaged children have not had equal opportunity to learn.
2. The items are scored improperly because the test author has arbitrarily decided on the only correct answer, and minority children are inappropriately penalized for giving answers that are correct in their own culture but not in that of the test maker.
3. The wording of the question is unfamiliar, and a minority child who may "know" the correct answer is unable to respond because she or he did not understand the question (Reynolds & Brown, 1984a).

Any of these criticisms, if accurate, would constitute bona fide evidence of test bias. However, merely stating a criticism does not comprise proof. Where these criticisms fall short is that they are seldom buttressed by empirical evidence.

Reynolds (1982) has offered a definition of **content bias** for aptitude tests that addresses the preceding points in empirically defined, testable terms:

> An item or subscale of a test is considered to be biased in content when it is demonstrated to be relatively more difficult for members of one group than another when the general ability level of the groups being compared is held constant and no reasonable theoretical rationale exists to explain group differences on the item (or subscale) in question.

This definition is useful because it proposes an empirical approach to the question of test bias.

In general, attempts to prove that expert-nominated items are culturally biased have not yielded the conclusive evidence that critics expect. McGurk (1953a, 1953b, 1967, 1975) has written extensively on this topic, and we will use his classic study to illustrate this point. For his doctoral dissertation, McGurk asked a panel of 78 judges (professors, educators, and graduate students in psychology and sociology) to classify each of 226 items from well-known standardized tests of intelligence into one of three categories: least cultural; neutral; most cultural. McGurk administered these test items to hundreds of high school students. His primary analysis involved the test results for 213 African-American students and 213 white students matched for curriculum, school, length of enrollment, and socioeconomic background.

McGurk (1953ab) discovered that the mean difference between African-American and white students for the total hybrid test, expressed in standard deviation units, was 0.50. More pertinent to the topic of test bias in content validity was his comparison of scores on the 37 "most cultural" items versus the 37 "least cultural" items. For the "most cultural" items—the ones nominated by the judges as highly culturally biased—the difference was .30. For the "least cultural" items—the ones judged to be more fair to African Americans and other cultural minorities—the difference was .58. In other words, the items nominated as most cultural were relatively easier for African Americans; the items nominated as least cultural were relatively harder. This finding held true even after item difficulty was partialled out. Furthermore, the item difficulties for the two groups were almost perfectly correlated ($r = .98$ for "most cultural" and $r = .96$ for "least cultural" items). There is an important lesson here which test critics often overlook: "Expert" judges cannot identify culturally biased test items based on an analysis of item characteristics.

In general, with respect to well-known standardized tests of ability and aptitude, research has not supported the popular belief that the specific content of test items is a source of cultural bias against minorities. This conclusion does not exonerate these tests with respect to other criteria of test bias, discussed in the following sections. Furthermore, we can point out that savvy test developers should be vigilant even to the impression of bias in test content, since the appearance of unfairness can affect public attitudes about psychological tests in quite tangible ways.

Bias in Predictive or Criterion-Related Validity

The prediction of future performance is one important use of intelligence, ability, and aptitude tests. For this application of psychological testing, predictive validity is the most crucial form of validity in relation to test bias. In general, an unbiased test will predict future performance equally well for persons from different subpopulations. For example, an unbiased scholastic aptitude test will predict future academic performance of African Americans and white Americans with near-identical accuracy.

Reynolds (1982) offers a clear, direct definition of test bias with regard to criterion-related or **predictive validity bias:**

> A test is considered biased with respect to predictive validity when the inference drawn from the test score is not made with the smallest feasible random error or if there is constant error in an inference or prediction as a function of membership in a particular group.

This definition of test bias invokes what might be referred to as the criterion of homogeneous regression. According to this viewpoint, a test is unbiased if the results for all relevant subpopulations cluster equally well around a single regression line. In order to clarify this point, we need to introduce concepts relevant to simple regression. The discussion is modeled after Cleary, Humphreys, Kendrick, and Wesman (1975).

Suppose we are using a scholastic aptitude test to predict first-year grade point average (gpa) in college. In the case of a simple regression analysis, prediction of future performance is made from an equation of the form:

$$Y = bX + a$$

where Y is the predicted college gpa, X is the score on the aptitude test, and b and a are constants derived from a statistical analysis of test scores and grades of prior students. We will not concern ourselves with how b and a are derived; the reader can find this information in any elementary statistics textbook.

The values of b and a correspond to important aspects of the regression line—the straight line which facilitates the most accurate prediction of the criterion (college grades) from the predictor (aptitude score) (Figure 7.4). In particular, b corresponds to the slope of the line, with higher values of b indicating a steeper slope and more accurate prediction. The value of a depicts the intercept on the vertical axis. The units of measurement for b and a cannot be specified in advance because they depend upon the underlying scales used for X and Y. Notice in Figure 7.4 that the regression line is the reference for predicting grades from observed aptitude score.

According to the criterion of homogeneous regression, in an unbiased test a single regression line can predict performance equally well for all relevant subpopulations, even though the means for the different groups might differ. For example, in Figure 7.5 group A performs better than group B on both predictor and criterion. Yet, the relationship between aptitude score and grades is the same for both groups. In this hypothetical instance, the graph

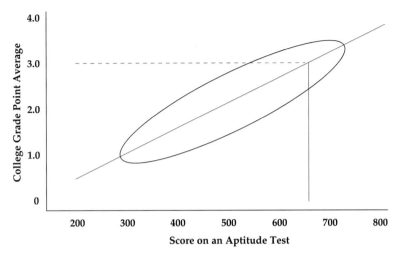

FIGURE 7.4

Test Scores, Grades, and Regression Line for a Hypothetical Large Group of College Students

Note: The dotted line shows how the regression line can be used to predict grade point average from the test score for a single, new subject.

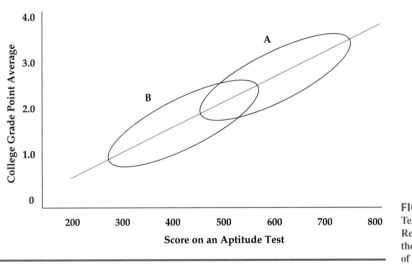

FIGURE 7.5

Test Scores, Grades, and Single Regression Line for Two Hypothetical, Large Subpopulations of College Students

depicts the absence of bias on the aptitude test with respect to criterion-related validity.

A more complicated situation known as intercept bias is shown in Figure 7.6. In this case, scores for the two groups do not cluster tightly around the single best regression line shown as a dotted line in the graph. Separate, parallel regression lines (and therefore separate regression equations) would be needed to facilitate accurate prediction. If a single regression line were used (the dotted line), criterion scores for group A would be overpredicted, whereas criterion scores for group B

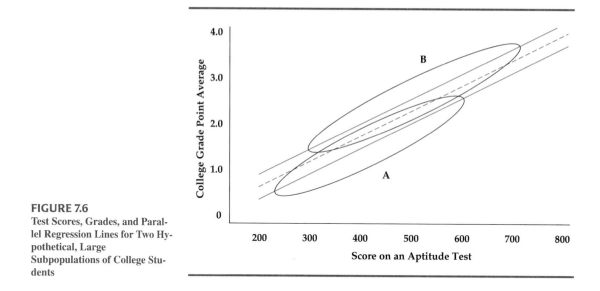

FIGURE 7.6

Test Scores, Grades, and Parallel Regression Lines for Two Hypothetical, Large Subpopulations of College Students

would be underpredicted. Thus, the use of a single regression line would constitute a clear instance of test bias, because the test has differential predictive validity for different subgroups.[1]

But what about using separate regression lines for each subgroup? Would this solve the problem and rescue the test from criterion-related test bias? Opinions differ on this point. Although there is no doubt that separate regression equations would maximize predictive accuracy for the combined sample, whether this practice would produce test fairness is debated. We return to this issue later, when we discuss the relevance of social values to test fairness.

The Scholastic Aptitude Test (now known as the Scholastic Assessment Test and discussed in a later chapter) has been analyzed by several researchers with regard to test bias in criterion-related validity (Cleary, Humphreys, Kendrick, & Wesman, 1975; Breland, 1979; Manning & Jackson, 1984). A consistent finding is that separate, parallel, regression lines are needed for African-

American and white examinees. For example, in one school the best regression equations for African-American, white, and combined students were as follows:

African-American: $Y = .055 + .0024V + .0025M$

White: $Y = .652 + .0026V + .0011M$

Combined: $Y = .586 + .0027V + .0012M$

where Y is the predicted college grade point, V is the SAT Verbal score, and M is the SAT Mathematics score (Cleary et al., 1975, p. 29). The effect of using the white or the combined formula is to overpredict college grades for African-American subjects based on SAT results. On the traditional four-point scale (A = 4, B = 3, etc.), the average amount of overprediction from 17 separate studies was .20 or one-fifth of a grade point (Manning & Jackson, 1984). What these results mean is open to debate, but it seems clear, at least, that the SAT and similar entrance examinations do not underpredict college grades for minorities.

The most peculiar regression outcome, known as slope bias, is depicted in Figure 7.7. In this case, the regression lines for separate subgroups are not even parallel. Using a single regression line (the dotted line) for prediction might therefore result in both

_____

1. Contrary to widely held belief, test bias in these cases actually favors the *lower*-scoring group because its performance on the criterion is overpredicted. On occasion, then, test bias can favor minority groups.

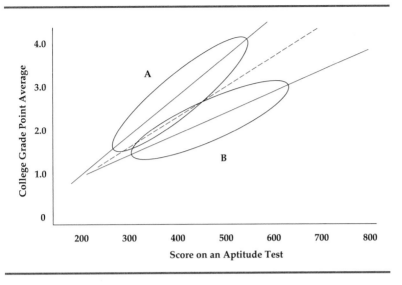

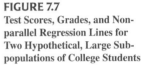

FIGURE 7.7

Test Scores, Grades, and Non-parallel Regression Lines for Two Hypothetical, Large Subpopulations of College Students

under- and overprediction of scores for selected subjects in both groups. Professional opinion would be unanimous in this case: This test possesses a high degree of test bias in criterion-related validity.

Bias in Construct Validity

The reader will recall that the construct validity of a psychological test can be documented by diverse forms of evidence, including appropriate developmental patterns in test scores, theory-consistent intervention changes in test scores, and confirmatory factor analysis. Because construct validity is such a broad concept, the definition of **bias in construct validity** requires a general statement amenable to research from a variety of viewpoints with a broad range of methods. Reynolds (1982) offers the following definition:

> Bias exists in regard to construct validity when a test is shown to measure different hypothetical traits (psychological constructs) for one group than another or to measure the same trait but with differing degrees of accuracy.

From a practical standpoint, two straightforward criteria for nonbias flow from this definition (Reynolds & Brown, 1984a). If a test is nonbiased,

then comparisons across relevant subpopulations should reveal a high degree of similarity for (1) the factorial structure of the test, and (2) the rank order of item difficulties within the test. Let us examine these criteria in more detail.

An essential criterion of nonbias is that the factor structure of test scores should remain invariant across relevant subpopulations. Of course, even within the same subgroup, the factor structure of a test might differ between age groups, so it is important that we restrict our comparison to same-aged persons from relevant subpopulations. For same-aged subjects, a nonbiased test will possess the same factor structure across subgroups. In particular, for a nonbiased test the number of emergent factors and the factor loadings for items or subscales will be highly similar for relevant subpopulations.

In general, when the items or subscales of prominent ability and aptitude tests are factor-analyzed separately in white and minority samples, the same factors emerge in the relevant subpopulations (Reynolds, 1982; Jensen, 1980, 1984). Although minor anomalies have been reported in a handful of studies (Scheuneman, 1987; Reschly, 1978; Gutkin & Reynolds, 1981; Johnston & Bolen, 1984) research in this area is more notable for its consistent findings with respect to factorial invariance across subgroups. An entirely typical result comparing white and Mexican-American children on the WISC-R (Geary & Whitworth, 1988) is reported in Table 7.5.

A second criterion of nonbias in construct validity is that the rank order of item difficulties within a test should be highly similar for relevant subpopulations. Since age is a major determinant of item difficulty, this standard is usually checked separately for each age group covered by a test. The reader should note what this criterion does not specify. It does not specify that relevant subgroups must obtain equivalent passing rates for test items. What is essential is that the items which are the most difficult (or least difficult) for one subgroup should be the most difficult (or least difficult) for other relevant subpopulations.

The criterion of similar rank order of item difficulties can be tested in a very straightforward and objective manner. If the difficulty level of each item is computed by means of the p value (percentage passing) for each relevant subpopulation, then it is possible to compare the relative item difficulties across same-aged subgroups. In fact, the similarity of the rank order of item difficulties for any two groups can be gauged objectively by means of a correlation coefficient (r_{xy}). The paired p values for the test items constitute the values of x and y used in the computation. The closer the value of r to 1.00, the more similar the rank ordering of item difficulties for the two groups.

In general, cross-group comparisons of relative item difficulties for prominent aptitude and ability tests have yielded correlations bordering on 1.00, that is, most tests show extremely similar rank orderings for item difficulties across relevant subpopulations (Jensen, 1980; Reynolds, 1982). In a representative study, Miele (1979) investigated the relative item difficulties of the WISC for African-American and white subjects at each of four grade levels (preschool, first, third, and fifth grades). He found that the average cross-racial correlations (holding grade level constant) for WISC item p values was .96 for males and .95 for females. These

TABLE 7.5 Comparative Factor Analysis of the WISC-R for 100 Anglo-American and 78 Mexican-American Children

| | Factor Loadings | | | | | |
| | Verbal Comprehension | | Perceptual Organization | | Freedom from Distractibility | |
Subtest	Ang	M-A	Ang	M-A	Ang	M-A
Information	.77	.77				
Similarities	.75	.85				
Arithmetic					.75	.75
Vocabulary	.86	.86				
Comprehension	.76	.76				
Picture Comp.			.58	.58		
Picture Arr.			.77	.61		
Block Design			.72	.61		
Object Assem.			.72	.72		
Coding					.52	.52

Ang = Anglo-American, N = 100

M-A = Mexican-American, N = 78

Source: Adapted with permission from Geary, D. C., and Whitworth, R. H. (1988). Is the factor structure of the WISC-R different for Anglo- and Mexican-American children? *Journal of Psychoeducational Assessment, 6,* 253–260.

values were hardly different from the cross-sex correlations (holding grade level constant) within race, which were .98 (whites) and .97 (African Americans). As noted, these findings are not unusual. In general, for prominent ability and aptitude tests, the rank order of item difficulties is virtually identical for all relevant subpopulations.

Reprise on Test Bias

Critics who hypothesize that tests are biased against minorities assert that the test scores underestimate the ability of minority members. As we have argued in the preceding sections, the hypothesis of test bias is a scientific question that can be answered empirically through such procedures as factor analysis, regression equations, intergroup comparisons of the difficulty levels for "biased" versus "unbiased" items, and rank ordering of item difficulties. In general, ability and aptitude tests fare quite well by these criteria. In fact, there is no domain of ability or aptitude testing where there has been cumulative evidence suggesting test bias. To the contrary, extensive reviews of the empirical studies provide overwhelming evidence disconfirming the bias hypothesis (Reynolds, 1982, 1994a; Jensen, 1980; Manning & Jackson, 1984).

We turn now to the broader concept of test fairness. How well do existing instruments meet reasonable criteria of test fairness? As the reader will learn, **test fairness** involves social values and is therefore an altogether more debatable—and more debated—topic than test bias.

▊ SOCIAL VALUES AND TEST FAIRNESS

Even an unbiased test might still be deemed unfair because of the social consequences of using it for selection decisions. In contrast to the narrow, objective notion of test bias, the concept of test fairness incorporates social values and philosophies of test use. We will demonstrate to the reader that, in the final analysis, the proper application of psychological tests is essentially an ethical conclusion which cannot be established on objective grounds alone.

In a classic article that deserves detailed scrutiny, Hunter and Schmidt (1976) proposed the first clear distinction between statistical definitions of test bias and social conceptions of test fairness. Although the authors reviewed the usual technical criteria of test bias with incisive precision, their article is most famous for its description of three mutually incompatible ethical positions that can and should affect test use.

Hunter and Schmidt (1976) noted that psychological tests are often used for institutional selection procedures such as employment or college admission. In this context, the application of test results must be guided by a philosophy of selection. Unfortunately, in many institutions the selection philosophy is implicit, not explicit. Nonetheless, when underlying values are made explicit, three ethical positions can be distinguished. These positions are unqualified individualism, quotas, and qualified individualism. Since these ethical stances are at the very core of public concerns about test fairness, we will review these positions in some detail.

Unqualified Individualism

In the American tradition of free and open competition, the ethical stance of **unqualified individualism** dictates that, without exception, the best qualified candidates should be selected for employment, admission, or other privilege. Hunter and Schmidt (1976) spell out the implications of this position:

> Couched in the language of institutional selection procedures, this means that an organization should use whatever information it possesses to make a scientifically valid prediction of each individual's performance and always select those with the highest predicted performance. This position looks appealing at first glance, but embraces some implications that most persons find troublesome. In particular, if race, sex, or ethnic group membership contributed to valid prediction of performance in a given situation over and above the contributions of test scores, then those who espouse unqualified individualism would be ethically bound to use such a predictor.

Quotas

The ethical stance of **quotas** acknowledges that many bureaucracies and educational institutions owe their very existence to the city or state in which they function. Since they exist at the will of the people, it can be argued that these institutions are ethically bound to act in a manner that is "politically appropriate" to their location. The logical consequence of this position is quotas. For example, in a location whose population is one-third African American and two-thirds white, selection procedures should admit candidates in approximately the same ratio. A selection procedure that deviates consistently from this standard would be considered unfair.

By definition, fair share quotas are based initially upon population percentages. Within relevant subpopulations, factors that predict future performance such as test scores would then be considered. However, one consequence of quotas is that those selected do not necessarily have the highest scores on the predictor test.

Qualified Individualism

Qualified individualism is a radical variant of individualism:

> This position notes that America is constitutionally opposed to discrimination on the basis of race, religion, national origin, or sex. A qualified individualist interprets this as an ethical imperative to refuse to use race, sex, and so on, as a predictor even if it were in fact scientifically valid to do so (Hunter & Schmidt, 1976).

For selection purposes, the qualified individualist would rely exclusively upon tested abilities, without reference to age, sex, race, or other demographic characteristics. This seems laudable, but examine the potential consequences. Suppose a qualified individualist used SAT scores for purposes of college admission. Even though SAT scores for African Americans and whites produce separate regression lines for the criterion of college grades, the qualified individualist would be ethically bound to use the single, less-accurate regression line derived for the entire sample of applicants.

As a consequence, the future performance of African Americans would be overpredicted, which would seemingly boost the proportion of persons selected from this applicant group. With respect to selection ratios, the practical impact of qualified individualism is therefore midway between quotas and unqualified individualism.

Reprise on Test Fairness

Which philosophy of selection is correct? The truth is, this problem is beyond the scope of rational solution. At one time or another, each of the ethical stances outlined previously has been championed by wise, respected, and thoughtful citizens. However, no consensus has emerged, and one is not likely to be found soon. The dispute reviewed here

> . . . is typical of ethical arguments—the resolution depends in part on irreconcilable values. Furthermore, even among those who agree on values there will be disagreements about the validity of certain relevant scientific theories that are not yet adequately tested. Thus, we feel that there is no way that this dispute can be objectively resolved. Each person must choose as he sees fit (and in fact we are divided) (Hunter & Schmidt, 1976).

When ethical stances clash—as they most certainly do in the application of psychological tests to selection decisions—the court system may become the final arbiter, as discussed later in this book.

GENETIC AND ENVIRONMENTAL DETERMINANTS OF INTELLIGENCE

Genetic Contributions to Intelligence

The nature-nurture debate regarding intelligence is a well-known and overworked controversy that we will largely sidestep here. We concur with McGue, Bouchard, Iacono, and Lykken (1993) that a substantial genetic component to intelligence has been proved by decades of adoption studies, familial research, and twin projects, even though individual studies may be faulted for particular reasons:

> When taken in aggregate, twin, family, and adoption studies of IQ provide a demonstration of the

existence of genetic influences on IQ as good as can be achieved in the behavioral sciences with nonexperimental methods. Without positing the existence of genetic influences, it simply is not possible to give a credible account for the consistently greater IQ similarity among monozygotic (MZ) twins than among like-sex dizygotic (DZ) twins, the significant IQ correlations among biological relatives even when they are reared apart, and the strong association between the magnitude of the familial IQ correlation and the degree of genetic relatedness [p. 60].

Of course, the demonstration of substantial genetic influence for a trait does not imply that heredity alone is responsible for differences between individuals—environmental factors are formative, too, as reviewed subsequently.

The genetic contribution to human characteristics such as intelligence (as measured by IQ tests) is usually measured in terms of a heritability index which can vary from 0.0 to 1.0. The **heritability index** is an estimate of how much of the total variance in a given trait is due to genetic factors. Heritability of 0.0 means that genetic factors make no contribution to the variance in a trait, whereas heritability of 1.0 means that genetic factors are exclusively responsible for the variance in a trait. Of course, for most measurable characteristics, heritability is somewhere between the two extremes. McGue et al. (1993) discuss the various methods for computing heritability, based upon twin and adoption studies.

It is important to stress that heritability is a population statistic that cannot be extended to explain an individual score. Furthermore, heritability for a given trait is not a constant. As Jensen (1969) notes, estimates of heritability "are specific to the population sampled, the point in time, how the measurements were made, and the particular test used to obtain the measurements." For IQ, most studies report heritability estimates right around .50, meaning that about half of the variability in IQ scores is from genetic factors. However, for some studies, the heritability of IQ is much higher, in the .70s (Bouchard, 1994; Bouchard, Lykken, McGue, Segal, & Tellegen, 1990; Pedersen, Plomin, Nesselroade, & McClearn, 1992).

Dozens of studies could be cited to demonstrate the importance of genetic factors in the determination of intelligence as measured by IQ tests. The relevant literature on this question is almost legion. For a basic initiation to the topic, the reader can consult Bouchard (1994) and McGue et al. (1993).

A most fascinating demonstration of the genetic contribution to IQ is found in the Minnesota Study of Twins Reared Apart (Bouchard et al., 1990). In this ongoing study, identical twins reared apart are reunited for extensive psychometric testing. Bouchard (1994) reports that the IQs of identical twins reared apart correlate almost as highly as those of identical twins reared together, even though the twins reared apart often were exposed to different environmental conditions (in some cases, sharply contrasting environments). In sum, differences in environment appeared to cause very little divergence in the IQs of identical twin pairs reared apart. These findings strongly corroborate a genetic contribution to intelligence, with heritability estimated in the vicinity of .70.

We can further illustrate the general thrust of research in this area with a classic study, Honzik's (1957) reanalysis of the data from the adoption study of Skodak and Skeels (1949). What this analysis showed is that when adopted children are repeatedly tested with an instrument such as the Stanford-Binet, their intelligence correlates more and more closely with the educational attainment of the biological parents; by age eight the correlation stabilizes at a value of approximately 0.35 (Figure 7.8). Interestingly enough, this is about the same level of correlation found between children's IQ and parent educational attainment for intact families. In contrast, Honzik (1957) determined that the intelligence of the adopted children correlated near zero with the educational attainment of their adoptive parents. The educational attainment of adults is a good proxy for their intelligence—the best estimate available under the circumstances. The results indicated that the intelligence of adoptive children parallels the intelligence of the biological parents—even in their absence—but showed no relationship to the intelligence of the adoptive parents—even in their constant, day-to-day presence.

What do these findings mean? We know that the biological parents provided the genetic subsidy to their children's intelligence whereas the adoptive parents furnished the environmental underpinnings. The dispassionate observer will find it difficult to avoid an obvious conclusion: Adoption studies such as reported by Honzik (1957) corroborate a robust—but not exclusive—genetic contribution to intelligence.

However, we must avoid the tendency to view any corpus of research in a simplistic either/or frame of mind. Even the most die-hard hereditarians acknowledge that a person's intelligence is shaped also by the quality of experience. The crucial question is: To what extent can enriched or deprived environments modify intelligence upward or downward from the genetically circumscribed potential? The reader is reminded that the genetic contribution to intelligence is indirect, most likely via the gene-coded physical structures of the brain and nervous system. Nonetheless, the brain is quite malleable in the face of environmental manipula-

tions which can even alter its weight and the richness of neuronal networks (Greenough, Black, & Wallace, 1987). How much can such environmental impacts sway intelligence as measured by IQ tests? We will review several studies indicating that environmental extremes help determine intellectual outcome within a range of approximately 20 IQ points, perhaps more.

Environmental Effects: Impoverishment and Enrichment

First we examine the effects of environmental disadvantage. Vernon (1979, chp. 9) has reviewed the early studies of severe deprivation, noting that children reared under conditions where they received little or no human contacts can show striking improvements in IQ—as much as 30 to 50 points—when transferred to a more normal environment. Yet we must regard this body of research with some skepticism, owing to the typically exceptional conditions under which the initial tests were adminis-

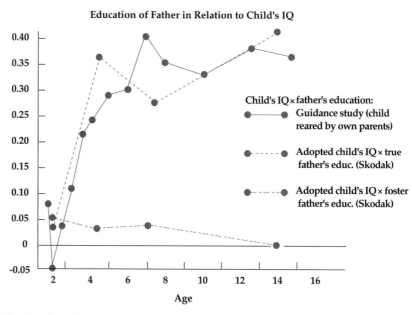

FIGURE 7.8

IQ Resemblance of Adopted Children to Foster and Biological Fathers

Source: Reprinted with permission from: Honzik, M. (1957). Developmental studies of parent-child resemblance in intelligence. *Child Development, 28,* 215–228. Copyright © by The Society for Research in Child Development, Inc.

Note: Data for mothers are quite similar.

tered. Can a meaningful test be administered to seven-year-old children raised almost like animals (Koluchova, 1972)?

Typical of this early research is the follow-up study by Skeels (1966) of 25 orphaned children originally diagnosed as mentally retarded (Skeels & Dye, 1939). These children were first tested at approximately 1½ years of age when living in a highly unstimulating orphanage. Thirteen of them were then transferred to another home where they received a great deal of supervised, doting attention from older mentally retarded girls. These children showed a considerable increase in IQ, whereas the 12 who remained behind decreased further in IQ. When traced at follow-up 26 years later, the 13 transferred cases were normal, self-supporting adults, or were married. The other subjects—the contrast group—were still institutionalized or in menial jobs. The enriched group showed an average increase of 32 IQ points when retested with the Stanford-Binet, whereas the contrast group fell below their original scores. Even though we are disinclined to place much credence in the original IQ scores and might therefore quarrel with the exact magnitude of the change, the Skeels (1966) study surely indicates that the difference between a severely depriving early environment and a more normal one might account for perhaps 15 to 20 IQ points.

A methodologically novel demonstration of environmentally induced IQ deficit has been reported by Jensen (1977). He tested 653 white children and 826 African-American children from a small rural town in the southeastern part of Georgia. The working hypothesis of his study was that older African-American children should score lower than their younger siblings, owing to the cumulative, intellect-depressing effects of their bleak, profoundly deprived environment. According to the cumulative deficit hypothesis, a consistent downward trend in IQ is a result of the cumulative effects of environmental disadvantages in factors related to mental development. In contrast, white children, who are less environmentally deprived, should not show a cumulative intellectual deficit as a linear function of age.

All children were administered the California Test of Mental Maturity (CTMM, 1963 revision), a standardized test of general intelligence, as part of a state-mandated testing program. The CTMM yielded carefully standardized deviation IQ scores (national mean of 100, standard deviation of 15) computed separately from national norms for each grade level from kindergarten through grade 12. Jensen (1977) noted that the sampled populations, particularly the African-American group, were not intended to be representative of the wider U.S. population, white or African-American:

> Blacks in the locality under study are probably as severely disadvantaged, educationally and economically, as can be found anywhere in the United States. If an age decrement does not exist in this group, it would seem most doubtful that it could be found in any subpopulation within our borders.

As predicted, older African-American children scored lower than their younger brothers and sisters, the magnitude of the difference being directly related to the difference in age. In particular, African-American children appeared to lose approximately one IQ point a year, on average, between the ages of 6 and 16, with the cumulative loss totalling 5 to 10 IQ points. The exact amount of the loss depends upon how we interpret some apparent sampling peculiarities in the data (Figure 7.9).

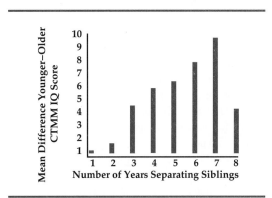

FIGURE 7.9   **Average Difference in CTMM IQ between Younger and Older African-American Siblings as a Function of the Difference in Age**
Source: Based on data from Jensen, A. R. (1977). Cumulative deficit in IQ of blacks in the rural south. *Developmental Psychology, 13,* 184–191.

Furthermore, if we factor in the probable IQ deficit that occurred between birth and age 5, we can surmise that the overall effect of a depriving environment is substantially more than the 5- to 10-point IQ decrement reported by Jensen (1977).

Scarr and Weinberg (1976, 1983) reversed the question probed by Jensen (1977), namely, they asked: What happens to their intelligence when African-American children are adopted into the relatively enriched environment provided by economically and educationally advantaged white families? As discussed later, it is well known that African-American children reared by their own families obtain IQ scores that average about 15 points below whites (Jensen, 1980). Some portion of this difference—perhaps all of it—is likely due to the many social, economic, and cultural differences between the two groups. We put that issue aside for now. Instead, we pursue a related question that bears on the malleability of IQ: What difference does it make when African-American children are adopted into a more economically and educationally advantaged environment?

Scarr and Weinberg (1976, 1983) found that 130 African-American and interracial children adopted into upper middle class white families averaged a Full Scale IQ of 106 on the Stanford-Binet or the WISC, a full 6 points higher than the national average and some 18 to 21 points higher than typically found with African-American examinees. African-American children adopted early in life, before one year of age, fared even better, with a mean IQ of 110. We can only wonder what the IQ scores would have been if the adoptions had taken place at birth, and if excellent prenatal care had been provided. This study indicates that when the early environment is optimal, IQ can be boosted by perhaps 20 points.

In addition to enriching the psychological environment, another approach to boosting IQ has been to enrich the nutritional status of children. An intriguing study by Schoenthaler, Amos, Eysenck, and others (1991) looked at the effects of controlled vitamin-mineral supplements on IQ in 615 high school students. Except that it employed an ex-

tremely tight experimental design with double-blind random assignment, this study would be easy to dismiss as a "crackpot" investigation of the implausible hypothesis that 12 weeks of vitamin-mineral enrichment will boost IQ. The researchers found that compared to a placebo control group, children who received 100 percent of the daily recommended vitamin/mineral supplements showed no incremental gains in Verbal IQ, but a significant average boost of 3.7 points in Performance IQ on the WISC-R. This intriguing result is badly in need of replication and extension by other researchers. Lynn (1993) reviews additional studies, including a reported nine-point IQ gain in nonverbal reasoning among normal 12- to 13-year-old British children who received a vitamin-mineral supplement over an eight-month period.

Limitations of space prevent us from further detailed discussion of environmental effects on IQ. It is worth noting, though, that a huge literature has emerged from early intervention and enrichment-stimulation studies of children at risk for school failure and mental retardation (e.g., Ramey & Ramey, 1998; Spitz, 1986; Sprigle & Schaeffer, 1985). In general, these studies show that intervention and enrichment can boost IQ in children at risk for school failure and mental retardation. Summarizing four decades of research, Ramey and Ramey (1998) extracted six principles from the research on early intervention for at-risk children. They refer to these as "remarkable consistencies in the major findings" on intervention studies:

1. Interventions that begin earlier (e.g., during infancy) and continue longer provide the best benefits to participating children.
2. More-intensive interventions (e.g., number of visits per week) produce larger positive effects than less-intensive interventions.
3. Direct enrichment experiences (e.g., working directly with the kids) provide greater impact than indirect experiences.
4. Programs with comprehensive services (e.g., multiple enhancements) produce greater positive changes than those with a narrow focus.

5. Some children (e.g., those with normal birth weight) show greater benefits from participation than other children.

6. Initial positive benefits diminish over time if the child's environment does not encourage positive attitudes and continued learning.

One concern about early intervention programs is their cost, which has been excessive for some of the demonstration projects. Skeptics wonder about the practicality and also the ultimate payoff of providing extensive, broad-based, continuing intervention virtually from birth onward for the millions of children at risk for developmental problems. This is a realistic concern because "relatively few early intervention programs have received long-term follow-up" (Ramey & Ramey, 1998). Critics also wonder if the programs merely teach children how to take tests without affecting their underlying intelligence very much (Jensen, 1981). Finally, there is the issue of cultural congruence. Intervention programs are mainly designed by white psychologists and then applied disproportionately to minority children. This a concern because programs need to be culturally relevant and welcomed by the consumers, otherwise the interventions are doomed to failure.

Teratogenic Effects on Intelligence and Development

In normal prenatal development, the fetus is protected from the external environment by the placenta, a vascular organ in the uterus through which the fetus is nourished. However, some substances known as **teratogens** cross the placental barrier and cause physical deformities in the fetus. Especially if the deformities involve the brain, teratogens may produce lifelong behavioral disorders, including low IQ and mental retardation. The list of potential teratogens is almost endless and includes prescription drugs, hormones, illicit drugs, smoking, alcohol, radiation, toxic chemicals, and viral infections (Berk, 1989; Martin, 1994). We will briefly highlight the most prevalent and also the most preventable teratogen of all, alcohol.

Heavy drinking by pregnant women causes their offspring to be at very high risk for **fetal alcohol syndrome** (FAS), a specific cluster of abnormalities first described by Jones, Smith, Ulleland, and Streissguth (1973). Intelligence is markedly lower in children with FAS. When assessed in adolescence or adulthood, about half of all persons with this disorder score in the retarded range on IQ tests (Olson, 1994). Prenatal exposure to alcohol is one of the leading known causes of mental retardation in the Western world. The defining criteria of FAS include the following:

1. Prenatal and/or postnatal growth retardation—weight below the 10th percentile after correcting for gestational age.
2. Central nervous system dysfunction—skull or brain malformations, mild to moderate mental retardation, neurological abnormalities, and behavior problems.
3. Facial dysmorphology—widely spaced eyes, short eyelid openings, small up-turned nose, thin upper lip, and minor ear deformities (Clarren & Smith, 1978; Sokol & Clarren, 1989).

The full-blown FAS previously described occurs mainly in offspring of women alcoholics—those who ingest many drinks per occasion. With lower levels of drinking, a more muted manifestation of the syndrome known as **fetal alcohol effect** may arise. A child with fetal alcohol effect typically has a normal physical appearance, but exhibits demonstrably impaired attentional capacities and is slower to respond in a reaction time paradigm (Streissguth, Martin, Barr, & Sandman, 1984). Furthermore, the effect is linear dose-related, that is, there may be no safe level of drinking during pregnancy (Streissguth, Bookstein, & Barr, 1996). For this reason, physicians now routinely advise women to abstain from alcohol during pregnancy. Nonetheless, a *conservative* estimate for the incidence of FAS (mild to severe forms) in the Western world is 1 per 1,000 live births, with most cases going undiagnosed and unrecognized (Abel, 1995). Spohr and Steinhausen

(1996) provide an excellent review of research on the FAS syndrome.

Effects of Environmental Toxins on Intelligence

Many industrial chemicals and byproducts may impair the nervous system temporarily, or even cause permanent damage that affects intelligence. Examples include lead, mercury, manganese, arsenic, thallium, tetra-ethyl lead, organic mercury compounds, methyl bromide, and carbon disulphide (Lishman, 1978, chp. 13). Certainly the most widely studied of these environmental toxins is lead, which we examine in modest detail here.

Sources of human lead absorption include eating of lead-pigmented paint chips by infants and toddlers; breathing of particulate lead from smelter emissions or automobile combustion of leaded gasoline; eating of food from lead-soldered cans or lead-glazed pottery; and the drinking of water that has passed through lead pipes. Because the human body excretes lead slowly, most citizens of the industrialized world carry a lead burden substantially higher—perhaps 500 times higher—than known in pre-Roman times (Patterson, 1980).

The hazards of high-level lead exposure are acknowledged by every medical and psychological researcher who has investigated this topic. High doses of lead are irrefutably linked to cerebral palsy, seizure disorders, blindness, mental retardation, even death. The more important question pertains to "asymptomatic" lead exposure: Can a level of absorption that is insufficient to cause obvious medical symptoms nonetheless produce a decrement in intellectual abilities?

Research findings on this topic are complex and controversial. Using tooth lead from shed teeth of young children as their index of cumulative lead burden, Needleman, Gunnoe, Leviton, Reed, Peresie, Maher, and Barrett (1979) reported that "asymptomatic" lead exposure was associated with decrements in overall intelligence (about 4 IQ points), and lowered performance on verbal subtests, auditory and speech processing tests, and a reaction time measure of attention. These differ-

ences persisted at follow-up 11 years later (Needleman, Schell, Bellinger, Leviton, & Allred, 1990). Yet, using a similar study method, Smith, Delves, Lansdown, Clayton, and Graham (1983) found a nonsignificant effect from children's lead exposure when social factors such as the parents' level of education and social status were controlled.

In part, research findings on this topic are contradictory because it is difficult to disentangle the effects of lead from those of poverty, stress, poor nutrition, and other confounding variables (Gregory & Mohan, 1977). Most likely, asymptomatic lead exposure has harmful effects upon the nervous system which translate to reduced intelligence, impaired attention, and a host of other undesirable behavioral consequences. Even in the absence of a scientific consensus on this point, prudence dictates that we should reduce lead exposure in humans to the lowest levels possible.

ORIGINS OF AFRICAN-AMERICAN AND WHITE IQ DIFFERENCES

African-American and White IQ Differences

As previously noted, African Americans score, on the average, about 15 points lower than white Americans on standardized IQ tests. This difference is not trivial, amounting to a full standard deviation. Although the IQ difference fluctuates from one analysis to the next—as small as 10 points in some studies but as large as 20 points in others—the disparity has been documented in numerous samples with a wide variety of tests. Controlling for social class reduces the difference but does not eliminate it. Furthermore, the magnitude of the difference apparently remained impervious to change throughout the mid- to late-twentieth century (Jensen, 1980; Kennedy, Van de Riet, & White, 1963; Shuey, 1966).

Figure 7.10 portrays an earlier study of IQ differences between African Americans and white Americans, based upon the 1960 edition of the Stanford-Binet. The reader will notice that, on average, the white sample ($M = 101.8$) outscored the African-American sample ($M = 80.7$) by slightly more than 20 IQ points. More recently, a similar pattern has emerged on the WAIS-R, with whites ($M = 101.4$) in the standardization sample outscoring African Americans ($M = 86.9$) by 14½ IQ points (Reynolds, Chastain, Kaufman, & McLean, 1987). The race difference also surfaces on the updated Stanford-Binet: Fourth Edition, with whites ($M = 103.5$) in the standardization sample outscoring African Americans ($M = 86.1$) by nearly 17½ points (Thorndike, Hagen, & Sattler, 1986).

When demographic variables such as socioeconomic status are taken into account, the size of the mean difference reduces to .5 to .7 standard deviations or 7 to 10 IQ points, but remains robust (Reynolds & Brown, 1984a). The actuality of a race difference in IQ scores has been replicated so many times that it is no longer the focus of serious dispute. However, the *interpretation* of the well-documented finding is fiercely debated.

One viewpoint (discussed previously) is that the observed IQ disparity is caused, partly or wholly, by test bias. This is a popular and widely held viewpoint which is rarely supported by technical studies of test bias, as noted previously. Test bias may play a minor role in race differences, but it cannot explain the large and persistent differences in IQ scores between African Americans and white Americans. Here we intend to examine a different hypothesis, namely: Is the IQ difference between African Americans and white Americans primarily genetic?

The Genetic Hypothesis for Race Differences in IQ

The hypothesis of a genetic basis for race differences in IQ first gained scholarly prominence in 1969 when Arthur Jensen published a provocative

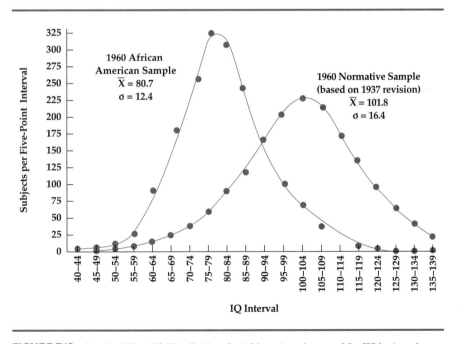

FIGURE 7.10   Stanford-Binet IQ Distributions for African Americans and for White Americans
Source: Reprinted with permission from Kennedy, W. A., Van de Riet, V., and White, Jr., J. C. (1963). A normative sample of intelligence and achievement of negro elementary school children in the southeast United States. *Monographs of the Society for Research in Child Development, 28* [No. 90], 68. Copyright © by The Society for Research in Child Development, Inc.

paper titled "How much can we boost IQ and scholastic achievement?" (Jensen, 1969). Jensen set the tone for his paper in the opening sentence when he asserted that "compensatory education has been tried and it apparently has failed." He further contended that compensatory education programs were based on two fallacious theoretical underpinnings, namely, the "average child concept" which views children as more or less homogeneous, and the "social deprivation hypothesis" which asserts that environmental deprivation is the primary cause of lowered achievement and IQ scores. Jensen argued forcefully against both suppositions. Furthermore, leaning heavily upon the literature in behavior genetics, Jensen implied that the reason whites scored higher than African Americans on IQ tests was probably related more to genetic factors than to the effects of environmental deprivation. The thrust of his paper was to suggest that, since compensatory education has proved ineffectual, and since the evidence suggests a strong genetic component to IQ, therefore it is appropriate to entertain a genetic explanation for the well-documented difference in favor of whites on IQ tests. He formulated the genetic hypothesis in a careful, tentative, scholarly manner:

> The fact that a reasonable hypothesis has not been rigorously proved does not mean that it should be summarily dismissed. It only means that we need more appropriate research for putting it to the test. I believe such definitive research is entirely possible but has not been done. So all we are left with are various lines of evidence, no one of which is definitive alone, but which, viewed all together, make it a not unreasonable hypothesis that genetic factors are strongly implicated in the average Negro-white intelligence difference. The preponderance of the evidence is, in my opinion, less consistent with a strictly environmental hypothesis than with a genetic hypothesis, which, of course, does not exclude the influence of environment or its interaction with genetic factors (Jensen, 1969).

With the articulation of a genetic hypothesis for race differences in IQ, Jensen provoked an intense debate that has raged on, with periodic lulls, to the present day.

In the mid-1990s the controversy over a genetic basis for race differences in IQ was intensified once again with the publication of *The Bell Curve* by Richard Herrnstein and Charles Murray (1994). This massive tome was primarily a book about the importance of IQ as a predictor of poverty, school leaving, unemployment, illegitimacy, crime, and a host of other social pathologies. But two chapters on ethnic differences in intelligence caused an uproar among social scientists and the lay public. The authors reviewed dozens of studies and concluded that the IQ gap between African Americans and whites has changed little in this century. They also argued that test bias cannot explain the race differences. Furthermore, they noted that races differ not just in average IQ scores but also in the profile of intellectual abilities. In addition, they concluded that intelligence is only slightly malleable even in the face of intensive environmental intervention. As did Jensen, Herrnstein and Murray (1994) stated their genetic hypothesis with considerable circumspection:

> It seems highly likely to us that both genes and the environment have something to do with racial differences [in cognitive ability]. What might the mix be? We are resolutely agnostic on that issue; as far as we can determine, the evidence does not yet justify an estimate.

Although the authors declined to provide an estimate of the genetic contribution to race differences in IQ, it is clear from the tone of their pessimistic book that they believe it to be substantial. Is such a disturbing conclusion warranted by the evidence?

Tenability of the Genetic Hypothesis

The genetic hypothesis for race IQ differences is an unpopular idea that is anathema to many laypersons and social scientists. But contempt for an idea does not constitute disproof, and superficiality is no substitute for a reasoned examination of evidence. In light of additional analysis and research, is the genetic hypothesis for IQ differences tenable? We will examine three lines of evidence here which indicate that the answer is "No."

Several critics have pointed out that the genetic hypothesis is based on the questionable assumption that evidence of IQ heritability within groups can be used to infer heritability between racial groups. Jensen (1969) expressed this premise rather explicitly, pointing to the substantial genetic component in IQ as suggestive evidence that differences in IQ between African Americans and white Americans are, in part, genetically based. Echoing earlier critics, Kaufman (1990) responds as follows:

> One cannot infer heritability between groups from studies that have provided evidence of the IQ's heritability within groups. Even if IQ is equally heritable within the black and white races separately, that does not prove that the IQ differences between the races are genetic in origin. Scarr-Salapatek's (1971, p. 1226) simple example explains this point well: Plant two randomly drawn samples of seeds from a genetically heterogeneous population in two types of soil—good conditions versus poor conditions—and compare the heights of the fully grown plants. Within each type of soil, individual variations in the heights are genetically determined; but the average difference in height between the two samples is solely a function of environment.

A second problem with the genetic hypothesis is that a crucial prediction derived from it does not hold up to empirical examination. Specifically, if racial IQ differences are genetically based, then the degree of African ancestry should help predict average IQs within African-American subgroups. In other words, African Americans with a fully African ancestry should, on average, score lower on IQ tests than African Americans with a mixed African and caucasian ancestry. However, using blood group markers as the index of African-caucasian admixture, Scarr, Pakstis, Katz, and Barker (1977) found no evidence of a relationship between degree of white ancestry and intellectual skills within the African-American population. Thus, their results failed to support a strong hypothesis of genetic racial differences in intelligence.

Another criticism of the genetic hypothesis is that careful analysis of environmental factors provides a sufficient explanation of race differences in IQ, that is, the genetic hypothesis is simply unnec-

essary. This is the approach taken by Brooks-Gunn, Klebanov, and Duncan (1996) in a study of 483 African-American and white low-birthweight children. What makes their study different from other similar analyses is the richness of their data. Instead of using only one or two measures of the environment (e.g., a single index of poverty level), they collected longitudinal data on income level and many other co-factors of poverty such as length of hospital stay, maternal verbal ability, home learning environment, neighborhood condition, and other components of family social class. When the IQ of the children was tested at age five with the WPPSI, the researchers found the usual disparity between the white children (mean IQ of 103) and the African-American children (mean IQ of 85). However, when poverty and its co-factors were statistically controlled, the IQ differences were almost completely eliminated. Their study suggests that previous research has underestimated the pervasive effects of poverty and its co-factors as a contribution to African-American and white IQ differences. Neisser, Boodoo, Bouchard, and others (1996) offer additional perspectives on race differences in IQ and related topics.

Before leaving the topic of race differences in IQ, we should point out that the emotion attached to this topic is largely undeserved, for two reasons. First, racial groups always show large overlaps in IQ—meaning that the peoples of the earth are much more alike than they are different. Second, as previously noted, the existing race differences in IQ certainly reflect cultural differences and environmental factors to a substantial degree. Wilson (1994) has catalogued the numerous differences in cultural background between African Americans and white Americans. In 1992, for example, 64 percent of African-American parents were divorced, separated, widowed, or never married; 63 percent of African-American births were to unmarried mothers; and 30 percent of African-American births were to adolescents (U.S. Bureau of the Census, 1993). On average, these realities of family life for many African Americans inevitably will lead to lowered performance on intelligence tests. Lest the reader conclude that we are hereby endorsing a subtle form of Anglocentric superiority, consider Lynn's (1987) conclusion that the mean IQ of the Japanese is 107, a full seven points higher than the average for American whites. So what?

AGE CHANGES IN INTELLIGENCE

We turn now to another controversial topic—whether intelligence declines with age. Certainly, one of the most pervasive stereotypes about aging is that we lose intellectual ability as we grow older. This stereotype is so pervasive that few laypersons question it. But we should question it.

In general, the empirical study of this topic provides a more optimistic conclusion than the common stereotype suggests. However, the research also reveals that age changes in intelligence are complex and multifaceted. The simple question "Does intelligence decline with age?" turns out to have several labyrinthine answers.

We can trace the evolution of research on age-related intellectual changes as follows:

1. Early cross-sectional research with instruments such as the WAIS painted a somber picture of a slow decline in general intelligence after age 15 or 20 and a precipitously accelerated descent after age 60.
2. Just a few years later, more sophisticated studies using sequential testing with multidimensional instruments such as the Primary Mental Abilities Test suggested a more optimistic trajectory for intelligence: minimal change in most abilities until at least age 60.
3. Parallel research utilizing the fluid-crystallized distinction posited a gradual increase in crystallized intelligence virtually to the end of life, juxtaposed against a rapid decline in fluid intelligence.
4. Most recently, a few psychologists have proposed that adult intelligence is qualitatively different, akin to a new Piagetian stage that might be called postformal reasoning. This research calls into question the ecological validity of using standard instruments with older examinees.

We examine each of these research epochs in more detail in the following sections.

Early Cross-Sectional Research

One of the earliest comprehensive studies of age trends on an individually administered intelligence test was reported by Wechsler (1944) shortly after publication of the Wechsler-Bellevue Form I. As is true of all the Wechsler tests designed for adults, raw scores on the W-B I subtests were first transformed into standard scores (referred to as scaled scores) with a mean of 10 and an SD of 3. Regardless of the age of the subject, these scaled scores were based on a fixed reference group of 350 subjects ages 20 to 34 included in the standardization sample. By consulting the appropriate age table, the sum of the 11 scaled scores was then used to find an examinee's IQ.

However, the sum of the scaled scores by itself is a direct index of an examinee's ability relative to the reference group. Wechsler used this index to chart the relationship between age and intelligence (Figure 7.11). His results indicated a rapid growth in general intelligence in childhood through age 15 or 20, followed by a slow decline to age 65. He was characteristically blunt in discussing his findings:

> If the fact that intellectual growth stops at about the age of fifteen has been a hard fact to accept, the indication that intelligence after attaining its maximum forthwith begins to decline just as any other physiological capacity, instead of maintaining itself at its highest level over a long period of time, has been an even more bitter pill to swallow. It has, in fact, proved so unpalatable that psychologists have generally chosen to avoid noticing it (Wechsler, 1952).

Normative studies with subsequent Wechsler adult tests revealed exactly the same pattern, both for the WAIS (Wechsler, 1955), the WAIS-R (Wechsler, 1981), and the WAIS-III (Tulsky, Zhu, & Ledbetter, 1997). Later investigators also extended the older age limit tested to age 70 and 80, finding a progressive and accelerating rate of decline in overall test performance that seemed to confirm Wechsler's belief that it was "normal" for

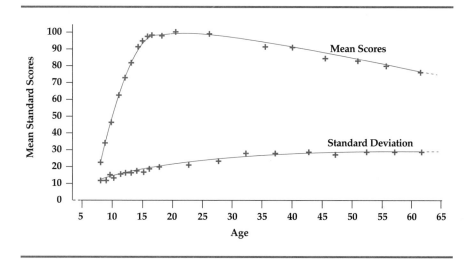

FIGURE 7.11   The Curve of Growth and Supposed Decline on the Wechsler-Bellevue Form I
Source: Reprinted with permission from: Wechsler, D. (1944). *Measurement of adult intelligence* (3rd ed.).
Baltimore, MD: Williams & Wilkins.

general intelligence to decline after young adulthood (Eisdorfer & Cohen, 1961).

Overlooked by Wechsler and many other **cross-sectional design** researchers was the influence of their methodology upon their findings. It has been recognized for quite some time that cross-sectional studies often confound age effects with educational disparities or other age group differences (see Baltes, Reese, & Nesselroade, 1977; Kausler, 1991). For example, in the normative studies of the Wechsler tests, it is invariably true that the younger standardization subjects are better educated than the older ones. In all likelihood, the lower scores of the older subjects are caused, in part, by these educational differences rather than signifying an inexorable age-related decline.

Sequential Studies of Intelligence

To control for age group differences, many researchers prefer a **longitudinal design** in which the same subjects are retested one or more times over periods of 5 to 10 years and, in rare cases, up to 40 years later. Because there is only one group of subjects, longitudinal designs eliminate age group disparities (e.g., more education in the young than the old subjects) as a confounding factor. However, the longitudinal approach is not without its shortcomings. Longitudinal studies suffer from four potential pitfalls:

1. Time of measurement is the most serious problem. Major historical events such as an economic depression can warp the intellectual and psychological development of entire generations. As a result, longitudinally measured age changes may reflect the peculiarities of the time of measurement rather than any universal age effects.
2. Selective attrition—the less capable subjects may be the most likely to drop out, artificially inflating the mean scores of retested subjects.
3. Practice effects—examinees improve when they take the same test two, three, even five times.
4. Regression to the mean—especially a problem when participants are selected because of their initial extreme scores such as very low IQ scores (Hayslip & Panek, 1989).

The most efficient research method for studying age changes in ability is a **cross-sequential**

design that combines cross-sectional and longitudinal methodologies (Schaie, 1977):

> In brief, the researchers begin with a cross-sectional study. Then, after a period of years, they retest these subjects, which provides longitudinal data on several cohorts—a longitudinal sequence. At the same time, they test a new group of subjects, forming a second cross-sectional study—and, together with the first cross-sectional study, a cross-sectional sequence. This whole process can be repeated over and over (every five or ten years, say) with retesting of old subjects (adding to the longitudinal data) and first-testing of new subjects (adding to the cross-sectional data) (Schaie & Willis, 1986).

In 1956, Schaie began the most comprehensive cross-sequential study ever conducted in what is referred to as the Seattle Longitudinal Study (Schaie, 1958, 1983, 1994). He administered Thurstone's test of five Primary Mental Abilities (PMA) and other intelligence-related measures to an initial cross-sectional sample of 500 community-dwelling adults. The PMA subtests include Verbal Meaning, Space, Reasoning, Number, and Word Fluency. In 1963, he retested these subjects and added a new cross-sectional cohort. Additional waves of data were collected in 1970, 1977, 1984, and 1991.

Three conclusions emerged from Schaie's cross-sequential study of adult mental abilities:

1. Each cross-sectional study indicated some degree of apparent age-related decrement in mental abilities, postponed until after age 50 for some abilities, but beginning after age 35 for others. In particular, Number skills and Word Fluency showed an age-related decrement only after age 50, whereas Verbal Meaning, Space, and Reasoning scores appeared to decline sooner, after age 35.
2. Successive cross-sectional studies—the cross-sectional sequence—revealed significant intergenerational differences in favor of those born most recently. Even holding age constant, those born and tested most recently performed better than those born and tested at an early time. For example, 30-year-old examinees tested in 1977 tended to score better than 30-year-old exami-

nees tested in 1970 who tended to score better than 30-year-old examinees tested in 1963 who, in turn, outperformed 30-year-old examinees tested in 1956. However, these cohort differences in intelligence were not uniform across the different abilities measured by the PMA. The pattern of rising abilities was most apparent for Verbal Meaning, Reasoning, and Space. Cohort changes for Number and Word Fluency were more complex and contradictory.

3. In contrast to the moderately pessimistic findings of the cross-sectional comparisons, the *longitudinal* comparisons showed a tendency for mean scores either to rise slightly or to remain constant until approximately age 60 or 70. The only exceptions to this trend involved highly speeded tests such as Word Fluency in which the examinee must name words in a given category as quickly as possible, and Number where the examinee must complete arithmetic computations quickly and accurately.

The results of the Schaie study are even more optimistic when individual longitudinal findings are disentangled from the group averages. As previously noted, the longitudinal findings differed from one mental ability to another. Nonetheless, taking the average of the five PMAs and using the 25th percentile for 25-year-olds as his standard of meaningful decline, Schaie has shown that no more than 25 percent of those studied had declined by age 67. From age 67 to age 74 about a third of the subjects had declined, whereas from age 74 to age 81, slightly more than 40 percent had declined (Schaie, 1980, 1994; Schaie & Willis, 1986). In sum, the vast majority of us show no meaningful decline in the skills measured by the Primary Mental Abilities Test until we are well into our seventies. Perhaps even more impressive is the fact that approximately 10 percent of the sample improved significantly when retested in their seventies and eighties. Based on his research and other longitudinal studies, Schaie arrives at this conclusion:

> If you keep your health and engage your mind with the problems and activities of the world around you, chances are good that you will experience lit-

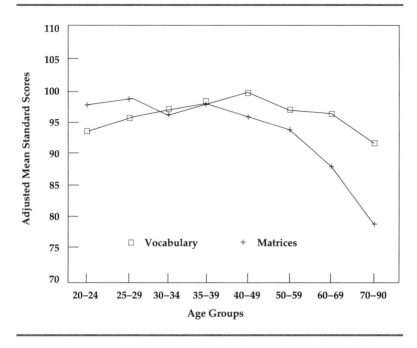

FIGURE 7.12
Mean Adjusted Standard Scores on the KBIT as a Function of Age
Source: Reprinted with permission from Wang, J., and Kaufman, A. (1993). Changes in fluid and crystallized intelligence across the 20- to 90-year age range on the K-BIT. *Journal of Psychoeducational Assessment, 11,* 29–37.

tle if any decline in intellectual performance in your lifetime. That's the promise of research in the area of adult intelligence (Schaie & Willis, 1986).

We concur with this resolution, but it would be unfair to leave the impression that all authorities in this area agree. Horn and Cattell have been the most vocal skeptics, arguing for a significant age-related decrement in fluid intelligence because of its reliance upon neural integrity, which is presumed to decline with advancing age (Horn & Cattell, 1966; Horn, 1985). Cross-sectional studies certainly support this view. For example, Wang and Kaufman (1993) plotted age differences in vocabulary and matrices scores from the Kaufman Brief Intelligence Test and found little change in vocabulary (crystallized measure) but a sharp drop in matrices (fluid measure). These results held true even when the scores were adjusted for educational level (Figure 7.12). Of course, cross-sectional studies are open to rival interpretations and can therefore only suggest longitudinal patterns. Readers who wish to pursue this controversy should consult Kausler (1991) and Lindenberger and Baltes (1994).

GENERATIONAL CHANGES IN INTELLIGENCE TEST SCORES

What happens to the intelligence of a population from one generation to the next? For example, how does the intelligence of Americans in the 1990s compare to the intelligence of their forebears in the early 1900s? We might expect that any differences would be small. After all, the human gene pool has remained essentially constant for centuries, perhaps millenia. Furthermore, only a small fraction of any generation is exposed to the extremes of environmental enrichment or deprivation that might stunt or boost intelligence dramatically. Thus, common sense dictates that any generational changes in population intelligence would be minimal.

On this issue, common sense appears to be incorrect. Flynn (1984, 1987, 1994) has charted the standardization data from the successive editions of the Stanford-Binet and the Wechsler tests from 1932 to 1981 and found that each edition established a higher standard than its predecessor (Table 7.6). The

TABLE 7.6 Comparative Average IQs from Successive Editions of the Stanford-Binet and Wechsler Tests

	Dates			Ages		Means		
Test Combinations	Test 1	Test 2	Years	Years	N	Test 1	Test 2	Gain
1. SB-L & WISC	1932	1947.5	15.5	5–15	1,563	107.13	101.64	5.49
2. SB-M & WISC	1932	1947.5	15.5	5	46	125.13	107.56	17.57
3. SB-LM & WISC	1932	1947.5	15.5	5–15	460	114.64	109.67	4.97
4. SB-L & WAIS	1932	1953.5	21.5	16–32	271	113.02	105.48	7.54
5. SB-LM & WAIS	1932	1953.5	21.5	16–48	79	109.08	101.75	7.33
6. SB-LM & WPPSI	1932	1964.5	32.5	4–6	416	101.74	92.78	8.96
7. SB-LM & SB-72	1932	1971.5	39.5	2–18	2,351	107.08	97.19	9.89
8. WB-I & WISC	1936.5	1947.5	11	11–14	110	103.51	105.54	−2.03
9. WB-I & WAIS	1936.5	1953.5	17	16–39	152	122.94	118.25	4.69
10. WISC & WAIS	1947.5	1953.5	6	14–17	436	101.76	99.12	2.64
11. WISC & WPPSI	1947.5	1964.5	17	5–6	108	93.56	90.86	2.70
12. WISC & SB-72	1947.5	1971.5	24	6–10	30	96.40	84.42	11.98
13. WISC & WISC-R	1947.5	1972	24.5	6–15	1,042	97.19	88.78	8.41
14. WAIS & WISC-R	1953.5	1972	18.5	16–17	40	102.94	96.29	6.65
15. WAIS & WAIS-R	1953.5	1978	24.5	35–44	72	109.69	101.65	8.04
16. WPPSI & SB-72	1964.5	1971.5	7	4–5	35	93.06	88.65	4.41
17. WPPSI & WISC-R	1964.5	1972	7.5	5–6	140	112.84	108.58	4.26
18. WISC-R & WAIS-R	1972	1978	6	16	80	99.61	98.65	0.96
19. WISC-R & WISC-III	1972	1988	16	6–16	206	108.20	102.90	5.30
20. WAIS-R & WISC-III	1978	1988	10	16	189	105.30	101.40	3.90
21. WPPSI-R & WISC-III	1986	1988	2	6	188	106.50	102.50	4.00
22. WISC-III & WAIS-III	1988	1996	8	16	184	104.60	103.90	.70

Note: *Dates* refers to dates of standardization for the comparison tests; *Years* refers to the years between standardization; *Ages* refers to the age range of tested subjects; *Gain* refers to the apparent gain in IQ.

Source: Adapted with permission from Flynn, J. R. (1984). The mean IQ of Americans: Massive Gains 1932 to 1978. *Psychological Bulletin, 95,* 29–51.

total gain amounts to an apparent rise in mean IQ of 13.8 points. Thus, a person who earned a Full Scale IQ of 100 in 1990 would have earned, on average, an IQ of 114 in 1932! A similar rising performance has been observed in many other industrialized nations using such tests as Raven's Progressive Matrices (Flynn, 1987).

Apparently, citizens of the Western industrialized nations have become better educated and more literate in this century, causing mean IQ levels to rise quite sharply. However, IQ gains of this magnitude pose a serious problem of causal explanation. Flynn (1994) is skeptical that any real and

meaningful intelligence of a population could vault upward so quickly. He concludes that current tests do not measure intelligence but rather a correlate with a weak causal link to intelligence:

> . . . psychologists should stop saying that IQ tests measure intelligence. They should say that IQ tests measure abstract problem-solving ability (APSA), a term that accurately conveys our ignorance. We know people solve problems on IQ tests; we suspect those problems are so detached, or so abstracted from reality, that the ability to solve them can diverge over time from the real-world problem-solving ability called intelligence; thus far we know little else (Flynn, 1987).

Although Flynn's radical prescription is not widely endorsed by experts in the field, he has sensitized psychometricians to the dangers of rendering conclusions based on ever-shifting intelligence test norms. IQ gains over time make it imperative to re-standardize tests frequently, otherwise examinees are being scored with obsolete norms and will receive inflated IQ scores (Flynn, 1994). Neisser (1998) has edited a book that explores possible explanations of the rising curve of IQ scores.

SUMMARY

1. Test bias is defined as differential validity of a given interpretation of a test score for any definable, relevant subgroup of test takers. As an example of test bias, an oral arithmetic test delivered in English might function well for English-speaking children, whereas for Hispanic children, the same test might predict arithmetic skill poorly.

2. Bias in content validity is demonstrated when an item or subscale of a test is relatively more difficult for members of one group than another after general ability level is held constant. In general, for the major standardized tests of ability and aptitude, evidence of bias in content validity is scant or nonexistent.

3. Bias in predictive or criterion-related validity is demonstrated when a test does not predict a relevant criterion equally well for persons from different subpopulations. An unbiased test possesses homogeneous regression: The results for all relevant subpopulations cluster equally well around a single regression line.

4. Bias in construct validity is demonstrated when a test is shown to measure different traits or constructs for one group than another. In comparisons across relevant subpopulations, a nonbiased test will reveal a high degree of similarity for the factorial structure of the test and the rank order of item difficulties within the test.

5. Test fairness incorporates social values and philosophies of test use. Three philosophies have been outlined: unqualified individualism (select the best person using all predictors), quotas (select by ratios), and qualified individualism (select the best person not using race, sex, etc., as predictors). Which of these philosophies is correct? This is an ethical question which is beyond objective solution.

6. The genetic contribution to human characteristics is usually measured in terms of a heritability index which can vary from 0.0 to 1.0. Heritability is an estimate of how much of the total variance in a given trait is due to genetic factors. Heritability is relative to the population sampled and does not explain individual scores. For IQ, most estimates of heritability are around .50.

7. Evidence of a genetic contribution to intelligence is documented by the Minnesota twin studies in which identical twins separated at birth are reunited for extensive psychometric testing. Even though many twin pairs were reared in dissimilar environments, their adult IQs are remarkably similar. These findings corroborate earlier adoption studies.

8. Jensen (1977) studied the cumulative effects of a bleak, deprived environment on the IQs of rural African-American children. He found that older African-American children scored lower than their younger brothers and sisters, apparently losing about one IQ point a year, on average, between the ages of 6 and 16.

9. Scarr and Weinberg studied the effects of environmental enrichment: They found that African-American children adopted into upper middle class white families showed above-average IQs.

10. Heavy drinking by pregnant women causes their offspring to be at very high risk for fetal alcohol syndrome, characterized by facial abnormalities, growth deficiencies, motor problems, hyperactivity, and mild to moderate mental retardation. With lower levels of drinking, offspring may show attentional impairment and other subtle problems known as fetal alcohol effect.

11. Environmental toxins may also affect intelligence. For example, children who absorb undue amounts of lead (such as by eating lead pigmented paint chips) may evidence long-term decrements in mental functioning (lowered IQ, problems with auditory and speech processing, and slowed reaction time).

12. On the average, African Americans score about 15 points lower than white Americans on standardized IQ tests. When demographic variables such as social class are accounted for, the difference reduces to 7 to 10 IQ points. Apparently, the magnitude of the difference has remained constant in the mid- to late-twentieth century.

13. Jensen (1969) and others have proposed that whites score higher than African Americans on IQ tests partly because of genetic factors. This hypothesis is based on the questionable assumption that evidence of IQ heritability within groups can be used to infer heritability between racial groups. Research on racial admixture and IQ does not support a genetic view.

14. Longitudinal research on age and intelligence provides a more optimistic perspective than does cross-sectional research. In longitudinal studies, most abilities change little until at least age 60. Fluid abilities—largely nonverbal and culture-reduced mental efficiency—show a greater age decline than other abilities.

15. Flynn has charted the standardization data for each edition of the Stanford-Binet and the Wechsler scales from 1932 to the present time. Each test established a higher standard than its predecessor, with a total gain of about 14 IQ points. These apparent IQ gains pose serious problems of explanation and indicate that norms for tests may shift very rapidly.

KEY TERMS AND CONCEPTS

test bias   p. 240

content bias   p. 243

predictive validity bias   p. 244

bias in construct validity   p. 247

test fairness   p. 249

unqualified individualism   p. 249

quotas   p. 250

qualified individualism   p. 250

heritability index   p. 251

teratogens   p. 255

fetal alcohol syndrome   p. 255

fetal alcohol effect   p. 255

cross-sectional design   p. 261

longitudinal design   p. 261

cross-sequential design   pp. 261–262

CHAPTER 8

Group Tests of Aptitude and Achievement

In this chapter, we examine a variety of instruments traditionally grouped under the headings of aptitude tests and achievement tests. The coverage includes relevant instruments, but also embraces issues and applications in aptitude and achievement testing. In Topic 8A, Aptitude Tests and Factor Analysis, the use of factor analysis in the development of aptitude measures is described. This is followed by a review of typical instruments, including multiple aptitude test batteries and tests used to predict academic performance in college. In Topic 8B, Group Tests of Achievement, we examine the educational achievement test batteries familiar to every student of American schooling. In addition, the reader will encounter a brief discussion of special purpose tests for achievement as well as a review of troubling social issues that

pertain to school system cheating on achievement tests.

Here we focus on aptitude tests, especially the multiple aptitude batteries commonly used to predict performance in school, employment, and military settings. Typically, multiple aptitude batteries perform a gatekeeper function. School admission, corporate employment, and military entry may hinge upon findings from the tests discussed here. Aptitude tests command great respect and therefore possess immense influence in modern society. The validity of aptitude tests is indeed consequential. The reader will learn more about the application of aptitude tests later in this topic.

Many aptitude tests arose as specialized offshoots of ability tests shortly after psychologists developed the necessary statistical tools for portioning general intelligence into its subcomponents. Put simply, most aptitude tests owe their origin to factor analysis, a family of procedures that researchers use to summarize relationships among variables that are correlated in highly complex ways. Because aptitude tests could not flourish without factor analysis, we begin this section with a primer of this useful statistical technique. The topic then continues with a discussion of prominent tests of aptitude, including multi-aptitude batteries useful for employment counseling (Differential Aptitude Test, General Aptitude Test Battery, and Armed Services Vocational Assessment Battery), tests used for college admission (Scholastic Assessment Tests and American College Test), and postgraduate admission tests (Graduate Record Exam, Medical College Admission Test, and Law School Admission Test).

A PRIMER OF FACTOR ANALYSIS

Broadly speaking, there are two forms of factor analysis: confirmatory and exploratory. In confirmatory factor analysis, the purpose is to confirm that test scores and variables fit a certain pattern predicted by a theory. For example, if the theory underlying a certain intelligence test prescribed that the subtests belong to three factors (e.g., verbal, performance, and attention factors), then a confirmatory factor analysis could be undertaken to evaluate the accuracy of this prediction. Confirmatory factor analysis is essential to the validation of many ability tests.

The central purpose of exploratory **factor analysis** is to summarize the interrelationships among a large number of variables in a concise and accurate manner as an aid in conceptualization (Gorsuch, 1983). For instance, factor analysis may help a researcher discover that a battery of 20 tests represents only four underlying variables, called **factors.** The smaller set of derived factors can be used to represent the essential constructs which underlie the complete group of variables.

Perhaps a simple analogy will clarify the nature of factors and their relationship to the variables or tests from which they are derived. Consider the track-and-field decathlon, a mixture of 10 diverse

events including sprints, hurdles, pole vault, shot put, and distance races, among others. In conceptualizing the capability of the individual decathlete, we do not think exclusively in terms of the participant's skill in specific events. Instead, we think in terms of more basic attributes such as speed, strength, coordination, and endurance, each of which is reflected to a different extent in the individual events. For example, the pole vault requires speed and coordination, while hurdle events demand coordination and endurance. These inferred attributes are analogous to the underlying factors of factor analysis. Just as the results from the 10 events of a decathlon may boil down to a small number of underlying factors (e.g., speed, strength, coordination, and endurance), so too may the results from a battery of 10 or 20 ability tests reflect the operation of a small number of basic cognitive attributes (e.g., verbal skill, visualization, calculation, and attention, to cite a hypothetical list). This example illustrates the goal of factor analysis: to help produce a parsimonious description of large, complex data sets.

We will illustrate the essential concepts of factor analysis by pursuing a classic example concerned with the number and kind of factors that best describe student abilities. Holzinger and Swineford (1939) gave 24 ability-related psychological tests to 145 junior high school students from Forest Park, Illinois. The factor analysis described below was based upon methods outlined in Kinnear and Gray (1997).

It should be intuitively obvious to the reader that any large battery of ability tests will reflect a smaller number of basic, underlying abilities (factors). Consider the 24 tests depicted in Table 8.1. Surely some of these tests measure common underlying abilities. For example, we would expect Sentence Completion, Word Classification, and Word Meaning (variables 7, 8, and 9) to assess a factor of general language ability of some kind. In like manner, other groups of tests seem likely to measure common underlying abilities. But how many abilities or factors? And what is the nature of these underlying abilities? Factor analysis is the ideal tool for answering these questions. We follow

TABLE 8.1   The 24 Ability Tests Used by Holzinger and Swineford (1939)

1. Visual Perception	13. Straight and Curved Capitals
2. Cubes	14. Word Recognition
3. Paper Form Board	15. Number Recognition
4. Flags	16. Figure Recognition
5. General Information	17. Object-Number
6. Paragraph Comprehension	18. Number-Figure
7. Sentence Completion	19. Figure-Word
8. Word Classification	20. Deduction
9. Word Meaning	21. Numerical Puzzles
10. Add Digits	22. Problem Reasoning
11. Code (Perceptual Speed)	23. Series Completion
12. Count Groups of Dots	24. Arithmetic Problems

the factor analysis of the Holzinger and Swineford (1939) data from beginning to end.

The Correlation Matrix

The beginning point for every factor analysis is the **correlation matrix,** a complete table of intercorrelations among all the variables.[1] The correlations between the 24 ability variables discussed here can be found in Table 8.2. The reader will notice that variables 7, 8, and 9 do, indeed, intercorrelate quite strongly (correlations of .62, .69, and .53), as we suspected above. This pattern of intercorrelations is presumptive evidence that these variables measure something in common, that is, it appears that these tests reflect a common underlying factor. However, this kind of intuitive factor analysis based upon a visual inspection of the correlation matrix is hopelessly limited; there are just too many intercorrelations for the viewer to discern the underlying patterns for all the variables. Here is where factor analysis can be helpful. Although we cannot elucidate the mechanics of the procedure,

factor analysis relies upon modern high-speed computers to search the correlation matrix according to objective statistical rules and determine the smallest number of factors needed to account for the observed pattern of intercorrelations. The analysis also produces the factor matrix, a table showing the extent to which each test loads on (correlates with) each of the derived factors, as discussed below.

The Factor Matrix and Factor Loadings

The **factor matrix** consists of a table of correlations called factor loadings. The factor loadings (which can take on values from −1.00 to +1.00) indicate the weighting of each variable on each factor. For example, the factor matrix in Table 8.3 shows that five factors (labeled I, II, III, IV, and V) were derived from the analysis. Note that the first variable, Series Completion, has a strong positive loading of .71 on factor I, indicating that this test is a reasonably good index of factor I. Note also that Series Completion has a modest negative loading of −.11 on factor II, indicating that, to a slight extent, it measures the opposite of this factor, that is, high scores on Series Completion tend to signify low scores on factor II, and vice versa.

The factors may seem quite mysterious, but in reality they are conceptually quite simple. A factor

---

1. In this example, the variables are tests that produce more or less continuous scores. But the variables in a factor analysis can take other forms, so long as they can be expressed as continuous scores. For example, all of the following could be variables in a factor analysis: height, weight, income, social class, and rating-scale results.

TABLE 8.2 The Correlation Matrix for 24 Ability Variables

	1	2	3	4	5	6	7	8	9	10	11	12	13	14	15	16	17	18	19	20	21	22	23
2	32																						
3	40	32																					
4	47	23	31																				
5	32	29	25	23																			
6	34	23	27	33	62																		
7	30	16	22	34	66	72																	
8	33	17	38	39	58	53	62																
9	33	20	18	33	72	71	69	53															
10	12	06	08	10	31	20	25	29	17														
11	31	15	09	11	34	35	23	30	28	48													
12	31	15	14	16	22	10	18	27	11	59	43												
13	49	24	32	33	34	31	35	40	28	41	54	51											
14	13	10	18	07	28	29	24	25	26	17	35	13	20										
15	24	13	07	13	23	25	17	18	25	15	24	17	14	37									
16	41	27	26	32	19	29	18	30	24	12	31	12	28	41	33								
17	18	01	18	19	21	27	23	26	27	29	36	28	19	34	35	32							
18	37	26	21	25	26	17	16	25	21	32	35	35	32	21	33	34	45						
19	27	11	31	14	19	25	23	27	27	19	29	11	26	21	19	26	32	36					
20	37	29	30	34	40	44	45	43	45	17	20	25	24	30	27	39	26	30	17				
21	37	31	17	35	32	26	31	36	27	41	40	36	43	18	23	35	17	36	33	41			
22	41	23	25	38	44	39	40	36	48	16	30	19	28	24	25	28	27	32	34	46	37		
23	47	35	38	34	44	43	41	50	50	26	25	35	38	24	26	36	29	27	30	51	45	50	
24	28	21	20	25	42	43	44	39	42	53	41	41	36	30	17	26	33	41	37	37	45	38	43

Note: Decimals omitted.

Source: Reprinted with permission from Holzinger, K., & Harman, H. (1941). *Factor analysis: A synthesis of factorial methods.* Chicago: University of Chicago Press.

is nothing more than a weighted linear sum of the variables, that is, each factor is a precise statistical combination of the tests used in the analysis. In a sense, a factor is produced by "adding in" carefully determined portions of some tests and perhaps "subtracting out" fractions of other tests. What makes the factors special is the elegant analytical methods used to derive them. Several different methods exist. These methods differ in subtle ways beyond the scope of this text; the reader can gather a sense of the differences by examining names of procedures: principal components factors, principal axis factors, method of unweighted least squares, maximum-likelihood method, image factoring, and alpha factoring (Tabachnick & Fidell, 1989). Most of the methods yield highly similar results.

The factor loadings depicted in Table 8.3 are nothing more than correlation coefficients between variables and factors. These correlations can be interpreted as showing the weight or loading of each factor on each variable. For example, variable 9, the test of Word Meaning, has a very strong loading (.69) on factor I, modest negative loadings (−.45 and −.29) on factors II and III, and negligible loadings (.08 and .00) on factors IV and V.

TABLE 8.3   The Principal-Axes Factor Analysis for 24 Variables

	Factors				
	I	*II*	*III*	*IV*	*V*
23. Series Completion	.71	−.11	.14	.11	.07
8. Word Classification	.70	−.24	−.15	−.11	−.13
5. General Information	.70	−.32	−.34	−.04	.08
9. Word Meaning	.69	−.45	−.29	.08	.00
6. Paragraph Comprehension	.69	−.42	−.26	.08	−.01
7. Sentence Completion	.68	−.42	−.36	−.05	−.05
24. Arithmetic Problems	.67	.20	−.23	−.04	−.11
20. Deduction	.64	−.19	.13	.06	.28
22. Problem Reasoning	.64	−.15	.11	.05	−.04
21. Numerical Puzzles	.62	.24	.10	−.21	.16
13. Straight and Curved Capitals	.62	.28	.02	−.36	−.07
1. Visual Perception	.62	−.01	.42	−.21	−.01
11. Code (Perceptual Speed)	.57	.44	−.20	.04	.01
18. Number-Figure	.55	.39	.20	.15	−.11
16. Figure Recognition	.53	.08	.40	.31	.19
4. Flags	.51	−.18	.32	−.23	−.02
17. Object-Number	.49	.27	−.03	.47	−.24
2. Cubes	.40	−.08	.39	−.23	.34
12. Count Groups of Dots	.48	.55	−.14	−.33	.11
10. Add Digits	.47	.55	−.45	−.19	.07
3. Paper Form Board	.44	−.19	.48	−.12	−.36
14. Word Recognition	.45	.09	−.03	.55	.16
15. Number Recognition	.42	.14	.10	.52	.31
19. Figure-Word	.47	.14	.13	.20	−.61

Geometric Representation of Factor Loadings

It is customary to represent the first two or three factors as reference axes in two- or three-dimensional space.[2] Within this framework the factor loadings for each variable can be plotted for examination. In our example, five factors were discovered, too many for simple visualization. Nonetheless, we can illustrate the value of geometric representation by oversimplifying somewhat and depicting just the first two factors (Figure 8.1). In this graph, each of the 24 tests has been plotted against the two factors which correspond to axes I and II. The reader will notice that the factor loadings on the first factor (I) are uniformly positive, whereas the factor loadings on the second factor (II) consist of a mixture of positive and negative.

The Rotated Factor Matrix

An important point in this context is that the position of the reference axes is arbitrary. There is

_____

2. Technically, it is possible to represent all the factors as reference axes in *n*-dimensional space, where *n* is the number of factors. However, when working with more than two or three reference axes, visual representation is no longer feasible.

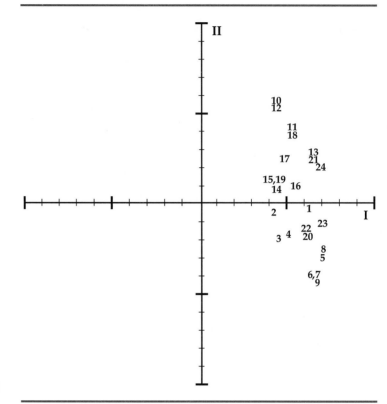

FIGURE 8.1
Geometric Representation of the First
Two Factors from 24 Ability Tests

nothing to prevent the researcher from rotating the axes so that they produce a more sensible fit with the factor loadings. For example, the reader will notice in Figure 8.1 that tests 6, 7, and 9 (all language tests) cluster together. It would certainly clarify the interpretation of factor I if it were to be redirected near the center of this cluster (Figure 8.2). This manipulation would also bring factor II alongside interpretable tests 10, 11, and 12 (all number tests).

Although rotation can be conducted manually by visual inspection, it is more typical for researchers to rely upon one or more objective statistical criteria to produce the final rotated factor matrix. Thurstone's (1947) criteria of positive manifold and simple structure are commonly applied. In a **rotation to positive manifold,** the computer program seeks to eliminate as many of the negative factor loadings as possible. Negative factor loadings make little sense in ability testing, because

they imply that high scores on a factor are correlated with poor test performance. In a **rotation to simple structure,** the computer program seeks to simplify the factor loadings so that each test has significant loadings on as few factors as possible. The goal of both criteria is to produce a rotated factor matrix that is as straightforward and unambiguous as possible.

The rotated factor matrix for this problem is shown in Table 8.4. The particular method of rotation used here is called varimax rotation. Varimax should not be used if the theoretical expectation suggests that a general factor may occur. Should we expect a general factor in the analysis of ability tests? The answer is as much a matter of faith as of science. One researcher may conclude that a general factor is likely and therefore pursue a different type of rotation. A second researcher may be comfortable with a Thurstonian viewpoint and seek

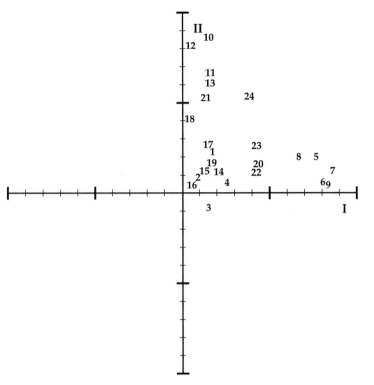

FIGURE 8.2
Geometric Representation of the First
Two Rotated Factors from 24 Ability
Tests

multiple ability factors using a varimax rotation. We will explore this issue in more detail later, but it is worth pointing out here that a researcher encounters many choice points in the process of conducting a factor analysis. It is not surprising, then, that different researchers may reach different conclusions from factor analysis, even when they are analyzing the same data set.

The Interpretation of Factors

Table 8.4 indicates that five factors underlie the intercorrelations of the 24 ability tests. But what shall we call these factors? The reader may find the answer to this question disquieting, because at this juncture we leave the realm of cold, objective statistics and enter the arena of judgment, insight, and presumption. In order to interpret or name a factor, the researcher must make a reasoned judgment

about the common processes and abilities shared by the tests with strong loadings on that factor. For example, in Table 8.4 it appears that factor I is verbal ability, because the variables with high loadings stress verbal skill (e.g., Sentence Completion loads .86, Word Meaning loads .84, and Paragraph Comprehension loads .81). The variables with low loadings also help sharpen the meaning of factor I. For example, factor I is not related to numerical skill (Numerical Puzzles loads .18) or spatial skill (Paper Form Board loads .16). Using a similar form of inference, it appears that factor II is mainly numerical ability (Add Digits loads .85, Count Groups of Dots loads .80). Factor III is less certain but appears to be a visual-perceptual capacity, and factor IV appears to be a measure of recognition. We would need to analyze the single test on factor V (Figure-Word) to surmise the meaning of this factor.

TABLE 8.4   The Rotated Varimax Factor Matrix for 24 Ability Variables

		Factors			
	I	*II*	*III*	*IV*	*V*
7. Sentence Completion	**.86**	.15	.13	.03	.07
9. Word Meaning	**.84**	.06	.15	.18	.08
6. Paragraph Comprehension	**.81**	.07	.16	.18	.10
5. General Information	**.79**	.22	.16	.12	−.02
8. Word Classification	**.65**	.22	.28	.03	.21
22. Problem Reasoning	**.43**	.12	.38	.23	.22
10. Add Digits	.18	**.85**	−.10	.09	−.01
12. Count Groups of Dots	.02	**.80**	.20	.03	.00
11. Code (Perceptual Speed)	.18	**.64**	.05	.30	.17
13. Straight and Curved Capitals	.19	**.60**	.40	−.05	.18
24. Arithmetic Problems	.41	**.54**	.12	.16	.24
21. Numerical Puzzles	.18	**.52**	.45	.16	.02
18. Number-Figure	.00	**.40**	.28	.38	.36
1. Visual Perception	.17	.21	**.69**	.10	.20
2. Cubes	.09	.09	**.65**	.12	−.18
4. Flags	.26	.07	**.60**	−.01	.15
3. Paper Form Board	.16	−.09	**.57**	−.05	.49
23. Series Completion	.42	.24	**.52**	.18	.11
20. Deduction	.43	.11	**.47**	.35	−.07
15. Number Recognition	.11	.09	.12	**.74**	−.02
14. Word Recognition	.23	.10	.00	**.69**	.10
16. Figure Recognition	.07	.07	.46	**.59**	.14
17. Object-Number	.15	.25	−.06	**.52**	.49
19. Figure-Word	.16	.16	.11	.14	**.77**

Note: Bold-faced entries signify subtests loading strongly on each factor.

These results illustrate a major use of factor analysis, namely, the identification of a small number of marker tests from a large test battery. Rather than using a cumbersome battery of 24 tests, a researcher could gain nearly the same information by carefully selecting several tests with strong loadings on the five factors. For example, the first factor is well represented by test 7, Sentence Completion (.86) and test 9, Word Meaning (.84); the second factor is reflected in test 10, Add Digits (.85), while the third factor is best illustrated by test 1, Visual Perception (.69). The fourth factor is captured by test 15, Number Recognition (.74) and Word Recognition (.69). Of course, the last factor loads well on only test 19, Figure-Word (.77).

Issues in Factor Analysis

Unfortunately, factor analysis is frequently misunderstood and often misused. Some researchers appear to use factor analysis as a kind of divining rod, hoping to find gold hidden underneath tons of dirt. But there is nothing magical about the technique. No amount of statistical analysis can rescue data based on trivial, irrelevant, or haphazard measures. If there is no gold to be found, then none will be found; factor analysis is not alchemy. Factor analysis will yield meaningful results only when the research was meaningful to begin with.

An important point is that a particular kind of factor can emerge from factor analysis only if the tests and measures contain that factor in the first place. For example, a short-term memory factor cannot possibly emerge from a battery of ability tests if none of the tests requires short-term memory. In general, the quality of the output depends upon the quality of the input. We can restate this point as the acronym GIGO or "garbage in, garbage out."

Sample size is crucial to a stable factor analysis. Comrey (1973) offers the following rough guide:

Sample Size	Rating
50	very poor
100	poor
200	fair
300	good
500	very good
1,000	excellent

In general, it is comforting to have at least five subjects for each test or variable (Tabachnick & Fidell, 1989).

Finally, we cannot overemphasize the extent to which factor analysis is guided by subjective choices and theoretical prejudices. A crucial question in this regard is the choice between orthogonal axes and oblique axes. With **orthogonal axes,** the factors are at right angles to one another, which means that they are uncorrelated (Figures 8.1 and 8.2 both depict orthogonal axes). In many cases the clusters of factor loadings are situated such that oblique axes provide a better fit. With **oblique axes,** the factors are correlated among themselves. Some researchers contend that oblique axes should always be used, whereas others take a more experimental approach. Tabachnick and Fidell (1989) recommend an exploratory strategy based on repeated factor analyses. Their approach is unabashedly opportunistic:

> During the next few runs, researchers experiment with different numbers of factors, different extraction techniques, and both orthogonal and oblique rotations. Some number of factors with some combination of extraction and rotation produces the so-

lution with the greatest scientific utility, consistency, and meaning; this is the solution that is interpreted.

With oblique rotations it is also possible to factor analyze the factors themselves. Such a procedure may yield one or more second-order factors. Second-order factors can provide support for the hierarchical organization of traits and may offer a rapprochement between ability theorists who posit a single general factor (e.g., Spearman) and those who promote several group factors (e.g., Thurstone). Perhaps both camps are correct, with the group factors sitting underneath the second-order general factor.

MULTIPLE APTITUDE TEST BATTERIES

As previously noted, aptitude tests did not flourish until the prerequisite statistical tools—factor-analytic procedures—were available. One of the major applications of factor analysis was the development of multiple aptitude test batteries. In a multiple aptitude test battery, the examinee is tested in several separate, homogeneous aptitude areas. The development of the subtests is dictated by the findings of factor analysis. For example, Thurstone developed one of the first multiple aptitude test batteries, the Primary Mental Abilities Test, a set of seven tests chosen on the basis of factor analysis (Thurstone, 1938).

More recently, several multiple aptitude test batteries have gained favor for educational and career counseling, vocational placement, and armed services classification (Gregory, 1994a). Each year hundreds of thousands of persons are administered one of these prominent batteries: The Differential Aptitude Test (DAT), the General Aptitude Test Battery (GATB), and the Armed Services Vocational Aptitude Battery (ASVAB). These batteries either used factor analysis directly for the delineation of useful subtests or were guided in their construction by the accumulated results of other factor-analytic research. The salient characteristics of each battery are briefly reviewed in the following sections.

The Differential Aptitude Test (DAT)

The DAT was first issued in 1947 to provide a basis for the educational and vocational guidance of students in grades seven through twelve. Subsequently, examiners have found the test useful in the vocational counseling of young adults out of school and in the selection of employees. Now in its fifth edition (1992), the test has been periodically revised and stands as one of the most popular multiple aptitude test batteries of all time (Bennett, Seashore, & Wesman, 1982, 1984).

The DAT consists of eight independent tests:

1. Verbal Reasoning (VR)
2. Numerical Reasoning (NR)
3. Abstract Reasoning (AR)
4. Perceptual Speed and Accuracy (PSA)
5. Mechanical Reasoning (MR)
6. Space Relations (SR)
7. Spelling (S)
8. Language Usage (LU)

A characteristic item from each test is shown in Figure 8.3.

The authors chose the areas for the eight tests based on experimental and experiential data rather than relying upon a formal factor analysis of their own. In constructing the DAT, the authors were guided by several explicit criteria:

- Each test should be an independent test: There are situations in which only part of the battery is required or desired.
- The tests should measure power: For most vocational purposes to which test results contribute, the evaluation of power—solving difficult problems with adequate time—is of primary concern.
- The test battery should yield a profile: The eight separate scores can be converted to percentile ranks and plotted on a common profile chart.
- The norms should be adequate: In the fifth edition, the norms are derived from 100,000 students for the fall standardization, 70,000 for the spring standardization.
- The test materials should be practical: With time limits of 6 to 30 minutes per test, the entire DAT can be administered in a morning or an afternoon school session.
- The tests should be easy to administer: Each test contains excellent "warm up" examples and can be administered by persons with a minimum of special training.
- Alternate forms should be available: For purposes of retesting, the availability of alternate forms (currently forms C and D) will reduce any practice effects.

The reliability of the DAT is generally quite high, with split-half coefficients largely in the .90s

---

VERBAL REASONING
Choose the correct pair of words to fill in the blanks.

_____ is to eye as eardrum is to _____

A. vision	—	sound		D. sight	—	cochlea
B. iris	—	hear		E. eyelash	—	earlobe
<u>C.</u> retina	—	ear				

NUMERICAL ABILITY
Choose the correct answer.

$4(-5)(-3) =$
A. −60   B. 27   C. −27   <u>D. 60</u>   E. none of these

FIGURE 8.3 Differential Aptitude Tests and Characteristic Items

ABSTRACT REASONING

The four figures in the row to the left make a series. Find the single choice on the right that would be next in the series.

<	<>	<<>	<<>>>		<>	<<<>	<<<>>>	<<<<>>>
					A	B	C	D

CLERICAL SPEED AND ACCURACY

In each test item, one of the combinations is underlined. Mark the same combination on the answer sheet.

1. AB Ab AA <u>BA</u> Bb   2. 5m 5M <u>M5</u> Mm m5

   Ab Bb AA BA AB   M5 m5 Mm 5m 5M

1. O O O O O   2. O O O O O

MECHANICAL REASONING

Which lever will require more force to lift an object of the same weight? If equal, mark C.

A   C (equal)   <u>B</u>

SPACE RELATIONS

Which of the figures on the right can be made by folding the pattern at the left? The pattern always displays the outside of the figure.

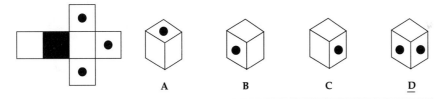

A   B   C   <u>D</u>

SPELLING

Mark whether each word is spelled right or wrong.

1. irelevant	R	<u>W</u>
2. parsimonious	<u>R</u>	W
3. excellant	R	<u>W</u>

LANGUAGE USAGE

Decide which part of the sentence contains an error and mark the corresponding letter on the answer sheet. Mark N (None) if there is no error.

In spite of public criticism, / the researcher studied /
       A   B

the affects of radiation / on plant growth.
    <u>C</u>   D

FIGURE 8.3   *continued*

and alternate-form reliabilities ranging from .73 to .90, with a median of .83. Mechanical Reasoning is an exception, with reliabilities as low as .70 for girls. The tests show a mixed pattern of intercorrelations with each other which is optimistically interpreted by the authors as establishing the independence of the eight tests. Actually, many of the correlations are quite high and it seems likely that the eight tests reflect a smaller number of ability factors. Certainly the Verbal Reasoning and Numerical Ability tests measure a healthy general factor, with correlations around .70 in various samples.

The manual presents extensive data demonstrating that the DAT tests, especially the VR + NR combination, are good predictors of other criteria such as school grades and scores on other aptitude tests (correlations in the .60s and .70s). For this reason, the combination of VR + NR often is considered an index of scholastic aptitude. Evidence for the *differential* validity of the other tests is rather slim. Bennett, Seashore, and Wesman (1974) do present results of several follow-up studies correlating vocational entry/success with DAT profiles, but their research methods are more impressionistic than quantitative; the independent observer will find it difficult to make use of their results. Schmitt (1995) notes that a major problem with the battery is the

> . . . lack of discriminant validity between the eight subtests. With the exception of the Perceptual Speed and Accuracy test, all of the subscales are highly intercorrelated (.50 to .75). If one wants only a general index of the person's academic ability, this is fine; if the scores on the subtests are to be used in some diagnostic sense, this level of intercorrelation makes statements about students' relative strengths and weaknesses highly questionable.

Even so, the revised DAT is better than previous editions. One significant improvement is the elimination of apparent sex bias on the Language Usage and Mechanical Reasoning tests—a source of criticism from earlier reviews. The publishers of the Fifth Edition conducted a careful study of sex, race, ethnic, and regional bias so as to eliminate items that might be stereotypic or offensive to identifiable subgroups. Furthermore, they conducted sophisticated statistical analyses to eliminate items of unequal difficulty across racial subgroups matched in terms of overall performance.

The General Aptitude Test Battery (GATB)

In the late 1930s, the U.S. Department of Labor developed aptitude tests to predict job performance in 100 specific occupations. In the 1940s, the department hired a panel of experts in measurement and industrial-organizational psychology to create a multiple aptitude test battery to assess the 100 occupations previously studied and many more. The outcome of this Herculean effort was the General Aptitude Test Battery (GATB), widely acknowledged as the premiere test battery for predicting job performance (Hunter, 1994).

The GATB was derived from a factor analysis of 59 tests administered to thousands of male trainees in vocational courses (United States Employment Service, 1970). The interpretive standards have been periodically revised and updated, so the GATB is a thoroughly modern instrument even though its content is little changed. One limitation is that the battery is available mainly to state employment offices, although nonprofit organizations, including high schools and certain colleges, can make special arrangements for its use.

The GATB is composed of eight paper-and-pencil tests and four apparatus measures. The entire battery can be administered in approximately two and a half hours and is appropriate for high school seniors and adults. The twelve tests yield a total of nine factor scores:

- *General Learning Ability* (intelligence) (G). This score is a composite of Vocabulary, Arithmetic Reasoning, and Three-Dimensional Space.
- *Verbal Aptitude* (V). Derived from a Vocabulary test which requires the examinee to indicate which two words in a set are either synonyms or antonyms.
- *Numerical Aptitude* (N). This score is a composite of both the Computation and Arithmetic Reasoning tests.

- *Spatial Aptitude* (S).   Consists of the Three-Dimensional Space test, a measure of the ability to perceive two-dimensional representations of three-dimensional objects and to visualize movement in three dimensions.
- *Form Perception* (P).   This score is a composite of Form Matching and Tool Matching, two tests in which the examinee must match identical drawings.
- *Clerical Perception* (Q).   A proofreading test called Name Comparison, the examinee must match names under pressure of time.
- *Motor Coordination* (K).   Measures the ability to quickly make specified pencil marks in the Mark Making test.
- *Finger Dexterity* (F).   A composite of the Assemble and Disassemble tests, two measures of dexterity with rivets and washers.
- *Manual Dexterity* (M).   A composite of Place and Turn, two tests requiring the examinee to transfer and reverse pegs in a board.

The nine factor scores on the GATB are expressed as standard scores with a mean of 100 and an SD of 20. These standard scores are anchored to the original normative sample of 4,000 workers obtained in the 1940s. Alternate-forms reliability coefficients for factor scores range from the .80s to the .90s. The GATB manual summarizes several studies of the validity of the test, primarily in terms of its correlation with relevant criterion measures. Hunter (1994) notes that GATB scores predict training success for all levels of job complexity. The average validity coefficient is a phenomenal .62.

The absolute scores are of less interest than their comparison to updated Occupational Aptitude Patterns (OAPs) for dozens of occupations. Based on test results for huge samples of applicants and employees in different occupations, counselors and employers now have access to a wealth of information about score patterns needed for success in a variety of jobs. Thus, one way of using the GATB is to compare an examinee's scores with OAPs believed necessary for proficiency in various occupations.

Hunter (1994) recommends an alternative strategy based on composite aptitudes (Figure 8.4). The nine specific factor scores combine nicely into three general factors: Cognitive, Perceptual, and Psychomotor. Hunter notes that different jobs require various contributions of the Cognitive, Perceptual, and Psychomotor aptitudes. For example, an assembly line worker in an automotive plant might need high scores on the Psychomotor and Perceptual composites, whereas the Cognitive score would be less important for this occupation. Hunter's research demonstrates that general factors dominate over specific factors in the prediction of job performance. Davison, Gasser, & Ding (1996) discuss additional approaches to GATB profile analysis and interpretation.

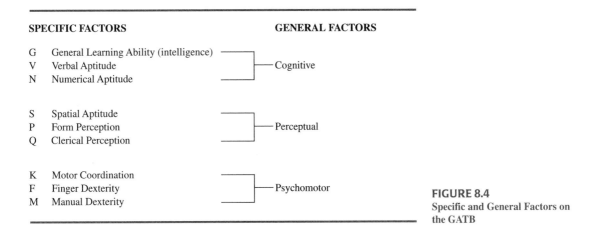

SPECIFIC FACTORS

G	General Learning Ability (intelligence)
V	Verbal Aptitude
N	Numerical Aptitude

S	Spatial Aptitude
P	Form Perception
Q	Clerical Perception

K	Motor Coordination
F	Finger Dexterity
M	Manual Dexterity

GENERAL FACTORS

Cognitive

Perceptual

Psychomotor

FIGURE 8.4
Specific and General Factors on the GATB

Van de Vijver and Harsveld (1994) investigated the equivalence of their computerized version of the GATB with the traditional paper-and-pencil version. Of course, only the cognitive and perceptual subtests were compared—tests of motor skills cannot be computerized. They found that the two versions were not equivalent. In particular, the computerized subtests produced faster and more inaccurate responses than the conventional subtests. Their research demonstrates once again that the equivalence of traditional and computerized versions of a test should not be assumed. This is an empirical question answerable only with careful research. Nijenhuis and van der Flier (1997) discuss a Dutch version of the GATB and its application in the study of cognitive differences between immigrants and majority group members in the Netherlands.

The Armed Services Vocational Aptitude Battery (ASVAB)

The ASVAB is probably the most widely used paper-and-pencil test in existence. This test is used by the Armed Services to screen potential recruits and to assign personnel to different jobs and training programs. More than 2 million examinees take the ASVAB each year. The current version consists of ten subtests, four of which produce the Armed Forces Qualification Test (AFQT), the common qualifying exam for all services (Table 8.5). Eight subtests are power tests with adequate time limits for most subjects, whereas two subtests (Numerical Operations and Coding Speed) are speeded tests which place a premium upon rapid performance. Alternate-forms reliability coefficients for ASVAB scores are in the mid-.80s to mid-.90s, and test-retest coefficients range from the mid-.70s to the mid-.80s (Larson, 1994). The one exception is Paragraph Comprehension with a reliability of only .50. The test is well normed on a representative sample of 12,000 persons between the ages of 16 to 23. The ASVAB manual reports a median validity coefficient of .60 with measures of training performance.

Decisions about ASVAB examinees are typically based upon composite scores, not subtest scores. For example, a Clerical Composite is derived by combining Word Knowledge, Paragraph Comprehension, Numerical Operations, and Coding Speed. Subjects scoring well on this composite might be assigned to secretarial positions. Since the composite scores are empirically derived, new ones can be developed for placement decisions at any time. Composite scores are continually updated and revised. For example, Ree and Carretta (1994) advocated three composites derived from a factor analysis of more than 11,000 participants in the

TABLE 8.5 The Armed Services Vocational Aptitude Battery (ASVAB) Subtests

Arithmetic Reasoning*	30-item test of arithmetic word problems based upon simple calculation
Mathematics Knowledge*	25-item test of algebra, geometry, fractions, decimals, and exponents
Paragraph Comprehension*	15-item test of reading comprehension in short paragraphs
Word Knowledge*	35-item test of vocabulary knowledge and synonyms
Coding Speed	84-item speeded test of substitution of numeric for verbal codes
General Science	25-item test of general knowledge in physical and biological science
Numerical Operations	50-item speeded test of ability to add, subtract, multiply, and divide
Electronics Information	20-item test of electronics, radio, and electrical principles
Mechanical Comprehension	25-item test of mechanical and physical principles
Auto and Shop Information	25-item test of basic knowledge of autos, shop practices, and tool usage

*Armed Forces Qualifying Test (AFQT).

ASVAB testing. These composites and their constitutent tests were as follows:

1. Speed: Numerical Operations and Coding Speed
2. Verbal/Math: Arithmetic Reasoning, Word Knowledge, Paragraph Comprehension, and Mathematics Knowledge
3. Technical Knowledge: General Science, Auto and Shop Information, Mechanical Comprehension, and Electronics Information

The reader will notice that the second factor is identical to the AFQT, mentioned previously.

At one point, the Armed Services relied heavily upon the seven composites listed below (Murphy, 1984). The first three constitute academic composites whereas the remaining are occupational composites. The reader will notice that individual subtests may appear in more than one composite:

1. Academic Ability: Word Knowledge, Paragraph Comprehension, and Arithmetic Reasoning
2. Verbal: Word Knowledge, Paragraph Comprehension, and General Science
3. Math: Mathematics Knowledge and Arithmetic Reasoning
4. Mechanical and Crafts: Arithmetic Reasoning, Mechanical Comprehension, Auto and Shop Information, and Electronics Information
5. Business and Clerical: Word Knowledge, Paragraph Comprehension, Mathematics Knowledge, and Coding Speed
6. Electronics and Electrical: Arithmetic Reasoning, Mathematics Knowledge, Electronics Information, and General Science
7. Health, Social, and Technology: Word Knowledge, Paragraph Comprehension, Arithmetic Reasoning, and Mechanical Comprehension

The problem with forming composites in this manner is that they are so highly correlated with one another as to be essentially redundant. In fact, the average intercorrelation among these seven composite scores is .86! (Murphy, 1984). Clearly, composites do not always provide differential information about specific aptitudes. Perhaps that is

why recent editions of the ASVAB have steered clear of multiple, complex composites. Instead, the emphasis is on simpler composites that are composed of highly related constructs. For example, a Verbal Ability composite is derived from Word Knowledge and Paragraph Comprehension, two highly interrelated subtests. In like manner, a Math Ability composite is obtained from the combination of Arithmetic Reasoning and Mathematics Knowledge.

Some researchers have concluded that the ASVAB does not function as a multiple aptitude test battery, but achieves success in predicting diverse vocational assignments because the composites invariably tap a general factor of intelligence. The ASVAB may be a good test of general intelligence, but it falls short as a multiple aptitude test battery. Another concern is that the test may possess different psychometric structures for men and women. Specifically, the Electronics Information subtest is a good measure of g (the general factor of intelligence) for men, but not women (Ree & Carretta, 1995). The likely explanation for this is that men are about nine times more likely to enroll in high school classes in electronics and auto shop, and men therefore have the opportunity for their general ability to shape what they learn about electronics information whereas women do not. Scores on this subtest will therefore function as a measure of achievement (what has already been learned) but not as an index of aptitude (forecasting future results).

Research on a computerized adaptive testing (CAT) version of the ASVAB has been underway since the 1980s. Computerized adaptive testing is discussed in Topic 15A, Computerized Assessment and the Future of Testing. We provide a brief overview here. In CAT, the examinee takes the test while sitting at a computer terminal. The difficulty level of the items presented on the screen is continually readjusted as a function of the examinee's ongoing performance. In general, an examinee who answers a subtest item correctly will receive a harder item, whereas an examinee who fails that item will receive an easier item. The computer uses item response theory as a basis for selecting items. Each examinee receives a unique set of test items tailored to his or her ability level.

The CAT-ASVAB is being tested at a limited number of sites. Larson (1994) lists the reasons for adopting the CAT-ASVAB as follows:

1. Shorten overall testing time (adaptive tests require roughly one-half the items of standard tests).
2. Increase test security by eliminating the possibility that test booklets could be stolen.
3. Increase test precision at the upper and lower ability extremes.
4. Provide a means for immediate feedback on test scores, since the computers used for testing can immediately score the tests and output the results.
5. Provide a means for flexible test start times (unlike group-administered paper-and-pencil tests, where everyone must start and stop at the same time, computer-based testing can be tailored to the examinees' personal schedules).

The success or failure of the CAT-ASVAB could have major implications for testing in general. If the project succeeds, the ASVAB and other tests likely will be expanded to measure new aspects of performance such as response latencies and to display unique item types such as visuospatial tests of objects in motion (Larson, 1994). The CAT-ASVAB has the potential to change the future of testing.

PREDICTING COLLEGE PERFORMANCE

As most every college student knows, a major use of aptitude tests is the prediction of academic performance. In most cases, applicants to college must contend with the Scholastic Assessment Tests (SAT) or the American College Test (ACT) assessment program. Institutions may set minimum standards on the SAT or ACT tests for admission, based on the knowledge that low scores foretell college failure. In this section we will explore the technical adequacy and predictive validity of the major college aptitude tests.

The Scholastic Assessment Tests (SAT)

Formerly known as the Scholastic Aptitude Tests, the Scholastic Assessment Tests or SAT is the oldest of the college admissions tests, dating back to 1926. The SAT is published by the College Board (formerly the College Entrance Examination Board), a group formed in 1899 to provide a national clearinghouse for admissions testing. As noted by historian Fuess (1950), the purpose of a nationally based admissions test was "to introduce law and order into an educational anarchy which towards the close of the nineteenth century had become exasperating, indeed almost intolerable, to schoolmasters." Over the years, the test has been extensively revised, continuously updated, and repeatedly renormed. In the early 1990s, the SAT was renamed the Scholastic Assessment Tests to emphasize changes in content and format. The new SAT assesses mastery of high school subject matter to a greater extent than its predecessor, but continues to tap reasoning skills. The SAT represents state of the art for aptitude testing.

The new SAT consists of the SAT-I Reasoning Tests and the SAT-II Subject Tests. The SAT-I Verbal Reasoning Test emphasizes vocabulary in context, reading comprehension, and critical reasoning. The SAT-I Math Reasoning emphasizes the application of mathematical concepts, the interpretation of data, and the actual construction of a response, as opposed to the typical multiple-choice format. A calculator is highly recommended but not required.

The SAT-I Verbal Reasoning and Math Reasoning scores are reported on a scale that ranges from 200 to 800. Characteristic item types for the Verbal portion include the following:

- Analogies: Select a pair of words that best expresses a relationship similar to that expressed in a stimulus pair.
- Sentence Completions: For a sentence with one or two blanks, choose a word or pair of words

that best fits the meaning of the sentence as a whole.
- Reading Comprehension: Read a passage and answer multiple-choice questions based on what is stated or implied in the passage.

Characteristic item types for the Math portion include the following:

- Regular Mathematics: Solve basic problems in geometry and algebra.
- Quantitative Comparisons: Choose from two quantities which is greater, or denote that they are equal, or denote that the problem is unsolvable from the information given.

A persistent misconception about SAT scores is that 500 and 100 represent the mean and standard deviation of the most recent sample of SAT test takers (Donlon, 1984). In fact, the numbers 500 and 100 refer to the mean and standard deviation of the anchor group of 10,654 students who took the Verbal portion of the SAT in April of 1941. (The Mathematics portion was equated to this verbal portion the next year.) All new scores are equated to the anchor scores by linking each new form of the SAT to one or more previous forms. For example, if a new form is slightly easier than previous forms, the test taker may need a few more correct answers in order to attain an equivalent score. This procedure guarantees that current SAT scores are based on the same measurement scale used at the inception of the anchoring procedure in 1941.[3] A rescaling and repositioning of SAT scores was scheduled for 1996. One purpose of the rescaling was to provide more reliable measurement in upper and lower score ranges by widening the item difficulty level (Johnson, 1994).

From year to year, the average score for SAT test takers may be substantially different from the original average of 500. In fact, SAT scores declined precipitously from 1963 to 1980. By 1980, the Mathematics average had declined from 500 to about 465, while the Verbal average reached a low of 420, nearly a full standard deviation below its starting point. Average scores on both scales have increased only slightly since then. This phenomenon has been the subject of intense scrutiny, and it is beyond the scope of this text to review all the explanations that have been proffered. The following findings are generally accepted:

- The decline was not an artifact of SAT difficulty or scaling; it was a real phenomenon that affected other major testing programs.
- The decline was significant, representing a sizable shift in test performance; the change represented a "serious deterioration of the learning process in America" (Wirtz, 1977).
- The decline did not lessen the predictive validity of the SAT; the test continued to correlate well with college performance.
- Population shifts such as increases in family size may explain part of the decline; if average family size continues to decrease, SAT scores are predicted to increase (Zajonc, Markus, & Markus, 1979).
- Social changes such as the expansion of television may have contributed to the decline; however, such hypotheses are difficult to prove (Donlon, 1984).

Great care is taken in the construction of new forms of the SAT Verbal and Math tests because unfailing reliability and a high degree of parallelism are essential to the mission of this testing program. The internal consistency reliability of both forms is repeatedly in the range of .91 to .93; with only a few exceptions, test-retest correlations vary between .87 and .89. The standard error of measurement is 30 to 35 points.

The primary evidence for SAT validity is criterion-related, in this case, the ability to predict freshman-year college grades. Donlon (1984, chp. VIII) reports a wealth of information on this point; we can only summarize trends here. In 685 studies, the

---

3. This practice differs from the procedure followed in the renorming of IQ tests. When a revision of an IQ test is newly standardized, the mean for the population is always set at 100, regardless of the comparative difficulty of the revised test and its predecessor.

combined SAT Verbal and Math scores correlated .42, on average, with college freshman grade point average. Interestingly, high school record (e.g., rank or grade point average) fares better than the SAT in predicting college grades ($r = .48$). But the combination of SAT and high school record proves even more predictive; these variables correlated .55, on average, with college freshman grade point average. Of course, these findings reflect a substantial restriction of range: low SAT-scoring high school students tend not to attend college. Donlon (1984) estimates that the real correlation without restriction of range (SAT + high school record) would be in the neighborhood of .65.

One issue of great practical concern is the effect of special study and coaching on SAT scores. Does it help to receive special coaching on vocabulary and mathematics or to read the numerous preparation guides available in most any bookstore? Messick and Jungeblut (1981) reviewed the available studies that employed an experimental versus control group format. They concluded that coaching boosts the combined Verbal and Math scores about 28 to 30 points, not a substantial increase compared to no coaching/preparation. However, for highly motivated students who seek out coaching and receive a rigorous, structured program, coaching effects are much larger, 45 to 110 points on the combined Verbal and Math scores (Johnson, 1994). A related issue pertains to the sizable proportion of students who take the SAT more than once. Do scores tend to rise with repeated testing? In cases where the retesting occurs within five to eight months, the average increase is about 12 points each for the Verbal and Mathematics scores (Donlon, 1984). The increase reflects, in part, familiarity with the test, but a factor overlooked by many is the active learning that might take place in the interim.

The American College Test (ACT)

The American College Test (ACT) assessment program is a recent program of testing and reporting designed for college-bound students. In addition to traditional test scores, the ACT assessment program includes a brief 90-item interest inventory (based on Holland's typology) and a student profile section (in which the student may list subjects studied, notable accomplishments, work experience, and community service). We will not discuss these ancillary measures here, except to note that they are useful in generating the Student Profile Report which is sent to the examinee and the colleges listed on the registration folder.

Initiated in 1959, the ACT is based on the philosophy that direct tests of the skills needed in college courses provide the most efficient basis for predicting college performance. In terms of the number of students who take it, the ACT occupies second place behind the SAT as a college admissions test. The four ACT tests require knowledge of a subject area, but emphasize the use of that knowledge:

- English (75 questions, 45 minutes). The examinee is presented with several prose passages excerpted from published writings. Certain portions of the text are underlined and numbered, and possible revisions for the underlined sections are presented; in addition, "no change" is one choice. The examinee must choose the best option.
- Mathematics (60 questions, 60 minutes). Here the examinee is asked to solve the kinds of mathematics problems likely to be encountered in basic college mathematics courses. The test emphasizes concepts rather than formulas and uses a multiple-choice format.
- Reading (40 questions, 35 minutes). This subtest is designed to assess the examinee's level of reading comprehension; subscores are reported for social studies/sciences and arts/literature reading skills.
- Science Reasoning (40 questions, 35 minutes). This test assesses the ability to read and understand material in the natural sciences. The questions are drawn from data representations, research summaries, and conflicting viewpoints.

In addition to the area scores listed previously, ACT results are also reported as an overall Composite score, which is the average of the four tests. ACT scores are reported on a standard score 36-point scale. In 1992, the average ACT Composite score of high school graduates was 20.7, with a standard deviation of about 5 points (Maxey, 1994). However, like the SAT, scores on the ACT are not fixed in any given year. ACT scores showed the same decline in the 1960s and 1970s as observed on the SAT.

Critics of the ACT program have pointed to the heavy emphasis upon reading comprehension that saturates all four tests. The average intercorrelation of the tests is typically around .60. These data suggest that a general achievement/ability factor pervades all four tests; results for any one test should not be overinterpreted. Fortunately, college admission officers probably place the greatest emphasis upon the Composite score, which is the average of the four separate tests. The ACT test appears to measure much the same thing as the SAT; the correlation between these two tests approaches .90. It is not surprising, then, that the predictive validity of the ACT Composite score rivals the SAT combined score, with correlations in the vicinity of .40 to .50 with college freshman grade point average. The predictive validity coefficients are virtually identical for advantaged and disadvantaged students, indicating that the ACT tests are not biased.

Kifer (1985) does not question the technical adequacy of the ACT and similar testing programs, but does protest the enormous symbolic power these tests have accrued. The heavy emphasis upon test scores for college admissions is not a technical issue, but a social, moral, and political concern:

> Selective admissions means simply that an institution cannot or will not admit each person who completes an application. Choices of who will or will not be admitted should be, first of all, a matter of what the institution believes is desirable and may or may not include the use of prediction equations. It is just as defensible to select on talent broadly construed as it is to use test scores however high. There are talented students in many areas—leaders, organizers, doers, musicians, athletes, science award winners, opera buffs—who may have moderate or low ACT scores but whose presence on a campus would change it.

The reader may wish to review Topic 7B, Test Bias and Other Controversies, for further discussion of this point.

POSTGRADUATE SELECTION TESTS

Graduate and professional programs also rely heavily upon aptitude tests for admission decisions. Of course, many other factors are considered when selecting students for advanced training, but there is no denying the centrality of aptitude test results in the selection decision. For example, Figure 8.5 depicts a fairly typical quantitative weighting system used in evaluating applicants for graduate training in psychology. The reader will notice that an overall score on the Graduate Record Exam (GRE) receives the single highest weighting in the selection process. We review the GRE in the following sections, as well as admission tests used by medical schools and law schools.

Graduate Record Exam

The GRE is a multiple-choice group test widely used by graduate programs in many fields as one component in the selection of candidates for advanced training. The GRE offers subject examinations in many fields (e.g., Biology, Computer Science, History, Mathematics, Political Science, Psychology), but the heart of the test is the general test designed to measure verbal, quantitative, and analytical aptitudes. The verbal section (GRE-V) includes verbal items such as analogies, sentence completion, antonyms, and reading comprehension. The quantitative section (GRE-Q) consists of problems in algebra, geometry, reasoning, and the interpretation of data, graphs, and diagrams. The analytical section (GRE-A) includes analytical and logical reasoning problems. All three GRE scores are reported as standard scores with an *approximate* mean of 500 and standard deviation of 100. Actually, the mean score may differ from year to year because all test results are anchored to a standard reference group of 2,095 college seniors tested in 1952 on the verbal and quantitative portions of the test. Graduate programs tend to pay attention to the combination of scores on the first two parts (GRE-V + GRE-Q), where combined scores above 1,000 would be considered above average.

The reliability of the GRE is strong, with internal consistency reliability coefficients typically

GRE Scores	0	6	12	18	24	30
GRE-V + GRE-Q total:		1000	1100	1200	1300	1400
Undergraduate GPA	0	5	10	15	20	25
		3.0	3.2	3.4	3.6	3.8
Psychology GPA	0	1	2	3	4	5
		3.0	3.2	3.4	3.6	3.9
Background in Statistics/Experimental	0	1	2	3	4	5
Background in Biology/Chemistry	0	1	2	3	4	5
Background in Math/Computer Science	0	1	2	3	4	5
Research Experience	0	1	2	3	4	5
Positive Interpersonal Skills	0	2	4	6	8	10
Ethnic/Linguistic/Cultural Diversity	0	2	4	6	8	10
				Maximum Total:		100

FIGURE 8.5

Representative Weighting Scheme Used by Graduate Program Admission Committees in Psychology

around .90 for the three components. The validity of the GRE commonly has been examined in relation to the ability of the test to predict performance in graduate school. Performance has been operationalized mainly as grade point average, although faculty ratings of student aptitude also have been used. For example, based upon a meta-analytic review of 22 studies with a total of 5,186 students, Morrison and Morrison (1995) concluded that GRE-V correlated .28 and GRE-Q correlated .22 with graduate grade point average. Thus, on average, GRE scores accounted for only 6.3 percent of the variance in graduate-level academic performance. In a recent study of 170 graduate students in psychology at Yale University, Sternberg and Williams (1997) also found minimal correlations between GRE scores and graduate grades. When GRE scores were correlated with faculty ratings on five variables (analytical, creative, practical, research, and teaching abilities) the correlations were even lower, for the most part hovering right around zero. The single exception was the GRE-A score,

which correlated modestly with almost all of the faculty ratings. However, this correlation was observed *only* for men (on the order of $r = .3$), whereas for women it was almost exactly zero in every case! Based upon these and similar studies, the consensus would appear to be that excessive reliance on the GRE for graduate school selection may overlook a talented pool of promising graduate students.

However, other researchers are more supportive in their evaluation of the GRE, noting that the correlation of GRE scores and graduate grades is not a good index of validity because of the restriction of range problem (Kuncel, Campbell, & Ones, 1998). Specifically, applicants with low GRE scores are unlikely to be accepted for graduate training in the first place, and thus relatively little information is available with respect to whether low scores predict poor academic performance. Put simply, the correlation of GRE scores with graduate academic performance is based *mainly* upon persons with middle to high levels of GRE scores, that is, GRE-V + GRE-Q totals of 1,000 and up. As such, the correlation will be attenuated precisely because those with low GREs are not included in the sample. Another problem with validating the GRE against grades in graduate school is the unreliability of the criterion (grades). Based upon the expectation that graduate students will perform at high levels, some professors may give blanket As such that grades do not reflect real differences in student aptitudes. This would lower the correlation between the predictor (GRE scores) and the criterion (graduate grades). When these factors are accounted for, many researchers find reason to believe the GRE is still a valid tool for graduate school selection (Melchert, 1998; Ruscio, 1998).

Medical College Admission Test

The MCAT is required of applicants to almost all medical schools in the United States. The test is designed to assess achievement of the basic skills and concepts that are prerequisites for successful completion of medical school. There are three multiple choice sections (Verbal Reasoning, Physical Sciences, Biological Sciences) and one essay section (Writing Sample). The Verbal Reasoning section is designed to evaluate the ability to understand and apply information and arguments presented in written form. Specifically, the test consists of several passages of about 500 to 600 words each, taken from humanities, social sciences, and natural sciences. Each passage is followed by several questions based on information included in the passage. The Physical Sciences section is designed to evaluate reasoning in general chemistry and physics. The Biological Sciences is designed to evaluate reasoning in biology and organic chemistry. These physical and biological science sections contain 10 to 11 problem sets described in about 250 words each, with several questions following. The Writing Sample test consists of two 30-minute essays. This test is designed to assess basic writing skills such as developing a central idea, synthesizing concepts and ideas, writing logically, and following accepted practices of grammar, syntax, and punctuation.

Each of the MCAT scores is reported on a scale from 1 to 15 (means of about 8.0 and standard deviations of about 2.5). The reliability of the test is lower than that of other aptitude tests used for selection, with internal consistency and split-half coefficients mainly in the low .80s (Gregory, 1994a). MCAT scores are mildly predictive of success in medical school, but once again the restriction of range conundrum (previously discussed in relation to the GRE) is at play. In particular, examinees with low MCAT scores who would presumably confirm the validity of the test by performing poorly in medical school are rarely admitted, which reduces the apparent validity of the test.

Law School Admission Test

The LSAT is a half-day standardized test required of applicants to virtually every law school in the United States. The test is designed to measure skills considered essential for success in law school, including the reading and understanding of complex material, the organization and management of information, and the ability to reason critically and draw correct inferences. The LSAT consists of multiple-choice questions in four areas: reading comprehension, analytical reasoning, and two logical reasoning sections. An additional section is used to pretest new test items and to preequate new test forms, but this section does not contribute to the LSAT score. The score scale for the LSAT extends from a low of 120 to a high of 180. In addition to the objective portions, a 30-minute writing sample is administered at the end of the test. The section is not scored, but copies of the writing sample are sent to all law schools to which the examinee applies.

The LSAT has acceptable reliability (internal consistency coefficients in the .90s) and is regarded as a moderately valid predictor of law school grades. Yet in one fascinating study, LSAT scores correlated more strongly with state bar test results than with law school grades (Melton, 1985). This speaks well for the validity of the test, insofar as it links LSAT scores with an important, real-world criterion.

SUMMARY

1. Aptitude and ability tests differ in focus and use. In general, ability is a broad concept whereas aptitude typically refers to homogeneous segments of ability. Also, ability tests attempt to gauge current functioning, whereas aptitude tests are typically used to help predict future performance.

2. Aptitude tests owe their origin to factor analysis, a family of procedures employed to summarize relationships among variables that are correlated in highly complex ways. For example, factor analysis might help a researcher discover that a battery of 24 ability tests represents only four underlying variables, called factors.

3. The beginning point for every factor analysis is the correlation matrix, a complete table of intercorrelations among all the variables. The variables in a factor analysis can include results for any more-or-less continuous dimension, such as test scores, social class, and behavior ratings.

4. The factor matrix consists of a table of factor loadings showing the weighting of each variable on each factor. A factor is a weighted linear sum of the variables. The factor loading for each variable is a correlation coefficient between the factor and that variable.

5. Factors can be represented as geometric reference axes, and the loadings for each variable on each factor can be plotted within this space. This allows the researcher to visualize the location of each variable on the two or three most important factors.

6. Because the position of the reference axes is arbitrary, the researcher is free to rotate the axes so that they produce a more sensible fit with the factor loadings for the variables. A number of different methods of rotation exist (e.g., rotation to positive manifold, rotation to simple structure).

7. The naming of factors requires judgment and inference. In particular, the researcher must attempt to determine the common processes and abilities shared by the tests or variables with strong loadings on a factor. Also, tests or variables with low loadings may help sharpen the definition and naming of a factor.

8. In order for a particular kind of factor to emerge from an analysis, some of the tests and measures must contain that factor in the first place. Large samples, in excess of 200 persons, are preferred. The choice of strategies for rotation is important: Orthogonal axes assume that factors are uncorrelated; oblique axes accept that factors are correlated.

9. Used for educational and vocational guidance in the high school years, the Differential Aptitude Test (DAT) consists of eight independent tests. A lack of discriminant validity between the eight tests is one concern with this respected battery.

10. The General Aptitude Test Battery (GATB) is typical of the multiple aptitude test batteries based upon factor analysis. The GATB consists of eight paper-and-pencil tests and four apparatus measures derived from a factor analysis of 59 tests. The test yields nine factor scores helpful in the prediction of job performance.

11. The Armed Services Vocational Aptitude Battery (ASVAB), used by the Armed Services to screen and assign recruits, is probably the most widely used paper-and-pencil test in existence. The test yields composite scores, each based upon two to four subtest scores. A limitation of the ASVAB is that the composites are highly correlated with one another.

12. The prediction of academic performance is facilitated by such tests as the Scholastic Assessment Tests (SAT), formerly the Scholastic Aptitude Tests, and the American College Test (ACT) assessment program.

13. The SAT yields separate Verbal and Mathematics scores anchored to a 1941 mean of 500 (SD of 100). The ACT yields four scores (in English, mathematics, reading, and science reasoning) reported on a 36-point standard score scale (mean of about 20.7, SD of 5).

14. Used for admission to many graduate programs, the GRE consists of three general tests (Verbal, Quantitative, and Analytical) as well as subject tests in specific areas (e.g., Biology, Computer Science, Psychology). Each exam is normed to a mean of about 500 and SD of 100.

15. The MCAT is required of applicants to almost all medical schools in the United States. There

are three multiple-choice sections (Verbal Reasoning, Physical Sciences, Biological Sciences) and one essay section (Writing Sample), all designed to assess basic skills needed for medical school.

16. The LSAT is a half-day standardized test required of applicants to virtually every law school in the United States. The LSAT consists of multiple-choice questions in four areas: reading comprehension, analytical reasoning, and two logical reasoning sections.

KEY TERMS AND CONCEPTS

factor analysis   p. 268

factors   p. 268

correlation matrix   p. 269

factor matrix   p. 269

rotation to positive manifold   p. 272

rotation to simple structure   p. 272

orthogonal axes   p. 275

oblique axes   p. 275

Topic **8B** Group Tests of Achievement

In this topic, we continue the discussion of group tests by surveying their use within educational systems. Beginning in the elementary grades, school districts use group achievement tests to track the progress of individual students and to gauge the success of educational programs. The ubiquitous practice of group achievement testing within American schools is largely a positive affair because it provides an objective basis for evaluation. However, there is on occasion a dark side as well, insofar as testing can become the tail that wags the dog. The negative impact falls into three general categories. First, teachers may teach to the tests rather than trying to impart genuine knowledge. Second, in a quest to obtain high scores for their school systems, administrators may foster an environment that encourages liberal, nonstandard testing. Worse yet, school personnel may engage in outright fraud such as "correcting" answer sheets. The third consequence is that individual examinees will find ingenious ways of cheating on nationally normed tests. We review a few of these disquieting trends at the end of this topic.

ESSENTIAL CONCEPTS IN ACHIEVEMENT TESTS

Achievement tests, known as attainment tests in the United Kingdom, are the most widely used of all types of tests. Although precise figures on usage do not exist, virtually every school-aged child in the United States encounters group standardized achievement testing on a yearly or bi-yearly basis. One estimate is that public schools administer an average of two and one-half tests per student per year (Medina & Neill, 1990). Beyond a doubt, the number of achievement tests administered surpasses all other forms of psychological and educational testing.

Achievement tests are designed to measure the attainment of skills taught within schools or training programs. These tests can be quite narrowly defined such as a test of punctuation skills, or more broadly conceived such as a test of reading comprehension. Even though achievement tests differ in their specificity, they all serve a related function: to measure current skill level in a well-defined domain.

As catalogued in the *Mental Measurements Yearbook* series (Conoley & Impara, 1995; Conoley & Kramer, 1989, 1992; Mitchell, 1985), literally hundreds of achievement tests have been published. It is not feasible to survey the vast panorama of these instruments. Instead, we review representative achievement tests and focus upon the issues raised by their use. We begin with a primer on essential concepts in achievement testing.

Group and Individual Achievement Tests

A fundamental distinction is drawn between group achievement tests and individual achievement tests. Group achievement tests are used mainly in the classroom, whereas individual achievement tests are employed one on one in clinical or educational settings. **Group achievement tests** might also be called educational achievement tests, since these instruments are commonly administered to entire school systems at the behest of state school superintendents or other administrators. Of course, group tests are given simultaneously to dozens or hundreds of students at the same time, with all the advantages and pitfalls attendant to this approach (see Topic 2B, The Testing Process).

Individual achievement tests play an essential role in the diagnosis of a learning disability (LD). Not only do these tests provide documentation of impaired performance in such crucial academic areas as reading, writing, and calculation, some achievement tests can help identify the particular skill deficits that underlie learning disabilities. Individual achievement tests are used in conjunction with other instruments, especially intelligence tests, as discussed in Topic 10A, School-Based Assessment.

Norm-Referenced and Criterion-Referenced Tests

In addition to the fundamental dichotomy which separates group from individual achievement tests, another important distinction is between norm-referenced and criterion-referenced achievement tests. The reader will recall from Topic 2A (The Nature and Uses of Psychological Tests) that norm-referenced tests allow for interpretation in reference to a large standardization sample. Norm-referenced tests facilitate the reporting of scores as percentile ranks, standard scores, and the like. In contrast, criterion-referenced tests allow for interpretation in reference to the specific content mastered by the individual examinee. For example, a criterion-referenced test might determine that an examinee knows how to spell correctly 94 out of 100 items from a designated list of essential words. Of course, these two approaches are not necessarily incompatible. In fact, most major achievement test batteries provide both norm-referenced and criterion-referenced interpretations.

Ability, Aptitude, and Achievement Tests

The distinction between ability, aptitude, and achievement tests merits brief review in this context.

Ability tests sample a broad assortment of skills in order to estimate general intellectual level. In contrast, aptitude tests usually measure homogeneous segments of ability and are often used to predict future performance. The exceptions here include multiple aptitude test batteries which sample abilities broadly; these instruments are very similar to ability tests. Finally, as noted, achievement tests measure current skill attainment, particularly in relation to school and training programs.

In the real world, the distinction between these three types of tests is often quite fuzzy (Gregory, 1994a). It has been known for some time that the correlation between an achievement test and an ability test may be nearly as high as that between any two ability tests. In many cases, achievement and ability tests tap similar underlying cognitive factors. However, the assumptions which underly these two forms of testing differ widely. Achievement tests are generally designed to measure the effects of relatively standardized educational experiences, whereas aptitude tests typically make fewer assumptions about specific prior learning experiences.

The applications of aptitude and achievement tests also differ widely. Aptitude tests are designed primarily to predict future performance in schools or training programs. For example, a scholastic aptitude test might be used to predict future academic performance in college; a clerical aptitude test might be used to predict future performance in the role of secretary. In contrast, achievement tests are used to gauge a student's current level of attainment in a given subject matter. In other words, aptitude tests are oriented to the future, whereas achievement tests are oriented to the present. The assessment of current skill level with achievement tests can serve several purposes, as outlined in the following section.

The Functions of Achievement Testing

Achievement tests permit a wide range of potential uses. Practical applications of individual and group achievement tests include the following:

- To identify children and adults with specific achievement deficits who might need more detailed assessment for learning disabilities.

- To help parents recognize the academic strengths and weaknesses of their children and thereby foster individual remedial efforts at home.
- To identify classwide or schoolwide achievement deficiencies as a basis for redirection of instructional efforts.
- To appraise the success of educational programs by measuring the subsequent skill attainment of students.
- To group students according to similar skill level in specific academic domains.
- To identify the level of instruction that is appropriate for individual students.

Thus, achievement tests serve institutional goals such as monitoring schoolwide achievement levels, but also play an important role in the assessment of individual learning difficulties. As previously noted, different kinds of achievement tests are used to pursue these two fundamental applications (institutional and individual). Institutional goals are best served by group achievement test batteries, whereas individual assessment is commonly pursued with individual achievement tests (even though group tests may play a role here, too). In this topic we focus on group educational achievement tests.

EDUCATIONAL ACHIEVEMENT TESTS

Virtually every school system in the nation uses at least one educational achievement test, so it is not surprising that test publishers have responded to the widespread need by developing a panoply of excellent instruments. In the following section, we describe several of the most widely used group standardized achievement tests. The tests to be described share several characteristics in common.

First, these instruments are multilevel batteries which contain comparable subtests for students in the different grades of primary and/or secondary school. Some of the batteries span kindergarten (K) through grade 12, whereas others are designed for elementary grades (K through 8) or secondary grades (9 through 12) only. In a multilevel battery, test booklets contain overlapping sections, and students at different grade levels enter and exit the test materials at grade-appropriate positions.

A second feature common to many educational test batteries is concurrent norming with an ability test. For example, the achievement battery known as the Sequential Tests of Educational Progress (STEP-III) is concurrently normed with the ability battery known as the School and College Ability Test (SCAT-III). Tests which are concurrently normed share the same standardization sample. As a result, average performance on one test can be directly equated with average performance on the other. Concurrent norming is helpful because it allows parents, teachers, and counselors to make precise, direct, and meaningful comparisons between achievement and ability. After all, the implications of an achievement score are moderated by knowledge of the student's ability. A student with high ability scores but low achievement scores might be a good candidate for educational intervention, including a more detailed assessment for learning disability (as discussed in Topic 10A, School-Based Assessment). In contrast, a student with low ability scores and low achievement scores might be working at full potential; specialized interventions may not be warranted.

The third commonality in group achievement tests is that they measure similar educational skills. Educational achievement tests tend to emphasize these skill areas:

- Reading, including comprehension and vocabulary
- Written language, including spelling, punctuation, and capitalization
- Mathematics, including computation and application

In addition, tests at the elementary grade levels often assess listening skills, including oral comprehension. Some test batteries also assess knowledge of basic concepts in science, social studies, and humanities.

Finally, the educational achievement tests discussed here possess generally excellent psychometric characteristics. Test contents are relevant and appropriate, that is, the instruments show good content validity; subscales possess excellent internal and alternate-forms reliability; standardization samples are invariably large and representative; and overt gender and race bias are nonexistent. The psychometric quality of the widely used educational achievement tests is typically respectable, if not extraordinary.

We survey several widely used tests of educational achievement subsequently. The reader will discover that a detailed analysis of psychometric properties—reliability, validity, norming, and the like—is encountered only for the first instrument reviewed, the Iowa Tests of Basic Skills. In general, the psychometric quality of the other tests is equally laudable, so for these test batteries we focus upon functions, applications, special features, and an occasional shortcoming or two. Readers who desire more information on these instruments should consult reviews in the *Mental Measurements Yearbook* (Conoley & Impara, 1995; Conoley & Kramer, 1989, 1992; Mitchell, 1985).

Iowa Tests of Basic Skills

First published in 1935, the Iowa Tests of Basic Skills (ITBS) were most recently revised and restandardized in 1992. The ITBS is a multilevel battery of achievement tests that covers grades K through 9. A companion test, the Tests of Achievement and Proficiency (TAP), covers grades 9 through 12. In order to expedite direct and accurate comparisons of achievement and ability, the ITBS and the TAP were both concurrently normed with the Cognitive Abilities Test (CogAT), a respected group test of general intellectual ability.

The ITBS is available in several levels which correspond roughly with the ages of the potential examinees: levels 5 and 6 (grades K–1), levels 7–9 (grades 1–3) and levels 9–14 (grades 3–9). The basic subtests for the older levels measure vocabulary, reading, language, mathematics, social studies, science, and sources of information.

From the first edition onward, the ITBS has been guided by a pragmatic philosophy of educational measurement. The *Manual* states the purpose of testing as follows:

The purpose of measurement is to provide information which can be used in improving instruction. Measurement has value to the extent that it results in better decisions which directly affect pupils.

To this end, the ITBS incorporates a criterion-referenced skills analysis to supplement the usual array of norm-referenced scores. For example, one feature available from the publisher's scoring service is item-level information. This information indicates topic areas, items sampling the topic, and correct or wrong response for each item. Teachers therefore have access to a wealth of diagnostic-instructional information for each student. Whether this information translates to better instruction—as the test authors desire—is very difficult to quantify. As Linn (1989) notes, "We must rely mostly on logic, anecdotes, and opinions when it comes to answering such questions."

The technical properties of the ITBS are beyond reproach. Internal consistency and equivalent-form reliability coefficients are mostly in the mid-.80s to low .90s. Stability coefficients for a one-year interval are almost all in the .70 to .90 range. The test is free from overt racial and gender bias, as determined by content evaluation and item bias studies. The standardization sample for the latest edition included 270,000 students roughly stratified according to school type (public/private/parochial), larger versus smaller cities, geographic regions, and socioeconomic classes.

Standardization of a previous form in 1988 revealed an intriguing trend in comparison to results for versions that were standardized several years earlier. The 1988 sample demonstrated higher achievement levels, on the order of 1 to 3 months of grade equivalent. This pattern of slowly rising test performance emphasizes the need for annual or biannual restandardization of achievement test batteries. What has happened in the absence of timely restandardization of major achievement tests is that all 50 states can report honestly that they exceed the national average on group standardized tests (Cannell, 1988).

Item content of the ITBS is judged relevant by curriculum experts and reviewers, which speaks to the content validity of the test (Lane, 1992; Linn,

1989; Raju, 1992; Willson, 1989). Although the predictive validity of the latest ITBS has not been studied extensively, evidence from prior editions is very encouraging. For example, ITBS scores correlate moderately with high school grades (*r*s around .60). The ITBS is not a perfect instrument, but it represents the best that modern test development methods can produce.

Metropolitan Achievement Test

The Metropolitan Achievement Test dates back to 1930 when the test was designed to meet the curriculum assessment needs of New York City. The stated purpose of the MAT is "to measure the achievement of students in the major skill and content areas of the school curriculum." The MAT is concurrently normed with the Otis-Lennon School Ability Test (OLSAT).

The MAT is a multilevel battery designed for grades K through 12. The instrument consists of two components that can be used separately or in combination. The two components include the Survey Battery and the Diagnostic Batteries. The Survey Battery provides norm-referenced information for traditional academic skills. For example, the subtests at the high school level (grades 10 through 12) include the following:

> Reading
> Mathematics
> Language
> Science
> Social Studies
> Research Skills

The Research Skills score is based upon relevant test items from the other subtests. Scores for the total battery are also provided.

The Diagnostic Batteries consist of three tests designed as instructional planning tools. These three tests encompass a criterion-referenced approach to measuring fundamental skills in reading, mathematics, and language skills. For example, the reading diagnostic test for grades K through 2 include measures of visual discrimination, letter recognition, auditory discrimination, sight vocabulary, phonemes/graphemes, vocabulary in context, and reading comprehension. The MAT possesses exceptional reliability, but reviewers have noted that additional evidence of criterion-related validity would be desirable (Nitko, 1989; Rogers, 1989).

The Iowa Tests of Educational Development

The widely used Iowa Tests of Educational Development were first released in 1942, then revised and restandardized every few years. The purpose of the ITED is: "To assess intellectual skills that are important in adult life and provide the basis for continued learning." Unlike many other achievement tests which emphasize skills linked to specific curricular goals, the intention of the ITED is to measure the fundamental goals or generalized skills of education that are independent of the curriculum. For this reason, the ITED items emphasize higher-order thinking skills. Rather than testing isolated bits of knowledge, questions on the ITED feature problems which require the synthesis of knowledge or a multiple-step solution (Figure 8.6).

The ITED is designed for high school students in grades 9 through 12. The test yields seven basic scores plus two derived scores:

> Correctness and Appropriateness of Expression
> Vocabulary
> Ability To Do Quantitative Thinking
> Analysis of Social Science Materials
> Analysis of Natural Science Materials
> Ability to Interpret Literary Materials
> Uses of Sources of Information
> Composite
> Reading Total

The Composite is based upon all the subtests, while the Reading Total is derived from the subtests that require analysis of reading material. The ITED is anchored to previous editions so that regardless of form, level, or edition a given score represents the same level of excellence. The purpose of anchoring the test to previous editions is to expedite longitu-

Social Studies
Advertisement

> Four out of five doctors surveyed favored
> BALM SOAP
> Tests show that Balm Soap clears up complexion problems
> faster than any other product!

On the basis of this advertisement, which of the following conclusions, if any, is valid?

A. It has been scientifically demonstrated that the quickest way to get rid of any complexion problem is to use Balm Soap.

B. Of the five leading brands of complexion soaps, only one is better than Balm Soap from a medical point of view.

C. Of all the doctors who recommended skin care products, four out of five recommended Balm Soap.

D. None of these conclusions is valid.

Natural Sciences

Soon after being bitten by a mosquito, a person became ill with yellow fever. Which conclusion, if any, is justified solely from these observations?

A. There is insufficient evidence to draw any of the conclusions that follow.

B. Mosquitoes are the direct cause of yellow fever.

C. The mosquito introduced a microorganism into the person's bloodstream.

D. The mosquito carried an organism that caused yellow fever.

FIGURE 8.6
Representative Items from the Iowa Tests of Educational Development
Source: Reprinted from *Teacher, Administrator, and Counselor Manual: Iowa Tests of Educational Development, Forms X-8 and Y-8* (1988). Chicago, IL: Riverside Publishing Co. Copyright © 1988. Reproduced with permission of the Riverside Publishing Company.

dinal growth comparisons within individuals and to facilitate the long-term investigation of historical and educational trends. In 1992, the ITED was restandardized on a large national sample of students in grades 9 through 12.

The Tests of Achievement and Proficiency

The Tests of Achievement and Proficiency (TAP) are designed to provide a comprehensive appraisal of student progress toward traditional academic goals in grades 9 through 12. The TAP is the second component in the Riverside Basic Skills Assessment Program; the first component is the Iowa Tests of Basic Skills (ITBS), used in grades K through 9 (previously discussed). Like the ITBS, the TAP is concurrently normed with the CogAT, an ability test which measures verbal, quantitative, and nonverbal reasoning abilities. The subtests from the TAP measure achievement in reading

comprehension, mathematics, written expression, using sources of information, social studies, and science. A total or composite score is also provided.

The TAP also yields an applied proficiency score that assesses the examinee's capacity to handle real-life situations. This score reflects student competence in applying mathematics and communication skills to solving problems of daily living. The items emphasize communication of ideas in writing, mathematical solution of problems, use of reference materials, and the interpretation of tabular and graphic material. The TAP was conormed with the ITED and the CogAT and restandardized in 1992.

Tests of General Educational Development (GED)

Another widely used achievement test battery is the Tests of General Educational Development (GED), developed by the American Council on Education and administered nationwide for high school equivalency certification (GED Testing Service, 1991). The GED consists of multiple-choice examinations in five educational areas: writing skills, social studies, science, interpreting literature and the arts, and mathematics. The writing skills section also contains an essay question which examinees must answer in writing. The essay question is scored independently by two trained readers according to a six-point holistic scoring method. The readers make a judgment about the essay based upon its overall effectiveness in comparison to the effectiveness of other essays.

The GED comes in 12 alternate forms. Internal consistency reliabilities for the subscales are mostly above .90, with only a few as low as .87. The latest edition of the GED does not report alternate-forms reliabilities, but results from earlier versions were largely in the mid- to high .80s, with the exception of reading skills (now called interpreting literature and the arts), for which the reliability was as low as .76. Interrater reliability of the writing samples was found to lie between .6 and .7; these findings indicate that a liberal criterion for passing this subtest is appropriate so as to reduce decision errors. Regarding validity, the GED correlates very strongly with the graduation reading test used in New York ($r = .77$). Furthermore, the standards for passing the GED are more stringent than those employed by most high schools: in 1985, between 27 percent and 33 percent of graduating high school seniors nationwide would have been unable to pass the GED Tests (Whitney, Malizio, & Patience, 1985).

The GED emphasizes broad concepts rather than specific facts and details. In general, the purpose of the GED is to allow adults who did not graduate from high school to prove that they have obtained an equivalent level of knowledge from life experiences or independent study. Employers regard the GED as equivalent (if not superior) to earning a high school diploma. Successful performance on the GED enables individuals to apply to colleges, seek jobs, and request promotions that require a high school diploma as a prerequisite.

Rogers (1992) and Trevisan (1992) provide unusually thorough reviews of the GED.

Additional Group Standardized Achievement Tests

In addition to the previously listed batteries, a few other widely used group standardized achievement tests deserve brief mention. Because these tests strongly resemble the instruments discussed previously, we provide only the barest listing here. The Sequential Tests of Educational Progress (STEP-III) are organized into two batteries, one used for grades K through 3, the other used for grades 3 through 12. The basic STEP-III battery assesses the following educational skills: reading, writing skills, vocabulary, mathematics computation, and mathematics concepts. Additional tests measure attainment in social studies, science, study skills, and oral comprehension (listening). The STEP-III is a companion test to the School and College Ability Tests (SCAT-III).

The widely used Stanford Achievement Series is one of the oldest and most prestigious testing programs in the United States. The series consists of three related test batteries covering grades K through 13: the Stanford Early School Achievement Test (SESAT) for kindergarteners and first graders; the Stanford Achievement Test (SAchT) for grades 1 through 9; and the Stanford Test of Academic Skills (TASK) for grades 8 through 13 (*grade 13* refers to the first year of college). Reviewers are cautious about the SESAT because the value of the test is predicated solely upon content validity. Little is known about test-retest reliability, criterion-related validity, and construct validity (Ackerman, 1992; Carpenter, 1992). The SAchT is lauded because of its excellent norm-referenced coverage of a representative and balanced national consensus curriculum (Brown, 1992; Stoker, 1992). The TASK has excellent psychometric characteristics, but in attempting to span high school and college achievement, this test undertakes a difficult assignment. After all, there is modest agreement about the curricular intentions of grade school and high school, but what are the educational goals of the first year in college?

SPECIAL-PURPOSE ACHIEVEMENT TESTS

Achievement tests can be used for many important applied purposes, including the appraisal of knowledge in advanced fields and the evaluation of professional competency. In this final section we will examine two special-purpose achievement tests. The College-Level Examination Program (CLEP) is a widely used program by which students can demonstrate college-level achievement and receive advance credit or exemption from certain college courses. The National Teacher Examination (NTE) is a controversial test required by many states for teacher certification.

College-Level Examination Program (CLEP)

CLEP is one of two national testing programs through which students can receive college credit by examination without enrolling in the courses. The other program is the ACT Proficiency Examination Program which we do not discuss here. CLEP is administered by the College Board with financial support from the Carnegie Corporation of New York. The original purpose of the program was to support nontraditional students such as returning veterans and older adults who had obtained valuable learning experiences outside of the classroom. However, it is mainly ambitious high school students enrolled in advanced classes who now register to take the CLEP examinations. Some students begin college with nearly a full semester of course credits obtained through CLEP and similar programs.

The CLEP consists of two categories of exams. Each of the five General Examinations is a test of material taught in basic courses taken by most students as part of the general education requirements. The areas tested include English Composition, Humanities, College Mathematics, Natural Sciences, and Social Sciences/History. Except for the English Composition test which includes a 45-minute essay, the general tests are 90-minute multiple-choice exams. Three to six hours of semester credit are usually awarded for satisfactory scores on each general test.

Each of the 30 Subject Examinations is a 90-minute multiple-choice test in two separately timed sections. Four of these tests also include an essay section that is required by some colleges. Sample tests include American literature, French, German, Spanish, American government, macroeconomics, introduction to psychology, algebra, biology, chemistry, computer science, and accounting. Three or more hours of semester credit are usually awarded for satisfactory scores on each subject test.

Scores on the CLEP General Examinations are reported on a scale from 200 to 800, with an average of 500 and standard deviation of 100. For the Subject Examinations, scores are reported on a scale from 20 to 80 with an average of 50 and a standard deviation of 10. The reference groups for these scores consisted of volunteer students completing courses in each of the specified areas. These students were recruited from a nonrandom but presumably representative selection of American colleges and universities. The CLEP scores are, in general, highly reliable, with split-half coefficients mainly in the .90s. The validity of the Subject Examinations has been evaluated by means of correlating CLEP scores with final grades in the relevant courses. Most of these correlation coefficients are in the .40s and .50s, which supports the concurrent validity of these tests. The validity of the General Examinations is presumably good but is less well established.

The CLEP program has received high marks from reviewers, but there is a potential negative side as well. In particular, some students might "test out" of college courses that would have proved enriching, inspiring, even life-changing. For example, it is possible to have factual knowledge about art, music, or drama and therefore pass a CLEP test in one or more of these areas. However, in the ambitious quest to finish college quickly, students could overlook important experiences for personal growth.

National Teacher Examination (NTE)

The National Teacher Examination is actually a series of tests published by the Educational Testing Service and known more formally as the Praxis Series. Of the 40 states that require testing as part of the licensure process, 36 use the Praxis Series, which explains why the test is known informally as the National Teacher Examination, or NTE. The Praxis Series is nationally administered and continually updated and improved. The three categories of assessment correspond to major milestones in teacher development:

- Praxis I (Academic Skills Assessments): Entering a teacher training program
- Praxis II (Subject Assessments): Graduating from college and entering the profession
- Praxis III (Classroom Performance Assessments): The first year of teaching

The initial test, Praxis I, is taken early in the student's college career to evaluate reading, writing, and math skills essential for the success of any teacher. A passing score on this multiple-choice test is required before the student can continue his or her major in education. These tests can be taken in the traditional paper-and-pencil format or as a computer-based test that is tailored to each candidate's ongoing performance. One advantage to the computer-based testing is year-round availability, whereas the traditional version is given only six times a year. Praxis II assesses knowledge of the subjects a candidate will teach, as well as how much he or she knows about teaching the subject. More than 120 content tests (all multiple choice) are available. Praxis III is an in-class evaluation by trained local assessors who use structured criteria that have been nationally validated.

The reliability of the Praxis I and Praxis II tests is beyond reproach. Similarly, the content validity of these tests is outstanding because they were carefully constructed and refined with the help of many experts and test consumers. What is less clear is the predictive validity of the Praxis Series, insofar as little information exists to show that good scores or Praxis evaluations predict good teaching and vice

versa. Of course, part of the difficulty here is finding a suitable definition and measure of "good teaching." The National Teaching Examination probably serves a useful purpose by requiring that prospective teachers possess minimum levels of knowledge in their disciplines, but the test also raises difficult questions with regard to how our society identifies promising teachers. Is factual knowledge enough? Should we not also insist that our teachers possess enthusiasm for their material and the capacity to inspire children? These are features not easily captured by objective tests.

CHEATING: THE DARK SIDE OF ACHIEVEMENT TESTING

The prevailing view in the general public is that cheating rarely or never occurs in nationally administered testing programs. We tend to think that the risks are too high and the opportunities too limited for cheaters to prevail. Therefore, we rest assured that test fraud must be a rare event. Unfortunately, this view is probably naive. After all, a growing number of people must pass a test to gain college entry, get a job, or obtain a promotion. Furthermore, school officials increasingly are evaluated on the basis of average test scores in their district. Precisely because the stakes are so high, unscrupulous individuals will try to beat the system.

Consider the case of superior test scores at an acclaimed elementary school in Connecticut (Associated Press, May 4, 1996, and March 15, 1997). The stellar reputation of the school was based upon high exam scores on the Iowa Test of Basic Skills given to first, third, and fifth graders. The school had won blue ribbons from the U.S. Education Department and was featured as one of the nation's best elementary schools in a prominent magazine. However, in a fluke discovery, school district personnel noted a high number of erasures on the tests from this school and notified the test publisher. On close inspection, the publishers found an exceedingly high number of erasures—9 percent—which was three to five times higher than two nearby schools. Even more suspicious was the fact that 89 percent of the erasures were changed from the wrong answer to the correct answer. Based upon retesting under close supervision, the test publisher found "clearly and conclusively" that tampering occurred. The principal resigned amid allegations that he was responsible for the tampering.

An especially flagrant instance of cheating on national tests was uncovered in Louisiana in 1997. This case involved wholesale circulation of the Educational Testing Service (ETS) exam administered to teachers who want to be school principals. As reported in the *New York Times* (September 28, 1997), copies of the 145-item test, along with correct answers, had circulated among teachers throughout southern Louisiana, most likely for several years. In a state ranked at or near the bottom on nearly every educational index, it appears that many potentially unqualified persons cheated their way into running the schools. ETS handled this case quietly by asking more than 200 teachers to retake the test so as to "confirm" their initial scores. Unfortunately, the Louisiana case was not an isolated instance. The *New York Times* article includes this disquieting conclusion:

> In numerous instances across the country, E. T. S. has confronted case after case of cheating but withheld information from the public and failed to take aggressive steps in time to insure the integrity of its tests, according to internal documents and interviews with current and former officials there.

Among the examples cited, ETS allegedly failed to monitor its handling of the federal government's test for immigrants who want to become citizens, with the likely result that test supervisors accepted bribes. English-proficiency tests for foreign students also were vulnerable to cheating. In 1994, ETS canceled the scores of 30,000 students from China after discovering a ring that was selling the examinations abroad. In another case, federal prosecutors uncovered a nationwide cheating ring involving hundreds of students who paid thousands of dollars each for answers to the GRE and similar exams. This scheme involved a well-known time-zone scam in which experienced test takers took the exams in New York City and then relayed the answers to paying customers taking the tests in the later time zones.

Dishonest and inappropriate practices by school officials are implicated in the recent inflation of scores on nationally normed group tests of achievement. By definition, for a norm-referenced test, 50 percent of the examinees should score above the 50th percentile, 50 percent below. If the same test is used in a large sample of typical and representative school systems, average scores for the school systems should be split evenly—about half above the nationally normed 50th percentile, half below.

According to a recent survey reported in the news media (Foster, 1990), virtually all states of the union claim that average achievement scores for their school systems exceed the 50th percentile. The resulting overly optimistic picture of student achievement is labeled the **Lake Wobegon Effect,** in reference to humorist Garrison Keillor's mythical Minnesota town where "all the children are above average."

How does inflation of achievement test scores arise? According to Cannell (1988), the major cause is educational administrators who are desperate to demonstrate the excellence of their school systems. Precisely because our society attaches so much importance to achievement test results, some educators apparently help students cheat on standardized tests. The alleged cheating includes the following:

- Teachers and principals coach students on test answers.
- Examiners give more than the allotted time to take tests.
- Administrators alter answer sheets.
- Teachers teach directly to the specific test items.
- Teachers make copies of the tests to give to their students.

Cannell notes that over 300 teachers and school administrators answered his trade journal advertisement, admitting that they or colleagues had tampered with tests or helped students improperly. These improprieties constitute a quiet crisis that continues unabated. Another consequence of the Lake Wobegon Effect is that test publishers and federal reviewers will likely increase their efforts to monitor test security. In sum, the importance that our society attaches to achievement test scores has caused a number of unappealing side effects that undermine the very foundations of nationally normed group-testing programs.

Moore (1994) reports on a special case in educational testing, namely, the districtwide consequences of court-ordered achievement testing. He surveyed 79 teachers from third- through fifth-grade level in a midwestern town in which the court required the use of a standardized test to determine the effectiveness of a desegregation effort. The test in question, the Iowa Tests of Basic Skills (ITBS) is a well-respected group achievement test that requires strict adherence to instructions and time limits for obtaining valid results (see above). Yet the teachers found little value in the testing program, complaining that its benefits did not offset the time and costs involved. As a consequence of their devaluing the effort, nonstandard testing was practically the rule rather than the exception. The teachers engaged in several nonstandard practices, most of which tended to inflate the test scores. Inappropriate testing practices included praising students who answered a question correctly during the test (67 percent), using last year's test questions for practice (44 percent), recoding a student's answer sheet because he or she just "miscoded" the answer (26 percent), giving students as much time as they needed (24 percent), giving students items that were directly off the test (24 percent), and giving hints or clues during the test (23 percent). In general, Moore (1994) notes that teachers modified their instructional efforts and curriculum in anticipation of having their students take the test. More than 90 percent of the teachers added test-related lessons to the curriculum, and more than 70 percent

eliminated topics so that they could spend more time on test-related skills. Whether these are desirable changes is surely open to debate. Moore (1994) concludes:

> Standardized testing has held a central role in education for many years. What studies of testing program impact have most recently demonstrated is the growing reliance on test scores for decision making and the increasing potential for misuse of test scores. Educational and political policymakers need to address the important link between instruction and testing and ensure that teachers are integrated into, not isolated from, the intent of testing (p. 365).

In sum, what this study demonstrates is that mandated educational testing can have the unanticipated consequence of polluting the validity of a worthy test—especially when crucial stakeholders have no voice in the process.

We cannot survey here all the unintended side effects of educational achievement tests, because the possibilities are nearly endless. For example, what about the warping effects of achievement-testing programs upon school curricula? As we have seen in Moore's (1994) study, teachers do modify their classroom practices with the intention of helping students score well on the tests. However, in teaching to the tests, educators may emphasize bits and pieces of factual knowledge rather than imparting a general ability to think clearly and solve problems. In conclusion, it appears that an excessive emphasis upon nationally normed achievement tests for selection and evaluation promotes inappropriate behavior, including outright fraud and cheating on the part of students and school officials. Just how widespread is the problem? Although we live with the optimistic assumption that fraud in nationally normed testing programs is rare, the disturbing truth is that we really don't know how often this occurs.

SUMMARY

1. Achievement tests are used to measure the attainment of skills taught within schools or training programs. Group achievement tests are used mainly in the classroom, whereas individual achievement tests are employed one-on-one in clinical or educational settings.

2. The distinction between ability, aptitude, and achievement tests is fuzzy. In fact, the correlations among these three kinds of measures are often very high. However, the typical applications of these tests differ: aptitude tests are used to predict future performance, whereas achievement tests gauge current functioning.

3. The functions of group achievement testing include screening for possible learning disability, identification of individual strengths and weaknesses, grouping of students, and appraising the success of educational programs.

4. Test publishers have developed several excellent multilevel test batteries to meet the needs of school systems for assessment of educational achievement. In a multilevel battery, test booklets contain overlapping sections, and students at different grade levels enter and exit the test materials at grade-appropriate places.

5. The Iowa Tests of Basic Skills is a multilevel battery of achievement tests that covers grades K through 9. Concurrently normed with the Cognitive Abilities Test (CogAT), the ITBS measures achievement in such basic areas as vocabulary, reading comprehension, spelling, and mathematics.

6. The Metropolitan Achievement Test (MAT) consists of two components which can be used separately or in combination. The two components include the Survey Battery (norm-referenced assessment for traditional academic skills), and the Diagnostic Batteries (criterion-referenced approach for educational planning purposes).

7. Unlike many other achievement tests that emphasize skills linked to specific curricular goals, the intention of the Iowa Tests of Educational Development (ITED) is to measure the fundamental goals or generalized skills of education that are independent of the curriculum. For this reason, the items used in the ITED stress higher-order thinking skills.

8. The Tests of Achievement and Proficiency (TAP) are designed to provide a comprehensive appraisal of student progress toward traditional academic goals in grades 9 through 12. Companion test to the ITBS, the TAP is concurrently normed with the CogAT, an ability test which measures verbal, quantitative, and nonverbal reasoning abilities.

9. Another widely used achievement test battery is the Tests of General Educational Development (GED), developed by the American Council on Education and administered nationwide for high school equivalency certification. The GED consists of multiple-choice examinations in five educational areas and includes an essay question to assess writing skills.

10. The College-Level Examination Program (CLEP) allows students to receive college credit by examination without enrolling in the courses. There are five general examinations (e.g., Humanities, College Mathematics) and 30 specific examinations (e.g., American literature, introduction to psychology, algebra, biology).

11. Published by the Educational Testing Service, the National Teacher Examination (NTE) is known more formally as the Praxis Series. This evaluation consists of three categories (academic skills, subject expertise, and classroom performance). The subject assessments are required by many states as a prerequisite for licensure.

12. The prevalence of cheating on nationally administered achievement tests is unknown. However, many reports have surfaced in recent years, including the alteration of answer sheets by school officials, wholesale circulation of some licensing examinations, and inappropriate testing practices by individual teachers (e.g., extra time to finish tests).

KEY TERMS AND CONCEPTS

group achievement tests   p. 290

individual achievement tests   p. 291

Lake Wobegon Effect   p. 299

CHAPTER 9

Neuropsychological and Geriatric Assessment

TOPIC 9A A Primer of Neuropsychology

Neuropsychological assessment is the application of specialized tests for purposes of diagnosing and treating individuals with known or suspected brain dysfunction. Neuropsychological tests are distinctive because of their demonstrated link to brain functions (Lezak, 1995). Specifically,

any test or technique that is highly sensitive to the effects of brain impairment—and especially a test or technique that permits inferences about the site, type, or degree of such impairment—would qualify as a neuropsychological procedure. The purpose of this chapter is to introduce the reader to neuropsychological tests, concepts, and methods. In addition, the chapter includes a secondary emphasis upon assessment of age-related disorders such as Alzheimer's disease, multi-infarct dementia (stroke), and late-life depression, because these problems are best understood within a neuropsychological context. In Topic 9A, A Primer of Neuropsychology, we provide a condensed review of human brain functions. We also give special consideration to disorders of aging and review medical approaches to brain imaging. The central purpose of this topic is to prepare the reader for the ensuing discussion of neuropsychological and geriatric assessment procedures. In Topic 9B, Neuropsychological and Geriatric Assessment, we examine the nature and use of major neuropsychological tests and geriatric assessment procedures.

Neuropsychology is the study of the relationship between brain function and behavior (Cytowic, 1996; Kolb & Whishaw, 1990). Human neuropsychology did not flourish until World War II, when psychologists and neurologists encountered thousands of brain-injured soldiers in need of assessment and rehabilitation (Aita, Armitage, Reitan, & Rabinowitz, 1947; Goldstein, 1944). It was a grim circumstance for innovation, but the carnage of war obliged psychologists to develop new tools for understanding the effects of brain damage. Thus, as humankind ravaged its own during the second world war, several specialists forged a new specialty, clinical neuropsychology, to help deal with the aftermath. The first and most fundamental goal of this fledgling discipline was to determine the relationships between brain injury and performance upon psychological tests (Case Exhibit 9.1).

The central focus of human neuropsychology is the advancement of a science of human behavior founded on human brain function (Kolb & Whishaw, 1990). Students of neuropsychological assessment must be familiar with the essentials of brain function if they are to appreciate the role of tests in the diagnosis of brain-impairing conditions. In this topic we present a primer of neurological terms and concepts, including a review of brain anatomy and function, with discussion of medical approaches to imaging the brain. We also touch briefly upon the major forms of neuropathology that might disrupt the normal functioning of the brain, with special emphasis upon the elderly.

ANATOMY OF THE BRAIN

By convention the nervous system is divided into the central nervous system consisting of the brain and spinal cord and the peripheral nervous system which includes the cranial nerves and the network of nerves emanating from the spinal cord. Neuropsychological assessment aims to determine the relationship between brain and behavior, so the brain will be the major focus of our discussion here.

The brain weighs roughly three pounds. It is composed principally of two components, neurons and glial cells. For decades it has been believed that neurons do not reproduce. However, recent research suggests that humans may have a limited capacity to reproduce neurons, especially in areas of the brain important for learning and memory (Associated Press, October 30, 1998). Capable of prolific reproduction, the more numerous glial cells provide various forms of structural support to the neurons.

The 10^{11} or 100 billion neurons in the brain are arranged in complex networks that largely have defied understanding. In part, the inscrutability of the brain derives from its computational complexity. Neurons communicate by sending all-or-none electrochemical impulses to one another. Each neuron might send transmissions to thousands, perhaps tens of thousands, of other neurons at near and distant sites called synapses. Chemical communications across the synapses can occur up to a thousand times a second. Even if we use a conservative estimate of 1,000 synapses per neuron, in theory the number of neural transmissions that could occur in just one second is a staggering 10^{17} or 100,000,000,000,000,000 (one hundred quadrillion). No wonder that staid neuroscientists such as Sir John Eccles (who received a Nobel Prize for his work in neurophysiology) resort to hyperbole and describe the brain as "without qualification the most highly organized and most complexly organized matter in the universe" (Eccles, 1973).

CASE EXHIBIT
9.1

BRAIN DYSFUNCTION AND TEST RESULTS

A consulting neuropsychologist was asked to evaluate a college junior whose poor grades were a source of bafflement to the student's advisor, parents, and even his psychiatrist. The student had functioned well for two years at the university, earning an A– average in a varied curriculum. However, he was now failing miserably in a premedical curriculum that included courses in organic chemistry and embryology. He complained that the material in his science courses was simply beyond his grasp. Yet, he was earning Bs in history and literature. Based on the inexplicable downturn in grades, the psychiatrist suspected that the student might suffer from subtle brain damage. A neuropsychological evaluation was requested.

We will not review the entire test battery here, but certain results will serve to introduce the link between test results and brain function. Perhaps the most intriguing finding was that the hapless student could not accurately copy the simple geometric pattern of a cross (see illustration). Another suggestive finding was a huge difference in fine motor control on the two sides of his body. Using a standardized finger-tapping apparatus, the neuropsychologist ascertained that the student could tap 56 times in 10 seconds with his right index finger, but only 42 times with his left index finger (Morrison, Gregory, & Paul, 1979). Finally, even though his Full Scale IQ was 122, the student performed poorly on the Category Test, a measure of abstract reasoning and concept formation that discriminates well between brain-damaged and neurologically intact persons (Reitan & Wolfson, 1993).

Greek Cross Drawing:

Finger Tapping: Right 56   Left 42

WAIS-R Full Scale IQ   122   Verbal IQ   133   Performance IQ   105

Category Test: 56 errors/208

Was this student brain-damaged? If so, what was the most likely site of the impairment? What would be the implications of this apparent dysfunction? We will return to the case of the failing premedical student at the end of this topic. By that point the reader should possess enough knowledge about brain-behavior relationships to understand a neuropsychological analysis of the test results shown above.

In spite of the difficulties in comprehending the brain, neuroscientists have formulated a few rudimentary and partial theories from the following sources:

1. Behavioral studies of patients with discrete brain lesions
2. Clinical observations of the effects of electrical stimulation of selected brain sites in conscious epileptic patients about to undergo therapeutic brain excisions
3. Laboratory studies of epileptic patients in whom the cerebral hemispheres have been surgically disconnected for purposes of seizure control
4. Research studies with new brain-imaging techniques that provide a real-time analysis of ongoing brain activity.

In the remainder of this topic, we provide the reader with a primer of the brain-behavior relationships discerned from these sources.

Functional Organization of the Brain

The functional organization of the human brain is difficult to comprehend because important structures are interwoven and folded over upon one another. In addition, the brain contains a complicated system of fluid-filled caverns called **ventricles.** Although they begin in the center of the brain, the ventricles consist of a canal system that ultimately extends outward and wraps around the entire brain and also down the spinal cord to act as a buffer for the extremely delicate structures of the central nervous system.

Even though the spatial arrangement of brain structures is very complex (Figure 9.1), from the perspective of neural interconnections, the divisions of the brain are linear successions of one another: hindbrain (myelencephalon and metencephalon), midbrain (mesencephalon), and forebrain (diencephalon and telencephalon). Structurally, the lowest brain centers (in the hindbrain) are the most simply organized, whereas the more forward brain centers (in the forebrain) are large, elaborate, and anatomically complex. Functional organization follows this pattern also: The lower brain centers mediate primitive, simple life functions such as breathing whereas the forward brain centers govern complex, higher functions such as thought and perception.

In the fully developed brain, each division consists of several important structures (Table 9.1). In

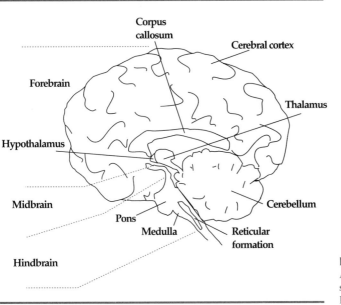

FIGURE 9.1
A Midline View of the Right Cerebral Hemisphere Showing Important Structures in the Hindbrain, Midbrain, and Forebrain

TABLE 9.1   The Divisions of the Human Brain

Forebrain

Telencephalon (endbrain)	Cerebral cortex
	Corpus callosum
	Basal ganglia
	Putamen
	Globus pallidus
	Caudate nucleus
	Amygdala
	Limbic lobe
	Hippocampus
	Septum
	Cingulate gyrus
	Olfactory bulbs
Diencephalon (between-brain)	Thalamus
	Hypothalamus
	Pineal body

Midbrain

Mesencephalon (midbrain)	Tectum
	Superior colliculi
	Inferior colliculi
	Tegmentum
	Cranial nerves

Hindbrain

Metencephalon (across-brain)	Cerebellum
	Pons
	Reticular formation*
Myelencephalon (spinal brain)	Medulla oblongata

*The reticular formation begins in the hindbrain and extends upward into the diencephalon.

the remainder of this unit, we review function and dysfunction in these major structural components of the human brain.

HINDBRAIN

The lowest part of the brain is the **hindbrain,** and its lowest section is the medulla oblongata. All of the nerve fibers from higher parts of the brain pass through the **medulla oblongata** on their way to the spinal cord. The crisscrossing of these fibers in the medulla explains why the two halves of the brain wind up controlling the opposites side of the body. The medulla mediates a number of essential bodily functions: breathing, swallowing, vomiting, blood pressure, and, partially, heart rate (Kandel, Schwartz, & Jessell, 1995). Aspects of talking and singing also are governed here, although higher brain sites are intimately involved in these functions as well.

Significant damage to the medulla usually is fatal. In rare cases, a small stroke in the medulla causes one or more of the following symptoms: opposite-sided paralysis, partial loss of pain and temperature sense, clumsiness, dizziness, same-sided paralysis and atrophy of the tongue, and partial loss of the gag reflex. The polio virus—rampant in the 1950s but now well controlled—may attack the medulla, shutting down the neural control of breathing and necessitating a mechanical respirator.

The **reticular formation,** a network of ascending and descending nerve cell bodies and fibers, begins in the spinal cord and extends through the medulla all the way up to the thalamus. Specific nuclei within the reticular formation project to wide areas of the brain and thereby help mediate complex postural reflexes and muscle tone. Based on the classic studies of Moruzzi and Magoun (1949) demonstrating that ascending nerve tracts within the reticular formation govern general arousal or consciousness, portions of this structure are also known as the reticular activating system. Damage to the reticular activating system gives rise to global diminution of consciousness ranging from chronic drowsiness to stupor or coma (Carpenter, 1991).

The pons and cerebellum are the highest structures in the hindbrain. Together they help coordinate muscle tone, posture, and hand and eye movements. Lesions of the pons may render the individual incapable of making coordinated lateral eye movements. For this reason, neurologists commonly ask patients to demonstrate left-right and up-down eye movements.

Although many brain sites are involved in motor control, the **cerebellum** plays an important role. The cerebellum receives sensory information from every part of the body and coordinates the details of automatic, skilled movements. Damage to the cerebellum may cause a variety of motor disturbances, depending upon the specific sites affected (Bradshaw & Mattingley, 1995). Muscles may become flabby and tire easily. Rapid, coordinated tapping of the index finger may prove difficult. Measures of finger-tapping speed (Reitan & Wolfson, 1993) are therefore an important component of neuropsychological test batteries.

Bodily movements may lose their coordination in cerebellar disease, becoming spasmodic and jerky. Even a simple gesture such as reaching for a cup may result in the inadvertent thrusting of cup and contents halfway across the room. The characteristic wide-based gait found in many chronic alcoholics—called ataxia—is a consequence of cerebellar degeneration (Ghez, 1991). Another symptom of cerebellar damage is intention tremor, so named because it is not present at rest but arises during voluntary, intentional movements of the hands. Nystagmus also is common in cerebellar disease. In this symptom, the eyes appear to jitter back and forth even when the individual attempts to hold a steady gaze.

In conjunction with the vestibular center in the inner ear, the cerebellum also helps coordinate the vestibuloocular reflex (VOR). The VOR acts to maintain the eyes on a fixed target when the head is rotated. Without the VOR, vision would be incredibly blurred whenever the head moved even a fraction of an inch. Instead, a small area of the cerebellum coordinates a rapid refixation of the eyes to compensate for head movements.

MIDBRAIN

The **midbrain** consists of two main divisions that wrap around a fluid-filled aqueduct. The tectum or roof lies above the aqueduct, and the tegmentum or floor lies below the aqueduct. The tectum consists mainly of two sets of bilaterally symmetrical nuclei, the superior colliculi and the inferior colliculi. The superior colliculi mediate head and eye movements used to localize and follow visual stimuli.

The inferior colliculi provide the same function for auditory stimuli.

The tegmentum is a relay station for sensory and motor fibers and also contains nuclei for many of the cranial nerves (some of which also emanate from the hindbrain). The 12 paired **cranial nerves** are major neural tracts whose functions are well understood and easily tested. Some are exclusively sensory, relaying information from the external world to the brain; some are exclusively motor, serving to execute commands from the brain; about a third of the cranial nerves possess both sensory and motor functions. Neurologists refer to the cranial nerves by number. The numbers correspond roughly to the top to bottom sequence of the nerves' emergence from the brain (Table 9.2). The reader will notice that many cranial nerves mediate aspects of vision and eye movement, basic sensory functions, and movement of jaw, tongue, face, and head. Over the centuries, neurologists have devised a variety of simple confrontational techniques to assess the cranial nerves. As peculiar as it may appear, asking the patient to stick out his or her tongue and move it left, right, up, or down can provide important information about the functioning of the hypoglossal (twelfth) cranial nerve. In like manner,

TABLE 9.2   The Cranial Nerves and Their Functions

1. Olfactory	Sense of smell
2. Optic	Vision
3. Oculomotor	Horizontal and vertical eye movement
4. Trochlear	Vertical eye movement
5. Trigeminal	Facial sensation, jaw movement
6. Abducens	Horizontal eye movement
7. Facial	Facial movement and taste
8. Auditory/vestibular	Hearing and balance
9. Glossopharyngeal	Taste, swallowing
10. Vagus	Visceral reflexes
11. Accessory	Head movement
12. Hypoglossal	Tongue movement

various simple tests of hearing, balance, eye movement, and so on, are used to complete the examination of the cranial nerves.

Although neuropsychologists have some tools and procedures suitable for the assessment of dysfunction in the hindbrain and midbrain, disabilities associated with these brain sites are more typically diagnosed and treated by medical specialists, particularly neurologists. In the main, neuropsychological tests and procedures were conceived for the assessment of function and dysfunction in the **forebrain.** Correspondingly, we devote the major share of our discussion to the forebrain structures. The forebrain consists of the diencephalon, a smaller-than-fist-sized set of structures roughly at the center of the brain, and the telencephalon, a more massive group of brain structures sitting astride the diencephalon (see Table 9.1).

DIENCEPHALON

The structures of the diencephalon include the thalamus, hypothalamus, and pineal body. The **pineal body** is a pea-sized structure that sits at the center of the brain. It is known that the pineal body secretes the hormone melatonin in a cyclic biological rhythm, but the exact function of this gland is unclear (Crapo, 1985). Owing to a lack of knowledge about its function, contemporary textbooks of neuroscience virtually ignore this structure. From a neuropsychological standpoint, the thalamus and hypothalamus are much more important.

The **thalamus** is a small bifurcated structure at the base of the brain. The importance of the thalamus cannot be exaggerated: It is the key structure that provides sensory input and information about ongoing movement to the cerebral cortex. In fact, all sensory information except for olfaction (the sense of smell) is sent to the thalamus first and then projected to specific regions of the cerebral cortex by neural tracts known collectively as the thalamocortical radiations. An extensive lesion on one side of the thalamus causes gross impairment of all forms of sensibility on the opposite side of the body. Smaller lesions may cause the threshold for pain to be raised; in addition, painful stimuli may cause an exaggerated response. Appreciation of posture and passive movement may dramatically diminish with thalamic lesions (Carpenter, 1991).

The thalamus is much more than just a relay station; it also plays a key role in the integration of neural systems. The thalamus contributes to memory functions, attention, speech, and emotional experience (Kandel, Schwartz, & Jessell, 1995). Carpenter (1991) asserts that the thalamus is the key to understanding the operation of the cerebral cortex.

The **hypothalamus** is a deceptively small structure that sits just below and in front of the thalamus. Even though it composes only about 0.3 percent of the brain's weight, the hypothalamus is involved in numerous aspects of motivated behavior and bodily regulation: feeding, sexual behavior, sleeping, temperature regulation, emotional behavior, and movement. Well studied in lower animals, the functions of the hypothalamus are less well known in humans (Kolb & Whishaw, 1990). It is known that the hypothalamus exerts proprietary control over the pituitary gland, thereby modulating a wide range of endocrine functions. The most common cause of a hypothalamic lesion is a severe head injury. Hypothalamic lesions often lead to disturbances of pituitary function, including excessive or deficient intake of food or water, and temperature and blood pressure disregulation (Kupfermann, 1991a).

The outermost formation of the forebrain is the telencephalon, a structure that is vastly larger than the diencephalon. Neuropsychological tests are particularly well suited to detecting dysfunction within the telencephalon. We present separate discussions of the following telencephalic structures: limbic lobe, basal ganglia, corpus callosum, and cerebral cortex. Please note that some degree of oversimplification is unavoidable when discussing brain functions. The reader is reminded that the brain is richly interconnected with complex and poorly understood functional systems. Individual brain sites rarely act in isolation.

LIMBIC LOBE

The **limbic lobe** consists of the hippocampus, septum, and cingulate gyrus. These structures line the inside wall of the cerebral cortex. The limbic lobe is commonly referred to as the limbic system, which is probably a misnomer based on early speculations now known to be incomplete. In particular, Papez (1937) proposed that the structures of the limbic lobe constitute a continuous neural circuit responsible for the elaboration of emotion and the control of visceral activity—hence the reference to the limbic system. This view has proved to be over-simplified, but the catchy reference to a functional system is still with us. It now seems clear that the separate structures of the limbic lobe may have many different functions, including a major role in the regulation of emotion (Kupfermann, 1991a).

One limbic structure, the **hippocampus,** is known to play a special role in memory. Humans possess two hippocampi, one in each temporal lobe. The hippocampi are part of a complex, ill-defined memory circuit that consolidates new experiences into long-term memories (Mishkin & Appenzeller, 1987). Damage to one hippocampus may cause mild deficits in memory. However, persons in whom both hippocampi have been damaged or surgically removed experience a catastrophic inability to remember anything new for more than a few seconds (Milner, Corkin, & Teuber, 1968). These unfortunate individuals retain long-term memories acquired before the bilateral hippocampal destruction, but possess no capacity to convert new short-term memories into long-term memories. Such persons are prisoners of the moment. They might read the same magazine time after time, and greet the doctor each day as if he or she were a total stranger. General intelligence is little affected. However, because of their memory deficits, these patients invariably require institutionalization or a high degree of supervision.

Unilateral destruction of the hippocampus causes selective memory impairments that correlate with well-known hemispheric specializations (verbal functions in the left hemisphere, spatial functions in the right hemisphere, discussed later). Loss of the left hippocampus impairs verbal memory, whereas destruction of the right hippocampus causes impairment in pictorial and auditory memory, particularly with visual and auditory patterns

that are not easily labeled (Smith & Milner, 1981). In contrast to the memory disturbances caused by bilateral hippocampal damage which are profound and long-lasting, the memory disturbances caused by unilateral damage tend to be transient and subtle. Sophisticated neuropsychological testing is required for their detection (Rausch, 1985).

BASAL GANGLIA

The **basal ganglia** consist of a collection of nuclei in the forebrain that make connections with the cerebral cortex above and the thalamus below. The basal ganglia are traditionally considered as part of the motor system. The main constituents of the basal ganglia are three large subcortical nuclei: the caudate, the putamen, and the globus pallidus. Some authorities also consider the amygdala to be part of the basal ganglia (Carpenter, 1991). These structures are interconnected with and functionally related to the subthalamic nucleus and the substantia nigra. Along with the cerebellum, the corticospinal system, and motor nuclei in the brain stem, the basal ganglia participate in the control of movement. Unlike the other components of the motor system, the basal ganglia do not have direct connections with the spinal cord. The motor functions of the basal ganglia are indirect, mediated via neural connections with the frontal cerebral cortex.

The most common syndrome caused by damage to the basal ganglia is **Parkinson's disease** (Cote & Crutcher, 1991). In Parkinson's disease, three characteristic types of motor disturbances are observed: involuntary movement, including tremor; poverty and slowness of movement without paralysis; and changes in posture and muscle tone. In its later stages, this disease is typified by an immobile, masklike facial expression, an extreme difficulty initiating movements, and a fine tremor that may disappear once a movement is under way.

Patients with Parkinson's disease also reveal specific cognitive deficits, suggesting that the basal ganglia contribute not just to movement, but thinking as well. Deficits observed in these patients include diminished cognitive flexibility and mildly reduced learning and recall (Koss, 1994). A loss of spontaneity and a lack of initiative also are observed (La Rue, 1992).

CORPUS CALLOSUM

The **corpus callosum** is the major commissure that serves to integrate the functions of the two cerebral hemispheres. This large bundle of subcortical nerve fibers is about four inches long and a quarter inch thick. The corpus callosum spans the brain from side to side just above the level of the thalamus. Although there are exceptions, the corpus callosum generally connects homologous brain sites in the left and right hemispheres.

The function of the corpus callosum was poorly understood until the 1960s when Sperry, Gazzaniga, and others initiated sophisticated laboratory studies of so-called split-brain patients (Sperry, 1964; Gazzaniga, 1970; Gazzaniga & LeDoux, 1978). These patients were persons with epilepsy whose corpus callosa had been severed to prevent the transport of epileptic discharges from one hemisphere to the other. Although outwardly normal, split-brain patients revealed a striking isolation of consciousness when visual information was restricted to one hemisphere or the other. For example, when a picture of an apple was tachistoscopically presented to the left side of the examinee's fixation point, this stimulus was processed only in the right hemisphere (on account of the normal crossing over of neural connections). Furthermore, because the corpus callosum was severed, the image of the apple remained trapped in the right hemisphere. As the reader will discover later, the right hemisphere is usually mute and does not subserve important language functions. Thus, when asked "What did you see?" the examinees, responding from the verbal left hemisphere, would honestly reply "Nothing." Yet, these patients could readily identify the object by pointing to it with the left hand (which is under the neural control of the right hemisphere). This suggests that although the right hemisphere cannot talk, it has a separate and independent capacity to perceive, learn, remember, and issue commands for motor tasks.

In a normal individual with intact corpus callosum, consciousness appears unitary because the two halves of the brain can communicate and forge a compromise as regards perception, thought, and action. Much of our knowledge of hemispheric specializations, discussed later, has been garnered from the detailed study of split-brain patients. Further insight has been gained from studies of persons afflicted with congenital absence of this structure, a condition known as agenesis of the corpus callosum. These patients usually have a variety of intellectual defects, indicating that the corpus callosum facilitates learning in many different cognitive spheres (Bradshaw & Mattingley, 1995).

CEREBRAL CORTEX

The **cerebral cortex,** the outermost layer of the brain, is the source of the highest levels of sensory, motor, and cognitive processing. Also called the neocortex, the cerebral cortex is a very recent evolutionary development. It is the functional capacity of this brain system—a uniform six layers deep—that most dramatically separates humans from the lower animals.

The tissue of the cerebral cortex is folded over into elaborate convolutions consisting of bulges and grooves. The prominent bulges are called gyri (singular *gyrus*), whereas the clefts, fissures, and grooves are called sulci (singular *sulcus*). This arrangement allows the brain to have a great deal more cerebral cortex than if the surface were smooth. Although the pattern of gyri and sulci is subtly unique for each person, certain major landmarks such as the central sulcus and the lateral sulcus (Figure 9.2) are always discernible in a normal brain.

A small portion of the cerebral cortex is committed cortex. These sites are dedicated to basic sensory processing of vision, hearing, touch, and motor control. Nonetheless, the specificity of committed cortex is relative, not absolute. For example, the precentral gyrus is regarded as the motor strip, yet only 40 percent of the primary motor cells subserving voluntary movement are located there; another 10 to 20 percent are located in the sensory

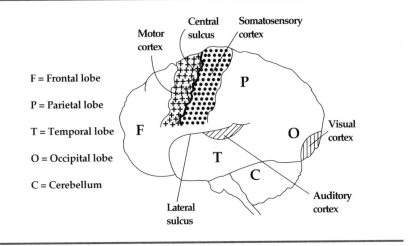

F = Frontal lobe

P = Parietal lobe

T = Temporal lobe

O = Occipital lobe

C = Cerebellum

FIGURE 9.2
Major Landmarks of
the Left Cerebral
Hemisphere

strip, and 40 to 50 percent are situated in adjoining brain sites (Brodal, 1981). Furthermore, the motor strip contains a sizable proportion of sensory cells, too. Thus, cells that subserve each specific sensory or motor function are highly concentrated in the respective committed area, but also thin out and overlap with nearby brain sites.

The majority of the cerebral cortex is uncommitted or association cortex. These sites are involved in the analysis of sensory information and the formulation of motor responses. It is the relatively large proportion of association cortex that distinguishes *homo sapiens* from lower animals. Abstract thought, creativity, and problem solving are, in large measure, underwritten by these evolutionary adaptations of the human brain.

Benson (1994) subdivides association cortex into three types: unimodal, heteromodal, and supramodal. The unimodal association areas are dedicated to a single modality (vision, hearing, somesthesis, or movement) and located adjacent to the committed cortical areas. Within each unimodal association area, incoming stimuli are categorized and compared with previous information. Damage to the unimodal areas tends to cause difficulties in discriminating and categorizing incoming stimuli within that modality. For example, a lesion in the unimodal visual area will leave vision intact but im-

pair visual recognition and discrimination. A variety of tests involving overlapping figures have been designed to assess impairment of this type. For example, a person with damage to the unimodal visual association area would be unable to recognize the individual shapes in Figure 9.3. The heteromodal association areas possess neural connections that travel across modalities. In these areas, cross-modal information involving sensory modalities (vision, hearing, touch) is intermixed and processed. Damage to heteromodal association cortex may cause a variety of well-known syndromes such as aphasia, discussed later. Finally, the supramodal association cortex, located exclusively in the frontal area, is responsible for the control of high-level cognition through a process of selection and, especially, inhibition. This cortex is phylogenetically the most recent and exerts executive control over other brain functions. Damage to this area of the brain may cause impairments of impulse control, planning, and other executive functions.

In the remainder of this section, we discuss two aspects of brain function that occur within the cerebral cortex: (1) localization of function within the four major lobes of each cerebral hemisphere, and (2) lateralization of function within the left and right cerebral hemispheres, with special attention to the language functions of the left hemisphere.

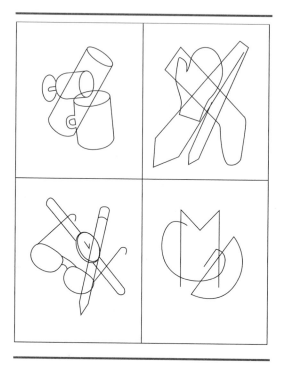

FIGURE 9.3   Examples of Overlapping Figures for Testing Visual-Perceptual Dysfunction
Source: Reprinted with permission from Gregory, R. J. (1987). *Adult intellectual assessment.* Boston, MA: Allyn & Bacon.

We will also introduce the reader to brain-imaging techniques and other clinical tests for brain dysfunction, because their use often goes hand in hand with a neuropsychological evaluation. This discussion is designed to help the reader understand the nature and purpose of the neuropsychological tests discussed in the next topic.

FUNCTIONS OF THE CEREBRAL LOBES

The cerebrum consists of the cerebral cortex and underlying structures of the telencephalon. A large midline sulcus extending from front to back separates the cerebrum into two roughly symmetrical structures known as the left cerebral hemisphere and the right cerebral hemisphere. In general, the cortex of each hemisphere receives sensory input from, and sends motor output to, the opposite or contralateral side of the body. This principle of contralateral regulation has only one real exception: the

sense of smell. Olfactory stimulation in each nostril is processed directly by the same-sided olfactory bulb sitting just above the nasal cavity. We should also mention that the contralateral regulation of vision is complex: each half of the visual field is processed in the opposite cerebral hemisphere. Furthermore, contralateral regulation is relative, not absolute. For example, the neural connections from the right ear extend mainly to the left hemisphere, but there are some same-side or ipsilateral projections as well.

Within each cerebral hemisphere, several prominent landmarks can be used to demarcate four major lobes. The occipital lobe is at the rear of the brain behind the parieto-occipital sulcus; the parietal lobe is behind the central sulcus; the temporal lobe is beneath the lateral sulcus; and the frontal lobe is in front of the central sulcus. The occipital-parietal and occipital-temporal boundaries are somewhat indistinct (see Figure 9.2).

The same-named lobes on the two sides of the brain are roughly symmetrical in structure and also share many functions in common. For the moment we will emphasize the operative similarities of the two halves of the brain as we review the functions of the four lobes. However, we should forewarn the reader that the left and right cerebral hemispheres also possess specialized functions, discussed later. Furthermore, these hemispheric specializations often correlate in a sensible way with structural variations. For example, certain hemispheric structures are larger on the left side of the brain, revealing the lateralization of language functions to this hemisphere.

Occipital Lobes

The primary sensory areas for vision are located in the **occipital lobes;** much of this projection area is on the mesial or midline surface that separates the two cerebral hemispheres. Each occipital lobe sees the opposite side of the visual world. Thus, all visual stimuli to the left of the reader's fixation point are ultimately processed in the right occipital lobe, and vice versa. The split visual world is shared across the splenium, the rearward portion of the corpus callosum, producing a unified perception of the entire visual field. Damage to the primary visual area produces a corresponding loss of visual field on the opposite side. For example, an extensive lesion in the left occipital lobe would render a person blind to the right half of the visual world. A very small lesion might produce a scotoma or blind spot.

A thorough visual field examination is crucial to the detective work of a comprehensive neuropsychological evaluation. Based on the pattern of visual field loss, a competent examiner can infer the location and extent of brain damage. The visual system can be likened to transmission cables that traverse the brain from the eyes in the front to the occipital lobes in the back. Particularly toward the rear of the brain, the cables radiate outward to occupy significant portions of the subcortical tissue. Subcortical lesions toward the rear of the brain stand a good chance of disrupting or damaging the neural transmission networks. This damage leads to a loss of the associated visual field (Figure 9.4). The pattern of visual field loss is a direct clue to the site of damage within the occipital lobes and surrounding tissue.

The forward portion of each occipital lobe is unimodal association cortex. These regions synthesize visual stimuli and produce meaning from them.

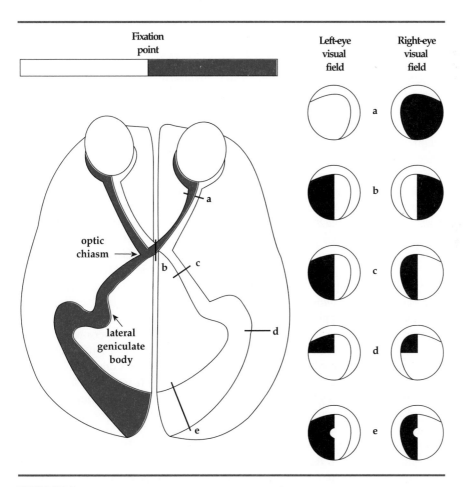

FIGURE 9.4   Schematic Diagram of the Visual System and the Effects of Lesions at Various Sites
Source: Adapted with permission from Gregory, R. J. (1987). *Adult intellectual assessment.* Boston: Allyn & Bacon.

This is where the high-level processing of visual information occurs. Damage to the association cortex of the occipital lobes may cause **visual agnosia,** a difficulty in the recognition of drawings, objects, or faces (Kandel, 1991). Luria (1973) described a typical case of a patient with such a lesion:

> The patient carefully examines the picture of a pair of spectacles shown to him. He is confused and does not know what the picture represents. He starts to guess. "There is a circle . . . and another circle . . . and a stick . . . a cross-bar . . . why, it must be a bicycle?"

The visual agnosias are especially linked to right-sided lesions of occipital association cortex, but may also involve impairment of the parietal and temporal lobes as well. A particularly dramatic form of visual agnosia is prosopagnosia, the inability to recognize familiar faces. Benson (1994) cites the example of a 70-year-old man who suffered a series of strokes affecting the forward portions of the occipital lobes. The patient's chief complaint was that he could not recognize his wife or his daughter by sight, although he immediately recognized them by their voices. In another case of visual agnosia known as object agnosia, a patient reproduced a drawing of a train with great skill, but had no idea what he had drawn. Benson (1988) describes the many fascinating symptoms of visual agnosia.

Parietal Lobes

Kolb and Whishaw (1990) note that the parietal lobes are an artifact of gross anatomical definition, that is, they do not reflect cytoarchitectural or physiological unity. A unitary theory of parietal lobe function is therefore impossible. In fact, two independent functions of the **parietal lobes** can be identified, one primarily concerned with the somatosensory strip located on the postcentral gyrus, the other primarily concerned with the rearward or association zones of the parietal lobes.

The postcentral gyrus of each parietal lobe mediates opposite-sided awareness of what is happening on the surface of our bodies. This tissue, appropriately referred to as the somatosensory (or somesthetic) strip, receives information about touch sensations and the position of the limbs (see Figure 9.2). The somatosensory strip and the motor strip of the frontal lobe are richly interlinked by subcortical neural networks; the topical organization of these intertwined functional systems is very similar. The amount of somatosensory tissue devoted to each body location corresponds to the functional importance of that area. For example, feedback from the lips and tongue is essential for speech; the amount of somatosensory tissue devoted to these structures is relatively large. Damage to the somatosensory strip results in loss of sensation for the corresponding parts of the body on the opposite side.

The rearward portion of each parietal lobe is heteromodal association cortex. This area seems specialized for integrating sensory information from nearby somatic, visual, and auditory regions. A common symptom of damage to this area is inability to recognize objects by touch, a symptom known as astereognosis. Many neuropsychological test batteries incorporate measures of astereognosis, such as recognizing coins (penny, nickel, dime) by touch. This is a cross-modal task, insofar as the patient must form a visual representation from touch alone. This region uses its polymodal information to provide visuomotor guidance to the limbs, hands, and eyes (Clarke, 1994).

Damage to the parietal association region on either side may impair the ability to draw. This is one form of construction dyspraxia, discussed subsequently. Left-sided damage to this area results in an impoverished drawing, as if the person has trouble getting the drawing hand to go in the correct direction. In contrast, right-sided damage to this area results in a perceptual deficit. The person has trouble integrating the individual parts into a consistent whole; the overall gestalt of the drawing is lost. The association areas of the left and right parietal lobes also subserve several lateralized functions, discussed later.

Temporal Lobes

Four basic functions of the **temporal lobes** can be identified (Kolb & Whishaw, 1990; Bear, 1986). These are primary processing of auditory sensations, secondary processing of auditory perceptions, long-term memory storage, and modulation of biological drives (especially aggression, fear, and sexuality). We discuss each of these functions in turn.

Each temporal lobe contains a primary auditory cortex on its upper portion. Much of the auditory cortex is tucked into the lateral sulcus and is not visible from a side view of the brain. The left auditory cortex receives sensory information primarily from the right ear and vice versa; however, there is some same-sided input as well. A lesion of the primary auditory region in one temporal lobe may cause a variety of audioperceptual deficits, including inability to detect brief sounds, impaired localization of sounds, and difficulty discriminating speech sounds. These deficits are especially likely in the case of damage to the left auditory cortex, as discussed below. In rare cases, damage to the auditory areas can cause deafness even though the auditory apparatus itself is intact.

The unimodal auditory association cortex occupies much of the external surface of the temporal lobe. This associational cortex is important in the analysis of complex sounds and rhythmic acoustic structures. The auditory association regions of the left and right temporal lobes are specialized for different functions, discussed later. In brief, the left side governs language comprehension, whereas the right side governs nonverbal auditory patterns and rhythms. Damage to this region in the left temporal lobe causes a disruption of language comprehension, while right-sided impairment causes auditory agnosia, a difficulty in recognizing and discriminating nonverbal sounds. Albert, Sparks, von Stockert, and Sax (1972) reported the fascinating case of a 57-year-old man who suffered a discrete stroke in the associational cortex of the right temporal lobe. This otherwise high-functioning gentleman could accurately note when a sound was made, but he could not distinguish a telephone ring, a dog bark, the clip-clop of horse hooves, whistling, clapping of hands, or snapping of fingers. Yet, his perception of language sounds (a left temporal lobe function) was intact.

In conjunction with the hippocampus, the centermost portions of the temporal cortex help sustain long-term memory functions. As discussed below, these memory functions are strongly asymmetrical, with verbal functions on the left and pictorial functions on the right. In brief, lesions of the left temporal lobe and/or the underlying hippocampal structure cause impairment in delayed recall of verbal material, such as paragraphs and word lists, whether presented visually or orally. Lesions of the right temporal lobe and/or the underlying hippocampal structure cause defects in the delayed recall of pictorial material, such as geometric drawings and faces. Typically, temporal lobe lesions do not disturb the *immediate* recall of verbal or nonverbal material.

Finally, in conjunction with underlying structures such as the amygdala, the temporal lobes also are involved in biological drives such as aggression, fear, and sexuality. Evidence for involvement of the temporal lobes in motivation and emotion comes from two sources: studies of direct electrical stimulation of this region, and investigations of behavioral alteration in persons with temporal lobe seizure disorders. For example, Penfield and Jasper (1959) reported that mild electrical stimulation of the front and middle temporal cortex produced feelings of fear, a response also obtained from the amygdala. Bear (1986) has catalogued the behavioral disorders that can result from the motivational and emotional dysfunction secondary to temporal lobe damage (Table 9.3). These symptoms portray the so-called temporal lobe personality, although few persons combine all these traits.

We close our discussion of the temporal lobes with a cautionary note. Because the temporal lobes are rich in subcortical connections to the parietal, frontal, limbic, and occipital lobes of the brain, lesions in this region can cause many diverse symptoms not catalogued in the preceding. For example, temporal lesions may interfere with visual recognition. This was first demonstrated by Milner (1958), who found that her patients were impaired at recognizing visual anomalies (e.g., a monkey in a cage with an oil painting on the wall). Kolb, Milner, and Taylor (1983) found that patients with right-sided temporal lesions failed to perceive that portion of a face falling in the left visual field. Kolb

TABLE 9.3 A Compilation of Symptoms that May Occur in Temporal Lobe Dysfunction

Compulsive and indiscriminant hypersexuality

Hyperirritability to trivial slights

Anxiety and phobic responses

Paranoid concerns that generalize widely

Depression and/or agitated euphoric periods

Preoccupation with religion, cosmology, or philosophy

Extensive but unproductive writing, drawing, or lecturing

Preoccupation with details

Circumstantiality, a roundabout loquacious style

Viscosity, a tendency to prolong social encounters

Source: Based on Bear, D. M. (1986). Behavioural changes in temporal lobe epilepsy. In M. R. Trimble and T. G. Bolwig (Eds.), *Aspects of epilepsy and psychiatry.* New York: John Wiley.

and Whishaw (1985) describe this interesting symptom:

> . . . right temporal lobe patients do not appear able to perceive subtle social signals such as discreet but obvious glances at one's watch, a gesture often intended as a cue to break off a conversation. Presumably the patients fail to perceive the significance of the visual signal.

The interested reader may consult Kolb and Whishaw (1990) for further discussion of temporal lobe dysfunction.

Frontal Lobes

The **frontal lobes** are required for the programming, regulation, and verification of executive functions and motor performance (Luria, 1973; Lezak, 1995). Executive functions include goal formulation, planning, carrying out goal-directed plans, and efficient performance. It is with the frontal lobes that humans create intentions, form plans, and regulate their behavior by comparing the effects of their actions with the original intentions.

Enacting a plan requires a bodily movement of some kind. People pursue their goals by physically manipulating the environment, whether with their hands or through the motor activity of speech. It is

not surprising, then, to find that the primary motor cortex is located in the frontal lobes—where plans and intentions are also formed.

The primary motor cortex is found on the precentral gyrus, at the rear of the frontal lobe, just in front of the central sulcus. Motor control is opposite-sided, with the left motor cortex controlling bodily movements on the right, and vice versa. The topical organization of the motor strip was first mapped by Penfield (1958) during a series of operations to remove damaged cortical tissue in persons with epilepsy. He stimulated different areas of the motor cortex with a harmless electrical current to map the correspondence between cortex and different body parts. Penfield found that those areas of the body requiring precise control, such as fingers and mouth, occupy a disproportionately large amount of cortical space.

Just in front of the primary motor cortex is the supplementary motor cortex. The supplementary motor cortex is involved in the serial ordering of complex motor chains, that is, movement programming. A portion of the frontal lobes just below the supplementary motor cortex is involved in the control of voluntary eye gaze. The left frontal lobe also mediates expressive language, discussed in detail below.

Damage to the primary motor cortex causes opposite-sided deficits in fine motor control and also reduces the speed and strength of limb movements. These effects are easily detected with simple motor tests such as finger-tapping speed. Severe damage to the motor cortex causes total paralysis of the affected bodily parts. Damage to the supplementary motor cortex causes deficits in the execution of motor sequences such as copying a series of arm or facial movements (Kolb & Milner, 1981).

The most common cause of frontal lobe damage is closed head injury, which is one type of traumatic brain injury. (Traumatic brain injury and other prominent causes of adult neuropathology, including age-related syndromes, are outlined in Table 9.4.) In a closed head injury, acceleration/deceleration forces are instantly applied to the entire brain, as when a person's head strikes the dashboard in an automobile accident. Because of the

TABLE 9.4   Major Neuropathological Conditions of Adulthood and Aging: Brief Synopsis and Essential References

Traumatic Brain Injury
Bigler (1990), Dikmen et al. (1995)

Description: Neurological consequences depend upon the severity of the injury, but all of the following are possible: contusions or bruising of the brain underneath the site of impact (coup injury); opposite-sided contusions (contrecoup injury); frequent contusions in the undersurfaces of the frontal lobes and the tips of the temporal lobes; diffuse axonal injury or nonspecific damage from shear-strain effects on neural pathways; brain tissue damage due to obstructed blood flow; hematoma or blood clot between the skull and the surface of the brain; edema or swelling of the brain; long-term consequences include possible shrinkage of the brain and corresponding enlargement of the ventricular system.

Potential Neurobehavioral Effects: The most common, and reliable, complaints are of concentration and memory problems; other generalizations are difficult because the nature and severity of the brain damage will not be the same in any two patients; focal damage may lead to specific symptoms, e.g., damage to the left hemisphere language areas may cause expressive aphasia; many studies suggest that traumatically brain-injured patients are more seriously handicapped by personality and emotional disturbances than by cognitive and physical disabilities (Lezak & O'Brien, 1990).

Neoplastic Disease (Tumor)
Reitan and Wolfson (1993)

Description: Neoplastic disease encompasses many different forms of tumorous growth; for example, gliomas are tendril-like tumors of the glial cells that infiltrate the brain over a period of weeks or months; meningiomas are slower-growing, globular-shaped tumors of the meninges (membranes encasing the brain) that press down upon the brain.

Potential Neurobehavioral Effects: Brain tumors produce a variety of effects, depending upon their location and size; rapidly infiltrating tumors may compromise many skills, e.g., language and problem-solving abilities, motor and sensory functions on the right side, if the left hemisphere is affected; slower-growing meningiomas may lead to focal symptoms that relate to the site of encroachment on the brain, e.g., deficits in spatial ability and impairment of motor and sensory functions on the left side if the right parieto-frontal area is affected.

Chronic Alcohol Abuse
Davila et al. (1994)

Description: Chronic alcohol ingestion leads to neuron changes that include a loss of dendritic branches and dendritic spines, especially in the hippocampus and dentate gyrus; enlargement of the ventricles and widening of the cerebral sulci is also observed; in severe cases, atrophy of the medial thalamus and mamillary bodies is found (Wernicke-Korsakoff's syndrome); the neuropathology of alcoholism may be exacerbated by vitamin and nutritional deficiencies.

Potential Neurobehavioral Effects: In cases of severe alcohol abuse in which the medial thalamus and mamillary bodies are compromised, the profound anterograde amnesia of Wernicke-Korsakoff's syndrome is noted; patients show an inability to retain memory of events for more than a short time even though immediate memory is intact and remote memory is only mildly impaired; confabulation or falsification of memory with clear consciousness is noted; other symptoms of severe abuse include gait disturbance and gaze difficulties; in neurologically intact alcoholics, neurobehavioral effects are more elusive, but may include subtle memory deficits and difficulties with novel problem solving.

Alzheimer's Disease
Knight (1992), Koss (1994)

Description: The most common degenerative neurological disease is Alzheimer's Disease (AD), which features an insidious degeneration of the brain; the pathophysiology includes clumplike deposits in the brain consisting of neuritic plaques and neurofibrillary tangles; additional brain changes include neuronal loss, shrinkage or atrophy of the brain, depletion of acetylcholine neurotransmitters involved in memory, and accumulation of foreign deposits in the cerebral vasculature; the course of the disease is invariably downhill. First described in 1907, Alois Alzheimer portrayed his initial case as follows:

> The first noticeable symptom of illness shown by this 51-year-old woman was suspiciousness of her husband. Soon, a rapidly increasing memory impairment became evident; she could no longer orient herself in her own dwelling, dragged objects here and there and hid them, and at times, believing that people were out to murder her, started to

(continued)

TABLE 9.4 Continued

scream loudly. On observation at the institution, her entire demeanor bears the stamp of utter bewilderment. She is completely disoriented to time and place (La Rue, 1992).

Although Alzheimer's Disease is not part of normal aging, advanced age is an important risk factor; rare before age 65, the disease afflicts 3 percent of persons 65 to 74 years of age, 18 percent of persons 75 to 84 years of age, and nearly half of those 85 years and older (Evans, Funkenstein, Albert, and others, 1989).

Potential Neurobehavioral Effects: As detailed by Storandt and Hill (1989), difficulty with the acquisition of new information (short-term memory dysfunction) is generally the most salient symptom in the early stages; patients may also show a prominent language dysfunction (e.g., pronounced word-finding difficulty) or a striking visuospatial disturbance; reports of personality change, including delusions and agitation, are also common; the late stages are characterized by severe, pervasive disability.

Vascular Dementia
  Mirsen and Hachinski (1988)

Description: The second most common cause of dementia in the elderly, vascular dementia is caused by blockage of an artery and subsequent death of brain tissue because of insufficient blood supply (infarction), or bleeding into or around the brain (hemorrhage); sudden onset is the rule, but the accumulation of small strokes over time, known as multi-infarct dementia (MID), may produce an apparently progressive disorder. The Hachinski Ischemic Score was developed to distinguish multi-infarct dementia from Alzheimer's Disease (Hachinski, Iliff, Zilha, and others, 1975). MID is indicated by the presence of several of the following factors: abrupt onset, somatic complaints, stepwise deterioration, emotional incontinence, fluctuating course, history of hypertension, nocturnal confusion, history of strokes, personality preserved, atherosclerosis present, depression, and focal neurological signs.

Because MID may be partially treatable, the differential diagnosis of MID versus AD is more than academic; the course of the illness in MID is shorter than in AD, but more variable from person to person.

Potential Neurobehavioral Effects: The stroke syndrome is defined by the acute onset of a focal deficit involving the central nervous system; symptoms depend upon the site of infarction but may include motor

weakness and impaired sensibility in the opposite limbs; nonfluent aphasia may result if the dominant hemisphere is affected; stroke in the rear of the brain may produce partial loss of the visual field; acute symptoms may partially abate and lead to a plateau of stable functioning.

Parkinson's Disease
  La Rue (1992)

Description: Parkinson's Disease (PD) is almost nonexistent before age 40 and affects only 1 or 2 in 1,000 persons ages 70 and over; primarily a movement disorder, but cognitive and emotional problems are common; late stages of PD may involve a clear dementia; symptoms include slowness of movement (bradykinesia), tremor at rest, shuffling gait, and postural rigidity; neuropathology involves depletion of dopamine and neuron loss in the basal ganglia.

Potential Neurobehavioral Effects: Tremor is the most common and the least debilitating early symptom; the rate of progression is quite variable, but movement disability in PD can become pronounced and lead to confinement; 10 to 20 percent of PD patients develop a clear dementia; PD patients reveal a deficit on neuropsychological tests requiring speed (e.g., Digit Symbol, Trail Making, reaction time measures); surprisingly, tests of visual discrimination and paired-associate learning which do not require speed also differentiate patients with moderate to severe PD from matched controls (Pirozzolo, Hansch, Mortimer, Webster, & Kuskowski (1982); about 40 to 60 percent of PD patients also experience depression.

Dementia Syndrome of Depression
  Blazer (1993)

Description: About 10 to 20 percent of depressed elderly show cognitive deficits which mimic organic dementia; memory loss in combination with severe complaints of disability are common features; Dementia Syndrome of Depression (also known as pseudodementia) is mainly a post hoc diagnosis defined by a return to normal cognitive performance after severe depression is treated.

Potential Neurobehavioral Effects: Memory loss for both recent and remote events is common; attention and concentration are preserved; social skills may show prominent early losses; marked variability of performance on cognitive tests, even across similar tasks, is noted.

irregular surfaces of the surrounding skull, the forward underside surfaces of the frontal lobes are almost always damaged (Jennett & Teasdale, 1981). The front ends of the temporal lobes also are highly vulnerable in closed head injury.

Nauta (1971) summarizes the effects of frontal lobe dysfunction as a "derangement of behavioral programming." Lezak (1983, 1995) has catalogued the behavioral disturbances that can result from generalized, bilateral frontal lobe damage:

1. Motivational-like problems involving decreased spontaneity, decreased productivity, reduced rate of behavior, and lack of initiative.
2. Difficulties in making mental shifts and perseveration of activities and responses.
3. Problems in stopping that are often described as impulsivity, overreactivity, and difficulty in holding back a wrong or unwanted response.
4. Deficits in self-awareness resulting in an inability to perceive performance errors or to size up social situations appropriately.
5. A concrete attitude (Goldstein, 1944) in which objects, experiences, and behavior are all taken at their most obvious face value.

Curiously, frontal lobe lesions may have little effect on old learning and well-established skills. Both Hebb and Penfield reported that surgical removal of frontal lobe tissue caused little change in IQ scores (Hebb, 1939; Penfield & Evans, 1935). Early studies of prefrontal lobotomy demonstrated much the same finding: no change in IQ or even a slight improvement after dysconnection of the frontal lobes.

Devising adequate measures of frontal lobe function has proved to be difficult. Lezak (1995) notes that frontal lobe disorders change how a persons responds, whereas most tests measure what a person knows. She has devised an ingenious method called the Tinkertoy® Test, discussed in the next topic, to assess the programming difficulties experienced by persons with frontal lobe lesions. More commonly, clinicians rely upon observation and checklists to diagnose frontal lobe dysfunction. A useful instrument for this purpose is the Checklist of Executive Functions (Pollens, McBratnie, & Burton, 1988). The items on this checklist define important aspects of frontal lobe functions: awareness, goal setting, planning, self-initiation, self-inhibition, self-monitoring, ability to change set, and strategic behavior. Each item is rated on a 1 to 5 scale so that the total score provides an index of the integrity of executive functions.

CEREBRAL LATERALIZATION OF FUNCTION

Up to this point, we have stressed the similarities of the two halves of the brain, particularly with respect to opposite-sided processing of sensory and motor functions. In many important respects, however, the two hemispheres of the human brain are anatomically and functionally asymmetrical (Cytowic, 1996; Geschwind & Galaburda, 1987). The important structural asymmetries include the following:

1. The top of the temporal lobe, the planum temporale, is larger in the left hemisphere.
2. The left hemisphere contains more gray matter, even though it is slightly smaller and lighter than the right hemisphere.
3. The lateral sulcus is much longer in the right hemisphere with the result that the parietal-temporal cortex is slightly enlarged on this side.

Of course, exceptions will occur in individual cases. The differences previously listed are most consistent and pronounced in right-handers and males. Left-handers and females show fewer structural and functional asymmetries of the brain (Weekes, 1994).

The structural asymmetries between the hemispheres correlate with the well-known functional differences between the two sides of the brain. Language is subserved, in part, by the temporal enlargements on the left side, whereas spatial thinking is subserved, in part, by the parietal-temporal enlargements on the right side. In the remainder of this section we will further catalogue the specialties of the left and right hemisphere, forewarning the reader that lateralization of function is relative, not absolute. For example, both hemispheres have some degree of verbal and spatial capacity. Furthermore, virtually any high-level intellectual activity requires the synthetic interaction of the entire brain (Efron, 1990). Speech is a case in point. While speech is primarily a left hemisphere function, the right cerebral hemisphere does provide the intonation patterns. As a result, patients with right-sided lesions (particularly in the frontal area) may speak in an eerie monotone (Gardner, 1975).

Language Functions of the Left Hemisphere

Language is primarily (but not exclusively) a left hemisphere function that involves widely separated cortical and subcortical structures. Because so many regions of the left hemisphere are involved in language, virtually any significant left hemisphere lesion will produce some kind of disturbance in the production or comprehension of language. For this reason a detailed profile of language skills offers a window to the integrity and functioning of the left hemisphere.

Modern conceptions of brain-language correlations actually stem from the late-nineteenth century. In 1861, Paul Broca observed that damage to a small region just in front of the motor cortex of the left hemisphere caused a language disorder originally called expressive aphasia and now more typically known as nonfluent aphasia. Persons with damage to this left hemisphere premotor area—aptly named Broca's area—speak in a slow, labored manner. They have difficulty enunciating words correctly; the act of speaking seems to be torturous for them. Speech takes on a frankly telegrammatic nature; adjectives, adverbs, articles, and conjunctions—the words that add color to speech—frequently are omitted. Writing also is difficult for these persons. Fortunately, persons who experience Broca's aphasia have little difficulty understanding either spoken or written language. In its pure form, the disorder involves expressive language only.

In 1874, Wernicke announced that damage to the upper and rearward portion of the left temporal lobe—a region now known as Wernicke's area—was linked to a language disorder originally called receptive aphasia and now more typically known as fluent aphasia. Affected individuals appear unable to comprehend spoken or written language. Apparently, persons with Wernicke's aphasia have no difficulty perceiving words, but cannot associate the words with their underlying meaning. As a consequence, the written and verbal expressions of persons with this aphasia are fluent but meaningless. For example, when asked to define *book,* a patient might respond, "Book, a husbelt, a king of prepator, find it in front of a car ready to be directed." The same person might define *scarecrow* as "We'll call that a three-minute resk witch, you'll find one in the country in three witches" (Williams, 1979).

Building on the observations of Broca and Wernicke, Geschwind (1972) proposed a structural, neurological model of left hemisphere language functions that has been highly influential in neuropsychological assessment. This model bears directly upon the assessment of language skills; the major elements are outlined below and depicted in Figure 9.5. Geschwind postulated the following:

1. Spoken language is perceived in the left auditory cortex at the top of the temporal lobe, then transferred to Wernicke's area.
2. In Wernicke's area, the meanings of words are activated and the auditory codes are transported to a subcortical bundle of transmission fibers called the arcuate fasciculus.
3. The arcuate fasciculus sends the auditory codes directly to Broca's area.
4. Upon reaching Broca's area, the auditory code activates the corresponding articulatory code that specifies the sequence of muscle actions required to pronounce a word.
5. In turn, the articulatory code is transmitted to the portions of the motor cortex governing tongue, lips, larynx, and so forth, in order to produce the desired spoken word.

Comprehending or speaking a written word involves most of the previously outlined pathways, but with a different starting point:

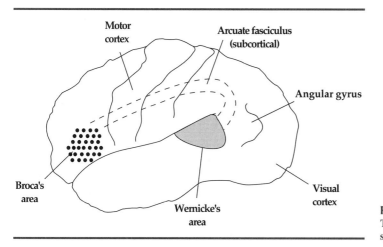

FIGURE 9.5
The Structural Model of Left Hemisphere Language Functions

6. Written words are first registered in the visual cortex, then relayed through the visual association cortex to the angular gyrus.

7. In the angular gyrus, the visual form of the word is mapped into the auditory code stored in Wernicke's area, thereby gaining access to the meaning of the written word, which can also be spoken (steps 2 through 5 previously).

The Geschwind model is helpful in explaining a number of clinical syndromes caused by discrete left hemisphere brain damage (Gregory, 1999):

• Lesions to Broca's area will cause slow, labored, telegraphic speech, but the comprehension of spoken or written language will not be affected.

• Damage to Wernicke's area will have more serious and pervasive implications for language comprehension; namely, the patient will be unable to understand spoken or written communications.

• Damage to the angular gyrus will cause serious reading disability, but there will be little problem in comprehending speech or in speaking.

• Impairment limited to the left auditory cortex will result in serious disruption of verbal comprehension. However, such persons will be able to speak and read normally.

In practice, few patients reveal aphasic symptoms that fall neatly into one or another of the preceding categories. Furthermore, modern conceptions of aphasia point to weaknesses in the classical model (e.g., its overly simplistic view of the structure of language) and propose a complex, nonlinear model of aphasia that is beyond the scope of coverage here (Cytowic, 1996; Whitaker & Kahn, 1994). Nonetheless, a thorough assessment of language functions is an essential part of every neuropsychological evaluation and the classical model of Broca, Wernicke, and Geschwind provides a useful starting point. Additional perspectives on aphasia and the structural model of language can be found in Benson (1994) and Mayeux and Kandel (1991).

SPECIALIZED FUNCTIONS OF THE RIGHT HEMISPHERE

Based on thousands of studies of normal and brain-damaged persons, it is now well established that the right hemisphere is dominant for a variety of cognitive and perceptual skills. However, a detailed discussion of specialized right hemisphere functions is beyond the scope of this section. Competent reviews of the extensive literature on this topic can be found in Bradshaw and Mattingley (1995),

Joseph (1988), Kupfermann (1991b), Dean (1986), and Springer and Deutsch (1985). In general, the right hemisphere appears to be dominant for the analysis of geometric and visual space, the comprehension and expression of emotion, the processing of music and nonverbal environmental sounds, the production of nonverbal and spatial memories, and the tactual recognition of complex shapes.

A frequent symptom of right hemisphere damage is **constructional dyspraxia,** the impaired ability to deal with spatial relationships either in a two- or three-dimensional framework (Reitan & Wolfson, 1993). This symptom is commonly exhibited by an impaired ability to copy simple shapes such as a cross. Left hemisphere lesions can also cause constructional dyspraxia, but the correlation is less consistent. Most neuropsychological test batteries include one or more copying tasks to screen for constructional dyspraxia. We include a summary of findings on cerebral lateralization in Table 9.5.

CLINICAL TESTS AND BRAIN-IMAGING TECHNIQUES

Several clinical tests and brain-imaging techniques have been invented to assist in neurological diagnosis (Cohen & Bookheimer, 1994; Kandel, Schwartz, & Jessell, 1995; Raichle, 1994). Because neuropsychological testing often goes hand in hand with these medical procedures, we provide a brief introduction to the most widely used clinical tests and brain-imaging techniques (Table 9.6). These procedures are authorized and used exclusively by neurologists and other medical practitioners who specialize in diseases of the nervous system. In ad-

TABLE 9.5   A Summary of Findings on Cerebral Lateralization

Functional System	Left Hemisphere Dominance	Right Hemisphere Dominance
Vision	Processing of the right visual field Recognition of letters, words	Processing of the left visual field Recognition of faces
Audition	Processing of right ear Processing of language-related sounds	Processing of left ear Processing of music and environmental sounds
Somatosensory	Sensory input from the right side	Sensory input from the left side
Movement	Motor output to the right side Complex voluntary movement, including speech	Motor output to the left side
Language	Speech, reading, writing, and arithmetic	Intonation and emotional patterning to speech
Memory	Verbal memory	Pictorial memory
Spatial processes		Analysis of geometric and visual space
Emotion		Comprehension and expression of emotion
Olfaction	Smell in left nostril	Smell in right nostril

TABLE 9.6   Clinical Tests and Brain-Imaging Techniques Useful in Neurological Diagnosis

Electroencephalography (EEG)

The EEG produces a record of electrical activity of the cortex from electrodes posted on specific areas of the skull. The fluctuations in activity are depicted as separate ink lines drawn on a continuous roll of paper. The EEG is a crude index, since the moment-to-moment fluctuations of each ink line reflect the synchronized activity of millions of neurons. The test is useful in diagnosing seizure disorders and localizing abnormal brain activity such as caused by a tumor.

Cerebral Angiography

In this technique a special radio-opaque dye is injected into a major artery that supplies the brain (vertebral or carotid artery) and then the brain is X-rayed. Because the dye blocks the X-rays, the arterial system of the brain stands out in stark relief on the negative. The physician therefore can locate vascular anomalies such as an aneurysm (a dangerous ballooning of an artery). Also, if an artery is displaced from its normal location, the specialist can infer underlying pathology such as a tumor. Traditional angiography presents a slight risk to the patient, because the injection of the dye can cause neurological complications. With continued advances in technique, magnetic resonance angiography will likely supplant traditional approaches.

Computerized Tomography (CT)

In a CT scan, a narrow beam of X-rays is passed through the brain from dozens of different angles; the machine detects the amount of X-rays emerging from the other side. The density of different internal structures appears on X-ray films in inverse proportion to their absorption of X-rays. A computer works out the mathematics to reconstruct a three-dimensional representation of internal brain densities, thereby revealing important structures. The computer prints eight or so two-dimensional cross-sectional X-rays of the brain, each from a different plane. CT produces a resolution of less than 1 millimeter; tumors, blood clots, and ventricular displacements are easily seen. CT is less harmful than a traditional chest X-ray.

Positron Emission Tomography (PET)

In a PET scan, the patient is injected with a radioactively tagged form of glucose, an essential metabolic fuel used by the brain. The level of radioactivity is extremely scant and not considered harmful. The radioactivity is then monitored by a special detector surrounding the patient's skull. Because the glucose goes to the most active parts of the brain, a PET scan measures activity level and not structure per se. Thus, a PET scan can be used to gauge regional cerebral activity, which can be helpful in the diagnosis of Alzheimer's disease, schizophrenia, and other brain-impairing conditions. PET scans also can be used to map receptor sites by having the patient inhale a radioactive gas which binds to specific receptor sites such as the dopamine receptors of the basal ganglia. The major drawback to PET is the level of technology required. Some applications require a nearby cyclotron for creation of short-lived isotopes.

Magnetic Resonance Imaging (MRI)

The functional principle of MRI is that certain atoms such as hydrogen behave like tiny spinning magnets. When placed in a strong magnetic field, these atoms will line up with one another. When radio waves are then beamed across the atoms at right angles to the magnetic field, the atoms wobble synchronously with one another. As the radio waves are turned off, a wire coil surrounding the skull will detect a voltage or magnetic resonance in the magnetic field, the voltage being stronger in areas that contain higher concentrations of hydrogen. Because many parts of the brain are hydrogen-rich (especially those that contain water or H_2O), the differential pattern of magnetic resonance helps reveal underlying brain structures. The spatial resolution of MRI is so keen that the images resemble fixed and sectioned anatomical material. A new procedure known as magnetic resonance angiography promises to replace the more dangerous and invasive procedures of traditional cerebral angiography.

dition to an office examination that focuses upon the patient's history, mental state, neural reflexes, sensory functioning, and motor skill, a neurologist commonly uses one or more clinical tests to help diagnose or rule out neurological disease. Clinical tests are essential in arriving at a correct diagnosis of the patient's medical condition. However, they do not replace neuropsychological testing which is needed to illuminate the functional consequences of neurological conditions.

APPLICATIONS OF NEUROPSYCHOLOGICAL TEST FINDINGS

Now that we have reviewed the essentials of human brain structure and function, the reader should be in a better position to comprehend the neurological meaning of psychological test results. But there is more to neuropsychological assessment than mere understanding of brain function. We concur with Kolb and Whishaw (1990) that the value of neuropsychology lies not only in its contribution to an understanding of brain function, but also in the applicability of this basic knowledge to human problems. To illustrate these interlocking points—that neuropsychologically based testing leads to understanding and that understanding leads to application—we return to the case of the failing premedical student.

The reader may wish to examine the test results for the failing premedical student introduced at the beginning of this chapter (Case Exhibit 9.1) in light of the knowledge gained from the preceding pages. By way of quick review, the student was failing courses such as organic chemistry and embryology in spite of his superior Full Scale IQ of 122. In addition to his suspiciously low score on a test of abstract thinking (Category Test), the student could not accurately copy a Greek cross, and his finger-tapping speed for the left hand was comparatively quite slow. The reader may recognize the first symptom—difficulty copying a shape—as constructional dyspraxia, which often indicates right hemisphere impairment. Because constructional dyspraxia signals a severe weakness in dealing with spatial relationships, this student's difficulty with organic chemistry and embryology was not surprising. Furthermore, the second symptom—motor slowing in the left hand—also suggests right hemisphere impairment. The nondominant hand should be about 10 percent slower than the dominant hand (Reitan & Wolfson, 1993). In this instance, the nondominant hand is 25 percent slower than the dominant hand (56 versus 42). Although the cause remains a mystery, a CT scan confirmed that the premedical student had incurred a static lesion in the frontal-parietal region of the right hemisphere. Of course, this fact could have been revealed by use of the CT scan alone, without reference to neuropsychological test results. Nonetheless, the test battery served a useful purpose by documenting the functional consequences of brain damage. Incidentally, the student switched majors to history—an academic pursuit more compatible with his left hemisphere strengths—and graduated with a degree in education.

SUMMARY

1. Neuropsychology is the study of the relationship between brain function and behavior. In neuropsychological assessment, tests sensitive to brain dysfunction are used for individual assessment.

2. The central nervous system consists of the brain and spinal cord. The peripheral nervous system includes the cranial nerves and the network of nerves emanating from the spinal cord. The brain consists of 10^{11} neurons and an even larger number of glial cells which provide structural support.

3. The lowest part of the brain is the hindbrain which contains the medulla oblongata. Nerve fibers from higher parts of the brain pass through here and cross over on their way to the spinal cord. The medulla helps control swallowing, vomiting, breathing, blood pressure, respiration, and heart rate.

4. The reticular formation passes through the medulla. Specific nuclei within the reticular formation project to wide areas of the brain and thereby help mediate complex postural reflexes and muscle tone. Portions of this structure known as the reticular activating system are known to govern general arousal or consciousness.

5. Located within the midbrain, the tegmentum is a relay station for sensory and motor fibers and also contains many of the cranial nerves. The 12 paired cranial nerves help govern the major senses (smell, vision, taste, hearing) and are also involved in the movement of the face and tongue.

6. The structures of the diencephalon include the thalamus, hypothalamus, and pineal body. The function of the pineal gland is obscure, although it is known to help regulate cyclic biologic rhythms through release of the hormone melatonin.

7. The thalamus is a key structure which provides sensory input and information about ongoing movement to the cerebral cortex. The thalamus may also be involved in memory, attention, speech, and emotional experience, either directly or indirectly through its role as a relay station to distant cerebral sites.

8. The hypothalamus is involved in numerous aspects of motivated behavior, including feeding, sexual behavior, sleeping, temperature regulation, emotional behavior, and movement. The hypothalamus also controls the pituitary gland, thereby modulating a wide range of endocrine functions.

9. The outermost formation of the forebrain is the telencephalon, which includes the limbic lobe, basal ganglia, corpus callosum, and cerebral cortex. The limbic lobe, including the hippocampus, septum, and cingulate gyrus, is involved in the regulation of emotion. The hippocampus plays a crucial role in the consolidation of new experiences into long-term memories.

10. The basal ganglia, including the caudate, putamen, and globus pallidus, help govern movement. Parkinson's disease is a degenerative disorder of the basal ganglia characterized by involuntary movement, including tremor; poverty and slowness

of movement without paralysis; and changes in posture and muscle tone.

11. The corpus callosum is the major commissure that serves to integrate the functions of the two hemispheres. Much has been learned about brain function by studying persons with epilepsy in whom the corpus callosum has been surgically severed for therapeutic purposes.

12. The outermost layer of the brain is the cerebral cortex or neocortex. Committed cerebral cortex consists of dedicated sites for basic sensory processing of vision, hearing, touch, and motor control. But the majority of the cerebral cortex is uncommitted or association cortex, used in the analysis of sensory information and the formulation of motor responses.

13. The frontal lobes are involved in programming and regulation of goal planning, including bodily movement; the parietal lobes mediate opposite-sided bodily awareness and help with spatial tasks; the occipital lobes are involved in vision; and the temporal lobes are involved in auditory processing, memory, and biological drives such as aggression, fear, and sexuality.

14. In most persons, the left cerebral hemisphere is dominant for language. Expressive components of language are subserved by Broca's area in the frontal lobe, while receptive components of language are mediated by Wernicke's area in the temporal lobe.

15. Specialized functions of the right cerebral hemisphere include the analysis of geometric and visual space, the comprehension and expression of emotion, the processing of music and nonverbal environmental sounds, the production of nonverbal memories, and the tactual recognition of complex shapes.

16. Several clinical tests and brain-imaging techniques can be used to help diagnose neurological diseases. These include EEG, cerebral arteriography, computerized tomography, positron emission tomography, magnetic resonance imaging, and magnetic resonance angiography.

KEY TERMS AND CONCEPTS

neuropsychology   p. 303

ventricles   p. 305

hindbrain   p. 306

medulla oblongata   p. 306

reticular formation   p. 306

cerebellum   p. 306

midbrain   p. 307

cranial nerves   p. 307

forebrain   p. 308

pineal body   p. 308

thalamus   p. 308

hypothalamus   p. 308

limbic lobe   p. 308

hippocampus   p. 309

basal ganglia   p. 309

Parkinson's disease   p. 309

corpus callosum   p. 310

cerebral cortex   p. 310

occipital lobes   p. 312

visual agnosia   p. 314

parietal lobes   p. 314

temporal lobes   p. 314

frontal lobes   p. 316

constructional dyspraxia   p. 322

europsychological tests and procedures encompass an eclectic assortment of methods and purposes. At one end of the spectrum are simple, 10-minute screening tests used to probe the need for further assessment. At the other end of the spectrum are exhaustive, six-hour test batteries designed to provide a comprehensive assessment. In between are hundreds of specialized instruments developed to measure particular neuropsychological abilities. At first glance, this multitude of tests would appear to resist simple categorization, as if researchers in this area had followed an incoherent philosophy of trial and error in the development of new instruments and procedures. However, with closer scrutiny it is evident that most neuropsychological tests fit within a simple, logical model of brain-behavior relationships. We will use this model as a framework for discussing well-known neuropsychological tests and procedures.

Neuropsychological assessment involves more than the administration and scoring of specialized tests. An important component of any assessment is an evaluation of the client's mental status. This is particularly true with elderly clients who may be experiencing Alzheimer's disease or other forms of dementia. Accordingly, we close this chapter with an emphasis upon mental status assessment in the elderly.

A CONCEPTUAL MODEL OF BRAIN-BEHAVIOR RELATIONSHIPS

Bennett (1988) has proposed a simplified model of brain-behavior relationships that is helpful in organizing the seemingly chaotic profusion of neuropsychological tests (Figure 9.6). His conceptualization is a slight expansion of the model presented by Reitan and Wolfson (1993). According to this view, each neuropsychological test or procedure evaluates one or more of the following categories:

1. Sensory input
2. Attention and concentration
3. Learning and memory
4. Language

5. Spatial and manipulatory ability
6. Executive functions:
   Logical analysis
   Concept formation

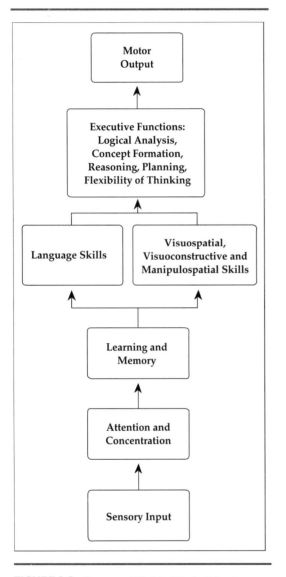

FIGURE 9.6 **Conceptual Model of Brain-Behavior Relationships**
Source: Based on Reitan and Wolfson (1993) and reprinted with permission from Bennett, T. (1988). Use of the Halstead-Reitan Neuropsychological Test Battery in the assessment of head injury. *Cognitive Rehabilitation, 6,* 18–25.

Reasoning
Planning
Flexibility of thinking
7. Motor output

The order of the categories listed corresponds roughly to the order in which incoming information is analyzed by the brain in preparation for a response or motor output.

In the remainder of this topic, the discussion of neuropsychological tests and procedures is organized around these seven categories. Within each category we will review established tests and also introduce new instruments that show promise of extending the horizons of neuropsychological assessment. However, the reader needs to know that neuropsychological assessment commonly involves a battery of tests. One approach is flexible or patient-centered testing in which an individualized test battery is fashioned for each client. These batteries are based upon the presenting complaints, referral issues, and an initial assessment (Goodglass, 1986; Kane, 1991). More typically, neuropsychologists employ a fixed battery of tests for most referrals. One of the most widely used fixed batteries, the Halstead-Reitan Neuropsychological Battery, is outlined in Table 9.7. The chapter closes with an illustration of how another well-known fixed battery, the Luria-Nebraska Neuropsychological Battery, is used in assessment.

ASSESSMENT OF SENSORY INPUT

The accuracy of sensory input is crucial to the proficiency of perception, thought, plans, and action. An individual who does not see stimuli correctly, hear sounds accurately, or process touch reliably may encounter additional handicaps at higher levels of perception and cognition. Neuropsychological assessment always incorporates a multimodal examination of sensory capacities.

Sensory-Perceptual Exam

The procedures developed by Reitan and Klove are entirely typical of sensory-perceptual proce-

TABLE 9.7   Tests and Procedures of the Halstead-Reitan Test Battery

Test	Description
Category Test*:	Measures abstract reasoning and concept formation; requires examinee to find the rule for categorizing pictures of geometric shapes
Tactual Performance Test*:	Measures kinesthetic and sensorimotor ability; requires blindfolded examinee to place blocks in appropriate cutout on an upright board with dominant hand, then nondominant hand, then both hands; also tests for incidental memory of blocks
Speech Sounds Perception Test*:	Measures attention and auditory-visual synthesis; requires examinee to pick from four choices the written version of taped nonsense words
Seashore Rhythm Test*:	Measures attention and auditory perception; requires examinee to indicate whether paired musical rhythms are same or different
Finger-Tapping Test*:	Measures motor speed; requires examinee to tap a telegraph key-like lever as quickly as possible for 10 seconds
Grip Strength:	Measures grip strength with dynamometer; requires examinee to squeeze as hard as possible; separate trials with each hand
Trail Making, parts A, B:	Measures scanning ability, mental flexibility, and speed; requires examinee to connect numbers (part A) or numbers and letters in alternating order (part B) with a pencil line under pressure of time
Tactile Form Recognition:	Measures sensory-perceptual ability; requires examine to recognize simple shapes (e.g., triangle) placed in the palm of the hand
Sensory-Perceptual Exam:	Measures sensory-perceptual ability; requires examinee to respond to simple bilateral sensory tasks, e.g., detecting which finger has been touched, which ear has received a brief sound; assesses the visual fields
Aphasia Screening Test:	Measures expressive and receptive language abilities; tasks include naming a pictured item (e.g., fork) repeating short phrases; copying tasks (not a measure of aphasia) included here for historical reasons
Supplementary:	WAIS-III, WRAT-3, MMPI-2, memory tests such as Wechsler Memory Scale-III or Rey Auditory Verbal Learning Test

*Strictly speaking, these five measures constitute the Halstead-Reitan Test Battery. However, in common parlance reference to the Halstead-Reitan includes all of the measures listed above.

dures (Reitan, 1984, 1985). The Reitan-Klove Sensory-Perceptual Examination consists of several methods for delivering unilateral and bilateral stimulation in the modalities of touch, hearing, and vision. The tasks are so simple that normal persons seldom make any errors at all. For example, the examinee is asked to say which hand has been touched (with eyes closed), or to report which ear has received a barely audible finger snap, or to identify which number has been traced on the fingertip. The results of this test are especially diagnostic if the examinee consistently makes more errors on one side of the body than the other. The reader will recall from the previous chapter that neural innervation is almost exclusively opposite-sided. Furthermore, certain areas of the cerebral cortex are devoted to primary processing of touch, hearing, and vision. Thus, an examinee who finds it difficult to process touch in the right hand may have a lesion in the postcentral gyrus of the left parietal lobe. Similarly, difficulty processing sound in the right ear may indicate a lesion in the superior portion of the left temporal lobe, and right-sided visual defects may indicate brain impairment in the left occipital lobe.

Finger Localization Test

Finger localization is a venerable procedure developed by neurologists to evaluate possible sensory losses caused by impairment of brain functions. Most neuropsychological test batteries employ a variant of this test, in which examinees must identify those fingers that have been touched (without benefit of sight). Benton has developed a well-normed 60-item test of finger localization that consists of three parts: (1) with the hand visible, identifying single fingers touched by the examiner with the pointed end of a pencil (10 trials each hand); (2) with the hand hidden from view, identifying single fingers touched by the examiner (10 trials each hand); (3) with the hand hidden from view, identifying pairs of fingers simultaneously touched by the examiner (10 trials each hand). The method of response is left to the patient: naming, touching, or pointing to fingers on a diagram (Benton, Sivan, Hamsher, Varney, & Spreen, 1994). Each stimulus presentation is scored right or wrong, and normal adults typically make very few errors in the 60 trials. Mean scores for normal adults are near perfect, ranging from 56 to 60 in various samples. In contrast, patients with brain disease find finger local-

ization to be a challenging task, particularly on the second and third parts of the test.

MEASURES OF ATTENTION AND CONCENTRATION

The attentional capacity of the brain makes it possible to attend to meaningful stimuli, screen irrelevant sensory input from the profusion of incoming stimuli, and flexibly shift to alternative stimuli when conditions demand it (Kinsbourne, 1994). While in theory it might be possible to make subtle distinctions between simple attention, concentration, mental shifting, mental tracking, vigilance, and other variants of attention/concentration, in practice these skills are difficult to separate. Only one attentional measure—the Test of Everyday Attention (TEA)—has succeeded in partitioning attention into its component sources. We discuss the TEA and other prominent measures of attentional impairment in the following sections.

Test of Everyday Attention

The Test of Everyday Attention (TEA) is a promising measure devised in Great Britain by Robertson, Ward, Ridgeway, and NimmoSmith (1994, 1996). The TEA measures the subcomponents of attention, including sustained attention, selective attention, divided attention, and attentional switching. The subtests of the TEA are outlined in Table 9.8. The test has three parallel versions and has been well validated with closed head injury clients, stroke patients, and persons with Alzheimer's disease. Normative data are based upon the performance of 154 healthy individuals between the ages of 18 and 80. Examinees enjoy the real-life scenarios of the TEA, which adds to the ecological validity of the instrument. The TEA is highly sensitive to normal age effects in the general population and is therefore well suited to geriatric assessment. With the exception of the Elevator Counting subtest, the eight subtests were standardized to yield

TABLE 9.8   Subtests of the Test of Everyday Attention (TEA)

Map Search: A two-minute speeded search for 80 symbols on a colored map; measures selective attention.

Elevator Counting: Simulation of elevator floor counting from tape-presented tones; measures sustained attention.

Elevator Counting with Distraction: Same as above but with auditory distractors; measures sustained attention.

Visual Elevator: Visual simulation of elevator floor counting with up-down reversals; measures attentional switching.

Auditory Elevator with Reversal: Same as visual elevator, except it is presented on tape; measures attentional switching.

Telephone Search: Search for key symbols while searching entries in a simulated classified telephone directory; measures divided attention.

Telephone Search Dual Task: Combines Telephone Search with simultaneous counting of auditory tones; measures divided attention.

Lottery: Subject listens for winning numbers known to end in 55 and then writes down preceding stimuli; measures sustained attention.

equivalent scores with a common mean of 10 and standard deviation of 3. Thus, the TEA allows for subtest analysis as a means of identifying an individual's particular strengths and weaknesses (Crawford, Sommerville, & Robertson, 1997).

Continuous Performance Test

The Continuous Performance Test (CPT) is not really a single test but rather a family of similar procedures that dates back to the pathbreaking research of Rosvold, Mirsky, Sarason, and others (1956). These authors devised a measure of sustained attention (also called vigilance) that involved continuous presentation of letters on a screen. In some cases, examinees were to press a key when a certain letter appeared (e.g., *x*). In other instances, examinees were to press a key when a certain letter appeared *after* another letter (e.g., *x* when it occurs after *a*). Errors of omission are noted when the examinee fails to press for a target stimulus. Errors of commission are noted when the examinee presses the key for a nontarget stimulus. Normal subjects make few errors. The method has proved especially effective in identifying brain-impairing conditions that include hyperactivity, drug effects, schizophrenia, and overt brain damage (Huhtaniemi, Haier, Fedio, & Buchsbaum, 1983; Sostek, Buchsbaum, & Rapoport, 1980).

The CPT is ideal for computerized adaptation, and dozens of different versions of it have appeared in the literature (e.g., Buchsbaum & Sostek, 1980; Gordon & Mettelman, 1988). Unfortunately, the proliferation of similar but not identical tests has hindered research on the practical utility of this promising measure of attention. Recently, Sandford and Turner (1997) have published a computerized CPT that uses both visual and auditory stimuli. The Intermediate Visual and Auditory Continuous Performance Test (IVA) is normed on 781 normal persons ranging from 5 to 90 years of age and screened for attention deficit, learning difficulties, emotional problems, and medication use. In one analysis, the IVA showed 92 percent sensitivity (i.e., an 8 percent rate of false negatives) and 90 percent specificity (i.e., a 10 percent rate of false positives) in differentiating children diagnosed with Attention-Deficit/Hyperactivity Disorder (ADHD) from normal children. This instrument is just one of many promising neuropsychological tests that takes advantage of microcomputer technology.

Paced Auditory Serial Addition Task

Considering its utter simplicity, the Paced Auditory Serial Addition Task (PASAT) is an extremely sensitive index of mental tracking (Gronwall & Wrightson, 1974; Gronwall & Sampson, 1974). The examinee listens to a series of digits presented by audiotape and adds together each successive pair of digits. Thus, if the numbers presented are "3-1-9-5-4" the examinee should respond "4-10-14-9."

The PASAT begins with a 10-digit practice series, with a new digit presented every 2.4 seconds. The actual test consists of 61 stimuli (hence requiring 60 additions) at each of four presentation speeds: 2.4, 2.0, 1.6, and 1.2 seconds between digits. By computing the percent correct at each of the presentation rates, the examiner obtains four scores on the PASAT.

Even though the format of the PASAT is simple, the information processing demands of this test are quite burdensome. In order to perform well, the examinee must hold two numbers in short-term memory, perform a mental addition, speak the answer, retain in short-term memory only the last of the two numbers, annex the latest digit to short-term memory, and then start the cycle over again. Persons with impaired brain functions find this mental juggling to be cognitively overwhelming.

Gronwall recommends the PASAT for serial testing of concussion patients (Gronwall, 1977; Gronwall & Wrightson, 1981). Briefly defined, a **concussion** is a transitory alteration of consciousness from a blow to the head. A concussion may be followed by temporary amnesia, dizziness, nausea, weak pulse, and slow respiration, yet there is no demonstrable organic brain damage (McMordie, 1988). It is widely recognized that the PASAT is very sensitive to the effects of concussion (Stuss, Stethem, Hugenholtz, and Richard, 1989). However, a crucial issue in concussion is how long the patient should recuperate. When successive PASAT scores finally return to the normal range—which might take several days or several weeks—the therapist can have increased confidence that the patient is ready to return to work.

Largely on humanistic grounds, Lezak (1995) warns against routine use of the PASAT. In her experience, even cognitively intact persons experience the test as very stressful, feeling that they are failing even when their performance is normal. Insofar as there are easier ways to demonstrate attentional impairment, she recommends use of the PASAT only in special circumstances:

> . . . I keep it available for those times when subtle attentional deficits need to be made obvious to the most hide-bound skeptics for some purpose very much in the patient's interest; and then I prepare these patients beforehand, letting them know that it can be an unpleasant procedure and that they may feel that they are failing when they are not.

In a field where testing is justified mainly on the basis of hit rates and the like, her patient-centered perpective is refreshing and welcome.

Subtracting Serial Sevens

A well-known task frequently included in a mental status examination is subtracting serial sevens (Strub & Black, 1985). The examinee is told to "subtract seven from 100." When this is completed, the examinee is then told "Now subtract 7 from 93 and keep on subtracting sevens until you can't go any further." The examiner records the number of individually incorrect subtractions, and may also score for time taken and pauses longer than five seconds.

Smith (1967) has reported one of the few normative studies of subtracting serial sevens. He tested 132 employed adults, most with college or professional degrees. Only 2 percent of his sample was unable to complete the test, while another 5 percent made more than five errors. Women were more error-prone than men, particularly women over 45 with no college education. Thus, examiners must not overinterpret minor problems with subtracting serial sevens. On the other hand, grossly defective performance—an inability to proceed, very high error rate, or very slow subtractions—is characteristic of individuals with brain impairment.

Additional Measures of Attentional Impairment

Many tests devised for other purposes possess a strong attentional factor. The Digit Span and Arithmetic subtests of the Wechsler intelligence scales are recognized as good indices of immediate auditory attention. The Coding or Digit Symbol subtests also load heavily on a freedom-from-distractibility factor.

Smith (1968, 1973) has devised an interesting extention of Wechsler's Digit Symbol, known as the Symbol Digit Modalities Test (SDMT). In this test, the symbols are printed on the page and the examinee writes corresponding numbers underneath (Figure 9.7). With this format the examiner can administer both a written and an oral trial which helps isolate the source of difficulty with the substitution task. For example, an examinee who was normatively impaired on the written portion but above average on the oral portion might suffer from an impairment of motor control. The correlation between SDMT and Digit Symbol scores is extremely high ($r = .91$) but the SDMT produces scores that are comparatively lower than Digit Symbol (Morgan & Wheelock, 1992).

Several tests from the Halstead-Reitan battery are good measures of attention (Bennett, 1988). In the Speech Sounds Perception Test, the examinee must pick from four choices the written version of taped nonsense words. For example, the voice on the tape might say "freep" while the examinee must read from four choices and underline the correct alternative:

freeb fleeb freep fleep

The SSPT is highly sensitive to attentional impairments from any kind of brain damage. The Seashore Rhythm Test, originally a test of musical aptitude in which paired musical rhythms must be compared, also turns out to be highly dependent upon attentional processes. The Trail Making Test, parts A and B, is also sensitive to attentional impairment. Shum, McFarland, and Bain (1990) discuss additional tests of attention.

TESTS OF LEARNING AND MEMORY

Learning and memory are intertwined processes that are difficult to discuss in isolation. Learning new material usually requires the exercise of memory. Furthermore, many tests of memory incorporate a learning curve through repeated administrations. The separation of learning and memory processes is theoretical possible, but of little practical value in clinical assessment. We make no tight distinction between these processes.

Memory tests can be categorized according to several dimensions, including short-term versus long-term, verbal versus pictorial, and learning curve versus no learning curve. These dimensions reflect neurological factors discussed in the previous section. For example, verbal memory is significantly lateralized to the left hemisphere, whereas pictorial memory is largely underwritten by the right hemisphere. The interested reader can consult

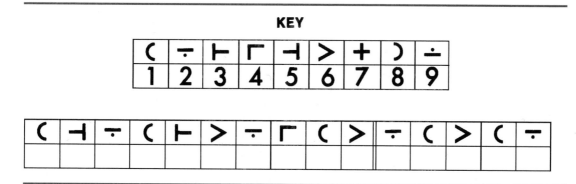

FIGURE 9.7 **The Symbol Digit Modalities Test (SDMT)**
Source: Reprinted with permission from Smith, A. (1973). *Symbol Digit Modalities Test Manual.* Los Angeles: Western Psychological Services. Material from the Symbol Digit Modalities Test copyright © 1973 by Western Psychological Services. Reprinted by permission of the publisher, Western Psychological Services, 12031 Wilshire Boulevard, Los Angeles, California 90025, United States of America.

Lezak (1995) and Reeves and Wedding (1994) for more detailed analyses of the neural substrates for different types of memory. Here, we will concentrate on the psychometric characteristics of four quite dissimilar memory tests.

Wechsler Memory Scale-III

The Wechsler Memory Scale-III (Tulsky, Zhu, & Ledbetter, 1997) is a substantial revision of a simple one-paged test published more than 50 years ago (Wechsler, 1945). The third edition is an extensive, multiphasic test of memory consisting of 17 subtests, including 7 that are optional. The 10 primary subtests are described in Table 9.9. These

---

TABLE 9.9   Wechsler Memory Scale-III Primary Subtests

Immediate Recall Subtests

Logical Memory I: Recall of essential elements from brief stories read to the examinee.

Faces I: Yes-no recall for 24 target faces each presented for two seconds.

Verbal Paired Associates I: Recall for a list of eight paired terms, (e.g., truck-arrow) when only the first term is presented (e.g., truck—?).

Family Pictures I: Recall of location and activities of persons depicted in pictures of family scenes.

Letter-Number Sequencing: Reordering of random digits and letters so that numbers and letters are in correct order (e.g.: "7, x, d, s, 4, 2" is reordered as "2, 4, 7, d, s, x").

Spatial Span: A visual analogue to Digit Span in which numbered blocks are tapped in a particular order; the examinee completes both a forward and a backward series.

*Delayed Recall Subtests**

Logical Memory II

Faces II

Verbal Paired Associates II

Family Pictures II

---
*30-minute delayed recall for stimuli in administration I.

---

subtests constitute the basis for obtained age-adjusted scaled scores (mean of 100 and SD of 15) for *eight* primary indices of memory:

Auditory immediate	Auditory delayed
Visual immediate	Visual delayed
Immediate memory	Auditory recognition delayed
General memory	Working memory

The WMS-III was co-normed with the WAIS-III in 1997. The standardization of the new instrument is superb, with 200 cases selected for each of these age bands: 16–17, 18–19, 20–24, 25–29, 30–34, 35–44, 45–54, 55–64, 65–69, 70–74, 75–79. For the two oldest age bands (80–84, 85–89), 150 cases and 100 cases, respectively, were included. Based upon 1995 census data, participants for the standardization sample were carefully stratified as to age, sex, race/ethnicity, educational level, and geographic region.

Validity studies of the WMS-III are strongly positive, although factor analytic investigation does not always support the designated breakdown into the various aspects of memory previously cited. The most powerful evidence for validity is that the instrument functions well in the detection of memory deficits. In the initial validation studies (Tulsky, Zhu, & Ledbetter, 1997), it was observed that clinical groups with neurological disorders (e.g., Alzheimer's disease, traumatic brain injury) scored significantly low on all eight of the WMS-III primary indices. For example, a sample of 35 individuals with probable early stage Alzheimer's disease obtained average scores in the mid- to high 60s on six of the eight indices. This is especially noteworthy because memory deficit is the initial complaint in the progression of Alzheimer's disease.

Validity research with the WMS-III is scant at this time. However, the latest edition retains the essential features of its predecessor, the WMS-R, for which a large body of validity research is available. For example, Ryan and Lewis (1988) found substantial memory deficits in recently detoxified alcoholics. This is an important finding because clinical studies with the original WMS did not reveal memory deficits in alcoholics, which caused researchers to doubt the validity of the first edition. The WMS-R also functions well in the identification of neuropsychological deficits caused by closed head injury (Reid & Kelly, 1993). In a related finding, Mittenberg, Azrin, Millsaps, and Heilbronner (1993) found that individuals who attempt to malinger head injury symptoms on the WMS-R produce a pattern of scores that can be discriminated from true cases of head injury. This is an important conclusion, because the accuracy of test results is usually contested when head-injured persons pursue litigation or worker's compensation. The WMS-R also reveals the expected memory deficits in patients with schizophrenia, which supports the validity of the test (Gold, Randolph, Carpenter, and others, 1992).

Rey Auditory Verbal Learning Test

This short, easily administered measure of verbal memory and learning first appeared in French (Rey, 1964), but an English-language adaptation has been provided by Lezak (1983, 1995) and others. In administering the Rey Auditory Verbal Learning Test (RAVLT), the examiner reads a list of 15 concrete nouns at the rate of one per second. The examinee recalls as many as possible in any order. Forewarning the examinee to recall all the words, including those previously recalled, the examiner reads the entire list a second time. A third, fourth, and fifth administration and recall then ensue; these are followed by an interference trial with a new list of words. Next, immediate recall of the original list is tested (without benefit of a new presentation). Finally, a recognition trial is included in which the examinee must underline the administered words from a longer written paragraph. The test yields a number of scores, including the number recalled (of 15) for each of the initial five trials, the total for the five trials (75 possible), the immediate recall after the distractor list is read, and the recognition score.

Rosenberg, Ryan, and Prifitera (1984) concluded that the RAVLT performs well in the identification of patients known to be memory impaired by other criteria. In addition to an overall reduction in performance, memory-impaired patients showed a reduced rate of improvement across the five learning trials. Adult norms for the RAVLT can be found in Geffen, Moar, O'Hanlon, Clark, and Geffen (1990), and Wiens, McMinn, and Crossen (1988). Norms for children ages 5 to 16 are provided by Bishop, Knights, and Stoddart (1990). Ivnik, Malec, Smith, and others (1992) contributed age-specific norms based on 530 cognitively normal persons 56 to 97 years of age. Schmidt (1996) has compiled, summarized, and synthesized available norms for the RAVLT.

Fuld Object-Memory Evaluation

The Fuld Object-Memory Evaluation is a useful test of memory impairment in the elderly (Fuld, 1977). The test begins by presenting the examinee a bag containing 10 common objects (ball, bottle, button, etc.). The task is not described as a memory test. The examinee is asked to determine whether he/she can identify objects by touch alone. Each object is felt and then named; the examinee then pulls it out of the bag to see if he/she was right. After all 10 items have been correctly identified, a distractor task is administered: rapidly naming words in a semantic category (e.g., names, foods, things that make people happy, vegetables, or things that make people sad). Then, the examinee is asked to recall as many of the objects as possible. After each recall, the subject is slowly and clearly reminded verbally of each item omitted on that trial, a procedure called selective reminding (Buschke & Fuld, 1974). The examinee is then administered four more chances to recall the list by selective reminding, with a distractor task after each trial. Delayed recall is tested after a 5-minute interval. Finally, the test closes with a multiple-choice recognition test.

The Fuld test is often used to help confirm a diagnosis of **Alzheimer's disease,** a degenerative neurological disorder described in the previous topic. In the early stages of Alzheimer's disease the most prominent symptom is memory loss. Elderly persons with memory impairment not only score lower than control subjects on the Fuld Object-Memory Evaluation, they also benefit very little from the selective reminding. Fuld (1977) has provided norms for community-active and healthy nursing-home residents in their 70s and 80s. Fuld, Masur, Blau, Crystal, and Aronson (1990) describe a prospective study in which the Fuld Object-Memory Evaluation demonstrated promise as a predictor of dementia in cognitively normal elderly. Lichtenberg, Manning, Vangel, and Ross (1995) describe a program of neuropsychological research using the Fuld test with older urban medical patients.

Additional Tests of Learning and Memory

Because of space limitations, we can do no more than briefly mention several other useful tests of learning and memory. The California Verbal Learning Test is patterned after the Rey AVLT but provides software to quantify and analyze the pattern of results (Schear & Craft, 1989). The Benton Visual Retention Test is a design-copying test of visual memory (Sivan, 1991). The Rivermead Behavioral Memory Test is a measure of everyday memory (e.g., route finding, remembering a name) in rehabilitation settings (Koltai, Bowler, & Shore, 1996). Good reviews of memory tests can be found in Lezak (1995), Reeves and Wedding (1994), and Spreen and Strauss (1998).

ASSESSMENT OF LANGUAGE FUNCTIONS

As noted in the previous section, language functioning offers a window to the integrity of the left cerebral hemisphere. Thus, neuropsychologists are keenly interested in an examinee's ability to speak, read, write, and comprehend what others say. Little wonder that a comprehensive neuropsychologi-

cal examination always includes one or more methods for assessing language functions.

Neuropsychologists exhibit a special interest in a variety of language dysfunctions known collectively as aphasia. Briefly stated, **aphasia** is any deviation in language performance caused by brain damage. In testing for aphasia, a neuropsychologist might use any or all of three approaches: (1) a nonstandardized clinical examination, (2) a standardized screening test, or (3) a comprehensive diagnostic test of aphasia. We will provide examples of each in our brief review of assessment methods in aphasia.

Clinical Examination for Aphasia

A clinical examination for aphasia has the advantages of simplicity, flexibility, and brevity. These are important attributes when assessing a severely impaired patient who may require bedside testing. Every practitioner has a slightly different version of the brief clinical exam (Lezak, 1995; Reitan, 1984, 1985). Nonetheless, certain elements commonly are assessed:

- *Spontaneous speech:* The examiner looks for distinctive symptoms of aphasia such as word-finding difficulty or neologisms (e.g., referring to a comb as a "planker").
- *Repetition of sentences and phrases:* The examiner asks the patient to repeat stimuli such as "No ifs, ands, or buts," and "Methodist Episcopal." The repetition tasks are so simple that normal subjects almost never fail them.
- *Comprehension of spoken language:* The examiner asks questions ("Does a car have handlebars?") and issues commands ("Take this paper, fold it in half, and put it on the floor"). Again, the tasks are so simple that normal subjects almost never fail them.
- *Word finding:* The examiner points to common, easily recognized objects and asks "What's this?" Typical items include watch, pen, pencil, glasses, ring, and shoes. The examiner may ask the patient to name numbers, letters, or colors.

- *Reading:* The examiner requests the patient to read and explain a short paragraph suited to prior level of education and intelligence. The examiner may ask the patient to follow written instructions (e.g., "Close your eyes" or "Clap your hands three times").
- *Writing and copying:* The examiner asks the patient to write spontaneously and from dictation. Also, the examiner may ask the patient to copy written matter and geometric shapes. The examiner is interested in grossly ungrammatical written productions and significant distortions in copying.
- *Calculation:* The examiner asks the patient to perform very simple mathematical calculations (e.g., 17 × 3) with and without aid of scratch paper. The tasks are so simple that normal subjects rarely fail.

Based on the clinical assessment, the examiner may fill out a rating scale for severity of aphasia. For example, the rating scale used in the Boston Diagnostic Aphasia Exam (Goodglass & Kaplan, 1983) includes the following speech characteristics: melodic line, phrase length, articulatory agility, grammatical form, word finding, and auditory comprehension.

Screening and Comprehensive Diagnostic Tests for Aphasia

Standardized screening tests for aphasia closely resemble the brief clinical exam. The essential difference is that standardized screening tests incorporate objective and precise instructions for administration and scoring. The weakness of screening tests is that they will not detect subtle forms of aphasia. The stimuli for a widely used screening test of aphasia are depicted in Figure 9.8.

Comprehensive diagnostic tests for aphasia are quite lengthy and used mainly when a patient is known to experience aphasia. These tests provide a profile of language skills that is helpful in treatment planning. We provide a brief description of several aphasia tests in Table 9.10.

Note: Tasks involve naming, spelling, reading, repeating, and calculation.

FIGURE 9.8 **Stimulus Figures for the Reitan-Indiana Aphasia Screening Test**
Source: Reprinted with permission from Reitan, R. M., and Wolfson, D. (1993). *The Halstead-Reitan Neuropsychological Test Battery: Theory and Clinical Interpretation* (2nd ed.). Tucson, AZ: Neuropsychology Press. The Reitan-Indiana Aphasia Screening Test is available from Reitan Neuropsychology Laboratories, 2920 S. Fourth Ave., South Tucson, AZ 85713.

TABLE 9.10   Brief Description of Several Aphasia Tests

Multilingual Aphasia Examination
  Benton, Hamsher, Rey, & Sivan (1994)

This respected, comprehensive battery consists of 11 subtests and rating scales that assess visual naming, repetition, fluency, articulation, spelling, and other language variables; available in a Spanish edition, too.

Western Aphasia Battery
  Kertesz (1979)

Comprehensive test of verbal fluency, auditory comprehension, and repetition that aims to identify aphasia syndromes and determine their severity.

Boston Diagnostic Aphasia Examination
  Goodglass & Kaplan (1983)

Comprehensive test with 46 subscales which include music, spatial, computation, and seven types of writing skill in addition to traditional aphasia measures; available in French and Hindi versions, too.

Aphasia Screening Test
  Reitan (1984, 1985)

Uses the pathognomic sign approach (error = aphasic symptom) and so does not yield a range of scores. A good screening test but may not detect subtle impairment.

Aphasia Language Performance Scales
  Keenan & Brassell (1975)

The four major language modalities (talking, listening, reading, writing) are each tested with 10 items of increasing complexity. Good reliability (.80s and .90s) and robust correlations (.94) with PICA, listed below.

Porch Index of Communicative Ability
  Porch (1967)

A battery containing eighteen 10-item subtests, four verbal, eight gestural, and six graphic. Very reliable test often used to measure small changes in patient performance.

Token Test
  Spreen & Strauss (1998)

An extremely sensitive test that presents little challenge to normal individuals. The examinee must complete oral commands with colored tokens, e.g., "Put the small red token on top of the large square token." Originally devised by Boller & Vignolo (1966), numerous versions of the Token Test are now available.

TESTS OF SPATIAL AND MANIPULATORY ABILITY

Tests of spatial and manipulatory ability are also known as tests of constructional performance. A constructional performance test combines perceptual activity with motor response and always has a spatial component (Lezak, 1995). Because constructional ability involves several complex functions, even mild forms of brain dysfunction will result in impaired constructional performance. However, careful observation is needed to distinguish the cause of the failed performance, which may include spatial confusion, perceptual deficiency, attentional difficulties, motivational problems, and apraxias. The term **apraxia** refers to a variety of dysfunctions characterized by a breakdown in the direction or execution of complex motor acts (Strub & Black, 1985). For example, a patient who could not demonstrate how to use a key would be diagnosed as suffering from ideomotor apraxia.

Tests of constructional performance embrace two large classes of activities: drawing and assembling. Owing to limitations of space, we will review only a few prominent instruments in each category.

Drawing Tests

Beyond any doubt, the most widely used drawing test is the Bender Visual Motor Gestalt Test, more commonly known as the Bender Gestalt Test (BGT, Bender, 1938). The BGT consists of nine stimulus figures (Figure 9.9); the examinee is instructed to copy one at a time on a sheet of blank paper. The examinee is told that the BGT " . . . is not a test of artistic ability, but try to copy the drawing as accurately as possible. Work as fast or as slowly as you wish" (Hutt, 1977).

Several scoring systems have been devised to determine whether an examinee's performance is more typical of brain-impaired or non-brain-impaired individuals (Hain, 1964; Hutt & Briskin, 1960; Lacks, 1999; Pascal & Suttell, 1951; Pauker, 1976). For adults the best of these scoring approaches is found in Lacks (1999). She identified 12 qualitative signs scored absent versus present for

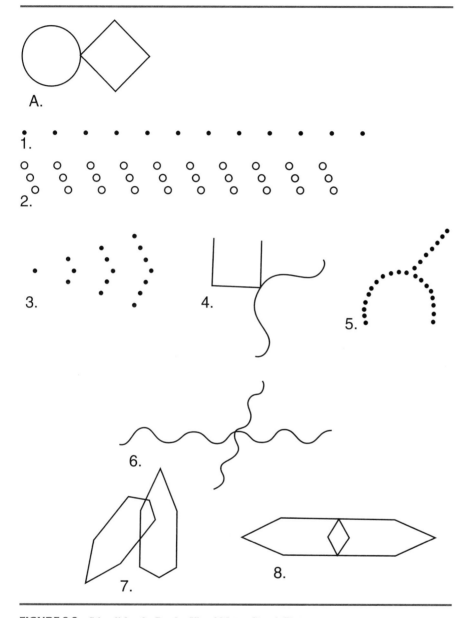

FIGURE 9.9   Stimuli for the Bender Visual Motor Gestalt Test
Source: Reprinted with permission from Bender, L. (1938). *A visual motor gestalt test and its clinical use.*
New York: American Orthopsychiatric Association. Copyright © American Orthopsychiatric Association.

the entire protocol. The presence of any 5 of the signs is indicative of brain damage (Table 9.11). Based on independent confirmation from other sources of information, Lacks reports hit rates of 82 percent to 86 percent in a mixed sample of admissions to the acute psychiatric treatment unit of an urban community mental health center (Lacks & Newport, 1980). Several interesting variations on

TABLE 9.11 Summary of Diagnostic Signs on the Bender Gestalt

1. *Rotation:* Figure is rotated 80 to 180 degrees.
2. *Overlapping difficulty:* Problem in drawing the portions of a single figure that should overlap.
3. *Simplification:* Figure is simplified.
4. *Fragmentation:* Figure is broken up so that the overall gestalt is lost.
5. *Retrogression:* Substitution of a more primitive gestalt form than the stimulus.
6. *Perseveration:* Features of a previous stimulus carry over in the current stimulus.
7. *Collision:* Two separate figures overlap or collide with each other.
8. *Impotence:* Numerous erasures and inability to finish a drawing to personal satisfaction.
9. *Closure difficulty:* Difficulty in getting adjacent parts of a figure to touch.
10. *Motor incoordination:* Tremor is evident in drawing.
11. *Angulation difficulty:* Severe difficulty in reproducing the angulation of drawings.
12. *Cohesion:* Isolated decrease or increase in size of subportion of one drawing.

Note: A 13th error can be counted if the entire test takes longer than 15 minutes.

Source: Based on Lacks, P. (1999). *Bender-Gestalt screening for brain dysfunction* (2nd ed.). New York: John Wiley.

the BGT are discussed in Gregory (1999). Groth-Marnat (1990) devotes an entire chapter to this instrument, including interpretive guidelines for children and adults.

The Greek Cross (Reitan & Wolfson, 1993) is a very simple drawing task that is surprisingly sensitive to brain impairment. The examinee is requested carefully to copy the figure without lifting the pencil, that is, by tracing the perimeter. The stimulus figure and examples of defective performance are shown in Figure 9.10. This test is most often evaluated on a qualitative basis, although scoring guides do exist (Swiercinsky, 1978; Gregory, 1999).

Assembly Tests

In his classic book on the parietal lobes, Critchley (1953) provided the rationale for including three-dimensional construction tasks in a neuropsychological test battery:

> It is possible, and indeed useful, to proceed to problems in three-dimensional space though tests of this character are only too rarely employed. This is a more difficult undertaking, and patients who respond moderately well to the usual procedures with sticks and pencil-and-paper may display gross

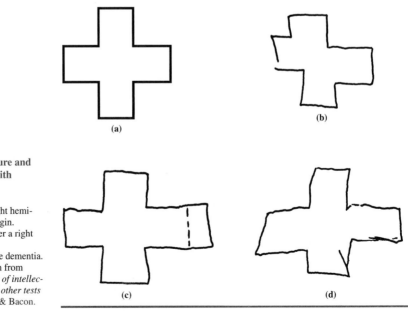

FIGURE 9.10

The Greek Cross Stimulus Figure and Reproductions from Persons with Known Brain Damage
(a) Stimulus figure.
(b) Clerical worker with diffuse right hemisphere dysfunction of unknown origin.
(c) College professor two years after a right hemisphere stroke.
(d) Patient with generalized, diffuse dementia.
Source: Reprinted with permission from Gregory, R. J. (1999). *Foundations of intellectual assessment: The WAIS-III and other tests in clinical practice.* Boston: Allyn & Bacon.

abnormalities when told to assemble bricks according to a three-dimensional pattern.

Benton, Sivan, Hamsher, Varney, and Spreen (1994) present a three-dimensional block construction test with excellent norms and scoring guide. The two forms of the test (Form A and Form B) consist of three block models that are presented one at a time to the patient. The patient is requested to construct an exact replica of the model by selecting the appropriate blocks from a set of loose blocks on a tray. Based on omissions, additions, substitutions, and displacements, the three models are scored from 0 to 6, 8, and 15 points, respectively. This test is quite sensitive to brain impairment, especially when the left or right parietal area is affected. Lezak (1995) discusses other assembly tasks. We should mention that the Tactual Performance Test from the Halstead-Reitan battery is, in part, an assembly task that measures spatial and manipulatory abilities (see Table 9.7).

ASSESSMENT OF EXECUTIVE FUNCTIONS

Executive functions include logical analysis, conceptualization, reasoning, planning, and flexibility of thinking. The assessment of executive functions presents an unusual quandary to neuropsychologists:

> A major obstacle to examining the executive functions is the paradoxical need to structure a situation in which patients can show whether and how well they can make structure for themselves. Typically in formal examinations, the examiner determines what activity the subject is to do with what materials, when, where, and how. Most cognitive tests, for example, allow the subject little room for discretionary behavior, including many tests thought to be sensitive to executive—or frontal lobe—disorders . . . The problem for clinicians who want to examine the executive functions becomes how to transfer goal setting, structuring, and decision making from the clinician to the subject within the structured examination (Lezak, 1995).

Many neuropsychologists resolve this quandary by using the clinical method to evaluate executive functions rather than administering formal

tests (Cripe, 1996). For example, Pollens, McBratnie, and Burton (1988) use interview and observations to fill out the structured checklist on executive functions mentioned in the previous topic.

Only a limited number of neuropsychological tests tap executive functions to any appreciable degree. Useful instruments in this regard include the Porteus Mazes, Wisconsin Card Sorting Test, and a novel approach known as the Tinkertoy® Test. We remind the reader that the Category Test from the Halstead-Reitan battery also captures executive functions to some extent (Table 9.7).

The Porteus Maze Test was devised as a culture-reduced measure of planning and foresight (Porteus, 1965). Without lifting the pencil and attempting to avoid dead ends, the examinee must trace a line through a series of increasingly difficult mazes. This underused instrument is quite sensitive to the effects of brain damage, particularly in the frontal lobes (Smith & Kinder, 1959; Smith, 1960; Tow, 1955).

The Wisconsin Card Sorting Test is a good measure of executive functions, although its differential sensitivity to frontal lobe damage is debated (Mountain & Snow, 1993). The instrument was devised to study abstract thinking and the ability to shift set (Berg, 1948; Heaton, Chelune, Talley, and others, 1993). The examinee is given a pack of 64 cards on which are printed one to four symbols (triangle, star, cross, or circle) in one of four colors (red, green, yellow, or blue). No two cards are identical. Thus, each card embodies a number, a particular shape, and a specific color. The examinee must sort these cards underneath four stimulus cards according to an unknown principle (Figure 9.11). For example, the unknown principle might be "sort according to color." As the examinee places cards, the examiner says "right" or "wrong." After the examinee has sorted a run of 10 correct placements in a row, the examiner shifts the principle without warning. The test continues until the examinee has made six runs of 10 correct placements. The test can be scored in several different ways, including total number of trials to criterion (Axelrod, Greve, & Goldman, 1994).

Lezak (1982) devised the Tinkertoy® Test to give patients the opportunity to demonstrate executive

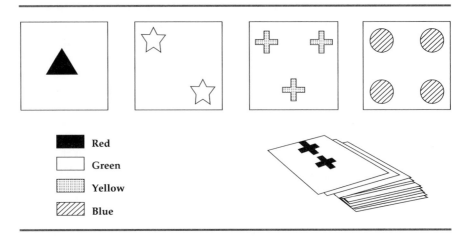

FIGURE 9.11 The Cards and Sorting Piles for the Wisconsin Card Sorting Test
Source: Reproduced by special permission from Psychological Assessment Resources, Inc. All rights reserved. Copyright © 1981 by Psychological Assessment Resources, Inc.

capacities within the structured format of an examination. Fifty pieces of a standard Tinkertoy® set are placed on a clean surface and the examinee is told "Make whatever you want with these. You will have at least five minutes and as much more time as you wish to make something." The test is scored from –1 to +12 based on several variables including the number of pieces used, the mobility of the construction, symmetry, and the naming of the construction. Head-injured patients produce impoverished designs consisting of a small number of pieces. These individuals often are unable to provide a name for their constructions.

Bayless, Varney, and Roberts (1989) studied the predictive validity of the Tinkertoy® Test by comparing the results of 50 patients with closed-head injuries versus 25 normal controls. Half of the head-injured individuals had returned to work while half had not. Whereas all but one of the head-injured who returned to work scored normally on the Tinkertoy® Test, nearly half of the nonreturnees performed below the level of the worst control subject. The researchers conclude:

> The test seems particularly well suited for demonstrating the presence of deficits in executive functioning, which have proven to be difficult to demonstrate with clinical tests even though they

have catastrophic sequelae in daily vocational or psychosocial endeavors (Bayless et al., 1989).

Neuropsychologists still need additional measures of executive functions. One promising approach in the early stages of development is real-world assessment of route finding. The ability to find an unfamiliar location in the city requires strategy, self-monitoring, and corrective maneuvers. These are executive functions applied to a realistic problem (Boyd & Sauter, 1993). Another promising approach is embodied in a recent battery called the Behavioral Assessment of the Dysexecutive System (Wilson, Alderman, Burgess, and others, 1996). The BADS battery consists of six new tests that are similar to real-life activities:

1. Rule shifting with playing cards
2. Problem solving with a water-filled beaker
3. Simulated search for a lost key
4. Judgment of time needed for activities, events
5. Route finding with a map
6. Organization task involving dictation, arithmetic, naming

The battery also includes a 20-item questionnaire rated on a 5-point (0 to 4) Likert scale. The items involve likely changes when executive functions are impaired, for example, "I have difficulty thinking ahead and planning for the future." Spreen and Strauss (1998) provide a helpful review of this promising test battery.

ASSESSMENT OF MOTOR OUTPUT

Most neuropsychological test batteries include measures of manipulative speed and accuracy. Lezak (1995) provides a comprehensive review. We will briefly summarize three approaches: finger tapping, pegboard performance, and line tracing.

Perhaps the most widely used test of motor dexterity is the Finger-Tapping Test from the Halstead-Reitan battery. This test consists of a tapping key that extends from a mechanical counting device attached to a flat board. With the index finger of each hand, the examinee completes a series of 10-second trials until five trials in a row are within a 5-point range. The score for each hand is the average of these five trials, rounded to the nearest whole number. With the dominant hand, males typically score about 54 taps (SD of 4) whereas females typically score about 51 taps (SD of 5, Dodrill, 1979; Morrison, Gregory, & Paul,1979).

In general, the absolute level of performance is of less interest than the relative abilities on the two sides of the body. Normative expectation is that the nondominant hand will yield a tapping rate about 90 percent of the dominant hand. Significant deviations from this pattern are thought to indicate a lesion in the hemisphere opposite that of the slowed hand (Haaland & Delaney, 1981). However, such inferences must be made with great caution owing to the very low reliability of the ratio score. Although test-retest and interexaminer reliabilities for either hand alone approach .80, the reliability of the ratio score is a dismal .44 to .54 (Morrison, Gregory, & Paul, 1979). The ratio score should be used with extreme caution in making clinical inferences about lateralization of damage.

The Purdue Pegboard Test requires the examinee to place pegs in holes with the left hand, right hand, and then both hands. Each trial lasts only 30 seconds, so the entire test can be administered in a matter of minutes. Tiffin (1968) reports normative scores for work applicants. Relative slowing in one

hand suggests a lesion in the opposite hemisphere, whereas bilateral slowing indicates diffuse or bilateral brain damage. Using the Purdue Pegboard Test in isolation, one study found an 80 percent accuracy in identifying brain impairment among a large group of normal subjects and neurological patients (Lezak, 1983). Other studies report much less favorable findings (Heaton, Smith, Lehman, & Vogt, 1978). The Purdue Pegboard Test is a useful addition to a comprehensive battery but should not be used in isolation for screening purposes. Spreen and Strauss (1998) provide an excellent summary of norms for this widely used test.

Klove has developed a variation on the pegboard test in which the pegs have a ridge along one side (Klove, 1963). Because each peg must be rotated into position, the Grooved Pegboard requires complex coordination in addition to motor dexterity. The Grooved Pegboard test is an excellent instrument for assessing lateralized brain damage (Haaland & Delaney, 1981).

Finally, we should mention that useful motor tests need not require sophisticated equipment. Lezak (1995) recommends a Line Tracing Task to assess difficulties in motor regulation (Figure 9.12). The examinee is given a brightly colored felt-tipped pen and a sheet of paper with several figures and told to draw over the lines as rapidly as possible. Difficulties with motor regulation show up in

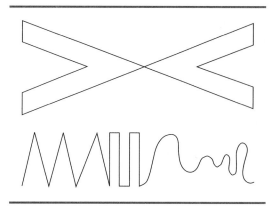

FIGURE 9.12   A Typical Line-Tracing Task (Reduced Size)

overshooting corners, perseveration of an ongoing response, and inability to follow the reduced curves in the bottom figure. Because this task is easily completed by most 10-year-olds, any noticeable deviations are suggestive of difficulties in motor regulation.

TEST BATTERIES IN NEUROPSYCHOLOGICAL ASSESSMENT

Now that we have completed a tour of some individual neuropsychological tests and procedures, it is time once again to remind the reader that many neuropsychologists prefer to use a fixed battery rather than an ever shifting, individualized assortment of instruments. Certainly one of the most widely used fixed batteries is the Luria-Nebraska Neuropsychological Battery (LNNB, Golden, 1989; Golden, Purish, & Hammeke, 1980, 1986).

The test consists of 269 discrete items, chosen from the work of Luria (e.g., 1966) and formally standardized. These items are scored 0, 1, or 2 according to precise criteria in the administration and scoring manual. Similar items are grouped together into 11 clinical scales, C1 through C11 (Table 9.12). Raw scores on each scale are converted into T-scores, with a mean of 50 and a standard deviation of 10. Higher scores reflect more psychopathology; scores above 70 are especially suggestive of brain impairment.

Three summary scales are also derived from test performance: S1 (Pathognomonic), S2 (Left Hemisphere), and S3 (Right Hemisphere). The Pathognomonic scale reflects the degree of compensation that has occurred since an injury, such as functional reorganization of the brain as well as actual physical recovery. Higher scores reflect less compensation. The Left Hemisphere and Right Hemisphere scales can be used to help determine whether an injury is diffuse or lateralized. A number of other scales and interpretive factors are also available (Golden, Purish, & Hammeke, 1986). The use of the LNNB is illustrated in Case Exhibit 9.2.

We cannot review the voluminous literature on the LNNB, but brief mention of a few key studies certainly is merited. The reliability of the LNNB

TABLE 9.12   Tests and Procedures of the Luria-Nebraska Neuropsychological Battery

Ability Scale: Tasks Included

C1 Motor: Coordination, speed, drawing, complex motor abilities

C2 Rhythm: Attend to, discriminate, and produce verbal and nonverbal rhythmic stimuli

C3 Tactile: Identify tactile stimuli, including stimuli traced on the wrists

C4 Visual: Identify drawings, including overlapping and unfocused objects; solve progressive matrices and other visuospatial skills

C5 Receptive Speech: Discriminate phonemes and comprehend words, phrases, sentences

C6 Expressive Speech: Articulate sounds, words, and sentences fluently; identify pictured or described objects

C7 Writing: Use motor writing abilities in general; copy and write from dictation

C8 Reading: Read letters, words, and sentences; synthesize letters into sounds and words

C9 Arithmetic: Complete simple mathematical computations; comprehend mathematical signs and number structure

C10 Memory: Remember verbal and nonverbal stimuli under both interference and noninterference conditions

C11 Intelligence: Reasoning, concept formation, and complex mathematical problem solving

has been evaluated from the usual perspectives (split-half, internal consistency, and test-retest), with excellent results. For example, the mean test-retest reliability for the clinical scales was near .90 (Bach, Harowski, Kirby, Peterson, & Schulein, 1981; Plaisted & Golden, 1982). In various validity studies of classification of brain-damaged persons versus other criterion groups, the LNNB has shown hit rates of 80 percent or better (Golden, Moses, Graber, & Berg, 1981; Hammeke, Golden, & Purish, 1978; Moses & Golden, 1979).

In spite of the positive findings reported by Golden and his colleagues, many neuropsychologists remain skeptical of the LNNB (Lezak, 1995; Kolb & Whishaw, 1990; Crosson & Warren, 1982; Delis & Kaplan, 1982, 1983). For example, Delis and Kaplan (1983) argued that the heterogeneity of

LURIA-NEBRASKA NEUROPSYCHOLOGICAL BATTERY

To illustrate the application of the LNNB, we present the case of a 56-year-old male with postcollege training (Golden, 1989). This patient experienced two strokes in the right hemisphere prior to administration of the LNNB. His scores on the clinical and summary scales are shown below. The reader will notice the marked elevation of S3 (Right Hemisphere, $T = 124$) in comparison to S2 (Left Hemisphere, $T = 81$), signalling a lesion that is strongly lateralized to the right side of the brain. Notice, too, that S1 is only moderately elevated ($T = 75$), indicating that the patient has made fair progress in compensating for his brain impairment. Language (C5 and C6) and intelligence (C11) are generally intact, but reading, writing, and memory (C7, C8, and C10) show possible subtle impairment ($T = 60, 60,$ and 65, respectively). The most severe disabilities are on C1 through C4, that is, Motor, Rhythm, Tactile, and Visual. This indicates severe sensorimotor impairment. Examination of the specific errors on the scales revealed that 74 percent of the errors involved vision. The patient showed a consistent left unilateral neglect, in which the left side of visual stimuli (such as words or sentences) was ignored. Overall, the results are quite consistent with a major stroke in the middle cerebral artery of the right hemisphere. The stroke has apparently damaged the sensorimotor areas and also the subcortical neural tracts that terminate in the visual areas of the brain.

Scale		T-Score
C1	Motor	99
C2	Rhythm	92
C3	Tactile	92
C4	Visual	85
C5	Receptive	39
C6	Expressive	40
C7	Writing	60
C8	Reading	60
C9	Arithmetic	45
C10	Memory	65
C11	Intelligence	53
S1	Pathognomonic	75
S2	Left Hemisphere	81
S3	Right Hemisphere	124

Note: Expected scores for normal subjects is about 50; higher scores reflect greater impairment.

the scales is so great that the scores do not quantify specific neuropsychological deficits:

In the "validation" of the battery, elevation on a scale was analyzed only in terms of differentiating a group of "brain-damaged" patients from "normals." The construct validity of whether elevation on a particular scale represented an impairment in that ability was not even considered.

The same authors demonstrated that the speech scales were not oriented to syndromes of aphasia and could therefore misdiagnose language deficits (Delis & Kaplan, 1982). Lezak (1995) points to the gap separating the evaluations of the LNNB made by Golden and his colleagues from those by other neuropsychologists. Based on their reading of the literature, Kolb and Whishaw (1990) conclude that the "usefulness and validity of this battery is far from proved." Snow (1992) and Van Gorp (1992) also recommend caution, noting that the LNNB is good at identifying brain-impaired subjects in general, but questionable at identifying the type, location, and consequences of brain damage. Another problem with the LNNB is the high rate of false positives with geriatric patients. With normal subjects 70 years of age and older, false positive rates ranged from 21 percent to 41 percent, depending upon the method of interpretation used (Roecker, House, & Graybill, 1992–93).

ASSESSMENT OF MENTAL STATUS IN THE ELDERLY

The mental status examination (MSE) is a loosely structured interview that usually precedes other forms of psychological and medical assessment. The purpose of the evaluation is to provide an accurate description of the patient's functioning in the realms of orientation, memory, thought, feeling, and judgment. The MSE is the psychological equivalent of the general physical examination: Just as the physician reviews all the major organ systems, looking for evidence of disease, the psychologist reviews the major categories of personal and intellectual functioning, looking for signs and symptoms of psychopathology (Gregory, 1999). Although there is some latitude as to the scope of the MSE, certain mental functions are almost always investigated. A typical evaluation touches upon the areas listed in Table 9.13.

Some of the elements in this list can be assessed with short screening tests. In particular, cognition, memory, and orientation are intellectual functions that can be tested in a formal, structured manner (Hodges, 1994). In this section, we review several brief measures of mental status used by clinicians to supplement interview impressions. These measures are most commonly used in the mental status evaluation of the elderly, especially when the client appears to have a dementia such as Alzheimer's disease. Formal tests of mental status are also helpful in the assessment of certain brain-impairing conditions such as head injury, schizophrenia, severe depression, and drug-induced delirium. It is important to emphasize that screening tests are supplementary—they do not replace clinical judgment in the evaluation of mental status. Some areas covered by the MSE are simply impossible to quantify. For example, the evaluation of a patient's insight requires

TABLE 9.13   Major Areas of a Typical Mental Status Exam

Appearance and Behavior
Grooming
Facial expressions
Gross motor behavior
Eye contact

Speech and Communication Processes
Speech content, rate, tone, volume
Word difficulty, confusion, misuse

Thought Content
Logic, clarity, appropriateness
Delusions

Cognitive and Memory Functioning
Calculating ability
Immediate recall
Recent and remote memory
Fund of information
Abstracting ability

Emotional Functioning
Predominant mood
Appropriateness of affect

Insight and Judgment
Awareness of problems

Orientation
Day, date, time, location

Source: Based on Gregory, R. J. (1999). *Foundations of intellectual assessment: The WAIS-III and other tests in clinical practice.* Boston, MA: Allyn & Bacon.

keen observation and sensitive interviewing skills. An MSE screening test for insight does not exist.

Mini-Mental State Exam

The most widely used mental status tool is the Mini-Mental State Examination (MMSE), a 5- to 10-minute screening test that yields an objective global index of cognitive functioning (Folstein, Folstein, & McHugh, 1975; Tombaugh, McDowell, Kristjansson, & Hubley, 1996). The test contains 30 scorable items having to do with orientation, immediate memory, attention, calculation, language production, language comprehension, and design copying. The items are so easy that normal adults almost always obtain scores in the range of 27 to 30 points (Figure 9.13).

The reliability of this simple instrument is excellent. Folstein et al. (1975) report a 24-hour test-retest reliability of .89 for 22 patients with varied depressive symptoms. Reliability over a 28-day period for 23 clinically stable patients with diagnoses of dementia, depression, and schizophrenia was an impressive .99. Normative data are available from several sources (e.g., Lindal & Stefansson, 1993; Tombaugh, McDowell, Kristjansson, & Hubley, 1996).

Using a cutting score of 23 or below as abnormal and 24 or above as normal, the MMSE is about 80 to 90 percent accurate in identifying elderly patients with suspected Alzheimer's disease or other dementia. This cutting score produces few false positives (normal patients classified as having dementia). The sensitivity of the instrument depends upon a number of factors, including the cutting score used, the educational level of the examinee, the extent of the dementia, the nature of the underlying pathology, and the type of setting in which assessments are undertaken (Anthony, LeResche, Niaz, Von Korff, & Folstein, 1982; Tombaugh, McDowell, Kristjansson, & Hubley, 1996; Tsai & Tsuang, 1979). In spite of its limitations, the MMSE remains the most reliable and practical screening test for dementia in the elderly (Ferris, 1992). Drebing, Van Gorp, Stuck, and others (1994) recommend its use as part of a short screening battery for cognitive decline in the elderly. Several additional measures of geriatric mental status are outlined in Table 9.14.

TABLE 9.14   Mental Status Tests Used with Geriatric Patients

Test	*Content*
Cognistat Kiernan, Mueller, & Langston (1997)	Language, construction (copying), memory, calculation, and reasoning/judgment
Information-Memory-Concentration Blessed, Tomlinson, and Roth (1968)	Information, orientation, concentration
Short Portable Mental Status Questionnaire Pfeiffer (1975)	Information, orientation, attention
Dementia Rating Scale Mattis (1976)	Attention, memory, construction (copying), conceptualization, verbal fluency
Test of Temporal Orientations Benton, Sivan, Hamsher, Varney, and Spreen (1994)	Orientation
Alzheimer's Disease Assessment Scale Rosen, Mohs, and Davis (1984)	Orientation, memory, language, construction (copying)
Cambridge Cognitive Examination Roth, Tym, Mountjoy, & others (1986)	Orientation, memory, language, construction (copying), attention, abstraction, perception, calculation
Severe Impairment Battery Saxton, McGonigle-Gibson, Swihart, and others (1990)	Orientation, memory, language, attention, social interaction, construction (copying), praxis, visuo-perception

MiniMental LLC

NAME OF SUBJECT _____ Age _____

NAME OF EXAMINER _____ Years of School Completed _____

Approach the patient with respect and encouragement.   Date of Examination _____
Ask: "Do you have any trouble with your memory?"   ☐ Yes ☐ No
"May I ask you some questions about your memory?   ☐ Yes ☐ No

SCORE   ITEM

5 ( )   **TIME ORIENTATION**
Ask:
"What is the year _____ (1), season _____ (1),
month of the year _____ (1), date _____ (1),
day of the week _____ (1)?"

5 ( )   **PLACE ORIENTATION**
Ask:
"Where are we now? What is the state _____ (1), city _____ (1),
part of the city _____ (1), building _____ (1),
floor of the building _____ (1)?"

3 ( )   **REGISTRATION OF THREE WORDS**
Say: "Listen carefully. I am going to say three words. You say them back after I stop.
Ready? Here they are . . . PONY (wait 1 second), QUARTER (wait 1 second), ORANGE (wait
1 second). What were those words?"
_____ (1)
_____ (1)
_____ (1)
Give 1 point for each correct answer, then repeat them until the patient learns all three.

5 ( )   **SERIAL 7's AS A TEST OF ATTENTION AND CALCULATION**
Ask: "Subtract 7 from 100 and continue to subtract 7 from each subsequent remainder until I tell
you to stop. What is 100 take away 7?" _____ (1)
Say:
"Keep Going." _____ (1), _____ (1),
_____ (1), _____ (1).

3 ( )   **RECALL OF THREE WORDS**
Ask:
"What were those three words I asked you to remember?"
Give one point for each correct answer. _____ (1),
_____ (1), _____ (1).

For more
information or
additional copies
of this exam,
call (617) 587-4215

© 1998 M. FOLSTEIN

FIGURE 9.13   **The Mini-Mental Status Examination**
Source: Folstein, M., Folstein, S., and McHugh, P. (1975). Mini-Mental State: A practical method for grading the cognitive state of patients for the clinician. *Journal of Psychiatric Research, 12,* 189–198. The copyright in the Mini-Mental State Examination is wholly owned by the Mini Mental LLC, a Massachusetts limited liability company. For information about how to obtain permission to use or reproduce the Mini-Mental State Examination, please contact John Gonsalves, Jr., Administrator of the Mini-Mental LLC, at 31 St. James Avenue, Suite 1, Boston, MA 02116. (617) 587-4215. © 1998 MMLLC.

2 ( )   NAMING
Ask:
"What is this?" (show pencil) _____ (1). "What is this?" (show watch) _____ (1).

1 ( )   REPETITION
Say:
"Now I am going to ask you to repeat what I say. Ready? No ifs, ands, or buts."
Now you say that." _____ (1)

3 ( )   COMPREHENSION
Say:
"Listen carefully because I am going to ask you to do something:
Take this paper in your left hand (1), fold it in half (1), and put it on the floor." (1)

1 ( )   READING
Say:
"Please read the following and do what it says, but do not say it aloud." (1)

Close your eyes

1 ( )   WRITING
Say:
"Please write a sentence." If patient does not respond, say: "Write about the weather." (1)

_____

_____

1 ( )   DRAWING
Say: "Please copy this design."

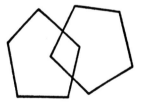

TOTAL SCORE _____   Assess level of consciousness along a continuum

Alert	Drowsy	Stupor	Coma

	YES	NO		YES	NO	**FUNCTION BY PROXY**			
Cooperative:	☐	☐	Deterioration from previous level of functioning:	☐	☐	Please record data when patient was last able to perform the following tasks. Ask caregiver if patient independently handles.			
Depressed:	☐	☐							
Anxious:	☐	☐							
Poor Vision:	☐	☐	Family History of Dementia:	☐	☐		YES	NO	DATE
Poor Hearing:	☐	☐	Head Trauma:	☐	☐	Money/Bills:	☐	☐	_____
Native Language:			Stroke:	☐	☐	Medication:	☐	☐	_____
_____			Alcohol Abuse:	☐	☐	Transportation:	☐	☐	_____
			Thyroid Disease:	☐	☐	Telephone:	☐	☐	_____

FIGURE 9.13   (Continued)

SUMMARY

1. For purposes of assessment, cognitive processing is viewed as proceeding sequentially through the following stages: sensory input, attention and concentration, learning and memory, language skills and/or visual-spatial/manipulatory skills, executive functions, and motor output (see Figure 9.6).

2. The assessment of sensory input is typically achieved through unilateral and bilateral stimulation in the modalities of touch, hearing, and vision. Typical tasks (e.g., finger localization) are so simple that normal persons rarely make errors.

3. Measures of attentional impairment include subtracting serial sevens; the Continuous Performance Test, a family of computerized vigilance tasks; and the Paced Auditory Serial Addition Test, a speeded test of mental arithmetic (adding successive pairs of digits) which is very sensitive to the effects of concussion.

4. A respected memory test is the Wechsler Memory Scale-III, a substantial revision of the original scale published nearly 50 years ago. Carefully standardized, the WMS-III consists of 17 subtests, including some with surprise recall a half hour after the original administration.

5. Another widely used memory test is the Rey Auditory Verbal Learning Test (RAVLT) in which the same list of 15 concrete nouns is read to the examinee for five successive trials. Recall is tested after each trial and also after an interpolated word list is administered.

6. Aphasia is any deviation in language performance caused by brain damage. Tests of aphasia (e.g., Reitan's Aphasia Screening Test or the Boston Diagnostic Aphasia Exam by Goodglass and Kaplan) typically assess spontaneous speech, repetition of sentences and phrases, comprehension of spoken language, word finding, reading, writing, copying, and calculation.

7. Tests of spatial and manipulatory ability include drawing or copying tests such as the Bender Visual Motor Gestalt Test, and three-dimensional block construction tests; both types are sensitive to the effects of brain damage.

8. Executive functions include logical analysis, conceptualization, reasoning, planning, and flexibility of thinking. Useful tests for the assessment of executive functions include the Porteus Maze Test; the Wisconsin Card Sorting Test; and the Tinkertoy® Test, so-named because of the materials used.

9. Neuropsychological test batteries commonly include measures of motor output such as the Finger-Tapping Test from the Halstead-Reitan battery. Typically, the nondominant hand is 10 percent slower than the dominant hand; deviations from this pattern may indicate a lesion in the hemisphere opposite that of the slowed hand.

10. Other useful motor tests include the Purdue Pegboard Test, which requires the examinee to place pegs in holes with the left hand, right hand, and then both hands; and simple line-tracing tasks easily completed by most 10-year-olds.

11. The Luria-Nebraska Neuropsychological Battery consists of 269 discrete items modeled upon the work of Luria and formally standardized. The test developer and his colleagues report excellent reliability and strong validity (e.g., hit rates of 80 percent or better in identification of brain damaged subjects).

12. The mental status examination (MSE) is a loosely structured interview that usually precedes other forms of psychological and medical assessment. Areas assessed in the MSE include orientation, memory, thought, feeling, and judgment.

13. A helpful mental status screening test particularly useful with the elderly is the Mini-Mental Status Examination. This 30-item test has high reliability and hit rates in some populations of 80 to 90 percent for the detection of dementia in the elderly.

KEY TERMS AND CONCEPTS

concussion   p. 332

Alzheimer's disease   p. 335

aphasia   p. 336

apraxia   p. 338

executive functions   p. 341

CHAPTER 10

Special Settings for Psychological Assessment

TOPIC 10A School-Based Assessment

In this chapter, we explore the applications of testing within two distinctive environments—schools and the legal system. Although disparate in many respects, these two settings for assessment share some essential features. In both arenas, legal guidelines exert a powerful and constraining influence upon the practice of testing. Issues of proper diagnosis and classification are especially pertinent. For example, in assessing a student for learning disability, the school psychologist observes federal guidelines that circumscribe the definition of these disorders. Similarly, in evaluating a client for competency to stand trial, the forensic psychologist follows published guidelines that determine

the boundaries of legal fitness. In both cases, the practice of assessment is shaped, informed, and guided by legal precepts.

School-based assessment and forensic assessment certainly comprise two of the more interesting arenas for psychological testing. In Topic 10A, School-Based Assessment, we consider the use of psychological tests within schools for purposes such as screening, assessment, and special placement. In Topic 10B, Forensic Applications of Assessment, we analyze the unique challenges encountered by forensic psychologists who perform court-based evaluations. Of course, relevant tests are surveyed and catalogued. But more important, we focus upon the special issues and challenges encountered within these distinctive milieus.

While it is true that a major application of school-based testing is evaluation for learning disabilities (discussed at length in the following), psychologists provide many other assessment services for schools. These include screening for school readiness, evaluation of attention deficit and other behavioral problems, and testing for giftedness. A survey of these topics is provided in the following sections. Additional school-based assessment practices such as evaluation for mental retardation and assessment of children with disabilities are described in Topic 7A, Testing Special Populations.

SCREENING FOR SCHOOL READINESS

The purpose of **screening** is to identify at-risk children so they can be referred for more comprehensive evaluation (Kamphaus, 1993). But "at-risk" for what? The general answer refers to likelihood of failure in the early elementary years of schooling. The notion of being at-risk is intimately linked to the concept of developmental delay, which refers to children whose cognitive development is well below age expectations. Some children identified with this label "catch up" later in life. For these children, developmental delay is an appropriate designation. Certainly it is a more optimistic and less-stigmatizing label than mental retardation—which is often the ultimate outcome of developmental delay.

Children with low intelligence are substantially at-risk for school failure, which explains why individual intelligence tests play an important role in the evaluation of preschool children. But individual intelligence tests require a substantial commitment of time (up to two hours) and must be administered by carefully trained practitioners. For practical reasons, then, individual intelligence tests are not suitable as screening instruments.

The ideal screening instrument is a short test that can be administered by teachers, school nurses, and other individuals who have received limited training in assessment. In addition, a sensible screening test is one that provides a cutoff score that is accurate in classifying children as normal or

at-risk. In the context of screening tests, two kinds of errors can occur. Normal children who fail the test would be referred to as false-positive cases (because they are falsely classified as positive for potential disability). At-risk children who pass the test would be referred to as false-negative cases (because they are falsely classified as negative for potential disability). The reader must keep in mind that the purpose of screening is merely to identify children in need of additional evaluation, which means that false-positive cases will receive further evaluation. Hence a false-positive misclassification rarely leads to undesirable consequences. However, false-negative cases typically do not receive further evaluation, so this kind of misclassification is potentially more serious—because a needy child is deemed to be normal. Glascoe (1991) recommends that a useful instrument should yield a false-negative rate of less than 20 percent (meaning that 80 percent of truly at-risk children are flagged by the test) and an even lower false-positive rate of less than 10 percent (meaning that 90 percent of normal children pass the test).

Screening tests are by definition brief and therefore prone to measurement errors. Even with the best tests available, deserving children will slip through the cracks (false-negative cases) and go unrecognized as needing intervention until they are well into their elementary years in school. However, if it identifies a high proportion of true-positive cases—preschoolers classified at-risk who turn out really to need special services or delayed school entrance—a screening test still serves a useful purpose.

Instruments for Preschool Screening

Although dozens of instruments have been produced to screen for developmental delays (Malcolm, 1998), we limit discussion here to just three tests: the DIAL-R (Developmental Indicators for the Assessment of Learning-Revised), the Denver II (a revision of the Denver Developmental Screening Test-Revised), and the HOME (Home Observation for the Measurement of the Environment). The first two tests use conventional approaches for the identification of developmental delay whereas the third instrument, the HOME, embodies a radical departure from traditional procedures.

DIAL-R

The Developmental Indicators for the Assessment of Learning-Revised (DIAL-R) is an individually administered screening procedure designed for the quick and efficient detection of developmental problems (or giftedness) in preschool children ages 2-0 through 5-11 (Mardell-Czudnowski & Goldenberg, 1990). The test screens the performance of children in three developmental domains: motor, concepts, and language. Each domain is assessed by eight items which are subdivided into discrete tasks. The DIAL-R also provides an observational assessment of social-emotional problems (e.g., crying or whining, distractibility, resistiveness, disruptiveness) but in a less rigorous manner. Examples of test items within the three developmental domains include the following:

1. *Motor:* Catching, hopping, building, cutting, copying shapes and letters, writing one's name
2. *Concepts:* Body part identification, color naming, counting blocks, position words, letter naming, sorting
3. *Language:* Speaking single words, giving personal data, naming nouns, classifying foods, oral problem solving, length of spoken sentence

Scoring for some items is discrete and objective whereas for other questions the scoring criteria in the manual leave room for subjective interpretation, which detracts from the reliability of the instrument. A total score is obtained by summing the three area scores. For each area score and also the total score the manual provides cutoff scores for assigning the child to one of three outcome groups labeled "okay," "potential problem," or "potential advanced." The DIAL-R cutoffs are available for three norm groups: Caucasian, Minority, and Census (combined groups). The standardization samples closely parallel the 1990 census with respect to parents' educational background.

Reliability of the DIAL-R is fair, given that it is a brief test for screening purposes. Test-retest reliability data ($N = 65$) indicate average coefficients ranging from .76 for the motor domain to .90 for concepts. Validity of the instrument has been evaluated along the familiar lines of content, construct, and criterion-related. Content validity is judged to be high insofar as a panel of eight experts provided content reviews and helped eliminate inappropriate and biased items. Construct validity is more questionable because factor-analytic evidence does not appear to support the validity of the three domains as independent subtests.

It is with regard to criterion-related validity that the DIAL-R has raised the greatest skepticism. The value of a screening test is best judged by the extent to which it *accurately* identifies children in need of further developmental assessment. A test with good criterion-related validity correctly classifies a high proportion of children currently scoring poorly on more extensive tests of developmental delay (concurrent validity) or later confirmed to display such problems (predictive validity). One statistic useful in evaluating criterion-related validity is **sensitivity,** which is the proportion of confirmed problem cases accurately "flagged" as problem cases. Unfortunately, the DIAL-R is not an efficient test in this regard. The *Manual* cites a variety of studies which reveal weak sensitivity, generally in the range of 25 to 57 percent. What this means is that of those children who really do have a problem, only 25 to 57 percent are identified as "potential problem" by the DIAL-R. The test functions better in correctly identifying normal children as normal, with a **specificity** of about 90 percent. However, the low sensitivity means that many children in need of special consideration will remain unrecognized by this test (Cooper & Shepard, 1992).

Denver II

The Denver II (Frankenburg, Dodds, Archer, and others, 1990) is an updated version of the highly popular Denver Developmental Screening Test-

Revised (Frankenburg, 1985; Frankenburg & Dodds, 1967). The Denver test is probably the most widely known and researched pediatric screening tool in the United States. The instrument is popular worldwide—it has been translated into 44 different languages. Suitable for infants and children ages 1 month to 6 years, the test consists of 125 items in four areas: personal-social, fine motor–adaptive, language, and gross motor. The items are a mix of parent report, direct elicitation, and observation. Each item is arranged chronologically on the test by age of the child and marked pass/fail. Testing begins at an age-appropriate level and continues until the child fails three items. Total time for evaluation is 20 minutes or less.

Unlike other screening tests, the Denver II does not produce a developmental quotient or score. Instead, results on about 30 age-appropriate items provide a score that can be interpreted as normal, questionable, or abnormal in reference to age-based norms. A category of "untestable" also is included. The standardization sample consisted of 2,096 children, all from the state of Colorado, stratified by age, race, and socioeconomic status.

Recognizing that no instrument is perfectly reliable and that children change over time, the developers of the Denver II recommend repeat testing at approximately six-month intervals up to age 2 years, and then yearly thereafter through age 5 years. Reliability of the Denver II is reported to be outstanding for a brief screening test. Interrater reliability among trained raters averaged an outstanding .99. Test-retest reliability for total score over a 7- to 10-day interval averaged .90.

The Denver possesses excellent content validity insofar as the behaviors tested are recognized by authorities in child development as important markers of development. However, the test interpretation categories (normal, questionable, abnormal) were based upon clinical judgment and therefore await additional study for validation. A few initial studies raise significant concerns. Glascoe and Byrne (1993) evaluated 89 children in daycare settings who were 7 to 70 months of age.

Based upon extensive independent evaluation, 18 of these 89 children were confirmed to have developmental delays according to federal definitions of disabling conditions (e.g., language delays, mental retardation, and autism). While the Denver II functioned well in correctly identifying 15 of the 18 at-risk children, the instrument performed poorly with the normal children. In fact, 38 of the 71 normal children failed the test and were classified as questionable or abnormal. Overall, almost 4 in 6 children taking the test would be referred for additional assessment, and of the 4, only 1 would have a true disability. The researchers conclude:

> This causes parents needless expense and anxiety, wastes precious diagnostic and intervention resources, and leaves professionals with unanswered questions about children's developmental status both before and after screening.

They recommend further validational study with recalibration and possible discarding of some test items before the test receives widespread use.

HOME

The Home Observation for Measurement of the Environment (HOME), popularly known as the HOME Inventory, is probably the most widely used index of children's environment. Based upon in-home observation and an interview with the primary caretaker, the instrument provides a measure of children's physical and social environments. The HOME Inventory comes in three forms: Infant and Toddler, Early Childhood, and Middle Childhood. The latest editions of the instrument, dated 1984, emerged after 15 years of methodical revision and refinement (Caldwell & Richmond, 1967; Caldwell & Bradley, 1984, 1994).

Background and Description

Prior to the development of the HOME Inventory, the measurement of children's environments was based largely upon demographic data such as parental education, occupation, income, and location of residence. Often, these indices were combined into a cumulative measure referred to as social class or socioeconomic status (SES). For example, Hollingshead and Redlich (1958) developed a continuum of social class derived from residence, occupation, and education of the head of the household. The SES score for a family whose household head worked at a clerical job, was a high school graduate, and lived in a middle-rank residential area would be computed as follows (Hollingshead & Redlich, 1958):

Factor	Scale Value	×	Factor Weight	=	Partial Score
Residence	3		6		18
Occupation	4		9		36
Education	4		5		20
Index of Socioeconomic Status			=		74

For research purposes, social scientists may categorize families into a fivefold hierarchy of social classes (classes I through V) based upon the total score. The reader will notice that the Hollingshead and Redlich measure was derived entirely from *status* indices. The unstated assumption is that these indices reflect, indirectly, meaningful environmental variation. Put bluntly, proponents of SES as an environmental measure believe that, on average, children from a higher social class will experience a richer and more nurturant environment than children from a lower social class.

In contrast to the SES approach, the HOME Index was developed to provide a direct *process* measure of children's environments. The guiding philosophy of this instrument is that direct assessment of children's experiences is a better index of the home environment than such indirect measures as parental occupation and education. Although it is true that social class—as embodied in occupation, education, residence—provides an oblique measure of environmental richness, the authors of the HOME Inventory would argue that direct assessment of children's experiences provides a more accurate index of variations in the home environ-

ment. Thus, assessment with the HOME involves, in part, direct observation of children's home environments to determine whether certain types of crucial interactions and experiences are present or absent. For example, during an hour-long visit, the examiner observes whether the parent spontaneously communicates with the child at least five times, determines whether the child has at least 10 children's books or story records, and assesses whether the neighborhood is aesthetically pleasing according to detailed standards, to cite just a few examples.

The purpose of the HOME Inventory is to measure the quality and quantity of stimulation and support for cognitive, social, and emotional development available to the child in the home. The scales and items of the HOME were derived from a list of environmental processes identified from existing research and theory as important for optimal childhood development (Caldwell & Bradley, 1984). These growth-promoting processes include basic need gratification; frequent contact with a relatively small number of adults; a positive emotional climate that fosters trust of self and others; appropriate, varied, and patterned sensory input; consistency in the physical, verbal, and emotional responses of others; a minimum of social restrictions on exploratory and motor behavior; structure and order in the daily environment; provision and adult interpretation of varied cultural experiences; appropriate play materials and environment; contact with adults who value achievement; and the cumulative programming of experiences to match the child's developmental level (Caldwell & Bradley, 1984). In brief, then, the purpose of the HOME is to measure specific, designated patterns of nurturance and stimulation available to children in the home.

In order to complete the HOME Inventory, the examiner must observe the child and caregiver (usually the mother) interacting in the home environment. Ratings for a few inventory items are derived from observation of the physical environment. In addition, completion of some items is based upon self-report of the caregiver. Items are dichotomously scored, 1 for present, 0 for absent. For example, one item asks whether the child is included in grocery store shopping at least once a week. The manual for the inventory encourages a relaxed, semistructured approach to observation and interview (Caldwell & Bradley, 1984). Completion of the inventory takes about an hour.

The HOME is available in three forms: Infant and Toddler (ages 0 to 3 years), Early Childhood (ages 3 to 6 years), and Middle Childhood (ages 6 to 10 years). The Infant and Toddler form consists of 45 items organized into the following six subscales:

Emotional and Verbal Responsivity of Parent
Acceptance of the Child's Behavior
Organization of the Environment
Provision of Appropriate Play Materials
Parent Involvement with Child
Variety of Stimulation

The Early Childhood version consists of 55 items organized into eight subscales, whereas the Middle Childhood version consists of 59 items organized into eight subscales. The items for the Infant and Toddler version of the HOME Inventory are listed in Table 10.1. Details on the specific items included in the HOME can be found in Caldwell and Bradley (1984).

Technical Features

Relevant norms for the HOME Inventory are available from several sources. For the Infant and Toddler version, Caldwell and Bradley (1984) report subscale means and standard deviations for 174 families from Little Rock, Arkansas. Compared to the general population, this sample appears to overrepresent lower-SES families. For example, 34 percent of the families were on welfare, and 29 percent were single-parent households. For the Early Childhood version, standardization data were available from 232 families in Little Rock, with lower-SES families similarly overrepresented. For the Middle Childhood version, Bradley

and Rock (1985) report subscale means and standard deviations for 141 families from Little Rock. Approximately half of these families were African-American, the remainder caucasian; boys and girls were sampled equally. These families were thought to be representative of all families rearing elementary-aged children in Little Rock, Arkansas. However, for all three versions it is clear that the standardization samples provide only local norms. These data may be useful as points of reference but should not be equated with a stratified, random, national sample.

The reliability of the HOME Inventory has been demonstrated in a variety of ways, particularly for the Infant and Toddler version, which we discuss here. The authors note that short-term test-retest studies are inappropriate, since a respondent is quite likely to remember a specific answer given to a question, which would artificially inflate test-retest correlations (Bradley & Caldwell, 1984). Methods used for the assessment of reliability included interobserver agreement, internal consistency, and long-range test-retest stability coefficients for 91 families from the standardization sample. By definition, interobserver agreement for the subscale items is reported to be 90 percent or higher, since this is the training criterion for new raters. Internal consistency estimates using Kuder-Richardson Formula 20 ranged from .67 to .89 for all subscales except Variety of Stimulation, which yielded a coefficient of only .44. This rather low reliability coefficient was due to the small number of items in the subscale (five). Test-retest data were available from 91 families tested when their infant/toddler was 6, 12, and 24 months of age. The coefficients indicated a moderate to high degree of stability for the subscales, with most correlations in the .50s, .60s, and .70s. The correlation between total score for testings at 12 and 24 months of age was a highly respectable .77.

The validity of the HOME Inventory has been bolstered by research findings that show modest correlations with SES indices. Because the inventory was proposed as a more meaningful, sensitive index of environment than social class, HOME

TABLE 10.1 List of Subscales and Items for the Infant and Toddler Version of the HOME Inventory

HOME Inventory

Place a plus (+) or minus (–) in the box alongside each item if the behavior is observed during the visit or if the parent reports that the conditions or events are characteristic of the home environment. Enter the subtotal and the total on the front side of the Record Sheet.

I. Emotional and Verbal RESPONSIVITY

☐ 1. Parent spontaneously vocalized to child twice.
☐ 2. Parent responds verbally to child's verbalizations.
☐ 3. Parent tells child name of object or person during visit.
☐ 4. Parent's speech is distinct and audible.
☐ 5. Parent initiates verbal exchanges with visitor.
☐ 6. Parent converses freely and easily.
☐ 7. Parent permits child to engage in "messy" play.
☐ 8. Parent spontaneously praises child at least twice.
☐ 9. Parent's voice conveys positive feelings toward child.
☐ 10. Parent caresses or kisses child at least once.
☐ 11. Parent responds positively to praise of child offered by visitor.
☐ Subtotal

II. ACCEPTANCE of Child's Behavior

☐ 12. Parent does not shout at child.
☐ 13. Parent does not express annoyance with or hostility to child.
☐ 14. Parent neither slaps nor spanks child during visit.
☐ 15. No more than one instance of physical punishment during past week.
☐ 16. Parent does not scold or criticize child during the visit.
☐ 17. Parent does not interfere or restrict child more than 3 times.
☐ 18. At least ten books are present and visible.
☐ 19. Family has a pet.
☐ Subtotal

III. ORGANIZATION of Environment

☐ 20. Substitute care is provided by one of three regular substitutes.
☐ 21. Child is taken to grocery store at least once/week.
☐ 22. Child gets out of house at least four times/week.
☐ 23. Child is taken regularly to doctor's office or clinic.
☐ 24. Child has a special place for toys and treasures.
☐ 25. Child's play environment is safe.
☐ Subtotal

IV. Provision of PLAY MATERIALS

☐ 26. Muscle activity toys or equipment.
☐ 27. Push or pull toy.
☐ 28. Stroller or walker, kiddie car, scooter, or tricycle.
☐ 29. Parent provides toys for child during visit.
☐ 30. Learning equipment appropriate to age—cuddly toys or role-playing toys.
☐ 31. Learning facilitators—mobile, table and chairs, high chair, play pen.
☐ 32. Simple eye-hand coordination toys.
☐ 33. Complex eye-hand coordination toys (those permitting combination).
☐ 34. Toys for literature and music.
☐ Subtotal

V. Parental INVOLVEMENT with Child

☐ 35. Parent keeps child in visual range, looks at often.
☐ 36. Parent talks to child while doing household work.
☐ 37. Parent consciously encourages developmental advance.
☐ 38. Parent invents maturing toys with value via personal attention.
☐ 39. Parent structures child's play periods.
☐ 40. Parent provides toys that challenge child to develop new skills.
☐ Subtotal

VI. Opportunities for VARIETY

☐ 41. Father provides some care daily.
☐ 42. Parent reads stories to child at least 3 times weekly.
☐ 43. Child eats at least one meal per day with mother and father.
☐ 44. Family visits relatives or receives visits once a month or so.
☐ 45. Child has 3 or more books of his/her own.
☐ Subtotal

☐ TOTAL SCORE

For complete wording of items, please refer to the Administration Manual.

Source: Reprinted with permission from Caldwell, B. M., and Bradley, R. H. (1984). *Home Observation for Measurement of the Environment.* Little Rock, AR: University of Arkansas at Little Rock.

scores should be significantly but not highly related to SES indices. For the Infant and Toddler version, HOME Inventory subscale correlations with SES are mainly in the .30s and .40s, while the total score-SES correlation is .45 (Bradley, Rock, Caldwell, & Brisby, 1989).

HOME scores also show strong, theory-confirming relationships with appropriate external criteria, including language and cognitive development, school failure, therapeutic intervention, and mental retardation (Caldwell & Bradley, 1984). The correlations between HOME scores and intellectual measures such as the Bayley Scales of Infant Development and the Stanford-Binet are particularly informative. Bradley and Caldwell (1984) conducted a longitudinal study with 174 families, administering the HOME at 6, 12, and 24 months of age and correlating these scores with the Bayley Mental Development Index (MDI) at 12 months and with Stanford-Binet IQ at 36 months and 54 months of age. The pattern of correlations indicated stronger predictive than concurrent validity, that is, HOME-IQ correlations at 36 months and 54 months of age were higher than HOME-MDI correlations at 12 months of age (Table 10.2). Factor-analytic studies of the HOME also support the construct validity of this instrument (Bradley, Mundfrom, Whiteside, and others, 1994; Mundfrom, Bradley, & Whiteside, 1993).

In addition to its usefulness as a research tool, the HOME shows promise as a clinical instrument. Because low HOME scores are predictive of risk for intellectual disability, the inventory can be used to identify children for whom remedial intervention would be appropriate. This kind of intervention is more than just a humanistic application of research findings—it may be required by law:

> Among the more compelling new reasons for investigating the environments of handicapped children is the requirement in P. L. 99–457 that all service plans for preschool-age handicapped children include a component for parents. It will no longer be sufficient to have a plan of remediation aimed exclusively at the child. Plans for parental

TABLE 10.2   Correlations between HOME Scores at 12 months and Cognitive Scores at 12, 36, and 54 Months

HOME Subscale	MDI at 12 months	IQ at 36 months	IQ at 54 months
Responsivity	.15	.39*	.34*
Restriction	.01	.24*	.21
Organization	.20	.39*	.34*
Play Materials	.28*	.56*	.52*
Involvement	.28*	.47*	.36*
Variety	.05	.28*	.32*
Total Score	.30*	.58*	.53*

*p <.05.

Note: MDI refers to the Mental Development Index from the Bayley Scales of Infant Development; IQ is from the Stanford-Binet.

Source: Reprinted with permission from Bradley, R. H., and Caldwell, B. M. (1984). 174 children: A study of the relationship between home environment and cognitive development during the first 5 years. In A. W. Gottfried (ed.), *Home environment and early cognitive development: Longitudinal research.* Orlando, FL: Academic Press.

involvement and for developing the capacities of parents must also be included (Bradley, Rock, Caldwell, & Brisby, 1989).

In sum, the HOME inventory shows promise not only in research, but also as a practical adjunct to intervention.

INTELLECTUAL EVALUATION OF PRESCHOOL CHILDREN

By definition screening tests are less accurate than comprehensive assessments, that is, they merely signal the need for further evaluation. As part of any follow-up evaluation, a practitioner would administer a variety of instruments, almost certainly including an individual intelligence test. Although test scores of preschoolers on intelligence measures are notoriously unstable in the long run, in the short run there is probably no better index of whether a child is at-risk for school failure.

Several individually administered intelligence tests are suitable for preschool children. The most widely used are the Stanford-Binet: Fourth Edition (SB:FE), the Wechsler Preschool and Primary Scale of Intelligence (WPPSI-R), the Kaufman Assessment Battery for Children (K-ABC), and the Differential Ability Scales (DAS). These instruments were reviewed in an earlier topic.

ASSESSMENT OF LEARNING DISABILITIES AND RELATED DISORDERS

The learning disability (LD) field is one the fastest growing areas within assessment. Paradoxically, it is also one of the most controversial and perplexing domains of psychological testing. Considerable background is needed to understand the role of psychological tests in the evaluation of learning disabilities. We begin by asking a seemingly simple question that turns out to have a complicated answer: What is a **learning disability**?

The Federal Definition of Learning Disabilities

For decades the essential nature of learning disabilities has been understood in terms of a definition embedded in federal law. In 1975, Congress passed Public Law 94–142, the Education for All Handicapped Children Act. One of the provisions of this act was a definition of learning disabilities as follows:

> The term "specific learning disability" means a disorder in one or more of the basic psychological processes involved in understanding or in using language, spoken or written, which may manifest itself in imperfect ability to listen, speak, read, write, spell, or to do mathematical calculations. The term includes such conditions as perceptual handicaps, brain injury, minimal brain dysfunction, dyslexia, and developmental aphasia. The

term does not include children who have learning disabilities which are primarily the result of visual, hearing, or motor handicaps, of mental retardation, or emotional disturbance, or of environmental, cultural, or economic disadvantage (USDE, 1977, p. 65083).

The commitment to a federally mandated definition was reaffirmed in 1990 by passage of Public Law 101–476, the Individuals with Disabilities Education Act (IDEA). Slightly more than half of the states in the United States now follow this model. The remaining states mandate similar approaches (Lerner, 1993).

The federal definition embodied in IDEA also stipulates an operational approach to the identification of children with learning disabilities. Specifically, candidates for an LD diagnosis must demonstrate a severe discrepancy between general ability (intelligence) and specific achievement in one or more of these seven areas:

Oral expression
Listening comprehension
Written expression
Basic reading skill
Reading comprehension
Mathematics calculation
Mathematics reasoning

The discrepancy model for the identification of LD children has functioned as a directive for school psychologists. In effect, the model mandates that psychologists should administer an individual intelligence test (general ability measure) and an individual achievement test (specific achievement measure) and then look for a discrepancy between Full Scale IQ and one or more areas of school achievement (e.g., reading, mathematics, written expression).

In practical terms, a severe discrepancy has been defined as a difference of one standard deviation or more between general intelligence and specific achievement. A common practice in identification of LD children is to compare Full Scale IQ on an individual intelligence test such as the

WISC-III with specific achievement scores on an individual achievement test such as the WIAT (Wechsler Individual Achievement Test) or similar instrument which has subtests normed with a mean of 100 and a standard deviation of 15. A difference of 15 points or more between Full Scale IQ and specific achievement in any of the previously listed areas would then raise the suspicion of learning disability.

Unfortunately, the federal definition has not served its intended purposes and, increasingly, school psychologists and other professionals look to other approaches for understanding and assessing learning disabilities in children. The fundamental problem is that many, many children who exhibit serious learning problems in school and who would benefit from services for LD simply do not meet the psychometric criteria of a severe discrepancy. This is because a learning disability may adversely affect performance on *both* the intelligence and the achievement measures used to diagnose it, resulting in a test profile that does not fit the discrepancy model but nonetheless is LD (Shaw, Cullen, McGuire, & Brinckerhoff, 1995). Another problem is that individual states have adopted different discrepancy formulas, such that a child is viewed as LD in one location, but not another. Not only does this create confusion, it undermines the integrity of the entire enterprise of LD identification.

Emerging Consensus: A New Definition of Learning Disabilities

After a lengthy period of confusion and struggle over the definition of learning disabilities, specialists and educators began to rally around a consensus view in the early 1990s. The new definition was proposed by the National Joint Committee on Learning Disabilities (NJCLD), a group of representatives from eight national organizations with a special interest in learning disabilities. Although similar to the federal definition, the new approach contains important contrasts:

> *Learning disabilities* is a general term that refers to a heterogeneous group of disorders manifested by significant difficulties in the acquisition and use of listening, speaking, reading, writing, reasoning, or mathematical abilities. These disorders are intrinsic to the individual, presumed to be due to central nervous system dysfunction, and may occur across the life span. Problems in self-regulatory behaviors, social perception and social interaction may exist with learning disabilities but do not by themselves constitute a learning disability. Although learning disabilities may occur concomitantly with other handicapping conditions (for example, sensory impairment, mental retardation (MR), serious emotional disturbance (ED)) or with extrinsic influences (such as cultural differences, insufficient or inappropriate instruction), they are not the result of those conditions or influences (NJCLD, 1988, p. 1).

The new definition avoids vague reference to "basic psychological processes," specifies that the disorder is intrinsic to the individual, identifies central nervous system dysfunction as the origin of LD problems, and states explicitly that learning disabilities may extend into adulthood.

Perhaps most important of all, the NJCLD approach abandons the excessive reliance upon discrepancy between ability and achievement as the hallmark of LD. Instead, the new model specifies that the necessary (but not sufficient) condition of LD is that the individual (child or adult) exhibit an intraindividual weakness in one or more of the core areas of academic functioning (listening, speaking, reading, writing, reasoning, or mathematical abilities). Shaw et al. (1995) illustrate how the NJCLD model might look in practice (Figure 10.1). In this approach, the first task is to identify one or more intraindividual weaknesses in the core areas. These are always relative to strengths in several other core areas. In other words, persons who are slow learners in all areas do not meet the criteria of LD. The second step is to trace the learning difficulties to central nervous system dysfunction, which may manifest as problems with information processing. For example, a young adult with a severe weakness in listening

Step 1. Intraindividual Discrepancy

The examiner identifies a significant difficulty in one or more core areas alongside relative strengths in several areas. Core Areas: Listening, Speaking, Reading, Writing, Reasoning, Math, Subject Area.

Step 2. Discrepancy Intrinsic to the Individual

The examiner traces the discrepancy to central nervous system dysfunction (e.g., brain injury) or links the discrepancy with information-processing problems (e.g., memory, organization, or learning efficiency).

Step 3. Related Considerations

The examiner evaluates the relevance of psychosocial skills, physical abilities, and sensory abilities to the learning disability.

Step 4. Alternative Explanations

The examiner rules out alternative explanations, e.g., environmental, cultural, or economic factors; or inappropriate or inadequate instruction.

Step 5. LD Diagnosis

The examiner determines that children who pass steps 1 through 4 meet the criteria for an LD diagnosis.

FIGURE 10.1 Operationalizing the NJCLD Definition of Learning Disability
Source: Based on Brinckerhoff, L., Shaw, S., & McGuire, J. (1993). *Promoting Postsecondary Education for Students with Learning Disabilities: A Handbook for Practitioners.* Austin, TX: PRO-ED.

(as judged by her inability to learn from the traditional lecture approach to teaching) might exhibit a deficit on a test of verbal memory—confirming that an information-processing problem was at the heart of her disability. The purpose of the third step (examining psychosocial skills, physical and sensory abilities) is to specify additional problems that may need to be addressed for program-planning purposes. Finally, in the fourth step the examiner rules out non-LD explanations for the learning difficulties (since these explanations would mandate a different strategy for remediation).

Hammill (1990) has noted wisely that political realities are such that the NJCLD definition may never replace the federally mandated approach. But this is less important than whether parents and professionals unite around one definition for purposes of research and communication with one another. At the present time, the NJCLD definition has received the strongest general support from professionals in the field of assessment.

Although we will not discuss additional viewpoints here, we can refer the reader to several other respected models of learning disabilities (*Special Education Today,* 1985; Lerner, 1993; Lyon, 1994). Offered many years ago, the wise counsel of Farnham-Diggory (1978) is still worth mentioning in this context. Shortly after Public Law 94–142 was activated in 1977 with its influential definition of learning disabilities, she wrote:

> Publishing this definition has amounted to waving a red flag in front of a herd of bulls—parents and professionals alike. Far from clarifying the situation, the definition inspired so much snorting and ground-pawing that the conceptual dust has grown thicker than ever. Part of the problem arises from the fact that we lose sight of what a definition is for. Definitions are not truth: they merely set up the conditions under which particular actions are to be taken (Farnham-Diggory, 1978).

The actions referred to may include research investigations, diagnostic assessments, and/or educational interventions. But whatever response is undertaken, we must guard against the proclivity to view definitions as true or false. Definitions are merely human inventions with greater or lesser utility, nothing more.

Essential Features of Learning Disabilities

Even though the definition of LD remains a point of contention, we can cite several features of these disorders which are less controversial. As the reader will discover, the features discussed in the following dictate, to some extent, the nature of testing practices in the assessment of learning disabilities. There is general agreement—with occasional dissenting votes—on the following features of learning disabilities:

1. A learning disability involves an intraindividual discrepancy in cognitive functioning. The child (or adult) with LD reveals a relative weakness in one area compared to strengths in most other areas. According to the federal definition followed within many school systems, the discrepancy is between general ability (intelligence) and specific achievement. We have described previously some of the pitfalls of this definition and prefer the NJCLD approach in which the discrepancy is not rigidly tied to a difference between IQ and achievement test scores.

2. An exclusionary clause is included in most definitions of learning disability. If the academic difficulties are primarily caused by other disabling conditions (mental retardation, emotional disturbance, visual or hearing impairment, cultural or social disadvantage), then a diagnosis of learning disability is typically ruled out. This clause is often misinterpreted. A person can be both learning disabled and impaired in other ways (e.g., mentally retarded). The important point is that the coexisting condition must not be the primary cause of the learning difficulties.

3. Learning disabilities are heterogeneous, that is, there are many different varieties. Research on the identification of subtypes is still in its infancy, but most researchers express optimism that meaningful subgroups of learning-disabled persons can be identified. Pending further research and refinement, only two broad categories of learning disability are recognized currently (Forster, 1994). These are as follows:

- Dyslexia or verbal learning disability
- Right hemisphere or nonverbal learning disability.

The characteristics of these two major categories of LD are outlined in Table 10.3. These patterns have emerged in many studies of LD children. For example, Blakely, Crinella, Fisher, Champaigne, and Beck (1994) distinguished

TABLE 10.3 Characteristics of Two Broad Categories of Learning Disability

	Dyslexia or Verbal Learning Disability	*Right Hemisphere or Nonverbal Learning Disability*
Primary Manifestation	Unexpected difficulty in learning to read or spell	Poor skills in mathematics, handwriting, or social cognition
Fundamental Deficiency	Problems in phonological coding (associating sounds with letter combinations)	Problems in spatial cognition (visuospatial perception of relationships)
Physiological Correlates	Subtle anomalies in the left cerebral hemisphere (revealed by brain scans and EEG studies)	Likely origin in right cerebral hemisphere dysfunction
Relative Prevalence	About 90% of all LD cases	About 10% of all LD cases
Ratio of boys to girls	3:1 or 4:1	1:1

Source: Based on Forster, A. (1994). Learning disabilities. In R. J. Sternberg (ed.), *Encyclopedia of human intelligence.* New York: Macmillan.

both a verbal LD and a nonverbal LD in a sophisticated analysis of neuropsychological test scores for 177 children 9 to 14 years of age. The sample consisted of 129 children with LD (including 37 with verified brain damage) and 48 children with no evidence of LD or brain damage. Six patterns of neuropsychological performance were identified by means of a complex statistical clustering method:

1. *Very Low IQ:* Children with very low IQ but otherwise nondiscrepant test scores
2. *Low IQ:* Children with low IQ but otherwise nondiscrepant test scores
3. *Clumsy/Lethargic:* Children whose test scores indicate clumsiness and lethargy
4. *Language Dysfunction:* Children with relatively low scores on language variables
5. *Spatial Dysfunction:* Children with good verbal function but faulty spatial orientation
6. *No Deficit:* Children with no detectable deficits

Groups 4 and 5 correspond to the major categories of LD listed previously (verbal and nonverbal LD), whereas the other groups signify normalcy (group 6), low intellectual ability (groups 1 and 2), or variant forms of possible LD (group 3). Of course, some of the children in groups 1 and 2 might meet the criteria for LD when assessed with additional tests.

4. A learning disability is a developmental phenomenon that is usually evident in early childhood and which may persist into adulthood. Even though remediation efforts should be based upon optimism—so as to avoid self-fulfilling prophecies—a dose of realism is needed, too. Longitudinal studies of severely learning-disabled children suggest that marked improvement in academic achievement is the exception, not the rule, even when these subjects receive intensive educational intervention. For example, Frauenheim and Heckerl (1983) retested 11 adults diagnosed as learning disabled in childhood. All the participants had received special help for reading; nine had graduated from high school, and two completed the tenth grade. Full Scale IQs were

typically in the low 90s, with Verbal IQ below average (mean of 85) and Performance IQ above average (mean of 104). In spite of the remedial intervention, when retested as adults on *exactly* the same achievement test (Wide Range Achievement Test), these examinees were scarcely improved from their elementary school results. These findings are corroborated by several other follow-up studies (see Kolb & Whishaw, 1990, chp. 29, for a review). Such results indicate that specialists who work with learning-disabled children should not become fixated solely upon academic concerns. Social and emotional problems—which may be more amenable to intervention—also cry out for notice.

5. Learning-disabled individuals frequently experience social and emotional difficulties that are as pervasive and consequential as the deficits in academic achievement. These problems may persist into adolescence and adulthood. In fact, the socioemotional sequelae often become the primary presenting complaint, which can complicate the testing process and obscure the diagnosis. For example, in a needs assessment study of 381 learning-disabled adults, Hoffman, Sheldon, Minskoff, and others (1987) identified several crucial nonacademic areas meriting intervention by service providers. These adults self-endorsed several social and emotional problems with high frequency: feeling frustrated (40 percent), talking or acting before thinking (33 percent), being shy (31 percent), no self-confidence (28 percent), controlling emotions and temper (28 percent), and dating (27 percent). Many other problems were also endorsed, but by less than 25 percent of the sample. These findings indicate that learning disability assessments should incorporate measures of social and emotional functioning. Vaughn and Haager (1994) provide an excellent overview on the measurement of social skills in persons with learning disability.

Causes and Correlates of Learning Disabilities

Approximately 4 percent of all school-aged children receive a diagnosis of LD, so this is not a rare problem (Chalfant, 1989). The most common form of LD is dyslexia, and boys outnumber girls by about 3:2 (Nass, 1992). In a minority of cases, the etiology is clear and can be attributed to a specific cause such as a known brain injury. The reader will recall from Chapter 9 that left hemisphere impairment is especially likely to result in verbal difficulties whereas right hemisphere impairment may lead to problems with spatial thinking or other nonverbal skills. Thus, head injury or other neurological problems can be the proximate cause of a child receiving an LD diagnosis.

However, in the majority of cases the direct etiology of LD problems is unclear. A number of possibilities have been proposed and these may explain some but not all cases of LD. For example, pathological neurodevelopmental processes have been identified in some persons with severe dyslexia (Culbertson & Edmonds, 1996). Individuals with this disorder appear to have alterations in brain structures such as the planum temporale (the flat surface on the top of the temporal lobes) known to be important for language processing. Whereas in normal individuals the planum temporale is much larger in the left temporal lobe than in the right, persons with severe dyslexia do not show this pattern of asymmetry (tending toward symmetry instead). Moreover, researchers have identified microscopic cortical malformations called polymicrogyria (numerous small convolutions) that parallel these structural differences. Several postmortem studies of persons with severe dyslexia have revealed these deviations at the cellular level. Dyslexia also appears to show a significant genetic component for some persons such that the idea of familial dyslexia needs to be taken seriously. However, what needs to be emphasized is that for most individuals the etiology of LD (whether dyslexia or other forms) remains a mystery.

Assessment of Learning Disabilities

Learning disabilities manifest primarily as academic problems, that is, an LD child is typically unable to master skills important for school success such as reading, mathematics, or written communication. Because school-based accomplishment is at the heart of the problem, an evaluation for LD must include relevant measures of academic achievement. Furthermore, the evaluation of school achievement—one small part of an LD assessment—must be based upon an *individual* test of achievement. Even though a group achievement test might raise the suspicion of a learning disability, practitioners must rely upon individual achievement tests for definitive assessment. We explain why this is so and then review useful instruments for achievement testing.

Individual achievement tests typically are administered one on one with the examiner sitting across from the respondent and posing structured questions and problems. Of course, any well-standardized achievement test will yield normative data about the functioning of a schoolchild. But the special virtue of individual achievement tests is that the examiner can observe the clinical details of deficient (or superior) performance and form hypotheses about the cognitive capacities of the examinee.

Consider the problem of poor spelling, widely observed in children and adults with verbal LD. Any good spelling achievement test will document the disability; however, little insight is gained from mere scores. What the examiner should seek to know is the qualitative nature of the problem, not just its quantitative dimensions. Individual achievement tests are invaluable in this regard. By observing the details of deficient performance, an astute examiner can form hypotheses about the origin of an achievement problem. For example, a child whose spelling is phonetically correct is at least *hearing* the words correctly, whereas a child with nonphonetic spelling might very well reveal a problem with auditory processing of speech sounds.

Individual Achievement Tests

More than a dozen individually administered achievement tests exist, but only a few are widely used in the assessment of learning difficulties. Prominent individual achievement tests include the Diagnostic Achievement Battery-Second Edition,

(DAB-2), the Kaufman Test of Educational Achievement (K-TEA), the Mini-Battery of Achievement (MBA), the Peabody Individual Achievement Test-Revised (PIAT-R), the Wechsler Individual Achievement Test (WIAT), the Woodcock-Johnson Psycho-Educational Battery-Revised (WJ-R) and the Wide Range Achievement Test-III (WRAT-III). The essential features of these tests are outlined in Table 10.4. Owing to limitations of space, we will select one test, the K-TEA, for more detailed presentation. Readers who seek further information about individual achievement tests are encouraged to consult Sattler (1988, chp. 13) and the *Mental Measurements Yearbook* series (Conoley & Impara, 1995; Conoley & Kramer, 1989, 1992; Mitchell, 1985).

TABLE 10.4 Survey of Widely Used Individual Achievement Tests

Diagnostic Achievement Battery-2 (DAB-2)
  Newcomer (1990)

Suitable for ages 6 through 14, the DAB-2 consists of 12 subtests used to compute eight diagnostic composites. The composite scores include Listening, Speaking, Reading, Writing, Mathematics, Spoken Language, Written Language, and total Achievement. More comprehensive than most achievement tests, the DAB-2 takes up to two hours to administer. The test was carefully normed on 2,600 children nationwide.

Kaufman Test of Educational Achievement (K-TEA)
  Kaufman & Kaufman (1985)

A well-normed individual test of educational achievement, a special feature of the K-TEA is the detailed error analysis (see text). Currently, norms extend only through high school age. A separate brief form that can be administered in 30 minutes or less is useful for screening purposes.

Mini-Battery of Achievement (MBA)
  Woodcock, McGrew, & Werder (1994)

Assesses four broad achievement areas—reading, writing, mathematics, and factual knowledge—for persons ages 4 through 90+. The complete battery can be administered in 30 minutes. The MBA provides a more extensive coverage of basic and applied skills than any other brief battery. For example, the reading component assesses letter-word identification, vocabulary, and comprehension.

Peabody Individual Achievement Test-Revised
  (PIAT-R)   Markwardt (1989)

For ages 5 through 18, this 60-minute test includes subtests of general information, reading recognition, reading comprehension, mathematics, and spelling. A new subtest, written expression, is now offered for screening written language skills. Administration of the PIAT-R requires minimal training; the test can be administered by properly trained classroom teachers.

Wechsler Individual Achievement Test (WIAT)
  Wechsler (1992)

The Wechsler Individual Achievement Test consists of eight subtests: basic reading, mathematics reasoning, spelling, reading comprehension, numerical operations, oral expression, listening comprehension, and written expression. Suitable for ages 5 through 19, the WIAT is co-normed with the WISC-III. Administration to older subjects can take up to 75 minutes. A shorter WIAT Screener (basic reading, mathematics reasoning, spelling) can be administered in 10 to 15 minutes.

Woodcock-Johnson-Revised (WJ-R)
  Woodcock & Johnson (1989)

The Woodcock-Johnson-Revised covers individuals from 2 years of age through adulthood. The full battery encompasses three areas of functioning: achievement, cognitive ability, and interest. The nine standard achievement tests yield cluster scores in areas labeled Broad Reading, Broad Mathematics, Broad Written Language, Broad Knowledge, and Skills. The achievement tests are widely respected, but some reviewers recommend caution in the use of the cognitive battery.

Wide Range Achievement Test-III (WRAT-III)
  Wilkinson (1993)

Well-normed for ages 5 through 75, the WRAT-III is widely used as a screening instrument. The subtests include reading, spelling, and arithmetic. The major weakness of the battery is the reading subtest, which is really only a measure of word recognition. The reading subtest consists of asking the examinee to pronounce aloud each word from a list ranging from simple to difficult. Because of the limited item content and the high intercorrelations among the subtests, the WRAT-R is unsuited for the identification of specific skill deficits.

Kaufman Test of Educational Achievement (K-TEA)

The K-TEA is an untimed test of educational achievement for children ages 6 through 18. A brief, three-subtest version exists, but for diagnostic assessment of learning difficulties the Comprehensive Form is preferred. The K-TEA Comprehensive Form consists of five subtests: Reading Decoding, Reading Comprehension, Mathematics Applications, Mathematics Computation, and Spelling. Testing time is approximately one hour for older examinees, but somewhat less for younger children.

Brief examples of K-TEA-like items are shown in Table 10.5. These examples would be at the upper end of the subtests, appropriate for high school students. The K-TEA utilizes entry and exit rules for each subtest to insure that students only

---

TABLE 10.5   Examples of Characteristic K-TEA Items Applicable to Older Children

Reading Decoding

The examiner points to each word in turn and says, "What word is this?"

duodecagon   obstreperous   correlative
indolence   perspicacity

Reading Comprehension

The examiner says, "Do what this says."

Utter a fallacious response to the question, "How many eyes does a cyclops have?"

Spelling

The examiner explains the rules for a traditional spelling test concluding with, "I want you to write the word on this sheet."

"Paramour. One's lover is called a paramour."

Mathematics Computation

The examiner says "Now I want you to work these problems."

$(X - 7)(X - 9) =$ 5 lb.   5 oz.
                           -2 lb. 14 oz.

Mathematics Application

The examiner says, "The Missoula Muggers played 80 ballgames last year. They won 16 games. What percentage of the games did they win?"

---

encounter items of appropriate difficulty. Scoring is completely objective, one for correct items, zero for incorrect items. Raw scores are converted to standard scores (mean of 100, SD of 15) for each subtest, the reading composite, the mathematics composite, and the entire battery composite.

In addition to formal scoring, the K-TEA provides a systematic method for evaluating the qualitative nature of subtest errors. For example, on the spelling subtest, errors can be classified according to whether they involve prefixes, suffixes, vowel digraphs (such as *ue* in *blue*) and diphthongs, consonant clusters (such as *scr* in *unscrupulous*), r-controlled patterns (such as *er* in *inferior*), and several other patterns.

Kaufman and Kaufman (1985) stress that the error analysis provides the diagnostician with a source of information from which instructional objectives can be developed. For example, a weakness in vowel digraphs and diphthongs on the spelling subtest translates directly to classroom objectives: practice in the spelling and reading of these elements in isolation, progressing to spelling and pronouncing words containing digraphs and diphthongs, and ending in writing and reading sentences containing words with vowel digraphs and diphthongs. The K-TEA *Manual* contains many useful clinical insights with educational ramifications.

Although the normative samples of the K-TEA and the description of their characteristics are a model of excellence, the technical characteristics of this instrument vary in adequacy. Split-half reliabilities for the five subtests range from .87 to .96, quite acceptable values for an achievement test. Stability data are less clear. Data for 172 students who were retested within 35 days were collapsed for grades 1 to 6 and grades 7 to 12. All correlations for subtests and composites exceeded .90, but these values are likely inflated because they confound stability of achievement with grade × achievement correlations.

The content validity of the K-TEA appears to be very strong, but this point may vary from one school system to another. After all, individual school systems may choose to emphasize different

CASE EXHIBIT
10.1

A TEST BATTERY IN LEARNING DISABILITY ASSESSMENT

Jimmy is a nine-year-old boy referred by his pediatrician for evaluation of possible learning disability. Parents and teachers characterized Jimmy as distractible, quiet, appealing, but lazy about doing his schoolwork, especially written assignments. Often it appeared that he was not paying attention to what the teacher was saying. The purpose of the assessment was to determine whether Jimmy could be characterized as LD and also to offer recommendations for remediation.

The examiner used standard instruments such as the WISC-III and the Woodcock-Johnson Psychoeducational Battery-Revised (WJ-R) but also supplemented these with measures tailored to specific referral concerns (e.g., problems with distractibility and auditory comprehension). What the test battery revealed was a picture of generally adequate intellectual ability (WISC-III Full Scale IQ of 100) with relative weakness in verbal areas (e.g., Verbal Comprehension Index of 89) and relative strength in nonverbal areas such as perceptual organization, visual memory, and visual-motor integration (e.g., Perceptual Organization Index of 110). Yet in spite of these areas of competence, Jimmy was functioning at a much lower level in at least one academic area (Writing Samples at the 5th percentile). These findings certainly corroborate impressions from the teacher and parents. Descriptively, these results strongly suggested a diagnosis of verbal learning disability, especially since other contributory factors could be ruled out (e.g., emotional disturbance, poor instruction).

The source of his difficulties no doubt had something to do with his extremely poor abilities in auditory comprehension. Jimmy performed in the lowest few percent for children his age on the Test for Auditory Comprehension of Language-Revised (TACL-R) and the Wepman Auditory Discrimination

(continued)

domains of achievement. Salvia and Ysseldyke (1991) warn that users must be sensitive to the correspondence of K-TEA content with the students' curriculum. As with any achievement test, the user should verify that the content of the K-TEA is appropriate within the curricular setting. Nonetheless, Kaufman and Kaufman (1985) offer sufficient evidence for the validity of the test to make a case for general adequacy.

Test Batteries in the Assessment of Learning Disability

Although experts agree that the assessment of a potential learning disability requires a multifaceted approach, there is little consensus as to the best instruments and techniques. Of course, the most essential tools in the assessment of learning-disabled children are reliable and valid measures of intelligence and achievement. Virtually every LD test battery includes mainstream instruments in both areas, for example, SB:FE, WPPSI-R, or WISC-III for intellectual assessment and PIAT-R, K-TEA, WJ-R, or WIAT for measurement of achievement. However, the choice of ancillary measures for examining language skills, specific forms of information processing, or visual-spatial processing will differ from one practitioner to another. Furthermore, many examiners will individualize each test battery in light of the referral issues. In Case Exhibit 10.1,

Test. On the TACL-R the examinee listens to a word or sentence and then points to the black-and-white drawing (from a group of three) that best depicts the meaning. On the Wepman Auditory Discrimination Test, the examiner reads a pair of similar words and the child responds by indicating whether they are the same or different. Difficulties on these two tests strongly indicated that Jimmy exhibited a fundamental deficit in the processing and comprehension of spoken words. This deficit helped explain his problem with written expression (Writing Samples percentile rank of 5). No doubt his attentional difficulties also contributed to the constellation of problems that he experienced.

One important conclusion that emerged from the test results was that Jimmy might learn better from written than verbal instructions. After all, he scored at exactly the average mark for reading skills (Passage Comprehension of 100). Another implication of the findings was that even though he showed some attentional difficulties, these were not so severe as to warrant further evaluation. The main focus for intervention was to accommodate his very significant weaknesses in auditory comprehension.

CASE EXHIBIT *(cont.)*

Summary of Jimmy's Test Results

	Scaled Score Equivalent	Percentile 0 10 30 50 70 90 100	
Verbal Skills			
WISC-III Verbal Comprehension Index	89		24
Test of Word Finding	88		22
Perceptual Organizational Skills			
WISC-III Perceptual Organization Index	110		74
Test of Nonverbal Intelligence-3	109		72
Visual-Motor Integration			
Bender Gestalt	120		91
Developmental Test of VMI	107		68
Auditory Comprehension			
TACL-R (Auditory Comprehension)	72		3
Wepman Auditory Discrimination Test	65		1
Memory			
WRAML Verbal Memory Index	82		12
WRAML Visual Memory Index	99		48
Attentional Skills			
WISC-III Distractibility Index	84		15
Vigilance Task (Gordon System)	82		12
Distractibility Task (Gordon System)	80		9
Academic Achievement			
WJ-R Passage Comprehension	100		50
WJ-R Writing Samples	75		5
WJ-R Calculation	95		37
WJ-R Applied Problems (Math)	110		74

we provide a representative test battery for the LD assessment of Jimmy, a nine-year-old boy with a history of school failure.

ASSESSMENT OF ADHD

Attention-deficit/hyperactivity disorder (ADHD) is the term proposed by the American Psychiatric Association to designate a behavioral syndrome previously known as attention-deficit disorder with hyperactivity, minimal brain dysfunction, and hyperkinesis (American Psychiatric Association, 1994). Children with this disorder often exhibit academic underachievement. Therefore, they are frequently referred for learning disability assessment. However, even though LD and ADHD often coexist and their symptoms overlap slightly, they are conceptually distinct syndromes. Here, we review certain useful instruments designed to help diagnose the ADHD syndrome.

ADHD comes in three varieties: predominantly inattentive, predominantly hyperactive-impulsive, and combined type. The inattentive type is defined by the presence of six or more symptoms of inattention, but fewer than six symptoms of hyperactivity-impulsivity. The hyperactive-impulsive type is defined by the presence of six or more symptoms of hyperactivity-impulsivity, but fewer than six symptoms of inattention. The combined type consists of six or more symptoms in both clusters. In all cases, the symptoms must be present for at least six months and lead to impairment in social, academic, or occupational functioning. The diagnostic symptoms for ADHD are summarized in Table 10.6.

Unfortunately, these official criteria are dispiritingly vague and relatively common even in normal children. No wonder that estimates of hyperactivity range from 3 percent to 20 percent in the school-age population (Cantwell, 1975). To further complicate matters, experts in this field emphasize other elements in the ADHD picture. For example, Barkley (1981) notes that ADHD children are mainly deficient in situations where instructions

TABLE 10.6   Diagnostic Symptoms of Attention-Deficit/Hyperactivity Disorder

**Inattentive Type
(Six or More Symptoms)**

Lack of attention to details

Difficulty sustaining attention

Does not seem to listen

Failure to follow through

Difficulty organizing tasks

Avoids sustained mental effort

Loses things

Easily distracted

Forgetful in daily activities

**Hyperactive-Impulsive Type
(Six or More Symptoms)**

Fidgets and/or squirms

Leaves seat in classroom

Inappropriate running or climbing

Difficulty playing quietly

Seems driven, always on the go

Talks excessively

Blurts out answers

Difficulty waiting turn

Interrupts or intrudes on others

Combined Type

Six or more of the symptoms in each of the above areas

Source: Based on American Psychiatric Association. (1994). *Diagnostic and statistical manual of mental disorders* (4th ed.). Washington, D.C.: Author.

require delayed responding and/or sustained responding according to tightly defined rule systems. He also emphasizes that these children perform poorly when reinforcements are delayed. Thus, in the typical testing environment with interesting tasks and immediate rewards, an ADHD child often will appear quite normal. The examiner who suspects that a child exhibits ADHD faces a daunting diagnostic challenge. Fortunately, several reliable and valid rating systems can be of assistance in making the diagnosis.

Conners (1990, 1991) has produced a family of rating scales that are useful for identifying hyperactivity and other behavioral problems in children. The Conners' Teacher Rating Scales are available in two forms, one containing 28 items (CTRS-28), the other 39 items (CTRS-39). The teacher rates the child on each item on a four-point scale. The two forms yield different scale scores and possess different psychometric properties. The CTRS-28 is normed on 383 children from 3 to 17 years of age and yields three scales: Conduct Problem, Inattentive Passivity, and Hyperactivity. The CTRS-39 is normed on 9,583 children from 4 to 12 years of age and yields six scales: Hyperactivity, Emotional Overindulgent, Asocial, Conduct Problem, Anxious-Passive, and Daydream-Attendance Problem.

The Conners' Parent Rating Scales also come in two forms, one containing 48 items (CPRS-48), the other 93 items (CPRS-93). The CPRS-48 is normed on 6- to 14-year-old children and yields five scales: Conduct Problems, Psychosomatic, Anxiety, Learning Problems, and Impulsive-Hyperactive. The CPRS-93, normed on children between 3 and 17 years of age, includes eight scales: Conduct Disorder, Restless Disorganized, Psychosomatic, Antisocial, Fearful Anxious, Learning Problem-Immature, Obsessional, and Hyperactive-Immature.

On all the Conners scales, parents, teachers, or parent-surrogates rate symptoms on a four-point scale (0–3). The format of the various Conners scales is of the following nature:

	Not at all	Just a little	Pretty much	Very much
Cries easily				
Restless and fidgety				
Acts without thinking				
Disobeys adults				
Gets into trouble				
Daydreams				

Trites, Blouin, and LaPrade (1982) conducted a factor analysis of the CTRS-39 using a large stratified random sample of 9,583 Canadian schoolchildren. The results yielded six factors. The first factor—by far the most prominent factor—was hyperactivity, which loaded on 17 of the 39 items and accounted for 36 percent of the variance. The hyperactivity factor also possessed excellent internal consistency (coefficient alpha of .94). In several other studies of childhood behavior checklists, hyperactivity emerges as the first and most robust factor when scale items are factor analyzed (Trites, 1979).

Validity evidence for the Conners scales is substantial and includes the following (Martens, 1992):

- Scale scores show appropriate changes when hyperactive children are treated with drugs known to improve attention.
- The rating scales possess strong, positive correlations with other rating scales, peer ratings, and independent observations.
- Scale scores discriminate appropriately among diagnostic groups.

In spite of the voluminous research base which supports these instruments, reviewers do express concern about the standardization samples. For example, norms for the CPRS-48 appear to be based on a sample of 529 almost exclusively white children in the Pittsburgh area, which may not be representative of the general population (Martens, 1992; Oehler-Stinnett, 1992).

Test publishers have released an almost dizzying array of checklists for ADHD and other childhood behavior problems in recent years. Most of these instruments are designed for use by parents and teachers in the context of school-based assessment. For example, Achenbach (1991, 1992) has published revised versions of his parent-informant Child Behavior Checklist (CBCL), a highly respected instrument that assesses social problems and academic competence in a wide variety of behavioral domains. We have summarized several newer, more restricted instruments in Table 10.7.

TABLE 10.7 Domains Assessed by Rating Scales for Attention Deficit and Related Disorders

Domains	Scales			
	ACTeRS	ADDES	ADHDT	CAAS
Inattention	*	*	*	*
Conduct/Aggressiveness				*
Hyperactivity	*	*	*	*
Impulsivity		*	*	*
Oppositional	*			
Social Skills	*			

ACTeRS = ADD-H: Comprehensive Teacher's Rating Scale-2nd Edition (Ullman, Sleator, & Sprague, 1988).

ADDES = Attention Deficit Disorders Evaluation Scales (McCarney, 1989).

ADHDT = Attention-Deficit Hyperactivity Disorder Test (Gilliam, 1994).

CAAS = Children's Attention and Adjustment Survey (Lambert, Hartsough, & Sandoval, 1990).

ASSESSMENT OF EMOTIONAL AND BEHAVIORAL DISORDERS

While most children are carefree and enjoy going to school, every teacher can cite cases similar to the following:

> Peter was a nine-year-old third grader whose academic performance was erratic. His parents expressed concern that he was anxious and withdrawn at home. His teacher noted certain "odd" social behaviors such as never looking other children in the eye, screaming and making odd sounds on the playground, and appearing too eager to please other children in games. Peter also seemed excessively concerned about keeping his books, papers, and pencils rigidly ordered on his desk. He would spend many minutes each day arranging and rearranging these materials.

Is something wrong with Peter? What is the role of the school psychologist in dealing with the apparent emotional problems of this child?

In addition to assessment for learning disability, school psychologists also perform evaluations to determine whether children meet the criteria for a serious emotional or behavioral disturbance.

Beginning in 1975 with Public Law 94–142, the U.S. Congress stipulated that children with serious emotional or behavioral disorders were eligible for special services funded indirectly by the federal government. Hence, for purposes of identification, funding, and treatment, school psychologists need to determine whether designated children are emotionally disturbed or behaviorally disordered.

The federal law classifies these children as "seriously emotionally disturbed" (SED). The process by which a student is identified as SED involves interviews with parents and teachers, evaluation with behavior rating scales, and direct classroom observation. The goal is to identify children who exhibit inappropriate behaviors, feelings, or patterns of social interaction. We focus here upon the role of behavior rating scales in this process, because they provide a relatively objective approach to assessment.

In a child behavior rating scale, key informants such as parents and teachers are asked to rate a child on relatively discrete behaviors such as *likes to be alone, gets in fights, talkative, accident-prone, gets along with others,* and the like. The ratings can be dichotomous (yes-no) but more commonly are along a three- or four-point continuum (e.g., never, occasionally, frequently, always). The items are grouped into factor-analytically derived scales which yield percentiles or other scores in reference to standardization samples of reasonably normal (i.e., nonreferred) children. Several dozen behavior rating scales have been developed according to this strategy. A few of the most widely used instruments of this nature are identified in Table 10.8. We focus here upon a tool with extensive empirical underpinnings, the Child Behavior Checklist (Achenbach, 1991).

TABLE 10.8 A Brief Listing of Representative Child Behavior Rating Scales

---

Revised Behavior Problem Checklist (Quay & Peterson, 1983)

This scale consists of 89 items, each rated on a three-point severity scale; the scale yields six primary dimensions: conduct problems, socialized aggression, attention problems, anxiety-withdrawal, psychotic behavior, and motor excess.

Behavior Assessment System for Children (Reynolds & Kamphaus, 1992)

This scale is an omnibus instrument that includes parent, teacher, and child versions; the scale yields scores in broad externalizing and internalizing domains as well as in specific content areas, including aggression, hyperactivity, conduct problems, attention problems, depression, anxiety, withdrawal, somatization, and social skills.

Home Situations Questionnaire (Barkley & Edelbrock, 1987)

This scale consists of 16 items pertaining to home situations in which noncompliant behavior may occur (e.g., child is asked to do chores); parents rate each item on a nine-point scale.

Social Skills Rating System (Gresham & Elliott, 1990)

Available in parent, teacher, and self-rating forms, this is a 55-item questionnaire that provides specific information in three domains (social skills, problem behaviors, and academic competence).

Child Behavior Checklist

The Child Behavior Checklist (CBCL) is one of the most carefully designed and thoroughly developed scales in all of clinical psychology. Actually, the instrument comes in several different forms depending upon the age of the child and whether it is to be filled out by parents or teachers. We restrict our discussion here to the CBCL/4–18, suitable for parents' reports of competencies and problems in children ages 4 through 18 (Achenbach, 1991). The origin of this multidimensional tool dates back to 1966 when Achenbach analyzed over 600 clinical case histories of children to identify discrete symptoms that were relatively easy to observe and also general as opposed to excessively specific. Further research and consultation resulted in the 100+ items that comprise the behavior-problem portion of the CBCL. These items are rated 0 (not true as far as you know), 1 (somewhat or sometimes true), or 2 (very true or often true). In addition, the instrument includes items that tap social competency in three broad categories: activities, social, and school.

Based upon numerous factor-analytic studies, Achenbach discovered that parents tend to portray children's problems along eight dimensions: Aggressive Behavior, Anxious/Depressed, Attention Problems, Delinquent Behavior, Social Problems, Somatic Complaints, Thought Problems, and Withdrawn. These scale patterns were derived from factor analysis of ratings for 4,455 clinically referred children. Results are reported as percentiles in comparison to a normative sample of 2,368 nonreferred children. In addition to individual scale scores, the CBCL yields an Internalizing score (problems are internalized), an Externalizing score (problems are externalized), and a Total Problem score (reflective of overall maladjustment).

Consider the test results for Peter, the troubled third grader described previously. One valuable feature of the CBCL is that ratings for both parents can be compared as a kind of reliability check. The percentile ranks for the ratings from his mother and father, respectively, are listed below, with higher scores indicating a greater problem:

Aggressive Behavior	52, 65
Anxious/Depressed	98, 91
Attention Problems	98, 98
Delinquent Behavior	34, 45
Social Problems	93, 91
Somatic Complaints	88, 89
Thought Problems	98, 77
Withdrawn	95, 95
Total Problem score	98, 98

Overall the results are within the clinical range (Total Problem score at the 98th percentile). The individual scales indicate that Peter is perceived as highly withdrawn, anxious/depressed, with possible thought problems (e.g., odd or peculiar thoughts) and a distinct difficulty paying attention. Further assessment by the school psychologist revealed an average range intelligence (Full Scale IQ of 94) with a huge discrepancy between verbal ability (VIQ of 110) and performance ability (PIQ of 79). In interview, Peter revealed loose, disordered thinking and marked distractibility. Overall the results indicated that he qualified as SED and was deserving of special psychological services at school.

TESTING FOR GIFTEDNESS

One ideal of Western societies is that each person should be educated to his or her potential. This ideal is not only consistent with prevailing egalitarianism, it is also shrewd policy insofar as suitable education of the very gifted pays huge dividends for society in general. It is the gifted who develop original and effective scientific concepts; discover cures for the ailments of humankind; produce great works of art; and invent new and useful products, tools, and machines. The early identification of gifted children is essential if we are to nurture their talents for the benefit of all.[1]

The designation of a person as **gifted** typically means that he or she has extraordinary ability in

some area (Horowitz, 1994). Renzulli (1986) notes that within this general definition, scholars have pursued two broad categories of giftedness. These might be referred to as "schoolhouse giftedness" and "creative-productive giftedness." The first variety is typified by students who excel at traditional academic pursuits such as writing, mathematics, or the sciences. These children would be described as possessing intellectual giftedness. Regarding this variety of talent, Renzulli (1986) notes:

> It exists in varying degrees; it can be identified through standardized assessment techniques; and we should therefore do everything in our power to make appropriate modifications for students who have the ability to cover regular curricular material at advanced rates and levels of understanding (p. 57).

This kind of giftedness is easily assessed by IQ or other ability and achievement tests. The second category of giftedness, creative-productive giftedness, is more difficult to evaluate. The identification of talent within this domain rests upon more subjective procedures—few tests are suited to this purpose.

Perhaps this is one reason why school systems often restrict the concept of giftedness to the intellectual realm and rely upon standardized tests for the identification of eligible children. The point at which intellectual ability is high enough to classify a child as mentally superior or gifted is, of course, a somewhat arbitrary decision. A typical approach is to reserve the label of giftedness (and access to enriched educational opportunities) for students scoring in the top 1 percent on standard intelligence tests such as the Stanford-Binet or Wechsler scales. This translates to an IQ of about 135 and above. In summary, one approach to the identification of talented children involves teacher or parent nomination, administration of an appropriate individual IQ test, and then selection of children for enriched educational experiences based upon a sufficiently high test score.

An extension of the test-based approach to the identification of schoolhouse or intellectual giftedness is the use of a quantitative rating system that incorporates test data, grades, and teacher recommendations (Table 10.9). This method provides a

---

1. As this is a book on psychological testing, there is not room to analyze trends in funding for the education of the gifted. Yet it is discouraging to note that in the 1990s less than *one-tenth of 1 percent* of all the federal funds spent on elementary and secondary education went to programs for the gifted (Irwin, 1992).

TABLE 10.9   Sample Guidelines for the Identification of Intellectual Giftedness

Category	Score Range	Weighted Value[a]
Intelligence Test Data	95th—99th percentile	10
	92–94	8
	89–91	7
	86–88	6
	80–85	5
Achievement Test Data	95th—99th percentile	8
	92–94	7
	89–91	6
	86–88	5
	80–85	4
School Grades	A or 96–99 or Superior	8
	B or 91–95 or Very Good	7
	C or 80–90 or Good	6
Teacher Rating	Most Promising in Class	5
	Excellent Student	4
	Above Average	3
	Average	2

[a]Maximum possible score = 31, and 28 points are needed to identify a student as gifted.

Source: Based on Gallagher, J. J., and Courtright, R. D. (1986). The educational definition of giftedness and its policy implications. In R. J. Sternberg & J. E. Davidson (eds.), *Conceptions of giftedness.* Cambridge: Cambridge University Press.

more stable platform for the identification of intellectual talent.

The Creative-Productive Conception of Giftedness

Based on suspicions that traditional tests rely too heavily on specific knowledge, experience, and content, educators have proposed an alternative approach to the definition and identification of talented children. Creative-productive giftedness refers to children (and adults) who excel in the development of original products and materials (Sternberg & Zhang, 1995). Finding these children mandates that we must "look below the top 3–5% on the normal curve of IQ scores" (Renzulli, 1986, p. 58). In fact, few tests are useful in locating creative-productive giftedness. The identification of these children relies heavily upon the subjective judgment of authorities (including teachers and psychologists) who must apply conceptual definitions of giftedness to the specific circumstances of individual children.

The view of giftedness offered by Renzulli (1978, 1986) serves to illustrate this alternative approach. He downplays the role of IQ, defining giftedness instead as the confluence of *three* elements:

1. Above-average ability
2. Evidence of creativity
3. Evidence of task commitment

The first element specifies above-average but not necessarily superior or gifted ability. According to this view, a gifted child is one with above-average general ability (say an IQ of 115 or higher) or recognized talent in a specific domain. Examples of specific domains include chemistry, ballet, mathematics, musical composition, sculpture, and photography. While general ability and many specific talents can be measured with standardized tests, some areas such as the arts must be evaluated through performance-based assessment techniques.

The second essential element is that gifted children reveal flashes of creativity in their activities. But what is creativity and how can it be assessed as an element of creative-productive giftedness? The assessment of creativity has fascinated psychologists and educators for decades—and it has also proved to be a vexing problem. Although researchers generally acknowledge that **creativity** is something different from intelligence, beyond this fundamental point there is little agreement as to the nature or assessment of creativity (Wallach, 1985).

Over the years creativity has been defined as a process, a personal characteristic, and a behavioral product (Amabile, 1983). An example of a process view is the idea that creative persons excel at a specific cognitive process called **divergent thinking:**

> Divergent thinking is defined as the kind that goes off in different directions. It makes possible changes of direction in problem solving and also leads to a diversity of answers, where more than one answer may be acceptable (Guilford, 1959).

An illustration of a measure of divergent thinking is the Consequences Test (Guilford & Hoepfner, 1971). Examples include: "What would be the consequences if clouds had strings hanging down from them?" or "What would be the consequences if lightbulbs cost $10 each?" or "What would be the consequences if the oceans rose by 10 feet?" The sheer number of answers given is considered an index of divergent thinking which, in turn, is considered evidence of creativity. Tests of divergent thinking have enjoyed periodic popularity, but their value as measures of creativity remains questionable.

Another view of creativity is that personal traits signify its likely presence. According to this perspective, creativity flows from the temperament, motivation, and character of the individual. This would suggest that there is a creative personality. Harrington (1975) has captured a not altogether flattering portrait of the creative person in his Com-

posite Creative Personality scale. This test is an adjective checklist: creative persons are distinguished by self-rated traits including argumentative, assertive, hurried, insightful, rebellious, spontaneous, and versatile, among others. This line of research indicates that creative persons are distinguished by interests, attitudes, and motivations, and not by intellectual ability alone. Yet the link is indirect and imperfect. As a consequence, personality measures rarely aid in the identification of talented students.

The final approach to creativity uses the product as the distinguishing sign of this capacity. According to this view, creative persons produce things (ideas, inventions, writings, artistic outputs, etc.) that meet certain criteria. For example, Jackson and Messick (1968) apply four criteria to a creative product:

- *Novelty:* Creative products are new, or at least represent a new application of the familiar.
- *Appropriateness:* The product must be appropriate to the context, not merely novel.
- *Transcendence of constraints:* A product transcends when it goes beyond the traditional.
- *Coalescence of meaning:* The value of creative products may not be apparent at first; the full significance may be appreciated only with time.

These criteria can be used to identify children who show promise of creativity, which is one element of creative-productive giftedness. Subjective judgment is needed to identify these elements of a creative product—no tests or rating scales are available for this purpose.

The third essential element in creative-productive giftedness is evidence of task commitment. In the dedication and passion for their pursuits, gifted children astonish parents and teachers alike. These talented children willingly spend as much time in quest of their giftedness as peers spend watching television (Renzulli, 1986). In case studies of talented children, qualities of persistence, endurance, engagement, perseverance, hard work, dedication, and self-confidence are mentioned over and over (Terman & Oden, 1959). The assessment of task commitment requires a subjective approach although one operational specification might be that the eligible candidate must have shown a passion for his or her area of giftedness over a specific period of time (say at least for one year or more).

Recently, several scholars have expressed concern that the notion of giftedness has been defined from a European-centered cultural perspective such that many minority students remain unrecognized (Hamilton, 1993; Maker, 1996). The heavy reliance upon test scores is considered particularly problematic insofar as existing tests are questionable predictors of success in nonacademic settings—especially for ethnic, cultural, and linguistic minority groups. As a remedy, Maker (1996) recommends that educators use identification practices that are process-oriented and based upon performance (as opposed to test scores). She developed an authentic approach for identification of gifted minority children, called DISCOVER, in which groups of elementary students solve problems with blocks, tangrams, puzzle books, and toys:

The intent is to create a problem solving situation similar to what might occur in a classroom appropriate for gifted students from varied cultural, ethnic, economic, and linguistic backgrounds (p. 45).

The children rotate through three or more activities while observers document problem-solving processes and skills. The observers then fill out an 82-item checklist for purposes of identifying gifted students. Because the children use concrete materials, they can express what Gardner (1992) refers to as "first order" knowledge, which involves the creation and understanding of stories, music, drawings, constructions, and explanations. This type of knowledge is less dependent on academic learning and proficiency in the symbol systems taught in school and is therefore considered a more accurate index of the abilities of children from diverse backgrounds. The DISCOVER approach reminds us that giftedness can be viewed from many perspectives—it is not necessarily one thing.

SUMMARY

1. Screening for school readiness is one important function of assessment within school systems. A useful screening test should yield false-negative rates of less than 20 percent and false-positive rates of less than 10 percent. Unfortunately, existing screening instruments rarely meet these criteria.

2. Useful instruments for preschool screening include the Developmental Indicators for the Assessment of Learning-Revised (DIAL-R), which assesses motor skills, cognitive concepts, and language skills; the Denver II, which assesses development in four areas—personal-social, fine motor–adaptive, language, and gross motor; and the Home Observation for the Measurement of the Environment (HOME).

3. HOME is an index of the child's environment based upon in-home observation and interview with the primary caretaker. The inventory measures the quality and quantity of stimulation and support for cognitive, social, and emotional development available to the child in the home.

4. In the short run, there is probably no better index of a child being at-risk for school failure than an individual test of intelligence such as the Stanford-Binet: Fourth Edition (SB:FE) or the Differential Ability Scales (DAS).

5. Based on Public Law 101–476, an extension of Public Law 94–142, the federal definition of learning disabilities (defined as a significant discrepancy between intelligence and achievement) has lost favor with experts in the LD field. A newer definition refers to an intraindividual weakness in one or more of the core areas of academic functioning (listening, speaking, reading, writing, reasoning, or mathematical abilities) as the essential feature of LD.

6. There is general agreement—with occasional dissenting votes—on the following features of learning disabilities. A learning disability involves an intraindividual discrepancy in cognitive functioning; an exclusion of other disabling conditions as the primary cause; heterogeneity, that is, the existence of many different subtypes;

a developmental continuity from childhood into adulthood; and a high incidence of social and emotional consequences.

7. Representative of individual achievement tests used in the assessment of LD is the Kaufman Test of Educational Achievement (K-TEA), an untimed test for children ages 6 through 18. The K-TEA consists of five subtests: Reading Decoding, Reading Comprehension, Mathematics Applications, Mathematics Computation, and Spelling.

8. K-TEA subtest scores can be converted to grade equivalents and standard scores with mean of 100 and SD of 15. A qualitative error analysis is also possible for subtests, which improves the educational utility of the K-TEA. Standardization, reliability, and content validity appear to be good, although additional test-retest studies would be desirable.

9. Because attention-deficit hyperactivity disorder (ADHD) often coexists with learning disability, practitioners need tools and concepts for assessment of ADHD. The DSM-IV criteria for ADHD stress fidgeting, distractibility, impulsivity, attentional deficits, poor social skills, and not considering consequences. Others emphasize deficiencies in delayed and/or sustained responding as diagnostic symptoms.

10. Conners has developed a family of rating scales for identifying hyperactivity and other behavioral problems in children. Teachers, parents, and caretakers rate symptoms on a four-point scale. These instruments and other rating scales such as Achenbach's Child Behavior Checklist are useful adjuncts in the assessment of problematic behavior in children.

11. A child with serious emotional disturbance (SED) exhibits inappropriate behaviors, feelings, or patterns of social interaction. Objective scales such as the Child Behavior Checklist (CBCL) are helpful in the assessment of SED. The items on the CBCL are rated 0 (not true), 1 (somewhat or sometimes true), or 2 (very true or often true) by one or both parents.

12. Another function of the school psychologist is testing for giftedness, which refers to extraordinary ability in some area. Eligible children are often identified by a high IQ on an individual intelligence test, but other approaches can be used. Some experts refer to above-average intelligence, creativity, and task commitment as the important ingredients of giftedness. This approach relies heavily upon the subjective judgment of authorities (administrators, psychologists) for the identification of gifted children.

KEY TERMS AND CONCEPTS

screening   p. 353

sensitivity   p. 354

specificity   p. 354

learning disability   p. 360

attention-deficit/hyperactivity disorder   p. 370

gifted   p. 374

creativity   p. 376

divergent thinking   p. 376

TOPIC 10B Forensic Applications of Assessment

Psychology and the legal system have had a long and uneasy alliance characterized by mistrust on both sides. Within the legal system, lawyers and judges maintain antipathy toward the testimony of psychologists because of a concern that their opinions are based upon "junk science" (or perhaps no science at all) and also because of a belief (not entirely unfounded) that some expert witnesses will profess almost any viewpoint that serves the interests of a defendant. Within the mental health profession, psychologists find the adversarial aspect of courtroom testimony—based upon the expectation of yes-no opinions expressed as virtual certainties—to be an impossible arena in which to pursue the truth about human behavior. As the reader will discover, this essential tension between law and psychology is a constant backdrop that shapes and informs the nature of psychological practice in the courtroom.

For better or for worse, psychologists do testify in court cases, and the focus of their testimony often pertains to the interpretation of psychological tests and assessment interviews. When are test results and psychological opinions based upon them admissible in court? What criteria do judges use in determining whether to admit psychological testimony? Psychologists who represent themselves as experts and who use tests to justify their opinions must have a firm grounding in legal issues that pertain to assessment. In this topic we examine the relevance of legal standards to testimony based upon psychological tests and evaluations. We also explore a few specialized instruments useful in forensic assessment.

The role of the psychological examiner can intersect with the legal system in a multitude of ways. The practitioner might be called upon for the following:

- Evaluation of possible malingering
- Assessment of mental state for the insanity plea
- Determination of competency to stand trial
- Prediction of violence and assessment of risk
- Evaluation of child custody in divorce
- Assessment of personal injury
- Interpretation of polygraph data

These are the primary applications of forensic practice which we examine here. A variety of additional applications are surveyed in Melton, Petrila, Poythress, and Slobogin (1998).

In addition to meeting the general guidelines for ethical practice required of any clinician, practitioners who offer expert testimony based upon psychological tests will encounter additional standards of practice unique to the American jurisprudence system. We summarize major concerns regarding psychological tests and courtroom testimony here. The reader can find extended discussions of this topic in Melton et al. (1998) and Wrightsman, Nietzel, and Fortune (1994).

Each of the previously listed topics raises unique questions about the role of the psychologist in the courtroom. However, one issue is common to all forms of courtroom testimony: When is a psychologist an expert witness? We discuss this general issue before returning to specific applications of psychological evaluation that intersect with the American legal system.

STANDARDS FOR THE EXPERT WITNESS

Just as psychologists are concerned with issues of standards and competence, so too are lawyers and judges. American jurisprudence has developed various guidelines for courtroom testimony, including several general principles regarding the testimony of an **expert witness.** These standards are found in *Federal Rules of Evidence* (1975) and have been upheld by various court decisions. We can summarize the principles of expert testimony as follows:

- The witness must be a qualified expert. Not all psychologists who are asked to testify will be allowed to do so. Based on a summary of the expert's education, training, and experience, the judge decides whether the testimony of the witness is to be admitted.
- The testimony must be about a proper subject matter. In particular, the expert must present information beyond the knowledge and experience of the average juror.
- The value of the evidence in determining guilt or innocence must outweigh its prejudicial effect. For example, if the expert's testimony might con-

fuse the issue at hand or might prejudice the members of the jury, it is generally not admissible.
- The expert's testimony should be in accordance with a generally accepted explanatory theory. In most courts, guidance on this matter is provided by *Frye v. United States,* a 1923 court case pertaining to the admissibility of expert testimony.

In *Frye v. United States,* the counsel for a murder defendant attempted to introduce the results of a systolic blood pressure deception test. The lawyer offered an expert witness to testify to the result of the deception test. It was asserted that emotionally induced activation of the sympathetic nervous system causes systolic blood pressure to rise gradually if the examinee attempts to deceive the examiner. In other words, the expert witness asserted that in the course of an interrogation about a crime, the pattern of change in systolic blood pressure could be used as a form of lie detector test. The defense counsel wanted their expert witness to testify in support of the client's innocence. Counsel for the prosecution objected, and the Court of Appeals of the District of Columbia upheld the objection, ruling:

> . . . while courts will go a long way in admitting expert testimony deduced from a well-recognized scientific principle or discovery, the thing from which the deduction is made must be sufficiently established to have gained general acceptance in the particular field in which it belongs (cited in Blau, 1984).

The court concluded that the systolic blood pressure deception test had not gained acceptance among physiological and psychological authorities and therefore refused to allow the testimony of the expert witness.

According to these guidelines, a test, inventory, or assessment technique must have been available for a fairly long period of time in order to have a history of general acceptance. For this reason, the prudent expert witness will choose well-established, extensively researched instruments as the basis for testimony, rather than relying upon recently developed tests that might not stand up to cross-examination under the constraints of *Frye v. United States.*

In 1993, the standards for expert testimony were refined further by a Supreme Court decision in *Daubert v. Merrell Dow Pharmaceuticals.* The Court's written opinion added extensive guidelines about factors to be considered in weighing scientific testimony in trials. In particular, the court ruled that an expert opinion must be based on "an inference or assertion . . . derived by the scientific method." The ramifications of this ruling for the expert testimony of psychologists are unclear at this time. However, some courts have used the *Daubert* ruling as a basis for denying testimony from mental health professionals, including psychologists. For example, one court ruled that psychological evaluations of sexually abused children were inadmissible as evidence. It appears likely that courts will increasingly demand proof that testimony from psychologists has a strict scientific basis (Melton et al., 1998).

EVALUATION OF SUSPECTED MALINGERING

In most settings, a psychologist safely can assume that clients will be reasonably honest about their mental and emotional state. Clients want to tell their stories and they want to get things right. At worst, they may overstate symptoms slightly so as to impress the clinician that help truly is deserved and needed. Yet outright deception and manipulation are uncommon—for the simple reason that clients rarely have incentive for these strategies.

However, the rules of clinical engagement are turned upside-down in forensic settings. The typical forensic client has much to gain from a case formulation that emphasizes illness and disability. Indeed, the context of the assessment almost guarantees that clients will seek to look "crazy" or disabled, whether by exaggeration or (more rarely) deceptive design. In the mind of the forensic client, fabrication of symptoms may serve to excuse unacceptable behavior (e.g., favoring the insanity plea), sway sentencing recommendations (e.g., against capital punishment), or gain entitlements (e.g., certification for disability). These client maneuvers clearly influence the validity of forensic assessments. Hovering in the background of every forensic assessment is this troubling question: Was the client reasonably honest and forthright?

The forensic examiner must make a judgment about the honesty of the client's self-portrayal during the evaluation. And yet while common sense dictates that the examiner should expect some degree of deception, the conclusion that a client has consciously malingered needs to be reached with caution:

> Given the significant potential for deception and the implications for the validity of their findings, mental health professionals should develop a low threshold for suspecting deceptive responding. At the same time, because the label of "malingerer" may carry considerable weight with legal decision-makers and potentially tarnish all aspects of the person's legal position, conclusions that a person is feigning should not be reached hastily (Melton et al., 1998).

The most common and venerable method for identifying dishonest clients is the clinical interview. However, a more objective approach should be preferred. The assessment of potential **malingering** with interview hinges upon the judgment of the clinician (e.g., "This client is inconsistent in his presentation of symptoms and appears eager to be sick, so I conclude that he is malingering"), which may prove erroneous. In contrast, an objective approach provides normative data, hit rates, and the like, for the evaluation. Not only might this improve the accuracy of the assessment, in addition a more standardized approach should find greater acceptability in many court systems.

Unfortunately, there are relatively few objective approaches for the assessment of malingering in forensic clients. One promising instrument is the Structured Interview of Reported Symptoms (SIRS), a 172-item interview schedule designed expressly for the evaluation of malingering (Rogers, Bagby, & Dickens, 1992). The approach embodied in the SIRS was based upon strategies identified in the clinical literature as potentially useful for detecting malingering. Using a structured interview method, malingering is assessed on eight primary scales:

- Rare Symptoms (overreporting of infrequent symptoms)
- Symptom Combinations (real psychiatric symptoms that rarely occur together)
- Improbable or Absurd Symptoms (symptoms reveal a fantastic quality)
- Blatant Symptoms (overendorsement of obvious signs of mental disorder)
- Subtle Symptoms (overendorsement of everyday problems)
- Severity of Symptoms (symptoms portrayed with extreme, unbearable severity)
- Selectivity of Symptoms (indiscriminant endorsement of psychiatric problems)
- Reported versus Observed Symptoms (comparison of observed and reported symptoms)

In addition to the eight primary scales, five supplementary scales are used to interpret response styles. Of the 172 questions, 32 are repeated inquiries to detect inconsistency of responding. Examples of the kinds of structured interview questions include: "Do you ever feel like the fillings in your teeth can pick up radio messages?" (Rare Symptoms); "Do you have severe headaches at the same time as you have a fear of germs?" (Symptom Combinations); "Does the furniture where you live seem to get bigger or smaller from day to day?" (Improbable or Absurd Symptoms). "Do you have any serious problems with thoughts about suicide?" (Blatant Symptoms). The scale takes less than an hour to administer.

Results allow for classification of examinees as definite feigning, probable feigning, and honest. Reliability of the instrument is good, with internal consistency reliability coefficients for subscales ranging from .66 to .92. Interrater reliability estimates are superb, ranging from .89 to 1.00.

Although the validity of the SIRS can be discussed along the familiar lines of content, criterion-related, and construct validity (and the test performs well in these domains), the real measure of its clinical utility pertains to the capacity of the test to discriminate known or suspected malingerers from psychiatric patients and normal controls. One recent study indicates that the test performs well in this ca-

pacity (Gothard, Viglione, Meloy, & Sherman, 1996). In a mixed sample of 125 males referred for competency evaluation (including 30 persons asked to simulate malingering, 7 individuals strongly suspected of malingering, and 88 persons for whom malingering appeared unlikely), the SIRS was overall 97.8 percent accurate in classifying participants as malingered or nonmalingered.

A few other studies reveal promising results, but these involve predominantly white and educated samples (Rogers, Gillis, Dickens, & Bagby, 1991; Rogers, Kropp, Bagby, & Dickens, 1992). In contrast, the population of the criminal justice system—the arena in which SIRS most likely would be used—is relatively uneducated, and minorities are heavily overrepresented. By one estimate, more than 80 percent of the urban jail population in the United States is African-American (Dixon, 1995). Unanswered is how well the SIRS would function in the detection of malingering within this sizable subpopulation.

ASSESSMENT OF MENTAL STATE FOR THE INSANITY PLEA

In criminal trials the defendant may invoke a variety of defenses including entrapment, diminished capacity (e.g., from mental subnormality), automatism (e.g., from hypnotic suggestion), and the insanity plea. Whenever a special defense is invoked, an evaluation of the defendant's **mental state at the time of the offense** (MSO) is required. In some courts, a psychologist is qualified to offer opinions about the MSO of a defendant. We restrict the discussion here to the insanity plea since this is the most common doctrine that would trigger the need for an MSO evaluation.

Almost everyone is familiar with the insanity defense, but only the exceptional person understands its provisions. Technically, the insanity defense is known as **not guilty by reason of insanity (NGRI).** Based on a few sensational and widely publicized trials such as the case of John Hinckley, who attempted to assassinate President Ronald Reagan, the lay public generally has concluded that the insanity defense is commonly employed by cynical lawyers to help dangerous clients evade legal responsibility for heinous crimes. Nothing could be further from the truth. In reality, the NGRI plea is widely respected by jurisprudence experts and is invoked in fewer than 1 in 1,000 trials (Blau, 1984). And in this tiny fraction of all criminal cases, the defense succeeds less than 1 time in 4 (Melton et al., 1998). The widespread belief that persons found NGRI "walk" away from their crimes also is inaccurate: Most receive hospital treatment that lasts several years. Recidivism rates are perhaps lower (and certainly not higher) than felons convicted of similar offenses (Melton et al., 1998). Even though outlawed in some states, the insanity defense has shown remarkable resiliency— probably because it performs a desirable role in a modern and compassionate society.

Several legal tests for insanity have had significant influence in the United States, including the M'Naughten rule, the Durham rule, the Model Penal Code rule, and the Guilty But Mentally Ill (GBMI) verdict (Wrightsman et al., 1994). Some jurisdictions include irresistible impulse as a supplement to the M'Naughten Rule. A few states have abolished the insanity defense altogether. We will survey the different standards briefly before commenting upon the role of psychological tests in determining legal insanity.

The **M'Naughten rule** is the oldest, stemming from an 1843 case in England. Daniel M'Naughten was plagued by paranoid delusions that the prime minister, Robert Peel, was part of a conspiracy against him. M'Naughten stalked the prime minister and, in a case of mistaken identity, shot his male secretary at No. 10, Downing Street. M'Naughten was found not guilty by reason of insanity, a verdict that touched off a national furor. In response to the furor, Queen Victoria commanded all 15 high judges of England to appear before the House of Lords and clarify the newly forged guidelines on insanity. The M'Naughten rule states:

> The jury ought to be told in all cases that every man is to be presumed to be sane, and to possess a sufficient degree of reason to be responsible for his crimes, until the contrary be proved to their satisfaction; and that to establish a defense on the grounds of insanity it must be clearly proved that, at the time of committing the act, the accused was laboring under such a defect of reason, from disease of the mind, as not to know the nature and quality of the act he was doing, or, if he did know it, that he did not know what he was doing was wrong (cited in Wrightsman et al., 1994).

Thus, the M'Naughten rule "excuses" criminal behavior if the defendant, as a consequence of a "disease of the mind," did not know what he was doing (e.g., a paranoid schizophrenic who believed he was shooting the literal devil) or did not know that what he was doing was wrong (e.g., a mentally retarded person who believed that it was acceptable to shoot an obnoxious panhandler). Approximately half of the states use the M'Naughten rule.

Some jurisdictions also allow "irresistible impulse" as a supplement to the M'Naughten rule. An irresistible impulse is generally defined as a behavioral response that is so strong that the accused could not resist it by will or reason. But when is an impulse irresistible as opposed to simply unresisted? This has proved difficult to define. For obvious reasons, legal experts are unhappy with the notion of irresistible impulse, and its use as part of an insanity plea appears to be waning.

The **Durham rule** was formulated in 1954 by the District of Columbia Federal Court of Appeals in *Durham v. United States.* Dissatisfied with the M'Naughten rule, Judge David Bazelon proposed a new test, known as the Durham rule, which provided for the defense of insanity if the criminal act was a "product" of mental disease or defect. The purpose of the Durham rule was to give mental health professionals a wider latitude in presenting information pertinent to the defendant's responsibility. Legal scholars hailed Durham as a great step forward, but in 1972 the rule was dropped by the circuit which had formulated it.

The Durham rule was replaced by the Model Penal Code rule proposed by the American Law Institute. Adopted in 1972, the Model Penal Code rule is as follows:

> A person is not responsible for criminal conduct if at the time of such conduct, as a result of mental disease or defect, he lacks substantial capacity

either to appreciate the criminality (wrongfulness) of his conduct or to conform his conduct to the requirements of the law (cited in Melton et al., 1998).

The Model Penal Code rule also contains provisions which prohibit the inclusion of the psychopath or antisocial personality within the insanity defense.

The **Model Penal Code** rule differs from the M'Naughten rule in three important ways:

1. By using the term *appreciate,* it acknowledges the emotional determinants of criminal action.
2. It does not require a total lack of appreciation by offenders for the nature of their conduct—only a lack of "substantial capacity."
3. It includes both a cognitive element and a volitional element, making defendants' inability to control their actions an independent criterion for insanity (Wrightsman et al., 1994).

About 20 states now follow the Model Penal Code rule or slight variants of it.

A recent development in the insanity plea is the **Guilty But Mentally Ill (GBMI)** verdict. Approximately one-fourth of the states allow juries to reach a verdict of GBMI in cases where the defendant pleads insanity. Typically, in states which allow the GBMI verdict, the judge instructs the jury to return with one of four verdicts:

- Guilty of the crime
- Not guilty of the crime
- Not guilty by reason of insanity
- Guilty but mentally ill

The intention of the last alternative is that a defendant found GBMI should receive the same sentence as if found guilty of the crime, but he or she begins the sentence in a psychiatric hospital. After treatment is completed, the defendant then serves the remainder of the sentence in a prison.

But the intention of GBMI and its reality are two different things. Initial support for the GBMI verdict as a humane variant of the insanity plea has waned in recent years. Wrightsman et al. (1994) point out that jurors express confusion when asked to make the difficult distinction between mental illness that results in insanity (GBMI) and mental ill-

ness that does not. Melton et al. (1998) find little virtue in the verdict:

> . . . the GBMI verdict is conceptually flawed, has significant potential for misleading the factfinder, and does not appear to achieve its goals of reducing insanity acquittals or prolonging confinement of offenders who are mentally ill and dangerous. The one goal it may achieve is relieving the anxiety of jurors and judges who otherwise would have difficulty deciding between a guilty verdict and a verdict of not guilty by reason of insanity. It is doubtful this goal is a proper one or worth the price (p. 215).

Empirical studies indicate that offenders found GBMI seldom receive adequate treatment. Furthermore, they may receive harsher sentences than their counterparts found merely guilty (Callahan, McGreevy, Cirincione, & Steadman, 1992). In fact, some defendants found GBMI have been sentenced to death!

Now that the reader has been introduced to variants of the insanity plea, we review the role of the psychologist in determining legal insanity. An important point is that psychologists are rightfully cautious in offering an interview-based opinion as to a person's mental state at the time of a criminal offense. After all, the crime usually occurred days, weeks, months, or even years before, and the client may be unable to assist in the accurate reconstruction of events and mental states. Consequently, psychological testimony regarding legal insanity should be cautious and conservative. Reliability studies of insanity evaluations also suggest that caution is appropriate. In a review of seven studies, Melton et al. (1998) determined that interrater agreement (as to whether a defendant was legally insane) ranged from a low of 64 percent (between prosecution and defense psychiatrists) to a high of 97 percent (between psychologists with forensic training who used structured instruments, discussed later).

In spite of controversy over the role of the psychologist in MSO determinations, some experts foresee an increased role for psychological assessment in cases involving the insanity plea. In particular, neuropsychological assessments may provide objective, valid data to help the courts decide the merits of an insanity defense. Recent court rulings affirm that neuropsychological test findings can be used to show that a defendant has impaired capability to choose right and refrain from wrong (Blau, 1984; Heilbrun, 1992). Martell (1992) has discussed the relevance of neuropsychological assessment to the insanity plea as defined by the Model Penal Code. The Model Penal Code defines a defendant as not guilty by reason of insanity if he or she "lacks substantial capacity" to appreciate the criminality of his or her conduct. Neuropsychological test results have a direct bearing upon this issue.

Rating scales such as the Rogers Criminal Responsibility Assessment Scales (R-CRAS) also provide a useful basis for evaluating criminal responsibility (Rogers, 1984, 1986). The R-CRAS is completed by the examiner immediately following a review of clinical records, police investigative reports, and the final clinical interview with the patient-defendant. The instrument consists of clear descriptive criteria for 25 items assessing both psychological and situational factors. The items are scored with respect to the time of the crime on five scales measuring these variables:

- Patient Reliability
- Organicity
- Psychopathology
- Cognitive Control
- Behavioral Control

The individual items on the R-CRAS were derived from the Model Penal Code standard of insanity (Table 10.10). Interrater reliabilities of the R-CRAS scales ranged from .48 (for a Malingering subscale) to 1.00 (for Organicity). Construct validity was established by comparing the disposition of 93 legal cases with R-CRAS data. Even though legal outcome is determined by many variables besides the psychological state of the person at the time of the crime, there was 95 percent agreement in the determination of sanity and 73 percent agreement in the determination of insanity.

TABLE 10.10   Sample Items from the R-CRAS

10. Amnesia about the alleged crime.
     (This refers to the examiner's assessment of amnesia, not necessarily the patient's reported amnesia)
    (0) No information.
    (1) None. Remembers the entire event in considerable detail.
    (2) Slight; of doubtful significance. The patient forgets a few minor details.
    (3) Mild. Patient remembers the substance of what happened but is forgetful of many minor details.
    (4) Moderate. The patient has forgotten a major portion of the alleged crime but remembers enough details to believe it happened.
    (5) Severe. The patient is amnesic to most of the alleged crime but remembers enough details to believe it happened.
    (6) Extreme. Patient is completely amnesic to the whole alleged crime.

11. Delusions at the time of the alleged crime.
    (1) No information.
    (2) Suspected delusions (e.g., supported only by questionable self-report).
    (3) Definite delusions but not actually associated with the commission of the alleged crime.
    (4) Definite delusions which contributed to, but were not the predominant force in, the commission of the alleged crime.
    (5) Definite controlling delusions on the basis of which the alleged crime was committed.

Source: Adapted and reproduced by special permission of the Publisher, Psychological Assessment Resources, Inc., Odessa, FL 33556, from the Rogers' Criminal Responsibility Assessment Scales by Richard Rogers, Ph.D. Copyright 1984 by PAR, Inc. Further reproduction is prohibited without permission from PAR, Inc.

Even though reviewers recognize the promise of the R-CRAS, for some a healthy skepticism still prevails. One concern is that the subscales of the instrument represent an *ordinal* level of measurement whereas an *interval* level of quantification is implied. Another concern is that the test developers claim to "quantify areas of judgment that are logical and/or intuitive in nature" which leads to a false sense of scientific certainty (Melton et al., 1998).

Certainly the R-CRAS performs a valuable function by helping clinicians organize their thinking and evaluation. The utility of the overall decision—sane versus insane—will rest upon additional validational research (Howell & Richards, 1989).

COMPETENCY TO STAND TRIAL

The Sixth Amendment to the U.S. Constitution, passed in 1791, guarantees every accused citizen the right to an impartial, speedy, and public trial with benefit of counsel. If the defendant is unable to exercise these constitutional rights for any reason, then a proper trial cannot take place. Specifically, if the defendant has a mental defect, illness, or condition that renders him or her unable to understand the proceedings or to assist in his or her defense, the defendant would be considered incompetent to stand trial. This standard was confirmed by the U.S. Supreme Court in *Dusky v. United States* (1960) as ". . . whether [the defendant] has sufficient present ability to consult with his lawyer with a reasonable degree of rational understanding—and whether he has a rational as well as factual understanding of the proceedings against him." In practice, **competency to stand trial** refers to four elements and distinctions (Melton et al., 1998):

1. The defendant's capacity to understand the criminal process, including the role of the participants in that process
2. The defendant's ability to function in that process, primarily through consulting with counsel in the preparation of a defense
3. The defendant's capacity, as opposed to willingness, to relate to counsel and understand the proceedings
4. The defendant's reasonable degree of understanding, as opposed to perfect or complete understanding

Most American courts follow this standard, which emphasizes *current* functioning of the accused.

The presiding judge may request a psychological or psychiatric evaluation to assist in determining a defendant's competency to stand trial. One recent report indicates that more than 25,000 evaluations of competency to stand trial are performed in the United States each year (McDonald, Nussbaum, & Bagby, 1992). It is important to emphasize that psychologists, psychiatrists, and other mental health professionals merely assist in a competency hearing by presenting expert opinions. Only the judge has the power to make a competency determination. Although there is no standard format for a competency determination, most judges request that the psychologist consider most or all of the 11 factors cited in Table 10.11.

Incompetency to stand trial is entirely separate from legal insanity; these two issues are judged by completely different standards. Legal insanity pertains to the moment of the criminal act, whereas incompetency implies a current, ongoing condition. Furthermore, incompetency is not synonymous with mental illness, although the two may occur together. In the event that the judge rules the defen-

TABLE 10.11   Factors Considered in Determining Competency to Stand Trial

1. Defendant's appreciation of the charges
2. Defendant's appreciation of the nature and range of penalties
3. Defendant's understanding of the adversary nature of the legal process
4. Defendant's capacity to disclose to attorney pertinent facts surrounding the alleged offense
5. Defendant's ability to relate to attorney
6. Defendant's ability to assist attorney in planning defense
7. Defendant's capacity to realistically challenge prosecution witnesses
8. Defendant's ability to manifest appropriate courtroom behavior
9. Defendant's capacity to testify relevantly
10. Defendant's motivation to help himself in the legal process
11. Defendant's capacity to cope with the stress of incarceration prior to trial

Source: Florida Rules of Criminal Procedure, cited in Wrightsman, L. S., Nietzel, M. T., and Fortune, W. H. (1994). *Psychology and the legal system* (3rd ed.). Pacific Grove, CA: Brooks/Cole.

dant incompetent, the trial is postponed, usually for a period of six months or so. In some cases, persons found incompetent are placed in a mental institution for treatment to restore their competency so that a trial can be held later. Individuals charged with less-serious crimes may receive outpatient treatment.

In addition to information obtained from the clinical interview, psychological test results are important components of a competency evaluation. For example, a low IQ may constitute evidence of incompetence in the eyes of the court. Although there are no firm guidelines, most courts rule that persons with significant intellectual deficits—say, an IQ in the moderately retarded range or lower—are incompetent to stand trial. Likewise, a pattern of test results indicating severe neuropsychological deficit may warrant a finding of legal incompetence, even if the client's IQ is in the normal range. For example, a defendant with severe stroke-induced deficits in language comprehension may be found incompetent to stand trial.

Several formalized screening tests and procedures are available to assist in competency evaluation. These instruments are summarized briefly in Table 10.12. We focus our attention here upon the Competency Screening Test, which is probably the most widely used adjunct to competency evaluation.

Lipsitt, Lelos, and McGarry (1971) developed the Competency Screening Test (CST) in an attempt to formalize the competency evaluation. The CST consists of 22 incomplete sentences which focus on courtroom procedures, attorney-client relationships, and thought processes of the defendant (Figure 10.2). Each response is scored 0 (poor), 1 (borderline but not clearly appropriate), or 2 (clearly appropriate) according to sample scoring standards. In a cross-validation study based on 50 male residents of a state forensic unit, the CST correctly predicted 82 percent of the competency recommendations rendered by the forensic team charged with determining legal competency or incompetency. The CST was found to gauge competence accurately, but overpredicted incompetence (Nottingham & Mattson, 1981). In general, the

TABLE 10.12 Competency Assessment Instruments

Competency Screening Test (Lipsitt, Lelos, & McGarry, 1971)

The CST is a 22-item sentence completion test with an objective scoring guide. Some reviewers find the scoring criteria to be vague and also complain that the test has poor face validity and weak content validity.

Competency Assessment Instrument (Laboratory for Community Psychiatry, 1974)

The CAI is a structured interview of 13 functions relevant to competent functioning at trial. One concern is that examiners use different approaches to administer the scale.

Interdisciplinary Fitness Interview (Golding, Roesch, & Schreiber, 1984)

The IFI is a semistructured interview of the defendant in 5 legal areas and 11 categories of psychopathology. Ideally, the defendant's attorney should be present during administration.

Fitness Interview Test (McDonald, Nussbaum, & Bagby, 1992)

The FIT is a semistructured rating of the defendant regarding 24 legal issues and 14 psychiatric areas. The FIT reveals excellent interrater reliability and discriminates well between groups of defendants rated as being fit and or unfit to stand trial. Pending its revision, caution is advised in the use of the scale.

Georgia Court Competency Test-Revised (Johnson & Mullett, 1987)

The GCCT-R is a 21-item oral test of understanding courtroom procedure, knowledge of the charge, knowledge of possible penalties, and ability to communicate rationally. Some reviewers warn that the test inadequately samples the domain of competence-related abilities.

CST and similar instruments are a useful beginning to a competency evaluation, but should not be the sole method of assessment. Additional competency screening tests are reviewed by Bagby, Nicholson, Rogers, and Nussbaum (1992), Melton et al. (1998), and Nicholson, Robertson, Johnson, and Jensen (1988).

A serious concern in competency evaluations is whether the client is malingering. After all, delaying

 1. The lawyer told Bill that _____

 2. When I go to court, the lawyer will _____

 3. Jack felt that the judge _____

 4. When Phil was accused of the crime, he _____

 5. When I prepare to go to court with my lawyer _____

 6. If the jury find me guilty, I _____

 7. The way a court trial is decided _____

 8. When the evidence in George's case was presented to the jury _____

 9. When the lawyer questioned his client in court, the client said _____

10. If Jack had to try his own case, he _____

11. Each time the D.A. asked me a question, I _____

12. While listening to the witnesses testify against me, I _____

13. When the witness testifying against Harry gave incorrect evidence, he _____

14. When Bob disagreed with his lawyer on this defense, he _____

15. When I was formally accused of the crime, I thought to myself _____

16. If Ed's lawyer suggests that he plead guilty, he _____

17. What concerns Fred most about his lawyer _____

18. When they say a man is innocent until proven guilty _____

19. When I think of being sent to prison, I _____

20. When Phil thinks of what he is accused of, he _____

21. When the jury hears my case, they will _____

22. If I had a chance to speak to the judge, I _____

 2. When I go to court the lawyer will
    (a) Legal criteria: ability to cooperate in own defense, communicate, relate.
    (b) Psychological criteria: ability to relate or trust

        Score 2:
        Examples: "defend me"
                    "be there to help me"
                    "do his best to get me off with a light sentence"
                    "represent me"
                    "present my case"

        Score 1:
        Examples: "be there"
                    "ask for a postponement"
                    "ask me to take the stand"

        Score 0:
        Examples: "put me away"
                    "keep his mouth shut"
                    "prosecute me"

FIGURE 10.2
Competency Screening Test
Source: Reprinted with permission from Lipsitt, P. D. (1970), *Competency Screening Test.* Boston: Competency to Stand Trial and Mental Illness Project.

a trial date for a long time provides a strong motive to appear incompetent. Clinicians have a variety of methods and tests (described previously) for identifying clients who might be malingering. Even so, the process of competency evaluation is not foolproof, as indicated by such high-profile cases as the Connecticut man who avoided prosecution for murder (Associated Press, June 30, 1998). This individual had allegedly murdered his former girlfriend and her current boyfriend with a handgun, then shot himself in the head. He suffered brain damage and partial paralysis and was declared incompetent to stand trial by *four* psychiatrists in four separate hearings. They argued that he was incapable of communicating effectively with his lawyer. A court order that he undergo yearly competency evaluations was overturned, dropping him through the cracks and leaving him a free man. Nine years later he was found attending college as a pre-med student with a 3.3 grade point average. Examples like this are reason for humility and caution when psychologists approach competency evaluations.[1]

PREDICTION OF VIOLENCE AND ASSESSMENT OF RISK

Psychologists occasionally serve as consultants during the sentencing phase of a trial to determine whether a convicted defendant poses a danger to fellow prisoners or to community members. This information may be pivotal in determining the length of a sentence or the placement of the defendant (e.g., in minimum-, medium-, or maximum-security facilities). Parole decisions also may rest upon a determination of dangerousness. In extreme cases, courtroom testimony of mental health professionals may influence the decision whether to invoke the death penalty.

Unfortunately, even though many researchers have attempted to devise psychological measures of dangerousness, no psychometric test or procedure has been developed which provides an accurate long-range prediction of violence (Blau, 1984; Horowitz & Willging, 1984; Melton et al., 1998). In fact, it is not even possible to *postdict* violence from psychological tests alone with any degree of accuracy.

Why is it so difficult to predict violence accurately? Melton et al. (1998) cite four factors that contribute to the challenge:

1. *Variability in the legal definition.* The outcome to be predicted is variously defined as violence, risk, or dangerousness, and the criteria of legal

relevance shift from one setting to another. Some statutes require proof of an overt act within a particular time period, whereas others might accept a clinical judgment of "explosive tendencies" as proof of violence.

2. *Complexity of the literature.* The research literature that examines the relationship between background factors and violence recidivism is enormous. However, the voluminous literature is "both overwhelming and disjointed" so that even conscientious professionals find it difficult to extract meaning from it.

3. *Judgment errors and biases.* Mental health professionals are prone to subtle cognitive errors in their evaluation of defendants. For example, one problem is the tendency to view dangerousness solely as a trait when, in fact, its appearance is always an interaction with environmental factors (e.g., the availability of a weapon). Another problem is that clinicians let the salience of a crime affect their judgment disproportionately.

4. *Political consequences for the practitioner.* Overpredicting violence is safer for clinicians than underpredicting. If a defendant is released on the basis of a clinician's prediction and then commits a violent crime, the practitioner is vulnerable to legal action for negligent release. In borderline cases, there is a very strong incentive to lean in the direction of a "dangerous" finding.

A recent study by Menzies, Webster, McMain, Staley, and Scaglione (1994) illustrates the difficulties in predicting violence. These researchers used a 15-item Dangerous Behavior Rating Scheme (DBRS) to predict violence over a six-year follow-up of 162 accused persons remanded for evaluation of dangerousness. The DBRS consisted of 15 seven-point Likert scale items measuring personality attributes (e.g., hostility, emotionality, capacity for empathy), environmental factors (e.g., support, stress), situational factors (e.g., dangerousness increased with alcohol), and general items (e.g., dangerous to others in the present). In addition, a variety of prediction indices based upon ratings by nurses, psychiatrists, social workers, and others were used to predict an assortment of violence outcome measures at intervals ranging from

---

1. Another (cynical) explanation is that even incompetent persons with severe brain damage will receive As and Bs when they attend college. Perhaps grade inflation has gone too far.

one year to six years. Most of the correlations were on the order of .2, and very few predictors managed to exceed an upper limit of .40. The highest correlation was .53, but this pertained to the restricted case of short-term prediction of violence in those hospitalized on a psychiatric ward. Overall, the results were so discouraging that the researchers advised against "clinical or psychometric involvement in the identification of potentially violent clinical or correctional subjects."

A particular concern in the prediction of violence is the very high false-positive rate usually observed in controlled studies. This means that large proportions of those predicted to be violent subsequently reveal no violent behaviors. Gardner, Lidz, Mulvey, and Shaw (1996) asked clinicians in a psychiatric emergency room to rate their concern (from 0, no concern, to 5, great concern) that 784 patients would engage in violence over the following six months. The ratings of the clinician and the attending psychiatrist were combined (a total of 10 points possible) to produce a more stable estimate. A total of 327 patients received total scores of 6 or greater, indicating a significant degree of clinical concern. Of this group, 49 percent were found to be completely free of violent behavior over the next six months! A simple statistical formula using background information was significantly more accurate in making predictions, but still yielded a 42 percent false-positive rate. Both methods—the clinical and the statistical—also yielded high levels of false negatives (patients not suspected of future violence who subsequently engaged in such acts).

Although the *long-range* prediction of dangerousness with psychological tests or rating scales has proved to be difficult, the *short-range* assessment of risk with violent offenders has met with moderate success. Analyzing the prior history of violent offenders, Hall (1987) demonstrated that the following variables can be used to derive a probability of violence in the three months ensuing a forensic evaluation:

- Recency of prior violent act(s)
- Number of previous serious acts of violence

- Substance abuse within the previous month
- Actual or threatened breakup of love relationship
- Work problems leading to discipline or termination
- Opportunity for violence, such as access to a handgun

By quantifying the preceding factors, the examiner arrives at a probability of continued violence in the short-range future (Hall, 1987). This strategy is useful mainly with examinees who have a past history of violence, so it has limited applicability in the forensic field. However, for particular persons who meet most or all of the previously listed criteria, a prediction of violence can be correct more often than not. The approach highlighted here demonstrates once again the potency of biodata in predicting behavior.

EVALUATION OF CHILD CUSTODY IN DIVORCE

Psychologists may testify in the child custody disputes which arise after divorce. Actually, these disputes are rare—in 90 percent of divorce cases, both parents agree upon custody arrangements without resort to legal intervention (Melton et al., 1998). The role of the consultant is to offer expert opinions on such matters as the suitability of the parents or the best interests of the child. These opinions usually are based upon an assessment of the child (or children) and both parents and may include psychological testing.

Unfortunately, testimony based upon psychological test results rarely provides a useful basis for helping a judge make the Solomonic decision required in a custody dispute (Blau, 1984). The essential weakness of psychological tests in this regard is that the link between test findings and effective parenting is weak or nonexistent. The Rorschach technique and other personality tests were not designed to assess parents' relationships to children and are therefore largely irrelevant to the real issues in child custody cases.

Unfortunately, clinicians have been slow to realize their forensic limitations in child custody disputes. As a result there "is probably no forensic question on which overreaching by mental health professionals has been so common and so egregious" (Melton et al., 1998, p. 484). Understandably, legal practitioners are skeptical about the value of psychological testimony in child custody cases.

The American Psychological Association has acknowledged the tension between psychology and the legal system by publishing guidelines for child custody evaluations in divorce proceedings (APA, 1994a). These guidelines refer to concerns about the "misuse of psychologists' influence" in custody proceedings and offer principles of practice for this increasingly complex area. The guidelines specify that the best interest of the child is paramount. They further specify that specialized training is required, including familiarity with applicable legal standards and procedures, and knowledge of laws governing divorce and custody adjudication in the local jurisdiction. The guidelines also prescribe a complete neutrality on the part of the psychologist:

> The psychologist, in a balanced, impartial manner, informs and advises the court and the prospective custodians of the child of the relevant psychological factors pertaining to the custody issue. The psychologist should be impartial regardless of whether he or she is retained by the court or by a party to the proceedings (APA, 1994, p. 678).

This last guideline is especially important for the profession insofar as it promotes dignity in the practice of psychology. Nonetheless, impartiality is a difficult quality to maintain insofar as subtle pressures arise when a partisan attorney retains a psychologist for custody evaluation.

In response to the absence of a scientific data base, a number of experimental assessment devices have been proposed for child custody forensic procedures, including rating scales which attempt to gauge the potential for effective child rearing. One such test is the Ackerman-Schoendorf Scales for Parent Evaluation of Custody (ASPECT, Ackerman & Schoendorf, 1992). The ASPECT is essentially a battery of standard tests (Rorschach, MMPI-2, WAIS-R, WRAT-R for the parents, and Draw-A-Family, CAT, and an IQ measure for the child) used

alongside open-ended questionnaires, interviews, observations, and court records (where necessary) as a data base from which the practitioner completes a 56-item yes-no inventory (separate inventories are completed for the father and the mother). Results from the 56 yes-no items yield three subscores and a total score, the Parental Custody Index (PCI) for each parent. All scores are reported as T scores with a mean of 50 and standard deviation of 10. The PCI is intended to identify which parent is more effective—and how much more. A T-score difference of 10 points or more on the PCI is interpreted as suggesting that the higher-scoring parent might be a better choice for custody. In general, T-score differences of 10 to 15 points are considered significant, differences of 16 to 20 points are very significant, and differences of more than 20 points are marked. When both parents have PCI scores above 60, it is thought likely that either would be an effective parent. If neither parent is effective (scores of 40 or below), the PCI is intended to reflect this finding as well.

For the total PCI score, interrater reliability ranges from .92 to .96 and is considered adequate. Reliability data for the three subscales consisting of

- Observational, or the parent's appearance and presentation
- Social, or the parent's interaction with others, including the child
- Cognitive-Emotional, or the parent's psychological and mental functioning

are substantially weaker, indicating that practitioners should rely upon the PCI score only. A large standardization sample was used ($N = 200$), but these families were predominantly white (97 percent), so that the ASPECT may not be appropriate for use with minority families.

Validity of the PCI score was assessed by comparing ASPECT recommendations with judges' decisions in custody cases. In those cases where there was a significant difference between the ASPECT scores of the mother and the father (10 points or more), the test showed 93 percent agreement with the judges' decisions. Even so, reviewers have recommended caution in the use of the ASPECT for several reasons. One concern is the dearth of independent research in refereed journals pertinent to the validity of the instrument. Melton (1995) notes that the validation study was based upon the same families as those used to develop the instrument, which could lead to inflated hit rates. Another concern is that some scale items (e.g., whether the parent's IQ is more than five points below that of the child; which parent the child is placed next to in the child's drawing) have not been shown to indicate parental competence or child outcome in divorce studies. Heinze and Grisso (1996) conclude that the ASPECT needs more normative, reliability, and validity data before practitioners can place confidence in the assessment battery.

One problem with ASPECT is the enormity of the entire battery, which includes lengthy tests with both parents and all children, as well as interviews and analysis of abundant (excessive?) test information. Perhaps the same kind of assessment information could be obtained in a manner less time-consuming. This is the approach taken by Gordon and Peek (1989), who developed the Custody Quotient™, a sophisticated item-based rating scale that yields a nine-point rating for each of the following parenting factors:

> Emotional needs of child now and in future
> Physical needs of the child now and in future
> No dangers to the child emotionally or physically
> Good parenting
> Parent assistance
> Planning for the child
> Home stability
> Prior caring
> Acts or omissions
> Values

The instrument also yields an overall custody quotient or CQ (mean of 100) designed to gauge parental competence. The authors report some empirical data about their instrument, including interrater agreement studies based on evaluation of videotaped interviews. For most scales, the two authors were within two points of each other (on the nine-point rating scales) 90 to 100 percent of the time. The validity of the instrument has been assessed, in part, by confirmatory factor analysis which reveals a "general good parenting factor" as predicted. An initial validation study revealed that parents with a CQ less than 100 rarely received custody of the child (except in cases where both parents received ratings below 100). Gordon and Peek (1989) acknowledge that their instrument needs additional research.

Another test for child custody evaluation is the Parent-Child Relationship Inventory (PCRI, Gerard, 1993). The PCRI is a 78-item self-report inventory suitable for mothers and fathers of children ages 3 to 15 years. The inventory includes seven scales:

- Parental Support
- Satisfaction
- Involvement
- Communication
- Limit Setting
- Autonomy
- Role Orientation

Norms are based on a nonclinical sample of more than 1,000 parents throughout the United States. Like most instruments relevant to child custody evaluation, more research is needed to determine the value of the PCRI in child custody evaluations. One special concern is that the test items are relatively transparent such that parents might consciously skew the test findings in a favorable direction.

Bricklin (1995) has devised four simple tests that may prove helpful in custody evaluation. Two of the tests assess skill and investment in parenting for the mother and father separately. Specifically, the Parent Awareness Skills Survey evaluates awareness of child-rearing skills, whereas the Parent Perception of Child Profile appraises a genuine interest in the child. We focus here on the remaining two instruments which examine the child's perception of the parents: The Bricklin Perceptual Scales (BPS) and the Perception-of-Relationships Test (PORT).

The Bricklin Perceptual Scales or BPS consists of 64 questions asked of each child (age four and above) involved in a custody dispute. Thirty-two questions pertain to the child's perception of mother and 32 to perceptions of father. The questions fall into four areas designed to identify the best interests of the child: competency, supportiveness, consistency, and possession of admirable traits. Examples of the kinds of questions asked are as follows:

- *Competency:* "If you were having trouble with a school report, how much would Mom be able to help you?"
- *Supportiveness:* "When you feel really upset, how much does Dad help you calm down?"
- *Consistency:* "If you tried to sleep in on a school day, how often would Mom make you get up at your regular time?"
- *Possession of Admirable Traits:* "If you had a pet, how well would Dad take care of it when you went to camp for a week?"

The 32 Mom questions and 32 Dad questions are identical; they are widely separated in the questionnaire so as to avoid immediate and obvious comparisons. The questions are asked verbally first and then repeated with a slightly different phrasing. For example, the examiner holds a test card up to the child: "If this (point to end of line marked 'Very Well') is Dad doing very well at helping you to calm down, and this is (pointing to end marked 'Not So Well') is Dad doing not so well at helping you to calm down, where on this line would Dad be?" The child responds by using a stylus to punch a hole in the card. Each card contains a scoring grid on the opposite side for immediate and objective scoring.

BPS scoring consists of an item-by-item comparison of Mom and Dad ratings. A parent-of-choice (POC) is identified in terms of which parent, the mother or father, obtains the higher score on the most items:

> It is assumed that this parent is the parent better able to operate in the child's "best interests" in the widest variety of situations as measured by the BPS (Bricklin, 1995, p. 77).

Of course, this result is just one point of information used by the examiner in arriving at a custody recommendation.

The BPS embodies a number of positive qualities in comparison to other approaches to custody evaluation. First, the test avoids asking the child to make a direct choice between the parents, which minimizes guilt. It also assesses important areas of caretaking presumed to be important for healthy child development. Furthermore, by focusing on the *child's* perceptions of parenting as opposed to the examiner's perceptions of parenting, the instrument provides a voice for those with the greatest stake in a custody decision. Bricklin (1995) notes that the BPS is not necessarily intended to be a direct measure of parental competency but instead is designed to identify the caretaker whose style is congruent with the child's ability to take in and profit from parental guidance.

Although evidence regarding the reliability of the BPS is not available in Bricklin (1995), initial validity findings are supportive. Specifically, the BPS yielded a 90 percent agreement rate with the caretaker choices of mental health professionals who had access to independent clinical and family history data collected over a period of several years. On a cautionary note, as is true of so many instruments in the field of custody evaluation, there are few (if any) empirical studies of the BPS published in refereed journals. Heinze and Grisso (1996) offer the following critique:

> A related issue is that the Bricklin Scales attempt to address the legal questions of preferred custody without direct assessment of parents' functional abilities and deficits, including how these interact with children's needs. In addition, the scales address the issue of two parents with significant deficits only in a very superficial way. Thus, because the child's perceptions of the two parents are compared only to each other and not those of other parents, the clinician may not glean much information regarding a specific parent's level of parental functioning as perceived by the child (p. 301).

Clearly, more research from independent sources would be desirable.

Another child-based test invented by Bricklin (1995) is the Perception-of-Relationships Test (PORT). The PORT is a projective drawing test that can be scored to determine the parent-of-choice. The child is asked to complete seven sets of drawings, beginning with a drawing of each parent. The test then proceeds to other drawings, including a self-representation on the same sheet as a drawing of Mom, and then of Dad. A complex scoring system is used to identify the parent with whom the child seeks psychological "closeness." This is thought to reveal which parent the child views as more supportive and better able to respond to the child's needs. In a series of seven validity studies spanning several decades (Bricklin, 1992), the PORT typically yielded a 90 percent accuracy in predicting the parent-of-choice as designated by a courtroom judge or independent clinicians.

One specialized application of the PORT mentioned by Bricklin (1995) is the detection of physical and sexual abuse. The scoring criteria that indicate abuse appear to have been derived from psychoanalytic lore. For example, all of the following are thought to signal abuse:

- A dramatic increase in the distance between the self-figure and the abusing parent in comparison to the nonabusing parent
- Wavy or broken lines in the area of bodily abuse (e.g., genital area, breasts)
- Distortion of one hand in the drawing of an abusing parent

Unfortunately, empirical support for these hypotheses is limited, as we discuss at length in a later topic (Topic 13B, Projective Techniques). Because allegations of sexual abuse are highly prejudicial in custody proceedings, examiners should exercise great caution in speculating about such matters, especially if the evidence consists solely of a few human figure drawings deemed to be suspicious.

In closing this section on **custody evaluation,** we remind the reader that expert testimony in child custody evaluations needs to be tempered with a large dose of humility on the part of the psychological examiner. Determining the best interests of the child is almost always a difficult and thorny assignment. The absence of well-validated tests and methods for this task assures that custody evalua-

tion will remain one of the most challenging responsibilities in all of psychological practice.

PERSONAL INJURY AND RELATED TESTIMONY

Personal injury as from an automobile accident is often a source of litigation for monetary compensation. In **personal injury** lawsuits, attorneys may hire psychologists to testify as to the lifelong consequences of traumatic stress or acquired brain damage. For example, a clinical neuropsychologist might administer a comprehensive test battery (see Chapter 9, Neuropsychological and Geriatric Assessment) and then testify as to the long-term functional implications of known brain damage.

In general, a consulting psychologist who testifies in court will encounter extremely high practice standards. We have already mentioned the Frye standard, which provides that testimony must be based upon tests and procedures that have "gained general acceptance" in the field. Thus, a test or procedure that is relevant or useful in everyday clinical practice—but which is not widely accepted in the field—might be greeted with skepticism in the courts. A judge may even rule that testimony is inadmissible if it is based upon tests or procedures with flimsy validation. Worse yet, the judge may allow such testimony, which opens the expert witness to criticism and ridicule by opposing attorneys. With these concerns in mind, Heilbrun (1992) has published guidelines for the practice of forensic assessment which we summarize here:

- Tests should be commercially available and well documented, such as in *Mental Measurements Yearbook.*
- Reliability should be well documented and .8 or higher, except in unusual circumstances.
- Tests should be relevant to the legal issue, or to a psychological construct underlying the legal issue.
- Standard administration should be used, with ideal testing conditions.

- Tests should have been validated in a population that is relevant to the individual being assessed.
- Where possible, practitioners should use objective tests with actuarial formulas for interpretation.
- Practitioners should check carefully for malingering, defensiveness, and other reasons to discount or ignore the test data.

Additional guidelines can be found in the "Specialty Guidelines for Forensic Psychologists" (Committee on Ethical Guidelines for Forensic Psychologists, 1991).

Increasingly, courts have been willing to compensate mental injuries in addition to physical injuries. The damage is variously referred to as "psychic trauma" or "emotional distress" or "emotional harm." The evaluation of emotional injury will rely somewhat on psychological test results (especially personality tests) but the assessment requires great clinical skill including "a longitudinal history of the impairment, its treatment, and attempts at rehabilitation, including the claimant's motivation to recover" (Melton et al., 1998, p. 381). We see once again that the question of malingering haunts most forms of forensic assessment.

INTERPRETATION OF POLYGRAPH RECORDS

Although polygraph results are not routinely admitted in court cases, about 20 states allow testimony if both parties in a trial agree that the evidence can be used. At least two states (Massachusetts and New Mexico) allow testimony even if the other side objects (Wrightsman et al., 1994). In cases involving polygraph records, psychologists may be asked to offer expert testimony. We provide here a brief review of the art and science of polygraph examination.

The polygraph was developed around 1917 by William Marston, a student of Hugo Munsterberg at Harvard University. Marston's crude approach consisted of measuring systolic blood pressure during questioning of a suspect. He believed that systolic blood pressure would rise gradually if the examinee attempted to deceive the examiner. His controversial technique was the procedure questioned in the landmark *Frye v. United States* (1923) case. The reader will recall that the Frye decision helped define the qualifications of an expert witness as one who uses an approach which has ". . . gained general acceptance in the particular field in which it belongs." In the Frye case, the court did not allow Marston's testimony because his "lie detector" approach was not widely accepted.

The modern **polygraph** is substantially more sophisticated than Marston's crude predecessor. In a modern polygraph test, the examinee has several monitors attached to his or her body: a blood pressure cuff, a heart rate monitor, a flexible ring around the chest to monitor breathing, and electrical leads to the fingers to detect changes in electrodermal activity. The polygraph monitors ongoing physiological responses, including changes in breathing, pulse rate, blood pressure, and perspiration. The changes in perspiration are not monitored directly, but are measured indirectly from a pair of electrodes that gauge changes in electrical conductivity on the surface of the skin. Even a very slight increase in moisture from perspiration facilitates conductivity of an electrical current across the surface of the skin. Polygraph translates literally as "many writings." The physiological responses are displayed as a set of fluctuating ink lines drawn on a continuously moving roll of paper.

The justification for using the polygraph as a lie detector derives from the observation that many persons do react with increased physiological arousal at the moment they tell a lie. In theory at least, truthful responses are accompanied by relatively flat ink lines, whereas a lie is presumed to cause significant, detectable fluctuations in heart rate, perspiration, and perhaps other measures as well. Thus, a common procedure in polygraph testing is to compare responses to a neutral or control question ("Is today Tuesday?") with responses to a relevant question ("Did you rob the First Interstate Bank last Friday?").

Although a polygraph is commonly referred to as a "lie detector," this colloquial designation is substantially inaccurate. Polygraphers themselves are largely to blame for promoting the informal appellation of "lie detector" for their instrument. As a consequence, a vast mythology now surrounds the polygraph. In fact, a polygraph detects physiological responses, not lies. A distinctive physiological response monitored from a polygraph may or may not signal a lie—this is an empirical question open to research.

The polygraph does not "beep" at the moment of a presumed lie; the pattern of physiological responses must be interpreted by an examiner. Herein resides a significant limitation of the instrument: A great degree of judgmental interpretation is required to determine which "blips" are significant and which are merely coincidental. Unfortunately, the "expert" judgments of experienced polygraphers do not stand up well to empirical tests in the real world (Carroll, 1988; Lykken, 1981, 1987). In a field study of the accuracy of polygraph interpretation, Kleinmuntz and Szucko (1984) painted what is perhaps the most unflattering portrait of polygrapher accuracy. The authors collected polygraph readings from 50 persons later substantiated to be thieves and 50 persons suspected of the same thefts who were later exonerated. In addition, 20 unverified cases were added as "buffer" or "filler" cases, but not included in the analyses.

The polygraph examinations were presented to six highly experienced polygraphers. These interpreters were told that half the sample was guilty and half innocent. The results of the study consisted of a tally of accurate and inaccurate identifications on the part of the interpreters. The reader will recognize that the interpreters would be correct 50 percent merely by guessing. Also, we should point out that several categories of classification were possible: valid positives (guilty persons identified as guilty), valid negatives (innocent persons identified as innocent), false positives (innocent persons identified as guilty), and false negatives (guilty persons identified as innocent). Kleinmuntz and Szucko (1984) also converted the polygraph readings to digital data for purposes of discriminant function analysis. In a discriminant function analysis, purely objective statistical factors are used to classify subjects with as much accuracy as possible.

The results of the study were unexpectedly discouraging. On average, the interpreters were accurate 69 percent of the time, only a 19 percent improvement over guessing. The discriminant function analysis performed slightly better at 73 percent. The single best interpreter was correct only 76 percent of the time. The error rates in this careful study were alarmingly high, especially for false positives—innocent persons identified as guilty. Even the best polygraph interpreter still classified 18 percent or 9 of the 50 innocent persons as guilty.

Blinkhorn (1988) summarizes a psychometrically informed perspective on the polygraph as follows:

> The polygraph used as a lie detector falls very far short of acceptable standards for psychological tests. It is essentially unstandardized; it is internally inconsistent; rescoring of charts is unreliable; no retest reliability information is available for examinees; it produces a disproportionate number of false positive results; it has not been investigated for adverse impact on social and ethnic subgroups; it involves measures sensitive to aspects of temperament (p. 39).

Other reviews are more favorable, but not so favorable that legal experts will rush forward to promote the polygraph as evidence in court. Saxe, Dougherty, and Cross (1985) reviewed 10 field studies of polygraph accuracy. In these studies, the average rate of correct classification of the innocent was 89 percent (range of 77 to 100 percent), whereas the average rate of correct classification of the guilty was only 82 percent (range of 47 to 100 percent). More recently, a major field study of polygraph testing by the U.S. Secret Service concluded that examiners correctly identified 96 percent of the truthful subjects and 95 percent of the suspects who lied (Raskin, 1989). Elaad, Ginton, and Jungman (1992) also analyzed the accuracy of the polygraph in real-life criminal investigations. They amassed polygraph records for paired subjects suspected of the same crime (e.g., theft of a videorecorder from a military base). In all, they used records for 40 innocent subjects and 40 guilty persons for whom actual truth was later established by voluntary confession. Using objective decision rules, 94 per-

cent of the innocent subjects were correctly classified and 76 percent of the guilty subjects were
correctly identified. Collectively, all of these studies support the use of the polygraph in the investigatory stages of a criminal case. However, the error
rates are still much too high for the polygraph to
be allowed as evidence in the courtroom (Honts &
Perry, 1992).

In recent years, the polygraph appears to be
making a limited comeback. For example, the state
of Texas keeps tabs on sex offenders with polygraph
tests, which pits civil liberties against the safety of
the public (Associated Press, May 16, 1997). In one
case, a 33-year-old man, who was on probation for
molesting a young boy, "failed" a lie-detector test
regarding sexual contact with children. When confronted with this, he confessed sexual activity with
a 15-year-old boy and then faced a prison sentence
for violation of his probation. Increasingly, court
systems are relying upon the lie detector to keep
track of sex offenders (50,000 in the state of Texas
alone), raising difficult legal and ethical questions.
One concern is the problem of false positives, in
which an innocent person is suspected of sex crimes
based upon the blips seen on the rolling ink lines of
a polygraph test. In a survey of 195 psychologists
from the Society for Psychophysiological Research, most respondents answered that polygraphic lie detection is not theoretically sound, that
the lie test can be beaten by easily learned counter-
measures, and that test results should not be admitted in courts of law (Iacono & Lykken, 1997).

CONTROVERSY OVER THE PSYCHOLOGIST AS EXPERT WITNESS

It should be evident from the previous topics that
the expert testimony of psychologists may alter
lives. As Faust and Ziskin (1988) observe: "Depending on the expert's opinion, an individual may
be confined to a mental institution, receive huge
monetary awards, obtain custody of a child, or lose
his or her life." These authors also note that clinicians participate in at least one million legal cases
annually, so the potential impact of expert testimony is far-reaching. It is fitting to conclude this
section on legal and courtroom issues with brief

mention of the controversy that surrounds the psychologist as expert witness.

In a three-volume book titled *Coping With Psychiatric and Psychological Testimony,* Ziskin and
Faust (1988) provide a completely skeptical view
of the clinician in the courtroom. These authors
summarize their main points in a shorter article
(Faust & Ziskin, 1988). Their critique rests upon
two assertions:

1. Expert witnesses in psychology (and psychiatry)
   cannot answer forensic questions with reasonable accuracy.
2. These experts do not help the judge and jury
   reach more accurate conclusions than would
   otherwise be possible.

The first contention, that expert witnesses cannot answer forensic questions with reasonable accuracy, rests in large measure upon the alleged
inability of clinicians to provide accurate psychiatric diagnoses. The argument goes like this: If clinicians cannot perform accurately an assignment so
fundamental as the classification or diagnosis of
patients, then how can they possibly perform the
more complex task of determining the prior, current, or future state of the person under examination? Thus, problems with diagnostic reliability are
used to illustrate the more general difficulty in
achieving interclinician agreement on descriptions
or predictions of past, current, and future status of
the examinee. To buttress their position, Ziskin and
Faust (1988) cite numerous studies that demonstrate the unreliability of psychiatric diagnosis, including a few analyses that show the rate of
disagreement for specific diagnostic categories to
equal or exceed the rate of agreement.

The second contention, that expert witnesses do
not help the judge and jury reach more accurate
conclusions than would otherwise be possible, is
based upon assembled research findings which suggest that professional clinicians do not in fact make
more accurate clinical judgments than laypersons
(Ziskin & Faust, 1988). For example, Faust and
Ziskin (1988) cite a classic study by Goldberg
(1959) in which office secretaries performed as well
as professional psychologists in distinguishing the
visual-motor productions of normal versus brain-

damaged subjects on the Bender Visual Motor Gestalt Test, a design copying test. In the Goldberg (1959) study, half of the Bender Gestalt drawings were from patients with confirmed organic brain disease, whereas the other half were from normal individuals; chance diagnostic accuracy was therefore 50 percent. For each subject's drawings, participants in the study were asked to make a dichotomous judgment: normal versus brain damaged. On average, Ph.D. psychology staff classified 65 percent of the protocols correctly, psychology graduate students 70 percent, and office secretaries 67 percent. Ziskin and Faust (1988) cite many other studies that illustrate the same general theme of no difference in the accuracy of clinical judgments for professional clinicians and laypersons.

In defense of expert testimony, several authors have criticized the Faust and Ziskin (1988) critique for its partisan scholarship and lack of balance (Brodsky, 1989; Fowler & Matarazzo, 1988; Heilbrun, 1992; Matarazzo, 1990). For example, in his reviews of studies of diagnostic accuracy, Matarazzo (1983, 1990) concluded that the findings indicate good to very good magnitudes of reliability; he cited many positive studies not mentioned by Faust and Ziskin (1988). Furthermore, Fowler and Matarazzo (1988) decry the lopsided emphasis upon diagnostic accuracy:

Diagnostic classification alone is rarely, if ever, the basis on which legal determinations are made. Such legal questions as insanity, disability, and competency are based more on the judge's or jury's understanding of an individual's behavior and ability to function in specific situations than on what specific diagnosis is assigned to that individual.

We concur that Faust and Ziskin (1988) produced a one-sided literature review which ignores the findings supportive of forensic psychology. For example, consider one small detail of the Goldberg (1959) study—not by coincidence, a detail that Faust and Ziskin (1988) failed to cite. In addition to using psychologists, trainees, and secretaries as judges, Goldberg (1959) also asked a renowned expert on the Bender Gestalt test to classify the test protocols. The expert achieved the best classification rates of all: an impressive 83 percent correct.[2] On the basis of a review of clinical judgment studies, Garb (1992) concludes that mental health professionals (and especially psychologists) are more accurate in their judgments than laypersons, that is, they *do* have something to offer judges and juries in forensic cases. Clearly, there is no denying the fallibility of the individual clinician. But this point does not justify the elimination of experts in the courtroom.

SUMMARY

1. The practice of psychology intersects with the legal system in several ways, including evaluation for malingering, assessment of mental state (for the insanity plea), assessment of competency to stand trial, prediction of violence, and child custody evaluation.

2. To qualify as an expert witness, a psychologist must be a qualified expert in the opinion of the court. In general, testimony is restricted to techniques that have been available for a fairly long time in order to have a history of general acceptance (*Frye v. United States,* 1923).

3. In forensic assessments, the practitioner should have a high suspicion of malingering, but should reach this conclusion cautiously because of

the consequences to the client. Tools such as the Structured Interview of Reported Symptoms can help in the assessment of malingering.

4. The insanity defense is widely respected by jurisprudence experts and is invoked in fewer than 1 in 1,000 trials. Currently, most states follow the M'Naughten rule or the Model Penal Code as legal tests for insanity. Some jurisdictions allow "irresistible impulse" as a supplement.

5. According to the M'Naughten rule, a person can be found not guilty by reason of insanity if "at the time of the committing of the act, the party

_____

2. The expert was Max Hutt, who later authored *The Hutt Adaptation of the Bender Gestalt Test* (1977).

accused was laboring under such a defect of reason, from disease of the mind, as not to know the nature and quality of the act he was doing; or, if he did know it, that he did not know he was doing what was wrong."

6. The Model Penal Code proposes that a "person is not responsible for criminal conduct if at the time of such conduct, as a result of mental disease or defect, he lacks substantial capacity either to appreciate the criminality (wrongfulness) of his conduct or to conform his conduct to the requirements of the law."

7. A recent addition to legal jurisprudence is the Guilty But Mentally Ill verdict. Use of this verdict has several liabilities, including confusion by jurors and harsher sentences than being found merely guilty.

8. Rating scales such as the Rogers Criminal Responsibility Scales provide a helpful basis for evaluating the mental state of the defendant at the time of the offense (MSO). However, reviewers suggest caution in the application of this and similar scales because they might lead to a false sense of scientific certainty about matters that are inherently intuitive and judgmental.

9. Courts often ask psychologists to help determine if a defendant is competent to stand trial. Competency generally implies that the defendant is capable of understanding the charges against him/her, can cooperate with the defense attorney, and can make a reasonable self-presentation during the trial.

10. The prediction of violence and assessment of risk is another court-based task that is occasionally asked of psychologists. Unfortunately, no psychometric test or procedure has been developed which provides an accurate long-range prediction of violence. In contrast, the short-range prediction of violence or risk has met with greater success.

11. Additional areas of sensitive assessment include child custody disputes, in which psychological test results rarely are helpful; and personal injury cases, in which psychological tests can play a crucial role in documenting the effects of injury.

12. Several assessment devices and scales have been proposed to provide an objective means for making child custody recommendations. While providing useful information, these tools may promise more than they deliver from the standpoint of psychometric validity.

13. A polygraph detects physiological responses such as electrodermal changes to interrogation questions and displays them as ink lines on paper. Research supports the use of the polygraph in the investigatory stages of a criminal case but error rates are still much too high for its use in the courtroom.

14. Skeptics argue that expert witnesses in psychology (and psychiatry) cannot answer forensic questions with reasonable accuracy and do not help the judge and jury reach more accurate conclusions than would otherwise be possible. These opinions appear to be based on one-sided reviews of the research.

KEY TERMS AND CONCEPTS

expert witness   p. 380

malingering   p. 381

mental state at the time of the offense (MSO)   p. 382

not guilty by reason of insanity (NGRI)   p. 382

M'Naughten rule   p. 383

Durham rule   p. 383

Model Penal Code   p. 384

Guilty But Mentally Ill (GBMI)   p. 399

competency to stand trial   p. 386

custody evaluation   p. 394

personal injury   p. 394

polygraph   p. 395

Industrial and Organizational Assessment

TOPIC 11A Personnel Assessment and Selection

Industrial and organizational psychology (I/O psychology) is the subspecialty of psychology that deals with behavior in work situations (Dunnette & Hough, 1990, 1991, 1992). In its broadest sense, I/O psychology includes diverse applications in business, advertising, and the military. For example, corporations typically consult I/O psychologists to help design and evaluate hiring procedures; businesses may ask I/O psychologists to appraise the effectiveness of advertising; and, military leaders rely heavily upon I/O psychologists in the testing and placement of recruits. Psychological testing in the service of decision making about personnel (hiring, placement, promotion, and evaluation) is thus a prominent focus of this profession. Of course, specialists in I/O psychology have broad skills and often handle many corporate responsibilities not previously mentioned. Nonetheless, there is no denying the centrality of assessment to their profession.

The purpose of this chapter is to review the numerous ways in which tests and assessment procedures can be used by I/O psychologists for the previously mentioned purposes. We will also introduce the reader to some of the issues and controversies that may arise in the selection and appraisal of employees. In Topic 11A, Personnel Assessment and Selection, testing practices for employee selection are discussed and relevant instruments are introduced. In Topic 11B, Appraisal of Work Performance, the vexatious problem of performance evaluation is addressed. Legal issues and the effects of government regulations upon industrial assessment are also reviewed here.

A FRAMEWORK FOR PERSONNEL ASSESSMENT AND SELECTION

Key Issues in Personnel Testing

It is important to have a framework for understanding the intricate, multifaceted role of the I/O psychologist in personnel assessment and selection. A crucial point—often overlooked in the coverage of tests and assessment approaches—is that I/O psychologists must be more than mere specialists in testing. This point is particularly important in personnel selection, which requires so much more than knowledge of the tests that might be used. In order to use tests wisely in this capacity, the I/O psychologist must be conversant with several complex issues. For example, detailed knowledge of decision theory, discussed in Topic 4A, Basic Concepts of Validity, is essential for the efficacious use of tests in personnel selection. Elements of decision theory such as the Taylor-Russell tables provide a basis for determining the expected proportion of successful applications selected with a test. An I/O psychologist would be foolish to embark on a new program of employee selection without considering Taylor-Russell tables and decision theory. In addition, the prudent consultant should be well grounded in the concepts of test bias, discussed in Topic 7B, Test Bias and Other Controversies. For legal and ethical reasons, businesses disdain the use of biased tests. Typically, it is the psychologist's responsibility to select or develop nonbiased tests for personnel selection. The I/O psychologist should be familiar with issues of test bias, including the objective criteria by which tests are evaluated for bias. Likewise, the personnel specialist must understand legal issues in employment testing, discussed at the end of this chapter.

The many concerns of the I/O psychologist in personnel selection are profiled in Table 11.1, which provides a synopsis of major issues in testing and assessment. This list of key issues is not meant to be exhaustive, but it does convey the breadth of concerns encountered in the application of tests to personnel selection. The reader will notice that one area of expertise needed by the I/O psychologist is job analysis, which is the identification of criteria for effective job performance. A thorough job analysis can provide the basic building blocks for personnel selection. For this reason, we discuss approaches to job analysis before turning to other issues in personnel selection.

TABLE 11.1   A Compilation of Key Issues in Testing and Assessing for Personnel Selection

---

Job analysis: What are the specific criteria for effective job performance?

Tests and assessments: Do the selection devices and procedures possess a demonstrated relationship to effective job performance?

Cutoff scores: What is the expected proportion of successful applicants selected with a test of known validity?

Cost effectiveness: Including the costs of testing and selection, which assessment procedures yield the greatest overall benefit?

Test bias: Do the tests and assessment procedures evidence bias against one or more minorities?

Legal guidelines: Do the tests and selection procedures meet federal guidelines for fair employment testing?

Validity studies: What is the ongoing validity of the personnel selection program?

Job Analysis

For large corporations and small businesses alike, the basic building blocks of organizational success are the individual jobs performed by specific employees at all levels—from management on down to neophyte recruit. The manner in which jobs are defined is crucial to organizational direction and growth. Cascio (1987) has outlined the questions which may be asked when new or existing organizations are scrutinized from the standpoint of employee positions:

> How many positions will we have to staff and what will be the nature of these positions? What abilities, skills, and personal characteristics will be required of the individual jobholders? How many individuals should we recruit? What factors (personal, social, and technical) should we be concerned with in the selection of these individuals? How should they be trained, and what criteria should we use to measure how well they have performed their jobs?

Before any of these questions can be answered, administrators must define the jobs in question, and then identify the employee skills and behaviors necessary to perform each job. This process, known as job analysis, properly falls within the province of the I/O psychologist. We will review here some of the assessment issues raised by job analysis and survey a few standardized questionnaires used for this purpose (Harvey, 1991).

Broadly speaking, **job analysis** consists of defining a job in terms of the behaviors necessary to perform it. Job analysis includes two major components: job description and job specification. The job description identifies the physical and environmental characteristics of the work to be done, whereas the job specification details the personal characteristics necessary to do that work. For example, a job description for office secretary might note that he or she must occasionally handle phone complaints, whereas the corresponding job specification might list tolerance with difficult people as essential. Another example: A job description for police officer might specify that he or she must be able to "Carry a person who has been arrested and is unable or refuses to walk by grasping the person under the arms, supporting his weight, and transporting him to the police car," whereas the corresponding job specification might refer to a minimum level of physical strength and stamina. We are getting ahead of the story here, but it would even be possible to operationalize "strength and stamina" as that which is needed to drag a 120-pound dummy a distance of 50 feet within one minute (Arvey, Landon, Nutting, & Maxwell, 1992).

The primary justification for job analysis is that it helps provide a valid basis for making personnel decisions. Not only is this desirable from an ethical standpoint, it also meets legal standards mandated by the courts and regulatory bodies. In *Albemarle v. Moody* (1975) the U.S. Supreme Court ruled that job analysis must be included in validation studies which purport to demonstrate a relationship between a selection device and job performance. Also, the *Uniform Guidelines on Employee Selection* (1978) require job analysis as a component of validation studies. As outlined by Cascio (1987), additional justifications for job analysis include: organizational resource planning, training and personnel development, safety and improvement of job methods, and personnel research.

Numerous methods can be used to perform a job analysis, and a full discussion would take us too far afield. Briefly, Cascio (1987) lists the following approaches:

- Direct observation of job incumbents
- Structured interview of workers
- Collection of critical incidents from supervisors
- Checklists of duties and skills
- Questionnaires

Another useful source of information for job analysis is the *Dictionary of Occupational Titles* or *DOT* (U.S. Department of Labor, 1991, 1993). The *DOT* provides standardized occupational information to support job placement activities. For example, the *DOT* listing for *psychometrist* consists of the following:

045.067–018 PSYCHOMETRIST (profess. & kin.)

Administers, scores, and interprets intelligence, aptitude, achievement and other psychological tests to provide test information to teachers, counselors, students, or other specified entitled party: Gives paper and pencil tests or utilizes testing equipment, such as picture tests and dexterity boards, under standard conditions. Times, tests and records results. Interprets test results in light of standard norms, and limitations of test in terms of validity and reliability (U.S. Department of Labor, 1991).

The *DOT* also provides occupational information pertinent to educational preparation, physical demands of the job, and environmental conditions typically encountered. For example, the position of psychometrist requires 2 to 4 years of higher education and is defined as a sedentary occupation with frequent need for reaching, handling, manipulating, and talking. Good hearing and good close-up vision are also listed as necessary physical characteristics of the position (U.S. Department of Labor, 1993). The *DOT* is an important source of information for job analysis, particularly for traditional positions which are well defined. Recently, the U.S. Department of Labor began an ambitious initiative to analyze virtually all jobs in the economy according to the content or work activities required (Peterson, Mumford, Borman, and others, 1995). The resulting database is called O*Net and it promises to be invaluable in matching people with jobs.

But not all jobs are clearly defined, which means that the I/O psychologist may need to conduct a formal job analysis. This is more difficult than it might appear. Morgeson and Campion (1997) have outlined the pitfalls of accurate job analysis, which include social factors such as conformity in job analysis committees and problems of information overload that stem from the complexity of the task. We focus here upon questionnaires for job analysis, because they raise a number of interesting issues in assessment.

Structured, quantifiable questionnaires for job analysis did not become popular until the Position Analysis Questionnaire (PAQ) appeared in the early 1970s (McCormick, Mecham, & Jeanneret, 1972). This instrument introduced a novel "worker-oriented" concept of job analysis that allowed I/O psychologists to make meaningful comparisons between different jobs. Still popular today, the PAQ

consists of 194 items or job elements from five categories:

- *Information input:* How and where does the worker get the information needed for the job?
- *Mental processes:* What kinds of reasoning, planning, and decision making are required by the job?
- *Work output:* What are the physical activities performed and the tools or devices used by the worker?
- *Personal relationships:* What kinds of relationships with others are inherent to the job?
- *Job context:* What are the physical and social contexts in which the work is performed?

Some of the individual job elements are simply checked "yes" or "no," whereas other items are rated on an appropriate scale such as importance, time, or difficulty. For example, in one subsection, job analysts rate (on a 1 to 5 scale) five aspects of oral communication (advising, negotiating, persuading, instructing, and interviewing) as to importance for a specific job.

The PAQ has respectable reliability when used by trained job analysts. Interrater reliability is typically around .80 for the overall instrument (McCormick et al., 1972; Mecham, McCormick, & Jeanneret, 1977). Validity is less well established, although Cascio (1987) has noted that PAQ results are not affected by the sex of the analyst, the interest level of the job incumbents, or the amount of information provided about the job. The instrument does have significant limitations, including the high reading level needed (college graduate for some items) and limited suitability for professional and managerial positions. Perhaps a more serious limitation is that the emphasis upon behavioral aspects of work may overlook important task differences between highly dissimilar jobs. For example, Arvey and Begalla (1975) have noted that a police officer's profile is quite similar to a housewife's profile. For example, both positions may involve conflict resolution—but in highly different contexts.

In response to the perceived shortcomings of the PAQ, Cornelius and Hakel (1978) developed the Job

Element Inventory (JEI). Similar in format to the PAQ, the JEI consists of 153 items with tenth-grade reading level. The most significant innovation is that the instrument is simple enough to be completed by job incumbents. Since professionally trained job analysts are not needed, the JEI is highly cost-efficient. In a factor-analytic study of the JEI with 2,000 Coast Guard incumbents, Harvey, Friedman, Hakel, and Cornelius (1988) discovered that the JEI factors closely paralleled those of the PAQ. The JEI appears to accomplish the same goals as the PAQ, but with much greater speed and efficiency.

Several standardized job analysis questionnaires have appeared in recent years, as outlined in Table 11.2. These instruments are really still in their infancy. However, with external regulations and the threat of discrimination lawsuits always lurking in the background, we can forecast confi-

dently that job analysis questionnaires will become commonplace—at least in large corporations which must assign diverse employees to specific jobs.

THE ROLE OF TESTING IN PERSONNEL SELECTION

Complexities of Personnel Selection

Based upon the assumption that psychological tests and assessments can provide valuable information about potential job performance, many businesses, corporations, and military settings have used test scores and assessment results for personnel selection. As Guion (1991) has noted, I/O research on personnel selection has emphasized criterion-related validity as opposed to content or construct validity. These other approaches to validity are certainly relevant, but usually take a back seat to criterion-related validity, which preaches that current assessment results must predict the future criterion of job performance.

From the standpoint of criterion-related validity, the logic of personnel selection is seductively simple. Whether in a large corporation or a small business, those who select employees should use tests or assessments which have documented, strong correlations with the criterion of job performance, and then hire the individuals who obtain the highest test scores or show the strongest assessment results. What could be simpler than that?

Unfortunately, the real-world application of employment selection procedures is fraught with psychometric complexities and legal pitfalls. The psychometric intricacies arise, in large measure, from the fact that job behavior is rarely simple, unidimensional behavior. There are some exceptions (such as assembly line production) but the general rule in our postindustrial society is that job behavior is complex, multidimensional behavior. Even jobs that seem simple may be highly complex. For example, consider what is required for effective performance in the delivery of the U.S. mail. The individual who delivers your mail six days a week must do more than merely place it in your mailbox. He or she must accurately sort mail on the run, interpret and enforce government regulations about

---

TABLE 11.2   Job Analysis Questionnaires

Professional and Managerial Position Questionnaire (PMPQ)   (Mitchell & McCormick, 1979)

A managerial-oriented instrument which assesses interpersonal activities, planning and decision making, processing information, technical activities, and prerequisite background factors such as relevant experience, special training, and second-language usage.

Occupation Analysis Inventory (OAI) (Cunningham, Boese, Neeb, & Pass, 1983)

A general-purpose 617-item instrument which assesses biological/health-related activities, botanical activities, electrical-electronic repair, working with animals, and food preparation/processing.

General Work Inventory (GWI) (Cunningham & Ballentine, 1982)

Essentially a short form of the Occupational Analysis Inventory which assesses similar work constructs.

Common Metric Questionnaire (CMQ) (Harvey, 1990)

The CMQ was designed to be applicable to all jobs; includes behaviorally referenced scales so that ratings mean the same thing across different jobs, e.g., interactions with others might be rated on: coordinate/ schedule their activities, sell to them or persuade them, train/instruct/educate them.

package size, manage pesky and even dangerous animals, recognize and avoid physical dangers, and exercise effective interpersonal skills in dealing with the public, to cite just a few of the complexities of this position.

Personnel selection is therefore a fuzzy, conditional, and uncertain task. Guion (1991) has highlighted the difficulty in predicting complex behavior from simple tests. For one thing, complex behavior is, in part, a function of the situation. This means that even an optimal selection approach may not be valid for all candidates. Quite clearly, personnel selection is not a simple matter of administering tests and consulting cutoff scores.

We must also acknowledge the profound impact of legal and regulatory edicts upon I/O testing practices. Given that such practices may have weighty consequences—determining who is hired or promoted, for example—it is not surprising to learn that I/O testing practices are rigorously constrained by legal precedents and regulatory mandates. We review these issues in the final section of this chapter.

Approaches to Personnel Selection

Acknowledging that the interview is a widely used form of personnel assessment, it is safe to conclude that psychological assessment is almost a universal practice in hiring decisions. Even by a narrow definition that includes only paper-and-pencil measures, at least two-thirds of the companies in the United States engage in personnel testing (Schmitt & Robertson, 1990). For purposes of personnel selection, the I/O psychologist may recommend one or more of the following:

• Autobiographical data
• Employment interview
• Cognitive ability tests
• Personality, temperament, and motivation tests
• Paper-and-pencil integrity tests
• Sensory, physical, and dexterity tests
• Work sample and situational tests

We turn now to a brief survey of typical tests and assessment approaches within each of these cate-

gories. We close this topic with a discussion of legal issues in personnel testing.

AUTOBIOGRAPHICAL DATA

According to Owens (1976), application forms which request personal and work history as well as demographic data such as age and marital status have been used in industry since at least 1894. Objective or scorable autobiographical data—sometimes called **biodata**—are typically secured by means of a structured form variously referred to as a biographical information blank, biographical data form, application blank, interview guide, individual background survey, or similar device. Although the lay public may not recognize these devices as true tests with predictive power, I/O psychologists have known for some time that biodata furnish an exceptionally powerful basis for the prediction of employee performance (Drakeley, Herriot, & Jones, 1988; Cascio, 1976; Ghiselli, 1966; Hunter & Hunter, 1984; Reilly & Chao, 1982). An important milestone in the biodata approach is the recent publication of the *Biodata Handbook,* a thorough survey of the use of biographical information in selection and the prediction of performance (Stokes, Mumford, & Owens, 1994).

The rationale for the biodata approach is that future work-related behavior can be predicted from past choices and accomplishments. Biodata have predictive power because certain character traits which are essential for success also are stable and enduring. The consistently ambitious youth with accolades and accomplishments in high school is likely to continue this pattern into adulthood. Thus, the job applicant who served as editor of the high school newspaper—and who answers a biodata item to this effect—is probably a better candidate for corporate management than the applicant who reports no extracurricular activities on a biodata form.

The Nature of Biodata

Biodata items usually call for "factual" data; however, items that tap attitudes, feelings, and value judgments are sometimes included. Except for demographic data such as age and marital status, biodata items always refer to past accomplishments and events. Examples of biodata questions include highest level of educational attainment, number of special awards or recognition, income on previous job, number of jobs held in the last 10 years, length of time at present address, number of publications, and number of projects managed in the last five years.

Once biodata are collected, the I/O psychologist must devise a means for predicting job performance from this information. The most common strategy is a form of empirical keying not unlike that used in personality testing. From a large sample of workers who are already hired, the I/O psychologist designates a successful group and an unsuccessful group, based on performance, tenure, salary, or supervisor ratings. Individual biodata items are then contrasted for these two groups to determine which items most accurately discriminate between successful and unsuccessful workers. Items which are strongly discriminative are assigned large weights in the scoring scheme. New applicants who respond to items in the keyed direction therefore receive high scores on the biodata instrument and are predicted to succeed. Cross-validation of the scoring scheme on a second sample of successful and unsuccessful workers is a crucial step in guaranteeing the validity of the biodata selection method. Readers who wish to pursue the details of empirical scoring methods for biodata instruments should consult Murphy and Davidshofer (1988) and Stokes et al. (1994).

The Validity of Biodata

The validity of biodata has been surveyed by several reviewers, with generally positive findings (Mumford & Owens, 1987; Reilly & Chao, 1982; Rothstein, Schmidt, Erwin, Owens, & Sparks, 1990; Russell, Mattson, Devlin, & Atwater, 1990; Stokes et al., 1994). An early study by Cascio (1976) is typical of the findings. He used a very simple biodata instrument—a weighted combination of 10 application blank items—to predict turnover for female clerical personnel in a medium-

sized insurance company. The cross-validated correlations between biodata score and length of tenure were .58 for minorities and .56 for nonminorities.[1] Drakeley et al. (1988) compared biodata and cognitive ability tests as predictors of training success. Biodata scores possessed the same predictive validity as the cognitive tests. Furthermore, when added to the regression equation, the biodata information improved the predictive accuracy of the cognitive tests.

In an extensive research survey, Reilly and Chao (1982) compared eight selection procedures as to validity and adverse impact on minorities. The procedures were biodata, peer evaluation, interviews, self-assessments, reference checks, academic achievement, expert judgment, and projective techniques. Noting that properly standardized ability tests provide the fairest and most valid selection procedure, Reilly and Chao (1982) concluded that only biodata and peer evaluations had validities substantially equal to those of standardized tests. For example, in the prediction of sales productivity, the average validity coefficient of biodata was a very healthy .62.

Certain cautions need to be mentioned with respect to biodata approaches in personnel selection. Employers may be prohibited by law from asking questions about age, race, sex, religion, and other personal issues—even when such biodata can be shown empirically to predict job performance. Also, even though the incidence of faking is very low, there is no doubt that shrewd respondents can falsify results in a favorable direction. As with any measurement instrument, biodata items will need periodic restandardization. Finally, a potential drawback to the biodata approach is that, by its nature, this method captures the organizational status quo and might therefore squelch innovation.

---

1. The curious reader may wish to know which 10 biodata items could possess such predictive power. The items were age, marital status, children's age, education, tenure on previous job, previous salary, friend or relative in company, location of residence, home ownership, and length of time at present address. Unfortunately, Cascio (1976) does not reveal the relative weights or direction of scoring for the items.

Becker and Colquitt (1992) discuss precautions in the development of biodata forms.

There is little doubt, then, that purely objective biodata information can predict aspects of job performance with fair accuracy. However, employers are perhaps more likely to rely upon subjective information such as interview impressions when making decisions about hiring. We turn now to research on the validity of the employment interview in the selection process.

THE EMPLOYMENT INTERVIEW

The employment interview is usually only one part of the evaluation process, but most administrators regard it as the crucial make-or-break component of hiring (Miner & Miner, 1978). Landy (1985) reports that companies typically interview from five to twenty persons for each person hired! Considering the importance of the interview and its tremendous costs to industry and the professions, the reader should not be surprised to learn that thousands of studies address the reliability and validity of the interview. We can only highlight a few trends here; more detailed reviews can be found in Conway, Jako, and Goodman (1995), Landy (1985), and Schmitt and Robertson (1990).

Early studies of interview reliability were quite sobering. In various studies and reviews, reliability was typically assessed by correlating evaluations of different interviewers who had access to the same job candidates (Wagner, 1949; Mayfield, 1964; Ulrich & Trumbo, 1965). The interrater reliability from dozens of these early studies was typically in the mid-.50s, much too low to provide accurate assessments of job candidates. This research also revealed that interviewers were prone to halo bias and other distorting influences upon their perceptions of candidates. Halo bias—discussed in the next topic—is the tendency to rate a candidate high or low on all dimensions because of a global impression.

Later, researchers discovered that interview reliability could be increased substantially if the interview was jointly conducted by a panel instead of a single interviewer (Landy, 1985). In addition,

structured interviews in which each candidate was asked the same questions by each interviewer also proved to be much more reliable than unstructured interviews (Borman, Hanson, & Hedge, 1997; Campion, Pursell, & Brown, 1988). In these studies, reliabilities in the .70s and higher were found.

Research on validity of the interview has followed the same evolutionary course noted for reliability: Early research that examined unstructured interviews was quite pessimistic, while later research using structured approaches produced more promising findings. In these studies, interview validity was typically assessed by correlating interview judgments with some measure of on-the-job performance. Early studies of interview validity yielded almost uniformly dismal results, with typical validity coefficients hovering in the mid-.20s (Arvey & Campion, 1982).

Mindful that interviews are seldom used in isolation, early researchers also investigated incremental validity, which is the potential increase in validity when the interview is used in conjunction with other information. These studies were predicated on the optimistic assumption that the interview would contribute positively to candidate evaluation when used alongside objective test scores and background data. Unfortunately, the initial findings were almost entirely unsupportive (Landy, 1985).

In some instances, attempts to prove incremental validity of the interview demonstrated just the opposite, what might be called decremental validity. For example, Kelly and Fiske (1951) established that interview information actually decreased the validity of graduate student evaluations. In this early and classic study, the task was to predict the academic performance of more than 500 graduate students in psychology. Various combinations of credentials (a form of biodata), objective test scores, and interview were used as the basis for clinical predictions of academic performance. The validity coefficients are reported in Table 11.3. The reader will notice that credentials alone provided a much better basis for prediction than credentials plus a one-hour interview. The best predictions were based upon credentials and objective test

TABLE 11.3   Validity Coefficients for Ratings Based on Various Combinations of Information

Basis for Rating	Correlation with Academic Performance
Credentials alone	.26
Credentials and one-hour interview	.13
Credentials and objective test scores	.36
Credentials, test scores, and two-hour interview	.32

Source: Based on data in Kelly, E. L., and Fiske, D. W. (1951). *The prediction of performance in clinical psychology.* Ann Arbor: University of Michigan Press.

scores; adding a two-hour interview to this information actually decreased the accuracy of predictions. These findings highlighted the superiority of actuarial prediction (based on empirically derived formulas) over clinical prediction (based on subjective impressions). We pursue the actuarial versus clinical debate in the last chapter of this text.

Recent studies using carefully structured interviews, including situational interviews, provide a more positive picture of interview validity (Borman, Hanson, & Hedge, 1997; Maurer & Fay, 1988; Schmitt & Robertson, 1990). When the findings are corrected for restriction of range and unreliability of job performance ratings, the mean validity coefficient for structured interviews turns out to be an impressive .63 (Wiesner & Cronshaw, 1988). In a recent meta-analysis, Conway, Jako, and Goodman (1995) concluded that the upper limit for the validity coefficient of structured interviews was .67, whereas for unstructured interviews the validity coefficient was only .34. Additional reasons for preferring structured interviews include their legal defensibility in the event of litigation (Williamson, Campion, Malo, and others 1997) and, surprisingly, their minimal bias across different racial groups of applicants (Huffcutt & Roth, 1998).

In order to reach acceptable levels of reliability and validity, structured interviews must be de-

signed with painstaking care. Consider the protocol used by Motowidlo et al. (1992) in their research on structured interviews for management and marketing positions in eight telecommunications companies. Their interview format was based upon a careful analysis of critical incidents in marketing and management. Prospective employees were asked a set of standard questions about how they had handled past situations similar to these critical incidents. Interviewers were trained to ask discretionary probing questions for details about how the applicants handled these situations. Throughout, the interviewers took copious notes. Applicants were then rated on scales anchored with behavioral illustrations. Finally, these ratings were combined to yield a total interview score used in selection decisions.

In summary, under carefully designed conditions, the interview can provide a reliable and valid basis for personnel selection. However, as noted by Schmitt and Robertson (1990), the prerequisite conditions for interview validity are not always available. The essential problem is that each interviewer may evaluate only a small number of applicants, so that standardization of interviewer ratings is not always realistic. While the interview is potentially valid as a selection technique, in its common, unstructured application there is probably substantial reason for concern.

Why are interviews used? If the typical, unstructured interview is so unreliable and ineffectual a basis for job candidate evaluation, why do administrators continue to value interviews so highly? In their review of the employment interview, Arvey and Campion (1982) outline several reasons for the persistence of the interview, including practical considerations such as the need to sell the candidate on the job, and social reasons such as the susceptibility of interviewers to the illusion of personal validity. Others have emphasized the importance of the interview for assessing a good fit between applicant and organization (Adams, Elacqua, & Colarelli, 1994; Latham & Skarlicki, 1995).

It is difficult to imagine that most employers would ever eliminate entirely the interview from the screening and selection process. After all, the interview does serve the simple human need of meeting the persons who might be hired. However, based on 50 years worth of research, it is evident that biodata and objective tests often provide a more powerful basis for candidate evaluation and selection than unstructured interviews.

COGNITIVE ABILITY TESTS

Cognitive ability can refer either to a general construct akin to intelligence or to a variety of specific constructs such as verbal skills, numerical ability, spatial perception, or perceptual speed (Kline, 1993). Tests of general cognitive ability and measures of specific cognitive skills have many applications in personnel selection, evaluation, and screening. Such tests are quick, inexpensive, and easy to interpret. A vast body of empirical research offers modest to strong support for the validity and fairness of standardized ability tests in personnel selection (Gottfredson, 1986). Certainly it seems clear that ability tests often provide an excellent basis for job selection, at least according to objective criteria such as the capacity to predict job performance. For example, Hunter and Hunter (1984) conducted a meta-analysis of research on the prediction of job performance and concluded that for entry-level jobs no predictor (except for the work sample) exceeded the validity of ability tests, which showed a mean validity coefficient of .54.

An ongoing debate within I/O psychology is whether employment testing is best accomplished with highly specific ability tests or with measures of general cognitive ability. The weight of the evidence seems to support the conclusion that a general factor of intelligence (the so-called g factor) is usually a better predictor of training and job success than are scores on specific cognitive measures—even when several specific cognitive measures are used in combination. Of course, this conclusion runs counter to common sense and anecdotal evidence. For example, Kline (1993) offers the following vignette:

The point is that the g factors are important but so also are these other factors. For example, high g is necessary to be a good engineer and to be a good journalist. However for the former high spatial ability is also required, a factor which confers little advantage on a journalist. For her or him, however, high verbal ability is obviously useful.

Curiously, empirical research provides only mixed support for this position (Gottfredson, 1986; Larson & Wolfe, 1995; Ree, Earles, & Teachout, 1994). Although the topic continues to be debated, most studies support the primacy of g in personnel selection (Borman et al., 1997). Perhaps the reason that g usually works better than specific cognitive factors in predicting job performance is that most jobs are factorially complex in their requirements, stereotypes notwithstanding (Guion, 1991). For example, the successful engineer must explain his or her ideas to others and so needs verbal ability as well as spatial skills. Since measures of general cognitive ability tap many specific cognitive skills, a general test often predicts performance in complex jobs as well as, or better than, measures of specific skills.

Literally hundreds of cognitive ability tests are available for personnel selection, so it is not feasible to survey the entire range of instruments here. Instead, we will highlight three representative tests: one that measures general cognitive ability, a second that is germane to assessment of mechanical abilities, and a third that taps a highly specific facet of clerical work. The three instruments chosen for review—the Wonderlic Personnel Evaluation, the Bennett Mechanical Comprehension Test, and the Minnesota Clerical Test—are merely exemplars of the hundreds of cognitive ability tests available for personnel selection. All three tests are often used in business settings and therefore worthy of specific mention. Representative cognitive ability tests encountered in personnel selection are listed in Table 11.4. Some classic viewpoints on cognitive ability testing for personnel selection are found in Ghiselli (1966, 1973), Guion (1991), Hunter and Hunter (1984), and Reilly and Chao (1982). Contemporary discussion of this issue is provided by Borman et al. (1997) and Murphy (1996).

TABLE 11.4   Representative Cognitive Ability Tests Used in Personnel Selection

General Ability Tests

Shipley Institute of Living Scale
Wonderlic Personnel Test
Wesman Personnel Classification Test
Personnel Tests for Industry

Multiple Aptitude Test Batteries

General Aptitude Test Battery
Armed Services Vocational Aptitude Battery
Differential Aptitude Test
Employee Aptitude Survey

Mechanical Aptitude Tests

Bennett Mechanical Comprehension Test
Minnesota Spatial Relations Test
Revised Minnesota Paper Form Board Test
SRA Mechanical Aptitudes

Motor Ability Tests

Crawford Small Parts Dexterity Test
Purdue Pegboard
Hand-Tool Dexterity Test
Stromberg Dexterity Test

Clerical Tests

Minnesota Clerical Test
Clerical Abilities Battery
General Clerical Test
SRA Clerical Aptitudes

Note: SRA denotes Science Research Associates. These tests are reviewed in the *Mental Measurements Yearbook* series.

Wonderlic Personnel Test

Even though it is described as a personnel test, the Wonderlic Personnel Test (WPT) is really a group test of general mental ability (Hunter, 1989; Wonderlic, 1983). What makes this instrument somewhat of an institution in personnel testing is its format (50 multiple-choice items), its brevity (a 12-minute time limit), and its numerous parallel forms (16 at last count). Item types on the Wonderlic are quite varied and include vocabulary, sentence rearrangement, arithmetic problem solving, logical induction, and interpretation of prov-

erbs. The following items capture the flavor of the Wonderlic:

1. REGRESS is the opposite of
   a. ingest   b. advance
   c. close   d. open
2. Two men buy a car which costs $550; X pays $50 more than Y. How much did X pay?
   a. $500   b. $300   c. $400   d. $275
3. HEFT CLEFT—Do these words have
   a. similar meaning   b. opposite meaning
   c. neither similar nor opposite meaning

The reliability of the WPT is quite impressive, especially considering the brevity of the instrument. Internal consistency reliabilities typically reach .90, while alternative-form reliabilities usually exceed .90. Normative data are available on 126,000 adults ages 20 to 65. Regarding validity, if the WPT is considered a brief test of general mental ability, the findings are quite positive (Dodrill & Warner, 1988). For example, Dodrill (1981) reports a correlation of .91 between scores on the WPT and scores on the WAIS. This correlation is as high as that found between any two mainstream tests of general intelligence. Hawkins, Faraone, Pepple, Seidman, and Tsuang (1990) report a similar correlation ($r = .92$) between WPT and WAIS-R IQ for 18 chronically ill psychiatric patients. However, in their study, one subject was unable to manage the format of the WPT, suggesting that severe visuospatial impairment can invalidate the test. A recent innovation with the Wonderlic is the addition of four forms of the test (called the Scholastic Level Exam) for use in educational selection and counseling. The validity of the Wonderlic in educational settings is not yet firmly established (Belcher, 1992).

Reviewers of the WPT do raise some concerns about the interpretive guidelines found in the test manual (Schoenfeldt, 1985). For example, the manual suggests that persons who earn raw scores between 16 and 22 have a limited capacity for anything other than routine tasks. These WPT scores correspond to IQs of 93 to 104, that is, such persons are completely within the normal range of intelligence. Thus, the interpretive guidelines seem both arbitrary and unnecessarily restrictive. The manual also lists cutting scores used in industry for over 75 occupations, which raises the specter of an undertrained personnel officer over-interpreting individual scores. This would be especially problematical to racial minorities, since race differences on the WPT are significant (Schoenfeldt, 1985).

Another concern about the Wonderlic is that examinees whose native language is not English will be unfairly penalized on the test (Belcher, 1992). The Wonderlic is a speeded test. In fact, it has such a heavy reliance on speed that points are added for subjects age 30 and older to compensate for the well-known decrement in speed that accompanies normal aging. However, no accommodation is made for nonnative English speakers who might also perform more slowly. One solution to the various issues of fairness cited above would be to provide norms for untimed performance on the Wonderlic. However, the publishers have resisted this suggestion.

Bennett Mechanical Comprehension Test

In many trades and occupations, the understanding of mechanical principles is a prerequisite to successful performance. Automotive mechanics, plumbers, mechanical engineers, trade school applicants, and persons in many other "hands-on" vocations need to comprehend basic mechanical principles in order to succeed in their fields. In these cases, a useful instrument for occupational testing is the Bennett Mechanical Comprehension Test (BMCT). This test consists of pictures about which the examinee must answer straightforward questions. The situations depicted emphasize basic mechanical principles that might be encountered in everyday life. For example, a series of belts and flywheels might be depicted, and the examinee would be asked to discern the relative revolutions per minute of two flywheels. The test includes two equivalent forms (S and T).

The BMCT has been widely used since World War II for military and civilian testing, so an extensive body of technical and validity data exist for this instrument. Split-half reliability coefficients range from the .80s to the low .90s. Comprehensive normative data are provided for several groups. Based on a huge body of earlier research, the concurrent and predictive validity of the BMCT appear to be well established (Wing, 1992). For example, in one study with 175 employees, the correlation between the BMCT and the DAT Mechanical Reasoning subtest was an impressive .80. An intriguing finding is that the test proved to be one of the best predictors of pilot success during World War II (Ghiselli, 1966).

In spite of its psychometric excellence, the BMCT is in need of modernization. The test looks old and many items are dated. By contemporary standards, some BMCT items are sexist or potentially offensive to minorities (Wing, 1992). The problem with dated and offensive test items is that they can subtly bias test scores. Modernization of the BMCT would be a straightforward project that could increase the acceptability of the test to women and minorities while simultaneously preserving its psychometric excellence.

Minnesota Clerical Test

The Minnesota Clerical Test (MCT), which purports to measure perceptual speed and accuracy relevant to clerical work, has remained essentially unchanged in format since its introduction in 1931, although the norms have undergone several revisions, most recently in 1979 (Andrew, Peterson, & Longstaff, 1979). The MCT is divided into two subtests: Number Comparison and Name Comparison. Each subtest consists of 100 identical and 100 dissimilar pairs of digit or letter combinations (Table 11.5). The dissimilar pairs generally differ in regard to only one digit or letter, so the comparison task is challenging. The examinee is required to check only the identical pairs, which are randomly intermixed with dissimilar pairs. The score depends predominantly upon speed, although the examinee is penalized for incorrect items (errors are subtracted from the number of correct items).

The reliability of the MCT is acceptable, with reported stability coefficients in the range of .81 to .87 (Andrew, Peterson, & Longstaff, 1979). The

TABLE 11.5 Items Similar to Those Found on the Minnesota Clerical Test

Number Comparison

1. 3496482 _____ 3495482
2. 17439903 _____ 17439903
3. 84023971 _____ 84023971
4. 910386294 _____ 910368294

Name Comparison

1. New York Globe _____ New York Globe
2. Brownell Seed _____ Brownel Seed
3. John G. Smith _____ John G Smith
4. Daniel Gregory _____ Daniel Gregory

manual also reports a wealth of validity data, including some findings that are not altogether flattering. In these studies, the MCT was correlated with measures of job performance, measures of training outcome, and scores from related tests. The job performance of directory assistants, clerks, clerk-typists, and bank tellers was correlated significantly but not robustly with scores on the MCT. The MCT is also highly correlated with other tests of clerical ability.

Nonetheless, questions still remain about the validity and applicability of the MCT. Ryan (1985) notes that the manual lacks a discussion of the significant versus the nonsignificant validity studies. In addition, the MCT authors fail to provide detailed information concerning the specific attributes of the jobs, tests, and courses used as criterion measures in the reported validity studies. For this reason, it is difficult to surmise exactly what the MCT measures. Both Thomas (1985) and Ryan (1985) complain that the new 1979 norms are difficult to use because the MCT authors provide so little information on how the various norm groups were constituted. Thus, even though the revised MCT manual presents new norms for 10 vocational categories, the test user may not be sure which norm group applies to his or her setting. Because of the marked differences in performance between the norm groups, the vagueness of definition poses a significant problem to potential users of this test.

PERSONALITY AND TEMPERAMENT TESTS

Several personality tests provide a useful basis for employee selection, when used appropriately. Citing bygone practices, Muchinsky (1990) warns against the wreckless use of personality tests for personnel selection:

> Personality inventories such as the MMPI [Minnesota Multiphasic Personality Inventory] were used for many years for personnel selection—in fact, overused or misused. They were used indiscriminately to assess a candidate's personality, even when there was no established relation between test scores and job success. Soon personality inventories came under attack.

Of course, it is essential that personality tests must possess a demonstrated link to job performance before they are used in personnel selection. Unfortunately, the literature on this topic is somewhat sobering for most personality scales. To illustrate this point, we have summarized key findings of a review by Hough, Eaton, Dunnette, Kamp, and McCloy (1990) in Table 11.6. The table reports the mean correlations between various categories of personality measures and several job-related criteria. The data are based upon hundreds of published studies from the time period 1960 to 1984.

The reader will notice that most of the correlations are too low to be of practical value. For example, the mean correlation between Adjustment scores (from various personality scales) and Job Proficiency (usually supervisor ratings) is only .13. Data for this cell are derived from 146 different studies, so the results are highly stable and indicate that, on average, measures of psychological adjustment are very, very weak predictors of job performance. Yet, there is some cause for limited optimism from these studies, as indicated by the healthy correlation of –.43 between Adjustment and Delinquency (e.g., neglect of work duties). Notice, too, that measures of Dependability correlate –.28, on average, with Substance Abuse. Apparently, it is easier to predict some job-related criteria than others.

Certain tests are known to have greater validity than others for specific applications in personnel

TABLE 11.6   Summary of Criterion-Related Validity Studies Using Personality Tests to Predict Job Criteria

Personality Construct	Job Criteria			
	Job Involvement	Job Proficiency	Delinquency	Substance Abuse
Surgency[a]	.04	.04	−.29	.06
Affiliation	.06	−.01	NA	−.03
Adjustment	.13	.13	−.43	−.07
Agreeableness	.02	−.01	−.31	−.04
Dependability	.17	.13	−.27	−.28
Intellectance[b]	−.10	.01	−.24	.18
Achievement	.24	NA	−.35	NA
Masculinity	.10	NA	.02	−.18
Locus of control	.25	NA	NA	NA

Note: NA signifies an absence of research on this predictor-criterion relationship.
[a]Personality trait characterized by sociability, cheerfulness, and social responsiveness.
[b]Personality trait characterized by intellectual analysis and thinking things through.
Source: Adapted with permission from Hough, L. M., Eaton, N., Dunnette, M., Kamp, J., and McCloy, R. (1990). Criterion-related validities of personality constructs and the effect of response distortion on those validities [Monograph]. *Journal of Applied Psychology, 75,* 581–595.

selection. For example, the California Psychological Inventory (CPI) provides an accurate measure of managerial potential (Gough, 1984, 1987). Certain scales of the CPI predict overall performance of military academy students reasonably well (Blake, Potter, & Sliwak, 1993). The Inwald Personality Inventory is well validated as a preemployment screening test for law enforcement (Inwald, 1988). The Minnesota Multiphasic Personality Inventory also bears mention as a selection tool for law enforcement (Hiatt & Hargrave, 1988). Finally, the Hogan Personality Inventory (HPI) is well validated for prediction of job performance in military, hospital, and corporate settings. The HPI was based upon the Big Five theory of personality (see Topic 13A, Theories and the Measurement of Personality). This instrument has cross-validated criterion-related validities as high as .60 for some scales (Hogan, 1986; Hogan & Hogan, 1986). Additional job-related applications of personality tests are discussed in Topic 14A, Self-Report Inventories. Borman et al. (1997) provide a good summary of recent studies on this topic.

PAPER-AND-PENCIL INTEGRITY TESTS

Several test publishers have introduced instruments designed to screen theft-prone individuals and other undesirable job candidates such as persons who are undependable or frequently absent from work (Hogan & Hogan, 1989; O'Bannon, Goldinger, & Appleby, 1989; Ones & Viswesvaran, 1998; Ones, Viswesvaran, & Schmidt, 1993; Sackett, Burris, & Callahan, 1989). These tests come in two clearly differentiated types: overt integrity tests and personality-based measures. We will discuss each type separately, concentrating upon issues raised by these tests rather than detailing the merits or demerits of individual instruments. Table 11.7 lists 20 of the more commonly used instruments.

One problem with integrity tests is that their proprietary nature makes it difficult to scrutinize them in the same manner as traditional instruments. In most cases, scoring keys are available only to in-house psychologists, which makes independent research difficult. Nonetheless, a sizable body of

---

TABLE 11.7   Commonly Used Integrity Tests

Overt Integrity Tests

    Accutrac Evaluation System

    Applicant Review

    Compuscan

    Employee Attitude Inventory

    Employee Reliability Inventory

    Integrity Interview

    Orion Survey

    PEOPLE Survey

    Personnel Selection Inventory

    Phase II Profile

    Reid Report and Reid Survey

    Rely

    Stanton Survey

    True Test

Personality-Based Integrity Tests

    Employment Productivity Index

    Hogan Personnel Selection Series

    Inwald Personality Inventory

    Personnel Decisions, Inc., Employment Inventory

    Personnel Outlook Inventory

    Personnel Reaction Blank

Note: Publishers and authors of these tests can be found in O'Bannon, R. M., Goldinger, L. A., and Appleby, G. S. (1989). *Honesty and integrity testing.* Atlanta, GA: Applied Information Resources.

research now exists on integrity tests, as discussed in the following section on validity.

Overt Integrity Tests

Overt **integrity tests** typically consist of two sections. The first is a section dealing with attitudes toward theft and other forms of dishonesty such as beliefs about extent of employee theft, degree of condemnation of theft, endorsement of common rationalizations about theft, and perceived ease of theft. The second is a section dealing with overt admissions of theft and other illegal activities such as items stolen in the last year, gambling, and drug use. The most widely researched tests of this type include the Personnel Selection Inventory, the Reid

Report, and the Stanton Survey. The interested reader can find addresses for the publishers of these and related instruments in O'Bannon et al. (1989).

Apparently, overt integrity tests can be more easily faked than personality-based integrity tests and might therefore be of less value in screening dishonest applicants. For example, Ryan and Sackett (1987) created a generic overt integrity test modeled upon existing instruments. The test contained 52 attitude and 11 admission items. In comparison to a contrast group asked to respond truthfully and another contrast group asked to respond as job applicants, subjects asked to "fake good" produced substantially superior scores (i.e., better attitudes and fewer theft admissions).

Personality-Based Integrity Tests

The personality-based integrity tests typically do not contain obvious references to theft or other forms of undesirable employee behavior. These measures are more subtle in their approach and therefore less offensive to most job candidates. In fact, some integrity tests are really nothing more than recycled parts of existing personality tests such as the California Psychological Inventory (CPI). For example, the Personnel Reaction Blank (Gough, 1971) is based on those portions of the CPI dealing with sociability, dependability, conscientiousness, internal values, self-restraint, and acceptance of convention. In general, paper-and-pencil measures of conscientiousness show strong relationships with work-related integrity (Collins & Schmidt, 1993).

One common test development strategy for personality-based integrity measures is empirical keying against a criterion of theft. The problem with this approach is the criterion: Theft is rarely apprehended and admissions of theft may or may not be accurate. The base rate for employee theft is almost impossible to nail down. For example, rates of self-reported theft range from 28 percent to 62 percent in different studies (Camara & Schneider, 1994). Thus, the criterion classification of some research subjects may not be valid. A second approach is to measure broad constructs such as general employee deviance as indicated by hostility toward authority, thrill seeking, irresponsibility, and social insensitivity. The instruments that employ this strategy show modest ability to predict global criteria such as supervisor ratings of effectiveness (Ones et al., 1993; Sackett et al., 1989).

A serious problem with most integrity tests is the very high fail rate, typically in the 30 percent to 60 percent range. Because integrity tests commonly are the final hurdle—used only with the small fraction of applicants who have the necessary ability and relevant experience—organizations that employ these tests must be in a position to turn away the majority of applicants. Of course, the high fail rate is, in part, a consequence of stringent cutting scores which cause rejection of potentially valuable employees (false positives) alongside real thieves and scoundrels (true positives). Actually, this is a validity issue, as discussed in the following section.

Validity of Integrity Tests

Publishers of integrity tests have responded to skeptical psychologists and a distrustful public with a barrage of criterion-related validity studies. Ones et al. (1993) requested data on integrity tests from publishers, authors, and colleagues. These sources proved highly cooperative: The authors collected 665 validity coefficients based upon 25 integrity tests administered to more than half a million employees. Using the intricate procedures of meta-analysis, Ones et al. (1993) computed an average validity coefficient of .41 when integrity tests were used to predict supervisory ratings of job performance. Interestingly, integrity tests predicted global disruptive behaviors (theft, illegal activities, absenteeism, tardiness, drug abuse, dismissals for theft, and violence on the job) better than they predicted employee theft alone. The authors concluded with a mild endorsement of these instruments:

> When we started our research on integrity tests, we, like many other industrial psychologists, were skeptical of integrity tests used in industry. Now, on the basis of analyses of a large database consisting of more than 600 validity coefficients, we conclude that integrity tests have substantial evidence of generalizable validity.

This conclusion is echoed in a series of ingenious studies by Cunningham, Wong, and Barbee (1994). Among other supportive findings, these researchers discovered that integrity test results were correlated with returning an overpayment—even when subjects were instructed to provide a positive impression on the integrity test.

Other reviewers are more cautious in their conclusions. In commenting on recent reviews by the American Psychological Association and the Office of Technology Assessment, Camara and Schneider (1994) concluded that integrity tests do not measure up to expectations of experts in assessment, but that they are probably better than hit-or-miss, unstandardized methods used by many employers to screen applicants.

Several concerns remain about integrity tests. Publishers may release their instruments to unqualified users, which is a violation of ethical standards of the American Psychological Association. A second problem arises from the unknown base rate of theft and other undesirable behaviors, which makes it difficult to identify optimal cutting scores on integrity tests. If cutting scores are too stringent, honest job candidates will be disqualified unfairly. Conversely, too lenient a cutting score renders the testing pointless. A final concern is that situational factors may moderate the validity of these instruments. For example, how a test is portrayed to examinees may powerfully affect their responses and therefore skew the validity of the instrument.

Increasingly, the fate of employment testing is being decided by legislatures and the courts. For test developers and the public, the stakes are high: Businesses in the United States administer an estimated 5 million integrity tests each year. As of 1994, Massachusetts was the only state to ban integrity tests, but legislation was pending in at least six other states (Camara & Schneider, 1994). Most likely, the use of integrity tests will be increasingly restrictive in the years ahead.

The debate about integrity tests juxtaposes the legitimate interests of business against the individual rights of workers. Certainly businesses have a right not to hire thieves, drug addicts, and malcontents. But in pursuing this goal, what is the ultimate cost to society of asking millions of job applicants about past behaviors involving drugs, alcohol, criminal behavior, and other highly personal matters? Hanson (1991) has asked rhetorically whether society is well served by the current balance of power—in which businesses can obtain proprietary information about who is seemingly worthy and who is not. It appears almost inevitable that Congress will enter the debate. In 1988, President Reagan signed into law the Employee Polygraph Protection Act which effectively eliminated polygraph testing in industry (see Topic 10B, Forensic Applications of Assessment). Perhaps in the years ahead we will see integrity testing sharply curtailed by an Employee Integrity Test Protection Act.

STRUCTURE AND MEASUREMENT OF PSYCHOMOTOR ABILITIES

Guion (1991) has noted the curious paradox that sensory, physical, and dexterity abilities are essential to success in many work situations, yet these abilities are almost never assessed as part of employee screening or selection. Not only is the lack of such testing unfortunate from the standpoints of efficiency and fairness in employee selection, it also raises concerns about litigation, as discussed below. In this section we briefly review relevant instruments and issues in the assessment of psychomotor abilities. Additional perspectives on this topic can be found in Hogan & Quigley (1994) and Blakley, Quinones, Crawford, & Jago (1994).

A proper understanding of the sensorimotor requirements of specific jobs is important for several reasons. First, physically disabled applicants have a legitimate basis for litigation if they are denied employment because of psychomotor limitations which have no bearing upon job performance. Employers are therefore in the position of needing to document, by means of job analysis and/or validity studies, that minimum levels of psychomotor skill are needed for efficient job performance. Conversely, employees may sue the company if they are injured or develop health problems on a job for which they do not possess a necessary level of physical skill. As Guion (1991) notes, questions of

psychomotor ability are too important to leave to the traditional medical screening examination.

Taxonomy of Psychomotor Skills

The measurement of psychomotor skills has received intense scrutiny over the years by Fleishman and his colleagues (Fleishman, 1975; Fleishman & Quaintance, 1984). Based upon numerous factor-analytic studies, these researchers have identified approximately 20 specific ability factors in the psychomotor domain (Fleishman, 1975). Eleven of these factors are designated as perceptual-motor abilities, whereas nine are referred to as physical proficiency abilities (Table 11.8). Fleishman has developed rating scales to help employers determine the physical abilities required for specific jobs—the interested reader may wish to consult Fleishman and Mumford (1988) for details. We restrict our coverage here to more traditional tests that can be used for assessment of the psychomotor capacities of potential employees.

For some occupations—particularly the manual trades—tests of psychomotor abilities can be used for screening or placement. However, test users should demonstrate the relevance of the

TABLE 11.8   A Taxonomy of Psychomotor Skills

Perceptual-Motor Abilities	Physical Proficiency Abilities
Control precision	Extent flexibility
Multilimb coordination	Dynamic flexibility
Response orientation	Static strength
Reaction time	Dynamic strength
Speed of arm movement	Explosive strength
Rate control (timing)	Trunk strength
Manual dexterity	Gross body coordination
Finger dexterity	Equilibrium
Arm-hand steadiness	Stamina
Wrist-finger speed	
Aiming	

Source: Fleishman, E. A. (1975). Toward a taxonomy of human performance. *American Psychologist, 30,* 1127–1149.

screening criteria to actual job performance (Hogan, 1991). Following, we review a sampling of such tests.

Employee Aptitude Survey

Two of the ten subtests from the Employee Aptitude Survey (EAS) can be used to assess perceptual-motor skills (Ruch & Ruch, 1980). The EAS is primarily a cognitive battery used for personnel selection in organizations. However, Test 3—Visual Pursuit and Test 9—Manual Speed and Accuracy capture several of the perceptual-motor skills proposed by Fleishman. The Visual Pursuit subtest consists of 30 lines interwoven with other lines. The task is to quickly trace each line from beginning to end, as in an electrical circuit diagram. Each line ends on one of five letters—the answer options. Both right (R) and wrong (W) answers are used to compute the score (S) from the formula $S = R - W/4$. The subtest has a five-minute time limit and would appear to capture such crucial perceptual-motor abilities as control precision, manual dexterity, and arm-hand steadiness (Table 11.8). This subtest is recommended in screening for positions such as draftsperson, design engineer, and technician. The Manual Speed and Accuracy subtest consists of placing a pencil dot in as many Os as possible in a five-minute time limit. Dots marked must be within the circle, and errors are heavily penalized. The formula for the corrected score is $S = R - (5 \times W)$. This subtest measures aiming and other perceptual-motor abilities and is recommended in screening for positions such as clerical worker, machine operator, and jobs that require precision or repetitive tasks.

The *Technical Report* (Ruch & Ruch, 1980) reports good test-retest reliabilities for the subtests (mainly in the .80s) and provides normative data for 57 specific jobs or job categories. Summary scores for more than 1,000 males employed by a manufacturing company are also provided. The brevity of the Visual Pursuit and Manual Speed and Accuracy subtests (5-minute time limit each) makes them highly attractive choices for initial screening in technical and clerical positions which require

precision in speeded tasks. For a recent review of the EAS, see Fitzpatrick (1984).

Minnesota Rate of Manipulation Test

The Minnesota Rate of Manipulation Test is a venerable, respected mainstay for the assessment of finger-hand-arm dexterity. This test has been used since the 1940s for employee screening in a wide variety of industrial settings. The test consists of a 60-hole board with round, fitted blocks that are red on one side and yellow on the other. The five subtests include: Placing, Turning, Displacing, One Hand Turning and Placing, and Two Hand Turning and Placing. For each subtest, examinees are instructed to place, turn, or move the round blocks in specific ways as quickly as possible. Reference norms are provided for a sample of 11,000 young adults and 3,000 older adults. This test would appear to measure the Fleishman variables of speed of arm movement, manual dexterity, and finger dexterity.

Purdue Pegboard

Another test of motor skills widely used in preemployment screening is the Purdue Pegboard test. This test was devised at Purdue University in 1948 as an aid in the selection of employees for various kinds of manual labor. The test measures dexterity for two types of activity: gross movement of hands, fingers, and arms; and fingertip dexterity needed in assembly tasks. This test would appear to assess a complex mixture of the perceptual-motor skills identified by Fleishman. A number of additional tests of perceptual-motor abilities are described briefly in Table 11.9.

From a practical standpoint, psychomotor tests such as the Purdue Pegboard can be very useful in establishing minimal levels of performance for purposes of preemployment screening. Nonetheless, their utility in employee selection and placement is limited. A major problem is that psychomotor tests typically show substantial practice effects. Moreover, these practice effects are highly variable from one subject to the next. What this means is that the reliability of psychomotor tests is typically only

TABLE 11.9 Tests of Perceptual-Motor Skills

Roeder Manipulative Aptitude Test: Sorting and assembling nuts, bolts, and washers

Pennsylvania Bi-Manual Worksample: Assembling nuts and bolts

O'Connor Finger Dexterity Test: Hand placement of pins in holes, as in assembly line work.

O'Connor Tweezer Dexterity Test: Use of tweezers in placing single pins in $\frac{1}{16}$-inch diameter holes

Grooved Pegboard: Rotating and placing pegs in slots which have random orientations

Stromberg Dexterity Test: Placing 54 round, colored discs (red, yellow, blue) in a prescribed sequence

Note: These tests are available from the Lafayette Instrument Company, among other sources.

modest—test-retest reliabilities rarely exceed .80 and are often much lower, in the .50s and .60s.

WORK SAMPLE AND SITUATIONAL EXERCISES

A **work sample** is a miniature replica of the job for which examinees have applied. Muchinsky (1990) points out that the I/O psychologist's goal in devising a work sample is "to take the content of a person's job, shrink it down to a manageable time period, and let applicants demonstrate their ability in performing this replica of the job." Guion (1991) has emphasized that work samples need not include every aspect of a job, but should focus upon the more difficult elements that effectively discriminate strong from weak candidates. For example, a position as clerk-typist may also include making coffee and running errands for the boss. However, these are trivial tasks demanding so little skill that it would be pointless to include them in a work sample. A work sample should test important job domains, not the entire job universe.

Campion (1972) devised an ingenious work sample for mechanics that illustrates the preceding point. Using the job analysis techniques discussed at the beginning of this topic, Campion determined that the essence of being a good mechanic was defined by successful use of tools, accuracy of work, and overall mechanical ability. With the help of skilled mechanics, he devised a work sample that incorporated these job aspects through typical tasks such as installing pulleys and repairing a gearbox. Points were assigned to component behaviors for each task. Example items and their corresponding weights were as follows:

Installing Pulleys and Belts	Scoring Weights
1. Checks key before installing against:	
____ shaft	2
____ pulley	2
____ neither	0

Disassembling and Repairing a Gear Box

10. Removes old bearing with:	
____ press and driver	3
____ bearing puller	2
____ gear puller	1
____ other	0

Pressing a Bushing into Sprocket and Reaming to Fit a Shaft

4. Checks internal diameter of bushing against shaft diameter:	
____ visually	1
____ hole gauge and micrometers	3
____ Vernier calipers	2
____ scale	1
____ does not check	0

Campion found that the performance of 34 male maintenance mechanics on the work sample measure was significantly and positively related to the supervisor's evaluations of their work performance, with validity coefficients ranging from .42 to .66.

A **situational exercise** is approximately the white-collar equivalent of a work sample. Situational exercises are largely used to select persons for managerial and professional positions. The main difference between a situational exercise and a work sample is that the former mirrors only part of the job, whereas the latter is a microcosm of the entire job (Muchinsky, 1990). In a situational exercise, the prospective employee is asked to perform under circumstances that are highly similar to the anticipated work environment. Measures of accomplishment can then be gathered as a basis for gauging likely productivity or other aspects of job effectiveness. The situational exercises with the highest validity show a close resemblance with the criterion, that is, the best exercises are highly realistic (Asher & Sciarrino, 1974; Muchinsky, 1990).

Work samples and situational exercises are based on the conventional wisdom that the best predictor of future performance in a specific domain is past performance in that same domain. Typically, a situational exercise requires the candidate to perform in a setting that is highly similar to the intended work environment. Thus, the resulting performance measures resemble those which make up the prospective job itself.

Hundreds of work samples and situational exercises have been proposed over the years. For example, in an earlier review, Asher and Sciarrino (1974) identified 60 procedures, including the following:

- Typing test for office personnel
- Mechanical assembly test for loom fixers
- Map-reading test for traffic control officers
- Tool dexterity test for machinists and riveters
- Headline, layout, and story organization test for magazine editors
- Oral fact-finding test for communication consultants
- Role-playing test for telephone salespersons
- Business letter–writing test for managers

A very effective situational exercise which we will discuss here is the in-basket technique, a procedure that simulates the work environment of an administrator.

The In-Basket Test

The classic paper on the **in-basket test** is the monograph by Frederiksen (1962). For this comprehensive study Frederiksen devised the Bureau of Business In-Basket Test, which consists of the letters, memoranda, records of telephone calls, and other documents which have collected in the in-basket of a newly hired executive officer of a business bureau. In this test, the candidate is instructed not to play a role, but to be himself.[2] The candidate is not to say what he would do, he is to do it.

The letters, memoranda, phone calls, and interviews completed by him in this simulated job environment constitute the record of behavior which is scored according to both content and style of the responses. *Response style* refers to how a task was completed—courteously, by telephone, by involving a superior, through delegation to a subordinate, and so on. *Content* refers to what was done, including making plans, setting deadlines, seeking information; several quantitative indices were also computed, including number of items attempted and total words written. For some scoring criteria such as imaginativeness—the number of courses of action which seemed to be good ideas—expert judgment was required.

Frederiksen (1962) administered his in-basket test to 335 subjects, including students, administrators, executives, and army officers. Scoring the test was a complex procedure that required the development of a 165-page manual. The odd-even reliability of the individual items varied considerably, but enough modestly reliable items emerged (rs of .70 and above) that Frederiksen (1962) could conduct several factor analyses and also make meaningful group comparisons.

When scores on the individual items were correlated with each other and then factor analyzed, the behavior of potential administrators could be described in terms of eight primary factors. When scores on these primary factors were themselves factor analyzed, three second-order factors emerged. These second-order factors describe administrative behavior in the most general terms possible. The first dimension is Preparing for Action, characterized by deferring final decisions until information and advice is obtained. The second dimension is simply Amount of Work, depicting the large individual differences in the sheer work output. The third major dimension is called Seeking Guidance,

---

2. We do not mean to promote a subtle sexism here, but in fact Frederiksen (1962) tested a predominantly (if not exclusively) male sample of students, administrators, executives, and army officers.

with high scorers appearing to be anxious and indecisive. These dimensions fit well with existing theory about administrator performance and therefore support the validity of Frederiksen's task.

A number of salient attributes emerged when Frederiksen compared the subject groups on the scorable dimensions of the in-basket test. For example, the undergraduates stressed verbal productivity, the government administrators lacked concern with outsiders, the business executives were highly courteous, the army officers exhibited strong control over subordinates, and school principals lacked firm control. These group differences speak strongly to the construct validity of the in-basket test, since the findings are consistent with theoretical expectations about these subject groups.

Early studies supported the predictive validity of in-basket tests. For example, Brass and Oldham (1976) demonstrated that performance on an in-basket test corresponded to on-the-job performance of foremen if the appropriate in-basket scoring categories are used. Specifically, based on the in-basket test, foremen who personally reward employees for good work, personally punish subordinates for poor work, set specific performance objectives, and enrich their subordinates' jobs, are also rated by their superiors as being effective managers. The predictive power of these in-basket dimensions was significant, with a multiple correlation coefficient of .54 between predictors and criterion. Standardized in-basket tests can now be purchased for use by private organizations. Unfortunately, most of these tests are "in-house" instruments not available for general review. In spite of an occasional cautionary review (e.g., Brannick et al., 1989), the in-basket technique is still highly regarded as a useful method of evaluating candidates for managerial positions.

Assessment Centers

An assessment center is not so much a place as a process. Many corporations and military branches—as well as a few progressive governments—have dedicated special sites to the application of in-basket and other simulation exercises in the training and selection of managers. The purpose of an **assessment center** is to evaluate managerial potential by exposing candidates to multiple simulation techniques, including group presentations, problem-solving exercises, group discussion exercises, interviews, and in-basket techniques. Results from traditional aptitude and personality tests also are considered in the overall evaluation. The various simulation exercises are observed and evaluated by successful senior managers who have been specially trained in techniques of observation and evaluation. Assessment centers are used in a variety of settings including business and industry, government, and the military. There is no doubt that a properly designed assessment center can provide a valid evaluation of managerial potential. Follow-up research has demonstrated that the performance of candidates at an assessment center is strongly correlated with supervisor ratings of job performance (Gifford, 1991). A more difficult question to answer is whether assessment centers are cost-effective in comparison to traditional selection procedures. After all, funding an assessment center is very expensive. The key question is whether the assessment center approach to selection boosts organizational productivity sufficiently to offset the expense of the selection process. Anecdotally, the answer would appear to be a resounding yes, since poor decisions from bad managers can be very expensive. However, there is little empirical data that addresses this issue.

Goffin, Rothstein, and Johnston (1996) compared the validity of traditional personality testing (with the Personality Research Form, Jackson, 1984b) and the assessment center approach in the prediction of the managerial performance of 68 managers in a forestry products company. Both methods were equivalent in predicting performance, which would suggest that the assessment center approach is not worth the (very substantial) additional cost. However, when both methods were used in combination, personality testing provided significant incremental validity over that of the assessment center alone. Thus, personality testing and assessment center findings each contribute unique information helpful in predicting performance. Case Exhibit 11.1 illustrates an assessment center in action.

CAREER ASSIGNMENT IN CANADA

Gifford (1991) has described at length how the Canadian government selects its top managers with an assessment center approach known as the Career Assignment Program (CAP). Based upon interviews with effective executives, the CAP research team determined that 13 attributes were vital to executive success:

Intelligence	Planning and Organization
Creativity	Delegation
Stress tolerance	Analysis and synthesis
Motivation	Judgment
Effective independence	Oral communication
Leadership	Written communication
Interpersonal relations	

For a few of these attributes (e.g., intelligence, creativity, written communication), standardized tests can provide a valid basis for assessment. However, most of these attributes can only be evaluated by means of management simulation exercises. The CAP research team came up with a grueling three-day program that included five simulation exercises, described below.

On arrival at the assessment center, candidates receive written materials describing a hypothetical government agency. Each candidate is to assume the role of senior executive in a newly formed unit within the agency. The assessment process consists of a series of five activities and meetings which simulate interactions (with trained actors) needed to administer the agency unit:

- *In-basket task*—responding to reports, phone messages, and memoranda directed to the executive.
- *Staff meeting*—the candidate meets with four subordinates to solve problems facing the unit and agency.
- *Briefing*—the candidate informs the president about the general state of the unit.
- *Budget presentation*—budget presentation and three-year forecast delivered to senior financial officers.
- *Taskforce*—the candidate helps study and recommend solutions to unit and agency problems.

All of these activities are observed and evaluated by CAP personnel and candidates are then rated on the 13 attributes listed above. These data are used to determine overall potential for management. Follow-up research indicates that the assessment center approach is predictively valid: CAP ratings are highly correlated with supervisor ratings of job performance up to four years later (Gifford, 1991).

SUMMARY

1. Industrial and organizational psychology (I/O psychology) deals with behavior in work situations (business, advertising, and the military). I/O psychologists use psychological testing and assessment for diverse purposes, including hiring, placement, promotion, and evaluation.

2. Job analysis consists of defining a job in terms of the behaviors necessary to perform it. Job analysis includes two major components: job description (physical and environmental characteristics of the work) and job specification (personal characteristics required).

3. The Position Analysis Questionnaire (PAQ) and similar instruments provide quantifiable information pertinent to job analysis. For example, the PAQ assesses the following components of a job: information input, mental processes, work output, personal relationships, and job context.

4. Psychological tests may play a major role in personnel selection, but they must be used with sensitivity to issues of predictive validity and legal concerns. I/O psychologists need to recognize that even an optimal selection approach may not be valid for all candidates.

5. Autobiographical data, known as biodata, possess substantial predictive validity for many kinds of personnel selection. In many studies the predictive validity of biodata (with values in the .50s) rivals that of standardized tests.

6. In the form in which it is typically used for personnel selection, the interview has low reliability and poor validity. Only when the interview is carefully designed and highly structured can it provide a reliable and valid basis for personnel selection.

7. Cognitive ability tests provide a good basis for personnel selection in most occupations. Rivalled only by the work sample, ability tests have a validity coefficient of .54 averaged over many tests and many samples.

8. Cognitive tests which measure general ability (g) often predict job performance better than measures of specific abilities. The reason is that most jobs are factorially complex in their requirements, which insures that measures of g will possess high predictive validity.

9. When validated for the intended use, personality and temperament tests may provide a useful basis for employee selection. For example, the Hogan Personality Inventory (HPI) is well validated for prediction of job performance in military, hospital, and corporate settings.

10. Paper-and-pencil integrity tests are designed to screen theft-prone individuals and other undesirable job candidates. Some of these instruments possess moderate predictive validity (e.g., personality-based measures), but their use raises many ethical concerns.

11. The assessment of psychomotor and sensorimotor skills can be important for some occupations. For example, the Minnesota Rate of Manipulation Test provides a measure of finger-hand-arm dexterity useful for employee screening in a variety of industrial settings.

12. A work sample is a miniature replica of the job for which examinees have applied. A properly designed work sample (e.g., prospective mechanics might be asked to install a pulley and repair a gearbox) can yield validity coefficients in the .40s, .50s, or .60s.

13. Situational exercises such as the in-basket test are used mainly to select persons for managerial and professional positions. Although very time-consuming and expensive, situational exercises provide a valid basis for selection of managers.

14. An assessment center is used to evaluate managerial potential by exposing candidates to multiple simulation techniques, including group presentations, problem-solving exercises, interviews, and in-basket techniques. Assessment center ratings help identify high-level managerial talent.

KEY TERMS AND CONCEPTS

job analysis   p. 402

biodata   p. 405

integrity tests   p. 414

work sample   p. 418

situational exercise   p. 418

in-basket test   p. 419

assessment center   p. 420

Topic **11B**   Appraisal of Work Performance

The appraisal of work performance is crucial to the successful operation of any business or organization. In the absence of meaningful feedback, employees have no idea how to improve. In the absence of useful assessment, administrators have no idea how to manage personnel. It is difficult to imagine how a corporation, business, or organization could pursue an institutional mission without evaluating the performance of its employees in one manner or another.

Industrial and organizational psychologists frequently help devise rating scales and other instruments used for performance appraisal (Landy & Farr, 1983). When done properly, employee evaluation rests upon a solid foundation of applied psychological measurement—hence its inclusion as a major topic in this text. In addition to introducing essential issues in the measurement of work performance, we also touch briefly upon the many legal issues which surround the selection and appraisal of personnel. We begin by discussing the context of performance appraisal.

FUNCTIONS OF PERFORMANCE APPRAISAL

The evaluation of work performance serves many organizational purposes. The short list includes

promotions, transfers, layoffs, and the setting of salaries—all of which may hang in the balance of performance appraisal. The long list includes the 20 common uses identified by Cleveland, Murphy, and Williams (1989):

Salary administration
Promotion
Retention or termination
Recognition of individual performance
Layoffs
Identify poor performance
Identify individual training needs
Performance feedback
Determine transfers and assignments
Identify individual strengths and weaknesses
Personnel planning
Determine organizational training needs
Evaluate goal achievement
Assist in goal identification
Evaluate personnel systems
Reinforce authority structure
Identify organizational development needs
Criteria for validation research
Document personnel decisions
Meet legal requirements

These applications of performance evaluation cluster around four major uses: comparing individuals in terms of their overall performance levels; identifying and using information about individual strengths and weaknesses; implementing and evaluating human resource systems in organizations; and documenting or justifying personnel decisions. Beyond a doubt, performance evaluation is essential to the maintenance of organizational effectiveness.

As the reader will soon discover, performance evaluation is a perplexing problem for which the simple and obvious solutions are usually incorrect. In part, the task is difficult because the criteria for effective performance are seldom so straightforward as "dollar amount of widgets sold" (e.g., for a salesperson) or "percentage of students passing a national test" (e.g., for a teacher). As much as we might prefer objective methods for assessing the effectiveness of employees, judgmental approaches are often the only practical choice for performance evaluation.

The problems encountered in the implementation of performance evaluation are usually referred to collectively as the criterion problem—a designation that first appeared in the 1950s (e.g., Flanagan, 1956; Landy & Farr, 1983). The phrase **criterion problem** is meant to convey the difficulties involved in conceptualizing and measuring performance constructs which are often complex, fuzzy, and multidimensional. For a thorough discussion of the criterion problem, the reader should consult comprehensive reviews by Austin and Villanova (1992) and Campbell, Gasser, and Oswald (1996). We touch upon some aspects of the criterion problem in the following review.

APPROACHES TO PERFORMANCE APPRAISAL

There are literally dozens of conceptually distinct approaches to the evaluation of work performance. In practice, these numerous approaches break down into four classes of information: performance measures such as productivity counts; personnel data such as rate of absenteeism; peer ratings and self-assessments; and supervisor evaluations such as rating scales. Rating scales completed by supervisors are by far the preferred method of performance

appraisal, as discussed later. First, we mention the other approaches briefly.

Performance Measures

Performance measures include seemingly objective indices such as number of bricks laid for a mason, total profit for a salesperson, or percent of students graduated for a teacher. Although production counts would seem to be the most objective and valid methods for criterion measurement, there are serious problems with this approach (Guion, 1965). The problems include the following:

- The rate of productivity may not be under the control of the worker. For example, the fast-food worker can only sell what people order, and the assembly line worker can only proceed at the same pace as coworkers.
- Production counts are not applicable to most jobs. For example, relevant production units do not exist for a college professor, a judge, or a hotel clerk.
- An emphasis upon production counts may distort the quality of the output. For example, pharmacists in a mail-order drug emporium may fill prescriptions with the wrong medicine if their work is evaluated solely upon productivity.

Another problem is that production counts may be unreliable, especially over short periods of time. Finally, production counts may tap only a small proportion of job requirements, even when they appear to be the definitive criterion. For example, sales volume would appear to be the ideal criterion for most sales positions. Yet, a salesperson can boost sales by misrepresenting company products. Sales may be quite high for several years—until the company is sued by unhappy customers. Productivity is certainly important in this example, but the corporation should also desire to assess interpersonal factors such as honesty in customer relations.

Personnel Data: Absenteeism

Personnel data such as rate of absenteeism provide another possible basis for performance evaluation. Certainly employers have good reason to keep tabs on absenteeism and to reduce it through appropriate incentives. Steers and Rhodes (1978) calculate that absenteeism costs about $25 billion a year in lost productivity! Little wonder that absenteeism is a seductive criterion measure which has been researched extensively (Harrison & Hulin, 1989).

Unfortunately, absenteeism turns out to be a largely useless measure of work performance, except for the extreme cases of flagrant work truancy. A major problem is defining absenteeism. Landy and Farr (1983) list 28 categories of absenteeism, many of which are uncorrelated with the others. Different kinds of absenteeism include scheduled versus unscheduled, authorized versus unauthorized, justified versus unjustified, contractual versus noncontractual, sickness versus nonsickness, medical versus personal, voluntary versus involuntary, explained versus unexplained, compensable versus noncompensable, certified illness versus casual illness, Monday/Friday absence versus midweek, and reported versus unreported. When is a worker truly absent from work? The criteria are very slippery.

In addition, absenteeism turns out to be an atrociously unreliable variable. The test-retest correlations (absentee rates from two periods of identical length) are as low as .20, meaning that employees display highly variable rates of absenteeism from one time period to the next. A related problem with absenteeism is that workers tend to underreport it for themselves and overreport it for others (Harrison & Shaffer, 1994). Finally, for the vast majority of workers, absenteeism rates are quite low. In short, absenteeism is a poor method for assessing worker performance, except for the small percentage of workers who are chronically truant.

Peer Ratings and Self-Assessments

Some researchers have proposed that peer ratings and self-assessments are highly valid and constitute an important complement to supervisor ratings. A substantial body of research pertains to this ques-

tion, but the results are often confusing and contradictory. Nonetheless, it is possible to list several generalizations (Harris & Schaubroeck, 1988; Smither, 1994):

- Peers give more lenient ratings than supervisors.
- The correlation between self-ratings and supervisor ratings is minimal.
- The correlation between peer ratings and supervisor ratings is moderate.
- Supervisors and subordinates have different ideas about what is important in jobs.

Overall, reviewers conclude that peer ratings and self-assessments may have limited application for purposes such as personal development, but their validity is not yet sufficiently established to justify widespread use (Smither, 1994).

Supervisor Rating Scales

Rating scales are the most common measure of job performance (Landy & Farr, 1983; Muchinsky, 1990). These instruments vary from simple graphic forms to complex scales anchored to concrete behaviors. In general, supervisor rating scales reveal only fair reliability, with a mean interrater reliability coefficient of .52 across many different approaches and studies (Viswesvaran, Ones, & Schmidt, 1996). In spite of their weak reliability, supervisor ratings still rank as the most widely used approach. About three-quarters of all performance evaluations are based upon judgmental methods such as supervisor rating scales (Landy, 1985).

The simplest rating scale is the graphic rating scale, introduced by Donald Paterson in 1922 (Landy & Farr, 1983). A **graphic rating scale** consists of trait labels, brief definitions of those labels, and a continuum for the rating. As the reader will notice in Figure 11.1, several types of graphic rating scales have been used.

The popularity of graphic rating scales is due, in part, to their simplicity. But this is also a central weakness because the dimension of work performance being evaluated may be vaguely defined. Dissatisfaction with graphic rating scales led to the

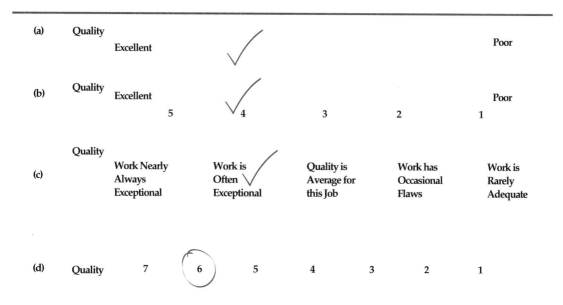

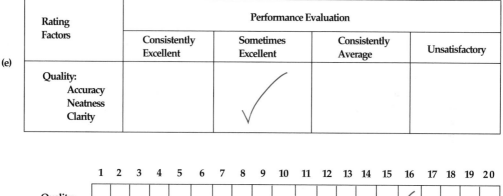

FIGURE 11.1   Examples of Graphic Rating Scales

development of many alternative approaches to performance appraisal, as discussed below.

A **critical incidents checklist** is based upon actual episodes of desirable and undesirable on-the-job behavior (Flanagan, 1954). Typically, a check-list developer will ask employees to help construct the instrument by submitting specific examples of desirable and undesirable job behavior. For example, suppose that we intended to develop a checklist to appraise the performance of resident advisers (RAs) in a dormitory. Modeling a study by Aamodt, Keller, Crawford, and Kimbrough (1981), we might ask current dormitory RAs the following question:

> Think of the best RA that you have ever known. Please describe in detail several incidents that reflect why this person was the best adviser. Please do the same for the worst RA you have ever known.

Based upon hundreds of nominated behaviors, checklist developers would then proceed to distill and codify these incidents into a smaller number of relevant behaviors, both desirable and undesirable. For example, the following items might qualify for the RA checklist:

_____ stays in dorm more than required

_____ breaks dormitory rules

_____ is fair about discipline

_____ plans special programs

_____ fails to discipline friends

_____ is often unfriendly

_____ shows concern about residents

_____ comes across as authoritarian

Of course, the full checklist would be much longer than the preceding. The RA supervisor would complete this instrument as a basis for performance appraisal. If needed, an overall summary score can be derived from an appropriate weighting of individual items. Harvey (1991) discusses the advantages and disadvantages of this approach.

Another form of criterion-referenced judgmental measure is the **behaviorally anchored rating scale** (BARS). The classic work on BARS dates back to Smith and Kendall (1963). These authors proposed a complex developmental procedure for producing criterion-referenced judgments. The procedure uses a number of experts to identify and define performance dimensions, generate behavior examples, and scale the behaviors meaningfully. Overall, the procedure is quite complex, time-consuming, and expensive. A number of variations and

improvements have been suggested (Harvey, 1991). An advantage to BARS and other behavior-based scales is their strict adherence to EEOC (Equal Employment Opportunity Commission) guidelines discussed later in this chapter. BARS and related approaches focus upon behaviors as opposed to personality or attitudinal characteristics. A behaviorally anchored scale for job performance of a sales supervisor is depicted in Figure 11.2. Of course, the comprehensive evaluation of a sales manager would include additional scales for other aspects of work.

Research on improving the accuracy of ratings with BARS is mixed. Some studies find fewer rating errors—especially a reduction in unwarranted leniency of evaluations—whereas other studies report no improvement with BARS compared to other evaluation methods (Murphy & Pardaffy, 1989). Overall, Muchinsky (1990) concludes that the BARS approach is not much better than graphic rating scales in reducing rating errors. Nonetheless, the scale development process of BARS may have indirect benefits in that supervisors are compelled to pay close attention to the behavioral components of effective performance.

A **behavior observation scale** (BOS) is a variation upon the BARS technique. The difference between the two is that the BOS approach uses a continuum from "almost never" to "almost always" to measure how often an employee performs the specific tasks on each behavioral dimension. As with the BARS technique, researchers question whether behavior observation scales are worth the extra effort (Guion, 1991).

A **forced-choice scale** is designed to eliminate bias and subjectivity in supervisor ratings by forcing a choice between options that are equal in social desirability. In theory, this approach makes it impossible for the supervisor to slant ratings in a biased or subjective manner. We will use the path-breaking research by Sisson (1948) to illustrate the features of this approach. He developed a scale to evaluate Army officers which consisted of tetrads of behavioral descriptors. Each tetrad contained two positive items matched for social desirability and two negative items also matched for social desirability. The four items in each tetrad were topi-

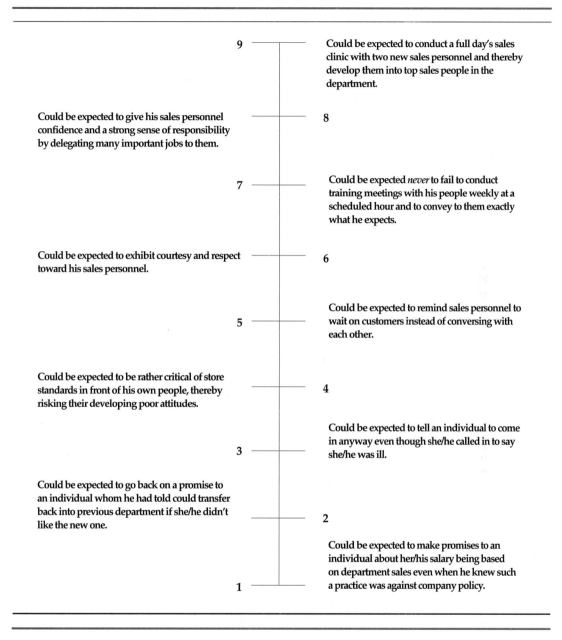

9 — Could be expected to conduct a full day's sales clinic with two new sales personnel and thereby develop them into top sales people in the department.

Could be expected to give his sales personnel confidence and a strong sense of responsibility by delegating many important jobs to them. — 8

7 — Could be expected *never* to fail to conduct training meetings with his people weekly at a scheduled hour and to convey to them exactly what he expects.

Could be expected to exhibit courtesy and respect toward his sales personnel. — 6

5 — Could be expected to remind sales personnel to wait on customers instead of conversing with each other.

Could be expected to be rather critical of store standards in front of his own people, thereby risking their developing poor attitudes. — 4

3 — Could be expected to tell an individual to come in anyway even though she/he called in to say she/he was ill.

Could be expected to go back on a promise to an individual whom he had told could transfer back into previous department if she/he didn't like the new one. — 2

1 — Could be expected to make promises to an individual about her/his salary being based on department sales even when he knew such a practice was against company policy.

FIGURE 11.2   Behaviorally Anchored Rating Scale for Sales Supervisor
Source: Reprinted with permission from Campbell, J. P., Dunnette, M. D., Arvey, R. D., and Hellervik, L. V. (1973). The development and evaluation of behaviorally based rating scales. *Journal of Applied Psychology, 57,* 15–22.

cally related to a single performance dimension. Unknown to the supervisors who completed the rating scale, one of the two positive items was judged very descriptive of effective Army officers and the other judged less so. Likewise, one of the two negative items was judged more descriptive of ineffective Army officers and the other judged less so. Here is a sample tetrad (Borman, 1991):

	Most Descriptive	**Least Descriptive**
A. Cannot assume responsibility	_____	_____
B. Knows how and when to delegate authority	_____	_____
C. Offers suggestions	_____	_____
D. Changes ideas too easily	_____	_____

Supervisors were asked to review the items in each tetrad and to check one item as most descriptive and one item as least descriptive of the officer being evaluated. A score of +1 was awarded for responding "most descriptive" to the positively keyed item (in this case, alternative B) or "least descriptive" to the negatively keyed item (in this case alternative A), whereas a score of –1 was awarded for responding "least descriptive" to the positively keyed item or "most descriptive" to the negatively keyed item. Responding to the nonkeyed items (alternatives C and D) as most or least descriptive earned a score of 0. Thus, each tetrad yielded a five-point continuum of scores: +2, +1, 0, –1, –2. The summary score used for performance appraisal consisted of the algebraic sum of the individual items.

The forced-choice approach has never really caught on, due largely to the effort required in scale construction. This is unfortunate, because the method does effectively reduce unwanted bias. Borman (1991) refers to this approach as a "bold initiative" that produces a relatively objective rating scale.

SOURCES OF ERROR IN PERFORMANCE APPRAISAL

The most difficult problem in the assessment of job performance is the proper definition of appraisal criteria. If the supervisor is using a poorly designed instrument that does not tap the appropriate dimensions of job behavior, then almost by definition the performance appraisal will be inaccurate, incomplete, and erroneous. Undoubtedly, the failure to identify appropriate criteria for acceptable and unacceptable performance is a major source of error in performance appraisal. But it is not the only source. Even when supervisors have access to excellent, well-designed measures of performance appraisal, various sorts of subtle errors can creep in. We discuss three such additional sources of rating error: halo effect, rater bias, and criterion contamination.

Halo Effect

The tendency to rate an employee high or low on all dimensions because of a global impression is called **halo effect.** Research on the halo effect can be traced back to the early part of this century (Thorndike, 1920). The most common halo effect is a positive halo effect. In this case, an employee receives a higher rating than deserved because the supervisor fails to be objective when rating specific aspects of the employee's behavior. A positive halo effect is usually based upon overgeneralization from one element of a worker's behavior. For example, an employee with perfect attendance may receive higher-than-deserved evaluations on productivity and work quality—even though attendance is not directly related to these job dimensions.

Smither (1994) lists the following approaches to control for halo effects:

- Provide special training for raters
- Supervise the supervisors during the rating
- Practice simulations before doing the ratings
- Keep a diary of information relevant to appraisal
- Provide supervisors with a short lecture on halo effects

Additional approaches to rater training are discussed by Goldstein (1991). An intriguing analysis of the nature and consequences of halo error can be found in Murphy, Jako, and Anhalt (1993). Contrary to the reigning prejudice against halo errors, these researchers conclude that the halo effect does not necessarily detract from the accuracy of ratings. They point out that a presumed halo effect is often the byproduct of true overlap on the dimensions being rated. The debate over halo effect is not likely to be resolved any time soon (Arvey & Murphy, 1998).

Rater Bias

The potential sources of **rater bias** are so numerous that we can only mention a few prominent examples here. Leniency or severity errors occur when a supervisor tends to rate workers at the extremes of the scale. Leniency may reflect social dynamics, as when the supervisor wants to be liked by employees. Leniency is also caused by extraneous factors such as the attractiveness of the employee. Severity errors refer to the practice of rating all aspects of performance as deficient. In contrast, central tendency errors occur when the supervisor rates everyone as nearly average on all performance dimensions. Context errors occur when the rater evaluates an employee in the context of other employees rather than based upon objective performance. For example, the presence of a workaholic salesperson with extremely high sales volume might cause the sales supervisor to rate other sales personnel lower than deserved.

Recently, researchers have paid considerable attention to the possible biasing effects of whether a supervisor likes or dislikes a subordinate. Surprisingly, the trend of the findings is that supervisor affect (liking or disliking) toward specific employees does not introduce rating bias. In general, strong affect in either direction represents valid information about an employee. Thus, ratings of affect often correlate strongly with performance ratings, but this is because both are a consequence of how well or poorly the employee does the job (Ferris, Judge, Rowland, & Fitzgibbons, 1994; Varma, DeNisi, & Peters, 1996). Other forms of rater bias are discussed by Goldstein (1991) and Smither (1994).

Criterion Contamination

Criterion contamination is said to exist when a criterion measure includes factors that are not demonstrably part of the job (Borman, 1991; Harvey, 1991). For example, if a performance measure includes appearance, this would most likely be a case of criterion contamination—unless appearance is relevant to job success. Likewise, evaluating an employee on "dealing with the public" is only appropriate if the job actually requires the employee to meet the public. Goldstein (1992) outlines three kinds of criterion contamination:

1. Opportunity bias occurs when workers have different opportunities for success, as when one salesperson is assigned to a wealthy neighborhood and others must seek sales in isolated, rural areas.
2. Group characteristic bias is present when the characteristics of the group affect individual performance, as when workers in the same unit agree to limit their productivity to maintain positive social relations.
3. Knowledge of predictor bias occurs when a supervisor permits personal knowledge about an employee to bias the appraisal, as when quality of the college attended by a new worker affects her evaluation.

Careful attention to job analysis as a basis for selection of appraisal criteria is the best way to reduce errors in performance appraisal. In addition, employers should follow certain guidelines in performance appraisal, as discussed in the following section.

Guidelines for Performance Appraisal

Performance appraisal is a formidable task. Not only must employers pay attention to the psychometric soundness of their approach, they must also design a practical system that meets organizational goals. For example, appraisal standards must be sufficiently difficult and detailed to ensure that organizational goals are accomplished. Another concern is that performance appraisal falls under the purview of Title VII of the Civil Rights Act of 1964. Hence, employers must develop fair systems that do not discriminate on the basis of race, sex, and other protected categories. To complicate matters, these standards—soundness, practicality, legality—may conflict with one another. The practical approach may be neither psychometrically sound nor legal. Often, appraisal methods which show the best measurement characteristics (e.g., strong interrater reliability) will fail to assess the most important aspects of performance, that is, they are not practical. This is a familiar refrain within the measurement field. Too often, psychologists must choose between rigor and relevance, rarely achieving both at the same time. Finally, legal considerations must be considered when exploring the limits of performance appraisal.

Smither (1994) has published guidelines for developing performance appraisal systems that we paraphrase here:

- Base the performance appraisal upon a careful job analysis
- Develop specific, contamination-free criteria for appraisal from the job analysis
- Determine that the instrument used to rate performance is appropriate for the appraisal situation
- Train raters to be accurate, fair, and legal in their use of the appraisal instrument
- Use performance evaluations at regular intervals of six months to a year
- Evaluate the performance appraisal system periodically to determine whether it is actually improving performance

The training of raters is an especially important guideline. An appraisal system that seems perfectly straightforward to the employer could easily be misunderstood by an untrained rater, resulting in biased evaluations. Borman (1991) notes that two kinds of rater training are effective: rater error training, in which the trainer seeks simply to alert raters to specific kinds of errors (e.g., halo effect); and frame-of-reference training, in which the trainer familiarizes the raters with the specific content of each performance dimension. Research indicates that these kinds of training improve the accuracy of ratings.

LEGAL ISSUES IN I/O ASSESSMENT

Nearly every aspect of the employment relationship is subject to the law: recruitment, screening, selection, placement, compensation, promotion, and performance appraisal all fall within the domain of legal interpretations (Cascio, 1987). However, courts and legislative bodies have reserved special scrutiny for employment-related testing. The practitioner who refuses to learn relevant legal guidelines in personnel testing does so at great peril, because unwise practices can lead to costly and time-consuming litigation (Case Exhibit 11.2).

Personnel testing is particularly sensitive because the consequences of an adverse decision are often grave: The applicant does not get the job, or an employee does not get the desired promotion or placement. Recognizing that employment testing performs a sensitive function as gatekeeper to economic advantage, Congress has passed laws sharply regulating the use of testing. The courts have also rendered decisions which help define unfair test discrimination. In addition, regulatory bodies have published guidelines which substantially impact testing practices. We will provide a current perspective on the regulation of personnel testing by tracing the development of laws, regulations, and major court cases.

It may surprise the reader to learn that employment testing has raised legal controversy only in the last 35 years (Arvey & Faley, 1988). During this period, several definitive court decisions and path-breaking governmental directives have helped define current legal trends. These landmarks are depicted in Table 11.10, beginning with The Civil Rights Act of 1964, proceeding through the federal regulations of the Equal Employment Opportunity Commission (EEOC), and concluding with very recent court cases and legislative developments. We will review these landmarks in chronological order.

Early Court Cases and Legislation

During the presidency of Lyndon Johnson, Congress passed the Civil Rights Act of 1964. This early civil rights legislation had a profound effect on employee testing procedures. In addition to broad provisions designed to prevent discrimination in many social contexts, Title VII of this Act prohibits employment practices that discriminate on the basis of

UNWISE TESTING PRACTICES IN EMPLOYEE SCREENING

According to the Associated Press of July 11, 1993, the Target discount chain agreed to settle out of court in a class-action lawsuit filed on behalf of an estimated 2,500 job applicants. Prospective security guards for Target were required to take the Rodgers Psychscreen, a 704-item condensed combination of the CPI and the MMPI. Several applicants objected to answering the test, which included questions about God, sex, and bowel movements. Target agreed to pay $1.3 million, including $60,000 to four plaintiffs named in the lawsuit. Although Target admitted no wrongdoing in the case, corporate officers agreed not to use the Psychscreen test for at least five years.

Sibi Soraka was one of the plaintiffs in the lawsuit. He found the questions to be "off-the-wall and bizarre." He claimed that the cumulative effect of answering the questions made him palpably ill. He added: "It doesn't take Einstein to figure out that these questions really don't have any bearing on our world and life today, or certainly on a job walking around looking for shoplifters." Target corporation defended the testing practice, noting that Psychscreen is commonly used in the evaluation of law enforcement officers. Attorneys for Soraka disagreed, citing a lack of evidence that the test helped identify good versus poor risks for employment. They noted that about 800 of the 2,500 applicants were denied employment based solely upon Psychscreen results.

This case illustrates that the psychometric soundness of an instrument is not the only criterion in test selection. In addition, test users must show that the instrument is relevant to their application. Furthermore, issues of acceptability to prospective examinees must be considered.

race, color, religion, sex, or national origin. The Act established several important general principles relevant to employment testing (Cascio, 1987):

- Discriminatory preference for any group, minority or majority, is barred by the Act.
- The employer bears the burden of proof that all requirements for employment, including test scores, are related to job performance.
- Professionally developed tests used in personnel testing must be job-related.
- In addition to open and deliberate discrimination, the law forbids practices that are fair in form but discriminatory in operation.
- Intent is irrelevant: the plaintiff need not show that discrimination was intentional.

- In spite of the above proscriptions, job-related tests and other measuring devices are deemed both legal and useful.

The 1964 legislation also created the Equal Employment Opportunity Commission (EEOC) to develop guidelines defining fair employee-selection procedures. The initial guidelines, published in 1966, were vague. Later revisions of these guidelines, including the Uniform Guidelines on Employee Selection (1978), were quite specific and have been used by the courts to help resolve legal disputes regarding employment testing practices (see the following section).

The 1964 *Myart v. Motorola* case marked the first involvement of the courts in employment

TABLE 11.10   Major Legal Landmarks in Employment Testing

1964   *Myart v. Motorola.*   This case set the precedent for courts to hear employment testing cases.

1964   Civil Rights Act.   This act prohibits job discrimination based on sex, race, color, religion, or national origin.

1966   EEOC Guidelines.   The first published guidelines on employment testing practices.

1971   *Griggs v. Duke Power.*   The Supreme Court rules that employment test results must have a demonstrable link to job performance.

1973   *United States v. Georgia Power.*   Ruling strengthens the authority of EEOC guidelines for studies of employment testing validity.

1975   *Albemarle v. Moody.*   EEOC guidelines strengthened; subjective supervisory ratings ruled a poor basis for validating tests.

1976   *Washington v. Davis.*   Court ruled that performance in a training program was a sufficient basis against which to validate a test.

1978   *Uniform Guidelines on Employee Selection.* These guidelines defined adverse impact by the four-fifths rule and incorporated criteria for validity in employee selection studies.

1988   *Watson v. Fort Worth Bank and Trust.*   The court ruled that subjective employment devices such as the interview can be validated; employees can claim disparate impact based on interview-based promotion policies.

1990   Americans with Disabilities Act.   This act sharply limits the reasons for not hiring a disabled person. One provision is that medical tests may not be administered prior to an offer of employment.

1991   Civil Rights Act.   This act outlaws subgroup norming of employee selection tests.

testing. The issues raised by this landmark case are still reverberating today. Leon Myart was an African-American applicant for a job at one of Motorola's television assembly plants. Even though he had highly relevant job experience, Mr. Myart was refused a position because his score on a brief screening test of intelligence fell below the company cutoff. Claiming racial discrimination, he filed an appeal with the Illinois Fair Employment Practices Commission. The state examiner found in

favor of the complainant and directed that the Motorola company should offer Mr. Myart a job. In addition, the examiner ruled that the particular test should not be used in the future and that any new test should "take into account the environmental factors which contribute to cultural deprivation." In essence, the examiner concluded that Motorola's employment testing practices were unfair because they acted as a barrier to the employment of culturally deprived and disadvantaged applicants. Even though the case was later overturned for lack of evidence, *Myart v. Motorola* did set the precedent to hear such complaints in the court system (Arvey & Faley, 1988).

Advent of EEOC Employment Testing Standards

During the 1970s, several court cases helped shape current standards and practices in employment testing. The focus of *Griggs v. Duke Power Company* (1971) was the use of tests—in this case the Wonderlic Personnel Test and the Bennett Mechanical Comprehension Test—as eligibility criteria for employees who wanted to transfer to other departments. In particular, employees at Duke Power Company who lacked a high school education could qualify for transfer if they scored above the national median on both tests. This policy appeared to discriminate against African-American employees since it was disproportionately difficult for them to gain eligibility for transfer. However, lower courts found no discriminatory intent and therefore found in favor of the power company.

In 1971, the Supreme Court reversed the lower court findings, ruling against the use of tests without their validation. The decision emphasized several points of current relevance (Arvey & Faley, 1988):

- Fairness in employment testing is determined by consequences, not motivations.
- Testing practices must have a demonstrable link to job performance.
- The employer has the burden of showing that an employment practice such as testing is job-related.

- Diplomas, degrees, or broad testing devices are not adequate as measures of job-related capability.
- The EEOC testing standards deserve considerable deference from employment testers.

These employment testing guidelines were further refined in a 1973 court decision, *United States v. Georgia Power Company.* In this case, the Georgia Power Company presented a validation study to support its employment testing practices when its policies were shown to have an adverse impact upon the hiring and transferring of African Americans. However, the validation study was weak, in part because it was based upon multiple discriminant analysis, a complex statistical technique rarely used for this purpose. The courts ruled that the validation study was inadequate since it did not adhere to EEOC guidelines for evaluating validity studies. This finding ensconced the EEOC guidelines as virtually the law of the land in employment testing practices.

Several other court cases in the 1970s and 1980s also served to strengthen the authority of EEOC testing guidelines. These cases were quite complex and involved multiple issues in addition to those cited here. In *Albemarle v. Moody* (1975), the Supreme Court deferred to EEOC guidelines in finding that subjective supervisory ratings are ambiguous and therefore constitute a poor basis for evaluating the validity of an employment selection test. The central issue in *Washington v. Davis* (1976) was whether performance in a training program (as opposed to actual on-the-job performance) was a sufficient basis for determining the job-relatedness of the employment selection procedures. In this case, the Supreme Court ruled that performance in a police officer training program was a sufficient criterion against which to validate a selection test.

In *State of Connecticut v. Teal,* the U.S. Supreme Court sided with four African-American state employees who had failed a written test that was used to screen applicants for the position of welfare eligibility supervisor. The workers claimed unfair discrimination, noting that only 54 percent of minority applicants passed, compared to 80 percent for whites. In its defense, the state of Connecticut argued that discrimination did not exist, since 23 percent of the successful African-American applicants were ultimately promoted, compared to 14 percent for whites. The Court was not impressed with this argument, noting that Title VII of the 1964 Civil Rights Act was specifically designed to protect individuals, not groups. Thus, any unfairness to an individual is unacceptable. Further analysis of fair employment court cases can be found in Arvey and Faley (1988), Cascio (1987), Kleiman and Faley (1985), and Russell (1984).

Uniform Guidelines on Employee Selection

During the 1970s several federal agencies and professional groups proposed revisions and extensions of the existing EEOC employment testing guidelines. The revisions were developed in response to court decisions which had interpreted EEOC guidelines in a narrow, inflexible, legalistic manner. However, the existence of several sets of competing guidelines was confusing, and strong pressures were exerted upon the involved parties to forge a compromise. These efforts culminated in a consensus document known as the 1978 *Uniform Guidelines on Employee Selection.*

The *Uniform Guidelines* quickly earned respect in court cases and were frequently cited in the resolution of legal disputes. The new guidelines contain interpretation and guidance not found in earlier versions, particularly regarding adverse impact, fairness, and the validation of selection procedures, as discussed below.

The *Uniform Guidelines* provide a very specific definition of adverse impact. In general, when selection procedures favor applicants from one group (usually males or whites), the basis for selection is said to have an **adverse impact** on other groups (usually females or nonwhites) with a lower selection proportion. The *Uniform Guidelines* define adverse impact with a four-fifths rule. Specifically, adverse impact exists if one group has a selection rate less than four-fifths of the rate of the group with the highest selection rate. For example, consider an employer who has 200 applicants in a year, 100 African-American and 100 white. If 120 persons were hired, including 80 whites and 40 African Americans, then the percentage of whites hired is 80 percent (80/100) whereas the percentage of African Americans hired is 40 percent (40/100). Since the selection rate for African Americans is only half that of whites (40 percent/80 percent), the employer might be vulnerable to charges of adverse impact. We should note that the *Uniform Guidelines* suggest caution about this rule when sample sizes are small.

The *Uniform Guidelines* also pay more attention to fairness than previous documents. Fairness is treated in the following manner:

> When members of one racial, ethnic, or sex group characteristically obtain lower scores on a selection procedure than members of another group, and the differences are not reflected in differences in a measure of job performance, use of the selection procedure may unfairly deny opportunities to members of the group that obtain the lower scores. Furthermore, in cases where two or more selection procedures are equally valid, the employer is obliged to use the method that produces the least adverse impact.

The *Uniform Guidelines* also establish a strong affirmative action responsibility on the part of employers. If an employer finds a substantial disparity in persons hired from a subgroup compared to their availability in the job market, several corrective steps are recommended. These corrective measures include specialized recruitment programs designed to attract qualified members of the group in question, on-the-job training programs so that affected minorities do not get locked into dead-end jobs, and a revamping of selection procedures to reduce or eliminate exclusionary effects.

Finally, the guidelines provide specific technical standards for evaluating validity studies of employee selection procedures. The courts will almost certainly consult these *Uniform Guidelines* if employees bring suit against the company for alleged unfairness in employee selection practices. Thus, is a foolish employer who does not pay special attention to these technical criteria. For example, one criterion concerns the use of performance scores obtained during training programs:

> Where performance in training is used as a criterion, success in training should be properly measured and the relevance of the training should be shown either through a comparison of the content of the training program with the critical or important work behavior(s) of the job(s), or through a demonstration of the relationship between measures of performance in training and measures of job performance.

Thus, preemployment evaluation of job candidates in a training program may constitute a valid method of employee selection, but only if a strong link exists between the task demands of training and the requirements of the actual job.

The *Uniform Guidelines* contain many other criteria which we cannot review here. We urge the reader to read this fascinating and influential document which is often cited in court cases on employment discrimination.

Legal Implications of Subjective Employment Devices

In many corporations, promotions are based upon the subjective judgment of senior managers. A common practice is for one or more managers to interview several qualified employees and offer a promotion to the one candidate who appears most promising. The selection of this candidate is typically based upon subjective appraisal of such factors as judgment, originality, ambition, loyalty, and tact. Until recently, these subjective employment devices appeared to be outside the scope of fair employment practices codified in the *Uniform Guidelines* and other sources.

However, in a recent civil rights case, *Watson v. Fort Worth Bank and Trust* (1988), the Supreme Court made it easier for employees to prove charges of race or sex discrimination against employers who use interview and other subjective assessment devices for employee selection or promotion. We outline the factual background of this important case before discussing the legal implications (Bersoff, 1988).

Clara Watson, an African-American employee at Fort Worth Bank and Trust, was rejected for promotion to supervisory positions four times in a row. Each time, a white applicant received the promotion. Watson obtained evidence showing that the bank had never had an African-American officer or director, had only one African-American supervisor, and paid African-American employees lower salaries than equivalent white employees. Furthermore, all supervisors had to receive approval from a white male senior vice president for their promotion decisions. The bank did not dispute that it made hiring and promotion decisions solely on the basis of subjective judgment. When an analysis of promotion patterns confirmed statistically significant racial disparities, Watson brought suit against the bank.

Two legal theories were available for Watson to litigate her claim under Title VII of the 1964 Civil Rights Act. The two theories are called "disparate treatment" and "disparate impact." A disparate treatment case is more difficult to litigate, since the plaintiff must prove that the employer engaged in intentional discrimination. In a disparate impact case, intention is irrelevant. Instead, the plaintiff need merely show that a particular employment practice—such as using a standardized test—results in an unnecessary and disproportionately adverse impact upon a protected minority.

The lower courts ruled that Watson was restricted to the more limited disparate treatment approach since the employer had used subjective evaluation procedures. Furthermore, the lower courts ruled that the bank had not engaged in intentional discrimination and did have legitimate reasons for not promoting Watson. Nonetheless, the Supreme Court agreed to hear the case in order to determine whether a disparate impact analysis could be applied to subjective employment devices such as interview. Relying heavily upon a brief from the American Psychological Association (APA, 1988), the Supreme Court ruled unanimously that the disparate impact analysis is applicable to subjective or discretionary promotion practices based on interview. In effect, the court ruled that subjective employment devices such as

interview can be validated. Thus, employers do not have unmonitored discretion to evaluate applications for promotion based on subjective interview. As a consequence of *Watson v. Fort Worth Bank and Trust,* employers must be ready to defend all their promotion practices—including subjective interview—against claims of adverse impact.

Recent Developments in Employee Selection

In 1990, Congress passed the Americans with Disabilities Act (ADA), which forbids discrimination against qualified individuals with disabilities. The ADA was discussed briefly in Topic 7A, Testing Special Populations. This act protects job applicants with disabilities by sharply limiting permissible reasons for refusing to hire them. Specifically, employers can decline to hire a disabled worker for *only* the following reasons (1) if hiring the applicant would cause the company undue hardship in terms of making accommodations for the disability; (2) business necessity; or (3) the presence of the disabled worker would pose a direct threat to the health or safety of the worker or others.

An important stipulation of ADA is that medical tests may not be administered prior to an offer of employment. Unfortunately, what constitutes a "medical test" is not well defined by the act. In particular, it is possible that intelligence tests might be construed as "medical" in nature, which could wreak havoc with employment testing:

> According to ADA requirements, if an attribute is not required for performing an essential task, then an applicant may request an accommodation or modification of either the testing process or the job if he or she claims a covered disability that is associated with that nonessential attribute. In practice, this might mean that unless it is demonstrated that intelligence is required for accomplishing an essential task, no test that measures intelligence (or any facet of intelligence) could be administered before offering employment to any applicant claiming an impairment that is associated with intellectual functioning (Landy, Shankster, & Kohler, 1994).

It is still too soon to determine the impact of ADA upon the practice of personnel selection.

CHAPTER 11   INDUSTRIAL AND ORGANIZATIONAL ASSESSMENT

There is confusion about which disabilities are covered by the act, uncertainty about which selection practices are forbidden, and anxiety over how many people will seek accommodation under the act (Klimoski & Palmer, 1994). Court decisions and administrative guidelines will be needed to sharpen the focus of this important legislation.

The Civil Rights Act of 1991 also contained important provisions relevant to employee selection and appraisal. Specifically, the act outlaws subgroup norming of test scores, which effectively eliminates the use of separate hiring and promotion lists. Subgroup norming refers to the practice of using identified subgroups (instead of a diversified national sample) for purposes of developing group-specific test norms. The prohibition of this practice presents a challenge to employers and I/O psychologists, since racial subgroup norming of test scores has been a popular and effective method for avoiding adverse impact.

Recent court cases also have impacted personnel testing. The issue in *Soraka v. Dayton Hudson* was whether corporations can use a personality test as a basis for preemployment screening for mental health problems in job applicants. As discussed previously, Soraka was required to take the Rodgers Psychscreen as part of the application process for a position as security guard. The Psychscreen is a true-false personality inventory intended to identify persons with psychological problems such as depression and anxiety. Soraka filed suit against the department store, claiming that individual questions about his sexual practices and religious beliefs were a violation of his civil rights. This case was interesting because it pertained to the value and validity of individual items as opposed to overall test scores. The courts have long held that preemployment testing must have demonstrated relevance to job performance or it cannot be used. However, the courts have not required validity evidence for individual test items. Soraka won his case, which was appealed by Dayton Hudson. In 1993, the company settled out of court. This litigation is summarized in Case Exhibit 11.2 found earlier in this section.

SUMMARY

1. Performance appraisal of employees is essential to the ongoing success of any business or organization. Applied psychological measurement is at the heart of performance appraisal.

2. Performance evaluation serves many organizational purposes, including promotions, transfers, layoffs, and the setting of salaries. Although objective methods for assessing the effectiveness of employees would appear to be preferable, judgmental approaches are often the only practical choice.

3. Methods for performance appraisal include performance measures such as productivity counts; personnel data such as rate of absenteeism; peer ratings and self-assessments; and supervisor evaluations such as rating scales. Rating scales are by far the most common approach.

4. About three-quarters of all performance evaluations are based upon judgmental methods such as supervisor rating scales. The simplest rating scale is the graphic rating scale, which consists of trait labels, brief definitions of those labels, and a continuum for the rating.

5. The behaviorally anchored rating scale (BARS) is a popular form of criterion-referenced performance measure. A BARS form contains explicit behavioral anchors along a continuum of excellence which the supervisor evaluates in terms of past observations of work performance.

6. Performance appraisal is subject to several sources of error including failure to identify appropriate criteria for acceptable and unacceptable performance, halo effect (rating an employee high or low on all dimensions because of a global impression), rater bias, and criterion contamination.

7. Criterion contamination occurs when a criterion measure includes factors that are not demonstrably part of the job, such as rating an employee on "dealing with the public" when this is not really part of the position.

8. Appropriate guidelines for the development of performance appraisal systems include basing the appraisal method upon a careful job analysis; training raters to be fair, accurate, and legal; and evaluating the performance appraisal system periodically.

9. Employee testing and appraisal is carefully circumscribed by legal and regulatory guidelines. For example, Title VII of the Civil Rights Act of 1964 prohibits employment practices that discriminate on the basis of race, color, religion, sex, or national origin.

10. Several court cases have helped to shape testing practices in personnel selection. For example, in *Griggs v. Duke Power* (1971) the Supreme Court ruled that fairness in employment testing is determined by consequences, not motivations; testing practices must have a demonstrable link to job performance; and the employer must show that a testing practice is job-related.

11. Several federal agencies and professional groups helped develop the *Uniform Guidelines on Employee Selection* (1978). This document provides guidance on many employee testing practices, including a very specific definition of adverse impact.

12. In general, when selection procedures favor applicants from one group (usually males or whites), the basis for selection is said to have an adverse impact on other groups (usually females or nonwhites) when they have a lower selection proportion (less than four-fifths of the majority group).

13. As a consequence of *Watson v. Fort Worth Bank and Trust* (1988), employers must now be ready to defend all their promotion practices— including subjective interview—against claims of adverse impact.

14. The Americans with Disabilities Act and the Civil Rights Act of 1991 also contained important provisions relevant to employee selection and appraisal. For example, the Civil Rights Act outlaws subgroup norming of tests.

KEY TERMS AND CONCEPTS

Vocational and Values Assessment

T O P I C **12A** Assessment of Interests and Work Values

An Overview of Interest Assessment
Inventories for Interest Assessment
Career and Work Values Assessment
Integrative Model of Career Assessment
Summary
Key Terms and Concepts

In this chapter we examine approaches to the assessment of interests and values, broadly defined. Because they are formative in everything from work to worship, interests and values are fundamental to the identity of each individual. It is no accident that the adolescent who values aesthetic harmony later reveals an interest in literature and then pursues a vocation as English teacher. Nor is it surprising when a shy teenager with an analytic bent shows a passion for mathematics and becomes a computer scientist. The values held by persons shape their interests in life which, in turn, shape career choices. Lives possess a coherency that is explained, in part, by the influence of interests and values.

Values not only link the individual to the world of work, they are intertwined in moral, spiritual, and religious matters as well. Whether we favor or oppose capital punishment, whether we find life meaningful or merely chaotic, whether we seek or avoid religious practice—these matters we resolve based upon personal values. In sum, the choices we make in matters of work, spiritual life, and personal conduct are not random, they are bound together by common threads that we call interests and values.

A problem faced by many young adults is that their values are unstated and their interests are unexplored. Furthermore, they lack knowledge about career options. In these cases, career selection can arouse anxiety, and perhaps it should. Lowman (1991) has noted that the process of finding a vocation can be as complex and as difficult as choosing a mate. The dilemma of career choice is not limited to young adults entering the job market, but also vexes older workers who are dissatisfied with their careers. Fortunately, a large array of tests and guidance approaches are available to help individuals identify values, interests, and potential career choices, as reviewed in this topic.

In Topic 12A, Assessment of Interests and Work Values, we survey the measurement of interests and work-related values. The focus here is on the world of work and the use of specialized tests for career assessment and advising. In Topic 12B, Values in Moral, Spiritual, and Religious Development, we introduce the reader to methods and concerns in the assessment of moral, spiritual, and religious dimensions of the individual.

AN OVERVIEW OF INTEREST ASSESSMENT

In most applications of psychological testing, the goals of assessment are reasonably clear. For example, intelligence testing helps predict school performance; aptitude testing foretells potential for accomplishment; and personality testing provides information about social and emotional functioning. But what is the purpose of interest assessment? Why would a psychologist recommend it? What can a client expect to gain from a survey of his or her interests?

Interest assessment promotes two compatible goals: life satisfaction and vocational productivity. It is nearly self-evident that a good fit between individual interests and chosen vocation will help foster personal life satisfaction. After all, when work is interesting we are more likely to experience personal fulfillment as well. In addition, persons who are satisfied with their work are more likely to be productive. Thus, employees and employers both stand to gain from the artful application of interest assessment. Several useful instruments exist for this purpose, and we will review the most widely used interest inventories later.

In the selection of employees, the consideration of personal interests may be of great practical significance to employers and therefore circumstantially relevant to the job candidates as well. We may sketch out a rough equation as follows: productivity = ability × interest. In other words, high ability

in a specific field does not guarantee success; neither does high interest level. The best predictions are possible when both variables are considered together. Thus, employers have good reason to determine if a potential employee is well matched to the position; the employee should like to know as well.

We begin this section with a critical examination of major interest tests. The six instruments chosen for review include the following:

- The Strong Interest Inventory (SII), the latest revision of the well-known Strong Vocational Interest Blank (SVIB).
- The Jackson Vocational Interest Survey (JVIS), a test that embodies modern methods for scale construction
- The Kuder General Interest Survey (KGIS), an instrument that incorporates a divergent philosophy of test construction
- The Vocational Preference Inventory (VPI), which measures six widely used vocational themes
- The Self-Directed Search (SDS), a self-administered and self-scored guide to exploring career options
- The Campbell Interest and Skill Survey (CISS), a recent and appealing test that is simple in format but sophisticated in execution

The review of prominent interest tests is followed by the related topic of assessment in career and work values.

INVENTORIES FOR INTEREST ASSESSMENT

Strong Interest Inventory (SII)

The Strong Interest Inventory (SII) is the latest revision of the Strong Vocational Interest Blank (SVIB), one of the oldest and most prominent instruments in psychological testing (Hansen, 1992). We can best understand the SII by studying the history of its esteemed predecessor, the SVIB. In particular, we need to review the guiding assumptions used in the construction of the SVIB which have been carried over into the SII.

The first edition of the SVIB appeared in 1927, eight years after E. K. Strong formulated the essential procedures for measuring occupational interests while attending a seminar at the Carnegie Institute of Technology (Campbell, 1971; Strong, 1927). In constructing the SVIB, Strong employed two little-used techniques in measurement. First, the examinee was asked to express liking or disliking for a large and varied sample of occupations, educational disciplines, personality types, and recreational activities. Second, the responses were empirically keyed for specific occupations. In an empirical key, a specific response (e.g., liking to roller skate) is assigned to the scale for a particular occupation only if successful persons in that occupation tend to answer in that manner more often than comparison subjects.

Although Strong did not express his underlying assumptions in a simple and straightforward manner, it is clear that the theoretical foundation for the SVIB derives from a typological, trait-oriented conception of personality. Tzeng (1987) has identified the following basic assumptions in the development and application of the SVIB:

1. Each occupation has a desirable pattern of interests and personality characteristics among its workers. The ideal pattern is represented by successful people in that occupation.
2. Each individual has relatively stable interests and personality traits. When such interests and traits match the desirable interest patterns of the occupation the individual has a high probability to enter that occupation and be more likely to succeed in it.
3. It is highly possible to differentiate individuals in a given occupation from others-in-general in terms of the desirable patterns of interests and traits for that occupation.

Strong constructed the scales of his inventory by contrasting the responses of several specific occupational criterion groups with those of a people-in-general group. The subjects for each criterion group were workers in that occupation who were satisfied with their jobs and who had been so employed for at least three years. The items which differentiated the two groups, keyed in the appropriate direction, were selected for each occupational scale. For example, if members of a specific occupational group disliked "buying merchandise for a store" more often than people-in-general, then that item (keyed in the dislike direction) was added to the scale for that occupation.

The first SVIB consisted of 420 items and a mere handful of occupational scales (Strong, 1927). Separate editions for men and women followed shortly. The inventory has undergone numerous revisions over the years (Tzeng, 1987), culminating in the modern instrument known as the Strong Interest Inventory (Campbell, 1974; Hansen, 1992; Hansen & Campbell, 1985).

Although the Strong Interest Inventory (SII) was fashioned according to the same philosophy as the SVIB, the latest revision departs from its predecessors in three crucial ways:

1. The SII merges the men's and women's forms into a single edition.
2. The SII introduces a theoretical framework to guide the organization and interpretation of scores, as discussed below.
3. The SII incorporates a substantial increase in the number of occupational scales, particularly in the vocational/technical areas underrepresented in the SVIB.

The SII consists of 317 items grouped into seven sections. In the first five sections, the examinee records "Like," "Indifferent," or "Dislike" for occupations, school subjects, activities, leisure activities, and contact with different types of persons (Table 12.1). A sixth part requires the examinee to express a preference between paired items (e.g., dealing with things versus dealing with people). The seventh section consists of self-descriptive statements which the examinee marks "Yes," "No," or "?".

The SII can only be scored by prepaid answer sheets or booklets that are mailed or faxed to the publisher, or through purchase of a software system that provides on-site scoring for immediate results. The results consist of a lengthy printout which is organized according to several themes. All scores are expressed as standard scores with a mean of 50 and an SD of 10. Normative results for men and women

TABLE 12.1   Characteristic Items from the Strong Interest Inventory

Mark *Like, Indifferent,* or *Dislike* next to the following items.

1. Driving a truck _____
2. Being a fish and game officer _____
3. Chemistry _____
4. Doing applied research _____
5. Acting in a drama _____
6. Magazines about music _____
7. Sociology _____
8. Fundraising for charities _____
9. Buying goods for a store _____
10. People who are leaders _____
11. Regular work hours _____
12. Assertive people _____

are reported separately, but cross-sex comparisons can be achieved by simple visual transposition.

At the most global level are the six General Occupational Theme Scores, namely, Realistic, Investigative, Artistic, Social, Enterprising, and Conventional. These theme scores were based upon the theoretical analysis of Holland (1966, 1985ab) whose work we discuss later. Each theme score pertains to a major interest area which describes both a work environment and a type of person. For example, persons scoring high on the Realistic theme are generally quite robust, have difficulty expressing their feelings, and prefer to work outdoors with heavy machinery. Within the theme scores can be found 25 Basic Interest Scales such as Adventure, Mathematics, and Social Science. The interest scales are empirically derived and consist of substantially intercorrelated items.

The most specific results consist of 211 scores for the Occupational Scales. In the 1985 revision of the SII, these scales were constructed in the usual manner by comparing responses of persons employed in the given occupation versus samples of men-in-general and women-in-general (Hansen, 1992; Hansen & Campbell, 1985). Sample sizes for the criterion groups ranged from 60 to 420, with most groups containing 200 or more persons. The criterion groups consisted of persons between the ages of 25 and 60, satisfied with their occupation, meeting certain minimum standards of successful employment, and employed in the given occupation for at least three years. Standardization of the 1985 version involved the testing of over 140,000 persons, of whom only 50,000 met the criteria for scale development.

A recent innovation on the SII is the addition of personal style scales (Harmon, Hansen, Borgen, & Hammer, 1994). These are designed to measure preferences for broad styles of living and working. These scales assist in vocational guidance by showing level of comfort with distinctive styles. The four style scales are:

1. *Work Style,* on which a high score indicates a preference to work with people and a low score signifies an interest in ideas, data, and things;
2. *Learning Environment,* on which a high score indicates a preference for academic learning environments and a low score indicates a preference for more applied learning activities;
3. *Leadership Style,* on which a high score indicates comfort in taking charge of others and a low score indicates uneasiness; and
4. *Risk Taking/Adventure,* on which a high score indicates a preference for risky and adventurous activities as opposed to safe and predictable activities.

The personal style scales each have a mean of 50 and a standard deviation of 10. Note that these are truly bipolar scales where each pole is distinct and meaningful.

Evaluation of the SII

The SII represents the culmination of over 50 years of study, involving literally thousands of research reports and hundreds of thousands of respondents. In evaluating this instrument, we can only outline basic trends in the research, referring the reader to other sources for details (Tzeng, 1987; Campbell, 1971; Campbell & Hansen, 1981; Hansen, 1984, 1987, 1992; Hansen & Campbell, 1985). We should also point out that evaluations of the reliability and validity of the SII are based in part upon its similarity to the SVIB, for which a huge amount of technical data exists.

Based upon test-retest studies, the reliability of the SII-SVIB has proved to be exceptionally good in the short run, with one- and two-week stability coefficients for the occupational scales generally in the .90s. When the test-retest interval is years or decades, the correlations drop to the .60s and .70s for the occupational scales, except for respondents who were older (over age 25) upon first testing. For younger respondents first tested as adolescents, the median test-retest correlation after 15 years is around .50 (Lubinski, Benbow, & Ryan, 1995). But for older respondents, first tested after the age of 25, the median test-retest correlation 10 to 20 years later is a phenomenal .80 (Campbell, 1971). Apparently, by the time we pass through young adulthood, personal interests become extremely stable. The questions on the SII-SVIB capture that stability in the occupational scores, providing support for the trait conception of personality upon which these instruments were based.

The validity of the SII-SVIB is premised largely on the ability of the initial occupational profile to predict the occupation eventually pursued. Strong (1955) reported that the chances were about two in three that people would be in occupations predicted by high occupational scale scores, and about one in five that respondents would be in occupations for which they had shown little interest when tested. Although other researchers have quibbled with the exact proportions (Dolliver, Irvin, & Bigley, 1972), it is clear that the SII-SVIB has impressive hit rates in predicting occupational entry. The instrument functions even better in predicting the occupations that an examinee will *not* enter. In a recent study, Donnay and Borgen (1996) provide evidence for construct validity by demonstrating strong overall differentiation between 50 occupational groups on the SII:

> The big picture is that people in diverse occupations show large and predictable differences in likes and dislikes, whether in terms of vocational interests or in terms of personal styles. And the Strong provides valid, structural, and comprehensive measures of these differences (p. 290).

The SII is used mainly with high school and college students, and adults seeking vocational guidance or advice on continued education. Because most students' interests are undeveloped and unstabilized prior to age 13 or 14, the SII is not recommended for use below high school level. As evident in the reliability data reported above, the SII becomes increasingly valuable with older subjects, and it is not unusual to see middle-aged persons use the results of this instrument for guidance in career change.

Jackson Vocational Interest Survey (JVIS)

The Jackson Vocational Interest Survey (JVIS) is a relatively new instrument that contrasts sharply in several respects with the SII (Jackson, 1977; Verhoeve, 1993). The 34 basic interest scales on the JVIS are composed of two different types, work role scales and work style scales. The 26 work role scales measure specific interests pertinent to broad occupational themes such as mathematics, life science, adventure, business, and teaching. The 8 work style scales were designed to measure preferences for working in environments that require particular modes of behavior, such as job security, dominant leadership, accountability, and stamina. The JVIS may be hand-scored, but computer scoring is probably preferable since the user then obtains several additional groups of scales, including data on examinees' similarity to college students majoring in specific academic disciplines. The JVIS is suited to high school age and older.

Several features distinguish the JVIS from the SII and other interest inventories. First, the JVIS employs a forced-choice ipsative format whereby examinees must select their preferred choice from two alternatives. Items on the JVIS resemble the following:

A. Acting in a school drama.
B. Teaching kids how to write.

A. Quilting bedspreads with ornate designs.
B. Buying furniture for a chain of stores.

A. Writing a mathematics text for grade school children.
B. Studying the financial growth of a local bank.

Although rarely used, the forced-choice item format has the advantage of reducing the impact of social desirability upon test results. A second distinctive feature of the JVIS is that Jackson used a rational and theory-guided method in the derivation of scales, as opposed to the empirical approach found in most other instruments. As a result of these two features, the JVIS scales possess a greater independence from one another than found on other instruments and are also quite factorially pure. As evidence of factorial homogeneity of the scales, biserial correlations between item endorsements and scale scores are typically in the high .60s and low .70s.

The JVIS is normed on a very large sample—approximately 8,000 high school and college students. However, these subjects consist mainly of students from Pennsylvania and the Province of Ontario, so their representation of the general population is questionable. Reliability is excellent, at least in the short range, with one- to two-week test-retest coefficients typically in the mid-.80s. Based on an eclectic group of studies reported in the *Manual,* concurrent and predictive validity appear promising, but additional studies are needed to bolster confidence in this instrument (Shepard, 1989).

Kuder General Interest Survey

The Kuder General Interest Survey (KGIS) represents the most recent evolution of a series of highly respected Kuder vocational interest inventories developed over the last 50 years. The first of these instruments, the Kuder Preference Record, was published in 1939. This instrument introduced an interesting forced-choice response format that has survived into the present (discussed below). The Preference Record underwent several revisions and emerged in 1979 as the Kuder Occupational Interest Survey-Revised (KOIS-R, Kuder & Diamond, 1979). The KOIS-R is a well-known test that produces scores for over 100 specific occupational groups and nearly 50 college majors. The target population for the KOIS-R is roughly the same as for the SII and the JVIB. For purposes of presenting a diversity of interest tests, it is more instructive to discuss the KGIS here.

The KGIS is unique among interest inventories in that its target population is restricted to adolescents in grades six through twelve (Kuder, 1975). The test requires only a sixth-grade reading level and may be administered by the classroom teacher and hand-scored on site. Thus, the KGIS is well suited to the development of educational and vocational goals in the early formative years of adolescence.

The KGIS is also unusual in its methodology: The inventory uses a forced-response triad format to measure interests. Specifically, each item on the test requires the examinee to indicate most- and least-liked alternatives from three statements. This forced-choice approach is particularly suited to identifying examinees who have not answered the items sincerely.

The 168-item inventory produces 10 interest scores that are largely ipsative in nature. The reader will recall that scores on an ipsative test reflect intraindividual variability rather than interindividual variability. With the KGIS, comparison to an external reference group is of secondary importance in determining scores.[1] Thus, a high score in one interest area mainly means that the examinee preferred that area more often than the others in the forced-choice items.

The 10 scales reflect broad areas of interest: Outdoor, Mechanical, Computational, Scientific, Persuasive, Artistic, Literary, Musical, Social Service, and Clerical. An eleventh scale, the Verification Scale, is designed to determine the sincerity of the responses. The manual reports extensive test-retest, internal consistency, and stability data based on a sample of 9,819 students in grades 6 through 12. The six-week test-retest and internal consistency data are generally acceptable, with the older students showing higher test-retest correlations. The possible exception to good reliability is the Persuasive Scale (pertinent to sales positions), which shows test-retest correlations of .69 and .73, respectively, for boys and girls in grades 6 through 8.

Stability data over a four-year follow-up are less impressive. The mean stability coefficient is only .50, and for low-IQ subjects (below 100) it is

---

1. In truth, the KGIS is only partially ipsative. Some of the item triads are scored for more than one scale.

even lower, as low as .19 for the Clerical Scale. This is unfortunate because low-IQ adolescents would be more likely to enter clerical fields than high-IQ adolescents. Yet, measurement of clerical interests is highly unstable for precisely this group.

Comment on the KGIS and Other Interest Inventories

Considering the difficulty of the task it undertakes—measuring the broad interest patterns of adolescents—the KGIS performs at an acceptable level. In grades 6 through 8, results of the KGIS may spur students to explore new experiences pertinent to their measured interests; in grades 9 and 10, results may help students plan high school courses; and in grades 11 and 12, the results can help students make tentative vocational choices.

But the KGIS suffers the same pivotal shortcoming of all existing interest inventories, a total inattention to opportunity. Williams and Williams (1985) have expressed this point well:

> . . . for those specifically looking for a measure of interest, the Kuder is definitely an acceptable measure. But interest is only one prong in the triumvirate of interest-ability-opportunity. The most important prong, opportunity, has generated the least psychometric interest. That this would be so is not surprising. Opportunity is by far the hardest construct to define, but those who deal in career counseling should never ignore it, regardless of the difficulty in measurement and definition.

We remind the reader that the inattention to opportunity is common to all interest measures, although it is perhaps a more serious problem for the KGIS because this instrument is used with persons who have not yet entered the job market.

Vocational Preference Inventory

The Vocational Preference Inventory is an objective, paper-and-pencil personality interest inventory used in vocational and career assessment (Holland, 1985c). The VPI measures eleven dimensions, including the six personality-environment themes of Realistic, Investigative, Artistic, Social, Enterprising, and Conventional, and five additional dimen-

sions of Self-Control, Masculinity/Femininity, Status, Infrequency, and Acquiescence. The test items consist of 160 occupational titles toward which the examinee expresses a feeling by marking *y* (yes) or *n* (no). The VPI is a brief test (15 to 30 minutes) and is intended for persons 14 years and older with normal intelligence.

Holland proposes that personality traits tend to cluster into a small number of vocationally relevant patterns, called types. For each personality type there is also a corresponding work environment best suited to that type. According to Holland, there are six types: Realistic, Investigative, Artistic, Social, Enterprising, and Conventional. This is sometimes known as the **RIASEC model,** in reference to the first letters of the six types. The types are idealizations which few people (or environments) fit completely. Nonetheless, Holland believes that most individuals tend to resemble one type more than the others. In addition, individuals show a lesser degree of resemblance to a second and third type as well.

We can summarize the personality-environment types as follows:

- *Realistic:* athletic, lacks verbal and interpersonal skills, and prefers "hands-on" or outdoors vocations such as mechanic, farmer, or electrician
- *Investigative:* task-oriented thinker with unconventional attitudes who fits well in scientific and scholarly positions such as chemist, physicist, or biologist
- *Artistic:* individualistic, avoids conventional situations, and prefers aesthetic pursuits
- *Social:* uses social competencies to solve problems, likes to help others, and prefers teaching or helping professions
- *Enterprising:* a leader with good selling skills who fits well in business and managerial positions
- *Conventional:* conforming and prefers structured roles such as bank teller or computer operator

The six themes in the RIASEC system can be arranged in a hexagon with similar themes side-by-side and dissimilar themes opposite one another, as depicted in Figure 12.1.

Test-retest reliability coefficients for the six major scales range from .89 to .97. VPI norms are

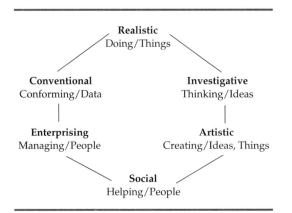

FIGURE 12.1   Holland's Hexagonal Model
of Occupational Themes
Source: Reprinted with permission from Lowman, R. L. (1991).
The clinical practice of career assessment: Interests, abilities,
and personality. Washington, DC: American Psychological
Association. Copyright © 1991 by the American Psychological
Association.

based upon large convenience samples of college students and employed adults from earlier VPI editions. The characteristics of the standardization sample are not well defined which makes the norms somewhat difficult to interpret (Rounds, 1985).

The validity of the VPI is essentially tied to the validity of Holland's (1985a) hexagonal model of vocational interests. Literally hundreds of studies have examined this model from different perspectives. We will cite trends and representative studies. The reader is referred to Holland (1985c) and Walsh and Holland (1992) for more details.

Several VPI studies have investigated a key assumption of Holland's theory—that individuals tend to move toward environments which are congruent with their personality types. If this assumption is correct, then the real-world match between work environments and personality types of employees should be substantial. We should expect to find that Realistic environments have mainly Realistic employees, Social environments have mainly Social employees, and so on. Research on this topic has followed a straightforward methodology: Subjects are tested with the VPI and classified by their Holland types (using up to six letters); the work environments of the subjects are then independently

classified by an appropriate environmental measure; finally, the degree of congruence between persons and environments is computed. In better studies, a correction for chance agreement is also applied.

Using his hexagonal model, Holland has developed occupational codes as a basis for classifying work environments (Gottfredson & Holland, 1989; Holland, 1966, 1978, 1985c). For example, landscape architect is coded as RIA (Realistic, Investigative, Artistic) because this occupation is known to be a technical, skilled trade (Realistic component) that requires scientific skills (Investigative component) and also demands artistic aptitude (Artistic component). The Realistic component is listed first because it is the most important for landscape architect, whereas the Investigative and Artistic components are of secondary and tertiary importance, respectively. Some other occupations and their codes are taxi driver (RSE), mathematics teacher (ISC), reporter (ASE), police officer (SRE), real estate appraiser (ECS), and secretary (CSA). In a similar manner, Holland has also worked out codes for different college majors.

One approach to congruence studies is to compare VPI results of students or workers with the Holland codes which correspond to their college majors or occupations. For example, VPI Holland codes for a sample of police officers should consist mainly of profiles that begin with S and should contain a larger-than-chance proportion of specifically SRE profiles. Furthermore, the degree of congruence should be related to the degree of expressed satisfaction with that line of work or study.

Research with college students provides strong support for the congruence prediction: Students tend to select and enter college majors which are congruent with their primary personality types (Holland, 1985a; Walsh & Holland, 1992). Thus, Artistic types tend to major in art, Investigative types tend to major in biology, and Enterprising types tend to major in business, to cite just a few examples. These results provide strong support for the VPI and the theory upon which it is based.

This short review has barely touched the surface of supportive validity studies with the VPI.

Walsh and Holland (1992) cite several additional lines of research which buttress the validity of this test. But not all studies of the VPI affirm its validity. Furnham, Toop, Lewis, and Fisher (1995) failed to find a relationship between person-environment (P-E) "fit" and job satisfaction, a key theoretical underpinning of the test. According to Holland's theory, the better the P-E fit, the greater should be job satisfaction. In three British samples, the relationships were weak or nonexistent, suggesting that the VPI does not "travel well" in cultures outside of the United States.

Although we have emphasized mainly the strengths of the VPI up to this point, even the authors of the test acknowledge that there is room for improvement. For example, Walsh and Holland (1992) cite the following weaknesses of the VPI: (1) the notions about vocational environments are only partially tested; (2) the hypotheses about the person-environment interactions need considerable additional research work; (3) the formulations about personal development have received some support but need more comprehensive examinations; (4) the classification of occupations may differ depending on the device used to assess the personality types; and (5) there are personal and environmental contingencies that are currently outside the scope of the theory.

The last weakness is perhaps the most serious. After all, the VPI assessment approach does not currently recognize any role for education, intelligence, and special aptitudes, except insofar as these factors might indirectly bear upon personality and vocational interests. Yet, common sense dictates that intellectual ability will have a great deal to do with vocational satisfaction for some professions, independent of the match between personality type and work environment. For further discussion of the VPI and the theory upon which it is based, the interested reader is referred to Gottfredson (1990), Holland (1990), and Holland and Gottfredson (1990).

Self-Directed Search

Holland has always shown a keen interest in the practical applications of his research on vocational development. Consistent with this interest, he developed the Self-Directed Search, a highly practical, brief test that is appealing in its simplicity (Holland, 1985ab). As the name suggests, the Self-Directed Search is designed to be a self-administered, self-scored, and self-interpreted test of vocational interest. The SDS measures the six RIASEC vocational themes described previously.

The SDS consists of dichotomous items which the examinee marks "like" or "dislike" (or "yes" or "no") in four sections: (1) Activities (six scales of 11 items each); (2) Competencies (six scales of 11 items each); (3) Occupations (six scales of 14 items each); and (4) Self-Estimates (two sets of six ratings). For each section, the face-valid items are grouped by RIASEC themes. For each theme, the total number of "like" and "yes" answers is combined with the self-estimates of ability to come up with a total theme score. The SDS takes 30 to 50 minutes for completion and is intended for persons 15 years and older.

The RIASEC themes on the SDS showed test-retest reliabilities that range from .56 to .95 and internal consistencies that range from .70 to .93. Norms for SDS scales and codes are reported for pooled convenience samples of 4,675 high school students, 3,355 college students, and 4,250 employed adults ages 16 through 24 (Holland, 1985ab). However, SDS results are typically interpreted in an individualized, ipsative manner ("Is this occupation a good fit for this client?"), so normative data are of limited relevance.

The SDS is available in a hand-scored paper-and-pencil version and a computerized version as well. Unfortunately, the paper-and-pencil version is prone to a 16 percent clerical error rate when used by high school students (Holland, 1985ab). The user-friendly microcomputer test is probably the preferred version because of the ease of administration and the error-free scoring and interpretation.

When a subject takes the SDS, the three highest theme scores are used to denote a summary code. For example, a person whose three highest scores were on Investigative, Artistic, and Realistic would have a summary code of IAR. In a separate booklet distributed with the test—the *Occupations Finder*—the examinee can look up his or her summary code and find a list of occupations which provide the best "fit." For example, an examinee with an IAR summary code would learn that he or she most closely resembles persons in the following occupations: anthropologist, astronomer, chemist, pathologist, and physicist. The test booklet contains additional information which helps the examinee explore relevant career options.

The SDS serves a very useful purpose in providing a quick and simple format for prompting young persons to examine career alternatives. By eliminating the time-consuming process of administration, scoring, interpretation, and counselor feedback, the test makes it possible for a wide audience to receive an introductory level of career counseling. Holland (1985ab) proposes that the SDS is appropriate for up to 50 percent of students and adults who might desire career guidance. Presumably, the other 50 percent would find the SDS an insufficient basis for career exploration. Holland (1985ab) rightfully warns users to consider many sources of information in career choice and not to rely too heavily on test scores per se. Levinson (1990) discusses the integration of SDS data with other psychoeducational data to make specific vocational recommendations for high school students.

The validity of the SDS is linked to the validity of the hexagonal model of personality and environments upon which the test is based. One aspect of validity, then, is whether the model makes predictions which are confirmed by SDS results in the real world. In general, the results from over 400 studies support the construct validity of the SDS (Dumenci, 1995; Holland, 1985ab, 1987).

One approach to construct validity is to determine whether the relationships between SDS scales make theoretical sense. As is true of the VPI, the six RIASEC themes of the SDS can be arranged in a hexagon with similar themes side by side and dissimilar themes opposite one another. For example, in Figure 12.2, Artistic and Investigative themes are adjacent. It is not difficult to imagine one person combining these two themes in personality and work environment, so we would predict a moder-

ate positive correlation between them. In a general reference sample of 175 women ages 26 to 65, Holland (1985ab) found that scores on these two themes correlated modestly, $r = .26$, as would be expected. The reader will also notice that the Investigative and Enterprising themes are opposite one another, signifying the huge disparities in these two occupational motifs. These themes should be uncorrelated. In fact, scores on these two themes correlated very little, $r = -.02$. In general, the correlations found in Figure 12.2 make theoretical sense; these findings support the construct validity of the SDS.

The predictive validity of the SDS has been investigated in several dozen studies which are summarized by Holland (1985ab, 1987). The typical methodology for these studies is that SDS high-point codes for large samples of students are compared with the first letter of their occupational choices (or aspirations) one to three years later. Overall, the findings indicate that the SDS has moderate to high predictive efficiency, depending upon the age of the sample (hit rates go up with age), the length of the time interval (hit rates go down with time), and the specific category predicted (hit rates are better for Investigative and Social predictions) (Gottfredson & Holland, 1975).

Correlations between SDS scales and a wide range of other psychological measures (e.g., personality, aptitudes, and values) also serve to define the meaning of SDS scales and therefore help to validate the test (Holland, 1985ab, 1987). For example, a study by Costa, McCrae, and Holland (1984) investigated the relationship between SDS scales and the NEO Personality Inventory for a sample of 217 men and 144 women ages 21 to 89. The Investigative and Artistic scales from the SDS showed strong positive correlations with the NEO Openness scale—a measure of openness to experience in the areas of fantasy, feelings, actions, and ideas. The Social and Enterprising scales from the SDS showed strong correlations with the NEO Extraversion scale—a measure of outward-directness and sociability. The Realistic and Conventional scales from the SDS revealed only trivial correlations with the NEO scales. Overall, the observed

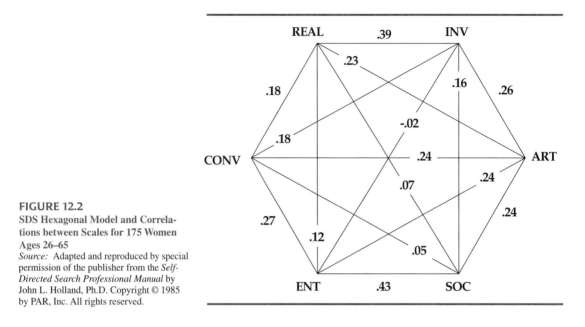

FIGURE 12.2
SDS Hexagonal Model and Correlations between Scales for 175 Women Ages 26–65
Source: Adapted and reproduced by special permission of the publisher from the *Self-Directed Search Professional Manual* by John L. Holland, Ph.D. Copyright © 1985 by PAR, Inc. All rights reserved.

correlations were consistent with the interpretation of the I, A, S, and E scales and provide good support for their validity. Although results for this study failed to support the validity of the R and C scales, many other investigations have yielded confirmatory findings (Holland, 1985ab). Schinka, Dye, and Curtiss (1997) provide a thoughtful analysis and discussion of the relationship between NEO dimensions and the SDS scales.

Campbell Interest and Skill Survey

The Campbell Interest and Skill Survey (CISS, Campbell, Hyne, & Nilson, 1992) is a newer measure of self-reported interests and skills. The test is designed to help individuals make better career choices by describing how their interests and skills match the occupational world. The primary target population for the CISS is students and young adults who have not entered the job market, but the test is also suitable for older workers who are considering a change in careers. The test is appropriate for persons 15 years of age and older with a sixth-grade reading level, although younger children can be tested in exceptional circumstances.

The CISS consists of 200 interest items and 120 skill items. The interest items include occupations, school subjects, and varied working activities which the examinee rates on a six-point scale from strongly like to strongly dislike. The interest items resemble the following:

A pilot, flying commercial aircraft
A biologist, working in a research lab
A police detective, solving crimes

The skill items include a list of activities which the examinee rates on a six-point scale from expert (widely recognized as excellent in this area) to none (have no skills in this area). The skill items resemble the following:

Helping a family resolve its conflicts
Making furniture, using woodworking and power tools
Writing a magazine story

CISS results are scored on several different kinds of scales: Orientation Scales, Basic Interest and Skill Scales, Occupational Scales, Special Scales, and Procedural Checks. All scale scores are reported as *T* scores, normed to a population average of 50, with a standard deviation of 10.

The Orientation Scales serve to organize the CISS profile—the interest, skill, and occupational scales are reported under the appropriate Orientations. The seven Orientations are as follows (Campbell et al., 1992, pp. 2–3):

- *Influencing*—influencing others through leadership, politics, public speaking, and marketing
- *Organizing*—organizing the work of others, managing, and monitoring financial performance
- *Helping*—helping others through teaching, healing, and counseling
- *Creating*—creating artistic, literary, or musical productions, and designing products or environments
- *aNalyzing*—analyzing data, using mathematics, and carrying out scientific experiments
- *Producing*—producing products, using "hands-on" skills in farming, construction, and mechanical crafts
- *Adventuring*—adventuring, competing, and risk taking through athletic, police, and military activities

There are 29 pairs of Basic Scales, each pair consisting of parallel interest and skill scales. The Basic Scales are clustered within the seven Orientations, based upon their intercorrelations. For example, the Helping Orientation contains the following Basic Scales, each with separate interest and skill components: Adult Development, Counseling, Child Development, Religious Activities, and Medical Practice.

The 58 pairs of Occupational Scales, each with separate interest and skill components, provide feedback on the degree of similarity between the examinee and satisfied workers in that occupation. These scales were constructed empirically by contrasting the responses of happily employed persons in specific occupations with responses of a general reference sample drawn from the working population at large.

In addition to Basic and Occupational Scales, the CISS incorporates three special scales: Academic Focus, a measure of interest and confidence in

intellectual, scientific, and literary activities; Extraversion, a measure of social extraversion; and Variety, a measure of the examinee's breadth of interests and skills. Finally, the CISS reports a variety of Procedural Checks to detect possible problems in test taking such as random responding or excessive omissions.

Overall, the reliability of CISS scales is exceptionally strong. For example, coefficient alpha for the Orientation Scales is typically in the high .80s, and three-month test-retest reliabilities for 324 respondents are in the mid- to high .80s. Similar findings for reliability are reported for the Basic and Occupational Scales. Norms for the CISS are based upon 5,000 subjects spread over the 58 occupations. The authors report extensive validity data for the Occupational Scales, including sample means for each occupational sample as well as lists of the three highest- and lowest-scoring occupations for each scale (Campbell et al., 1992). These data document that the scales do discriminate between occupations in an effective and meaningful way. For example, the average *T* score on Accountant by accountants is 75.8. Statisticians, bookkeepers, and financial planners achieve the next three highest scores for this scale, with average *T* scores in the low 60s. Commercial artists, professors, and social workers obtain the three lowest scores, with average *T* scores around 40. Because these results fit well with our expectations about occupational interest and skill patterns, they provide support for the validity of the CISS.

This instrument will almost certainly receive increased attention in the years ahead. One noteworthy feature of the CISS is the comprehensiveness and clarity of the profile report form. The report consists of 11 user-friendly pages. We have reprinted two pages in Figure 12.3 for illustrative purposes. This format is preferable to the detail-rich but eye-straining graphs encountered with many instruments. The CISS does not yet have a strong foundation of empirical findings from independent researchers. Nonetheless, confirmatory research is just around the corner, and the CISS promises to rival the Strong Interest Inventory for vocational guidance of young adults.

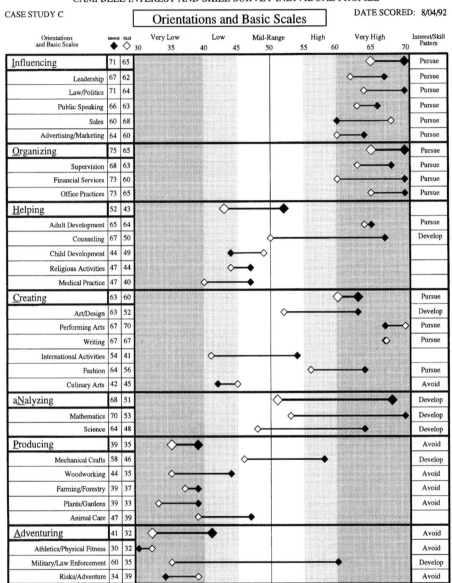

FIGURE 12.3 **Representative Sections from the Campbell Interest and Skill Survey**
Source: Reprinted with permission from Campbell, D. P., Hyne, S., and Nilsen, D. (1992). *Manual for the Campbell Interest and Skill Survey.* Minneapolis, MN: National Computer Systems. Copyright © by David Campbell, Ph.D.

CAMPBELL INTEREST AND SKILL SURVEY INDIVIDUAL PROFILE

CASE STUDY C

| Influencing Orientation |

DATE SCORED: 8/04/92

Orientation Scale

	Standard Scores	Very Low 30 35	Low 40 45	Mid-Range 50 55	High 60	Very High 65 70	Interest/Skill Pattern
Influencing	I 71 / S 65					◆ / ◊	Pursue

Basic Interest and Skill Scales

	Standard Scores	Very Low 30 35	Low 40 45	Mid-Range 50 55	High 60	Very High 65 70	Interest/Skill Pattern
Leadership	I 67 / S 62					◆ / ◊	Pursue
Law/Politics	I 71 / S 64					◆ / ◊	Pursue
Public Speaking	I 66 / S 63					◆ / ◊	Pursue
Sales	I 60 / S 68				◆	◊	Pursue
Advertising/Marketing	I 64 / S 60					◆ / ◊	Pursue

Occupational Scales

	Orientation Code	Standard Scores	Very Low 25 30 35	Low 40 45	Mid-Range 50 55	High 60 65	Very High 70 75	Interest/Skill Pattern
Attorney	I	I 54 / S 70				◆	◊	Explore
Financial Planner	IO	I 66 / S 73					◆ / ◊	Pursue
Hotel Manager	IO	I 60 / S 68					◆ / ◊	Pursue
Manufacturer's Representative	IO	I 63 / S 68					◆ / ◊	Pursue
Marketing Director	IO	I 72 / S 69					◆ / ◊	Pursue
Realtor	IO	I 58 / S 72				◆	◊	Pursue
CEO/President	IOA	I 79 / S 67					◆ / ◊	Pursue
Human Resources Director	IOH	I 63 / S 66					◆ / ◊	Pursue
School Superintendent	IOH	I 73 / S 74					◆ / ◊	Pursue
Advertising Account Executive	IC	I 49 / S 72			◆		◊	Explore
Media Executive	IC	I 61 / S 70					◆ / ◊	Pursue
Public Relations Director	IC	I 58 / S 70				◆	◊	Pursue
Corporate Trainer	ICH	I 75 / S 65					◆ / ◊	Pursue

The Influencing Orientation covers the general area of leading and influencing others. People who score high are interested in making things happen. They want to take charge and are willing to accept responsibility for the results. Influencers are generally confident of their ability to persuade others to their viewpoints, and they enjoy the give and take of verbal jousting. They typically work in organizations, and often want to take charge of the specific activities that particularly interest them. They enjoy public speaking, and like to be visible in public. Typical high-scoring occupations include company presidents, corporate managers, and school superintendents.

You have expressed a strong interest in the area of organizational leadership -- for being in charge and accepting the responsibility for the outcome. You would probably be comfortable in situations where you were responsible for directing the work of others, setting organizational policies and motivating people around you.

Further, you have also reported a high level of confidence in your abilities in leading and motivating other people. You would probably enjoy being in charge of your own department, division, or organization, and are quite confident that you could perform well. Because both your Interest and Skill scores are high, this is an appealing area for you.

Your scores on the Influencing Basic Scales, which provide more detail about your Interests and Skills in this area, are reported above on the left-hand side of the page. Your scores on the Influencing Occupational Scales, which show how your pattern of interests and skills compares with those of people employed in Influencing occupations, are reported above on the right-hand side of the page. Each occupation has a one to three-letter code which indicates its highest Orientation score(s). The more similar the Orientation code is to your highest Orientation scores (which are reported on page 2), the more likely you will find satisfaction working in that occupation.

* Standard Scores: I (◆) = Interests; S (◊) = Skills
** Interest/Skill Pattern: Pursue = High Interests, High Skills; Develop = High Interests, Lower Skills; Explore = High Skills, Lower Interests; Avoid = Low Interests, Low Skills
*** Orientation Code: I=Influencing; O=Organizing; H=Helping; C=Creating; N=aNalyzing; P=Producing; A=Adventuring
Range of middle 50% of people in the occupation: Solid Bar = Interests; Hollow Bar = Skills

FIGURE 12.3   Continued

CAREER AND WORK VALUES ASSESSMENT

In *Working,* his monumental discourse about Americans on the job, Studs Terkel concluded that work is a search:

> . . . for daily meaning as well as daily bread, for recognition as well as cash, for astonishment rather than torpor; in short, for a sort of life rather than a Monday through Friday sort of dying. Perhaps immortality, too, is part of the quest. To be remembered was the wish, spoken and unspoken, of the heroes and heroines of this book (Terkel, 1974).

People seek meaning in their work. After interviewing hundreds of workers, Terkel concluded that only a lucky few find this meaning. Everyone can recall such fulfilled souls: the minister who is adored by his flock, the landscaper who proudly leaves an enduring legacy, the auto mechanic who delights in the perfectly tuned engine, or the oral historian who rescues a piece of the past. But contrasted with these few, Terkel discovered that the vast majority harbor a "hardly concealed discontent" about work.

Whether we agree or disagree with this pessimistic position, it is clear that values play an important role in work satisfaction, career choice, and career development. This is especially evident when a mismatch arises between personal values and the dominant values required by a career. In her book on career changes, Jones (1980) relates the story of an advertiser who came to a painful midlife realization: "I disliked the focus of my work. The advertising of bad products is damaging the country. . . . The whole idea of advertising seemed wrong" (p. 27). This person was so dissatisfied with his vocation that he switched to another field in midlife. Apparently, he valued service to others—a work value which collided head-on with the amoral stance prevalent in advertising. We can only wonder how he picked such a mismatched career in the first place, but it seems unlikely that it was a rational choice based on an assessment of his work values.

It is also worth asking about the source of the discontent that Terkel discovered. Is this discontent largely unavoidable, inherent to the very nature of work? Or, does it arise, at least in part, from the millions of individual mismatches between what a job offers and what a worker needs?

In this section we expand upon the theme developed in the preceding topic—that career choice can be enhanced through the appropriate application of career assessment tools. The reader will first encounter individual tests of work values and career development. Next, we discuss the integrative career assessment model. In this approach, abilities, interests, and personality characteristics are integrated in vocational guidance. The chapter closes on the related topic of consumer assessment.

Work values refer to needs, motives, and values that influence vocational choice, job satisfaction, and career development. Even when background factors such as intelligence, education, and ability are held constant, it is clear that individuals differ in their work values. What one person desires from his or her work might be positively poisonous to another individual of equal intelligence, education, and ability.

Here is a true story to illustrate this point. On behalf of several families, an attorney specializing in personal injury filed a lawsuit against a large mining corporation. The mining company was accused of spewing poisonous lead smelter emissions into the air breathed by hundreds of small town residents, causing subtle neurological damage to dozens of children. The lawsuit involved more than 20 expert witnesses and dragged on for years. The lawyer was deep in debt from financing the protracted litigation—he faced bankruptcy if the lawsuit failed. Yet, he was ecstatic as he approached the final showdown in U.S. Federal Court, his entire career on the line. For this individual, perilous risk taking was a cherished work value. In contrast, most persons would actively avoid this kind of high-stakes gamble with their careers.

A proper match between work values and career choice is essential for job satisfaction. Some people succeed in finding such a match. For example, the intrepid lawyer mentioned above was well suited to his career path. But for those uncertain about career choice, feedback about work values can provide much needed guidance. There are several assessment tools which might be helpful in this regard, but three instruments deserve special mention: the Minnesota Importance Questionnaire, the Work Values Inventory, and the Values Scale are reviewed in the following sections.

Minnesota Importance Questionnaire

The Minnesota Importance Questionnaire (MIQ) was developed to measure vocational needs and values of adults from high school age on up. The test has a solid foundation in a theory of work adjustment that emphasizes the importance of person-environment correspondence in determining satisfaction from work (Dawis, England, & Lofquist, 1964; Dawis & Lofquist, 1984; Lofquist & Dawis, 1991). According to the theory, work satisfaction is directly related to the correspondence between the worker's needs and the rewards or reinforcers available from the job. For example, a prospective employee who has a strong need to help other people will probably find satisfaction in a job that provides plentiful opportunities for social service; conversely, he or she might be miserable in a position that emphasizes solitary work.

In its most popular form—which consists of paired-comparison items—the MIQ measures 20 needs organized into six underlying values relevant to work satisfaction. The test also comes in a ranked format which we do not discuss here. The six values emerged from factor analyses of the needs. The values and their component needs are listed in Table 12.2. It is important to emphasize that each need "scale" actually consists of a single need statement. For example, the Independence need "scale" actually consists of a single statement resembling the following: "Could make my own decisions."

The MIQ consists of 210 items. These include 190 items which pair each of the 20 needs with every other need. An additional 20 items require absolute judgments of the importance of each need

TABLE 12.2   Values and Components of the Minnesota Importance Questionnaire

Values	Components
Achievement	Ability Utilization
	Achievement
Comfort	Activity
	Independence
	Variety
	Compensation
	Security
	Working Conditions
Status	Advancement
	Recognition
	Authority
Altruism	Coworkers
	Social Service
	Moral Feelings
Safety	Company Policies
	Supervision—Human Relations
	Supervision—Technical
Autonomy	Creativity
	Responsibility

dimension. The paired-comparison items are in reference to the examinee's "ideal job" and resemble the following:

_____ Could give me a sense of accomplishment OR
_____ Could make my own decisions

The examinee is instructed to select the alternative of greater personal importance in a job—hence the reference to Importance in the title of the instrument. In the preceding example, the achievement need (Could give me a sense of accomplishment) is matched with the responsibility need (Could make my own decisions). In order to pair each need with every other need, 190 items are required.[2] Each of the 20 work needs is also rated individually on an absolute scale of importance, which results in a

---

2. The total number of paired comparisons for N statements (when order is not relevant) can be calculated from the formula $N(N-1)/2$ which is $20(19)/2$ or 190.

total of 210 items. These absolute judgments permit comparisons across examinees or across scales within examinees.

The MIQ is interpreted in reference to **occupational reinforcer patterns** (ORPs) for nearly 200 occupations. The ORPs were derived from a parallel research program using the Minnesota Job Description Questionnaire (MJDQ), a scale which resembles the MIQ. The MJDQ requires current job holders to rate the perceived presence or absence of reinforcers in a given job. Of course, these reinforcers are simply the 20 work needs appropriately restated so as to capture occupational requirements.

By comparing the profile of examinee needs and values with known reinforcer patterns for representative occupations, MIQ results can be used to predict satisfaction in specific jobs. This is done by means of the C-Index or correspondence index, which is the correlation coefficient between the individual's MIQ profile and the ORP for each occupation. Satisfaction is predicted in an occupation when the correlation exceeds .50.

The paired-comparison format of the MIQ permits the examiner to evaluate the consistency of responses. Consider any three needs, designated as *A, B,* and *C*. Suppose an examinee prefers *A* to *B* and also prefers *B* to *C*. Logically, this person also should prefer *A* to *C* (transitivity). This is an example of a Logically Consistent Triad (LCT). The LCT score is the percentage of all triads which are logically consistent. This score provides an index of response consistency which is one measure of test-taking validity. LCT scores below 33 raise a suspicion that the examinee has responded carelessly or randomly. In test-retest studies, the higher the LCT the more stable the examinee's MIQ profile.

Reliability of the MIQ is fair to excellent, depending upon the retesting interval. The median test-retest correlation for the 20 scales is reported to be .89 for immediate retesting, but only .53 for retesting after 10 months. Internal consistency reliabilities are typically around .80 (Rounds et al., 1981).

Approximately 200 studies bear upon the validity of the MIQ, so it is difficult to summarize trends (Layton, 1992). The results indicate that the 20 MIQ scales discriminate among distinct occupational groups; that correlations with the Strong Vocational Interest Blank are significant and theory-consistent; and that the MIQ has appropriately low correlations with abilities as measured by the General Aptitude Test Battery (Benson, 1985; Layton, 1992). In an affirming study, scores on the MIQ Independence scale moderately predicted whether graduate students in counseling psychology would become scientists or practitioners when they entered the job market (Tinsley, Tinsley, Boone, & Shim-Li, 1993).

The MIQ is a well-respected instrument that deserves to be broadly used. Curiously, the test has never really captured wide attention. Perhaps this is due to the format of the instrument, which might be an impediment to its adoption by human service personnel. The problem is that examinees encounter the same need statements time and again. In order to pair each need with every other need, it is necessary to use each individual need statement in 19 separate test items. Examinees feel like they encounter the same questions over and over, even though each item on the MIQ is, in fact, unique. Regardless of its psychometric soundness, from the standpoint of the examinee the MIQ is an unappealing instrument.

Work Values Inventory

The Work Values Inventory (WVI) is a short and simple instrument designed to measure 15 work values in individuals from junior high level through high school (Super, 1968, 1970). The test is the end product of decades of research on the goals that motivate individuals to work. The 15 work values were identified through a literature review that included the early, classic work of Spranger (1928) on *Types of Men*. Items, scales, and test formats were continually revised and refined until the current 5-point rating approach was selected (Super, 1970, 1973).

The WVI is a self-report instrument consisting of 45 items rated on a 5-point scale from "Very Important" to "Unimportant." Test items resemble the following: "Become famous in your field," "Make your own job decisions," "Feel you have helped other people," and "Have a boss who is considerate." There are three items for each of the 15 scales.

The 15 work values measured by the test include the following:

Altruism	Economic Returns
Esthetic	Security
Creativity	Surroundings
Intellectual Stimulation	Supervisory Relations
Achievement	Associates
Independence	Way of Life
Prestige	Variety
Management	

These work values are described in detail in the manual. For example, Altruism is described as "present in work that enables one to contribute to the welfare of others" and Prestige is described as "associated with work that gives one standing in the eyes of others and evokes respect." The items and scales are transparent. For example, the item "Become famous in your field" would belong on the Prestige scale.

Results for the WVI are reported as 15 scale raw scores, each ranging from 3 (low score) to 15 (endorsing "Very Important" for all three items on the scale). These scores permit three strategies of interpretation. In a clinical analysis, the three highest scores are highlighted for purposes of discussion by counselor and examinee. The data can also be analyzed normatively with respect to results for other students of the same age. Most importantly, it is also possible to predict satisfaction in various occupations by use of occupational reinforcer patterns (ORPs). The approach is similar to that previously discussed for the MIQ, in which the counselor determines the degree of match between the examinee's work values and the known reinforcers available in various occupations.

The technical aspects of the WVI are commendable. In a sample of 99 tenth-grade students, the instrument revealed two-week test-retest reliabilities in the .80s for all scales except Prestige ($r = .76$). The manual provides extensive normative data for junior and senior high school students. Validity also looks strong, as judged by correlations with other measures of work values, factor analysis of scales and items, and theory-confirming relationships with external criteria. Bolton (1985) provides an excellent review of validity evidence for the WVI. Perhaps the only cautionary note about the WVI is that the instrument is now somewhat dated. New norms and reliability data need to be provided.

Values Scale

The Values Scale (VS) was developed by a consortium of researchers under the direction of Super and Nevill (1986) to assess 21 values relevant to work and life roles. The test consists of five items per value, each rated from 1 ("Of little or no importance") to 4 ("Very important"). A final item is used when the scale is administered cross-culturally for a total of 106 items. The values measured by the VS include the following:

Ability Utilization	Personal Development
Achievement	Physical Activity
Advancement	Prestige
Aesthetics	Risk
Altruism	Social Interaction
Authority	Social Relations
Autonomy	Variety
Creativity	Working Conditions
Economic Rewards	Cultural Identity
Life Style	Physical Prowess
	Economic Security

An unusual but highly desirable aspect to the VS is that the test was developed explicitly for use in cross-cultural research. An informal consortium of research teams from dozens of countries in North America, Europe, Australia, Asia, and Africa was involved in the definition, revision, and refinement of values measured by the test. Each national team translated the test into its own language and pilot-tested the items.

The reliability of the VS is only fair, which is understandable since the instruments contain only five items per scale. Alpha coefficients are above .70 for all scales, and test-retest reliabilities are above .50 in college student samples. Norms are provided for a convenience sample of 3,000 American students and adults. Initial validity studies are promising, but more studies are needed before the test is used for individual guidance (Rousseau, 1989; Slaney, 1989).

The Values Scale represents the very best in test development ideals. By involving dozens of research teams around the globe, Super and Nevill (1986) have conceived a test with true cross-cultural appeal and utility. Perhaps their efforts will help forge a global perspective on the nature and value of work. Too often, test development has been a parochial activity restricted to Western industrialized cultures. We can only hope that other test developers will also value the cross-cultural perspective in assessment.

Assessment of Career Development

Super (1957, 1990) has emphasized that career choice is not a discrete decision but a continuing process. He argues that vocational development is characterized by stages: growth, exploration, establishment, maintenance, and decline. In the growth stage, an individual entertains fantasies, develops interests, and discovers his or her capacities. During the exploration stage in adolescence and early adulthood, the individual engages in tentative examination of careers. This is followed by stabilization and consolidation of a career in the establishment phase. At the age of approximately 50, most individuals enter the maintenance stage, characterized by innovation and updating for some, but stagnation and deceleration for others. The decline stage features disengagement for most, but career specialization for a few.

In the beginning stages of career development—the growth and exploration stages—traditional vocational tests may not provide the best kinds of guidance information, since they are usually founded on the premise that the examinee is knowledgeable about work and has well-established interest patterns. However, it is typical of individuals in these stages to have limited information about careers and minimal knowledge of their vocational interests and values. In these situations, specialized instruments are needed for effective career assessment.

Several vocational measures are based upon a recognition that career choice is an ongoing process rather than a single decision. These alternative instruments focus upon maturity of career knowledge, vocational planning, and decision-making skills. Several representative career development and career maturity tests are mentioned briefly in Table 12.3. For a more extended discus-

TABLE 12.3   Representative Measures of Career Development

**Career Directions Inventory
(Jackson, 1986)**

Consisting of 100 triads of statements describing job-related activities, the examinee marks his/her most-preferred and least-preferred activity. The 15 basic interest scales include both work roles and work styles, e.g, administration, food service, sales, outdoors, writing, assertive, persuasive, systematic. Excellent reliability and validity; norms based upon 12,000 individuals from more than 150 educational and occupational specialties.

**Career Decision Scale
(Osipow, 1980)**

A short inventory consisting of 19 items, the examinee indicates on a scale of 1 to 4 how closely each statement describes his/her thinking about careers. This scale provides a measure of career indecision that is especially useful in pretest-posttest studies of career interventions.

**Career Beliefs Inventory
(Krumboltz, 1991)**

Comprised of 96 items rated on a five-point scale from "strongly agree" to "strongly disagree," this inventory is intended to identify client beliefs that may be blocking his/her career goals. Examples of the 25 scales include: career plans, acceptance of uncertainty, intrinsic satisfaction, control, approval of others.

**Career Development Inventory
(Super, Thompson, Lindeman, and others, 1981)**

A comprehensive measure of career development and maturity, the CDI consists of five subtests: Career Planning, which measures extent of, and engagement in, career planning; Career Exploration, which evaluates current and prospective attempts to obtain career information; Decision Making, which measures ability to apply knowledge and insight to career planning; World of Work Information, a measure of knowledge of occupational structure; and Knowledge of the Preferred Occupational Group, which provides an in-depth assessment of knowledge about the examinee's single, preferred occupational group.

sion, the reader is urged to consult Walsh and Betz (1995).

INTEGRATIVE MODEL OF CAREER ASSESSMENT

Practitioners of career assessment rarely rely upon information from a single source such as a survey of interests or work values. The effective vocational counselor uses an **integrative model** in which information from interest, ability, and personality domains is considered simultaneously. Lowman (1991) has presented the elements of this approach, and much of our discussion is based upon his analysis. Practitioners of this method do not minimize the importance of interests in determining career choice and satisfaction. However, they tend to assign primary importance to ability patterns and certain personality characteristics in vocational assessment and guidance. We discuss ability patterns first.

Ability Patterns in Career Assessment

Depending upon the career goals of the client, several ability dimensions might be relevant to career assessment. A partial list includes general intelligence (*g*), mechanical and physical abilities, spatial analysis, verbal intelligence, investigative skills, artistic abilities, and social intelligence (Gottfredson, 1986; Lowman, 1991). The importance of broad or primary mental abilities such as spatial analysis or verbal intelligence is fairly obvious. For example, architecture requires high levels of spatial analysis for success. In a prospective architect, no amount of interest in the field can compensate for low ability in spatial analysis. Likewise, verbal abilities are essential for journalism and other professions that demand language proficiency. The relevance of specialized aptitudes such as mechanical abilities (for a prospective mechanic) and artistic abilities (for a prospective artist) is likewise straightforward. But what about social intelligence? Is this relevant to career assessment? Can social intelligence be measured?

First identified by Thorndike (1920b), **social intelligence** refers to the capacity to understand other people and to relate effectively to them. Although there has been much ongoing controversy about the validity of the social intelligence construct, recent studies indicate that simple paper-and-pencil measures can be used to isolate this dimension of ability from other aspects of intelligence (Lowman & Leeman, 1988). We will review two studies to illustrate this point.

Getter and Nowinski (1981) developed the Interpersonal Problem Solving Assessment Technique (IPSAT), a semistructured free-response test of interpersonal effectiveness. In this test, the respondent is presented with a series of 46 problematic interpersonal situations and asked to imagine being in each situation. Examinees are instructed to write alternative ways of handling each situation and to indicate which of these potential solutions they would actually choose. An example of a situation is as follows:

> Your boss (or teacher) has just criticized a piece of work that you've done, and you think the criticism is unjustified and unfair. What do you do?

Based upon a detailed scoring manual, each response chosen by the examinee is scored in one of these categories: Effective, Avoidant, Inappropriate, Dependent, and unscorable. The grand total number of responses is first tallied to provide an index of the examinee's ability to think of alternative courses of action. Then, the number of chosen solutions scored in each category is counted, providing a profile of the types of solutions preferred by the examinee. Interscorer reliability of IPSAT subscales is quite high, and correlations with other instruments strongly support the convergent and discriminant validity of this instrument.

A more recent and promising inventory of social intelligence is the 128-item, true-false Social Relations Survey (SRS) developed by Lorr, Youniss, and Stefic (1991). They used a rational scale construction method buttressed with factor analysis to produce an instrument that measures eight factors of social intelligence. The subscales and illustrative items are depicted in Table 12.4. For 49 subjects retested after two weeks, the median

TABLE 12.4 Scales and Illustrative Items from the Social Relations Survey

Social Assertiveness

I find it easy to talk with other people that I have just met. (T)

When I meet new people I usually let them bring up things to talk about. (F)

Directiveness

I am at my best when I am the person in charge. (T)

I am comfortable letting others take the lead in a group. (F)

Defense of Rights

If someone breaks in line in front of me, I speak up. (T)

I am uncomfortable returning merchandise to a store. (F)

Confidence

I feel confident most of the time. (T)

I feel dissatisfied with my abilities. (F)

Perceived Approval

I am sure that people I know think well of me. (T)

I sometimes feel a sense of disapproval from others around me. (F)

Expression of Positive Feelings

I like to show my positive feelings for others. (T)

I am uncomfortable showing affection for a friend in public. (F)

Social Approval Need

I make a deliberate effort to make myself popular. (T)

I am unconcerned with what people say about me. (F)

Empathy

I am strongly affected when friends tell me about their problems. (T)

I usually maintain an objective and detached feeling toward others. (F)

Source: Based on Lorr, M., Youniss, R., and Stefic, E. (1991). An inventory of social skills. *Journal of Personality Assessment, 57,* 506–520.

test-retest reliability of the subscales is an impressive .89. Norms are provided for 260 college women and 355 high school women. Several approaches to concurrent and construct validity indicate that the SRS provides a useful and valid approach to the self-report assessment of social skills.

Beyond a doubt, social intelligence is highly relevant to career guidance. For example, a prospective nurse will need high levels of social intelligence to function effectively on the job. In contrast, a computer technician may need little in the way of social skills to excel in the work environment. Lowman (1991) presents a hypothetical taxonomy of social intelligence to illustrate its relevance to career assessment (Table 12.5). Although the measurement of social intelligence remains a challenge, practitioners would be foolish to ignore this ability factor in career assessment.

Personality Patterns in Career Assessment

Several personality dimensions are also highly relevant to career assessment. Personality testing is discussed in detail in later chapters, so we will only mention a few occupationally relevant personality dimensions here:

- Need for achievement is important for persons with business and managerial aspirations (e.g., Orpen, 1983).
- Ascendance or dominance is also important for success in managerial ranks (e.g., Bentz, 1985).
- Emotional stability predicts positive performance in a wide range of traditional jobs, whereas neuroticism is associated with success in some artistic professions (e.g., Wills, 1984).
- Masculinity and femininity differ significantly between various occupational groups (e.g., Gough, 1987).

Research on the relevance of personality dimensions to career assessment is still in its infancy. Nonetheless, preliminary trends such as those previously noted clearly demonstrate the relevance of personality variables to job success. Practitioners are advised to consider occupationally relevant personality dimensions in career assessment. In sum, career assessment is a multifaceted enterprise that must take into account not just interests, but also ability patterns and personality traits as well.

TABLE 12.5   Hypothetical Taxonomy of Social Demands of Jobs

Degree of Social Involvement	Social Job Dimensions
Very high	Therapeutic, educational or management roles such as business manager, nurse, or psychotherapist; high degree of social interaction
High	Social contact is not always primary, e.g., college professor, social science researcher; moderate degree of social interaction.
Moderate	Minimal social interaction, but social facilitation needed, e.g., high-level executive
Slight	Minimal social interaction and minimal need for concern with feelings and reactions of others, e.g., clerk in discount department store
Low	Very limited interaction with people and no requirement for therapeutic or influencing roles, e.g., laboratory scientist or novelist
Very low	Social skills not needed; the work setting may be unsociable, such as computer programmer

Source: Based on Lowman, R. L. (1991). *The clinical practice of career assessment: Interests, abilities, and personality.* Washington, DC: American Psychological Association.

SUMMARY

1. The purpose of interest inventories is to identify a person's vocational and related interests in order to facilitate career choices. A good fit between personal interests and the identified interest patterns of an occupation promotes success in, and satisfaction with, occupational choice.

2. The Strong Interest Inventory (SII) is the latest revision of the Strong Vocational Interest Blank (SVIB), which first appeared in 1927. Like its predecessor, the SII uses empirical keys for occupations.

3. Short-run stability coefficients for the 211 occupational scales on the SII are generally in the .90s. The validity of the test is bolstered by the generally good fit between the initial occupational profile and the occupation eventually pursued.

4. The Jackson Vocational Interest Scale (JVIS) uses a forced-choice item format to reduce the impact of social desirability. The derivation of the 34 basic interest scales was rational and theory-guided. The scales are reasonably independent of one another and possess short-run stability coefficients in the mid-.80s. Validity studies are promising.

5. The 168-item Kuder General Interest Survey (KGIS), used with adolescents in grades 6 through 12, produces 10 broad interest scores. Users must be cautious not to overinterpret the Kuder: the mean four-year stability coefficient for scales is only .50.

6. The 160-item Vocational Preference Inventory (VPI) is an objective, paper-and-pencil personality interest inventory that assesses eleven dimensions, including the six personality-environment themes of Realistic, Investigative, Artistic, Social, Enterprising, and Conventional (RIASEC).

7. The reliability of the VPI is very good, with scale test-retest reliabilities largely in the .90s. The validity of the test is supported by a key finding that individuals tend to move toward environments which are congruent with their personality types, for example, students tend to select and enter college majors which match their VPI codes.

8. The Self-Directed Search (SDS) is a self-administered and self-scored test of vocational interest. The SDS is also based upon the RIASEC model; each theme of this model characterizes not only a type of person but also the type of work environment that such a person finds most compatible.

9. A newer measure of self-reported skills and interests is the Campbell Interest and Skill Survey (CISS). The test consists of 200 interest items and 120 skill items which are rated upon a six-point scale. The test yields *T* scores on numerous scales, including the seven Orientation Scales: Influencing, Organizing, Helping, Creating, Analyzing, Producing, and Adventuring.

10. The CISS also provides separate interest and skill measures for 29 Basic Scales and 58 Occupational Scales. The reliability of CISS scales is exceptionally strong. Initial validity data reported by the test authors is very promising, such as, the scales do discriminate between occupations in an effective and meaningful way.

11. Work values refer to needs, motives, and values that influence vocational choice, job satisfaction, and career development. A proper match between work values and career choice is important for job satisfaction.

12. A useful measure of work values is the Minnesota Importance Questionnaire (MIQ). One version of the test consists of paired-comparison items (e.g., Could give me a sense of accomplishment versus Could make my own decisions) which

assess 20 needs organized into six underlying values relevant to work satisfaction.

13. Super's 45-item Work Values Inventory (WVI) is a short instrument designed to measure 15 work values in junior and senior high school students. Reliability and validity of the instrument are good. Like the MIQ, the WVI is interpreted in relation to occupational reinforcer patterns.

14. The Values Scale (VS) is a cross-culturally derived instrument designed to assess 21 values relevant to work and life roles. The test consists of five items per value rated on a four-point scale. Primarily a research instrument, applications for individual guidance should be approached cautiously.

15. For some persons, career choice is not a discrete decision but a continuing process. Super outlines five stages of career development: growth, exploration, establishment, maintenance, and decline. In the growth and exploration stages, specialized instruments are helpful for effective career assessment.

16. Lowman has proposed an integrative model of career assessment that includes simultaneous consideration of interest, ability, and personality domains. Ability patterns, including social intelligence, can be very important in some vocations.

KEY TERMS AND CONCEPTS

RIASEC model   p. 446

work values   p. 454

occupational reinforcer patterns   p. 456

integrative model   p. 459

social intelligence   p. 459

TOPIC 12B Values in Moral, Spiritual, and Religious Development

In the popular media we find frequent reference to values and changes in values at the individual and national level. Politicians deplore the decline of family values, magazine editors denounce the absence of altruistic volunteerism, and columnists disparage the reemergence of materialism and careerism. Religious leaders enter the fray, too. As an antidote to global cynicism, they call for a return to spiritual values that affirm the meaning of life. Practically everyone has an opinion about values—especially in regard to the presumed values of other persons or groups.

But what are values and how can they be measured? Although a huge amount of literature exists on the nature and definition of values, there is surprisingly little empirical research on their measurement. In general, psychologists define a **value** as a shared, enduring belief about ideal modes of behavior or end states of existence (Rokeach, 1980). Values instill action, shape attitudes, and guide efforts to influence others. Values also arise in response to societal conditions and are therefore malleable to some degree (Ball-Rokeach, Rokeach, & Grube, 1984).

In this topic, we examine key issues and important tests that pertain to the assessment of personal values, broadly defined. We begin with a critique of wideband instruments that assess life values—the social ends or goals considered desirable of achievement. The chapter then reviews assessment approaches in the moral, spiritual, and religious domains. This includes lengthy coverage of Kohlberg's (1981, 1984) classic method for the measurement of moral reasoning. We close with brief coverage of the overlooked literature on the measurement of spiritual and religious concepts.

THE ASSESSMENT OF LIFE VALUES

Values are important because they provide a pervasive framework for personal actions and judgments. When we know the life values of an individual, we can predict typical behaviors and surmise likely attitudes. In a classic work on the topic, Rokeach (1968) underscores the importance of values:

> To say that a person "has a value" is to say that he has an enduring belief that a specific mode of conduct or end-state of existence is personally and socially preferable to alternative modes of conduct or end-states of existence. Once a value is internalized it becomes, consciously or unconsciously, a standard or criterion for guiding action, for developing and maintaining attitudes toward relevant objects and situations, for justifying one's own and others' actions and attitudes, for morally judging self and others, and for comparing self with others. Finally, a value is a standard employed to influence the values, attitudes, and actions of at least some others— our children's, for example (pp. 159–160).

This view that values are in some sense primary and formative also has been advanced by Kluckhohn (1951) and Smith (1963).

Values are more easily defined than measured. Few value scales have withstood the test of time. We survey three instruments here: the Study of Values is an interesting test mainly of historical importance; the Rokeach Value Survey is a highly respected research tool; the Values Inventory provides a cautionary illustration that bad tests occasionally do make their way into publication.

Study of Values

Psychologists have been interested in the assessment of personal values since early in this century. However, it is only in the last 30 years that psychometrically sound self-report measures of values have been developed. An early instrument in this vein was the Study of Values (SOV), an inventory designed to measure six basic evaluative attitudes: Theoretical (T), Economic (E), Aesthetic (A), Social (S), Political (P), and Religious (R) (Allport & Vernon, 1931; Allport, Vernon, & Lindzey, 1960). These six values were patterned directly after Spranger's (1928) *Types of Men*. In this influential book, the German intellectual Eduard Spranger argued that most people display one of the following as a dominant value which defines their personality:

- *Theoretical (T)*: The dominant interest of the theoretical person is the discovery of truth.
- *Economic (E)*: The economic person is primarily interested in what is useful.
- *Aesthetic (A)*: The aesthetic person sees the highest value in form and harmony.
- *Social (S)*: Love of people is the highest value for the social person.
- *Political (P)*: The political person is interested primarily in power.
- *Religious (R)*: The religious person places the highest value upon mystical unity with the cosmos.

The SOV scale consists of 30 questions which pit one value against another, and another 15 questions which require the rank ordering of values. Examples of the questions include the following:

- When you visit a church are you more impressed by a pervading sense of reverence and worship or by the architectural features and stained glass? [Religious versus Aesthetic]
- In your opinion, has general progress been advanced more by the freeing of slaves, with the enhancement of the value placed on individual life, or by the discovery of the steam engine, with the consequent industrialization and economic rivalry of European and American countries? [Social versus Economic]

From answers to the forced-choice questions and the rank ordering of values, a profile of values is plotted in ipsative manner, displaying the relative strength of the six values for each individual.

Lubinski, Schmidt, and Benbow (1996) demonstrated the merit of testing values with the SOV in a 20-year follow-up study of 203 intellectually gifted adolescents. Their gifted sample was first tested at age 13 and then again as adults at age 33. In general, the six themes revealed significant stability over this time period, with mean interindividual correlations of .37 for the various themes. This is remarkable, given that the teenage and young adult years are assumed to be a period of turmoil and change, especially in personal values, as young persons struggle to find an identity. Sex differences were notable: Males tended to shift toward a T-E-P profile as adults whereas females tended to shift toward an A-S-R profile. Even so, a common pattern was observed for all participants, with Aesthetic and Economic values taking on more saliency in young adulthood and Political and Social values revealing less dominance.

The Study of Values has provoked considerable discussion as a classroom demonstration tool in psychology courses, but otherwise has not been an influential test. A major problem with the instrument is that the six values are vaguely defined and too general to be of practical use. Nonetheless, the test did inspire others to develop more sophisticated and comprehensive approaches to values assessment. One of those who acknowledged a debt to Allport and the Study of Values was Milton Rokeach.

Rokeach Value Survey

Rokeach (1973) defined two kinds of values, instrumental and terminal. Instrumental values are desirable modes of conduct, whereas terminal values are desirable end states of existence. For example, ambition is an instrumental value, whereas family security is a terminal value. In devising the Rokeach Value Survey, a final list of 18 instrumental values was arrived at by condensing 555 "personality-trait" names into near-synonyms. The final list of 18 terminal values was derived from literature survey and other subjective, impressionistic approaches. The 36 values are listed in Table 12.6.

Although the individual values are not defined in detail, each is accompanied by a short phrase or synonyms to clarify the item for respondents. For example, the first of the terminal values reads as follows: "A COMFORTABLE LIFE (a prosperous life)." Completing the survey is extremely simple.

TABLE 12.6   The 36 Value Constructs from the Rokeach Value Survey, Form D

Terminal Values

A Comfortable Life	Inner Harmony
An Exciting Life	Mature Love
A Sense of Accomplishment	National Security
A World at Peace	Pleasure
A World of Beauty	Salvation
Equality	Self-respect
Family Security	Social Recognition
Freedom	True Friendship
Happiness	Wisdom

Instrumental Values

Ambitious	Imaginative
Broadminded	Independent
Capable	Intellectual
Cheerful	Logical
Clean	Loving
Courageous	Obedient
Forgiving	Polite
Helpful	Responsible
Honest	Self-Controlled

Respondents are asked to rank separately the 18 terminal and 18 instrumental values based on "their importance to you, as guiding principles in your life." The values are printed on gummed labels (for Form D). Subjects merely peel off the labels and arrange them in order of importance, removing and reattaching as needed. The rank for each item becomes the score for that value. Ties are not allowed, so value scores will range from 1 to 18, with lower scores indicating greater importance.

Reliability of the Value Survey can be approached in two ways. The first is the temporal stability of rank orderings for individual subjects. For this approach, the scale is administered twice and the two sets of rank orderings are correlated for each individual. Using this approach with four groups of college students (retest intervals of three weeks to four months) Rokeach (1973) reported median test-retest correlations ranging from .76 to .80 for terminal values, and .65 to .72 for instrumental values. The second way to examine reliability is to calculate the test-retest reliability of individual value scores separately, across all respondents. Using this approach, reliability of the individual scales is lower, about .65 for the terminal values and .56 for the instrumental values (Rokeach, 1973). These reliabilities are rather low in comparison to instruments with more items per scale—which is not surprising. After all, the "scales" on the Value Survey each consist of a single item. Nonetheless, with reliabilities this low, the Value Survey should be used only for research purposes such as description or comparison of group values. Individual interpretation for counseling purposes cannot be supported.

In an intriguing example of its application in research, Rokeach and his colleagues used the Value Survey to measure the effects of viewing a single 30-minute television program on values, attitudes, and behaviors (Ball-Rokeach, Rokeach, & Grube, 1984). The television program, hosted by Ed Asner and known as "The Great American Values Test," was specially designed to influence viewers' ratings of the importance of the terminal values of freedom and equality. For example, over a full-screen graphic display indicating that Americans had ranked freedom third and equality twelfth, on average, among 18 terminal values, Asner commented:

> Americans feel that freedom is very important. They rank it third. But they also feel that equality is considerably less important . . . they rank it twelfth. Since most Americans value freedom far higher than they value equality, the question is: what does that mean? Does it suggest that Americans as a whole are much more interested in their own freedom than they are in freedom for other people? Is there a contradiction in the American people between their love of freedom and their lesser love for equality?
>
> By comparing your values with these results, you should be able to decide for yourself whether you agree with the average American's feelings about freedom and equality (Ball-Rokeach et al., 1984).

A full discussion of this study would involve a lengthy detour away from the topic of psychological testing. However, the reader may appreciate a quick summary. The authors used a tightly controlled pretest-posttest design with experimental and control cities to determine the effects of viewing the program. For viewers who watched the show without interruption, mean rankings on equality went from 11.0 to 9.3, whereas for nonviewers the ratings on this value were quite stable. A number of other experimental checks (e.g., soliciting donations to provide cultural opportunities for African-American children) also confirmed a real change in values. This study is a good example of the kind of social research for which the Value Survey is well suited.

Limitations of the Rokeach Value Survey

We have already mentioned that the individual scales of the Value Survey possess marginal reliability—which means that the instrument should not be used for individual guidance. Several additional limitations stem from the ipsative nature of the test. The reader will recall that an ipsative test is one in which the average of the scales is always the same for every examinee. In particular, the average rank for the 18 instrumental values will always be 9.5, and likewise for the terminal values. By definition,

when an examinee gives some scales a high ranking, others must receive a low ranking. What is lost in this process is any absolute measure of the value for that individual. Suppose, for example, that we could measure the absolute strength of the 18 instrumental values on a scale from 1 to 100 (note: this is not possible with the Value Survey). Consider the case where individual A has an absolute strength of 99 for ambitious and 98 for obedient with all other values below 90, whereas individual B has an absolute strength of 39 for ambitious and 19 for obedient with all other values below 10. Most likely, individual A would value ambition and obedience to a high degree, whereas individual B modestly values ambition and devalues obedience. In fact, individual B could be characterized as almost valueless. Yet, both persons would receive scores of 1 for ambitious and 2 for obedient. The Value Survey is not sensitive to magnitude differences within individual subjects, nor does it capture scaling differences between individuals.

Braithwaite and Law (1985) call attention to additional weaknesses of the Value Survey. They note that the inventory omits several important values, including physical wellbeing, individual rights, thriftiness, and carefreeness. Perhaps more significant, they criticize the Rokeach test for relying upon a single item for each value instead of using multi-item indices for the value constructs. They propose an alternative instrument (based on the Rokeach approach) that would presumably embody improved psychometric qualities in the measurement of personal values.

Values Inventory

The Values Inventory is designed to assess six values in professional managers: theoretical, power, achievement, human, industry, and financial. The instrument consists of 28 sets of three quotations resembling the following:

- The smallest grain of truth represents some man's bitter toil and agony.
- We never do anything well if we think about the manner of doing it.
- All work is noble and only work is noble.

The examinee indicates the extent to which he or she agrees with each statement. Three points are distributed between each set of three quotations: one point for each quote if all are equally endorsed, three points for one quote if it is the only one endorsed, and so on. As the reader might have guessed, each statement represents a specific value. By summing the number of points awarded to each of the six values across the 28 sets of items, a profile of value scores is obtained.

Reviewers have been scathingly critical of the Values Inventory, noting that the test lacks a theoretical rationale and does not even possess face validity let alone technical validity (Muchinsky, 1985; Tziner, 1985). We mention the instrument here not out of any mean-spiritedness, but simply to illustrate that questionable tests do occasionally make their way to publication. Test users must exercise judgment before adopting new instruments.

THE ASSESSMENT OF MORAL JUDGMENT

The Moral Judgment Scale

Kohlberg has proposed one of the few theories of moral development that is both comprehensive and empirically based (Colby, Kohlberg, Gibbs, & Lieberman, 1983; Kohlberg, 1958, 1981, 1984; Kohlberg & Kramer, 1969). Although he was more concerned with theory-based problems of moral development than with the nuances of standardized measurement, Kohlberg did generate a method of assessment that is widely used and intensely debated. We will review the underlying rationale for his measurement tool and discuss the psychometric properties of the instrument as well. In addition, we will take a brief look at a more objectively based adaptation of Kohlberg's approach known as the Defining Issues Test (Rest, 1979, Rest & Thoma, 1985).

Stages of Moral Development

Kohlberg's theory grew out of Piaget's (1932) stage theory of moral development in childhood. Kohlberg extended the stages into adolescence and adulthood. In order to explore reasoning about difficult moral issues, he devised a series of **moral dilemmas.** One of the most famous is the dilemma of Heinz and the druggist:

> In Europe, a woman was near death from a special kind of cancer. There was one drug that the doctors thought might save her. It was a form of radium that a druggist in the same town had recently discovered. The drug was expensive to make, but the druggist was charging ten times what the drug cost him to make. He paid $200 for the radium and charged $2000 for a small dose of the drug. The sick woman's husband, Heinz, went to everyone he knew to borrow the money, but he could only get together about $1000 which is half of what it cost. He told the druggist that his wife was dying, and asked him to sell it cheaper or let him pay later. But the druggist said, "No, I discovered the drug and I'm going to make money from it." So Heinz got desperate and broke into the man's store to steal the drug for his wife (Kohlberg & Elfenbein, 1975).

After reading or hearing this story, the respondent is asked a series of probing questions. The questions might be as follows: Should Heinz have stolen the drug? What if Heinz didn't love his wife? Would that change anything? What if the person dying was a stranger? Should Heinz steal the drug anyway? Based on answers to this and other dilemmas, Kohlberg concluded that there are three main levels of moral reasoning, with two substages within each level (Table 12.7). One use of his measurement instrument, the Moral Judgment Scale, is to determine a respondent's stage of moral reasoning.[1]

The Moral Judgment Scale consists of several hypothetical dilemmas such as Heinz and the druggist, presented one at a time (Colby, Kohlberg, Gibbs, & others, 1978). In its latest revision, the Scale comes in three versions called Forms A, B, and C. Scoring is quite complex, based on the examiner's judgment of responses in relation to extensive criteria outlined in a detailed scoring

---

1. Even though the Moral Judgment Scale has been widely used for empirical research, Kohlberg (1981, 1984) suggests that its most valuable application is for the promotion of self-understanding and the development of moral reasoning in the individual respondent.

TABLE 12.7   Kohlberg's Levels and Stages of Moral Development

Level 1: Preconventional

Stage 1.   Punishment and obedience orientation: The physical consequences determine what is good or bad.

Stage 2.   Instrumental relativism orientation: What satisfies one's own needs is good.

Level 2: Conventional

Stage 3.   Interpersonal concordance orientation: What pleases or helps others is good.

Stage 4.   "Law-and-order" orientation: Maintaining the social order and doing one's duty is good.

Level 3: Postconventional or Principled

Stage 5.   Social contract-legalistic orientation: Values agreed upon by society determine what is good.

Stage 6.   Universal ethical-principle orientation: What is right is a matter of conscience derived from universal principles.

Source: Based on Kohlberg (1984).

manual (Colby & Kohlberg, 1987). Although there are several different dimensions to scoring, the one element most frequently cited in research studies is the overall stage of moral reasoning that characterizes a respondent.

Critique of the Moral Judgment Scale

Early versions of the Moral Judgment Scale suffered serious shortcomings of scoring and interpretation. For example, in his doctoral dissertation, Kohlberg (1958) proposed two scoring systems: one using the sentence or completed thought as the unit of scoring, the other relying upon a global rating of all the subject's utterances as the unit of analysis. Neither approach was fully satisfactory, and early reviews of the scale were justifiably critical of its reliability and validity (Kurtines & Greif, 1974).

In response to these criticisms, Kohlberg and his associates developed a scoring system that is unparalleled in its clarity, detail, and sophistication (Rest, 1986). Fortuitously, since the moral dilem-

mas of the Moral Judgment Scale have remained constant over the years, it is possible to apply the new scoring system to old data. The capacity to re-analyze old data and compare it with new data is invaluable in determining the reliability and validity of an existing scale. A most important study in this regard has been published by Kohlberg and associates (Colby et al., 1983).

This investigation reports the results of using the new scoring system in a longitudinal study spanning more than 20 years. The results are impressive and offer strong support for the reliability and validity of the instrument. Test-retest correlations for the three forms were in the high .90s, as were interrater correlations. Longitudinal scores of subjects tested at three- to four-year intervals over 20 years revealed theory-consistent trends. Fifty-six of 58 subjects showed upward change, with no subjects skipping any stages. Furthermore, only 6 percent of the 195 comparisons showed backward shifts between two testing sessions. The internal consistency of scores was also excellent: about 70 percent of the scores were at one stage, and only 2 percent of the scores were spread further than two adjacent stages. Cronbach's alpha was in the mid-.90s for the three forms. These findings have been corroborated by Nisan and Kohlberg (1982). Heilbrun and Georges (1990) also report favorably upon the validity of the Moral Judgment Scale, insofar as postconventional development is correlated with higher levels of self-control, as would be predicted from the fact that morally mature persons often oppose social pressure or legal constraints. In sum, the Moral Judgment Scale is reliable, internally consistent, and possesses a theory-confirming developmental coherence.

The Defining Issues Test

The Defining Issues Test is similar to the Moral Judgment Scale, but incorporates a much simpler and completely objective scoring format (Rest, 1979, 1986). The examinee reads a series of moral dilemmas similar to those designed by Kohlberg, and then chooses a proper action for each. For example, one dilemma involves a patient dying a painful death from cancer. In her lucid moments, she requests an overdose of morphine to hasten her death. What should the doctor do? Three options of the following kind are listed:

_____ He should give the woman a fatal overdose

_____ Should not give the overdose

_____ Can't decide

The examinee's choice does not enter directly into the determination of the moral judgment score. The real purpose in forcing a choice is to cause the examinee to think about the importance of various factors in making the decision. Following the choice of proper action, the examinee rates the importance of several factors on a five-point Likert scale: great, much, some, little, or no importance. The factors are distinct for each dilemma. The factors differ in the level of moral judgment they signify, ranging from Kohlberg's stage 1 through stage 6. In the case of the preceding dilemma, the factors include such matters as follows:

_____ Whether the doctor can make it look like an accident

_____ Can society afford to let people end their lives when they want to

_____ Whether the woman's family favors giving the overdose or not

These ratings form the basis for generating several quantitative scores that pertain to the moral judgment of the examinee. The most widely used score is the P score, which is a percentage of principled thinking. Reliability of the P score ranges from .71 to .82 in test-retest studies (Rest, 1979, 1986). Validity has been studied by contrasting groups known to differ on principled thinking. For example, graduate students in moral philosophy and political science, general college students, high school seniors, and ninth-grade students were found to differ appropriately and systematically on the P score. In longitudinal studies, significant upward trends were found over six years and four testings. Recently, Rest has recommended a new measure of moral judgment, the N2 index, calculated on the basis of several complex formulas that use both ranking and rating data. The two indices are highly correlated in the .90s. Nonetheless, in a retrospective analysis of previous studies, the N2 index outperformed the P index by a substantial margin (Rest, Thoma, Narvaez, & Bebeau, 1997).

Over 600 articles have been published on the Defining Issues Test (McCrae, 1985; Moreland, 1985; Sutton, 1992). In general, the instrument is considered a useful alternative to Kohlberg's Moral Judgment Scale, particularly for research on group differences in moral reasoning. However, reviewers do note several cautions about the DIT (Sutton, 1992; Westbrook & Bane, 1992). First, the test uses two moral dilemmas from the Vietnam War and is therefore somewhat dated. Many young examinees have little knowledge of (and perhaps no interest in) this topic and may find it difficult to identify with these questions. Another dilemma—the classic case of whether Heinz should steal a drug to save his wife's life—is also of dubious value since it has been widely publicized and reprinted in college textbooks. A significant proportion of prospective examinees are no longer naive about this moral dilemma.

Richards and Davison (1992) have pressed the point that the DIT is biased against conservatively religious individuals. Certainly it is well established that conservative or fundamentalist religious people tend to score lower than average on the P score of the Defining Issues Test (Getz, 1984; Richards, 1991). According to Richards and Davison (1992), the reason for this is that Stage 3 and Stage 4 items (unintentionally) possess strong theological implications that cause fundamentalist individuals to endorse the items, thereby lowering their score on the test. Consider items that tap stage 4 reasoning, which is the "law and order" orientation that equates "moral" with doing one's duty and maintaining the social order. Whereas nonreligious persons might support the laws of the land (and endorse Stage 4 items) because they believe that legal authorities define what is right and moral, religious minorities such as Mormons believe that supporting the laws of the land is a theological and religious obligation that flows directly from articles of faith in their religion:

. . . while Mormons place a high value on obeying the law and supporting legal authorities, this value is due to their theological belief that God has commanded them to do so, and not because they believe, as do true Stage 4 thinkers, that the laws of the land or legal authorities *define* what is right or moral (Richards & Davison, 1992, 470).

These researchers demonstrate empirically that certain DIT items measure a different construct for conservative religious persons than for the general population. As a consequence, the validity of the test in these groups is open to question.

A related criticism of the DIT is the dearth of norms pertinent to minority groups. Finally, Westbrook and Bane (1992) argue that the technical manual for the DIT lacks essential details needed to evaluate the adequacy of the test. In spite of these criticisms, the DIT is a widely respected test, particularly for research on moral reasoning.

THE ASSESSMENT OF SPIRITUAL AND RELIGIOUS CONCEPTS

Within the field of psychology, transcendent topics such as spiritual well-being or faith maturity never have received mainstream attention. Fifty years ago, Gordon Allport (1950) lamented that the subject of religion "seems to have gone into hiding" among intellectuals and academic researchers:

> Whatever the reason may be, the persistence of religion in the modern world appears as an embarrassment to the scholars of today. Even psychologists, to whom presumably nothing of human concern is alien, are likely to retire into themselves when the subject is broached (p. 1).

The situation is little improved in contemporary times. For example, except for a few specialty journals, spiritual and religious topics are virtually absent from the psychological literature.

Yet researchers have no right to retire from the field, given its significance to the average person. Consider these statistics on religious belief in the United States, stable since 1944 when national polls first came into use (Hoge, 1996):

- Belief in God has remained constant at about 95 percent of the population.
- Belief in the divinity of Jesus Christ has been endorsed by 75 to 77 percent of adults.
- Belief in an afterlife has remained at about 75 percent of the population.

Comparable statistics are not available worldwide, but it seems likely that the percentage of believing individuals (whether Muslim, Buddhist, Hindu, Jew, or other) is very high. Most people embrace a spiritual perspective in life, and surely this must have some bearing on their adjustment, behavior, and outlook.

Unfortunately, the field of psychology, including the specialty area of testing, largely has maintained an indifference to this important aspect of human experience. Worse yet, in many intellectual circles the endorsement of spiritual or religious sentiments is seen as evidence of psychopathology. Among others, Sigmund Freud endorsed a cynical view of religion in his aptly titled essay, *The Future of an Illusion* (1927/1961). Yet for many persons, a connection with the transcendent is essential to meaning in life. This is especially so in times of extreme duress, as when personal annihilation knocks at the front door. Consider the experience of Viktor Frankl (1963), a Nazi death camp survivor and founding figure of existential psychology. At one point during World War II he had to surrender his coat with a cherished manuscript in the pockets in exchange for the worn-out rags of an inmate sent to the gas chamber:

> Instead of the many pages of my manuscript, I found in a pocket of the newly acquired coat a single page torn out of a Hebrew prayer book, which contained the main Jewish prayer, *Shema Yisrael*. How should I have interpreted such a "coincidence" other than as a challenge to live my thoughts instead of merely putting them on paper?

In the remainder of this topic, we take the view that spiritual and religious dimensions to life often serve constructive purposes and that assessment within these domains is worthy of additional study.

The Rationale for Religious and Spiritual Assessment

Academic researchers justify the assessment of religious and spiritual dimensions as a means of pursuing the truth about human behavior. Their primary motive is intellectual curiosity and their goal is to understand the role of religion and spirituality in human affairs. But is there any practical reason for seeking to measure religious or spiritual dimensions in the *individual*? For example, would clinical practitioners such as psychologists or social workers gain anything useful by assessing the religious and spiritual backgrounds of their clients?

Richards and Bergin (1997) offer several compelling arguments in favor of therapists' assessment of the religious and spiritual backgrounds of their clients. Specifically, this form of assessment could serve to

1. Increase empathy by helping therapists to better understand the worldview of their clients
2. Identify and assess the impact of healthy and unhealthy religious-spiritual orientations in clients
3. Determine whether religious and spiritual beliefs and community can provide support to clients
4. Identify possible spiritual interventions that can be used in therapy to help clients
5. Determine whether clients possess unresolved spiritual doubts or concerns that need to be addressed

In general, Richards and Bergin (1997) argue that clinicians need to address the whole person in order to provide the best possible response to emotional and psychological problems. Because most clients bring religious and spiritual concerns to the therapy session, clinicians who assess these dimensions of human existence may be better prepared to provide effective service.

Historical Overview on Religious Assessment

Interest in the psychology of religion can be traced to the early 1900s when William James (1902) composed his masterpiece, *The Varieties of Religious Experience*. In this book, James catalogued the manifold ways in which humans reveal their interest in transcendent matters. His overall conclusion was that religion is "an essential organ of our life, performing a function which no other portion of our nature can so successfully fulfill."

Although many writers have offered psychological analyses of religion since the seminal writings of James, it was not until the 1960s that scales for the assessment of religious variables began to appear (Wulff, 1996). One of the first such measures was the Allport-Ross Religious Orientation scales, which proposed to assess two dimensions of religious expression, the **intrinsic** and the **extrinsic** (Allport & Ross, 1967). Intrinsically religious persons were thought to *live* their religion (e.g., to find meaning, direction, outlook) whereas extrinsically religious persons were believed to *use* their religion (e.g., to seek security, status, sociability). In his earlier writings on this topic, Allport referred to the intrinsic form as a genuine or mature religious orientation whereas the extrinsic form was viewed as immature. Later he dropped the mature-immature designations because the labels seemed overly judgmental.

The impetus for development of these scales was Allport's distressing observation of a positive relationship between religiosity (in certain forms) and authoritarian, bigoted, prejudicial attitudes. As a devoutly religious person, Allport was convinced that intrinsically oriented religious individuals rarely would harbor these attitudes. After all, an essential precept of almost every religious faith is an attitude of love toward one's neighbors. In the Christian faith, this view is summed up in the famous dictum "Love your neighbor as yourself" (Mark 12:31). Yet the evidence was overwhelming to Allport that at least some religious individuals did reveal hatred, bigotry, and prejudice toward their neighbors. The usual targets of these malicious attitudes were racial minorities, Jews, and homosexual persons, among others. He reasoned that religious persons with intolerant attitudes possessed a predominantly extrinsic religious orientation, that is, their faith served external goals such as status in the community, belonging to an in-group, and the like. The investigation of this hypothesis (that extrinsically religious persons would be more authoritarian, bigoted, and prejudiced than intrinsically religious persons) required appropriate tools. For this purpose, Allport and colleagues developed the Religious Orientation scales.

Examples of the kinds of items on the 11-item Extrinsic scale and the 9-item Intrinsic scale are as follows:

- The church is important as a place to develop good social relationships. (Extrinsic)
- Sometimes I find it necessary to compromise my religious beliefs for economic reasons. (Extrinsic)
- I try hard to carry my religion over into other aspects of my life. (Intrinsic)
- My religion is important because it provides meaning to my life. (Intrinsic)

Although originally devised in a yes-no format, modern applications of these scales utilize a nine-point continuum from (1) strongly disagree to (9) strongly agree (Batson, Schoenrade, & Ventis, 1993).

Research on the Religious Orientation scales has not provided strong support for Allport's original hypothesis (Wulff, 1996). In fact, several studies have shown that persons scoring high on the Intrinsic scale actually reveal *higher* levels of authoritarianism, close-mindedness, and prejudice toward African Americans, gays, and lesbians. Hunsberger (1995) concludes that it is not religion per se that makes for prejudice, nor is it intrinsic/extrinsic religious orientation. Instead, "it is the way in which religious beliefs are held that seems most directly associated with prejudice, and this is best explained by the tendency for fundamentalism and right-wing authoritarianism to be closely linked." Specifically, he links prejudice against minorities with authoritarian religious traditions that promote an absolute truth, divide the world into "Good" and "Evil," and shun complexity or doubt in their belief systems. These aspects of religious expression are not typically measured by paper-and-pencil tests.

In a recent study, Genia (1993a) concluded that the combined Religious Orientation scales (consisting of 20 items) measure *three* factors of religious expression and not the two proposed by Allport (Intrinsic and Extrinsic). She conducted a factor analysis of test results for 309 persons ages 17 to 83 (mean age of 29 years) from diverse religious traditions. The nine items on the original Intrinsic scale held together very well substantiating a robust factor of intrinsic religious orientation. But the eleven items on the original Extrinsic scale broke down into two separate subfactors which Genia (1993a) labeled use of religion for personal benefits (Ep) and use of religion for social reward (Es). She recommended transforming the original instrument into a three-factor test (Intrinsic, Extrinsic-personal, Extrinsic-social) by adding and dropping a few items. However, most authorities in the field have concluded that Allport's scales served a valuable function by identifying key dimensions of religious experience and spurring research but have now outlived their usefulness.

Religion as Quest

Increasingly, the conceptual basis for the distinction between Intrinsic and Extrinsic religious orientation has been questioned. Kirkpatrick and Hood (1990) summarized the major theoretical and methodological criticisms of the scales as follows:

- A lack of conceptual clarity in what the Intrinsic-Extrinsic scales are supposed to be measuring. Are these types of motivation (i.e., the motives associated with religious belief and practice), or personality variables (i.e., pervasive aspects of institutional behavior or involvement), or something else?
- A confusion over the relationship between the Intrinsic-Extrinsic scales. In particular, are these opposite ends of a single bipolar dimension, or do the scales measure separate dimensions (so that conceivably some persons could score high on *both*)?

Other problems cited include weaknesses in the factorial structure, reliability, and construct validity of the scales; excessive reliance on a "good religion" versus "bad religion" dichotomy; and the folly of defining and studying religiousness independent of belief content (Kirkpatrick & Hood, 1990).

In response to the limitations of the Religious Orientation scales, Batson and his associates (1993) developed a measure of a third religious orientation known as Quest. These researchers consider Quest to be a more mature and flexible religious outlook than the Intrinsic and Extrinsic orientations. Actually, Allport recognized the elements inherent to this orientation, but failed to incorporate them in his Intrinsic scale. **Quest** is characterized by complexity, doubt, and tentativeness as ways of being religious. This orientation suggests

> . . . an approach that involves honestly facing existential questions in all their complexity, while at the same time resisting clear-cut, pat answers. An individual who approaches religion in this way recognizes that he or she does not know, and probably never will know, the final truth about such matters. Still, the questions are deemed important, and however tentative and subject to change, answers are sought. There may or may not be a clear belief in a transcendent reality, but there is a transcendent, religious aspect to the individual's life. We shall call this open-ended, questioning approach *religion as quest* (Batson et al., 1993, p. 166).

Examples of the kinds of items on the 12-item Quest scale are as follows:

- My life experiences have led me to reconsider my religious convictions.
- I find religious doubts upsetting [reverse scored].
- As I grow and mature, I expect my religious beliefs to change.
- Questions are more important to my religious faith than answers.

Items are scored on the same nine-point continuum from (1) strongly disagree to (9) strongly agree. Results are reported as an average rating. Research with 424 undergraduates interested in religion indicates that Quest is, indeed, a dimension of religious experience independent from both Intrinsic and Extrinsic orientations. Whereas Intrinsic and Extrinsic scores correlated .72, Quest revealed negligible relationships with both scales (−.05 with Intrinsic and .16 with Extrinsic).

But exactly what does the Quest scale measure? The intention of its authors was that it assess "the degree to which an individual's religion involves an open-ended, responsive dialogue with existential questions raised by the contradictions and tragedies of life" (p. 169). The three components of the quest orientation are (1) readiness to face existential questions without reducing their complexity, (2) self-criticism and perception of religious doubts as positive, and (3) openness to change. But critics have charged that the scale may not measure anything religious at all, that instead it may assess agnosticism, anti-orthodoxy, religious doubt, or religious conflict.

In response to these criticisms, Batson et al. (1993) note the following:

- Students at Princeton Theological Seminary scored significantly higher ($p < .001$) on the Quest scale (mean of 6.7) than undergraduates at the same institution (mean of 5.2). This finding supports the view that the scale is a valid measure of something religious.
- The 32 members of a charismatic Bible study group scored significantly higher ($p < .001$) on the Quest scale (mean of 5.5) than the 26 members of a traditional Bible study group (mean of 4.6). The charismatic group placed emphasis on religion as a shared search; most prayed with hands raised, and some members spoke in tongues.

Quest is its own dimension of religious expression, and substantial research on the meaning and correlates of this faith orientation has been completed. Batson et al. (1993) summarize research with the Quest scale by noting that it appears to measure a religion of less faith but more works.

Quest arose as a response to the limitations of the Intrinsic and Extrinsic approach to the measurement of religious orientation. But this brief 12-item scale possesses its own limitations, chief among them its brevity and factorial simplicity. Several other instruments have been proposed to measure aspects of religious experience. We survey a few prominent and representative approaches in the following sections.

The Spiritual Well-Being Scale

The concept of spiritual well-being can be traced to a paper by Moberg (1971) that proposed this form of well-being as an essential component of healthy aging. Spiritual well-being was conceptualized as a two-dimensional construct consisting of a vertical dimension and a horizontal dimension. The vertical dimension concerned well-being in relation to God or a higher power, whereas the horizontal dimension involved existential well-being which is a sense of purpose in life without any specific religious reference. The challenge of developing a scale to measure these components of well-being was taken up by Ellison (1983) and Paloutzian and Ellison (1982).

Their instrument was designated the Spiritual Well-Being Scale (SWB Scale). The SWB Scale consists of two subscales: Religious Well-Being (RWB), which assesses the vertical dimension of well-being in relation to God; and Existential Well-Being (EWB), which measures the horizontal dimension of well-being in relation to life purpose and life satisfaction. Each subscale consists of 10 items which are scored from 1 (strongly disagree) to 6 (strongly agree). The items from the two subscales are combined on the SWB Scale, with odd-numbered items assessing religious well-being and even-numbered items assessing existential well-being. Some items are worded negatively; these are reverse scored so that a higher score always indicates greater well-being. Items similar to those found on the SWB Scale are reproduced in Table 12.8.

The SWB Scale provides three scores: a total SWB score (maximum 120), a subscore for RWB (maximum 60), and a subscore for EWB (maximum 60). Initial reliability and validity studies were based upon 206 students from three religiously oriented colleges and one secular university. Test-retest reliability coefficients were .93 for SWB, .96 for RWB, and .86 for EWB. Factor analysis tended to support the construct validity of the instrument by revealing that all of the religious items loaded on a religious factor, whereas existential items appeared to load on two subfactors, one connoting life direction and the other indicating life satisfaction. The correlation between the RWB and EWB subscales was modest ($r = .32$), indicating that they tap separate aspects of spiritual well-being.

In later writings, Ellison described the SWB Scale as a measure of psychospiritual personality integration and resultant well-being (Ellison & Smith, 1991). According to this view, well-being

---

TABLE 12.8 Items Similar to Those Found on the Spiritual Well-Being Scale

For each statement circle the choice that best indicates the degree of your agreement or disagreement.

SA = Strongly Agree	D = Disagree
MA = Moderately Agree	MD = Moderately Disagree
A = Agree	SD = Strongly Disagree

I don't find much reward in private prayer (reverse scored)	SA	MA	A	D	MD	SD
My relationship with God helps me through hard times	SA	MA	A	D	MD	SD
Life is inherently without meaning (reverse scored)	SA	MA	A	D	MD	SD
I feel good about where my life is headed	SA	MA	A	D	MD	SD

consists of "the integral experience of a person who is functioning as God intended, in consonant relationship with Him, with others, and within one's self" (p. 36). This is the biblical notion of *shalom,* which denotes being harmoniously at peace within and without. If this conceptualization is correct, healthy spirituality as measured by the SWB Scale should show positive relationships with independent measures of health and subjective well-being. Literally dozens of studies have investigated this broad-range hypothesis, with generally positive findings. Representative studies are summarized in Table 12.9.

The one identified shortcoming of the SWB Scale is an apparent low ceiling, especially in religious samples. Ledbetter, Smith, Vosler-Hunter, and Fischer (1991) caution that the clinical usefulness of the scale is limited to low scores (since high-functioning religious persons tend to "top out" on the scale). They also offer suggestions for revision (e.g., rewording items in more extreme directions) toward the goal of increasing the ceiling level of the SWB Scale. Bufford, Paloutzian, and

---

TABLE 12.9   Summary of Findings with the Spiritual Well-Being Scale

Spiritual Well-Being Scale Scores Correlate Positively With:

Being closer to ideal body weight (Hawkins & Larson, 1984)

Perceived health in rural elderly (DeCrans, 1990)

Overall adjustment to hemodialysis (Campbell, 1988)

Hope in cancer patients (Mickley, 1990)

Measures of self-esteem (Paloutzian & Ellison, 1982)

Spiritual Well-Being Scale Scores Correlate Negatively With:

Diastolic and systolic blood pressure (Hawkins, 1988)

Frequency and amount of pain in cancer patients (Granstrom, 1987)

Social isolation and despair (Bonner, 1988)

Aggressiveness and conflict avoidance (Bufford & Parker, 1985)

Depression scores on the MMPI (Fehring, Brennan, & Keller, 1987)

Ellison (1991) have published norms for the test, but caution that in many religious samples the typical individual receives the maximum score. This would indicate that the scale is helpful in research, but is not useful for distinguishing among individuals with high levels of spiritual well-being.

The Faith Maturity Scale

In 1987, six major Protestant denominations undertook a national four-year study of personal faith, denominational allegiance, and their determinants (Benson, Donahue, & Erickson, 1993). Funded in part by the Lilly Endowment, this project spawned what is undoubtedly the most sophisticated measure of spiritual maturity ever conceived. The Faith Maturity Scale (FMS) arose as a practical tool to serve three research purposes:

1. Provide baseline data on the vitality of faith in mainstream Protestant congregations
2. Identify the contributions of demographic, personal, and congregational variables to faith development
3. Furnish a criterion variable for evaluating the impact of religious education in mainstream denominations

The development of the scale was a time-consuming and careful process that began with a working definition:

> Faith maturity is the degree to which a person embodies the priorities, commitments, and perspectives characteristic of vibrant and life-transforming faith, as they have been understood in "mainline" Protestant traditions (Benson, Donahue, & Erickson, 1993, p. 3).

Using open-ended questionnaires with a convenience sample of 410 mainline Protestant adults, the test developers next identified eight core dimensions of faith maturity. Three advisory panels provided ongoing counsel during this stage and the next phase of item writing. These interactions assured that the scale possessed face and content validity.

The resulting FMS is a 38-item test that embodies key indicators of faith maturity in eight core areas (Table 12.10). Items are answered on a

TABLE 12.10 The Eight Core Dimensions and
Sample Items from the Faith Maturity Scale

A. Trusts and believes (5 items)
   Every day I see evidence that God is at work in the world

B. Experiences the fruits of faith (5 items)
   I feel weighed down by all my responsibilities (reverse scored)

C. Integrates faith and life (5 items)
   My faith influences how I think and act every day

D. Seeks spiritual growth (4 items)
   I take time to meditate or pray

E. Experiences and nurtures faith in community (4 items)
   I talk with others about my faith

F. Holds life-affirming values (6 items)
   I tend to be critical of other persons (reverse scored)

G. Advocates social change (4 items)
   I believe the churches of this nation should get involved in political issues

H. Acts and serves (5 items)
   I offer significant amounts of time to help others

Note: The sample items are similar to those on the Faith Maturity Scale.
Source: Based on Benson, P., Donahue, M., & Erickson, J. (1993). The Faith Maturity Scale: Conceptualization, Measurement, and Empirical Validation. In M. L. Lynn & D. O. Moberg (eds.), *Research in the social scientific study of religion* (vol. 5). Greenwich, CT: JAI Press.

seven-point scale from 1 = never true to 7 = always true. Based upon the areas assessed, the reader will notice that right belief is only one aspect of a mature faith. In large measure, faith maturity is defined by value and behavioral consequences. As the authors note, the Faith Maturity Scale "parts company with more traditional ways of defining and measuring personal religion." Yet it does embody the kinds of behaviors and attitudes that derive from a dynamic, life-transforming faith. These behaviors and attitudes are consistent with the theology found in most religious traditions, but are especially pertinent for the particular purpose of assessing faith maturity in the Protestant context.

The FMS is scored as the mean of the 38 items, which yields a potential range of 1 to 7. The average score for 3,040 adults in five Protestant denominations was 4.63, which indicates that the instrument avoids the "ceiling effect" found on other scales such as the Spiritual Well-Being Scale, discussed previously. The estimated reliability of the scale is very robust across age, gender, occupation, and denomination, with typical coefficient alphas of .88 (Benson et al., 1993). Test-retest reliability was not reported.

The validity of the scale is supported by several lines of evidence, beginning with the careful approach to item selection, by which face validity and content validity were built-in. Construct validity was demonstrated in several ways. First, it was predicted and confirmed that groups presumed to differ in levels of faith maturity would obtain significantly different mean scores on the FMS. Indeed, pastors scored the highest (5.3), followed by church education coordinators (4.9), teachers (4.7), adults (4.6), and youth (4.1)—each group in respective order scoring significantly lower than the others. Second, pastors' ratings of the faith maturity of 123 congregation members on a 1 to 10 scale correlated very substantially ($r = .61$) with the FMS scores of these persons, indicating a correspondence between independent expert ratings and self-report. The scale also revealed predictive utility. Specifically, FMS scale scores were strongly related to a variety of prosocial behaviors such as donating time to help those who are poor, hungry, or sick; promoting a greater role for women in the church; and endorsing the use of foreign policy to challenge apartheid.

One cautionary note is that the susceptibility of the scale to response sets (e.g., "fake good") is simply unknown. The authors of the test call for further research to examine yea-saying, social desirability, and other response sets. They also offer a refreshing modesty in discussing their 38-item test:

> It would be presumptuous to claim that these 38 are the final word on what defines mature faith. Over time, we hope that the Faith Maturity Scale itself matures, being further informed and modified through interaction with an expanded range of researchers and reactors representing a widening circle of religious traditions (Benson et al., 1993, p. 24).

Overall, the FMS holds great promise as a measure of faith maturity. A special virtue of the test is that it avoids the ceiling effect so common in other measures of spiritual variables. This feature guarantees that the instrument will prove useful in examining the effects of educational programs as well as changes over time in religiously devout individuals.

The Spiritual Experience Index

Measures of spiritual and religious functioning largely have been developed from a Christian interpretation of faith, with the result that applications cannot be extended to persons whose spiritual beliefs are rooted in any other ideology. A notable exception is the Spiritual Experience Index (SEI), which derives from a developmental view of faith. This test is based upon the theory that faith is a developmental phenomenon that progresses from the highly egocentric religiosity of childhood to the transcendent faith of middle adulthood—when nurtured by favorable psychosocial conditions. The developmental theory was first elucidated by Fowler (1981) and later revised by Genia (1990). A summary of Genia's five stages of faith is included in Table 12.11.

This highest level of religious maturity (found in all the major faiths) is characterized by ten criteria (Genia, 1993b):

1. Transcendent relationship to something greater than oneself
2. Consistency of lifestyle and behavior with spiritual values
3. Commitment without absolute certainty
4. Openness to spiritually diverse viewpoints
5. Lack of magical thinking and anthropomorphic God concepts
6. Inclusion of both rational and emotional components
7. Social interest and humanitarian concern
8. Mature faith is life-enhancing and growth-producing
9. Provision of meaning and purpose in life
10. Lack of dependence upon particular practices or formal religious structure

TABLE 12.11 The Stages of Religious Faith

Stage 1: Egocentric faith

Characteristic of persons with immature personality development, egocentric faith is narcissistic, based on anticipated reward or punishment. The divine image is anthropomorphic, and prayer is petitionary.

Stage 2: Dogmatic faith

Religious dogma is used rigidly and defensively as a means of psychological support. Scripture is interpreted literally and absolutely. Prayer may take the form of bargaining with God.

Stage 3: Transitional faith

Characteristic of many adolescents, the individual recognizes a freedom to engage in questioning and doubt. Religious experimentation such as "trying on" different ideologies or switching denominations may occur.

Stage 4: Reconstructed Internalized Faith

There is commitment to a self-chosen faith that transcends egocentric concerns. The chosen ideology provides a sense of purpose and meaning in life. Religious doctrine is more complex and prayers feature thanksgiving, praise, and devotion.

Stage 5: Transcendent Faith

The individual maintains a transcendent relationship to something greater than the self. There is commitment without absolute certainty, and the person's style of living is consistent with his/her religious values.

Source: Based on Genia, V. (1990). Religious development: A synthesis and reformulation. *Journal of Religion and Health, 29,* 85–99.

The purpose of the SEI scale is to assess the degree of spiritual maturity (conceived as a unidimensional construct) for persons from diverse religious and spiritual traditions. The items of the scale were developed from these 10 criteria by means of rational scale construction (meaning that the test author devised several items pertinent to each of the criteria). A try-out sample of 75 persons (40 percent Roman Catholic, 28 percent Protestant, 23 percent Jewish, and 9 percent unaffiliated) completed a preliminary scale of 50 items. Twelve items were dropped due to low item-total correlations, leaving a scale of 38 items.

Examples of items similar to those on the SEI include the following:

- My faith provides meaning and purpose to my life.
- Usually a moral dilemma has only one right solution. (reverse scored)
- I sense a strong spiritual connection with all of humankind.
- My faith helps me to deal with tragedy and suffering.

The item format is a six-point Likert-type scale from 1 = strongly disagree to 6 = strongly agree. The score is reported as the total raw score, with a range of 38 to 228. For the initial sample, scores formed a normal distribution ranging from 103 to 211 with a mean of 166.

Internal consistency of the SEI is reported to be .87 (coefficient alpha) whereas test-retest stability was not tested. When the 38 items were entered into a Principle Axis Factoring Analysis, the scale held up as a unidimensional construct—no factors emerged that explained a meaningful portion of the variance. Thus, the findings indicate good internal reliability for the SEI and support its use as a unidimensional measure.

Validity inspection consisted of correlational analyses with a variety of other tests and measures. Strong correlations were noted with several variables: dogmatism ($r = -.52$), which indicates that high scale scores go with low dogmatism; Quest scores ($r = .44$), which suggests that the scale includes aspects of complexity and doubt; intrinsic religiosity ($r = .43$), which indicates that strong spiritual experience promotes a mature religious faith; intolerance of ambiguity ($r = -.40$), which argues that strong spiritual experience allows for tolerance of ambiguity; and frequency of worship ($r = .24$), which is intriguing because none of the SEI test items pertain to this behavioral index of faith.

Overall, these findings support the reliability and validity of this scale, but additional research is needed to examine its psychometric properties. Further analysis is especially desirable insofar as the SEI occupies a special niche in the assessment of spiritual variables—it is one of the few scales that is applicable across diverse religious traditions.

SUMMARY

1. A value is a shared, enduring belief about ideal modes of behavior or end states of existence. The assessment of values is important because values instill action, shape attitudes, and guide efforts to influence others.

2. One of the first inventories to assess values was the Study of Values, a test consisting of 30 questions pitting one value against another, and 15 questions involving the rank ordering of values. This scale produced an inventory of six values: Theoretical, Economic, Aesthetic, Social, Political, and Religious.

3. The Rokeach Value Survey is another tool to measure values. This test defines and measures two kinds of values: instrumental (e.g., Ambitious, Imaginative, Broad-minded) and terminal (e.g., a comfortable life, inner harmony, an exciting life).

4. With Kohlberg's Moral Judgment Scale, the examinee is asked a series of structured questions pertaining to several moral dilemmas. Responses are categorized according to six stages and three levels of development: preconventional, conventional, and postconventional.

5. Rest's Defining Issues Test is a spinoff of the Moral Judgment Scale that uses a completely objective scoring format. The test yields several quantitative indices, including the P score (percentage of principled thinking) and the N2 index (based on complex formulas), both of which show good reliability and validity.

6. A relatively neglected area in assessment is the evaluation of spiritual and religious dimensions. This is unfortunate because assessment of these variables could have important implications for individual clients.

7. One of the first forms of religious assessment was the Allport-Ross Religious Orientation scales. These scales popularized the concepts of intrinsic religiousness (persons *live* their religion to find meaning and direction) versus extrinsic religiousness (persons *use* their religion to seek security or status).

8. The Quest scale seeks to measure a third religious orientation (beyond intrinsic and extrinsic) characterized by complexity, doubt, and tentativeness as ways of being religious. This simple 12-item scale appears to measure a religion of less faith but more works.

9. The Spiritual Well-Being Scale is a mainstay in the field of religious assessment. It consists of two subscales, Religious Well-Being (a vertical dimension of well-being in relation to God) and Existential Well-Being (a horizontal dimension of well-being in relation to life purpose and satisfaction. A problem with this scale is its low ceiling.

10. The Faith Maturity Index is an ambitious scale devised at the behest of six major Protestant denominations. The 38 items are answered on a seven-point scale, providing an index of a vibrant and life-transforming faith, as understood in mainline Protestant faiths.

11. The Spiritual Experience Index was designed to measure spiritual maturity from a developmental view of faith, independent of any particular creed or religion. The 38 items are answered on a six-point scale, yielding a unitary index of spiritual maturity, broadly defined.

KEY TERMS AND CONCEPTS

value   p. 463

moral dilemmas   p. 467

intrinsic religious expression   p. 471

extrinsic religious expression   p. 471

religion as Quest   p. 473

CHAPTER 13

Origins of Personality Testing

TOPIC **13A** Theories and the Measurement of Personality

In psychological testing a fundamental distinction often is drawn between ability tests and personality tests. Defined in the broadest sense, ability tests include the plethora of instruments for measuring intelligence, achievement, aptitude, and neuropsychological functions. In the preceding 12 chapters we have explored the nature, construction, application, reliability, and validity of these instruments. In the next two chapters we shift the emphasis to personality tests. Personality tests seek to measure one or more of the following: personality traits, dynamic motivation, personal adjustment, psychiatric symptomatology, social skills, and attitudinal characteristics. This chapter investigates the origins of personality testing. In Topic 13A, Theories and the Measurement of Personality, the different ways in which researchers have conceptualized personality are surveyed to illustrate how their theories have impacted the design of personality tests and assessments. In Topic 13B, Projective Techniques, we examine the multiplicity of instruments based upon the turn-of-the-century psychoanalytic hypothesis that responses to ambiguous stimuli reveal the innermost, unconscious mental processes of the examinee. The coverage of personality assessment continues in the next chapter with a review of objective tests and procedures, including self-report inventories and behavioral assessment approaches.

PERSONALITY: AN OVERVIEW

Although personality is difficult to define, we can distinguish two fundamental features of this vague construct. First, each person is consistent to some extent; we have coherent traits and action patterns that arise repeatedly. Second, each person is distinctive to some extent; behavioral differences exist between individuals. Consider the reactions of three graduate students when their midterm examinations were handed back. Although all three students received nearly identical grades (solid Bs), personal reactions were quite diverse. The first student walked off sullenly and was later overheard to say that a complaint to the departmental administrator was in order. The second student was pleased, stating out loud that a B was, after all, a respectable grade. The third student was disappointed but stoical. He blamed himself for not studying harder.

How are we to understand the different reactions of these three persons, each of whom was responding to an identical stimulus? Psychologists and laypersons alike invoke the concept of **personality** to make sense out of the behavior and expressed feelings of others. The notion of personality is used to explain behavioral differences between persons (for example, why one complains and another is stoical) and to understand the behavioral consistency within each individual (for example, why the complaining student noted previously was generally sour and dissatisfied).

In addition to understanding personality, psychologists also seek to measure it. Literally hundreds of personality tests are available for this purpose; we will review historically prominent instruments and also discuss some promising new approaches. However, in order that the reader can better comprehend the diversity of instruments and

approaches, we begin with a more fundamental question: How is personality best conceptualized? As the reader will discover, in order to measure personality we must first envision what it is we seek to measure. The reader will better appreciate the multiplicity of tests and procedures if we also briefly describe the personality theories which comprise the underpinnings for these instruments. We close out this topic by raising a general question pertinent to all theories and testing approaches: How stable and predictable is behavior?

Although we partition personality tests separately from the ability tests, the distinction between these two kinds of instruments is far from absolute. Intellectual ability is, in part, a characterological feature based on such attributes as perseverance and self-control. Thus, ability tests inevitably tap important dimensions of personality, albeit in an indirect and imperfect manner. Often, the converse is also true: Personality tests may be saturated with ability factors. For example, certain personality dimensions such as openness to experience probably correlate positively with intelligence. As the reader will discover in the next chapter, some true-false personality inventories incorporate a very robust intelligence factor (e.g., Cattell, Eber, & Tatsuoka, 1970).

PSYCHOANALYTIC THEORIES OF PERSONALITY

Psychoanalysis was the original creation of Sigmund Freud (1856–1939). While it is true that many others have revised and adapted his theories, the changes have been slight in comparison to the substantial foundations which can be traced to this singular genius of the Victorian and early-twentieth-century era. Freud was enormously prolific in his writing and theorizing. We restrict our discussion to just those aspects of psychoanalysis that have influenced psychological testing. In particular, the Rorschach, the Thematic Apperception Test, and most of the projective techniques critiqued in the next topic dictate a psychoanalytic framework for interpretation. Readers who wish a more thorough review of Freud's contributions can start with the New Introductory Lectures on Psychoanalysis (Freud, 1933). Reviews and interpretations of Freud's theories can be found in Stafford-Clark (1971) and Fisher and Greenberg (1984).

Origins of Psychoanalytic Theory

Freud began his professional career as a neurologist, but was soon specializing in the treatment of hysteria, an emotional disorder characterized by histrionic behavior and physical symptoms of psychic origin such as paralysis, blindness, and loss of sensation. With his colleague Joseph Breuer, Freud postulated that the root cause of hysteria was buried memories of traumatic experiences such as childhood sexual molestation. If these memories could be brought forth under hypnosis, a release of emotion called abreaction would take place and the hysterical symptoms would disappear, at least briefly (*Studies on Hysteria,* Breuer & Freud, 1893–1895).

From these early studies Freud developed a general theory of psychological functioning with the concept of the unconscious as its foundation. He believed that the unconscious was the reservoir of instinctual drives and a storehouse of thoughts and wishes that would be unacceptable to our conscious self. Thus, Freud argued that our most significant personal motivations are largely beyond conscious awareness. The concept of the unconscious was discussed in elaborate detail in his first book (*The Interpretation of Dreams,* Freud, 1900). Freud believed that dreams portray our unconscious motives in a disguised form. Even a seemingly innocuous dream might actually have a hidden sexual or aggressive meaning, if it is interpreted correctly.

Freud's concept of the unconscious penetrated the very underpinnings of psychological testing early in this century. An entire family of projective techniques emerged, including inkblot tests, word association approaches, sentence completion techniques, and story-telling (apperception) techniques (Frank, 1939; 1948). Each of these methods was predicated on the assumption that unconscious motives could be divined from an examinee's responses to ambiguous and unstructured stimuli. In fact, Rorschach (1921) likened his inkblot test to an X ray of the unconscious mind. Although he patently overstated the power of projective techniques, it is evident from Rorschach's view that the psychoanalytic conception of the unconscious had a strong influence on testing practices.

The Structure of the Mind

Freud's views on the structure of the mind and the operation of defense mechanisms also influenced psychological testing and assessment (*New Introductory Lectures on Psychoanalysis,* Freud, 1933). Several tests and assessment approaches discussed in this chapter are predicated upon the psychoanalytic conception of defense mechanisms, so this topic deserves brief summary.

Freud divided the mind into three structures: the id, the ego, and the superego. The id is the obscure and inaccessible part of our personality that Freud likened to "a chaos, a cauldron of seething excitement." Because the **id** is entirely unconscious, we must infer its characteristics indirectly by analyzing dreams and symptoms such as anxiety. From such an analysis, Freud concluded that the id is the seat of all instinctual needs such as for food, water, sexual gratification, and avoidance of pain. The id has only one purpose, to obtain immediate satisfaction for these needs in accordance with the pleasure principle. The **pleasure principle** is the impulsion toward immediate satisfaction without regard for values, good or evil, or morality. The id is also incapable of logic and possesses no concept of time. The chaotic mental processes of the id are therefore unaltered by the passage of time, and impressions which have been pushed down into the id "are virtually immortal and are preserved for whole decades as though they had only recently occurred" (Freud, 1933).

If our personality consisted only of an id striving to gratify its instincts without regard for reality, we would soon be annihilated by outside forces. Fortunately, soon after birth part of the id develops into the **ego** or conscious self. The purpose of the ego is to mediate between the id and reality. The ego is part of the id and servant to it, but the ego "interpolates between desire and action the procrastinating factor of thought" (Freud, 1933). Thus, the ego is largely conscious and obeys the **reality principle;** it seeks realistic and safe ways of discharging the instinctual tensions which are constantly pushing forth from the id.

The ego must also contend with the **superego,** the ethical component of personality which starts to emerge in the first five years of life. The superego is roughly synonymous with conscience and is comprised of the societal standards of right and wrong which are conveyed to us by our parents. The superego is partly conscious, but a large part of it is unconscious, that is, we are not always aware of its existence or operation. The function of the superego is to restrict the attempts of the id and ego to obtain gratification. Its main weapon is guilt, which it uses to punish the wrongdoings of the ego and id. Thus, it is not enough for the ego to find a safe and realistic way for the gratification of id strivings. The ego must also choose a morally acceptable outlet, or it will suffer punishment from its overseer, the superego. This explains why we may feel guilty for immoral behavior such as theft even when getting caught is impossible. Another part of the superego is the ego ideal which consists of our aims and aspirations. The ego measures itself against the ego ideal and strives to fulfill its demands for perfection. If the ego falls too far short of meeting the standards of the ego ideal, a feeling of guilt may result. We commonly interpret this feeling as a sense of inferiority (Freud, 1933).

The Role of Defense Mechanisms

The ego certainly has a difficult task, acting as mediator and servant to three tyrants: id, superego, and external reality. It may seem to the reader that the task would be essentially impossible and that the individual would therefore be in a constant state of anxiety. Fortunately, the ego has a set of tools at its disposal to help carry out its work, namely, mental strategies collectively labeled **defense mechanisms.**

Defense mechanisms come in many varieties, but they all share three characteristics in common. First, their exclusive purpose is to help the ego reduce anxiety created by the conflicting demands of id, superego, and external reality. In fact, Freud felt that anxiety was a signal telling the ego to invoke one or more defense mechanisms in its own behalf. Defense mechanisms and anxiety are therefore complementary concepts in psychoanalytic theory, one existing as a counterforce to the other. The second common feature of defense mechanisms is that they operate unconsciously. Thus, even though defense mechanisms are controlled by the ego, we are not aware of their operation. The third characteristic of defense mechanisms is that they distort inner or outer reality. This property is what makes them capable of reducing anxiety. By allowing the ego to view a challenge from the id, superego, or external reality in a less-threatening manner, defense mechanisms help the ego avoid crippling levels of anxiety. Of course, because they distort reality, the rigid, excessive application of defense mechanisms may create more problems than it solves.

Assessment of Defense Mechanisms and Ego Functions

Although Freud introduced the concept of defense mechanisms, it was left to his followers to elucidate these unconscious mental strategies in more detail (Paulhus, Fridhandler, & Hayes, 1997). An early portrayal of defense mechanisms was provided by Freud's daughter, Anna (*The Ego and the Mechanisms of Defense,* A. Freud, 1946). However, the application of these concepts to psychological measurement and assessment is much more recent. For example, Loevinger (1976, 1979, 1984) has produced a sentence completion technique for measuring ego development that is based, indirectly, on the analysis of defense mechanisms. This interesting approach to personality measurement is outlined briefly in the next unit. Here we will present Vaillant's (1977, 1992) work to illustrate the measurement of defense mechanisms and the application of this information to the understanding of personality.

Vaillant (1971) developed a hierarchy of ego adaptive mechanisms based on the assumption that some defensive mechanisms are intrinsically healthier than others. In his view, defense mechanisms can be grouped into four different types. Listed in order of increasing healthiness, the types are psychotic, immature, neurotic, and mature (Table 13.1). Psychotic mechanisms such as gross denial of external reality are the least healthy because they distort reality to an extreme degree. They appear "crazy" to the beholder. Immature mechanisms such as the projection of one's own unacknowledged feelings to others are healthier than psychotic mechanisms. Nonetheless, they are easily detected by outside observers and seen as undesirable. Neurotic defense mechanisms typically alter private feelings so that they are less threatening. An example is intellectualization, a defense mechanism in which threatening matters are analyzed in bland terms that are void of feelings. For example, a physician whose mother died recently might talk at great length about the medical characteristics of her cancer, thereby easing his sense of loss. Mature mechanisms of defense appear to the beholder as convenient virtues. An example is certain forms of humor which do not distort reality but which case ease the burden of matters "too terrible to be borne" (Vaillant, 1977).

The application of defense mechanisms to the understanding of personality is illustrated in the Grant Study, a 45-year follow-up study conducted by Vaillant and others (Vaillant, 1977; Vaillant & Vaillant, 1990). These researchers used structured interviews to obtain evidence of unconscious adaptive mechanisms from a sample of 95 men. The subjects were from an original sample of 268 students from Harvard University's classes of 1939 through 1944. At follow-up, Vaillant interviewed each participant for two hours, using a semistructured interview schedule (Vaillant, 1977, App. B). In addition, the subjects filled out autobiographical questionnaires and provided other sources of information. The entire protocol for each subject was then evaluated by Vaillant and other raters according to the extent that each defense mechanism characterized the individual's adaptation to life.

Defense mechanisms were scored from 1 (absent) to 5 (major). Here is an example of one unconscious adaptive behavior:

> A California hematologist developed a hobby of cultivating living cells in test tubes. In a recent interview, he described with special interest and animation an unusually interesting culture that he had grown from a tissue biopsy from his mother. Only toward the end of the interview did he casually reveal that his mother had died from a stroke only three weeks previously. His mention of her death was as bland as his description of her still-living tissue culture had been affectively colored. Ingeniously and unconsciously, he had used his hobby and his special skills as a physician to mitigate temporarily the pain of his loss. Although his mother was no longer alive, by shifting his attention he was still able to care for her. There was nothing morbid in the way he told the story; and because ego mechanisms are unconscious, he had no idea of his defensive behavior. Many of the healthiest men in the Study used similar kinds of attention shifts or displacement. Unless specifically looked for by a trained observer, such behavior goes unnoticed more often than not (Vaillant, 1977).

Most likely, this individual would receive a rating of 5 (major) for the neurotic defense mechanism of displacement.

Considering the degree of skilled judgment required by the evaluation task, the interrater reliability of the defense mechanism ratings was—with a few exceptions—respectable. The individual defense mechanisms possessed reliabilities that ranged from .53 (Fantasy) to .96 (Projection); most reliabilities were in the .70s and .80s. Reliability of a global rating (reflecting the ratio of mature to immature ratings) was .77.

The validity of defense mechanism ratings hinges mainly on the demonstration that developmental changes and group differences are consistent with psychoanalytic theory regarding these constructs. We would expect, for example, that the Grant Study subjects would use fewer immature and more mature defense mechanisms as they grew into middle age, and this is precisely what Vaillant discovered. In addition, we would expect that persons found to be maladjusted by other

TABLE 13.1   Levels of Defense Mechanisms Proposed by Vaillant (1977)

I. Psychotic

Delusional Projection: frank delusions about external reality, usually of a persecutory nature

Denial: denial of external reality; e.g., failing to acknowledge that one has a terminal illness

Distortion: grossly reshaping external reality to suit inner needs; e.g., wish-fulfilling delusions

II. Immature

Projection: attributing one's own unacknowledged feelings to others; e.g., "You're angry, not me!"

Schizoid Fantasy: use of fantasy and inner retreat for the purpose of conflict resolution and gratification

Hypochondriasis: transforming reproach toward others first into self-reproach then into complaints of physical illness

Passive-Aggressive Behavior: aggression toward others expressed indirectly and ineffectively through passivity or directed against the self

Acting Out: direct expression of an unconscious wish or impulse in order to avoid being conscious of the feeling that accompanies it

III. "Neurotic"

Intellectualization: thinking about wishes in formal, unfeeling terms, but not acting upon them

Repression: seemingly inexplicable memory lapses or failure to acknowledge information; e.g., "forgetting" a dental appointment

Displacement: directing of feelings toward something or someone other than the real object; e.g., kicking the dog when angry with the boss

Reaction Formation: unconsciously turning an impulse into its opposite, e.g., over-solicitousness to a hated coworker

Dissociation: temporary but drastic modification of one's character to avoid emotional distress; e.g., a brief devil-may-care attitude

IV. Mature

Altruism: vicarious but constructive and gratifying service to others; e.g., philanthropy

Humor: playful acknowledgment of ideas and feelings without discomfort and without unpleasant effects on others; does not include sarcasm

Suppression: conscious or semiconscious decision to postpone paying attention to a conscious conflict or impulse

Anticipation: realistic anticipation of or planning for future inner discomfort; e.g., realistic anticipation of surgery or separation

Sublimation: indirect expression of instinctual wishes without adverse consequences or loss of pleasure; e.g., channeling aggression into sports

Source: Based on Vaillant, G. (1977). *Adaptation to life: How the best and the brightest came of age.* Boston, MA: Little, Brown.

criteria (e.g., frequent divorce, underachievement) would rate less favorably on defense mechanisms in comparison to adjusted persons, and this is also what Vaillant observed. In sum, the analysis of defense mechanisms is a promising approach to personality assessment. However, this approach does have two drawbacks: The examiner needs specialized training to recognize defense mechanisms, and the process of collecting relevant information from examinees is very time-consuming.

TYPE THEORIES OF PERSONALITY

The earliest personality theories attempted to sort individuals into discrete categories or types. For example, the Greek physician Hippocrates (ca. 460–377 B.C.) proposed a humoral theory with four personality types (sanguine, choleric, melancholic, and phlegmatic) that was too simplistic to be useful. In the 1940s, Sheldon and Stevens (1942) proposed a type theory based upon the relationship between body build and temperament. Their approach stimulated a flurry of research and then faded into obscurity. Nonetheless, typological theories have continued to capture intermittent interest among personality researchers. We will illustrate type theories by reviewing contemporary research on coronary-prone personality types.

Type A Coronary-Prone Behavior Pattern

Friedman and Rosenman (1974) investigated the psychological variables that put individuals at higher risk of coronary heart disease. They were the first to identify a **Type A coronary-prone behavior pattern,** which they described as "an action-emotion complex that can be observed in any person who is aggressively involved in a chronic, incessant struggle to achieve more and more in less and less time, and if required to do so, against the opposing efforts of other things or persons" (Friedman & Rosenman, 1974). At the opposite extreme is the Type B behavior pattern, characterized by an easygoing, noncompetitive, relaxed lifestyle. Of course, people vary along a continuum from "pure" Type A to "pure" Type B.

Friedman and Ulmer (1984) have listed the specific components of the full-fledged Type A behavior pattern:

- *Insecurity of status:* A hidden lack of self-esteem seems to plague many Type A persons. No matter how successful, they often compare themselves unfavorably to other superachievers.
- *Hyperaggressiveness:* A desire to dominate others and damage their self-esteem is part of the pattern. Type A persons are often indifferent to the feelings or rights of competitors.
- *Free-floating hostility:* The Type A person finds too many things to get upset about, and the anger is out of proportion to the situation.
- *Sense of time urgency (hurry sickness):* This includes two basic strategems: speeding up daily activities (one Type A used an electric shaver in each hand!), and doing two things at once such as conversing on the phone while reviewing correspondence.

Type A behavior can be diagnosed from a short interview consisting of questions about habits of working, talking, eating, reading, and thinking (Friedman & Ulmer, 1984). The more flagrant cases of Type A behavior can also be detected by paper-and-pencil tests (Jackson & Gray, 1987; Jenkins, Zyzanski, & Rosenman, 1971, 1979) which we discuss in the next chapter. However, the questionnaire approach is limited because it cannot reveal the facial, vocal, and psychomotor indices of hostility and time urgency that are usually evident in interview (Friedman & Ulmer, 1984).

Early studies indicated that persons who exhibited the Type A behavior pattern were at greatly increased risk of coronary disease and heart attack. In one 9-year study of more than 3,000 healthy men, persons with the Type A behavior pattern were 2½ times more likely to suffer heart attacks than those with Type B behavior pattern (Friedman & Ulmer, 1984). In fact, not one of the "pure" Type Bs—the extremely relaxed, easygoing, and noncompetitive members of the study—had suffered a heart attack. In the famous Framingham longitudinal study, Type A men ages 55 to 64 were about twice as likely at 10-year follow-up to develop coronary heart disease as Type B men (Haynes, Feinleib, & Eaker, 1983). In this study, the link between Type A behavior and heart disease was especially strong for white-collar workers.

In more recent studies, researchers have found only a weak relationship—or no relationship at all—between Type A behavior and coronary heart disease (e.g., Eaker & Castelli, 1988; Mathews & Haynes, 1986). Other researchers have found that heart disease is linked not so much with the full-blown Type A behavior pattern as it is with specific components such as being anger-prone (Dembroski, MacDougall, Williams, & Haney, 1985) or possessing time urgency (Wright, 1988). Certainly there is a need to sort out the specific risk factors in this area of investigation. Good reviews of the complex and confusing research on Type A behavior can be found in Brannon and Feist (1992) and Wiebe and Smith (1997).

Research on Type A behavior has sparked a renewed and more sophisticated interest in typological conceptions of personality. Rather than viewing types as separate pigeonholes, psychologists have come to view them as idealized examples that occupy the end points of continuous dimensions. Individuals can thus differ with respect to how much of an idealized personality type that they possess. This is similar to the trait conception of personality discussed later. Perhaps the main difference is that modern type theorists tend to believe that most individuals are near to the idealized types at the end of each dimension, whereas trait theorists argue that people are more likely to be found at all points along each personality continuum. In practice, then, the modern distinction between types and traits is relative, not absolute.

PHENOMENOLOGICAL THEORIES OF PERSONALITY

Phenomenological theories of personality emphasize the importance of immediate, personal, subjective experience as a determinant of behavior. Some of the theoretical positions subsumed under this title have been given other labels also, such as humanistic theories, existential theories, construct theories, self theories, and fulfillment theories (Maddi, 1989). Nonetheless, these approaches share a common focus on the person's subjective experience, personal worldview, and self-concept as the major wellsprings of behavior.

Origins of the Phenomenological Approach

The orientation briefly reviewed in this section has numerous sources that reach back to turn-of-the-century European philosophy and literature. Nonetheless, two persons, one a philosopher and the other a writer, stand out as seminal contributors to the modern phenomenological viewpoint. The German philosopher Edmund Husserl (1859–1938) invented a complex philosophy of phenomenology that was concerned with the description of pure mental phenomena. Husserl's approach was heavily introspective and nearly inscrutable. More approachable was the Danish writer Soren Kierkegaard (1813–1855), well known for his contributions to existentialism. Existentialism is the literary and philosophical movement concerned with the meaning of life and an individual's freedom to choose personal goals. The phenomenology of Husserl and the existentialism of Kierkegaard influenced dozens of prominent philosophers and psychologists. Vestiges of these early viewpoints are evident in virtually every contemporary phenomenological personality theory (Maddi, 1989).

Carl Rogers, Self-Theory, and the Q-Technique

The most influential phenomenological theorist was Carl Rogers (1902–1987). His contributions to personality theory, known as self-theory, are extensive and generally well appreciated by students of psychology (Rogers, 1951, 1961, 1980). But it is also true, albeit little recognized, that Rogers helped shape a small part of psychological testing by popularizing the Q-technique.

The **Q-technique** is a procedure for studying changes in the self-concept, a key element in Rogers's self-theory. The technique was developed by Stephenson (1953) but a series of studies by

Rogers and his colleagues served to popularize this measurement approach (Rogers & Dymond, 1954). Also known as a Q-Sort, the Q-technique is a generalized procedure that is especially useful for studying changes in self-concept.[1] The Q-sort consists of a large number of cards, each containing a printed statement such as:

I am poised
I put on a false front
I make strong demands on myself
I am a submissive person
I am likeable

The examinee is asked to sort a hundred or so statements into nine piles, putting a prescribed number of cards into each, thus forcing a near-normal distribution. The instructions specify that the examinee put the cards most descriptive of him or her at one end, those least descriptive at the opposite end, and those about which he or she is indifferent or undecided around the middle of the distribution. The required distribution might look like this:

	Least Like Me					**Most Like Me**			
Pile No.	1	2	3	4	5	6	7	8	9
No. of cards	1	4	11	21	26	21	11	4	1

The nature of the items is determined by the needs of the researcher or practitioner. Rogers used a set of items devised by Butler and Haigh (Rogers & Dymond, 1954, chp. 4) to tap the self-concept. These statements were taken at random from available therapeutic protocols; their Q-sort items represented actual client statements, reworded for clarity. But a special virtue of the Q-technique is that other researchers or practitioners are free to craft their own items. For example, Marks and Seeman (1963) used a psychodynamic perspective in devising items for the therapist description of patient groups. Examples of their items include the following:

Utilizes acting out as a defense mechanism
Tends to be flippant in both word and gesture
Genotype has paranoid features
Appears to be poised, self-assured, socially at ease
Exhibits depression (manifest sad mood)

Scoring a Q-sort is usually a matter of comparing or correlating the distribution of items against an established norm. For example, well-adjusted persons might be asked to sort the items so as to derive an average pile placement number (ranging from 1 to 9) for each item. An individual examinee would be considered more- or less-adjusted according to the resemblance between his or her sortings and the average sorting for adjusted persons. We will refer the reader to Block (1961) for details.

Another way to use the Q-sort is to compare an examinee's self-sort with his or her ideal sort. Rogers used the discrepancy between these two sortings as an index of adjustment. His subjects were required to sort the items twice, according the following instructions:

1. *Self-sort.* Sort these cards to describe yourself as you see yourself today, from those that are least like you to those that are most like you.
2. *Ideal sort.* Now sort these cards to describe your ideal person—the person you would most like within yourself to be (Rogers & Dymond, 1954).

Using the item pile numbers, Rogers then correlated the two sorts for each subject separately. Consider what these data mean: If the self-sort and the ideal sort are highly similar, the correlation of Q-sort data will approach 1.0; if the two sorts are opposite one another, the correlation will approach –1.0. Of course, most sorts will be somewhere in between but typically on the positive side. Butler and Haigh found that psychotherapy clients increased their congruence between self and ideal (Rogers & Dymond, 1954, chp. 4). Even so, adjusted control subjects possessed a greater congruence (Table 13.2).

---

1. The Q-technique has additional applications as well. Marks and Seeman (1963) employed Q-sorts by therapists to describe patients with specific MMPI profiles. Bem and Funder (1978) recommend a Q-sort to derive a profile of characteristics associated with successful performance of a specific task. Persons whose self-descriptions match the derived profile can be predicted to succeed at the selected task.

TABLE 13.2   Average Self-Ideal Correlations for Client and Control Groups

	Precounseling	Postcounseling	Follow-Up
Client Group (N = 25)	−.01	.36	.32
Control Group (N = 16)	.58		.59

Source: Based on Rogers, C. R., and Dymond, R. F. (eds.) (1954). *Psychotherapy and personality change: Co-ordinated research studies in the client-centered approach.* Chicago: The University of Chicago Press.

BEHAVIORAL AND SOCIAL LEARNING THEORIES

Behavioral and social learning theories have their origins in laboratory studies on operant learning and classical conditioning. A fundamental assumption of all behavioral theorists is that many of the behaviors that make up personality are learned. To understand personality, then, we must know about the learning history of the individual. Behavioral theorists also believe that the environment is of supreme importance in shaping and maintaining behavior. Behavioral inquiry therefore seeks to identify the specific components of the current environment that are controlling a person's behavior. The behavioral approach to personality has produced a variety of direct assessment methods which we discuss in the next chapter.

Behavioral theorists disagree mainly on the role that cognitions play in determining behavior. Cognitions are inferred mental processes such as problem solving, judging, or reasoning. Radical behaviorists believe that resorting to mentalistic explanations of any kind is futile: "When what a person does is attributed to what is going on inside him, investigation is brought to an end" (Skinner, 1974). By contrast, social learning theorists make cautious reference to cognitions in explaining what it is, specifically, that a person learns. A social learning theorist might argue that we learn expectations or rules about the environment, not just stimulus and response connections.

Modern social learning theory can be viewed as a cognitive variant of the strict behaviorism that was dominant in American psychology early in this century. Social learning theorists accept the Skin-nerian premise that external reinforcement is an important determinant of behavior. But they also maintain that cognitions have a critical influence on our actions as well. For example, Rotter (1972) has popularized the view that our expectations about future outcomes are the primary determinants of behavior. The probability that a person will behave self-assertively, for example, depends upon his or her expectations about the likely results of self-assertiveness. If the expected outcome is valued by the person, the behavior is more likely. Of course, expectations are a function of the person's history of reinforcement, so Rotter's social learning perspective is similar to the behavioral viewpoint. But the implication of social learning theory is that behavior is the result of a belief, in particular, a belief that the behavior will result in a desired outcome. Thus, cognitions are assumed to affect actions.

Based on his social learning views, Rotter (1966) developed the Internal-External (I-E) Scale, an interesting measure of internal versus external locus of control. The construct of **locus of control** refers to the perceptions that individuals have about the source of things that happen to them. In particular, the I-E Scale seeks to assess the examinee's generalized expectancies for internal versus external control of reinforcement. The purpose of the I-E Scale is to determine the extent to which the examinee believes that reinforcement is contingent upon his/her behavior (internal locus of control) as opposed to the outside world (external locus of control). The instrument is a forced-choice self-report inventory. For each item, the examinee chooses the single statement (from a pair) with which he/she more strongly concurs. Items resemble the following:

In general, most people get the respect they deserve.

OR

In reality, a person's worth often passes unrecognized.

For the preceding item, the first alternative indicates an internal locus of control, whereas the second alternative signifies an external locus of control. The balance of internal to external responses determines the overall score on the scale. The I-E Scale is a reliable and valid instrument that has stimulated a huge body of research on the nature and meaning of locus of control and related variables. Research indicates that locus of control has a strong relationship to occupational success, physical health, academic achievement, and numerous other variables. As the reader might suspect, an internal locus of control generally predicts a more positive outcome than an external locus of control. The interested reader can consult Lefcourt (1982) and Wall, Hinrichsen, and Pollack (1989) for further details.

Important contributions to social learning theory have also been made by Albert Bandura. In his early studies, Bandura examined the role of observational learning and vicarious reinforcement in the development of behavior (Bandura, 1965, 1971; Bandura & Walters, 1963). More recently, he has proposed that perceived self-efficacy is a central mechanism in human action (Bandura, 1982; Bandura, Taylor, Ewart, Miller, & DeBusk, 1985). **Self-efficacy** is a personal judgment of "how well one can execute courses of action required to deal with prospective situations" (Bandura, 1982). The concept of self-efficacy is useful in explaining why correct knowledge does not necessarily predict efficient action. For example, two boys may be equally convinced that a garden snake in the bathtub presents no hazard, but one will pick it up while the other runs out the door. These differences in behavior illustrate the role of self-referential thought as a mediator between knowledge and action. The boy who ran out the door did not believe he could deal with the situation effectively. He had little perceived self-efficacy for snake handling. Bandura would argue that the primary determinant of the boy's behavior is a self-judgment about

personal capabilities. Cognitions are therefore assumed to be a major determinant of behavior.

Bandura has developed an interesting instrument for the assessment of self-efficacy expectancies (Bandura, Taylor, Ewart, Miller, & BeBusk, 1985). For a variety of situations that might arouse anxiety, annoyance, or anger, the examinee checks whether he or she "can do" the task, and also rates the degree of confidence using a number from 10 to 100. The format of the checklist is as follows:

10	20	30	40	50	60	70	80	90	100
Quite Uncertain			Moderately Certain						Certain

Can Do Confidence

Go to a party at which there is no one you know. _____ _____
Complain about poor food at a restaurant. _____ _____

Bandura's instrument is essentially a criterion-referenced tool for use in psychotherapy and research.

TRAIT CONCEPTIONS OF PERSONALITY

A **trait** is any "relatively enduring way in which one individual differs from another" (Guilford, 1959). Psychologists developed the concept of trait from the ways people describe other people in everyday life. As language evolved, people found words to portray the consistencies and differences they encountered in their daily interactions with others. Thus, when we say one person is sociable and another is shy we are using trait names to describe consistencies within individuals and also differences between them (Goldberg, 1981a; Fiske, 1986).

Trait conceptions of personality have been enormously popular throughout the history of psychological testing, so the coverage here is necessarily selective. We will review three prominent and influential positions from the dozens of trait theories that have been proposed. These approaches differ primarily in terms of whether traits are split off into finely discriminable variants or grouped together into a small number of broad dimensions:

1. Cattell's factor-analytic viewpoint identifies 16 to 20 bipolar trait dimensions.
2. Eysenck's trait-dimensional approach coalesces dozens of traits into two overriding dimensions.
3. Goldberg and others have sought a modern synthesis of all trait approaches by proposing a five-factor model of personality.

For readers who desire a more detailed discussion of this topic, Pervin (1993) and Wiggins (1997) provide an excellent review of trait approaches to personality theory.

Cattell's Factor-Analytic Trait Theory

Cattell (1950, 1973) refined existing methods of factor analysis to help reveal the basic traits of personality. He referred to the more obvious aspects of personality as **surface traits.** These would typically emerge in the first stages of factor analysis when individual test items were correlated with each other. For example, true-false items such as "I enjoy a good prize fight," "Getting stuck behind a slow driver really bothers me," and "It's important to let people know who is in charge" might be answered similarly by subjects, revealing a surface trait of aggressiveness.

But surface traits themselves tended to come in clusters, as revealed by Cattell's more sophisticated application of factor analysis. For Cattell, this was evidence of the existence of **source traits,** the stable and constant sources of behavior. Source traits are therefore less visible than surface traits but are more important in accounting for behavior.

Cattell (1950) was unrivaled in his use of factor analysis to discover how traits were organized and how they were related to each other. One approach was to have persons rate others they knew well by checking various adjectives such as *aggressive, thoughtful,* and *dominating* from a list of 171 choices. When the results from 208 subjects were subsequently factor analyzed, about 20 underlying personality factors or traits were tentatively identified. Another approach was to have thousands of persons answer questions about themselves and then factor analyze their responses. Six-

teen of the original 20 personality traits were independently confirmed by this second approach (Cattell, 1973). These 16 source traits have been incorporated into the Sixteen Personality Factor Questionnaire, a trait-based paper-and-pencil test of personality that is discussed in the next chapter.

Eysenck's Trait-Dimensional Theory

Eysenck used factor analysis to produce a parsimonious rapprochement between trait and dimensional approaches to personality (Eysenck & Eysenck, 1975, 1985). According to his system, personality consists of two basic dimensions, introverted-extraverted and emotionally stable–emotionally unstable. These two dimensions are presumed to be biologically and genetically based. Furthermore, the dimensions subsume numerous specific traits (Figure 13.1). The positions of the 32 traits correspond to the direction and amount of the two basic dimensions. For example, a moderately extraverted person who was also moderately unstable might be characterized by these traits: aggressive, excitable, changeable. An extremely introverted person who was also midway on the stable–unstable dimension might be viewed as unsociable, quiet, passive, and careful. Eysenck's trait-dimensional theory is incorporated in his personality inventory, the Eysenck Personality Questionnaire, which we review in the next chapter.

The Five-Factor Model of Personality

The five-factor model of personality has its origins in a review chapter by Goldberg (1981b). In his analysis of factor-analytic trait research, Goldberg identified several consistencies which he referred to as the "Big Five" dimensions. Although researchers have used slightly different terms for these factors, the most common labels are

Neuroticism
Extraversion
Openness to Experience
Agreeableness
Conscientiousness

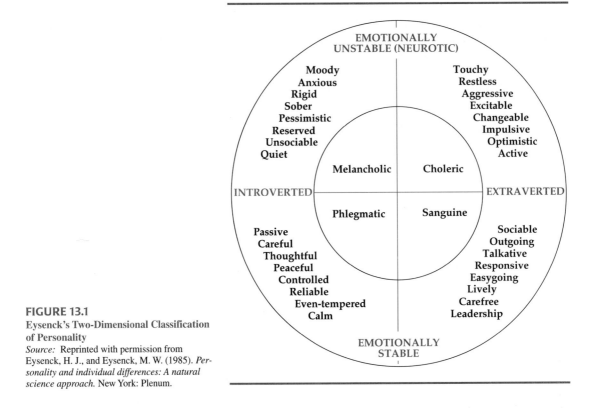

FIGURE 13.1
Eysenck's Two-Dimensional Classification
of Personality
Source: Reprinted with permission from
Eysenck, H. J., and Eysenck, M. W. (1985). *Personality and individual differences: A natural
science approach.* New York: Plenum.

Rearranging the factors yields a simple acronym: OCEAN. The five-factor model is rapidly becoming the consensus model of personality. Support for the five-factor approach comes from several sources, including factor analysis of trait terms in language and the analysis of personality from an evolutionary perspective. Following, we discuss these perspectives.

The use of trait terms in the analysis of personality is based upon the **fundamental lexical hypothesis.** The essential point of this hypothesis is that trait terms have survived in language because they convey important information about our dealings with others:

> The variety of individual differences is nearly boundless, yet most of these differences are insignificant in people's daily interactions with others and have remained largely unnoticed. Sir Francis Galton may have been among the first scientists to recognize explicitly the fundamental lexi-

cal hypothesis—namely that the most important individual differences in human transactions will come to be encoded as single terms in some or all of the world's languages (Goldberg, 1990).

When trait terms in English are distilled down to a reasonably distinct and nonoverlapping set of adjectives, a few hundred characteristics typically emerge (Allport, 1937). For decades, researchers have been asking individuals to rate themselves or others on these or similar traits. When these ratings are subjected to factor analysis, the "Big Five" dimensions previously listed usually appear in one guise or another. In sum, a mounting body of research indicates that the five-factor model captures a valid and useful representation of the structure of human traits.

The five-factor approach also possesses evolutionary plausibility. Specifically, the five factors of personality previously listed capture individual differences which relate to such basic evolutionary functions as survival and reproductive success (Buss, 1997; Pervin, 1993). Goldberg (1981b) has theorized that people implicitly ask the following questions in their interactions with others:

1. Is X active and dominant or passive and submissive? (Can I bully X or will X try to bully me?)
2. Is X agreeable (warm and pleasant) or disagreeable (cold and distant)?
3. Can I count on X? (Is X responsible and conscientious or undependable and negligent?)
4. Is X crazy (unpredictable) or sane (stable)?
5. Is X smart or dumb? (How easy will it be for me to teach X?)

Directly or indirectly, each of these evaluations has a bearing upon survival and reproductive success. For example, point 3 (conscientiousness) involves a trait that might insure group survival in a hostile world. A person low on this trait (undependable) would be poor choice for guarding the food supply. The ability to discern conscientiousness in others therefore has adaptive value. Not surprisingly, the five points previously listed correspond to the five-factor personality model.

Costa and McCrae have developed two personality tests based upon the five-factor model (Costa, 1991; McCrae & Costa, 1987). The Revised NEO Personality Inventory (NEO-PI-R) contains 240 items rated on a five-point scale. In addition to the five major domains of personality, the inventory measures six specific traits (called facets) within each domain. A shortened 60-item version known as the NEO Five-Factor Inventory (NEO-FFI) also is available. Trull, Widiger, Useda, and others (1998) have published a semistructured interview for the assessment of the five-factor model of personality. These tests are discussed in the next chapter.

Comment on the Trait Concept

The challenge faced by trait theorists is that psychologists have long known that thousands of trait names can be found in any standard English dictionary. For example, in an early and influential study, Allport and Odbert (1936) tallied over 18,000 trait names. This is obviously too many to be useful in any theory of personality or testing, so theorists are required to search for a smaller, more manageable number of basic traits. Until recently, there was no consensus whatever on the number of fundamental traits. Some theorists proposed two or three overriding trait factors whereas others divided the personality domain into sixteen or twenty trait dimensions. Many personality theorists—perhaps a majority—now concede that the five factors previously noted (Neuroticism, Extraversion, Openness, Agreeableness, Conscientiousness) provide a parsimonious and useful way to look at personality. But this model is very recent, and it will take time to confirm its utility. For example, there is still debate about whether Openness to Experience belongs on the list of fundamental dimensions of personality (Digman, 1990). Also, why is Intellect not included in the five-factor model?

All trait approaches to personality share certain problems in common. First, there is disagreement whether traits cause behavior or merely describe behavior (Fiske, 1986). It can be persuasively argued that invoking traits as causes is an empty form of circular reasoning. For example, a person with extremely high standards might be said to possess the trait of perfectionism. But when asked to explain what is meant by perfectionism, we invariably end up referring to a pattern of extremely high standards. Thus, when we assert that someone is perfectionistic, are we really doing anything more than providing a short-hand description of their past behavior? Miller (1991) has voiced this criticism of the five-factor approach, noting that the model merely describes psychopathology but does not explain it.

A second problem with traits is their apparently low predictive validity. Mischel (1968) is credited with the first effective disparagement of the trait concept in his influential book *Personality and Assessment*. He stated that "while trait theory predicts behavioral consistency, it is behavior inconsistency that is typically observed" (Mischel, 1968). In a wide-ranging review of existing research, Mischel noted that trait scales produced validity coefficients with an upper limit of $r = .30$. He coined the term

personality coefficient to describe these low correlations. Undoubtedly significant for large samples of subjects, correlations of $r = .30$ are of minimal value in the prediction of individual behavior.

Trait researchers responded to Mischel's attack by refining and limiting the trait concept. Researchers sought to identify subgroups of persons whose behavior could be accurately predicted on the basis of trait scores and also attempted to distinguish the kinds of situations in which behavior is largely determined by traits (Amelang & Borkenau, 1986; Bem & Allen, 1974; Houts, Cook, & Shadish, 1986; Moskowitz, 1982; Wright & Mischel, 1987). These efforts met with modest success, raising the validity of some trait questionnaires—in some contexts with some persons—substantially beyond the ominous $r = .30$ barrier posited by Mischel (1968). But gone forever are the days of simplistic, generalized assertions such as "trait X predicts behavior Y."

SUMMARY

1. Personality is a vague construct that we invoke to explain behavioral consistency within persons and behavioral distinctiveness between persons. In order to appreciate the nature of personality tests, it is helpful to review theories of personality.

2. Psychoanalytic theories of personality originated with the seminal work of Sigmund Freud. According to Freud's tripartite theory of mind, behavior is the dynamic outcome of the struggle between id, ego, and superego. The id is completely unconscious, pleasure-oriented, and is the seat of all instinctual needs such as for food, water, sexual gratification, and avoidance of pain.

3. Soon after birth, part of the id develops into the ego or conscious self. The ego is servant to the id but obeys the reality principle. The ego must also contend with the superego, the ethical component of personality which is modeled upon parental and societal standards of right and wrong.

4. To aid in its difficult task, the ego uses defense mechanisms, which consist of a variety of unconscious cognitive strategies for warding off anxiety. Defense mechanisms such as projection (attributing one's faults to others) work because they distort reality.

5. In a longitudinal interview study, Vaillant has shown that defense mechanisms tended toward greater maturity in middle age. Also, the use of mature defense mechanisms in young adulthood predicted better adult outcome as measured by independent criteria such as marital stability, absence of drug problems, and the like.

6. Type theories attempt to sort individuals into discrete categories or types. For example, the Type A coronary-prone behavior pattern consists of insecurity of status, hyperaggressiveness, free-floating hostility, and a sense of time urgency (hurry sickness). Type A persons—especially those with anger proneness or time urgency—may be at increased risk of coronary disease and heart attack.

7. Phenomenological theories of personality emphasize the importance of immediate, personal, subjective experience as a determinant of behavior. The phenomenological viewpoint originated with the German philosopher Husserl and the Danish existential writer Kierkegaard.

8. The most influential phenomenological theorist was Carl Rogers who believed that the self or self-concept was central to personality. Rogers invented the Q-sort to measure the self-concept and the ideal self. In a Q-sort, the examinee sorts self-referential statements in nine or so piles (least like me to most like me).

9. A fundamental assumption of all behavioral and social learning theories is that many of the behaviors that comprise personality are learned. Radical behavior theorists such as Skinner see no role for cognitions in explaining behavior. In contrast, social learning theorists such as Rotter believe that expectations (cognitions) about environmental reinforcers are the primary determinants of behavior.

10. Guilford defines a trait as any relatively enduring way in which one individual differs from another. Trait theories evolved from the ways in which people describe other people in everyday life. Mischel has pointed out a major weakness of the trait approach: Traits possess low predictive validity, seldom exceeding $r = .30$.

11. Cattell's factor-analytic trait theory refers to the more obvious aspects of personality as surface traits, such as aggressiveness. These emerge in the first stages of factor analysis. Source traits—more important and predictive of behavior than surface traits—are revealed by the clusterings of surface traits. Cattell's 16PF is based upon this model.

12. The five-factor model proposes a modern synthesis of trait approaches in terms of five dimensions of personality: Neuroticism, Extraversion, Openness, Agreeableness, and Conscientiousness. Costa and McCrae have developed two inventories based upon this approach (NEO-PI-R and NEO-FFI).

KEY TERMS AND CONCEPTS

personality   p. 481

id   p. 482

pleasure principle   p. 482

ego   p. 482

reality principle   p. 483

superego   p. 483

defense mechanisms   p. 483

Type A coronary-prone behavior pattern   p. 486

Q-technique   p. 487

locus of control   p. 489

self-efficacy   p. 490

trait   p. 490

surface traits   p. 491

source traits   p. 491

fundamental lexical hypothesis   p. 492

personality coefficient   p. 494

Topic 13B Projective Techniques

Frank (1939, 1948) introduced the term *projective method* to describe a category of tests for studying personality with unstructured stimuli. In a **projective test** the examinee encounters vague, ambiguous stimuli and responds with his or her own constructions. Disciples of projective testing are heavily vested in psychoanalytic theory and its postulation of unconscious aspects of personality. These examiners believe that unstructured, vague, ambiguous stimuli provide the ideal circumstance for revelations about inner aspects of personality. The central assumption of projective testing is that responses to the test represent projections from the innermost unconscious mental processes of the examinee. We introduce this topic with some preliminary concepts and distinctions relevant to projective testing.

THE PROJECTIVE HYPOTHESIS

The assumption that personal interpretations of ambiguous stimuli must necessarily reflect the unconscious needs, motives, and conflicts of the examinee is known as the **projective hypothesis.** Frank (1939) is generally credited with popularizing the projective hypothesis:

When we scrutinize the actual procedures that may be called projective methods we find a wide variety of techniques and materials being employed for the same general purpose, to obtain from the subject, "what he cannot or will not say," frequently because he does not know himself and is not aware what he is revealing about himself through his projections.

The challenge of projective testing is to decipher underlying personality processes (needs, motives, and conflicts) based on the individualized, unique, subjective responses of each examinee. In the sections that follow we will examine how well projective tests have met this portentous assignment.

A PRIMER OF PROJECTIVE TECHNIQUES

Origins of Projective Techniques

Projective techniques date back to the previous century. By way of quick review, Galton (1879) developed the first projective technique, a word association test. This procedure was adapted to testing by Kent and Rosanoff (1910) and used in therapy by C. G. Jung and others. Meanwhile, Ebbinghaus (1897) used a sentence completion test as a measure of intelligence, but others soon realized the method was better suited to personality assessment (Payne, 1928; Tendler, 1930). Heavily influenced by psychoanalytic formulations of personality, Rorschach published his famous inkblot test in 1921. In 1905, Binet invented a precursor to story telling or thematic apperception techniques when he used verbal responses to pictures as a measure of intelligence. These and other endeavors form the cornerstone of modern projective testing.

The Popularity of Projective Tests: A Paradox

The widespread use of projective tests has continued unabated from the early twentieth century to present times (Louttit & Browne, 1947; Lubin, Wallis, & Paine, 1971; Watkins, Campbell, & McGregor, 1988). Recently, Watkins, Campbell, Nieberding, & Hallmark (1995) surveyed more than 400 psychologists who practiced assessment to estimate the frequency of use of various prominent tests. They discovered that 5 of 15 most frequently used tests are projective techniques (Table 13.3).

Paradoxically, from the standpoint of traditional psychometric criteria, projective tests do not fare nearly as well as the objective tests discussed in the next chapter. The essential puzzle of projective tests is how to explain the enduring popularity of these instruments in spite of their sometimes questionable psychometric quality. After all, psychologists are not uniformly dense, nor are they dumb to issues of test quality. So why do projective techniques persist? We return to this puzzle—which might be called the projective paradox—after we familiarize the reader with prominent approaches to projective testing.

A Classification of Projective Techniques

Lindzey (1959) has offered a classification of projective techniques which we will follow here. Based on the response required, he divided projectives into five categories:

- Association to inkblots or words
- Construction of stories or sequences

TABLE 13.3   The 15 Most Frequently Used Tests in the United States

Test	Rank
Wechsler Adult Intelligence Scale-Revised	1
Minnesota Multiphasic Personality Inventory-2	2
Sentence Completion Methods*	3
Thematic Apperception Test*	4
Rorschach*	5
Bender-Gestalt	6
Projective Drawings*	7
Beck Depression Inventory	8
Wechsler Intelligence Scale for Children-III	9
Wide Range Achievement Test-Revised	10
Wechsler Memory Scale-Revised	11
Peabody Picture Vocabulary Test-Revised	12
Millon Clinical Multiaxial Inventory-II	13
Wechsler Preschool and Primary Scale of Intelligence-R	14
Children's Apperception Test*	15

*Denotes a projective test. Some examiners use the Bender as a projective test.
Source: Adapted with permission from Watkins, C., Campbell, V., Nieberding, R., & Hallmark, R. (1995). Contemporary practice of psychological assessment by clinical psychologists. *Professional Psychology: Research and Practice, 26,* 54–60.

- Completions of sentences or stories
- Arrangement/selection of pictures or verbal choices
- Expression with drawings or play

Association techniques include the widely used Rorschach inkblot test and its psychometrically superior cousin the Holtzman Inkblot Test, as well as word association tests. Construction techniques include the Thematic Apperception Test and the many variations upon this early instrument. Completion techniques consist mainly of sentence completion tests, discussed later. Arrangement/ selection procedures such as the Szondi test (discussed in the first chapter) are currently seldom used. Finally, expression techniques such as the Draw-A-Person or House-Tree-Person test are very popular among clinicians in spite of dubious validity data.

We will review prominent techniques within each category except the antiquated arrangement/selection approaches, which are almost never used. However, the literature on major projective techniques is simply overwhelming, running to perhaps tens of thousands of articles on the Rorschach alone. We can suggest major trends in the research, but the reader will need to consult other sources for comprehensive reviews.

ASSOCIATION TECHNIQUES

The Rorschach

The Rorschach consists of 10 inkblots devised by Herman Rorschach (1884–1922) in the early 1900s. He formed the inkblots by dribbling ink on a sheet of paper and folding the paper in half, producing relatively symmetrical bilateral designs. Five of the inkblots are black or shades of gray, while five contain color; each is displayed on a white background. An inkblot of the type employed by Rorschach is shown in Figure 13.2. The Rorschach is suited to persons age five and up, but is most commonly used with adults.

In administering the Rorschach, the examiner sits by the examinee's side to minimize body language communication. Administration consists of two phases. In the free association phase, the examiner presents the first blot and asks "What might this be?" If the examinee asks for clarification (e.g., "Should I use the whole blot or only part of it?"), the examiner always responds in a nondirective manner ("It's up to you"). The test proceeds at a leisurely pace, so there is an implicit expectation that the examinee will give more than one response per card. However, this is not required; it is even permissible for the examinee to reject a card entirely, although this rarely happens. All 10 cards are presented in a similar manner.

Next, the examiner begins the inquiry phase. In this phase the examiner asks questions to clarify the exact blot location of each percept and to determine which aspects of the blot, such as the form or color, played a part in the creation of the response. Based on the information collected during the inquiry

FIGURE 13.2 An Inkblot Similar to Those Found on the Rorschach

phase, the examiner can then code the location, determinants, form quality, and content of each response according to one or more formal scoring systems. For example, if the examinee used the entire blot for a percept, the response is coded W (whole); if the form of the blot was important in the percept, the response is further coded F (form); if human movement is depicted in the percept, the response is coded M (movement); the use of color in a percept is coded C (color), CF (color/form), or FC (form/color), depending upon whether form is totally absent, primary, or secondary to color as a determinant. The content of the percept is also coded, for example H (human), Hd (human detail), An (anatomy), Cg (clothing), and so on (Table 13.4). Proper scoring of the Rorschach requires extensive training and supervision; we have touched on just a few basic aspects here.

Regrettably, Rorschach died before he could complete his scoring methods, so the systematization of Rorschach scoring was left to his followers. Five American psychologists produced overlapping

TABLE 13.4   Summary of Major Rorschach Scoring Criteria

I. Location: Where on the blot was the percept located?

W	Whole	Entire inkblot used
D	Common detail	Well-defined part used
Dd	Unusual detail	Unusual part used
S	Space	Percept defined by white space

II. Determinant: What feature of the blot determined the response?

F	Form	Shape or outline used
F+	Form+	Excellent match of percept and inkblot
F–	Form–	Very poor match of percept and inkblot
M	Movement	Movement seen or implied in percept
C	Color	Color helped determine the response
T	Texture	Shading involved in the response

III. Content: What was the percept?

H	Human	Percept of a whole human form
Hd	Human detail	Human form incomplete in any way
Ex	Explosion	An actual explosion
Xy	X-ray	X-ray of any human part; involves shading

IV. Popular versus Original

P	Popular	Response given by many normal persons
O	Original	Rare and creative response

Note: This table represents a consensus of all the major scoring systems. The list is incomplete and illustrative only. Full scoring systems are very complex and allow for blends, e.g., FM, CF, WS-, Do. For examples, see Exner, J. E., Jr. (1993). *The Rorschach: A comprehensive system, Volume 1. Basic foundations* (3rd ed.). New York: Wiley.

but independent approaches to the test—Samuel Beck, Marguerite Hertz, Bruno Klopfer, Zygmunt Piotrowski, and David Rapaport (Erdberg, 1985). Predictably, the nuances of scoring vary from one scoring method to another. Fortunately, Exner and his colleagues have synthesized these earlier approaches into the Comprehensive Scoring System (Exner, 1991, 1993; Exner & Weiner, 1994). The Comprehensive Scoring System is better grounded in empirical research and clearly has supplanted all other approaches to Rorschach scoring.

Once the entire protocol has been coded, the examiner can compute a number of summary scores that form the primary basis for hypothesizing about the personality of the examinee. For example, the F+ percent is the proportion of the total responses which use pure form as a determinant. A voluminous literature exists on the meaning of this index, but it seems safe to hypothesize that when the F+ percent falls below 70 percent, the examiner should consider the possibility of severe psychopathology,

brain impairment, or intellectual deficit in the examinee (Exner, 1993). The F+ percent is also considered to be an index of ego strength with higher scores indicating a greater capacity to deal effectively with stress. However, support for this conjecture is mixed at best.

Frank (1990) has emphasized that formal scoring of the Rorschach is insufficient for some purposes such as the diagnosis of schizophrenia. He stresses that an analysis of the patient's thinking for the presence of highly personal, illogical, and bizarre associations to the blots is essential for psychodiagnosis. In his approach, the Rorschach is really an adjunct to the interview, and not a test per se.

Comment on the Rorschach

For a variety of reasons, it is difficult to offer concise generalizations about the reliability, validity, and clinical utility of the Rorschach. Even simple questions provoke complex answers. For example,

What is the purpose of a Rorschach evaluation? In successive research epochs, the Rorschach has been used to derive a psychiatric diagnosis, estimate prognosis for psychotherapy, obtain an index of primary process thinking, predict suicide, and formulate complex personality structures, to name just a few applications (Peterson, 1978). The purpose of the Rorschach is so ill-defined that some adherents even decline to regard it as a test, preferring instead to call it a method for generating information about personality functioning (Weiner, 1994). When the purpose of an instrument is unclear, objective research on its psychometric attributes is both risky and difficult. Worse yet, objective research may be pointless since supporters will ignore contrary findings and detractors don't use the test anyway.

A study by Albert, Fox, and Kahn (1980) on the susceptibility of the Rorschach to faking is typical of research on this instrument. We remind the reader that thousands of research studies exist in the literature, including many with positive, supportive findings (e.g., Hilsenroth, Fowler, Padawer, & Handler, 1997; Smith, Gacono, & Kaufman, 1997; Weiner, 1996). But the mixed results reported by Albert, Fox, and Kahn (1980) are not unusual. They submitted the Rorschach protocols of 24 persons to a panel of experts, asking for psychiatric diagnoses of each examinee. The 24 Rorschach protocols consisted of results from four groups of six persons each:

- Mental hospital patients with a diagnosis of paranoid schizophrenia
- Uninformed fakers given instructions to fake the responses of a paranoid schizophrenic
- Informed fakers who listened to a detailed audiotape about paranoid schizophrenia
- Normal controls who took the test under standard instructions

The uninformed fakers, informed fakers, and normal controls were students who had passed an MMPI screening and were judged reasonably normal during interview. Each protocol was rated by six to nine judges, all fellows of the Society for Personality Assessment. The judges were told to pro-

vide a psychiatric diagnosis as well as other information not reported here. The judges were not informed as to the purpose of the study, but were told to assess whether any profiles appeared to be malingered.

The informed fakers must have done an excellent job, for they were more likely to be diagnosed psychotic than the real patients themselves (72 percent versus 48 percent, respectively). The uninformed fakers were fairly convincing, too, with a 46 percent rate of diagnosed psychosis. The normal controls were diagnosed as psychotic 24 percent of the time. Granted that the diagnostic challenge in this study was immense, it is still disturbing to find that the expert judges rated 24 percent of the normal protocols as psychotic, while correctly identifying psychosis in only 48 percent of the actual psychotic protocols. A more recent study by Netter and Viglione (1994) also concluded that the Rorschach was susceptible to the faking of psychosis.

Although there are noteworthy exceptions in Rorschach testing, a substantial number of studies point to low reliability and a general lack of predictive validity (Carlson, Kula, & St. Laurent, 1997; Peterson, 1978; Lanyon, 1984; Wood, Nezworski, & Stejskal, 1996). In a meta-analytic review, Garb, Florio, & Grove (1998) concluded that the Rorschach explained a dismal 8 percent to 13 percent of the variance in client characteristics, as compared to the MMPI which explained 23 percent to 30 percent of the variance. On the positive side, recent studies based upon improvements in scoring offered by the Exner approach are more optimistic in outcome (see Exner, 1995; Exner & Andronikof-Sanglade, 1992; Meyer, 1997; Ornberg & Zalewski, 1994; Piotrowski, 1996). Even so, the Rorschach has not yet gained the status of scientific respectability enjoyed by many other personality tests, and perhaps it never will.

Holtzman Inkblot Technique

Wayne H. Holtzman sought to overcome the major limitations in the Rorschach by developing a completely new technique using more inkblots with simplified procedures for administration and scoring. In the Holtzman Inkblot Technique, the examinee is limited to one response per card, but views a series of 45 cards. Each response is followed with a very simple twofold question: Where was the percept represented in the blot, and what about the blot suggested the percept?

The HIT comes in two carefully constructed parallel forms. The existence of parallel forms is invaluable for test-retest studies, since examinees often remember their responses to a card and therefore mechanically offer the same answer when retested. The 45 responses to the HIT are scored for 22 different variables derived from early Rorschach

scoring systems. The HIT scoring variables are described in Table 13.5.

The scoring system for the HIT is highly reliable, and the standardization of the instrument appears to be adequate. When well-trained scorers are used, interscorer agreement for the different categories is .95 to 1.00 for most categories; only Penetration and Integration fall below these standards. Split-half reliabilities are also acceptable, with median values in the .70s and .80s. Test-retest stability with parallel forms is generally fair, although some categories (Location, with r of .81) perform better than others (Popular, with r of .36). Percentile norms for each scoring category are re-

---

TABLE 13.5   Names and Descriptions of the Holtzman Inkblot Technique Variables

Reaction Time:	Time in seconds from the presentation of the inkblot to the beginning of the primary response.
Rejection:	Subject fails to report anything or returns the inkblot to the examiner.
Location:	Scored on a 3-point system: 0—whole blot, 1—large area, 2—smaller area.
Space:	Scored when there is a true figure-ground reversal; the white part is the figure.
Form Definiteness:	Scored on a 5-point system from 0 (formless concept—e.g., paint splatter) to 4 (highly formed concept—e.g., centaur).
Form Appropriateness:	Goodness of fit of the concept to the form of the inkblot; 0—poor, 1—fair, 2—good.
Color:	Color is a primary determinant, usually mentioned by the subject; scored 0 to 3.
Shading:	Subject refers to shading (fuzziness, texture) as a determinant; scored 0 to 2.
Movement:	Scored when the response implies energy or dynamic movement quality; scored 0 to 4.
Pathognomic Verbalization:	Incoherent, queer, absurd, self-referential, etc., verbalizations to cards.
Integration:	Scored 1 if two or more blot elements are effectively integrated in the response; otherwise scored 0.
Content Scores:	Each category (Human, Animal, Anatomy, Sex, Abstract) is scored 0 to 2 based on absence, partial, or full presence of the concept.
Anxiety:	Each response is scored 0 to 2 for signs of anxiety (e.g., dark and dangerous cave).
Hostility:	Each response is scored 0 to 3 for signs of hostility (e.g., mangled butterfly).
Barrier:	Barrier refers to any protective covering, membrane, shell, or skin that might be symbolically related to body-image boundaries; 1 if present, 0 if absent.
Penetration:	Scored 1 if the concept is symbolic of an examinee's feeling that his or her body exterior can be easily penetrated; otherwise 0.
Balance:	Scored 1 if examinee refers to presence or absence of symmetry in the design; otherwise scored 0.
Popular:	Scored 1 if the response is common, observed in 1 of 7 normative protocols.

Source: Based on Holtzman, W. H. (1961). *Guide to administration and scoring: Holtzman Inkblot Technique.* New York: The Psychological Corporation.

ported separately for college students ($N = 206$), average adults ($N = 252$), seventh graders ($N = 197$), elementary school children ($N = 132$), five-year-olds ($N = 122$), chronic schizophrenics ($N = 140$), depressed patients ($N = 90$), and mentally retarded persons ($N = 100$).

The validity of the HIT has been addressed in several hundred research studies reporting on the relationships between HIT scores and independent measures of personality (Hill, 1972; Holtzman, 1988; Swartz, Reinehr, & Holtzman, 1983). In general, the relationships are modest but supportive of HIT validity, especially as an aid to psychodiagnosis.

A recent variant of the HIT requires two responses to each of a carefully selected subset of 25 cards from Form A. Called the HIT 25 to distinguish it from the standard HIT, this new test holds exceptional promise for helping make the diagnosis of schizophrenia. Using completely objective scoring criteria and simple decision rules, the HIT 25 correctly classified 26 of 30 schizophrenics and 28 of 30 normal college students (Holtzman, 1988). The decision criteria consist of four rules for normal findings scored +1 each, and 13 rules for schizophrenic findings scored –1 each. The total results are summed algebraically, yielding the "normalcy" score. This score is the basis for simple diagnostic decisions. Scores above zero suggest normalcy, whereas scores below zero indicate schizophrenia; a score of zero is indeterminate. The HIT 25 looks

promising but cross-validation studies would be especially welcome.

COMPLETION TECHNIQUES

Sentence Completion Tests

In a sentence completion test, the respondent is presented with a series of stems consisting of the first few words of a sentence, and the task is to provide an ending. As with any projective technique, the examiner assumes that the completed sentences reflect the underlying motivations, attitudes, conflicts, and fears of the respondent. Usually, sentence completion tests can be interpreted in two different ways: subjective-intuitive analysis of the underlying motivations projected in the subject's responses, or objective analysis by means of scores assigned to each completed sentence.

An example of a sentence completion test is shown in Figure 13.3. This test is quite similar to existing instruments in that the stems are very short and restricted to a small number of basic themes. The reader will notice that three topics reoccur in this short test (the respondent's self-concept, mother, and father). In this manner the examinee has multiple opportunities to reveal underlying motivations about each topic. Of course, most sentence completion tests are much longer—anywhere from 40 to 100 stems—and contain more themes—anywhere from 4 to 15 topics.

Directions: Finish these sentences to indicate how you feel.

1. My best characteristic is _____

2. My mother _____

3. My father _____

4. My greatest fear is _____

5. The best thing about my mother was _____

6. The best thing about my father was _____

7. I am proudest about _____

8. I only wish my mother had _____

9. I only wish my father had _____

FIGURE 13.3
Example of a Short Sentence Completion Test

Dozens of sentence completion tests have been developed; most are unpublished and unstandardized instruments produced to meet a specific clinical need. Some of the more prominent sentence completion tests still in use are outlined in Table 13.6. Of these instruments, Loevinger's Washington University Sentence Completion Test is the most sophisticated and theory-bound (e.g., Weiss, Zilberg, & Genevro, 1989). However, the Rotter Incomplete Sentences Blank has the strongest empirical underpinnings and is the most widely used in clinical settings. We examine this instrument in more detail.

Rotter Incomplete Sentences Blank

The Rotter Incomplete Sentences Blank (RISB) consists of three similar forms—high school, college, and adult—each containing 40 sentence stems written mostly in the first person (Rotter & Rafferty, 1950; Rotter, Lah, & Rafferty, 1992). Although the test can be subjectively interpreted in the usual manner through qualitative analysis of needs projected in the subject's responses, it is the objective and quantitative scoring of the RISB that has drawn the most attention.

In the objective scoring system each completed sentence receives an adjustment score from 0 (good adjustment) to 6 (very poor adjustment). These scores are based initially on the categorizing of each response as follows:

* *Omission*—no response or response too short to be meaningful
* *Conflict response*—indicative of hostility or unhappiness
* *Positive response*—indicative of positive or hopeful attitude
* *Neutral response*—declarative statement with neither positive nor negative affect

Examples of the last three categories include:

> I hate . . . the entire world (conflict response)
> The best . . . is yet to come (positive response)
> Most girls . . . are women (neutral response)

Conflict responses are scored 4, 5, or 6, from lowest to highest degree of the conflict expressed.

TABLE 13.6 Brief Outline of Prominent Sentence Completion Tests

Bloom Sentence Completion Survey (1974–1975), Stoelting Co.

The BSCS comes in one form with two levels (student or adult). Forty stems yield scores in eight areas: age mates (student) or people (adults), physical self, family, psychological self, self-directedness, education (students) and work (adults), accomplishment, and irritants.

Activity Completion Technique (1984), Psychological Assessment Resources

Consisting of 60 sentence stems, the ACT covers four areas: Family, Interpersonal, Affect, and Self-Concept. The manual discusses a clinically oriented content analysis of responses within each area. The test also uses a semiobjective scoring system to yield an Adjustment Rating Scale.

Incomplete Sentences Task (1979–1980), Stoelting Co.

The IST consists of two forms (grades 7–12 and college) with 39 highly structured, behaviorally anchored items specially designed to assess hostility, anxiety, and dependency.

Geriatric Sentence Completion Form (1982), Psychological Assessment Resources

The GSCF is a 30-item form specifically developed for use with older adult clients. The GSCF elicits personal responses to four content domains: physical, psychological, social, and temporal orientation. The test manual includes a number of clinical case illustrations.

Washington University Sentence Completion Test, Privately published by Loevinger (1976, 1979)

The WUSC uses separate forms for men, women, and younger male and female subjects. This test is highly theory-bound; responses are classified according to seven stages of ego development: presocial and symbiotic, impulsive, self-protective, conformist, conscientious, autonomous, integrated.

Miner Sentence Completion Scale (Miner, 1964, 1986), Organizational Measurement Systems Press

The MSCS consists of three forms, including the original Form H, first published in 1964. The test is geared toward management, professional, and sales-oriented occupations. Form H is unique in providing a multiple-choice option; the nine subscales include work-relevant dimensions such as Authority Figures, Competitive Situations, and Assertive Role.

Positive responses are scored 2, 1, or 0, from least to most positive response. Neutral responses and omissions receive no score. The manual gives examples of each scoring category. The overall adjustment score is obtained by adding the weighted ratings in the conflict and positive categories. The adjustment score can vary from 0 to 240, with higher scores indicating greater maladjustment.

The reliability of the adjustment score is exceptionally good, even when derived by assistants with minimal psychological expertise. Typically, interscorer reliabilities are in the .90s and split-half coefficients are in the .80s (Rotter, Lah, & Rafferty, 1992; Rotter, Rafferty, & Schachtitz, 1965). The validity of this index has been investigated in numerous studies using the RISB as a screening device with a "maladjustment" cutoff score. For example, a cutoff score of 135 has been found to correctly screen delinquent youths 60 percent of the time while identifying nondelinquent youths correctly 73 percent of the time (Fuller, Parmelee, & Carroll, 1982). The same cutoff identifies heavy drug users 80 to 100 percent of the time (Gardner, 1967). These and similar findings support the construct validity of the adjustment index, but also indicate that classification rates are much lower than needed for individual decision making or effective screening. It also appears that the norms for the adjustment index are outdated. Lah and Rotter (1981) found that current student scores differ significantly from those obtained in the original study by Rotter and Rafferty (1950). Lah (1989) and Rotter, Lah, & Rafferty (1992) provide new normative, scoring, and validity data for the RISB.

As discussed by P. Goldberg (1965), the simplicity of the single adjustment score is both the test's strength and weakness. True, the test provides a quick and efficient method for obtaining an overall index of how respondents are functioning on a day to day basis. However, a single score cannot possibly capture any nuances of personality functioning. In addition, the RISB is subject to the same types of bias as other self-report measures, namely, the information will reflect mainly what the respondent wants the examiner to know (Phares, 1985).

Rosenzweig Picture Frustration Study

Often considered a semiprojective technique, the Rosenzweig Picture Frustration Study (P-F Study) requires the examinee to produce a verbal response to highly structured verbal-pictorial stimuli. The P-F Study comes in three forms—child, adolescent, and adult—each consisting of 24 comic-strip pictures depicting a frustrating circumstance (Rosenzweig, 1977, 1978a). Each picture contains two people, with the person on the left uttering words that provoke or describe a frustrating situation to the person on the right (Figure 13.4). The examinee is requested to indicate, by writing in the balloon above the frustrated person's head, the first verbal response that comes to mind as being uttered by the anonymous cartoon figure. In the case of younger examinees, the examiner writes down the subject's response.

The purpose of the P-F Study is to assess the examinee's characteristic manner of reacting to frustration. **Frustration** is defined as occurring whenever the organism encounters an obstacle or obstruction en route to the satisfaction of a need

FIGURE 13.4   **Sample Item from the Rosenzweig Picture-Frustration Study**
Copyright © by Saul Rosenzweig. Reproduced by permission.

(Rosenzweig, 1944). In a general sense, it is well known that persons react to frustration with aggression. The value of the P-F Study is its multi-faceted conceptualization of aggression according to three directions and three types. The direction of aggression can be extraggressive, it is turned onto the environment; intraggressive, it is turned by the examinee onto the self; or imaggressive, it is evaded in an attempt to gloss over the frustration. The type of aggression can be obstacle-dominant, in which the barrier that occasions the frustration stands out in the response; ego-defensive, in which the organizing capacity of the examinee predominants in the response; or need-persistent, in which the solution of the frustrating situation is emphasized by pursuing the goal despite the obstacle (Rosenzweig, 1978b). It is important to point out that aggression is not necessarily a negative construct. Need-persistent types of aggression represent constructive, sometimes creative, forms of aggression while ego-defensive aggression is frequently destructive (of others or oneself).

The P-F Study is scored by detecting one or two of the factors in each individual response. Deep interpretations are avoided; the manual contains scoring samples to aid in decision making. When the item scores have been tallied, the scoring blank is completed by computing the percentages of the nine scoring categories which occur in the protocol of the examinee. The overall types and directions of aggression are also tallied, resulting in 15 indices. In addition, a Group Conformity Rating (GCR) can be computed. The GCR indicates how closely the examinee's responses correspond to those given most frequently by a norm sample. All the indices can be compared to results from appropriate standardization samples. Of course, in addition to quantitative scoring, responses to the P-F Study can be evaluated impressionistically.

The interscorer reliability of the P-F Study is reportedly in the range of .80 to .85 for well-trained, conscientious examiners. However, the test-retest stability of the instrument is somewhere between fair and marginal. For example, retest correlations for scoring categories on the adult form of the P-F Study range from .21 to .71, with most values in the

.40s (Rosenzweig, 1978b). A huge body of validational research has been summarized in several publications (Rosenzweig, 1977, 1978b; Rosenzweig & Adelman, 1977). Based on the very modest reliabilities of the scoring categories, we concur that the P-F Study is more appropriate for research than individual assessment (Graybill & Heuvelman, 1993).

CONSTRUCTION TECHNIQUES

The Thematic Apperception Test (TAT)

The TAT consists of 30 pictures that portray a variety of subject matters and themes in black-and-white drawings and photographs; one card is blank. Most of the cards depict one or more persons engaged in ambiguous activities. Some cards are used for adult males (M), adult females (F), boys (B), or girls (G), or some combination (e.g., BM). As a consequence, exactly 20 cards are appropriate for every examinee.

A picture similar to those on the TAT is shown in Figure 13.5. In administering the TAT, the examiner requests the examinee to make up a

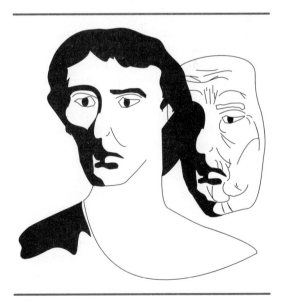

FIGURE 13.5   A Picture Similar to Those on the Thematic Apperception Test

dramatic story for each picture, telling what led up to the current scene, what is happening at the moment, how the characters are thinking and feeling, and what the outcome will be. The examiner writes down the story verbatim for later scoring and analysis.

The TAT was developed by Henry Murray and his colleagues at the Harvard Psychological Clinic (Morgan & Murray, 1935; Murray, 1938). The test was originally designed to assess constructs such as needs and press, elements central to Murray's personality theory. According to Murray, needs organize perception, thought, and action and energize behavior in the direction of their satisfaction. Examples of needs include the needs for achievement, affiliation, and dominance. In contrast, press refers to the power of environmental events to influence a person. Alpha press is objective or "real" external forces, whereas beta press concerns the subjective or perceived components of external forces. Murray (1938, 1943) developed an elaborate TAT scoring system for measuring 36 different needs and various aspects of press, as revealed by the examinee's stories.

Almost as soon as Murray released the TAT, other clinicians began to develop alternative scoring systems (e.g., Dana, 1959; Eron, 1950; Shneidman, 1951; Tomkins, 1947). Literature on the administration, scoring, and interpretation of the TAT burgeoned extensively, as documented by recent reviews (Aiken, 1989, chp. 12; Groth-Marnat, 1997; Ryan, 1987; Weiner & Kuehnle, 1998). By the 1950s, there was no single preferred mode of administration, no single preferred system of scoring, and no single preferred method of interpretation, a predicament that still endures today. Clinicians even vary the wording of the instructions and commonly select an individualized subset of TAT cards for each client. Indeed, the absence of standardized procedures is such that we should rightly regard the TAT as a method, not a test.

It is worth mentioning that Murray's instructions included a statement that the TAT was "a test of imagination, one form of intelligence" and further stipulated:

I am going to show you some pictures, one at a time; and your task will be to make up as dramatic a story as you can for each. Tell what has led up to the event shown in the picture, describe what is happening at the moment, what the characters are feeling and thinking; and then give the outcome. Speak your thoughts as they come to your mind. Do you understand? Since you have fifty minutes for ten pictures, you can devote about five minutes to each story. Here is the first picture (Murray, 1943).

Currently, clinicians downplay the emphasis upon imagination and intelligence when giving instructions. Surely this omission must influence the quality of the stories produced.

Even though more than a dozen scoring systems have been proposed, interpretation of the TAT is usually based upon a clinical-qualitative analysis of the story productions. A central consideration harks back to Murray's "hero" assumption. According to this viewpoint, the hero is the protagonist of the examinee's story. It is assumed that the examinee clearly identifies with this character and projects his or her own needs, strivings, and feelings onto the hero. Conversely, thoughts, feelings, or actions avoided by the hero may represent areas of conflict for the examinee. A specific example will help clarify these points. Consider the response to Card 3BM given by a depressed examinee[1]:

Looks like . . . I can't tell if it's a girl or boy. Could be either. I guess it doesn't matter. This person just had a hard physical workout. I guess it's a her. She's just tired. No trauma happened or anything. She was sitting around a table with friends and she got real tired. She's not in a health danger or anything. These are her keys. Her friends drag her back to her room and put her to bed. She's O.K. the next day. No trauma. She's tired physically, not mentally (Ryan, 1987).

What stands out in this response is the repetitive denial of danger or trauma. But later in the testing, the

---

1. Card 3BM depicts one person—arguably male or female—kneeling or slumped over on a couch with head bowed on one arm. In the corner is a vaguely drawn object interpreted by some examinees to be a handgun or other weapon.

denial of trauma is no longer maintained. Read how the examinee responded to the blank card, relating a story of a young man, traumatized at school, who takes his car down to the river:

> He sees the bridge, he's really down. He remembers that he's heard stories about people jumping off and killing themselves. He could never understand why they did that. Now he understands, he jumps and dies . . . he should have waited 'cause things always get better sometime. But he didn't wait, he died (Ryan, 1987).

Most clinicians would conclude that the examinee who produced these stories had been traumatized and was defending against self-destructive impulses. Correspondingly, the clinician would be well advised to explore these issues in psychotherapy.

The psychometric adequacy of the TAT is difficult to evaluate because of the abundancy of scoring and interpretation methods. Clinicians defend the test on an anecdotal basis, pointing out remarkable and confirmatory findings such as illustrated above. However, data-minded researchers are more cautious. One problem is that formally scored TAT protocols possess very low test-retest reliability, with a reported median value of $r = .28$ (Winter & Stewart, 1977). Furthermore, 82 percent of test users employ "personalized" procedures for interpreting the TAT and other projective tests (Wade & Baker, 1977). In large measure, then, the interpretation of the TAT is based on strategies with unknown and untested reliability and validity. In response to these concerns, several researchers have devised new TAT scoring approaches that show promise of providing this instrument a solid psychometric foundation (McGrew & Teglasi, 1990; Ronan, Colavito, & Hammontree, 1993). However, there is surprisingly little ongoing research on TAT scoring systems.

The Picture Projective Test

The Picture Projective Test (PPT) is a long overdue attempt to construct a general purpose instrument with improved psychometric qualities (Ritzler, Sharkey, & Chudy, 1980; Sharkey & Ritzler, 1985).

The developers of the PPT note that the majority of the TAT pictures exert a strong negative stimulus "pull" on story telling. The TAT cards are cast in dark, shaded tones and most scenes portray persons in low-key or gloomy situations. It is not surprising, then, that projective responses to the TAT are strongly channeled toward negative, melancholic stories (Goldfried & Zax, 1965).

In contrast, the PPT uses a new set of pictures taken from the *Family of Man* photo essay published by the Museum of Modern Art (1955). The following criteria were used in selecting 30 pictures:

- The pictures had to show promise of eliciting meaningful projective material.
- Most but not all of the pictures had to include more than one human character.
- About half of the pictures had to depict humans showing positive affective expression (e.g., smiling, embracing, dancing).
- About half of the pictures had to depict humans in active poses, not simply standing, sitting, or lying down.

In an initial pilot study, the authors compared TAT and PPT story productions of eight undergraduates on several variables such as length of stories, emotional tone, and activity level (Ritzler, Sharkey, & Chudy, 1980). Compared to the TAT productions, the PPT stories were of comparable length but were much more positive in thematic content and emotional tone. The PPT stories were also much more active, meaning that the central character had an active, self-determined effect on the situation in the story. Furthermore, the PPT stories placed greater emphasis upon interpersonal rather than intrapersonal themes. In other words, the PPT stories placed more emphasis on "healthy," adaptive aspects of personality adjustment than did the TAT productions.

The PPT developers also compared their instrument against the TAT in a diagnostic validity study (Sharkey & Ritzler, 1985). PPT and TAT story productions of 50 subjects were compared: normals, nonhospitalized depressives, hospitalized depressives, hospitalized psychotics with good pre-morbid histories, and hospitalized psychotics with poor premorbid histories (10 subjects in each group). Although the TAT and PPT were essentially equal in their capacity to discriminate normal from depressed subjects, the PPT was superior in differentiating psychotics from normals and depressives. On the PPT, depressives told stories with gloomier emotional tone and psychotics made more perceptual distortions, and thematic/interpretive deviations. The PPT appears to be a very promising instrument, although it is obvious that further research is needed on its psychometric qualities. One noteworthy feature is that anyone can purchase the PPT stimuli at their local bookstore. The requisite materials are found in the *Family of Man* photo collection (Museum of Modern Art, 1955).

Children's Apperception Test

Designed as a direct extension of the TAT, the Children's Apperception Test (CAT) consists of 10 pictures and is suitable for children 3 to 10 years of age. The preferred version for younger children (CAT-A) depicts animals in unmistakably human social settings (Bellak & Bellak, 1991). The test developers used animal drawings on the assumption that young children would identify better with animals than humans. A human figure version (CAT-H) is available for older children (Bellak & Bellak, 1994). No formal scoring system exists for the CAT and no statistical information is provided on reliability or validity. Instead, the examiner prepares a diagnosis or personality description based upon a synthesis of 10 variables recorded for each story: (1) main theme; (2) main hero; (3) main needs and drives of hero; (4) conception of environment (or world); (5) perception of parental, contemporary, and junior figures; (6) conflicts; (7) anxieties; (8) defenses; (9) adequacy of superego; (10) integration of ego (including originality of story and nature of outcome) (Bellak, 1992). The lack of attention to psychometric issues of scoring, reliability, and validity of the CAT is troublesome to most testing specialists.

Other Variations on the TAT

The TAT has inspired a number of similar tests designed for children and older adults (Table 13.7). In addition, modifications and variations of the TAT have been developed for ethnic, racial, and linguistic minorities. One of the first was the Thompson TAT (T-TAT) in which 21 of the original TAT pictures were redrawn with African-American figures (Thompson, 1949). This TAT modification incorporated certain unintended changes—for example, in facial expressions and the situations portrayed. As a result, the T-TAT should be considered a new test and not just a TAT translation suited to African-American individuals (Aiken, 1989).

Another specialized TAT-like test is the TEMAS, which consists of 23 colorful drawings that depict Hispanic persons interacting in contemporary, inner-city settings (Aiken, 1989; Constantino, Malgady, & Rogler, 1988). TEMAS is Spanish for *theme* and an acronym for "tell me a story." The thematic content of TEMAS stories is scored for 18 cognitive functions, 9 personality (ego) functions, and 7 affective functions. The test can also be scored for various objective indices such as reaction time, fluency, unanswered inquiries and stimulus transformations (e.g., a letter is transformed into a bomb). Hispanic children respond well to the TEMAS, even though they may be inarticulate in response to traditional projective tests.

The inconsistent reliability of the TEMAS is a source of concern, because reliability constrains validity. The manual reports that Cronbach's alpha for the 34 scoring functions ranged from .31 to .98 with half below .70. Test-retest reliabilities were even lower; the highest correlation was $r = .53$ and for 26 of the 34 functions the correlations were near zero! In spite of the questionable reliability of the instrument, several studies provide support for its concurrent and predictive validity. For example, in a clinical sample of 210 Puerto Rican children, TEMAS scale scores predicted independent criteria of ego development, trait anxiety, and adaptive behavior reasonably well, with correlations ranging from .27 to .51 (Malgady, Constantino, & Rogler, 1984). A steady stream of research has continued to

TABLE 13.7

TABLE 13.7 Thematic Apperception Tests for Specific Populations

Adolescent Apperception Cards

This is the only thematic apperception test designed specifically for adolescents (12- to 19-year-olds). The 11 cards represent contemporary issues relevant to adolescents; themes include loneliness, parenting styles, domestic violence, gang activity, and drug abuse (Silverton, 1993). Problems with this instrument include the negative themes depicted in the cards (which preclude positive associations) and the absence of any objective approach to scoring. Like many thematic apperception techniques, the AAC is really an idiographic clinical tool, not a test.

Blacky Pictures

For children ages 5 and older, the Blacky Pictures test was also based on the premise that children identify more readily with animals than humans. The 11 cartoon stimuli depict the adventures of the dog Blacky and his family (Mama, Papa, and sibling Tippy). In addition to requesting a story for each card, the examiner also presents multiple-choice questions based on stages of psychosexual development derived from psychoanalytic theory (Blum, 1950). Although the test was originally developed with adults, children enjoy taking the Blacky and are quite responsive to the pictures. Problems with this test include the absence of norms, especially for children, and poor stability of scores (LaVoie, 1987).

Michigan Picture Test-Revised

For older children ages 8 to 14 years, the MPT-R consists of 15 pictures and a blank card. Responses are scored for Tension Index (e.g., portrayal of personal adequacy), Direction of Force (whether the central figure acts or is acted upon), and Verb Tense (e.g., past, present, future). These three scores can be combined to yield a Maladjustment Index. Reliability and norms are adequate, although evidence of validity is unsatisfactory. A major problem with this test is that the cards portray interpersonal relationships so vividly that little is left to the child's imagination (Aiken, 1989).

Senior Apperception Test (SAT)

Although the 16 situations depicted on the SAT cards include some positive circumstances, the majority of pictures were designed to reflect themes of helplessness, abandonment, disability, family problems, loneliness, dependence, and low self-esteem (Bellak, 1992). Critics complain that the SAT stereotypes the elderly and therefore discourages active responding (Schaie, 1978; Klopfer & Taulbee, 1976).

bolster the utility of this instrument, as surveyed by Constantino & Malgady (1996). Ritzler (1993) provides a supportive review of the test, whereas others recommend that the TEMAS should be used for research purposes only (Lang, 1992).

EXPRESSION TECHNIQUES

The Draw-A-Person Test

As the reader will recall from an earlier chapter, Goodenough (1926) used the Draw-A-Man task as a basis for estimating intelligence. Subsequently, psychodynamically minded psychologists adapted the procedure to the projective assessment of personality. Karen Machover (1949, 1951) was the pioneer in this new field. Her procedure became known as the Draw-A-Person Test (DAP). Her test enjoyed early popularity and is still widely used as a clinical assessment tool. Watkins, Campbell, Nieberding, and Hallmark (1995) report that projective drawings such as the DAP rank eighth in popularity among clinicians in the United States.

The DAP is administered by presenting the examinee with a blank sheet of paper and a pencil with eraser, then asking the examinee to "draw a person." When the drawing is completed the examinee usually is directed to draw another person of the sex opposite that of the first figure. Finally, the examinee is asked to "make up a story about this person as if he [or she] were a character in a novel or a play" (Machover, 1949).

Interpretation of the DAP proceeds in an entirely clinical-intuitive manner, guided by a number of tentative psychodynamically based hypotheses (Machover, 1949, 1951). For example, Machover maintained that examinees were likely to project acceptable impulses onto the same-sex figure and unacceptable impulses onto the opposite-sex figure. She also believed that the relative sizes of the male and female figures revealed clues about the sexual identification of the examinee. Several of Machover's interpretive hypotheses are listed in Table 13.8.

These interpretive premises are colorful, interesting, and plausible. However, they are based en-

TABLE 13.8   Illustrative Interpretations of the Draw-A-Person Test

Sign	Hypothesized Interpretive Significance
Disproportionately large head	Organic brain disease; previous brain surgery; preoccupation with headaches
Deliberate omission of facial features	Evasive about highly conflictual interpersonal relationships
Mouth drawn with heavy line slash	Verbally aggressive, over-critical, and sometimes sadistic personality
Chin changed, erased, or reinforced	Compensation for weakness, indecision, and fear of responsibility
Large male eyes with lashes	Homosexually inclined male, often very extraverted
Hair emphasis, e.g., a beard	An indication of a striving for virility
Graphic emphasis of the neck	Disturbed about the lack of control over impulses
Conspicuous treatment of index finger, thumb	Preoccupation with masturbation
Anatomical indications of internal organs	Found only in schizophrenic or actively manic patients

Source: Based on Machover, K. (1949). *Personality projection in the drawing of the human figure.* Springfield, IL: Charles C. Thomas.

tirely upon psychodynamic theory and anecdotal observations. Machover made little effort to validate the interpretations. The empirical support for her hypotheses is somewhere between meager and nonexistent (Swensen, 1957, 1968). In favor of the DAP, the overall quality of drawings does weakly predict psychological adjustment (Lewinsohn, 1965; Yama, 1990). However, judged by contemporary standards of evidence, the sweeping and cavalier assessments of personality so often derived from the DAP are embarrassing. Some reviewers have concluded that the DAP is an unworthy test that should no longer be used (Gresham, 1993; Motta, Little, & Tobin, 1993).

Rather than using the DAP to infer nuances of personality, a more appropriate application of this test is in the screening of children suspected of behavior disorder and emotional disturbance. For this purpose, Naglieri, McNeish, and Bardos (1991) developed the Draw A Person: Screening Procedure for Emotional Disturbance (DAP:SPED). In one study, diagnostic accuracy of problem children was significantly improved by application of the

DAP:SPED scoring approach (Naglieri & Pfeiffer, 1992).

The House-Tree-Person Test

The H-T-P is a projective test that uses freehand drawings of a house, tree, and person (Buck, 1948, 1981). The examinee is given almost complete freedom in sketching the three objects; separate pencil and crayon drawings are requested. Although the examiner can improvise an H-T-P test with mere blank pieces of paper, Buck (1981) recommends the use of a four-page drawing form with identification information on the first page. Pages two, three, and four are titled House, Tree, and Person. Two drawing forms are needed for each examinee, one for pencil drawings and the other for crayon drawings. Buck (1981) also provides a separate four-page form for a postdrawing interrogation phase which consists of 60 questions designed to elicit the examinee's opinions about elements of the drawings. Many practitioners feel the postdrawing interrogation phase is not worth the extended effort. Also, the value of separate crayon drawings is questioned (Killian, 1987).

The House-Tree-Person Test has much the same familial lineage as the Draw-A-Person Test. Like the DAP Test, the H-T-P Test was originally conceived as a measure of intelligence, complete with a quantitative scoring system to appraise an approximate level of ability (Buck, 1948). However, clinicians soon abandoned the use of the H-T-P as a measure of intelligence, and it is now used almost exclusively as a projective measure of personality.

Although we will not delve into any details here, the interpretation of the H-T-P rests upon three general assumptions: the House drawing mirrors the examinee's home life and intrafamilial relationships; the Tree drawing reflects the manner in which the examinee experiences the environment; and the Person drawing echoes the examinee's interpersonal relationships. Buck (1981) provides numerous interpretive hypotheses for both quantitative and qualitative aspects of the three drawings.

The H-T-P is an alluring test that has fascinated clinicians for more than 40 years. Unfortunately, Buck (1948, 1981) has never provided any evidence to support the reliability or validity of this instrument. Indeed, he is perhaps his own worst critic. At one point in his test manual, he even asserts that validational research is not possible with the H-T-P (Buck, 1981, p. 164). Among the impediments to such research, he cites the following points:

1. No single sign itself is an infallible indication of any strength or weakness in the S.
2. No H-T-P sign has but one meaning.
3. The significance of a sign may differ markedly from one constellation to another.
4. The amount of diagnostic and prognostic data derivable from each of the points of analysis may vary greatly from S to S.
5. Colors do not have any absolute and universal meaning.
6. Nothing in the quantitative scoring system can be taken automatically at face value (Buck, 1981).

In general, attempts to validate the H-T-P as a personality measure have failed miserably (for reviews see Ellis, 1970; Hayworth, 1970; Krugman, 1970; Killian, 1987). Thoughtful reviewers have repeatedly recommended the abandonment of the H-T-P and similar figure-drawing approaches to personality assessment. But these pronouncements apparently fall on deaf ears. The popularity of the H-T-P and other projective techniques continues unabated. In the final section of this chapter, we offer some reflections on the continued acceptance of projective techniques.

REPRISE: THE PROJECTIVE PARADOX

The evidence is quite clear that personality inferences drawn from projective tests often are wrong. In the face of negative validational findings, the enduring practitioner acceptance of these tests constitutes what we have referred to as the projective paradox. How do we explain the continued popularity of instruments for which the validity evidence is at best mixed, often marginal, occasionally nonexistent, or even decisively negative?

We offer two explanations for the projective paradox. The first is that human beings cling to pre-existing stereotypes even when exposed to contradictory findings. Decades ago, Chapman and Chapman (1967) demonstrated this phenomenon with projective tests, naming it **illusory validation.** These researchers asked college students to observe several human figure drawings similar to those obtained from the Draw-A-Person Test (DAP). The students were naive with respect to projective tests and knew nothing about traditional DAP interpretive hypotheses. Each drawing was accompanied by brief descriptions of two symptoms which supposedly characterized the patient who produced the drawing. Actually, the symptoms were assigned randomly to drawings and consisted of the bits and pieces of DAP clinical lore that had been gleaned from an earlier mail questionnaire to clinical psychologists. For example, two of the symptoms used were:

1. is worried about how manly he is.
2. is suspicious of other people.

CASE EXHIBIT 13.1

PROJECTIVE TESTS AS ANCILLARY TO THE INTERVIEW

A specific example may help to clarify the role of projective techniques as ancillary to the clinical interview. During the Vietnam War, a Veteran's Administration psychologist tested a young soldier who had accidentally shot himself in the leg with a forty-five calibre pistol while practicing quick draw in the jungle. Surgeons found it necessary to amputate the soldier's leg from the knee down. He was quite depressed, and everyone assumed that he suffered from grief and guilt over his great personal tragedy. He was virtually mute and nearly untestable. However, he was persuaded to complete a series of figure drawings. In one drawing he depicted himself as a helicopter gunner, spraying bullets indiscriminantly into the jungle below. When questioned about this drawing, he became quite animated and confessed that he relished combat. Guided by the possible implications of the morbid drawing, the psychologist sought to learn more about the veteran's attitudes toward combat. In the course of several interviews, the veteran revealed that he particularly enjoyed firing upon moving objects—animals, soldiers, civilians—it made no difference to him. Gradually, it became clear that the young veteran was an incipient war criminal who was depressed because his injury would prevent him from returning to the front lines. Needless to say, this information had quite an impact on the tenor of the psychological report.

Each student received a different combination of drawings and randomly assigned symptoms.

Later, the students were asked to demonstrate what they had learned by describing, for several drawings, the symptoms they had observed to be linked with that kind of drawing. Of course, in reality there was no learning to be demonstrated, since symptoms and drawings were randomly combined. Nonetheless, the participants responded in terms of popular clinical stereotypes (e.g., unusual eyes indicate suspiciousness, large head suggests a concern with intelligence). Apparently, the commonsense stereotypes held by participants emerged robust and unscathed—in spite of an abundance of disconfirming examples. Perhaps something similar occurs in all fields of projective testing: clinicians notice the confirming instances, but ignore the more numerous findings which contradict expectations.

The second explanation for the projective paradox is that many clinicians do not use projective methods as tests at all, but as auxiliary approaches to the clinical interview. These practitioners use projective techniques as clinical tools to derive tentative hypotheses about the examinee. Most of these hypotheses will turn out to be false when examined more closely. However, the few that are confirmed may have important implications for the clinical management of the examinee. Furthermore, we suspect that these fruitful hypotheses might not emerge—or might emerge more slowly—if the practitioner relied entirely upon the interview or used only formal tests with established reliability and validity (Case Exhibit 13.1). However, this assertion is difficult to test empirically. We remain open to the possibility that clinically successful applications of projective techniques largely provide further evidence of illusory validation.

SUMMARY

1. Projective tests are based upon the projective hypothesis: Personal interpretations of ambiguous stimuli must necessarily reflect the unconscious needs, motives, and conflicts of the examinee. Popular projectives include the Rorschach inkblot test, the Thematic Apperception Test, sentence completion tests, and drawing tests (e.g., Draw-A-Person).

2. The Rorschach, released in 1921, consists of 10 roughly symmetrical inkblots. For each card, the examiner asks "What might this be?" In the inquiry phase, the examiner clarifies which aspects of the blot (e.g., form or color) played a part in the creation of each response.

3. The preferred Rorschach scoring method by Exner codes each response for location, form, human movement, the use of color, content, and other variables. Summary scores and ratios of variables provide hypotheses about personality functioning. In spite of its enduring popularity, the Rorschach is still haunted by questions about reliability and validity.

4. The Holtzman Inkblot test consists of 45 cards; a single response to each is required. Scoring categories for the HIT are highly reliable, with interscorer agreement generally in the .90s. Validity studies using simple decision rules support the use of the HIT as an aid to psychodiagnosis, especially in schizophrenia.

5. The Rotter Incomplete Sentences Blank (RISB) contains 40 sentence stems written mostly in the first person. Each completed sentence receives an adjustment score from 0 (good) to 6 (poor); the sum is the overall adjustment score. Correct classification rates (e.g., adjusted versus maladjusted) are too low for individual decision making.

6. The Rosenzweig Picture Frustration Study (P-F Study) consists of 24 drawings, each showing two persons in a highly frustrating circumstance. The examinee provides the first verbal response that comes to mind. Objective ratings indicate typical modes of reacting to frustration. Owing to its low reliability, the P-F Study is suited mainly to research.

7. The Thematic Apperception Test (TAT) consists of 30 black-and-white drawings and photographs; one card is blank. The examinee is asked to make up a dramatic story for each picture, including past, present, future, and feelings of the main characters. TAT interpretation usually rests upon clinical-qualitative analysis of story productions.

8. Variations on the TAT include the Picture Projective Test, based upon photographs from the *Family of Man* photo essay; the Thompson TAT for African Americans; the Children's Apperception Test (CAT) which utilizes drawings of animals; TEMAS, an apperception test designed for Hispanic persons; and apperception tests for elderly citizens.

9. In Machover's Draw-A-Person (DAP), the examinee is asked simply to "draw a person." Interpretation proceeds in a clinical-intuitive manner based upon published hypotheses, for example, a redrawn chin indicates indecision. Another test in a similar vein is the House-Tree-Person (the examinee draws these) for which validity evidence is also meager.

10. The projective paradox (enduring popularity of projective tests in spite of questionable validity) can be explained, in part, by the phenomenon of illusory validation. Illusory validation is demonstrated when subjects ignore disconfirming instances and cling to their preexisting stereotypes.

KEY TERMS AND CONCEPTS

projective test   p. 496

projective hypothesis   p. 496

frustration   p. 504

illusory validation   p. 511

CHAPTER 14

Structured Personality Assessment

TOPIC **14A** Self-Report Inventories

Theory-Guided Inventories
Factor-Analytically Derived Inventories
Criterion-Keyed Inventories
Summary
Key Terms and Concepts

The history of personality assessment can be characterized by two overlapping trends. First, unstructured projective techniques such as the Rorschach test dominated personality testing in the early twentieth century and then waned in popularity. Second, structured approaches such as self-report inventories and behavioral ratings gained prominence in midcentury and then rapidly expanded in popularity. In the previous topic we introduced the reader to the many varieties of projective techniques. These methods are resplendent in the richness of the hypotheses they yield; however, projective techniques largely lack the approval of psychometrically oriented clinicians. In this chapter, we focus on the more objective methods for personality assessment favored by measurement-minded psychologists. In Topic 14A, Self-Report Inventories, we review true-false and forced-choice instruments, including the most widely used personality test ever, the Minnesota Multiphasic Personality Inventory (MMPI) and its recent revision, the MMPI-2. In Topic 14B, Behavioral Assessment and Related Approaches, we examine more recent approaches that rely upon behavioral observations and ratings.

Contemporary psychometricians have relied upon three tactics for test development: theory-bounded approaches, factor-analytic strategies, and criterion-key methods. We will organize the discussion of self-report inventories around these three categories. Of course, the boundaries are somewhat artificial and many test developers use a combination of methods.

The structured approaches to personality testing discussed in the following sections are steeped in the details of psychometric methodology. These tests feature prominent references to reliability indices, criterion keying, factor analysis, construct validation, and other forms of technical craftsmanship. For this reason, the approaches discussed here are often considered objective—as contrasted with projective. However, whether they are objective in any meaningful sense is really an empirical question that must be answered on the basis of research. Perhaps it is more accurate to call these methods *structured*. They are structured in the sense that highly specific rules are followed in the administration, scoring, and interpretation of the tests. In fact, some of the approaches are so completely structured that an examinee can answer questions presented on a computer screen and observe a computer-generated narrative report spewed forth from the printer seconds later.[1]

THEORY-GUIDED INVENTORIES

The construction of several self-report inventories was guided closely by formal or informal theories of personality. In these cases, the test developer designed the instrument around a preexisting theory. Theory-guided inventories stand in contrast to factor-analytic approaches which often produce a retrospective theory based upon initial test findings. Theory-guided inventories also differ from the stark atheoretical empiricism found in criterion-key instruments such as the MMPI and MMPI-2. Examples of theory-guided inventories include the Edward Personal Preference Schedule (EPPS) and the Personality Research Form (PRF), both based on Murray's (1938) need-press theory of personality. Further examples include the Myers-Briggs Type Indicator (MBTI), which represents an application of Carl Jung's theory of personality types. The Jenkins Activity Survey, designed to assess the Type-A coronary-prone behavior pattern, also epitomizes a theory-guided instrument. Finally, some theory-guided inventories such as the State-Trait Anxiety Inventory (STAI) attempt to measure very

specific components of personality. Following, we review each of these tests in more detail.

Edwards Personal Preference Schedule

The Edwards Personal Preference Schedule (EPPS) was the first attempt to measure Murray's (1938) manifest needs with a structured personality inventory (Edwards, 1959; Helms, 1983). The reader will recall from an earlier discussion that Murray posited 15 needs and developed a projective test, the Thematic Apperception Test, to tap those needs. Edwards, a consummative psychometrician well versed in the nuances of measurement theory, sought to develop an objective, structured test to measure those 15 needs in a more reliable and valid manner. The 15 needs are listed next to an EPPS profile in Figure 14.1.

The EPPS consists of 210 pairs of statements in which items from each of the 15 scales are paired with items from the other 14. The inventory uses a forced-choice format in which the examinee must choose the one statement from each pair that is most personally representative. The forced-choice format of the EPPS is peculiar and uncomfortable to most test takers, because it often serves up the proverbial choice between a rock and a hard place. Here are three EPPS-like items; for each item, the examinee must choose the one statement that is most personally characteristic:

1. A. I like to talk in front of a group.
    B. I like to work toward self-chosen goals.
2. A. I feel sad when I watch a tragic news story on TV.
    B. I feel nervous when I have to speak before a group.
3. A. I wouldn't mind mopping up ten gallons of syrup.
    B. I wouldn't mind scaling a steep cliff on a safety rope.

Why did Edwards adopt this awkward format for his test? The answer has to do with the problem of social desirability response set. **Social desirability response set** is the tendency of examinees to react to the perceived desirability (or

---

1. Computerized narrative reports may not be altogether a positive development. We discuss the benefits and pitfalls of computer-generated reports in the next chapter.

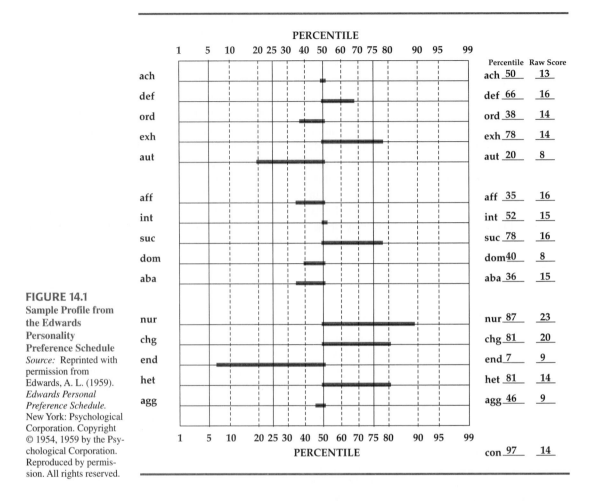

FIGURE 14.1
Sample Profile from the Edwards Personality Preference Schedule
Source: Reprinted with permission from Edwards, A. L. (1959). *Edwards Personal Preference Schedule.* New York: Psychological Corporation. Copyright © 1954, 1959 by the Psychological Corporation. Reproduced by permission. All rights reserved.

undesirability) of a test item rather than responding accurately to its content. Put simply, examinees tend to endorse socially desirable statements and tend not to endorse socially undesirable statements—regardless of the truth value of the responses.[2] Most persons would respond true to a statement such as "I enjoy helping older persons across the street" because the item sanctions a socially desirable attribute; and most persons would respond false to a statement such as "At times I have fantasized about the death of my parents" because the item authorizes a socially undesirable quality. But for some persons, the socially desirable answer is not really accurate. After all, in truth many persons really do not enjoy helping others, and most individuals have fantasized about unpleasant possibilities.

The elegance of the EPPS is that pairs of statements in each item are matched for social desirability (Edwards, 1957). Because each statement in an item pair is of equal social desirability, the content of each statement will exert more "pull" in de-

2. We should mention here that a social desirability response set is a natural human tendency found in nearly every examinee. The extreme form of this tendency is the conscious, deliberate attempt to "fake good" on personality tests. But social desirability need not betoken deliberate deception on the part of the respondent. Social desirability is always present to some degree, even when the examinee adopts a "good faith" perspective in taking a personality test.

termining the examinee's choice. Of course, Edwards carefully designed the content of the statements to incorporate Murray's needs. By making all possible pair-wise comparisons between statements embodying the 15 needs, the EPPS produces a measure of the relative strength of each of Murray's needs.

Because each need is paired twice with the other 14 needs, the maximum possible raw score on each scale is 2 × 14 or 28. This score would occur if the examinee chose the statement for a given need as being more personally characteristic than all the other needs it was paired with. Of course, the lowest possible score on a need scale would be zero. The EPPS also incorporates a consistency check by repeating 15 items in identical format.

The reader should recognize that the EPPS is an **ipsative test.** On an ipsative measure, the overall score—averaged across all subtests—is always the same for every examinee. For example, because the EPPS is an ipsative measure, the overall average scale score is always 14, and high scale scores must be counterbalanced by low ones. Remember, too, that on an ipsative scale, high scores are relative, not absolute. In other words, the strength of each need is expressed not absolutely but relative to the strength of the examinee's other needs. It is therefore confusing that Edwards (1959) also recommends reporting EPPS scores in a normative format. The manual provides T scores and percentiles by which an examinee's raw scale scores can be compared to results from college and general adult samples (see Figure 14.1). By combining two incompatible test methodologies (ipsative and normative) in the same instrument, Edwards makes the interpretation of his test confusing.

The EPPS is widely used in college counseling as a means of personal discovery and receives occasional activity as a research tool. However, some reviewers regard the EPPS as an exercise in test construction rather than a serious entry into the market of validated tests (Heilbrun, 1972; Drummond, 1987). Many clients become frustrated and bored when taking the test. Furthermore, the standardization is outdated and the reliability findings are not particularly exciting. For example, the test-retest reliability of the 15 scale scores ranges from .55 to .87, with a median of .73. Cooper (1990) concluded that the norms reported in Edwards (1959) do not correspond to more recent normative studies.

Early attempts to validate the EPPS by comparing ratings of the strength of Murray's needs with scores on the EPPS met with mixed success (Drummond, 1987). However, a recent study by Piedmont, McCrae, and Costa (1992) provides strong support for the validity of the EPPS. These investigators correlated EPPS scores with NEO Personality Inventory (NEO PI) scores for 330 undergraduate subjects. The NEO PI, discussed later, measures five constructs: Neuroticism, Extraversion, Openness to Experience, Agreeableness, and Conscientiousness. The pattern of relationships was supportive of the convergent validity of both instruments, with scales showing appropriate and theory-confirming correlations. For example, EPPS Aggression correlated .47 with NEO PI Neuroticism and −.53 with NEO PI Agreeableness. The relationships were strongest and most theory-confirming when the EPPS was scored in the normative fashion. The ipsative, forced-choice format of the EPPS apparently lowered validity coefficients and decreased convergent and discriminant validity.

Personality Research Form

Another test based on Murray's need system is the Personality Research Form (Jackson, 1970, 1984b). This test is available in several forms that differ in the number of scales or number of items per scale. In addition to parallel short tests (forms A and B), the PRF also exists as parallel long forms (forms AA and BB). These forms, used primarily with college students, consist of 440 true-false items. The long forms yield 20 personality scale scores and two validity scores, Infrequency and Desirability (Table 14.1). The most popular version of the PRF is form E, which consists of all 22 scales in a modified 352-item test.

In constructing the PRF long forms, Jackson first developed precise and detailed descriptions of the constructs to be measured. Next, for each scale

TABLE 14.1 Personality Research Form Scales

Scale	Interpretation of High Score
Abasement	Self-effacing, humble, blame-accepting
Achievement	Goal striving, competitive
Affiliation	Friendly, accepting, sociable
Aggression	Argues, combative, easily annoyed
Autonomy	Independent, avoids restrictions
Change	Avoids routine, seeks change
Cognitive Structure	Prefers certainty, dislikes ambiguity
Defendence	On guard, takes offense easily
Dominance	Influential, enjoys leading
Endurance	Persevering, hard-working
Exhibition	Dramatic, enjoys attention
Harm Avoidance	Avoids risk and excitement
Impulsivity	Impulsive, speaks freely
Nurturance	Caring, sympathetic, comforting
Order	Organized, dislikes confusion
Play	Playful, light-hearted, enjoys jokes
Sentience	Notices, remembers sensations
Social Recognition	Concern for reputation and approval
Succorance	Insecure, seeks reassurance
Understanding	Values logical thought
Desirability	Validity Scale: favorable presentation
Infrequency	Validity Scale: infrequent responses

over 100 items were written to tap the traits underlying the hypothesized needs. After editorial review, these items were administered to large samples of college students. Based upon high biserial correlations with total scale scores and low correlation with scores on the other scales and the Desirability scale, 20 items were selected for each scale.

Unlike many other personality inventories, the PRF scales have no item overlap. As a result, the scales are exceptionally independent, with most intercorrelation coefficients in the vicinity of ± .30 (Gynther & Gynther, 1976). Furthermore, the rigorous scale construction procedures employed by Jackson (1970) yielded scales with exceptionally good internal consistency, with a range of .80 to .94 and median of .92. A desirable feature of the PRF is its readability: The test requires only a fifth- or sixth-grade reading level (Reddon & Jackson, 1989). MacLennan (1992) has prepared an annotated bibliography of over 375 citations to the PRF.

The construct validity of the PRF rests especially upon confirmatory factor analyses corroborating the grouping of the items into 20 scales (Jackson, 1970, 1984b). In addition, research indicates positive correlations with comparable scales on other inventories (Mungas, Trontel, & Weingardner, 1981). For example, Edwards and Abbott (1973) found exceptionally strong and confirmatory correlations between similar scales on the PRF and the Edwards Personality Inventory (EPI, Edwards, 1967). The EPI is a respected but little-used test consisting of 1,200 (!) true-false questions. Some of the confirmatory correlations between PRF and EPI scales for 218 male and female college students are reported as follows:

Achievement (PRF) × Is a Hard Worker (EPI)   .74
Change (PRF) × Likes a Set Routine (EPI)   −.54
Nurturance (PRF) × Helps Others (EPI)   .64
Succorance (PRF) × Dependent (EPI)   .73

Because these instruments were developed independently according to different test construction philosophies, the findings bolster the validity of both tests.

Myers-Briggs Type Indicator (MBTI)

Originally published in 1962, the MBTI is a forced-choice, self-report inventory that attempts to classify persons according to an adaptation of Carl Jung's theory of personality types (Myers & Mc-Caulley, 1985; Tzeng, Ware, & Chen, 1989). The instrument comes in a 166-item version (Form F) and a 126-item version (Form G). We mainly discuss Form F here, because it is the most widely used. In fact, the MBTI may be the most widely used personality test of any kind with nonpsychiatric populations (DeVito, 1985).

The MBTI is scored on four theoretically independent dimensions: Extraversion-Introversion, Sensing-iNtuition, Thinking-Feeling, Judging-Perceptive. Although scores on each bipolar dimension are continuous, it is common practice to summarize an examinee's scores in a typological manner. For example, an examinee might score more toward Extraversion, iNtuition, Feeling, and Perceptive, and thereby obtain a summary type of ENFP.[3] Such a profile would suggest the following personality characteristics: a greater relatedness to the outer world of people and things than to the inner world of ideas (E); a tendency to look for possibilities rather than to work with known facts (N); a bias for basing judgments on personal values rather than analysis and logic (F); and preference for a flexible, spontaneous way of life rather than a planned, orderly existence (P).

Standardization data for the MBTI consists of percentile norms for the four indicators scores, de-

rived from small samples of high school and college students. Split-half reliabilities for the four scales are listed in the .70s and .80s. Perhaps in part because supportive validity studies are scant, the typological interpretation of the MBTI is generally not well received by measurement-oriented psychologists. One problem with this approach is that the interpretations seem too slick and simple, possessing an almost horoscope-like quality. In fairness to the MBTI, there are more sophisticated ways to interpret the instrument, as revealed by an explosion of recent research. Kaufman, McClean, and Lincoln (1996) list relevant references.

Measures of Type A Behavior

Several questionnaire measures of Type A behavior are available for research purposes. The most recent is the Time Urgency and Perpetual Activation (TUPA) scale (Wright, McCurdy, & Rogoll, 1992). The TUPA scale is respected by researchers in behavioral medicine because of its psychometric excellence. However, the best-known and most widely used instrument of this type is the Jenkins Activity Survey.

The Jenkins Activity Survey is a 52-item, multiple-choice, self-report questionnaire designed to identify the Type A coronary-prone behavior pattern discussed in the previous chapter (Jenkins, Zyzanski, & Rosenman, 1979). Items on the JAS resemble the following:

Currently, do you consider yourself to be:

A. Definitely competitive and ambitious?
B. Probably competitive and ambitious?
C. Probably more relaxed and easygoing?
D. Definitely more relaxed and easygoing?

In addition to the composite Type A behavior score, the JAS yields three factor-analytically derived subscales: Speed and Impatience, Job Involvement, and Hard-driving/Competitiveness. Correlations between the composite Type A scale and the three subscales are modest (.42 to .67), indicating that the factor scores may provide independent contributions to the assessment of Type A tendencies. The JAS is normed on 2,588 employed middle-class

---

3. Because there are two poles to each of the four dimensions, the number of possible personality types is 2^4 which is 16.

males ages 48 through 65 years. The instrument was standardized to have a mean of 0.0 and standard deviation of 10.0, with positive scores indicating Type A tendencies, negative scores indicating the opposite, Type B tendencies.

By way of quick review, the Type A behavior pattern consists of insecurity of status, hyperaggressiveness, free-floating hostility, and a sense of time urgency (Friedman & Ulmer, 1984). Some studies indicate that persons with this behavior pattern are at increased risk of coronary heart disease (CHD). Early identification of high-risk individuals therefore might have portentous implications for intervention. Prior to the JAS, a lengthy structured interview provided the only means for identifying persons with the Type A behavior pattern. The JAS was developed in an attempt to duplicate the structured interview, thereby providing a quick and economical method of screening for Type A behavior.

Unfortunately, the JAS has not fulfilled its ambitious aspirations. The test-retest reliability of the three subscales is marginal at best, with values as low as .58 for Speed and Impatience, .66 for Job Involvement, and .71 for Hard-Driving/Competitiveness (Bishop, Hailey, & O'Rourke, 1989; Igbokwe, 1989). Furthermore, the level of agreement between the structured interview and JAS scores is only fair, not strong enough to warrant the use of this test for individual diagnosis (Yarnold & Bryant, 1988). Another problem with the JAS is that patients with CHD do not differ from general medical patients on its subscales. In comparing 40 patients with CHD and 40 patients with other medical problems, Wright (1992) found that the Speed and Impatience scale produced a significant and appropriate difference, but Hard-Driving/Competitiveness yielded a significant difference in the wrong direction—the CHD patients scored lower than the non-CHD medical patients.

In addition, the norms are obviously not representative, because they do not include women, young or elderly, or persons from lower social strata. The JAS also is difficult to score by hand because of the complex weighting system used. Blumenthal (1985) offers a not too flattering review of the JAS and recommends its use only for clinical and experimental research. Nonetheless, researchers continue to find value in the JAS, although it is now recognized that specific subscores are more predictive of health problems than the overall global score (Hart, 1997).

State-Trait Anxiety Inventory (STAI)

The STAI is a short, quick measure of state and trait anxiety that has received high marks for technical merit (Spielberger and others, 1983). **State anxiety** is the transitory feelings of fear or worry that most of us experience on occasion. **Trait anxiety** is the relatively stable tendency of an individual to respond anxiously to a stressful predicament. These two constructs are separate but related: The level of trait anxiety reflects the proneness to display state anxiety.

The STAI is a 40-item measure which assesses both types of anxiety separately. Items on the STAI are simple, descriptive terms such as "high-strung," "secure," and "relaxed." The 20 State-anxiety items are each rated on a four-point intensity scale, labeled "Not At All," "Somewhat," "Moderately So," and "Very Much So." Examinees are instructed to rate these items for how they feel "right now." The 20 Trait-anxiety items are each rated on a four-point intensity scale that is labeled "Almost Never," "Sometimes," "Often," and "Almost Always." Examinees are instructed to rate these items for how they "generally feel."

The STAI is used with high school students, college students, and adults. A similar children's version, the State-Trait Anxiety Inventory for Children, is targetted for elementary and junior high school students. The technical aspects of this test are generally good, and the standardization samples are large and representative. For example, retest reliability is in the high .70s for trait anxiety and predictably lower for state anxiety (.27 to .62 in various studies). Two weak points of the STAI should be mentioned. First, the construct of trait anxiety is not well defined and seems to include unrelated traits such as a general feeling of dissatisfaction with oneself (Chaplin, 1984). In addition, the STAI is a totally face valid instrument that can be faked with impunity. For this reason, results of the STAI must be interpreted with considerable caution, particularly when situational demands for "healthy" test results are strong. Spielberger (1984) has published a comprehensive bibliography of STAI research studies.

FACTOR-ANALYTICALLY DERIVED INVENTORIES

Sixteen Personality Factor Questionnaire (16PF)

The 16PF is a widely used forced-choice test of personality that is currently available in five separate forms. Each form consists of declarative stems that require the examinee to respond to a specific situation by choosing from among two (Form E) or three forced-choice options (Forms A, B, C, and D). Examples of 16PF-like items include the following:

I make decisions based on
  a. feelings
  b. feelings and reason equally
  c. reason
Which of the following items is different from the others?[4]
  a. candle
  b. star
  c. lightbulb
I find it hard to give a speech to strangers.
  a. yes
  b. somewhat
  c. no

The forms contain from 105 to 187 items and differ mainly in reading level (from third-grade to seventh-grade level). The test is untimed and is usually completed in 30 to 60 minutes.

---

4. The inclusion of what appear to be intelligence test items in the 16PF may seem curious to the reader. In fact, psychologists have long recognized that personality and intelligence are complexly intertwined. Most test builders have addressed this quandary by attempting to tease personality and intelligence apart. Cattell decided instead to exploit the overlaps between personality and intelligence by including elements of both in the same test.

The 16PF is intended for high school seniors and adults. Most norms date back to 1970, a significant shortcoming of this test. However, Form E has been recently normed for highly diverse populations, including prison inmates, patients with schizophrenia, culturally disadvantaged individuals, and physical rehabilitation clients. Nonetheless, most practitioners would concede that the 16PF is more suited to a "normal" rather than an "emotionally disturbed" population. The 16PF also is useful for cross-cultural applications (e.g., Argentero, 1989).

The 16PF is predicated on Cattell's factor-analytic conception of personality (Cattell, Eber, & Tatsuoka, 1970). According to this model, surface traits—the more obvious aspects of personality—emerge from simple cluster analyses of test responses. In contrast, source traits—the stable, constant, but less-visible wellsprings of behavior—emerge only from specialized factor analyses of the surface traits (Cattell, 1950). In a series of studies, Cattell determined that 16 personality factors or source traits are needed to explain the structure of test responses, hence the name for his instrument.

The 16PF yields a total of 20 indices or attributes of personality. In addition to the 16 basic scales, four second-order indices of personality are computed from weighted linear sums of the previous 16 indices, yielding a total of 20 bipolar scales. Over the years, the meaning of extreme scores in either direction has been well established (Table 14.2).

The major thrust of application for the 16PF is career guidance, vocational exploration, and occupational testing. One reason for the popularity of the instrument—it is second in use only to the MMPI/MMPI-2—is that answer sheets can be mailed in for quick-turnaround machine scoring. Most practitioners also request a computer-generated narrative report. An attractive feature of these reports is the wealth of information provided. Reports include a capsule personality description, score profile, and summary of clinical signs, cognitive factors, and need patterns.

A major shortcoming of the 16PF is that the 16 surveyed personality attributes are based upon as few as 10 to 13 items each. Inevitably, a test with scales as short as these will possess diminished

TABLE 14.2 The 16 Personality Factors and 4 Second-Order Indices from the 16PF

Factor Name	Interpretation of Low Score	Interpretation of High Score
Warmth	reserved, detached, cool, impersonal	warm, outgoing, likes people
Intelligence	concrete thinking	abstract thinking, bright
Emotional Stability	emotionally less stable, changeable	emotionally stable, calm, mature
Dominance	submissive, conforming, mild	dominant, assertive, competitive
Impulsivity	serious, prudent, sober, taciturn	enthusiastic, cheerful, heedless
Conformity	expedient, disregards rules	conforming, persevering, moralistic
Boldness	shy, timid, restrained	bold, uninhibited, spontaneous
Sensitivity	tough-minded, self-reliant	tender-minded, sensitive
Suspiciousness	trusting, adaptable	suspicious, hard to fool, opinionated
Imagination	practical, conventional	impractical, absent-minded, unconventional
Shrewdness	forthright, genuine, unpretentious	calculating, polished, socially alert
Insecurity	confident, self-satisfied, secure	self-blaming, worrying, troubled
Radicalism	conservative, resisting change	liberal, analytical, innovative
Self-sufficiency	group-oriented, sociable	resourceful, self-sufficient
Self-discipline	undisciplined, impulsive	compulsive, socially precise
Tension	relaxed, tranquil, low drive	frustrated, driven, tense
Extraversion (Q_I)	introversion	extraversion
Anxiety (Q_{II})	low anxiety	high anxiety
Tough Poise (Q_{III})	sensitivity, emotionalism	tough poise
Independence (Q_{IV})	dependence	independence

Source: Based on Wholeben, B. E. (1987). Sixteen Personality Factor Questionnaire. In D. J. Keyser and R. C. Sweetland (eds.), *Test critiques compendium.* Kansas City, MO: Test Corporation of America. Also, Cattell, R. B. (1986). *The handbook for the 16 Personality Factor Questionnaire.* Champaign, IL: Institute for Personality and Ability Testing.

reliability. Not surprisingly, the split-half reliabilities of the 16 factors are as low as .54; correlations between the same scales for different forms of the test typically hover around .50; and test-retest coefficients for scales on the same form are .70 to .80 for same or next-day administrations, but much lower for longer intervals.

Most of the validity evidence for the 16PF consists of statistical demonstrations that items "belong" on their respective scales and that the scales consist of relatively pure factors. The evidence in this regard is reasonably encouraging (Cattell, Eber, & Tatsuoka, 1970). In addition, some studies with the 16PF demonstrate that the real-world correlates of test results are theory-consistent. For example, Cattell and Nesselroade (1967) studied the similarity of 16PF profiles in 102 stably and 37 un-

stably married couples. These authors discovered that stably married couples are much, much more similar on the 16PF than unstably married couples. In Table 14.3, the reader will notice that scale correlations for stably married couples are almost uniformly positive—meaning that these couples produce similar 16PF scale scores—whereas more than half the scale correlations for unstably married couples are negative—meaning that these couples often produce dissimilar 16PF scale scores. These findings support the viewpoint that likeness facilitates stable marriages.[5] More importantly, the results bolster the validity of the 16PF by showing

_____
5. Another possibility is that in stable marriages the personalities of the partners evolve toward increasing similarity over the years. Of course, both factors could operate simultaneously.

TABLE 14.3 **Intercorrelations of 16PF Factors for Stably and Unstably Married Spouses**

16PF Factor		Correlation for Stably Married (N = 102)	Correlation for Unstably Married (N = 37)	p-Value for Difference
A	Warmth	.16	−.50	<.001
B	Intelligence	.31	.21	ns
C	Ego Strength	.32	.05	ns
E	Dominance	.13	.31	ns
F	Impulsivity	.23	−.40	<.001
G	Conformity	.33	.19	ns
H	Boldness	.23	.12	ns
I	Sensitivity	−.15	−.13	ns
L	Suspiciousness	.18	−.33	<.01
M	Imagination	.22	−.01	ns
N	Shrewdness	.18	.27	ns
O	Insecurity	.11	.36	ns
Q_1	Radicalism	.27	.34	ns
Q_2	Self-Sufficiency	.15	−.32	<.01
Q_3	Self-Discipline	.27	−.02	ns
Q_4	Tension	.16	−.11	ns
Q_I	Extraversion	.22	−.30	<.01
Q_{II}	Anxiety	.31	.23	ns

Source: Adapted with permission from Cattell, R. B., and Nesselroade, J. R. (1967). Likeness and completeness theories examined by Sixteen Personality factor measures on stably and unstably married couples. *Journal of Personality and Social Psychology, 7,* 351–361.

that test results carry meaningful and predictable real-world implications.

Eysenck Personality Questionnaire

The Eysenck Personality Questionnaire (EPQ) is the latest in a series of tests designed to measure the major dimensions of normal and abnormal personality (Eysenck & Eysenck, 1975). Based on a lifelong program of factor-analytic questionnaire research and laboratory experiments on learning and conditioning, Eysenck isolated three major dimensions of personality: Psychoticism (P), Extraversion (E), and Neuroticism (N). The EPQ consists of scales to measure these dimensions and also incorporates a Lie (L) scale to assess the validity of an examinee's responses. The EPQ contains 90

statements answered "yes" or "no" and is designed for persons aged 16 and older. A Junior EPQ containing 81 statements is suitable for children ages 7 to 15.

Items on the P scale resemble the following:

Do you often break the rules? (T)
Would you worry if you were in debt? (F)
Do you take risks just for fun? (T)

High scores on the P scale indicate aggressive and hostile traits, impulsivity, a preference for liking odd or unusual things, and empathy defects. Antisocial and schizoid patients often obtain high scores on this dimension. In contrast, low scores on P foretell more desirable characteristics such as empathy and interpersonal sensitivity. Items on the E scale resemble the following:

Do you like to meet new people? (T)
Are you quiet when with others? (F)
Do you like lots of excitement? (T)

High scores on the E scale indicate a loud, gregarious, outgoing, fun-loving person. Low scores on the E scale indicate introverted traits such as a preference for solitude and quiet activities. Items on the N scale resemble the following:

Are you a moody person? (T)
Do you feel that life is dull? (T)
Are your feelings easily hurt? (T)

The N scale reflects a dimension of emotionality which ranges from nervous, maladjusted, and overemotional (high scores) to stable and confident (low scores).

The reliability of the EPQ is excellent. For example, the one-month test-retest correlations were .78 (P), .89 (E), .86 (N), and .84 (L). Internal consistencies were in the .70s for P and the .80s for the other three scales. The construct validity of the EPQ is also well established through dozens of studies using behavioral, emotional, learning, attentional, and therapeutic criteria (reviewed in Eysenck & Eysenck, 1976, 1985). Friedman (1987) provides a short but thorough introduction to other sources on the EPQ.

A major focus of research with the EPQ has been on the empirical correlates of **extraversion** and its polar opposite, **introversion.** Eysenck and Eysenck (1975) describe the typical extravert as follows:

The typical extravert is sociable, likes parties, has many friends, needs to have people to talk to, and does not like reading or studying by himself. He craves excitement, takes chances, often sticks his neck out, acts on the spur of the moment, and is generally an impulsive individual.

They describe the typical introvert as follows:

The typical introvert is a quiet, retiring sort of person, introspective, fond of books rather than people; he is reserved and distant except to intimate friends. He tends to plan ahead, "looks before he leaps," and mistrusts the impulse of the moment.

Eysenck and his followers have linked a number of perceptual and physiological factors to the extraversion/introversion dimension. Because of space limitations, we can only list representative findings here:

- Introverts are more vigilant in watchkeeping.
- Introverts do better at signal-detection tasks.
- Introverts are less tolerant of pain but more tolerant of sensory deprivation.
- Extraverts are more easily conditioned to stimuli associated with sexual arousal.
- Extraverts have a greater need for external stimulation.

Aiken (1989) summarizes additional research on the real-world correlates of the EPQ extraversion/introversion dimension.

In general, the technical characteristics of the EPQ are very strong, certainly stronger than found in most self-report inventories. The practical utility of the instrument is supported by voluminous research literature. Nonetheless, the EPQ has never caught on among American psychologists, who seem enamoured of multiphasic instruments that produce 10, 20, or 30 scores, not a simple trio of basic dimensions.

Comrey Personality Scales

For practitioners who desire a short self-report inventory suitable for college students and other adults, the Comrey Personality Scales (Comrey, 1970, 1980) would be a good choice. As a protege of Guilford, Comrey pursued a factor-analytic strategy in developing his 180-item test. Comrey relied exclusively upon college students in the development and standardization of his test, so the CPS is well suited to assessment of personality in this subpopulation.

A special virtue of the CPS is its brevity. Consisting of 180 statements, the test is only one-third as long as competing instruments such as the MMPI-2. The eight CPS personality scales consist of 20 items each, divided equally between positively and negatively worded statements. Another

20 items are devoted to a validity check and the assessment of social desirability response bias.

The following description of CPS scales is based upon Merenda (1985):

(V) *Validity Check.* A score of 8 is the expected raw score. Any score on the V scale which gives a *T*-score equivalent below 70 is still within the normal range, however. Higher scores are suggestive of an invalid record.

(R) *Response Bias.* High scores indicate a tendency to answer questions in a socially desirable way, making the respondent look like a "nice" person.

(T) *Trust versus Defensiveness.* High scores indicate a belief in the basic honesty, trustworthiness, and good intentions of other people.

(O) *Orderliness versus Lack of Compulsion.* High scores are characteristic of careful, meticulous, orderly, and highly organized individuals.

(C) *Social Conformity versus Rebelliousness.* Individuals with high scores accept society as it is, resent nonconformity in others, seek the approval of society, and respect the law.

(A) *Activity versus Lack of Energy.* High-scoring individuals have a great deal of energy and endurance, work hard, and strive to excel.

(S) *Emotional Stability versus Neuroticism.* High-scoring persons are free from depression, optimistic, relaxed, stable in mood, and confident.

(E) *Extraversion versus Introversion.* High-scoring individuals meet people easily, seek new friends, feel comfortable with strangers, and do not suffer from stage fright.

(M) *Masculinity versus Femininity.* High-scoring individuals tend to be rather tough-minded people who are not bothered by blood, crawling creatures, vulgarity, and who do not cry easily or show much interest in love stories.

(P) *Empathy versus Egocentrism.* High-scoring individuals describe themselves as helpful, generous, sympathetic people who are interested in devoting their lives to the service of others.

Reflecting its careful factor-analytic derivation, the CPS scales possess exceptional internal consistencies, which range from .91 to .96. These findings indicate that the CPS is most likely a reliable test, but traditional test-retest data are scant. Cross-cultural studies with the CPS are highly supportive of its validity. Brief and Comrey (1993) report that the eight-factor solution to CPS item responses is found in factor analyses with Russian, American, Brazilian, Israeli, Italian, and New Zealand samples. Other validational studies with the CPS are not straightforward in their interpretation. On the one hand, the correlations between CPS scale scores and personality-relevant biographical data are very small (Comrey & Backer, 1970; Comrey & Schiebel, 1983). On the other hand, extreme scores on the CPS scales are strongly associated with psychological disturbance (Comrey & Schiebel, 1985). This is particularly true for low scores on Trust versus Defensiveness, Activity versus Lack of Energy, Emotional Stability versus Neuroticism, Extraversion versus Introversion, and high scores on Orderliness versus Lack of Compulsion. In general, reviewers conclude that the CPS is a promising test that needs updated standardization and additional documentation on its technical qualities.

NEO Personality Inventory-Revised

The NEO Personality Inventory-Revised (NEO PI-R) embodies decades of factor-analytic research with clinical and normal adult populations (Costa & McCrae, 1992). The test is based upon the five-factor model of personality described in the previous chapter. It is available in two parallel forms consisting of 240 items rated on a five-point dimension. An additional three items are used to check validity. A shorter version, the NEO Five-Factor Inventory (NEO-FFI) is also available (Costa & McCrae, 1989). We limit our discussion to the NEO PI-R. Form S is for self-reports whereas Form R is for outside observers (e.g., the spouse of a client). The item format consists of five-point ratings: strongly disagree, disagree, neutral, agree, strongly agree. The items assess emotional, interpersonal, experiential, attitudinal, and motivational variables.

The five domain scales of the NEO PI-R are each based upon six facet (trait) scales (Table 14.4). The internal consistency of the scales is superb: .86 to .95 for the domain scales, and .56 to .90 for the facet scales. Stability coefficients range from .51 to .83 in three- to seven-year longitudinal studies. Validity evidence for the NEO PI-R is substantial, based upon the correspondence of ratings between self and spouse, correlations with other tests and checklists, and the construct validity of the five-factor model itself (Costa & McCrae, 1992; Piedmont & Weinstein, 1993; Trull, Useda, Costa, & McCrae, 1995).

The NEO PI-R is an excellent measure of personality that is especially useful in research. The test also shows promise as a measure of clinical psychopathology. For example, Clarkin, Hull, Cantor, and Sanderson (1993) found that patients diagnosed with borderline personality disorder scored very high on Neuroticism and very low on Agreeableness, which resonates strongly with every clin-

ician's response to these challenging patients. One minor concern about the instrument is that it lacks substantial validity scales—only three items assess validity. The administration of the NEO PI-R assumes that subjects are cooperative and reasonably honest. This is usually a safe assumption in research settings but may not hold true in forensic, personnel, or psychiatric settings.

CRITERION-KEYED INVENTORIES

The final self-report inventories that we will review embody a criterion-keyed test development strategy. In a criterion-keyed approach, test items are assigned to a particular scale if, and only if, they discriminate between a well-defined criterion group and a relevant control group. For example, in devising a self-report scale for depression, items endorsed by depressed persons significantly more (or less) frequently than by normal controls would be assigned to the depression scale, keyed in the appropriate direction. A similar approach might be used to develop scales for other constructs of interest to clinicians such as schizophrenia, anxiety re-

TABLE 14.4 Domain and Facet (Trait) Scales of the NEO PI-R

Domains	Facets	
Neuroticism	Anxiety	Self-Consciousness
	Angry Hostility	Impulsiveness
	Depression	Vulnerability
Extraversion	Warmth	Activity
	Gregariousness	Excitement Seeking
	Assertiveness	Positive Emotions
Openness to Experience	Fantasy	Actions
	Aesthetics	Ideas
	Feelings	Values
Agreeableness	Trust	Compliance
	Straightforwardness	Modesty
	Altruism	Tender-Mindedness
Conscientiousness	Competence	Achievement Striving
	Order	Self-Discipline
	Dutifulness	Deliberation

action, and the like. Notice that the test developer does not consult any theory of schizophrenia, depression, or anxiety reaction to determine which items belong on the respective scales. The essence of the criterion-keyed procedure is, so to speak, to let the items fall where they may.[6]

Minnesota Multiphasic Personality Inventory-2 (MMPI-2)

First published in 1943, the MMPI was a 566-item true-false personality inventory designed originally as an aid in psychiatric diagnosis (Hathaway & McKinley, 1940, 1942, 1943: McKinley & Hathaway, 1940, 1944; McKinley, Hathaway, & Meehl, 1948). The test authors followed a strict empirical keying approach in the construction of the MMPI scales. The clinical scales were developed by contrasting item responses of carefully defined psychiatric patient groups (average *N* of about 50) with item responses of 724 control subjects. The result was a remarkable test useful both in psychiatric assessment and the description of normal personality. Within a few years, the MMPI became the most widely used personality test in the United States.

At first the MMPI aged gracefully; what appeared to be minor flaws were tolerated by practitioners. But as the MMPI reached middle age, the need for rejuvenation became increasingly obvious. The most serious problem was the original control group, which consisted primarily of relatives and visitors of medical patients at the University of Minnesota Hospital. The narrow choice of control subjects, tested mainly in the 1930s, proved to be a persistent source of criticism for the MMPI. All of the control subjects were white, and most were young (average age about 35), married, and from a small town or rural area. This was a sample of convenience that was significantly unrepresentative of the population at large.

The item content of the MMPI also raised concerns (Graham, 1993). Several items used archaic and obsolete terminology, referring to "drop the handkerchief" (a parlor game from the 1930s), sleeping powders (sleeping pills), and streetcars (electric-powered buses). Other items used sexist language. Examinees found some items objectionable, especially those dealing with Christian religious beliefs. These items were the source of occasional lawsuits alleging invasion of privacy. Finally, a few items dealing with bowel functions and sexual behavior were just downright offensive.

From the standpoint of measurement, a more serious problem with item content was that of omission. The MMPI item pool was not broad enough to assess many important characteristics, including suicidal tendencies, drug abuse, and treatment-related behaviors. An additional motive for MMPI revision was to extend the range of item coverage.

The MMPI-2 was released in 1989 after nearly a decade of revision and restandardization. The new, improved MMPI-2 incorporates a contemporary normative sample of 2,600 individuals who are loosely representative of the general population on major demographic variables (geographic location, race, age, occupational level, and income). Although higher educational levels are overrepresented, the MMPI-2 normative sample is still a vast improvement over the MMPI normative sample. The item pool has been significantly improved by revision of obsolete items, deletion of offensive items, and addition of new items to extend content coverage.

The MMPI-2 is a significant improvement upon the MMPI, but maintains substantial continuity with its esteemed predecessor. The test developers retained the same titles and measurement objectives for the traditional validity and clinical scales. The restandardization provides a better calibration for scale elevations, a much-needed improvement (Tellegen & Ben-Porath, 1992). Although dozens of items were rewritten, most of these revisions are cosmetic and do not affect the psychometric characteristics of the test (Ben-Porath & Butcher, 1989). In fact, when large samples of subjects complete the MMPI and the MMPI-2, scores on the individual

---

6. We are glossing over certain complexities here. Some items reflecting general psychopathology might discriminate *all* the contrast groups from the control group. The test developer might discard these in favor of items that are *differentially* discriminating for just one contrast group but not the others.

validity and clinical scales typically correlate near .99.

The MMPI-2 consists of 567 items carefully designed to assess a wide range of concerns. The examinee is asked to mark "true" or "false" for each statement as it applies to himself or herself. Most of the items are self-referential. The items encompass these general themes (Dahlstrom, Welsh, & Dahlstrom, 1972; Graham, 1993):

health concerns
neurologic symptoms
family problems
marital relations
work problems
depressive and manic symptoms
obsessive and compulsive states
delusions and hallucinations
anxiety and phobias
anger control
antisocial practices
alcohol and drug abuse
self-esteem
social discomfort
Type A behavior
masculinity-femininity
negative treatment indicators
response validity, for example, improbable virtues

The MMPI requires a sixth-grade reading level and is completed by most persons in 1 to 1½ hours.

The original MMPI scales were developed by contrasting item responses of carefully defined psychiatric patient groups (average N of about 50) with item responses of about 700 controls. The psychiatric patient groups included the following diagnostic categories: hypochondriasis, depression, hysteria, psychopathy, male homosexuality, paranoia, psychasthenia,[7] schizophrenia, and the early phase of mania (hypomania). In addition, samples of socially introverted and socially extraverted college students were used to construct a scale for social introversion. The MMPI-2 retains the basic

clinical scales with only minor item deletions and revisions. Ben-Porath and Butcher (1989) investigated the characteristics of the rewritten items on the MMPI-2 and discovered that they are psychometrically equivalent to the original items.

The MMPI-2 can be scored for four validity scales, 10 standard clinical scales, and dozens of supplementary scales. In practice, clinicians place the greatest emphasis upon the validity and standard clinical scales. The supplementary scales are just that—supplementary. They provide information helpful in fine-tuning the interpretation of the traditional validity and clinical scales. MMPI-2 scale raw scores are converted to T scores, with a mean of 50 and a standard deviation of 10. Scores that exceed T of 65 merit special consideration. These elevated scores are statistically uncommon in the general population and may signify the presence of psychiatric symptomatology. We will concentrate upon the traditional scales here, beginning with a review of the four validity scales, known as Cannot Say (or ?), L, F, and K.

The Cannot Say score is simply the total number of items omitted or double-marked in completion of the answer sheet. The instructions for the test encourage examinees to mark all items, but omissions or double-marked items will occur. However, this is rare—the modal number of items omitted is zero (Tamkin & Scherer, 1957). Omission of up to 10 items appears to have little effect on the overall test results—one of the benefits of having a huge pool of statements in the MMPI-2. A very high score on this scale may indicate a reading problem, opposition to authority, defensiveness, or indecisiveness caused by depression.

The L Scale is composed of 15 items all scored in the false direction. By answering "false" to L Scale items, the examinee asserts that he or she possesses a degree of personal virtue that is rarely observed in our culture (e.g., never gets angry, likes everyone, never lies, reads every newspaper editorial, and would rather lose than win). The L Scale was designed to identify a general, deliberate, evasive test-taking attitude. A high score on the L Scale indicates that the examinee is not only defensive, but naively so. Persons with any degree of psycho-

---

7. This outdated diagnostic term is quite similar to what would now be labeled obsessive-compulsive disorder.

logical sophistication can adopt a defensive test-taking attitude and still score in the normal range on the L Scale.

The F Scale consists of 60 items answered by normal subjects in the scored direction no more than 10 percent of the time. These items reflect a broad spectrum of serious maladjustment, including peculiar thoughts, apathy, and social alienation. Even though F Scale items seem to indicate psychiatric pathology, they are seldom endorsed by patients. Fewer than 50 percent of these items appear on the clinical scales. Many persons with significant psychiatric disturbance do produce elevated scores in the range of $T = 70$ or 80 on the F Scale. On the other hand, exceptionally high scores suggest additional hypotheses: insufficient reading ability, random or uncooperative responding, a motivated attempt to "fake bad" on the test, or an exaggerated "cry for help" in a distressed client.

The K Scale was designed to help detect a subtle form of defensiveness. The 30-item scale is composed, in part, of 22 items which differentiated normal profiles produced by defensive hospitalized psychiatric patients from those produced by normal controls. Additionally, eight items which improved discrimination of depressive and schizophrenic symptoms were added (McKinley, Hathaway & Meehl, 1948). An elevated score on the K Scale may indicate a defensive test-taking attitude. Normal range elevations on the K Scale suggest good ego strength—the presence of useful psychological defenses which allow the person to function well in spite of internal conflict.

The combined use of F and K may be useful in the detection of MMPI-2 profiles which have been faked or malingered. In one study, 81 percent of fake-good profiles were identified by a simple decision rule (using raw scores) of F-K < −12, whereas 87 percent of fake-bad profiles were identified by a simple decision rule (using raw scores) of F-K > 7 (Bagby, Rogers, Buis, Kalemba, 1994). Studies in which subjects are coached on how to fake the MMPI-2 raise troubling ethical concerns (Ben-Porath, 1994; Wetter, Baer, Berry, & Reynolds, 1994).

Several clinical scales are "K-corrected" to improve their discriminatory power. The rationale for this practice is that elevations on K betoken an artificial reduction of scores on these clinical scales. Portions of the raw score on K are thus added to these clinical scale scores prior to computation of the T scores. The K-corrected scales, discussed below, include Hypochondriasis, Psychopathic Deviate, Psychasthenia, Schizophrenia, and Hypomania. Whether K-correction actually improves the MMPI-2 is debatable, but the test publishers continued the tradition from the MMPI for the sake of continuity. Separate norms for non-K-corrected scale score transformations are also available.

In addition to the validity scales, the MMPI-2 is always scored for 10 clinical scales. With the exception of Social Introversion, these clinical scales were constructed in the usual criterion-keyed manner by contrasting responses of clinical subjects and normal controls. As noted previously, Social Introversion was developed by contrasting the responses of college students high and low in social introversion. The 10 clinical scales and common interpretations of elevated scores are outlined in Table 14.5.

Dozens of supplementary scales can also be scored on the MMPI-2. Some of the supplementary scales are based upon rational identification of symptom clusters and subsequent scale purification by empirical means. Fifteen useful MMPI-2 Content Scales were developed in this manner (Butcher, Graham, Williams, & Ben-Porath, 1990). Many of the supplementary scales were developed by independent investigators; these scales vary widely in quality. In practice, only about 30 of the additional scales are routinely scored. Examples of the supplementary scales include Anxiety, Repression, Ego Strength, and the MacAndrew Alcoholism Scale-Revised. Anxiety (A) and Repression (R) are the first two major factors that always emerge from factor analysis of MMPI-2 responses. An interesting supplementary scale is Barron's (1953) Ego Strength (Es) Scale, which purports to predict positive response to psychotherapy. However, not all studies confirm this use of the scale (Graham, 1987). The MacAndrew Alcoholism Scale-Revised (MAC-R, MacAndrew, 1965) is a useful index of alcohol or other substance abuse. The MAC-R is not only useful in assessment of alcoholism but is

TABLE 14.5   The 10 Clinical Scales from the Minnesota Multiphasic Personality Inventory-2

Scale No. and Abbreviation	Scale Name	K-Correction	Typical Interpretation of Elevation
1 Hs	Hypochondriasis	.5K	Excessive physical preoccupation
2 D	Depression		Sad feelings, hopelessness
3 Hy	Hysteria		Immaturity, use of repression, denial
4 Pd	Psychopathic deviate	.4K	Authority conflict, impulsivity
5 Mf	Masculinity-femininity		Masculine interests [women], Feminine interests [men]
6 Pa	Paranoia		Suspiciousness, hostility
7 Pt	Psychasthenia	1K	Anxiety and obsessive thinking
8 Sc	Schizophrenia	1K	Alienation, unusual thought processes
9 Ma	Hypomania	.2K	High energy, possible agitation
0 Si	Social introversion		Shyness and introversion

also helpful in the identification of heavy drinkers and drug-dependent individuals (Wolf, Schubert, Patterson, Grande, & Pendleton, 1990). We cannot possibly review all the useful supplementary scales here. The interested reader should consult Butcher and Williams (1992) and Graham (1993).

MMPI-2 Interpretation

The interpretation of an MMPI-2 profile can proceed along two different paths: scale by scale or configural. In the simplest possible approach, scale by scale, the examiner determines the validity of the test, as discussed previously, by inspecting the four validity scales. If the test appears reasonably valid by these criteria, the examiner consults a relevant resource book and proceeds scale by scale to produce a series of hypotheses. For example, Lachar (1974) has distilled the meaning of various elevations on the Pa or Paranoia scale as follows:

$T = 27-44$ examinee may be stubborn, touchy, or difficult

$T = 45-59$ no undue sensitivity and adequate regard for others

$T = 60-69$ increasing probability of rigidity and oversensitivity

$T = 70-79$ rigid, touchy, projects blame and hostility

$T = 79-100$ frankly delusional paranoid features may be present

The configural approach to MMPI-2 interpretation is somewhat more complicated and consists of classifying the profile as belonging to one or another loosely defined code type that has been studied extensively. Code types are usually defined by a combination of elevation (two or more clinical scales elevated beyond a certain criterion) and definition (two or more clinical scales clearly standing out from the others). For example, in its full-blown manifestation, the 4–9 code type can be defined by a valid profile in which scale 4 (Psychopathic De-viate) and scale 9 (Hypomania) are the high-point elevations, both exceed *T* of 65 (elevation), and both exceed the next highest clinical scale by at least 5 *T*-score points (definition). Here is how Graham (1993) describes persons who fit this code type:

> The most salient characteristics of 49/94 individu-als is a marked disregard for social standards and values. They frequently get in trouble with the au-thorities because of antisocial behavior. They have a poorly developed conscience, easy morals, and fluctuating ethical values. Alcoholism, fighting, marital problems, sexual acting out, and a wide array of delinquent acts are among the difficulties in which they may be involved. This is a common code type among persons who abuse alcohol and other substances.

The most likely diagnosis for such individuals is antisocial personality disorder.

We should mention briefly that several comput-erized interpretation systems are available for the MMPI and the MMPI-2 (Fowler, 1985; Butcher, 1987). The Minnesota Report™ (Butcher, 1993) is the best. This system generates a very cautious and methodical 16-page report that includes discussion of profile validity, symptomatic patterns, interper-sonal relations, diagnostic considerations, and treat-ment considerations. The Minnesota Report™ also provides a variety of figures and tables to illustrate test results.

The adequacy of computerized MMPI-2 narra-tive reports is generally good, but the reader should realize that computer programs are written by fal-lible human beings. There is a danger that com-puter-generated test reports will be erroneous. Furthermore, some less-reputable interpretive sys-tems can be purchased on microcomputer diskette for a few hundred dollars. This increases the risk that computer-based test interpretations will be misused by unqualified persons. We discuss the pit-falls of computerized test interpretation in the final chapter of the book.

Technical Properties of the MMPI-2

From the standpoint of traditional psychometric criteria, the MMPI-2 presents a mixed picture. Re-liability data are generally positive, with median in-ternal consistency coefficients (alpha) typically in the .70s and .80s, but as low as the .30s for some scales in some samples. One-week test-retest coef-ficients range from the high .50s to the low .90s, with a median in the .80s (Butcher, Dahlstrom, Graham, Tellegen, & Kaemmer, 1989). These are good figures considering that some attributes—such as those measured by the Depression scale—change so quickly that the test-retest methodology is of questionable suitability.

A shortcoming of the MMPI-2 is that intercor-relations among the clinical scales are extremely high. For example, in the case of scales 7 and 8, the Psychasthenia and Schizophrenia scales, the corre-lation is commonly in the .70s. In part, this reflects the item overlap between MMPI scales—scales 7 and 8 share 17 items in common. But it is also true that the criterion-keyed approach is not well suited to the development of independent measures. A high intercorrelation of basic scales is one price to be paid for using this test development strategy.

The validity of the MMPI-2 is difficult to sum-marize, owing to the sheer volume of research on this instrument and its predecessor, the MMPI. As of 1975, over 6,000 studies employing the MMPI had been completed (Dahlstrom, Welsh, & Dahlstrom, 1975). Of course, thousands of addi-tional studies have been published since then. Gra-ham (1993) provides a brief but excellent review of validity studies on the MMPI/MMPI-2. He notes that the average validity coefficient for MMPI stud-ies conducted between 1970 and 1981 was a healthy .46. He also points out the confirming pat-tern of extratest correlates in dozens of studies of identified patient groups. Research also indicates that the MMPI-2 is highly comparable to the MMPI, for which a substantial body of validity data has been compiled (Hargrave, Hiatt, Ogard, & Karr, 1994; Harrell, Honaker, & Parnell, 1992). Finally, bias studies comparing MMPI-2 results for cau-casian and African-American clients indicate that slight racial differences do exist in average profiles. However, these differences validly reflect emo-tional functioning, that is, the MMPI-2 is not racially biased (McNulty, Graham, Ben-Porath, & Stein, 1997).

The MMPI/MMPI-2 has been shown to be of value for a wide range of diagnostic problems, including the assessment of antisocial, borderline, and narcissistic personality disorders (Castlebury, Hilsenroth, Handler, & Durham, 1997), the evaluation of sexual abuse history and sexual orientation in women (Griffith, Myers, Cusick, & Tankersley, 1997), the prediction of outcome from surgery for back pain (Uomoto, Turner, & Herron, 1988), and the empirical classification of homicide offenders (Kalichman, 1988), to cite just a few examples. The MMPI-2 likely will maintain its status as the premiere instrument for assessment of psychopathology in adulthood for many years to come.

California Psychological Inventory (CPI)

Originally published in 1957, the recently revised CPI is an MMPI-like instrument designed expressly to measure the dimensions of normal personality (Gough, 1987; McAllister, 1986). The test consists of 462 true-false items, including nearly 200 items borrowed directly from the MMPI. The revised CPI yields scores on 20 scales, including three measures designed to assess test-taking attitudes. These validity scales are Sense of well-being (Wb), derived from normals asked to "fake bad"; Good impression (Gi), derived from normals asked to "fake good"; and Communality (Cm), which consists of items endorsed by 95 percent of normals. Thus, Wb, Gi, and Cm are designed, respectively, to detect subjects who fake bad, fake good, or respond randomly.

The clinical scales are based on "folk" concepts of personality; they measure dimensions of personality that are meaningful and easily recognized by laypersons and psychologists alike. For 13 of the 17 clinical scales, Gough used a criterion-keyed approach in test development. Extreme groups of subjects (mainly college students) were formed on such scale-relevant criteria as school grades, sociability, and participation in extracurricular activities. Item endorsement frequencies were then contrasted to ferret out the best statements for each scale. The remaining four scales were constructed on a rational basis backed up by indices of internal consistency. The CPI scales are described in Table 14.6.

Reflecting the care with which the scales were constructed, reliability data for the CPI are quite satisfactory. Most test-retest scale correlations are in the .80s, with a range from about the .50s to the low .90s, depending upon the sample and the time interval between administrations. The CPI is also well standardized; scores are based on a normative sample of 6,000 males and 7,000 females of widely varying age, social class, and geographic region. All scale scores are reported as T scores, with a mean of 50 and standard deviation of 10.

The CPI scales were cross-validated to determine their ability to discriminate new samples of subjects rated on the relevant dimension. These validity coefficients are quite mixed; some values are acceptable, but other criterion correlations are very low. For example, scores on the Flexibility scale typically correlate only about .2 with staff ratings of flexibility (Domino, 1987).

The CPI is heir to a long history of empirical research that substantiates a number of real-world correlates for distinctive test profiles. Due to space limitations, we can only list several prominent areas in which the value of the test has been empirically confirmed. The CPI is useful for helping predict the following:

- high school and college achievement
- effectiveness of student-teachers
- grade point average in medical school
- effectiveness of police and military personnel
- leadership and executive success

The CPI is particularly effective at identifying adolescents or adults who follow a delinquent or criminal life style (Gough & Bradley, 1992b). The reader can find further details on the real-world empirical correlates of CPI profiles in Groth-Marnat (1990) and Hargrave and Hiatt (1989).

Millon Clinical Multiaxial Inventory-III (MCMI-III)

The MCMI-III is a personality inventory designed for the same purposes as the MMPI-2, namely, to provide useful information for psychiatric diagnosis (Millon, 1983, 1987, 1994). The MCMI-III has

TABLE 14.6   Brief Description of California Psychological Inventory Scales

	Scale	Common Interpretation of High Score
Do	Dominance	dominant, persistent, good leadership ability
Cs	Capacity for Status	personal qualities that underlie and lead to status
Sy	Sociability	outgoing, sociable, participative temperament
Sp	Social Presence	poise, spontaneity, and self-confidence in social situations
Sa	Self-Acceptance	self-acceptance and sense of personal worth
In	Independence	high sense of personal independence, not easily influenced
Wb	Sense of Well-being	not worrying or complaining, free from self-doubt
Em	Empathy	good capacity to empathize with other persons
Re	Responsibility	conscientious, responsible, and dependable
So	Socialization	strong social maturity and high integrity
Sc	Self-Control	good self-control, freedom from impulsivity and self-centeredness
To	Tolerance	permissive, accepting, and nonjudgmental social beliefs
Gi	Good Impression	concerned about creating a good impression
Cm	Communality	valid and thoughtful response pattern
Ac	Achievement via Conformance	achieves well in settings where conformance is necessary
Ai	Achievement via Independence	achieves well in settings where independence is necessary
Ie	Intellectual Efficiency	high degree of personal and intellectual efficiency
Py	Psychological-Mindedness	interested in and responsive to the inner needs, motives, and experiences of others
Fx	Flexibility	flexible and adaptable in thought and social behavior
Fe	Femininity	high degree of feminine interests

Source: Based on Gough, H. G. (1987). *California Psychological Inventory manual.* Palo Alto, CA: Consulting Psychologists Press. Also, Megargee, E. (1972). *The California Psychological Inventory handbook.* San Francisco: Jossey-Bass.

two advantages over the MMPI-2. First, it is much shorter (175 true-false items) and therefore more palatable to clinical referrals; second, it is planned and organized to identify clinical patterns in a manner that is compatible with the *Diagnostic and Statistical Manual (DSM-IV)* of the American Psychiatric Association.

The MCMI-III is a highly theory-driven test, incorporating Millon's elaborate theoretical formulations on the nature of psychopathology and personality disorder (Millon, 1969, 1981, 1986; Millon & Davis, 1996). The test includes 27 scales, listed in Table 14.7. The first 11 scales measure personality styles or traits such as narcissism and antisocial tendencies; the next three assess more severe personality pathology (schizotypal, borderline, and paranoid disorders); the following seven scales as-

sess clinical syndromes such as anxiety and depression; the next three scales assess severe clinical syndromes such as thought disorder; the last three scales are validity (response style) indices. Scores on these scales (Disclosure, Desirability, and Debasement) are used to adjust the other scale scores upward or downward, based on defensiveness or exaggeration of symptoms, respectively.

Scale development for the MCMI-III and its precursors was careful and methodical. We can only portray the broad outline here, in which 3,500 initial items were culled to 175 statements in three stages of test development: a theoretical-substantive stage (theory-guided item writing), an internal-structural stage (item-scale correlations), and an external-criterion stage (contrast of diagnostic groups with the reference group). A special feature

TABLE 14.7 Scales of the Millon Clinical Multiaxial Inventory-III

Clinical Personality Patterns		Clinical Syndromes	
1	Schizoid	A	Anxiety
2A	Avoidant	H	Somatoform
2B	Depressive	N	Bipolar: Manic
3	Dependent	D	Dysthymia
4	Histrionic	B	Alcohol Dependence
5	Narcissistic	R	Post-Traumatic Stress Disorder
6A	Antisocial		
6B	Aggressive (Sadistic)	**Severe Syndromes**	
7	Compulsive	SS	Thought Disorder
8A	Passive-Aggressive (Negativistic)	CC	Major Depression
8B	Self-Defeating	PP	Delusional Disorder
Severe Personality Pathology		**Validity (Modifying) Indices**	
S	Schizotypal	X	Disclosure
C	Borderline	Y	Desirability
P	Paranoid	Z	Debasement

of the last stage was Millon's use of general psychiatric patients instead of normal controls as the reference group. The purpose of this strategy was to enhance the capacity of MCMI scales to differentiate specific diagnostic groups from one another. Unfortunately, one side effect of this particular criterion-keyed approach was a rather substantial degree of item overlap for the clinical scales. Millon planned for and expected the item overlap, but probably did not anticipate that some pairs of scales on the MCMI would share the majority of their items in common. Some of this overlap was eliminated with the further refinement of the test for the second and third editions. The revised instrument also incorporates an item-weighting procedure. In this approach, individual questions are weighted 2 or 1 to reflect their importance in discriminating the prototype for each scale. The item-weighting approach has been criticized as unnecessary and unwieldy (Streiner, Goldberg, & Miller, 1993).

The normative sample for the MCMI-III consisted of about a thousand men and women patients from across the United States. This is an unusual and controversial approach to the collection of a normative sample. More typically, population proportion-ate sampling of reasonably normal individuals is used. Millon offers the arguable justification that a patient sample is adequate for the normative sample because the base rates (in the general population) for specific personality and clinical disorders were consulted to calibrate the cutting points on the individual scales (Millon & Davis, 1996). But this approach is complex, experimental, and difficult to understand. The reliability of the individual scales is good: Internal consistency coefficients average .82 to .90, and test-retest coefficients for one week range from .81 to .87. Support for the validity of the MCMI-III is mixed (Haladyna, 1992; Piersma & Boes, 1997).

The MCMI-III is unlikely to replace the MMPI-2, which is better suited to the diagnosis of acute clinical syndromes. However, the MCMI-III shows promise in the diagnosis of personality disorders and therefore can supplement the MMPI-2 in this capacity (Antoni, 1993). Nonetheless, several recent independent studies have called into question the value of the MCMI-III and especially its precursors in determining diagnoses within the framework of the Diagnostic and Statistical Manual of Mental Disorders (Smith, Carroll, & Fuller, 1988; Patrick, 1988; McCann & Suess, 1988).

Also, Choca, Shanley, Peterson, and Van Denburg (1990) found evidence of racial bias against African Americans on the MCMI. Reynolds (1992) captures what must be the shared opinion of many clinicians when he describes the MCMI as "a conceptual gem and psychometrically somewhere between a nightmare and an enigma." For other reviews, see Dana and Cantrell (1988) and Overholser (1990). Craig (1993) has assembled a series of articles that are largely supportive of the MCMI.

Personality Inventory for Children (PIC)

Using the general methodological approach embodied in the MMPI, the PIC was designed to provide clinically relevant descriptions of child behavior and family characteristics (Lachar, 1982; Wirt & Lachar, 1981; Wirt, Lachar, Klinedinst, & Seat, 1984). The PIC is applicable to children and adolescents ages 3 through 16 years. In its original form, the instrument consisted of 600 true-false statements which a parent or caregiver completes. The questions resemble the following:

> My child finds it difficult to fall asleep.
> My child is a finicky eater.
> My child has threatened to kill himself (herself).
> Sometimes my child swears at other adults.
> Our marriage has been full of turmoil.

The test is also available in three shorter versions (131, 280, or 420 items). The four versions of the test differ in the number of scales that can be scored. The full 600-item version yields four factor scales, four validity scales, 12 clinical scales, and 17 experimental scales. The 280-item and 420-item versions do not provide scores on the experimental scales, while the 131-item version, useful mainly for screening purposes, yields only four factor scores and a single validity index. We will limit our discussion to the 420-item version.

The scales of the PIC are listed in Table 14.8. As with the MMPI, scale raw scores are converted to T scores with a mean of 50 and standard deviation of 10. Higher T scores indicate increased probability of psychopathology or deficit. Norms for children ages 6 through 16 years are based on a

TABLE 14.8   Scales of the Personality Inventory for Children

Factor Scales
Undisciplined/Poor Self-Control
Social Incompetence
Internalization/Somatic Symptoms
Cognitive Development

Validity and Screening Scales
Lie
Frequency
Defensiveness
Adjustment

Clinical Scales
Achievement
Intellectual Screening
Development
Somatic Concern
Depression
Family Relations
Delinquency
Withdrawal
Anxiety
Psychosis
Hyperactivity
Social Skills

sample of 2,390 children and adolescents collected mainly in the Minneapolis school system. These subjects were from highly varied social class backgrounds and provide a reasonable basis for generalization of test results. Norms for preschool children ages 3 through 5 are much more limited (102 boys and 90 girls) and the test should be used with caution in this age range.

With the possible exception of the validity scales, the scale names are self-explanatory. The validity scales include Lie, a 15-item scale designed to identify parents/caregivers who are naively defensive about their child; Frequency, a 42-item scale designed to identify deliberate exaggeration about symptoms or random responding; Defensiveness, a 23-item scale used to identify defensiveness about the child's problems; and Adjustment, a 42-item scale which provides a general index of poor psychological adjustment.

Most of the PIC scales were constructed by means of a statistically sophisticated variant of the empirical criterion-keyed approach (Darlington, 1964; Darlington & Bishop, 1966). This iterative procedure adds prospective scale items according to their correlation with the relevant criterion (e.g., delinquency, psychosis, cerebral dysfunction) and also considers inter-item correlations in choosing the combination of items that yields the highest correlation between the scale score and the criterion. Eight of the profile scales were constructed in a purely rational method based on item nominations by experts. These scales were: Lie, Development, Somatic Concern, Depression, Family Relations, Withdrawal, Anxiety, and Social Skills.

The reliability of PIC scale scores is exceptionally good, with test-retest coefficients averaging in the high .80s for three different samples (Wirt, Lachar, Klinedinst, & Seat, 1984). A separate monograph by Lachar and Gdowski (1979) reports the confirmatory results of a comprehensive validity study used to establish descriptive interpretations for elevated PIC scale scores. The study correlated the PIC results of 431 child-guidance clients with criterion data provided by parents, teachers, and psychiatric residents. Based on these findings, a number of descriptive interpretations were confirmed for elevated PIC scores. The Lachar and Gdowski (1979) study was also the impetus for development of a computerized narrative report, available on a mail-in basis from the PIC publishers. An on-site microcomputer version of the program is available. This program administers, scores, and interprets the PIC. Seconds after the test is completed, the program prints an extensive summary of data and a lengthy narrative report.

Although the PIC has a history dating back to the 1950s (Wirt & Broen, 1958), the instrument did not attract the attention of empirically minded researchers until quite recently. As a consequence, validity research on the PIC is really still in its infancy. Nonetheless, contemporary findings are quite encouraging. For example, Keenan and Lachar (1988) proved the effectiveness of the PIC in identifying preschool children in need of special education services. Using a very simple decision rule (two or more scales elevated beyond $T = 70$), 91 percent of a mixed clinical and nonclinical sample of 120 children was correctly classified. The PIC is also highly effective in identifying elementary school children with special education needs (Kline, Lachar, & Boersma, 1993; Kline, Lachar, Gruber, & Boersma, 1994). Lachar, Kline, and Gdowski (1987) investigated the accuracy of PIC results as a function of maternal psychopathology. Contrary to commonsense expectations, mothers with clinically elevated MMPI profiles were just as accurate in depicting their children as mothers with normal MMPI profiles. One discouragement with the PIC is that a code type approach—so successful with the MMPI—has proved futile (Kline, Lachar, Gdowski, 1992). However, the PIC is still a useful instrument when interpreted on a scale-by-scale basis. For additional reviews, see Kline and Lachar (1992) and Rothermel and Lovell (1985).

SUMMARY

1. Theory-guided self-report inventories rely upon explicit personality theories for their development. A good example of a theory-guided inventory is the Edwards Personal Preference Schedule (EPPS), a 210-item forced-choice instrument that attempts to measure Murray's manifest needs by self-report.

2. Jackson's Personality Research Form (PRF) is also based upon Murray's need system. The 20 personality scales on the PRF possess no item overlap and show exceptional internal consistency (median of .92). PRF validity is buttressed by confirmatory factor analysis and appropriate correlations with similar scales on other instruments.

3. The Myers-Briggs Type Indicator (MBTI) is a forced-choice self-report inventory based loosely upon Carl Jung's theory of personality types. The MBTI is scored for four dimensions: Extraversion-Introversion, Sensing-iNtuition, Thinking-Feeling, and Judging-Perceptive, yielding 16 different types, such as ENFP.

4. The Jenkins Activity Survey (JAS) is a 52-item multiple-choice questionnaire designed to identify the Type A coronary-prone behavior pattern. The three subscales include: Speed and Impatient, Job Involvement, and Hard-Driving and Competitive. The JAS has several limitations (e.g., unrepresentative norms, scoring complexities) and is therefore best suited to research.

5. A short, simple test that has received high marks for technical merit is the State-Trait Anxiety Inventory (STAI). The 40 items of the STAI are each rated on a four-point intensity scale. The STAI measures state anxiety, or transitory feelings of fear or worry; and trait anxiety, the relatively stable tendency to respond anxiously to stressful situations.

6. Cattell's Sixteen Personality Factor Questionnaire (16PF) is typical of factor-analytically derived instruments. The five forms of the 16PF (for different age groups) all encompass a forced-choice format. The 16 surveyed personality attributes (and four higher-order dimensions) have been repeatedly confirmed by factor analysis.

7. The Eysenck Personality Questionnaire (EPQ) proposes three major factor-analytically derived dimensions of personality: Psychoticism, Extraversion, and Neuroticism. Scale reliabilities are quite strong and the construct validity of the instrument is supported by dozens of studies.

8. The Comrey Personality Scales embody a short self-report instrument suitable for college students. The eight CPS scales consist of 20 items each and possess no overlap. The scales show excellent internal consistency. Extreme scores are especially predictive of psychological disturbance.

9. The NEO Personality Inventory-Revised (NEO PI-R) is based upon the five-factor model of personality described earlier. The five constructs measured by the test are Neuroticism, Extraversion, Openness to Experience, Agreeableness, and Conscientiousness. The NEO PI-R is available in two parallel forms consisting of 240 items rated on a five-point dimension.

10. The MMPI-2 consists of 567 true-false questions. The test is scored for four validity scales (?, L, F, and K) which assess unanswered questions, naive defensiveness, deviant responses, and subtle defensiveness, respectively. The 10 clinical scales are Hypochondriasis, Depression, Hysteria, Psychopathic Deviate, Masculinity-Femininity, Paranoia, Psychasthenia, Schizophrenia, Hypomania, and Social Introversion.

11. The California Psychological Inventory (CPI) is an MMPI-like instrument designed to measure the dimensions of normal personality. Three scales measure test-taking attitudes (e.g., "fake good" and "fake bad" tendencies). The 17 clinical scales are based upon "folk" concepts of personality easily recognized by laypersons.

12. The Millon Clinical Multiaxial Inventory, now in its third edition (MCMI-III) is a short test (175 true-false items) designed as an aid to psychiatric diagnosis. The 27 scales are organized into four broad categories relevant to DSM-IV: clinical personality patterns, severe personality pathology, clinical syndromes, and severe clinical syndromes.

13. The Personality Inventory for Children (PIC) was designed to provide clinically relevant descriptions of child behavior and family characteristics. The most common form consists of 420 items concerning the child and family which the parent or caretaker fills out. Four scales provide validity and screening data. Most of the 12 clinical scales were derived by the criterion-keyed approach.

KEY TERMS AND CONCEPTS

social desirability response set   p. 515

ipsative test   p. 517

state anxiety   p. 520

trait anxiety   p. 520

extraversion   p. 524

introversion   p. 524

In this topic the reader will encounter a variety of straightforward, innovative, and occasionally nontraditional approaches to personality evaluation collectively known as behavioral assessment. **Behavioral assessment** concentrates on behavior itself rather than on underlying traits, hypothetical causes, or presumed dimensions of personality. The many methods of behavioral assessment offer a practical alternative to projective tests, self-report inventories, and other unwieldy techniques aimed at global personality assessment.

Typically, behavioral assessment is designed to meet the needs of therapists and their clients in a quick and uncomplicated manner. But behavioral assessment differs from traditional assessment in more than its simplicity. The basic assumptions, practical aspects, and essential goals of behavioral and traditional approaches are as different as night and day. Traditional assessment strategies tend to be complex, indirect, psychodynamic, and often extraneous to treatment. In contrast, behavioral assessment strategies tend to be simple, direct, behavior-analytic, and continuous with treatment.

Behavior therapists use a wide range of modalities to evaluate their clients, patients, and subjects. The methods of behavioral assessment include, but are not limited to, behavioral observations, self-reports, parent ratings, staff ratings, sibling ratings, judges' ratings, teacher ratings, therapist ratings, nurses' ratings, physiological assessment, biochem-

ical assessment, biological assessment, structured interviews, semistructured interviews, and analogue tests. In their *Dictionary of Behavioral Assessment Techniques,* Hersen and Bellack (1988) list 286 behavioral tests used in widely diverse problems and disorders in children, adolescents, adults, and the geriatric population. Dozens more are referenced in a more recent compendium (Hersen & Bellack, 1998). So that the reader can appreciate the diversity of techniques available, we provide a sampling of these tests in Table 14.9.

Behavioral assessment is often—but not always—an integral part of **behavior therapy** designed to change the duration, frequency, or intensity of a well-defined target behavior. For example, one therapy goal for a shy college student might be that she initiate a minimum of five conversations lasting two minutes or more each day. The therapist might recommend that she approach this goal incrementally, beginning with a few brief social exchanges before proceeding to lengthier conversations with strangers. In this example, behavioral assessment might take the form of self-monitoring in which the student uses a wristwatch for timing and a diary for keeping track of conversations.

As noted, behavioral assessment often exists in service of behavior therapy. In many cases, the nature of behavioral assessment is dictated by the procedures and goals of behavior therapy. For this

TABLE 14.9   A Sampling of Behavioral Assessment Tests and Techniques

Abnormal Involuntary Movement Scale	Expired Air Carbon Monoxide Measurement
Activities of Daily Living-Modular Assessment	Family Interaction Coding System
Agoraphobic Cognitions Questionnaire	Fire Emergency Behavioral Situations Scale
Alcohol Beliefs Scale	Georgia Court Competency Test-Revised
Antidepressive Activity Questionnaire	Goal Attainment Scaling
Assertion Situations	Height Avoidance Test
Assertiveness Self-Statement Test	Irrational Beliefs Inventory
Automated Matching Familiar Figures Test	Leyton Obsessional Inventory
Behavior Profile Rating Scale	McGill Pain Questionnaire
Behavioral Assessment of Bruxism	Michigan Alcohol Screening Test
Behavioral Avoidance Slide Test	Musical Performance Anxiety Self-Statement Scale
Behavioral Measures of Severe Depression	Panic Attack Questionnaire
Behavioral Visual Acuity Test	Parent-Adolescent Interaction Coding System
Binge Eating Questionnaire	Penile Volume Responses
Blood Alcohol Level	Rape Aftermath Symptom Test
Blood Pressure Reactivity	Self-Control Rating Scale
Body Sensations Questionnaire	Self-Statement Assessment via Thought Listing
Client Resistance Coding System	Sensation Seeking Scale-Form VI
Clinical Dementia Rating	Sexual Experience Scales
Combat Exposure Scale	Spouse Verbal Problem Checklist
Compulsive Activity Checklist	Standardized Walk
Conflict Behavior Questionnaire	Subjective Probability of Consequences Inventory
Daily Sleep Diary	Test Meals in the Assessment of Bulimia Nervosa
Derogatis Sexual Functioning Inventory	Treatment Evaluation Inventory
Dieter's Inventory of Eating Temptations	Type A Structured Interview
Dysfunctional Attitudes Scale	Visual Analogue Scale

Source: Based on entries in Hersen, M., and Bellack, A. S. (eds.) (1988). *Dictionary of behavioral assessment techniques.* New York: Pergamon.

reason, the reader will better appreciate behavioral assessment tools if we interweave this topic with a discussion of behavior therapy methods.

FOUNDATIONS OF BEHAVIOR THERAPY

Behavior therapy, also called behavior modification, is the application of the methods and findings of experimental psychology to the modification of maladaptive behavior (Plaud & Eifert, 1998). The roots of behavior therapy can be traced to Skinner's (1953) seminal book, *Science and Human Behavior,* which detailed the application of operant conditioning to the problems of human behavior. Skinner shunned any reference to private, nonobservable events such as thoughts or feelings; he emphasized the importance of identifying observable

behaviors and methodically altering the environmental consequences of those behaviors.

Research by Wolpe (1958) on the systematic behavioral treatment of phobias also was influential in founding the methods of behavior therapy. Wolpe's clinical procedures were derived from his laboratory work on the conditioning and counterconditioning of fear in cats. Like Skinner, Wolpe deemphasized the significance of thoughts and beliefs. He viewed fear as a learned phenomenon that could be unlearned by following a strict protocol of graduated exposure to the feared object or situation.

More recently, Bandura (1977), Mahoney and Arnkoff (1978), and Meichenbaum (1977) reintroduced cognitive factors into the ever changing behavioral framework. For example, Bandura (1977) demonstrated that persons are perfectly capable of cognitively based learning. In particular, he showed that individuals can learn from mere observation of the response contingencies experienced by models. Since this learning occurs in the absence of personal consequences, it must be cognitively mediated. As a consequence of this paradigm shift, practically all modern-day behavior therapists concern themselves—at least to some extent—with the thoughts and beliefs of their clients. This new emphasis is reflected in a family of very popular treatment procedures known collectively as cognitive behavior therapy (McMullin, 1986).

BEHAVIOR THERAPY AND BEHAVIORAL ASSESSMENT

At present, the specific techniques of behavior therapy can be classified into five overlapping categories (Johnston, 1986): exposure-based methods, contingency management procedures, cognitive behavior therapies, self-control procedures, and social skills training. Behavioral assessment is used in all of these approaches, as reviewed in the following sections. However, there are relatively few behaviorally based tools for the evaluation of social skills, so this category is not discussed. Readers who desire limited coverage of instruments for the behavioral evaluation of social skills training (including assertiveness) should consult Meier and Hope (1998).

Exposure-Based Methods

Exposure-based methods of behavioral therapy are well suited to the treatment of phobias, which include intense and unreasonable fears (e.g., of spiders, blood, public speaking). One approach to phobic avoidance is systematic exposure of the client to the feared situation or object. Wolpe (1973) favored gradual exposure with minimal anxiety in a procedure known as systematic desensitization. In this therapeutic approach, the client first learns total relaxation and then proceeds from imagined exposure to actual or in vivo exposure to the feared stimulus. Another exposure-based method is flooding or implosion in which the client is immediately and totally immersed in the anxiety-inducing situation.

The therapist needs some type of behavioral assessment to gauge the continuing progress of a client undergoing an exposure-based treatment for a phobia. In the simplest possible assessment approach, known as a **behavioral avoidance test** (BAT), the therapist measures how long the client can tolerate the anxiety-inducing stimulus. Here is one classic example of a standardized BAT used to evaluate patients with agoraphobia, a disabling fear of open spaces often accompanied by panic attacks:

> The standardized Behavioral Avoidance Test (BAT) was conducted a week after intake. All anxiolytics, antidepressants, or other psychotropic medication had been taken away at least 4 days before the test. The test was administered by the first author, who was blind to the patients' diagnoses [and] not involved in the treatment. The patients were asked to walk alone as far as they could from the hospital along a mildly trafficated road that was 2 km long. The route was divided into eight intervals of equal length, and the patients rated their anxiety level on a 0–10 scale at the end of each interval. Uncompleted intervals were given a score of 10. An avoidance-anxiety score was computed by summing the anxiety scores for all intervals (Hoffart, Friis, Strand, and Olsen, 1994).

The researchers discovered that the avoidance-anxiety score from the BAT technique was strongly related to self-reports of catastrophic thoughts (e.g., choking to death, having a heart attack, acting foolish, becoming helpless). This finding illustrates that behavioral assessment approaches often encompass a cognitive component as well. Notice, too, the direct relationship between the goal of therapy and the behavioral avoidance test. In agoraphobia, the primary treatment goal is to reduce patients' anxiety about walking alone in open spaces—which is exactly what the BAT measures.

The BAT approach is predicated on the reasonable assumption that the client's fear is the main determinant of behavior in the testing situation. Unfortunately, demand characteristics for desirable behavior may exert a strong influence on the client's behavior. The client's tolerance of the anxiety-inducing stimulus will bear some relationship to experienced fear, but also has much to do with the situational context of assessment (McGlynn &

Rose, 1998). The results of BAT assessments may not generalize, and the therapist must be wary of foreclosing treatment too soon.

A **fear survey schedule** is another type of behavioral assessment useful in the identification and quantification of fears. Fear survey schedules are face valid devices which require respondents to indicate the presence and intensity of their fears in relation to various stimuli, typically on a 5- or 7-point Likert scale. Dozens of these instruments have been published, including versions by Wolpe (1973), Ollendick (1983), and Cautela (1977). Tasto, Hickson, and Rubin (1971) used factor analysis to develop a 40-item survey that yields a profile of fear scores in five categories. A generic fear survey schedule is shown in Table 14.10. Fear survey schedules are often used in research projects to screen large samples of persons in search of subjects who share a common fear. Another use of these schedules is to monitor changes in fears, including those that have been targeted for clinical intervention.

Klieger and Franklin (1993) have raised a number of cautions about the use of fear survey schedules in clinical research. These authors note that reliability data for fear surveys are almost nonexistent. A more serious problem has to do with the validity of these instruments. Using the Wolpe and Lang (1977) Fear Survey Schedule-III (FSS-III), a highly respected and widely used schedule, Klieger and Franklin (1993) found no relationship between reported fears on the FSS-III and BAT measures of the same fears. For example, subjects who reported a high fear of blood on the FSS-III were just as likely to approach a bloody white towel and touch it as were subjects who reported no fear of blood. Similar results were found for subjects who feared snakes, spiders, and fire. The researchers concluded that the FSS-III and similar instruments are a poor choice for identifying experimental groups and a poor basis for measuring the outcome of therapeutic interventions. The essential downfall seems to be that fear survey schedules possess such "obvious" validity that few researchers have bothered to evaluate the traditional psychometric characteristics of reliability and validity. Fear survey schedules should be used with caution.

Contingency Management Procedures

Contingency management is predicated on the assumption that all behavior—including disturbed or

---

TABLE 14.10 Example of a Fear Survey Schedule

Please check the column that best describes your current response to these situations or objects.

	Degree to which you would be disturbed				
	Not at All	Just a Little	Moderate Amount	Very Much	Extremely Bothered
Being in a strange place					
Speaking in public					
Walking into a party					
Getting an injection					
People watching me work					
Large open spaces					
Being fat					
Spider on the wall					
Cat in the room					
Reprimand from the boss					

Note: Most fear survey schedules consist of several dozen items.

maladaptive behavior—is maintained by its consequences. A contingency management approach to behavior change proceeds in two steps. In step one, the therapist attempts to identify the positively reinforcing consequences of the unwanted behavior. For example, in the case of an agoraphobic housewife, the therapist might determine that she receives attention from her family mainly when she is panicky and housebound. In this instance, the maladaptive behavior of housebound panic is being maintained—at least in part—by the untimely solicitousness of family members. Step two consists of changing the contingencies for the unwanted behavior. The therapist might recommend that family members not attend to the housewife during her panicky episodes and that they do reinforce her small steps toward independence. For example, if the housewife walks to the mailbox and back, the family members should shower her with attention.

One form of contingency management widely used in institutional settings is the token economy. This approach is particularly well suited to clients with limited behavioral repertoires. In a **token economy,** many different forms of prosocial behavior are rewarded with tokens which can be later exchanged for material rewards or privileges (Kazdin, 1988).

Behavioral assessment in a token economy mainly takes the form of direct behavioral observation (Foster, Bell-Dolan, & Burge, 1988). The application of a direct behavioral observation system is much more demanding than it sounds. The researcher or therapist must identify target behaviors, define them precisely, produce a system for data recording, calibrate appropriate rewards, and train staff members (Paul, 1986). If the program works, the observed frequency of targeted prosocial behaviors will increase gradually over a period of weeks or months.

Token economies were enormously popular in the 1970s when they were even used by entire school systems to facilitate the improvement of social skills in disadvantaged elementary school children (Bushell, 1978). Token economies are still popular, but the initial uncritical enthusiasm has been replaced by a less sanguine view. Kazdin (1988) discusses the limitations of token economies

which include (1) poor generalization of the target behaviors beyond the treatment program, (2) difficulties in training staff to properly implement token economies, and (3) client resistance to participation. In addition, reactivity can be a problem in direct behavioral observation: Clients may not behave naturally when they know they are being observed.

Cognitive Behavior Therapies

The one factor common to all cognitive behavior therapies is an emphasis on changing the belief structure of the client. The three best-known variants of **cognitive behavior therapy** are Ellis's (1962) rational emotive therapy (RET), Meichenbaum's (1977) self-instructional training, and Beck's (1976) cognitive therapy. Ellis postulates that most disturbed behavior is caused by irrational beliefs, such as the widespread belief that one must have the love and approval of all significant persons at all times. Ellis attempts to alter such core irrational beliefs, primarily by logical argument and forceful exhortation. Meichenbaum's self-instructional technique consists of teaching the client to use coping self-statements to combat stressful situations. For example, a college student suffering from intense test-taking anxiety might be taught to use the following self-talk during examinations: "You have a strategy this time. . . . Take a deep breath and relax. . . . Just answer one question at a time. . . ." Beck's cognitive therapy concentrates mainly on the role of cognitive distortions in the maintenance of depression and other emotional disturbances. Beck (1983) regards depression as primarily a cognitive disorder characterized by the negative cognitive triad: a pessimistic view of the world, a pessimistic self-concept, and a pessimistic view of the future. In therapy, he uses a gentle form of cognitive restructuring to help the client perceive his or her problems in alternative, solvable terms.

Cognitive behavior therapists need not use formal assessment tools in their clinical practice. Typically, these therapists monitor the belief structure of their clients on an informal session-to-session basis. Irrational and distorted thoughts are challenged as they arise during therapy. In the end, the client's self-report of improvement may constitute the main index of therapeutic success. Nonetheless, several straightforward measures of cognitive distortion are available. We have outlined a few prominent instruments in Table 14.11. Other examples can be found in Clark (1988) and Haynes (1998). These instruments are mainly research questionnaires suitable to the testing of group differences, but not sufficiently validated for individual assessment. Clark (1988) faults the developers of cognitive distortion questionnaires for premature release of their instruments. In particular, he notes the absence of research on the concurrent and discriminant validity of most self-statement measures. Another problem is that existing questionnaires were designed to validate constructs in research and consequently do not work well in clinical practice.

An exceptional and well-validated measure not listed in Table 14.11 is the Beck Depression Inventory (BDI). The BDI is a short, simple, self-report questionnaire that focuses, in part, on the cognitive distortions that underlie depression (Beck & Steer, 1987; Beck, Ward, Mendelsohn, Mock, & Erbaugh, 1961). One reason for its popularity is that most patients can complete the 21 items on the BDI in 10 minutes or less. The test has been widely used: More than 1,900 articles using the BDI have been published (Conoley, 1992). A second edition of the inventory was released in 1996 (Beck, Steer, & Brown, 1996). On the BDI-II, several items were revised so as to bring the inventory into closer conformity with prevailing diagnostic criteria for depression. The 21 items are of the following form:

Check the statement from this group that you feel is most true about you:

0 I am upbeat about the future
1 I feel slightly discouraged about the future
2 I feel the future has little to offer for me
3 I feel that the future is utterly hopeless

Thirteen items cover cognitive and affective components of depression such as pessimism, guilt, crying, indecision, and self-accusations; eight items assess somatic and performance variables such as sleep problems, body image, work difficulties, and loss of interest in sex. The examinee re-ceives a score of 0 to 3 for each item; the total raw score is the sum of the endorsements for the 21 items; the highest possible score is 63.

In a meta-analysis of BDI research studies, the internal consistency of the scale (coefficient alpha) ranged from .73 to .95, with a mean of .86 in nine psychiatric populations (Beck, Steer, & Garbin, 1988). The BDI-II possesses excellent internal consistency with a coefficient alpha of .92 (Beck, Steer, & Brown, 1996). Test-retest reliability of the BDI is modest, with a range of .60 to .83 in nonpsychiatric samples and .48 to .86 in psychiatric samples. However, the test-retest methodology is not well suited to phenomena such as depression which are naturally unstable. Subjective depression fluctuates dramatically from week to week, day to day, even hour to hour. A lackluster value for test-retest reliability might signify valid change in the construct being measured rather than unwanted measurement error.

A variety of normative results are available, with BDI data for samples of patients with major depression, dysthymia, alcoholism, heroin addiction, and mixed problems. The manual also provides guidelines for degree of depression based upon BDI score (0 to 9, normal; 10 to 19, mild to moderate; 20 to 29 moderate to severe; 30 and above, extremely severe). These ratings are based upon clinical evaluations of patients.

The BDI has been extensively validated against other measures of depression and independent criteria of depression. For example, correlations with clinical ratings and scales of depression such as from the MMPI are typically in the range of .60 to .76 (Conoley, 1992). Sex differences are minimal, although there may be slight differences in the expression of depression between men and women (Steer, Beck, & Brown, 1989).

The only shortcoming of the BDI is its transparency. Patients who wish to hide their despair or exaggerate their depression can do so easily. However, for patients who are motivated to accurately reflect their emotional status, the BDI and BDI-II are probably unbeatable as an index of the presence and degree of depression (Stehouwer, 1987). Some practitioners ask patients to complete the BDI after

TABLE 14.11 Questionnaire Measures of Cognitive Distortion

Anxious Self-Statements Questionnaire (ASSQ)
Kendall and Hollon (1989)

Examinee rates how often specific anxious thoughts occurred over the last week. Items are of the form:

> I can't stand it anymore.
> What's going to happen to me now?
> I'm not going to make it.

A psychometrically sound instrument, the ASSQ can be used to assess changes in the frequency of anxious self-talk.

Automatic Thoughts Questionnaire (ATQ)
Hollon and Kendall (1980); Kazdin (1990)

The ATQ is a frequency measure of depression-related cognitions that assesses personal maladjustment, negative self-concept and expectations, low self-esteem, and giving up/helplessness. The 30-item ATQ correlates very well with the MMPI Depression scale and the Beck Depression Inventory (Ross, Gottfredson, Christensen, & Weaver, 1986).

Cognitive Errors Questionnaire (CEQ)
Lefebvre (1981)

The CEQ assesses the degree of maladaptive thinking in general situations and also situations related to chronic low back pain. Discrete vignettes concerning chronic back pain and general scenes are each followed by an illogical dysphoric cognition. The respondent indicates on a 5-point scale how similar the cognition is to the thought he or she would have in the same situation. For example: "You just finished spending three hours cleaning the basement. Your spouse, however, doesn't say anything about it. You think to yourself, 'S(he) must think I did a poor job.' " Smith, Follick, Ahern, and Adams (1986) found that overgeneralization was the specific CEQ cognitive error most consistently correlated with chronic low back pain disability.

Attribution Styles Questionnaire (ASQ)
Seligman, Abramson, Semmel, and Von Baeyer (1979)

The ASQ measures three attributional dimensions relevant to Seligman's learned helplessness model of depression: internal-external, stable-unstable, and global-specific. Depressed persons attribute bad outcomes to internal, stable, and global causes; they attribute good outcomes to external, unstable causes. The questionnaire consists of 12 hypothetical situations, 6 describing good outcomes, 6 describing bad outcomes (e.g., "You have been looking for a job unsuccessfully for some time"). The respondents rate each vignette on a 7-point scale for degree of internality, stability, and globality.

Hopelessness Scale (HS)
Beck (1987), Dyce (1996)

A 20-item true/false scale, the HS is designed to quantify hopelessness, one component of the negative cognitive triad found in depressed persons. (The triad consists of negative views of self, world, and future.) The scale is sensitive to changes in the patient's state of depression. In a validational study, Beck, Riskind, Brown, and Steer (1988) found that HS scores had a negligible relationship to anxiety or general psychopathology when the influence of coexisting depression was partialed out. Thus, the HS appears to measure a specific attribute of depression rather than general psychopathology.

each therapy session; they use the BDI much as a physician might use a thermometer.

Self-Monitoring Procedures

A common misconception about behavior therapy is that it consists of authoritarian therapists applying powerful rewards and punishments to passive clients. Although this stereotypical model may be true for some impaired clients with limited behavioral repertoires, for the most part behavior therapy consists of humane practitioners teaching their clients methods of self-control. An emphasis upon self-monitoring is fundamental to all forms of behavior therapy. In **self-monitoring,** the client chooses the goals and actively participates in supervising, charting, and recording progress toward the endpoint(s) of therapy. According to this model, the therapist is relegated to the status of expert consultant.

Self-monitoring procedures are especially useful in the treatment of depression, a prevalent behavior disorder consisting of sad mood, low activity level, feelings of worthlessness, concentration problems, and physical symptoms (sleep loss, appetite disturbance, reduced interest in sex). Several self-monitoring programs for depression have been reported (Lewinsohn & Talkington, 1979; Rehm, 1984; Rehm, Kornblith, O'Hara, and others, 1981). In order to illustrate the self-monitoring approach to the control of depression, we will summarize one small corner of the program advocated by Lewinsohn and his colleagues (Lewinsohn, Munoz, Youngren, & Zeiss, 1986).

Lewinsohn observed that depression goes hand in hand with a marked reduction in the experiencing of pleasant events. Depressed persons retreat from engaging in pleasant activities; the behavioral withdrawal only contributes further to their depression, inciting a continuous downward spiral. Fortunately, it is possible to replace the downward spiral with an upward one. To help reverse the downward spiral of depression, Lewinsohn and his colleagues devised the Pleasant Events Schedule (PES, MacPhillamy & Lewinsohn, 1982). The purpose of the PES is twofold. First, in the baseline assessment phase, the PES is used to self-monitor the frequency (F) and pleasantness (P) of 320 largely ordinary, everyday events. Examples of the kinds of events listed on the PES include the following:

> reading magazines
> going for a walk
> being with pets
> playing a musical instrument
> making food for charity
> listening to the radio
> reading poetry
> attending a church service
> watching a sports event
> playing catch with a friend
> working on my job

The frequency and pleasantness of these everyday events are both rated 0 to 2.[1] The mean rate of pleasant activities is then calculated from the sum of the $F \times P$ scores, that is, mean rate = $F \times P/320$. Normative findings for mean F, mean P, and mean $F \times P$ are reported in Lewinsohn, Munoz, Youngren, and Zeiss (1986) and serve as a basis for treatment planning. Participants in the Lewinsohn program also monitor their daily mood on a simple 1 (worst) to 9 (best) basis.

The second use of the PES is to self-monitor therapeutic progress. Based on the initial PES results, clients identify 100 or so potentially pleasant events and strive to increase the frequency of these events, monitoring daily mood along the way. Clients who increase the frequency of pleasant events generally show an improvement in mood and other depressive symptoms.

---

1. The Frequency Scale is calibrated as follows:

0—This has *not* happened in the past 30 days.
1—This has happened a *few times* (1 to 6 times) in the past 30 days.
2—This has happened *often* (7 times or more) in the past 30 days.

The Pleasantness Scale is calibrated as follows:

0—This was *not* pleasant.
1—This was *somewhat* pleasant.
2—This was *very* pleasant.

The PES is a highly useful tool for clinicians who wish to implement a self-monitoring approach to the assessment and treatment of depression. MacPhillamy and Lewinsohn (1982) report favorably on the technical qualities of the PES and discuss a variety of rational, factorial, and empirical subscales which we cannot review here. The instrument has fair to good test-retest reliability (one-month correlations in the range of .69 to .86), excellent concurrent validity with trained observers, and promising construct validity. In general, the subscales behave as one would predict on the basis of the constructs they purport to measure—we refer the reader to MacPhillamy and Lewinsohn (1982) for details.

Self-monitoring approaches to behavioral assessment have applications in many subspecialties of psychology and the health professions. We will briefly outline one other assessment device to illustrate the diversity of methods available. Schlundt and Bell (1993) developed a microcomputer-based Body Image Testing System (BITS) to assess body image in persons with eating disorders. The eating disorder known as anorexia nervosa is characterized by refusal to maintain normal body weight, an intense fear of gaining weight, and a significant disturbance in the perception of the shape or size of the body. The majority of patients with anorexia nervosa are young females—the average age of onset is 17 years. A person with this disorder perceives her body to be much fatter than is actually true. But how can this misperception be measured and quantified? The BITS program is one approach to self-monitoring of distortions in body image. Briefly, the subject uses a menu to change a computer-generated body image until it resembles her self-perception.

Instructions for the BITS program specify that the subject is to adjust the individual body parts until the image resembles her actual body dimensions. In a second trial, the subject generates ideal body dimensions. The discrepancy between actual and ideal dimensions represents the subject's degree of satisfaction with her body. In addition, the BITS program yields an index of perceptual distortion based upon a regression analysis of height and weight versus the self-generated (actual) body image.

Using data from 94 undergraduate females retested again after two to four weeks, BITS measures were found to have acceptable reliability. For example, the overall satisfaction rating for the nine body parts showed a test-retest reliability of .80. Normative data for 528 subjects drawn mainly from undergraduate samples are also available. The construct validity of the procedure was found to be very promising, based upon three sources of information: strong correlations between BITS scores and actual body size, strong correlations between BITS variables and other measures of body image, and the ability of the measure to predict disturbances in eating behavior such as dieting, binge eating, and emotional eating.

The BITS procedure is an excellent example of a new generation of psychological tests made possible by recent developments in microcomputer technology. Tests that make creative use of computer graphics for stimulus and/or response display will become commonplace in the future. Additional approaches to computer-assisted psychological assessment are discussed in Topic 15A.

ASSESSMENT OF NONVERBAL BEHAVIOR

Nonverbal behavior includes the subtler forms of human communication contained in glance, gesture, body language, tone of voice, and facial expression. Although nonverbal communication plays a crucial role in human behavior, our knowledge of it is very incomplete. In part, this ignorance reflects the strong verbal orientation of our society; we equate communication with the successful use of words. But there are other, more subtle reasons for the lack of scientific knowledge about nonverbal communication:

> Different types of nonverbal communication are so embedded in our daily lives that we use the nonverbal messages without being aware of them. When we form an opinion of what someone is like, for example, the opinion is probably based in part upon a complex analysis of nonverbal information. When

we conclude that someone we have just met is angry or jealous or anxious to leave, we may have reached this conclusion as much by listening to the person's tone of voice and by observing how agitated the person's movements were, or by forming an impression of the warmth of his or her facial expression, as by interpreting what was actually said (Rosenthal, Hall, DiMatteo, Rogers, & Archer, 1979).

In this section we will investigate the scientific study of nonverbal communication, focusing on tools and methods that can be used for purposes of assessment. We begin by reviewing methods for discerning the nature of underlying personality from such external behavioral signs as visual interaction, paralinguistic cues (e.g., tone of voice), and facial expression. The chapter closes with an analysis of the Profile of Nonverbal Sensitivity (PONS), a fascinating film or video test for assessing personal sensitivity to the nonverbal communication of others.

Visual Interaction

Visual interaction has long been recognized as a key to other aspects of personality, although it is only in the last few decades that systematic research on this topic has appeared. Nielsen (1962) carried out the first empirical investigation of gaze in social behavior. His study was a purely observational analysis of social confrontation and visual interaction. Shortly thereafter, other researchers embarked on programmatic studies, using standard experimental designs, with visual contact as the dependent variable, and later as the independent variable (summarized in Argyle & Cook, 1976; Fehr & Exline, 1987; Exline & Fehr, 1982). In large measure, this research has sought to determine the implications of individual differences in such variables as initiation of, maintenance of, and comfort with individual and mutual eye contact. A few fragile generalizations have emerged from this research, which we summarize below. More noteworthy, however, is a dawning consensus as to the difficulty of obtaining meaningful measurements about visual interaction. Let us briefly review the findings and then summarize the obstacles to serviceable research on this important topic.

Visual interaction is best viewed as a social behavior that acts as a powerful signal from one person to another. The meaning of the signal is determined in many complex ways, so the interpretation of another person's gaze pattern is very difficult. Nonetheless, several consistent findings do emerge from research on this topic (Argyle & Cook, 1976; Fehr & Exline, 1987):

1. Gaze often acts as a signal for liking, especially from dependent persons.
2. Mutual gaze, especially if prolonged, may signify a special kind of intimacy.
3. Extraverts and self-confident persons establish visual contact more often and for longer periods of time.
4. Aversion of gaze increases when persons are close together or discussing intimate topics.
5. Dishonest persons reduce visual interaction during episodes of deception.
6. Females look more often, even in infancy.
7. The amount of gaze is high during childhood, falls during adolescence, and then rises again.
8. Affiliative persons gaze more in cooperative situations, but less in competitive situations.
9. Lower-status persons gaze more than higher-status persons.
10. Marked cultural differences exist; Arabs and Latin Americans gaze more, certain American Indians gaze less.
11. Autistic, schizophrenic, and depressive persons tend to avoid looking at other persons.

It should be obvious from the preceding list that the interpretation of gaze depends on numerous variables and is also influenced by the interaction between variables (e.g., affiliation and competition).

The practitioner who wishes to interpret individual differences in visual interaction must first implement a data-gathering paradigm of some sort. Exline and Fehr (1982) have drawn attention to the difficulties involved in the assessment of gaze and mutual gaze. These difficulties include the reactivity of measurements made in laboratory settings and problems of reliability of measurements. The pragmatic problems of assessing and interpreting visual interaction are substantial. In fact, the obstacles most likely preclude the development of standardized tests for the measurement of gaze and mutual gaze. Nonetheless, knowledge of the findings in this area can be used in conjunction with other nonverbal cues in practical clinical applications such as the detection of deception (Ekman & Friesen, 1975).

Paralinguistics

Paralinguistics refers to tone of voice, rate of speaking, and other nonverbal aspects of speech. Often, paralinguistic cues are more powerful than the overt spoken message, as when we declare "It wasn't what he said; it was the way he said it." An essential maxim of paralinguistic research is that the content of speech must be separated from its affective nuances.

An important area for paralinguistic assessment has been emotion judged from "content-filtered" speech. In content-filtered speech, a person's voice is recorded (or a tape is rerecorded) through a low-pass filter to remove high-frequency sounds and thereby render the words themselves unrecognizable. Content-filtered speech maintains the essential paralinguistic aspects of speech (pitch variation and contour, tempo, volume, tonality, and rhythm) but eliminates the potential distraction of the content. Trained judges can then rate the content-filtered speech for affective components such as anger or anxiety.

Milmoe, Rosenthal, Blane, Chafetz, and Wolf (1967) conducted a pathbreaking study that illustrates the practical application of content-filtered speech. They recorded the voices of resident physicians who had completed a tour of duty in an alcoholism clinic. In particular, the researchers excerpted the doctors' replies to the interview question, "What has been your experience with alcoholics?" These replies were content-filtered, and then rated along a six-point scale (1 = none, 6 = a lot) by a panel of judges for anger, sympathy, anxiety, and matter-of-factness.[2] The interrater relia-

bility of the emotional dimensions varied quite markedly and was also affected by the sex of the judge. For example, the agreement between male and female judges was good for anxiety ($r = .84$) but nonexistent for matter-of-factness ($r = -.07$).

The researchers also collected post hoc information on the doctors' success in getting alcoholic patients to seek treatment. The paralinguistic data (ratings of anger, sympathy, anxiety, and matter-of-factness) were then correlated with objective data on referral effectiveness. The relationship between judges' ratings of anger for the content-filtered speech correlated strongly with effectiveness in referring alcoholic patients ($r = -.67, p = .06$). Other variables were unrelated to effectiveness. In sum, doctors with high paralinguistic ratings for anger were ineffective in convincing alcoholic patients to seek treatment. The same research team has shown that ratings of the mother's voice (content-filtered) are correlated with aspects of baby's behavior as such as irritability, insecurity, and attentiveness (Milmoe, Novey, Kagan, & Rosenthal, 1974).

Facial Expression

Nonverbal communication is often mediated through facial expression. Indeed, the facial-expressive apparatus is in large measure dedicated to facial displays of emotion. Additionally, the face helps regulate several nonemotional functions such as speech production, eating, respiration, smell, and protection of the eyes.

The crucial role of the face in communication via the display of emotions has prompted researchers to develop objective methods for observing and quantifying facial action. Two major methods for this purpose have emerged: (1) measurement of visible facial actions using facial coding systems, and (2) the measurement of electrical discharges from the contraction of facial muscles. Ekman (1982) and Fridlund, Ekman, and Oster (1987) review both developments in detail. We will highlight the best-known facial-coding system here.

The Facial Action Coding System (FACS; Ekman & Friesen, 1978) was developed as a general purpose evaluation tool suitable to a wide

---

2. Two other dimensions were rated from the *content* of the tapes: sophistication and psychological-mindedness. We do not discuss these findings here.

range of research and assessment purposes. Based upon an elaborate electrophysiological analysis of the precise role of each facial muscle in visible facial expression, Ekman and Friesen derived 44 action units (AUs) that can, singly or in combination, account for all visible facial movement. All of the AUs are scoreable on a five-point intensity scale. For example, AU 1 concerns brow raising, which is controlled by one large muscle in the forehead area. Ekman and Friesen (1978) provide detailed instructions for rating each AU from video recordings. FACS also allows for coding onset, apex, and offset time of each AU.

FACS is difficult to learn and use because it requires repeated, slow-motion viewing of facial actions. However, once the system is mastered, competent judges produce highly reliable ratings of facial actions. Furthermore, the ratings predict emotional states with considerable accuracy. In one important validity study, Ekman, Friesen, and Ancoli (1980) recorded the facial action of persons viewing both pleasant and unpleasant films. The FACS accurately predicted the subjects' retrospective reports of emotional experience (happiness, negative feelings, disgust). At least in some contexts, particular facial actions do signal particular emotions. What needs to be sorted out in future research is the generality of the link between coded facial actions from FACS and the experience of predicted emotions.

Profile of Nonverbal Sensitivity (PONS)

The PONS was developed in the 1970s by Robert Rosenthal and colleagues to study the ability to comprehend nonverbal cues transmitted by facial expressions, body movements, and tone of voice (Rosenthal, Hall, DiMatteo, Rogers, & Archer, 1979). One impetus for inventing this new assessment instrument was Rosenthal's earlier discovery of the experimenter expectancy effect (Rosenthal, 1967). Research on the experimenter expectancy effect showed that the experimenter can unintentionally influence subjects to change their behavior in the direction of the experimenter's expectations, thereby creating self-fulfilling prophecies in the research laboratory and the classroom. Rosenthal rea-

soned that the experimenter expectancy effect must be facilitated by the unwitting communication of nonverbal information from the experimenter to the subject. The PONS was developed, in part, to study the manner in which these nonverbal communications might be decoded.

The stimuli for the PONS are administered by means of film or videotape and consist of 220 two-second segments of one female's nonverbal behavior.[3] For each stimulus item, the examinee must choose which affective or emotional situation is being portrayed; two alternatives are listed on the answer sheet. For example, one visual item shows the portrayer's face for two seconds as she depicts an emotional scene. The test taker is asked to choose between two descriptions of what the person is doing: (a) nagging a child, or (b) expressing jealous anger. The audio has been "cut" for this item so the examinee must decode the information purely from facial expression. Since the portrayer is on camera for only two seconds, there is little chance that the subject can use lip reading to obtain useful verbal information.

The PONS assesses the examinee's ability to decode nonverbal behavior from 11 different channels. These include three that are "pure" visual channels, two different auditory (paralanguage) channels, and six combined (visual plus auditory) channels. The visual channels include the following:

1. The face
2. The body from the neck to the knees
3. The entire figure

The auditory channels include the following:

4. The randomized-spliced (RS) voice of the speaker
5. The content-filtered (CF) voice of the speaker

The combined channels include:

6. The face plus RS voice
7. The body plus RS voice
8. The figure plus RS voice

---

3. The PONS comes in five versions, including audio only, video only, brief PONS, and nonverbal discrepancy test. We discuss only the full PONS here.

9.   The face plus CF voice
10.   The body plus CF voice
11.   The figure plus CF voice

The portrayer in the PONS is shown expressing 20 different affective or emotional situations, ranging from relatively subtle emotions (e.g., "expressing motherly love") to more dramatic situations (e.g., "threatening someone"). Since each of the 20 scenes appears in each of the 11 channels, the test consists of a total of 220 scenes. The PONS takes about 45 minutes to complete.

The main standardization sample for the PONS consists of 492 public senior high school students from three locations (West Coast, Midwest, and East Coast) in the United States. These subjects were of average intelligence and from primarily middle-class families. Using the KR-20 formula, the authors computed internal consistency correlations for test results of these students. The results indicate generally adequate homogeneity for the individual channels, with the blatant exception of the randomized-spliced voice channel ($r = .06$). Unfortunately, the test-retest stability coefficients for PONS channel scores were found to be marginal at best (Table 14.12). Based upon 293 students retested after 10 days to 10 weeks, most of the test-retest correlations for individual channel scores were in the .20s and .30s. The only stability coefficient that was even marginally passable was based on the entire scale ($r = .69$).

The validity of the PONS has been investigated in dozens of studies summarized by the authors (Rosenthal et al., 1979). In general, correlations

TABLE 14.12   Median PONS Test-Retest Reliability Coefficients from Six Samples ($N = 293$)

Audio Channel	Video Channel				
	None	Face	Body	Figure	Total
None		.24	.34	.24	.52
Randomized-Spliced	.18	.43	.26	.20	.50
Content-Filtered	.27	.20	.24	.27	.50
Total	.32	.49	.54	.51	.69

Source: Reprinted with permission from Rosenthal, R., Hall, J. A., DiMatteo, M. R., Rogers, P. L., and Archer, D. (1979). *Sensitivity to nonverbal communication: The PONS test.* Baltimore, MD: Johns Hopkins University Press.

with other indices of interpersonal sensitivity are appropriately positive (support for criterion validity), whereas correlations with cognitive variables such as IQ are suitably low (support for discriminant validity). In one interesting study, the effectiveness of foreign service officers was found to correlate .30 with scores on the audio version of the PONS, that is, the more-effective officers were better than the less-effective officers at decoding nonverbal information contained in content-filtered and random-spliced voices. We may conclude, then, that the PONS total score is a fair index of sensitivity to nonverbal communication. However, the individual channels of the PONS test possess such marginal reliability that they should be used for research purposes only.

SUMMARY

1. Behavioral assessment concentrates on behavior itself rather than on underlying traits, hypothetical causes, or presumed dimensions of personality. Behavioral assessment is usually an integral part of behavior therapy designed to change the duration, frequency, or intensity of a well-defined target behavior.

2. One assessment approach useful in exposure-based methods of behavior therapy is the behavioral avoidance test (BAT), in which the therapist charts how long the client can tolerate the anxiety-inducing stimulus. Fear survey schedules, based upon self-ratings of commonly feared objects and situations, are also useful, but there are reasons to question their validity.

3. In contingency management, the therapist attempts to modify maladaptive behavior by identifying the reinforcing consequences and eliminating them. Conversely, adaptive behaviors can be strengthened by arranging for the delivery of rewards when these behaviors occur, such as in a token economy.

4. In cognitive behavior therapy, the therapist attempts to change the belief structure of the client. For example, Meichenbaum teaches clients to use coping self-statements (e.g., "You have a strategy . . . you can do it") to combat stressful situations.

5. An excellent index of depression—including the cognitive distortions—is the Beck Depression Inventory (BDI), which consists of 21 quartets of hierarchically ordered statements, each scored 0 to 3. The BDI is recognized as an excellent self-report index of depression and is extensively validated against external criteria.

6. Lewinsohn and his colleagues have published the Pleasant Events Schedule for self-monitoring the frequency and pleasantness of up to 320 largely ordinary, everyday behaviors. Depressed patients who increase their self-monitored frequency of pleasant events generally show improved mood.

7. Self-monitoring has many applications in psychology and medicine. One example is the Body Image Testing System (BITS) used to assess the distortions in body image found in anorexia nervosa and other eating disorders. BITS provides the subject with a menu to change a computer-generated body image until it resembles her (or his) self-perception.

8. A number of tools and methods exist for the assessment of nonverbal behavior such as visual interaction. Unfortunately, the assessment of visual interaction is beset with practical and methodological pitfalls; the application of this approach is restricted to research studies.

9. Paralinguistics refers to tone of voice, rate of speaking, and other nonverbal aspects of speech. An important area for paralinguistic assessment has been emotion judged from "content-filtered" speech. For example, paralinguistic anger in a physician's voice (judged from content-filtered speech) predicts poor effectiveness in referring alcoholic patients for treatment.

10. Facial expression is another nonverbal behavior useful in assessment. The Facial Action Coding System (FACS) is a systematic approach to the coding of facial expression from slow-motion videotapes. The system consists of 44 action units (AUs) that account for all visible facial movement. With FACS, trained judges can produce highly reliable ratings of facial actions.

11. The Profile of Nonverbal Sensitivity (PONS) is a comprehensive assessment of the ability to perceive nonverbal cues in a series of 220 two-second segments (film or videotape) of one female's nonverbal behavior. Although the reliability of PONS channels is low, the global PONS score is a fair index of sensitivity to nonverbal communication.

KEY TERMS AND CONCEPTS

behavioral assessment   p. 538

behavior therapy   p. 538

behavioral avoidance test   p. 540

fear survey schedule   p. 541

contingency management   p. 541

token economy   p. 542

cognitive behavior therapy   p. 542

self-monitoring   p. 545

nonverbal behavior   p. 546

paralinguistics   p. 548

CHAPTER 15

Special Topics and Issues in Testing

In the previous chapters the myriads of ways that tests are used in decision making were outlined. Further, we have established that psychological testing is not only pervasive, it is also consequential. Test results matter. Test findings may warrant a passage to privilege. Conversely, test findings may sanction the denial of opportunity. For many reasons, then, it is appropriate to close the book with two special topics bearing upon the potential repercussions of psychological testing. In Topic 15A, Computerized Assessment and the Future of Testing, current applications of the computer in psychological assessment are surveyed and then the professional and social issues raised by this practice are discussed. This topic closes with thoughts on the future of testing—which will be forged in large measure by increasingly sophisticated applications of computer technology. The theme of professional issues is continued in Topic 15B, Ethical and Social Issues in Testing. We begin with an overview and history of the computer in testing.

COMPUTERS IN TESTING: OVERVIEW AND HISTORY

Introduction to Computer-Aided Assessment

In many counseling centers it is possible for a client to make an appointment with a microcomputer to explore career options. Other than a brief interaction with the receptionist to schedule time at the computer, the client need not interact with any other human being during the entire assessment process. The exact scenario will differ from one setting to the next, but might resemble the following. Instructions on the computer screen encourage the user to press any key. The computer then prompts the client to answer a series of questions about activities and interests by pressing designated numeric keys. After completion of the inventory, the computer calculates raw scores for a long list of occupational scales and makes appropriate statistical transformations. Next, a brief report appears on the screen. The report provides a list of careers which best fit the interests of the client. A hard copy is also printed for later review. Presumably, the client is better informed about compatible career options and therefore more likely to choose a satisfying line of work. This scenario is a simple example of computer-assisted psychological assessment (CAPA), a recent development hailed by many psychologists but criticized by others.

It is common knowledge that computers are now used widely in psychological testing. However, the breadth of these applications might surprise the reader. In addition to straightforward applications such as presenting test questions, scoring test data, and printing test results (as above), computers can be used to: (1) design individualized tests based upon real-time feedback during testing, (2) interpret test results according to complex decision rules, (3) write lengthy and detailed narrative reports, and (4) present test stimuli in an engaging and realistic video format by means of multimedia. We touch upon all of these topics in our review. The umbrella term **computer-assisted psychological assessment** (CAPA) refers to the entire range of computer applications in psychological assessment. CAPA holds great promise to the practice of psychology, but also presents a variety of practical and ethical problems which demand careful and thoughtful consideration. A brief history of CAPA is a good backdrop to the discussion of practical and ethical concerns.

Brief History of CAPA

The scoring of psychological tests by hand is tedious, time-consuming, and error-prone. Psychologists therefore eagerly embraced technology in their quest to improve the efficiency and accuracy of testing. The use of mechanical scoring machines for psychological tests such as the Strong Vocational Interest Blanks (SVIB) first occurred in the 1920s. In 1946, Elmer Hankes built an analog computer for automatic scoring and profiling of the SVIB (Moreland, 1992). By the early 1960s, the combination of optical scanners and mainframe computers provided quick, error-free scoring and profile printing of tests such as the SVIB and the MMPI.

The use of computers to provide test interpretations—not just scores and profiles—can be traced to the Mayo Clinic in the early 1960s (Swenson, Rome, Pearson, & Brannick, 1965). The Mayo group needed a rapid and efficient system for screening thousands of medical patients for psychological problems with the MMPI. Patients answered the MMPI items on special IBM cards that could be read into the computer by a scanner. The first interpretive system was crude by contemporary standards:

A program was written that scored 14 MMPI scales, converted them into standard scores, and printed a series of descriptive statements. These statements were selected from a collection of 62 statements, most of which were associated with the elevations on the MMPI scales. The program had some configural statements, but scale combinations, on which most of the literature is based, were largely ignored [Fowler, 1985].

Configural statements refer to interpretations based upon specific patterns of scale scores, such as high-point elevations on two designated scales. The success of the Mayo system served as an impetus for computer-based test interpretation of many other psychological tests. For example, in the early 1960s, Piotrowski (1964) developed a computer-based Rorschach interpretation system. The Rorschach system required considerable "pre-processing" by a technician. The individual responses were first coded according to a list of 320 parameters. The interpretation was based upon these parameter scores, not upon the raw responses.

By the 1970s, psychologists realized that computers could be integrated into the entire process of psychological assessment. Johnson and Williams (1975) described the use of a mainframe computer with several remote terminals to assess an average of 17 psychiatric inpatient admissions per day. Typically, patients completed the following computer-administered tests: MMPI, Beck Depression Inventory, intelligence test, memory test, and online social history. A structured mental status exam was conducted by an interviewer and entered directly into the computer. The computer scored the tests and generated a comprehensive narrative report. In a series of research studies, the Utah group demonstrated that these reports were generated in half the time and at half the cost of traditional evaluations (Klingler, Miller, Johnson, & Williams, 1977).

By the 1980s, CAPA was so prevalent that virtually every psychological test in existence could be interpreted by computer. A detailed chronology of developments is beyond the scope of this text. We have summarized major historical landmarks in Table 15.1.

TABLE 15.1   Historical Landmarks in CAPA

1946	Hankes develops an analog computer to score the SVIB (Moreland, 1992).
1954	Meehl's (1954) book *Clinical Versus Statistical Prediction* sets the stage for automated test interpretation.
1962	Optical scanner and digital computer are used to score SVIB and MMPI and also to print profiles (Moreland, 1992).
1962	First computer-based test interpretation system is developed for the MMPI at the Mayo Clinic (Swenson et al., 1965).
1964	Piotrowski publishes a system for computer-based interpretation of the Rorschach (Piotrowski, 1964).
1960s	Computer-based interpretive systems for the MMPI proliferate; Fowler, Finney, and Caldwell develop popular systems (Fowler, 1985).
1971	A mainframe computer with terminals is used to automate the entire assessment process for psychiatric inpatients at the VA Hospital in Salt Lake City, Utah (Klingler, Miller, Johnson, & Williams, 1977).
1970s	Computerized adaptive testing (CAT) is introduced; CAT allows for flexible, individualized test batteries which produce a given level of measurement accuracy with the fewest possible test items (Weiss, 1982).
1975	First automated interpretation of a neuropsychological test battery (Adams & Heaton, 1985).
1979	Lachar publishes an actuarially based interpretive system for the Personality Inventory for Children (Lachar & Gdowski, 1979).
1985	A special series on computerized psychological assessment appears in the *Journal of Consulting and Clinical Psychology* (Butcher, 1985).
1986	American Psychological Association publishes *Guidelines for Computer-Based Tests and Interpretations.*
1987	Publication of the first resource book titled *Computerized Psychological Assessment: A Practitioner's Guide* (Butcher, 1987).
1994	Introduction of multimedia assessment batteries; for example, at IBM, a multimedia test is used to assess the real-life problem-solving skills of prospective employees (*APA Monitor,* June 1994).
1997	Educational Testing Service and other testing giants move to computerized testing for major admissions tests such as the Graduate Management Admission Test (GMAT) and Graduate Record Examinations (GRE).

COMPUTER-BASED TEST INTERPRETATION: CURRENT STATUS

Computer-based test interpretation or CBTI refers to test interpretation and report writing by computer. Every major test publisher now offers computer-based test interpretations. These services are available by mail-in, on-line computer with modem or on-site microcomputer package. Moreover, the market for computer-based testing and report writing is so lucrative that we can anticipate massive growth in this field for many years to come. Butcher (1987, App. A) listed 169 vendors as of 1986. Conoley, Plake, and Kemmerer (1991) note that the number of computerized psychological test interpretations had increased to more than 400 by 1990. New computerized test systems are reported virtually every month in trade magazines and newspapers (e.g., *APA Monitor*). Computer-based test interpretation is here to stay.

In this section we will provide an overview of the types of computer-based test interpretations currently available. A comprehensive review of products could easily span several volumes, so the reader will have to settle for a discussion of diverse and representative examples of CBTI. We will examine four approaches to CBTI: scoring reports, descriptive reports, actuarial reports, and computer-assisted clinical reports (Moreland, 1992).

Scoring Reports

Scoring reports consist of scores and/or profiles. In addition, a scoring report may include statistical significance tests and confidence intervals plotted for the test scores. By definition, scoring reports do not include narrative text or explanation of scores. Moreland (1992) discusses the appeal of scoring reports:

> These kinds of data make it possible to identify especially meaningful scores and meaningful differences among scores at a glance. They should also increase a user's confidence that those scores are in fact important. Statistical significance tests are undoubtedly superior to "clinical rules of thumb" when it comes to accurate interpretation of test scores. And who has time to hand calculate confidence intervals—especially for tests with dozens of scales?

An example of a scoring report for the Jackson Vocational Interest Survey (Jackson, 1991) is shown in Figure 15.1. The reader will notice that a great deal of information is presented in an efficient, condensed manner. This is typical of scoring reports. In a single page, this hypothetical respondent would learn that his interests are highly similar to majors in liberal arts, education, and business. In terms of occupational fit, he also learns that he is highly compatible with counselors, teachers, lawyers, administrators, and other professions with an emphasis upon human relations.

Descriptive Reports

A descriptive report goes one step further than a scoring report by providing brief scale-by-scale interpretation of test results. Descriptive reports are especially useful when test findings are conveyed to mental health professionals who have little knowledge of the test in question. For example, most clinical psychologists know that a high score on the MMPI Psychasthenia scale signifies worry and dissatisfaction with social relationships—but other mental health practitioners may not have a clue as to the meaning of an elevation on this scale. A descriptive report can convey invaluable information in a half page or less. One of the first descriptive reports published is portrayed in Figure 15.2. The reader will notice that the 20-year-old male patient is described as shy, sensitive, worried, and severely depressed. Referral of this medical patient to a psychologist or psychiatrist clearly is warranted. This report is a model of simplicity and clarity. By comparison, most contemporary computer-based descriptive reports provide excessive detail. Typically, the clinician must wade through several pages of narrative to extract essential features about the client.

Actuarial Reports: Clinical versus Actuarial Prediction

The actuarial approach to computer-based test interpretation is based upon the empirical determination

SIMLIARITY TO COLLEGE AND UNIVERSITY STUDENT GROUPS

	FEMALES	MALES	
AGRICULTURE	-0.67	-0.57	(VERY LOW)
ARTS & ARCHITECTURE	-0.18	-0.08	(LOW)
BUSINESS	+0.53	+0.65	(VERY HIGH)
EARTH AND MINERAL SCIENCE		-0.72	(VERY LOW)
EDUCATION	+0.64	+0.65	(VERY HIGH)
ENGINEERING	-0.53	-0.61	(VERY LOW)
HEALTH, PHYSICAL EDUC. & RECREATION	-0.40		
HUMAN DEVELOPMENT	+0.39	+0.70	(VERY HIGH)
LIBERAL ARTS	+0.71	+0.77	(VERY HIGH)
SCIENCE	-0.66	-0.60	(VERY LOW)
NURSES	+0.17		
MEDICAL STUDENTS	+0.08	-0.12	(VERY LOW)
TECHNICAL COLLEGE		-0.43	(VERY LOW)

SIMILARITY TO OCCUPATIONAL CLASSIFICATIONS

BELOW ARE RANKED THE OCCUPATIONAL CLASSIFICATION FOUND TO BE SIMILAR TO YOUR INTEREST PROFILE. A POSITIVE SCORE INDICATES THAT YOUR PROFILE SHOWS SOME DEGREE OF SIMILARITY TO THOSE ALREADY WORKING IN THE OCCUPATIONAL CLUSTER, WHILE A NEGATIVE SCORE INDICATES DISSIMILARITY.

SCORE	SIMILARITY	OCCUPATIONAL CLASSIFICATION
+0.78	VERY SIMILAR	COUNSELORS/STUDENT PERSONNEL WORKERS
+0.74	VERY SIMILAR	TEACHING AND RELATED OCCUPATIONS
+0.74	VERY SIMILAR	OCCUPATIONS IN RELIGION
+0.71	VERY SIMILAR	ADMINSTRATIVE AND RELATED OCCUPATIONS
+0.68	VERY SIMILAR	OCCUPATIONS IN LAW AND POLITICS
+0.60	VERY SIMILAR	PERSONNEL/HUMAN MANAGEMENT
+0.57	SIMILAR	OCCUPATIONS IN SOCIAL WELFARE
+0.55	SIMILAR	OCCUPATIONS IN SOCIAL SCIENCE
+0.55	SIMILAR	OCCUPATIONS IN PRE-SCHOOL & ELEMENTARY TEACHING
+0.50	SIMILAR	SALES OCCUAPTIONS
+0.50	SIMILAR	OCCUPATIONS IN MERCHANDISING
+0.49	SIMILAR	CLERICAL SERVICES
+0.48	SIMILAR	OCCUAPTIONS IN WRITING
+0.44	SIMILAR	OCCUPATIONS IN ACCOUNTING, BANKING AND FINANCE
+0.05	NEUTRAL	SERVICE OCCUAPTIONS
+0.03	NEUTRAL	OCCUPATIONS IN MUSIC
+0.02	NEUTRAL	ASSEMBLY OCCUPATIONS-INSTRUMENTS & SMALL PRODUCTS
-0.30	NEUTRAL	OCCUPATIONS IN ENTERTAINMENT
-0.24	NEUTRAL	OCCUPATIONS IN COMMERCIAL ART
-0.35	DISSIMILAR	PROTECTIVE SERVICES OCCUPATIONS
-0.38	DISSIMILAR	AGRICULTURALISTS
-0.39	DISSIMILAR	MILITARY OFFICERS
-0.41	DISSIMILAR	OCCUPATIONS IN FINE ART
-0.58	DISSIMILAR	SPORT AND RECREATION OCCUPATIONS
-0.59	DISSIMILAR	MATHEMATICAL AND RELATED OCCUPATIONS
-0.62	VERY DISSIMILAR	MACHINING/MECHANICAL & RELATED OCCUPATIONS
-0.63	VERY DISSIMILAR	HEALTH SERVICE WORKERS
-0.65	VERY DISSIMILAR	OCCUPATIONS IN THE PHYSICAL SCIENCES
-0.65	VERY DISSIMILAR	CONSTRUCTION/SKILLED TRADES
-0.68	VERY DISSIMILAR	MEDICAL DIAGNOSIS AND TREATMENT OCCUPATIONS
-0.71	VERY DISSIMILAR	ENGINEERING & TECHNICAL SUPPORT WORKERS
-0.76	VERY DISSIMILAR	LIFE SCIENCES

FIGURE 15.1 A Scoring Report for the Jackson Vocational Interest Survey

Source: Reprinted with permission from Jackson, D. N. (1991). *Jackson Vocational Interest Survey Manual* (3rd ed.). Port Huron, MI: Sigma Assessment Systems, Inc. (800) 265-1285.

Sex: Male.   Education: 20.   Age: 34.   Marital Status: Married.   Outpatient.

MMPI Code: 27″5′8064–391/ –KLF/

D	2	Severely depressed, worrying, indecisive, and pessimistic
Pt	7	Rigid and meticulous. Worrisome and apprehensive. Dissatisfied with social relationships. Probably very religious and moralistic.
Mf	5	Probably sensitive and idealistic with high esthetic, cultural, and artistic interests
Sc	8	Tends toward abstract interests such as science, philosophy, and religion
Si	0	Probably retiring and shy in social situations
Pa	6	Sensitive. Alive to opinions of others
Pd	4	Independent or mildly nonconformist
Hy	3	
Ma	9	Normal energy and activity level
Hs	1	Number of physical symptoms and concern about bodily functions fairly typical for clinic patients

Consider psychiatric evaluation

FIGURE 15.2

Mayo Clinic MMPI Descriptive Report

Source: Reprinted with permission from Dahlstrom, W. G., Welsh, G. S., and Dahlstrom, L. E. (1972). *An MMPI handbook. Volume 1: Clinical interpretation* (rev. ed.). Minneapolis, MN: University of Minnesota Press. Copyright © 1960, 1972 by the University of Minnesota.

of relationships between test results and the criteria of interest. The nature of this approach is best understood in the context of the longstanding debate on clinical versus actuarial prediction. A brief detour is needed here to introduce relevant concepts and issues before discussing actuarial reports.

Many computer-based test interpretations make predictions about the test taker. These predictions are often disguised in the language of classification or diagnosis, but they are predictions nonetheless. For example, when a computer-based neuropsychological test report tentatively classifies a client as brain-damaged, this is actually an implicit prediction which can be confirmed or disconfirmed by external criteria such as brain scans and neurological consultation. Likewise, when a computer-based MMPI-2 report provides a tentative DSM-IV diagnosis of a clinic referral, this is also a prediction that can be validated or invalidated by external criteria such as intensive clinical interview. A final example: When a computer-based CPI screening report for police candidates warns that an applicant will make a poor adjustment in law enforcement, this is also a prediction that could be proved correct or incorrect by an inspection of personnel records at a later date.

The use of computers for test-based prediction highlights an essential distinction known as clinical versus actuarial judgment (Dawes, Faust, & Meehl, 1989; Garb, 1994; Meehl, 1954, 1965, 1986). In **clinical judgment,** the decision maker processes information in his or her head to diagnose, classify, or predict behavior. An example: A clinical psychologist uses experience, intuition, and textbook knowledge to determine whether an MMPI profile indicates psychosis. Psychosis is a broad category that includes serious mental disorders often characterized by hallucinations, delusions, and disordered thinking. Thus, a clinician's prediction of psychosis (or lack thereof) can be validated against external criteria such as detailed interview.

In **actuarial judgment,** an empirically derived formula is used to diagnose, classify, or predict behavior. An example: A clinical psychologist merely plugs scale scores into a research-based formula to determine whether an MMPI profile indicates psychosis. The actuarial prediction, too, can be validated against appropriate external criteria.

The essence of actuarial judgment is the careful development and subsequent use of an empirically based formula for diagnosis, classification, or prediction of behavior. A common type of actuarial formula is the regression equation in which subtest scores are combined in a weighted linear sum to predict a relevant criterion. But other statistical approaches may work well for decision making, too, including simple cutoff scores and rule-based flow charts. Of course, statistical rules lend themselves to computer implementation, so it is fitting to discuss clinical versus actuarial judgment in this section on computer-based test interpretation.

Although computers facilitate the use of the actuarial method, we need to emphasize that "actuarial" and "computerized" are not synonymous. To be truly actuarial, test interpretations must be automatic (prespecified or routinized) and based on empirically established relations (Dawes, Faust, & Meehl, 1989). If a computer program incorporates such automatic, empirically based decision-making rules, then it is making an actuarial prediction. Conversely, if a computer program embodies the thinking and judgment of a clinician—no matter how wise that person be—then it is making a clinical prediction.

Meehl (1954) was the first to introduce the issue of clinical versus actuarial judgment to a broad range of social scientists. He stated the issue with pure simplicity: "When shall we use our heads instead of the formula?" Consider the practical problem of distinguishing between neurosis and psychosis on the basis of MMPI results. *Neurosis* is an outdated (but still used) diagnostic term that refers to a milder form of mental disorder in which symptoms of anxiety or dysphoria predominate. As noted previously, psychosis is a more serious form of mental disorder which may include hallucinations, delusions, and disordered thinking. The differential diagnosis between these two broad classes of mental disorder is important. Persons with neurosis often respond well to individual psychotherapy whereas a patient with psychosis may need powerful antipsychotic medications which produce adverse side effects. Which is superior for MMPI-based diagnostic decision making, the head of the well-trained psychologist or an appropriate formula based upon prior research? We return to this issue later.

Meehl (1954) specified two conditions for a fair comparison of these contrasting approaches to decision making. First, both methods should base judgments on the same data. For example, in comparing the experienced clinician against an actuarial equation, both approaches should prognosticate from the same pool of MMPI profiles and only those profiles. Second, we must avoid conditions that can artificially inflate the accuracy of the actuarial approach. For example, the actuarial equation should be derived on an initial sample, prior to the comparison with clinical decision making on a new sample of MMPI profiles. Otherwise, the actuarial decision rules will capitalize upon chance relations among variables and produce a spuriously high rate of correct decisions.

When the conditions are met for a fair test of clinical versus actuarial decision making, the latter method is superior in virtually every case. The actuarial approach is clearly better for the task cited previously—differential diagnosis of neurosis or psychosis from the MMPI. L. R. Goldberg (1965) determined that a simple linear sum of selected MMPI scale scores resulted in 70 percent correct classifications, whereas Ph.D. psychologists averaged only 62 percent, with the single best psychologist achieving 67 percent correct decisions. The decision rule that defeated all human contenders was: if the T-score sum on L + Pa + Sc – Hy – Pt exceeds 44, diagnose psychosis, otherwise diagnose neurosis.[1]

Dawes, Faust, and Meehl (1989) cited nearly 100 comparative studies in the social sciences. In almost every case, the actuarial method equaled or surpassed the clinical method, sometimes substantially. The research by Leli and Filskov (1984) is typical in this regard. They studied the diagnosis of progressive brain dysfunction based upon neuropsychological testing. An actuarial decision rule derived from one set of cases was applied to a new sample with 83 percent correct identification. Working from precisely the same test data, groups of inexperienced and experienced clinicians correctly identified only 63 percent and 58 percent of the new cases, respectively. The reader will notice

---

1. Respectively, the full names for these scales are L (validity scale), Paranoia, Schizophrenia, Hysteria, and Psychasthenia.

the disturbing and embarrassing fact that experience did not improve hit rates for this clinical decision-making task.

The lesson to be learned from this literature is that computerized narrative test reports should incorporate actuarial methods, where possible. For example, computer-generated reports should use existing actuarial formulas to determine the likelihood of various psychiatric diagnoses, rather than relying upon the programmed logic of a master clinician. Unfortunately, as the reader will discover in the following, most computerized narrative test reports are clinically based—which raises concerns about their validity.

Actuarial Interpretation: Sample Approach

Sines (1966) defined an actuarial interpretation as based upon "the empirical determination of the regularities that may exist between specified psychological test data and equally clearly specified socially, clinically, or theoretically significant nontest characteristics of the person tested." In other words, the statements in an actuarial interpretation are not derived from conjecture or clinical lore, they are based upon specific, quantified research findings.

Because of the investigative effort required, actuarial approaches to computer-based test interpretation are rare. The first actuarial systems were based upon the MMPI (e.g., Gilberstadt & Duker, 1965; Marks & Seeman, 1963). More recently, actuarial interpretive systems have been applied to the Personality Inventory for Children (Lachar & Gdowski, 1979; Lachar, 1987), the Marital Satisfaction Inventory (Snyder, Lachar, & Wills, 1988), and the California Psychological Inventory (Gough, 1987). A specific example will clarify this method.

The developers of the Personality Inventory for Children (PIC) have produced an exemplary system for computer-based actuarial test interpretation which we will describe for illustrative purposes. The reader will recall from the previous chapter that the PIC is a true-false inventory which the parent or caregiver completes with respect to the child's behavior. Based upon these responses, a profile of T-scores (mean of 50, SD of 10) is produced for four validity scales (e.g., Defensiveness), 12 clinical scales (e.g., Delinquency), and four factor scales (e.g., Social Incompetence). In total, T-scores are reported for 20 scales on the PIC. Of course, higher T-scores indicate a greater likelihood of psychopathology.

Actuarial interpretation of the PIC rests upon the empirically derived correlations between individual scales and important nontest criteria. Research subjects for the Lachar and Gdowski (1979) study consisted of 431 children referred to a busy teaching clinic. As part of the evaluation process for each child, the staff members, parents, and teachers completed a comprehensive questionnaire which listed 322 descriptive statements concerning behavior and other variables. In addition, parents or caretakers filled out the PIC.

In the first phase of the actuarial study, the 322 descriptive statements were correlated with the 20 PIC scales to identify significant scale correlates. In the second phase, the significant correlates were analyzed further to determine the relationship between descriptive statements and T-score ranges on the PIC scales. The outcome of this prodigious effort was a series of actuarial tables not unlike the tables used by insurance companies to predict the likelihood of illness, death, accidents, and the like, based upon population demographics such as age, sex, and residence. Some examples of actuarial correlates of the Delinquency or DLQ Scale are depicted in Table 15.2.

Actuarial tables capture a wealth of information useful in clinical practice. Consider two hypothetical 12-year-old children, Jimmy and Johnny, each referred to a clinician with the same presenting problem: school underachievement. As part of the intake procedure, the clinician asks each mother to fill out the PIC. Suppose that the Delinquency or DLQ Scale score for Jimmy is highly elevated at a T-score of 114, whereas Johnny obtains an average range T-score of 54. Based upon these scores, the clinician would know the likelihood—listed below

TABLE 15.2 Occurrence Rates for Actuarial Descriptors of the PIC Delinquency Scale

Descriptor	Base Rate[a]	T-Score Ranges							
		30–59	60–69	70–79	80–89	90–99	100–109	110–119	>120
Refuses to go to bed	30	18	26	23	33	36	33	42	38
Lies	62	44	36	48	73	71	79	90	91
Uses drugs	12	0	2	6	7	11	18	32	53
Rejects school	40	16	26	40	42	50	47	56	67
Involved with police	17	0	4	6	10	21	19	58	63

[a]Percentage of all children rated as displaying the characteristic.
Note: These five descriptors are merely a representative sample of the 51 actuarial correlates of the Delinquency Scale.

Source: Material from *Actuarial Assessment of Child and Adolescent Personality: An Interpretive Guide for the Personality Inventory for Children Profile* copyright © 1979 by Western Psychological Services. Reprinted by permission of the publisher, Western Psychological Services, 12031 Wilshire Boulevard, Los Angeles, CA 90025, United States of America.

as percentages—that certain behavioral descriptions apply to each child:

	Jimmy (DLQ = 114)	Johnny (DLQ = 54)
Refuses to go to bed	42%	18%
Lies	90%	44%
Uses drugs	32%	0%
Rejects school	56%	16%
Involved with police	58%	0%

The reader will immediately recognize that Jimmy fits a pattern of pervasive conduct disorder, whereas Johnny appears to have few such behavior problems. In Jimmy's case, the underachievement is most likely secondary to a pattern of antisocial behavior, whereas for Johnny the clinician must look elsewhere to understand the school failure. Of course, this is only a small fraction of the information that would be available from a computer-based actuarial interpretation of the PIC. In a full report, the clinician would receive statistics and narrative statements pertinent to all 20 scales from the PIC.

Computer-Assisted Clinical Reports

In a computer-assisted clinical report, the interpretive statements assigned to test results are based upon the judgment of one or more expert clinicians.

The expert clinicians formalize their thought processes and develop automated decision rules which are then translated into computer code. This method differs crucially from the computer-assisted actuarial approach in which interpretive statements are based strictly upon formal research findings. Superficially, the two approaches may appear to be identical insofar as each is rule-based and automated. The difference has to do with the origin of the rules: empirical research (actuarial approach) versus clinician judgment (clinical approach).

Even though clinicians generally recognize the superiority of the actuarial method, there is one significant advantage to the computer-assisted clinical approach. The advantage is that the clinical approach can be designed to interpret all test profiles whereas some test profiles will be uninterpretable by means of an actuarial approach. The discouraging truth about actuarial "cookbook" systems for test interpretation is that the classification rate usually plummets when a system is used in a new setting. The classification rate refers to the percentage of test results which fit the complex profile classification rules necessary for actuarial interpretation. For example, in the Gilberstadt and Duker (1965) actuarial MMPI system, the 1-2-3 code type is defined by these rules for the Hs (Hypochondriasis), D (Depression), Hysteria (Hs) and L, F, K (validity) scales:

1. Hs, D, and Hy over *T*-score 70
2. Hs > D > Hy
3. No other scales over *T*-score 70
4. L < *T* score 66, F < *T*-score 86, and K < *T*-score 71

Persons who produce this kind of MMPI profile often suffer from psychophysiological overreactivity, not to mention a host of other empirically confirmed characteristics. Of course, there are several additional code types, each defined by a set of complex decision rules, and each accompanied by an elaborate, actuarially based description of personality and psychopathology. A typical finding is that a computer-assisted actuarial system developed within one client population will be capable of interpreting up to 85 percent of the test profiles encountered in that setting. However, when the actuarial system is applied to a new client population, perhaps 50 percent of the test profiles will fit the decision rules. This means that about half of the test profiles do not fit the rules. At best, these clients will receive a superficial, scale-by-scale interpretation rather than a more sophisticated actuarial interpretation based upon code types. The problem of shrinkage in classification rate is observed in virtually all studies of actuarial interpretation (Moreland, 1992).

Computer-assisted clinical reports tend to be lengthy and detailed, full of scale scores, item indices, and graphs. Of course, these reports also include several pages of narrative report, usually phrased in terms of hypotheses as opposed to confirmed findings. The shortest such report is about six pages (e.g., the Karson Clinical Report for the 16 PF), whereas longer ones can run to 10 or 20 pages (e.g., MMPI-2 interpretations).

MULTIMEDIA AND VIRTUAL REALITY: THE NEW HORIZONS OF CAPA

With recent improvements in technology, the modern microcomputer has opened up a whole new world for psychological assessment. The ordinary desktop computer is now capable of presenting video segments that possess the visual clarity of television. Built-in stereo sound systems produce exquisite audio output, including synthesized human speech that passes for the real thing. With CD-ROM accessories, instantaneous access to huge repositories of information—including still images, live video segments, music, tables, charts, animation—is possible. Collectively, these capacities are known as **multimedia**—especially when used for interactive and educational applications. Multimedia is one new horizon of computer-assisted psychological assessment. Another is virtual reality, discussed below.

At IBM, researchers have been developing a computerized multimedia test that can be used to assess job applicants for manufacturing positions (*APA Monitor,* June 1994). What is unique about this test is the nature of the stimuli. Rather than merely describing a work situation, the multimedia computer displays the actual scene. As the applicant watches different vignettes, the computer freezes at crucial points and asks what the candidate should do in that situation. The scenes have a highly realistic feeling to them, which enhances the face validity of the test. Multimedia promises to provide a more accurate assessment than paper-and-pencil tests of how people would actually perform on the job. Multimedia tests are especially good at tapping the examinee's ability to deal with complex, real-life problems, such as decision making under time pressure or conflict resolution in the workplace.

Another potential application of multimedia is in personnel screening for entry-level police officers. Law enforcement personnel must have good observational and evaluative skills, which can be assessed realistically with video stimuli. For example, an assessment might consist, in part, of a videotape of witnesses at a crime scene. Police candidates might be asked to determine the truth of the witnesses and to draw conclusions about the crime based upon their observational powers (*APA Monitor,* June 1994). This example—currently hypothetical—illustrates the potential for multimedia to revolutionize psychological assessment.

It is worth noting that multimedia tests can be virtually language free. Talented job candidates who do not possess good reading or writing abilities but who do have practical job skills can be identified by means of multimedia tests. For some jobs, multimedia might be fairer than the paper-and-pencil approach.

Finally, a very recent high-tech approach to computer-based assessment deserves brief mention. In virtual reality, the participant wears a pair of goggles that transmit realistic, three-dimensional images of a simulated environment. By manipulating simple control devices, the participant can navigate through the environment even though standing still. Of course, the visual environment, known as a **virtual reality,** is based on sophisticated computerized output. New assessment tools that utilize virtual reality are in their infancy, but show great promise. For example, it is possible to evaluate a client's body image using virtual reality, as described in a recent article in a new journal titled *CyberPsychology and Behavior.*

EVALUATION OF COMPUTER-BASED TEST INTERPRETATION

Computerized testing has clear advantages but also some potentially serious disadvantages in comparison to the traditional clinical approach to psychological testing. We offer a brief survey here, stressing both the advantages and disadvantages of computer-based testing, diagnosis, and report writing. More detail on this topic can be found in Butcher (1987), Kramer (1988), Moreland (1992), Roid and Johnson (1998), Tallent (1987), and the special issue of *Journal of Consulting and Clinical Psychology,* December (1985).

Advantages of Computerized Testing and Report Writing

The main advantages of computer-based testing are quick turnaround, inexpensive cost, near perfect reliability, and complete objectivity. In addition, some measurement applications such as flexible adaptive testing virtually require the use of computers for their implementation. We explore these points in more detail later.

In a busy clinical practice, delays between testing and submission of the consulting report are common, almost inevitable. These delays not only tarnish the reputation of the consultant, they may also adversely affect the treatment outcome for the client. For example, a learning-disabled college student may need immediate intervention in order to avert an academic disaster. A delay of two or three weeks in submission of a consulting report could spell, indirectly, the difference between failure and success in academic performance. Computer-based reports can speed up the entire consultation process. Many software systems produce reports that can be transferred into a standard word-processing program for immediate customized editing, thereby speeding up the turnaround time (e.g., Psychological Corporation, 1994; Tanner, 1992).

Cost is another consideration in computer-based testing. Although there are no definitive studies on this topic, most authorities assert that computer-scored and interpreted psychological tests cost considerably less than those produced entirely by clinician effort (Butcher, 1987). In their studies of automated testing at the Salt Lake City VA Hospital, Klingler, Miller, Johnson, and Williams (1977) concluded that the computer cut the cost of testing in half. Certainly as the computerized testing programs become more sophisticated and are used by larger numbers of clinicians, the cost per consultation will plummet.

Reliability and objectivity are the hallmarks of the computer. Assuming that the software is accurate and error-free, computers simply do not make clerical scoring errors, nor do they vary their methods of stimulus presentation from one day to the next, nor do they yield different narrative reports based on the same input. The product is the same no matter how many times the computer program is used. Furthermore, because computerized reports are based on objective rules, they are not distorted by halo effects or other subjective biases that might enter into a clinically derived report. Butcher (1987) asserts that computerized reports could have special significance in court cases, because they would be viewed as "untouched by human hands." This is an intriguing possibility, but perhaps somewhat overly optimistic. Lawyers and judges will still want to know who programmed the software, how the narrative statements were developed, and so on.

Disadvantages of Computerized Testing and Report Writing

Consider the following illustration, hypothetical yet realistic and probably not a rare occurrence. A hospital physician refers a difficult medical patient to the psychology service for a personality evaluation. The patient is escorted to the testing center where a receptionist seats him at a table in front of a microcomputer. Instructions appear on the computer monitor to answer a series of self-statements true or false by pressing the T or F key. The patient completes the computerized objective personality inventory and is escorted back to the medical service. Seconds later, a narrative report based on the patient's responses emerges from the printer. The consulting psychologist peruses the report briefly, then sends it (unsigned) through departmental mail to the physician. The report is handsome, ever so crisp in its laser-printed appearance, with a graphic summary of scales on the cover page. Furthermore, the narrative is valid-sounding and reads as if it were copyedited by a professional writer (in fact, it was). The physician is impressed and takes the report to heart, making treatment decisions based on the personality evaluation.

This scenario illustrates an essential quandary with computer-based testing and report writing: Computers can so dominate the testing process that the clinical psychologist is demoted to a mere clerk—or is removed from the assessment loop entirely. Although most psychologists acknowledge that computers are a welcome addition to the practice of psychological testing, critics have raised a number of disquieting concerns about recent assessment practices such as those depicted above. Computerization of the testing process raises prac-

tical, legal, ethical, and measurement issues which deserve thoughtful review.

In general, skeptics do not attack the practice of computerizing the mechanics of test administration and scoring; these computer applications are seen as efficient and appropriate uses of modern technology. Nonetheless, even the most ardent proponents acknowledge the need to investigate test-form equivalency when an existing test is adapted to computerized administration. In particular, practitioners should not assume that the computerized adaptation and the original version of a test produce identical results. Equivalency is an empirical issue that must be demonstrated by appropriate research. For most tests, equivalency can be demonstrated, but this must not be taken for granted (Lukin, Dowd, Plake, & Kraft, 1985; Schuldberg, 1988).

Some tests do not maintain score equivalency when translated to computer. The Category Test (CT) from the Halstead-Reitan Neuropsychological Battery is a case in point. In a comparison of computerized and standard versions of the Category Test with rehabilitation patients, Berger, Chibnall, and Gfeller (1994) found a huge difference in error rate for two groups of subjects who had equivalent backgrounds: an average of 84 errors on the computerized CT versus an average of 66 errors on the standard CT test. Apparently, the computerized CT test is much more difficult than the standard version, which means that separate norms must be developed for its interpretation. Much smaller differences between computerized and standard test administration have also been reported for the MMPI, with computer-based scores tending to underestimate (very slightly) the booklet-based scores (Watson, Thomas, & Anderson, 1992).

The main focus of controversy in computer-based test interpretation is computerized report writing. Several prominent experts in psychological testing have expressed grave reservations about the routine practice of automating the narrative reports that must accompany any clinical assessment (Faust & Ziskin, 1989; Lanyon, 1984; Matarazzo, 1986, 1990; Tallent, 1987). The primary concerns include the following:

- Computerized psychological testing is a poor substitute for psychological assessment.
- Computerized narrative reports are rarely validated prior to use.
- Computerized clinical psychological interpretations are unsigned.

These points are embellished below.

Matarazzo (1986) has emphasized that a computer-based evaluation is so easy to accomplish and so impressive in appearance that both users and recipients of a computerized narrative report may confuse it with a comprehensive assessment. But there is a difference between testing and assessment. The experienced clinician knows that psychological testing—whether traditional or computerized—is just the first step in a comprehensive assessment. In performing a comprehensive assessment, the competent clinician goes beyond the test results to integrate the findings into the examinee's total life situation and psychological history. In contrast, a computerized narrative report rarely makes reference to nontest information such as the purpose of the assessment, the client's recent adaptive functioning, or interview impressions which might strongly contradict test-based inferences about personality.

In his critique of computer-based testing, Lanyon (1984) has emphasized that the printed interpretations lack demonstrated validity. Indeed, most automated test interpretations are based upon clinical lore rather than empirical validation—that is, they are clinical rather than actuarial in nature. Although vendors may conduct customer satisfaction studies (e.g., "How satisfied are you with narrative statement X on client Y?") these analyses are no substitute for careful scrutiny of interpretive validity. Lanyon (1984) also notes with alarm that commercially available automated test interpretation systems are growing exponentially. Some systems can be purchased by almost anyone for home installation on a microcomputer. These developments portend a dark future:

> There is a real danger that the few satisfactory services will be squeezed out by the many unsatisfactory ones, since the consumer professionals are generally unable to discriminate among them and are predisposed to believe whatever is printed. Particularly distressing is that the lack of demonstrated program validity has now become the norm, and there appear to be no checks against the further development of this untenable situation. Perhaps the time has now come when federal regulations for this industry are necessary for consumer protection (Lanyon, 1984).

Matarazzo (1986) sounds a similar note, warning that the profession of psychology must regulate itself or risk federal incursion into the practice of psychological testing.

Another problem with computerized testing is that automated narrative reports are rarely signed. Unsigned reports raise horrendous issues with regard to professional responsibility and legal culpability. Suppose a client is harmed by an inaccurate computerized report. Who is to blame? Who is legally responsible? Fault could rest with the psychologist who used the computer program, the for-profit company that sold it, or the individual programmer who incorporated the offending statement(s) into the software logic. But legal responsibility usually settles upon the individual psychologist. The lesson is that using an automated system does not absolve the practitioner of responsibility for the consequences of a computerized report (Case Exhibit 15.1).

In the mid-1980s, the American Psychological Association adopted *Guidelines for Computer-Based Tests and Interpretations* (1986). These guidelines are reprinted in Butcher (1987, App. B). The general purpose of the guidelines is to interpret the *Standards for Educational and Psychological Testing* (AERA, APA, NCME, 1985) as they relate to computer-based testing and test interpretation. Two important guidelines include the following:

1. The extent to which statements in an interpretive report are based on quantitative research versus expert clinical opinion should be delineated.
2. When statements in an interpretive report are based on expert clinical opinion, users should be provided with information that will allow them to weigh the credibility of such opinion (Butcher, 1987).

UNWISE RELIANCE UPON A COMPUTERIZED MMPI REPORT

In one court case, a clinical psychologist was sued by a mechanic because of inappropriate reliance upon a computer-based test interpretation. The mechanic worked for a large corporation that owned a private fleet of helicopters. His work consisted mainly of maintenance and safety checks on the helicopters. As part of a progressive corporate policy, the mechanic consulted with a company-hired psychologist about a relatively minor issue involving a family conflict. The psychologist administered the MMPI to the mechanic and sent the answer sheet to a prominent MMPI interpretation service. A few days later, a computer-based test interpretation arrived in the mail. The computerized report was laced with alarming narrative prose. The report referred to the high likelihood of drug or alcohol problems, the distinct possibility of explosive outbursts, and the strong probability of overt paranoid thinking. The client was characterized as unstable, vindictive, paranoid, and possibly dangerous to self or others. Understandably, the psychologist became alarmed. Claiming to have the client's permission, the psychologist informed corporate officers about the MMPI report. The mechanic's supervisor demanded that he undergo additional evaluations for alcohol abuse and psychological disorder. When the mechanic refused, he was placed on medical leave and eventually fired. At this point he filed suit against the psychologist and the corporation. The case was settled out of court for a substantial sum of money.

What makes this case pertinent is that the computerized report was largely discrepant with the documented functioning of the client. Although the mechanic acknowledged a previous drinking problem, he no longer used drugs or alcohol. No evidence of explosive outbursts was found in his work history. His yearly evaluations were always satisfactory. Supervisors and coworkers described him as humorless but they did not regard him as unstable or vindictive or paranoid or dangerous in any manner. Apparently, the psychologist placed unwarranted faith in the validity of the computer-based test interpretation. The report was excessively pathological in tone. The essential error of the psychologist was accepting this report uncritically rather than checking its validity against other sources of information about the mechanic. We are reminded here of Lanyon's (1984) cynical but accurate conclusion about computerized reports (noted previously) that "consumer professionals are generally . . . predisposed to believe whatever is printed." We should also mention that the MMPI interpretation service was not held liable. Ultimately, it was the practitioner who was responsible for the consequences of the computer-based test interpretation.

The guidelines also detail the many other requirements that test producers, test publishers, and test users should meet. Perhaps these steps toward self-regulation will help increase the respectability and acceptability of computerized report writing. If not, increased federal incursion into the practice of psychological testing would appear to be inevitable.

COMPUTERIZED ADAPTIVE TESTING

A final advantage of computer-based testing is its application to flexible adaptive testing. Adaptive testing is nothing new—Binet used it when he worked out the methods for finding the basal and ceiling items on his famous intelligence test. Binet placed his items along a continuum of difficulty so that the examiner could test downward to find the examinee's basal level and test upward to find the ceiling level. This procedure eliminated the need to administer irrelevant items—those so easy (below the basal level) that the examinee would surely pass them, or those so hard (above the ceiling level) that the examinee would surely fail them. Another example of adaptive testing is the two-stage procedure whereby results on an initial routing test are used to determine the entry level for subsequent scales. For example, on the Stanford-Binet: Fourth Edition, results of the initial vocabulary subtest determine the starting point for subsequent subtests. By reducing the time needed to obtain an accurate measure of ability, adaptive testing fulfills a very constructive purpose.

Computerized adaptive testing (CAT) is a family of procedures that allows for accurate and efficient measurement of ability (Weiss, 1985; Weiss & Vale, 1987). Although details differ from one method to another, most forms of computerized adaptive testing share the following features:

1. Based on extensive pretesting, the item response characteristics of each item (e.g., percentage passing versus ability) are appraised precisely.
2. These item response characteristics and a CAT item-selection strategy are programmed into the computer.
3. In selecting the next item for presentation, the computer uses the examinee's total history of responses up to that point.
4. The computer recalculates the examinee's estimated ability level after each response.
5. The computer also estimates the precision of measurement (e.g., standard error of measurement) after each response.
6. Testing continues until a predetermined level of measurement precision is reached.

7. The examinee's score is based on the difficulty level and other measurement characteristics of items passed, not on the total number of items correct.

The measurement advantages of CAT can be summarized in two words: precision and efficiency (Weiss & Vale, 1987). Regarding precision, CAT guarantees that each examinee is measured with the same degree of precision because testing continues until this criterion is met. This is not so with traditional tests where scores at both tails of the distribution reflect greater levels of measurement error than scores in the middle of the distribution. Regarding efficiency, the CAT approach requires far fewer test items than are needed in traditional testing. For example, written certification examinations usually include 200 to 500 items while CAT examinations are always shorter, often including fewer than 100 items to achieve a more accurate level of measurement (Lunz & Bergstrom, 1994). In one analysis, the reliability of alternative computer-adaptive tests for certification in medical technology was .96 (Lunz, Bergstrom, & Wright, 1994). This is remarkable because shorter tests (the goal in CAT testing) tend to have lower reliability than longer tests (such as found in traditional testing programs).

The CAT approach to psychological testing has been used mainly by large organizations such as the U.S. Army and the Educational Testing Service for assessment of intelligence and special abilities. In recent years, national licensing boards (e.g., in medicine) have begun to implement CAT testing because of convenience in scheduling tests, tighter control over test security, reduced costs, and the opportunity for better data collection (Lunz & Bergstrom, 1994). Technical information on CAT systems is proprietary and difficult to obtain. Nonetheless, it is clear that the efficiency of the CAT approach is substantial. CAT uses fewer items of better quality than a conventional test of the same length. A general finding is that CAT reduces test length by about 50 percent, with reductions for individual examinees of up to 80 percent, with no loss in measurement accuracy (Laatsch & Choca, 1994; Weiss & Vale, 1987).

As the cost of computing continues to plummet, more and more large-scale applications of CAT will be developed. In the late 1990s, the Educational Testing Service moved toward near total reliance on CAT versions of the Graduate Record Examination and other selection tests. Licensing and certification boards such as the National Council of State Boards of Nursing also have introduced CAT versions of their certification tests. Mills and Stocking (1996) discuss practical issues in large-scale computerized testing.

THE FUTURE OF TESTING

As the twenty-first century begins, what is the future of psychological testing? We will hazard a few speculations here, cognizant that prognostications about the future often are wrong. Forecasting developments in testing is especially difficult because the enterprise is increasingly constrained, directly or indirectly, by public opinion. For example, at one point in the 1980s the legislature of the state of California made it *illegal* for school psychologists to use traditional intelligence tests as a basis for placing students in special education classes. These restraints on testing were driven by public outrage over the excessive placement of minority students in special education classes. Thus, even when a particular technology of testing is feasible and promoted by psychologists, there exists the possibility that it might be strictly controlled or even banned.

A case in point is Matarazzo's (1992) prediction that biological measures of intelligence will gain prominence in the twenty-first century. Certainly it appears true that biological measures of ability such as averaged evoked potential (gauged from EEG waves), or glucose metabolic rate in the brain (gauged from PET scans), or relative brain size (gauged from MRI scans) will prove to be effective approaches to assessment (see Topic 5A, Theories and the Measurement of Intelligence). But Matarazzo (1992) goes further in asserting that these and other biological approaches actually will receive common usage:

> Therefore, another of my predictions is that in the early decades of the 21st century we may see the

further development and *use in practice* of these and other biological indices of brain function and structure in a test (or a test battery) for the measurement of individual differences in mental ability, thus heralding the first clear break from test items and tests in the Binet tradition in a century [p. 1012, italics in the original].

While Matarazzo's prediction could come true, a more likely scenario is that the general public will be threatened when biological indices are used in assessment and will therefore take steps (e.g., pressure on legislators) to insure that such measures receive limited (if any) application. The public will be threatened because, rightly or wrongly, biological characteristics such as glucose metabolic rate in the brain are perceived to be relatively permanent and immutable. The fear will arise that biological tests will sort people into a caste system. Even if (or when) the validity of biological tests is firmly established, it will be decades (if ever) until they are found acceptable by the general public.

The computerization of testing, on the other hand, is already a fixture of industrialized societies and this trend can only increase in the future. Existing tests will be adapted to the desktop computer with increasing regularity. An example of this trend is Fepsy (Ferrum + Psyche), a system for automated neuropsychological testing that is available on-line at 220 sites throughout the Netherlands and most of Europe. Fepsy is described on the internet at www.euronet.nl. Fepsy consists of the following subtests:

- Auditory reaction time
- Binary choice reaction time
- Tapping task
- Visual searching task
- Recognition tasks
- Vigilance task
- Rhythm task
- Classification task
- 6 Visual Half field tasks
- Corsi block tapping

A common use is pre- and post-operative testing of patients who undergo epilepsy surgery for relief of seizures. The system has even been used with fully conscious patients *during* surgery. Under local anesthesia, the patient works on a subtest while simultaneously receiving harmless electrical stimulation at distinctive sites on the cortex. The purpose is to determine whether specific cognitive functions might be affected when scar tissue is excised from the brain. The advantage of using a multicenter, multinational, computerized testing system is that the examiner has access to normative data for *thousands* of patients with specific conditions.

Another prediction is that fewer and fewer wide-spectrum tests (e.g., personality inventories and individual intelligence tests) will be released by test publishers (Gregory, 1998). Instead, publishers will concentrate on tests designed to assess particular areas of functioning for specific target populations (e.g., measures of memory functioning for elderly suspected of dementia). The reasons for these complementary trends are economic:

> Test publishing is big business, a respectable way for large corporations to earn a profit. Publishers

will be reluctant to make the major investment needed to develop new instruments that have the grandiose ambition of assessing many aspects of personality or intellect for a wide range of subjects. The cost is too high and—in light of the existing competition—the risk is too great [Gregory, 1998, pp. 76–77].

Test publishers likely will focus on less-expensive and less-risky forms of test development such as instruments that embody distinctive constructs relevant to specific target groups. Examples might include tests to measure risky behaviors in adolescents, mental decline in the elderly, faulty cognitions in depressed persons, or communication problems in maritally distressed couples. These kinds of instruments will flourish whereas publishers will rarely invest in new omnibus tests of personality or ability, preferring instead to revise and recycle existing instruments.

SUMMARY

1. The term *computer-assisted psychological assessment* (CAPA) refers to the entire range of computer applications in psychological assessment. This includes administration, scoring, and interpretation of tests; computerized adaptive testing; and sophisticated multimedia applications.

2. The first use of computers to provide test interpretations can be traced to the Mayo Clinic in the early 1960s. This MMPI interpretive system supplied brief scale-by-scale statements based upon clinical lore.

3. Computer-based test interpretation (CBTI) is now available for virtually every published psychological test. Four approaches to CBTI are recognized: scoring reports, descriptive reports, actuarial reports, and computer-assisted clinical reports.

4. Scoring reports consist only of scores and/or profiles, but may include statistical significance tests and confidence intervals plotted for the test scores. These reports highlight meaningful scores and score differences at a glance.

5. A descriptive report provides brief scale-by-scale interpretation of test results. These reports are especially useful when test findings are conveyed to mental health professionals who have little knowledge of the test in question.

6. In actuarial test interpretation, an empirically derived formula is used to diagnose, classify, or predict behavior. This is in contrast to the clinical approach in which the psychologist processes information in his or her head to diagnose, classify, or predict behavior.

7. Empirical comparisons of clinical versus actuarial test interpretation find the latter to be superior in virtually every case. Computerized test interpretations should incorporate actuarial methods, where possible.

8. In a computer-assisted clinical report, the interpretive statements are based upon the automated and computerized judgment of one or more expert clinicians. This approach allows for interpretation of all test profiles, not just those that fit certain actuarial patterns.

9. The advantages of computer-based test interpretation include objectivity, speed, and low cost. A major disadvantage is the danger that the psychologist could be excluded from the assessment process entirely, which increases the risk that test results will be misused.

10. Multimedia includes realistic, interactive presentation of test stimuli via computer (e.g., video display of a work situation). Multimedia allows for the testing of complex, real-life problems, such as conflict resolution in the workplace.

11. Computerized adaptive testing (CAT) is a family of procedures that allows for accurate and efficient measurement of ability. In this approach, the computer guides item selection based upon prior examinee answers.

12. The purpose of CAT is to reach a predetermined level of measurement accuracy with as few test items as possible. A typical finding is that CAT reduces test length by about 50 percent with no loss in measurement accuracy.

13. The future of testing is difficult to predict. Whereas some authorities predict an increase in use of biological measures of intelligence, this is uncertain. Certainly the increased computerization of testing is one clear trend that can only intensify.

KEY TERMS AND CONCEPTS

computer-assisted psychological
    assessment   p. 553

computer-based test interpretation   p. 555

clinical judgment   p. 557

actuarial judgment   p. 557

multimedia   p. 561

virtual reality   p. 562

computerized adaptive testing   p. 566

TOPIC **15B** Ethical and Social Issues in Testing

The general theme of this book is that psychological testing is a beneficial influence in modern society. When used ethically and responsibly, testing provides a basis for arriving at sensible inferences about individuals and groups. After all, the intention of the enterprise is to promote proper guidance, effective treatment, accurate evaluation, and fair decision making—whether in one-on-one clinic testing or institutional group testing. Who could possibly complain about these goals?

Thankfully, tests generally are applied in an ethical and responsible manner by psychologists, educators, administrators, and others. But there are exceptions. Almost everyone has heard the horrific anecdotes: the minority grade schooler casually labeled as retarded on the basis of a single IQ score; the college student implausibly diagnosed as schizophrenic from a projective test; the job applicant wrongfully screened from employment based upon an irrelevant measure; the aspiring teacher given unfair advantage when a competency test is mysteriously leaked beforehand; or the minority child penalized in testing because English is not her first language. Exceptions such as these illustrate the need for ethical and professional standards in testing.

A major purpose of this topic is to introduce the reader to the ethical and professional standards that inform the practice of psychological testing.

We also pursue the related theme of special considerations in the testing of cultural and linguistic minorities. The two topics share substantial overlap: When an examinee is not from the majority Anglo-American culture (predominantly caucasian, English-speaking, individualistic, future-oriented), ethical and professional concerns in testing rise to the forefront.

THE RATIONALE FOR PROFESSIONAL TESTING STANDARDS

Testing is generally applied in a responsible manner, but as previously noted, there are exceptions. On rare occasion, testing is irresponsible by design rather than by accident. Consider, with shuddering amazement, the advertisement for Mind Prober featured in a pop psychology magazine:

> Read Any Good Minds Lately? With the Mind Prober you can. In just minutes you can have a scientifically accurate personality profile of anyone. This new expert systems software lets you discover the things most people are afraid to tell you. The strengths, weaknesses, sexual interests and more (Eyde & Primhoff, 1992).

In this case the irresponsibility is so blatant that discussion of ethical and professional guidelines is almost superfluous.

ETHICAL AND PROFESSIONAL QUANDARIES IN TESTING

1. A consulting psychologist agrees to perform preemployment screening for psychopathology in police officer candidates. At the beginning of each consultation, the psychologist asks the candidate to read and sign a detailed consent form that openly and honestly describes the evaluation process. However, the consent form explains that specific feedback about the test results will not be provided to job candidates. Question: Is it ethical for the psychologist to deny such feedback to the candidates?

2. A competent counselor who has received extensive training in the interpretation of the MMPI continues to use this instrument even though it has been superceded by the MMPI-2. His rationale is simply that there is a huge body of research on the MMPI and he feels secure about the meaning of elevated MMPI test profiles, whereas he knows very little about the MMPI-2. He intends to switch over to the MMPI-2 at some undetermined future date, but finds no compelling reason to do so immediately. Question: Is the counselor's refusal to use the MMPI-2 a breach of professional standards?

3. A consulting psychologist is asked to evaluate a nine-year-old boy of Puerto Rican descent for possible learning disability. The child's primary language is Spanish and his secondary language is English. The psychologist intends to use the Wechsler Intelligence Scale for Children-III (WISC-III) and other tests. Because he knows almost no Spanish, the psychologist asks the child's after-school babysitter to act as translator when this is required to communicate test directions, specific questions, or the child's responses. Question: Is it an appropriate practice to use a translator when administering an individual test such as the WISC-III?

4. In the midst of taking a test battery for learning disability, a distraught 20-year-old female college student confides a terrifying secret to the psychologist. The client has just discovered that her 25-year-old brother, who died three months ago, was most likely a pedophile. She shows the psychologist photographs of naked children posing in the brother's bedroom. To complicate matters, the brother lived with his mother—who is still unaware of his well-concealed sexual deviancy. Question: Is the psychologist obligated to report this case to law enforcement?

However, testing practices do not always present in sharply contrasting shades, responsible or irresponsible. The real challenge of competent assessment is to determine the boundaries of ethical and professional practice. As usual, it is the borderline cases that provide pause for thought. The reader is encouraged to read the quandaries of testing described in Case Exhibit 15.2, and form an opinion about each. These examples are based upon first-hand reports to the author. At the close of this chapter, we will return to these problematic vignettes.

The dilemmas of psychological testing do not always have simple, obvious answers. Even thoughtful and experienced psychologists may disagree as to what is ethical or professional in a given instance. Nonetheless, the scope of ethical and professional practice is not a matter of individual taste or personal judgment. Responsible test use is defined by written guidelines published by professional associations such as the American Psychological Association, the American Counseling Association, the National Association of School Psychologists, and other groups. Whether they know it or not, all practitioners owe allegiance to these guidelines, which we review below.

In general, the evolution of professional and ethical standards has been almost uniformly restrictive, providing an ever narrowing demarcation of where, when, and how psychological tests may be used. Writing from a legal background, Bersoff (1984) summarized the historical trend as follows:

> At one time, the work of academic and applied psychometricians went virtually unexamined by the law, but as the use of tests increased in the United States, so did their potential for causing legally cognizable injury to test takers. As a result, there is probably no current activity performed by psychologists so closely scrutinized and regulated by the legal system as testing.

Partly in response to the modern climate of litigation, organizations concerned with psychological testing have published guidelines which collectively define the ethical and professional standards relevant to the practice of assessment.

These standards also pertain to corporations and individuals who publish tests. We begin with a survey of guidelines for test publishers before examining the responsibilities of test users. The chapter closes with a review of special concerns in the testing of cultural and linguistic minorities.

RESPONSIBILITIES OF TEST PUBLISHERS

The responsibilities of publishers pertain to the publication, marketing, and distribution of their tests. In particular, it is expected that publishers will release tests of high quality, market their product in a responsible manner, and restrict distribution of tests only to persons with proper qualifications. We consider each of these points in turn.

Publication and Marketing Issues

Regarding the publication of new or revised instruments, the most important guideline is to guard against premature release of a test. Testing is a noble enterprise but it is also big business driven by the profit motive, which provides an inherent pressure toward early release of new or revised materials. Perhaps this is why the American Psychological Association and other organizations have published standards that relate to test publication (AERA/APA/NCME, 1985, 1999). These standards pertain especially to the technical manuals and user guides that typically accompany a test. These sources must be sufficiently complete so that a qualified user or reviewer can evaluate the appropriateness and technical adequacy of the test. This means that manuals and guides will report detailed statistics on reliability analyses, validity studies, normative samples, and other technical aspects.

Marketing tests in a responsible manner refers not only to advertising (which should be accurate and dignified) but also to the way in which information is portrayed in manuals and guides. In particular, test authors should strive for a balanced presentation of their instruments and refrain from a one-sided presentation of information. For example, if some preliminary studies reflect poorly on a test, these should be given fair weight in the manual alongside positive findings. Likewise, if a potential misuse or inappropriate use of a test can be anticipated, the test author needs to discuss this matter as well.

Competence of Test Purchasers

Test publishers recognize the broad responsibility that only qualified users should be able to purchase their products. By way of brief review (see Topic 2A, The Nature and Uses of Psychological Tests) the reasons for restricted access include the potential for harm if tests fall into the wrong hands (e.g., an undergraduate psychology major administers the MMPI-2 to his friends and then makes frightful pronouncements about the results) and the obvious fact that many tests are no longer valid if potential examinees have previewed them (e.g., a teacher memorizes the correct answers to a certification exam).

These examples illustrate that access to psychological tests needs to be limited. But limited to whom? The answer, it turns out, depends upon the complexity of the specific test under consideration. Guidelines proposed many years ago by the American Psychological Association (APA) are still relevant today, even though they are not enforced by all publishers. The APA proposed that tests fall into three levels of complexity (Levels A, B, and C) that require different degrees of expertise from the examiner.

Level A: These instruments are straightforward paper-and-pencil measures that can be administered, scored, and interpreted with minimal training. With the aid of a manual, these tests can be used by responsible nonpsychologists such as business executives or educational administrators. This category includes vocational proficiency and group educational achievement tests.

Level B: These tests require knowledge of test construction and training in statistics and psychology. These products are available to persons who have completed an advanced-level course in testing from an accredited college or university, or equivalent training under the supervision of a qualified psychologist. This category includes aptitude tests and personality inventories applicable to normal populations.

Level C: These tests require substantial understanding of testing and supporting topics. Supervised experience is essential for the proper administration, scoring, and interpretation of these instruments. Typically, Level C tests are available only to persons with a minimum of a master's degree in psychology or an allied field. These instruments include individual tests of intelligence, projective personality tests, and neuropsychological test batteries (American Psychological Association, 1953).

In general, test publishers try to screen out inappropriate requests by requiring that purchasers have the necessary credentials. For example, the Psychological Corporation, one of the major suppliers of test materials in the United States, requires prospective customers to fill out a registration form detailing their training and experience with tests. Buyers who do not hold an advanced degree in psychology must list details of courses in the administration and interpretation of tests and in statistics. References are required, too.

Most test publishers also specify that individuals or groups who provide testing and counseling by mail are not allowed to purchase materials. On a related note, ethical standards now discourage practitioners from giving "take home" tests to clients. Until recent years, this has been an occasional practice with lengthy personality tests such as the MMPI. The ethics committee endorsed the following points:

1. Nonmonitored administration of the MMPI generally does not represent sound testing practice and may result in invalid assessment for a variety of reasons (e.g., influence from other people or completion of the test while intoxicated).
2. Test security cannot be guaranteed when the MMPI is allowed outside the clinical setting.
3. There is debate as to whether there are ever any circumstances in which it might be reasonable and appropriate to allow an MMPI to be completed away from the clinical setting.
4. These issues are not unique to the MMPI, but must be considered in conducting any assessment.
5. In judging the ethicality of at-home administration of tests, it is important to consider such things as the nature and purpose of the test and available information regarding reliability, validity, and standardization procedures [APA, 1994b, pp. 665–666].

In general, users are advised to refrain from giving "take home" tests and publishers are counseled to deny access to practitioners or groups who promote this practice.

Even though publishers attempt to filter out unqualified purchasers, there may still be instances in which sensitive tests are sold to unscrupulous individuals. Oles and Davis (1977) discovered that graduate students in psychology could purchase the WISC-R, MMPI, TAT, Stanford-Binet, and 16-PF if they typed their orders on college stationery, placed the letters *Ph.D.* after their names, enclosed payment, and used a post office box return address. Although illicit test orders are few in number, they do occur.

RESPONSIBILITIES OF TEST USERS

The psychological assessment of personality, interests, brain functioning, aptitude, or intelligence is a sensitive professional action that should be completed with utmost concern for the well-being of the examinee, his or her family, employers, and the wider network of social institutions that might be affected by the results of that particular clinical assessment (Matarazzo, 1986, 1990). Over the years, the profession of psychology has proposed, clarified, and sharpened a series of thorough and thoughtful standards to provide guidance for the individual practitioner. Professional organizations publish formal ethical principles which bear upon test use, including the American Psychological Association (APA, 1992a), the American Association for Counseling and Development (AACD, 1988), the American Speech-Language-Hearing Association (ASHA, 1991), and the National Association of School Psychologists (NASP, 1992).

In addition to ethical principles, several testing organizations have published practice guidelines to help define the scope of responsible test use. Sources of test use guidelines include teaching groups (AFT, NCME, NEA, 1990), the American Psychological Association (APA, 1992b), the Educational Testing Service (ETS, 1987, 1988, 1989), the Joint Committee on Testing Practices (JCTP, 1988), the Society for Industrial and Organizational Psychology (SIOP, 1987), and professional alliances (AERA, APA, NCME, 1985, 1999). Finally, we should mention that the principles of responsible test use have been distilled in an illuminating casebook published jointly by several testing groups (Eyde, Robertson, Krug, & others, 1993).

The dozens of guidelines relevant to testing are quite specific, for example:

> Standard 6.8: When test results are released to the news media, those responsible for releasing the results should provide information to help minimize the possibility of the misinterpretation of the test results (AERA, APA, NCME, 1985).

Because of their specificity, a detailed analysis of relevant ethical and professional standards is beyond the scope of this text. What follows is a summary of the general provisions that pertain to the responsible practice of psychological testing and clinical psychological assessment.

These principles apply to psychologists, students of psychology, and others who work under the supervision of a psychologist. We restrict our discussion to those principles that are directly pertinent to the practice of psychological testing. Proper adherence to these principles would eliminate most—but not all—legal challenges to testing.

Best Interests of the Client

Several ethical principles recognize that all psychological services, including assessment, are provided within the context of a professional relationship. Psychologists are therefore enjoined to accept the responsibility implicit in this relationship. In general, the practitioner is guided by one overriding question: What is in the best interests of the client? The functional implication of this guideline is that assessment should serve a constructive purpose for the individual examinee. If it does not, the practitioner is probably violating one or more specific ethical principles. For example, Standard 6.5 in the *Standards* manual (AERA, APA, NCME, 1985) warns testers to avoid actions that have unintended negative consequences. Allowing a client to attach unsupported surplus meanings to test results would not be in the best interests of the client and would therefore constitute an unethical testing practice. In fact, with certain worry-prone and self-doubting clients, a psychologist may choose not to use an appropriate test, since these clients are almost certain to engage in self-destructive misinterpretation of virtually any test findings.

Confidentiality and the Duty to Warn

Practitioners have a primary obligation to safeguard the confidentiality of information, including test results, that they obtain from clients in the course of consultations (Principle 5, APA, 1992a). Such information can be ethically released to others only after the client or a legal representative gives unambiguous consent, usually in written form. The only exceptions to confidentiality involve those unusual circumstances in which the withholding of information would present a clear danger to the client or other persons. For example, most states have passed laws which mandate that health care practitioners must report all cases of suspected abuse in children and vulnerable elderly. In most states, a psychologist who learns in the course of testing that the client has physically or sexually abused a child is obligated to report that information to law enforcement.

Psychologists also have a **duty to warn** that stems from the 1976 decision in the Tarasoff case (Wrightsman, Nietzel, & Fortune, 1994). Tanya Tarasoff was a young college student in California who was murdered by Prosenjit Poddar, a student from India. What makes the case relevant to the practice of psychology is that Poddar had made death threats regarding Tarasoff to his campus-based therapist. Although the therapist warned the police that Poddar had made death threats, he did not warn Tarasoff. Two months later, Poddar stabbed Tarasoff to death at her home. The parents of Tanya Tarasoff sued, and the California Supreme Court later agreed that therapists have a duty to use "reasonable care" to protect potential victims from their clients. Although the Tarasoff ruling has been modified by legislation in many states, the thrust of the case still stands: Clinicians must communicate any serious threat to the potential victim, law enforcement agencies, or both.

Finally, the clinician should consider the client's welfare in deciding whether to release information, especially when the client is a minor who is unable to give voluntary, informed consent. Where appropriate, practitioners are advised to inform their clients of the legal limits of confidentiality.

Expertise of the Test User

A number of principles acknowledge that the test user must accept ultimate responsibility for the proper application of tests. From a practical standpoint, this means that the test user must be well trained in assessment and measurement theory. The user must possess the expertise needed to evaluate psychological tests for proper standardization, reliability, validity, interpretive accuracy, and other psychometric characteristics. This guideline has special significance in areas such as job screening, special education, testing of persons with disabilities, or other situations where potential impact is strong.

Psychologists who are poorly trained in their chosen instruments can make serious errors of test interpretation that harm examinees. Furthermore, inept test usage may expose the examiner to professional sanctions and civil lawsuits. A common error observed among inexperienced test users is the overzealous, pathologized interpretation of personality test results (Case Exhibit 15.3).

The expertise of the psychologist is particularly relevant when test scoring and interpretation services are used. The Ethical Principles of the American Psychological Association leave no room for doubt:

> Psychologists retain appropriate responsibility for the appropriate application, interpretation, and use of assessment instruments, whether they score and interpret such tests themselves or use automated or other services (APA, 1992a).

The reader is referred to Topic 15A, Computerized Assessment and the Future of Testing, for further discussion of this point.

Informed Consent

Before testing commences, the test user needs to obtain informed consent from test takers or their legal representatives. Exceptions to informed consent can be made in certain instances, for example, legally mandated statewide testing programs, school-based group testing, and when consent is clearly implied

---

CASE EXHIBIT | **OVERZEALOUS INTERPRETATION OF THE MMPI**
15.3

An inexperienced consulting psychologist routinely used the MMPI for pre-employment screening of law enforcement candidates. One candidate subsequently filed a lawsuit, alleging that she had been harmed by the psychologist's report. The plaintiff, a young woman with extensive training and background in law enforcement, was denied a position as police officer because of a supposedly "defensive" MMPI profile. Her profile was entirely within normal limits, although she did obtain a *T*-score of 72 on the K-scale. The K-scale is usually considered a good index of defensive test-taking attitudes, especially for mental health evaluations with clinic or hospital referrals. By way of quick review, MMPI *T*-scores of approximately 50 are average, whereas elevations of 70 or higher are considered noteworthy. The consulting psychologist noticed the candidate's elevated score on the K-scale, surmised hastily that the candidate was unduly defensive, and cautioned the police chief not to hire her.

What the psychologist did not know is that elevated K-scale scores are extremely common among law enforcement job applicants. For example, Hiatt and Hargrave (1988) found that about 25 percent of a sample of peace officers produced MMPI profiles with K-scales at or above a *T*-score of 70. In fact, successful police officers tend to have higher K-scale scores than "problem" peace officers! In this case the test user did not possess sufficient expertise to use the MMPI for job screening. His ignorance on this point constituted a breach of professional ethics. Incidentally, the case was settled out of court for a substantial sum of money, showing that trespasses of responsible test use can have serious legal consequences.

(e.g., college admissions testing). The principle of **informed consent** is so important that the *Standards* manual devotes a separate standard to it:

> Informed consent implies that the test takers or representatives are made aware, in language that they can understand, of the reasons for testing, the type of tests to be used, the intended use and the range of material consequences of the intended use, and what testing information will be released and to whom (AERA et al., 1985).

Even young children or test takers with limited intelligence deserve an explanation of the reasons for assessment. For example, the examiner might explain, "I'm going to ask you some questions and have you work on some puzzles so I can see what you can do and find out what things you need more help with."

From a legal standpoint, the three elements of informed consent include disclosure, competency, and voluntariness (Melton, Petrila, Poythress, & Slobogin, 1998). The heart of disclosure is that the client receive sufficient information (e.g., about risks, benefits, release of reports) to make a thoughtful decision about continued participation in the testing. Competency refers to the mental capacity of the examinee to provide consent. In general, there is a presumption of competency unless the examinee is a child, very elderly, or mentally disabled (e.g., mentally retarded). In these cases, a guardian will need to provide legal consent. Finally, the standard of voluntariness implies that the choice to undergo an assessment battery is given freely and not based on subtle coercion (e.g., inmates are promised release time if they participate in research testing). In most cases, the examiner uses a written informed consent form such as that found in Figure 15.3.

Obsolete Tests and the Standard of Care

Standard of care is a loose concept that often arises in the professional or legal review of specific health practices, including psychological testing. The prevailing **standard of care** is one that is "usual, customary or reasonable" (Rinas & Clyne-Jackson, 1988). To cite an extreme example, in medicine the standard of care for a fever might include the administration of aspirin—but would not include the antiquated practice of bleeding the patient.

Practitioners of psychological testing must be wary of obsolete tests, because their use might violate the prevailing standard of care. A case in point is the MMPI versus the MMPI-2. Even though the MMPI-2 is a relatively conservative revision of the highly esteemed MMPI, the improvements in norming and scale construction are substantial. The MMPI-2 is now the standard of care in MMPI-based assessment of psychopathology. Practitioners who continue to rely upon the original MMPI could be liable for malpractice suits, especially if the test interpretation resulted in misleading interpretive statements or an incorrect diagnosis.

Another concern relevant to the standard of care is reliance upon test results that are outdated

---

This is an agreement between [Client's name] and [Practitioner's Name], Ph.D., a licensed psychologist in the state of Illinois. You are encouraged to ask questions about experience or professional credentials at any time.

1. General Information: The purpose of this assessment is to provide your [physician, counselor, therapist] with information about your psychological functioning that may prove helpful in his/her work with you. The assessment will involve a brief interview and psychological testing. This will take 3–4 hours of your time.

2. Test Report: The relevant information from the interview and the test results will be summarized in a written report which will be sent to your [physician, counselor, therapist]. The test results and the report will be reviewed with you in approximately one week.

3. Confidentiality: The report will not be released to any other source unless you request this formally in writing. Exceptions to this rule include these situations: your life or another person's life is in danger, child or elder abuse is reported, or a court orders the disclosure of the report.

4. Cost: An hourly rate of $___ is used in arriving at the total fee. Some or all of this cost may be covered by your health insurance policy. The estimated total cost for your assessment is $___.

5. Side Effects: Although most individuals enjoy the process of psychological consultation, some persons find it uncomfortable, especially if the test results indicate psychological problems. It is appropriate for you to discuss your feelings with the examiner. You are free to withdraw your consent for ongoing testing at any time.

6. Refusal of Assessment: You have the right to refuse this assessment. You are not required to complete this evaluation in order to continue working with your [physician, counselor, therapist]. However, your treatment is more likely to be effective if you participate in this assessment. Upon request, I will discuss referral options with you.

_____   _____
Client's Name   Date

FIGURE 15.3
Abbreviated Example of Informed Consent for Psychological Assessment
Source: Adapted and abbreviated with permission from Gregory, R. J. (1999). *Foundations of intellectual assessment: The WAIS-III and other tests in clinical practice.* Boston: Allyn & Bacon.

for the current purpose. After all, individual characteristics and traits show valid change over time. A student who meets the criteria for learning disability in the fourth grade might show large gains in academic achievement, such that the LD diagnosis is no longer accurate in the fifth grade. Personality test results are especially prone to quixotic change. A short-term personal crisis might cause an MMPI-2 profile to look like a range of mountains. A week later, the test profile could be completely normal. It is difficult to provide comprehensive guidelines as to the "shelf life" of psychological test results. For example, GRE test scores that are years old still might be validly predictive of performance in graduate school, whereas Beck Depression Inventory test results from yesterday could mislead a therapist as to the current level of depression. Practitioners must evaluate the need for retesting on an individual basis.

Responsible Report Writing

Except for group testing, the practice of psychological testing invariably culminates in a written report which constitutes a semipermanent record of test findings and examiner recommendations. Effective report writing is an important skill because of the potential lasting impact of the written document. It is beyond the scope of this text to illuminate the qualities of effective report writing, although we can refer the reader to a few sources (Gregory, 1999; Tallent, 1993).

Responsible reports typically use simple and direct writing that steers clear of jargon and technical terms. The proper goal of a report is to provide helpful perspectives on the client, not to impress the referral source that the examiner is a learned person! When Tallent (1993) surveyed more than one thousand health practitioners who made referrals for testing, one respondent declared his disdain toward psychologists who "reflect their needs to shine as a psychoanalytic beacon in revealing the dark, deep secrets they have observed." On a related note, effective reports stay within the bounds of expertise of the examiner. For example:

> ... it is never appropriate for a psychologist to recommend that a client undergo a specific medical procedure (such as a CT scan for an apparent brain tumor) or receive a particular drug (such as Prozac for depression). Even when the need for a special procedure seems obvious (e.g., the symptoms strongly attest to the rapid onset of a brain disease), the best way to meet the needs of the client is to recommend immediate consultation with the appropriate medical profession (e.g., neurology or psychiatry) [Gregory, 1999].

Additional advice on effective report writing can be found in Ownby (1991) and Sattler (1988).

Communication of Test Results

Individuals who take psychological tests anticipate that the results will be shared with them. Yet practitioners often do not include one-to-one feedback as part of the assessment. A major reason for reluctance is a lack of training in how to provide feedback, especially when the test results appear to be negative. For example, how does a clinician tell a college student that her IQ is 93 when most students in that milieu score 115 or higher?

Providing effective and constructive feedback to clients about their test results is a challenging skill to learn. Pope (1992) emphasizes the responsibility of the clinician to determine that the client has understood adequately and accurately the information that the clinician was attempting to convey. Furthermore, it is the responsibility of the clinician to check for adverse reactions:

> Is the client exceptionally depressed by the findings? Is the client inferring from findings suggesting a learning disorder that the client—as the client has always suspected—is "stupid"? Using scrupulous care to conduct this assessment of the client's understanding of and reactions to the feedback is no less important than using adequate care in administering standardized psychological tests; test administration and feedback are equally important, fundamental aspects of the assessment process [p. 271].

Proper and effective feedback involves give-and-take dialogue in which the clinician ascertains how the client has perceived the information and seeks to correct potentially harmful interpretations.

Destructive feedback often arises when the clinician fails to challenge a client's incorrect perceptions about the meaning of test results. Consider IQ tests in particular—a case where many persons deify test scores and consider them an index of personal worth. Prior to providing test results, a clinician is advised to investigate the client's understanding of what IQ scores mean. After all, IQ is a limited slice of intellectual functioning: It does not evaluate drive or character of any kind, it is accurate only to about ±5 points, it may change over time, and it does not assess many important attributes such as creativity, social intelligence, musical ability, or athletic skill. But a client may have an unrealistic perspective about IQ and hence might jump to erroneous conclusions when hearing that her score is "only" 93. The careful practitioner will elicit the client's views and challenge them when needed before proceeding. Further thoughts on feedback can be found in Gass & Brown (1992) and Pope (1992).

Going beyond the general pronouncement to avoid harm when providing test feedback, Finn and Tonsager (1997) present the intriguing view that information about test results should be directly and immediately therapeutic to individuals experiencing psychological problems. In other words, they propose that psychological assessment is a form of short-term intervention, not just a basis for gathering information which is *later* used for therapeutic purposes. In one study (Finn & Tonsager, 1992), they examined the effects of a brief psychological assessment on clients at a university counseling center. Thirty-two students took part in an initial interview, completed the MMPI-2, and then received a one-hour feedback session conducted according to a method developed by Finn (1996). A comparison group of 29 students were interviewed and received an equal amount of supportive, nondirective psychotherapy instead of the test feedback. The clients in the MMPI-2 assessment group showed a greater decline in symptomatic distress and a greater increase in self-esteem, immediately

following their feedback session and also two weeks later, than the clients in the comparison group. The feedback group also felt more hopeful about their problems after the brief assessment. These findings illustrate the importance of providing thoughtful and constructive test feedback instead of rushing through a perfunctory review of the results.

Consideration of Individual Differences

Knowledge of and respect for individual differences is highlighted by all professional organizations that deal with psychological testing. The American Psychological Association lists this as one of six guiding principles:

> Principle D: Respect for People's Rights and Dignity
>
> . . . Psychologists are aware of cultural, individual, and role differences, including those due to age, gender, race, ethnicity, national origin, religion, sexual orientation, disability, language, and socioeconomic status. Psychologists try to eliminate the effect on their work of biases based on those factors, and they do not knowingly participate in or condone unfair discriminatory practices (APA, 1992a).

The relevance of this principle to psychological testing is that practitioners are expected to know when a test or interpretation may not be applicable because of factors such as age, gender, race, ethnicity, national origin, religion, sexual orientation, disability, language, and socioeconomic status. We can illustrate this point with a case study reported in Eyde et al. (1993). A psychologist evaluated a 75-year-old man at the request of his wife, who had noticed memory problems. The psychologist administered a mental status examination and a prominent intelligence test. Performance on the mental status examination was normal, but standard scores on the intelligence test revealed a large discrepancy between verbal subtests and subtests measuring spatial ability and processing speed. The psychologist interpreted this pattern as indicating a deterioration of intellectual functioning in the husband. Unfortunately, this interpretation was based upon faulty use of non-age-corrected standard scores. Also, the psychologist did not assess for depression, which is known to cause visuospatial performance to drop sharply (Wolff & Gregory, 1992). In fact, a series of further evaluations revealed that the husband was a perfectly healthy 75-year-old man. The psychologist failed to consider the relevance of the gentleman's age and emotional status when interpreting the intelligence test. This was a costly oversight that caused the client and his wife substantial unnecessary worry.

TESTING OF CULTURAL AND LINGUISTIC MINORITIES

Background and Historical Notes

Persons of ethnic minority descent (non-European origin) currently constitute about 25 percent of the U.S. population and it is estimated that they will comprise more than 50 percent within several decades (Dana, 1993). Yet the enterprise of testing is based almost entirely upon the efforts of white psychologists who bring an Anglo-American viewpoint to their work. The suitability of existing tests for the evaluation of diverse populations cannot be taken for granted. The assessment of ethnic minority individuals raises important questions, especially when test results translate to placement decisions or other sensitive outcomes, as is commonly the case within educational institutions.

As noted in Chapter 1 (The History of Psychological Testing), early pioneers in the testing movement largely ignored the impact of cultural background on test results. For example, in the 1920s Henry Goddard concluded that the intelligence of the average immigrant was alarmingly low, "perhaps of moron grade." Yet he downplayed the likelihood that language and cultural differences could explain the low test scores of immigrants.

Perhaps as a rebound against these early methods, beginning in the 1930s psychologists displayed an increased sensitivity to cultural variables in the practice of testing. A shining example in this regard was Stanley Porteus, who undertook a wide-ranging investigation of the temperament and intelligence of Australian aboriginal peoples. Porteus (1931) used many traditional instruments (block designs, mazes, digit span) but to his credit he also devised an ecologically valid measure of intelligence for this group, namely, footprint recognition. Whereas the aboriginal examinees performed poorly on the Eurocentric tests, their ability to recognize photographed footprints was on a par with other racial groups studied. Even so, Porteus displayed an acute awareness that his procedures *still* might have handicapped the aboriginals:

> The photograph of a footprint is not the same as the footprint itself, and quite probably a number of cues that are made use of by the aboriginal tracker are absent from a photograph. The varying depths of parts of the foot impression are not visible in the photograph, and the individual peculiarities other than general shape and size of the footprint may not be brought out clearly. Hence we must expect that the aboriginal subjects would be under some disadvantage in matching these photographs of footprints, as against recognition of the footprints themselves [p. 399–400].

In a similar vein, DuBois (1939) found that Pueblo Indian children displayed superior ability on his specially devised horse drawing test of mental ability whereas they performed less well on the mainstream Goodenough (1926) Draw-a-Man test. From these early studies onward, psychologists have maintained a keen interest in the impact of language and culture on the meaning of test results.

The Impact of Cultural Background on Test Results

Practitioners need to appreciate that the cultural background of examinees will impact the entire process of assessment. For this reason, Sattler (1988) advises assessment psychologists to approach their task from a pluralistic standpoint:

> Cultural groups may vary with respect to cultural values (stemming in part from cultural shock, discontinuity, or conflict); language and nuances in language style; views of life and death; roles of family members; problem-solving strategies; atti-

tudes toward education, mental health, and mental illness; and stage of acculturation (the group may follow traditional values, accept the dominant group's values, or be at some point between the two). You should adopt a frame of reference that will enable you to understand how particular behaviors make sense within each culture [p. 565].

While acknowledging the impact of cultural differences on testing, it is also important to avoid stereotypical overgeneralization. For example, it is often noted that Native Americans display a distinctive conception of time, emphasizing *present-time* as opposed to the *future-time* orientation that is so powerfully formative in white, middle-class America (Panigua, 1994). A possible implication of this cultural difference is that time limits might not mean the same thing for a Native American child as for a child from the mainstream culture. Perhaps the minority child will disregard the subtest instructions and work at a careful, measured pace rather than seeking quick solutions. Of course, this child would then obtain a misleadingly low score on that measure.

Yet in affirming cultural differences, examiners need to avoid the danger of stereotyping. Culture is not monolithic. Every person is unique. Some Native Americans will exhibit a distinctive orientation to time but perhaps most will not. The challenge for the practitioner is to observe the clinical details of performance and to identify the culture-based nuances of behavior that help determine the test results.

An ingenious study by Moore (1986) powerfully illustrates the relevance of cultural background for understanding the test performance of ethnic minority examinees. She compared not only the intelligence test scores but also *the qualitative manner* of responding to test demands in two groups of adopted African-American children. One group of 23 children had been transracially adopted into middle-class white families. The other group of 23 children had been intraracially adopted into middle class African-American families. All children were adopted prior to age 2 and the backgrounds of the adoptive families were similar in terms of education and social class. Thus, group

difference in test scores and test behaviors could be attributed mainly to differences in cultural background arising from the fact that one group was adopted into African-American families, the other adopted into white families. Testing and observations were completed by two female African-American examiners who were "blind" to the purposes of the study. Tested at 7 to 10 years of age, the transracially adopted children scored an average IQ of 117 on the WISC compared to an average IQ of 104 for the traditionally adopted children. These IQ results were not remarkable, insofar as Scarr and Weinberg reported similar findings years before.

The surprising and informative outcome of the study was that the two groups of children showed very different *qualitative* behaviors during testing. As a group, the children with lower IQ scores (those adopted by African-American families) were less likely to spontaneously elaborate on their work responses and more likely simply to refuse to respond when presented with a test demand. Moore (1986) offered the following interpretations:

> Children's tendency to spontaneously elaborate on their work responses may be a very important index of their level of involvement in task performance, strategies for problem solving, level of motivation to generate a correct response, and level of adjustment to the standardized test situation . . . Although the terminal not-work response is treated as an incorrect response, it does not actually provide any empirical documentation of what the child does or does not know or of what the child can and cannot do. The only information available is that the child did not respond to the demand [p. 322].

The essential lesson of this study is that culturally based differences in response style may function to conceal the underlying competence of some examinees. Cautious interpretation of test results is always advisable, but this is especially important for examinees from culturally or linguistically diverse backgrounds.

The influence of cultural factors is not limited to the test performance of children, but extends to adults as well. Terrell, Terrell, and Taylor (1981) investigated the effects of racial trust/mistrust on the intelligence test scores of African-American college students. They identified African-American students with high and low levels of mistrust of whites. Using a 2 × 2 design, half of each group was then administered an individual intelligence test by a white examiner, the other half by an African-American examiner. As predicted, the analysis of variance revealed no differences for the main effects of race of examiner (white versus African-American) or level of mistrust (high versus low) (Figure 15.4). But a substantial interaction was revealed, namely, the high-mistrust group with an African-American examiner scored much better than the high-mistrust group with a white examiner (average IQs of 96 versus 86, respectively). Put simply, cultural mistrust among African Americans was associated with significantly lower IQ scores, but *only* when the examiner was white.

Further illustrating cultural influences, Steele (1997) has proposed a theory that societal stereotypes about groups influence the immediate intellectual performance and also the long-term identity development of individual group members. He has applied this theory both to women—where stereotypes affect their achievement in math and

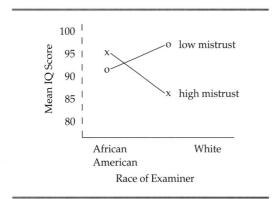

FIGURE 15.4   Mean IQ Scores of African-American Students as a Function of Race of Examiner and Cultural Mistrust
Source: Based on data in Terrell, F., Terrell, S., & Taylor, J. (1981). Effects of race of examiner and cultural mistrust on the WAIS performance of Black students. *Journal of Consulting and Clinical Psychology, 49,* 750–751.

sciences—and to African Americans—where stereotypes apparently depress their performance on standardized tests. Here we discuss his research on stereotype threat with African-American college students (Steele & Aronson, 1995).

The idea of stereotype threat is essentially a sophisticated version of a self-fulfilling prophecy. The researchers define **stereotype threat** as the threat of confirming, as self-characteristic, a negative stereotype about one's group. For example, based upon published data and media coverage about race and IQ scores, African Americans are stereotyped as possessing less intellectual ability than others. As a consequence, whenever they encounter tests of intelligence or academic achievement, individuals from this group may perceive a risk that they will confirm the stereotype. In the short run, stereotype threat is hypothesized to depress test performance through heightened anxiety and other mechanisms. In the long run, it may have the further impact of pressuring African-American students to "protectively disidentify" with achievement in school and related intellectual domains.

Steele and Aronson (1995) conducted a series of four studies to evaluate the hypothesis of stereotype threat. All the investigations supported the hypothesis. We focus here upon the first study, in which African-American and white college students were given a 30-minute test composed of challenging items from the verbal Graduate Record Examination. Students from both racial groups were randomly assigned to one of three test conditions: stereotype-threat, in which the test was described as diagnostic of individual verbal ability; control, in which the test was described as a research tool only; and, control-challenge, in which the test was described as a research tool only but participants were exhorted to "take this challenge seriously." Scores on the verbal test were adjusted (covariate analysis) on the basis of prior achievement scores so as to eliminate the effects of preexisting differences between groups.

Race differences were small and nonsignificant in the control and control-challenge conditions, whereas African Americans scored much lower

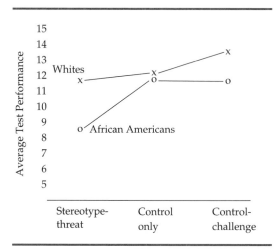

Stereotype-threat   Control only   Control-challenge

FIGURE 15.5   **Average Verbal Items Correct for Whites and African Americans under Three Conditions**
Source: Based on data in Steele, C. M., & Aronson, J. (1995). Stereotype threat and the intellectual test performance of African Americans. *Journal of Personality and Social Psychology, 69,* 797–811.

than whites in the stereotype-threat condition (Figure 15.5). In other studies, Steele and Aronson (1995) investigated the mechanism of mediation by which stereotype threat caused African Americans to score lower on standardized tests. The details are beyond the scope of this text, but the overall conclusion is not:

> Our best assessment is that stereotype threat caused an inefficiency of processing much like that caused by other evaluative pressures. Stereotype-threatened participants spent more time doing fewer items more inaccurately—probably as a result of alternating their attention between trying to answer the items and trying to assess the self-significance of their frustration (Steele & Aronson, 1995, 809).

In sum, the authors propose a social-psychological perspective on the meaning of lower test scores in African Americans and perhaps other stereotype-threatened groups as well. Their viewpoint emphasizes that test results do not reside within individuals. Test scores occur within a complex social-psychological field that is potentially influenced by national history, predicaments of race, and many other subtle factors.

Assessment of Cultural and Linguistic Minorities

Increasingly in the last 50 years, the field of psychology has recognized that specialized practices may be needed to accomplish equitable testing with cultural and linguistic minorities. Sensitivity to the unique issues encountered in minority assessment first emerged in the 1960s when the Society for the Psychological Study of Social Issues published guidelines for testing minority children. More recently, the profession of psychology has reiterated its concern for validity in the assessment of cultural and linguistic minorities by publishing guidelines for providers of psychological services to minority populations (APA, 1993). These broad guidelines provide aspirational goals (e.g., examiners are expected to recognize cultural diversity) but they furnish little in the way of specific advice for the practitioner of assessment. A flurry of influential books and articles has ensued, each offering thoughtful commentary on multicultural assessment (e.g., Lam, 1993; Suzuki, Meller, & Ponterotto, 1996; Rogers, 1998). Certain cautionary themes can be identified in this literature, as discussed below.

An overriding consideration is that linguistic barriers may inhibit test performance of minority individuals. Valdes and Figueroa (1994) express the problem as follows:

> When a bilingual individual confronts a monolingual test, developed by monolingual individuals, and standardized and normed on a monolingual population, both the test taker and the test are asked to do something that they cannot. The bilingual test taker cannot perform like a monolingual. The monolingual test can't "measure" in the other language [p. 172].

What this means from a practical standpoint is that even when a bilingual minority child is fluent in English, an English-language test might still underestimate his or her true level of ability. The sensitive examiner will acknowledge this possibility when interpreting test results.

It might appear that a native language interpreter could be used to facilitate testing of examinees whose first language is not English. In general, testing specialists advise against this practice because interpreters may substitute words, speak in a different dialect, or engage in subtle prompting that influences the examinees' responses (Rogers, 1998). A well-trained bilingual psychologist would be preferable, but even this practice is considered problematic by some (Figueroa, 1990).

The preferred option is to use tests translated into the examinee's native language and normed on relevant subpopulations. Unfortunately, there are relatively few instruments available for this purpose. Spanish versions of prominent tests are the exceptions to this trend. Examples include the Escala de Inteligencia Wechsler Para Ninos-Revisada de Puerto Rico (EIWN-R PR), a Spanish version of the WISC-R, and TEMAS, a Spanish version of the Thematic Apperception Test composed of new and culturally relevant stimulus cards. The EIWN-R PR is a 1993 Spanish adaptation of the WISC-R. This test was normed on 2,200 Puerto Rican children between the ages of 6 years and 16 years and 11 months. The EIWN-R PR retains the original structure and content of the WISC-R while providing directions in Spanish for administration and scoring of all 12 subtests. TEMAS was discussed briefly in Topic 13B, Projective Techniques.

In addition to possible linguistic barriers, minority examinees may exhibit a lack of sophistication about test taking that further compounds their disadvantage. Writing from a Hispanic background, Padilla and Medina (1996) make the following observations:

> It is quite probable that minority students are less familiar with standardized achievement testing and thus less testwise than majority students, most of whom have been exposed to standardized testing over an extended time. Another consideration is that more educated parents who are more testwise themselves engage in more coaching with their children to instruct them on strategies known to be useful on multiple-choice tests and in the importance of balancing speed and accuracy in objective type tests. This type of coaching and practice is generally not found in the homes of lower socioeconomic status children because their parents may not be knowledgeable themselves of good test-taking practices [p. 14].

There is no immediate redress to this kind of problem other than to acknowledge that minority test scores *may* reflect a lack of test sophistication.

The likelihood that linguistic barriers and lack of test sophistication will influence test results of minorities is a strong argument in favor of using a careful *multidisciplinary* assessment approach. When assessment embodies the multiple perspectives of several disciplines (e.g., psychology, speech, reading specialists) it is less likely that erroneous assessment results from any single discipline will prove damaging. This is especially true in school-based assessment of culturally and linguistically diverse children. Rogers (1998) recommends that assessment of minority children proceed along these lines:

1. Multidisciplinary assessments involving information gathered from a variety of sources and methods;
2. Assessments conducted in the child's native language as well as English;
3. Assessments that protect children from selection and administration practices that are racially and culturally discriminatory;
4. Clearly specified procedures for assessing linguistically diverse children;
5. Informed parental consent and notification of rights to due process [p. 357].

These points remind us once again that the practice of assessment occurs within a value-laden social context. The competent examiner displays a sensitivity to cultural and linguistic diversity in the application and interpretation of psychological tests.

REPRISE: RESPONSIBLE TEST USE

We return now to the real-life quandaries of testing mentioned at the beginning of the topic. The reader will recall that the first quandary had to do with whether a consulting psychologist responsibly could refuse to provide feedback to police officer candidates referred for preemployment screening. Surprisingly, the answer to this query is "Yes." Under normal circumstances, a practitioner must explain assessment results to the client. But there are exceptions, as explained by Principle 2.09 of the APA Ethical Code:

> Unless the nature of the relationship is clearly explained to the person being assessed in advance and precludes provision of an explanation of results (such as in some organizational consulting, preemployment or security screenings, and forensic evaluations), psychologists ensure than an explanation of the results is provided using language that is reasonably understandable to the person assessed or to another legally authorized person on behalf of the client (APA, 1992a).

The second quandary concerned a counselor who continued to use the MMPI even though the MMPI-2 has been available for several years. Is the counselor's refusal to use the MMPI-2 a breach of professional standards? The answer to this query is probably "Yes." The MMPI-2 is well validated and constitutes a significant improvement upon the MMPI. As mentioned previously, the MMPI-2 is now the standard of care in MMPI-based assessment of psychopathology. The counselor who continued to rely upon the original MMPI could be liable for malpractice suits, especially if his test interpretations resulted in misleading interpretive statements or a false diagnosis.

The third predicament involved the use of a neighborhood friend as translator in the administration of the WISC-III to a nine-year-old boy whose first language was Spanish. This is usually a mistake as it sacrifices strict control of the testing material. The examiner was not bilingual and therefore he would have no way of knowing whether the translator was remaining faithful to the original text or was possibly supplying additional cues. In an ideal world, the proper procedure would be to enlist a Spanish-speaking examiner who would use a test formally translated and also standardized with Hispanic examinees. For example, the Escala de Inteligencia Wechsler Para Ninos-Revisada de Puerto Rico (EIWN-R PR), discussed previously, would be a good choice.

The final quandary concerned the client who informed a psychologist that her recently deceased brother was most likely a pedophile. Is the psychologist obligated to report this case to law enforcement? The answer to this query is probably "Yes," but it may depend upon the jurisdiction of the psychologist and the wording of the relevant statutes. In fact, the psychologist did report the case to authorities, with unexpected consequences. Police obtained a search warrant, went to the home of the client's mother (where the brother had lived), and ransacked the brother's bedroom. The mother was traumatized by the unexpected visit from the police and blamed the fiasco on her daughter. A bitter estrangement followed, and the client then sued the psychologist for violation of confidentiality!

SUMMARY

1. As is true of all professional activities of psychologists, testing is guided by ethical and professional standards. Responsible test use is defined by written guidelines published by professional associations such as the American Psychological Association and other groups.

2. Test publishers also follow professional guidelines, including the expectation that they will release tests of high quality, market their products in a responsible manner, and restrict distribution of tests only to persons with proper qualifications.

3. Although there are exceptions, testing is generally guided by one overriding question: What is in the best interests of the client? The functional implication of this guideline is that assessment should serve a constructive purpose for the individual examinee.

4. Psychologists have a primary obligation to safeguard the confidentiality of information, including test results, that they obtain from clients in the course of consultations. Exceptions include those unusual circumstances in which the withholding of information would present a clear danger to the client or other persons.

5. Psychologists have a duty to warn that stems from the 1976 decision in the Tarasoff case.

Clinicians must communicate any serious threat to a potential victim, law enforcement agencies, or both.

6. The ultimate responsibility for the proper application of tests always rests with the test user. From a practical standpoint, this means that the test user must be well trained in assessment and measurement theory.

7. The professional standard on informed consent provides that test takers must be informed of the reasons for testing, the types of tests to be used, the possible consequences of the testing, and what testing information will be released and to whom.

8. The prevailing standard of care is one that is usual, customary, or reasonable. Meeting the standard of care means that psychologists should refrain from using outdated tests, especially when a new edition is available.

9. Other guidelines for the responsible use of tests include thoughtful and effective report writing, as well as a reflective and sensitive delivery of feedback to examinees in which their misconceptions are carefully dispelled.

10. Another expectation is that assessment will be guided by a knowledge of, and respect for, individual differences. For example, practitioners should know about the effects of age, gender, race, ethnicity, and other background variables on test results.

11. Cultural factors that may influence test results include the *qualitative* manner of approaching a test, racial trust/mistrust, and stereotype threat, which is the threat of confirming, as self-characteristic, a negative stereotype about one's group.

12. Linguistic barriers also may inhibit test performance of minority individuals. Bilingual persons, and individuals whose first language is not English, may encounter subtle problems on tests developed for use in the dominant culture.

13. A lack of sophistication about the nature of tests is another factor encountered by some minority individuals. Linguistic barriers and a lack of sophistication about testing are strong arguments in favor of using a *multidisciplinary* approach to assessment (e.g., psychology, speech, reading specialists).

KEY TERMS AND CONCEPTS

duty to warn   p. 575

informed consent   p. 576

standard of care   p. 577

stereotype threat   p. 582

Major Landmarks in the History of Psychological Testing

2200 B.C. Chinese begin civil service examinations.

1838 Jean Esquirol distinguishes between mental illness and mental retardation.

1862 Wilhelm Wundt uses a calibrated pendulum to measure the "speed of thought."

1866 O. Edouard Seguin writes the first major textbook on the assessment and treatment of mental retardation.

1869 Wundt founds the first experimental laboratory in psychology in Leipzig, Germany.

1884 Francis Galton administers the first test battery to thousands of citizens at the International Health Exhibit.

1890 James McKeen Cattell uses the term *mental test* in announcing the agenda for his Galtonian test battery.

1896 Emil Kraepelin provides the first comprehensive classification of mental disorders.

1901 Clark Wissler discovers that Cattellian "brass instruments" tests have no correlation with college grades.

1904 Charles Spearman proposes that intelligence consists of a single general factor g and numerous specific factors, s_1, s_2, s_3, and so forth.

1904 Karl Pearson formulates the theory of correlation.

1905 Alfred Binet and Theodore Simon invent the first modern intelligence test.

1908 Henry H. Goddard translates the Binet-Simon scales from French into English.

1912 Stern introduces the IQ or intelligence quotient: the mental age divided by chronological age.

1916 Lewis Terman revises the Binet-Simon scales, publishes the Stanford-Binet; revisions appear in 1937, 1960, and 1986.

1917 Robert Yerkes spearheads the development of the Army Alpha and Beta examinations used for testing WWI recruits.

1917 Robert Woodworth develops the Personal Data Sheet, the first personality test.

1920 The Rorschach Inkblot test is published.

1921 Psychological Corporation—the first major test publisher—is founded by Cattell, Thorndike, and Woodworth.

1926 Florence Goodenough publishes the Draw-A-Man Test.

1926   The first Scholastic Aptitude Test is published by the College Entrance Examination Board.

1927   The first edition of the Strong Vocational Interest Blank is published.

1935   The Thematic Apperception Test is released by Morgan and Murray at Harvard University.

1936   Lindquist and others publish the precursor to the Iowa Tests of Basic Skills.

1936   Edgar Doll publishes the Vineland Social Maturity Scale for assessment of adaptive behavior in the mentally retarded.

1938   L. L. Thurstone proposes that intelligence consists of about seven group factors known as primary mental abilities.

1938   Raven publishes the Raven's Progressive Matrices, a nonverbal test reasoning intended to measure Spearman's *g* factor.

1938   Lauretta Bender publishes the Bender Visual Motor Gestalt Test, a design-copying test of visual-motor integration.

1938   Oscar Buros publishes the first *Mental Measurements Yearbook.*

1938   Arnold Gesell releases his scale of infant development.

1939   The Wechsler-Bellevue Intelligence Scale is published; revisions are published in 1955 (WAIS), 1981 (WAIS-R), and 1997 (WAIS-III).

1939   Taylor-Russell tables published for determining the expected proportion of successful applicants with a test.

1939   The Kuder Preference Record, a forced-choice interest inventory, is published.

1942   The Minnesota Multiphasic Personality Inventory is published.

1948   Office of Strategic Services (OSS) uses situational techniques for selection of officers.

1949   The Wechsler Intelligence Scale for Children is published; revisions are published in 1974 (WISC-R) and 1991 (WISC-III).

1950   The Rotter Incomplete Sentences Blank is published.

1951   Lee Cronbach introduces coefficient alpha as an index of reliability (internal consistency) for tests and scales.

1952   American Psychiatric Association publishes the *Diagnostic and Statistical Manual (DSM I).*

1953   Stephenson develops the Q-technique for studying the self-concept and other variables.

1954   Paul Meehl publishes *Clinical vs. Statistical Prediction.*

1956   The Halstead-Reitan Test Battery begins to emerge as the premiere test battery in neuropsychology.

1957   C. E. Osgood describes the semantic differential.

1958   Lawrence Kohlberg publishes the first version of his Moral Judgment Scale; research with it expands until the mid-1980s.

1959   Campbell and Fiske publish a test validation approach known as the multitrait-multimethod matrix.

1963   Raymond Cattell proposes the theory of fluid and crystallized intelligence.

1967   In *Hobson v. Hansen* the court rules against the use of group ability tests to "track" students on the grounds that such tests discriminate against minority children.

1968   American Psychiatric Association publishes *DSM-II.*

1969   Nancy Bayley publishes the Bayley Scales of Infant Development (BSID). The revised version (BSID-2) is published in 1993.

1969   Arthur Jensen proposes the genetic hypothesis of African-American versus white IQ differences in the *Harvard Educational Review.*

1971   In *Griggs v. Duke Power* the Supreme Court rules that employment test results must have a demonstrable link to job performance.

1971   George Vaillant popularizes a hierarchy of 18 ego adaptive mechanisms and describes a methodology for their assessment.

1971   Court decision requires that tests used for personnel selection must be job relevant (*Griggs v. Duke Power*).

1972   The Model Penal Code rule for legal insanity is published and widely adopted in the United States.

1974   Rudolf Moos begins publication of the Social Climate Scales to assess different environments.

1974   Friedman and Rosenman popularize the Type A coronary-prone behavior pattern; their assessment is interview-based.

1975   The U.S. Congress passes Public Law 94–142, the Education for All Handicapped Children Act.

1978   Jane Mercer publishes SOMPA (System of Multicultural Pluralistic Assessment), a test battery designed to reduce cultural discrimination.

1978   In the *Uniform Guidelines on Employee Selection* adverse impact is defined by the four-fifths rule; also guidelines for employee selection studies are published.

1979   In *Larry P. v. Riles* the court rules that standardized IQ tests are culturally biased against low-functioning Black children.

1980   In *Parents in Action on Special Education v. Hannon* the court rules that standardized IQ tests are not racially or culturally biased.

1985   The American Psychological Association and other groups jointly publish the influential *Standards for Educational and Psychological Testing.*

1985   Sparrow and others publish the Vineland Adaptive Behavior Scales, a revision of the pathbreaking 1936 Vineland Social Maturity Scale.

1987   American Psychiatric Association publishes *DSM-III-R*

1989   The "Lake Wobegon Effect" is noted: Virtually all states of the union claim that their achievement levels are above average.

1989   The Minnesota Multiphasic Personality Inventory-2 is published.

1992   American Psychological Association publishes a revised *Ethical Principles of Psychologists and Code of Conduct* (*American Psychologist,* December 1992)

1994   American Psychiatric Association publishes *DSM-IV.*

1994   Herrnstein and Murray revive the race and IQ heritability debate in *The Bell Curve.*

APPENDIX B

Test Publisher Addresses

American Association on Mental Retardation
444 North Capitol Street, N.W., Suite 846
Washington, DC 20001-1512

American College Testing Program
P.O. Box 168
Iowa City, IA 52243-0168

American Guidance Service
P.O. Box 99
Circle Pines, MN 55014-1796

C.P.S., Inc.
P.O. Box 83
Larchmont, NY 10538

Consulting Psychologists Press
P.O. Box 10096
Palo Alto, CA 94303

CTB/Macmillan/McGraw-Hill
20 Ryan Ranch Road
Monterey, CA 93940

Denver Developmental Materials
P.O. Box 20037
Denver, CO 80220

DLM Teaching Resources
One DLM Park
Allen, TX 75002

Educational and Industrial Testing
   Service (EdITS)
P.O. Box 7234
San Diego, CA 92167

Educational Testing Service
ETS Test Collection (30-B)
Rosedale Road
Princeton, NJ 08541-001

GED Testing Service
One Dupont Circle, N. W.
Washington, DC 20036

Harvard University Press
79 Garden Street
Cambridge, MA 02138

Hawthorne Educational Services
800 Gray Oak Drive
Columbia, MO 65201

Marshal S. Hiskey
5640 Baldwin
Lincoln, NE 68507

Hogrefe & Huber Publishers
P. O. Box 2487
Kirkland, WA 98083

Institute for Personality and Ability Testing
P.O. Box 1188
Champaign, IL 61824-1188

Jastak Associates, Inc.
P.O. Box 3410
Wilmington, DE 19804-0250

Jossey-Bass
615 Montgomery Street
San Francisco, CA 94111

Mind Garden
P.O. Box 60669
Palo Alto, CA 94306

National Computer Systems
P.O. Box 1416
Minneapolis, MN 55440

National Rehabilitation Services
P.O. Box 1247
Gaylord, MI 49735

Oxford University Press
200 Madison Avenue
New York, New York 10016

Pro-Ed
8700 Shoal Creek Boulevard
Austin, TX 78757-6897

Psychological Assessment Resources, Inc.
P.O. Box 998
Odessa, FL 33556-0998

Psychological Corporation
555 Academic Court
San Antonio, TX 78204-2498

Reitan Neuropsychology Laboratories
2920 South 4th Avenue
Tucson, AZ 85713-4819

Riverside Publishing Company
3 O'Hare Towers
8420 Bryn Mawr Avenue
Chicago, IL 60631

Saul Rosenzweig
8029 Washington Avenue
St. Louis, MO 63114

Scholastic Testing Service
480 Meyer Road
P.O. Box 1056
Bensenville, IL 60106-1617

Sigma Assessment Systems, Inc.
P.O. Box 610984
Port Huron, MI 48061-0984

SRA/London House
9701 W. Higgins Road
Rosemont, IL 60018

Slosson Educational Publications, Inc.
P.O. Box 280
East Aurora, NY 14052

Stoelting Company
620 Wheat Lane
Wood Dale, IL 60191

Charles C. Thomas
2600 South First Street
Springfield, IL 62794-9265

U.S. Employment Service
Western Assessment Research
    and Development Center
140 East 300 South
Salt Lake City, UT 84111

U.S. Military Entrance
    Processing Command
Testing Directorate
2500 Green Bay Road
North Chicago, IL 60064

University of Illinois Press
1325 South Oak Street
Champaign, IL 61820

Western Psychological Services
12031 Wilshire Boulevard
Los Angeles, CA 90025-1251

West Virginia Rehabilitation Center
509 Allen Hall
West Virginia University
Morgantown, WV 26506

Wilmington Institute
13315 Wilmington Drive
Dallas, TX 75234

Wonderlic Personnel Test, Inc.
1509 North Milwaukee Avenue
Libertyville, IL 60048-1380

APPENDIX C

Major Tests and Their Publishers

Individual Tests of Intelligence and Adaptive Behavior

Adaptive Behavior Inventory for Children	Psychological Corporation
AAMR Adaptive Behavior Scale	Pro-Ed
AAMR Adaptive Behavior Scale—School Edition	Pro-Ed
Balthazar Scales of Adaptive Behavior	Consulting Psychologists Press
Bayley Scales of Infant Development-II	Psychological Corporation
The Blind Learning Aptitude Test	University of Illinois Press
Bruininks-Oseretsky Test of Motor Proficiency	American Guidance Service
Columbia Mental Maturity Scale	Psychological Corporation
Denver-2	Denver Developmental Materials
Detroit Tests of Learning Aptitude-3	Pro-Ed
Developmental Indicators for the Assessment of Learning-Revised	American Guidance Service
Differential Ability Scales	Psychological Corporation
Draw A Person: Quantitative Scoring System	Psychological Corporation
Goodenough-Harris Drawing Test	Psychological Corporation
Hiskey-Nebraska Test of Learning Aptitude	Marshal S. Hiskey
Independent Living Behavior Checklist	West Virginia Rehabilitation Center
Kaufman Assessment Battery for Children	American Guidance Service
Kaufman Brief Intelligence Test	American Guidance Service
Kaufman Adolescent and Adult Intelligence Test	American Guidance Service
Leiter International Performance Scale-Revised	Stoelting Company
McCarthy Scale of Children's Ability	Psychological Corporation
Miller Assessment for Preschoolers	Psychological Corporation

Ordinal Scales of Psychological Development	Uzgiriz & Hunt (1989)
Peabody Picture Vocabulary Test—Revised	American Guidance Service
Scales of Independent Behavior-R	DLM Teaching Resources
Stanford-Binet: Fourth Edition	Riverside Publishing Co.
Test of Nonverbal Intelligence-3	Pro-Ed
T. M. R. School Competency Scales	Consulting Psychologists Press
Vineland Adaptive Behavior Scales	American Guidance Service
Wechsler Adult Intelligence Scale-III	Psychological Corporation
Wechsler Intelligence Scale for Children-III	Psychological Corporation
Wechsler Preschool and Primary Scale of Intelligence—Revised	Psychological Corporation

Group Intelligence Tests

Cognitive Abilities Test	Riverside Publishing Co.
Culture Fair Intelligence Test	Institute for Personality and Ability Testing
Henmon-Nelson Tests of Mental Ability	Riverside Publishing Co.
Kuhlmann-Anderson Tests of Mental Ability	Scholastic Testing Service
Miller Analogies Test	Psychological Corporation
Multidimensional Aptitude Battery	Sigma Assessment Systems
Otis-Lennon School Ability Test	Psychological Corporation
Raven Progressive Matrices	Psychological Corporation [distributor]
School and College Ability Tests—Series III	Educational Testing Service
Shipley Institute of Living Scale	Western Psychological Services
Wonderlic Personnel Evaluation	Wonderlic Personnel Test

Aptitude Tests and Batteries

American College Testing Assessment Program	American College Testing Program
Armed Services Vocational Aptitude Battery	U.S. Military Entrance Processing Command
Differential Aptitude Tests	Psychological Corporation
General Aptitude Test Battery	U.S. Employment Service
Graduate Record Examinations	Educational Testing Service
Scholastic Assessment Tests	Educational Testing Service

Group Achievement Tests

California Achievement Tests	CTB/Macmillan/McGraw-Hill
Comprehensive Tests of Basic Skills	CTB/Macmillan/McGraw-Hill
Iowa Tests of Basic Skills	Riverside Publishing Co.
Iowa Tests of Educational Development	Riverside Publishing Co.
Metropolitan Achievement Tests	Psychological Corporation

Sequential Tests of Educational Progress, Series III	Educational Testing Service
SRA Achievement Series	SRA/London House
Stanford Achievement Series	SRA/London House
Stanford Test of Academic Skills	Psychological Corporation
Tests of Achievement and Proficiency	Riverside Publishing Co.
Tests of General Educational Development (GED)	GED Testing Service

Individual Achievement Tests

Kaufman Test of Educational Achievement	American Guidance Service
Mini-Battery of Achievement	DLM Teaching Resources
Peabody Individual Achievement Test-Revised	American Guidance Service
Wechsler Individual Achievement Test	Psychological Corporation
Wide Range Achievement Test-III	Jastak Associates, Inc.
Woodcock-Johnson Psycho-Educational Battery-Revised	Riverside Publishing Co.

Psychomotor and Dexterity Tests

Crawford Small Parts Dexterity Test	Psychological Corporation
Hand-Tool Dexterity Test	Psychological Corporation
Purdue Pegboard	SRA/London House
Stromberg Dexterity Test	Psychological Corporation

Clerical Tests

Clerical Abilities Battery	Psychological Corporation
General Clerical Test	Psychological Corporation
Minnesota Clerical Test	Psychological Corporation
SRA Clerical Aptitudes	SRA/London House

Mechanical Aptitude Tests

Bennett Mechanical Comprehension Test	Psychological Corporation
Minnesota Spatial Relations Test	American Guidance Service
Revised Minnesota Paper Form Board Test	Psychological Corporation
SRA Mechanical Aptitudes	SRA/London House

Interest Inventories

Campbell Interest and Skill Survey	National Computer Systems
Jackson Vocational Interest Survey	Sigma Assessment Systems
Kuder General Interest Survey	SRA/London House

Kuder Occupational Interest Survey, Revised	SRA/London House
Kuder Preference Record	SRA/London House
Self-Directed Search	Psychological Assessment Resources, Inc.
Strong Interest Inventory	Consulting Psychologists Press

Neuropsychological Tests

Bender Visual Motor Gestalt Test	Western Psychological Services
Benton Revised Visual Retention Test	Psychological Corporation
Finger Localization Test	Oxford University Press
Halstead-Reitan Neuropsychological Test Battery	Reitan Neuropsychology Laboratories
Luria-Nebraska Neuropsychological Battery	Western Psychological Services
Porteus Maze Test	Psychological Corporation
Serial Digit Learning Test	Oxford University Press
Symbol Digit Modalities Test	Western Psychological Services
Three-Dimensional Block Construction Test	Oxford University Press
Wechsler Memory Scale-Revised	Psychological Corporation
Wisconsin Card Sorting Test	Psychological Assessment Resources

Projective Personality Tests

Children's Apperception Test	C. P. S., Inc.
Draw-A-Person Test	Charles C. Thomas
Holtzman Inkblot Test	Psychological Corporation
Rorschach	Hogrefe & Huber Publishers
Rosenzweig Picture-Frustration Study (P-F Study)	Saul Rosenzweig
Rotter Incomplete Sentences Blank	Psychological Corporation
Senior Apperception Technique	C. P. S., Inc.
Thematic Apperception Test (TAT)	Harvard University Press
Washington University Sentence Completion Test	Jossey-Bass

Self-Report Personality Inventories

Beck Depression Inventory, Revised	Psychological Corporation
California Psychological Inventory	Consulting Psychologists Press
Comrey Personality Scales	EdITS, Educational and Industrial Testing Service
Edwards Personal Preference Schedule	Psychological Corporation
Eysenck Personality Questionnaire	EdITS, Educational and Industrial Testing Service
Jenkins Activity Survey	Psychological Corporation

Millon Clinical Multiaxial Inventory-3	National Computer Services
Minnesota Multiphasic Personality Inventory-2	National Computer Systems
Myers-Briggs Type Indicator	Consulting Psychologists Press
NEO Five Factor Inventory	Sigma Assessment Systems
NEO Personality Inventory-Revised	Sigma Assessment Systems
Personality Inventory for Children	Western Psychological Services
Personality Research Form	Sigma Assessment Systems
Sixteen Personality Factor Questionnaire (16PF)	Institute for Personality and Ability Testing
State-Trait Anxiety Inventory	Mind Garden
Survey of Work Styles	Sigma Assessment Systems

Forensic Tests

Custody Quotient™	Wilmington Institute
Parent-Child Relationship Inventory	Western Psychological Services
Rogers Criminal Responsibility Assessment Scales	Psychological Assessment Resources, Inc.

APPENDIX D

Standard and Standardized-Score Equivalents of Percentile Ranks in a Normal Distribution

This table lists the equivalence between percentile ranks and four other types of scores: z scores (mean of 0, SD of 1.00), deviation IQs (mean of 100, SD of 15), T-scores (mean of 50, SD of 10), and GRE-like scores (mean of 500, SD of 100). The application of the table assumes that the distribution of scores on a test or variable is normally distributed.

We illustrate how this appendix can be used with two examples. Suppose that we desire to know the WAIS-R IQ that is equivalent to a percentile rank of 97. Reading across the row that begins with PR 97, we discover that the equivalent IQ is 128. Suppose that we desire to know the percentile rank that is equivalent to a GRE score of 675. In the far right column, we locate a score of 675 and read across to the left-hand column to discover that the equivalent percentile rank is 96.

	z	Deviation IQ	T-Score	GRE-like Score		z	Deviation IQ	T-Score	GRE-like Score
Mean	0.00	100	50	500	PR 93	1.48	122	65	648
St. Dev.	1.00	15	10	100	92	1.41	121	64	641
					91	1.34	120	63	634
PR 99	2.33	135	73	733	90	1.28	119	63	628
98	2.05	131	71	705	89	1.22	118	62	622
97	1.88	128	69	688	88	1.18	118	62	618
96	1.75	126	68	675	87	1.13	117	61	613
95	1.64	125	66	664	86	1.08	116	61	608
94	1.55	123	66	655	85	1.04	116	60	604

(continued)

	z	Deviation IQ	T-Score	GRE-like Score		z	Deviation IQ	T-Score	GRE-like Score
PR 84	0.99	115	60	599	PR 42	−0.20	97	48	480
83	0.95	114	60	595	41	−0.23	96	48	477
82	0.91	114	59	591	40	−0.25	96	47	475
81	0.88	113	59	588	39	−0.28	96	47	472
80	0.84	113	58	584	38	−0.31	95	47	469
79	0.80	112	58	580	37	−0.33	95	47	467
78	0.77	112	58	577	36	−0.36	95	46	464
77	0.74	111	57	574	35	−0.39	94	46	461
76	0.71	111	57	571	34	−0.41	94	46	459
75	0.67	110	57	567	33	−0.44	93	46	456
74	0.64	110	56	564	32	−0.47	93	45	453
73	0.61	110	56	561	31	−0.49	93	45	451
72	0.58	109	56	558	30	−0.52	92	45	448
71	0.55	108	56	555	29	−0.55	92	44	445
70	0.52	108	55	552	28	−0.58	91	44	442
69	0.49	107	55	549	27	−0.61	90	44	439
68	0.47	107	55	547	26	−0.64	90	44	436
67	0.44	107	54	544	25	−0.67	90	43	433
66	0.41	106	54	541	24	−0.71	89	43	429
65	0.39	106	54	539	23	−0.74	89	43	426
64	0.36	105	54	536	22	−0.77	88	42	423
63	0.33	105	53	533	21	−0.80	88	42	420
62	0.31	105	53	531	20	−0.84	87	42	416
61	0.28	104	53	528	19	−0.88	87	41	412
60	0.25	104	53	525	18	−0.91	86	41	409
59	0.23	104	52	523	17	−0.95	86	40	405
58	0.20	103	52	520	16	−0.99	85	40	401
57	0.18	103	52	518	15	−1.04	84	40	396
56	0.15	102	52	515	14	−1.08	84	39	392
55	0.12	102	51	512	13	−1.13	83	39	387
54	0.10	102	51	510	12	−1.18	82	38	382
53	0.07	101	51	507	11	−1.22	82	38	378
52	0.05	101	51	505	10	−1.28	81	37	372
51	0.03	100	50	503	9	−1.34	80	37	366
50	0.00	100	50	500	8	−1.41	79	36	359
49	−0.03	100	50	497	7	−1.48	78	35	352
48	−0.05	99	49	495	6	−1.55	77	34	345
47	−0.07	99	49	493	5	−1.64	75	34	336
46	−0.10	98	49	490	4	−1.75	74	32	325
45	−0.12	98	49	488	3	−1.88	72	31	312
44	−0.15	98	48	485	2	−2.05	69	29	295
43	−0.18	97	48	482	1	−2.33	65	27	267

Glossary

accommodation in Piaget's theory, the adjustment of an unsuccessful schema so that it works.

achievement test a test that measures the degree of learning, success, or accomplishment in a subject matter.

actuarial judgment the kind of automated judgment in which an empirically derived formula is used to diagnose or predict behavior.

adverse impact in hiring, adverse impact is said to exist if one group has a selection rate less than four-fifths of the rate of the group with the highest selection rate (*Uniform Guidelines on Employee Selection,* 1978).

age norm a type of standardization that depicts the level of test performance for each separate age group in the normative sample.

alternate-forms reliability a form of reliability in which alternate forms of the same test are given to a group of heterogeneous and representative subjects; scores for the two forms are then correlated.

Alzheimer's disease a degenerative neurological disorder; in the early stages, the most prominent symptom is memory loss.

Americans with Disabilities Act an act passed by Congress in 1990 that forbids discrimination against qualified individuals with disabilities.

aphasia any deviation in language performance caused by brain damage.

apraxia variety of dysfunctions characterized by a breakdown in the direction or execution of complex motor acts.

aptitude test a test that measures one or more clearly defined and relatively homogeneous segments of ability.

assessment appraising or estimating the level or magnitude of some attribute of a person; testing is one small part of assessment which also incorporates observations, interviews, rating scales, and checklists.

assessment center an approach to assessment of managerial talent which consists of multiple simulation techniques, including group presentations, problem-solving exercises, group discussion exercises, interviews, and in-basket techniques.

assimilation in Piaget's theory, the application of a schema to an object, person, or event.

attention-deficit hyperactivity disorder a behavioral syndrome characterized by fidgeting, distractibility, impulsivity, attentional deficits, poor social skills, and not considering consequences.

basal ganglia a collection of nuclei in the forebrain that make connections with the cerebral cortex above and the thalamus below; the basal ganglia participate in the control of movement.

basal level for tests in which subtest items are ranked from easiest to hardest, the level below which the examinee would almost certainly answer all questions correctly.

base rate in decision theory, the proportion of successful applicants who would be selected using current methods, without benefit of the new test.

behavior observation scale a variation upon the BARS technique which uses a continuum from "almost never" to "almost always" to measure how often an employee performs specific tasks on each behavioral dimension.

behavior sample in testing, the notion that a test is just a sample of behaviors that permits the examiner to make inferences about a larger domain of relevant behaviors.

behavior therapy the application of the methods and findings of experimental psychology to the modification of maladaptive behavior; also called behavior modification.

behavioral assessment a variety of techniques that concentrate on behavior itself rather than on underlying traits, hypothetical causes, or presumed dimensions of personality.

behavioral avoidance test a behavioral procedure in which the therapist measures how long the client can tolerate an anxiety-inducing stimulus.

behavioral procedure a procedure for assessing the antecedents and consequences of behavior; behavioral procedures include checklists, rating scales, interviews, and structured observations.

behaviorally anchored rating scale a criterion-referenced rating scale.

bias in construct validity a type of bias demonstrated when a test is shown to measure different hypothetical traits (psychological constructs) for one group than another or to measure the same trait but with differing degrees of accuracy.

bias in content validity a type of bias demonstrated when an item or subscale is relatively more difficult for members of one group than another after the general ability level of the two groups is held constant.

bias in predictive validity a type of bias demonstrated when the inference drawn from the test score is not made with the smallest feasible random error or if there is constant error in an inference or prediction as a function of membership in a particular group.

biodata objective or scorable autobiographical data; recognized as a valid adjunct to personnel selection.

C scale a variant on the stanine scale with 11 units.

ceiling level for tests in which subtest items are ranked from easiest to hardest, the level above which the examinee would almost certainly fail all remaining questions.

cerebellum part of the hindbrain responsible for helping to coordinate muscle tone, posture, and skilled movements.

cerebral cortex the outermost layer of the brain which is the source of the highest levels of sensory, motor, and cognitive processing.

certification testing to determine that a person has at least a minimum proficiency in some discipline or activity.

classical theory of measurement the dominant theory in psychological testing; the theory assumes that an observed score consists of a true score plus measurement error.

classification in testing, the process of using tests to assign a person to one category rather than another.

clerical scoring error in testing, an error in test scoring related to the mechanics of scoring, such as adding subscores incorrectly or consulting the wrong conversion table.

clinical judgment the kind of judgment in which the decision maker processes information in his or her head to diagnose or predict behavior.

coaching in testing, the attempt to boost test scores by providing the examinee with extra practice on test-like materials, review of fundamental concepts likely to be covered by the test, and advice about optimal test-taking strategies.

coefficient alpha an index of reliability that may be thought of as the mean of all possible split-half coefficients, corrected by the Spearman-Brown formula.

cognitive behavior therapy an approach to behavior change that emphasizes changing the client's belief structure.

competency to stand trial the determination by the presiding judge that a defendant does not have a mental defect, illness, or condition that renders him or her unable to understand the proceedings or to assist in his or her defense.

componential intelligence in Sternberg's theory, the internal mental mechanisms that are responsible for intelligent behavior.

computer-assisted psychological assessment CAPA refers to the entire range of computer applications in psychological assessment and includes testing, scoring, report writing, and individualized test administration.

computer-based test interpretation CBTI refers to test interpretation and report writing by computer, which is a major component of computer-assisted psychological assessment (CAPA).

computerized adaptive testing a family of procedures that allows for accurate and efficient measurement of ability; individualized testing continues until a predetermined level of measurement precision is reached.

concurrent validity a type of criterion-related validity in which the criterion measures are obtained at approximately the same time as the test scores.

concussion a transitory alteration of consciousness from a blow to the head; may be followed by temporary amnesia, dizziness, nausea, weak pulse, and slow respiration, yet there is no demonstrable organic brain damage.

conservation in Piaget's theory, the awareness that physical quantities do not change in amount when they are superficially altered in appearance.

construct a theoretical, intangible quality or trait in which individuals differ.

construct validity a type of validity that refers to the appropriateness of test-based inferences about the underlying construct purportedly measured by the test.

constructional dyspraxia impairment of the ability to deal with spatial relationships either in a two- or three-dimensional framework.

consumer psychology the branch of industrial/ organizational psychology that deals with the development, advertising, and marketing of products and services.

content validity the type of validity that is determined by the degree to which the questions, tasks, or items on a test are representative of the universe of behavior the test was designed to sample.

contextual intelligence in Sternberg's theory, the mental activity involved in purposive adaptation to, shaping of, and selection of real-world environments relevant to one's life.

contingency management procedure an approach to behavior therapy in which the therapist identifies and alters the consequences of unwanted behaviors.

convergent validity a type of validity that is demonstrated when a test correlates highly with other variables or tests with which it shares an overlap of constructs.

corpus callosum the major commissure that serves to integrate the functions of the two cerebral hemispheres.

correction for guessing in group testing, the practice of revising a subject's final score in light of apparent guessing.

correlation coefficient a numerical index of the degree of linear relationship between two sets of scores; correlation coefficients can vary between –1.00 and +1.00.

correlation matrix a complete table of intercorrelations between all the variables that is the beginning point of factor analysis.

cranial nerves twelve paired neural tracts that help govern basic sensory and motor functions such as vision, smell, facial movement, taste, and hearing.

creativity test a test that assesses the ability to produce new ideas, insights, or artistic creations that are accepted as being of social, aesthetic, or scientific value.

criterion contamination a source of error in test validation when the criterion is "contaminated" by its artificial commonality with the test, such as test and criterion contain nearly identical items. Also, a form of evaluation error in which a criterion measure includes factors that are not demonstrably part of the job, for example, rating appearance when it is not job-related.

criterion-keyed approach a test development approach in which test items are assigned to a particular scale if, and only if, they discriminate between a well-defined criterion group and a relevant control group.

criterion problem the difficult problem of conceptualizing and measuring work performance constructs which are often complex, fuzzy, and multidimensional.

criterion-referenced test a test in which the objective is to determine where the examinee stands with respect to very tightly defined educational objectives; no comparison is made to the performance of other examinees.

criterion-related validity the type of validity that is demonstrated when a test is shown to be effective in estimating an examinee's performance on some outcome measure.

critical incidents checklist a form of performance evaluation based upon actual episodes of desirable and undesirable on-the-job behavior.

cross-sectional design a research design in which subjects of different ages are tested at one point in time.

cross-sequential design a research design that combines cross-sectional and longitudinal methods.

cross-validation for predictive tests, the practice of using the original regression equation in a new sample to determine whether the test predicts the criterion as well as it did in the original sample.

crystallized intelligence in Cattell and Horn's theory, what one has already learned through the investment of fluid intelligence in cultural settings (e.g., learning algebra in school).

culture fair test a test designed to minimize irrelevant influences of cultural learning and social climate and thereby produce a cleaner separation of natural ability from specific learning.

custody evaluation in divorce cases, the psychological evaluation of a child (or children) and both parents so as to offer an opinion to the court as to the best interests of the child (or children) in custody arrangements.

decision theory an approach to psychological measurement that considers the costs and benefits of test-based decisions, for example, in personnel selection.

defense mechanisms unconscious mental strategies available to the ego in dealing with the conflicting demands of id, superego, and external reality.

diagnosis determining the nature and source of a person's abnormal behavior, and classifying the behavior pattern within an accepted diagnostic system.

discriminant validity a type of validity that is demonstrated when a test does not correlate with variables or tests from which it should differ.

divergent production the creation of numerous appropriate responses to a single stimulus situation.

divergent thinking the kind of thinking that goes off in different directions.

Durham rule the legal provision for the defense of insanity if the criminal act was a "product" of mental disease or defect; dropped in 1972 and replaced by the Model Penal Code.

duty to warn stemming from the Tarasoff case, the responsibility of clinicians to communicate any serious threat to the potential victim, law enforcement agencies, or both.

ego in psychoanalytic theory, the conscious self that mediates between the id and reality.

equilibration in Piaget's theory, the entire process of assimilation, accommodation, and equilibrium.

executive functions brain functions that include logical analysis, conceptualization, reasoning, planning, and flexibility of thinking.

expectancy table a table that portrays the established relationship between test scores and expected outcome on a relevant task.

experiential intelligence in Sternberg's theory, the ability to deal effectively with novel tasks.

expert rankings a scaling method that relies upon the judgment of experts to determine the rankings for individual components.

expert witness in court cases, a witness whom the judge deems qualified to testify about a proper subject matter.

extra-validity concerns the side effects and unintended consequences of testing.

extraversion a sociable, outgoing, excitement-seeking personality disposition.

extrinsic religious expression the use of religion for external goals such as security, status, and friendship.

face validity for tests, the appearance of validity to test users, examiners, and especially the examinees; not a technical form of validity, but important for the social acceptability of a test.

factor an underlying construct or variable that helps explain the correlations between several tests or measures.

factor analysis a family of statistical procedures that researchers use to summarize relationships among variables that are correlated in highly complex ways; the goal of factor analysis is to derive a parsimonious set of derived factors.

factor loading in factor analysis, the correlation between an individual test and a single factor.

factor matrix a table of correlations between variables and factors; the correlations are called factor loadings.

false negative in decision theory, a subject who is incorrectly predicted to fail on the criterion.

false positive in decision theory, a subject who is incorrectly predicted to succeed on the criterion.

fear survey schedule a behavioral assessment device which requires respondents to indicate the presence and intensity of their fears in relation to various stimuli, typically on a 5- or 7-point Likert scale.

fetal alcohol effect a subtle version of fetal alcohol syndrome in which physical abnormalities are not observed, but behavioral problems such as attentional difficulties are noted.

fetal alcohol syndrome a cluster of physical and behavioral abnormalities, including mental retardation, caused by the mother's drinking of alcohol during pregnancy.

fluid intelligence in Cattell and Horn's theory, a largely nonverbal and relatively culture-reduced form of mental efficiency.

forced-choice method in personality test development, an item-writing method in which the alternatives are matched for social desirability.

forced-choice scale a performance evaluation scale designed to eliminate bias and subjectivity in supervisor ratings by forcing a choice between options that are equal in social desirability.

forebrain the large, outermost portion of the brain consisting of the cerebral cortex and underlying structures such as the corpus callosum, basal ganglia, limbic lobe, thalamus, and hypothalamus.

freedom from distractibility the third factor on the WISC-III consisting of Arithmetic and Digit Span.

frequency distribution a method of summarizing data or test scores by specifying a small number of usually equal-sized class intervals and then tallying how many scores fall within each interval.

frequency polygon a method of summarizing data or test scores in graphic form; similar to a histogram, except that the frequency of the class intervals is represented by single points rather than columns.

frontal lobe   the part of the cerebral cortex at the front of the brain that is required for the programming, regulation, and verification of executive functions and motor performance.

frustration   in Rosenzweig's system, the state that occurs whenever an organism encounters an obstacle or obstruction en route to the satisfaction of a need.

functionalist definition of validity   the view that a test is valid if it serves the purpose for which it is used.

fundamental lexical hypothesis   in personality theory, the notion that trait terms have survived in language because they convey important information about our dealings with others.

general factor   according to Spearman, the single general factor of intelligence that must exist to account for the observed correlations between a large number of tests.

generalizability theory   a domain sampling model of reliability that recognizes several alternatives of generalization for test results.

gifted   the designation of a person as gifted typically means that he or she has extraordinary ability in some area.

grade norm   a type of standardization that depicts the level of test performance for each separate school grade in the normative sample.

graphic rating scale   a scale that consists of trait labels, brief definitions of those labels, and a continuum for the rating.

group achievement tests   also called educational achievement tests, these instruments are commonly administered to dozens or hundreds of students at the same time to gauge achievement levels in one or more well-defined academic domains.

group tests   mainly pencil-and-paper measures suitable to the testing of large groups of persons at the same time.

guilty but mentally ill   a verdict allowed in some states in which the intention is for the accused to begin his or her sentence in a psychiatric hospital.

halo effect   the tendency to rate an employee high or low on all dimensions because of a global impression.

heritability index   an estimate of how much of the total variance in a given trait is due to genetic factors; the index can vary from 0.0 to 1.0.

hindbrain   the lowest, most simply organized, brain structures; the hindbrain consists of the myelencephalon and metencephalon.

hippocampus   part of a complex, ill-defined memory circuit that consolidates new experiences into long-term memories.

histogram   a method of summarizing data or test scores in graphic form; a histogram contains the same information as a frequency distribution.

homogeneous scale   a scale in which the individual items tend to measure the same thing; homogeneity is gauged by item-total correlations.

hypothalamus   a small structure at the center of the brain that helps govern motivated behavior and bodily regulation: feeding, sexual behavior, sleeping, temperature regulation, emotional behavior, and movement.

id   in psychoanalytic theory, the unconscious part of personality that is the seat of all instinctual needs such as for food, water, sexual gratification, and avoidance of pain.

illusory validation   in projective testing, the finding that subjects ignore disconfirming instances and cling to their preexisting stereotypes.

in-basket technique   a realistic work sample test that simulates the work environment of an administrator.

index of intellectual deterioration   on the Shipley Institute of Living Scale, an index based on the discrepancy between verbal and abstractions ability which was intended to gauge the effects of organic brain impairment.

individual achievement tests   achievement tests administered one-on-one to gauge achievement levels; these tests are essential in the assessment of potential learning disabilities.

individual tests   instruments which by their design and purpose must be administered one on one.

informed consent   in testing, the principle that test takers or their representatives are made aware, in language that they can understand, of the purposes and likely consequences of testing.

insanity plea   in court cases, a defense based upon reference to legal insanity as spelled out by the Model Penal Code or other legal statutes.

integrative model   a model of career assessment in which information from interest, ability, and personality domains is considered simultaneously.

integrity test   an instrument designed to screen potential employees for theft-proneness and other undesirable qualities; overt integrity tests contain questions about attitudes toward theft and items dealing with admission of theft and other illegal activities.

intelligence   according to experts, (1) the capacity to learn from experience, and (2) the capacity to adapt to one's environment.

intelligence test   although there are exceptions, an intelligence test generally yields an overall summary score based on results from a heterogeneous sample of items (e.g., verbal skills, reasoning, spatial thinking).

interest inventory   a test that measures the preference for certain activities or topics and thereby helps determine occupational choice.

interscorer reliability   for tests that involve judgmental scoring, the typical degree of agreement between scorers.

interval scale   a measurement scale that provides information about ranking and the relative strength of ranks; based on the assumption of equal-sized units or intervals for the underlying scale.

intrinsic religious expression   the use of religion for internal goals such as finding meaning and direction in life.

introversion   a quiet, "bookish," reserved personality disposition.

ipsative test   a test in which the average of the subscales is always the same for every examinee; thus, for an individual examinee, high scores on subscales must be balanced by low scores on other subscales.

IQ constancy   On the Wechsler tests, the axiomatic assumption that IQ must remain constant with normal aging, even though raw intellectual ability might shift or decline.

item-characteristic curve   a graphical display of the relationship between the probability of a correct response and the examinee's position on the underlying trait measured by the test.

item-difficulty index   for a single test item, the proportion of examinees in a large tryout sample who get that item correct.

item-discrimination index   a statistical index of how efficiently an item discriminates between persons who obtain high and low scores on the entire test.

item-reliability index $s_i r_{iT}$, the product of a test item's internal consistency as indexed by the correlation with the total score (r_{iT}) and its variability as indexed by the standard deviation (s_i).

item-validity index $s_i r_{iC}$ consists of the product of a test item's standard deviation (s_i) and the point-biserial correlation with the criterion r_{iC}.

job analysis   the process of defining a job in terms of the behaviors necessary to perform it; includes job description (physical characteristics of the work) and job specification (personal characteristics needed).

Kuder-Richardson formula 20   an index of reliability that is relevant to the special case where each test item is scored 0 or 1 (e.g., right or wrong).

Lake Wobegon effect   the observation that virtually all states of the union claim that average achievement scores for their school systems exceed the 50th percentile.

learning disability   an indistinct concept that typically refers to a severe discrepancy between general ability and individual achievement that cannot be explained by sensory/motor handicaps, mental retardation, emotional problems, or cultural deprivation.

Likert scale   a scale that presents the examinee with five responses ordered on an agree/disagree or approve/disapprove continuum.

limbic lobe   a group of subcortical structures responsible for elaboration of emotion and the control of visceral activity.

local norms   norms derived from a representative local sample, as opposed to a national sample.

locus of control   a construct that refers to perceptions that people have about the source of things that happen to them (e.g., internal versus external).

longitudinal design   a research design in which the same subjects are tested at several points in time.

mean   the arithmetic average of a group of scores.

measurement error   everything other than the true score that makes up an examinee's obtained test score.

median   the middlemost score when all the scores in a sample have been ranked.

medulla oblongata   part of the hindbrain that helps mediate swallowing, vomiting, breathing, the control of blood pressure, respiration, and, partially, heart rate.

mental retardation   significantly subaverage general intellectual functioning resulting in or associated with concurrent impairments in adaptive behavior and manifested during the developmental period.

mental state at the time of the offense (MSO)   the mental state of a defendant at the time of the offense is relevant in special pleadings such as the insanity defense; psychologists and psychiatrists may offer opinions as to the MSO of defendants.

method of absolute scaling   a procedure for obtaining a measure of absolute item difficulty based upon results for different age groups of test takers.

method of empirical keying   a scale development method in which test items are selected based entirely on how well they contrast a criterion group from a normative sample.

method of equal-appearing intervals   a method for constructing interval-level scales from attitude statements.

method of rational scaling   a scale construction method in which all scale items correlate positively with each other and also with the total score for the scale; also known as the internal consistency approach.

midbrain   the middle portion of the brain consisting of cranial nerves and relay stations for vision and hearing.

mixed-standard scale   a complex approach to performance evaluation designed to minimize rating errors in performance appraisal; items for performance dimensions are randomly ordered on the scale.

M'Naughten rule   one of several standards of legal insanity; essentially, "the party accused was laboring under such a defect of reason, from disease of the mind, as not to know the nature and quality of the act he was doing. . . ."

mode   the most frequently occurring score.

Model Penal Code rule   a standard of legal insanity—"A person is not responsible for criminal conduct if at the time of such conduct, as a result of mental disease or defect, he lacks substantial capacity either to appreciate the criminality [wrongfulness] of his conduct or to conform his conduct to the requirements of the law."

moral dilemma   a brief story that involves a difficult moral choice such as whether to steal to prolong someone's life; used in the study of moral reasoning.

multimedia   the collective capacity of the modern computer to use still images, live video segments, music, tables, charts, animation, and other approaches in interactive format.

multitrait-multimethod matrix   a research design for assessing convergent and discriminant validity that calls for the assessment of two or more traits by two or more methods.

neuropsychological tests   tests and procedures with proven sensitivity to the effects of brain damage.

neuropsychology   the study of the relationship between brain function and behavior.

nominal scale   a measurement scale in which the categories are arbitrary and do not designate "more" or "less" of anything; the simplest and lowest level of measurement.

nonverbal behavior   the subtler forms of human communication contained in glance, gesture, body language, tone of voice, and facial expression.

norm group   a sample of examinees who are representative of the population for whom the test is intended.

norm-referenced test   a test in which the performance of each examinee is interpreted in reference to a relevant standardization sample.

normal distribution   a symmetrical, mathematically defined, bell-shaped frequency distribution.

normal ogive   the normal distribution graphed in cumulative form.

normalized standard score   a score obtained by a transformation that renders a skewed distribution into a normal distribution.

norms   a summary of test results for a large and representative group of subjects.

not guilty by reason of insanity (NGRI)   a verdict allowed in some states in which the defendant is found not guilty because his or her criminal act was the result of mental disease or defect.

oblique axes   in factor analysis, the assumption that factors are correlated with one another, that is, not at right angles.

occipital lobe   the part of the cerebral cortex at the rear of the brain that contains the vision centers.

occupational reinforcer patterns   an evaluation of jobs in terms of the worker-perceived reinforcers which are present or absent.

operational definition   a definition of a concept in terms of the way it is measured, such as, intelligence is "what the tests test."

ordinal scale   a measurement scale which allows for ranking; ordinal scales do not provide information about the relative strength of ranking.

orthogonal axes   in factor analysis, the assumption that the factors are at right angles to one another, which means that they are uncorrelated.

overt integrity test   an employment test that seeks to assess attitudes toward theft; these instruments may also contain a section dealing with overt admissions of theft.

paralinguistics   the nonverbal aspects of speech such as tone of voice and rate of speaking.

parietal lobe   the part of the cerebral cortex that mediates spatial integration and sensory awareness of what is happening on the surface of the body.

Parkinson's disease a degenerative brain disease characterized by three types of motor disturbance: involuntary movement, including tremor; poverty and slowness of movement without paralysis; and changes in posture and muscle tone.

percentile the percentage of persons in the standardization sample who scored below a specific raw score; percentiles vary from 0 to 100.

perceptual organization the second factor on the WISC-III consisting of Picture Arrangement, Picture Completion, Block Design, and Object Assembly.

personal injury in personal injury lawsuits, attorneys may hire psychologists to testify as to the lifelong consequences of traumatic stress or acquired brain damage.

personality an inexplicit construct which is invoked to explain behavioral consistency within persons and behavioral distinctiveness between persons.

personality coefficient a term used to refer to the finding that the predictive validity of personality scales rarely exceeds .30.

personality test a test that measures the traits, qualities, or behaviors that determine a person's individuality; this information helps predict future behavior.

pineal body a pea-sized structure that sits at the center of the brain; it secretes the hormone melatonin in a cyclic biological rhythm, but its functions are not well understood.

placement in testing, the sorting of persons into different programs appropriate to their needs or skills.

polygraph a device that monitors ongoing physiological responses, including changes in breathing, pulse rate, blood pressure, and perspiration; inaccurately referred to as a "lie detector."

power test a test that allows enough time for test takers to attempt all items; however, the test is difficult enough that no test taker is able to obtain a perfect score.

predictive validity a type of criterion-related validity in which the criterion measures are obtained in the future, usually months or years after the test scores are obtained, such as when college grades are predicted from an entrance exam.

primary mental abilities the seven group factors of intelligence posited by Thurstone.

processing speed the fourth factor on the WISC-III consisting of Coding and Symbol Search.

projective hypothesis the assumption that personal interpretations of ambiguous stimuli must necessarily reflect the unconscious needs, motives, and conflicts of the examinee.

projective test a test in which the examinee encounters vague, ambiguous stimuli and responds with his or her own constructions.

psychometrician a specialist in psychology or education who develops and evaluates psychological tests.

Public Law 93-112 is a "Bill of Rights" for handicapped persons that outlawed discrimination based upon handicap.

Public Law 94-142 the Education for All Handicapped Children Act (Public Law 94-142) which mandated that handicapped schoolchildren receive appropriate assessment and educational opportunities.

Public Law 99-457 legislation which requires states to provide a free appropriate public education to handicapped children ages 3 through 5.

Q-technique a technique for studying changes in self-concept and other variables by the sorting of statements into a near-normal distribution for assigned categories.

qualified individualism in testing for selection, the ethical stance that age, sex, race, or other demographic characteristics must not be used, even if knowledge of these factors would improve the validity of selection.

quotas in testing for selection, the ethical stance that the best-qualified candidates within definable subgroups should be selected in proportion to their representation in the population.

random sampling a selection strategy in which every subject has an equal chance of being chosen.

rapport in testing, a comfortable, warm atmosphere that serves to motivate examinees and elicit cooperation.

rater bias the tendency for supervisor ratings to be inaccurate because of leniency, severity, and other forms of evaluation errors.

ratio scale a measurement scale that yields equal-sized units or intervals and that possesses a conceptually meaningful zero point; the highest level of measurement.

raw score the most basic level of information provided by a psychological test, for example, the number of questions answered correctly.

real definition a definition that seeks to tell us the true nature of the thing being defined.

regression equation an equation that describes the best-fitting straight line for estimating the criterion from the test; the best-fitting line is one that minimizes the sum of the squared deviations from the line.

reliability the attribute of consistency in measurement.

reliability coefficient the ratio of true score variance to the total variance of test scores.

religion as Quest the view that complexity, doubt, and tentativeness are aspects of mature religious expression.

restriction of range a phenomenon in which the range on a variable is restricted, causing correlations with other variables to be artificially low.

reticular formation a network of ascending and descending nerve cell bodies and fibers that governs general arousal or consciousness.

RIASEC model a theory of person-environment types which proposes six themes: Realistic, Investigative, Artistic, Social, Enterprising, and Conventional (RIASEC).

rotation to positive manifold in factor analysis, a method of rotating the factor matrix that seeks to eliminate as many of the negative factor loadings as possible.

rotation to simple structure in factor analysis, a method of rotating the factor matrix that seeks to simplify the factor loadings so that each test has significant loadings on as few factors as possible.

routing test an initial subtest used to determine the entry level for all remaining subtests; used with individual intelligence tests such as the SB:FE.

savant a mentally deficient individual who has a highly developed talent in a single area such as art, rapid calculation, memory, or music.

schema in Piaget's theory, an organized pattern of behavior or a well-defined mental structure that leads to knowing how to do something.

screening the use of quick and simple tests or procedures to identify persons who might have special characteristics or needs.

self-efficacy in Bandura's theory, the personal judgment of how well one can execute courses of action required to deal with prospective situations.

self-monitoring a therapeutic approach in which the client chooses the goals and actively participates in supervising, charting, and recording progress toward the endpoint(s) of therapy.

semantic differential a rating technique in which the subject uses a seven-point continuum to rate a concept on a number of bipolar adjectives such as good-bad, strong-weak, active-passive.

simultaneous processing a form of information processing characterized by the simultaneous execution of several different mental operations.

situational exercise an assessment procedure in which the prospective employee is asked to perform under circumstances that are highly similar to the anticipated work environment.

skewness the symmetry or asymmetry of a frequency distribution; positive skew indicates that scores are piled up at the low end and negative skew indicates that scores are piled up at the high end.

social desirability response set the tendency of examinees to react to the perceived desirability (or undesirability) of a test item rather than responding accurately to its content.

social intelligence the capacity to understand other people and to relate effectively to them.

source traits the stable and constant sources of behavior which are less visible than surface traits but more important in accounting for behavior.

Spearman-Brown formula a formula for adjusting split-half correlations so that they reflect the full length of a scale.

specific factor according to Spearman, a factor of intelligence specific to an individual test.

speed test a timed test that contains items of uniform and generally simple level of difficulty; the time limit is strict enough that few subjects finish a speed test.

split-half reliability a form of reliability in which scores from the two halves of a test (e.g., even items versus odd items) are correlated with one another; the correlation is then adjusted for test length.

standard deviation a statistical index that reflects the degree of dispersion in a group of scores; the square root of the variance.

standard error of measurement an index of measurement error which indicates the extent to which an examinee's score might vary over a number of parallel tests.

standard error of the difference a statistical index that can help a test user determine whether, for an individual examinee, the difference between scores on two tests or subtests is significant.

standard error of estimate SE_{est} is the margin of error to be expected in the predicted criterion score; the error of estimate is derived from the following formula:

$$SE_{est} = SD_y \sqrt{1 - r_{xy}^2}$$

standard of care   the standard of care that is usual, customary, or reasonable.

standard score   a transformed score in which the original score is expressed as the distance from the mean in standard deviation units.

standardization fallacy   the fallacious view that a test standardized on one population is ipso facto unfair when used in any other population.

standardization sample   a large and representative group of subjects representative of the population for whom the test is intended.

standardized procedure   in testing, the attempt through carefully written instructions to insure that the procedures for administering a test are uniform from one examiner and setting to another.

stanine scale   a scale in which all raw scores are converted to a single-digit system of scores ranging from 1 to 9.

state anxiety   the transitory feelings of fear or worry which most persons experience on occasion.

sten scale   a 10-unit scale with five units above and five units below the mean.

stereotype threat   the threat of confirming, as self-characteristic, a negative stereotype about one's group.

stratified random sampling   a selection strategy in which subjects are chosen randomly, with the constraint that the sample matches the population on relevant background variables such as race, sex, occupation, and so on.

subgroup norms   norms derived from an identified subgroup, as opposed to a diversified national sample.

successive processing   a form of information processing in which a proper sequence of mental operations must be followed.

superego   in psychoanalytic theory, that part of personality that is roughly synonymous with conscience and is comprised of the societal standards of right and wrong which are conveyed to us by our parents.

surface traits   in Cattell's theory, the more obvious aspects of personality that typically emerge in the first stages of factor analysis when individual test items are correlated with each other.

systematic measurement error   a type of measurement error that arises when, unknown to the test developer, a test consistently measures something other than the trait for which it was intended.

table of specifications   in test development, a table that lists the exact number of items in relevant content areas; such a table also specifies the precise number of items which must embody different cognitive processes.

technical manual   in testing, the manual that summarizes the technical data about a new instrument.

temporal lobe   the part of the cerebral cortex involved in processing of auditory sensations, long-term memory storage, and modulation of biological drives such as aggression, fear, and sexuality.

teratogen   a substance that crosses the placental barrier and causes physical deformities in the fetus.

test   a standardized procedure for sampling behavior and describing it with categories or scores. In addition, most tests have norms or standards by which the results can be used to predict other, more important, behaviors.

test anxiety   a constellation of phenomenological, physiological, and behavioral responses that accompany concern about possible failure on a test.

test bias   in popular usage, a test is biased if it discriminates unfairly against racial and ethnic minorities, women, and the poor; technically, *test bias* refers to differential validity for definable, relevant subgroups of persons.

test fairness   the extent to which the social consequences of test usage are considered fair to relevant subgroups; a matter of social values, test fairness is especially pertinent when tests are used for selection decisions.

test-retest reliability   a form of reliability in which the same test is given twice to the same group of heterogeneous and representative subjects; scores for the two sessions are then correlated.

thalamus   a key structure that provides sensory input and information about ongoing movement to the cerebral cortex; the thalamus is the major relay station in the brain.

token economy   a behavioral approach in which many different forms of prosocial behavior are rewarded with tokens which can be later exchanged for material rewards or privileges.

trait   any relatively enduring way in which one individual differs from another.

trait anxiety   the relatively stable tendency of an individual to respond anxiously to a stressful predicament.

true score   an examinee's hypothetical real score on a test; the true score can be estimated probabilistically, but is never directly known.

T-score   a transformed score with mean of 50 and standard deviation of 10.

Type A coronary-prone behavior pattern a behavior pattern consisting of insecurity of status, hyperaggressiveness, free-floating hostility, and a sense of time urgency (hurry sickness).

unqualified individualism in testing for selection, the ethical stance that, without exception, the best-qualified candidates should be selected for employment, admission, or other privilege.

user's manual in testing, the manual which gives instructions for administration and also provides guidelines for test interpretation.

validity a test is valid to the extent that inferences made from it are appropriate, meaningful, and useful.

validity coefficient the correlation between test and criterion (r_{xy}).

validity shrinkage the common discovery in cross-validation research that a test predicts the relevant criterion less accurately with the new sample of examinees than with the original tryout sample.

value according to Rokeach and others, a shared and enduring belief about ideal modes of behavior or end states of existence.

variance a statistical index that reflects the degree of dispersion in a group of scores.

ventricles fluid-filled caverns within the brain.

verbal comprehension the first factor on the WISC-III consisting of Information, Similarities, Vocabulary, and Comprehension.

virtual reality the use of sophisticated computer images projected to wrap-around goggles to portray a moving, changing, three-dimensional environment.

visual agnosia a difficulty in the recognition of drawings, objects, or faces caused by brain damage.

work sample an assessment procedure which uses a miniature replica of the job for which examinees have applied.

work values the needs, motives, and values that influence vocational choice, job satisfaction, and career development.

References

Aamodt, M. G., Keller, R., Crawford, K., & Kimbrough, W. (1981). A critical incident job analysis of the university housing resident assistant position. *Psychological Reports, 49,* 983–986.

Abel, E. L. (1995). An update on incidence of FAS: FAS is not an equal opportunity birth defect. *Neurobehavioral Toxicology, 17,* 437–443.

Abell, S. C., Briesen, P., & Watz, L. (1996). Intellectual evaluations of children using human figure drawings: An empirical investigation of two methods. *Journal of Clinical Psychology, 52,* 67–74.

Achenbach, T. M. (1991). *Manual for the Teacher's Report Form and 1991 Profile.* Burlington, VT: University of Vermont, Department of Psychiatry.

Achenbach, T. M. (1992). *Manual for the Child Behavior Checklist/2–3 and 1992 Profile.* Burlington, VT: University of Vermont, Department of Psychiatry.

Ackerman, M. J., & Schoendorf, K. (1992). *Ackerman-Schoendorf Scales for Parent Evaluation of Custody (ASPECT).* Los Angeles: Western Psychological Services.

Ackerman, P. L. (1992). Review of Stanford Early School Achievement Test. *Eleventh Mental Measurements Yearbook.* Lincoln, NE: University of Nebraska Press.

Adams, G. A., Elacqua, T., & Colarelli, S. (1994). The employment interview as a sociometric selection technique. *Journal of Group Psychotherapy, Psychodrama, and Sociometry.* Fall, 99–113.

Adams, K. M., and Heaton, R. K. (1985). Automated interpretation of neuropsychological test data. *Journal of Consulting and Clinical Psychology, 53,* 790–802.

Ahrens, J., Evans, R., & Barnett, R. (1990). Factors related to dropping out of school in an incarcerated population. *Educational and Psychological Measurement, 50,* 611–617.

Aiken, L. R. (1989). *Assessment of personality.* Boston: Allyn & Bacon.

Aita, J. A., Armitage, S. G., Reitan, R. M., & Rabinowitz, A. (1947). The use of certain psychological tests in the evaluation of brain injury. *Journal of General Psychology, 37,* 25–44.

Albert, M., Sparks, R., von Stockert, T., & Sax, D. (1972). A case study of auditory agnosia: linguistic and non-linguistic processing. *Cortex, 8,* 427–455.

Albert, S., Fox, H. M., & Kahn, M. W. (1980). Faking psychosis on the Rorschach: Can expert judges detect malingering? *Journal of Personality Assessment, 44,* 115–119.

Allen, M. J., & Yen, W. M. (1979). *Introduction to measurement theory.* Monterey, CA: Brooks/Cole.

Allport, G. W. (1937). *Personality: A psychological interpretation.* New York: Holt, Rinehart & Winston.

Allport, G., & Ross, J. (1967). Personal religious orientation and prejudice. *Journal of Personality and Social Psychology, 5,* 432–443.

Allport, G., Vernon, P. E., & Lindzey, G. (1960). *Study of Values* (3rd ed.): Manual. Chicago: Riverside Publishing Company.

Allport, G. W. (1950). *The individual and his religion.* New York: Macmillan.

Allport, G. W., & Odbert, H. (1936). Trait names, a psycholexical study. *Psychological Monographs, 47* (Whole No. 211).

Allport, G. W., & Vernon, P. E. (1931). *Study of values: A scale for measuring the dominant interests in personality.* Boston: Houghton Mifflin.

Altepeter, T. S. (1989). The PPVT-R as a measure of psycholinguistic functioning: A caution. *Journal of Clinical Psychology, 45,* 935–941.

Altepeter, T. S., & Johnson, K. A. (1989). Use of the PPVT-R for intellectual screening with adults: A caution. *Journal of Psychoeducational Assessment, 7,* 39–45.

Amabile, T. M. (1983). *The social psychology of creativity.* New York: Springer-Verlag.

Amelang, M., & Borkenau, P. (1986). The trait concept: Current theoretical considerations, empirical facts, and implications for personality inventory construction. In A. Angleitner & J. S. Wiggins (eds.), *Personality assessment via questionnaires: Current issues in theory and measurement.* Berlin: Springer-Verlag.

American Association for Counseling and Development. (1988). *Ethical standards.* Washington, DC: Author.

American Association on Mental Retardation. (1992). *Mental retardation: Definition, classification, and systems of supports.* Washington, DC: Author.

American Educational Research Association, American Psychological Association, & National Council on Measurement in Education. (1985). *Standards for educational and psychological testing.* Washington, DC: American Psychological Association.

American Educational Research Association, American Psychological Association, & National Council on Measurement in Education. (1999). *Standards for educational and psychological testing* (2nd ed.). Washington, DC: American Psychological Association.

American Federation of Teachers, National Council on Measurement in Education, and National Education Association. (1990). *Standards for teacher competence in educational assessment of students.* Washington, DC: Author.

American Psychiatric Association (1994). *Diagnostic and statistical manual of mental disorders* (4th ed.). Washington, DC: Author.

American Psychological Association. (1953). *Ethical standards of psychologists.* Washington, DC: Author.

American Psychological Association. (1986). *Guidelines for computer-based tests and interpretations.* Washington, DC: Author.

American Psychological Association. (1988). In the Supreme Court of the United States: *Clara Watson v. Fort Worth Bank & Trust. American Psychologist, 43,* 1019–1028.

American Psychological Association. (1992a). Ethical principles of psychologists and code of conduct. *American Psychologist, 47,* 1597–1611.

American Psychological Association. (1992b). *Psychological testing of language minority and culturally different children.* Washington, DC: Author.

American Psychological Association. (1993). Guidelines for providers of psychological services to ethnic, linguistic, and culturally diverse populations. *American Psychologist, 48,* 45–48.

American Psychological Association. (1994a). Guidelines for child custody evaluations in divorce proceedings. *American Psychologist, 49,* 677–680.

American Psychological Association. (1994b). Report of the ethics committee, 1993. *American Psychologist, 49,* 659–666.

American Speech-Language-Hearing Association. (1991). *Code of ethics of the American Speech-Language Hearing Association.* Rockville, MD: Author.

Anastasi, A. (1975). Review of the Goodenough-Harris Drawing Test. *The Seventh Mental Measurements Yearbook.* Lincoln, NE: University of Nebraska Press.

Anastasi, A. (1981). Coaching, test sophistication, and developed abilities. *American Psychologist, 36,* 1086–1093.

Anastasi, A. (1985). *Psychological testing* (6th ed.). New York: Macmillan.

Anastasi, A. (1986). Emerging concepts of test validation. *Annual Review of Psychology, 37,* 1–15.

Anastasi, A. (1988). *Psychological testing* (6th ed.). New York, NY: Macmillan.

Andersson, H. W. (1996). The Fagan Test of Infant Intelligence: Predictive validity in a random sample. *Psychological Reports, 78,* 1015–1026.

Andrew, D. M., Peterson, D. G., Longstaff, H. P. (1979). *Minnesota Clerical Test Manual.* San Antonio, TX: The Psychological Corporation.

Ansorge, C. J. (1985). Review of the Cognitive Abilities Test. *Ninth Mental Measurements Yearbook.* Lincoln, NE: University of Nebraska Press.

Anthony, J. C., LeResche, L., Niaz, U., Von Korff, M., & Folstein, M. (1982). Limits of the Mini-Mental State as a screening test for dementia and delirium among hospital patients. *Psychological Medicine, 12,* 397–408.

Antoni, M. (1993). The combined use of the MCMI and MMPI. In R. J. Craig (ed.), *The Millon Clinical Multiaxial Inventory: A clinical research information synthesis.* Hillsdale, NJ: Erlbaum.

Argentero, P. (1989). Second-order factor structure of Cattell's 16 Personality Factor Questionnaire. *Perceptual and Motor Skills, 68,* 1043–1047.

Argyle, M., & Cook, M. (1976). *Gaze and mutual gaze.* Cambridge: Cambridge University Press.

Arthur, G. (1950). *The Arthur adaptation of The Leiter International Performance Scale.* Chicago: Stoelting Co.

Arvey, R. D., & Begalla, M. E. (1975). Analyzing the homemaker job using the Position Analysis Questionnaire (PAQ). *Journal of Applied Psychology, 60,* 513–517.

Arvey, R. D., & Campion, J. E. (1982). The employment interview: A summary and review of recent research. *Personnel Psychology, 35,* 281–332.

Arvey, R. D., & Faley, R. H. (1988). *Fairness in selecting employees.* Reading, MA: Addison-Wesley.

Arvey, R. D., & Murphy, K. R. (1998). Performance evaluation in work settings. *Annual Review of Psychology, 49,* 141–168.

Arvey, R. D., Landon, T., Nutting, S., & Maxwell, S. (1992). Development of physical ability tests for police officers: A construct validation approach. *Journal of Applied Psychology, 77,* 996–1009.

Asher, J. J., & Sciarrino, J. A. (1974). Realistic work samples: A review. *Personnel Psychology, 27,* 519–533.

Auer, S., & Reisberg, B. (1996). Reliability of the modified Ordinal Scales of Psychological Development: A cognitive assessment battery for severe dementia. *International Psychogeriatrics, 8,* 225–231.

Austin, J. T., & Villanova, P. (1992). The criterion problem: 1917–1992. *Journal of Applied Psychology, 77,* 836–874.

Axelrod, B. N., Greve, K., & Goldman, R. (1994). Comparison of four Wisconsin Card Sorting Test Scoring guides with novice raters. *Assessment, 1,* 115–121.

Bach, P. J., Harowski, K., Kirby, K., Peterson, P., & Schulein, M. (1981). The interrater reliability of the Luria-Nebraska Neuropsychological Battery. *Clinical Neuropsychology, 3,* 19–21.

Bagby, R. M., Nicholson, R., Rogers, R., and Nussbaum, D. (1992). Domains of competency to stand trial: A factor analytic study. *Law and Human Behavior, 16,* 491–507.

Bagby, R. M., Rogers, R., Buis, T., & Kalemba, V. (1994). Malingered and defensive response styles on the MMPI-2: An examination of validity scales. *Assessment, 1,* 31–38.

Ballard, J., & Zettel, J. (1977). Public Law 94–142 and Sec. 504: What they say about rights and protections. *Exceptional Children, 44,* 177–185.

Ball-Rokeach, S., Rokeach, M., & Grube, J. (1984). *The great American values test.* New York: Free Press.

Baltes, P. B., Reese, H., & Nesselroade, J. (1977). *Life-span developmental psychology: Introduction to research methods.* Belmont, CA: Wadsworth.

Balthazar, E. E. (1976). *Balthazar Scales of Adaptive Behavior.* Palo Alto, CA: Consulting Psychologists Press.

Bandura, A. (1965). Vicarious processes: A case of no-trial learning. In L. Berkowitz (ed.), *Advances in experimental social psychology* (vol. 2). New York: Academic Press.

Bandura, A. (1971). *Social learning theory.* Morristown, NJ: General Learning Press.

Bandura, A. (1977). *Social learning.* Englewood Cliffs, NJ: Prentice-Hall.

Bandura, A. (1982). Self-efficacy mechanism in human agency. *American Psychologist, 37,* 122–147.

Bandura, A., & Walters, R. H. (1963). *Social learning and personality development.* New York: Holt, Rinehart & Winston.

Bandura, A., Taylor, C. B., Ewart, C. K., Miller, N. M., & BeBusk, R. F. (1985). Exercise testing to enhance wives' confidence in their husbands' cardiac capability soon after clinically uncomplicated acute myocardial infarction. *American Journal of Cardiology, 55,* 635–638.

Banerji, M. (1992). An integrated study of the predictive properties of the Gesell School Readiness Test. *Journal of Psychoeducational Assessment, 10,* 240–256.

Barkley, R. A. (1981). *Hyperactive children: A handbook for diagnosis and treatment.* New York: Guilford Press.

Barkley, R. A., & Edelbrock, C. S. (1987). Assessing situational variation in children's behavior problems: The home and school situations questionnaires. In R. Prinz (ed.), *Advances in behavioral assessment of children and families* (vol. 3). Greenwich, CT: JAI Press.

Barron, F. (1953). An ego-strength scale which predicts response to psychotherapy. *Journal of Consulting Psychology, 17,* 327–333.

Batson, C. D., Schoenrade, P., & Ventis, W. (1993). *Religion and the individual: A Social-psychological perspective.* New York: Oxford University Press.

Bausell, R. B. (1986). *A practical guide to conducting empirical research.* New York: Harper & Row.

Bayless, J. D., Varney, N. R., & Roberts, R. J. (1989). Tinker Toy Test performance and vocational outcome in patients with closed-head injuries. *Journal of Clinical and Experimental Neuropsychology, 11,* 913–917.

Bayley, N. (1969). *Bayley Scales of Infant Development.* San Antonio, TX: The Psychological Corporation.

Bayley, N. (1993). *Bayley Scales of Infant Development-II.* San Antonio, TX: The Psychological Corporation.

Bear, D. M. (1986). Behavioural changes in temporal lobe epilepsy. In M. R. Trimble & T. G. Bolwig (eds.), *Aspects of epilepsy and psychiatry.* New York: Wiley.

Beck, A. T. (1976). *Cognitive therapy and the emotional disorders.* New York: New American Library.

Beck, A. T. (1983). Negative cognitions. In E. Levitt, B. Lubin, & J. Brooks (eds.), *Depression: Concepts, controversies, and some new facts* (2nd ed.). Hillsdale, NJ: Erlbaum.

Beck, A. T. (1987). Cognitive models of depression. *Journal of Cognitive Psychotherapy, An International Quarterly, 1,* 5–37.

Beck, A. T., & Steer, R. A. (1987). *Manual for the revised Beck Depression Inventory.* San Antonio, TX: Psychological Corporation.

Beck, A. T., Steer, R. A., & Brown, G. K. (1996). *Manual for the Beck Depression Inventory-II.* San Antonio, TX: Psychological Corporation.

Beck, A. T., Steer, R. A., & Garbin, M. G. (1988). Psychometric properties of the Beck Depression Inventory: Twenty-five years of evaluation. *Clinical Psychology Review, 8,* 77–100.

Beck, A. T., Ward, C. H., Mendelsohn, M., Mock, J., & Erbaugh, J. (1961). An inventory for measuring depression. *Archives of General Psychiatry, 4,* 561–571.

Becker, T. E., & Colquitt, A. L. (1992). Potential versus actual faking of a biodata form: An analysis along several dimensions of item type. *Personnel Psychology, 45,* 389–406.

Belcher, M. J. (1992). Review of the Wonderlic Personnel Test. *The Eleventh Mental Measurements Yearbook.* Lincoln, NE: University of Nebraska Press.

Bellak, L. (1992). *The Thematic Apperception Test, the Children's Apperception Test, and the Senior Apperception Technique in clinical use* (5th ed.). Orlando, FL: Grune & Stratton.

Bellak, L., & Bellak, S. S. (1991). *Children's Apperception Test Manual (CAT)* (8th rev. ed.). Larchmont, NY: C. P. S.

Bellak, L., & Bellak, S. S. (1994). *Children's Apperception Test Human Figures (CAT-H)* (11th ed.). Larchmont, NY: C. P. S.

Bem, D. J., & Allen, A. (1974). On predicting some of the people some of the time: The search for cross-situational consistencies in behavior. *Psychological Review, 81,* 506–520.

Bem, D., & Funder, D. (1978). Predicting more of the people more of the time: Assessing the personality of situations. *Psychological Review, 85,* 485–501.

Bender, L. (1938). *A visual motor gestalt test and its clinical use.* New York: American Orthopsychiatric Association.

Bennett, G. K., Seashore, H. G., & Wesman, A. G. (1974). *Fifth edition manual for the Differential Aptitude Tests, Forms S and T.* San Antonio, TX: Psychological Corporation.

Bennett, G. K., Seashore, H. G., & Wesman, A. G. (1982). *Differential Aptitude Tests: Administrator's handbook.* San Antonio, TX: Psychological Corporation.

Bennett, G. K., Seashore, H. G., & Wesman, A. G. (1984). *Differential Aptitude Tests: Technical Supplement.* San Antonio, TX: Psychological Corporation.

Bennett, T. (1988). Use of the Halstead-Reitan Neuropsychological Test Battery in the assessment of head injury. *Cognitive Rehabilitation, 6,* 18–25.

Ben-Porath, Y. S. (1994). The ethical dilemma of coached malingering research. *Psychological Assessment, 6,* 16–17.

Ben-Porath, Y. S., & Butcher, J. N. (1989). Psychometric stability of rewritten MMPI items. *Journal of Personality Assessment, 53,* 645–653.

Benson, D. F. (1988). Disorders of visual gnosis. In J. W. Brown (ed.), *The neuropsychology of visual perception.* Hillsdale, NJ: Erlbaum.

Benson, D. F. (1994). *The neurology of thinking.* New York: Oxford University Press.

Benson, P. G. (1985). Minnesota Importance Questionnaire. In D. J. Keyser & R. C. Sweetland (eds.), *Test critiques* (vol. 2). Kansas City, MO: Test Corporation of America.

Benson, P., Donahue, M., & Erickson, J. (1993). The Faith Maturity Scale: Conceptualization, Measurement, and Empirical Validation. In M. L. Lynn & D. O. Moberg (eds.), *Research in the social scientific study of religion* (vol. 5). Greenwich, CN: JAI Press.

Benton, A., Hamsher, K., Rey, G., & Sivan, A. (1994). *Multilingual Aphasia Examination* (3rd ed.). Iowa City, IA: AJA Associates.

Benton, A., Sivan, A., Hamsher, K., Varney, N., & Spreen, O. (1994). *Contributions to neuropsychological assessment* (2nd ed). New York: Oxford University Press.

Bentz, V. J. (1985). Research findings from personality assessment of executives. In H. J. Bernardin & D. A. Bownas (eds.), *Personality assessment in organizations.* New York: Praeger.

Berg, E. A. (1948). A simple objective test for measuring flexibility in thinking. *Journal of General Psychology, 39,* 15–22.

Berger, S. G., Chibnall, J., & Gfeller, J. (1994). The Category Test: A comparison of computerized and standard versions. *Assessment, 3,* 255–258.

Berk, L. E. (1989). *Child development.* Boston: Allyn & Bacon.

Berk, R. A. (ed.). (1984). *A guide to criterion-referenced test construction.* Baltimore: Johns Hopkins University Press.

Bernreuter, R. G. (1931). *The personality inventory.* Stanford, CA: Stanford University Press.

Bersoff, D. N. (1984). Social and legal influences on test development and usage. In B. S. Plake (ed.), *Social and technical issues in testing: Implications for test construction and usage.* Hillsdale, NJ: Erlbaum.

Bersoff, D. N. (1988). Should subjective employment devices be scrutinized? Its elementary, my dear Ms. Watson. *American Psychologist, 43,* 1016–1018.

Bigler, E. D. (ed.). (1990). *Traumatic brain injury: Mechanisms of damage, assessment, intervention, and outcome.* Austin, TX: PRO-ED.

Binet, A., & Simon, T. (1905). Methodes nouvelles pour le diagnostic du niveau intellectuel des anormaux. *Annee Psychologique, 11,* 191–244.

Bishop, E. G., Hailey, B. J., & O'Rourke, D. F. (1989). Reliability of the Jenkins Activity Survey—Form T: Temporal stability and internal consistency. *Journal of Personality Assessment, 53,* 60–65.

Bishop, J., Knights, R. M., Stoddart, C. (1990). Rey Auditory-Verbal Learning Test: Performance of English and French children aged 5 to 16. *The Clinical Neuropsychologist, 4,* 133–140.

Blake, R. J., Potter, E., III, Sliwak, R. (1993). Validation of the structural scales of the CPI for predicting the performance of junior officers in the U.S. Coast Guard. *Journal of Business Psychology, 7,* 431–448.

Blakley, B. R., Quinones, M., Crawford, M., & Jago, I. (1994). The validity of isometric strength tests. *Personnel Psychology, 47,* 247–274.

Blakely, T., Jr., Crinella, F., Fisher, T., Champaigne, L., & Beck, F. (1994). Neuropsychological correlates of learning disabilities: Identification by the Tryon clustering method. *Journal of Developmental and Physical Disabilities, 6,* 1–22.

Blau, T. (1984). *The psychologist as expert witness.* New York: Wiley.

Blazer, D. G. (1993). *Depression in late life* (2nd ed.). St. Louis, MO: Mosby.

Blin, Dr. (1902). Les debilites mentales. *Revue de Psychiatrie, 8,* 337–345.

Blinkhorn, S. (1988). Lie detection as a psychometric procedure. In A. Gale (ed.), *The polygraph test: Lies, truth and science.* London: SAGE.

Block, J. (1961). *The Q-sort method in personality assessment and psychiatric research.* Springfield, IL: Charles C. Thomas.

Blum, G. (1950). *The Blacky Pictures.* New York: Psychological Corporation.

Blumenthal, J. A. (1985). Review of Jenkins Activity Survey. In: J. V. Mitchell, Jr. (ed.). *The ninth mental measurements yearbook* (vol. 1). Lincoln, NE: Buros Institute of Mental Measurements of the University of Nebraska-Lincoln.

Boggs, D. H., & Simon, J. R. (1968). Differential effect of noise on tasks of varying complexity. *Journal of Applied Psychology, 52,* 148–153.

Bolton, B. (1985). Work Values Inventory. In D. J. Keyser & R. C. Sweetland (eds.), *Test critiques* (vol. 2). Kansas City, MO: Test Corporation of America.

Bond, L. (1989). The effects of special preparation on measures of scholastic ability. In R. L. Linn (ed.), *Educational measurement* (3rd ed.). New York: American Council on Education/Macmillan.

Bondy, M. (1974). Psychiatric antecedents of psychological testing (before Binet). *Journal of the History of the Behavioral Sciences, 10,* 180–194.

Bonner, C. M. (1988). *Utilization of spiritual resources by patients experiencing a recent cancer diagnosis.* Unpublished master's thesis, University of Pittsburgh.

Boring, E. G. (1923, June). Intelligence as the tests test it. *New Republic,* 35–37.

Boring, E. G. (1950). *A history of experimental psychology* (2nd ed.). New York: Appleton-Century-Crofts.

Borman, W. C. (1991). Job behavior, performance, and effectiveness. In M. D. Dunnette & L. M. Hough (eds.), *Handbook of industrial and organizational psychology* (vol. 2). Palo Alto, CA: Consulting Psychologists Press.

Borman, W. C., Hanson, M., & Hedge, J. (1997). Personnel selection. *Annual Review of Psychology, 48,* 299–337.

Bornstein, M. H. (1994). Infancy. In R. J. Sternberg (ed.), *Encyclopedia of human intelligence.* New York: Macmillan.

Borstelmann, L. J., & Klopfer, W. G. (1953). The Szondi Test: A review and critical evaluation. *Psychological Bulletin, 50,* 112–132.

Bouchard, T. J., Jr. (1994). Twin studies. In R. J. Sternberg (ed.), *Encyclopedia of human intelligence.* New York: Macmillan.

Bouchard, T. J., Jr., Lykken, D., McGue, M., Segal, N., & Tellegen, A. (1990). Sources of human psychological differences: The Minnesota Study of Twins Reared Apart. *Science, 250,* 223–228.

Bowers, T., & Pantle, M. (1998). Shipley Institute for Living Scale and the Kaufman Brief Intelligence Test as screening instruments for intelligence. *Assessment, 5,* 187–195.

Boyd, T. M., & Sauter, S. (1993). Route-finding: A measure of everyday executive functioning in the head-injured adult. *Applied Cognitive Psychology, 7,* 171–181.

Bracken, B. A., and Fagan, T. K. (1990). Guest editors' introduction to the conference "Intelligence: Theories and Practice." *Journal of Psychoeducational Assessment, 8,* 221–222.

Bracken, B. A., Prasse, D. P., & McCallum, R. S. (1984). Peabody Picture Vocabulary Test-Revised: An appraisal and review. *School Psychology Review, 13,* 49–60.

Bradley, R. H., & Caldwell, B. M. (1984). 174 children: A study of the relationship between home environment and cognitive development during the first 5 years. In A. W. Gottfried (ed.), *Home environment and early cognitive development: Longitudinal research.* Orlando, FL: Academic Press.

Bradley, R. H., Mundfrom, D., Whiteside, L., Case, P., & Barrett, K. (1994). A factor analytic study of the

Infant-Toddler and Early Childhood versions of the HOME Inventory administered to white, Black, and Hispanic American parents of children born preterm. *Child Development, 65,* 880–888.

Bradley, R. H., & Rock, S. L. (1985). The HOME Inventory: Its relation to school failure and development of an elementary-age version. In W. K. Frankenburg, R. N. Emde, & J. W. Sullivan (eds.), *Early identification of children at risk.* New York: Plenum.

Bradley, R. H., Rock, S. L., Caldwell, B. M., & Brisby, J. A. (1989). Use of the HOME Inventory for families with handicapped children. *American Journal on Mental Retardation, 94,* 313–330.

Bradshaw, J. L., & Mattingley, J. B. (1995). *Clinical neuropsychology: Behavioral and brain science.* San Diego, CA: Academic Press.

Braithwaite, V., & Law, H. (1985). Structure of human values: Testing the adequacy of the Rokeach Value Survey. *Journal of Personality and Social Psychology, 49,* 250–263.

Brannick, M. T., Michaels, C. E., & Baker, D. P. (1989). Construct validity of in-basket scores. *Journal of Applied Psychology, 74,* 957–963.

Brannon, L., & Feist, J. (1992). *Health psychology: An introduction to behavior and health* (2nd ed.). Belmont, CA: Wadsworth.

Brass, D. J., & Oldham, G. R. (1976). Validating an in-basket test using an alternative set of leadership scoring dimensions. *Journal of Applied Psychology, 61,* 652–657.

Breland, H. M. (1979). *Population validity and college entrance measures.* Research Monograph No. 8. New York: The College Board.

Breuer, J., & Freud, S. (1893–1895). Studies on hysteria. In J. Strachey, (ed., in collaboration with A. Freud). *The standard edition of the complete psychological works of Sigmund Freud.* London: Hogarth, 1955, vol. 2.

Bricklin, B. (1992). Data-based tests in custody evaluations. *American Journal of Family Therapy, 20,* 254–265.

Bricklin, B. (1995). *The custody evaluation handbook: Research-based solutions and applications.* New York: Brunner/Mazel.

Brief, D. E., & Comrey, A. L. (1993). A profile of personality for a Russian sample: As indicated by the Comrey Personality Scales. *Journal of Personality Assessment, 60,* 267–284.

Brigham, C. C. (1923). *A study of American intelligence.* Princeton, NJ: Princeton University Press.

Brigham, C. C. (1930). Intelligence tests of immigrant groups. *Psychological Review, 37,* 158–165.

Brinckerhoff, L., Shaw, S., & McGuire, J. (1993). *Promoting Postsecondary Education for Students with Learning Disabilities: A Handbook for Practitioners.* Austin, TX: PRO-ED.

Brodal, A. (1981). *Neurological anatomy* (3rd ed.). New York: Oxford University Press.

Brodsky, S. L. (1989). Advocacy in the guise of scientific advocacy: An examination of Faust and Ziskin. *Computers in Human Behavior, 5,* 261–264.

Brody, E. B., and Brody, N. (1976). *Intelligence: Nature, determinants and consequences.* New York: Academic Press.

Bromberg, W. (1959). *The mind of man: A history of psychotherapy and psychoanalysis.* New York: Harper & Row.

Brooks-Gunn, J., Klebanov, P., & Duncan, G. (1996). Ethnic differences in children's intelligence test scores: Role of economic deprivation, home environment, and maternal characteristics. *Child Development, 67,* 396–408.

Brown, F. G. (1992). Review of Stanford Achievement Test. *Eleventh Mental Measurements Yearbook.* Lincoln, NE: University of Nebraska Press.

Brown, L., Sherbenou, R., & Johnsen, S. (1998). *Test of Nonverbal Intelligence-3.* Austin, TX: Pro-Ed.

Bruininks, R. H. (1978). *Bruininks-Oseretsky Test of Motor Proficiency.* Circle Pines, MN: American Guidance Service.

Bruininks, R. H., Woodcock, R. W., Weatherman, R. F., & Hill, B. K. (1996). *Scales of Independent Behavior-Revised, Interviewer's Manual.* Allen, TX: DLM Teaching Resources.

Bruyere, S. M., & O'Keeffe, J. (eds.). (1994). *Implications of the Americans with Disabilities Act for psychology.* New York: Springer.

Buchsbaum, M. S., & Sostek, A. J. (1980). An adaptive-rate continuous performance test: Vigilance characteristics and reliability for 400 male students. *Perceptual and Motor Skills, 51,* 707–713.

Buck, J. (1948). The H-T-P technique, a qualitative and quantitative scoring method. *Journal of Clinical Psychology Monograph Supplement* No. *5,* 1–120.

Buck, J. (1981). *The House-Tree-Person technique: A revised manual.* Los Angeles: Western Psychological Services.

Bufford, R., & Parker, T., Jr. (1985). *Religion and well-being: Concurrent validation of the Spiritual Well-Being Scale.* Paper presented at the annual meeting of the American Psychological Association, Los Angeles.

Bufford, R., Paloutzian, R., & Ellison, C. (1991). Norms for the Spiritual Well-Being Scale. *Journal of Psychology and Theology, 19,* 56–70.

Burgemeister, B. B., Blum, L. H., & Lorge, I. (1972). *Columbia Mental Maturity Scale* (3rd ed.). New York: Harcourt Brace Jovanovich.

Burke, H. R. (1958). Raven's Progressive Matrices: A review and critical evaluation. *Journal of Genetic Psychology, 93,* 199–228.

Buros, O. K. (1978). *Eighth Mental Measurements Yearbook.* Lincoln, NE: University of Nebraska Press.

Buschke, H., & Fuld, P. A. (1974). Evaluating storage, retention, and retrieval in disordered memory and learning. *Neurology, 24,* 1019–1025.

Bushell, D., Jr. (1978). An engineering approach to the elementary classroom: The Behavior Analysis Follow Through project. In A. C. Catania & T. A. Brigham (eds.), *Handbook of applied behaviour analysis: Social and instructional processes.* New York: Irvington.

Buss, A. (1997). Evolutionary perspectives on personality traits. In R. Hogan, J. Johnson, & S. Briggs (eds.), *Handbook of personality psychology.* San Diego, CA: Academic Press.

Butcher, J. N. (1985). Introduction to the special series. *Journal of Consulting and Clinical Psychology, 53,* 746–747.

Butcher, J. N. (1993). *The Minnesota Report user's guide.* Minneapolis, MN: National Computer System.

Butcher, J. N. (ed.). (1987). *Computerized psychological assessment: A practitioner's guide.* New York: Basic Books.

Butcher, J. N., & Williams, C. L. (1992). *Essentials of MMPI-2 and MMPI-A interpretation.* Minneapolis, MN: University of Minnesota Press.

Butcher, J. N., Dahlstrom, W. G., Graham, J. R., Tellegen, A., & Kaemmer, B. (1989). *Minnesota Multiphasic Personality Inventory-2: Manual for administration and scoring.* Minneapolis, MN: University of Minnesota Press.

Butcher, J. N., Graham, J. R., Williams, C. L., & Ben-Porath, Y. S. (1990). *Development and use of the MMPI-2 content scales.* Minneapolis, MN: University of Minnesota Press.

Caldwell, B. M., & Bradley, R. H. (1984). *Home Observation for Measurement of the Environment.* Little Rock, AR: University of Arkansas at Little Rock.

Caldwell, B. M., & Bradley, R. H. (1994). Environmental issues in developmental follow-up research. In S. L. Friedman & H. C. Haywood (eds.), *Developmental follow-up: Concepts, domains, and methods.* San Diego, CA: Academic Press.

Caldwell, B. M., & Richmond, J. (1967). Social class level and the stimulation potential of the home. In J. Hellmuth (ed.), *The exceptional infant* (vol. 1). Seattle, WA: Special Child Publications.

Callahan, L. A., McGreevy, M., Cirincione, C., and Steadman, H. (1992). Measuring the effects of the Guilty But Mentally Ill (GBMI) verdict. *Law and Human Behavior, 16,* 447–462.

Camara, W. J., & Schneider, D. L. (1994). Integrity tests: Facts and unresolved issues. *American Psychologist, 49,* 112–119.

Campbell, C. D. (1988). Coping with hemodialysis: Cognitive appraisals, coping behaviors, spiritual well-being, assertiveness, and family adaptability and cohesion as correlates of adjustment (Doctoral dissertation, Western Conservative Baptist Seminary, 1983). *Dissertation Abstracts International, 49,* 538B.

Campbell, D. P. (1971). *Handbook for the Strong Vocational Interest Blank.* Stanford, CA: Stanford University Press.

Campbell, D. P. (1974). *Manual for the Strong-Campbell Vocational Interest Blank.* Stanford, CA: Stanford University Press.

Campbell, D. P., & Hansen, J. C. (1981). *Manual for the SVIB-SCII* (3rd ed.). Stanford, CA: Stanford University Press.

Campbell, D. P., Hyne, S., & Nilsen, D. (1992). *Manual for the Campbell Interest and Skill Survey.* Minneapolis, MN: National Computer Systems.

Campbell, D. T., & Fiske, D. W. (1959). Convergent and discriminant validation by the multitrait-multimethod matrix. *Psychological Bulletin, 56,* 81–105.

Campbell, J., & McCord, D. (1996). The WAIS-R Comprehension and Picture Arrangement Subtests as measures of social intelligence: Testing traditional interpretations. *Journal of Psychoeducational Assessment, 14,* 240–249.

Campbell, J. P., Dunnette, M. D., Arvey, R. D., & Hellervik, L. V. (1973). The development and evaluation of behaviorally based rating scales. *Journal of Applied Psychology, 57,* 15–22.

Campbell, J. P., Gasser, M., & Oswald, F. (1996). The substantive nature of job performance variability. In K. R. Murphy (ed.), *Individual differences and behavior in organizations.* San Francisco: Jossey-Bass.

Campion, J. E. (1972). Work sampling for personnel selection. *Journal of Applied Psychology, 56,* 40–44.

Campion, M. A., Pursell, E. D., & Brown, B. K. (1988). Structured interviewing: Raising the psychometric properties of the employment interview. *Personnel Psychology, 41,* 25–42.

Canfield, A. A. (1951). The "sten" scale—A modified C-scale. *Educational and Psychological Measurement, 11,* 295–297.

Canivez, G. L. (1995). Validity of the Kaufman Brief Intelligence Test: Comparisons with the Wechsler Intelligence Scale for Children-Third Edition. *Assessment, 2,* 101–111.

Cannell, J. J. (1988). Nationally normed elementary achievement testing in America's public schools: How all 50 states are above the national average. *Educational Measurement: Issues and Practice, 7,* 5–9.

Cantwell, D. P. (ed.). (1975). *The hyperactive child: Diagnosis, management, current research.* New York: Spectrum.

Carlson, C. F., Kula, M., & St. Laurent, C. (1997). Rorschach revised DEPI and CDI with inpatient major depressives and borderline personality disorder with major depression: Validity issues. *Journal of Clinical Psychology, 53,* 51–58.

Carlson, J. S., & Jensen, C. M. (1980). The factorial structure of the Raven Coloured Progressive Matrices Test: A reanalysis. *Educational and Psychological Measurement. 40,* 1111–1116.

Carpenter, C. D. (1992). Review of Stanford Early School Achievement Test. *The Eleventh Mental Measurements Yearbook.* Lincoln, NE: University of Nebraska Press.

Carpenter, M. B. (1991). *Core text of neuroanatomy* (4th ed.). Baltimore, MD: Williams & Wilkins.

Carroll, D. (1988). How accurate is polygraph lie detection? In A. Gale (ed.), *The polygraph test: Lies, truth and science.* London: Sage Publications.

Cascio, W. F. (1976). Turnover, biographical data, and fair employment practice. *Journal of Applied Psychology, 61,* 576–580.

Cascio, W. F. (1987). *Applied psychology in personnel management* (3rd ed.). Englewood Cliffs, NJ: Prentice-Hall.

Castlebury, F., Hilsenroth, M., Handler, L., & Durham, T. (1997). Use of the MMPI-2 Personality Disorder Scales in the assessment of DSM-IV Antisocial, Borderline, and Narcissistic Personality Disorders. *Assessment, 4,* 155–168.

Cattell, J. McK. (1890). Mental tests and measurements. *Mind, 15,* 373–380.

Cattell, R. (1950). *Personality: A systematic theoretical and factual study.* New York: McGraw-Hill.

Cattell, R. B. (1940). A culture free intelligence test, Part I. *Journal of Educational Psychology, 31,* 161–179.

Cattell, R. B. (1941). Some theoretical issues in adult intelligence testing. *Psychological Bulletin,* 38, 592 (abstract).

Cattell, R. B. (1971). *Abilities: Their structure, growth, and action.* Boston: Houghton Mifflin.

Cattell, R. B. (1973). Personality pinned down. *Psychology Today, 7,* 40–46.

Cattell, R. B. (1986). *The handbook for the 16 Personality Factor Questionnaire.* Champaign, IL: Institute for Personality and Ability Testing.

Cattell, R. B., & Nesselroade, J. R. (1967). Likeness and completeness theories examined by Sixteen Personality factor measures on stably and unstably married couples. *Journal of Personality and Social Psychology, 7,* 351–361.

Cattell, R. B., Eber, H. W., & Tatsuoka, M. M. (1970). *Handbook for the Sixteen Personality Factor Questionnaire.* Champaign, IL: Institute for Personality and Ability Testing.

Cautela, J. R. (1977). *Behavioral analysis forms for clinical intervention.* Champaign, IL: Research Press.

Ceci, S. J. (1994). Bioecological theory of intellectual development. In R. J. Sternberg (ed.), *Encyclopedia of human intelligence.* New York: Macmillan.

Chaffee, J. W. (1985). *The thorny gates of learning in Sung China: A social history of examinations.* Cambridge: Cambridge University Press.

Chalfant, J. C. (1989). Learning disabilities: Policy issues and promising approaches. *American Psychologist, 44,* 392–398.

Chaplin, W. F. (1984). State-Trait Anxiety Inventory. In: D. J. Keyser & R. C. Sweetland (eds.). *Test critiques* (vol. 1). Kansas City, MO: Test Corporation of America.

Chapman, L. J., & Chapman, J. P. (1967). Genesis of popular but erroneous psychodiagnostic observations. *Journal of Abnormal Psychology, 74,* 271–280.

Choca, J. P., Shanley, L. A., Peterson, C. A., & Van Denburg, E. (1990). Racial bias and the MCMI. *Journal of Personality Assessment, 54,* 479–490.

Choi, H., & Proctor, T. (1994). Error-prone subtests and error types in the administration of the Stanford-Binet Intelligence Scale: Fourth Edition. *Journal of Psychoeducational Assessment,* 12, 165–171.

Cicerelli, V. G. (1969). *The impact of Head Start.* Athens, OH: Westinghouse Learning Corporation and Ohio University.

Clark, D. A. (1988). The validity of measures of cognition: A review of the literature. *Cognitive Therapy and Research, 12,* 1–20.

Clarke, J. M. (1994). Neuroanatomy: Brain structure and function. In D. W. Zaidel (ed.), *Neuropsychology* (2nd ed.). San Diego, CA: Academic Press.

Clarke-Stewart, A., & Friedman, S. (1987). *Child development: Infancy through adolescence.* New York: Wiley.

Clarkin, J. F., Hull, J., Cantor, J., & Sanderson, C. (1993). Borderline personality disorder and personality traits: A comparison of SCID-II BPD and NEO-PI. *Psychological Assessment, 5,* 472–476.

Clarren, S. K., & Smith, D. W. (1978). The fetal alcohol syndrome. *New England Journal of Medicine, 298,* 1063–1067.

Cleary, T. A., Humphreys, L. G., Kendrick, S. A., & Wesman, A. (1975). Educational uses of tests with disadvantaged students. *American Psychologist, 30,* 15–41.

Cleckley, H. (1976). *The mask of sanity* (5th ed.). St. Louis, MO: Mosby.

Clemans, W. V. (1971). Test administration. In R. L. Thorndike (ed.), *Educational measurement* (2nd ed.). Washington, DC: American Council on Education.

Cleveland, J. N., Murphy, K. R., & Williams, R. E. (1989). Multiple uses of performance appraisal: Prevalence and correlates. *Journal of Applied Psychology, 74,* 130–135.

Cohen, M. S., & Bookheimer, S. (1994). Localization of brain function using magnetic resonance imaging. *Trends in Neurosciences, 17,* 268–277.

Colby, A., & Kohlberg, L. (1987). *The measurement of moral judgment* (vol. I). Cambridge: Cambridge University Press.

Colby, A., Kohlberg, L., Gibbs, J. C., & others. (1978). *Measuring moral judgment: Standardized scoring manual.* Cambridge, MA: Harvard University, Moral Education Research Foundation.

Colby, A., Kohlberg, L., Gibbs, J., & Lieberman, M. (1983). A longitudinal study of moral judgment. *Monographs for the Society for Research in Child Development, 48* 1, 2.

Cole, N. S., & Moss, P. A. (1989). Bias in test use. In Linn, R. L. (ed.), *Educational measurement* (3rd ed.). New York: ACE/Macmillan.

Collins, J. M., & Schmidt, F. L. (1993). Personality, integrity, and white collar crime: A construct validity study. *Personnel Psychology, 46,* 295–311.

Committee on Ethical Guidelines for Forensic Psychologists. (1991). Specialty guidelines for forensic psychologists. *Law and Human Behavior, 15,* 655–665.

Comrey, A. L. (1970). *Manual for the Comrey Personality Scales.* San Diego, CA: EdITS.

Comrey, A. L. (1973). *A first course in factor analysis.* New York: Academic Press.

Comrey, A. L. (1980). *Handbook of interpretations for the Comrey Personality Scales.* San Diego, CA: EdITS.

Comrey, A. L., & Backer, T. (1970). Construct validation of the Comrey Personality Scales. *Multivariate Behavior Research, 5,* 469–477.

Comrey, A. L., & Schiebel, D. (1983). Personality test correlates of psychiatric outpatient status. *Journal of Consulting and Clinical Psychology, 51,* 756–762.

Comrey, A. L., & Schiebel, D. (1985). Personality test correlates of psychiatric case history data. *Journal of Consulting and Clinical Psychology, 53,* 470–479.

Conners, C. K. (1990). *Conners' Rating Scales.* Los Angeles: Western Psychological Services.

Conners, C. K. (1991). *Conners' Teacher Rating Scales-39.* North Tonawanda, NY: Multi-Health Systems, Inc.

Conoley, C. W. (1992). Review of Beck Depression Inventory. *The Eleventh Mental Measurements Yearbook.* Lincoln, NE: University of Nebraska Press.

Conoley, C. W., Plake, B., and Kemmerer, B. (1991). Issues in computer-based test interpretive systems. *Computers in Human Behavior, 7,* 97–101.

Conoley, J. C., & Impara, J. C. (eds.). (1995). *The Twelfth Mental Measurements Yearbook.* Lincoln, NE: The University of Nebraska Press.

Conoley, J. C., & Kramer, J. J. (eds.). (1989). *The Tenth Mental Measurements Yearbook.* Lincoln, NE: The Buros Institute of Mental Measurements.

Conoley, J. C., & Kramer, J. J. (eds.). (1992). *The Eleventh Mental Measurements Yearbook.* Lincoln, NE: The Buros Institute of Mental Measurements.

Conry, R., & Plant, W. T. (1965). WAIS and group test predictions of an academic success criterion: High School and college. *Educational and Psychological Measurement, 25,* 493–500.

Constantino, G., & Malgady, R. (1996). Development of TEMAS, a multicultural thematic apperception test: Psychometric properties and clinical utility. In G. R. Sodowsky & J. C. Impara (eds.), *Multicultural assessment in counseling and clinical psychology.* Lincoln, NE: The Buros Institute of Mental Measurements.

Constantino, G., Malgady, R., & Rogler, L. (1988). *Tell-Me-A-Story (TEMAS): manual.* Los Angeles: Western Psychological Services.

Conway, J. M., Jako, R., & Goodman, D. (1995). A meta-analysis of interrater and internal consistency reliability of selection interviews. *Journal of Applied Psychology, 80,* 565–579.

Cooley, E. J., and Ayres, R. (1985). Convergent and discriminant validity of the Mental Processing Scales of the Kaufman Assessment Battery for Children. *Psychology in the Schools, 22,* 373–377.

Cooper, D. (1990). Factor structure of the Edwards Personal Preference Schedule in a vocational rehabilitation sample. *Journal of Clinical Psychology, 46,* 421–424.

Cooper, D., & Shepard, K. (1992). Review of DIAL-R. *Learning Disabilities Research & Practice, 7,* 171–174.

Corcoran, K., & Fischer, J. (1994). *Measures for clinical practice: A sourcebook, Vol. 1, 2.* (2nd ed.). New York: Free Press.

Cornelius, E. T., & Hakel, M. D. (1978). *A study to develop an improved enlisted performance evaluation system for the U.S. Coast Guard.* Washington, DC: Department of Transportation, USCG.

Cornelius, S. W., and Caspi, A. (1987). Everyday Problem Solving in Adulthood and Old Age. *Psychology and Aging, 2,* 144–153.

Cortina, J. M. (1993). What is coefficient alpha? An examination of theory and applications. *Journal of Applied Psychology, 78,* 98–104.

Cosden, M. (1992). Review of the Draw A Person: A Quantitative Scoring System. *The Eleventh Mental Measurements Yearbook.* Lincoln, NE: University of Nebraska Press.

Costa, P. T., Jr. (1991). Clinical use of the five-factor model. *Journal of Personality Assessment, 57,* 393–398.

Costa, P. T., Jr., & McCrae, R. (1989). *NEO Five-Factor Inventory test manual.* Port Huron, MI: Sigma Assessment Systems.

Costa, P. T., Jr., & McCrae, R. (1992). *NEO PI-R test manual.* Port Huron, MI: Sigma Assessment Systems.

Costa, P. T., Jr., McCrae, R. R., & Holland, J. L. (1984). Personality and vocational interests in an adult sample. *Journal of Applied Psychology, 69,* 390–400.

Cote, L., & Crutcher, M. D. (1991). The basal ganglia. In E. R. Kandel, J. H. Schwartz, & T. M. Jessell (eds.), *Principles of neural science* (3rd ed.). New York: Elsevier.

Coveny, T. E. (1972). A new test for the visually handicapped: Preliminary analysis of reliability and validity of the Perkins-Binet. *Education of the Handicapped, 4,* 97–101.

Cowdery, K. M. (1926–27). Measurement of professional attitudes: Differences between lawyers, physicians, and engineers. *Journal of Personnel Research, 5,* 131–141.

Craig, R. J. (ed.). (1993). *The Millon Clinical Multiaxial Inventory: A clinical research information synthesis.* Hillsdale, NJ: Erlbaum.

Crandall, J. E. (1981). *Theory and measurement of social interest: Empirical tests of Alfred Adler's concept.* New York: Columbia University Press.

Crandall, J. E. (1984). Social interest as a moderator of life stress. *Journal of Personality and Social Psychology, 47,* 164–174.

Crapo, L. (1985). *Hormones: The messengers of life.* New York: Freeman.

Crawford, J. R., Sommerville, J., & Robertson, I. (1997). Assessing the reliability and abnormality of subtest differences on the Test of Everyday Attention. *British Journal of Clinical Psychology, 36,* 609–617.

Cripe, L. (1996). The ecological validity of executive function testing. In R. J. Sbordone & C. J. Long (eds.), *Ecological validity of neuropsychological testing.* Delray Beach, FL: GR Press/St. Lucie Press.

Critchley, M. (1953). *The parietal lobes.* London: Edward Arnold.

Cronbach, L. J. (1951). Coefficient alpha and the internal structure of tests. *Psychometrika, 16,* 297–334.

Cronbach, L. J. (1970). *Essentials of psychological testing* (3rd ed.). New York: Harper & Row.

Cronbach, L. J. (1971). Test validation. In R. L. Thorndike (ed.), *Educational Measurement* (2nd ed.). Washington, DC: American Council on Education.

Cronbach, L. J. (1984). *Essentials of psychological testing* (4th ed.). New York: Harper & Row.

Cronbach, L. J. (1988). Five perspectives on the validity argument. In H. Wainer & H. I. Braun (eds.), *Test validity.* Hillsdale, NJ: Lawrence Erlbaum.

Cronbach, L. J., & Gleser, G. C. (1965). *Psychological tests and personnel decisions.* Urbana, IL: University of Illinois Press.

Cronbach, L. J., & Meehl, P. E. (1955). Construct validity in psychological tests. *Psychological Bulletin, 52,* 281–302.

Cronbach, L. J., Gleser, G. C., Nanda, H., & Rajaratnam, N. (1972). *The dependability of behavioral measurements: Theory of generalizability for scores and profiles.* New York: Wiley.

Crosson, B., & Warren, R. L. (1982). Use of the Luria-Nebraska Neuropsychological Battery. *Journal of Consulting and Clinical Psychology, 50,* 22–31.

Culbertson, J., & Edmonds, A. (1996). Learning Disabilities. In R. Adams, O. Parsons, J. Culbertson, & S. Nixon, (eds.). *Neuropsychology for clinical practice: Etiology, assessment, and treatment of common neurological disorders.* Washington, DC: American Psychological Association.

Cunningham, J. W., & Ballentine, R. D. (1982). *The General Work Inventory.* Raleigh, NC: Authors.

Cunningham, J. W., Boese, R, Neeb, R., & Pass, J. (1983). Systematically derived work dimensions: Factor analyses of the Occupation Analysis Inventory. *Journal of Applied Psychology, 68,* 232–252.

Cunningham, M., Wong, D., & Barbee, A. (1994). Self-presentation dynamics on overt integrity tests: Experimental studies with the Reid Report. *Journal of Applied Psychology, 79,* 643–658.

Cureton, E. E. (1950). Validity, reliability, and baloney. *Educational and Psychological Measurement, 10,* 94–96.

Cytowic, R. E. (1996). *The neurological side of neuropsychology.* Cambridge, MA: MIT Press.

Dahlstrom, W. G., Welsh, G. S., & Dahlstrom, L. E. (1972). *An MMPI handbook. Volume I: Clinical interpretation* (rev. ed.). Minneapolis, MN: University of Minnesota Press.

Dahlstrom, W. G., Welsh, G. S., & Dahlstrom, L. E. (1975). *An MMPI handbook: Vol. II. Research applications.* Minneapolis, MN: University of Minnesota Press.

Dana, R. H. (1959). Proposal for objective scoring of the TAT. *Perceptual and Motor Skills,* 10, 27–43.

Dana, R. H. (1993). *Multicultural assessment perspectives for professional psychology.* Boston: Allyn & Bacon.

Dana, R. H., & Cantrell, J. D. (1988). An update on the Millon Clinical Multiaxial Inventory (MCMI). *Journal of Clinical Psychology, 44,* 760–763.

Darlington, R. B. (1964). Increasing test validity through the use of interitem correlations (doctoral dissertation, University of Minnesota, 1963). *Dissertation Abstracts International, 24,* 4778. (University Microfilms No. 64–4089).

Darlington, R. B., & Bishop, C. H. (1966). Increasing test validity by considering interitem correlations. *Journal of Applied Psychology, 50,* 322–330.

Das, J. P. (1994). Serial and parallel processing. In R. J. Sternberg (ed.), *Encyclopedia of human intelligence.* New York: Macmillan.

Das, J. P., and Mensink, D. (1989). K-ABC Simultaneous-Sequential Scales and prediction of achievement in reading and mathematics. *Journal of Psychoeducational Assessment, 7,* 103–111.

Das, J. P., and Naglieri, J. A. (1993). *Cognitive assessment system: Standardization version.* Chicago, IL: Riverside.

Das J. P., Naglieri, J., & Kirby, J. (1994). *Assessment of cognitive processes: The PASS theory of intelligence.* Boston: Allyn & Bacon.

Das, J. P., Kirby, J. R., & Jarman, R. F. (1979). *Simultaneous and successive cognitive processes.* Orlando, FL: Academic Press.

Davila, M., Shear, P., Lane, B., Sullivan, E., & Pfefferbaum, A. (1994). Mamillary body and cerebellar shrinkage in chronic alcoholics: An MRI and neuropsychological study. *Neuropsychology, 8,* 433–444.

Davis, C. (1980). *Perkins-Binet Tests of Intelligence for the blind.* Watertown, MA: Perkins School for the Blind.

Davison, M., Gasser, M., & Ding, S. (1996). Identifying major profile patterns in a population: An exploratory study of WAIS and GATB patterns. *Psychological Assessment, 1,* 26–31.

Dawes, R. M., Faust, D., and Meehl, P. E. (1989). Clinical versus actuarial judgment. *Science, 243,* 1668–1674.

Dawis, R. V., & Lofquist, L. H. (1984). *A psychological theory of work adjustment: An individual-differences model and its applications.* Minneapolis, MN: University of Minnesota Press.

Dawis, R. V., England, G. W., & Lofquist, L. H. (1964). A theory of work adjustment. *Minnesota Studies in Vocational Rehabilitation,* 15.

Dean, R. S. (1986). Lateralization of cerebral functions. In D. Wedding, A. M. Horton, & J. Webster (eds.), *The neuropsychology handbook.* New York: Springer.

Deary, I. J., Hendrickson, A. E., and Burns, A. (1987). Serum calcium levels in Alzheimer's disease: A finding and an aetiological hypothesis. *Personality and Individual Differences, 8,* 75–80.

DeCrans, M. (1990). *Spiritual well-being in the rural elderly.* Unpublished manuscript, Marquette University, Milwaukee, WI.

Delis, D. C., & Kaplan, E. (1982). Assessment of aphasia with the Luria-Nebraska Neuropsychological Battery: A conceptual critique. *Journal of Consulting and Clinical Psychology, 50,* 32–39.

Delis, D. C., & Kaplan, E. (1983). Hazards of a standardized neuropsychological test with low content validity. *Journal of Consulting and Clinical Psychology, 51,* 396–398.

Dembroski, T., MacDougall, J., Williams, B., & Haney, T. (1985). Components of Type A, hostility, and anger-in: Relationship to angiographic findings. *Psychosomatic Medicine, 47,* 219–233.

Deri, S. (1949). *Introduction to the Szondi Test.* New York: Grune & Stratton.

Detterman, D. K. (1984). Understand cognitive components before postulating metacomponents, etc., part 2. *Behavioral and Brain Sciences, 7,* 289–290.

DeVito, A. J. (1985). Review of Myers-Briggs Type Indicator. *Ninth mental measurements yearbook.* Lincoln, NE: University of Nebraska Press.

Diamond, S. (1980). Wundt before Leipzig. In R. W. Rieber (ed.), *Wilhelm Wundt and the making of a scientific psychology.* New York: Plenum Press.

Digman, J. (1990). Personality structure: Emergence of the five-factor model. *Annual Review of Psychology, 41,* 417–440.

Dikmen, S., Machamer, J., Winn, H., & Temkin, N. (1995). Neuropsychological outcome at 1-year post head injury. *Neuropsychology, 9,* 80–90.

DiLalla, L. F., Thompson, L. A., Plomin, R., and others. (1990). Infant predictors of preschool and adult IQ: A study of infant twins and their parents. *Developmental Psychology, 26,* 759–769.

Dillon, H. J. (1949). *Early school leavers: A major educational problem.* New York: National Child Labor Committee.

Dillon, R. F., Pohlmann, J. T., & Lohman, D. F. (1981). A factor analysis of Raven's Advanced Progressive Matrices freed of difficulty factors. *Educational and Psychological Measurement, 41,* 1295–1302.

Dixon, D. (1995). Review of Structured Interview of Reported Symptoms. *Twelfth Mental Measurements Yearbook.* Lincoln, NE: University of Nebraska Press.

Dodrill, C. B. (1979). Sex differences on the Halstead-Reitan Neuropsychological Battery and on other neuropsychological measures. *Journal of Clinical Psychology, 35,* 236–241.

Dodrill, C. B. (1981). An economical method of measuring general intelligence in adults. *Journal of Consulting and Clinical Psychology, 49,* 668–673.

Dodrill, C. B., & Warner, M. H. (1988). Further studies of the Wonderlic Personnel Test as a brief measure of intelligence. *Journal of Consulting and Clinical Psychology, 56,* 145–147.

Doll, E. A. (1935). The Vineland Social Maturity Scale. *Training School Bulletin, 32,* 1–7, 25–32, 48–55, 68–74.

Doll, E. A. (1936). Preliminary standardization of the Vineland Social Maturity Scale. *American Journal of Orthopsychiatry, 6,* 283–293.

Dolliver, R. H., Irvin, J. A., & Bigley, S. E. (1972). Twelve-year follow-up of the Strong Vocational Interest Blank. *Journal of Counseling Psychology, 19,* 212–217.

Donders, J. (1995). Validity of the Kaufman Brief Intelligence Test (K-BIT) in children with traumatic brain injury. *Assessment, 2,* 219–224.

Donlon, T. F. (ed.). (1984). *The College Board technical handbook for the Scholastic Aptitude Test and Achievement Tests.* New York: College Entrance Examination Board.

Donnay, D., & Borgen, F. (1996). Validity, structure, and content of the 1994 Strong Interest Inventory. *Journal of Counseling Psychology, 43,* 275–291.

Doppelt, W. E. (1956). Estimating the full scale score on the Wechsler Adult Intelligence Scale from scores on four subtests. *Journal of Consulting Psychology, 20,* 63–66.

Drakeley, R. J., Herriot, P., & Jones, A. (1988). Biographical data, training success and turnover. *Journal of Occupational Psychology, 61,* 145–152.

Drebing, C., Van Gorp, W., Stuck, A., Mitrushina, M., & Beck, J. (1994). Early detection of cognitive decline in higher cognitively functioning older adults: Sensitivity and specificity of a neuropsychological screening battery. *Neuropsychology, 8,* 31–37.

Drummond, R. J. (1987). Edwards Personal Preference Schedule. In D. J. Keyser & R. C. Sweetland (eds.), *Test critiques compendium.* Kansas City, MO: Test Corporation of America.

DuBois, P. E. (1939). A test standardized on Pueblo Indian children. *Psychological Bulletin, 36,* 523.

DuBois, P. H. (1970). *A history of psychological testing.* Boston: Allyn & Bacon.

Dumenci, L. (1995). Construct validity of the Self-Directed Search using hierarchically nested structural models. *Journal of Vocational Behavior, 47,* 21–34.

Dumont, R., & Hagberg, C. (1994). Kaufman Adolescent and Adult Intelligence Test (KAIT). *Journal of Psychoeducational Assessment, 12,* 190–196.

Dumont, R., Cruse, C., Price, L., & Whelley, P. (1996). The relationship between the Differential Ability Scales (DAS) and the Wechsler Intelligence Scale for Children-Third Edition (WISC-III). *Psychology in the Schools, 33,* 203–209.

Dunn, L. M., & Dunn, L. M. (1981). *Peabody Picture Vocabulary Test-Revised.* Circle Pines, MN: American Guidance Service.

Dunn, L. M., & Dunn, L. M. (1998). *Examiner's Manual: Peabody Picture Vocabulary Test-III.* Circle Pines, MN: American Guidance Service.

Dunnette, M. D., & L. M. Hough (eds.). (1990–1992). *Handbook of industrial and organizational psychology* (vols. 1–3). Palo Alto, CA: Consulting Psychologists Press.

Dunst, C. J. (1980). *A clinical and educational manual for use with the Uzgiris and Hunt Scales of Infant Psychological Development.* Baltimore: University Park Press.

Dyce, J. A. (1996). Factor structure of the Beck Hopelessness Scale. *Journal of Clinical Psychology, 52,* 555–558.

Eaker, E. D., & Castelli, W. P. (1988). Type A behavior and coronary heart disease in women: Fourteen-year incidence from the Framingham study. In B. K. Houston & C. R. Snyder (eds.), *Type A behavior pattern: Research, theory, and interventions.* New York: Wiley.

Ebbinghaus, H. (1897). Ueber eine neue Methode zur Pruefung geistiger Faehigkeiten und ihre Anwendung bei Schulkindern. *Zeitschrift fuer Angewandte Psychologie, 13,* 401–459.

Eccles, J. C. (1973). *The understanding of the brain.* New York: McGraw-Hill.

Educational Testing Service. (1987). *ETS standards for quality and fairness.* Princeton, NJ: Author.

Educational Testing Service. (1988). *Guidelines for proper use of NTE tests.* Princeton, NJ: Author.

Educational Testing Service. (1989). *Guidelines for proper use of GRE scores.* Princeton, NJ: Author.

Edwards, A. L. (1957). *The social desirability variable in personality assessment and research.* New York: Dryden Press.

Edwards, A. L. (1959). *Edwards Personal Preference Schedule.* New York: The Psychological Corporation.

Edwards, A. L. (1961). Social desirability or acquiescence in the MMPI? A case study with the SD Scale. *Journal of Abnormal and Social Psychology, 63,* 351–359.

Edwards, A. L. (1967). *Edwards Personality Inventory.* Chicago: Science Research Associates.

Edwards, A. L., & Abbott, R. D. (1973). Relationships among the Edwards Personality Inventory Scales, the Edwards Personality Preference Schedule, and the Personality Research Form Scales. *Journal of Consulting and Clinical Psychology, 40,* 27–32.

Efron, R. (1990). *The decline and fall of hemispheric specialization.* Hillsdale, NJ: Erlbaum.

Eisdorfer, C., & Cohen, L. D. (1961). The generality of the WAIS standardization for the aged: A regional comparison. *Journal of Abnormal and Social Psychology, 62,* 520–527.

Eisenson, J. (1954). *Examining for aphasia.* New York: Psychological Corporation.

Eisenstein, N., & Engelhart, C. (1997). Comparison of the K-BIT with short forms of the WAIS-R in a neuropsychological population. *Psychological Assessment, 9,* 57–62.

Ekman, P. (1982). Methods for measuring facial action. In K. R. Scherer & P. Ekman (eds.), *Handbook of methods in nonverbal behavior research.* Cambridge: Cambridge University Press.

Ekman, P., & Friesen, W. V. (1975). *Unmasking the face.* Englewood Cliffs, NJ: Prentice-Hall.

Ekman, P., & Friesen, W. V. (1978). *The Facial Action Coding System: A technique for the measurement of facial movement.* Palo Alto, CA: Consulting Psychologists Press.

Ekman, P., & Friesen, W. V., & Ancoli, S. (1980). Facial signs of emotional experience. *Journal of Personality and Social Psychology, 39,* 1125–1134.

Elaad, E., Ginton, A., & Jungman, N. (1992). Detection measures in real-life criminal guilty knowledge tests. *Journal of Applied Psychology, 77,* 757–767.

Elliott, C. D. (1990). *The Differential Ability Scales: Introductory and technical handbook.* San Antonio, TX: Psychological Corporation.

Elliott, C. D. (1997). The Differential Ability Scales. In D. P. Flanagan, J. Genshaft, & P. Harrison (eds.), *Contemporary intellectual assessment: Theories, tests, and issues.* New York: Guilford.

Ellis, A. (1962). *Reason and emotion in psychotherapy.* New York: Lyle Stuart.

Ellis, A. (1970). H-T-P: A projective device and a measure of adult intelligence. In O. K. Buros (ed.), *Personality tests and reviews.* Highland Park, NJ: The Gryphon Press.

Ellison, C. W. (1983). Spiritual well-being: Conceptualization and measurement. *Journal of Psychology and Theology, 11,* 330–340.

Ellison, C. W., & Smith, J. (1991). Toward an integrative measure of health and well-being. *Journal of Psychology and Theology, 19,* 35–48.

Erdberg, P. (1985). The Rorschach. In C. S. Newmark (ed.), *Major psychological assessment instruments.* Boston: Allyn & Bacon.

Eron, L. D. (1950). A normative study of the Thematic Apperception Test. *Psychological Monographs, 64* (9, Whole No. 315).

Ertl, J. P., and Schafer, E. W. P. (1969). Brain response correlates of psychometric intelligence. *Nature, 223,* 421–422.

Esquirol, J. E. D. (1845/1838). *Mental maladies.* (trans. E. K. Hunt). Philadelphia: Lea & Blanchard.

Estes, W. K. (1974). Learning theory and intelligence. *American Psychologist, 29,* 740–749.

Evans, D. A., Funkenstein, H., Albert, M., & others (1989). Prevalence of Alzheimer's Disease in a community population of older persons. *Journal of the American Medical Association, 262,* 2551–2556.

Exline, R. V., & Fehr, B. J. (1982). The assessment of gaze and mutual gaze. In K. R. Scherer & P. Ekman (eds.), *Handbook of methods in nonverbal behavior research.* Cambridge: Cambridge University Press.

Exner, J. E., Jr. (1991). *The Rorschach: A comprehensive system, Volume 2. Current research and advanced interpretation* (2nd ed.). New York: Wiley.

Exner, J. E., Jr. (1993). *The Rorschach: A comprehensive system, Volume 1. Basic foundations* (3rd ed.). New York: Wiley.

Exner, J. E., Jr. (1995). *Issues and methods in Rorschach research.* Mahwah, NJ: Erlbaum.

Exner, J. E., Jr., & Andronikof-Sanglade, A. (1992). Rorschach changes following brief and short-term psychotherapy. *Journal of Personality Assessment, 59*, 59–71.

Exner, J. E., Jr., & Weiner, I. B. (1994). *The Rorschach: A comprehensive system, Volume 3. Assessment of children and adolescents* (2nd ed.). New York: Wiley.

Eyde, L. D., and Primhoff, E. S. (1992). Responsible test use. In M. Zeidner and R. Most (eds.), *Psychological testing: An inside view.* Palo Alto, CA: Consulting Psychologists Press.

Eyde, L. D., Robertson, G. J., Krug, S., and others. (1993). *Responsible test use: Case studies for assessing human behavior.* Washington, DC: American Psychological Association.

Eysenck, H. J. (1986). Is intelligence? In R. J. Sternberg and D. K. Detterman (eds.), *What is intelligence? Contemporary viewpoints on its nature and definition.* Norwood, NJ: Ablex.

Eysenck, H. J. (1994). EEG evoked potentials. In R. J. Sternberg (ed.), *Encyclopedia of human intelligence.* New York: Macmillan.

Eysenck, H. J. (ed.). (1982). *A model for intelligence.* Heidelberg: Springer-Verlag.

Eysenck, H. J., & Eysenck, M. W. (1975). *Manual of the Eysenck Personality Questionnaire.* San Diego: Educational and Industrial Testing Service.

Eysenck, H. J., & Eysenck, M. W. (1985). *Personality and individual differences: A natural science approach.* New York: Plenum.

Eysenck, H. J., & Eysenck, S. B. G. (1976). *Psychoticism as a dimension of personality.* London: Hodder & Stoughton.

Fagan, J. F. III. (1984). Infant memory. In M. Moscovitch (ed.), *Infant memory.* New York: Plenum Press.

Fagan, J. F. III, & Haiken-Vasen, J. (1997). Selective attention to novelty as a measure of information processing across the lifespan. In J. Burack & J. Enns (eds.), *Attention, development, and psychopathology.* New York: Guilford.

Fagan, J. F. III, & McGrath, S. K. (1981). Infant recognition memory and later intelligence. *Intelligence, 5*, 121–130.

Fagan, J. F. III, & Shepherd, P. A. (1986). *The Fagan Test of Infant Intelligence: Training manual.* Cleveland, OH: Infantest Corporation.

Fancher, R. E. (1985). *The intelligence men: Makers of the IQ controversy.* New York: Norton.

Farnham-Diggory, S. (1978). *Learning disabilities: A psychological perspective.* Cambridge, MA: Harvard University Press.

Faust, D., and Ziskin, J. (1988). The expert witness in psychology and psychiatry. *Science, 241*, 31–35.

Faust, D., and Ziskin, J. (1989). Computer-assisted psychological evaluation as legal evidence: Some day my prints will come. *Computers in Human Behavior, 5*, 23–36.

Federal Rules of Evidence for United States Courts and Magistrates. (1975). St. Paul, MN: West Publishing Company.

Fehr, B. J., & Exline, R. V. (1987). Social visual interaction: A conceptual and literature review. In A. W. Siegman & S. Feldstein (eds.), *Nonverbal behavior and communication* (2nd ed.). Hillsdale, NJ: Erlbaum.

Fehring, R., Brennan, P., & Keller, M. (1987). Psychological and spiritual well-being in college students. *Research in Nursing and Health, 10*, 391–398.

Feldman, R. D. (1982). *Whatever happened to the quiz kids?* Chicago: Chicago Review Press.

Feldt, L. S., & Brennan, R. L. (1989). In R. L. Linn (ed.), *Educational Measurement* (3rd ed.). New York: American Council on Education/Macmillan.

Ferris, G., Judge, T., Rowland, K., & Fitzgibbons, D. (1994). Subordinate influence and the performance evaluation process: Test of a model. *Organizational Behavior and Human Decision Processes, 58*, 101–135.

Ferris, S. H. (1992). Diagnosis by specialists: Psychological testing. *Acta Neurologica Scandinavica, 85*, 32–35.

Figueroa, R. A. (1990). Best practices in the assessment of bilingual children. In A. Thomas & J. Grimes (eds.), *Best practices in school psychology II.* Washington, DC: National Association of School Psychologists.

Finn, S. E. (1996). *A manual for using the MMPI-2 as a therapeutic intervention.* Minneapolis: University of Minnesota Press.

Finn, S. E., & Tonsager, M. E. (1992). Therapeutic effects of providing MMPI-2 test feedback to college students awaiting therapy. *Psychological Assessment, 4*, 278–287.

Finn, S. E., & Tonsager, M. E. (1997). Information-gathering and therapeutic models of assessment: Complementary paradigms. *Psychological Assessment, 9*, 374–385.

Fisher, G. L., Jenkins, S. J., Bancroft, M. J., and Kraft, L. M. (1988). The effects of K-ABC-based remedial teaching strategies on word recognition skills. *Journal of Learning disabilities, 21*, 307–312.

Fisher, S., & Greenberg, R. P. (1984). *The scientific credibility of Freud's theories and therapy.* New York: Columbia University Press.

Fiske, D. W. (1986). The trait concept and the personality questionnaire. In A. Angleitner & J. S. Wiggins (eds.), *Personality assessment via questionnaires: Current issues in theory and measurement.* Berlin: Springer-Verlag.

Fitzpatrick, R. (1984). Employee Aptitude Survey Tests. In D. J. Keyser & R. C. Sweetland (eds.), *Test Critiques* (vol. 1). Kansas City, MO: Test Corporation of America.

Flanagan, J. C. (1954). The critical incident technique. *Psychological Bulletin, 51,* 327–358.

Flanagan, J. C. (1956). The evaluation of methods in applied psychology and the problem of criteria. *Occupational Psychology, 30,* 1–9.

Fleishman, E. A. (1975). Toward a taxonomy of human performance. *American Psychologist, 30,* 1127–1149.

Fleishman, E. A., & Mumford, M. D. (1988). Ability requirement scales. In S. Gael (ed.), *Job analysis handbook for business, industry, and government* (vol. 2). New York: Wiley.

Fleishman, E. A., & Quaintance, M. K. (1984). *Taxonomies of human performance.* New York: Academic Press.

Flynn, J. R. (1984). The mean IQ of Americans: Massive gains 1932 to 1978. *Psychological Bulletin, 95,* 29–51.

Flynn, J. R. (1987). Massive IQ gains in 14 nations: What IQ tests really measure. *Psychological Bulletin, 101,* 171–191.

Flynn, J. R. (1994). IQ gains over time. In R. J. Sternberg (ed.), *Encyclopedia of human intelligence.* New York: Macmillan.

Folstein, M., Folstein, S., & McHugh, P. (1975). Mini-Mental State: A practical method for grading the cognitive state of patients for the clinician. *Journal of Psychiatric Research, 12,* 189–198.

Forns-Santacana, M., and Gomez-Benito, J. (1990). Factor structure of the McCarthy Scales. *Psychology in the Schools, 27,* 111–115.

Forrest, D. W. (1974). *Francis Galton: The life and work of a Victorian genius.* New York: Taplinger Publishing.

Forster, A. A. (1994). Learning Disability. In R. J. Sternberg (ed.), *Encyclopedia of human intelligence.* New York: Macmillan.

Foster, C. (1990). Achievement tests put pressure on students and schools. *Christian Science Monitor,* May 24, 7.

Foster, R. W. (1974). *Camelot Behavioral Checklist manual.* Bellevue, WA: Edmark Associates.

Foster, S. L., Bell-Dolan, D. J., & Burge, D. A. (1988). Behavioral observation. In A. S. Bellack & M. Hersen (eds.), *Behavioral assessment: A practical handbook* (3rd ed.). New York: Pergamon Press.

Fowler, J. (1981). *Stages of faith: The psychology of human development and the quest for meaning.* San Francisco: Harper & Row.

Fowler, P. C., Zillmer, E., & Macciocchi, S. N. (1990). Confirmatory factor analytic models of the WAIS-R for neuropsychiatric patients. *Journal of Clinical Psychology, 46,* 324–332.

Fowler, R. D. (1985). Landmarks in computer-assisted psychological assessment. *Journal of Consulting and Clinical Psychology, 53,* 748–759.

Fowler, R. D., & Matarazzo, J. D. (1988). Psychologists and psychiatrists as expert witnesses. *Science, 241,* 1143.

Frank, G. (1983). *The Wechsler enterprise: An assessment of the development, structure, and use of the Wechsler tests of intelligence.* New York: Pergamon Press.

Frank, G. (1990). Research on the clinical usefulness of the Rorschach: 1. The diagnosis of schizophrenia. *Perceptual and Motor Skills, 71,* 573–578.

Frank, L. K. (1939). Projective methods for the study of personality. *Journal of Psychology, 8,* 389–413.

Frank, L. K. (1948). *Projective methods.* Springfield, IL: Thomas.

Franke, W. (1963). *The reform and abolition of the traditional Chinese examination system.* Cambridge, MA: Harvard University Press.

Frankenburg, W. K. (1985). The Denver approach to early case finding: A review of the Denver Developmental Screening Test and a brief training program in developmental diagnosis. In W. K. Frankenburg, R. M. Emde, and J. W. Sullivan (eds.), *Identification of children at risk: An international perspective.* New York: Plenum Press.

Frankenburg, W. K., and Dodds, J. B. (1967). The Denver developmental screening tests. *Journal of Pediatrics, 71,* 181–191.

Frankenburg, W. K., Dodds, J., Archer, P., and others. (1990). *Denver II: Technical manual.* Denver, CO: Denver Developmental Materials.

Frankl, V. (1963). *Man's search for meaning: An introduction to logotherapy.* New York: Washington Square Press.

Frauenheim, J. G., & Heckerl, J. R. (1983). A longitudinal study of psychological and achievement test performance in severe dyslexic adults. *Journal of Learning Disabilities, 16,* 339–347.

Frechtling, J. A. (1989). Administrative uses of school testing programs. In R. L. Linn (ed.), *Educational measurement* (3rd ed.). New York: American Council on Education/Macmillan.

Frederickson, L. C. (1985). Goodenough-Harris Drawing Test. In Keyser, D. J., & Sweetland, R. C. (eds.). *Test critiques* (vol. 2). Kansas City, MO: Test Corporation of America.

Frederiksen, N. (1962). Factors in In-basket Performance. *Psychological Monographs, 76,* Whole No. 541.

Freud, A. (1946). *The ego and the mechanisms of defense.* New York: International Universities Press.

Freud, S. (1900). The interpretation of dreams. In J. Strachey, (ed., in collaboration with A. Freud). *The standard edition of the complete psychological works of Sigmund Freud.* London: Hogarth, 1955, vols. 4 and 5.

Freud, S. (1927/1961). *The future of an illusion* (J. Strachey, trans.). New York: Basic Books. (Originally published 1900).

Freud, S. (1933). *New introductory lectures on psychoanalysis.* New York: Norton.

Fridlund, A. J., Ekman, P., & Oster, H. (1987). Facial expressions of emotion: Review of literature 1970–1983. In A. W. Siegman & S. Feldstein (eds.), *Nonverbal behavior and communication* (2nd ed.). Hillsdale, NJ: Erlbaum.

Friedman, A. F. (1987). Eysenck Personality Questionnaire. In D. J. Keyser & R. C. Sweetland (eds.), *Test critiques compendium.* Kansas City, MO: Test Corporation of America.

Friedman, M., & Rosenman, R. (1974). *Type A behavior and your heart.* New York: Fawcett Crest.

Friedman, M., & Ulmer, D. (1984). *Treating Type A behavior and your heart.* New York: Alfred A. Knopf.

Fuess, C. M. (1950). *The College Board: Its first fifty years.* New York: Columbia University Press.

Fuld, P. A. (1977). *Fuld Object-Memory Evaluation.* Chicago: Stoelting Co.

Fuld, P. A., Masur, D. M., Blau, A. D., Crystal, H., & Aronson, M. K. (1990). Object-Memory Evaluation for prospective detection of dementia in normal functioning elderly: predictive and normative data. *Journal of Clinical and Experimental Neuropsychology, 12,* 520–528.

Fuller, G. B., Parmelee, W. M., & Carroll, J. L. (1982). Performance of delinquent and nondelinquent high school boys on the Rotter Incomplete Sentences Blank. *Journal of Personality Assessment, 46,* 506–510.

Furnham, A., Toop, A., Lewis, C., & Fisher, A. (1995). P-E fit and job satisfaction: A failure to support Holland's theory in three British samples. *Personality and Individual Differences, 19,* 677–690.

Gale, A., and Edwards, J. (1983). Cortical correlates of intelligence. In A. Gale and J. Edwards (eds.), *Physiological correlates of human behaviour* (vol. 3). New York: Academic Press.

Gallagher, J. J., & Courtright, R. D. (1986). The educational definition of giftedness and its policy implications. In R. J. Sternberg and J. E. Davidson (eds.), *Conceptions of giftedness.* Cambridge: Cambridge University Press.

Galton, F. (1879). Psychometric experiments. *Brain, 2,* 149–162.

Galton, F. (1883). *Inquiries into human faculty and its development.* London: Macmillan.

Galton, F. (1888). *Natural inheritance.* London: Macmillan.

Garb, H. N. (1992). The trained psychologist as expert witness. *Clinical Psychology Review, 12,* 451–467.

Garb, H. N. (1994). Judgment research: Implications for clinical practice and testimony in court. *Applied and Preventive Psychology, 3,* 173–183.

Garb, H. N., Florio, C., & Grove, W. (1998). The validity of the Rorschach and the MMPI: Results from meta-analyses. *Psychological Science, 9,* 402–404.

Gardner, H. (1975). *The shattered mind: The person after brain damage.* New York: Alfred A. Knopf.

Gardner, H. (1983). *Frames of mind: The theory of multiple intelligence.* New York: Basic Books.

Gardner, H. (1986). The waning of intelligence tests. In R. J. Sternberg and D. K. Detterman (eds.), *What is intelligence? Contemporary viewpoints on its nature and definition.* Norwood, NJ: Ablex.

Gardner, H. (1992). Assessment in context: The alternative to standardized testing. In B. R. Gifford & M. C. O'Connor (eds.), *Alternative views of aptitude, achievement, and instruction.* Boston: Klummer.

Gardner, H. (1993). *Multiple intelligences: The theory in practice.* New York: Basic Books.

Gardner, H. (1998). Are there additional intelligences? The case for naturalistic, spiritual, and existential intelligences. In J. Kane (ed.), *Education, information, and transformation.* Englewood Cliffs, NJ: Prentice-Hall.

Gardner, J. (1967). The adjustment of drug addicts as measured by the sentence completion test. *Journal of Projective Techniques and Personality Assessment, 31,* 28–29.

Gardner, R. A. (1981). Digits forward and digits backward as two separate tests: Normative data on 1567 school children. *Journal of Clinical Child Psychology, 10,* 131–135.

Gardner, W., Lidz, C., Mulvey, E., & Shaw, E. (1996). Clinical versus actuarial predictions of violence in patients with mental illnesses. *Journal of Consulting and Clinical Psychology, 64,* 602–609.

Gass, C., & Brown, M. (1992). Neuropsychological test feedback to patients with brain dysfunction. *Psychological Assessment, 4,* 272–277.

Gazzaniga, M. S. (1970). *The bisected brain.* New York: Appleton-Century-Crofts.

Gazzaniga, M. S., & LeDoux, J. E. (1978). *The integrated mind.* New York: Plenum Press.

Geary, D. C., & Whitworth, R. H. (1988). Is the factor structure of the WISC-R different for Anglo- and Mexican-American children? *Journal of Psychoeducational Assessment, 6,* 253–260.

GED Testing Service (1991). *Examiner's manual: Test of General Educational Development.* Washington, DC: GED Testing Service of the American Council on Education.

Geffen, G., Moar, K. J., O'Hanlon, A. P., Clark, C. R., & Geffen, L. B. (1990). Performance measures of 16- to 86-year-old males and females on the Auditory Verbal Learning Test. *The Clinical Neuropsychologist, 4,* 45–64.

Gelb, S. (1986). Henry H. Goddard and the immigrants, 1910–1917: The studies and their social context. *Journal of the History of the Behavioral Sciences, 22,* 324–332.

Genia, V. (1990). Religious development: A synthesis and reformulation. *Journal of Religion and Health, 29,* 85–99.

Genia, V. (1993a). A psychometric evaluation of the Allport-Ross I/E Scales in a religiously heterogeneous sample. *Journal for the Scientific Study of Religion, 32,* 284–290.

Genia, V. (1993b). The Spiritual Experience Index: A measure of spiritual maturity. *Journal of Religion and Health, 30,* 337–347.

Gerard, A. B. (1993). *Manual for Parent-Child Relationship Inventory.* Los Angeles, CA: Western Psychological Services.

Geschwind, N. (1972). Language and the brain. *Scientific American, 226,* 76–83.

Geschwind, N., & Galaburda, A. M. (1987). *Cerebral lateralization: Biological mechanisms, associations, and pathology.* Cambridge, MA: MIT Press.

Gesell, A., Ilg, F. L., and Ames, L. B. (1974). *Infant and child in the culture of today* (rev. ed.). New York: Harper & Row.

Getter, H., & Nowinski, J. (1981). A free response test of interpersonal effectiveness. *Journal of Personality Assessment, 45,* 301–308.

Getz, I. R. (1984). Moral judgment and religion: A review of the literature. *Counseling and Values, 28,* 94–116.

Ghez, C. (1991). The cerebellum. In E. R. Kandel, J. H. Schwartz, & T. M. Jessell (eds.), *Principles of neural science* (3rd ed.). New York: Elsevier.

Ghiselli, E. E. (1966). *The validity of occupational aptitude tests.* New York: Wiley.

Ghiselli, E. E. (1973). The validity of aptitude tests in personnel selection. *Personnel Psychology, 26,* 461–477.

Ghiselli, E. E., Campbell, J. P., & Zedeck, S. (1981). *Measurement theory for the behavioral sciences.* San Francisco: W. H. Freeman.

Gifford, R. (1991). *Applied psychology: Variety and opportunity.* Boston: Allyn & Bacon.

Gilberstadt, H., and Duker, J. (1965). *A handbook for clinical and actuarial MMPI interpretation.* Philadelphia: W. B. Saunders.

Gilliam, J. E. (1994). *Attention-Deficit/Hyperactivity Disorder Test examiner's manual.* Austin, TX: PRO-ED.

Ginsburg, H., and Opper, S. (1988). *Piaget's theory of intellectual development* (3rd ed.). Englewood Cliffs, NJ: Prentice-Hall.

Glascoe, F. P. (1991). Developmental screening: Rationale, methods and application. *Infants and Young Children, 4,* 1–10.

Glascoe, F. P., & Byrne, K. E. (1993). The accuracy of three developmental screening tests. *Journal of Early Intervention, 17,* 368–379.

Glaser, R. (1963). Instructional technology and the measurement of learning outcomes. *American Psychologist, 18,* 519–522.

Goddard, H. H. (1910a). A measuring scale for intelligence. *The Training School, 6,* 146–155.

Goddard, H. H. (1910b). Four hundred feebleminded children classified by the Binet method. *Pedagogical Seminary, 17,* 387–397.

Goddard, H. H. (1911). Two thousand normal children measured by the Binet measuring scale of intelligence. *Pedagogical Seminary, 18,* 232–259.

Goddard, H. H. (1912). *Feeble-mindedness and immigration.* Training School Bulletin, *9,* 91.

Goddard, H. H. (1917). The mental level of a group of immigrants. *Psychological Bulletin, 14,* 68–69.

Goddard, H. H. (1928). Feeblemindedness: A question of definition. *Journal of Psycho-Asthenics, 33,* 219–227.

Goffin, R. D., Rothstein, M., & Johnston, N. (1996). Personality testing and the assessment center: Incremental validity for managerial selection. *Journal of Applied Psychology, 81,* 746–756.

Gold, J., Randolph, C., Carpenter, C., and others (1992). The performance of patients with schizophrenia on the Wechsler Memory Scale-Revised. *Clinical Neuropsychologist, 6,* 367–373.

Goldberg, L. R. (1959). The effectiveness of clinicians' judgments: The diagnosis of organic brain damage from the Bender-Gestalt Test. *Journal of Consulting Psychology, 23,* 25–33.

Goldberg, L. R. (1965). Diagnosticians vs. diagnostic signs: The diagnosis of psychosis vs. neurosis from the MMPI. *Psychological Monographs, 79* (9, Whole No. 602).

Goldberg, L. R. (1981a). Developing a taxonomy of trait-descriptive terms. In D. Fiske (ed.), *New directions for methodology of social and behavioral science: Problems with language imprecision* (no. 9). San Francisco: Jossey-Bass.

Goldberg, L. R. (1981b). Language and individual differences: The search for universals in personality lexicons. In L. Wheeler (ed.), *Review of personality and social psychology.* Beverly Hills, CA: Sage.

Goldberg, L. R. (1990). An alternative "description of personality": The big-five factor structure. *Journal of Personality and Social Psychology, 59,* 1216–1229.

Goldberg, P. (1965). A review of sentence completion methods in personality assessment. In B. I. Murstein (ed.), *Handbook of projective techniques.* New York: Basic Books.

Golden, C. J. (1989). The Luria-Nebraska Neuropsychological Battery. In C. S. Newmark (ed.), *Major psychological assessment instruments* (vol. II). Boston: Allyn & Bacon.

Golden, C. J., Moses, J. A., Graber, B., & Berg, R. A. (1981). Objective clinical rules for interpreting the Luria-Nebraska Neuropsychological Battery: Derivation, effectiveness, and validation. *Journal of Consulting and Clinical Psychology, 49,* 616–618.

Golden, C. J., Purish, A. D., & Hammeke, T. A. (1980). *Luria-Nebraska Neuropsychological Battery: Manual.* Los Angeles: Western Psychological Services.

Golden, C. J., Purish, A. D., & Hammeke, T. A. (1986). *Luria-Nebraska Neuropsychological Battery: Forms I and II.* Los Angeles: Western Psychological Services.

Goldfried, M. R., & Zax, M. (1965). The stimulus value of the TAT. *Journal of Projective Techniques, 29,* 46–57.

Golding, S. L., Roesch, R., and Schreiber, J. (1984). Assessment and conceptualization of competency to stand trial: Preliminary data on the Interdisciplinary Fitness Interview. *Law and Human Behavior, 8,* 321–334.

Goldstein, D., Fogle, E., Wieber, J., & O'Shea, T. (1995). Comparison of the Bayley Scales of Infant Development-Second Edition and the Bayley Scales of Infant Development with premature infants. *Journal of Psychoeducational Assessment, 13,* 391–396.

Goldstein, I. L. (1991). Training in work organizations. In M. D. Dunnette & L. M. Hough (eds.), *Handbook of industrial and organizational psychology* (vol. 2). Palo Alto, CA: Consulting Psychologists Press.

Goldstein, I. L. (1992). *Training* (3rd ed.). Monterey, CA: Brooks/Cole.

Goldstein, K. (1944). The mental changes due to frontal lobe damage. *Journal of Psychology, 17,* 187–208.

Gonzales, E. (1986). *Human figure drawing test.* Austin, TX: PRO-ED.

Goodenough, F. L. (1926). *Measurement of intelligence by drawings.* New York: Harcourt, Brace & World.

Goodenough, F. L. (1949). *Mental testing: Its history, principles, and applications.* New York: Rinehart.

Goodglass, H. (1986). The flexible battery in neuropsychological assessment. In T. Incagnoli, G. Goldstein, & C. J. Golden (eds.), *Clinical applications of neuropsychological test batteries.* New York: Plenum Press.

Goodglass, H., & Kaplan, E. (1983). *The assessment of aphasia and related disorders.* Philadelphia: Lea & Febiger.

Goodman, J. (1990). Infant intelligence: Do we, can we, should we assess it? In C. C. Reynolds, and R. W. Kamphaus (eds.), *Handbook of psychological and educational assessment of children: Intelligence and achievement.* New York: Guilford.

Goodman, J., Malizia, K., Durieux-Smith, A., MacMurray, B., and Bernard, P. (1990). Bayley Developmental Performance at two years of age of neonates at risk for hearing loss. *Developmental Medicine and Child Neurology, 32,* 689–697.

Gordon, M., & Mettelman, B. B. (1988). The assessment of attention: I. Standardization and reliability of a behavior-based measure. *Journal of Clinical Psychology, 44,* 688–690.

Gordon, R., and Peek, L. A. (1989). *The Custody Quotient.* Dallas, TX: Wilmington Institute.

Gorsuch, R. L. (1983). *Factor analysis* (2nd ed.). Hillsdale, NJ: Erlbaum.

Goslin, D. A. (1963). *The search for ability: Standardized testing in social perspective.* New York: Russell Sage Foundation.

Gothard, S., Viglione, D., Meloy, J. R., & Sherman, M. (1996). Detection of malingering in competency to stand trial evaluations. *Law and Human Behavior, 19,* 493–505.

Gottfredson, G. D. (1990). *Applications and research using Holland's theory of careers: Where we would like to be and suggestions for getting there.* Paper presented at the annual meeting of the American Psychological Association, Boston, MA.

Gottfredson, G. D., & Holland, J. L. (1975). Vocational choices of men and women: A comparison of predictors from the Self-Directed Search. *Journal of Counseling Psychology, 22,* 28–34.

Gottfredson, G. D., & Holland, J. L. (1989). *Dictionary of Holland Occupational Codes* (2nd ed.). Odessa, FL: Psychological Assessment Resources.

Gottfredson, L. S. (1986). Societal consequences of the *g* factor in employment. *Journal of Vocational Behavior, 29,* 379–410.

Gough, H. G. (1971). The assessment of wayward impulse by means of the Personnel Reaction Blank. *Personnel Psychology, 24,* 669–677.

Gough, H. G. (1984). A managerial potential scale for the California Psychological Inventory. *Journal of Applied Psychology, 69,* 233–244.

Gough, H. G. (1987). *California Psychological Inventory manual.* Palo Alto, CA: Consulting Psychologists Press.

Gough, H. G., & Bradley, P. (1992a). Comparing two strategies for developing personality scales. In M. Zeidner & R. Most (eds.), *Psychological testing: An inside view.* Palo Alto, CA: Consulting Psychologists Press.

Gough, H. G., & Bradley, P. (1992b). Delinquent and criminal behavior as assessed by the Revised California Psychological Inventory. *Journal of Clinical Psychology, 48,* 298–307.

Gould, S. J. (1981). *The mismeasure of man.* New York: Norton.

Graham, J. R. (1987). *The MMPI: A practical guide* (2nd ed.). New York: Oxford University Press.

Graham, J. R. (1993). *MMPI-2: Assessing personality and psychopathology.* New York: Oxford.

Granstrom, S. L. (1987). *A comparative study of loneliness, Buberian religiosity and spiritual well-being in cancer patients.* Paper presented at the conference of the National Hospice Organization.

Graybill, D., & Heuvelman, L. (1993). Validity of the Children's Picture-Frustration Study: A social-cognitive perspective. *Journal of Personality Assessment, 60,* 379–389.

Greenough, W. T., Black, J. E., & Wallace, C. S. (1987). Experience and brain development. *Child Development, 58,* 539–559.

Gregory, R. J. (1987). *Adult intellectual assessment.* Boston, MA: Allyn & Bacon.

Gregory, R. J. (1994a). Aptitude tests. In R. J. Sternberg (ed.), *Encyclopedia of human intelligence.* New York: Macmillan.

Gregory, R. J. (1994b). Profile interpretation. In R. J. Sternberg (ed.), *Encyclopedia of human intelligence.* New York: Macmillan.

Gregory, R. J. (1998). Testing in clinical psychology. In S. Cullari (ed.), *Foundations of clinical psychology.* Boston: Allyn & Bacon.

Gregory, R. J. (1999). *Foundations of intellectual assessment: The WAIS-III and other tests in clinical practice.* Boston: Allyn & Bacon.

Gregory, R. J., & Gernert, C. H. (1990). Age trends for fluid and crystallized intelligence in an able subpopulation. Unpublished manuscript.

Gregory, R. J., & Mohan, P. J. (1977). Effects of asymptomatic lead exposure on childhood IQ: A review. *Intelligence, 1,* 381–400.

Gregory, R. J., Alley, P., & Morris, L. (1980). Left-handedness and spatial reasoning abilities: The deficit hypothesis revisited. *Intelligence, 4,* 151–159.

Gregory, R. J., Lehman, R. E., & Mohan, P. J. (1976). Intelligence scores for children with and without undue lead absorption. In G. Wegner (ed.), *Shoshone lead health project* (pp. 120–150). Boise: Idaho Department of Health and Welfare.

Gresham, F. M. (1993). "What's wrong in this picture?": Response to Motta et al.'s review of human figure drawings. *School Psychology Quarterly, 8,* 182–186.

Gresham, F. M., & Elliott, S. N. (1990). *Social skills rating system manual.* Circle Pines, MN: American Guidance Service.

Griffith, P., Myers, R., Cusick, G., & Tankersley, M. (1997). MMPI-2 profiles of women differing in sexual abuse history and sexual orientation. *Journal of Clinical Psychology, 53,* 791–800.

Gronwall, D. M. A. (1977). Paced auditory serial-addition task: a measure of recovery from concussion. *Perceptual and Motor Skills, 44,* 367–373.

Gronwall, D. M. A., & Sampson, H. (1974). *The psychological effects of concussion.* Auckland, NZ: Auckland University Press/Oxford University Press.

Gronwall, D. M. A., & Wrightson, P. (1974). Delayed recovery of intellectual function after minor head injury. *Lancet, 2,* 605–609.

Gronwall, D. M. A., & Wrightson, P. (1981). Memory and information processing capacity after closed head injury. *Journal of Neurology, Neurosurgery, and Psychiatry, 44,* 889–895.

Groth-Marnat, G. (1990). *Handbook of psychological assessment.* New York: Wiley.

Groth-Marnat, G. (1997). *Handbook of psychological assessment* (2nd ed.). New York: Wiley.

Gudjonsson, G. H. (1995). The Standard Progressive Matrices: methodological problems associated with the administration of the 1992 adult standardisation sample. *Personality and Individual Differences, 18,* 441–442.

Guilford, J. P. (1959). *Personality.* New York: McGraw-Hill.

Guilford, J. P. (1967). *The nature of human intelligence.* New York: McGraw-Hill.

Guilford, J. P. (1985). The Structure-of-Intellect model. In B. B. Wolman (ed.), *Handbook of intelligence: Theories, measurements, and applications.* New York: Wiley.

Guilford, J. P., & Fruchter, B. (1978). *Fundamental statistics in psychology and education* (6th ed.). New York: McGraw-Hill.

Guilford, J. P., & Hoepfner, R. (1971). *The analysis of intelligence.* New York: McGraw-Hill.

Guion, R. M. (1965). *Personnel testing.* New York: McGraw-Hill.

Guion, R. M. (1980). On trinitarian doctrines of validity. *Professional Psychology, 11,* 385–398.

Guion, R. M. (1991). Personnel Assessment, selection, and placement. In M. D. Dunnette & L. M. Hough (eds.), *Handbook of industrial and organizational psychology* (vol. 2). Palo Alto, CA: Consulting Psychologists Press.

Gulliksen, H. (1950). *Theory of mental tests.* New York: Wiley.

Gutkin, R. B., & Reynolds, C. R. (1981). Factorial similarity of the WISC-R for white and black children from the standardization sample. *Journal of Educational Psychology, 73,* 227–231.

Guttman, L. (1944). A basis for scaling qualitative data. *American Sociological Review, 9,* 139–150.

Guttman, L. (1947). The Cornell technique for scale and intensity analysis. *Educational and Psychological Measurement, 7,* 247–280.

Gynther, M. D., & Gynther, R. A. (1976). Personality inventories. In I. B. Weiner (ed.), *Clinical methods in psychology.* New York: Wiley.

Haaland, K. Y., & Delaney, H. D. (1981). Motor deficits after left or right hemisphere damage due to stroke or tumor. *Neuropsychologia, 19,* 17–27.

Hachinski, V. C., Iliff, L., Zilha, E., & others (1975). Cerebral blood flow in dementia. *Archives of Neurology, 32,* 632–637.

Haddad, F. A. (1986). Comparison of the WISC-R, PPVT-R, and PPVT for learning disabled children. *Psychological Reports, 58,* 659–662.

Haier, R. J., Nuechterlein, K., Hazlett, E., and others. (1988). Cortical glucose metabolic rate correlates of abstract reasoning and attention studied with positron emission tomography. *Intelligence, 12,* 199–217.

Haier, R. J., Siegel, B., Tang, C., and others. (1992). Intelligence and changes in regional cerebral glucose metabolic rate following learning. *Intelligence, 16,* 415–426.

Hain, J. (1964). The Bender-Gestalt Test: A scoring method for identifying brain damage. *Journal of Consulting and Clinical Psychology, 28,* 34–40.

Haladyna, T. M. (1992). Review of the Millon Clinical Multiaxial Inventory-II. *Eleventh mental measurements yearbook.* Lincoln, NE: University of Nebraska Press.

Hall, H. V. (1987). *Violence prediction: Guidelines for the forensic practitioner.* Springfield, IL: Charles C. Thomas.

Halpern, D. F. (1986). *Sex differences in cognitive abilities.* Hillsdale, NJ: Erlbaum.

Hambleton, R. K. (1984). Validating the test scores. In R. A. Berk (ed.), *A guide to criterion-referenced test construction.* Baltimore, MD: The Johns Hopkins University Press.

Hambleton, R. K. (1989). Principles and selected applications of item response theory. In R. L. Linn (ed.), *Educational measurement* (3rd ed.). New York: American Council on Education/Macmillan.

Hamilton, S. E. (1993). Identifying African American gifted children using a behavioral assessment technique: The Gifted Child Locator. *Journal of Black Psychology, 19,* 63–76.

Hammeke, T. A., Golden, C. J., & Purish, A. D. (1978). A standardized, short and comprehensive neuropsychological test battery based on the Luria neuropsychological evaluation. *International Journal of Neuroscience, 8,* 135–141.

Hammill, D. D. (1990). On defining learning disabilities: An emerging consensus. *Journal of Learning Disabilities, 23,* 74–84.

Hammill, D. D. (1999). *Detroit Tests of Learning Aptitude-4 (DTLA-4).* Austin, TX: PRO-ED.

Hansen, J. C. (1984). *User's guide for the SVIB-SCII.* Stanford, CA: Stanford University Press.

Hansen, J. C. (1987). Computer-assisted interpretation of the Strong-Campbell Interest Inventory. In J. N. Butcher (ed.), *Computerized psychological assessment.* New York: Basic Books.

Hansen, J. C. (1992). *Strong user's guide, Revised edition.* Palo Alto, CA: Consulting Psychologists Press.

Hansen, J. C., & Campbell, D. P. (1985). *Manual for the Strong Interest Inventory Form T325 of the Strong Vocational Interest Blanks, Fourth Edition.* Stanford, CA: Stanford University Press.

Hanson, G. A. (1991). To catch a thief: The legal and policy implications of honesty testing in the workplace. *Law and Inequality, 9,* 497–531.

Hargrave, G. E. (1985). Using the MMPI and CPI to screen law enforcement applicants: A study of reliability and validity of clinicians' decisions. *Journal of Police Science and Administration, 13,* 221–224.

Hargrave, G., & Hiatt, D. (1989). Use of the California Psychological Inventory in law enforcement officer selection. *Journal of Personality Assessment, 53,* 267–277.

Hargrave, G., Hiatt, D., Ogard, E., & Karr, C. (1994). Comparison of the MMPI and the MMPI-2 for a sample of peace officers. *Psychological Assessment, 6,* 27–32.

Harmon, L. W. (1989). Counseling. In R. L. Linn (ed.), *Educational measurement* (3rd ed.). New York: American Council on Education/Macmillan.

Harmon, L. W., Hansen, J. C., Borgen, F., & Hammer, A. (1994). *Strong Interest Inventory applications and technical guide.* Palo Alto, CA: Consulting Psychologists Press.

Harrell, T. H., Honaker, L., & Parnell, T. (1992). Equivalence of the MMPI-2 with the MMPI in psychiatric patients. *Psychological Assessment, 4,* 460–465.

Harrington, D. M. (1975). Effect of explicit instructions to "be creative" on the psychological meaning of divergent thinking test scores. *Journal of Personality, 43,* 434–454.

Harrington, R. G. (ed.). (1986). *Testing adolescents.* Kansas City, MO: Test Corporation of America.

Harris, D. B. (1963). *Children's drawings as measures of intellectual maturity.* New York: Harcourt, Brace & World.

Harris, M. M., & Schaubroeck, J. (1988). A meta-analysis of self-supervisor, self-peer, and peer-supervisor ratings. *Personnel Psychology, 38,* 43–62.

Harrison, D. A., & Hulin, C. L. (1989). Investigations of absenteeism: Using event history models to study the absence-taking process. *Journal of Applied Psychology, 74,* 300–316.

Harrison, D. A., & Shaffer, M. (1994). Comparative examinations of self-reports and perceived absenteeism norms: Wading through Lake Wobegon. *Journal of Applied Psychology, 79,* 240–251.

Harrison, P. L., & Schock, H. H. (1994). Draw-A-Figure test. In R. J. Sternberg (ed.), *Encyclopedia of human intelligence.* New York: Macmillan.

Hart, K. E. (1997). A moratorium on research using the Jenkins Activity Survey for Type A behavior? *Journal of Clinical Psychology, 53,* 905–907.

Harvey, R. J. (1990). *The common-metric questionnaire for the analysis and evaluation of jobs* (field test version 1.12). San Antonio, TX: The Psychological Corporation.

Harvey, R. J. (1991). Job analysis. In M. D. Dunnette & L. M. Hough (eds.), *Handbook of industrial and organizational psychology* (vol. 2). Palo Alto, CA: Consulting Psychologists Press.

Harvey, R. J., Friedman, L., Hakel, M., & Cornelius, E. (1988). Dimensionality of the Job Element Inventory,

a simplified worker-oriented job analysis questionnaire. *Journal of Applied Psychology, 73,* 639–646.

Hathaway, S. R., & McKinley, J. C. (1940). A multiphasic personality schedule (Minnesota): I. Construction of the schedule. *Journal of Psychology, 10,* 249–254.

Hathaway, S. R., & McKinley, J. C. (1942). A Multiphasic Personality Schedule (Minnesota): III. The measurement of symptomatic depression. *Journal of Psychology, 14,* 73–84.

Hathaway, S. R., & McKinley, J. C. (1943). *The Minnesota Multiphasic Personality Inventory* (rev. ed.). Minneapolis, MN: University of Minnesota Press.

Hawkins, D. B. (1988). Interpersonal behavior traits, spiritual well-being, and their relationships to blood pressure (doctoral dissertation, Western Conservative Baptist Seminary, 1986). *Dissertation Abstracts International, 48,* 3680B.

Hawkins, D. B., & Larson, R. (1984). *The relationship between measures of health and spiritual well-being.* Unpublished manuscript, Western Conservative Baptist Seminary, Portland, OR.

Hawkins, K. A., Faraone, S. V., Pepple, J. R., Seidman, L. J., & Tsuang, M. T. (1990). WAIS-R validation of the Wonderlic Personnel Test as a brief intelligence measure in a psychiatric sample. *Psychological Assessment: A Journal of Consulting and Clinical Psychology, 2,* 198–201.

Haynes, S. G., Feinleib, M., & Eaker, E. (1983). Type A behavior and the ten-year incidence of coronary heart disease in the Framingham heart study. In R. H. Rosenman (ed.), *Psychosomatic risk factors and coronary heart disease.* Bern, Switzerland: Huber.

Haynes, S. N. (1998). Principles and practices of behavioral assessment with adults. In A. S. Bellack & M. Hersen (eds.), *Comprehensive clinical psychology* (vol. 4). Amsterdam: Elsevier.

Hayslip, B., & Panek, P. E. (1989). *Adult development and aging.* New York: Harper & Row.

Hayworth, M. (1970). H-T-P: A projective device. In O. K. Buros (ed.), *Personality tests and reviews.* Highland Park, NJ: The Gryphon Press.

Heaton, R. K., Chelune, G., Talley, J., and others (1993). *Wisconsin Card Sorting Test manual: Revised and expanded.* Odessa, FL: Psychological Assessment Resources.

Heaton, R. K., Smith, H. H., Jr., Lehman, R. A. W., & Vogt, A. T. (1978). Prospects for faking believable deficits on neuropsychological testing. *Journal of Consulting and Clinical Psychology, 46,* 892–900.

Hebb, D. O. (1939). Intelligence in man after large removals of cerebral tissue: Report of four left frontal lobe cases. *Journal of General Psychology, 21,* 73–87.

Heilbrun, A. B., Jr. (1972). Edwards Personal Preference Schedule. *The Seventh mental measurements yearbook.* Lincoln, NE: University of Nebraska Press.

Heilbrun, A. B., Jr., & Georges, M. (1990). The measurement of principled morality by the Kohlberg Moral Dilemma Questionnaire. *Journal of Personality Assessment, 55,* 183–194.

Heilbrun, K. (1992). The role of psychological testing in forensic assessment. *Law and Human Behavior, 16,* 257–272.

Heinemann, A. W., Harper, R. G., Friedman, L. C., & Whitney, J. (1985). The relative utility of the Shipley-Hartford Scale: Prediction of WAIS-R IQ. *Journal of Clinical Psychology, 41,* 547–551.

Heinze, M., & Grisso, T. (1996). Review of instruments assessing parenting competencies used in child custody evaluations. *Behavioral Sciences and the Law, 14,* 293–313.

Helms, J. E. (1983). *A practitioners guide to the Edwards Personal Preference Schedule.* Springfield, IL: Charles C. Thomas.

Hendrickson, A. E. (1982). The biological basis of intelligence. Part 1: Theory. In H. J. Eysenck, (ed.), *A model for intelligence.* Berlin: Springer-Verlag.

Hendrickson, D. E. (1982). The biological basis of intelligence Part II: Measurement. In H. J. Eysenck (ed.). A model for intelligence. New York: Springer-Verlag.

Herman, D. O. (1988). Blind Learning Aptitude Test. In D. J. Keyser & R. C. Sweetland (eds.), *Test critiques* (vol. 5). Kansas City, MO: Test Corporation of America.

Herrnstein, R. J., & Murray, C. (1994). *The bell curve: Intelligence and class structure in American life.* New York: Free Press.

Hersen, M., & Bellack, A. S. (eds.). (1988). *Dictionary of behavioral assessment techniques.* New York: Pergamon.

Hersen, M., & Bellack, A. S. (eds.). (1998). *Behavioral assessment: A practical handbook* (2nd ed.). Boston: Allyn & Bacon.

Hiatt, D., & Hargrave, G. E. (1988). MMPI profiles of problem peace officers. *Journal of Personality Assessment, 52,* 722–731.

Hill, E. F. (1972). *The Holtzman Inkblot Technique: A handbook for clinical application.* San Francisco: Jossey-Bass.

Hilliard, A. G. (1984). IQ testing as the emperor's new clothes: A critique of Jensen's Bias in Mental Testing. In C. R. Reynolds & R. T. Brown (eds.), *Perspectives on bias in mental testing.* New York: Plenum.

Hilsenroth, M. J., Fowler, J., Padawer, J., & Handler, L. (1997). Narcissism in the Rorschach revisited: Some reflections on empirical data. *Psychological Assessment, 9,* 113–121.

Hiskey, M. S. (1966). *Manual for the Hiskey-Nebraska Test of Learning Aptitude.* Lincoln, NE: Union College Press.

Hodges, J. R. (1994). *Cognitive assessment for clinicians.* Oxford: Oxford University Press.

Hoffart, A., Friis, S., Strand, J., & Olsen, B. (1994). Symptoms and cognitions during situational and hyperventilatory exposure in agoraphobic patients with and without panic. *Journal of Psychopathology and Behavioral Assessment, 16,* 15–32.

Hoffman, F. J., Sheldon, K. L., Minskoff, E. H., and others (1987). Needs of learning disabled adults. *Journal of Learning Disabilities, 20,* 43–52.

Hogan, J., & Hogan, R. (1986). *Manual for the Hogan Personnel Selection System.* Minneapolis, MN: National Computer Systems.

Hogan, J., & Hogan, R. (1989). How to measure employee reliability. *Journal of Applied Psychology, 74,* 273–279.

Hogan, J., & Quigley, A. (1994). Effects of preparing for physical ability tests. *Public Personnel Management, 23,* 85–104.

Hogan, R. T. (1986). *Manual for the Hogan Personality Inventory.* Minneapolis, MN: National Computer Systems.

Hogan, R. T. (1991). Personality and personality measurement. In M. D. Dunnette & L. M. Hough (eds.), *Handbook of industrial and organizational psychology* (vol. 2). Palo Alto, CA: Consulting Psychologists Press.

Hoge, D. R. (1996). Religion in America: The demographics of belief and affiliation. In E. P. Shafranske (ed.), *Religion and the clinical practice of psychology.* Washington, DC: American Psychological Association.

Holland, J. L. (1966). *The psychology of vocational choice.* Waltham, MA: Blaisdell.

Holland, J. L. (1978). *The occupations finder.* Palo Alto, CA: Consulting Psychologists Press.

Holland, J. L. (1985a). *Making vocational choices: A theory of vocational personalities and work environments* (2nd ed.). Englewood Cliffs, NJ: Prentice-Hall.

Holland, J. L. (1985b). *Self-Directed Search: Professional manual—1985 edition.* Odessa, FL: Psychological Assessment Resources, Inc.

Holland, J. L. (1985c). *Vocational Preference Inventory (VPI) manual—1985 edition.* Odessa, FL: Psychological Assessment Resources, Inc.

Holland, J. L. (1987). *1987 manual supplement for the Self-Directed Search.* Odessa, FL: Psychological Assessment Resources.

Holland, J. L. (1990). *Applications and research using Holland's theory of careers: Where are we now?* Paper presented at the annual meeting of the American Psychological Association, Boston, MA.

Holland, J. L., & Gottfredson, G. D. (1990). *An annotated bibliography for Holland's theory of vocational personalities and work environments.* Paper presented at the annual meeting of the American Psychological Association, Boston, MA.

Hollingshead, A., & Redlich, F. (1958). *Social class and mental illness.* New York: Wiley.

Hollon, S. D., & Kendall, P. C. (1980). Cognitive self-statements in depression: Development of an automatic thoughts questionnaire. *Cognitive Therapy and Research, 4,* 383–397.

Holmes, T., & Rahe, R. (1967). The Social Readjustment Rating Scale. *Journal of Psychosomatic Research, 11,* 213–218.

Holtzman, W. (1988). Beyond the Rorschach. *Journal of Personality Assessment, 52,* 578–609.

Holtzman, W. H. (1961). *Guide to administration and scoring: Holtzman Inkblot Technique.* New York: The Psychological Corporation.

Holzinger, K. J., & Swineford, F. (1939). *A study in factor analysis: The stability of a bi-factor solution.* University of Chicago, Supplementary Educational Monographs, No. 48.

Holzinger, K., & Harman, H. (1941). *Factor analysis: A synthesis of factorial methods.* Chicago: University of Chicago Press.

Honts, C. R., and Perry, M. V. (1992). Polygraph admissibility: Changes and challenges. *Law and Human Behavior, 16,* 357–379.

Honzik, M. (1957). Developmental studies of parent-child resemblance in intelligence. *Child Development, 28,* 215–228.

Honzik, M. (1983). Measuring mental abilities in infancy: The value and limitations. In M. Lewis (ed.), *Origins of intelligence: Infancy and early childhood* (2nd ed.). New York: Plenum.

Horn, J. L. (1968). Organization of abilities and the development of intelligence. *Psychological Review, 75,* 242–259.

Horn, J. L. (1982). The theory of fluid and crystallized intelligence in relation to concepts of cognitive psychology and aging in adulthood. In: F. I. M. Craik and S. Trehub (eds.). *Aging and cognitive processes.* New York: Plenum Press.

Horn, J. L. (1985). Remodeling old models of intelligence. In B. B. Wolman (ed.), *Handbook of intelligence: Theories, measurements, and applications.* New York: Wiley.

Horn, J. L. (1994). Theory of fluid and crystallized intelligence. In R. J. Sternberg (ed.), *Encyclopedia of human intelligence.* New York: Macmillan.

Horn, J. L., & Cattell, R. B. (1966). Refinement and test of the theory of fluid and crystallized general intelligences. *Journal of Educational Psychology, 57,* 253–270.

Horowitz, F. D. (1994). Giftedness. In R. J. Sternberg (ed.), *Encyclopedia of human intelligence* (vol. 1). New York: Macmillan.

Horowitz, I., and Willging, T. (1984). *The psychology of law.* Boston: Little, Brown.

Hough, L. M., Eaton, N., Dunnette, M., Kamp, J., & McCloy, R. (1990). Criterion-related validities of personality constructs and the effect of response distortion on those validities [Monograph]. *Journal of Applied Psychology, 75,* 581–595.

Houts, A. C., Cook, T. D., & Shadish, W. R., Jr. (1986). The person-situation debate: A critical multiplist perspective. *Journal of Personality, 54,* 52–105.

Howell, R. J., and Richards, L. (1989). Review of the Rogers Criminal Responsibility Assessment Scales. *The Tenth Mental Measurements Yearbook.* Lincoln, NE: University of Nebraska Press.

Huffcutt, A. I., & Roth, P. (1998). Racial group differences in employment interview evaluations. *Journal of Applied Psychology, 83,* 179–189.

Hughes, J. L., & McNamara, W. J. (1959). *Manual for the revised Programmer Aptitude Test.* New York: The Psychological Corporation.

Huhtaniemi, P., Haier, R. J., Fedio, P., & Buchsbaum, M. S. (1983). Neuropsychological characteristics of college males who show attention dysfunction. *Perceptual and Motor Skills, 51,* 707–713.

Humphreys, L. G. (1971). Theory of intelligence. In R. Cancro (ed.), *Intelligence: genetic and environmental influences.* New York: Grune & Stratton.

Hunsberger, B. (1995). Religion and prejudice: The role of religious fundamentalism, quest, and right-wing authoritarianism. *Journal of Social Issues, 51,* 113–129.

Hunter, J. E. (1989). *The Wonderlic Personnel Test as a predictor of training success and job performance.* Northfield, IL: E. F. Wonderlic Personnel Test, Inc.

Hunter, J. E. (1994). General Aptitude Test Battery. In R. J. Sternberg (ed.), *Encyclopedia of human intelligence.* New York: Macmillan.

Hunter, J. E., & Hunter, R. F. (1984). Validity and utility of alternative predictors of job performance. *Psychological Bulletin, 96,* 72–98.

Hunter, J. E., & Schmidt, F. L. (1976). Critical analysis of the statistical and ethical implications of various definitions of test bias. *Psychological Bulletin, 83,* 1053–1071.

Hutt, M. L. (1977). *The Hutt Adaptation of the Bender-Gestalt Test.* New York: Grune & Stratton.

Hutt, M. L., & Briskin, G. J. (1960). *The clinical use of the revised Bender-Gestalt Test.* New York: Grune & Stratton.

Hynd, G. W., & Willis, W. G. (1985). Neurological foundations of intelligence. In B. B. Wolman (ed.), *Handbook of intelligence: Theories, measurements, and applications.* New York: Wiley.

Iacono, W. G., & Lykken, D. T. (1997). The validity of the lie detector: Two surveys of scientific opinion. *Journal of Applied Psychology, 82,* 426–433.

Igbokwe, N. U. (1989). Reliability of the Jenkins Activity Survey in assessing Type A behavior pattern in middle-aged Nigerians. *Perceptual and Motor Skills, 69,* 1330.

Inwald, R. E. (1988). Five-year follow-up of departmental terminations as predicted by 16 preemployment psychological indicators. *Journal of Applied Psychology, 73,* 703–710.

IPAT (1973). *Measuring intelligence with the Culture Fair Tests: Manual for Scales 2 and 3.* Champaign, IL: Institute for Personality and Ability Testing.

Irwin, P. M. (1992). *Elementary and Secondary Education Act of 1965: FY 1993 Guide To Programs.* Congressional Research Service. Washington, DC: Government Printing Office.

Itard, J. M. G. (1932/1801). The *wild boy of Aveyron.* Trans. by G. & M. Humphrey. New York: Appleton-Century-Crofts.

Ivnik, R., Malec, J., Smith, G., & others (1992). Mayo's Older Americans Normative Studies: Updated AVLT norms for ages 56 to 97. *Clinical Neuropsychologist, 6,* 83–104.

Jackson, D. N. (1970). A sequential system for personality scale development. In C. D. Spielberger (ed.), *Current topics in clinical and community psychology* (vol. 2). Orlando, FL: Academic Press.

Jackson, D. N. (1977). *Jackson Vocational Interest Survey Manual.* Ontario: Research Psychologists Press.

Jackson, D. N. (1984a). *Manual for the Multidimensional Aptitude Battery.* Port Huron, MI: Research Psychologists Press.

Jackson, D. N. (1984b). *Personality Research Form manual.* Port Huron, MI: Research Psychologists Press.

Jackson, D. N. (1986). *Career Directions Inventory manual.* Port Huron, MI: Sigma Assessment Systems.

Jackson, D. N. (1991). *Jackson Vocational Interest Survey Manual* (3rd ed.). Port Huron, MI: Research Psychologists Press.

Jackson, D. N., & Gray, A. (1987). *The Survey of Work Styles.* Port Huron, MI: Research Psychologists Press.

Jackson, D. N., & Messick, S. (1968). Creativity. In P. London & D. Rosenhan (eds.). *Foundations of abnormal psychology.* New York: Holt.

James, W. (1902). *The varieties of religious experience.* New York: Longman.

Jenkins, C. D., Zyzanski, S., & Rosenman, R. (1971). Progress toward validation of a computer-scored test for the Type A coronary-prone behavior pattern. *Psychosomatic Medicine, 33,* 193–201.

Jenkins, C. D., Zyzanski, S., & Rosenman, R. (1979). *Jenkins Activity Survey: Manual.* New York: The Psychological Corporation.

Jenkins, J. J., & Paterson, D. G. (eds.). (1961). *Studies in individual differences.* New York: Appleton-Century-Crofts.

Jennett, B., & Teasdale, G. (1981). *Management of head injuries.* Philadelphia, PA: F. A. Davis.

Jennett, B., Teasdale, G. M., & Knill-Jones, R. P. (1975). Predicting outcome after head injury. *Journal of Royal College of Physicians of London, 9,* 231–237.

Jensen, A. R. (1969). How much can we boost IQ and scholastic achievement? *Harvard Educational Review, 39,* 1–123.

Jensen, A. R. (1977). Cumulative deficit in IQ of blacks in the rural south. *Developmental Psychology,* 13, 184–191.

Jensen, A. R. (1979). g: outmoded theory or unconquered frontier? *Creative Science and Technology, 2,* 16–29.

Jensen, A. R. (1980). *Bias in mental testing.* New York: Free Press.

Jensen, A. R. (1981). Raising the IQ: The Ramey and Haskins Study. *Intelligence, 5,* 29–40.

Jensen, A. R. (1982). The chronometry of intelligence. In R. J. Sternberg (ed.), *Advances in the psychology of human intelligence.* Hillsdale, NJ: Erlbaum.

Jensen, A. R. (1984). Test bias: Concepts and criticisms. In C. R. Reynolds & R. T. Brown (eds.), *Perspectives on bias in mental testing.* New York: Plenum.

Jensen, A. R., & Osborne, R. T. (1979). *Forward and backward digit span interaction with race and IQ: A longitudinal developmental comparison.* Berkeley: University of California. (ERIC Document Reproduction Service No. ED 173 384).

Johnson, J. H., and Williams, T. A. (1975). The use of on-line computer technology in a mental health admitting system. *American Psychologist, 30,* 388–390.

Johnson, N. E., Saccuzzo, D., & Guertin, T. (1994). The development and validation of a reliable alternate form for Raven's Standard Progressive Matrices. *Assessment, 1,* 315–319.

Johnson, R. C., McClearn, G. E., Yuen, S., Nagoshi, C. T., Ahern, F. M., & Cole, R. E. (1985). Galton's data a century later. *American Psychologist, 40,* 875–892.

Johnson, R. G. (1987). Shipley Institute of Living Scale. In D. J. Keyser & R. C. Sweetland (eds.), *Test critiques compendium.* Kansas City, MO: Test Corporation of America.

Johnson, S. T. (1994). Scholastic Assessment Tests. In R. J. Sternberg (ed.), *Encyclopedia of human intelligence.* New York: Macmillan.

Johnson, W. G., and Mullett, N. (1987). Georgia Court Competency Test-Revised. In M. Hersen and A. S. Bellack (eds.), *Dictionary of behavioral assessment techniques.* Elmsford, NY: Pergamon.

Johnston, D. W. (1986). Behavior therapy. In R. Harre & R. Lamb (eds.), *The dictionary of physiological and clinical psychology.* Cambridge, MA: The MIT Press.

Johnston, W. T., & Bolen, R. M. (1984). A comparison of the factor structures of the WISC-R for Blacks and Whites. *Psychology in the Schools, 21,* 42–44.

Joint Committee on Testing Practices (1988). *Code of fair testing practices in education.* Washington, DC: Author.

Jones, K. L., Smith, D. W., Ulleland, C. N., & Streissguth, A. P. (1973). Patterns of malformation in offspring of chronic alcoholic mothers. *Lancet, 1,* 1267–1271.

Jones, R. (1980). *The big switch: New careers, new lives after 35.* New York: McGraw-Hill.

Joseph, R. (1988). The right cerebral hemisphere: Emotion, music, visual-spatial skills, body-image, dreams, and awareness. *Journal of Clinical Psychology, 44,* 630–763.

Jung, C. G. (1910). The association method. *American Journal of Psychology, 21,* 219–269.

Kaiser, H. F., & Michael, W. B. (1975). Domain validity and generalizability. *Educational and Psychological Measurement, 35,* 31–35.

Kalichman, S. C. (1988). Empirically derived MMPI profile subgroups of incarcerated homicide offenders. *Journal of Clinical Psychology, 44,* 733–738.

Kamphaus, R., Beres, K., Kaufman, A., & Kaufman, N. (1996). The Kaufman Assessment Battery for Children. In C. S. Newmark (ed.), *Major psychological assessment instruments* (2nd ed.). Boston: Allyn & Bacon.

Kamphaus, R. W. (1990). K-ABC theory in historical and current contexts. *Journal of Psychoeducational Assessment, 8,* 356–368.

Kamphaus, R. W. (1993). *Clinical assessment of children's intelligence.* Boston: Allyn & Bacon.

Kandel, E. R. (1991). Perception of motion, depth, and form. In E. R. Kandel, J. H. Schwartz, & T. M. Jessell (eds.), *Principles of neural science* (3rd ed.). New York: Elsevier.

Kandel, E. R., Schwartz, J. H., & Jessell, T. M. (1995). *Essentials of neural science and behavior.* Norwalk, CN: Appleton & Lange.

Kane, R. L. (1991). Standardized and flexible batteries in neuropsychology: An assessment update. *Neuropsychology Review, 2,* 281–339.

Kaplan, C. (1996). Predictive validity of the WPPSI-R: A four year follow-up study. *Psychology in the Schools, 33,* 211–219.

Kaplan, S. L., & Alfonso, V. C. (1997). Confirmatory factor analysis of the Stanford-Binet Intelligence Scale: Fourth Edition with preschoolers with developmental delays. *Journal of Psychoeducational Assessment, 15,* 226–237.

Karr, S., Carvajal, H., Elser, D., & Bays, K. (1993). Concurrent validity of the WPPSI-R and the McCarthy Scales of Children's Abilities. *Psychological Reports, 72,* 940–942.

Kaufman, A. S. (1975). Factor structure of the McCarthy Scales at five age levels between 2 ½ and 8 ½. *Educational and Psychological Measurement, 35,* 641–656.

Kaufman, A. S. (1978). Review of Columbia Mental Maturity Scale. *The Eighth Mental Measurements Yearbook.* Lincoln, NE: University of Nebraska Press.

Kaufman, A. S. (1983). Test review: WAIS-R. *Journal of Psychoeducational Assessment, 1,* 309–319.

Kaufman, A. S. (1990). *Assessing adolescent and adult intelligence.* Boston: Allyn & Bacon.

Kaufman, A. S., & Kaufman, N. L. (1983). *K-ABC administration and scoring manual.* Circle Pines, MN: American Guidance Service.

Kaufman, A. S., & Kaufman, N. L. (1985). *Kaufman Test of Educational Achievement: Comprehensive Form Manual.* Circle Pines, MN: American Guidance Service.

Kaufman, A. S., & Kaufman, N. L. (1990). *Kaufman Brief Intelligence Test manual.* Circle Pines, MN: American Guidance Service.

Kaufman, A. S., & Kaufman, N. L. (1997). The Kaufman Adolescent and Adult Intelligence Test. In D. P. Flanagan, J. Genshaft, & P. Harrison (eds.), *Contemporary intellectual assessment: Theories, tests, and issues.* New York: Guilford.

Kaufman, A. S., & Wang, J. (1992). Gender, race, and education differences on the K-BIT at ages 4 to 90. *Journal of Psychoeducational Assessment, 10,* 219–229.

Kaufman, A. S., Kamphaus, R. W., & Kaufman, N. L. (1985). The Kaufman Assessment Battery for Children (K-ABC). In C. S. Newmark (ed.), *Major psychological assessment instruments.* Boston: Allyn & Bacon.

Kaufman, A. S., Kaufman, N. L., & Goldsmith, B. Z. (1984). *Kaufman sequential or simultaneous: Leader's kit.* Circle Pines, MN: American Guidance Service.

Kaufman, A. S., Kaufman, N. L., Kamphaus, R. W., & Naglieri, J. A. (1982). Sequential and simultaneous factors at ages 3–12 ½: Developmental changes in neuropsychological dimensions. *Clinical Neuropsychology, 4,* 74–81.

Kaufman, A. S., McLean, J. E., & Lincoln, A. (1996). The relationship of the Myers-Briggs Type Indicator (MBTI) to IQ level and the fluid and crystallized IQ discrepancy on the Kaufman Adolescent and Adult Intelligence Test (KAIT). *Assessment, 3,* 225–239.

Kaufman, A. S., McLean, J. E., & Reynolds, C. R. (1988). Sex, race, residence, region, and education differences on the 11 WAIS-R subtests. *Journal of Clinical Psychology, 44,* 231–248.

Kausler, D. (1991). *Experimental psychology, cognition, and human aging* (2nd ed.). New York: Springer-Verlag.

Kazdin, A. E. (1988). The token economy: A decade later. In G. Davey & C. Cullen (eds.), *Human operant conditioning and behavior modification.* New York: Wiley.

Kazdin, A. E. (1990). Evaluation of the Automatic Thoughts Questionnaire: Negative cognitive processes and depression among children. *Psychological Assessment: A Journal of Consulting and Clinical Psychology.* 2, 73–79.

Keenan, J., & Brassell, E. (1975). *Aphasia Language Performance Scales.* Murfreesboro, TN: Pinnacle Press.

Keenan, P. A., & Lachar, D. (1988). Screening preschoolers with special problems: Use of the Personality Inventory for Children (PIC). *Journal of School Psychology, 26,* 1–11.

Keith, T. Z., and Bolen, L. M. (1980). Factor structure of the McCarthy Scales for children experiencing problems in school. *Psychology in the Schools, 17,* 320–326.

Kelley, T. L. (1928). *Crossroads in the mind of man: A study of differentiable mental abilities.* Stanford, CA: Stanford University Press.

Kelly, E. L., & Fiske, D. W. (1951). *The prediction of performance in clinical psychology.* Ann Arbor: University of Michigan Press.

Kendall, P. C., & Hollon, S. D. (1989). Anxious self-talk: Development of the Anxious Self-Statements Questionnaire (ASSQ). *Cognitive Therapy and Research,* 13, 81–93.

Kennedy, W. A., Van de Riet, V., & White, J. C., Jr. (1963). A normative sample of intelligence and achievement of negro elementary school children in the southeast United States. *Monographs of the Society for Research in Child Development, 28* [No. 90], 68.

Kent, G. H., & Rosanoff, A. J. (1910). A study of association in insanity. *American Journal of Insanity, 67,* 37–96; 317–390.

Kertesz, A. (1979). *Aphasia and associated disorders: Taxonomy, localization, and recovery.* New York: Grune & Stratton.

Keyser, D. J., & Sweetland, R. C. (eds.). (1984–1988). *Test Critiques* (volumes I–VI). Kansas City, MO: Test Corporation of America.

Kifer, E. (1985). Review of ACT Assessment Program. *Ninth Mental Measurements Yearbook.* Lincoln, NE: University of Nebraska Press.

Killian, G. A. (1987). House-Tree-Person technique. In D. J. Keyser & R. C. Sweetland, (eds.), *Test critiques compendium.* Kansas City, MO: Test Corporation of America.

Kinnear, P. R., & Gray, C. D. (1997). *SPSS for Windows made simple* (2nd ed.). Trowbridge, UK: Psychology Press.

Kinsbourne, M. (1994). Neuropsychology of attention. In D. W. Zaidel (ed.), *Neuropsychology.* San Diego, CA: Academic Press.

Kirkpatrick, L., & Hood, R. (1990). Intrinsic-Extrinsic Religious Orientation: The boon or bane of contemporary psychology of religion? *Journal for the Scientific Study of Religion, 29,* 442–462.

Kleinmuntz, B., and Szucko, J. J. (1984). A field study of the fallibility of polygraphic lie detection. *Nature, 308,* 449–450.

Klieger, D. M., & Franklin, M. E. (1993). Validity of the fear survey schedule in phobia research: A laboratory test. *Journal of Psychopathology and Behavioral Assessment, 15,* 207–218.

Klimoski, R., & Palmer, S. (1994). The ADA and the hiring process in organizations. In S. M. Bruyere & J. O'Keeffe (eds.), *Implications of the Americans with Disabilities Act for psychology.* New York: Springer.

Kline, P. (1986). *A handbook of test construction.* New York: Metheun.

Kline, P. (1993). *The handbook of psychological testing.* London: Routledge.

Kline, R. B. (1989). Is the Fourth Edition Stanford-Binet a four-factor test? Confirmatory factor analysis of alternative models for ages 2 through 23. *Journal of Psychoeducational Assessment, 7,* 4–13.

Kline, R. B., & Lachar, D. (1992). Evaluation of age, sex, and race bias in the Personality Inventory for Children (PIC). *Psychological Assessment, 4,* 333–339.

Kline, R. B., Guilmette, S., Snyder, J., & Castellanos, M. (1992). Relative cognitive complexity of the Kaufman Assessment Battery for Children (K-ABC) and the WISC-R. *Journal of Psychoeducational Assessment, 10,* 141–152.

Kline, R. B., Lachar, D., & Boersma, D. (1993). Identification of special education needs with the personality inventory for children (PIC): A hierarchical classification model. *Psychological Assessment, 5,* 307–316.

Kline, R. B., Lachar, D., & Gdowski, C. L. (1992). Clinical validity of a Personality Inventory for Children (PIC) profile typology. *Journal of Personality Assessment, 58,* 691–705.

Kline, R. B., Lachar, D., Gruber, C., & Boersma, D. (1994). Identification of special education needs with the Personality Inventory for Children (PIC): A profile-matching strategy. *Assessment, 1,* 301–314.

Klingler, D. E., Miller, D., Johnson, J., and Williams, T. (1977). Process evaluation of an on-line computer-assisted unit for intake assessment of mental health patients. *Behavior Research Methods and Instrumentation, 9,* 110–116.

Klopfer, W. G., & Taulbee, E. S. (1976). Thematic Apperception Test. *Annual Review of Psychology, 27,* 543–567.

Klove, H. (1963). Clinical neuropsychology. In: F. M. Forster (ed.). *The Medical Clinics of North America.* New York: Saunders.

Kluckhohn, C. (1951). Values and value orientations in the theory of action. In T. Parsons and E. A. Shils (eds.), *Toward a general theory of action.* Cambridge, MA: Harvard University Press.

Knight, B. C., Baker, E. H., and Minder, C. C. (1990). Concurrent validity of the Stanford-Binet: Fourth Edition and Kaufman Assessment Battery for Children with learning-disabled students. *Psychology in the Schools, 27,* 116–125.

Knight, R. G. (1992). *The neuropsychology of degenerative brain diseases.* Hillsdale, NJ: Erlbaum.

Knobloch, H., Stevens, F., and Malone, A. (1987). *Manual of developmental diagnosis: The administration and interpretation of the Revised Gesell and Amatruda Developmental and Neurologic Examination.* Houston, TX: Developmental Evaluation Materials, Inc.

Knox, H. A. (1914). A scale, based on the work at Ellis Island, for estimating mental defect. *Journal of the American Medical Association, 62,* 741–747.

Koch, W. R. (1984). Culture Fair Intelligence Test. In D. J. Keyser & R. C. Sweetland (eds.), *Test Critiques* (vol. I). Kansas City, MO: Test Corporation of America.

Kohlberg, L. (1958). *The development of modes of moral thinking and choice in the years ten to sixteen.* Unpublished doctoral dissertation, University of Chicago.

Kohlberg, L. (1981). *Essays on moral development: Vol. 1. The philosophy of moral development.* San Francisco: Harper & Row.

Kohlberg, L. (1984). *Essays on moral development: Vol. 2. The psychology of moral development.* San Francisco: Harper & Row.

Kohlberg, L., & Elfenbein, D. (1975). The development of moral judgments concerning capital punishment. *American Journal of Orthopsychiatry, 45,* 614–639.

Kohlberg, L., & Kramer, R. (1969). Continuities and discontinuities in children and adult moral development. *Human Development, 12,* 225–252.

Kohs, S. C. (1920). The block-design tests. *Journal of Experimental Psychology, 3,* 357–376.

Kolb, B., & Milner, B. (1981). Performance of complex arm and facial movements after focal brain lesions. *Neuropsychologia, 19,* 491–503.

Kolb, B., & Whishaw, I. Q. (1985). *Fundamentals of human neuropsychology* (2nd ed.). New York: Freeman.

Kolb, B., & Whishaw, I. Q. (1990). *Fundamentals of human neuropsychology* (3rd ed.). New York: Freeman.

Kolb, B., Milner, B., & Taylor, L. (1983). Perception of faces by patients with localized cortical excisions. *Canadian Journal of Psychology, 37,* 8–18.

Koltai, D., Bowler, R., & Shore, M. (1996). The Rivermead Behavioral Memory Test and Wechsler Memory Scale-Revised: Relationship to everyday memory impairment. *Assessment, 3,* 443–448.

Koluchova, J. (1972). Severe deprivation in twins: A case study. *Journal of Child Psychology and Psychiatry, 13,* 107–114.

Konold, T. R., Kush, J., & Canivez, G. (1997). Factor replication of the WISC-III in three independent samples of children receiving special education. *Journal of Psychoeducational Assessment, 15,* 123–137.

Koss, E. (1994). Neuropsychology of aging and dementia. In D. W. Zaidel (ed.), *Neuropsychology* (2nd ed.). San Diego, CA: Academic Press.

Kramer, J. J. (1988). Computer-based test interpretation in psychoeducational assessment: An initial appraisal. *Journal of School Psychology, 26,* 143–153.

Krieshok, T. S., & Harrington, R. G. (1985). A review of the Multidimensional Aptitude Battery. *Journal of Counseling and Development, 64,* 87–89.

Krugman, M. (1970). H-T-P: House, Tree, and Person. In O. K. Buros (ed.), *Personality tests and reviews.* Highland Park, NJ: The Gryphon Press.

Krumboltz, J. D. (1991). *Manual for the Career Beliefs Inventory.* Palo Alto, CA: Consulting Psychologists Press.

Kuder, G. F. (1934). *Kuder preference record.* Chicago: Science Research Associates.

Kuder, G. F. (1966). The Occupational Interest Survey. *Personnel and Guidance Journal, 45,* 72–77.

Kuder, G. F. (1975). *General Interest Survey (Form E)— Manual.* Chicago: Science Research Associates.

Kuder, G. F., & Diamond, E. E. (1979). *Kuder Occupational Interest Survey: General manual.* Chicago: Science Research Associates.

Kuder, G. F., & Richardson, M. W. (1937). The theory of estimation of test reliability. *Psychometrika, 2,* 151–160.

Kuncel, N., Campbell, J., & Ones, D. (1998). Validity of the Graduate Record Examination: Estimated or tacitly known? *American Psychologist, 53,* 567–568.

Kupfermann, I. (1991a). Hypothalamus and limbic system: Peptidergic neurons, homeostasis, and emotional behavior. In E. R. Kandel, J. H. Schwartz, & T. M. Jessell (eds.), *Principles of neural science* (3rd ed.). New York: Elsevier.

Kupfermann, I. (1991b). Localization of higher cognitive and affective functions: The association cortices. In E. R. Kandel, J. H. Schwartz, & T. M. Jessel (eds.), *Principles of neural science* (3rd ed.). New York: Elsevier.

Kurtines, W., & Greif, E. B. (1974). The development of moral thought: Review and evaluation of Kohlberg's approach. *Psychological Bulletin, 81,* 453–470.

La Rue, A. (1992). *Aging and neuropsychological assessment.* New York: Plenum.

Laatsch, L., & Choca, J. (1994). Cluster-branching methodology for adaptive testing and the development of the Adaptive Category Test. *Psychological Assessment, 6,* 345–351.

Laboratory for Community Psychiatry (1974). *Competency to stand trial and mental illness.* Northvale, NJ: Jason Aronson.

Lachar, D. (1974). *The MMPI: Clinical assessment and automated interpretation.* Los Angeles: Western Psychological Services.

Lachar, D. (1982). *Personality Inventory for Children: Revised format manual supplement.* Los Angeles: Western Psychological Services.

Lachar, D. (1987). Automated assessment of child and adolescent personality. In J. N. Butcher (ed.), *Computerized psychological assessment: A practitioner's guide.* New York: Basic Books.

Lachar, D., & Gdowski, C. L. (1979). *Actuarial assessment of child and adolescent personality: An interpretive guide for the Personality Inventory for Children profile.* Los Angeles: Western Psychological Services.

Lachar, D., Kline, R. B., & Gdowski, C. L. (1987). Respondent psychopathology and interpretive accuracy of the Personality Inventory for Children: The evaluation of a "most reasonable" assumption. *Journal of Personality Assessment, 51,* 165–177.

Lacks, P. (1999). *Bender-Gestalt screening for brain dysfunction* (2nd ed.). New York: Wiley.

Lacks, P., & Newport, K. (1980). A comparison of scoring systems and level of scorer experience on the Bender-Gestalt Test. *Journal of Personality Assessment, 44,* 351–357.

Lah, M. I. (1989). New validity, normative, and scoring data for the Rotter Incomplete Sentences Blank. *Journal of Personality Assessment, 53,* 607–620.

Lah, M. I., & Rotter, J. B. (1981). Changing college student norms on the Rotter Incomplete Sentences Blank. *Journal of Consulting and Clinical Psychology, 49,* 985.

Lai, T. C. (1970). *A scholar in imperial China.* Hong Kong: Kelly & Walsh.

Lam, T. C. M. (1993). Testability: A critical issue in testing language minority students with standardized achievement tests. *Measurement and Evaluation in Counseling and Development, 26,* 179–191.

Lambert, N., Hartsough, C., & Sandoval, J. (1990). *Manual for the Children's Attention and Adjustment Survey.* Circle Pines, MN: American Guidance Service.

Landy, F. J. (1985). *The psychology of work behavior* (3rd ed.). Homewood, IL: Dorsey Press.

Landy, F. J., & Farr, J. L. (1983). *The measurement of work performance: Methods, theory and applications.* New York: Academic Press.

Landy, F. J., Shankster, L. J., & Kohler, S. S. (1994). Personnel selection and placement. *Annual Review of Psychology, 45,* 261–296.

Lane, S. (1992). Review of the Iowa Tests of Basic Skills. *Eleventh Mental Measurements Yearbook.* Lincoln, NE: University of Nebraska Press.

Lang, W. (1995). Review of Gesell Child Developmental Age Scale. *Twelfth Mental Measurements Yearbook.* Lincoln, NE: University of Nebraska Press.

Lang, W. S. (1992). Review of TEMAS (Tell-Me-A-Story). *The Eleventh Mental Measurements Yearbook.* Lincoln, NE: University of Nebraska Press.

Lansdell, H., & Donnelly, E. F. (1977). Factor analysis of the Wechsler Adult Intelligence Scale Subtests and the Halstead-Reitan Category and Tapping Tests. *Journal of Consulting and Clinical Psychology, 45,* 412–416.

Lanyon, R. I. (1984). Personality assessment. *Annual Review of Psychology, 35,* 667–701.

Larson, G. E. (1994). Armed Services Vocational Aptitude Battery. In R. J. Sternberg (ed.), *Encyclopedia of human intelligence.* New York: Macmillan.

Larson, G. E., & Wolfe, J. (1995). Validity results for *g* from an expanded test base. *Intelligence, 20,* 15–25.

Lassiter, K., & Bardos, A. (1995). The relationship between young children's academic achievement and measures of intelligence. *Psychology in the Schools, 32,* 170–177.

Latham, G. P., & Skarlicki, D. (1995). Criterion-related validity of the situational and patterned behavior description interviews with organizational citizenship behavior. *Human Performance, 8,* 67–80.

Laurent, J., Swerdlik, M., and Ryburn, M. (1992). Review of validity research on the Stanford-Binet Intelligence Scale: Fourth Edition. *Psychological Assessment, 4,* 102–112.

Lavin, C. (1996). The WISC-III and the Stanford-Binet: Fourth Edition: A preliminary study of validity. *Psychological Reports, 78,* 491–496.

LaVoie, A. L. (1987). The Blacky Pictures. In D. J. Keyser & R. C. Sweetland (eds.), *Test critiques compendium.* Kansas City, MO: Test Corporation of America.

Lawshe, C. H. (1975). A quantitative approach to content validity. *Personnel Psychology, 28,* 563–575.

Layton, W. (1992). Review of Minnesota Importance Questionnaire. *Eleventh Mental Measurements Yearbook.* Lincoln, NE: University of Nebraska Press.

Ledbetter, M., Smith, L., Vosler-Hunter, W., & Fischer, J. (1991). An evaluation of the research and clinical usefulness of the Spiritual Well-Being Scale. *Journal of Psychology and Theology, 19,* 49–55.

Lee, M. S., Wallbrown, F., & Blaha, J. (1990). Note on the construct validity of the Multidimensional Aptitude Battery. *Psychological Reports, 67,* 1219–1222.

Lefcourt, H. M. (1982). *Locus of control: Current trends in theory and research* (2nd ed.). Hillsdale, NJ: Erlbaum.

Lefebvre, M. F. (1981). Cognitive distortion and cognitive errors in depressed psychiatric and low back pain patients. *Journal of Consulting and Clinical Psychology, 49,* 517–525.

Lehman, R. E. (1978). Symptom contamination of the Schedule of Recent Events. *Journal of Consulting and Clinical Psychology, 46,* 1564–1565.

Leiter, R. G. (1948). *Leiter International Performance Scale.* Chicago: Stoelting Co.

Leiter, R. G. (1979). *Leiter International Performance Scale: Instruction manual.* Chicago: Stoelting Co.

Leli, D. A., and Filskov, S. B. (1984). Clinical detection of intellectual deterioration associated with brain damage. *Journal of Clinical Psychology, 40,* 1435–1441.

Lerner, J. (1993). *Learning disabilities: Theories, diagnosis & teaching strategies.* Boston, MA: Houghton Mifflin.

Levine, S., Elzey, F. F., Thormahlen, P., & Cain, L. F. (1976). *Manual for the T. M. R. School Competency Scales.* Palo Alto, CA: Consulting Psychologists Press.

Levinson, E. M. (1990). Vocational assessment involvement and use of the Self-Directed Search by school psychologists. *Psychology in the Schools, 27,* 217–228.

Lewinsohn, P. M. (1965). Psychological correlates of overall quality of figure drawings. *Journal of Consulting Psychology, 29,* 504–512.

Lewinsohn, P. M., Munoz, R. F., Youngren, M. A., & Zeiss, A. M. (1986). *Control your depression: Reducing depression through learning self-control techniques, relaxation training, pleasant activities, social skills, constructed thinking, planning ahead, and more* (rev. ed.). New York: Prentice-Hall.

Lewis, M., and Brooks-Gunn, J. (1981). Visual attention at three months as a predictor of cognitive functioning at two years of age. *Intelligence, 5,* 131–140.

Lewis, M., and Sullivan, M. W. (1985). Infant intelligence and its assessment. In B. B. Wolman (ed.), *Handbook of intelligence: Theories, measurements, and applications.* New York: Wiley.

Lezak, M. (1982). The problem of assessing executive functions. *International Journal of Psychology, 17,* 281–297.

Lezak, M. (1983). *Neuropsychological assessment* (2nd ed.). New York: Oxford University Press.

Lezak, M. (1995). *Neuropsychological assessment* (3rd ed.). New York: Oxford University Press.

Lezak, M. D., & O'Brien, K. P. (1990). Chronic emotional, social, and physical changes after traumatic brain injury. In E. D. Bigler (ed.), *Traumatic brain injury: Mechanisms of damage, assessment, intervention, and outcome.* Austin, TX: PRO-ED.

Lichtenberg, P., Manning, Vangel, S., & Ross. T. (1995). Normative and ecological validity data in older urban medical patients: A program of neuropsychological research. *Advances in Medical Psychotherapy, 8,* 121–136.

Lichtenstein, R. (1990). Psychometric characteristics and appropriate use of the Gesell School Readiness Screening Test. *Early Childhood Research Quarterly, 5,* 359–378.

Likert, R. (1932). A technique for the measurement of attitudes. *Archives of Psychology,* No. 140.

Lindal, E., & Stefansson, J. (1993). Mini-Mental State Examination scores: Gender and lifetime psychiatric disorders. *Psychological Reports, 72,* 631–641.

Lindenberger, U., & Baltes, P. (1994). Aging and intelligence. In R. J. Sternberg (ed.), *Encyclopedia of human intelligence.* New York: Macmillan.

Lindvall, C. M. (1967). *Measuring pupil achievement and aptitude.* New York: Harcourt, Brace & World.

Lindzey, G. (1959). On the classification of projective techniques. *Psychological Bulletin, 56,* 158–168.

Linn, R. L. (1989). Review of the Iowa Tests of Basic Skills. *Tenth Mental Measurements Yearbook.* Lincoln, NE: University of Nebraska Press.

Lipsitt, P. D. (1970). *Competency Screening Test.* Boston: Competency to Stand Trial and Mental Illness Project.

Lipsitt, P. D., Lelos, D., and McGarry, A. L. (1971). Competency for trial: A screening instrument. *American Journal of Psychiatry, 128,* 137–141.

Lipsitz, J. D., Dworkin, R., & Erlenmeyer-Kimling, L. (1993). Wechsler Comprehension and Picture Arrangement subtests and social adjustment. *Psychological Assessment, 5,* 430–437.

Lishman, W. A. (1978). *Organic psychiatry: The psychological consequences of cerebral disorder.* Oxford: Blackwell Scientific Publications.

Loevinger, J. (1976). *Ego development.* San Francisco: Jossey-Bass.

Loevinger, J. (1979). Construct validity of the sentence completion test of ego development. *Applied Psychological Measurement, 3,* 281–311.

Loevinger, J. (1984). On the self and predicting behavior. In R. A. Zucker, J. Aronoff, & A. I. Rabin (eds.), *Personality and the prediction of behavior.* New York: Academic Press.

Lofquist, L. H., & Dawis, R. V. (1991). *Essentials of person-environment correspondence counseling.* Minneapolis, MN: University of Minnesota Press.

Lord, F. M., & Novick, M. R. (1968). *Statistical theories of mental test scores.* Menlo Park, CA: Addison-Wesley.

Lorr, M., Youniss, R., and Stefic, E. (1991). An inventory of social skills. *Journal of Personality Assessment, 57,* 506–520.

Louttit, C. M., & Browne, C. G. (1947). Psychometric instruments in psychological clinics. *Journal of Consulting Psychology, 11,* 49–54.

Lowman, R. L. (1991). *The clinical practice of career assessment: Interests, abilities, and personality.* Washington, DC: American Psychological Association.

Lowman, R. L., & Leeman G. (1988). The dimensionality of social intelligence: Social abilities, interests, and needs. *Journal of Psychology, 122,* 279–290.

Lubin, B., Wallis, R., & Paine, C. (1971). Patterns of psychological test use in the United States: 1935–1969. *Professional Psychology, 2,* 70–74.

Lubinski, D., Benbow, C., & Ryan, J. (1995). Stability of vocational interests among the intellectually gifted from adolescence to adulthood: A 15-year longitudinal study. *Journal of Applied Psychology, 80,* 196–200.

Lubinski, D., Schmidt, D., Benbow, C. (1996). A 20-year stability analysis of the Study of Values for intellectually gifted individuals from adolescence to adulthood. *Journal of Applied Psychology, 81,* 443–451.

Lukens, J., & Hurrell, R. (1996). A comparison of the Stanford-Binet: IV and the WISC-III with mildly retarded children. *Psychological in the Schools, 33,* 24–27.

Lukin, M. E., Dowd, E. T., Plake, B., and Kraft, R. (1985). Comparing computerized vs. traditional psychological assessment. *Computers in Human Behavior, 1,* 49–58.

Lunz, M., & Bergstrom, B. (1994). Computer adaptive testing: A national pilot study. In M. Wilson (ed.), *Objective measurement: Theory into practice* (vol. 2). Norwood, NJ: Ablex.

Lunz, M., Bergstrom, B., & Wright, B. (1994). Reliability of alternate computer-adaptive tests. In M. Wilson (ed.), *Objective measurement: Theory into practice* (vol. 2). Norwood, NJ: Ablex.

Luria, A. R. (1966). *Higher cortical functions in man.* New York: Basic Books.

Luria, A. R. (1973). *The working brain.* New York: Basic Books.

Lykken, D. T. (1981). *A tremor in the blood: Uses and abuses of the lie detector.* New York: McGraw-Hill.

Lykken, D. T. (1987, Spring). The validity of tests: Caveat emptor. *Jurimetrics Journal, 263–270.*

Lynn, R. (1987). Japan: Land of the rising IQ. A reply to Flynn. *Bulletin of the British Psychological Society, 40,* 464–468.

Lynn, R. (1993). Nutrition and intelligence. In P. A. Vernon (ed.), *Biological approaches to the study of human intelligence.* Norwood, NJ: Ablex.

Lyon, G. R. (ed.). (1994). *Frames of reference for the assessment of learning disabilities: New views on measurement issues.* Baltimore, MD: Brookes Publishing.

MacAndrew, C. (1965). The differentiation of male alcoholic out-patients from nonalcoholic psychiatric patients by means of the MMPI. *Quarterly Journal of Studies on Alcohol, 26,* 238–246.

Maccoby, E. E., & Jacklin, C. N. (1974). *The psychology of sex differences.* Stanford, CA: Stanford University Press.

Machover, K. (1949). *Personality projection in the drawing of the human figure.* Springfield, IL: Charles C. Thomas.

Machover, K. (1951). Drawing of the human figure: A method of personality investigation. In H. Anderson & G. Anderson (eds.), *An introduction to projective techniques.* New York: Prentice-Hall.

MacLennan, R. N. (1992). *PRF annotated bibliography.* Port Huron, MI: Sigma Assessment Systems.

MacPhillamy, D. J., & Lewinsohn, P. M. (1982). The Pleasant Events Schedule: Studies on reliability, validity, and scale intercorrelation. *Journal of Consulting and Clinical Psychology, 50,* 363–380.

Maddi, S. R. (1989). *Personality theories: A comparative analysis* (5th ed.). Chicago: Dorsey Press.

Mahoney, M., & Arnkoff, D. (1978). Cognitive and self-control therapies. In S. Garfield & A. Bergin (eds.), *Handbook of psychotherapy and behavior change: An empirical analysis.* New York: Wiley.

Maker, C. J. (1996). Identification of gifted minority students: A national problem, needed changes and a promising solution. *Gifted Child Quarterly, 40,* 41–50.

Malcolm, K. K. (1998). Developmental Assessment: Evaluation of Infants and Preschoolers. In H. B. Vance (ed.), *Psychological assessment of children: Best practices for schools and clinical settings* (2nd ed.). New York: Wiley.

Malgady, R. G., Constantino, G., & Rogler, L. H. (1984). Development of a Thematic Apperception Test (TEMAS) for urban Hispanic children. *Journal of Consulting and Clinical Psychology, 52,* 986–996.

Maloney, M. P., & Ward, M. P. (1979). *Mental retardation and modern society.* New York: Oxford University Press.

Manning, W. H., & Jackson, R. (1984). College entrance examinations: Objective selection or gatekeeping for the economically privileged. In C. R. Reynolds & R. T. Brown (eds.), *Perspectives on bias in mental testing.* New York: Plenum.

Mardell-Czudnowski, C., & Goldenberg, D. S. (1990). *DIAL-R: Developmental Indicators for the Assessment of Learning-Revised.* Circle Pines, MN: American Guidance Service.

Marks, P. A., & Seeman, W. (1963). *The actuarial description of abnormal personality.* Baltimore, MD: Williams & Wilkins.

Markwardt, F. C. (1989). *Manual for the Peabody Individual Achievement Test-Revised.* Circle Pines, MN: American Guidance Service.

Martell, D. A. (1992). Forensic neuropsychology and the criminal law. *Law and Human Behavior, 16,* 313–336.

Martens, B. K. (1992). Review of Conners' Rating Scales. *Eleventh Mental Measurements Yearbook.* Lincoln, NE: University of Nebraska Press.

Martin, J. C. (1994). Birth defects. In R. J. Sternberg (ed.), *Encyclopedia of human intelligence.* New York: Macmillan.

Martuza, V. R. (1977). *Applying norm-referenced and criterion-referenced measurement in education.* Boston: Allyn & Bacon.

Mason, C. F., Lemmon, D., Wayne, K., & Schmidt, R. (1991). Shipley Institute of Living Scale: Formulas for Abstraction Quotients from a normative sample of 580. Sex and Socioeconomic status considered as additional moderating variables. *Psychological Assessment, 3,* 412–417.

Massoth, N. A. (1985). The McCarthy Scales of Children's Abilities as a predictor of achievement: A five-year follow-up. *Psychology in the Schools, 22,* 10–13.

Massoth, N. A., and Levenson, R. L. (1982). The McCarthy Scales of Children's Abilities as a predictor of reading readiness and reading achievement. *Psychology in the Schools, 19,* 293–296.

Matarazzo, J. D. (1972). *Wechsler's measurement and appraisal of adult intelligence* (5th ed.). Baltimore: Williams & Wilkins.

Matarazzo, J. D. (1983). Computerized psychological testing. *Science, 221,* 323.

Matarazzo, J. D. (1986). Computerized clinical psychological test interpretations: Unvalidated plus all mean and no sigma. *American Psychologist, 41,* 14–24.

Matarazzo, J. D. (1990). Psychological assessment versus psychological testing: Validation from Binet to the school, clinic, and courtroom. *American Psychologist, 45,* 999–1017.

Matarazzo, J. D. (1992). Psychological testing and assessment in the 21st century. *American Psychologist, 47,* 1007–1018.

Matarazzo, J. D., & Herman, D. O. (1984). Relationship of Education and IQ in the WAIS-R standardization sample. *Journal of Consulting and Clinical Psychology, 52,* 631–634.

Matey, C. (1984). Leiter International Performance Scale. In D. J. Keyser & R. C. Sweetland (eds.), *Test critiques* (vol. 1). Kansas City, MO: Test Corporation of America.

Mathews, K. A., & Haynes, S. G. (1986). Type A behavior pattern and coronary risk: Update and critical evaluation. *American Journal of Epidemiology, 123,* 923–960.

Maurer, S. D., & Fay, C. (1988). Effect of situational interviews, conventional structured interviews, and training on interview rating agreement: an experimental analysis. *Personnel Psychology, 41,* 329–344.

Maxey, J. (1994). American College Test. In R. J. Sternberg (ed.), *Encyclopedia of human intelligence.* New York: Macmillan.

Maxwell, J. K., & Wise, F. (1984). PPVT IQ validity in adults: A measure of vocabulary, not of intelligence. *Journal of Clinical Psychology, 40,* 1048–1053.

Mayeux, R., & Kandel, E. R. (1991). Disorders of language: The aphasias. In E. R. Kandel, J. H. Schwartz, & T. M. Jessel (eds.), *Principles of neural science* (3rd ed.). New York: Elsevier.

Mayfield, E. C. (1964). The selection interview: A reevaluation of published research. *Personnel Psychology, 17,* 239–260.

McAllister, L. W. (1986). *A practical guide to CPI interpretation.* Palo Alto, CA: Consulting Psychologists Press.

McCall, R. B. (1976). Toward an epigenetic conception of mental development in the first three years of life. In M. Lewis (ed.), *Origins of intelligence: Infancy and early childhood.* New York: Plenum.

McCall, R. B. (1979). The development of intellectual functioning in infancy and the prediction of later IQ. In J. D. Osofsky (ed.), *Handbook of infant development.* New York: Wiley.

McCall, R. B. (1983). A conceptual approach to early mental development. In M. Lewis (ed.), *Origins of intelligence* (2nd ed.). New York: Plenum.

McCall, W. A. (1939). *Measurement.* New York: Macmillan.

McCallum, R. S. (1990). Determining the factor structure of the Stanford-Binet: Fourth Edition—the right choice. *Journal of Psychoeducational Assessment, 8,* 436–442.

McCallum, R. S., & Bracken, B. (1997). The Universal Nonverbal Intelligence Test. In D. P. Flanagan, J. Genshaft, & P. Harrison (eds.), *Contemporary intellectual assessment: Theories, tests, and issues.* New York: Guilford.

McCallum, R. S., Karnes, F. A., and Oehler-Stinnett, J. (1985). Construct validity of the K-ABC for gifted children. *Psychology in the Schools, 22,* 254–259.

McCann, J. T., & Suess, J. F. (1988). Clinical applications of the MCMI: The 1–2—3–8 Codetype. *Journal of Clinical Psychology, 44,* 181–185.

McCarney, S. B. (1989). *The Attention Deficit Disorders Evaluation Scale: School version technical manual.* Columbia, MO: Hawthorne Educational Services.

McCarthy, D. A. (1972). *Manual for the McCarthy Scales of Children's Abilities.* San Antonio, TX: The Psychological Corporation.

McCormick, E. J., Mecham, R., & Jeanneret, P. (1972). A study of job characteristics and job dimensions as based on the Position Analysis Questionnaire (PAQ). *Journal of Applied Psychology, 56,* 347–368.

McCrae, R. R. (1985). Review of the Defining Issues Test. *Ninth mental measurements yearbook.* Lincoln, NE: University of Nebraska Press.

McCrae, R. R., & Costa, P. T., Jr. (1987). Validation of the five-factor model of personality across instruments and observers. *Journal of Personality and Social Psychology, 2,* 81–90.

McCrowell, K. L., and Nagle, R. (1994). Comparability of the WPPSI-R and the SB:IV among preschool children. *Journal of Psychoeducational Assessment, 12,* 126–134.

McDermott, P. A., Fantuzzo, J. W., & Glutting, J. J. (1990). Just say no to subtest analysis: A critique on Wechsler theory and practice. *Journal of Psychoeducational Assessment, 8,* 290–302.

McDonald, A., Nussbaum, D. and Bagby, R. (1992). Reliability, validity, and utility of the Fitness Interview Test. *Canadian Journal of Psychiatry, 36,* 480–484.

McGlynn, F. D., & Rose, M. P. (1998). Assessment of anxiety and fear. In A. S. Bellack & M. Hersen (eds.), *Behavioral assessment: A practical handbook* (4th ed.). Boston: Allyn & Bacon.

McGrew, M. W., & Teglasi, H. (1990). Formal characteristics of Thematic Apperception Test stories as indices of emotional disturbance in children. *Journal of Personality Assessment, 54,* 639–655.

McGue, M., Bouchard, T., Iacono, W., & Lykken, D. (1993). Behavior genetics of cognitive ability: A lifespan perspective. In R. Plomin & G. McClearn (eds.), *Nature, nurture, and psychology.* Washington, DC: American Psychological Association.

McGurk, F. C. J. (1953a). On white and Negro test performance and socio-economic factors. *Journal of Abnormal and Social Psychology, 48,* 448–450.

McGurk, F. C. J. (1953b). Socioeconomic status and culturally-weighted test scores of Negro subjects. *Journal of Applied Psychology, 37,* 276–277.

McGurk, F. C. J. (1967). The culture hypothesis and psychological tests. In R. E. Kuttner (ed.), *Race and modern science.* New York: Social Science Press.

McGurk, F. C. J. (1975). Race differences—twenty years later. *Homo, 26,* 219–239.

McKeachie, W. J. (1984). Does anxiety disrupt information processing or does poor information processing lead to anxiety? *International Review of Applied Psychology, 33,* 187–203.

McKey, R. H. and others (1985). *The impact of Head Start on children, families and communities.* Washington, DC: U.S. Government Printing Office.

McKinley, J. C., & Hathaway, S. R. (1940). A Multiphasic Personality Schedule (Minnesota): II. A differential study of hypochondriasis. *Journal of Psychology, 10,* 255–268.

McKinley, J. C., & Hathaway, S. R. (1944). The MMPI: V. Hysteria, hypomania and psychopathic deviate. *Journal of Applied Psychology, 28,* 153–174.

McKinley, J. C., Hathaway, S. R., & Meehl, P. E. (1948). The MMPI: VI. The K scale. *Journal of Consulting Psychology, 12,* 20–31.

McLean, J. E., Kaufman, A. S., & Reynolds, C. R. (1989). Base rates of WAIS-R subtest scatter as a guide for clinical and neuropsychological assessment. *Journal of Clinical Psychology, 45,* 919–925.

McMordie, W. R. (1988). Twenty-year follow-up of the prevailing opinion on the posttraumatic or postconcussional syndrome. *The Clinical Neuropsychologist, 2,* 198–212.

McMullin, R. E. (1986). *Handbook of cognitive therapy techniques.* New York: Norton.

McNemar, Q. (1964). Lost: Our intelligence? Why? *American Psychologist, 19,* 871–882.

McNulty, J., Graham, J., Ben-Porath, Y., & Stein, L. (1997). Comparative validity of MMPI-2 scores of African American and caucasian mental health center clients. *Psychological Assessment, 9,* 464–470.

Mecham, R. C., McCormick, E., & Jeanneret, P. (1977). *Technical manual for the Position Analysis Questionnaire* (PAQ) (System II). West Lafayette, IN: Purdue University Book Store.

Medina, N., & Neill, D. M. (1990). *Fallout from the testing explosion.* Cambridge, MA: Fairtest.

Meehl, P. E. (1954). *Clinical versus statistical prediction.* Minneapolis, MN: University of Minnesota Press.

Meehl, P. E. (1965). Seer over sign: The first good example. *Journal of Experimental Research in Personality, 1,* 29–32.

Meehl, P. E. (1986). Causes and effects of my disturbing little book. *Journal of Personality Assessment, 50,* 370–375.

Megargee, E. (1972). *The California Psychological Inventory handbook.* San Francisco: Jossey-Bass.

Meichenbaum, D. (1977). *Cognitive-behavior modification: An integrative approach.* New York: Plenum.

Meier, S. T. (1984). The construct validity of burnout. *Journal of Occupational Psychology, 57,* 211–219.

Meier, V. J., & Hope, D. A. (1998). Assessment of social skills. In A. S. Bellack & M. Hersen (eds.), *Behavioral assessment: A practical handbook* (4th ed.). Boston: Allyn & Bacon.

Melchert, T. P. (1998). Support for the validity of the Graduate Record Examination. *American Psychologist, 53,* 573–574.

Melton, G. B. (1985). Review of Law School Admissions Test. In J. V. Mitchell, Jr. (ed.), *The ninth mental measurements yearbook.* Lincoln, NE: The Buros Institute of Mental Measurements.

Melton, G. B. (1995). Review of the Ackerman-Schoendorf Scales for Parent Evaluation of Custody. *The Twelfth Mental Measurements Yearbook.* Lincoln, NE: University of Nebraska Press.

Melton, G. B., Petrila, J., Poythress, N., & Slobogin, C. (1998). *Psychological evaluation for the courts* (2nd ed.). New York: Guilford.

Menzies, R. J., Webster, C., McMain, S., Staley, S., and Scaglione, R. (1994). The dimensions of dangerousness revisited: Assessing forensic predictions about violence. *Law and Human Behavior, 18,* 1–28.

Mercer, J. R., & Lewis, J. F. (1978). *System of Multicultural Pluralistic Assessment.* San Antonio, TX: The Psychological Corporation.

Merenda, P. F. (1985). Comrey Personality Scales. In D. J. Keyser & R. C. Sweetland (eds.), *Test critiques* (vol. 4). Kansas City, MO: Test Corporation of America.

Messick, S. (1980). Test validity and the ethics of assessment. *American Psychologist, 35,* 1012–1027.

Messick, S. (1995). Validity of psychological assessment: Validation of inferences from persons' responses and performances as scientific inquiry into score meaning. *American Psychologist, 50,* 741–749.

Messick, S., & Jungeblut, A. (1981). Time and method in coaching for the SAT. *Psychological Bulletin, 89,* 191–216.

Meyer, G. J. (1997). Assessing reliability: Critical corrections for a critical examination of the Rorschach Comprehensive System. *Psychological Assessment, 9,* 480–489.

Mickley, J. (1990). *Spiritual well-being, religiousness, and hope: Some relationships in a sample of women with breast cancer.* Unpublished master's thesis, University of Maryland, School of Nursing, College Park, MD.

Miele, F. (1979). Cultural bias in the WISC. *Intelligence, 3,* 149–164.

Miller, L. K. (1989). *Musical savants: Exceptional skill in the mentally retarded.* Hillsdale, NJ: Erlbaum.

Miller, L. T., & Lee, C. (1993). Construct validation of the Peabody Picture Vocabulary Test-Revised: A structural equation model of the acquisition order of words. *Psychological Assessment, 5,* 438–441.

Miller, T. R. (1991). Personality: A clinician's experience. *Journal of Personality Assessment, 57,* 415–433.

Millman, J., & Greene, J. (1989). The specification and development of tests of achievement and ability. In R. L. Linn (ed.), *Educational measurement* (3rd ed.). New York: ACE/Macmillan.

Millon, T. (1969). *Modern psychopathology: A biosocial approach to maladaptive learning and functioning.* Philadelphia: Saunders.

Millon, T. (1981). *Disorders of personality: DSM-III, Axis II.* New York: Wiley.

Millon, T. (1983). *Millon Clinical Multiaxial Inventory manual* (2nd ed.). Minneapolis, MN: National Computer Systems.

Millon, T. (1986). A theoretical derivation of pathological personalities. In T. Millon & G. Klerman (eds.), *Contemporary directions in psychopathology: Toward the DSM-IV.* New York: Guilford.

Millon, T. (1987). *Manual for the Millon Clinical Multiaxial Inventory-II (MCMI-II)* (2nd ed.). Minneapolis, MN: National Computer Systems.

Millon, T. (1994). *Manual for the Millon Clinical Multiaxial Inventory-III (MCMI-III)* (3rd ed.). Minneapolis, MN: National Computer Systems.

Millon, T., & Davis, R. (1996). The Millon Clinical Multiaxial Inventory-III (MCMI-III). In C. S. Newmark (ed.), *Major psychological assessment instruments* (2nd ed.). Boston: Allyn & Bacon.

Mills, C. N., & Stocking, M. L. (1996). Practical issues in large-scale computerized adaptive testing. *Applied Psychological Measurement, 9,* 287–304.

Mills, C., & Tissot, S. (1995). Identifying academic potential in students from underrepresented populations: Is using the Ravens Progressive Matrices a good idea? *Gifted Child Quarterly, 39,* 209–217.

Milmoe, S., Novey, M. S., Kagan, J., & Rosenthal, R. (1974). The mother's voice: postdictor of aspects of her baby's behavior. In S. Weitz (ed.), *Nonverbal communication: Readings with commentary.* New York: Oxford University Press.

Milmoe, S., Rosenthal, R., Blane, H. T., Chafetz, M. E., & Wolf I. (1967). The doctor's voice: Postdictor of successful referral of alcoholic patients. *Journal of Abnormal of Psychology, 72,* 78–84.

Milner, B. (1958). Psychological defects produced by temporal lobe excision. *Research Publications of the Association for Research in Nervous and Mental Disease, 38,* 244–257.

Milner, B., Corkin, S., & Teuber, H-L. (1968). Further analysis of the hippocampal amnesic syndrome: 14-year follow-up of H. M. *Neuropsychologia, 6,* 215–234.

Miner, J. B. (1964). *Scoring guide for the Miner Sentence Completion Scale.* New York: Springer.

Miner, M. G., & Miner, J. B. (1978). *Employee selection within the law.* Washington, DC: Bureau of National Affairs.

Mirsen, T., & Hachinski, V. (1988). Epidemiology and classification of vascular and multi-infarct dementia. In J. S. Meyer, J. Marshall, H. Lechner, & J. Toole (eds.), *Vascular and multi-infarct dementia.* Mount Kisco, NY: Futura Publishing.

Mischel, W. (1968). *Personality and assessment.* New York: Wiley.

Mishkin, M., & Appenzeller, T. (1987). The anatomy of memory. *Scientific American, 256,* 80–89.

Mishra, S. P., & Brown, K. (1983). The comparability of WAIS and WAIS-R IQs and subtest scores. *Journal of Clinical Psychology, 39,* 754–757.

Mitchell, J. L., & McCormick, E. J. (1979). *Development of the PMPQ: A structural job analysis questionnaire for the study of professional and managerial positions.* (Report No. 1). West Lafayette, IN: Occupational Research Center, Department of Psychological Studies, Purdue University.

Mitchell, J. V. (ed.). (1985). *The Ninth Mental Measurements Yearbook.* Lincoln, NE: University of Nebraska Press.

Mitchell, T. W., & Klimoski, R. J. (1986). Estimating the validity of cross-validity estimation. *Journal of Applied Psychology, 71,* 311–317.

Mittenberg, W., Azrin, R., Millsaps, C., & Heilbronner, R. (1993). Identification of malingered head injury on the Wechsler Memory Scale-Revised. *Psychological Assessment, 5,* 34–40.

Moberg, D. O. (1971). *Spiritual well-being: Background and issues.* Washington, DC: White House Conference on Aging.

Moore, E. G. J. (1986). Family socialization and the IQ-test performance of traditionally and transracially adopted children. *Developmental Psychology, 22,* 317–326.

Moore, W. P. (1994). The devaluation of standardized testing: One district's response. *Applied Measurement in Education, 7,* 343–368.

Moreland, K. L. (1985). Review of the Defining Issues Test. *Ninth mental measurements yearbook.* Lincoln, NE: University of Nebraska Press.

Moreland, K. L. (1992). Computer-assisted psychological assessment. In M. Zeidner and R. Most (eds.), *Psychological testing: An inside view.* Palo Alto, CA: Consulting Psychologists Press.

Morgan, C. D., & Murray, H. A. (1935). A method for investigating phantasies: The Thematic Apperception Test. *Archives of Neurology and Psychiatry, 34,* 289–306.

Morgan, S., & Wheelock, J. (1992). Digit Symbol and Symbol Digit Modalities Tests: Are they directly interchangeable? *Neuropsychology, 6,* 327–330.

Morgeson, F. P., & Campion, M. A. (1997). Social and cognitive science sources of potential inaccuracy in job analysis. *Journal of Applied Psychology, 82,* 627–655.

Morris, L. W., Davis, M. A., & Hutchings, C. A. (1981). Cognitive and emotional components of anxiety: Literature review and a revised worry-emotionality scale. *Journal of Educational Psychology, 73,* 541–555.

Morrison, M. W., Gregory, R. J., & Paul, J. J. (1979). Reliability of the Finger Tapping Test and a note on sex differences. *Perceptual and Motor Skills, 48,* 139–142.

Morrison, T., & Morrison, M. (1995). A meta-analytic assessment of the predictive validity of the quantitative and verbal components of the Graduate Record

Examination with graduate grade point average representing the criterion of graduate success. *Educational and Psychological Measurement, 55,* 309–316.

Moruzzi, G., & Magoun, H. W. (1949). Brain stem and reticular formation and activation of the EEG. *Electroencephalography and Clinical Neurophysiology, 1,* 455–473.

Moses, J. A., & Golden, C. J. (1979). Cross validation of the discriminative effectiveness of the standardized Luria Neuropsychological Battery. *International Journal of Neuroscience, 9,* 149–155.

Moskowitz, D. S. (1982). Coherence and cross-situational generality in personality: A new analysis of old problems. *Journal of Personality and Social Psychology, 43,* 754–768.

Motowidlo, S. J., Carter, G., Dunnette, M., Tippins, N., Werner, S., Burnett, J., & Vaughan, M. (1992). Studies of the structured behavioral interview. *Journal of Applied Psychology, 77,* 571–587.

Motta, R. W., Little, S., & Tobin, M. (1993). The use and abuse of human figure drawings. *School Psychology Quarterly, 8,* 162–169.

Mountain, M., & Snow, W. (1993). Wisconsin Card Sorting Test as a measure of frontal pathology: A review. *Clinical Neuropsychologist, 7,* 108–118.

Muchinsky, P. (1985). Review of Values Inventory. *Ninth Mental Measurements Yearbook.* Lincoln, NE: University of Nebraska Press.

Muchinsky, P. M. (1990). *Psychology applied to work: An introduction to industrial and organizational psychology* (3rd ed.). Chicago: Dorsey Press.

Mumford, M. D., & Owens, W. A. (1987). Methodology review: principles, procedures, and findings in the application of background data measures. *Applied Psychological Measurement, 11,* 1–31.

Mundfrom, D., Bradley, R., & Whiteside, L. (1993). A factor analytic study of the Infant-Toddler and Early Childhood versions of the HOME Inventory. *Educational and Psychological Measurement, 53,* 479–489.

Mungas, D. M., Trontel, E. H., & Weingardner, J. (1981). Multivariable-multimethod analysis of the dimensions of interpersonal behavior. *Journal of Research in Personality, 15,* 107–121.

Murphy, K. R. (1984). Review of Armed Services Vocational Aptitude Battery. In D. Keyser & R. Sweetland (eds.), *Test critiques* (vol. 1). Kansas City, MO: Test Corporation of America.

Murphy, K. R. (1992). Review of TONI-2. *The Eleventh Mental Measurements Yearbook.* Lincoln, NE: University of Nebraska Press.

Murphy, K. R. (ed.). (1996). *Individual differences and behavior in organizations.* San Francisco: Jossey-Bass.

Murphy, K. R., & Davidshofer, C. O. (1988). *Psychological testing.* Englewood Cliffs, NJ: Prentice-Hall.

Murphy, K. R., & Pardaffy, V. A. (1989). Bias in behaviorally anchored rating scales: Global or scale-specific? *Journal of Applied Psychology, 74,* 343–346.

Murphy, K. R., Jako, R., & Anhalt, R. (1993). Nature and consequences of halo error: A critical analysis. *Journal of Applied Psychology, 78,* 218–225.

Murray, H. A. (1938). *Explorations in personality.* New York: Oxford University Press.

Murray, H. A. (1943). *Thematic Apperception Test—Manual.* Cambridge: Harvard University Press.

Museum of Modern Art (1955). *The family of man.* New York: Maco Magazine Corporation.

Myers, I. B., & McCaulley, M. H. (1985). *Manual: A guide to the development and use of the Myers-Briggs Type Indicator.* Palo Alto, CA: Consulting Psychologists Press.

Naglieri, J. A. (1981). Concurrent validity of the Revised Peabody Picture Vocabulary Test. *Psychology in the Schools, 18,* 286–289.

Naglieri, J. A. (1985). Use of the WISC-R and K-ABC with learning disabled, borderline mentally retarded, and normal children. *Psychology in the Schools, 22,* 133–141.

Naglieri, J. A. (1988). *Draw A Person: A quantitative scoring system.* San Antonio, TX: The Psychological Corporation.

Naglieri, J. A., & Pfeiffer, S. (1983). Stability, concurrent and predictive validity of the PPVT-R. *Journal of Clinical Psychology, 39,* 965–967.

Naglieri, J. A., & Pfeiffer, S. (1992). Performance of disruptive behavior disordered and normal samples on the Draw A Person: Screening Procedure for Emotional Disturbance. *Psychological Assessment, 4,* 156–159.

Naglieri, J. A., & Yazzie, C. (1983). Comparison of the WISC-R and PPVT-R with Navajo children. *Journal of Clinical Psychology, 39,* 598–600.

Naglieri, J., McNeish, T., & Bardos, A. (1991). *Draw-A-Person: Screening Procedure for Emotional Disturbance.* Austin, TX: ProEd.

Nass, R. (1992). Developmental dyslexia: An update. *Pediatrics in Review, 13,* 231–235.

National Association of School Psychologists. (1992). *Principles for professional ethics.* Silver Spring, MD: Author.

National Joint Committee on Learning Disabilities. (1988). A position paper of the National Trust Committee on Learning Disabilities. *Journal of Learning Disabilities, 21,* 53–55.

Naugle, R. I., Chelune, G., & Tucker, G. (1993). Validity of the Kaufman Brief Intelligence Test. *Psychological Assessment, 5,* 182–186.

Nauta, W. J. H. (1971). The problem of the frontal lobe. *Journal of Psychiatric Research, 8,* 167–187.

Naveh-Benjamin, M., McKeachie, W. J., & Lin, Y. (1987). Two types of test-anxious students: Support for an information processing model. *Journal of Educational Psychology, 79,* 131–136.

Needleman, H. L., Gunnoe, C., Leviton, A., Reed, R., Peresie, H., Maher, C., & Barrett, P. (1979). Deficits in psychologic and classroom performance of children with elevated dentine lead levels. *The New England Journal of Medicine, 300,* 689–695.

Needleman, H. L., Schell, A., Bellinger, D., Leviton, A., & Allred, E. (1990). The long-term effects of exposure to low doses of lead in childhood. *New England Journal of Medicine, 322,* 83–88.

Neisser, U. (ed.). (1998). *The rising curve: Long-term gains in IQ and related measures.* Washington, DC: American Psychological Association.

Neisser, U., Boodoo, G., & Bouchard, T., and others (1996). Intelligence: Knowns and unknowns. *American Psychologist, 51,* 77–101.

Nellis, L., & Gridley, B. (1994). Review of the Bayley Scales of Infant Development-Second Edition. *Journal of School Psychology, 32,* 201–209.

Nester, M. A. (1994). Psychometric testing and reasonable accommodation for persons with disabilities. In S. M. Bruyere & J. O'Keeffe (eds.), *Implications of the Americans with Disabilities Act for psychology.* New York: Springer.

Netter, B., & Viglione, D., Jr. (1994). An empirical study of malingering schizophrenia on the Rorschach. *Journal of Personality Assessment, 62,* 45–57.

Nevo, B. (1985). Face validity revisited. *Journal of Educational Measurement, 22,* 287–293.

Nevo, B. (1992). Examinee feedback: Practical guidelines. In M. Zeidner & R. Most (eds.), *Psychological testing: An inside view.* Palo Alto, CA: Consulting Psychologists Press.

Newcomer, P. (1990). *Diagnostic Achievement Battery manual* (2nd ed.) Austin, TX: ProEd.

Newland, T. E. (1971). *Blind Learning Aptitude Test.* Champaign, IL: University of Illinois Press.

Nicholson, R. A., Robertson, H., Johnson, W., & Jensen, G. (1988). A comparison of instruments for assessing competency to stand trial. *Law and Human Behavior, 12,* 313–321.

Nielsen, G. (1962). *Studies in self confrontation*. Copenhagen: Monksgaard.

Nihira, K. (1985). Assessment of mentally retarded individuals. In B. B. Wolman (ed.), *Handbook of intelligence: Theories, measurements, and applications*. New York: Wiley.

Nihira, K., Leland, H., & Lambert, N. (1993). *Adaptive Behavior Scale-Residential and Community: 2nd Ed.* Washington, DC: American Association on Mental Retardation.

Nijenhuis, J., & van der Flier, H. (1997). Comparability of GATB scores for immigrants and majority group members: Some Dutch findings. *Journal of Applied Psychology, 82,* 675–687.

Nisan, M., & Kohlberg, L. (1982). Universality and cross-cultural variation in moral development: A longitudinal and cross-sectional study in Turkey. *Child Development, 53,* 865–876.

Nitko, A. J. (1989). Review of Metropolitan Achievement Test, Sixth Edition. *The Tenth Mental Measurements Yearbook*. Lincoln, NE: University of Nebraska Press.

Nolan, R. F., Watlington, D. K., & Willson, V. L. (1989). Gifted and nongifted race and gender effects on item functioning on the Kaufman Assessment Battery for Children. *Journal of Clinical Psychology, 45,* 645–650.

Nottingham, E. J., & Mattson, R. E. (1981). A validation study of the Competency Screening Test. *Law and Human Behavior, 5,* 329–335.

Novick, M. R., & Lewis, C. (1967). Coefficient alpha and the reliability of composite measurements. *Psychometrika, 32,* 1–13.

Nunnally, J. C. (1978). *Psychometric theory* (2nd ed.). New York: McGraw-Hill.

Nunnally, J. C., & Bernstein, I. H. (1994). *Psychometric theory* (3rd ed.). New York: McGraw-Hill.

Nuttall, E. V., Romero, I., & Kalesnik, J. (1992). *Assessing and screening preschoolers: Psychological and educational dimensions*. Boston, MA: Allyn & Bacon.

O'Neill, J., Jacobson, S., & Jacobson, J. (1994). Evidence of observer reliability for the Fagan Test of Infant Intelligence (FTII). *Infant Behavior and Development, 17,* 465–469.

Oakland, T. D., & Dowling, L. (1983). The Draw-A-Person test: Validity properties for nonbiased assessment. *Learning Disability Quarterly, 6,* 526–534.

O'Bannon, R. M., Goldinger, L. A., & Appleby, G. S. (1989). *Honesty and integrity testing*. Atlanta, GA: Applied Information Resources.

Obrzut, A., Obrzut, J. E., & Shaw, D. (1984). Construct validity of the Kaufman Assessment Battery for

Children with learning disabled and mentally retarded. *Psychology in the Schools, 21,* 417–424.

Oehler-Stinnett, J. (1992). Review of Conners' Rating Scales. *Eleventh Mental Measurements Yearbook*. Lincoln, NE: University of Nebraska Press.

Oles, H. J., & Davis, G. D. (1977). Publishers violate APA standards on test distribution. *Psychological Reports, 41,* 713–714.

Ollendick, T. H. (1983). Reliability and validity of the Revised Fear Survey Schedule for Children (FSSC-R). *Behavior Research and Therapy, 21,* 685–692.

Olson, H. C. (1994). Fetal alcohol syndrome. In R. J. Sternberg (ed.), *Encyclopedia of human intelligence*. New York: Macmillan.

Ones, D. S., & Viswesvaran, C. (1998). Gender, age, and race differences on overt integrity tests: Results across four large-scale job applicant data sets. *Journal of Applied Psychology, 83,* 35–42.

Ones, D. S., Viswesvaran, C., & Schmidt, F. (1993). Comprehensive meta-analysis of integrity test validities: Findings and implications for personnel selection and theories of job performance. *Journal of Applied Psychology, 78,* 679–703.

Ornberg, B., & Zalewski, C. (1994). Assessment of adolescents with the Rorschach: A critical review. *Assessment, 1,* 209–217.

Orpen, C. (1983). The development and validation of an adjective check-list measure of managerial need for achievement. *Psychology: A Quarterly Journal of Human Behavior, 20,* 38–42.

Osipow, S. H. (1980). *Manual for the Career Decision Scale*. Columbus, OH: Marathon Consulting and Press.

OSS Assessment Staff. (1948). *Assessment of men: Selection of personnel for the Office of Strategic Services*. New York: Rinehart.

Otis, A. S. (1918). An absolute point scale for the group measure of intelligence. *Journal of Educational Psychology, 9,* 238–261, 333–348.

Overholser, J. C. (1990). Retest reliability of the Millon Clinical Multiaxial Inventory. *Journal of Personality Assessment, 55,* 202–208.

Owens, W. A. (1976). Background data. In M. D. Dunnette (ed.), *Handbook of industrial and organizational psychology*. Chicago: Rand McNally.

Ownby, R. L. (1991). *Psychological reports: A guide to report writing in professional psychology* (2nd ed.). Brandon, VT: Clinical Psychology Publishing Co.

Padilla, A., & Medina, A. (1996). Cross-cultural sensitivity in assessment: Using tests in culturally appropriate ways. In L. A. Suzuki, P. J. Meller, & J. G. Ponterotto (eds.), *Handbook of multicultural assess-*

ment: *Clinical, psychological, and educational applications.* Englewood Cliffs, NJ: Prentice-Hall.

Paget, K. D. (1990). Assessment of intellectual competence in preschool-age children: Conceptual issues and challenges. In C. R. Reynolds and R. W. Kamphaus (eds.). *Handbook of psychological and educational assessment of children: Intelligence and achievement.* New York: Guilford.

Paloutzian, R. F., & Ellison, C. W. (1982). Loneliness, spiritual well-being and the quality of life. In L. A. Peplau & D. Perlman (eds.), *Loneliness: A sourcebook of current theory, research and therapy.* New York: Wiley.

Panigua, F. (1994). *Assessing and treating culturally diverse clients: A practical guide.* Thousand Oaks, CA: Sage.

Papez, J. W. (1937). A proposed mechanism of emotion. *Archives of Neurology and Psychiatry, 38,* 724–744.

Parker, K. C., & Atkinson, L. (1994). Factor space of the Wechsler Intelligence Scale for Children-Third Edition: Critical thoughts and recommendations. *Psychological Assessment, 6,* 201–208.

Pascal, G. R., & Suttell, B. J. (1951). *The Bender-Gestalt Test.* New York: Grune & Stratton.

Patrick, J. (1988). Concordance of the MCMI and the MMPI in the diagnosis of three DSM-III Axis I disorders. *Journal of Clinical Psychology, 44,* 186–190.

Patterson, C. (1980). An alternative perspective—lead pollution in the human environment. In *Lead in the human environment.* Washington, DC: National Academy of Sciences.

Patton, J. R., Payne, J. S., & Beirne-Smith, M. (1986). *Mental retardation* (2nd ed.). Columbus, OH: Merrill.

Pauker, J. D. (1976). A quick-scoring system for the Bender-Gestalt: Interrater reliability and scoring validity. *Journal of Clinical Psychology, 32,* 86–89.

Paul, G. L. (ed.). (1986). *Assessment in residential treatment settings.* Champaign, IL: Research Press.

Paulhus, D., Fridhandler, B., & Hayes, S. (1997). Psychological defense: Contemporary theory and research. In R. Hogan, J. Johnson, & S. Briggs (eds.), *Handbook of personality psychology.* San Diego: Academic Press.

Paulman, R. G., & Kennelly, K. J. (1984). Test anxiety and ineffective test taking: Different names, same construct? *Journal of Educational Psychology, 76,* 279–288.

Payne, A. F. (1928). *Sentence completions.* New York: New York Guidance Clinic.

Pearson, K. (1914, 1924, 1930ab). *The life, letters, and labours of Francis Galton* (Volumes I, II, III, IIIb). Cambridge: Cambridge University Press.

Pedersen, N. L., Plomin, R., Nesselroade, J., & McClearn, G. (1992). A quantitative genetic analysis of cognitive abilities during the second half of the life span. *Psychological Science, 3,* 346–353.

Penfield, W. (1958). Functional localization in temporal and deep sylvian areas. *Research Publication, Association of Nervous and Mental Disease, 36,* 210–217.

Penfield, W., & Evans, J. (1935). The frontal lobe in man: A clinical study of maximum removals. *Brain, 58,* 115–133.

Penfield, W., & Jasper, H. (1959). *Epilepsy and the functional anatomy of the human brain.* Boston: Little, Brown.

Perleth, C., Hofmann, U., Schauer, S., & Wernberger, H. (1994). Intelligence testing in a Bavarian school. *School Psychology International, 15,* 261–275.

Pervin, L. A. (1993). *Personality: Theory and research* (6th ed.). New York: Wiley.

Petersen, N. S., Kolen, M. J., & Hoover, H. D. (1989). Scaling, norming, and equating. In R. L. Linn (ed.), *Educational Measurement* (3rd ed.). New York: American Council on Education/Macmillan.

Peterson, N. G., Mumford, M., Borman, W., and others (1995). *Development of prototype occupational information network (O*NET) content model* (vols. 1 & 2). Salt Lake City, UT: Utah Department of Employment Security.

Peterson, R. A. (1978). Review of the Rorschach. *The Eighth Mental Measurements Yearbook.* Lincoln, NE: University of Nebraska Press.

Phares, E. J. (1985). Incomplete sentences. In R. J. Corsini (ed.), *Encyclopedia of psychology* (vol. 2). New York: Wiley.

Phelps, L., & Ensor, A. (1986). Concurrent validity of the WISC-R using deaf norms and the Hiskey-Nebraska. *Psychology in the Schools, 23,* 138–141.

Phillips, S. E. (1994). High-stakes testing accommodations: Validity versus disabled rights. *Applied Measurement in Education, 7,* 93–120.

Piaget, J. (1926). *Judgment and reasoning in the child.* New York: Harcourt, Brace & World.

Piaget, J. (1932). *The moral judgment of the child.* London: Kegan Paul.

Piaget, J. (1952). *The origins of intelligence in children.* New York: International Universities Press.

Piaget, J. (1972). *The psychology of intelligence.* Totowa, NJ: Littlefield Adams.

Piedmont, R. L., & Weinstein, H. P. (1993). A psychometric evaluation of the new NEO-PIR Facet Scales for Agreeableness and Conscientiousness. *Journal of Personality Assessment, 60,* 302–318.

Piedmont, R. L., McCrae, R. R., & Costa, P. T., Jr. (1992). An assessment of the Edwards Personal Preference Schedule from the perspective of the five-factor model. *Journal of Personality Assessment, 58,* 67–78.

Piersma, H., & Boes, J. (1997). MCMI-III as a treatment outcome measure for psychiatric inpatients. *Journal of Clinical Psychology, 53,* 825–832.

Pintner, R. (1917). The mentality of the dependent child. *Journal of Educational Psychology, 8,* 220–238.

Pintner, R. (1921). Intelligence. In E. L. Thorndike (ed.), Intelligence and its measurement: A symposium. *Journal of Educational Psychology, 12,* 123–147, 195–216.

Pintner, R., & Paterson, D. G. (1917). *A scale of performance tests.* New York: Appleton.

Piotrowski, C. (1996). The status of Exner's Comprehensive System in contemporary research. *Perceptual and Motor Skills, 82,* 1341–1342.

Piotrowski, Z. A. (1964). A digital computer administration of inkblot test data. *Psychiatric Quarterly, 38,* 1–26.

Pirozzolo, F. J., Hansch, E., Mortimer, J., Webster, D., & Kuskowski, A. (1982). Dementia in Parkinson disease: A neuropsychological analysis. *Brain and Cognition, 1,* 71–83.

Plaisted, J. R., & Golden, C. J. (1982). Test-retest reliability of the clinical, factor and localization scales of the Luria-Nebraska Neuropsychological Battery. *International Journal of Neuroscience, 17,* 163–167.

Plaud, J. J., & Eifert, G. (eds.). (1998). *From behavior theory to behavior therapy.* Boston: Allyn & Bacon.

Pollack, R. H. (1971). Binet on perceptual-cognitive development or Piaget-come-lately. *Journal of the History of the Behavioral Sciences, 7,* 370–374.

Pollens, R., McBratnie, B., & Burton, P. (1988). Beyond cognition: Executive functions. *Cognitive Rehabilitation, 6,* 26–33.

Pope, K. S. (1992). Responsibilities in providing psychological test feedback to clients. *Psychological Assessment, 4,* 268–271.

Popham, W. J. (1978). *Criterion-referenced measurement.* Englewood Cliffs, NJ: Prentice-Hall.

Porch, B. E. (1967). *Porch Index of Communicative Ability.* Palo Alto, CA: Consulting Psychologists Press.

Porteus, S. D. (1915). Mental tests for the feebleminded: A new series. *Journal of Psycho-Asthenics, 19,* 200–213.

Porteus, S. D. (1931). *The psychology of a primitive people: A study of the Australian aborigine.* London: Edward Arnold & Co.

Porteus, S. D. (1965). *Porteus Maze Test. Fifty years' application.* Palo Alto, CA: Pacific Books.

Powers, D. E., & Swinton, S. S. (1984). Effects of self-study for coachable test item types. *Journal of Educational Psychology, 76,* 266–278.

Prewett, P. N. (1995). A comparison of two screening tests (the Matrix Analogies Test-Short Form and the Kaufman Brief Intelligence Test) with the WISC-III. *Psychological Assessment, 7,* 69–72.

Prewett, P. N., & Matavich, M. (1994). A comparison of referred students' performance on the WISC-III and the Stanford-Binet Intelligence Scale-Fourth Edition. *Journal of Psychoeducational Assessment, 12,* 42–48.

Prout, H., & Schwartz, J. (1984). Validity of the PPVT-R with mentally retarded adults. *Journal of Clinical Psychology, 40,* 584–587.

Psychological Corporation (1994). *WISC-III Writer manual.* San Antonio, TX: Author.

Pyle, W. H. (1913). *The examination of school children.* New York: Macmillan.

Quay, H., & Peterson, D. (1983). *Interim manual for the Revised Behavior Problem Checklist.* Unpublished manuscript, University of Miami.

Raichle, M. E. (1994). Visualizing the mind. *Scientific American,* April, 36–42.

Raju, N. S. (1992). Review of Iowa Tests of Basic Skills. *The Eleventh Mental Measurements Yearbook.* Lincoln, NE: University of Nebraska Press.

Ramey, C. T., & Ramey, S. (1998). Early intervention and early experience. *American Psychologist, 53,* 109–10.

Rasch, G. (1966). *Probabilistic models for some intelligence and attainment tests.* Copenhagen: The Danish Institute for Educational Research.

Raskin, D. C. (1989). *Psychological methods in criminal investigation and evidence.* New York: Springer.

Rausch, H. R. (1985). Differences in cognitive function with left and right temporal lobe dysfunction. In D. F. Benson & E. Zaidel (eds.), *The dual brain: Hemispheric specialization in humans.* New York: Guilford.

Raven, J. C. (1938). *Progressive Matrices.* London: Lewis.

Raven, J. C. (1965). *The Coloured Progressive Matrices Test.* London: Lewis.

Raven, J. C., & Summers, B. (1986). *Manual for Raven's Progressive Matrices and Vocabulary Scales—research supplement no. 3.* London: Lewis.

Raven, J. C., Court, J. H., & Raven, J. (1983). *Manual for Raven's Progressive Matrices and Vocabulary Scales (Section 3)—Standard Progressive Matrices (1983 edition).* London: Lewis.

Raven, J. C., Court, J. H., & Raven, J. (1986). *Manual for Raven's Progressive Matrices and Vocabulary Scales (Section 2)—Coloured Progressive Matrices* (1986 edition, with U.S. norms). London: Lewis.

Raven, J. C., Court, J. H., & Raven, J. (1992). *Standard Progressive Matrices. 1992 Edition.* Oxford: Oxford Psychologists Press.

Reddon, J. R., & Jackson, D. N. (1989). Readability of three adult personality tests: Basic Personality Inventory, Jackson Personality Inventory, and Personality Research Form-E. *Journal of Personality Assessment, 53,* 180–183.

Ree, M. J., & Carretta, T. R. (1994). Factor analysis of the ASVAB: Confirming a Vernon-like structure. *Educational and Psychological Measurement, 54,* 459–463.

Ree, M. J., & Carretta, T. R. (1995). Group differences in aptitude factor structure on the ASVAB. *Educational and Psychological Measurement, 55,* 268–277.

Ree, M. J., Earles, J., & Teachout, M. (1994). Predicting job performance: not much more than g. *Journal of Applied Psychology, 79,* 518–524.

Reed, M. T., & McCallum, R. S. (1995). Construct validity of the Universal Nonverbal Intelligence Test (UNIT). *Psychology in the Schools, 32,* 277–290.

Reeve, R. R., French, J. L., & Hunter, M. (1983). A validation of the Leiter International Performance Scale with kindergarten children. *Journal of Consulting and Clinical Psychology, 51,* 331–337.

Reeves, D., & Wedding, D. (1994). *The clinical assessment of memory: A practical guide.* New York: Springer.

Rehm, L. P. (1984). Self-management therapy for depression. *Advances in Behavior Research and Therapy, 6,* 83–98.

Rehm, L. P., Kornblith, S. J., O'Hara, M. W., and others (1981). An evaluation of major components in a self-control therapy program for depression. *Behavior Modification, 5,* 459–490.

Reid, D. B., & Kelly, M. P. (1993). Wechsler Memory Scale-Revised in closed head injury. *Journal of Clinical Psychology, 49,* 245–254.

Reilly, R. R., & Chao, G. T. (1982). Validity and fairness of some alternative employee selection procedures. *Personnel Psychology, 35,* 1–63.

Reitan, R. M. (1984). *Aphasia and sensory-perceptual deficits in adults.* Tucson, AZ: Neuropsychology Press.

Reitan, R. M. (1985). *Aphasia and sensory-perceptual deficits in children.* Tucson, AZ: Neuropsychology Press.

Reitan, R. M., & Wolfson, D. (1985). *The Halstead-Reitan Neuropsychological Test Battery: Theory and clinical interpretation.* Tucson, AZ: Neuropsychology Press.

Reitan, R. M., & Wolfson, D. (1993). *The Halstead-Reitan Neuropsychological Test Battery: Theory and clinical interpretation* (2nd ed.). Tucson, AZ: Neuropsychology Press.

Renzulli, J. S. (1978). What makes giftedness? Reexamining a definition. *Phi Delta Kappan, 60,* 180–184.

Renzulli, J. S. (1986). The three-ring conception of giftedness: A developmental model for creative productivity. In R. J. Sternberg & J. E. Davidson (eds.), *Conceptions of giftedness.* Cambridge: Cambridge University Press.

Reschly, D. J. (1978). WISC-R factor structures among Anglos, Blacks, Chicanos, and Native-American Papagos. *Journal of Consulting and Clinical Psychology, 3,* 417–422.

Reschly, D. J. (1990). Adaptive behavior. In A. Thomas & J. Grimes (eds.), *Best practices in school psychology* (2nd ed.). Washington, DC: National Association of School Psychologists.

Rest, J. R. (1979). *The Defining Issues Test: Manual.* Minneapolis: University of Minnesota Press.

Rest, J. R. (1986). Moral research methodology. In S. Modgil & C. Modgil (eds.), *Lawrence Kohlberg: Consensus and controversy.* Philadelphia, PA: Taylor & Francis.

Rest, J. R., & Thoma, S. J. (1985). Relation of moral judgment to formal education. *Developmental Psychology, 21,* 709–714.

Rest, J. R., Thoma, S., Narvaez, D., & Bebeau, M. (1997). Alchemy and beyond: Indexing the Defining Issues Test. *Journal of Educational Psychology, 89,* 498–507.

Rey, A. (1964). *L'examen clinique en psychologie.* Paris: Presses Universitaires de France.

Reynolds, C. R. (1982). The problem of bias in psychological assessment. In C. R. Reynolds & T. B. Gutkin (eds.), *The handbook of school psychology.* New York: Wiley.

Reynolds, C. R. (1992). Review of the Millon Clinical Multiaxial Inventory-II. *Eleventh Mental Measurements Yearbook.* Lincoln, NE: University of Nebraska Press.

Reynolds, C. R. (1994a). Bias in testing. In R. J. Sternberg (ed.), *Encyclopedia of human intelligence.* New York: Macmillan.

Reynolds, C. R. (1994b). Kaufman Assessment Battery for Children (K-ABC). In R. J. Sternberg (ed.), *Encyclopedia of human intelligence.* New York: Macmillan.

Reynolds, C. R., & Brown, R. T. (1984a). Bias in mental testing: An introduction to the issues. In Reynolds, C. R., & Brown, R. T. (eds.), *Perspectives on bias in mental testing.* New York: Plenum.

Reynolds, C. R., & Brown, R. T. (eds.). (1984b). *Perspectives on bias in mental testing.* New York: Plenum.

Reynolds, C. R., & Kamphaus, R. (1992). *Behavior assessment system for children.* Circle Pines, MN: American Guidance Service.

Reynolds, C. R., Chastain, R. L., Kaufman, A. S., & McLean, J. E. (1987). Demographic characteristics and IQ among adults: Analysis of the WAIS-R standardization sample as a function of the stratification variables. *Journal of School Psychology, 25,* 323–342.

Reynolds, C. R., Willson, V. L., and Chatman, S. (1984). Relationships between age and raw score increases on the Kaufman-Assessment Battery for Children. *Psychology in the Schools, 21,* 19–24.

Rhodes, L., Bayley, N., and Yow, B. (1983). *Manual supplement: Bayley Scales of Infant Development.* San Antonio, TX: Psychological Corporation.

Riccio, C. A., Cohen, M., Hall, J., & Ross, C. (1997). The third and fourth factors of the WISC-III: What they don't measure. *Journal of Psychoeducational Assessment, 15,* 27–39.

Ricciuti, H. N. (1994). Infant tests as measures of early competence. In R. J. Sternberg (ed.), *Encyclopedia of human intelligence.* New York: Macmillan.

Richards, P. S. (1991). The relation between conservative religious ideology and principled moral reasoning: A review. *Review of Religious Research, 32,* 359–368.

Richards, P. S., & Bergin, A. E. (1997). *A spiritual strategy for counseling and psychotherapy.* Washington, DC: American Psychological Association.

Richards, P. S., & Davison, M. L. (1992). Religious bias in moral development research: A psychometric investigation. *Journal for the Scientific Study of Religion, 31,* 467–485.

Rieber, R. W. (ed.). (1980). *Wilhelm Wundt and the making of a scientific psychology.* New York: Plenum Press.

Rinas, J., & Clyne-Jackson, S. (1988). *Professional conduct and legal concerns in mental health practice.* Norwalk, CT: Appleton & Lang.

Ritzler, B. A. (1993). TEMAS (Tell-Me-A-Story): Review. *Journal of Psychoeducational Assessment, 11,* 381–389.

Ritzler, B. A., Sharkey, K. J., & Chudy, J. (1980). A comprehensive projective alternative to the TAT. *Journal of Personality Assessment, 44,* 358–362.

Robertson, I. H., Ward, T., Ridgeway, V., & Nimmo-Smith, I. (1994). *Test of Everyday Attention (TEA).* Gaylord, MI: National Rehabilitation Services.

Robertson, I. H., Ward, T., Ridgeway, V., & Nimmo-Smith, I. (1996). The structure of normal human attention: The Test of Everyday Attention. *Journal of the International Neuropsychological Society, 2,* 525–534.

Robinson, R. (1950). *Definition.* Oxford: Oxford University Press.

Roecker, C., House, A., & Graybill, D. (1992–93). Luria-Nebraska Neuropsychological Battery: High rates of false positives for geriatric subjects. *Current Psychology: Research and Practice, 11,* 354–359.

Rogers, B. (1989). Review of Metropolitan Achievement Test, Sixth Edition. *The Tenth Mental Measurements Yearbook.* Lincoln, NE: University of Nebraska Press.

Rogers, B. G. (1992). Review of GED. *The Eleventh Mental Measurements Yearbook.* Lincoln, NE: University of Nebraska Press.

Rogers, C. R. (1951). *Client-centered therapy: Its current practice, implications, and theory.* Boston: Houghton Mifflin.

Rogers, C. R. (1961). *On becoming a person: A therapist's view of psychotherapy.* Boston: Houghton Mifflin.

Rogers, C. R. (1980). *A way of being.* Boston: Houghton Mifflin.

Rogers, C. R., & Dymond, R. F. (eds.). (1954). *Psychotherapy and personality change: Co-ordinated research studies in the client-centered approach.* Chicago: University of Chicago Press.

Rogers, M. R. (1998). Psychoeducational assessment of culturally and linguistically diverse children and youth. In H. B. Vance (ed.), *Psychological assessment of children: Best practices for schools and clinical settings* (2nd ed.). New York: Wiley.

Rogers, R. (1984). *Rogers Criminal Responsibility Assessment Scales.* Odessa, FL: Psychological Assessment Resources.

Rogers, R. (1986). *Conducting insanity evaluations.* Odessa, FL: Psychological Assessment Resources.

Rogers, R., Bagby, M., & Dickens, S. (1992). *Structured Interview of Reported Symptoms (SIRS) manual.* Odessa, FL: Psychological Assessment Resources.

Rogers, R., Gillis, J., Dickens, S., & Bagby, R. (1991). Standardized assessment of malingering: Validation of the SIRS. *Psychological Assessment, 3,* 89–96.

Rogers, R., Kropp, P., Bagby, R., & Dickens, S. (1992). Faking specific disorders: A study of the SIRS. *Journal of Clinical Psychology, 48,* 643–648.

Rogoff, B. (1984). What are the interrelations among the three subtheories of Sternberg's triarchic theory of intelligence? *Behavioral and Brain Sciences, 7,* 300–301.

Roid, G. H., & Johnson, W. B. (1998). Computer assisted psychological assessment. In A. S. Bellack & M. Hersen (eds.), *Comprehensive clinical psychology* (vol. 4). Amsterdam: Elsevier.

Roid, G., & Miller, L. (1997). *Leiter-R Manual.* Wood Dale, IL: Stoelting Co.

Roid, G., & Worrall, W. (1997). Replication of the Wechsler Intelligence Scale for Children-Third Edition four-factor model in the Canadian normative sample. *Psychological Assessment, 9,* 512–515.

Rokeach, M. (1968). *Beliefs, attitudes, and values.* San Francisco: Jossey-Bass.

Rokeach, M. (1973). *The nature of human values.* New York: Free Press.

Rokeach, M. (1980). Some unresolved issues in theories of beliefs, attitudes, and values. In H. E. Howe, Jr., & M. M. Page (eds.), *Nebraska symposium on motivation.* Lincoln, NE: University of Nebraska Press.

Ronan, G. F., Colavito, V., & Hammontree, S. (1993). Personal Problem-Solving System for scoring TAT responses: Preliminary validity and reliability data. *Journal of Personality Assessment, 61,* 28–40.

Rorschach, H. (1921). *Psychodiagnostik.* Berne: Birchen.

Rosenberg, S., Ryan, J., & Prifitera, A. (1984). Rey Auditory-Verbal Learning Test performance of patients with and without memory impairment. *Journal of Clinical Psychology, 40,* 785–787.

Rosenthal, R. (1967). Covert communication in the psychological experiment. *Psychological Bulletin, 67,* 356–367.

Rosenthal, R., Hall, J. A., DiMatteo, M. R., Rogers, P. L., & Archer, D. (1979). *Sensitivity to nonverbal communication: The PONS test.* Baltimore, MD: Johns Hopkins University Press.

Rosenzweig, S. (1944). An outline of frustration theory. In J. McV. Hunt (ed.), *Personality and the behavior disorders* (vol. 1). New York: Ronald Press.

Rosenzweig, S. (1977). *Manual for the Children's Form of the Rosenzweig Picture-Frustration (P-F) Study.* St. Louis: Rana House.

Rosenzweig, S. (1978a). *The Rosenzweig Picture-Frustration (P-F) Study: Basic manual.* St. Louis: Rana House.

Rosenzweig, S. (1978b). *Aggressive behavior and the Rosenzweig Picture-Frustration Study.* New York: Praeger.

Rosenzweig, S., & Adelman, S. (1977). Construct validity of the Picture-Frustration Study. *Journal of Personality Assessment, 41,* 578–588.

Ross, S. M., Gottfredson, D. K., Christensen, P., & Weaver, R. (1986). Cognitive self-statements in depression: Findings across clinical populations. *Cognitive Therapy and Research, 10,* 159–166.

Rosvold, H. E., Mirsky, A. E., Sarason, I., and others (1956). A continuous performance test of brain damage. *Journal of Consulting Psychology, 20,* 343–350.

Rothermel, R. D., & Lovell, M. R. (1985). Personality Inventory for Children. In D. J. Keyser & R. C. Sweetland (eds.), *Test critiques* (vol. 2). Kansas City, MO: Test Corporation of America.

Rothstein, H. R., Schmidt, F. L., Erwin, F. W., Owens, W. A., & Sparks, C. P. (1990). Biographical data in employment selection: Can validities be made generalizable? *Journal of Applied Psychology, 75,* 175–184.

Rotter, J. B. (1966). Generalized expectancies for internal versus external control of reinforcement. *Psychological Monographs, 80* (Whole No. 609).

Rotter, J. B. (1972). Beliefs, social attitudes, and behavior: A social learning analysis. In J. B. Rotter, J. Chances, & E. J. Phares (eds.), *Applications of a social learning theory of personality.* New York: Holt, Rinehart & Winston.

Rotter, J. B., & Rafferty, J. E. (1950). *Manual for the Rotter Incomplete Sentences Blank: College Form.* New York: The Psychological Corporation.

Rotter, J. B., Lah, M., & Rafferty, J. (1992). *Manual—Rotter Incomplete Sentences Blank* (2nd ed.). Orlando, FL: The Psychological Corporation.

Rotter, J. B., Rafferty, J. E., & Schachtitz, E. (1965). Validation of the Rotter Incomplete Sentences Test. In B. I. Murstein (ed.), *Handbook of projective techniques.* New York: Basic Books.

Rounds, J. B. (1985). Vocational Preference Inventory. *The Ninth Mental Measurements Yearbook.* Lincoln, NE: University of Nebraska Press.

Rounds, J. B., Jr., Henly, G. A., Dawis, R. V., Lofquist, L. H., & Weiss, D. J. (1981). *Manual for the Minnesota Importance Questionnaire: A measure of vocational needs and values.* Minneapolis, MN: Vocational Psychology Research, University of Minnesota.

Rousseau, D. M. (1989). Review of the Values Scale, Research Edition. *The Tenth Mental Measurements Yearbook.* Lincoln, NE: University of Nebraska Press.

Ruch, F. L., & Ruch, W. W. (1980). *Employee Aptitude Survey technical report.* Los Angeles: Psychological Services, Inc.

Ruscio, J. (1998). Gatekeeping, compensation, and fallibility. *American Psychologist, 53,* 568–569.

Russell, C. J., Mattson, J., Devlin, S. E., & Atwater, D. (1990). Predictive validity of biodata items generated from retrospective life experience essays. *Journal of Applied Psychology, 75,* 569–580.

Russo, J. (1994). Thurstone's scaling model applied to the assessment of self-reported depressive severity. *Psychological Assessment, 6,* 159–171.

Rust, J., & Lindstrom, A. (1996). Concurrent validity of the WISC-III and Stanford-Binet-IV. *Psychological Reports, 79,* 618–620.

Ryan, A. M., & Sackett, P. R. (1987). Pre-employment honesty testing: Fakability, reactions of test takers, and company image. *Journal of Business and Psychology, 1,* 248–256.

Ryan, J. J., & Lewis, C. V. (1988). Comparison of normal controls and recently detoxified alcoholics on the Wechsler Memory Scale-Revised. *The Clinical Neuropsychologist, 2,* 173–180.

Ryan, J. J., Prifitera, A., & Powers, L. (1983). Scoring reliability on the WAIS-R. *Journal of Consulting and Clinical Psychology, 51,* 460.

Ryan, M. (1985). Review of the Minnesota Clerical Test. *The Ninth Mental Measurements Yearbook* (vol. I). Lincoln, NE: University of Nebraska Press.

Ryan, R. M. (1987). Thematic Apperception Test. In D. J. Keyser & R. C. Sweetland (eds.), *Test critiques compendium.* Kansas City, MO: Test Corporation of America.

Saccuzzo, D. P., & Johnson, N. E. (1995). Traditional psychometric tests and proportionate representation: An intervention and program evaluation study. *Psychological Assessment, 7,* 183–194.

Sackett, P. R., Burris, L. R., & Callahan, C. (1989). Integrity testing for personnel selection: An update. *Personnel Psychology, 42,* 491–529.

Salvia, J., & Ysseldyke, J. (1988). *Assessment in special and remedial education* (4th ed.). Boston: Houghton Mifflin.

Salvia, J., & Ysseldyke, J. (1991). *Assessment* (5th ed.). Boston, MA: Houghton Mifflin.

Samelson, F. (1977). World War I intelligence testing and the development of psychology. *Journal of the History of the Behavioral Sciences, 13,* 274–282.

Sandford, J. A., & Turner, A. (1997). *Intermediate Visual and Auditory Continuous Performance Test* (IVA). Los Angeles: Western Psychological Services.

Sarason, I. G. (1961). Test anxiety, experimental instructions, and verbal learning. *American Psychologist, 16,* 374.

Sarason, I. G. (ed.). (1980). *Test anxiety: Theory, research, and applications.* Hillsdale, NJ: Erlbaum.

Sattler, J. M. (1982). Age effects on Wechsler Adult Intelligence Scale-Revised tests. *Journal of Consulting and Clinical Psychology, 50,* 785–786.

Sattler, J. M. (1988). *Assessment of children* (3rd ed.). San Diego, CA: Jerome M. Sattler, Publisher.

Sattler, J., & Ryan, J. (1999). *Assessment of children, revised and updated third edition, WAIS-III supplement.* San Diego: Jerome M. Sattler, Publisher.

Saxe, L., Dougherty, D., and Cross, T. (1985). The validity of polygraph testing: Scientific analysis and public controversy. *American Psychologist, 40,* 355–366.

Scarr, S. (1981). Testing for children: Assessment and the many determinants of intellectual competence. *American Psychologist, 36,* 1159–1168.

Scarr, S. (1994). Culture-Fair and Culture-Free tests. In R. J. Sternberg (ed.), *Encyclopedia of human intelligence.* New York: Macmillan.

Scarr, S., & Weinberg, R. A. (1976). IQ test performance of black children adopted by white families. *American Psychologist, 31,* 726–739.

Scarr, S., & Weinberg, R. A. (1983). The Minnesota Adoption Studies: Genetic differences and malleability. *Child Development, 54,* 260–267.

Scarr, S., Pakstis, A., Katz, S., & Barker, W. (1977). The absence of a relationship between degree of white ancestry and intellectual skills within a white population. *Human Genetics, 39,* 69–86.

Scarr-Salapatek, S. (1971). Unknowns in the IQ equation. *Science, 174,* 1223–1228.

Schaie, K. W. (1958). Rigidity-flexibility and intelligence: A cross-sectional study of the adult life span from 20–70. *Psychological Monographs, 72,* no. 9 (Whole No. 462).

Schaie, K. W. (1977). Quasi-experimental designs in the psychology of aging. In J. E. Birren & K. W. Schaie (eds.), *Handbook of the psychology of aging.* New York: Van Nostrand Reinhold.

Schaie, K. W. (1978). Review of Senior Apperception Techniques. *The Eighth Mental Measurements Yearbook.* Lincoln, NE: University of Nebraska Press.

Schaie, K. W. (1980). Cognitive development in aging. In L. K. Obler & M. Alpert (eds.), *Language and communication in the elderly.* Lexington, MA: Heath.

Schaie, K. W. (1983). The Seattle Longitudinal Study: A twenty-one year exploration of psychometric intelligence in adulthood. In: K. W. Schaie (ed.), *Longitudinal studies of adult psychological development.* New York: Guilford Press.

Schaie, K. W. (1985). *Manual for the Schaie-Thurstone Adult Mental Abilities Test (STAMAT).* Palo Alto, CA: Consulting Psychologists Press.

Schaie, K. W. (1994). The course of adult intellectual development. *American Psychologist, 49,* 305–313.

Schaie, K. W., & Willis, S. L. (1986). *Adult development and aging.* Boston, MA: Little, Brown & Co.

Schakel, J. A. (1986). Cognitive assessment of preschool children. *School Psychology Review, 15,* 200–215.

Schear, J. M., & Craft, R. B. (1989). Examination of the concurrent validity of the California Verbal Learning Test. *The Clinical Neuropsychologist, 3,* 162–168.

Scheuneman, J. D. (1987). An argument opposing Jensen on test bias: The psychological aspects. In S. Modgil & C. Modgil (eds.), *Arthur Jensen: Consensus and controversy.* New York: Falmer Press.

Schinka, J., Dye, D., & Curtiss, G. (1997). Correspondence between five-factor and RIASEC models of personality. *Journal of Personality Assessment, 68,* 355–368.

Schlundt, D. G., & Bell, C. (1993). Body Image Testing System: A microcomputer program for assessing body image. *Journal of Psychopathology and Behavioral Assessment, 15,* 267–285.

Schmidt, F. L., Hunter, J. E., McKenzie, R. C., & Muldrow, T. W. (1979). Impact of valid selection procedures on work-force productivity. *Journal of Applied Psychology, 64,* 609–626.

Schmidt, F. L., Hunter, J. E., Outerbridge, A. N., & Trattner, M. H. (1986). The economic impact of job selection methods on size, productivity, and payroll costs of the federal work force: An empirically based demonstration. *Personnel Psychology, 39,* 1–29.

Schmidt, K. L. (1994). Detroit Tests of Learning Aptitude-Third Edition. *Journal of Psychoeducational Assessment, 12,* 87–91.

Schmidt, M. (1996). *Rey Auditory-Verbal Learning Test.* Los Angeles: Western Psychological Services.

Schmitt, N. (1996). Uses and abuses of coefficient alpha. *Psychological Assessment, 8,* 350–353.

Schmitt, N. (1995). Review of the Differential Aptitude Tests, Fifth Edition. *The Twelfth Mental Measurements Yearbook.* Lincoln, NE: University of Nebraska Press.

Schmitt, N., & Robertson, I. (1990). Personnel selection. *Annual Review of Psychology, 41,* 289–320.

Schoenfeldt, L. F. (1985). Review of Wonderlic Personnel Test. *The Ninth Mental Measurements Yearbook* (vol. II). Lincoln, NE: University of Nebraska Press.

Schoenthaler, S. J., Amos, S., Eysenck, H., Peritz, E., & Yudin, J. (1991). Controlled trial of vitamin-mineral supplementation: Effects on intelligence and performance. *Personality and Individual Differences, 12,* 351–362.

Schuldberg, D. (1988). The MMPI is less sensitive to the automated testing format than it is to repeated testing: Item and scale effects. *Computers in Human Behavior, 4,* 285–298.

Schwab, L. O. (1979). *The Nebraska assessment for independent living* (Project 93–013). Lincoln, NE: Department of Human Development and the Family, University of Nebraska.

Scott, L. H. (1981). Measuring intelligence with the Goodenough-Harris Drawing Test. *Psychological Bulletin, 89,* 483–505.

Seashore, C. E. (1938). *The psychology of musical talent.* Boston: Silver, Burdett.

Self, P. A., and Horowitz, F. D. (1979). The behavioral assessment of the neonate: An overview. In J. D. Osofsky (ed.), *Handbook of infant development.* New York: Wiley.

Seligman, M. E. P., Abramson, L. Y., Semmel, A., & Von Baeyer, C. (1979). Depressive attributional style. *Journal of Abnormal Psychology, 88,* 242–247.

Sharkey, K. J., & Ritzler, B. A. (1985). Comparing diagnostic validity of the TAT and a new Picture Projective Test. *Journal of Personality Assessment, 49,* 406–412.

Shaughnessy, M., & Moore, J. (1994). The KAIT with developmental students, honor students, and freshmen. *Psychology in the Schools, 31,* 286–287.

Shavelson, R. J., & Webb, N. M. (1991). *Generalizability theory: A primer.* Thousand Oaks, CA: Sage.

Shaw, S., Cullen, J., McGuire, J., & Brinckerhoff, L. (1995). Operationalizing a definition of learning disabilities. *Journal of Learning Disabilities, 28,* 586–597.

Sheldon, W., & Stevens, S. (1942). *The varieties of temperament: A psychology of constitutional differences.* New York: Harper & Brothers.

Shepard, J. W. (1989). Review of the Jackson Vocational Interest Survey. *The Tenth Mental Measurements Yearbook.* Lincoln, NE: University of Nebraska Press.

Shipley, W. C. (1940). A self-administering scale for measuring intellectual impairment and deterioration. *Journal of Psychology, 9,* 371–377.

Shipley, W. C. (1983). *Shipley Institute of Living Scale.* Los Angeles: Western Psychological Services.

Shneidman, E. S. (ed.). (1951). *Thematic test analysis.* New York: Grune & Stratton.

Shucard, D. W., and Horn, J. L. (1972). Evoked cortical potential and measurement of human abilities.

Journal of Comparative and Physiological Psychology, 78, 59–68.

Shuey, A. M. (1966). *The testing of Negro intelligence* (2nd ed.). New York: Social Science Press.

Shum, D., McFarland, K. A., & Bain, J. D. (1990). Construct validity of eight tests of attention: Comparison of normal and closed head injured samples. *The Clinical Neuropsychologist, 4,* 151–162.

Shurrager, H. C. (1961). *A haptic intelligence scale for adult blind.* Chicago: Illinois Institute of Technology.

Shurrager, H. C., & Shurrager, P. S. (1964). *Manual for the Haptic Intelligence Scale for the Blind.* Chicago: Psychology Research Technology Center, Illinois Institute of Technology.

Siegman, A. W. (1956). The effect of manifest anxiety on a concept formation task, a nondirected learning task, and on timed and untimed intelligence tests. *Journal of Consulting Psychology, 20,* 176–178.

Silverstein, A. B. (1982a). Factor structure of the Wechsler Adult Intelligence Scale-Revised. *Journal of Consulting and Clinical Psychology, 50,* 661–664.

Silverstein, A. B. (1986). Organization and Structure of the Detroit Tests of Learning Aptitude (DTLA-2). *Educational and Psychological Measurement, 46,* 1061–1066.

Silverton, L. (1993). *Adolescent Apperception Cards: manual.* Los Angeles: Western Psychological Services.

Sines, J. O. (1966). Actuarial methods in personality assessment. In B. Maher (ed.), *Progress in experimental personality research* (vol. 3). New York: Academic Press.

Sipps, G. J., Berry, G. W., & Lynch, E. M. (1987). WAIS-R and social intelligence: A test of established assumptions that uses the CPI. *Journal of Clinical Psychology, 43,* 499–504.

Sisson, E. D. (1948). Forced-choice: The new Army rating. *Personnel Psychology, 1,* 365–381.

Sivan, A. B. (1991). *Revised Visual Retention Test: Clinical and experimental applications* (5th ed.). San Antonio, TX: The Psychological Corporation.

Skeels, H. M. (1966). Adult status of children with contrasting early life experiences. *Monographs of the Society for Research in Child Development, 31*(3, Serial No. 105).

Skeels, H. M., & Dye, H. B. (1939). A study of the effects of differential stimulation on mentally retarded children. *Proceedings and Addresses of the American Association on Mental Deficiency, 44,* 114–136.

Skinner, B. F. (1953). *Science and human behavior.* New York: Macmillan.

Skinner, B. F. (1974). *About behaviorism.* New York: Alfred A. Knopf.

Skodak, M., & Skeels, H. M. (1949). A final follow-up study of one hundred adopted children. *Journal of Genetic Psychology, 75,* 85–125.

Slaney, R. B. (1989). Review of the Values Scale, Research Edition. *The Tenth Mental Measurements Yearbook.* Lincoln, NE: University of Nebraska Press.

Smith, A. (1960). Changes in Porteus Maze scores of brain-operated schizophrenics after an eight year interval. *Journal of Mental Science, 106,* 967–978.

Smith, A. (1967). The serial sevens subtraction test. *Archives of Neurology, 17,* 78–80.

Smith, A. (1968). The Symbol Digit Modalities Test: A neuropsychologic test for economic screening of learning and other cerebral disorders. *Learning Disorders, 3,* 83–91.

Smith, A. (1973). *Symbol Digit Modalities Test. Manual.* Los Angeles: Western Psychological Services.

Smith, A., & Kinder, E. (1959). Changes in psychological test performances of brain-operated subjects after eight years. *Science, 129,* 149–150.

Smith, A. M., Gacono, C., & Kaufman, L. (1997). A Rorschach comparison of psychopathic and nonpsychopathic conduct disordered adolescents. *Journal of Clinical Psychology, 53,* 289–300.

Smith, C. R. (1983). *Learning disabilities: The interaction of learner, task, and setting.* Boston, MA: Little, Brown.

Smith, D., Carroll, J. L., & Fuller, G. B. (1988). The relationship between the Millon Clinical Multiaxial Inventory and the MMPI in a private outpatient mental health clinic population. *Journal of Clinical Psychology, 44,* 165–174.

Smith, M. B. (1963). Personal values in the study of lives. In R. W. White (ed.), *The study of lives.* New York: Atherton Press.

Smith, M. L., & Milner, B. (1981). The role of the right hippocampus in the recall of spatial location. *Neuropsychologia, 19,* 781–793.

Smith, M., Delves, T., Lansdown, R., Clayton, B., & Graham, P. (1983). The effects of lead exposure on urban children: The Institute of Child Health/Southampton Study. *Developmental Medicine and Child Neurology, 25,* 1–54.

Smith, P. C., & Kendall, L. M. (1963). Retranslation of expectations: An approach to the construction of unambiguous anchors for rating scales. *Journal of Applied Psychology, 47,* 149–155.

Smith, T. W., Follick, M. J., Ahern, D. K., & Adams, A. (1986). Cognitive distortion and disability in chronic low back pain. *Cognitive Therapy and Research, 10,* 201–210.

Smither, R. D. (1994). *The psychology of work and human performance* (2nd ed.). New York: Harper-Collins.

Snow, J. H. (1992). Review of Luria-Nebraska Neuropsychological Battery: Forms I and II. *The Eleventh Mental Measurements Yearbook.* Lincoln, NE: University of Nebraska Press.

Snyder, D. K., Lachar, D., and Wills, R. M. (1988). Computer-based interpretation of the Marital Satisfaction Inventory: Use in treatment planning. *Journal of Marital and Family Therapy, 14,* 397–409.

Society for Industrial and Organizational Psychology, Inc. (1987). *Principles for the validation and use of personnel selection procedures* (3rd ed.). College Park, MD: Author.

Sokol, R. J., & Clarren, S. K. (1989). Guidelines for use of terminology describing the impact of prenatal alcohol on the offspring. *Alcoholism: Clinical and Experimental Research, 13,* 597–598.

Sontag, L. W., Baker, C., and Nelson, V. (1958). Mental growth and personality development: A longitudinal study. *Monographs of the Society for Research in Child Development, 23* (Whole No. 68).

Sostek, A. J., Buchsbaum, M. S., & Rapoport, J. L. (1980). Effects of amphetamine on vigilance performance in normal and hyperactive children. *Journal of Abnormal Child Psychology, 8,* 491–500.

Sparrow, S. S., Balla, D. A., & Cicchetti, D. V. (1984). *Vineland Adaptive Behavior Scales.* Circle Pines, MN: American Guidance Service.

Spearman, C. (1904). "General intelligence," objectively determined and measured. *American Journal of Psychology, 15,* 201–293.

Spearman, C. (1923). *The nature of 'intelligence' and the principles of cognition.* London: Macmillan.

Spearman, C. (1927). *The abilities of man.* New York: Macmillan.

Special Education Today. (1985). ACALD definition of learning disabilities. 2, 1–20.

Sperry, R. W. (1964). The great cerebral commissure. *Scientific American, 210,* 42–52.

Spielberger, C. D. (1984). *State-Trait Anxiety Inventory: A comprehensive bibliography.* Palo Alto, CA: Consulting Psychologists Press.

Spielberger, C. D., and others (1983). *Manual for the State-Trait Anxiety Inventory (STAI, Form Y).* Palo Alto, CA: Consulting Psychologists Press.

Spitz, H. H. (1986). *The raising of intelligence: A selected history of attempts to raise retarded intelligence.* Hillsdale, NJ: Erlbaum.

Spohr, H., & Steinhausen, H. (eds.). (1996). *Alcohol, pregnancy, and the developing child.* Cambridge: Cambridge University Press.

Spranger, E. (1928). *Types of men.* Germany: Max Niemeyer Verlag.

Spreen, O., & Strauss, E. (1998). *A compendium of neuropsychological tests: Administration, norms, and commentary* (2nd ed.). New York: Oxford University Press.

Sprigle, J. E., & Schaefer, L. (1985). Longitudinal evaluation of the effects of two compensatory preschool programs on fourth- through sixth-grade students. *Developmental Psychology, 21,* 702–708.

Springer, S. P., & Deutsch, G. (1985). *Left brain, right brain.* San Francisco: W. H. Freeman.

Stafford-Clark, D. (1971). What Freud really said. New York: Schocken Books.

Stanley, J. C. (1971). Reliability. In R. L. Thorndike (ed.), *Educational measurement.* Washington, DC: American Council on Education.

Steele, C. M. (1997). A threat in the air: How stereotypes shape intellectual identity and performance. *American Psychologist, 6,* 613–629.

Steele, C. M., & Aronson, J. (1995). Stereotype threat and the intellectual test performance of African Americans. *Journal of Personality and Social Psychology, 69,* 797–811.

Steer, R. A., Beck, A. T., & Brown, G. (1989). Sex differences on the Revised Beck Depression Inventory for outpatients with affective disorders. *Journal of Personality Assessment, 53,* 693–702.

Steers, R. M., & Rhodes, S. R. (1978). Major influences on employee attendance: A process model. *Journal of Applied Psychology, 63,* 391–407.

Stehouwer, R. S. (1987). Beck Depression Inventory. In D. J. Keyser & R. C. Sweetland (eds.), *Test critiques compendium.* Kansas City, MO: Test Corporation of America.

STEP manual and technical report. (1980). Princeton, NJ: Educational Testing Service.

Stephenson, W. (1953). *The study of behavior: Q-technique and its methodology.* Chicago: University of Chicago Press.

Stern, W. L. (1912). Uber die psychologischen Methoden der Intelligenzprufung. American translation by G. M. Whipple (1914). The psychological methods of testing intelligence. *Educational Psychology Monographs,* no. 13, Baltimore: Warwick & York.

Sternberg, R. J. (1981). Intelligence and nonentrenchment. *Journal of Educational Psychology, 73,* 1–16.

Sternberg, R. J. (1985a). Componential analysis: A recipe. In D. K. Detterman (ed.), *Current topics in human intelligence* (vol. 1). Norwood, NJ: Ablex.

Sternberg, R. J. (1985b). *Beyond IQ: A triarchic theory of human intelligence.* Cambridge: Cambridge University Press.

Sternberg, R. J. (1986). *Intelligence applied: Understanding and increasing your intellectual skills.* San Diego, CA: Harcourt Brace Jovanovich.

Sternberg, R. J. (1994). The triarchic theory of intelligence. In R. J. Sternberg (ed.), *Encyclopedia of human intelligence.* New York: Macmillan.

Sternberg, R. J. (1996). *Successful intelligence.* New York: Simon & Schuster.

Sternberg, R. J. (ed.). (1994). *Encyclopedia of human intelligence* (vol. 1, 2). New York: Macmillan.

Sternberg, R. J., & Detterman, D. K. (eds.). (1986). *What is intelligence? Contemporary viewpoints on its nature and definition.* Norwood, NJ: Ablex.

Sternberg, R. J., & Kaufman, J. C. (1998). Human abilities. *Annual Review of Psychology, 49,* 479–502.

Sternberg, R. J., & Williams, W. (1997). Does the Graduate Record Examination predict meaningful success in the graduate training of psychologists? A case study. *American Psychologist, 52,* 630–641.

Sternberg, R. J., & Zhang, L. (1995). What do we mean by giftedness? A pentagonal implicit theory. *Gifted Child Quarterly, 39,* 88–94.

Sternberg, R. J., Conway, B. E., Ketron, J. L., and Bernstein, M. (1981). People's conceptions of intelligence. *Journal of Personality and Social Psychology, 41,* 37–55.

Stevens, S. S. (1946). On the theory of scales and measurement. *Science, 103,* 677–680.

Stoker, H. (1992). Review of Stanford Achievement Test. *Eleventh Mental Measurements Yearbook.* Lincoln, NE: University of Nebraska Press.

Stokes, G., Mumford, M., & Owens (eds.). (1994). *Biodata handbook: Theory, research, and use of biographical information in selection and performance prediction.* Palo Alto, CA: Consulting Psychologists Press.

Stone, B. J. (1994). Group ability test versus teachers' ratings for predicting achievement. *Psychological Reports, 75,* 1487–1490.

Storandt, M., & Hill, R. D. (1989). Very mild senile dementia of the Alzheimer type: 2. Psychometric test performance. *Archives of Neurology, 46,* 383–386.

Streiner, D. L., Goldberg, J. O., & Miller, H. R. (1993). MCMI-II item weights: Their lack of effectiveness. *Journal of Personality Assessment, 60,* 471–476.

Streissguth, A., Bookstein, F., & Barr, H. (1996). A dose-response study of the enduring effects of prenatal alcohol exposure: birth to 14 years. In H. Spohr & H. Steinhausen (eds.), *Alcohol, pregnancy, and the developing child.* Cambridge: Cambridge University Press.

Streissguth, A., Martin, D., Barr, H., & Sandman, B. (1984). Intrauterine alcohol and nicotine exposure: Attention and reaction time in 4-year-old children. *Developmental Psychology, 20,* 533–541.

Strommen, E. (1988). Confirmatory factor analysis of the Kaufman Assessment Battery for Children: A reevaluation. *Journal of School Psychology, 26,* 13–23.

Strong, E. K. (1927). *Vocational Interest Blank.* Stanford, CA: Stanford University Press.

Strong, E. K. (1955). *Vocational interests 18 years after college.* Minneapolis, MN: University of Minnesota Press.

Strub, R. L., & Black, F. W. (1985). *The mental status examination in neurology* (2nd ed.). Philadelphia: F. A. Davis.

Stuss, D. T., Stethem, L. L., Hugenholtz, H., & Richard, M. T. (1989). Traumatic brain injury: A comparison of three clinical tests, and analysis of recovery. *The Clinical Neuropsychologist, 3,* 145–156.

Super, D. E. (1957). *The psychology of careers.* New York: Harper.

Super, D. E. (1968). *Work Values Inventory.* Chicago, IL: Riverside Publishing Company.

Super, D. E. (1970). *Work Values Inventory manual.* Chicago, IL: Riverside Publishing Company.

Super, D. E. (1973). The Work Values Inventory. In D. G. Zytowski (ed.), *Contemporary approaches to interest measurement.* Minneapolis, MN: University of Minnesota Press.

Super, D. E. (1990). A life-span, life-space approach to career development. In D. Brown, L. Brooks, and associates (eds.), *Career choice and development* (2nd ed.). San Francisco, CA: Jossey-Bass.

Super, D. E., & Nevill, D. D. (1986). *The Values Scale, research edition.* Palo Alto, CA: Consulting Psychologists Press.

Super, D. E., Thompson, A. S., Lindeman, R. H., and others (1981). *Career Development Inventory.* Palo Alto, CA: Consulting Psychologists Press.

Sutton, R. S. (1992). Review of the Defining Issues Test. *Eleventh Mental Measurements Yearbook.* Lincoln, NE: The Buros Institute.

Suzuki, L., Meller, P., & Ponterotto, J. (eds.). (1996). *Handbook of multicultural assessment: Clinical, psychological, and educational applications.* Englewood Cliffs, NJ: Prentice-Hall.

Swartz, J. D., Reinehr, R. C., & Holtzman, W. H. (1983). *Holtzman Inkblot Technique, 1956–1982: An annotated bibliography.* Austin, TX: Hogg Foundation for Mental Health.

Sweetland, R. C., & Keyser, D. J. (1987). *Tests: A comprehensive reference for assessments in psychology, education, and business.* Kansas City, MO: Test Corporation of America.

Swensen, C. (1957). Empirical evaluations of human figure drawings. *Psychological Bulletin, 54,* 431–466.

Swensen, C. (1968). Empirical evaluations of human figure drawings: 1957–1966. *Psychological Bulletin, 70,* 20–44.

Swenson, W. M., Rome, H., Pearson, J., and Brannick, T. (1965). A totally automated psychological test: Experience in a medical center. *Journal of the American Medical Association, 191,* 925–927.

Swiercinsky, D. (1978). *Manual for the adult neuropsychological evaluation.* Springfield, IL: Charles C. Thomas.

Swiercinsky, D. (1985). *Testing adults.* Kansas City, MO: Test Corporation of America.

Swinton, S. S., & Powers, D. E. (1983). A study of special preparation on GRE analytical scores and item types. *Journal of Educational Psychology, 75,* 104–115.

Sylvester, R. H. (1913). *The form board test.* Psychological Monographs, 15, no. 65.

Tabachnick, B. G., & Fidell, L. S. (1989). *Using multivariate statistics* (2nd ed.). New York: Harper & Row.

Tallent, N. (1987). Computer-generated psychological reports: A look at the modern psychometric machine. *Journal of Personality Assessment, 51,* 95–108.

Tallent, N. (1993). *Psychological report writing* (4th ed.). Englewood Cliffs, NJ: Prentice-Hall.

Tamkin, A. S., & Scherer, I. W. (1957). What is measured by the "Cannot Say" scale of the group MMPI? *Journal of Consulting Psychology, 21,* 413–417.

Tanner, B. A. (1992). Computer-aided reporting of the results of neuropsychological evaluations of traumatic brain injury. *Computers in Human Behavior, 9,* 51–56.

Tasbihsazan, R., Nettelbeck, T., & Kirby, N. (1997). Increasing Mental Development Index in Australian children: A comparative study of two versions of the Bayley Mental Scale. *Australian Psychologist, 32,* 120–125.

Tasto, D. L., Hickson, R., & Rubin, S. E. (1971). Scaled profile analysis of fear survey schedule factors. *Behavior Therapy, 2,* 543–549.

Taylor, H. C., & Russell, J. T. (1939). The relationship of validity coefficients to the practical effectiveness of tests in selection. *Journal of Applied Psychology, 23,* 565–578.

Teacher, Administrator, and Counselor Manual: Iowa Tests of Educational Development. Forms X-8 and Y-8. 1988.

Teare, J. F., & Thompson, R. W. (1982). Concurrent validity of the Perkins-Binet tests of intelligence for the blind. *Journal of Visual Impairment and Blindness, 76,* 279–280.

Teasdale, G., & Jennett, B. (1974). The Glasgow Coma Scale. *Lancet, 2,* 81.

Tellegen, A., & Ben-Porath, Y. (1992). The new uniform *T* scores for the MMPI-2: Rationale, derivation, and appraisal. *Psychological Assessment, 4,* 145–155.

Tendler, A. D. (1930). A preliminary report on a test for emotional insight. *Journal of Applied Psychology, 14,* 123–126.

Teng, S. (1942–43). Chinese influence on the western examination system. *Harvard Journal of Asiatic Studies, 7,* 267–312.

Terkel, S. (1974). *Working: People talk about what they do all day and how they feel about what they do.* New York: Random House.

Terman, L. M. (1916). *The measurement of intelligence.* Boston: Houghton Mifflin.

Terman, L. M., & Oden, M. H. (1959). *Genetic studies of genius: The gifted group at mid-life.* Stanford, CA: Stanford University Press.

Terrell, F., Terrell, S., & Taylor, J. (1981). Effect of race of examiner and cultural mistrust on the WAIS performance of Black students. *Journal of Consulting and Clinical Psychology, 49,* 750–751.

Thomas, R. G. (1985). Review of the Minnesota Clerical Test. *The Ninth Mental Measurements Yearbook* (vol. I). Lincoln, NE: University of Nebraska Press.

Thompson, C. (1949). The Thompson modification of the Thematic Apperception Test. *Journal of Projective Techniques, 13,* 469–478.

Thorndike, E. L. (1912). The permanence of interests and their relation to abilities. *Popular Science Monthly, 81,* 449–456.

Thorndike, E. L. (1918). *The seventeenth yearbook of the National Society for the Study of Education. Pt. II.* Bloomington, IL: Public School Publishing Co.

Thorndike, E. L. (1920a). A constant error in psychological ratings. *Journal of Applied Psychology, 4,* 25–29.

Thorndike, E. L. (1920b). Intelligence and its use. *Harper's Magazine, 140,* 227–235.

Thorndike, E. L. (ed.). (1921). Intelligence and Its Measurement: A Symposium. *Journal of Educational Psychology, 12,* 123–147, 195–216.

Thorndike, R. L., & Hagen, E. P. (1993). *Cognitive Abilities Test, Form 5; Examiner's manual.* Boston: Houghton Mifflin.

Thorndike, R. L., Hagen, E. P., and Sattler, J. M. (1986). *The Stanford-Binet Intelligence Scale: Fourth*

Edition, Guide for administering and scoring. Chicago: Riverside Publishing Company.

Thorndike, R. M. (1990). Would the real factors of the Stanford-Binet Fourth Edition please come forward? *Journal of Psychoeducational Assessment, 8,* 412–435.

Thurstone, L. L. (1921). Intelligence. In E. L. Thorndike (ed.), Intelligence and Its Measurement: A Symposium. *Journal of Educational Psychology, 12,* 123–147, 195–216.

Thurstone, L. L. (1925). A method of scaling psychological and educational tests. The *Journal of Educational Psychology, 16,* 433–451.

Thurstone, L. L. (1929). Theory of attitude measurement. *Psychological Review, 36,* 222–241.

Thurstone, L. L. (1931). Multiple factor analysis. *Psychological Review, 38,* 406–427.

Thurstone, L. L. (1938). Primary mental abilities. *Psychometric Monographs,* no. 1. Chicago: University of Chicago Press.

Thurstone, L. L. (1947). *Multiple factor analysis.* Chicago: University of Chicago Press.

Thurstone, L. L., & Thurstone, T. (1930). A neurotic inventory. *Journal of Social Psychology, 1,* 3–30.

Thurstone, L. L., & Thurstone, T. (1941). Factorial studies in intelligence. *Psychometric Monographs, No. 2.* Chicago: University of Chicago Press.

Tiffin, J. (1968). *Purdue Pegboard Examiner's Manual.* Chicago: Science Research Associates.

Tinsley, D., Tinsley, H., Boone, S., & Shim-Li, C. (1993). Prediction of scientist-practitioner behavior using personality scores obtained during graduate school. *Journal of Counseling Psychology, 40,* 511–517.

Tombaugh, T., McDowell, I., Kristjansson, B., & Hubley, A. (1996). Mini-Mental State Examination (MMSE) and the Modified MMSE (3MS): A psychometric comparison and normative data. *Psychological Assessment, 8,* 48–59.

Tomkins, S. S. (1947). *The Thematic Apperception Test.* New York: Grune & Stratton.

Tow, P. M. (1955). *Personality changes following frontal leucotomy.* London: Oxford University Press.

Traxler, A. E. (1951). Administering and scoring the objective test. In E. F. Lindquist (ed.), *Educational measurement.* Washington, DC: American Council on Education.

Treffert, D. A. (1989). *Extraordinary people.* London: Bantam Press.

Trevisan, M. S. (1992). Review of GED. *The Eleventh Mental Measurements Yearbook.* Lincoln, NE: University of Nebraska Press.

Trites, R. L. (ed.). (1979). *Hyperactivity in children: Etiology, measurement, and treatment implications.* Baltimore, MD: University Park Press.

Trites, R. L., Blouin, A. G. A., & LaPrade, K. (1982). Factor analysis of the Conners Teacher Rating Scale based on a large normative sample. *Journal of Consulting and Clinical Psychology, 50,* 615–623.

Trull, T. J., Useda, J., Costa, Jr., P., & McCrae, R. (1995). Comparison of the MMPI-2 Personality Psychopathology Five (PSY-5), the NEO-PI, and the NEO-PI-R. *Psychological Assessment, 7,* 508–516.

Trull, T. J., Widiger, T., Useda, J., and others (1998). A structured interview for the assessment of the five-factor model of personality. *Psychological Assessment, 10,* 229–240.

Tryon, R. C. (1957). Reliability and behavior domain validity: Reformulation and historical critique. *Psychological Bulletin, 54,* 229–249.

Tsai, L., & Tsuang, M. (1979). The Mini-Mental State Test and computerized tomography. *American Journal of Psychiatry, 136,* 436–439.

Tulsky, D., Zhu, J., & Ledbetter, M. (1997). *WAIS-III WMS-III technical manual.* San Antonio, TX: The Psychological Corporation.

Tupa, D. J., Wright, M., & Fristad, M. (1997). Confirmatory factor analysis of the WISC-III with child psychiatric inpatients. *Psychological Assessment, 9,* 302–306.

Tweedie, D., & Shroyer, E. H. (eds.). (1982). *The multihandicapped hearing impaired: Identification and instruction.* Washington, DC: Gallaudet College Press.

Tzeng, O. C. S. (1987). Strong-Campbell Interest Inventory. In D. J. Keyser & R. C. Sweetland (eds.). *Test critiques compendium.* Kansas City, MO: Test Corporation of America.

Tzeng, O., Ware, R., & Chen, J. (1989). Measurement and utility of continuous unipolar ratings for the Myers-Briggs Type Indicator. *Journal of Personality Assessment, 53,* 727–738.

Tziner, A. (1985). Review of Values Inventory. *Ninth Mental Measurements Yearbook.* Lincoln, NE: University of Nebraska Press.

Ullman, R. K., Sleator, E., & Sprague, R. (1988). *ADD-H Comprehensive Teacher's Rating Scale* (ACTeRS) (2nd ed.). Champaign, IL: MetriTech, Inc.

Ulrich, L., & Trumbo, D. (1965). The selection interview since 1949. *Psychological Bulletin, 63,* 100–116.

Umberger, F. G. (1987). Peabody Picture Vocabulary Test-Revised. In D. J. Keyser & R. C. Sweetland (eds.), *Test critiques compendium.* Kansas City, MO: Test Corporation of America.

United States Employment Service. (1970). *Manual for the USES General Aptitude Test Battery.* Washington, DC: United States Department of Labor.

Uomoto, J. M., Turner, J. A., & Herron, L. D. (1988). Use of the MMPI and MCMI in predicting outcome of lumbar laminectomy. *Journal of Clinical Psychology, 44,* 191–197.

U.S. Department of Labor. (1991). *Dictionary of occupational titles* (4th ed.). Washington, DC: Author.

U.S. Department of Labor. (1993). *Selected characteristics of occupations defined in the revised dictionary of occupational titles* (4th ed.). Washington, DC: Author.

U.S. Department of Education. (1977). Definition and criteria for defining students as learning disabled. *Federal Register, 42(250),* 65083.

Uzgiris, I. C. (1976). Organization of sensorimotor intelligence. In M. Lewis (ed.), *Origins of intelligence: Infancy and early childhood.* New York: Plenum Press.

Uzgiris, I. C. (1983). Organization of sensorimotor intelligence. In M. Lewis (ed.), *Origins of intelligence: Infancy and early childhood* (2nd ed.). New York: Plenum Press.

Uzgiris, I. C., and Hunt, J. M. (1989). *Assessment in infancy: Ordinal scales of psychological development.* Urbana, IL: University of Illinois Press.

Vaillant, G. (1971). Theoretical hierarchy of adaptive ego mechanisms. *Archives of General Psychiatry, 24,* 107–118.

Vaillant, G. (1977). *Adaptation to life: How the best and the brightest came of age.* Boston, MA: Little, Brown.

Vaillant, G. (1992). *Ego mechanisms of defense: A guide for clinicians and researchers.* Washington, DC: American Psychiatric Press.

Vaillant, G., & Vaillant, C. (1990). Natural history of male psychosocial health, XII: A 45-year study of predictors of successful aging at age 65. *American Journal of Psychiatry, 147,* 31–37.

Valdes, G., & Figueroa, R. A. (1994). *Bilingualism and testing: A special case of bias.* Norwood, NJ: Ablex.

Valencia, R. R., & Rankin, R. J. (1988). Evidence of bias in predictive validity on the Kaufman Assessment Battery for Children in samples of Anglo and Mexican American children. *Psychology in the Schools, 25,* 257–263.

Van de Vijver, F., & Harsveld, M. (1994). The incomplete equivalence of the paper-and-pencil and computerized versions of the General Aptitude Test Battery. *Journal of Applied Psychology, 79,* 852–859.

Van Gorp, W. (1992). Review of Luria-Nebraska Neuropsychological Battery: Forms I and II. *The Eleventh Mental Measurements Yearbook.* Lincoln, NE: University of Nebraska Press.

Vance, B., Kitson, D., & Singer, M. (1985). Relationship between the standard scores of PPVT-R and Wide Range Achievement Test. *Journal of Clinical Psychology, 41,* 691–693.

Vance, H., Maddux, C., Fuller, G., & Awadh, A. (1996). A longitudinal comparison of WISC-III and WISC-R scores of special education students. *Psychology in the Schools, 33,* 113–118.

VanderVeer, B., and Schweid, E. (1974). Infant assessment: Stability of mental functioning in young retarded children. *American Journal of Mental Deficiency, 79,* 1–4.

Varma, A., DeNisi, A., & Peters, L. (1996). Interpersonal affect and performance appraisal: A field study. *Personnel Psychology, 49,* 341–360.

Vaughn, S., & Haager, D. (1994). The measurement and assessment of social skills. In G. R. Lyon (ed.), *Frames of reference for the assessment of learning disabilities: New views on measurement issues.* Baltimore, MD: Brookes Publishing.

Verhoeve, M. (1993). *JVIS applications handbook.* Port Huron, MI: Research Psychologists Press.

Vernon, M. C., & Alles, B. F. (1986). Psychoeducational assessment of deaf and hard-of-hearing children and adolescents. In P. J. Lazarus & S. S. Strichart (eds.), *Psychoeducational evaluation of children and adolescents with low-incidence handicaps.* New York: Grune & Stratton.

Vernon, M. C., & Brown, D. W. (1964). A guide to psychological tests and testing procedures in the evaluation of deaf and hard-of-hearing children. *Journal of Speech and Hearing Disorders, 29,* 414–423.

Vernon, P. A. (1994). Reaction time. In R. J. Sternberg (ed.), *Encyclopedia of human intelligence.* New York: Macmillan.

Vernon, P. A., & Mori, M. (1990). Physiological approaches to the assessment of intelligence. In C. R. Reynolds and R. W. Kamphaus (eds.), *Handbook of psychological and educational assessment of children: Intelligence and achievement.* New York: Guilford.

Vernon, P. E. (1950). *The structure of human abilities.* London: Methuen.

Vernon, P. E. (1979). *Intelligence: Heredity and environment.* San Francisco: Freeman.

Viswesvaran, C., Ones, D., & Schmidt, F. (1996). Comparative analysis of the reliability of job performance ratings. *Journal of Applied Psychology, 81,* 557–574.

Wade, T. C., & Baker, T. B. (1977). Opinions and use of psychological tests. *American Psychologist, 32,* 874–882.

Wagner, R. (1949). The employment interview: A critical review. *Personnel Psychology, 2,* 17–46.

Wall, R. E., Hinrichsen, G. A., & Pollack, S. (1989). Psychometric characteristics of the Multidimensional Health Locus of Control Scales among psychiatric patients. *Journal of Clinical Psychology, 45,* 94–98.

Wallach, M. A. (1985). Creativity testing and giftedness. In F. D. Horowitz & M. O'Brien (eds.). *The gifted and talented: Developmental perspectives.* Washington, DC: American Psychological Association.

Wallbrown, F. H., Carmin, C. N., & Barnett, R. W. (1988). Investigating the construct validity of the Multidimensional Aptitude Battery. *Psychological Reports, 62,* 871–878.

Walls, R. T., Werner, T. J., Bacon, A., & Zane, T. (1977). Behavior checklist. In J. D. Cone & R. P. Hawkins (eds.), *Behavioral assessment: New directions in clinical psychology.* New York: Bruner/Mazel.

Walls, R. T., Zane, T., & Thvedt, J. E. (1979). *The Independent Living Behavior Checklist.* Dunbar, WV: West Virginia Research and Training Center.

Walsh, W. B., & Holland, J. L. (1992). A theory of personality types and work environments. In W. Walsh, R. Price, & K. Craik (eds.), *Person-environment psychology: Models and perspectives.* Hillsdale, NJ: Erlbaum.

Wang, J., & Kaufman, A. (1993). Changes in fluid and crystallized intelligence across the 20- to 90-year age range on the K-BIT. *Journal of Psychoeducational Assessment, 11,* 29–37.

Ward, L. C. (1990). Prediction of verbal, performance, and full scale IQs from seven subtests of the WAIS-R. *Journal of Clinical Psychology, 46,* 436–440.

Watkins, C. E., Jr., Campbell, V., & McGregor, P. (1988). Counseling psychologists' uses of the opinions about psychological tests: A contemporary perspective. *The Counseling Psychologist, 16,* 476–486.

Watkins, C., Campbell, V., Nieberding, R., & Hallmark, R. (1995). Contemporary practice of psychological assessment by clinical psychologists. *Professional Psychology: Research and Practice, 26,* 54–60.

Watson, B. U., & Goldgar, D. E. (1985). A note on the use of the Hiskey-Nebraska Test of Learning Aptitude with deaf children. *Language, Speech, and Hearing Services in the Schools, 16,* 53–57.

Watson, C. G., Thomas, D., & Anderson, P. (1992). Do computer-administered Minnesota Multiphasic Personality Inventories underestimate booklet-based scores? *Journal of Clinical Psychology, 48,* 744–748.

Weaver, S. J. (ed.). (1984). *Testing children.* Kansas City, MO: Test Corporation of America.

Wechsler, D. (1932). Analytic use of the Army Alpha examination. *Journal of Applied Psychology, 16,* 254–256.

Wechsler, D. (1939). *The measurement of adult intelligence.* Baltimore, MD: William & Wilkins.

Wechsler, D. (1941). *The measurement of adult intelligence* (2nd ed.). Baltimore, MD: William & Wilkins.

Wechsler, D. (1944). *Measurement of adult intelligence* (3rd ed.). Baltimore: Williams & Wilkins.

Wechsler, D. (1945). A standardized memory scale for clinical use. *Journal of Psychology, 19,* 87–95.

Wechsler, D. (1949). *Manual for the Wechsler Intelligence Scale for Children.* New York: Psychological Corporation.

Wechsler, D. (1952). *The range of human capacities* (2nd ed.). Baltimore: Williams & Wilkins.

Wechsler, D. (1955). *Manual for the Wechsler Adult Intelligence Scale.* New York: Psychological Corporation.

Wechsler, D. (1974). *Manual for the Wechsler Intelligence Scale for Children-Revised.* San Antonio, TX: Psychological Corporation.

Wechsler, D. (1981). *Manual for the Wechsler Adult Intelligence Scale-Revised.* San Antonio, TX: Psychological Corporation.

Wechsler, D. (1989). *Manual for the Wechsler Preschool and Primary Scale of Intelligence-Revised.* San Antonio, TX: Psychological Corporation.

Wechsler, D. (1991). *Manual for the Wechsler Intelligence Scale for Children-III.* San Antonio, TX: Psychological Corporation.

Wechsler, D. (1992). *Wechsler Individual Achievement Test manual.* San Antonio, TX: Psychological Corporation.

Wechsler, D. (1997). *Manual for the Wechsler Adult Intelligence Scale-III.* San Antonio, TX: Psychological Corporation.

Weekes, N. Y. (1994). Sex differences in the brain. In D. W. Zaidel (ed.), *Neuropsychology* (2nd ed.). San Diego, CA: Academic Press.

Weiner, I. B. (1994). The Rorschach Inkblot Method (RIM) is not a test: implications for theory and practice. *Journal of Personality Assessment, 62,* 498–504.

Weiner, I. B. (1996). Some observations on the validity of the Rorschach inkblot method. *Psychological Assessment, 8,* 206–213.

Weiner, I. B., & Kuehnle, K. (1998). Projective assessment of children and adolescents. In A. S. Bellack, & M. Hersen (eds.), *Comprehensive clinical psychology,* (vol. 4). Amsterdam: Elsevier.

Weiss, D. J. (1985). Adaptive testing by computer. *Journal of Consulting and Clinical Psychology, 53,* 774–789.

Weiss, D. J. (ed.). (1983). *New horizons in testing: Latent trait theory and computerized adaptive testing.* New York: Academic Press.

Weiss, D. J., & Vale, C. D. (1987). Computerized adaptive testing for measuring abilities and other psychological variables. In J. N. Butcher (ed.), *Computerized psychological assessment: A practitioner's guide.* New York: Basic Books.

Weiss, D. S., Zilberg, N. J., & Genevro, J. L. (1989). Psychometric properties of Loevinger's Sentence Completion Test in an adult psychiatric outpatient sample. *Journal of Personality Assessment, 53,* 478–486.

Wesman, A. G. (1971). Writing the test item. In R. L. Thorndike (ed.), *Educational measurement* (2nd ed.). Washington, DC: American Council on Education.

Westbrook, B. W., & Bane, K. D. (1992). Review of Defining Issues Test. *Eleventh mental measurements yearbook.* Lincoln, NE: University of Nebraska Press.

Wetter, M. W., Baer, R., Berry, D., & Reynolds, S. (1994). The effect of symptom information on faking on the MMPI-2. *Assessment, 2,* 199–208.

Whipple, G. M. (1910). *Manual of mental and physical tests.* Baltimore: Warwick and York.

Whitaker, H. A., & Kahn, H. J. (1994). Brain and language. In D. W. Zaidel (ed.), *Neuropsychology* (2nd ed.). San Diego, CA: Academic Press.

Whitney, D. R., Malizio, A. G., Patience, W. M. (1985). The reliability and validity of the GED Tests. *American Council on Education GED Research Brief,* May, No. 6.

Wholeben, B. E. (1987). Sixteen Personality Factor Questionnaire. In D. J. Keyser & R. C. Sweetland (eds.), *Test critiques compendium.* Kansas City, MO: Test Corporation of America.

Wiebe, D. J., & Smith, T. (1997). Personality and health: Progress and problems in psychosomatics. In R. Hogan, J. Johnson, & S. Briggs (eds.), *Handbook of personality psychology.* San Diego, CA: Academic Press.

Wiedl, K. H., & Carlson, J. S. (1976). The factorial structure of the Raven Coloured Progressive Matrices Test. *Educational and Psychological Measurement, 36,* 409–413.

Wiens, A. N., McMinn, M. R., & Crossen, J. R. (1988). Rey Auditory-Verbal Learning Test: Development of norms for healthy young adults. *The Clinical Neuropsychologist, 2,* 67–87.

Wiesner, W. H., & Cronshaw, S. F. (1988). A meta-analytic investigation of the impact of interview format and degree of structure on the validity of the employment interview. *Journal of Occupational Psychology, 61,* 275–290.

Wiggins, J. (1997). In defense of traits. In R. Hogan, J. Johnson, & S. Briggs (eds.), *Handbook of personality psychology.* San Diego, CA: Academic Press.

Wilkinson, G. S. (1993). *Wide Range Achievement Test-III: Administration manual.* Wilmington, DE: Wide Range, Inc.

Willard, L. S. (1968). A comparison of Culture Fair Test scores with group and individual intelligence test scores of disadvantaged negro children. *Journal of Learning Disabilities, 1,* 30–35.

Williams, J. A., & Williams, J. D. (1985). Kuder General Interest Survey, Form E. In D. J. Keyser & R. C. Sweetland (eds.), *Test critiques* (vol. 2). Kansas City, MO: Test Corporation of America.

Williams, M. (1979). *Brain damage, behaviour, and the mind.* New York: Wiley.

Williamson, L., Campion, J., Malo, S., & others. (1997). Employment interview on trial: Linking interview structure with litigation outcomes. *Journal of Applied Psychology, 82,* 900–912.

Willingham, W. W., Ragosta, M., Bennett, R., and others (1988). *Testing handicapped people.* Boston: Allyn & Bacon.

Willis, S., & Schaie, K. W. (1986). Training the elderly on the ability factors of spatial orientation and inductive reasoning. *Psychology and Aging, 1,* 239–247.

Wills, G. I. (1984). A personality study of musicians working in the popular field. *Personality and Individual Differences, 5,* 359–360.

Willson, V. L. (1989). Review of the Iowa Tests of Basic Skills. *The Tenth Mental Measurements Yearbook.* Lincoln, NE: University of Nebraska Press.

Wilson, B., Alderman, N., Burgess, P., Emslie, H., & Evans, J. (1996). *Behavioral Assessment of the Dysexecutive Syndrome.* Bury St. Edmunds, England: Thames Valley Test Company.

Wilson, M. N. (1994). African Americans. In R. J. Sternberg (ed.), *Encyclopedia of human intelligence.* New York: Macmillan.

Wilson, R. S. (1983). The Louisville Twin Study: Developmental synchronies in behavior. *Child Development, 54,* 298–316.

Wing, H. (1992). Review of the Bennett Mechanical Comprehension Test. *The Eleventh Mental Measurements Yearbook.* Lincoln, NE: University of Nebraska Press.

Winter, D. G., & Stewart, A. J. (1977). Power motive reliability as a function of retest instructions. *Journal of Consulting and Clinical Psychology, 45,* 436–440.

Wirt, R. D., & Broen, W. E., Jr. (1958). *Booklet for the Personality Inventory for Children.* Minneapolis, MN: Authors.

Wirt, R. D., & Lachar, D. (1981). The Personality Inventory for Children: Development and clinical applications. In P. McReynolds (ed.), *Advances in psychological assessment* (vol. 5). San Francisco: Jossey-Bass.

Wirt, R. D., Lachar, D., Klinedinst, J. K., & Seat, P. D. (1984). *Multidimensional description of child personality: A manual for the Personality Inventory for Children, Revised 1984.* Los Angeles: Western Psychological Services.

Wirtz, W. (ed.). (1977). *On further examination: Report of the advisory panel on the Scholastic Aptitude Test score decline.* New York: College Entrance Examination Board.

Wisniewski, J. J., & Naglieri, J. A. (1989). Validity of the Draw A Person: A Quantitative Scoring System with the WISC-R. *Journal of Psychoeducational Assessment, 7,* 346–351.

Wissler, C. (1901). The correlation of mental and physical tests. *The Psychological Review,* Monograph Supplement 3(6).

Witkin, H. A. (1949). Perception of body position and of the position of the visual field. *Psychological Monographs, 63,* (Whole No. 302).

Wolf, A. W., Schubert, D., Patterson, M., Grande, T., & Pendleton, L. (1990). The use of the MacAndrew Alcoholism Scale in detecting substance abuse and antisocial personality. *Journal of Personality Assessment, 54,* 747–755.

Wolf, T. H. (1973). *Alfred Binet.* Chicago, IL: The University of Illinois Press.

Wolff, K. C., and Gregory, R. J. (1992). The effects of a temporary dysphoric mood upon selected WAIS-R subtests. *Journal of Psychoeducational Assessment, 9,* 340–344.

Wolpe, J. (1958). *Psychotherapy by reciprocal inhibition.* Stanford, CA: Stanford University Press.

Wolpe, J. (1973). *The practice of behavior therapy* (2nd ed.). New York: Pergamon.

Wolpe, J., & Lang, P. J. (1977). *Manual for the Fear Survey Schedule (revised).* San Diego, CA: Educational and Industrial Testing Service.

Wonderlic, E. F. (1983). *Wonderlic Personnel Test manual.* Northfield, IL: E. F. Wonderlic & Associates.

Wood, J. M., Nezworski, M., & Stejskal, W. (1996). The Comprehensive System for the Rorschach: A critical examination. *Psychological Science, 7,* 3–10.

Woodcock, R. W., & Johnson, M. B. (1989). *Woodcock-Johnson Psycho-Educational Battery-Revised.* Allen, TX: DLM Teaching Resources.

Woodcock, R. W., McGrew, K. S., & Werder, J. K. (1994). *Mini-Battery of Achievement: Examiner's manual.* Chicago, IL: Riverside.

Woodworth, R. S. (1919). Examination of emotional fitness for warfare. *Psychological Bulletin, 16,* 59–60.

Woodworth, R. S. (1951). Autobiography. In C. Murchison (ed.), *History of psychology in autobiography,* vol. 2. New York: Russell and Russell.

Wright, B. D., & Stone, M. (1979). *Best test design.* Chicago, IL: MESA Press.

Wright, J. C., & Mischel, W. (1987). A conditional approach to dispositional constructs: The local predictability of social behavior. *Journal of Personality and Social Psychology, 53,* 1159–1177.

Wright, L. (1988). The Type A behavior pattern and coronary artery disease: Quest for the active ingredients and the elusive mechanism. *American Psychologist, 43,* 2–14.

Wright, L. (1992). Are the physical and TABP risk factors for heart disease unique to CHD? *Journal of Clinical Psychology, 48,* 705–710.

Wright, L., McCurdy, S., & Rogoll, G. (1992). The TUPA Scale: A self-report measure for the Type A subcomponent of time urgency and perpetual activation. *Psychological Assessment, 4,* 352–356.

Wrightsman, L. S., Nietzel, M. T., and Fortune, W. H. (1994). *Psychology and the legal system* (3rd ed.). Pacific Grove, CA: Brooks/Cole.

Wulff, D. M. (1996). The psychology of religion: An overview. In E. P. Shafranske (ed.), *Religion and the clinical practice of psychology.* Washington, DC: American Psychological Association.

Wundt, W. (1862). Die Geschwindigkeit des Gedankens. *Gartenlaube,* 263–265.

Yama, M. (1990). The usefulness of human figure drawings as an index of overall adjustment. *Journal of Personality Assessment, 54,* 78–86.

Yarnold, P. R., & Bryant, F. B. (1988). A note on measurement issues in Type A research: Let's not throw out the baby with the bath water. *Journal of Personality Assessment, 52,* 410–419.

Yates, A. (1954). The validity of some psychological tests of brain damage. *Psychological Bulletin, 51,* 359–379.

Yerkes, R. M. (1919). Report of the psychology Committee of the National Research Council. *Psychological Review, 26,* 83–149.

Yerkes, R. M. (ed.) (1921). *Psychological examining in the United States Army. Memoirs of the National Academy of Sciences,* vol. 15.

Zachary, R. A. (1986). *Shipley Institute of Living Scale.* Los Angeles: Western Psychological Services.

Zachary, R. A., Crumpton, E., & Spiegel, D. (1985). Estimating WAIS-R IQ from the Shipley Institute of Living Scale. *Journal of Clinical Psychology, 41,* 532–540.

Zajonc, R. B., Markus, H., & Markus, G. B. (1979). The birth order puzzle. *Journal of Personality and Social Psychology, 37,* 1324–1341.

Zavala, A. (1965). Development of the forced-choice rating scale technique. *Psychological Bulletin, 63,* 117–124.

Ziskin, J., and Faust, D. (1988). *Coping with psychiatric and psychological testimony* (vols. 1–3, 4th ed.). Marina Del Ray, CA: Law & Psychology Press.

Zytowski, D. G. (1985). *Kuder Occupational Interest Survey manual supplement.* Chicago: Science Research Associates.

Name Index

Subject Index